Pro C# with .NET 3.0

Special Edition

■ ■ ■

Andrew Troelsen

Apress®

Pro C# with .NET 3.0, Special Edition

Copyright © 2007 by Andrew Troelsen

ISBN-13: 978-1-59059-823-8

ISBN-10: 1-59059-823-7

Printed and bound in the United States of America 9 8 7 6 5 4 3 2

Lead Editor: Ewan Buckingham
Technical Reviewer: Christophe Nasarre
Editorial Board: Steve Anglin, Ewan Buckingham, Gary Cornell, Jason Gilmore, Jonathan Gennick,
    Jonathan Hassell, James Huddleston, Chris Mills, Matthew Moodie, Dominic Shakeshaft,
    Jim Sumser, Matt Wade
Project Manager: Grace Wong
Copy Edit Manager: Nicole Flores
Copy Editors: Nicole Flores, Ami Knox
Assistant Production Director: Kari Brooks-Copony
Senior Production Editor: Kelly Winquist
Compositor: Dina Quan
Proofreader: Linda Seifert
Indexer: Broccoli Information Management
Artist: April Milne
Cover Designer: Kurt Krames
Manufacturing Director: Tom Debolski

Distributed to the book trade worldwide by Springer-Verlag New York, Inc., 233 Spring Street, 6th Floor, New York, NY 10013. Phone 1-800-SPRINGER, fax 201-348-4505, e-mail orders-ny@springer-sbm.com, or visit http://www.springeronline.com.

For information on translations, please contact Apress directly at 2855 Telegraph Avenue, Suite 600, Berkeley, CA 94705. Phone 510-549-5930, fax 510-549-5939, e-mail info@apress.com, or visit http://www.apress.com.

The source code for this book is available to readers at http://www.apress.com in the Source Code/ Download section. You will need to answer questions pertaining to this book in order to successfully download the code.

I would like to dedicate this book to my mother, Mary Troelsen.
Mom, thanks for all of your support over the years and the years to come.
Oh yeah, and thanks for not busting my chops when I came home
with the red Mohawk.
Luv ya,
Pooch

Contents at a Glance

PART 1 ■ ■ ■ Introducing C# and the .NET Platform

PART 2 ■ ■ ■ The C# Programming Language

PART 3 ■ ■ ■ Programming with .NET Assemblies

PART 4 ■■■ Programming with the .NET Libraries

PART 5 ■■■ Web Applications and XML Web Services

PART 6 ■■■ Programming with .NET 3.0 Extensions

Contents

PART 1 ■■■ Introducing C# and the .NET Platform

PART 2 ■■■ The C# Programming Language

PART 3 ■ ■ ■ Programming with .NET Assemblies

PART 4 ■ ■ ■ Programming with the .NET Libraries

■CHAPTER 20　Rendering Graphical Data with GDI+

PART 5 ■■■ Web Applications and XML Web Services

■**CHAPTER 24**   **ASP.NET 2.0 Web Applications**

PART 6 ■ ■ ■ Programming with .NET 3.0 Extensions

About the Author

ANDREW TROELSEN is a Microsoft MVP (Visual C#) and a partner, trainer, and consultant with Intertech Training (http://www.Intertech.com), a .NET and J2EE developer education center. He is the author of numerous books, including *Developer's Workshop to COM and ATL 3.0* (Wordware Publishing, 2000), *COM and .NET Interoperability* (Apress, 2002), *Pro VB 2005 and the .NET 2.0 Platform* (Apress, 2005), and the award-winning *C# and the .NET Platform* (Apress, 2003). Andrew has also authored numerous articles on .NET for MSDN online, DevX.com, and MacTech (where he explored the platform-independent aspects of the .NET platform), and he is a frequent speaker at various .NET conferences and user groups.

Andrew currently lives in Minneapolis, Minnesota, with his wife, Amanda. He spends his free time waiting for the Wild to win the Stanley Cup, the Vikings to win the Super Bowl (which he thinks may never happen), and the Timberwolves to grab numerous NBA championship titles (where he has similar doubts).

About the Technical Reviewer

CHRISTOPHE NASARRE is a development architect for Business Objects, a company that develops desktop and web-based business intelligence solutions. In his spare time, Christophe writes articles for *MSDN* magazine, MSDN/Vista, and ASP Today, and he has been reviewing books on Win32, COM, MFC, .NET, and WPF since 1996.

Acknowledgments

While completing a "special edition" of an existing text is far less painful than authoring a new book beginning with page 1, this manuscript would not have been possible without the assistance and talent offered by numerous individuals. First of all, many thanks to the entire Apress crew. As always, each of you did an outstanding job massaging my raw manuscript into a polished product. Next, I must thank my technical reviewers, who did a truly wonderful job of keeping me honest. Of course, any remaining errors (spelling, coding, or otherwise) that may have snuck into this book are my sole responsibility.

Thanks to my friends and family who (yet again) tolerated my lack of time and sometimes grumpy demeanor. More thanks to my friends and coworkers at Intertech Training. Your support (directly and indirectly) is greatly appreciated. Finally, thanks to my wife, Mandy, and "all the kids" for their love and encouragement.

Introduction

I remember a time years ago when I proposed a book to Apress regarding a forthcoming software SDK code-named Next Generation Windows Services (NGWS). As you may be aware, NGWS eventually became what we now know as the .NET platform. My research of the C# programming language and the .NET platform took place in parallel with the authoring of the initial manuscript. It was a fantastic project; however, I must confess that it was more than a bit nerve-racking writing about a technology that was undergoing drastic changes over the course of its development. Thankfully, after many sleepless nights, the first edition of *C# and the .NET Platform* was published in conjunction with the release of .NET 1.0 Beta 2, circa the summer of 2001.

Since that point, I have been extremely happy and grateful to see that this text was very well received by the press and, most important, by readers. Over the years it was nominated as a Jolt Award finalist (I lost . . . crap!) and for the 2003 Referenceware Excellence Award in the programming book category (I won? Cool!).

The second edition of this text (*C# and the .NET Platform, Second Edition*) provided me the opportunity to expand upon the existing content with regard to version 1.1 of the .NET platform. Although the second edition of the book did offer a number of new topics, a number of chapters and examples were unable to make it into the final product.

Once the text entered its third edition (*Pro C# 2005 and the .NET 2.0 Platform*), the manuscript was updated to account for the numerous bells and whistles brought about by .NET 2.0 (new C# programming constructs, generics, updates to core APIs, etc.), and it included new material that had long been written but not yet published (such as content on the common intermediate language [CIL] and dynamic assemblies, and expanded ASP.NET coverage).

In this special edition of the text, I have added six new chapters dedicated to the new programming APIs brought about with the release of .NET 3.0. Over these chapters, you will come to understand the role of Windows Presentation Foundation (WPF), Windows Communication Foundation (WCF), and Windows Workflow Foundation (WF). As well, this new text provides details regarding the forthcoming C# 3.0 programming language and LINQ programming technologies (LINQ to SQL and LINQ to XML). While C# 3.0 and LINQ are currently beta technologies, the final two chapters of this text will provide a solid road map for the changes to come.

As with the earlier editions, this special edition presents the C# programming language and .NET base class libraries using a friendly and approachable tone. I have never understood the need some technical authors have to spit out prose that reads more like a GRE vocabulary study guide than a readable book. As well, this new edition remains focused on providing you with the information you need to build software solutions today, rather than spending too much time examining esoteric details that few individuals will ever actually care about.

We're a Team, You and I

Technology authors write for a demanding group of people (I should know—I'm one of them). You know that building software solutions using any platform is extremely detailed and is very specific to your department, company, client base, and subject matter. Perhaps you work in the electronic publishing industry, develop systems for the state or local government, or work at NASA or a branch of the military. Speaking for myself, I have developed children's educational software, various n-tier systems, and numerous projects within the medical and financial industries. The chances are almost 100 percent that the code you write at your place of employment has little to do with the code I write at mine (unless we happened to work together previously!).

Therefore, in this book, I have deliberately chosen to avoid creating examples that tie the example code to a specific industry or vein of programming. I choose to explain C#, OOP, the CLR, and the .NET 2.0/3.0 base class libraries using industry-agnostic examples. Rather than having every blessed example fill a grid with data, calculate payroll, or whatnot, I'll stick to subject matter we can all relate to: automobiles (with some geometric structures and employees thrown in for good measure). And that's where you come in.

My job is to explain the C# programming language and the core aspects of the .NET platform the best I possibly can. As well, I will do everything I can to equip you with the tools and strategies you need to continue your studies at this book's conclusion.

Your job is to take this information and apply it to your specific programming assignments. I obviously understand that your projects most likely don't revolve around automobiles with pet names, but that's what applied knowledge is all about! Rest assured, once you understand the concepts presented within this text, you will be in a perfect position to build .NET solutions that map to your own unique programming environment.

An Overview of This Book

Pro C# with .NET 3.0, Special Edition is logically divided into six distinct parts, each of which contains some number of chapters that somehow "belong together." If you've read the third edition of this text (*Pro C# 2005 and the .NET 2.0 Platform*), you will notice that the first 25 chapters of this special edition are identical (beyond a number of errata integrations) to those. However, Part 6 of this book (which is devoted to building .NET 3.0/C# 3.0 and LINQ applications) is indeed entirely new. This being said, here is a part-by-part and chapter-by-chapter breakdown of the text.

Part 1: Introducing C# and the .NET Platform

The purpose of Part 1 is to acclimate you to the core aspects of the .NET platform, the .NET type system, and various development tools (many of which are open source) used during the construction of .NET applications. Along the way, you will also check out some basic details of the C# programming language.

Chapter 1: The Philosophy of .NET

This first chapter functions as the backbone for the remainder of the text. We begin by examining the world of traditional Windows development and uncover the shortcomings with the previous state of affairs. The primary goal of this chapter, however, is to acquaint you with a number of .NET-centric building blocks, such as the common language runtime (CLR), Common Type System (CTS), Common Language Specification (CLS), and the base class libraries. Also, you will also take an initial look at the C# programming language and the .NET assembly format, and you'll examine the platform-independent nature of the .NET platform and the role of the Common Language Infrastructure (CLI).

Chapter 2: Building C# Applications

The goal of this chapter is to introduce you to the process of compiling and debugging C# source code files using various tools and techniques. First, you will learn how to make use of the command-line compiler (`csc.exe`) and C# response files. Over the remainder of the chapter, you will examine numerous IDEs, including TextPad, SharpDevelop, Visual C# 2005 Express, and (of course) Visual Studio 2005. As well, you will be exposed to a number of open source tools (Vil, NAnt, NDoc, etc.), which any .NET developer should have in his or her back pocket.

Part 2: The C# Programming Language

This part explores all the gory details of the C# programming language, including the new syntactical constructs introduced with .NET 2.0. As well, Part 2 exposes you to each member of the CTS (classes, interfaces, structures, enumerations, and delegates) and the construction of generic types.

Chapter 3: C# Language Fundamentals

This chapter examines the core constructs of the C# programming language. Here you will come to understand basic class construction techniques, the distinction between value types and reference types, boxing and unboxing, and the role of everybody's favorite base class, System.Object. Also, Chapter 3 illustrates how the .NET platform puts a spin on various commonplace programming constructs, such as enumerations, arrays, and string processing. Finally, this chapter examines a number of 2.0-specific topics, including "nullable data types."

Chapter 4: Object-Oriented Programming with C#

The role of Chapter 4 is to examine the details of how C# 2.0 accounts for each "pillar" of OOP: encapsulation, inheritance, and polymorphism. Once you have examined the keywords and the syntax used to build class hierarchies, you will then look at the role of XML code comments.

Chapter 5: Understanding Object Lifetime

This chapter examines how the CLR manages memory using the .NET garbage collector. Here you will come to understand the role of application roots, object generations, and the System.GC type. Once you understand the basics, the remainder of this chapter covers the topics of "disposable objects" (via the IDisposable interface) and the finalization process (via the System.Object. Finalize() method).

Chapter 6: Understanding Structured Exception Handling

The point of this chapter is to discuss how to handle runtime anomalies in your code base through the use of structured exception handling. Not only will you learn about the C# keywords that allow you to handle such problems (try, catch, throw, and finally), but you will also come to understand the distinction between application-level and system-level exceptions. In addition, this chapter examines various tools within Visual Studio 2005 that allow you to debug the exceptions that have escaped your view.

Chapter 7: Interfaces and Collections

The material in this chapter builds upon your understanding of object-based development by covering the topic of interface-based programming. Here you will learn how to define types that support multiple behaviors, how to discover these behaviors at runtime, and how to selectively hide particular behaviors using *explicit interface implementation*. To showcase the usefulness of interface types, the remainder of this chapter examines the System.Collections namespace.

Chapter 8: Callback Interfaces, Delegates, and Events

The purpose of Chapter 8 is to demystify the delegate type. Simply put, a .NET *delegate* is an object that "points" to other methods in your application. Using this pattern, you are able to build systems that allow multiple objects to engage in a two-way conversation. After you have examined the use of .NET delegates (including numerous 2.0-specific features such as anonymous methods), you will then be introduced to the C# event keyword, which is used to simplify the manipulation of raw delegate programming.

Chapter 9: Advanced C# Type Construction Techniques

This chapter deepens your understanding of the C# programming language by introducing a number of advanced programming techniques. For example, you will learn how to overload operators and create custom conversion routines (both implicit and explicit), build type indexers, and manipulate C-style pointers within a *.cs code file.

Chapter 10: Understanding Generics

As of .NET 2.0, the C# programming language has been enhanced to support a new feature of the CTS termed *generics*. As you will see, generic programming greatly enhances application performance and type safety. Not only will you explore various generic types within the System.Collections. Generic namespace, but you will also learn how to build your own generic methods and types (with and without constraints).

Part 3: Programming with .NET Assemblies

Part 3 dives into the details of the .NET assembly format. Not only will you learn how to deploy and configure .NET code libraries, but you will also come to understand the internal composition of a .NET binary image. This part also explains the role of .NET attributes and the construction of mutilthreaded applications. Later chapters examine some fairly low-level details (such as object context) and the syntax and semantics of CIL.

Chapter 11: Introducing .NET Assemblies

From a very high level, *assembly* is the term used to describe a managed *.dll or *.exe file. However, the true story of .NET assemblies is far richer than that. Here you will learn the distinction between single-file and multifile assemblies, and how to build and deploy each entity. You'll examine how private and shared assemblies may be configured using XML-based *.config files and publisher policy assemblies. Along the way, you will investigate the internal structure of the global assembly cache (GAC) and the role of the .NET Framework 2.0 configuration utility.

Chapter 12: Type Reflection, Late Binding, and Attribute-Based Programming

Chapter 12 continues our examination of .NET assemblies by checking out the process of runtime type discovery via the System.Reflection namespace. Using these types, you are able to build applications that can read an assembly's metadata on the fly. You will learn how to dynamically activate and manipulate types at runtime using *late binding*. The final topic of this chapter explores the role of .NET attributes (both standard and custom). To illustrate the usefulness of each of these topics, the chapter concludes with the construction of an extendable Windows Forms application.

Chapter 13: Processes, AppDomains, Contexts, and CLR Hosts

Now that you have a solid understanding of assemblies, this chapter dives much deeper into the composition of a loaded .NET executable. The first goal is to illustrate the relationship between processes, application domains, and contextual boundaries. Once these terms have been qualified, you will then understand exactly how the CLR itself is hosted by the Windows operating system and deepen your understanding of mscoree.dll. The information presented here is a perfect lead-in to Chapter 14.

Chapter 14: Building Multithreaded Applications

This chapter examines how to build multithreaded applications and illustrates a number of techniques you can use to author thread-safe code. The chapter opens by revisiting the .NET delegate type in order to understand a delegate's intrinsic support for asynchronous method invocations. Next, you will investigate the types within the System.Threading namespace. You will look at numerous types (Thread, ThreadStart, etc.) that allow you to easily create additional threads of execution.

Chapter 15: Understanding CIL and the Role of Dynamic Assemblies

The goal of this chapter is twofold. In the first half (more or less), you will examine the syntax and semantics of CIL in much greater detail than in previous chapters. The remainder of this chapter covers the role of the System.Reflection.Emit namespace. Using these types, you are able to build software that is capable of generating .NET assemblies in memory at runtime. Formally speaking, assemblies defined and executed in memory are termed *dynamic assemblies.*

Part 4: Programming with the .NET Libraries

By this point in the text, you have a solid handle on the C# language and the details of the .NET assembly format. Part 4 leverages your newfound knowledge by exploring a number of namespaces within the base class libraries, including file I/O, the .NET remoting layer, Windows Forms development, and database access using ADO.NET.

Chapter 16: The System.IO Namespace

As you can gather from its name, the System.IO namespace allows you to interact with a machine's file and directory structure. Over the course of this chapter, you will learn how to programmatically create (and destroy) a directory system as well as move data into and out of various streams (file based, string based, memory based, etc.).

Chapter 17: Understanding Object Serialization

This chapter examines the object serialization services of the .NET platform. Simply put, *serialization* allows you to persist the state of an object (or a set of related objects) into a stream for later use. *Deserialization* (as you might expect) is the process of plucking an object from the stream into memory for consumption by your application. Once you understand the basics, you will then learn how to customize the serialization process via the ISerializable interface and a set of new attributes introduced with .NET 2.0.

Chapter 18: The .NET Remoting Layer

Contrary to popular belief, XML web services are not the only way to build distributed applications under the .NET platform. Here you will learn about the .NET remoting layer. As you will see, the CLR supports the ability to easily pass objects between application and machine boundaries using marshal-by-value (MBV) and marshal-by-reference (MBR) semantics. Along the way, you will learn how to alter the runtime behavior of a distributed .NET application in a declarative manner using XML configuration files.

Chapter 19: Building a Better Window with System.Windows.Forms

This chapter begins your examination of the System.Windows.Forms namespace. Here you will learn the details of building traditional desktop GUI applications that support menu systems, toolbars, and status bars. As you would hope, various design-time aspects of Visual Studio 2005 will be examined, as well as a number of .NET 2.0 Windows Forms types (MenuStrip, ToolStrip, etc.).

Chapter 20: Rendering Graphical Data with GDI+

This chapter covers how to dynamically render graphical data in the Windows Forms environment. In addition to discussing how to manipulate fonts, colors, geometric images, and image files, this chapter examines hit testing and GUI-based drag-and-drop techniques. You will learn about the new .NET resource format, which as you may suspect by this point in the text is based on XML data representation.

Chapter 21: Programming with Windows Forms Controls

This final Windows-centric chapter will examine numerous GUI widgets that ship with the .NET Framework 2.0. Not only will you learn how to program against various Windows Forms controls, but you will also learn about dialog box development and Form inheritance. As well, this chapter examines how to build *custom* Windows Forms controls that integrate into the IDE.

Chapter 22: Database Access with ADO.NET

ADO.NET is the data access API of the .NET platform. As you will see, you are able to interact with the types of ADO.NET using a connected and disconnected layer. Over the course of this chapter, you will have the chance to work with both modes of ADO.NET, and you'll learn about several new .NET 2.0 ADO.NET topics, including the data provider factory model, connection string builders, and asynchronous database access.

Part 5: Web Applications and XML Web Services

Part 5 is devoted to the construction of ASP.NET web applications and XML web services. As you will see in the first two chapters of this section, ASP.NET 2.0 is a major upgrade from ASP.NET 1.*x* and includes numerous new bells and whistles.

Chapter 23: ASP.NET 2.0 Web Pages and Web Controls

This chapter begins your study of web technologies supported under the .NET platform using ASP.NET. As you will see, server-side scripting code is now replaced with "real" object-oriented languages (such as C#, VB .NET, and the like). This chapter will introduce you to key ASP.NET topics such as working with (or without) code-behind files, the role of ASP.NET web controls, validations controls, and interacting with the new "master page" model provided by ASP.NET 2.0.

Chapter 24: ASP.NET 2.0 Web Applications

This chapter extends your current understanding of ASP.NET by examining various ways to handle state management under .NET. Like classic ASP, ASP.NET allows you to easily create cookies, as well as application-level and session-level variables. However, ASP.NET also introduces a new state management technique: the application cache. Once you have looked at the numerous ways to handle state with ASP.NET, you will then come to learn the role of the System.HttpApplication base class (lurking within the Global.asax file) and how to dynamically alter the runtime behavior of your web application using the Web.config file.

Chapter 25: Understanding XML Web Services

This chapter examines the role of .NET XML web services. Simply put, a *web service* is an assembly that is activated using standard HTTP requests. The beauty of this approach is the fact that HTTP is the one wire protocol almost universal in its acceptance, and it is therefore an excellent choice for building platform- and language-neutral distributed systems. You will also check out numerous surrounding technologies (WSDL, SOAP, and UDDI) that enable a web service and external client to communicate in harmony.

Part 6: Programming with .NET 3.0 Extensions

The bulk of Part 6 is devoted to the new APIs introduced with .NET 3.0: WPF, WCF, and WF. In addition, you will examine the details of C# 3.0 and the LINQ programming model, both of which (at the time of this writing) are in beta.

Chapter 26: Establishing a .NET 3.0 Programming Environment

Before you can build .NET 3.0–aware software, or explore C# 3.0 and LINQ development, your very first task is to install a number of freely downloadable SDKs and Visual Studio 2005 CTP modules. In this chapter, you'll be provided with a blow-by-blow account of setting up a .NET 3.0/C# 3.0/LINQ development machine, and you'll learn how to repair a critical installation bug along the way.

Chapter 27: Introducing Windows Presentation Foundation

Windows Presentation Foundation, or simply WPF, is a brand-new model for building .NET desktop applications. This chapter takes you behind the scenes of this new API by examining the problems WPF attempts to solve, the role of desktop markup (aka XAML), and the use of code-behind files. Along the way, you will come to understand the major services found within WPF (graphical rendering, animations, etc.), examine the new control programming model, and be introduced to the concept of an XBAP application.

Chapter 28: Introducing Windows Communication Foundation

Windows Communication Foundation (WCF) is a .NET 3.0 programming API specifically geared toward the development of distributed applications. As you will learn in this chapter, WCF's major goal is to integrate a number of previously independent APIs (COM+, MSMQ, .NET remoting, XML web services, etc.) into a single unified (and extendable) object model. Although WCF is indeed a new API, you will be happy to know that your current knowledge of the .NET remoting layer (Chapter 18) and XML web services (Chapter 25) will greatly increase your understanding of what is taking place behind the curtains.

Chapter 29: Introducing Windows Workflow Foundation

Windows Workflow Foundation (WF) is the final major component of .NET 3.0. This chapter begins by defining exactly what workflows are and where you may wish to make use of them in your programming assignments. Then this chapter examines a number of WF activities, the role of the WF runtime engine, and how to make use of the Visual Studio 2005 "Orcas" workflow designer.

Chapter 30: C# 3.0 Language Features

At the time of this writing, C# 3.0 is still a beta product. However, once you have installed the correct development tools (described in Chapter 26), you are able to explore all of the new constructs you will find in the future release of .NET's flagship programming language. In this chapter, you will learn about implicitly typed local variables, object initialization syntax, extension methods, anonymous types, and the role of lambda expressions. The information presented here will be a perfect (and, quite frankly, mandatory) foundation for the final chapter of this book.

Chapter 31: An Introduction to LINQ

The final chapter of this text dives into the details of the LINQ programming model, which will be released in conjunction with C# 3.0, sometime in the middle of 2007 (or so we hope!). Simply put, LINQ attempts to provide a single symmetrical model to access "data," regardless of its location. As you will see, LINQ allows you to build query expressions (which have been purposely designed to look like SQL queries) to access and manipulate data located in arrays, collections, relational databases, and XML documents.

What's Included in the Free Bonus Download

This special edition includes bonus materials with additional content in PDF. This content includes:

- A carefully selected sampler of chapters from 18 other *Pro* and *Expert* books from the Apress library, including advanced books about ASP.NET 2.0 and SQL Server 2005. These chapters total more than 1,500 information-rich pages in eBook form, with complementary examples at http://www.apress.com.
- A full selection of our .NET 2.0 road maps that illustrate how you, the reader, can link together Apress books to chart a path for custom learning.

Obtaining This Book's Source Code

All of the code examples contained within this book (minus small code snippets here and there) are available for free and immediate download from the Source Code/Download area of the Apress website. Simply navigate to http://www.apress.com, select the Source Code/Download link, and look up this title by name. Once you are on the "homepage" for *Pro C# with .NET 3.0, Special Edition*, you may download a self-extracting *.zip file. After you unzip the contents, you will find that the code has been logically divided by chapter.

Do be aware that Source Code notes like the following in the chapters are your cue that the example under discussion may be loaded into Visual Studio 2005 for further examination and modification:

■**Source Code** This is a source code note referring you to a specific directory!

Simply double-click the `*.sln` file found in the correct subdirectory to load the project into Visual Studio 2005.

Obtaining Updates for This Book

As you read through this text, you may find an occasional grammatical or code error (although I sure hope not). If this is the case, my apologies. Being human, I am sure that a glitch or two may be present, despite my best efforts. You can obtain the current errata list from the Apress website (located once again on the "homepage" for this book) as well as information on how to notify me of any errors you might find.

Contacting Me

If you have any questions regarding this book's source code, are in need of clarification for a given example, or simply wish to offer your thoughts regarding the .NET platform, feel free to drop me a line at the following e-mail address (to ensure your messages don't end up in my junk mail folder, please include "C# SpEd" in the Subject line somewhere): `atroelsen@Intertech.com`.

  Please understand that I will do my best to get back to you in a timely fashion; however, like yourself, I get busy from time to time. If I don't respond within a week or two, do know I am not trying to be a jerk or don't care to talk to you. I'm just busy (or, if I'm lucky, on vacation somewhere).

  So, then! Thanks for buying this text (or at least looking at it in the bookstore while you try to decide if you will buy it). I hope you enjoy reading this book and putting your newfound knowledge to good use.

Take care,
Andrew Troelsen

PART 1

■ ■ ■

Introducing C# and the .NET Platform

■■■

## CHAPTER 1

The Philosophy of .NET

Every few years or so, the modern-day programmer must be willing to perform a self-inflicted knowledge transplant to stay current with the new technologies of the day. The languages (C++, Visual Basic 6.0, Java), frameworks (MFC, ATL, STL), and architectures (COM, CORBA, EJB) that were touted as the silver bullets of software development eventually become overshadowed by something better or at the very least something new. Regardless of the frustration you can feel when upgrading your internal knowledge base, it is unavoidable. The .NET platform is Microsoft's current offering within the landscape of software engineering.

The point of this chapter is to lay the conceptual groundwork for the remainder of the book. It begins with a high-level discussion of a number of .NET-related topics such as assemblies, the common intermediate language (CIL), and just-in-time (JIT) compilation. In addition to previewing some key features of the C# programming language, you will also come to understand the relationship between various aspects of the .NET Framework, such as the common language runtime (CLR), the Common Type System (CTS), and the Common Language Specification (CLS). As you would hope, all of these topics are explored in further detail throughout the remainder of this text.

This chapter also provides you with an overview of the functionality supplied by the .NET base class libraries, sometimes abbreviated as the "BCL" or alternatively as the "FCL" (being the Framework class libraries). Finally, this chapter investigates the language-agnostic and platform-independent nature of the .NET platform (yes it's true, .NET is not confined to the Windows operating system).

Understanding the Previous State of Affairs

Before examining the specifics of the .NET universe, it's helpful to consider some of the issues that motivated the genesis of Microsoft's current platform. To get in the proper mind-set, let's begin this chapter with a brief and painless history lesson to remember our roots and understand the limitations of the previous state of affairs (after all, admitting you have a problem is the first step toward finding a solution). After completing this quick tour of life as we knew it, we turn our attention to the numerous benefits provided by C# and the .NET platform.

Life As a C/Win32 API Programmer

Traditionally speaking, developing software for the Windows family of operating systems involved using the C programming language in conjunction with the Windows application programming interface (API). While it is true that numerous applications have been successfully created using this time-honored approach, few of us would disagree that building applications using the raw API is a complex undertaking.

The first obvious problem is that C is a very terse language. C developers are forced to contend with manual memory management, ugly pointer arithmetic, and ugly syntactical constructs. Furthermore, given that C is a structured language, it lacks the benefits provided by the object-oriented approach (can anyone say *spaghetti code*?) When you combine the thousands of global functions and data types defined by the Win32 API to an already formidable language, it is little wonder that there are so many buggy applications floating around today.

Life As a C++/MFC Programmer

One vast improvement over raw C/API development is the use of the C++ programming language. In many ways, C++ can be thought of as an object-oriented *layer* on top of C. Thus, even though C++ programmers benefit from the famed "pillars of OOP" (encapsulation, inheritance, and poly-morphism), they are still at the mercy of the painful aspects of the C language (e.g., manual memory management, ugly pointer arithmetic, and ugly syntactical constructs).

Despite its complexity, many C++ frameworks exist today. For example, the Microsoft Foundation Classes (MFC) provides the developer with a set of C++ classes that facilitate the construction of Win32 applications. The main role of MFC is to wrap a "sane subset" of the raw Win32 API behind a number of classes, magic macros, and numerous code-generation tools (aka *wizards*). Regardless of the helpful assistance offered by the MFC framework (as well as many other C++-based windowing toolkits), the fact of the matter is that C++ programming remains a difficult and error-prone experience, given its historical roots in C.

Life As a Visual Basic 6.0 Programmer

Due to a heartfelt desire to enjoy a simpler lifestyle, many programmers have shifted away from the world of C(++)-based frameworks to kinder, gentler languages such as Visual Basic 6.0 (VB6). VB6 is popular due to its ability to build complex user interfaces, code libraries (e.g., COM servers), and data access logic with minimal fuss and bother. Even more than MFC, VB6 hides the complexities of the raw Win32 API from view using a number of integrated code wizards, intrinsic data types, classes, and VB-specific functions.

The major downfall of VB6 (which has been rectified given the advent of Visual Basic .NET) is that it is not a fully object-oriented language; rather, it is "object aware." For example, VB6 does not allow the programmer to establish "is-a" relationships between types (i.e., no classical inheritance) and has no intrinsic support for parameterized class construction. Moreover, VB6 doesn't provide the ability to build multithreaded applications unless you are willing to drop down to low-level Win32 API calls (which is complex at best and dangerous at worst).

Life As a Java/J2EE Programmer

Enter Java. The Java programming language is (almost) completely object oriented and has its syntac-tic roots in C++. As many of you are aware, Java's strengths are far greater than its support for platform independence. Java (as a language) cleans up many unsavory syntactical aspects of C++. Java (as a platform) provides programmers with a large number of predefined "packages" that contain various type definitions. Using these types, Java programmers are able to build "100% Pure Java" applications complete with database connectivity, messaging support, web-enabled front ends, and a rich user interface.

Although Java is a very elegant language, one potential problem is that using Java typically means that you must use Java front-to-back during the development cycle. In effect, Java offers little hope of language integration, as this goes against the grain of Java's primary goal (a single program-ming language for every need). In reality, however, there are millions of lines of existing code out there in the world that would ideally like to commingle with newer Java code. Sadly, Java makes this task problematic.

Pure Java is simply not appropriate for many graphically or numerically intensive applications (in these cases, you may find Java's execution speed leaves something to be desired). A better approach for such programs would be to use a lower-level language (such as C++) where appropriate. Alas, while Java does provide a limited ability to access non-Java APIs, there is little support for true cross-language integration.

Life As a COM Programmer

The Component Object Model (COM) was Microsoft's previous application development framework. COM is an architecture that says in effect, "If you build your classes in accordance with the rules of COM, you end up with a block of *reusable binary code.*"

The beauty of a binary COM server is that it can be accessed in a language-independent manner. Thus, C++ programmers can build COM classes that can be used by VB6. Delphi programmers can use COM classes built using C, and so forth. However, as you may be aware, COM's language independence is somewhat limited. For example, there is no way to derive a new COM class using an existing COM class (as COM has no support for classical inheritance). Rather, you must make use of the more cumbersome "has-a" relationship to reuse COM class types.

Another benefit of COM is its location-transparent nature. Using constructs such as application identifiers (AppIDs), stubs, proxies, and the COM runtime environment, programmers can avoid the need to work with raw sockets, RPC calls, and other low-level details. For example, consider the following VB6 COM client code:

```
' This block of VB6 code can activate a COM class written in
' any COM-aware language, which may be located anywhere
' on the network (including your local machine).
Dim c as MyCOMClass
Set c = New MyCOMClass     ' Location resolved using AppID.
c.DoSomeWork
```

Although COM can be considered a very successful object model, it is extremely complex under the hood (at least until you have spent many months exploring its plumbing—especially if you happen to be a C++ programmer). To help simplify the development of COM binaries, numerous COM-aware frameworks have come into existence. For example, the Active Template Library (ATL) provides another set of C++ classes, templates, and macros to ease the creation of COM types.

Many other languages also hide a good part of the COM infrastructure from view. However, language support alone is not enough to hide the complexity of COM. Even when you choose a relatively simply COM-aware language such as VB6, you are still forced to contend with fragile registration entries and numerous deployment-related issues (collectively termed *DLL hell*).

Life As a Windows DNA Programmer

To further complicate matters, there is a little thing called the Internet. Over the last several years, Microsoft has been adding more Internet-aware features into its family of operating systems and products. Sadly, building a web application using COM-based Windows Distributed interNet Applications Architecture (DNA) is also quite complex.

Some of this complexity is due to the simple fact that Windows DNA requires the use of numerous technologies and languages (ASP, HTML, XML, JavaScript, VBScript, and COM(+), as well as a data access API such as ADO). One problem is that many of these technologies are completely unrelated from a syntactic point of view. For example, JavaScript has a syntax much like C, while VBScript is a subset of VB6. The COM servers that are created to run under the COM+ runtime have an entirely different look and feel from the ASP pages that invoke them. The result is a highly confused mishmash of technologies.

Furthermore, and perhaps more important, each language and/or technology has its own type system (that may look nothing like another's type system). An "int" in JavaScript is not quite the same as an "Integer" in VB6.

The .NET Solution

So much for the brief history lesson. The bottom line is that life as a Windows programmer has been tough. The .NET Framework is a rather radical and brute-force approach to making our lives easier. The solution proposed by .NET is "Change everything" (sorry, you can't blame the messenger for the message). As you will see during the remainder of this book, the .NET Framework is a completely new model for building systems on the Windows family of operating systems, as well as on numerous non-Microsoft operating systems such as Mac OS X and various Unix/Linux distributions. To set the stage, here is a quick rundown of some core features provided courtesy of .NET:

- *Full interoperability with existing code*: This is (of course) a good thing. Existing COM binaries can commingle (i.e., interop) with newer .NET binaries and vice versa. Also, Platform Invocation Services (PInvoke) allows you to call C-based libraries (including the underlying API of the operating system) from .NET code.

- *Complete and total language integration*: Unlike COM, .NET supports cross-language inheritance, cross-language exception handling, and cross-language debugging.

- *A common runtime engine shared by all .NET-aware languages*: One aspect of this engine is a well-defined set of types that each .NET-aware language "understands."

- *A base class library*: This library provides shelter from the complexities of raw API calls and offers a consistent object model used by all .NET-aware languages.

- *No more COM plumbing*: IClassFactory, IUnknown, IDispatch, IDL code, and the evil VARIANT-compliant data types (BSTR, SAFEARRAY, and so forth) have no place in a native .NET binary.

- *A truly simplified deployment model*: Under .NET, there is no need to register a binary unit into the system registry. Furthermore, .NET allows multiple versions of the same *.dll to exist in harmony on a single machine.

As you can most likely gather from the previous bullet points, the .NET platform has nothing to do with COM (beyond the fact that both frameworks originated from Microsoft). In fact, the only way .NET and COM types can interact with each other is using the interoperability layer.

■**Note** Coverage of the .NET interoperability layer (including PInvoke) is beyond the scope of this book. If you require a detailed treatment of these topics, check out my book *COM and .NET Interoperability* (Apress, 2002).

Introducing the Building Blocks of the .NET Platform (the CLR, CTS, and CLS)

Now that you know some of the benefits provided by .NET, let's preview three key (and interrelated) entities that make it all possible: the CLR, CTS, and CLS. From a programmer's point of view, .NET can be understood as a new runtime environment and a comprehensive base class library. The runtime layer is properly referred to as the *common language runtime*, or *CLR*. The primary role of the CLR is to locate, load, and manage .NET types on your behalf. The CLR also takes care of a number of low-level details such as memory management and performing security checks.

Another building block of the .NET platform is the *Common Type System*, or *CTS*. The CTS specification fully describes all possible data types and programming constructs supported by the runtime, specifies how these entities can interact with each other, and details how they are represented in the .NET metadata format (more information on metadata later in this chapter).

Understand that a given .NET-aware language might not support each and every feature defined by the CTS. The *Common Language Specification* (*CLS*) is a related specification that defines a subset of common types and programming constructs that all .NET programming languages can agree on. Thus, if you build .NET types that only expose CLS-compliant features, you can rest assured that all .NET-aware languages can consume them. Conversely, if you make use of a data type or programming construct that is outside of the bounds of the CLS, you cannot guarantee that every .NET programming language can interact with your .NET code library.

The Role of the Base Class Libraries

In addition to the CLR and CTS/CLS specifications, the .NET platform provides a base class library that is available to all .NET programming languages. Not only does this base class library encapsulate various primitives such as threads, file input/output (I/O), graphical rendering, and interaction with various external hardware devices, but it also provides support for a number of services required by most real-world applications.

For example, the base class libraries define types that facilitate database access, XML manipulation, programmatic security, and the construction of web-enabled (as well as traditional desktop and console-based) front ends. From a high level, you can visualize the relationship between the CLR, CTS, CLS, and the base class library, as shown in Figure 1-1.

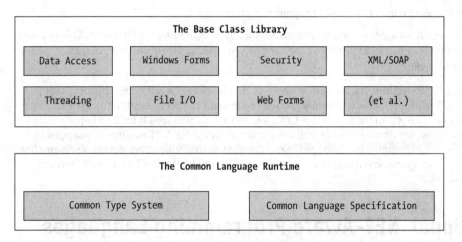

Figure 1-1. *The CLR, CTS, CLS, and base class library relationship*

What C# Brings to the Table

Given that .NET is such a radical departure from previous technologies, Microsoft has developed a new programming language, C# (pronounced "see sharp"), specifically for this new platform. C# is a programming language that looks *very* similar (but not identical) to the syntax of Java. However, to call C# a Java rip-off is inaccurate. Both C# and Java are based on the syntactical constructs of C++. Just as Java is in many ways a cleaned-up version of C++, C# can be viewed as a cleaned-up version of Java—after all, they are all in the same family of languages.

The truth of the matter is that many of C#'s syntactic constructs are modeled after various aspects of Visual Basic 6.0 and C++. For example, like VB6, C# supports the notion of formal type properties (as opposed to traditional getter and setter methods) and the ability to declare methods taking varying number of arguments (via parameter arrays). Like C++, C# allows you to overload operators, as well as to create structures, enumerations, and callback functions (via delegates).

Due to the fact that C# is a hybrid of numerous languages, the result is a product that is as syntactically clean—if not cleaner—than Java, is about as simple as VB6, and provides just about as much power and flexibility as C++ (without the associated ugly bits). In a nutshell, the C# language offers the following features (many of which are shared by other .NET-aware programming languages):

- No pointers required! C# programs typically have no need for direct pointer manipulation (although you are free to drop down to that level if absolutely necessary).

- Automatic memory management through garbage collection. Given this, C# does not support a delete keyword.

- Formal syntactic constructs for enumerations, structures, and class properties.

- The C++-like ability to overload operators for a custom type, without the complexity (e.g., making sure to "return *this to allow chaining" is not your problem).

- As of C# 2005, the ability to build generic types and generic members using a syntax very similar to C++ templates.

- Full support for interface-based programming techniques.

- Full support for aspect-oriented programming (AOP) techniques via attributes. This brand of development allows you to assign characteristics to types and their members to further qualify their behavior.

Perhaps the most important point to understand about the C# language shipped with the Microsoft .NET platform is that it can only produce code that can execute within the .NET runtime (you could never use C# to build a native COM server or a unmanaged Win32 API application). Officially speaking, the term used to describe the code targeting the .NET runtime is *managed code*. The binary unit that contains the managed code is termed an *assembly* (more details on assemblies in just a bit). Conversely, code that cannot be directly hosted by the .NET runtime is termed *unmanaged code*.

Additional .NET-Aware Programming Languages

Understand that C# is not the only language targeting the .NET platform. When the .NET platform was first revealed to the general public during the 2000 Microsoft Professional Developers Conference (PDC), several vendors announced they were busy building .NET-aware versions of their respective compilers. At the time of this writing, dozens of different languages have undergone .NET enlightenment. In addition to the five languages that ship with Visual Studio 2005 (C#, J#, Visual Basic .NET, Managed Extensions for C++, and JScript .NET), there are .NET compilers for Smalltalk, COBOL, and Pascal (to name a few).

Although this book focuses (almost) exclusively on C#, Table 1-1 lists a number of .NET-enabled programming languages and where to learn more about them (do note that these URLs are subject to change).

Table 1-1. *A Sampling of .NET-Aware Programming Languages*

.NET Language Web Link	Meaning in Life
`http://www.oberon.ethz.ch/oberon.net`	Homepage for Active Oberon .NET.
`http://www.usafa.af.mil/df/dfcs/bios/mcc_html/a_sharp.cfm`	Homepage for A# (a port of Ada to the .NET platform).
`http://www.netcobol.com`	For those interested in COBOL .NET.
`http://www.eiffel.com`	For those interested in Eiffel .NET.
`http://www.dataman.ro/dforth`	For those interested in Forth .NET.
`http://www.silverfrost.com/11/ftn95/ftn95_fortran_95_for_windows.asp`	For those interested in Fortran .NET.
`http://www.vmx-net.com`	Yes, even Smalltalk .NET is available.

Please be aware that Table 1-1 is not exhaustive. Numerous websites maintain a list of .NET-aware compilers, one of which would be `http://www.dotnetpowered.com/languages.aspx` (again, the exact URL is subject to change). I encourage you to visit this page, as you are sure to find many .NET languages worth investigating (LISP .NET, anyone?).

Life in a Multilanguage World

As developers first come to understand the language-agnostic nature of .NET, numerous questions arise. The most prevalent of these questions would have to be, "If all .NET languages compile down to 'managed code,' why do we need more than one compiler?" There are a number of ways to answer this question. First, we programmers are a *very* particular lot when it comes to our choice of programming language (myself included). Some of us prefer languages full of semicolons and curly brackets, with as few language keywords as possible. Others enjoy a language that offers more "human-readable" syntactic tokens (such as Visual Basic .NET). Still others may want to leverage their mainframe skills while moving to the .NET platform (via COBOL .NET).

Now, be honest. If Microsoft were to build a single "official" .NET language that was derived from the BASIC family of languages, can you really say all programmers would be happy with this choice? Or, if the only "official" .NET language was based on Fortran syntax, imagine all the folks out there who would ignore .NET altogether. Because the .NET runtime couldn't care less which language was used to build a block of managed code, .NET programmers can stay true to their syntactic preferences, and share the compiled assemblies among teammates, departments, and external organizations (regardless of which .NET language others choose to use).

Another excellent byproduct of integrating various .NET languages into a single unified software solution is the simple fact that all programming languages have their own sets of strengths and weaknesses. For example, some programming languages offer excellent intrinsic support for advanced mathematical processing. Others offer superior support for financial calculations, logical calculations, interaction with mainframe computers, and so forth. When you take the strengths of a particular programming language and then incorporate the benefits provided by the .NET platform, everybody wins.

Of course, in reality the chances are quite good that you will spend much of your time building software using your .NET language of choice. However, once you learn the syntax of one .NET language, it is very easy to master another. This is also quite beneficial, especially to the consultants of the world. If your language of choice happens to be C#, but you are placed at a client site that has committed to Visual Basic .NET, you should be able to parse the existing code body almost instantly (honest!) while still continuing to leverage the .NET Framework. Enough said.

An Overview of .NET Assemblies

Regardless of which .NET language you choose to program with, understand that despite the fact that .NET binaries take the same file extension as COM servers and unmanaged Win32 binaries (*.dll or *.exe), they have absolutely no internal similarities. For example, *.dll .NET binaries do not export methods to facilitate communications with the COM runtime (given that .NET is *not* COM). Furthermore, .NET binaries are not described using COM type libraries and are not registered into the system registry. Perhaps most important, .NET binaries do not contain platform-specific instructions, but rather platform-agnostic *intermediate language* (*IL*) and type metadata. Figure 1-2 shows the big picture of the story thus far.

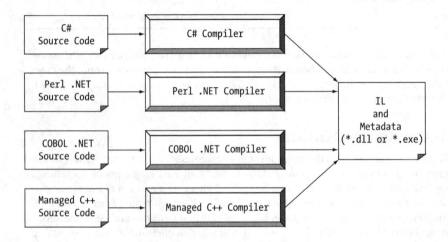

Figure 1-2. *All .NET-aware compilers emit IL instructions and metadata.*

■**Note** There is one point to be made regarding the abbreviation "IL." During the development of .NET, the official term for IL was Microsoft intermediate language (MSIL). However with the final release of .NET, the term was changed to common intermediate language (CIL). Thus, as you read the .NET literature, understand that IL, MSIL, and CIL are all describing the same exact entity. In keeping with the current terminology, I will use the abbreviation "CIL" throughout this text.

When a *.dll or *.exe has been created using a .NET-aware compiler, the resulting module is bundled into an *assembly*. You will examine numerous details of .NET assemblies in Chapter 11. However, to facilitate the discussion of the .NET runtime environment, you do need to understand some basic properties of this new file format.

As mentioned, an assembly contains CIL code, which is conceptually similar to Java bytecode in that it is not compiled to platform-specific instructions until absolutely necessary. Typically, "absolutely necessary" is the point at which a block of CIL instructions (such as a method implementation) is referenced for use by the .NET runtime.

In addition to CIL instructions, assemblies also contain *metadata* that describes in vivid detail the characteristics of every "type" living within the binary. For example, if you have a class named SportsCar, the type metadata describes details such as SportsCar's base class, which interfaces are implemented by SportsCar (if any), as well as a full description of each member supported by the SportsCar type.

.NET metadata is a dramatic improvement to COM type metadata. As you may already know, COM binaries are typically described using an associated type library (which is little more than a binary version of Interface Definition Language [IDL] code). The problems with COM type information are that it is not guaranteed to be present and the fact that IDL code has no way to document the externally referenced servers that are required for the correct operation of the current COM server. In contrast, .NET metadata is always present and is automatically generated by a given .NET-aware compiler.

Finally, in addition to CIL and type metadata, assemblies themselves are also described using metadata, which is officially termed a *manifest*. The manifest contains information about the current version of the assembly, culture information (used for localizing string and image resources), and a list of all externally referenced assemblies that are required for proper execution. You'll examine various tools that can be used to examine an assembly's types, metadata, and manifest information over the course of the next few chapters.

Single-File and Multifile Assemblies

In a great number of cases, there is a simple one-to-one correspondence between a .NET assembly and the binary file (*.dll or *.exe). Thus, if you are building a .NET *.dll, it is safe to consider that the binary and the assembly are one and the same. Likewise, if you are building an executable desktop application, the *.exe can simply be referred to as the assembly itself. As you'll see in Chapter 11, however, this is not completely accurate. Technically speaking, if an assembly is composed of a single *.dll or *.exe module, you have a *single-file assembly*. Single-file assemblies contain all the necessary CIL, metadata, and associated manifest in an autonomous, single, well-defined package.

Multifile assemblies, on the other hand, are composed of numerous .NET binaries, each of which is termed a *module*. When building a multifile assembly, one of these modules (termed the *primary module*) must contain the assembly manifest (and possibly CIL instructions and metadata for various types). The other related modules contain a module level manifest, CIL, and type metadata. As you might suspect, the primary module documents the set of required secondary modules within the assembly manifest.

So, why would you choose to create a multifile assembly? When you partition an assembly into discrete modules, you end up with a more flexible deployment option. For example, if a user is referencing a remote assembly that needs to be downloaded onto his or her machine, the runtime will only download the required modules. Therefore, you are free to construct your assembly in such a way that less frequently required types (such as a type named HardDriveReformatter) are kept in a separate stand-alone module.

In contrast, if all your types were placed in a single-file assembly, the end user may end up downloading a large chunk of data that is not really needed (which is obviously a waste of time). Thus, as you can see, an assembly is really a *logical grouping* of one or more related modules that are intended to be initially deployed and versioned as a single unit.

The Role of the Common Intermediate Language

Now that you have a better feel for .NET assemblies, let's examine the role of the common intermediate language (CIL) in a bit more detail. CIL is a language that sits above any particular platform-specific instruction set. Regardless of which .NET-aware language you choose, the associated compiler emits CIL instructions. For example, the following C# code models a trivial calculator. Don't concern yourself with the exact syntax for now, but do notice the format of the Add() method in the Calc class:

```
// Calc.cs
using System;

namespace CalculatorExample
{
    // This class contains the app's entry point.
    public class CalcApp
    {
        static void Main()
        {
            Calc c = new Calc();
            int ans = c.Add(10, 84);
            Console.WriteLine("10 + 84 is {0}.", ans);

            // Wait for user to press the Enter key before shutting down.
            Console.ReadLine();
        }
    }

    // The C# calculator.
    public class Calc
    {
        public int Add(int x, int y)
        { return x + y; }
    }
}
```

Once the C# compiler (csc.exe) compiles this source code file, you end up with a single-file
*.exe assembly that contains a manifest, CIL instructions, and metadata describing each aspect of
the Calc and CalcApp classes. For example, if you were to open this assembly using ildasm.exe
(examined a little later in this chapter), you would find that the Add() method is represented using
CIL such as the following:

```
.method public hidebysig instance int32  Add(int32 x, int32 y) cil managed
{
    // Code size       8 (0x8)
    .maxstack  2
    .locals init ([0] int32 CS$1$0000)
    IL_0000:  ldarg.1
    IL_0001:  ldarg.2
    IL_0002:  add
    IL_0003:  stloc.0
    IL_0004:  br.s       IL_0006
    IL_0006:  ldloc.0
    IL_0007:  ret
} // end of method Calc::Add
```

Don't worry if you are unable to make heads or tails of the resulting CIL for this method—
Chapter 15 will describe the basics of the CIL programming language. The point to concentrate on
is that the C# compiler emits CIL, not platform-specific instructions.

Now, recall that this is true of all .NET-aware compilers. To illustrate, assume you created this
same application using Visual Basic .NET (VB .NET), rather than C#:

```
' Calc.vb
Imports System

Namespace CalculatorExample
    ' A VB .NET 'Module' is a class that only contains
    ' static members.
    Module CalcApp
        Sub Main()
            Dim ans As Integer
            Dim c As New Calc
            ans = c.Add(10, 84)
            Console.WriteLine("10 + 84 is {0}.", ans)
            Console.ReadLine()
        End Sub
    End Module

    Class Calc
        Public Function Add(ByVal x As Integer, ByVal y As Integer) As Integer
            Return x + y
        End Function
    End Class
End Namespace
```

If you examine the CIL for the Add() method, you find similar instructions (slightly tweaked by the VB .NET compiler):

```
.method public instance int32  Add(int32 x, int32 y) cil managed
{
  // Code size       9 (0x9)
  .maxstack  2
  .locals init ([0] int32 Add)
  IL_0000:  nop
  IL_0001:  ldarg.1
  IL_0002:  ldarg.2
  IL_0003:  add.ovf
  IL_0004:  stloc.0
  IL_0005:  br.s       IL_0007
  IL_0007:  ldloc.0
  IL_0008:  ret
} // end of method Calc::Add
```

Benefits of CIL

At this point, you might be wondering exactly what is gained by compiling source code into CIL rather than directly to a specific instruction set. One benefit is language integration. As you have already seen, each .NET-aware compiler produces nearly identical CIL instructions. Therefore, all languages are able to interact within a well-defined binary arena.

Furthermore, given that CIL is platform-agnostic, the .NET Framework itself is platform-agnostic, providing the same benefits Java developers have grown accustomed to (i.e., a single code base running on numerous operating systems). In fact, there is an international standard for the C# language, and a large subset of the .NET platform and implementations already exist for many non-Windows operating systems (more details at the conclusion of this chapter). In contrast to Java, however, .NET allows you to build applications using your language of choice.

Compiling CIL to Platform-Specific Instructions

Due to the fact that assemblies contain CIL instructions, rather than platform-specific instructions, CIL code must be compiled on the fly before use. The entity that compiles CIL code into meaningful CPU instructions is termed a *just-in-time* (*JIT*) *compiler*, which sometimes goes by the friendly name of *Jitter*. The .NET runtime environment leverages a JIT compiler for each CPU targeting the runtime, each optimized for the underlying platform.

For example, if you are building a .NET application that is to be deployed to a handheld device (such as a Pocket PC), the corresponding Jitter is well equipped to run within a low-memory environment. On the other hand, if you are deploying your assembly to a back-end server (where memory is seldom an issue), the Jitter will be optimized to function in a high-memory environment. In this way, developers can write a single body of code that can be efficiently JIT-compiled and executed on machines with different architectures.

Furthermore, as a given Jitter compiles CIL instructions into corresponding machine code, it will cache the results in memory in a manner suited to the target operating system. In this way, if a call is made to a method named PrintDocument(), the CIL instructions are compiled into platform-specific instructions on the first invocation and retained in memory for later use. Therefore, the next time PrintDocument() is called, there is no need to recompile the CIL.

The Role of .NET Type Metadata

In addition to CIL instructions, a .NET assembly contains full, complete, and accurate metadata, which describes each and every type (class, structure, enumeration, and so forth) defined in the binary, as well as the members of each type (properties, methods, events, and so on). Thankfully, it is always the job of the compiler (not the programmer) to emit the latest and greatest type metadata. Because .NET metadata is so wickedly meticulous, assemblies are completely self-describing entities—so much so, in fact, that .NET binaries have no need to be registered into the system registry.

To illustrate the format of .NET type metadata, let's take a look at the metadata that has been generated for the Add() method of the C# Calc class you examined previously (the metadata generated for the VB .NET version of the Add() method is similar):

```
TypeDef #2 (02000003)
-------------------------------------------------------
  TypDefName: CalculatorExample.Calc  (02000003)
  Flags     : [Public] [AutoLayout] [Class]
  [AnsiClass] [BeforeFieldInit]  (00100001)
  Extends   : 01000001 [TypeRef] System.Object
  Method #1 (06000003)
-------------------------------------------------------
  MethodName: Add (06000003)
  Flags     : [Public] [HideBySig] [ReuseSlot]  (00000086)
  RVA       : 0x00002090
  ImplFlags : [IL] [Managed]  (00000000)
  CallCnvntn: [DEFAULT]
  hasThis
  ReturnType: I4
    2 Arguments
    Argument #1:  I4
    Argument #2:  I4
    2 Parameters
    (1) ParamToken : (08000001) Name : x flags: [none] (00000000)
    (2) ParamToken : (08000002) Name : y flags: [none] (00000000)
```

Metadata is used by numerous aspects of the .NET runtime environment, as well as by various development tools. For example, the IntelliSense feature provided by Visual Studio 2005 is made possible by reading an assembly's metadata at design time. Metadata is also used by various object browsing utilities, debugging tools, and the C# compiler itself. To be sure, metadata is the backbone of numerous .NET technologies including remoting, reflection, late binding, XML web services, and object serialization.

The Role of the Assembly Manifest

Last but not least, remember that a .NET assembly also contains metadata that describes the assembly itself (technically termed a *manifest*). Among other details, the manifest documents all external assemblies required by the current assembly to function correctly, the assembly's version number, copyright information, and so forth. Like type metadata, it is always the job of the compiler to generate the assembly's manifest. Here are some relevant details of the CSharpCalculator.exe manifest:

```
.assembly extern mscorlib
{
  .publickeytoken = (B7 7A 5C 56 19 34 E0 89 )
  .ver 2:0:0:0
}
.assembly CSharpCalculator
{
  .hash algorithm 0x00008004
  .ver 0:0:0:0
}
.module CSharpCalculator.exe
.imagebase 0x00400000
.subsystem 0x00000003
.file alignment 512
.corflags 0x00000001
```

In a nutshell, this manifest documents the list of external assemblies required by CSharpCalculator.exe (via the .assembly extern directive) as well as various characteristics of the assembly itself (version number, module name, and so on).

Understanding the Common Type System

A given assembly may contain any number of distinct "types." In the world of .NET, "type" is simply a generic term used to refer to a member from the set {class, structure, interface, enumeration, delegate}. When you build solutions using a .NET-aware language, you will most likely interact with each of these types. For example, your assembly may define a single class that implements some number of interfaces. Perhaps one of the interface methods takes an enumeration type as an input parameter and returns a structure to the caller.

Recall that the Common Type System (CTS) is a formal specification that documents how types must be defined in order to be hosted by the CLR. Typically, the only individuals who are deeply concerned with the inner workings of the CTS are those building tools and/or compilers that target the .NET platform. It is important, however, for all .NET programmers to learn about how to work with the five types defined by the CTS in their language of choice. Here is a brief overview.

CTS Class Types

Every .NET-aware language supports, at the very least, the notion of a *class type*, which is the corner-stone of object-oriented programming (OOP). A class may be composed of any number of members (such as properties, methods, and events) and data points (fields). In C#, classes are declared using the class keyword:

```
// A C# class type.
public class Calc
{
    public int Add(int x, int y)
    { return x + y; }
}
```

Chapter 4 examines the process of building CTS class types with C#; however, Table 1-2 documents a number of characteristics pertaining to class types.

Table 1-2. *CTS Class Characteristics*

Class Characteristic	Meaning in Life
Is the class "sealed" or not?	Sealed classes cannot function as a base class to other classes.
Does the class implement any interfaces?	An *interface* is a collection of abstract members that provide a contract between the object and object user. The CTS allows a class to implement any number of interfaces.
Is the class abstract or concrete?	*Abstract* classes cannot be directly created, but are intended to define common behaviors for derived types. *Concrete* classes can be created directly.
What is the "visibility" of this class?	Each class must be configured with a visibility attribute. Basically, this trait defines if the class may be used by external assemblies, or only from within the defining assembly (e.g., a private helper class).

CTS Structure Types

The concept of a structure is also formalized under the CTS. If you have a C background, you should be pleased to know that these user-defined types (UDTs) have survived in the world of .NET (although they behave a bit differently under the hood). Simply put, a *structure* can be thought of as a lightweight class type having value-based semantics. For more details on the subtleties of structures, see Chapter 3. Typically, structures are best suited for modeling geometric and mathematical data, and are created in C# using the struct keyword:

```
// A C# structure type.
struct Point
{
    // Structures can contain fields.
    public int xPos, yPos;

    // Structures can contain parameterized constructors.
    public Point(int x, int y)
    { xPos = x; yPos = y;}

    // Structures may define methods.
    public void Display()
    {
        Console.WriteLine("({0}, {1}", xPos, yPos);
    }
}
```

CTS Interface Types

Interfaces are nothing more than a named collection of abstract member definitions, which may be supported (i.e., implemented) by a given class or structure. Unlike COM, .NET interfaces do *not* derive a common base interface such as IUnknown. In C#, interface types are defined using the interface keyword, for example:

```
// A C# interface type.
public interface IDraw
{
    void Draw();
}
```

On their own, interfaces are of little use. However, when a class or structure implements a given interface in its unique way, you are able to request access to the supplied functionality using an interface reference in a polymorphic manner. Interface-based programming will be fully explored in Chapter 7.

CTS Enumeration Types

Enumerations are a handy programming construct that allows you to group name/value pairs. For example, assume you are creating a video-game application that allows the player to select one of three character categories (Wizard, Fighter, or Thief). Rather than keeping track of raw numerical values to represent each possibility, you could build a custom enumeration using the enum keyword:

```
// A C# enumeration type.
public enum CharacterType
{
    Wizard = 100,
    Fighter = 200,
    Thief = 300
}
```

By default, the storage used to hold each item is a 32-bit integer; however, it is possible to alter this storage slot if need be (e.g., when programming for a low-memory device such as a Pocket PC). Also, the CTS demands that enumerated types derive from a common base class, System.Enum. As you will see in Chapter 3, this base class defines a number of interesting members that allow you to extract, manipulate, and transform the underlying name/value pairs programmatically.

CTS Delegate Types

Delegates are the .NET equivalent of a type-safe C-style function pointer. The key difference is that a .NET delegate is a *class* that derives from System.MulticastDelegate, rather than a simple pointer to a raw memory address. In C#, delegates are declared using the delegate keyword:

```
// This C# delegate type can 'point to' any method
// returning an integer and taking two integers as input.
public delegate int BinaryOp(int x, int y);
```

Delegates are useful when you wish to provide a way for one entity to forward a call to another entity, and provide the foundation for the .NET event architecture. As you will see in Chapters 8 and 14, delegates have intrinsic support for multicasting (i.e., forwarding a request to multiple recipients) and asynchronous method invocations.

CTS Type Members

Now that you have previewed each of the types formalized by the CTS, realize that most types take any number of *members*. Formally speaking, a *type member* is constrained by the set {constructor, finalizer, static constructor, nested type, operator, method, property, indexer, field, read only field, constant, event}.

The CTS defines various "adornments" that may be associated with a given member. For example, each member has a given visibility trait (e.g., public, private, protected, and so forth). Some members may be declared as abstract to enforce a polymorphic behavior on derived types as well as virtual to define a canned (but overridable) implementation. Also, most members may be configured as static (bound at the class level) or instance (bound at the object level). The construction of type members is examined over the course of the next several chapters.

■**Note** As described in Chapter 10, .NET 2.0 supports the construction of generic types and generic members.

Intrinsic CTS Data Types

The final aspect of the CTS to be aware of for the time being is that it establishes a well-defined set of core data types. Although a given language typically has a unique keyword used to declare an intrinsic CTS data type, all language keywords ultimately resolve to the same type defined in an assembly named mscorlib.dll. Consider Table 1-3, which documents how key CTS data types are expressed in various .NET languages.

Table 1-3. *The Intrinsic CTS Data Types*

CTS Data Type	VB .NET Keyword	C# Keyword	Managed Extensions for C++ Keyword
System.Byte	Byte	byte	unsigned char
System.SByte	SByte	sbyte	signed char
System.Int16	Short	short	short
System.Int32	Integer	int	int or long
System.Int64	Long	long	__int64
System.UInt16	UShort	ushort	unsigned short
System.UInt32	UInteger	uint	unsigned int or unsigned long
System.UInt64	ULong	ulong	unsigned __int64
System.Single	Single	float	Float
System.Double	Double	double	Double
System.Object	Object	object	Object^
System.Char	Char	char	wchar_t
System.String	String	string	String^
System.Decimal	Decimal	decimal	Decimal
System.Boolean	Boolean	bool	Bool

Understanding the Common Language Specification

As you are aware, different languages express the same programming constructs in unique, language-specific terms. For example, in C# you denote string concatenation using the plus operator (+), while in VB .NET you typically make use of the ampersand (&). Even when two distinct languages express the same programmatic idiom (e.g., a function with no return value), the chances are very good that the syntax will appear quite different on the surface:

```
' VB .NET method returning nothing.
Public Sub MyMethod()
    ' Some interesting code...
End Sub

// C# method returning nothing.
public void MyMethod()
{
    // Some interesting code...
}
```

As you have already seen, these minor syntactic variations are inconsequential in the eyes of the .NET runtime, given that the respective compilers (vbc.exe or csc.exe, in this case) emit a similar set of CIL instructions. However, languages can also differ with regard to their overall level of functionality. For example, a .NET language may or may not have a keyword to represent unsigned data, and may or may not support pointer types. Given these possible variations, it would be ideal to have a baseline to which all .NET-aware languages are expected to conform.

The Common Language Specification (CLS) is a set of rules that describe in vivid detail the minimal and complete set of features a given .NET-aware compiler must support to produce code that can be hosted by the CLR, while at the same time be accessed in a uniform manner by all languages that target the .NET platform. In many ways, the CLS can be viewed as a *subset* of the full functionality defined by the CTS.

The CLS is ultimately a set of rules that compiler builders must conform to, if they intend their products to function seamlessly within the .NET universe. Each rule is assigned a simple name (e.g., "CLS Rule 6") and describes how this rule affects those who build the compilers as well as those who (in some way) interact with them. The crème de la crème of the CLS is the mighty Rule 1:

- *Rule 1*: CLS rules apply only to those parts of a type that are exposed outside the defining assembly.

Given this rule, you can (correctly) infer that the remaining rules of the CLS do not apply to the logic used to build the inner workings of a .NET type. The only aspects of a type that must conform to the CLS are the member definitions themselves (i.e., naming conventions, parameters, and return types). The implementation logic for a member may use any number of non-CLS techniques, as the outside world won't know the difference.

To illustrate, the following Add() method is not CLS-compliant, as the parameters and return values make use of unsigned data (which is not a requirement of the CLS):

```
public class Calc
{
    // Exposed unsigned data is not CLS compliant!
    public ulong Add(ulong x, ulong y)
    { return x + y;}
}
```

However, if you were to simply make use of unsigned data internally as follows:

```
public class Calc
{
    public int Add(int x, int y)
    {
        // As this ulong variable is only used internally,
        // we are still CLS compliant.
        ulong temp;
        ...
        return x + y;
    }
}
```

you have still conformed to the rules of the CLS, and can rest assured that all .NET languages are able to invoke the Add() method.

Of course, in addition to Rule 1, the CLS defines numerous other rules. For example, the CLS describes how a given language must represent text strings, how enumerations should be represented internally (the base type used for storage), how to define static members, and so forth. Luckily, you don't have to commit these rules to memory to be a proficient .NET developer. Again, by and large, an intimate understanding of the CTS and CLS specifications is only of interest to tool/compiler builders.

Ensuring CLS Compliance

As you will see over the course of this book, C# does define a number of programming constructs that are not CLS-compliant. The good news, however, is that you can instruct the C# compiler to check your code for CLS compliance using a single .NET attribute:

```
// Tell the C# compiler to check for CLS compliance.
[assembly: System.CLSCompliant(true)]
```

Chapter 12 dives into the details of attribute-based programming. Until then, simply understand that the [CLSCompliant] attribute will instruct the C# compiler to check each and every line of code against the rules of the CLS. If any CLS violations are discovered, you receive a compiler error and a description of the offending code.

Understanding the Common Language Runtime

In addition to the CTS and CLS specifications, the final TLA (three letter abbreviation) to contend with at the moment is the CLR. Programmatically speaking, the term *runtime* can be understood as a collection of external services that are required to execute a given compiled unit of code. For example, when developers make use of the Microsoft Foundation Classes (MFC) to create a new application, they are aware that their program requires the MFC runtime library (i.e., mfc42.dll). Other popular languages also have a corresponding runtime. VB6 programmers are also tied to a runtime module or two (e.g., msvbvm60.dll). Java developers are tied to the Java Virtual Machine (JVM) and so forth.

The .NET platform offers yet another runtime system. The key difference between the .NET runtime and the various other runtimes I just mentioned is the fact that the .NET runtime provides a single well-defined runtime layer that is shared by *all* languages and platforms that are .NET-aware.

The crux of the CLR is physically represented by a library named mscoree.dll (aka the Common Object Runtime Execution Engine). When an assembly is referenced for use, mscoree.dll is loaded automatically, which in turn loads the required assembly into memory. The runtime engine is responsible for a number of tasks. First and foremost, it is the entity in charge of resolving the location of an assembly and finding the requested type within the binary by reading the contained metadata. The CLR then lays out the type in memory, compiles the associated CIL into platform-specific instructions, performs any necessary security checks, and then executes the code in question.

In addition to loading your custom assemblies and creating your custom types, the CLR will also interact with the types contained within the .NET base class libraries when required. Although the entire base class library has been broken into a number of discrete assemblies, the key assembly is mscorlib.dll. mscorlib.dll contains a large number of core types that encapsulate a wide variety of common programming tasks as well as the core data types used by all .NET languages. When you build .NET solutions, you automatically have access to this particular assembly.

Figure 1-3 illustrates the workflow that takes place between your source code (which is making use of base class library types), a given .NET compiler, and the .NET execution engine.

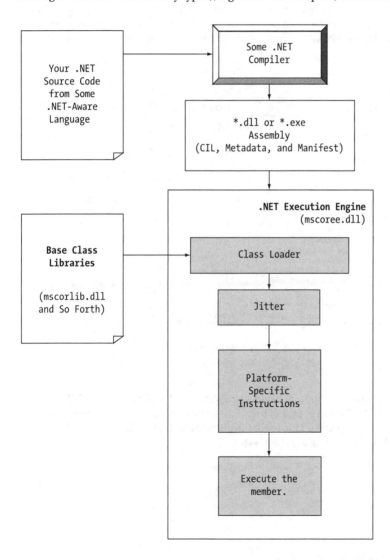

Figure 1-3. *mscoree.dll in action*

The Assembly/Namespace/Type Distinction

Each of us understands the importance of code libraries. The point of libraries such as MFC, J2EE, and ATL is to give developers a well-defined set of existing code to leverage in their applications. However, the C# language does not come with a language-specific code library. Rather, C# developers leverage the language-neutral .NET libraries. To keep all the types within the base class libraries well organized, the .NET platform makes extensive use of the *namespace* concept.

Simply put, a namespace is a grouping of related types contained in an assembly. For example, the System.IO namespace contains file I/O related types, the System.Data namespace defines basic database types, and so on. It is very important to point out that a single assembly (such as mscorlib.dll) can contain any number of namespaces, each of which can contain any number of types.

To clarify, Figure 1-4 shows a screen shot of the Visual Studio 2005 Object Brower utility. This tool allows you to examine the assemblies referenced by your current project, the namespaces within a particular assembly, the types within a given namespace, and the members of a specific type. Note that mscorlib.dll contains many different namespaces, each with its own semantically related types.

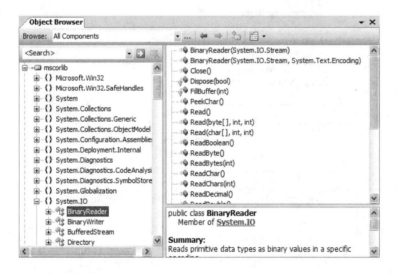

Figure 1-4. *A single assembly can have any number of namespaces.*

The key difference between this approach and a language-specific library such as MFC is that any language targeting the .NET runtime makes use of the *same* namespaces and *same* types. For example, the following three programs all illustrate the ubiquitous "Hello World" application, written in C#, VB .NET, and Managed Extensions for C++:

```
// Hello world in C#
using System;

public class MyApp
{
    static void Main()
    {
        Console.WriteLine("Hi from C#");
    }
}
```

```
' Hello world in VB .NET
Imports System

Public Module MyApp
    Sub Main()
        Console.WriteLine("Hi from VB .NET")
    End Sub
End Module
```

```
// Hello world in Managed Extensions for C++
#include "stdafx.h"
using namespace System;

int main(array<System::String ^> ^args)
{
    Console::WriteLine(L"Hi from managed C++");
    return 0;
}
```

Notice that each language is making use of the Console class defined in the System namespace. Beyond minor syntactic variations, these three applications look and feel very much alike, both physically and logically.

Clearly, your primary goal as a .NET developer is to get to know the wealth of types defined in the (numerous) .NET namespaces. The most fundamental namespace to get your hands around is named System. This namespace provides a core body of types that you will need to leverage time and again as a .NET developer. In fact, you cannot build any sort of functional C# application without at least making a reference to the System namespace. Table 1-4 offers a rundown of some (but certainly not all) of the .NET namespaces.

Table 1-4. *A Sampling of .NET Namespaces*

.NET Namespace	Meaning in Life
System	Within System you find numerous useful types dealing with intrinsic data, mathematical computations, random number generation, environment variables, and garbage collection, as well as a number of commonly used exceptions and attributes.
System.Collections System.Collections.Generic	These namespaces define a number of stock container objects (ArrayList, Queue, and so forth), as well as base types and interfaces that allow you to build customized collections. As of .NET 2.0, the collection types have been extended with generic capabilities.
System.Data System.Data.Odbc System.Data.OracleClient System.Data.OleDb System.Data.SqlClient	These namespaces are used for interacting with databases using ADO.NET.
System.Diagnostics	Here, you find numerous types that can be used to programmatically debug and trace your source code.
System.Drawing System.Drawing.Drawing2D System.Drawing.Printing	Here, you find numerous types wrapping graphical primitives such as bitmaps, fonts, and icons, as well as printing capabilities.

Continued

Table 1-4. *(Continued)*

.NET Namespace	Meaning in Life
System.IO System.IO.Compression System.IO.Ports	These namespaces include file I/O, buffering, and so forth. As of .NET 2.0, the IO namespaces now include support compression and port manipulation.
System.Net	This namespace (as well as other related namespaces) contains types related to network programming (requests/responses, sockets, end points, and so on).
System.Reflection System.Reflection.Emit	These namespaces define types that support runtime type discovery as well as dynamic creation of types.
System.Runtime. InteropServices	This namespace provides facilities to allow .NET types to interact with "unmanaged code" (e.g., C-based DLLs and COM servers) and vice versa.
System.Runtime.Remoting	This namespace (among others) defines types used to build solutions that incorporate the .NET remoting layer.
System.Security	Security is an integrated aspect of the .NET universe. In the security-centric namespaces you find numerous types dealing with permissions, cryptography, and so on.
System.Threading	This namespace defines types used to build multithreaded applications.
System.Web	A number of namespaces are specifically geared toward the development of .NET web applications, including ASP.NET and XML web services.
System.Windows.Forms	This namespace contains types that facilitate the construction of traditional desktop GUI applications.
System.Xml	The XML-centric namespaces contain numerous types used to interact with XML data.

Accessing a Namespace Programmatically

It is worth reiterating that a namespace is nothing more than a convenient way for us mere humans to logically understand and organize related types. Consider again the System namespace. From your perspective, you can assume that System.Console represents a class named *Console* that is contained within a namespace called *System*. However, in the eyes of the .NET runtime, this is not so. The runtime engine only sees a single entity named *System.Console*.

In C#, the using keyword simplifies the process of referencing types defined in a particular namespace. Here is how it works. Let's say you are interested in building a traditional desktop application. The main window renders a bar chart based on some information obtained from a back-end database and displays your company logo. While learning the types each namespace contains takes study and experimentation, here are some obvious candidates to reference in your program:

```
// Here are all the namespaces used to build this application.
using System;                  // General base class library types.
using System.Drawing;          // Graphical rendering types.
using System.Windows.Forms;    // GUI widget types.
using System.Data;             // General data-centric types.
using System.Data.SqlClient;   // MS SQL Server data access types.
```

Once you have specified some number of namespaces (and set a reference to the assemblies that define them), you are free to create instances of the types they contain. For example, if you are interested in creating an instance of the Bitmap class (defined in the System.Drawing namespace), you can write:

```
// Explicitly list the namespaces used by this file.
using System;
using System.Drawing;

class MyApp
{
    public void DisplayLogo()
    {
        // Create a 20_20 pixel bitmap.
        Bitmap companyLogo = new Bitmap(20, 20);
        ...
    }
}
```

Because your application is referencing System.Drawing, the compiler is able to resolve the Bitmap class as a member of this namespace. If you did not specify the System.Drawing namespace, you would be issued a compiler error. However, you are free to declare variables using a *fully qualified name* as well:

```
// Not listing System.Drawing namespace!
using System;

class MyApp
{
    public void DisplayLogo()
    {
        // Using fully qualified name.
        System.Drawing.Bitmap companyLogo =
            new System.Drawing.Bitmap(20, 20);
        ...
    }
}
```

While defining a type using the fully qualified name provides greater readability, I think you'd agree that the C# using keyword reduces keystrokes. In this text, I will avoid the use of fully qualified names (unless there is a definite ambiguity to be resolved) and opt for the simplified approach of the C# using keyword.

However, always remember that this technique is simply a shorthand notation for specifying a type's fully qualified name, and each approach results in the *exact* same underlying CIL (given the fact that CIL code always makes use of fully qualified names) and has no effect on performance or the size of the assembly.

Referencing External Assemblies

In addition to specifying a namespace via the C# using keyword, you also need to tell the C# compiler the name of the assembly containing the actual CIL definition for the referenced type. As mentioned, many core .NET namespaces live within mscorlib.dll. However, the System.Drawing. Bitmap type is contained within a separate assembly named System.Drawing.dll. A vast majority of the .NET Framework assemblies are located under a specific directory termed the *global assembly cache (GAC)*. On a Windows machine, this can be located under %windir%\Assembly, as shown in Figure 1-5.

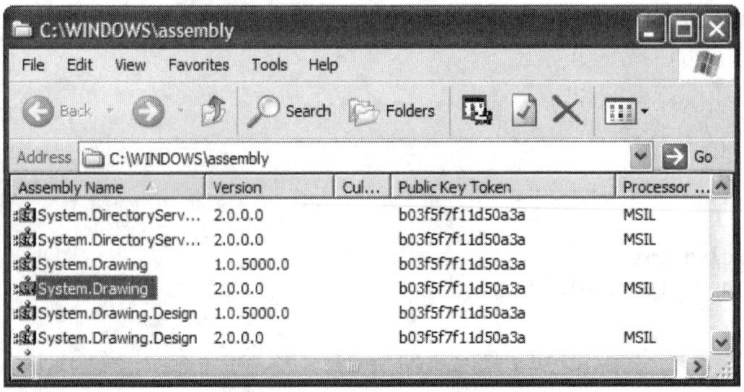

Figure 1-5. *The base class libraries reside in the GAC.*

Depending on the development tool you are using to build your .NET applications, you will have various ways to inform the compiler which assemblies you wish to include during the compilation cycle. You'll examine how to do so in the next chapter, so I'll hold off on the details for now.

Using ildasm.exe

If you are beginning to feel a tad overwhelmed at the thought of gaining mastery over every namespace in the .NET platform, just remember that what makes a namespace unique is that it contains types that are somehow *semantically related*. Therefore, if you have no need for a user interface beyond a simple console application, you can forget all about the System.Windows.Forms and System.Web namespaces (among others). If you are building a painting application, the database namespaces are most likely of little concern. Like any new set of prefabricated code, you learn as you go.

The Intermediate Language Disassembler utility (ildasm.exe) allows you to load up any .NET assembly and investigate its contents, including the associated manifest, CIL code, and type metadata. By default, ildasm.exe should be installed under C:\Program Files\Microsoft Visual Studio 8\SDK\v2.0\Bin (if you cannot find ildasm.exe in this location, simply search your machine for a file named "ildasm.exe").

Once you locate and run this tool, proceed to the File ➤ Open menu command and navigate to an assembly you wish to explore. By way of illustration, here is the CSharpCalculator.exe assembly shown earlier in this chapter (see Figure 1-6). ildasm.exe presents the structure of an assembly using a familiar tree-view format.

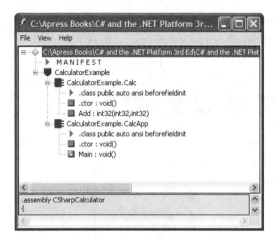

Figure 1-6. *Your new best friend, ildasm.exe*

Viewing CIL Code

In addition to showing the namespaces, types, and members contained in a given assembly, `ildasm.exe` also allows you to view the CIL instructions for a given member. For example, if you were to double-click the `Main()` method of the `CalcApp` class, a separate window would display the underlying CIL (see Figure 1-7).

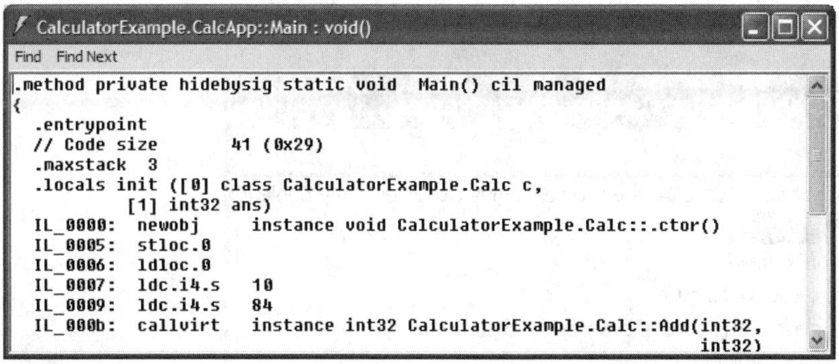

```
CalculatorExample.CalcApp::Main : void()

Find  Find Next

.method private hidebysig static void  Main() cil managed
{
  .entrypoint
  // Code size       41 (0x29)
  .maxstack  3
  .locals init ([0] class CalculatorExample.Calc c,
           [1] int32 ans)
  IL_0000:  newobj     instance void CalculatorExample.Calc::.ctor()
  IL_0005:  stloc.0
  IL_0006:  ldloc.0
  IL_0007:  ldc.i4.s   10
  IL_0009:  ldc.i4.s   84
  IL_000b:  callvirt   instance int32 CalculatorExample.Calc::Add(int32,
                                                                  int32)
```

Figure 1-7. *Viewing the underlying CIL*

Viewing Type Metadata

If you wish to view the type metadata for the currently loaded assembly, press Ctrl+M. Figure 1-8 shows the metadata for the Calc.Add() method.

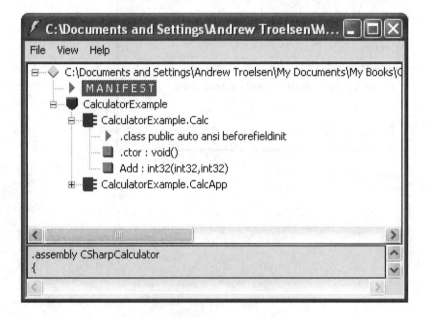

```
 MetaInfo                                                    _  □  X
Find   Find Next
        Method #1 (06000003)
        -------------------------------------------------------
            MethodName: Add (06000003)
            Flags      : [Public] [HideBySig] [ReuseSlot]  (00000086)
            RVA        : 0x00002090
            ImplFlags  : [IL] [Managed]  (00000000)
            CallCnvntn : [DEFAULT]
            hasThis
            ReturnType: I4
            2 Arguments
                Argument #1:  I4
                Argument #2:  I4
            2 Parameters
                (1) ParamToken : (08000001) Name : x flags: [none] (00000000)
                (2) ParamToken : (08000002) Name : y flags: [none] (00000000)
```

Figure 1-8. *Viewing type metadata via ildasm.exe*

Viewing Assembly Metadata

Finally, if you are interested in viewing the contents of the assembly's manifest, simply double-click the MANIFEST icon (see Figure 1-9).

```
 C:\Documents and Settings\Andrew Troelsen\M...  _  □  X
File   View   Help

□─◇  C:\Documents and Settings\Andrew Troelsen\My Documents\My Books\C
    ▶ MANIFEST
□─■  CalculatorExample
    □─■ CalculatorExample.Calc
        ▶ .class public auto ansi beforefieldinit
        ■ .ctor : void()
        ■ Add : int32(int32,int32)
    □─■ CalculatorExample.CalcApp

.assembly CSharpCalculator
{
```

Figure 1-9. *Double-click here to view the assembly manifest.*

To be sure, `ildasm.exe` has more options than shown here, and I will illustrate additional features of the tool where appropriate in the text. As you read through this text, I strongly encourage you to open your assemblies using `ildasm.exe` to see how your C# code is processed into platform-agnostic CIL code. Although you do *not* need to become an expert in CIL code to be a C# superstar, understanding the syntax of CIL will only strengthen your programming muscle.

Deploying the .NET Runtime

It should come as no surprise that .NET assemblies can be executed only on a machine that has the .NET Framework installed. As an individual who builds .NET software, this should never be an issue, as your development machine will be properly configured at the time you install the freely available .NET Framework 2.0 SDK (as well as commercial .NET development environments such as Visual Studio 2005).

However, if you deploy an assembly to a computer that does not have .NET installed, it will fail to run. For this reason, Microsoft provides a setup package named `dotnetfx.exe` that can be freely shipped and installed along with your custom software. This installation program is included with the .NET Framework 2.0 SDK, and it is also freely downloadable from Microsoft.

Once `dotnetfx.exe` is installed, the target machine will now contain the .NET base class libraries, .NET runtime (`mscoree.dll`), and additional .NET infrastructure (such as the GAC).

■Note Do be aware that if you are building a .NET web application, the end user's machine does not need to be configured with the .NET Framework, as the browser will simply receive generic HTML and possibly client-side JavaScript.

The Platform-Independent Nature of .NET

To close this chapter, allow me to briefly comment on the platform-independent nature of the .NET platform. To the surprise of most developers, .NET assemblies can be developed and executed on non-Microsoft operating systems (Mac OS X, numerous Linux distributions, BeOS, and FreeBSD, to name a few). To understand how this is possible, you need to come to terms to yet another abbreviation in the .NET universe: CLI (Common Language Infrastructure).

When Microsoft released the C# programming language and the .NET platform, it also crafted a set of formal documents that described the syntax and semantics of the C# and CIL languages, the .NET assembly format, core .NET namespaces, and the mechanics of a hypothetical .NET runtime engine (known as the Virtual Execution System, or VES). Better yet, these documents have been submitted to Ecma International as official international standards (http://www.ecma-international.org). The specifications of interest are

- ECMA-334: The C# Language Specification

- ECMA-335: The Common Language Infrastructure (CLI)

The importance of these documents becomes clear when you understand that they enable third parties to build distributions of the .NET platform for any number of operating systems and/or processors. ECMA-335 is perhaps the more "meaty" of the two specifications, so much so that is has been broken into five partitions, as shown in Table 1-5.

Table 1-5. *Partitions of the CLI*

Partitions of ECMA-335	Meaning in Life
Partition I: Architecture	Describes the overall architecture of the CLI, including the rules of the CTS and CLS, and the mechanics of the .NET runtime engine
Partition II: Metadata	Describes the details of .NET metadata
Partition III: CIL	Describes the syntax and semantics of CIL code
Partition IV: Libraries	Gives a high-level overview of the minimal and complete class libraries that must be supported by a .NET distribution.
Partition V: Annexes	A collection of "odds and ends" details such as class library design guidelines and the implementation details of a CIL compiler

Be aware that Partition IV (Libraries) defines only a *minimal* set of namespaces that represent the core services expected by a CLI distribution (collections, console I/O, file I/O, threading, reflection, network access, core security needs, XML manipulation, and so forth). The CLI does *not* define namespaces that facilitate web development (ASP.NET), database access (ADO.NET), or desktop graphical user interface (GUI) application development (Windows Forms).

The good news, however, is that the mainstream .NET distributions extend the CLI libraries with Microsoft-compatible equivalents of ASP.NET, ADO.NET, and Windows Forms in order to provide full-featured, production-level development platforms. To date, there are two major implementations of the CLI (beyond Microsoft's Windows-specific offering). Although this text focuses on the creation of .NET applications using Microsoft's .NET distribution, Table 1-6 provides information regarding the Mono and Portable .NET projects.

Table 1-6. *Open Source .NET Distributions*

Distribution	Meaning in Life
http://www.mono-project.com	The Mono project is an open source distribution of the CLI that targets various Linux distributions (e.g., SuSE, Fedora, and so on) as well as Win32 and Mac OS X.
http://www.dotgnu.org	Portable.NET is another open source distribution of the CLI that runs on numerous operating systems. Portable.NET aims to target as many operating systems as possible (Win32, AIX, BeOS, Mac OS X, Solaris, all major Linux distributions, and so on).

Both Mono and Portable.NET provide an ECMA-compliant C# compiler, .NET runtime engine, code samples, documentation, as well as numerous development tools that are functionally equivalent to the tools that ship with Microsoft's .NET Framework 2.0 SDK. Furthermore, Mono and Portable.NET collectively ship with a VB .NET, Java, and C complier.

■**Note** If you wish to learn more about Mono or Portable.NET, check out *Cross-Platform .NET Development: Using Mono, Portable.NET, and Microsoft .NET* by M. J. Easton and Jason King (Apress, 2004).

Summary

The point of this chapter was to lay out the conceptual framework necessary for the remainder of this book. I began by examining a number of limitations and complexities found within the technologies prior to .NET, and followed up with an overview of how .NET and C# attempt to simplify the current state of affairs.

.NET basically boils down to a runtime execution engine (`mscoree.dll`) and base class library (`mscorlib.dll` and associates). The common language runtime (CLR) is able to host any .NET binary (aka assembly) that abides by the rules of managed code. As you have seen, assemblies contain CIL instructions (in addition to type metadata and the assembly manifest) that are compiled to platform-specific instructions using a just-in-time (JIT) compiler. In addition, you explored the role of the Common Language Specification (CLS) and Common Type System (CTS).

This was followed by an examination of the `ildasm.exe` utility, as well as coverage of how to configure a machine to host .NET applications using `dotnetfx.exe`. I wrapped up by briefly addressing the platform-independent nature of C# and the .NET platform.

■ ■ ■

## CHAPTER 2

Building C# Applications

As a C# programmer, you may choose among numerous tools to build .NET applications. The point of this chapter is to provide a tour of various .NET development options, including, of course, Visual Studio 2005. The chapter opens, however, with an examination of working with the C# command-line compiler, csc.exe, and the simplest of all text editors, Notepad (notepad.exe). Along the way, you will also learn about the process of debugging .NET assemblies at the command line using cordbg.exe. Once you become comfortable compiling and debugging assemblies "IDE-free," you will then examine how the TextPad application allows you to edit and compile C# source code files in a (slightly) more sophisticated manner.

While you could work through this entire text using nothing other than csc.exe and Notepad/ TextPad, I'd bet you are also interested in working with feature-rich integrated development environments (IDEs). To this end, you will be introduced to an open source IDE named SharpDevelop. This IDE rivals the functionality of many commercial .NET development environments (and it's free!). After briefly examining the Visual C# 2005 Express IDE, you will turn your attention to Visual Studio 2005. This chapter wraps up with a quick tour of a number of complementary .NET development tools (many of which are open source) and describes where to obtain them.

Installing the .NET Framework 2.0 SDK

Before you are able to build .NET applications using the C# programming language and the .NET Framework, the first step is to install the freely downloadable .NET Framework 2.0 Software Development Kit (SDK). Do be aware that the .NET Framework 2.0 SDK is automatically installed with Visual Studio 2005 as well as Visual C# 2005 Express; therefore, if you plan to use either of these IDEs, there is no need to manually download or install this software package.

If you are not developing with Visual Studio 2005/Visual C# 2005 Express, navigate to http://msdn.microsoft.com/netframework and search for ".NET Framework 2.0 SDK". Once you have located the appropriate page, download setup.exe and save it to a location on your hard drive. At this point, double-click the executable to install the software.

After the installation process has completed, your development machine will not only be configured with the necessary .NET infrastructure, but also now contain numerous development tools, a very robust help system, sample code, and tutorials, as well as various white papers.

By default, the .NET Framework 2.0 SDK is installed under C:\Program Files\Microsoft Visual Studio 8\SDK\v2.0. Here you will find StartHere.htm, which (as the name suggests) serves as an entry point to other related documentation. Table 2-1 describes the details behind some of the core subdirectories off the installation root.

Table 2-1. *Subdirectories of the .NET Framework 2.0 SDK Installation Root*

Subdirectory	Meaning in Life
\Bin	Contains a majority of the .NET development tools. Check out `StartTools.htm` for a description of each utility.
\Bootstrapper	Although you can ignore most of the content in the directory, be aware that `dotnetfx.exe` (see Chapter 1) resides under the `\Packages\DotNetFx` subdirectory.
\CompactFramework	Contains the installer program for the .NET Compact Framework 2.0.
\Samples	Provides the setup program (and core content) for the .NET Framework 2.0 SDK samples. To learn how to install the samples, consult `StartSamples.htm`.

In addition to the content installed under C:\Program Files\Microsoft Visual Studio 8\SDK\v2.0, the setup program also creates the Microsoft.NET\Framework subdirectory under your Windows directory. Here you will find a subdirectory for each version of the .NET Framework installed on your machine. Within a version-specific subdirectory, you will find command-line compilers for each language that ships with the Microsoft .NET Framework (CIL, C#, Visual Basic .NET, J#, and JScript .NET), as well as additional command-line development utilities and .NET assemblies.

The C# Command-Line Compiler (csc.exe)

There are a number of techniques you may use to compile C# source code. In addition to Visual Studio 2005 (as well as various third-party .NET IDEs), you are able to create .NET assemblies using the C# command-line compiler, csc.exe (where csc stands for *C-Sharp Compiler*). This tool is included with the .NET Framework 2.0 SDK. While it is true that you may never decide to build a large-scale application using the command-line compiler, it is important to understand the basics of how to compile your *.cs files by hand. I can think of a few reasons you should get a grip on the process:

- The most obvious reason is the simple fact that you might not have a copy of Visual Studio 2005.
- You plan to make use of automated build tools such as MSBuild or NAnt.
- You want to deepen your understanding of C#. When you use graphical IDEs to build applications, you are ultimately instructing csc.exe how to manipulate your C# input files. In this light, it's edifying to see what takes place behind the scenes.

Another nice by-product of working with csc.exe in the raw is that you become that much more comfortable manipulating other command-line tools included with the .NET Framework 2.0 SDK. As you will see throughout this book, a number of important utilities are accessible only from the command line.

Configuring the C# Command-Line Compiler

Before you can begin to make use of the C# command-line compiler, you need to ensure that your development machine recognizes the existence of csc.exe. If your machine is not configured correctly, you are forced to specify the full path to the directory containing csc.exe before you can compile your C# files.

To equip your development machine to compile *.cs files from any directory, follow these steps (which assume a Windows XP installation; Windows NT/2000 steps will differ slightly):

1. Right-click the My Computer icon and select Properties from the pop-up menu.

2. Select the Advanced tab and click the Environment Variables button.

3. Double-click the Path variable from the System Variables list box.

4. Add the following line to the end of the current Path value (note each value in the Path variable is separated by a semicolon):

```
C:\Windows\Microsoft.NET\Framework\v2.0.50215
```

Of course, your entry may need to be adjusted based on your current version and location of the .NET Framework 2.0 SDK (so be sure to do a sanity check using Windows Explorer). Once you have updated the Path variable, you may take a test run by closing any command windows open in the background (to commit the settings), and then opening a new command window and entering

```
csc /?
```

If you set things up correctly, you should see a list of options supported by the C# compiler.

■**Note** When specifying command-line arguments for a given .NET development tool, you may use either a – or / (e.g., csc -? or csc /?).

Configuring Additional .NET Command-Line Tools

Before you begin to investigate csc.exe, add the following additional Path variable to the System Variables list box (again, perform a sanity check to ensure a valid directory):

```
C:\Program Files\Microsoft Visual Studio 8\SDK\v2.0\Bin
```

Recall that this directory contains additional command-line tools that are commonly used during .NET development. With these two paths established, you should now be able to run any .NET utility from any command window. If you wish to confirm this new setting, close any open command windows, open a new command window, and enter the following command to view the options of the GAC utility, gacutil.exe:

```
gacutil /?
```

■**Tip** Now that you have seen how to manually configure your machine, I'll let you in on a shortcut. The .NET Framework 2.0 SDK provides a preconfigured command window that recognizes all .NET command-line utilities out of the box. Using the Start button, activate the SDK Command Prompt located under the All Programs ➤ Microsoft .NET Framework SDK v2.0 menu selection.

Building C# Applications Using csc.exe

Now that your development machine recognizes csc.exe, the next goal is to build a simple single file assembly named TestApp.exe using the C# command-line compiler and Notepad. First, you need some source code. Open Notepad and enter the following:

```
// A simple C# application.
using System;

class TestApp
{
    public static void Main()
    {
        Console.WriteLine("Testing! 1, 2, 3");
    }
}
```

Once you have finished, save the file in a convenient location (e.g., C:\CscExample) as TestApp.cs. Now, let's get to know the core options of the C# compiler. The first point of interest is to understand how to specify the name and type of assembly to create (e.g., a console application named MyShell.exe, a code library named MathLib.dll, a Windows Forms application named MyWinApp.exe, and so forth). Each possibility is represented by a specific flag passed into csc.exe as a command-line parameter (see Table 2-2).

Table 2-2. *Output-centric Options of the C# Compiler*

Option	Meaning in Life
/out	This option is used to specify the name of the assembly to be created. By default, the assembly name is the same as the name of the initial input *.cs file (in the case of a *.dll) or the name of the type containing the program's Main() method (in the case of an *.exe).
/target:exe	This option builds an executable console application. This is the default file output type, and thus may be omitted when building this application type.
/target:library	This option builds a single-file *.dll assembly.
/target:module	This option builds a *module*. Modules are elements of multifile assemblies (fully described in Chapter 11).
/target:winexe	Although you are free to build Windows-based applications using the /target:exe flag, the /target:winexe flag prevents a console window from appearing in the background.

To compile TestApp.cs into a console application named TestApp.exe, change to the directory containing your source code file and enter the following command set (note that command-line flags must come before the name of the input files, not after):

```
csc /target:exe TestApp.cs
```

Here I did not explicitly specify an /out flag, therefore the executable will be named TestApp.exe, given that TestApp is the class defining the program's entry point (the Main() method). Also be aware that most of the C# compiler flags support an abbreviated version, such as /t rather than /target (you can view all abbreviations by entering csc /? at the command prompt):

```
csc /t:exe TestApp.cs
```

Furthermore, given that the /t:exe flag is the default output used by the C# compiler, you could also compile TestApp.cs simply by typing

```
csc TestApp.cs
```

TestApp.exe can now be run from the command line (see Figure 2-1).

Figure 2-1. TestApp *in action*

Referencing External Assemblies

Next up, let's examine how to compile an application that makes use of types defined in a separate .NET assembly. Speaking of which, just in case you are wondering how the C# compiler understood your reference to the System.Console type, recall from Chapter 1 that mscorlib.dll is *automatically referenced* during the compilation process (if for some strange reason you wish to disable this behavior, you may specify the /nostdlib flag).

To illustrate the process of referencing external assemblies, let's update the TestApp application to display a Windows Forms message box. Open your TestApp.cs file and modify it as follows:

```
using System;

// Add this!
using System.Windows.Forms;

class TestApp
{
    public static void Main()
    {
        Console.WriteLine("Testing! 1, 2, 3");

        // Add this!
        MessageBox.Show("Hello...");
    }
}
```

Notice the reference to the System.Windows.Forms namespace via the C# using keyword (introduced in Chapter 1). Recall that when you explicitly list the namespaces used within a given *.cs file, you avoid the need to make use of fully qualified names (which can lead to hand cramps).

At the command line, you must inform csc.exe which assembly contains the "used" namespaces. Given that you have made use of the MessageBox class, you must specify the System.Windows. Forms.dll assembly using the /reference flag (which can be abbreviated to /r):

```
csc /r:System.Windows.Forms.dll testapp.cs
```

If you now rerun your application, you should see what appears in Figure 2-2 in addition to the console output.

Figure 2-2. *Your first Windows Forms application*

Compiling Multiple Source Files with csc.exe

The current incarnation of the TestApp.exe application was created using a single *.cs source code file. While it is perfectly permissible to have all of your .NET types defined in a single *.cs file, most projects are composed of multiple *.cs files to keep your code base a bit more flexible. Assume you have authored an additional class contained in a new file named HelloMsg.cs:

```
// The HelloMessage class
using System;
using System.Windows.Forms;

class HelloMessage
{
    public void Speak()
    {
        MessageBox.Show("Hello...");
    }
}
```

Now, update your initial TestApp class to make use of this new type, and comment out the previous Windows Forms logic:

```
using System;

// Don't need this anymore.
// using System.Windows.Forms;

class TestApp
{
    public static void Main()
    {
        Console.WriteLine("Testing! 1, 2, 3");

        // Don't need this anymore either.
        // MessageBox.Show("Hello...");

        // Exercise the HelloMessage class!
        HelloMessage h = new HelloMessage();
        h.Speak();
    }
}
```

You can compile your C# files by listing each input file explicitly:

```
csc /r:System.Windows.Forms.dll testapp.cs hellomsg.cs
```

As an alternative, the C# compiler allows you to make use of the wildcard character (*) to inform csc.exe to include all *.cs files contained in the project directory as part of the current build:

```
csc /r:System.Windows.Forms.dll *.cs
```

When you run the program again, the output is identical. The only difference between the two applications is the fact that the current logic has been split among multiple files.

Referencing Multiple External Assemblies

On a related note, what if you need to reference numerous external assemblies using csc.exe? Simply list each assembly using a semicolon-delimited list. You don't need to specify multiple external assemblies for the current example, but some sample usage follows:

```
csc /r:System.Windows.Forms.dll;System.Drawing.dll *.cs
```

Working with csc.exe Response Files

As you might guess, if you were to build a complex C# application at the command prompt, your life would be full of pain as you type in the flags that specify numerous referenced assemblies and *.cs input files. To help lessen your typing burden, the C# compiler honors the use of *response files*.

C# response files contain all the instructions to be used during the compilation of your current build. By convention, these files end in a *.rsp (response) extension. Assume that you have created a response file named TestApp.rsp that contains the following arguments (as you can see, comments are denoted with the # character):

```
# This is the response file
# for the TestApp.exe app
# of Chapter 2.

# External assembly references.
/r:System.Windows.Forms.dll

# output and files to compile (using wildcard syntax).
/target:exe /out:TestApp.exe *.cs
```

Now, assuming this file is saved in the same directory as the C# source code files to be compiled, you are able to build your entire application as follows (note the use of the @ symbol):

```
csc @TestApp.rsp
```

If the need should arise, you are also able to specify multiple *.rsp files as input (e.g., csc @FirstFile.rsp @SecondFile.rsp @ThirdFile.rsp). If you take this approach, do be aware that the compiler processes the command options as they are encountered! Therefore, command-line arguments in a later *.rsp file can override options in a previous response file.

Also note that flags listed explicitly on the command line before a response file will be overridden by the specified *.rsp file. Thus, if you were to enter

```
csc /out:MyCoolApp.exe @TestApp.rsp
```

the name of the assembly would still be TestApp.exe (rather than MyCoolApp.exe), given the /out:TestApp.exe flag listed in the TestApp.rsp response file. However, if you list flags after a response file, the flag will override settings in the response file.

■**Note** The /reference flag is cumulative. Regardless of where you specify external assemblies (before, after, or within a response file) the end result is a summation of each reference assembly.

The Default Response File (csc.rsp)

The final point to be made regarding response files is that the C# compiler has an associated default response file (csc.rsp), which is located in the same directory as csc.exe itself (e.g., C:\Windows\Microsoft.NET\Framework\v2.0.50215). If you were to open this file using Notepad, you will find that numerous .NET assemblies have already been specified using the /r: flag.

When you are building your C# programs using csc.exe, this file will be automatically referenced, even when you supply a custom *.rsp file. Given the presence of the default response file, the current TestApp.exe application could be successfully compiled using the following command set (as System.Windows.Forms.dll is referenced within csc.rsp):

```
csc /out:TestApp.exe *.cs
```

In the event that you wish to disable the automatic reading of csc.rsp, you can specify the /noconfig option:

```
csc @TestApp.rsp /noconfig
```

Obviously, the C# command-line compiler has many other options that can be used to control how the resulting .NET assembly is to be generated. If you wish to learn more details regarding the functionality of csc.exe, look up my article titled "Working with the C# 2.0 Command Line Compiler" online at http://msdn.microsoft.com.

The Command-Line Debugger (cordbg.exe)

Before moving on to our examination of building C# applications using TextPad, I would like to briefly point out that the .NET Framework 2.0 SDK does ship with a command-line debugger named cordbg.exe. This tool provides dozens of options that allow you to debug your assembly. You may view them by specifying the /? flag:

```
cordbg /?
```

Table 2-3 documents some (but certainly not all) of the flags recognized by cordbg.exe (with the alternative shorthand notation) once you have entered a debugging session.

Table 2-3. *A Handful of Useful* cordbg.exe *Command-Line Flags*

Flag	Meaning in Life
b[reak]	Set or display current breakpoints.
del[ete]	Remove one or more breakpoints.
ex[it]	Exit the debugger.
g[o]	Continue debugging the current process until hitting next breakpoint.
o[ut]	Step out of the current function.
p[rint]	Print all loaded variables (local, arguments, etc.).
si	Step into the next line.
so	Step over the next line.

As I assume that most of you will choose to make use of the Visual Studio 2005 integrated debugger, I will not bother to comment on each flag of cordbg.exe. However, for those of you who are interested, the following section presents a minimal walk-through of the basic process of debugging at the command line.

Debugging at the Command Line

Before you can debug your application using `cordbg.exe`, the first step is to generate debugging symbols for your current application by specifying the `/debug` flag of `csc.exe`. For example, to generate debugging data for `TestApp.exe`, enter the following command set:

```
csc @testapp.rsp /debug
```

This generates a new file named (in this case) `testapp.pdb`. If you do not have an associated `*.pdb` file, it is still possible to make use of `cordbg.exe`; however, you will not be able to view your C# source code during the process (which is typically no fun whatsoever, unless you wish to complicate matters by reading CIL code).

Once you have generated a `*.pdb` file, open a session with `cordbg.exe` by specifying your .NET assembly as a command-line argument (the `*.pdb` file will be loaded automatically):

```
cordbg.exe testapp.exe
```

At this point, you are in debugging mode and may apply any number of `cordbg.exe` flags at the (`cordbg`) command prompt (see Figure 2-3).

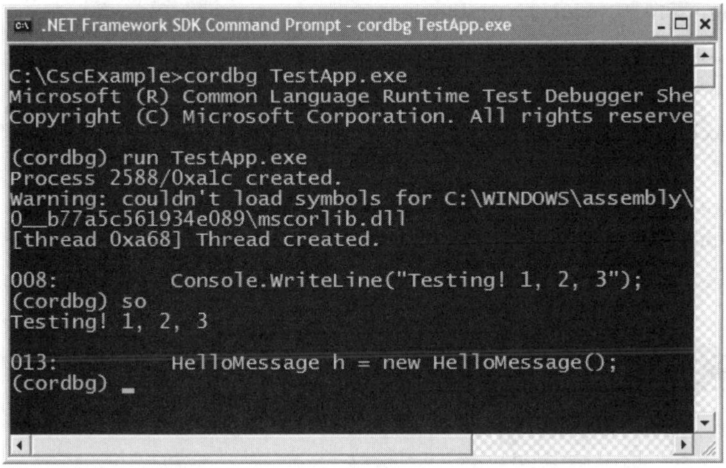

Figure 2-3. *Debugging with* `cordbg.exe`

When you wish to quit debugging with `cordbg.exe`, simply type `exit` (or the shorthand `ex`). Again, unless you are a command-line junkie, I assume you will opt for the graphical debugger provided by your IDE. If you require more information, look up `cordbg.exe` in the .NET Framework 2.0 SDK documentation.

Building .NET Applications Using TextPad

While Notepad is fine for creating simple .NET programs, it offers nothing in the way of developer productivity. It would be ideal to author `*.cs` files using an editor that supports (at a minimum) keyword coloring, code snippets, and integration with a C# compiler. As luck would have it, such a tool does exist: TextPad.

TextPad is an editor you can use to author and compile code for numerous programming languages, including C#. The chief advantage of this product is the fact that it is very simple to use and provides just enough bells and whistles to enhance your coding efforts.

To obtain TextPad, navigate to `http://www.textpad.com` and download the current version (4.7.3 at the time of this writing). Once you have installed the product, you will have a feature-complete version of TextPad; however, this tool is not freeware. Until you purchase a single-user license (for around US$30.00 at the time of this writing), you will be presented with a "friendly reminder" each time you run the application.

Enabling C# Keyword Coloring

TextPad is not equipped to understand C# keywords or work with `csc.exe` out of the box. To do so, you will need to install an additional add-on. Navigate to `http://www.textpad.com/add-ons/syna2g.html` and download `csharp8.zip` using the "C# 2005" link option. This add-on takes into account the new keywords introduced with C# 2005 (in contrast to the "C#" link, which is limited to C# 1.1).

Once you have unzipped `csharp8.zip`, place a copy of the extracted `csharp8.syn` file in the Samples subdirectory of the TextPad installation (e.g., C:\Program Files\TextPad 4\Samples). Next, launch TextPad and perform the following tasks using the New Document Wizard.

1. Activate the Configure ➤ New Document Class menu option.

2. Enter the name **C# 2.0** in the "Document class name" edit box.

3. In the next step, enter `*.cs` in the "Class members" edit box.

4. Finally, enable syntax highlighting, choose `csharp8.syn` from the drop-down list box, and close the wizard.

You can now tweak TextPad's C# support using the Document Classes node accessible from the Configure ➤ Preferences menu (see Figure 2-4).

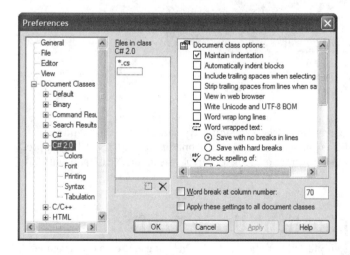

Figure 2-4. *Setting TextPad's C# preferences*

Configuring the *.cs File Filter

The next configuration detail is to create a filter for C# source code files displayed by the Open and Save dialog boxes:

1. Activate the Configure ➤ Preferences menu option and select File Name Filters from the tree view control.

2. Click the New button, and enter **C#** into the Description field and *.cs into the Wild cards text box.

3. Move your new filter to the top of the list using the Move Up button and click OK.

Create a new file (using File ➤ New) and save it in a convenient location (such as C:\TextPadTestApp) as TextPadTest.cs. Next, enter a trivial class definition (see Figure 2-5).

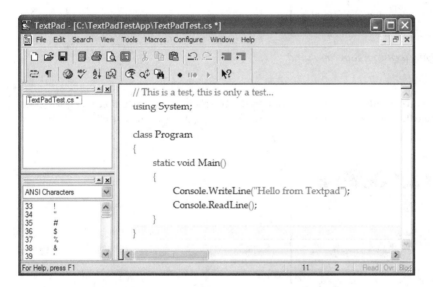

Figure 2-5. TextPadTest.cs

Hooking Into csc.exe

The last major configuration detail to contend with is to associate csc.exe with TextPad so you can compile your C# files. The first way to do so is using the Tools ➤ Run menu option. Here you are presented with a dialog box that allows you to specify the name of the tool to run and any necessary command-line flags. To compile TextPadTest.cs into a .NET console-based executable, follow these steps:

1. Enter the full path to csc.exe into the Command text box (e.g., C:\Windows\Microsoft.NET\ Framework\v2.0. 50215\csc.exe).

2. Enter the command-line options you wish to specify within the Parameters text box (e.g., /out:myApp.exe *.cs). Recall that you can specify a custom response file to simplify matters (e.g., @myInput.rsp).

3. Enter the directory containing the input files via the Initial folder text box (C:\TextPadTestApp in this example).

4. If you wish TextPad to capture the compiler output directly (rather than within a separate command window), select the Capture Output check box.

Figure 2-6 shows the complete compilation settings.

Figure 2-6. *Specifying a custom Run command*

At this point, you can either run your program by double-clicking the executable using Windows Explorer or leverage the Tools ➤ Run menu option to specify myApp.exe as the current command (see Figure 2-7).

Figure 2-7. *Instructing TextPad to run* myApp.exe

When you click OK, you should see the program's output ("Hello from TextPad") displayed in the Command Results document.

Associating Run Commands with Menu Items

TextPad also allows you to create custom menu items that represent predefined run commands. Let's create a custom item under the Tools menu named "Compile C# Console" that will compile all C# files in the current directory:

1. Activate the Configure ➤ Preferences menu option and select Tools from the tree view control.

2. Using the Add button, select Program and specify the full path to csc.exe.

3. If you wish, rename `csc.exe` to a more descriptive label (Compile C#) by clicking the tool name and then clicking OK.

4. Finally, activate the Configure ➤ Preferences menu option once again, but this time select Compile C# from the Tools node, and specify `*.cs` as the sole value in the Parameters field (see Figure 2-8).

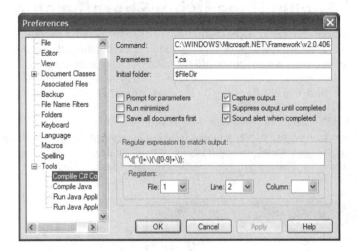

Figure 2-8. *Creating a Tools menu item*

With this, you can now compile all C# files in the current directory using your custom Tools menu item.

Enabling C# Code Snippets

Before leaving behind the world of TextPad, there is one final free add-on you might wish to install. Navigate to `http://www.textpad.com/add-ons/cliplibs.html` and download `csharp_1.zip` using the C# clip library provided by Sean Gephardt. Extract the contained `csharp.tcl` file and place it in the Samples subdirectory. When you restart TextPad, you should find a new clip library named C Sharp Helpers available from the Clip Library drop-down list (see Figure 2-9). Double-clicking any item will insert the related C# code in the active document at the location of the cursor.

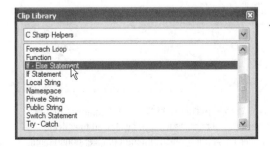

Figure 2-9. *C# code snippets à la TextPad*

As you may agree, TextPad is a step in the right direction when contrasted to Notepad and the command prompt. However, TextPad does not (currently) provide IntelliSense capabilities for C# code, GUI designers, project templates, or database manipulation tools. To address such needs, allow me to introduce the next .NET development tool: SharpDevelop.

Building .NET Applications Using SharpDevelop

SharpDevelop is an open source and feature-rich IDE that you can use to build .NET assemblies using C#, VB .NET, Managed Extensions for C++, or CIL. Beyond the fact that this IDE is completely free, it is interesting to note that it was written entirely in C#. In fact, you have the choice to download and compile the *.cs files manually or run a setup.exe program to install SharpDevelop on your development machine. Both distributions can be obtained from http://www.icsharpcode.net/OpenSource/SD/Download.

Once you have installed SharpDevelop, the File ➤ New ➤ Combine menu option allows you to pick which type of project you wish to generate (and in which .NET language). In the lingo of SharpDevelop, a *combine* is a collection of individual projects (analogous to a Visual Studio *solution*). Assume you have created a C# Windows Application named MySDWinApp (see Figure 2-10).

Figure 2-10. *The SharpDevelop New Project dialog box*

■**Note** Be aware that version 1.0 of SharpDevelop is configured to make use of the C# 1.1 compiler. To make use of the new C# 2005 language features and .NET Framework 2.0 namespaces, you will need to activate the Project ➤ Project options menu item and update the compiler version from the Runtime/Compiler option page.

Learning the Lay of the Land: SharpDevelop

SharpDevelop provides numerous productivity enhancements and in many cases is as feature rich as Visual Studio .NET 2003 (but not currently as powerful as Visual Studio 2005). Here is a hit list of some of the major benefits:

- Support for the Microsoft and Mono C# compilers
- IntelliSense and code expansion capabilities
- An Add Reference dialog box to reference external assemblies, including assemblies deployed to the GAC
- A visual Windows Forms designer
- Various project perspective windows (termed *scouts*) to view your projects
- An integrated object browser utility (the Assembly Scout)
- Database manipulation utilities
- A C# to VB .NET (and vice versa) code conversion utility
- Integration with the NUnit (a .NET unit test utility) and NAnt (a .NET build utility)
- Integration with the .NET Framework SDK documentation

Impressive for a free IDE, is it not? Although this chapter doesn't cover each of these points in detail, let's walk through a few items of interest. If you require further details of SharpDevelop, be aware that it ships with very thorough documentation accessible from the Help ➤ Help Topics menu option.

The Project and Classes Scouts

When you create a new combine, you can make use of the Project Scout to view the set of files, referenced assemblies, and resource files of each project (see Figure 2-11).

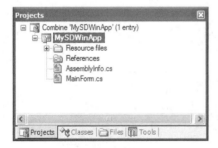

Figure 2-11. *The Project Scout*

When you wish to reference an external assembly for your current project, simply right-click the References icon within the Project Scout and select the Add Reference context menu. Once you do, you may select assemblies directly from the GAC as well as custom assemblies via the .NET Assembly Browser tab (see Figure 2-12).

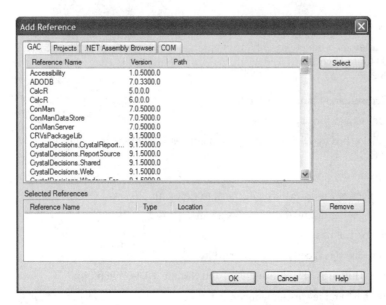

Figure 2-12. *The SharpDevelop Add Reference dialog box*

The Classes Scout provides a more object-oriented view of your combine in that it displays the namespaces, types, and members within each project (see Figure 2-13).

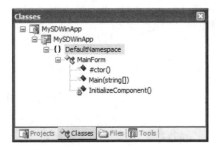

Figure 2-13. *The Classes Scout*

If you double-click any item, SharpDevelop responds by opening the corresponding file and placing your mouse cursor at the item's definition.

The Assembly Scout

The Assembly Scout utility (accessible from the View menu) allows you to graphically browse the assemblies referenced within your project. This tool is split into two panes. On the left is a tree view control that allows you to drill into an assembly and view its namespaces and the contained types (see Figure 2-14).

Figure 2-14. *Viewing referenced assemblies using the Assembly Scout*

The right side of the Assembly Scout utility allows you to view details of the item selected on the left pane. Not only can you view the basic details using the Info tab, but also you can also view the underlying CIL code of the item and save its definition to an XML file.

Windows Forms Designers

As you will learn later in this book, Windows Forms is a toolkit used to build desktop applications. To continue tinkering with SharpDevelop, click the Design tab located at the bottom of the MainForm.cs code window. Once you do, you will open the integrated Windows Forms designer.

Using the Windows Forms section of your Tools window, you can create a GUI for the Form you are designing. To demonstrate this, place a single Button type on your main Form by selecting the Button icon and clicking the designer. To update the look and feel of any GUI item, you can make use of the Properties window (see Figure 2-15), which you activate from the View ➤ Properties menu selection. Select the Button from the drop-down list and change various aspects of the Button type (e.g., BackColor and Text).

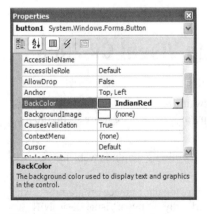

Figure 2-15. *The Properties window*

Using this same window, you can handle events for a given GUI item. To do so, click the lightning bolt icon at the top of the Properties window. Next, select the GUI item you wish to interact with from the drop-down list (your Button in this case). Finally, handle the Click event by typing in the name of the method to be called when the user clicks the button (see Figure 2-16).

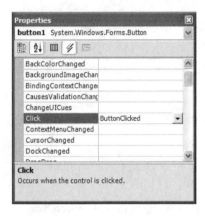

Figure 2-16. *Handing events via the Properties window*

Once you press the Enter key, SharpDevelop responds by generating stub code for your new method. To complete the example, enter the following statement within the scope of your event handler:

```
void ButtonClicked(object sender, System.EventArgs e)
{
    // Update the Form's caption with a custom message.
    this.Text = "Stop clicking my button!";
}
```

At this point, you can run your program (using the Debug ➤ Run menu item). Sure enough, when you click your Button, you should see the Form's caption update as expected.

That should be enough information to get you up and running using the SharpDevelop IDE. I do hope you now have a good understanding of the basics, though obviously there is much more to this tool than presented here.

Building .NET Applications Using Visual C# 2005 Express

During the summer of 2004, Microsoft introduced a brand-new line of IDEs that fall under the designation of "Express" products (http://msdn.microsoft.com/express). To date, there are six members of the Express family:

- *Visual Web Developer 2005 Express*: A lightweight tool for building dynamic websites and XML web services using ASP.NET 2.0

- *Visual Basic 2005 Express*: A streamlined programming tool ideal for novice programmers who want to learn how to build applications using the user-friendly syntax of Visual Basic .NET

- *Visual C# 2005 Express, Visual C++ 2005 Express, and Visual J# 2005 Express*: Targeted IDEs for students and enthusiasts who wish to learn the fundamentals of computer science in their syntax of choice
- *SQL Server 2005 Express*: An entry-level database management system geared toward hobbyists, enthusiasts, and student developers

---

■**Note** At the time of this writing, the Express family products are available as public betas free of charge.

By and large, Express products are slimmed-down versions of their Visual Studio 2005 counterparts and are primarily targeted at .NET hobbyists and students. Like SharpDevelop, Visual C# 2005 Express provides various browsing tools, a Windows Forms designer, the Add References dialog box, IntelliSense capabilities, and code expansion templates. As well, Visual C# 2005 Express offers a few (important) features currently not available in SharpDevelop, including

- An integrated graphical debugger
- Tools to simplify access to XML web services

Because the look and feel of Visual C# 2005 Express is so similar to that of Visual Studio 2005 (and, to some degree, SharpDevelop) I do not provide a walk-through of this particular IDE here. If you do wish to learn more about the product, look up my article "An Introduction to Programming Using Microsoft Visual C# 2005 Express Edition" online at `http://msdn.microsoft.com`.

The Big Kahuna: Building .NET Applications Using Visual Studio 2005

If you are a professional .NET software engineer, the chances are extremely good that your employer has purchased Microsoft's premier IDE, Visual Studio 2005, for your development endeavors (`http://msdn.microsoft.com/vstudio`). This tool is far and away the most feature-rich and enterprise-ready IDE examined in this chapter. Of course, this power comes at a price, which will vary based on the version of Visual Studio 2005 you purchase. As you might suspect, each version supplies a unique set of features.

My assumption during the remainder of this text is that you have chosen to make use of Visual Studio 2005 as your IDE of choice. Do understand that owning a copy of Visual Studio 2005 is *not* required for you to use this edition of the text. In the worst case, I may examine an option that is not provided by your IDE. However, rest assured that all of this book's sample code will compile just fine when processed by your tool of choice.

■**Note** Once you download the source code for this book from the Downloads area of the Apress website (`http://www.apress.com`), you may load the current example into Visual Studio 2005 by double-clicking the example's `*.sln` file. If you are not using Visual Studio 2005, you will need to manually configure your IDE to compile the provided `*.cs` files.

Learning the Lay of the Land: Visual Studio 2005

Visual Studio 2005 ships with the expected GUI designers, database manipulation tools, object and project browsing utilities, and an integrated help system. Unlike the IDEs we have already examined, Visual Studio 2005 provides numerous additions. Here is a partial list:

- Visual XML editors/designers
- Support for mobile device development (such as Smartphones and Pocket PC devices)
- Support for Microsoft Office development
- The ability to track changes for a given source document and view revisions
- Integrated support for code refactoring
- An XML-based code expansion library
- Visual class design tools and object test utilities
- A code definition window (which replaces the functionality of the Windows Forms Class Viewer, `wincv.exe`, which shipped with .NET 1.1 and earlier)

To be completely honest, Visual Studio 2005 provides so many features that it would take an entire book (a large book at that) to fully describe every aspect of the IDE. This is not that book. However, I do want to point out some of the major enhancements in the pages that follow. As you progress through the text, you'll learn more about the Visual Studio 2005 IDE where appropriate.

The Solution Explorer Utility

If you are following along, create a new C# console application (named Vs2005Example) using the File ➤ New ➤ Project menu item. The Solution Explorer utility (accessible from the View menu) allows you to view the set of all content files and referenced assemblies that comprise the current project (see Figure 2-17).

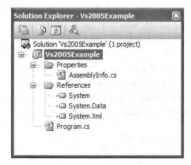

Figure 2-17. *Solution Explorer*

Notice that the References folder of Solution Explorer displays a list of each assembly you have currently referenced (console projects reference `System.dll`, `System.Data.dll`, and `System.Xml.dll` by default). When you need to reference additional assemblies, right-click the References folder and select Add Reference. At this point, you can select your assembly from the resulting dialog box.

■Note Visual Studio 2005 now allows you to set references to executable assemblies (unlike Visual Studio .NET 2003, in which you were limited to *.dll code libraries).

Finally, notice an icon named Properties within Solution Explorer. When you double-click this item, you are presented with an enhanced project configuration editor (see Figure 2-18).

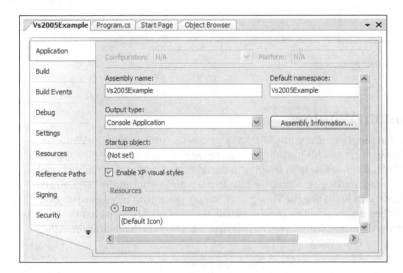

Figure 2-18. *The Project Properties window*

You will see various aspects of the Project Properties window as you progress through this text. However, if you take some time to poke around, you will see that you can establish various security settings, strongly name your assembly, insert string resources, and configure pre- and postbuild events.

The Class View Utility

The next tool to examine is the Class View utility, which you can load from the View menu. Like SharpDevelop, the purpose of this utility is to show all of the types in your current project from an object-oriented perspective. The top pane displays the set of namespaces and their types, while the bottom pane displays the currently selected type's members (see Figure 2-19).

Figure 2-19. *The Class View utility*

The Code Definition Window

If you have a background in programming with .NET 1.1, you may be familiar with the Windows Forms Class Viewer utility, `wincv.exe`. This tool allowed you to type in the name of a .NET type and view its C# definition. While `wincv.exe` is deprecated with the release of .NET 2.0, an enhanced version of this tool has been integrated within Visual C# 2005 Express and Visual Studio 2005. You can activate the Code Definition window using the View menu. Simply place your mouse cursor over any type in your C# code files, and you will be presented with a snapshot of the type in question. For example, if you click the word "string" within your `Main()` method, you find the definition of the `System.String` class type (see Figure 2-20).

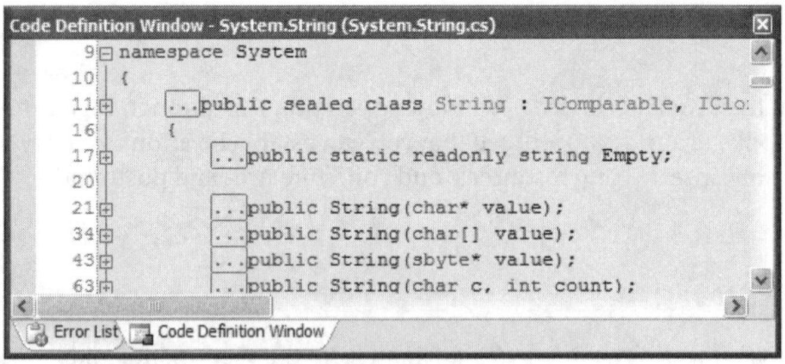

```
Code Definition Window - System.String (System.String.cs)
     9  namespace System
    10  {
    11      ...public sealed class String : IComparable, IClo
    16      {
    17          ...public static readonly string Empty;
    20
    21          ...public String(char* value);
    34          ...public String(char[] value);
    43          ...public String(sbyte* value);
    63          ...public String(char c, int count);

  Error List   Code Definition Window
```

Figure 2-20. *The Code Definition window*

The Object Browser Utility

As you may recall from Chapter 1, Visual Studio 2005 also provides a utility to investigate the set of referenced assemblies within your current project. Activate the Object Browser using the View ➤ Other Windows menu, and then select the assembly you wish to investigate (see Figure 2-21).

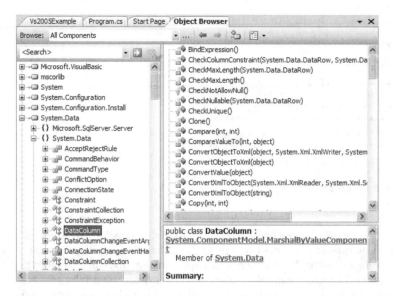

Figure 2-21. *The Visual Studio 2005 Object Browser utility*

Integrated Support for Code Refactoring

One major enhancement that ships with Visual Studio 2005 is intrinsic support to refactor existing code. Simply put, *refactoring* is a formal and mechanical process whereby you improve an existing code base. In the bad old days, refactoring typically involved a ton of manual labor. Luckily, Visual Studio 2005 does a great deal to automate the refactoring process. Using the Refactor menu, related keyboard shortcuts, smart tags, and/or context-sensitive mouse clicks, you can dramatically reshape your code with minimal fuss and bother. Table 2-4 defines some common refactorings recognized by Visual Studio 2005.

Table 2-4. *Visual Studio 2005 Refactorings*

Refactoring Technique	Meaning in Life
Extract Method	Allows you to define a new method based on a selection of code statements
Encapsulate Field	Turns a public field into a private field encapsulated by a C# property
Extract Interface	Defines a new interface type based on a set of existing type members
Reorder Parameters	Provides a way to reorder member arguments
Remove Parameters	Removes a given argument from the current list of parameters (as you would expect)
Rename	Allows you to rename a code token (method name, field, local variable, and so on) throughout a project
Promote Local Variable to Parameter	Moves a local variable to the parameter set of the defining method

To illustrate refactoring in action, update your Main() method with the following code:

```
static void Main(string[] args)
{
    // Set up Console UI (CUI)
    Console.Title = "My Rocking App";
    Console.ForegroundColor = ConsoleColor.Yellow;
    Console.BackgroundColor = ConsoleColor.Blue;
    Console.WriteLine("***********************************");
    Console.WriteLine("***** Welcome to My Rocking App *****");
    Console.WriteLine("***********************************");
    Console.BackgroundColor = ConsoleColor.Black;

    // Wait for key press to close.
    Console.ReadLine();
}
```

While there is nothing wrong with the preceding code as it now stands, imagine that you want to display this prompt at various places throughout your program. Rather than retyping the same exact console user interface logic, it would be ideal to have a helper function that could be called to do so. Given this, you will apply the Extract Method refactoring to your existing code. First, select each code statement (except the final call to Console.ReadLine()) within the editor. Now, right-click and select the Extract Method option from the Refactor context menu. Name your new method ConfigureCUI() in the resulting dialog box. When you have finished, you will find that your Main() method calls the newly generated ConfigureCUI() method, which now contains the previously selected code:

```
class Program
{
    static void Main(string[] args)
    {
        ConfigureCUI();

        // Wait for key press to close.
        Console.ReadLine();
    }

    private static void ConfigureCUI()
    {
        // Set up Console UI (CUI)
        Console.Title = "My Rocking App";
        Console.ForegroundColor = ConsoleColor.Yellow;
        Console.BackgroundColor = ConsoleColor.Blue;
        Console.WriteLine("***********************************");
        Console.WriteLine("***** Welcome to My Rocking App *****");
        Console.WriteLine("***********************************");
        Console.BackgroundColor = ConsoleColor.Black;
    }
}
```

■**Note** If you are interested in more information on the refactoring process and a detailed walk-through of each refactoring supported by Visual Studio 2005, look up my article "Refactoring C# Code Using Visual Studio 2005" online at http://msdn.microsoft.com.

Code Expansions and Surround with Technology

Visual Studio 2005 (as well as Visual C# 2005 Express) also has the capability to insert complex blocks of C# code using menu selections, context-sensitive mouse clicks, and/or keyboard shortcuts. The number of available code expansions is impressive and can be broken down into two main groups:

- *Snippets*: These templates insert common code blocks at the location of the mouse cursor.

- *Surround With*: These templates wrap a block of selected statements within a relevant scope.

To see this functionality firsthand, right-click a blank line within your Main() method and activate the Insert Snippet menu. Once you select a given item, you will find the related code is expanded automatically (press the Esc key to dismiss the pop-up menu).

If you were to right-click and select the Surround With menu, you would likewise be presented with a list of options. Be sure to take time to explore these predefined code expansion templates, as they can radically speed up the development process.

■**Note** All code expansion templates are XML-based descriptions of the code to generate within the IDE. Using Visual Studio 2005 (as well as Visual C# 2005 Express), you can create your own custom code templates. Details of how to do so can be found in my article "Investigating Code Snippet Technology" at http://msdn.microsoft.com.

The Visual Class Designer

Visual Studio 2005 gives us the ability to design classes visually (but this capability is not included in Visual C# 2005 Express). The Class Designer utility allows you to view and modify the relationships of the types (classes, interfaces, structures, enumerations, and delegates) in your project. Using this tool, you are able to visually add (or remove) members to (or from) a type and have your modifications reflected in the corresponding C# file. As well, as you modify a given C# file, changes are reflected in the class diagram.

To work with this aspect of Visual Studio 2005, the first step is to insert a new class diagram file. There are many ways to do so, one of which is to click the View Class Diagram button located on Solution Explorer's right side (see Figure 2-22).

Figure 2-22. *Inserting a class diagram file*

Once you do, you will find class icons that represent the classes in your current project. If you click the arrow image, you can show or hide the type's members (see Figure 2-23).

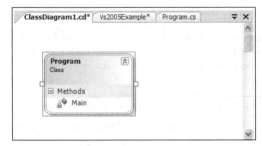

Figure 2-23. *The Class Diagram viewer*

This utility works in conjunction with two other aspects of Visual Studio 2005: the Class Details window (activated using the View ➤ Other Windows menu) and the Class Designer Toolbox (activated using the View ➤ Toolbox menu item). The Class Details window not only shows you the details of the currently selected item in the diagram, but also allows you to modify existing members and insert new members on the fly (see Figure 2-24).

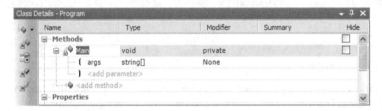

Figure 2-24. *The Class Details window*

The Class Designer Toolbox (see Figure 2-25) allows you to insert new types into your project (and create relationships between these types) visually. (Be aware you must have a class diagram as the active window to view this toolbox.) As you do so, the IDE automatically creates new C# type definitions in the background.

Figure 2-25. *Inserting a new class using the visual Class Designer*

By way of example, drag a new class from the Class Designer Toolbox onto your Class Designer. Name this class Car in the resulting dialog box. Now, using the Class Details window, add a public string field named petName (see Figure 2-26).

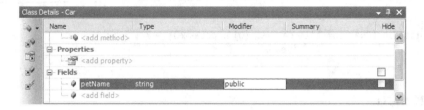

Figure 2-26. *Adding a field with the Class Details window*

If you now look at the C# definition of the Car class, you will see it has been updated accordingly:

```
public class Car
{
    // Public data is typically a bad idea; however,
    // it keeps this example simple.
    public string petName;
}
```

Add another new class to the designer named SportsCar. Now, select the Inheritance icon from the Class Designer Toolbox and click the top of the SportsCar icon. Without releasing the left mouse button, move the mouse on top of the Car class icon. If you performed these steps correctly, you have just derived the SportsCar class from Car (see Figure 2-27).

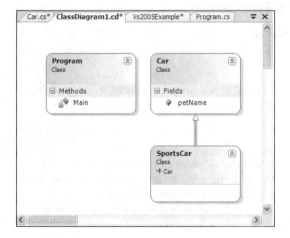

Figure 2-27. *Visually deriving from an existing class*

To complete this example, update the generated `SportsCar` class with a public method named `PrintPetName()` as follows:

```csharp
public class SportsCar : Car
{
    public void PrintPetName()
    {
        petName = "Fred";
        Console.WriteLine("Name of this car is: {0}", petName);
    }
}
```

Object Test Bench

Another nice visual tool provided by Visual Studio 2005 is Object Test Bench (OTB). This aspect of the IDE allows you to quickly create an instance of a class and invoke its members without the need to compile and run the entire application. This can be extremely helpful when you wish to test a specific method, but would rather not step through dozens of lines of code to do so.

To work with OTB, right-click the type you wish to create using the Class Designer. For example, right-click the `SportsCar` type, and from the resulting context menu select Create Instance ➤ Sports-Car(). This will display a dialog box that allows you to name your temporary object variable (and supply any constructor arguments if required). Once the process is complete, you will find your object hosted within the IDE. Right-click the object icon and invoke the `PrintPetName()` method (see Figure 2-28).

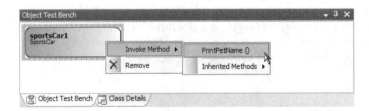

Figure 2-28. *The Visual Studio 2005 Object Test Bench*

You will see the message "Name of this car is: Fred" appear within the Visual Studio 2005 Quick Console.

The Integrated Help System

The final aspect of Visual Studio 2005 you *must* be comfortable with from the outset is the fully integrated help system. The .NET Framework 2.0 SDK documentation is extremely good, very readable, and full of useful information. Given the huge number of predefined .NET types (which number well into the thousands), you must be willing to roll up your sleeves and dig into the provided documentation. If you resist, you are doomed to a long, frustrating, and painful existence as a .NET developer.

Visual Studio 2005 provides the Dynamic Help window, which changes its contents (dynamically!) based on what item (window, menu, source code keyword, etc.) is currently selected. For example, if you place the cursor on the Console class, the Dynamic Help window displays a set of links regarding the System.Console type.

You should also be aware of a very important subdirectory of the .NET Framework 2.0 SDK documentation. Under the .NET Development ➤ .NET Framework SDK➤ Class Library Reference node of the documentation, you will find complete documentation of each and every namespace in the .NET base class libraries (see Figure 2-29).

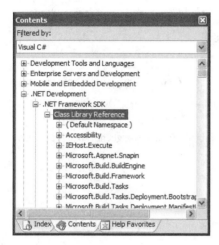

Figure 2-29. *The .NET base class library reference*

Each "book" defines the set of types in a given namespace, the members of a given type, and the parameters of a given member. Furthermore, when you view the help page for a given type, you will be told the name of the assembly and namespace that contains the type in question (located at the top of said page). As you read through the remainder of this book, I assume that you will dive into this *very, very* critical node to read up on additional details of the entity under examination.

A Partial Catalogue of Additional .NET Development Tools

To conclude this chapter, I would like to point out a number of .NET development tools that complement the functionality provided by your IDE of choice. Many of the tools mentioned here are open source, and all of them are free of charge. While I don't have the space to cover the details of these utilities, Table 2-5 lists a number of the tools I have found to be extremely helpful as well as URLs you can visit to find more information about them.

Table 2-5. *Select .NET Development Tools*

Tool	Meaning in Life	URL
FxCop	This is a must-have for any .NET developer interested in .NET best practices. FxCop will test any .NET assembly against the official Microsoft .NET best-practice coding guidelines.	`http://www.gotdotnet.com/team/fxcop`
Lutz Roeder's Reflector for .NET	This advanced .NET decompiler/object browser allows you to view the implementation of any .NET type using CIL, C#, Object Pascal .NET (Delphi), and Visual Basic .NET.	`http://www.aisto.com/roeder/dotnet`
NAnt	NAnt is the .NET equivalent of Ant, the popular Java automated build tool. NAnt allows you to define and execute detailed build scripts using an XML-based syntax.	`http://sourceforge.net/projects/nant`
NDoc	NDoc is a tool that will generate code documentation files for C# code (or a compiled .NET assembly) in a variety of popular formats (MSDN's *.chm, XML, HTML, Javadoc, and LaTeX).	`http://sourceforge.net/projects/ndoc`
NUnit	NUnit is the .NET equivalent of the Java-centric JUnit unit testing tool. Using NUnit, you are able to facilitate the testing of your managed code.	`http://www.nunit.org`
Vil	Think of Vil as a friendly "big brother" for .NET developers. This tool will analyze your .NET code and offer various opinions as to how to improve your code via refactoring, structured exception handling, and so forth.	`http://www.1bot.com`

■**Note** The functionality of FxCop has now been integrated directly into Visual Studio 2005. To check it out, simply double-click the Properties icon within Solution Explorer and activate the Code Analysis tab.

Summary

So as you can see, you have many new toys at your disposal! The point of this chapter was to provide you with a tour of the major programming tools a C# programmer may leverage during the development process. You began the journey by learning how to generate .NET assemblies using nothing other than the free C# compiler and Notepad. Next, you were introduced to the TextPad application and walked though the process of enabling this tool to edit and compile *.cs code files.

You also examined three feature-rich IDEs, starting with the open source SharpDevelop, followed by Microsoft's Visual C# 2005 Express and Visual Studio 2005. While this chapter only scratched the surface of each tool's functionality, you should be in a good position to explore your chosen IDE at your leisure. The chapter wrapped up by examining a number of open source .NET development tools that extend the functionality of your IDE of choice.

PART 2

■ ■ ■

The C# Programming Language

■ ■ ■

## CHAPTER 3

C# Language Fundamentals

Consider this chapter a potpourri of core topics regarding the C# language and the .NET platform. Unlike forthcoming chapters, there is no overriding example or theme; rather, the following pages illustrate a number of bite-size topics you must become comfortable with, including value-based and reference-based data types, decision and iteration constructs, boxing and unboxing mechanisms, the role of System.Object, and basic class-construction techniques. Along the way, you'll also learn how to manipulate CLR strings, arrays, enumerations, and structures using the syntax of C#.

To illustrate these language fundamentals, you'll take a programmatic look at the .NET base class libraries and build a number of sample applications, making use of various types in the System namespace. This chapter also examines a new C# 2005 language feature, nullable data types. Finally, you'll learn how to organize your types into custom namespaces using the C# namespace keyword.

The Anatomy of a Simple C# Program

C# demands that all program logic is contained within a type definition (recall from Chapter 1 that *type* is a term referring to a member of the set {class, interface, structure, enumeration, delegate}). Unlike in C(++), in C# it is not possible to create global functions or global points of data. In its simplest form, a C# program can be written as follows:

```
// By convention, C# files end with a *.cs file extension.
using System;

class HelloClass
{
    public static int Main(string[] args)
    {
        Console.WriteLine("Hello World!");
        Console.ReadLine();
        return 0;
    }
}
```

Here, a definition is created for a class type (HelloClass) that supports a single method named Main(). Every executable C# application must contain a class defining a Main() method, which is used to signify the entry point of the application. As you can see, this signature of Main() is adorned with the public and static keywords. Later in this chapter, you will be supplied with a formal definition of "public" and "static." Until then, understand that public members are accessible from other types, while static members are scoped at the class level (rather than the object level) and can thus be invoked without the need to first create a new class instance.

Note C# is a case-sensitive programming language. Therefore, "Main" is not the same as "main", and "Read-line" is not the same as "ReadLine". Given this, be aware that all C# keywords are in lowercase (`public`, `lock`, `global`, and so on), while namespaces, types, and member names begin (by convention) with an initial capital letter and have capitalized any embedded words (e.g., `Console.WriteLine`, `System.Windows.Forms.MessageBox`, `System.Data.SqlClient`, and so on).

In addition to the `public` and `static` keywords, this `Main()` method has a single parameter, which happens to be an array of strings (`string[] args`). Although you are not currently bothering to process this array, this parameter may contain any number of incoming command-line arguments (you'll see how to access them momentarily).

The program logic of `HelloClass` is within `Main()` itself. Here, you make use of the `Console` class, which is defined within the `System` namespace. Among its set of members is the static `WriteLine()` which, as you might assume, pumps a text string to the standard output. You also make a call to `Console.ReadLine()` to ensure the command prompt launched by Visual Studio 2005 remains visible during a debugging session until you press the Enter key.

Because this `Main()` method has been defined as returning an integer data type, we return zero (success) before exiting. Finally, as you can see from the `HelloClass` type definition, C- and C++-style comments have carried over into the C# language.

Variations on the Main() Method

The previous iteration of `Main()` was defined to take a single parameter (an array of strings) and return an integer data type. This is not the only possible form of `Main()`, however. It is permissible to construct your application's entry point using any of the following signatures (assuming it is contained within a C# class or structure definition):

```
// No return type, array of strings as argument.
public static void Main(string[] args)
{
}

// No return type, no arguments.
public static void Main()
{
}

// Integer return type, no arguments.
public static int Main()
{
}
```

Note The `Main()` method may also be defined as `private` as opposed to `public`. Doing so ensures other assemblies cannot directly invoke an application's entry point. Visual Studio 2005 automatically defines a program's `Main()` method as private.

Obviously, your choice of how to construct `Main()` will be based on two questions. First, do you need to process any user-supplied command-line parameters? If so, they will be stored in the array of strings. Second, do you want to return a value to the system when `Main()` has completed? If so, you need to return an integer data type rather than `void`.

Processing Command-Line Arguments

Assume that you now wish to update HelloClass to process possible command-line parameters:

```
// This time, check if you have been sent any command-line arguments.
using System;

class HelloClass
{
    public static int Main(string[] args)
    {
        Console.WriteLine("***** Command line args *****");
        for(int i = 0; i < args.Length; i++)
            Console.WriteLine("Arg: {0} ", args[i]);
...
    }
}
```

Here, you are checking to see if the array of strings contains some number of items using the Length property of System.Array (as you'll see later in this chapter, all C# arrays actually alias the System.Array type, and therefore have a common set of members). As you loop over each item in the array, its value is printed to the console window. Supplying the arguments at the command line is equally as simple, as shown in Figure 3-1.

Figure 3-1. *Supplying arguments at the command line*

As an alternative to the standard for loop, you may iterate over incoming string arrays using the C# foreach keyword. This bit of syntax is fully explained later in this chapter, but here is some sample usage:

```
// Notice you have no need to check the size of the array when using 'foreach'.
public static int Main(string[] args)
{
...
    foreach(string s in args)
        Console.WriteLine("Arg: {0} ", s);
...
}
```

Finally, you are also able to access command-line arguments using the static GetCommand-LineArgs() method of the System.Environment type. The return value of this method is an array of strings. The first index identifies the current directory containing the application itself, while the remaining elements in the array contain the individual command-line arguments (when using this technique, you no longer need to define the Main() method as taking a string array parameter):

```
public static int Main(string[] args)
{
...
    // Get arguments using System.Environment.
    string[] theArgs = Environment.GetCommandLineArgs();
    Console.WriteLine("Path to this app is: {0}", theArgs[0]);
...
}
```

Specifying Command-Line Arguments with Visual Studio 2005

In the real world, the end user supplies the command-line arguments used by a given application when starting the program. However, during the development cycle, you may wish to specify possible command-line flags for testing purposes. To do so with Visual Studio 2005, double-click the Properties icon from Solution Explorer and select the Debug tab on the left side. From here, specify values using the "Command line arguments" text box (see Figure 3-2).

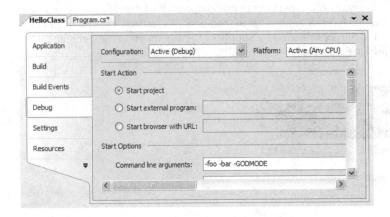

Figure 3-2. *Setting command arguments via Visual Studio 2005*

An Interesting Aside: The System.Environment Class

Let's examine the System.Environment class in greater detail. This class allows you to obtain a number of details regarding the operating system currently hosting your .NET application using various static members. To illustrate this class's usefulness, update your Main() method with the following logic:

```
public static int Main(string[] args)
{
...
    // OS running this app?
    Console.WriteLine("Current OS: {0} ", Environment.OSVersion);

    // Directory containing this app?
    Console.WriteLine("Current Directory: {0} ",
        Environment.CurrentDirectory);
```

```
// List the drives on this machine.
string[] drives = Environment.GetLogicalDrives();
for(int i = 0; i < drives.Length; i++)
    Console.WriteLine("Drive {0}  : {1} ",  i, drives[i]);

// Which version of the .NET platform is running this app?
Console.WriteLine("Executing version of .NET: {0} ",
    Environment.Version);
...
}
```

Possible output can be seen in Figure 3-3.

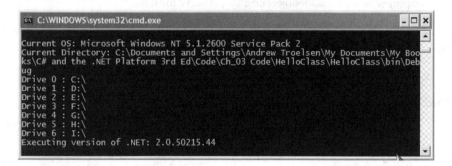

Figure 3-3. *Various environment variables at work*

The System.Environment type defines members other than those presented in the previous example. Table 3-1 documents some additional properties of interest; however, be sure to check out the .NET Framework 2.0 SDK documentation for full details.

Table 3-1. *Select Properties of* System.Environment

Property	Meaning in Life
MachineName	Gets the name of the current machine
NewLine	Gets the newline symbol for the current environment
ProcessorCount	Returns the number of processors on the current machine
SystemDirectory	Returns the full path to the system directory
UserName	Returns the name of the entity that started this application

Defining Classes and Creating Objects

Now that you have the role of Main() under your belt, let's move on to the topic of object construction. All object-oriented (OO) languages make a clear distinction between classes and objects. A *class* is a definition (or, if you will, a *blueprint*) for a user-defined type (UDT). An *object* is simply a term describing a given instance of a particular class in memory. In C#, the new keyword is the de facto way to create an object. Unlike other OO languages (such as C++), it is not possible to allocate a class type on the stack; therefore, if you attempt to use a class variable that has not been "new-ed," you are issued a compile-time error. Thus the following C# code is *illegal*:

```
using System;

class HelloClass
{
    public static int Main(string[] args)
    {
        // Error!  Use of unassigned local variable!  Must use 'new'.
        HelloClass c1;
        c1.SomeMethod();
...
    }
}
```

To illustrate the proper procedures for object creation, observe the following update:

```
using System;

class HelloClass
{
    public static int Main(string[] args)
    {
        // You can declare and create a new object in a single line...
        HelloClass c1 = new HelloClass();

        // ...or break declaration and creation into two lines.
        HelloClass c2;
        c2 = new HelloClass();
...
    }
}
```

The new keyword is in charge of calculating the correct number of bytes for the specified object and acquiring sufficient memory from the managed heap. Here, you have allocated two objects of the HelloClass class type. Understand that C# object variables are really a *reference* to the object in memory, not the actual object itself. Thus, in this light, c1 and c2 each reference a unique HelloClass object allocated on the managed heap.

The Role of Constructors

The previous HelloClass objects have been constructed using the *default constructor*, which by definition never takes arguments. Every C# class is automatically provided with a free default constructor, which you may redefine if need be. The default constructor ensures that all member data is set to an appropriate default value (this behavior is true for all constructors). Contrast this to C++, where uninitialized state data points to garbage (sometimes the little things mean a lot).

Typically, classes provide additional constructors beyond the default. In doing so, you provide the object user with a simple way to initialize the state of an object at the time of creation. Like in Java and C++, in C# constructors are named identically to the class they are constructing, and they never provide a return value (not even void). Here is the HelloClass type once again, with a custom constructor, a redefined default constructor, and a point of public string data:

```
// HelloClass, with constructors.
using System;

class HelloClass
{
    // A point of state data.
    public string userMessage;
```

```
    // Default constructor.
    public HelloClass()
    { Console.WriteLine("Default ctor called!"); }

    // This custom constructor assigns state data
    // to a user-supplied value.
    public HelloClass (string msg)
    {
        Console.WriteLine("Custom ctor called!");
        userMessage = msg;
    }

    // Program entry point.
    public static int Main(string[] args)
    {
        // Call default constructor.
        HelloClass c1 = new HelloClass();
        Console.WriteLine("Value of userMessage: {0}\n", c1.userMessage);

        // Call parameterized constructor.
        HelloClass c2;
        c2 = new HelloClass("Testing, 1, 2, 3");
        Console.WriteLine("Value of userMessage: {0}", c2.userMessage);
        Console.ReadLine();
        return 0;
    }
}
```

■**Note** Technically speaking, when a type defines identically named members (including constructors) that differ only in the number of—or type of—parameters, the member in question is *overloaded*. Chapter 4 examines member overloading in detail.

On examining the program's output, you can see that the default constructor has assigned the string field to its default value (null), while the custom constructor has assigned the member data to the user-supplied value (see Figure 3-4).

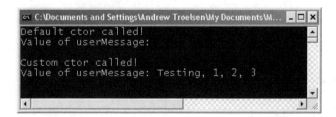

Figure 3-4. *Simple constructor logic*

■**Note** As soon as you define a custom constructor for a class type, the free default constructor is removed. If you wish to allow your object users to create an instance of your type using the default constructor, you will need to explicitly redefine it as in the preceding example.

Is That a Memory Leak?

If you have a background in C++, you may be alarmed by the previous code samples. Specifically, notice how the Main() method of the previous HelloClass type has no logic that explicitly destroys the c1 and c2 references.

This is not a horrible omission, but the way of .NET. Like Visual Basic and Java developers, C# programmers never explicitly destroy a managed object. The .NET garbage collector frees the allocated memory automatically, and therefore C# does not support a delete keyword. Chapter 5 examines the garbage collection process in more detail. Until then, just remember that the .NET runtime environment automatically destroys the managed objects you allocate.

Defining an "Application Object"

Currently, the HelloClass type has been constructed to perform two duties. First, the class defines the entry point of the application (the Main() method). Second, HelloClass maintains a point of field data and a few constructors. While this is all well and good, it may seem a bit strange (although syntactically well-formed) that the static Main() method creates an instance of the very class in which it was defined:

```
class HelloClass
{
...
    public static int Main(string[] args)
    {
        HelloClass c1 = new HelloClass();
        ...
    }
}
```

Many of my initial examples take this approach, just to keep focused on illustrating the task at hand. However, a more natural design would be to refactor the current HelloClass type into two distinct classes: HelloClass and HelloApp. When you build C# applications, it becomes quite common to have one type functioning as the "application object" (the type that defines the Main() method) and numerous other types that constitute the application at large.

In OO parlance, this is termed the *separation of concerns*. In a nutshell, this design principle states that a class should be responsible for the least amount of work. Thus, we could reengineer the current program into the following (notice that a new member named PrintMessage() has been added to the HelloClass type):

```
class HelloClass
{
    public string userMessage;

    public HelloClass()
    { Console.WriteLine("Default ctor called!"); }

    public HelloClass(string msg)
    {
        Console.WriteLine("Custom ctor called!");
        userMessage = msg;
    }

    public void PrintMessage()
    {
        Console.WriteLine("Message is: {0}", userMessage);
    }
}
```

```
class HelloApp
{
    public static int Main(string[] args)
    {
        HelloClass c1 = new HelloClass("Hey there...");
        c1.PrintMessage();
...
    }
}
```

■**Source Code** The HelloClass project is located under the Chapter 3 subdirectory.

The System.Console Class

Many of the example applications created over the course of these first few chapters make extensive use of the System.Console class. While a console user interface (CUI) is not as enticing as a Windows or web UI, restricting the early examples to a CUI will allow us to keep focused on the concepts under examination, rather than dealing with the complexities of building GUIs.

As its name implies, the Console class encapsulates input, output, and error stream manipulations for console-based applications. With the release of .NET 2.0, the Console type has been enhanced with additional functionality. Table 3-2 lists some (but not all) new members of interest.

Table 3-2. *Select .NET 2.0–Specific Members of* System.Console

Member	Meaning in Life
BackgroundColor ForegroundColor	These properties set the background/foreground colors for the current output. They may be assigned any member of the ConsoleColor enumeration.
BufferHeight BufferWidth	These properties control the height/width of the console's buffer area.
Clear()	This method clears the buffer and console display area.
Title	This property sets the title of the current console.
WindowHeight WindowWidth WindowTop WindowLeft	These properties control the dimensions of the console in relation to the established buffer.

Basic Input and Output with the Console Class

In addition to the members in Table 3-2, the Console type defines a set of methods to capture input and output, all of which are defined as static and are therefore called at the class level. As you have seen, WriteLine() pumps a text string (including a carriage return) to the output stream. The Write() method pumps text to the output stream without a carriage return. ReadLine() allows you to receive information from the input stream up until the carriage return, while Read() is used to capture a single character from the input stream.

To illustrate basic I/O using the Console class, consider the following Main() method, which prompts the user for some bits of information and echoes each item to the standard output stream. Figure 3-5 shows a test run.

```
// Make use of the Console class to perform basic I/O.
static void Main(string[] args)
{
    // Echo some stats.
    Console.Write("Enter your name: ");
    string s = Console.ReadLine();
    Console.WriteLine("Hello, {0} ", s);

    Console.Write("Enter your age: ");
    s = Console.ReadLine();
    Console.WriteLine("You are {0} years old", s);
}
```

Figure 3-5. *Basic I/O using* System.Console

Formatting Console Output

During these first few chapters, you have seen numerous occurrences of the tokens {0}, {1}, and the like embedded within a string literal. .NET introduces a new style of string formatting, slightly reminiscent of the C printf() function, but without the cryptic %d, %s, or %c flags. A simple example follows (see the output in Figure 3-6):

```
static void Main(string[] args)
{
...
    int theInt = 90;
    double theDouble = 9.99;
    bool theBool = true;

    // The '\n' token in a string literal inserts a newline.
    Console.WriteLine("Int is: {0}\nDouble is: {1}\nBool is: {2}",
        theInt, theDouble, theBool);
}
```

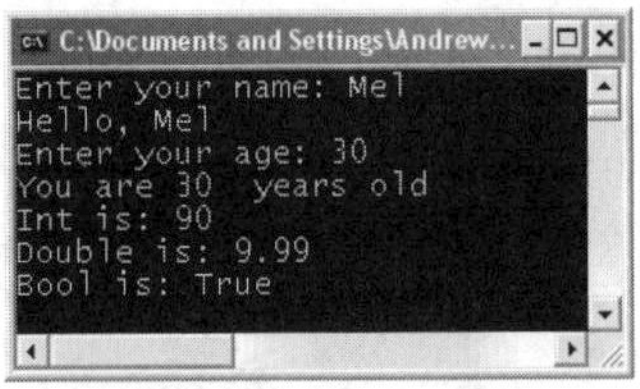

Figure 3-6. *Multiple string literal placeholders*

The first parameter to WriteLine() represents a string literal that contains optional placeholders designated by {0}, {1}, {2}, and so forth (curly bracket numbering always begins with zero). The remaining parameters to WriteLine() are simply the values to be inserted into the respective place-holders (in this case, an int, a double, and a bool).

Also be aware that WriteLine() has been overloaded to allow you to specify placeholder values as an array of objects. Thus, you can represent any number of items to be plugged into the format string as follows:

```
// Fill placeholders using an array of objects.
object[] stuff = {"Hello", 20.9, 1, "There", "83", 99.99933} ;
Console.WriteLine("The Stuff: {0} , {1} , {2} , {3} , {4} , {5} ", stuff);
```

It is also permissible for a given placeholder to repeat within a given string. For example, if you are a Beatles fan and want to build the string "9, Number 9, Number 9" you would write

```
// John says...
Console.WriteLine("{0}, Number {0}, Number {0}", 9);
```

■**Note** If you have a mismatch between the number of uniquely numbered curly-bracket placeholders and fill arguments, you will receive a FormatException exception at runtime.

.NET String Formatting Flags

If you require more elaborate formatting, each placeholder can optionally contain various format characters (in either uppercase or lowercase), as seen in Table 3-3.

Table 3-3. *.NET String Format Characters*

String Format Character	Meaning in Life
C or c	Used to format currency. By default, the flag will prefix the local cultural symbol (a dollar sign [$] for U.S. English).
D or d	Used to format decimal numbers. This flag may also specify the minimum number of digits used to pad the value.
E or e	Used for exponential notation.
F or f	Used for fixed-point formatting.
G or g	Stands for *general*. This character can be used to format a number to fixed or exponential format.
N or n	Used for basic numerical formatting (with commas).
X or x	Used for hexadecimal formatting. If you use an uppercase X, your hex format will also contain uppercase characters.

These format characters are suffixed to a given placeholder value using the colon token (e.g., {0:C}, {1:d}, {2:X}, and so on). Assume you have updated Main() with the following logic:

```
// Now make use of some format tags.
static void Main(string[] args)
{
...
    Console.WriteLine("C format: {0:C}", 99989.987);
    Console.WriteLine("D9 format: {0:D9}", 99999);
    Console.WriteLine("E format: {0:E}", 99999.76543);
    Console.WriteLine("F3 format: {0:F3}", 99999.9999);
```

```
    Console.WriteLine("N format: {0:N}", 99999);
    Console.WriteLine("X format: {0:X}", 99999);
    Console.WriteLine("x format: {0:x}", 99999);
}
```

Be aware that the use of .NET formatting characters is not limited to console applications. These same flags can be used within the context of the static `String.Format()` method. This can be helpful when you need to build a string containing numerical values in memory for use in any application type (Windows Forms, ASP.NET, XML web services, and so on):

```
static void Main(string[] args)
{
...
    // Use the static String.Format() method to build a new string.
    string formatStr;
    formatStr =
        String.Format("Don't you wish you had {0:C} in your account?",
            99989.987);
    Console.WriteLine(formatStr);
}
```

Figure 3-7 shows a test run.

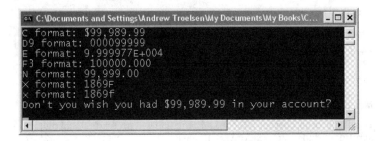

Figure 3-7. *String format flags in action*

■**Source Code**   The BasicConsoleIO project is located under the Chapter 3 subdirectory.

Establishing Member Visibility

Before we go much further, it is important to address the topic of *member visibility*. Members (methods, fields, constructors, and so on) of a given class or structure must specify their "visibility" level. If you define a member without specifying an accessibility keyword, it automatically defaults to `private`. C# offers the method access modifiers shown in Table 3-4.

Table 3-4. *C# Accessibility Keywords*

C# Access Modifier	Meaning in Life
public	Marks a member as accessible from an object variable as well as any derived classes.
private	Marks a method as accessible only by the class that has defined the method. In C#, all members are private by default.
protected	Marks a method as usable by the defining class, as well as any derived classes. Protected methods, however, are not accessible from an object variable.
internal	Defines a method that is accessible by any type in the same assembly, but not outside the assembly.
protected internal	Defines a method whose access is limited to the current assembly or types derived from the defining class in the current assembly.

As you may already know, members that are declared public are directly accessible from an object reference via the dot operator (.). Private members cannot be accessed by an object reference, but instead are called internally by the object to help the instance get its work done (i.e., private helper functions).

Protected members are only truly useful when you create class hierarchies, which is the subject of Chapter 4. As far as internal or internal protected members are concerned, they are only truly useful when you are creating .NET code libraries (such as a managed *.dll, a topic examined in Chapter 11).

To illustrate the implications of these keywords, assume you have created a class (SomeClass) using each of the possible member access modifiers:

```
// Member visibility options.
class SomeClass
{
    // Accessible anywhere.
    public void PublicMethod(){}

    // Accessible only from SomeClass types.
    private void PrivateMethod(){}

    // Accessible from SomeClass and any descendent.
    protected void ProtectedMethod(){}

    // Accessible from within the same assembly.
    internal void InternalMethod(){}

    // Assembly-protected access.
    protected internal void ProtectedInternalMethod(){}

    // Unmarked members are private by default in C#.
    void SomeMethod(){}
}
```

Now assume you have created an instance of SomeClass and attempt to invoke each method using the dot operator:

```
static void Main(string[] args)
{
    // Make an object and attempt to call members.
    SomeClass c = new SomeClass();
    c.PublicMethod();
```

```
    c.InternalMethod();
    c.ProtectedInternalMethod();
    c.PrivateMethod();          // Error!
    c.ProtectedMethod();        // Error!
    c.SomeMethod();             // Error!
}
```

If you compile this program, you will find that the protected and private members are *not* accessible from an object.

■**Source Code** The MemberAccess project is located under the Chapter 3 subdirectory.

Establishing Type Visibility

Types (classes, interfaces, structures, enumerations, and delegates) can also take accessibility modifiers, but are limited to public or internal. When you create a public type, you ensure that the type can be accessed from other types in the current assembly as well as external assemblies. Again, this is useful only when you are creating a code library (see Chapter 11); however, here is some example usage:

```
// This type can be used by any assembly.
public class MyClass{}
```

An internal type, on the other hand, can be used only by the assembly in which it is defined. Thus, if you created a .NET code library that defines three internal types, assemblies that reference the *.dll would not be able to see, create, or in anyway interact with them.

Because internal is the default accessibility for types in C#, if you do not specifically make use of the public keyword, you actually create an internal type:

```
// These classes can only be used by the defining assembly.
internal class MyHelperClass{}
class FinalHelperClass{}          // Types are internal by default in C#.
```

■**Note** In Chapter 4 you'll learn about nested types. As you'll see, nested types can be declared private as well.

Default Values of Class Member Variables

The member variables of class types are automatically set to an appropriate default value. This value will differ based on the exact data type; however, the rules are simple:

- bool types are set to false.
- Numeric data is set to 0 (or 0.0 in the case of floating-point data types).
- string types are set to null.
- char types are set to '\0'.
- Reference types are set to null.

Given these rules, ponder the following code:

```
// Fields of a class type receive automatic default assignments.
class Test
{
    public int myInt;              // Set to 0.
```

```
    public string myString;      // Set to null.
    public bool myBool;          // Set to false.
    public object myObj;         // Set to null.
}
```

Default Values and Local Variables

The story is very different, however, when you declare local variables within a member scope. When you define local variables, you *must* assign an initial value before you use them, as they do not receive a default assignment. For example, the following code results in a compiler error:

```
// Compiler error! Must assign 'localInt' to an initial value before use.
static void Main(string[] args)
{
    int localInt;
    Console.WriteLine(localInt);
}
```

Fixing the problem is trivial. Simply make an initial assignment:

```
// Better; everyone is happy.
static void Main(string[] args)
{
    int localInt = 0;
    Console.WriteLine(localInt);
}
```

■**Note** There's one exception to the mandatory assignment of local variables. If the variable is used as an *output parameter* (you'll examine this a bit later in this chapter), the variable doesn't need to be assigned an initial value.

Member Variable Initialization Syntax

Class types tend to have numerous member variables (aka fields). Given that a class may define multiple constructors, you can find yourself in the annoying position of having to write the same initialization code in each and every constructor implementation. This is particularly true if you do not wish to accept the member's default value. For example, if you wish to ensure that an integer member variable (myInt) always begins life with the value of 9, you could write

```
// This is OK, but redundant...
class Test
{
    public int myInt;
    public string myString;

    public Test() { myInt = 9; }
    public Test(string s)
    {
        myInt = 9;
        myString = s;
    }
}
```

An alternative would be to define a private helper function for your class type that is called by each constructor. While this will reduce the amount of repeat *assignment* code, you are now stuck with the following redundancy:

```
// This is still rather redundant...
class Test
{
    public int myInt;
    public string myString;

    public Test() { InitData(); }
    public Test(string s)
    {
        myString = s;
        InitData();
    }

    private void InitData()
    { myInt = 9; }
}
```

While both of these techniques are still valid, C# allows you to assign a type's member data to an initial value at the time of declaration (as you may be aware, other OO languages [such as C++] do not allow you to initialize a member in this way). Notice in the following code blurb that member initialization may be used with internal object references as well as numerical data types:

```
// This technique is useful when you don't want to accept default values
// and would rather not write the same initialization code in each constructor.
class Test
{
    public int myInt = 9;
    public string myStr = "My initial value.";
    public SportsCar viper = new SportsCar(Color.Red);
    ...
}
```

■**Note** Member assignment happens *before* constructor logic. Thus, if you assign a field within the scope of a constructor, it effectively cancels out the previous member assignment.

Defining Constant Data

Now that you have seen how to declare class variables, let's see how to define data that should never be reassigned. C# offers the const keyword to define variables with a fixed, unalterable value. Once the value of a constant has been established, any attempt to alter it results in a compiler error. Unlike in C++, in C# the const keyword cannot be used to qualify parameters or return values, and is reserved for the creation of local or instance-level data.

It is important to understand that the value assigned to a constant variable must be known at *compile time*, and therefore a constant member cannot be assigned to an object reference (whose value is computed at runtime). To illustrate the use of the const keyword, assume the following class type:

```
class ConstData
{
    // The value assigned to a const must be known
    // at compile time.
    public const string BestNbaTeam = "Timberwolves";
    public const double SimplePI = 3.14;
    public const bool Truth = true;
    public const bool Falsity = !Truth;
}
```

Notice that the value of each constant is known at the time of compilation. In fact, if you were to view these constants using ildasm.exe, you would find the value hard-coded directly into the assembly, as shown in Figure 3-8. (You can't get much more constant than this!)

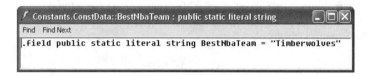

Figure 3-8. *The* const *keyword hard-codes its value into the assembly metadata.*

Referencing Constant Data

When you wish to reference a constant defined by an external type, you must prefix the defining type name (e.g., ConstData.Truth), as constant fields are *implicitly static*. However, if you are referencing a piece of constant data defined in the current type (or within the current member), you are not required to prefix the type name. To solidify these points, observe the following additional class:

```
class Program
{
    public const string BestNhlTeam = "Wild";

    static void Main(string[] args)
    {
        // Print const values defined by other type.
        Console.WriteLine("Nba const: {0}", ConstData.BestNbaTeam);
        Console.WriteLine("SimplePI const: {0}", ConstData.SimplePI);
        Console.WriteLine("Truth const: {0}", ConstData.Truth);
        Console.WriteLine("Falsity const: {0}", ConstData.Falsity);

        // Print member-level const.
        Console.WriteLine("Nhl const: {0}", BestNhlTeam);

        // Print local-scoped const.
        const int LocalFixedValue = 4;
        Console.WriteLine("Local const: {0}", LocalFixedValue);
        Console.ReadLine();
    }
}
```

Notice that when the Program class accesses the constants within ConstData, the type name must be specified. However, Program has direct access to the BestNhlTeam constant as it was defined within its own class scope. The LocalFixedValue constant defined within Main() would, of course, be accessible only from the Main() method.

Source Code The Constants project is located under the Chapter 3 subdirectory.

Defining Read-Only Fields

As mentioned earlier, the value assigned to a constant must be known at compile time. However, what if you wish to create an unchangeable field whose initial value is not known until *runtime*? Assume you have created a class named Tire, which maintains a manufacture ID. Furthermore, assume you wish to configure this class type to maintain a pair of well-known Tire instances whose value should never change. If you use the const keyword, you will receive compiler errors, given that the address of an object in memory is not known until *runtime*:

```
class Tire
{
    // Given that the address of objects is determined at
    // runtime, we cannot use the 'const' keyword here!
    public const Tire GoodStone = new Tire(90);    // Error!
    public const Tire FireYear = new Tire(100);    // Error!

    public int manufactureID;
    public Tire() {}
    public Tire(int ID)
    { manufactureID = ID; }
}
```

Read-only fields allow you to establish a point of data whose value is not known at compile time, but that should never change once established. To define a read-only field, make use of the C# read-only keyword. Unlike const however, read-only fields are not implicitly static; therefore if you wish to expose such data at class level, the static keyword must be included.

```
class Tire
{
    public readonly static Tire GoodStone = new Tire(90);
    public readonly static Tire FireYear = new Tire(100);

    public int manufactureID;
    public Tire() {}
    public Tire(int ID)
    { manufactureID = ID; }
}
```

With this update, you not only compile, but also ensure that if the GoodStone or FireYear fields are changed within your program, you receive a compilation error:

```
static void Main(string[] args)
{
    // Error!  Can't change the value of a read-only field.
    Tire t = new Tire();
    t.FireYear = new Tire(33);
}
```

Read-only fields have another distinction from constant data: their value may be assigned within the scope of a constructor. This can be very useful if the value to assign to a read-only field must be read from an external source (such as a text file or database). Assume another class named Employee, which defines a read-only string representing a U.S. Social Security number (SSN). To ensure the object user can specify this value, you may author the following code:

```
class Employee
{
    public readonly string SSN;
```

```
    public Employee(string empSSN)
    {
        SSN = empSSN;
    }
}
```

Again, because SSN is readonly, any attempt to change this value after the constructor logic results in a compiler error:

```
static void Main(string[] args)
{
    Employee e = new Employee("111-22-1111");
    e.SSN = "222-22-2222";  // Error!
}
```

Static Read-Only Fields

Unlike constant data, read-only fields are not implicitly static. If you wish to allow object users to obtain the value of a read-only field from the class level, simply make use of the static keyword:

```
class Tire
{
    public static readonly Tire GoodStone = new Tire(90);
    public static readonly Tire FireYear = new Tire(100);
...
}
```

Here is an example of working with the new Tire type:

```
static void Main(string[] args)
{
    Tire myTire = Tire.FireYear;
    Console.WriteLine("ID of my tire is: {0}", myTire.manufactureID);
}
```

Source Code The ReadOnlyFields project is included under the Chapter 3 subdirectory.

Understanding the static Keyword

As shown throughout this chapter, C# class (and structure) members may be defined using the static keyword. When you do so, the member in question must be invoked directly from the class level, rather than from a type instance. To illustrate the distinction, consider our good friend System.Console. As you have seen, you do not invoke the WriteLine() method from the object level:

```
// Error!  WriteLine() is not an instance level method!
Console c = new Console();
c.WriteLine("I can't be printed...");
```

but instead simply prefix the type name to the static WriteLine() member:

```
// Correct!  WriteLine() is a static method.
Console.WriteLine("Thanks...");
```

Simply put, static members are items that are deemed (by the type designer) to be so commonplace that there is no need to create an instance of the type. When you are designing custom class types, you are also able to define any number of static and/or instance-level members.

Static Methods

Assume a class named Teenager that defines a static method named Complain(), which returns a random string, obtained in part by calling a private helper function named GetRandomNumber():

```
class Teenager
{
    private static Random r = new Random();
    private static int GetRandomNumber(short upperLimit)
    { return r.Next(upperLimit); }

    public static string Complain()
    {
        string[] messages = new string[5]{ "Do I have to?",
            "He started it!", "I'm too tired...",
            "I hate school!", "You are sooo wrong." } ;
        return messages[GetRandomNumber(5)];
    }
}
```

Notice that the System.Random member variable and the GetRandomNumber() helper function method have also been declared as static members of the Teenager class, given the rule that static members can operate *only* on other static members.

■**Note** Allow me to repeat myself. *Static members can operate* only *on static class members*. If you attempt to make use of nonstatic class members (also called *instance data*) within a static method, you receive a compiler error.

Like any static member, to call Complain(), prefix the name of the defining class:

```
// Call the static Complain method of the Teenager class.
static void Main(string[] args)
{
    for(int i = 0; i < 10; i++)
        Console.WriteLine("-> {0}", Teenager.Complain());
}
```

And like any nonstatic method, if the Complain() method was *not* marked static, you would need to create an instance of the Teenager class before you could hear about the gripe of the day:

```
// Nonstatic data must be invoked at the object level.
Teenager joe = new Teenager();
joe.Complain();
```

■**Source Code** The StaticMethods application is located under the Chapter 3 subdirectory.

Static Data

In addition to static methods, a type may also define static data (such as the Random member variable seen in the previous Teenager class). Understand that when a class defines nonstatic data, each object of this type maintains a private copy of the field. For example, assume a class that models a savings account:

```
// This class has a single piece of nonstatic data.
class SavingsAccount
{
    public double currBalance;
    public SavingsAccount(double balance)
    { currBalance = balance;}
}
```

When you create SavingsAccount objects, memory for the currBalance field is allocated for each instance. Static data, on the other hand, is allocated once and shared among all object instances of the same type. To illustrate the usefulness of static data, assume you add piece of *static* data named currInterestRate to the SavingsAccount class:

```
class SavingsAccount
{
    public double currBalance;
    public static double currInterestRate = 0.04;
    public SavingsAccount(double balance)
    { currBalance = balance;}
}
```

If you were to create three instances of SavingsAccount as so:

```
static void Main(string[] args)
{
    // Each SavingsAccount object maintains a copy of the currBalance field.
    SavingsAccount s1 = new SavingsAccount(50);
    SavingsAccount s2 = new SavingsAccount(100);
    SavingsAccount s3 = new SavingsAccount(10000.75);
}
```

the in-memory data allocation would look something like Figure 3-9.

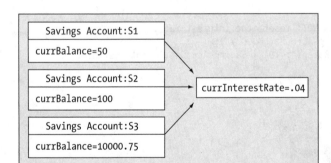

Figure 3-9. *Static data is shared for all instances of the defining class.*

Let's update the SavingsAccount class to define two static methods to get and set the interest rate value. As stated, static methods can operate only on static data. However, a nonstatic method can make use of both static and nonstatic data. This should make sense, given that static data is available to all instances of the type. Given this, let's also add two instance-level methods to interact with the interest rate variable:

```
class SavingsAccount
{
    public double currBalance;
    public static double currInterestRate = 0.04;
    public SavingsAccount(double balance)
    { currBalance = balance;}

    // Static methods to get/set interest rate.
    public static void SetInterestRate(double newRate)
    { currInterest Rate = newRate;}

    public static double GetInterestRate()
    { return currInterestRate;}

    // Instance method to get/set current interest rate.
    public void SetInterestRateObj(double newRate)
    { currInterestRate = newRate;}

    public double GetInterestRateObj()
    { return currInterestRate;}
}
```

Now, observe the following usage and the output in Figure 3-10:

```
static void Main(string[] args)
{
    Console.WriteLine("***** Fun with Static Data *****");
    SavingsAccount s1 = new SavingsAccount(50);
    SavingsAccount s2 = new SavingsAccount(100);

    // Get and set interest rate.
    Console.WriteLine("Interest Rate is: {0}", s1.GetInterestRateObj());
    s2.SetInterestRateObj(0.08);

    // Make new object, this does NOT 'reset' the interest rate.
    SavingsAccount s3 = new SavingsAccount(10000.75);
    Console.WriteLine("Interest Rate is: {0}", SavingsAccount.GetInterestRate());
    Console.ReadLine();
}
```

Figure 3-10. *Static data is allocated only once.*

Static Constructors

As you know, constructors are used to set the value of a type's data at the time of construction. If you were to assign the value to a piece of static data within an instance-level constructor, you would be saddened to find that the value is reset each time you create a new object! For example, assume you have updated the SavingsAccount class as so:

```
class SavingsAccount
{
    public double currBalance;
    public static double currInterestRate;
    public SavingsAccount(double balance)
    {
        currBalance = balance;
        currInterestRate = 0.04;
    }
...
}
```

If you execute the previous Main() method, you will see a very different output (see Figure 3-11). Specifically notice how the currInterestRate variable is reset each time you create a new SavingsAccount object.

Figure 3-11. *Assigning static data in a constructor "resets" the value.*

While you are always free to establish the initial value of static data using the member initialization syntax, what if the value for your static data needed to be obtained from a database or external file? To perform such tasks requires a method scope to author the code statements. For this very reason, C# allows you to define a *static constructor*:

```
class SavingsAccount
{
...
    // Static constructor.
    static SavingsAccount()
    {
        Console.WriteLine("In static ctor!");
        currInterestRate = 0.04;
    }
}
```

Here are a few points of interest regarding static constructors:

- A given class (or structure) may define only a single static constructor.
- A static constructor executes exactly one time, regardless of how many objects of the type are created.
- A static constructor does not take an access modifier and cannot take any parameters.
- The runtime invokes the static constructor when it creates an instance of the class or before accessing the first static member invoked by the caller.
- The static constructor executes before any instance-level constructors.

Given this modification, when you create new SavingsAccount objects, the value of the static data is preserved, and the output is identical to Figure 3-10.

Static Classes

C# 2005 has widened the scope of the static keyword by introducing *static classes*. When a class has been defined as static, it is not creatable using the new keyword, and it can contain only static members or fields (if this is not the case, you receive compiler errors).

At first glance, this might seem like a very *useless* feature, given that a class that cannot be created does not appear all that helpful. However, if you create a class that contains nothing but static members and/or constant data, the class has no need to be allocated in the first place. Consider the following type:

```
// Static classes can only
// contain static members and constant fields.
static class UtilityClass
{
    public static void PrintTime()
    { Console.WriteLine(DateTime.Now.ToShortTimeString()); }
    public static void PrintDate()
    { Console.WriteLine(DateTime.Today.ToShortDateString()); }
}
```

Given the static modifier, object users cannot create an instance of UtilityClass:

```
static void Main(string[] args)
{
    UtilityClass.PrintDate();

    // Compiler error! Can't create static classes.
    UtilityClass u = new UtilityClass();
...
}
```

Prior to C# 2005, the only way to prevent an object user from creating such a type was to either redefine the default constructor as private or mark the class as an abstract type using the C# abstract keyword (full details regarding abstract types are in Chapter 4):

```
class UtilityClass
{
    private UtilityClass(){}
...
}
```

```
abstract class UtilityClass
{
...
}
```

While these constructs are still permissible, the use of static classes is a cleaner solution and more type-safe, given that the previous two techniques allowed nonstatic members to appear within the class definition.

■**Source Code** The StaticData project is located under the Chapter 3 subdirectory.

Method Parameter Modifiers

Methods (static and instance level) tend to take parameters passed in by the caller. However, unlike some programming languages, C# provides a set of parameter modifiers that control how arguments are sent into (and possibly returned from) a given method, as shown in Table 3-5.

Table 3-5. *C# Parameter Modifiers*

Parameter Modifier	Meaning in Life
(none)	If a parameter is not marked with a parameter modifier, it is assumed to be *passed by value,* meaning the called method receives a copy of the original data.
out	Output parameters are assigned by the method being called (and therefore *passed by reference*). If the called method fails to assign output parameters, you are issued a compiler error.
params	This parameter modifier allows you to send in a variable number of identically typed arguments as a single logical parameter. A method can have only a single params modifier, and it must be the final parameter of the method.
ref	The value is initially assigned by the caller, and may be *optionally* reassigned by the called method (as the data is also passed by reference). No compiler error is generated if the called method fails to assign a ref parameter.

The Default Parameter-Passing Behavior

The default manner in which a parameter is sent into a function is *by value*. Simply put, if you do not mark an argument with a parameter-centric modifier, a copy of the variable is passed into the function:

```
// Arguments are passed by value by default.
public static int Add(int x, int y)
{
    int ans = x + y;

    // Caller will not see these changes
    // as you are modifying a copy of the
    // original data.
    x = 10000;
    y = 88888;
    return ans;
}
```

Here, the incoming integer parameters will be passed by value. Therefore, if you change the values of the parameters within the scope of the member, the caller is blissfully unaware, given that you are changing the values of copies of the caller's integer data types:

```
static void Main(string[] args)
{
    int x = 9, y = 10;
    Console.WriteLine("Before call: X: {0}, Y: {1}", x, y);
    Console.WriteLine("Answer is: {0}", Add(x, y));
    Console.WriteLine("After call: X: {0}, Y: {1}", x, y);
}
```

As you would hope, the values of x and y remain identical before and after the call to Add().

The out Modifier

Next, we have the use of *output* parameters. Methods that have been defined to take output parameters are under obligation to assign them to an appropriate value before exiting the method in question (if you fail to ensure this, you will receive compiler errors).

To illustrate, here is an alternative version of the Add() method that returns the sum of two integers using the C# out modifier (note the physical return value of this method is now void):

```
// Output parameters are allocated by the member.
public static void Add(int x, int y, out int ans)
{
    ans = x + y;
}
```

Calling a method with output parameters also requires the use of the out modifier. Recall that local variables passed as output variables are not required to be assigned before use (if you do so, the original value is lost after the call), for example:

```
static void Main(string[] args)
{
    // No need to assign local output variables.
    int ans;
    Add(90, 90, out ans);
    Console.WriteLine("90 + 90 = {0} ", ans);
}
```

The previous example is intended to be illustrative in nature; you really have no reason to return the value of your summation using an output parameter. However, the C# out modifier does serve a very useful purpose: it allows the caller to obtain multiple return values from a single method invocation.

```
// Returning multiple output parameters.
public static void FillTheseValues(out int a, out string b, out bool c)
{
    a = 9;
    b = "Enjoy your string.";
    c = true;
}
```

The caller would be able to invoke the following method:

```
static void Main(string[] args)
{
    int i;
    string str;
    bool b;

    FillTheseValues(out i, out str, out b);
    Console.WriteLine("Int is: {0}", i);
    Console.WriteLine("String is: {0}", str);
    Console.WriteLine("Boolean is: {0}", b);
}
```

The ref Modifier

Now consider the use of the C# ref parameter modifier. Reference parameters are necessary when you wish to allow a method to operate on (and usually change the values of) various data points declared in the caller's scope (such as a sorting or swapping routine). Note the distinction between output and reference parameters:

- Output parameters do not need to be initialized before they passed to the method. The reason for this? The method must assign output parameters before exiting.

- Reference parameters *must* be initialized before they are passed to the method. The reason for this? You are passing a reference to an existing variable. If you don't assign it to an initial value, that would be the equivalent of operating on an unassigned local variable.

Let's check out the use of the ref keyword by way of a method that swaps two strings:

```
// Reference parameter.
public static void SwapStrings(ref string s1, ref string s2)
{
    string tempStr = s1;
    s1 = s2;
    s2 = tempStr;
}
```

This method can be called as so:

```
static void Main(string[] args)
{
    string s = "First string";
    string s2 = "My other string";
    Console.WriteLine("Before: {0}, {1} ", s, s2);
    SwapStrings(ref s, ref s2);
    Console.WriteLine("After: {0}, {1} ", s, s2);
}
```

Here, the caller has assigned an initial value to local string data (s and s2). Once the call to SwapStrings() returns, s now contains the value "My other string", while s2 reports the value "First string".

The params Modifier

The final parameter modifier is the params modifier, which allows you to create a method that may be sent to a set of identically typed arguments *as a single logical parameter*. Yes, this can be confusing. To clear the air, assume a method that returns the average of any number of doubles:

```
// Return average of 'some number' of doubles.
static double CalculateAverage(params double[] values)
{
    double sum = 0;
    for (int i = 0; i < values.Length; i++)
        sum += values[i];
    return (sum / values.Length);
}
```

This method has been defined to take a parameter array of doubles. What this method is in fact saying is, "Send me *any number of doubles* and I'll compute the average." Given this, you can call CalculateAverage() in any of the following ways (if you did not make use of the params modifier in the definition of CalculateAverage(), the first invocation of this method would result in a compiler error):

```
static void Main(string[] args)
{
    // Pass in a comma-delimited list of doubles...
    double average;
    average = CalculateAverage(4.0, 3.2, 5.7);
    Console.WriteLine("Average of 4.0, 3.2, 5.7 is: {0}",
        average);
```

```
// ...or pass an array of doubles.
double[] data = { 4.0, 3.2, 5.7 };
average = CalculateAverage(data);
Console.WriteLine("Average of data is: {0}", average);
Console.ReadLine();
}
```

That wraps up our initial look at parameter modifiers. We'll revisit this topic later in the chapter when we examine the distinction between value types and reference types. Next up, let's check out the iteration and decision constructs of the C# programming language.

■**Source Code** The SimpleParams project is located under the Chapter 3 subdirectory.

Iteration Constructs

All programming languages provide ways to repeat blocks of code until a terminating condition has been met. Regardless of which language you have used in the past, the C# iteration statements should not raise too many eyebrows and should require little explanation. C# provides the following four iteration constructs:

- for loop
- foreach/in loop
- while loop
- do/while loop

Let's quickly examine each looping construct in turn.

The for Loop

When you need to iterate over a block of code a fixed number of times, the for statement is the construct of champions. In essence, you are able to specify how many times a block of code repeats itself, as well as the terminating condition. Without belaboring the point, here is a sample of the syntax:

```
// A basic for loop.
static void Main(string[] args)
{
    // Note! 'i' is only visible within the scope of the for loop.
    for(int i = 0; i < 10; i++)
    {
        Console.WriteLine("Number is: {0} ", i);
    }
    // 'i' is not visible here.
}
```

All of your old C, C++, and Java tricks still hold when building a C# for statement. You can create complex terminating conditions, build endless loops, and make use of the goto, continue, and break keywords. I'll assume that you will bend this iteration construct as you see fit. Consult the .NET Framework 2.0 SDK documentation if you require further details on the C# for keyword.

The foreach Loop

The C# foreach keyword allows you to iterate over all items within an array, without the need to test for the array's upper limit. Here are two examples using foreach, one to traverse an array of strings and the other to traverse an array of integers:

```
// Iterate array items using foreach.
static void Main(string[] args)
{
    string[] books = {"Complex Algorithms",
        "Do you Remember Classic COM?",
        "C# and the .NET Platform"};
    foreach (string s in books)
        Console.WriteLine(s);

    int[] myInts = { 10, 20, 30, 40 };
    foreach (int i in myInts)
        Console.WriteLine(i);
}
```

In addition to iterating over simple arrays, foreach is also able to iterate over system-supplied or user-defined collections. I'll hold off on the details until Chapter 7, as this aspect of the foreach keyword entails an understanding of interface-based programming and the role of the IEnumerator and IEnumerable interfaces.

The while and do/while Looping Constructs

The while looping construct is useful should you wish to execute a block of statements until some terminating condition has been reached. Within the scope of a while loop, you will, of course, need to ensure this terminating event is indeed established; otherwise, you will be stuck in an endless loop. In the following example, the message "In while loop" will be continuously printed until the user terminates the loop by entering **yes** at the command prompt:

```
static void Main(string[] args)
{
    string userIsDone = "no";

    // Test on a lower class copy of the string.
    while(userIsDone.ToLower() != "yes")
    {
        Console.Write("Are you done? [yes] [no]: ");
        userIsDone = Console.ReadLine();
        Console.WriteLine("In while loop");
    }
}
```

Closely related to the while loop is the do/while statement. Like a simple while loop, do/while is used when you need to perform some action for an undetermined number of times. The difference is that do/while loops are guaranteed to execute the corresponding block of code at least once (in contrast, it is possible that a simple while loop may never execute if the terminating condition is false from the onset).

```
static void Main(string[] args)
{
    string userIsDone = "";

    do
```

```
    {
        Console.WriteLine("In do/while loop");
        Console.Write("Are you done? [yes] [no]: ");
        userIsDone = Console.ReadLine();
    }while(userIsDone.ToLower() != "yes");    // Note the semicolon!
}
```

Decision Constructs and the Relational/Equality Operators

Now that you can iterate over a block of statements, the next related concept is how to control the flow of program execution. C# defines two simple constructs to alter the flow of your program, based on various contingencies:

- The if/else statement
- The switch statement

The if/else Statement

First up is our good friend the if/else statement. Unlike in C and C++, however, the if/else statement in C# operates only on Boolean expressions, not ad hoc values such as –1, 0. Given this, if/else statements typically involve the use of the C# operators shown in Table 3-6 in order to obtain a literal Boolean value.

Table 3-6. *C# Relational and Equality Operators*

C# Equality/Relational Operator	Example Usage	Meaning in Life
==	if(age == 30)	Returns true only if each expression is the same
!=	if("Foo" != myStr)	Returns true only if each expression is different

>
<=
>=
	if(bonus < 2000)
	if(bonus > 2000)
	if(bonus <= 2000)
	if(bonus >= 2000)
		Returns true if expression A is less than, greater than, less than or equal to, or greater than or equal to expression B

Again, C and C++ programmers need to be aware that the old tricks of testing a condition for a value "not equal to zero" will not work in C#. Let's say you want to see if the string you are working with is longer than zero characters. You may be tempted to write

```
// This is illegal, given that Length returns an int, not a bool.
string thoughtOfTheDay = "You CAN teach an old dog new tricks";
if(thoughtOfTheDay.Length)
{
    ...
}
```

If you wish to make use of the String.Length property to determine if you have an empty string, you need to modify your conditional expression as follows:

```
// Legal, as this resolves to either true or false.
if( 0 != thoughtOfTheDay.Length)
{
    ...
}
```

An if statement may be composed of complex expressions as well and can contain else statements to perform more-complex testing. The syntax is identical to C(++) and Java (and not too far removed from Visual Basic). To build complex expressions, C# offers an expected set of conditional operators, as shown in Table 3-7.

Table 3-7. *C# Conditional Operators*

Operator	Example	Meaning in Life
&&	if((age == 30) && (name == "Fred"))	Conditional AND operator
||	if((age == 30) || (name == "Fred"))	Conditional OR operator
!	if(!myBool)	Conditional NOT operator

The switch Statement

The other simple selection construct offered by C# is the switch statement. As in other C-based languages, the switch statement allows you to handle program flow based on a predefined set of choices. For example, the following Main() logic prints a specific string message based on one of two possible selections (the default case handles an invalid selection):

```
// Switch on a numerical value.
static void Main(string[] args)
{
    Console.WriteLine("1 [C#], 2 [VB]");
    Console.Write("Please pick your language preference: ");

    string langChoice = Console.ReadLine();
    int n = int.Parse(langChoice);

    switch (n)
    {
        case 1:
            Console.WriteLine("Good choice, C# is a fine language.");
        break;
        case 2:
            Console.WriteLine("VB .NET: OOP, multithreading, and more!");
        break;
        default:
            Console.WriteLine("Well...good luck with that!");
        break;
    }
}
```

■ **Note** C# demands that each case (including default) that contains executable statements have a terminating break or goto to avoid fall-through.

One nice feature of the C# switch statement is that you can evaluate string data in addition to numeric data. Here is an updated switch statement that does this very thing (notice we have no need to parse the user data into a numeric value with this approach):

```
static void Main(string[] args)
{
    Console.WriteLine("C# or VB");
    Console.Write("Please pick your language preference: ");

    string langChoice = Console.ReadLine();
    switch (langChoice)
    {
        case "C#":
            Console.WriteLine("Good choice, C# is a fine language.");
        break;
        case "VB":
            Console.WriteLine("VB .NET: OOP, multithreading and more!");
        break;
        default:
            Console.WriteLine("Well...good luck with that!");
        break;
    }
}
```

■**Source Code** The IterationsAndDecisions project is located under the Chapter 3 subdirectory.

Understanding Value Types and Reference Types

Like any programming language, C# defines a number of keywords that represent basic data types such as whole numbers, character data, floating-point numbers, and Boolean values. If you come from a C++ background, you will be happy to know that these intrinsic types are fixed constants in the universe, meaning that when you create an integer data point, all .NET-aware languages understand the fixed nature of this type, and all agree on the range it is capable of handling.

Specifically speaking, a .NET data type may be *value-based* or *reference-based*. Value-based types, which include all numerical data types (int, float, etc.), as well as enumerations and structures, are allocated *on the stack*. Given this factoid, value types can be quickly removed from memory once they fall out of the defining scope:

```
// Integers are value types!
public void SomeMethod()
{
    int i = 0;
    Console.WriteLine(i);
} // 'i' is popped off the stack here!
```

When you assign one value type to another, a member-by-member copy is achieved by default. In terms of numerical or Boolean data types, the only "member" to copy is the value of the variable itself:

```
// Assigning two intrinsic value types results in
// two independent variables on the stack.
public void SomeMethod()
{
```

```
    int i = 99;
    int j = i;

    // After the following assignment, 'i' is still 99.
    j = 8732;
}
```

While the previous example is no major newsflash, understand that .NET structures (and enumerations, which are examined later in this chapter) are also value types. Structures, simply put, provide a way to achieve the bare-bones benefits of object orientation (i.e., encapsulation) while having the efficiency of stack-allocated data. Like a class, structures can take constructors (provided they have arguments) and define any number of members.

All structures are implicitly derived from a class named System.ValueType. Functionally, the only purpose of System.ValueType is to "override" the virtual methods defined by System.Object (described in just a moment) to honor value-based, versus reference-based, semantics. In fact, the instance methods defined by System.ValueType are identical to those of System.Object:

```
// Structures and enumerations extend System.ValueType.
public abstract class ValueType : object
{
    public virtual bool Equals(object obj);
    public virtual int GetHashCode();
    public Type GetType();
    public virtual string ToString();
}
```

Assume you have created a C# structure named MyPoint, using the C# struct keyword:

```
// Structures are value types!
struct MyPoint
{
    public int x, y;
}
```

To allocate a structure type, you may make use of the new keyword, which may seem counterintuitive given that we typically think new always implies heap allocation. This is part of the smoke and mirrors maintained by the CLR. As programmers, we can assume everything is an object and new value types. However, when the runtime encounters a type derived from System.ValueType, stack allocation is achieved:

```
// Still on the stack!
MyPoint p = new MyPoint();
```

As an alternative, structures can be allocated without using the new keyword:

```
MyPoint p1;
p1.x = 100;
p1.y = 100;
```

If you take this approach, however, you *must* initialize each piece of field data before use. Failing to do so results in a compiler error.

Value Types, References Types, and the Assignment Operator

Now, ponder the following Main() method and observe the output shown in Figure 3-12:

```
static void Main(string[] args)
{
    Console.WriteLine("***** Value Types / Reference Types *****");
    Console.WriteLine("-> Creating p1");
    MyPoint p1 = new MyPoint();
    p1.x = 100;
    p1.y = 100;
    Console.WriteLine("-> Assigning p2 to p1\n");
    MyPoint p2 = p1;

    // Here is p1.
    Console.WriteLine("p1.x = {0}", p1.x);
    Console.WriteLine("p1.y = {0}", p1.y);

    // Here is p2.
    Console.WriteLine("p2.x = {0}", p2.x);
    Console.WriteLine("p2.y = {0}", p2.y);

    // Change p2.x. This will NOT change p1.x.
    Console.WriteLine("-> Changing p2.x to 900");
    p2.x = 900;

    // Print again.
    Console.WriteLine("-> Here are the X values again...");
    Console.WriteLine("p1.x = {0}", p1.x);
    Console.WriteLine("p2.x = {0}", p2.x);
    Console.ReadLine();
}
```

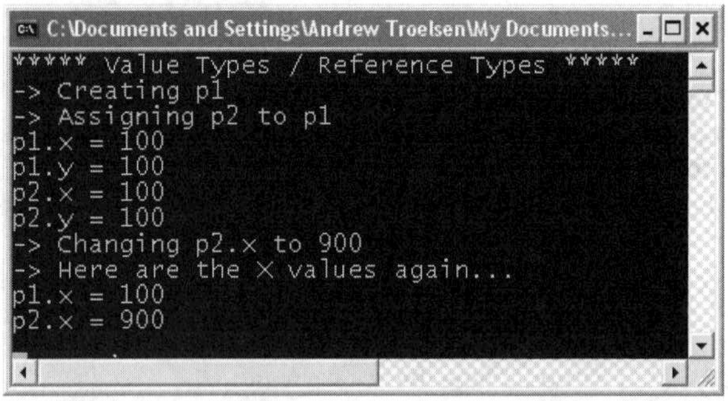

Figure 3-12. *Assignment of value types results in a verbatim copy of each field.*

Here you have created a variable of type MyPoint (named p1) that is then assigned to another MyPoint (p2). Because MyPoint is a value type, you have two copies of the MyPoint type on the stack, each of which can be independently manipulated. Therefore, when you change the value of p2.x, the value of p1.x is unaffected (just like the behavior seen in the previous integer example).

In stark contrast, reference types (classes) are allocated on the managed heap. These objects stay in memory until the .NET garbage collector destroys them. By default, assignment of reference types results in a new reference to the *same* object on the heap. To illustrate, let's change the definition of the MyPoint type from a C# structure to a C# class:

```
// Classes are always reference types.
class MyPoint // <= Now a class!
{
    public int x, y;
}
```

If you were to run the test program once again, you would notice a change in behavior (see Figure 3-13).

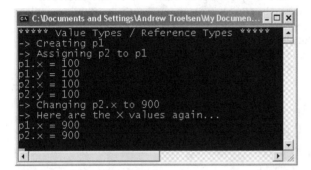

Figure 3-13. *Assignment of reference types copies the reference.*

In this case, you have two references pointing to the same object on the managed heap. Therefore, when you change the value of x using the p2 reference, p1.x reports the same value.

Value Types Containing Reference Types

Now that you have a better feeling for the differences between value types and reference types, let's examine a more complex example. Assume you have the following reference (class) type that maintains an informational string that can be set using a custom constructor:

```
class ShapeInfo
{
    public string infoString;
    public ShapeInfo(string info)
    { infoString = info; }
}
```

Now assume that you want to contain a variable of this class type within a value type named MyRectangle. To allow the outside world to set the value of the inner ShapeInfo, you also provide a custom constructor (as explained in just a bit, the default constructor of a structure is reserved and cannot be redefined):

```
struct MyRectangle
{
    // The MyRectangle structure contains a reference type member.
    public ShapeInfo rectInfo;

    public int top, left, bottom, right;
```

```
    public MyRectangle(string info)
    {
        rectInfo = new ShapeInfo(info);
        top = left = 10;
        bottom = right = 100;
    }
}
```

At this point, you have contained a reference type within a value type. The million-dollar question now becomes, what happens if you assign one MyRectangle variable to another? Given what you already know about value types, you would be correct in assuming that the integer data (which is indeed a structure) should be an independent entity for each MyRectangle variable. But what about the internal reference type? Will the object's state be fully copied, or will the *reference* to that object be copied? Ponder the following code and check out Figure 3-14 for the answer.

```
static void Main(string[] args)
{
    // Create the first MyRectangle.
    Console.WriteLine("-> Creating r1");
    MyRectangle r1 = new MyRectangle("This is my first rect");

    // Now assign a new MyRectangle to r1.
    Console.WriteLine("-> Assigning r2 to r1");
    MyRectangle r2;
    r2 = r1;

    // Change values of r2.
    Console.WriteLine("-> Changing all values of r2");
    r2.rectInfo.infoString = "This is new info!";
    r2.bottom = 4444;

    // Print values
    Console.WriteLine("-> Values after change:");
    Console.WriteLine("-> r1.rectInfo.infoString: {0}", r1.rectInfo.infoString);
    Console.WriteLine("-> r2.rectInfo.infoString: {0}", r2.rectInfo.infoString);
    Console.WriteLine("-> r1.bottom: {0}", r1.bottom);
    Console.WriteLine("-> r2.bottom: {0}", r2.bottom);
}
```

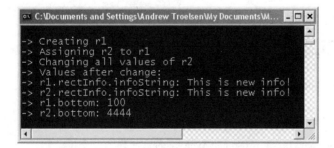

Figure 3-14. *The internal references point to the same object!*

As you can see, when you change the value of the informational string using the r2 reference, the r1 reference displays the same value. By default, when a value type contains other reference types, assignment results in a copy *of the references*. In this way, you have two independent structures, each of which contains a reference pointing to the same object in memory (i.e., a "shallow copy"). When you want to perform a "deep copy," where the state of internal references is fully copied into a new object, you need to implement the ICloneable interface (as you will do in Chapter 7).

■Source Code The ValAndRef project is located under the Chapter 3 subdirectory.

Passing Reference Types by Value

Reference types can obviously be passed as parameters to type members. However, passing an object by reference is quite different from passing it by value. To understand the distinction, assume you have a Person class, defined as follows:

```
class Person
{
    public string fullName;
    public int age;
    public Person(string n, int a)
    {
        fullName = n;
        age = a;
    }
    public Person(){}
    public void PrintInfo()
    { Console.WriteLine("{0} is {1} years old", fullName, age); }
}
```

Now, what if you create a method that allows the caller to send in the Person type by value (note the lack of parameter modifiers):

```
public static void SendAPersonByValue(Person p)
{
    // Change the age of 'p'?
    p.age = 99;

    // Will the caller see this reassignment?
    p = new Person("Nikki", 99);
}
```

Notice how the SendAPersonByValue() method attempts to reassign the incoming Person reference to a new object as well as change some state data. Now let's test this method using the following Main() method:

```
static void Main(string[] args)
{
    // Passing ref-types by value.
    Console.WriteLine("***** Passing Person object by value *****");
    Person fred = new Person("Fred", 12);
    Console.WriteLine("Before by value call, Person is:");
    fred.PrintInfo();
    SendAPersonByValue(fred);
    Console.WriteLine("After by value call, Person is:");
    fred.PrintInfo();
}
```

Figure 3-15 shows the output of this call.

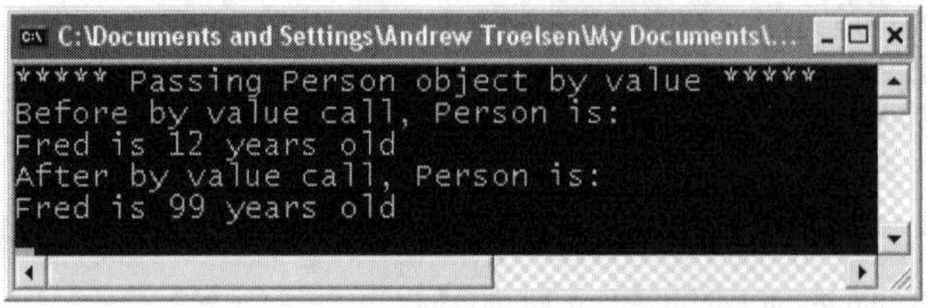

Figure 3-15. *Passing reference types by value locks the reference in place.*

As you can see, the value of age has been modified. This behavior seems to fly in the face of what it means to pass a parameter "by value." Given that you were able to change the state of the incoming Person, what was copied? The answer: a copy of the *reference* to the caller's object. Therefore, as the SendAPersonByValue() method is pointing to the same object as the caller, it is possible to alter the object's state data. What is *not* possible is to reassign what the reference is pointing to (slightly akin to a constant pointer in C++).

Passing Reference Types by Reference

Now assume you have a SendAPersonByReference() method, which passes a reference type by reference (note the ref parameter modifier):

```
public static void SendAPersonByReference(ref Person p)
{
    // Change some data of 'p'.
    p.age = 555;

    // 'p' is now pointing to a new object on the heap!
    p = new Person("Nikki", 999);
}
```

As you might expect, this allows complete flexibility of how the callee is able to manipulate the incoming parameter. Not only can the callee change the state of the object, but if it so chooses, it may also reassign the reference to a new Person type. Now ponder the following usage:

```
static void Main(string[] args)
{
    // Passing ref-types by ref.
    Console.WriteLine("\n***** Passing Person object by reference *****");
    Person mel = new Person("Mel", 23);
    Console.WriteLine("Before by ref call, Person is:");
    mel.PrintInfo();
    SendAPersonByReference(ref mel);
    Console.WriteLine("After by ref call, Person is:");
    mel.PrintInfo();
}
```

As you can see from Figure 3-16, an object named Mel returns after the call as a type named Nikki.

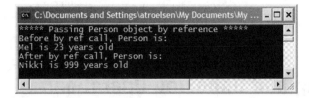

Figure 3-16. *Passing reference types by reference allows the reference to be redirected.*

The golden rule to keep in mind when passing reference types by reference is as follows:

- If a reference type is passed by reference, the callee may change the values of the object's state data *as well as the object it is referencing.*

■**Source Code** The RefTypeValTypeParams project is located under the Chapter 3 subdirectory.

Value and Reference Types: Final Details

To wrap up this topic, ponder the information in Table 3-8, which summarizes the core distinctions between value types and reference types.

Table 3-8. *Value Types and Reference Types Side by Side*

Intriguing Question	Value Type	Reference Type
Where is this type allocated?	Allocated on the stack.	Allocated on the managed heap.
How is a variable represented?	Value type variables are local copies.	Reference type variables are pointing to the memory occupied by the allocated instance.
What is the base type?	Must derive from `System.ValueType`.	Can derive from any other type (except `System.ValueType`), as long as that type is not "sealed" (more details on this in Chapter 4).
Can this type function as a base to other types?	No. Value types are always sealed and cannot be extended.	Yes. If the type is not sealed, it may function as a base to other types.
What is the default parameter passing behavior?	Variables are passed by value (i.e., a copy of the variable is passed into the called function).	Variables are passed by reference (e.g., the address of the variable is passed into the called function).
Can this type override `System.Object.Finalize()`?	No. Value types are never placed onto the heap and therefore do not need to be finalized.	Yes, indirectly (more details on this in Chapter 4).
Can I define constructors for this type?	Yes, but the default constructor is reserved (i.e., your custom constructors must all have arguments).	But of course!
When do variables of this type die?	When they fall out of the defining scope.	When the managed heap is garbage collected.

Despite their differences, value types and reference types both have the ability to implement interfaces and may support any number of fields, methods, overloaded operators, constants, properties, and events.

Understanding Boxing and Unboxing Operations

Given that .NET defines two major categories of types (value based and reference based), you may occasionally need to represent a variable of one category as a variable of the other category. C# provides a very simple mechanism, termed *boxing*, to convert a value type to a reference type. Assume that you have created a variable of type short:

```
// Make a short value type.
short s = 25;
```

If, during the course of your application, you wish to represent this value type as a reference type, you would "box" the value as follows:

```
// Box the value into an object reference.
object objShort = s;
```

Boxing can be formally defined as the process of explicitly converting a value type into a corresponding reference type by storing the variable in a System.Object. When you box a value, the CLR allocates a new object on the heap and copies the value type's value (in this case, 25) into that instance. What is returned to you is a reference to the newly allocated object. Using this technique, .NET developers have no need to make use of a set of wrapper classes used to temporarily treat stack data as heap-allocated objects.

The opposite operation is also permitted through *unboxing*. Unboxing is the process of converting the value held in the object reference back into a corresponding value type on the stack. The unboxing operation begins by verifying that the receiving data type is equivalent to the boxed type, and if so, it copies the value back into a local stack-based variable. For example, the following unboxing operation works successfully, given that the underlying type of the objShort is indeed a short (you'll examine the C# casting operator in detail in the next chapter, so hold tight for now):

```
// Unbox the reference back into a corresponding short.
short anotherShort = (short)objShort;
```

Again, it is mandatory that you unbox into an appropriate data type. Thus, the following unboxing logic generates an InvalidCastException exception (more details on exception handling in Chapter 6):

```
// Illegal unboxing.
static void Main(string[] args)
{
...
    try
    {
        // The type contained in the box is NOT a int, but a short!
        int i = (int)objShort;
    }
    catch(InvalidCastException e)
    {
        Console.WriteLine("OOPS!\n{0} ", e.ToString());
    }
}
```

Some Practical (Un)Boxing Examples

So, you may be thinking, when would you really need to manually box (or unbox) a data type? The previous example was purely illustrative in nature, as there was no good reason to box (and then unbox) the short data point. The truth of the matter is that you will seldom—if ever—need to manually box data types. Much of the time, the C# compiler automatically boxes variables when appropriate. For example, if you pass a value type into a method requiring an object parameter, boxing occurs behind the curtains.

```
class Program
{
    static void Main(string[] args)
    {
        // Create an int (value type).
        int myInt = 99;

        // Because myInt is passed into a
        // method prototyped to take an object,
        // myInt is 'boxed' automatically.
        UseThisObject(myInt);
        Console.ReadLine();
    }

    static void UseThisObject(object o)
    {
        Console.WriteLine("Value of o is: {0}", o);
    }
}
```

Automatic boxing also occurs when working with the types of the .NET base class libraries. For example, the System.Collections namespace (formally examined in Chapter 7) defines a class type named ArrayList. Like most collection types, ArrayList provides members that allow you to insert, obtain, and remove items:

```
public class System.Collections.ArrayList : object,
    System.Collections.IList,
    System.Collections.ICollection,
    System.Collections.IEnumerable,
    ICloneable
{
...
    public virtual int Add(object value);
    public virtual void Insert(int index, object value);
    public virtual void Remove(object obj);
    public virtual object this[int index] {get; set; }
}
```

As you can see, these members operate on generic System.Object types. Given that everything ultimately derives from this common base class, the following code is perfectly legal:

```
static void Main(string[] args)
{
...
    ArrayList myInts = new ArrayList();
    myInts.Add(88);
    myInts.Add(3.33);
    myInts.Add(false);
}
```

However, given your understanding of value types and reference types, you might wonder exactly what was placed into the ArrayList type. (References? Copies of references? Copies of structures?) Just like with the previous UseThisObject() method, it should be clear that each of the System.Int32 data types were indeed boxed before being placed into the ArrayList type. To retrieve an item from the ArrayList type, you are required to unbox accordingly:

```
static void BoxAndUnboxInts()
{
    // Box ints into ArrayList.
    ArrayList myInts = new ArrayList();
    myInts.Add(88);
    myInts.Add(3.33);
    myInts.Add(false);

    // Unbox first item from ArrayList.
    int firstItem = (int)myInts[0];
    Console.WriteLine("First item is {0}", firstItem);
}
```

To be sure, boxing and unboxing types takes some processing time and, if used without restraint, could hurt the performance of your application. However, with this .NET technique, you are able to symmetrically operate on value-based and reference-based types.

■**Note** Under C# 2.0, boxing and unboxing penalties can be eliminated using *generics*, which you'll examine in Chapter 10.

Unboxing Custom Value Types

When you pass custom structures or enumerations into a method prototyped to take a System.Object, a boxing operation also occurs. However, once the incoming parameter has been received by the called method, you will not be able to access any members of the struct (or enum) until you unbox the type. Recall the MyPoint structure defined previously in this chapter:

```
struct MyPoint
{
    public int x, y;
}
```

Assume you now send a MyPoint variable into a new method named UseBoxedMyPoint():

```
static void Main(string[] args)
{
...
    MyPoint p;
    p.x = 10;
    p.y = 20;
    UseBoxedMyPoint(p);
}
```

If you attempt to access the field data of MyPoint, you receive a compiler error, as the method assumes you are operating on a strongly typed System.Object:

```
static void UseBoxedMyPoint(object o)
{
    // Error!  System.Object does not have
    // member variables named 'x' or 'y'.
    Console.WriteLine("{0}, {1}", o.x, o.y);
}
```

To access the field data of MyPoint, you must first unbox the parameter. As a sanity check, you can leverage the C# is keyword to ensure the parameter is indeed a MyPoint variable. The is keyword is further examined in Chapter 4; however, here is some example usage:

```
static void UseBoxedMyPoint(object o)
{
    if (o is MyPoint)
    {
        MyPoint p = (MyPoint)o;
        Console.WriteLine("{0}, {1}", p.x, p.y);
    }
    else
        Console.WriteLine("You did not send a MyPoint.");
}
```

■**Source Code** The Boxing project is included under the Chapter 3 subdirectory.

Working with .NET Enumerations

In addition to structures, *enumerations* (or simply *enums*) are the other member of the .NET value type category. When you build a program, it is often convenient to create a set of symbolic names for underlying numerical values. For example, if you are creating an employee payroll system, you may wish to use the constants Manager, Grunt, Contractor, and VP rather than simple numerical values such as {0, 1, 2, 3}. C# supports the notion of custom enumerations for this very reason. For example, here is the EmpType enumeration:

```
// A custom enumeration.
enum EmpType
{
    Manager,       //  = 0
    Grunt,         //  = 1
    Contractor,    //  = 2
    VP             //  = 3
}
```

The EmpType enumeration defines four named constants corresponding to specific numerical values. In C#, the numbering scheme sets the first element to zero (0) by default, followed by an $n + 1$ progression. You are free to change this behavior as you see fit:

```
// Begin numbering at 102.
enum EmpType
{
    Manager = 102,
    Grunt,         //  = 103
    Contractor,    //  = 104
    VP             //  = 105
}
```

Enumerations do not necessarily need to follow a sequential order. If (for some reason) it made good sense to establish your EmpType as follows, the compiler continues to be happy:

```
// Elements of an enumeration need not be sequential!
enum EmpType
{
```

```
    Manager = 10,
    Grunt = 1,
    Contractor = 100,
    VP = 9
}
```

Under the hood, the storage type used for each item in an enumeration maps to a System.Int32 by default. You are also free to change this to your liking. For example, if you want to set the underlying storage value of EmpType to be a byte rather than an int, you would write the following:

```
// This time, EmpType maps to an underlying byte.
enum EmpType : byte
{
    Manager = 10,
    Grunt = 1,
    Contractor = 100,
    VP = 9
}
```

■**Note** C# enumerations can be defined in a similar manner for any of the numerical types (byte, sbyte, short, ushort, int, uint, long, or ulong). This can be helpful if you are programming for low-memory devices such as Pocket PCs or .NET-enabled cellular phones.

Once you have established the range and storage type of your enumeration, you can use them in place of so-called magic numbers. Assume you have a class defining a static function, taking EmpType as the sole parameter:

```
static void AskForBonus(EmpType e)
{
    switch(e)
    {
        case EmpType.Contractor:
            Console.WriteLine("You already get enough cash...");
        break;
        case EmpType.Grunt:
            Console.WriteLine("You have got to be kidding...");
        break;
        case EmpType.Manager:
            Console.WriteLine("How about stock options instead?");
        break;
        case EmpType.VP:
            Console.WriteLine("VERY GOOD, Sir!");
        break;
        default: break;
    }
}
```

This method can be invoked as so:

```
static void Main(string[] args)
{
    // Make a contractor type.
    EmpType fred;
    fred = EmpType.Contractor;
    AskForBonus(fred);
}
```

■**Note** The value of an enum must always be referenced by prefixing the enum name (e.g., EmpType.Grunt, not simply Grunt).

The System.Enum Base Class

The interesting thing about .NET enumerations is that they implicitly derive from System.Enum. This base class defines a number of methods that allow you to interrogate and transform a given enumeration. Table 3-9 documents some items of interest, all of which are static.

Table 3-9. *Select Static Members of* System.Enum

Member	Meaning in Life
Format()	Converts a value of a specified enumerated type to its equivalent string representation according to the specified format
GetName() GetNames()	Retrieves a name (or an array containing all names) for the constant in the specified enumeration that has the specified value
GetUnderlyingType()	Returns the underlying data type used to hold the values for a given enumeration
GetValues()	Retrieves an array of the values of the constants in a specified enumeration
IsDefined()	Returns an indication of whether a constant with a specified value exists in a specified enumeration
Parse()	Converts the string representation of the name or numeric value of one or more enumerated constants to an equivalent enumerated object

You can make use of the static Enum.Format() method and the same exact string formatting flags examined earlier in the chapter during our examination of System.Console. For example, you may extract the string name (by specifying G), the hexadecimal value (X), or numeric value (D, F, etc.) of a given enum.

System.Enum also defines a static method named GetValues(). This method returns an instance of System.Array (examined later in this chapter), with each item in the array corresponding to name/value pairs of the specified enumeration. To illustrate these points, ponder the following:

```
static void Main(string[] args)
{
    // Print information for the EmpType enumeration.
    Array obj = Enum.GetValues(typeof(EmpType));
    Console.WriteLine("This enum has {0} members.", obj.Length);

    foreach(EmpType e in obj)
    {
        Console.Write("String name: {0},", e.ToString());
        Console.Write(" int: ({0}),", Enum.Format(typeof(EmpType), e, "D"));
        Console.Write(" hex: ({0})\n", Enum.Format(typeof(EmpType), e, "X"));
    }
}
```

As you can guess, this code block prints out the name/value pairs (in decimal and hexadecimal) for the EmpType enumeration.

Next, let's explore the IsDefined() method. This property allows you to determine if a given string name is a member of the current enumeration. For example, assume you wish to know if the value SalesPerson is part of the EmpType enumeration. To do so, you must send it the type information of the enumeration (which can be done via the C# typeof operator) and the string name of the value you wish to query (type information will be examined in much greater detail in Chapter 12):

```
static void Main(string[] args)
{
...
    // Does EmpType have a SalesPerson value?
    if(Enum.IsDefined(typeof(EmpType), "SalesPerson"))
        Console.WriteLine("Yep, we have sales people.");
    else
        Console.WriteLine("No, we have no profits...");
}
```

It is also possible to generate an enumeration set to the correct value from a string literal via the static Enum.Parse() method. Given that Parse() returns a generic System.Object, you will need to cast the return value into the correct enum type:

```
// Prints: "Sally is a Manager"
EmpType sally = (EmpType)Enum.Parse(typeof(EmpType), "Manager");
Console.WriteLine("Sally is a {0}", sally.ToString());
```

Last but not least, it is worth pointing out that C# enumerations support the use of various operators, which test against the assigned values, for example:

```
static void Main(string[] args)
{
...
    // Which of these two EmpType variables has the greatest numerical value?
    EmpType Joe = EmpType.VP;
    EmpType Fran = EmpType.Grunt;

    if(Joe < Fran)
        Console.WriteLine("Joe's value is less than Fran's value.");
    else
        Console.WriteLine("Fran's value is less than Joe's value.");
}
```

■**Source Code** The Enums project is located under the Chapter 3 subdirectory.

The Master Class: System.Object

■**Tip** The following examination of System.Object requires you to understand the concept of virtual methods and method overriding. If you are new to the world of OOP, you may wish to reread this section once you complete Chapter 4.

In .NET, every type is ultimately derived from a common base class: System.Object. The Object class defines a common set of members supported by every type in the .NET universe. When you create a class that does not explicitly specify its base class, you implicitly derive from System.Object:

```
// Implicitly deriving from System.Object.
class HelloClass
{...}
```

If you wish to be more clear with your intension, the C# colon operator (:) allows you to explicitly specify a type's base class (such as System.Object):

```
// In both cases we are explicitly deriving from System.Object.
class ShapeInfo : System.Object
{...}

class ShapeInfo : object
{...}
```

System.Object defines a set of instance-level and class-level (static) members. Note that some of the instance-level members are declared using the virtual keyword and can therefore be *overridden* by a derived class:

```
// The topmost class in the .NET universe: System.Object
namespace System
{
    public class Object
    {
        public Object();
        public virtual Boolean Equals(Object obj);
        public virtual Int32 GetHashCode();
        public Type GetType();
        public virtual String ToString();
        protected virtual void Finalize();
        protected Object MemberwiseClone();
        public static bool Equals(object objA, object objB);
        public static bool ReferenceEquals(object objA, object objB);
    }
}
```

Table 3-10 offers a rundown of the functionality provided by each instance-level method.

Table 3-10. *Core Members of* System.Object

Instance Method of Object **Class**	**Meaning in Life**
Equals()	By default, this method returns true only if the items being compared refer to the exact same item in memory. Thus, Equals() is used to compare object references, not the state of the object. Typically, this method is overridden to return true only if the objects being compared have the same internal state values (that is, value-based semantics). Be aware that if you override Equals(), you should also override GetHashCode().
GetHashCode()	This method returns an integer that identifies a specific object in memory. If you intend your custom types to be contained in a System.Collections.Hashtable type, you are well-advised to override the default implementation of this member.
GetType()	This method returns a System.Type object that fully describes the details of the current item. In short, this is a Runtime Type Identification (RTTI) method available to all objects (this is discussed in greater detail in Chapter 12).

Continued

Table 3-10. *(Continued)*

Instance Method of Object Class	Meaning in Life
ToString()	This method returns a string representation of a given object, using the namespace.typename format (i.e., fully qualified name). If the type has not been defined within a namespace, typename alone is returned. This method can be overridden by a subclass to return a tokenized string of name/value pairs that represent the object's internal state, rather than its fully qualified name.
Finalize()	For the time being, you can understand that this protected method (when overridden) is invoked by the .NET runtime when an object is to be removed from the heap. We investigate the garbage collection process in Chapter 5.
MemberwiseClone()	This protected method exists to return a new object that is a member-by-member copy of the current object. Thus, if your object contains references to other objects, the *references* to these types are copied (i.e., it achieves a shallow copy). If the object contains value types, full copies of the values are achieved.

The Default Behavior of System.Object

To illustrate some of the default behavior provided by the System.Object base class, assume a class named Person defined in a custom namespace named ObjectMethods:

```
// The 'namespace' keyword is fully examined at the end of this chapter.
namespace ObjectMethods
{
    class Person
    {
        public Person(string fname, string lname, string s, byte a)
        {
            firstName = fname;
            lastName = lname;
            SSN = s;
            age = a;
        }
        public Person(){}

        // The state of a person.
        public string firstName;
        public string lastName;
        public string SSN;
        public byte age;
    }
}
```

Now, within our Main() method, we make use of the Person type as so:

```
static void Main(string[] args)
{
    Console.WriteLine("***** Working with Object *****\n");

    Person fred = new Person("Fred", "Clark", "111-11-1111", 20);
    Console.WriteLine("-> fred.ToString: {0}", fred.ToString());
    Console.WriteLine("-> fred.GetHashCode: {0}", fred.GetHashCode());
    Console.WriteLine("-> fred's base class: {0}", fred.GetType().BaseType);
```

```
// Make some other references to 'fred'.
Person p2 = fred;
object o = p2;

// Are all 3 instances pointing to the same object in memory?
if(o.Equals(fred) && p2.Equals(o))
    Console.WriteLine("fred, p2 and o are referencing the same object!");
Console.ReadLine();
}
```

Figure 3-17 shows a test run.

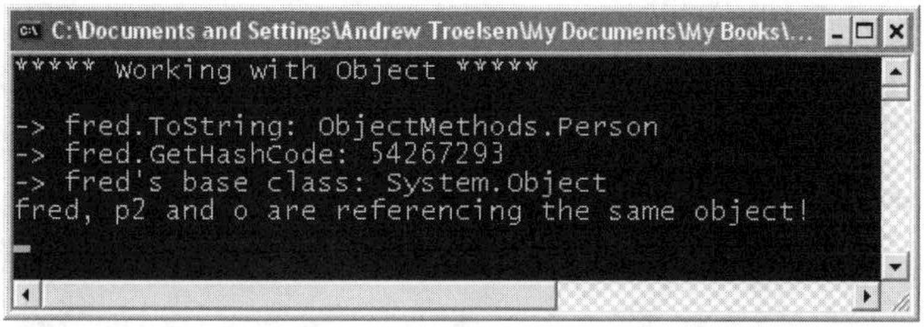

Figure 3-17. *Default implementation of select* System.Object *members*

First, notice how the default implementation of ToString() simply returns the fully qualified name of the type (e.g., namespace.typename). GetType() retrieves a System.Type object, which defines a property named BaseType (as you can guess, this will identify the fully qualified name of the type's base class).

Now, reexamine the code that leverages the Equals() method. Here, a new Person object is placed on the managed heap, and the reference to this object is stored in the fred reference variable. p2 is also of type Person, however, you are not creating a *new* instance of the Person class, but assigning p2 to fred. Therefore, fred and p2 are both pointing to the same object in memory, as is the variable o (of type object, which was thrown in for good measure). Given that fred, p2, and o all point to the same object in memory, the equality test succeeds.

Overriding Some Default Behaviors of System.Object

Although the canned behavior of System.Object can fit the bill in most cases, it is quite common for your custom types to override some of these inherited methods. Chapter 4 provides a complete examination of OOP under C#, but in a nutshell, *overriding* is the process of redefining the behavior of an inherited *virtual* member in a derived class. As you have just seen, System.Object defines a number of virtual methods (such as ToString() and Equals()) that do define a canned implementation. However, if you want to build a custom implementation of these virtual members for a derived type, you make use of the C# override keyword.

Overriding System.Object.ToString()

Overriding the ToString() method provides a way to quickly gain a snapshot of an object's current state. As you might guess, this can be helpful during the debugging process. To illustrate, let's override System.Object.ToString() to return a textual representation of a person's state (note we are using a new namespace named System.Text):

```
// Need to reference System.Text to access StringBuilder type.
using System;
using System.Text;

class Person
{
    // Overriding System.Object.ToString().
    public override string ToString()
    {
        StringBuilder sb = new StringBuilder();
        sb.AppendFormat("[FirstName={0};", this.firstName);
        sb.AppendFormat(" LastName={0};", this.lastName);
        sb.AppendFormat(" SSN={0};", this.SSN);
        sb.AppendFormat(" Age={0}]", this.age);
        return sb.ToString();
    }
...
}
```

How you format the string returned from System.Object.ToString() is largely a matter of personal choice. In this example, the name/value pairs have been contained within square brackets, with each pair separated by a semicolon (a common technique within the .NET base class libraries).

Also notice that this example makes use of a new type, System.Text.StringBuilder (which is also a matter of personal choice). This type is described in greater detail later in the chapter. The short answer, however, is that StringBuilder is a more efficient alternative to C# string concatenation.

Overriding System.Object.Equals()

Let's also override the behavior of System.Object.Equals() to work with *value-based semantics*. Recall that by default, Equals() returns true only if the two references being compared are pointing to the same object on the heap. In many cases, however, you don't necessary care if two references are pointing to the same object in memory, but you are more interested if the two objects have the same state data (name, SSN, and age in the case of a Person):

```
public override bool Equals(object o)
{
    // Make sure the caller sent a valid
    // Person object before proceeding.
    if (o != null && o is Person)
    {
        // Now see if the incoming Person
        // has the exact same information as
        // the current object (this).
        Person temp = (Person)o;
        if (temp.firstName == this.firstName &&
            temp.lastName == this.lastName &&
            temp.SSN == this.SSN &&
            temp.age == this.age)
            return true;
    }
```

```
    return false;    // Not the same!
}
```

Here you are first verifying the caller did indeed pass in a Person object to the Equals() method using the C# is keyword. After this point, you go about examining the values of the incoming parameter against the values of the current object's field data (note the use of the this keyword, which refers to the current object).

The prototype of System.Object.Equals() takes a single argument of type object. Thus, you are required to perform an explicit cast within the Equals() method to access the members of the Person type. If the name, SSN, and age of each are identical, you have two objects with the same state data and therefore return true. If any point of data is not identical, you return false.

If you override System.Object.ToString() for a given class, you can take a very simple shortcut when overriding System.Object.Equals(). Given that the value returned from ToString() should take into account all of the member variables of the current class (and possible data declared in base classes), Equals() can simply compare the values of the string types:

```
public override bool Equals(object o)
{
    if (o != null && o is Person)
    {
        if (this.ToString() == o.ToString())
            return true;
        else
            return false;
    }
    return false;
}
```

Now, for the sake of argument, assume you have a type named Car, and attempt to pass in a Car instance to the Person.Equals() method as so:

```
// Cars are not people!
Car c = new Car();
Person p = new Person();
p.Equals(c);
```

Given your runtime check for a true-blue Person object (via the is operator) the Equals() method returns false. Now consider the following invocation:

```
// Oops!
Person p = new Person();
p.Equals(null);
```

This would also be safe, given your check for an incoming null reference.

Overriding System.Object.GetHashCode()

When a class overrides the Equals() method, best practices dictate that you should also override System.Object.GetHashCode(). If you fail to do so, you are issued a compiler warning. The role of GetHashCode() is to return a numerical value that identifies an object based on its internal state data. Thus, if you have two Person objects that have an identical first name, last name, SSN, and age, you should obtain the same hash code.

By and large, overriding this method is only useful if you intend to store a custom type within a hash-based collection such as System.Collections.Hashtable. Under the hood, the Hashtable type calls the Equals() and GetHashCode() members of the contained types to determine the correct object to return to the caller. Due to the fact that System.Object has no clue about the state data of derived types, you should override this member for any type you wish to store in a Hashtable.

There are many algorithms that can be used to create a hash code—some fancy, others not so fancy. As mentioned, an object's hash value will be based on its state data. As luck would have it, the System.String class has a very solid implementation of GetHashCode() that is based on the string's character data. Therefore, if you can identify a string field that should be unique among objects (such as the Person's SSN field), you can simply call GetHashCode() on the field's string representation:

```
// Return a hash code based on the person's SSN.
public override int GetHashCode()
{
    return SSN.GetHashCode();
}
```

If you cannot identify a single point of data in your class, but have overridden ToString(), you can simply return the hash code of the string returned from your custom ToString() implementation:

```
// Return a hash code based our custom ToString().
public override int GetHashCode()
{
    return ToString().GetHashCode();
}
```

Testing the Overridden Members

You can now test your updated Person class. Add the following code to your Main() method and check out Figure 3-18 for output:

```
static void Main(string[] args)
{
    // NOTE:  We want these to be identical for testing purposes.
    Person p3 = new Person("Fred", "Jones", "222-22-2222", 98);
    Person p4 = new Person("Fred", "Jones", "222-22-2222", 98);

    // Should have same hash code and string at this point.
    Console.WriteLine("-> Hash code of p3 = {0}", p3.GetHashCode());
    Console.WriteLine("-> Hash code of p4 = {0}", p4.GetHashCode());
    Console.WriteLine("-> String of p3 = {0}", p3.ToString());
    Console.WriteLine("-> String of p4 = {0}", p4.ToString());

    // Should be equal at this point.
    if (p3.Equals(p4))
        Console.WriteLine("-> P3 and p4 have same state!");
    else
        Console.WriteLine("-> P3 and p4 have different state!");

    // Change age of p4.
    Console.WriteLine("\n-> Changing the age of p4\n");
    p4.age = 2;

    // No longer equal, different hash values and string data.
    Console.WriteLine("-> String of p3 = {0}", p3.ToString());
    Console.WriteLine("-> String of p4 = {0}", p4.ToString());
    Console.WriteLine("-> Hash code of p3 = {0}", p3.GetHashCode());
    Console.WriteLine("-> Hash code of p4 = {0}", p4.GetHashCode());
    if (p3.Equals(p4))
        Console.WriteLine("-> P3 and p4 have same state!");
    else
        Console.WriteLine("-> P3 and p4 have different state!");
}
```

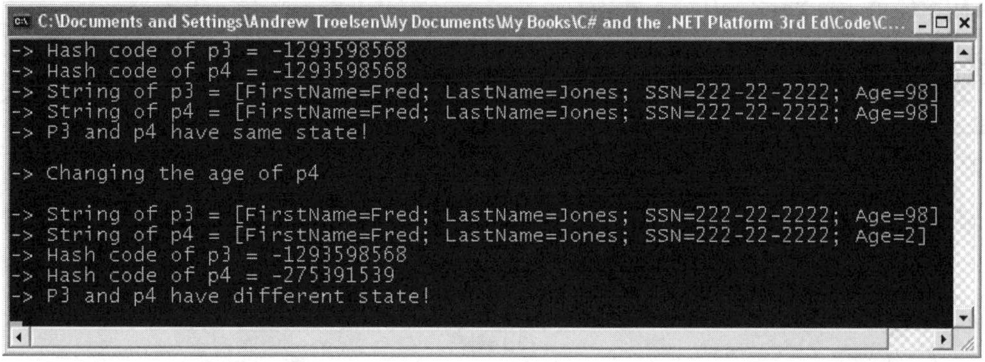

```
C:\Documents and Settings\Andrew Troelsen\My Documents\My Books\C# and the .NET Platform 3rd Ed\Code\C...
-> Hash code of p3 = -1293598568
-> Hash code of p4 = -1293598568
-> String of p3 = [FirstName=Fred; LastName=Jones; SSN=222-22-2222; Age=98]
-> String of p4 = [FirstName=Fred; LastName=Jones; SSN=222-22-2222; Age=98]
-> P3 and p4 have same state!

-> Changing the age of p4

-> String of p3 = [FirstName=Fred; LastName=Jones; SSN=222-22-2222; Age=98]
-> String of p4 = [FirstName=Fred; LastName=Jones; SSN=222-22-2222; Age=2]
-> Hash code of p3 = -1293598568
-> Hash code of p4 = -275391539
-> P3 and p4 have different state!
```

Figure 3-18. *Overridden* System.Object *members in action*

Static Members of System.Object

To wrap up our examination of this supreme base class of .NET, it is worth pointing out that System.Object does define two static members (Object.Equals() and Object.ReferenceEquals()) that test for value-based or reference-based equality. Consider the following code:

```csharp
static void Main(string[] args)
{
    // Assume two identically configured objects.
    Person p3 = new Person("Fred", "Jones", "222-22-2222", 98);
    Person p4 = new Person("Fred", "Jones", "222-22-2222", 98);

    // Do p3 and p4 have the same state? TRUE!
    Console.WriteLine("Do P3 and p4 have same state: {0} ", object.Equals(p3, p4));

    // Are they the same object in memory? FALSE!
    Console.WriteLine("Are P3 and p4 are pointing to same object: {0} ",
        object.ReferenceEquals(p3, p4));
}
```

■**Source Code** The ObjectMethods project is located under the Chapter 3 subdirectory.

The System Data Types (and C# Shorthand Notation)

As you may have begun to notice, every intrinsic C# data type is actually a shorthand notation for defining an existing type defined in the System namespace. Table 3-11 lists each system data type, its range, the corresponding C# alias, and the type's compliance with the Common Language Specification (CLS).

Table 3-11. *System Types and C# Shorthand*

C# Shorthand	CLS Compliant?	System Type	Range	Meaning in Life
sbyte	No	System.SByte	−128 to 127	Signed 8-bit number
byte	Yes	System.Byte	0 to 255	Unsigned 8-bit number
short	Yes	System.Int16	−32,768 to 32,767	Signed 16-bit number
ushort	No	System.UInt16	0 to 65,535	Unsigned 16-bit number
int	Yes	System.Int32	−2,147,483,648 to 2,147,483,647	Signed 32-bit number
uint	No	System.UInt32	0 to 4,294,967,295	Unsigned 32-bit number
long	Yes	System.Int64	−9,223,372,036,854,775,808 to 9,223,372,036,854,775,807	Signed 64-bit number
ulong	No	System.UInt64	0 to 18,446,744,073,709,551,615	Unsigned 64-bit number
char	Yes	System.Char	U0000 to Uffff	A single 16-bit Unicode character
float	Yes	System.Single	1.5×10^{-45} to 3.4×10^{38}	32-bit floating point number
double	Yes	System.Double	5.0×10^{-324} to 1.7×10^{308}	64-bit floating point number
bool	Yes	System.Boolean	true or false	Represents truth or falsity
decimal	Yes	System.Decimal	10^0 to 10^{28}	A 96-bit signed number
string	Yes	System.String	Limited by system memory	Represents a set of Unicode characters
object	Yes	System.Object	Any type can be stored in an object variable	The base class of all types in the .NET universe

■**Note** By default, a real numeric literal on the right-hand side of the assignment operator is treated as double. Therefore, to initialize a float variable, use the suffix f or F (5.3F).

It is very interesting to note that even the primitive .NET data types are arranged in a class hierarchy. The relationship between these core system types (as well as some other soon-to-be-discovered types) can be represented as shown in Figure 3-19.

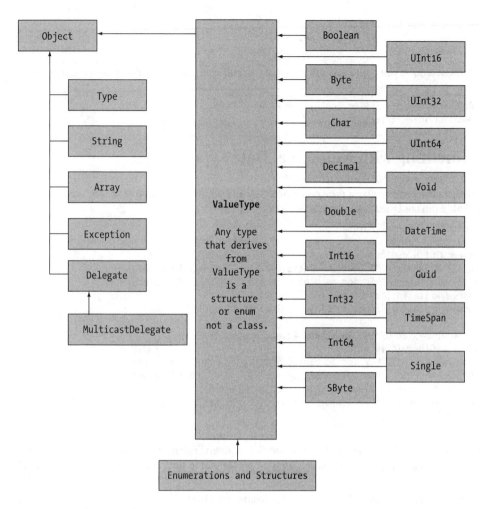

Figure 3-19. *The hierarchy of* System *types*

As you can see, each of these types ultimately derives from System.Object. Because data types such as int are simply shorthand notations for the corresponding system type (in this case, System.Int32), the following is perfectly legal syntax:

```
// Remember! A C# int is really a shorthand for System.Int32.
Console.WriteLine(12.GetHashCode());
Console.WriteLine(12.Equals(23));
Console.WriteLine(12.ToString());
Console.WriteLine(12);        // ToString() called automatically.
Console.WriteLine(12.GetType().BaseType);
```

Furthermore, given that all value types are provided with a default constructor, it is permissible to create a system type using the new keyword, which sets the variable to its default value. Although it is more cumbersome to use the new keyword when creating a System data type, the following is syntactically well-formed C#:

```
// These statements are identical.
bool b1 = new bool();     // b1 = false.
bool b2 = false;
```

On a related note, you could also create a system data type using the fully qualified name:

```
// These statements are also semantically identical.
System.Boolean b1 = new System.Bool();    // b1 = false.
System.Boolean sb2 = false;
```

Experimenting with Numerical Data Types

The numerical types of .NET support MaxValue and MinValue properties that provide information regarding the range a given type can store. Assume you have created some variables of type
System.UInt16 (an unsigned short) and exercised it as follows:

```
static void Main(string[] args)
{
    System.UInt16 myUInt16 = 30000;
    Console.WriteLine("Max for an UInt16 is: {0} ", UInt16.MaxValue);
    Console.WriteLine("Min for an UInt16 is: {0} ", UInt16.MinValue);
    Console.WriteLine("Value is: {0} ", myUInt16);
    Console.WriteLine("I am a: {0} ", myUInt16.GetType());

    // Now in System.UInt16 shorthand (e.g., a ushort).
    ushort myOtherUInt16 = 12000;
    Console.WriteLine("Max for an UInt16 is: {0} ", ushort.MaxValue);
    Console.WriteLine("Min for an UInt16 is: {0} ", ushort.MinValue);
    Console.WriteLine("Value is: {0} ", myOtherUInt16);
    Console.WriteLine("I am a: {0} ", myOtherUInt16.GetType());
    Console.ReadLine();
}
```

In addition to the MinValue/MaxValue properties, a given system type may define further useful members. For example, the System.Double type allows you to obtain the values for Epsilon and
infinity values:

```
Console.WriteLine("-> double.Epsilon: {0}", double.Epsilon);
Console.WriteLine("-> double.PositiveInfinity: {0}", double.PositiveInfinity);
Console.WriteLine("-> double.NegativeInfinity: {0}", double.NegativeInfinity);
Console.WriteLine("-> double.MaxValue: {0}", double.MaxValue);
Console.WriteLine("-> double.MinValue: {0}",double.MinValue);
```

Members of System.Boolean

Next, consider the System.Boolean data type. Unlike C(++), the only valid assignment a C# bool can
take is from the set {true | false}. You cannot assign makeshift values (e.g., –1, 0, 1) to a C# bool,
which (to most programmers) is a welcome change. Given this point, it should be clear that
System.Boolean does not support a MinValue/MaxValue property set, but rather TrueString/FalseString:

```
// No more ad hoc Boolean types in C#!
bool b = 0;        // Illegal!
bool b2 = -1;      // Also illegal!
bool b3 = true;    // No problem.
bool b4 = false;   // No problem.
Console.WriteLine("-> bool.FalseString: {0}", bool.FalseString);
Console.WriteLine("-> bool.TrueString: {0}", bool.TrueString);
```

Members of System.Char

C# textual data is represented by the intrinsic C# string and char data types. All .NET-aware languages map textual data to the same underlying types (System.String and System.Char), both of which are Unicode under the hood.

The System.Char type provides you with a great deal of functionality beyond the ability to hold a single point of character data (which must be placed between single quotes). Using the static methods of System.Char, you are able to determine if a given character is numerical, alphabetical, a point of punctuation, or whatnot. To illustrate, check out the following:

```
static void Main(string[] args)
{
...
    // Test the truth of the following statements...
    Console.WriteLine("-> char.IsDigit('K'): {0}", char.IsDigit('K'));
    Console.WriteLine("-> char.IsDigit('9'): {0}", char.IsDigit('9'));
    Console.WriteLine("-> char.IsLetter('10', 1): {0}", char.IsLetter("10", 1));
    Console.WriteLine("-> char.IsLetter('p'): {0}", char.IsLetter('p'));
    Console.WriteLine("-> char.IsWhiteSpace('Hello There', 5): {0}",
        char.IsWhiteSpace("Hello There", 5));
    Console.WriteLine("-> char.IsWhiteSpace('Hello There', 6): {0}",
        char.IsWhiteSpace("Hello There", 6));
    Console.WriteLine("-> char.IsLetterOrDigit('?'): {0}",
        char.IsLetterOrDigit('?'));
    Console.WriteLine("-> char.IsPunctuation('!'): {0}",
        char.IsPunctuation('!'));
    Console.WriteLine("-> char.IsPunctuation('>'): {0}",
        char.IsPunctuation('>'));
    Console.WriteLine("-> char.IsPunctuation(','): {0}",
        char.IsPunctuation(','));
...
}
```

As you can see, each of these static members of System.Char has two calling conventions: a single character or a string with a numerical index that specified the position of the character to test.

Parsing Values from String Data

Also understand that the .NET data types provide the ability to generate a variable of their underlying type given a textual equivalent (e.g., *parsing*). This technique can be extremely helpful when you wish to convert a bit of user input data (such as a selection from a drop-down list) into a numerical value. Ponder the following parsing logic:

```
static void Main(string[] args)
{
...
    bool myBool = bool.Parse("True");
    Console.WriteLine("-> Value of myBool: {0}", myBool);
    double myDbl = double.Parse("99.884");
    Console.WriteLine("-> Value of myDbl: {0}", myDbl);
    int myInt = int.Parse("8");
    Console.WriteLine("-> Value of myInt: {0}", myInt);
    char myChar = char.Parse("w");
    Console.WriteLine("-> Value of myChar: {0}\n", myChar);
...
}
```

System.DateTime and System.TimeSpan

To wrap up our examination of core data types, allow me to point out the fact that the System name-space defines a few useful data types for which there is no C# keyword—specifically, the DateTime and TimeSpan structures (I'll leave the investigation of System.Guid and System.Void, as shown in Figure 3-19, to interested readers).

The DateTime type contains data that represents a specific date (month, day, year) and time value, both of which may be formatted in a variety of ways using the supplied members. By way of a simple example, ponder the following statements:

```
static void Main(string[] args)
{
...
    // This constructor takes (year, month, day)
    DateTime dt = new DateTime(2004, 10, 17);

    // What day of the month is this?
    Console.WriteLine("The day of {0} is {1}", dt.Date, dt.DayOfWeek);
    dt = dt.AddMonths(2);   // Month is now December.
    Console.WriteLine("Daylight savings: {0}", dt.IsDaylightSavingTime());
...
}
```

The TimeSpan structure allows you to easily define and transform units of time using various members, for example:

```
static void Main(string[] args)
{
...
    // This constructor takes (hours, minutes, seconds)
    TimeSpan ts = new TimeSpan(4, 30, 0);
    Console.WriteLine(ts);

    // Subtract 15 minutes from the current TimeSpan and
    // print the result.
    Console.WriteLine(ts.Subtract(new TimeSpan(0, 15, 0)));
...
}
```

Figure 3-20 shows the output of the DateTime and TimeSpan statements.

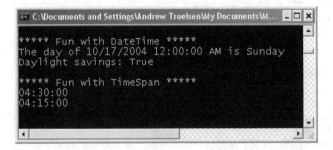

Figure 3-20. *Working with* DateTime *and* TimeSpan

■**Source Code** The DataTypes project is located under the Chapter 3 subdirectory.

The System.String Data Type

The C# string keyword is a shorthand notation of the System.String type, which provides a number of members you would expect from such a utility class. Table 3-12 lists some (but not all) of the interesting members.

Table 3-12. *Select Members of* System.String

Member	Meaning in Life
Length	This property returns the length of the current string.
Contains()	This method is used to determine if the current string object contains a specified string.
Format()	This static method is used to format a string literal using other primitives (i.e., numerical data and other strings) and the {0} notation examined earlier in this chapter.
Insert()	This method is used to receive a copy of the current string that contains newly inserted string data.
PadLeft() PadRight()	These methods return copies of the current string that has been padded with specific data.
Remove() Replace()	Use these methods to receive a copy of a string, with modifications (characters removed or replaced).
Substring()	This method returns a string that represents a substring of the current string.
ToCharArray()	This method returns a character array representing the current string.
ToUpper() ToLower()	These methods create a copy of a given string in uppercase or lowercase.

Basic String Operations

To illustrate some basic string operations, consider the following Main() method:

```
static void Main(string[] args)
{
    Console.WriteLine("***** Fun with Strings *****");
    string s = "Boy, this is taking a long time.";
    Console.WriteLine("--> s contains 'oy'?: {0}", s.Contains("oy"));
    Console.WriteLine("--> s contains 'Boy'?: {0}", s.Contains("Boy"));
    Console.WriteLine(s.Replace('.', '!'));
    Console.WriteLine(s.Insert(0, "Boy O' "));
    Console.ReadLine();
}
```

Here, we are creating a string type invoking the Contains(), Replace(), and Insert() methods. Figure 3-21 shows the output.

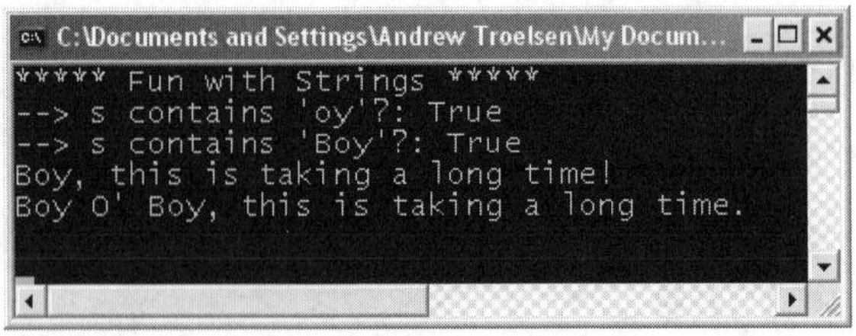

Figure 3-21. *Basic string operations*

You should be aware that although string is a reference type, the equality operators (== and !=) are defined to compare the *value* with the string objects, not the memory to which they refer. Therefore, the following comparison evaluates to true:

```
string s1 = "Hello ";
string s2 = "Hello ";
Console.WriteLine("s1 == s2: {0}", s1 == s2);
```

whereas this comparison evaluates to false:

```
string s1 = "Hello ";
string s2 = "World!";
Console.WriteLine("s1 == s2: {0}", s1 == s2);
```

When you wish to concatenate existing strings into a new string that is the sum of all its parts, C# provides the + operator as well as the static String.Concat() method. Given this, the following statements are functionally equivalent:

```
// Concatenation of strings.
string newString = s + s1 + s2;
Console.WriteLine("s + s1 + s2 = {0}", newString);
Console.WriteLine("string.Concat(s, s1, s2) = {0}", string.Concat(s, s1, s2));
```

Another helpful feature of the string type is the ability to iterate over each individual character using an arraylike syntax. Formally speaking, objects that support arraylike access to their contents make use of an *indexer method*. You'll learn how to build indexers in Chapter 9; however, to illustrate the concept, the following code prints each character of the s1 string object to the console:

```
// System.String also defines an indexer to access each
// character in the string.
for (int k = 0; k < s1.Length; k++)
    Console.WriteLine("Char {0} is {1}", k, s1[k]);
```

As an alternative to interacting with the type's indexer, the string class can also be used within the C# foreach construct. Given that System.String is maintaining an array of individual System.Char types, the following code also prints each character of s1 to the console:

```
foreach(char c in s1)
    Console.WriteLine(c);
```

Escape Characters

Like in other C-based languages, in C# string literals may contain various escape characters, which qualify how the character data should be printed to the output stream. Each escape character begins with a backslash, followed by a specific token. In case you are a bit rusty on the meanings behind these escape characters, Table 3-13 lists the more common options.

Table 3-13. *String Literal Escape Characters*

Character	Meaning in Life
\'	Inserts a single quote into a string literal.
\"	Inserts a double quote into a string literal.
\\	Inserts a backslash into a string literal. This can be quite helpful when defining file paths.
\a	Triggers a system alert (beep). For console applications, this can be an audio clue to the user.
\n	Inserts a new line (on Win32 platforms).
\r	Inserts a carriage return.
\t	Inserts a horizontal tab into the string literal.

For example, to print a string that contains a tab between each word, you can make use of the \t escape character:

```
// Literal strings may contain any number of escape characters.
string s3 = "Hello\tThere\tAgain";
Console.WriteLine(s3);
```

As another example, assume you wish to create a string literal that contains quotation marks, another that defines a directory path, and a final string literal that inserts three blank lines after printing the character data. To do so without compiler errors, you would need to make use of the \", \\, and \n escape characters:

```
Console.WriteLine("Everyone loves \"Hello World\"");
Console.WriteLine("C:\\MyApp\\bin\\debug");
Console.WriteLine("All finished.\n\n\n");
```

Working with C# Verbatim Strings

C# introduces the @-prefixed string literal notation termed a *verbatim string*. Using verbatim strings, you disable the processing of a literal's escape characters. This can be most useful when working with strings representing directory and network paths. Therefore, rather than making use of \\ escape characters, you can simply write the following:

```
// The following string is printed verbatim
// thus, all escape characters are displayed.
Console.WriteLine(@"C:\MyApp\bin\debug");
```

Also note that verbatim strings can be used to preserve white space for strings that flow over multiple lines:

```
// White space is preserved with verbatim strings.
string myLongString = @"This is a very
    very
        very
            long string";
Console.WriteLine(myLongString);
```

You can also insert a double quote into a literal string by doubling the " token, for example:

```
Console.WriteLine(@"Cerebus said ""Darrr! Pret-ty sun-sets""");
```

The Role of System.Text.StringBuilder

While the `string` type is perfect when you wish to represent basic string variables (first name, SSN, etc.), it can be inefficient if you are building a program that makes heavy use of textual data. The reason has to do with a very important fact regarding .NET strings: the value of a string cannot be modified once established. C# strings are immutable.

On the surface, this sounds like a flat-out lie, given that we are always assigning new values to string variables. However, if you examine the methods of `System.String`, you notice that the methods that *seem* to internally modify a string in fact return a modified *copy* of the original string. For example, when you call `ToUpper()` on a string object, you are not modifying the underlying buffer of an existing string object, but receive a new string object in uppercase form:

```
static void Main(string[] args)
{
...
    // Make changes to strFixed?  Nope!
    System.String strFixed = "This is how I began life";
    Console.WriteLine(strFixed);
    string upperVersion = strFixed.ToUpper();
    Console.WriteLine(strFixed);
    Console.WriteLine("{0}\n\n", upperVersion);
...
}
```

In a similar vein, when you assign an existing string object to a new value, you have actually allocated a *new* string in the process (the original string object will eventually be garbage collected). A similar process occurs with string concatenation.

To help reduce the amount of string copying, the `System.Text` namespace defines a class named `StringBuilder` (first seen during our examination of `System.Object` earlier in this chapter). Unlike `System.String`, `StringBuilder` provides you direct access to the underlying buffer. Like `System.String`, `StringBuilder` provides numerous members that allow you to append, format, insert, and remove data from the object (consult the .NET Framework 2.0 SDK documentation for full details).

When you create a `StringBuilder` object, you may specify (via a constructor argument) the initial number of characters the object can contain. If you do not do so, the default capacity of a `StringBuilder` is 16. In either case, if you add more character data to a `StringBuilder` than it is able to hold, the buffer is resized on the fly.

Here is an example of working with this class type:

```
using System;
using System.Text;        // StringBuilder lives here.

class StringApp
{
    static void Main(string[] args)
    {
        StringBuilder myBuffer = new StringBuilder("My string data");
        Console.WriteLine("Capacity of this StringBuilder: {0}",
            myBuffer.Capacity);
        myBuffer.Append(" contains some numerical data: ");
        myBuffer.AppendFormat("{0}, {1}.", 44, 99);
        Console.WriteLine("Capacity of this StringBuilder: {0}",
            myBuffer.Capacity);
        Console.WriteLine(myBuffer);
    }
}
```

Now, do understand that in many cases, System.String will be your textual object of choice. For most applications, the overhead associated with returning modified copies of character data will be negligible. However, if you are building a text-intensive application (such as a word processor program), you will most likely find that using System.Text.StringBuilder improves performance.

■**Source Code** The Strings project is located under the Chapter 3 subdirectory.

.NET Array Types

Formally speaking, an *array* is a collection of data points, of the *same* defined data type, that are accessed using a numerical index. Arrays are references types and derive from a common base class named System.Array. By default, .NET arrays always have a lower bound of zero, although it is possible to create an array with an arbitrary lower bound using the static System.Array.CreateInstance() method.

C# arrays can be declared in a handful of ways. First of all, if you are creating an array whose values will be specified at a later time (perhaps due to yet-to-be-obtained user input), specify the size of the array using square brackets ([ ]) at the time of its allocation, for example:

```
// Assign a string array containing 3 elements {0 - 2}
string[] booksOnCOM;
booksOnCOM = new string[3];
```

```
// Initialize a 100 item string array, numbered {0 - 99}
string[] booksOnDotNet = new string[100];
```

Once you have declared an array, you can make use of the indexer syntax to fill each item with a value:

```
// Create, populate, and print an array of three strings.
string[] booksOnCOM;
booksOnCOM = new string[3];
booksOnCOM[0] = "Developer's Workshop to COM and ATL 3.0";
booksOnCOM[1] = "Inside COM";
booksOnCOM[2] = "Inside ATL";
foreach (string s in booksOnCOM)
    Console.WriteLine(s);
```

As a shorthand notation, if you know an array's values at the time of declaration, you may specify these values within curly brackets. Note that in this case, the array size is optional (as it is calculated on the fly), as is the new keyword. Thus, the following declarations are identical:

```
// Shorthand array declaration (values must be known at time of declaration).
int[] n = new int[] { 20, 22, 23, 0 };
int[] n3 = { 20, 22, 23, 0 };
```

There is one final manner in which you can create an array type:

```
int[] n2 = new int[4] { 20, 22, 23, 0 };  // 4 elements, {0 - 3}
```

In this case, the numeric value specified represents the *number of elements* in the array, not the value of the upper bound. If there is a mismatch between the declared size and the number of initializers, you are issued a compile time error.

Regardless of how you declare an array, be aware that the elements in a .NET array are automatically set to their respective default values until you indicate otherwise. Thus, if you have an array of numerical types, each member is set to 0 (or 0.0 in the case of floating-point numbers), objects are set to null, and Boolean types are set to false.

Arrays As Parameters (and Return Values)

Once you have created an array, you are free to pass it as a parameter and receive it as a member return value. For example, the following PrintArray() method takes an incoming array of ints and prints each member to the console, while the GetStringArray() method populates an array of strings and returns it to the caller:

```
static void PrintArray(int[] myInts)
{
    for(int i = 0; i < myInts.Length; i++)
        Console.WriteLine("Item {0} is {1}", i, myInts[i]);
}

static string[] GetStringArray()
{
    string[] theStrings = {  "Hello", "from", "GetStringArray" };
    return theStrings;
}
```

These methods may be invoked from a Main() method as so:

```
static void Main(string[] args)
{
    int[] ages = {20, 22, 23, 0} ;
    PrintArray(ages);
    string[] strs = GetStringArray();
    foreach(string s in strs)
        Console.WriteLine(s);
    Console.ReadLine();
}
```

Working with Multidimensional Arrays

In addition to the single-dimension arrays you have seen thus far, C# also supports two varieties of multidimensional arrays. The first of these is termed a *rectangular array*, which is simply an array of multiple dimensions, where each row is of the same length. To declare and fill a multidimensional rectangular array, proceed as follows:

```
static void Main(string[] args)
{
...
    // A rectangular MD array.
    int[,] myMatrix;
    myMatrix = new int[6,6];

    // Populate (6 * 6) array.
    for(int i = 0; i < 6; i++)
        for(int j = 0; j < 6; j++)
            myMatrix[i, j] = i * j;

    // Print (6 * 6) array.
    for(int i = 0; i < 6; i++)
```

```
    {
        for(int j = 0; j < 6; j++)
            Console.Write(myMatrix[i, j] + "\t");
            Console.WriteLine();
    }
...
}
```

Figure 3-22 shows the output (note the rectangular nature of the array).

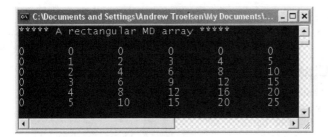

Figure 3-22. *A multidimensional array*

The second type of multidimensional array is termed a *jagged array*. As the name implies, jagged arrays contain some number of inner arrays, each of which may have a unique upper limit, for example:

```
static void Main(string[] args)
{
...
    // A jagged MD array (i.e., an array of arrays).
    // Here we have an array of 5 different arrays.
    int[][] myJagArray = new int[5][];

    // Create the jagged array.
    for (int i = 0; i < myJagArray.Length; i++)
        myJagArray[i] = new int[i + 7];

    // Print each row (remember, each element is defaulted to zero!)
    for(int i = 0; i < 5; i++)
    {
        Console.Write("Length of row {0}  is {1} :\t", i, myJagArray[i].Length);
        for(int j = 0; j < myJagArray[i].Length; j++)
            Console.Write(myJagArray[i][j] + " ");
        Console.WriteLine();
    }
}
```

Figure 3-23 shows the output (note the jaggedness of the array).

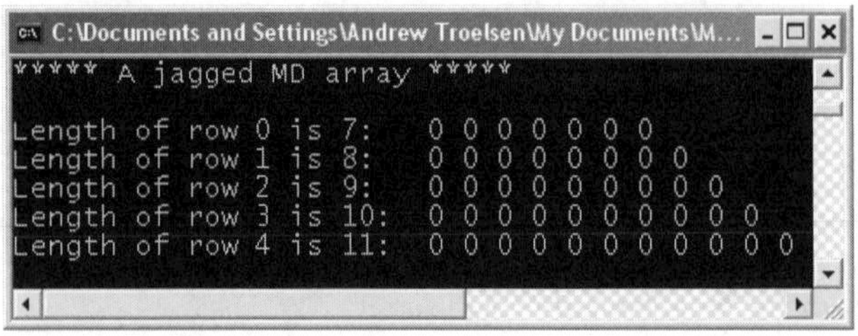

Figure 3-23. *A jagged array*

Now that you understand how to build and populate C# arrays, let's turn our attention to the ultimate base class of any array: System.Array.

The System.Array Base Class

Every .NET array you create is automatically derived from System.Array. This class defines a number of helpful methods that make working with arrays much more palatable. Table 3-14 gives a rundown of some (but not all) of the more interesting members.

Table 3-14. *Select Members of* System.Array

Member	Meaning in Life
BinarySearch()	This static method searches a (previously sorted) array for a given item. If the array is composed of custom types you have created, the type in question must implement the IComparer interface (see Chapter 7) to engage in a binary search.
Clear()	This static method sets a range of elements in the array to empty values (0 for value types; null for reference types).
CopyTo()	This method is used to copy elements from the source array into the destination array.
Length	This read-only property is used to determine the number of elements in an array.
Rank	This property returns the number of dimensions of the current array.
Reverse()	This static method reverses the contents of a one-dimensional array.
Sort()	This method sorts a one-dimensional array of intrinsic types. If the elements in the array implement the IComparer interface, you can also sort your custom types (again, see Chapter 7).

Let's see some of these members in action. The following code makes use of the static Reverse() and Clear() methods (and the Length property) to pump out some information about an array of strings named firstNames to the console:

```
// Create some string arrays and exercise some System.Array members.
static void Main(string[] args)
{
    // Array of strings.
    string[] firstNames = {  "Steve", "Dominic", "Swallow", "Baldy"} ;

    // Print names as declared.
```

```
Console.WriteLine("Here is the array:");
for(int i = 0; i < firstNames.Length; i++)
    Console.Write("Name: {0}\t", firstNames[i]);
Console.WriteLine("\n");

// Reverse array and print.
Array.Reverse(firstNames);
Console.WriteLine("Here is the array once reversed:");
for(int i = 0; i < firstNames.Length; i++)
    Console.Write("Name: {0}\t", firstNames[i]);
Console.WriteLine("\n");

// Clear out all but Baldy.
Console.WriteLine("Cleared out all but Baldy...");
Array.Clear(firstNames, 1, 3);
for(int i = 0; i < firstNames.Length; i++)
    Console.Write("Name: {0}\t", firstNames[i]);
Console.ReadLine();
}
```

Do note that when you call the Clear() method on an array type, the items are *not* compacted into a smaller array. Rather, the emptied elements are simply set to default values. If you require a dynamically allocated container type, you will need to check out the types within the System.Collections namespace (among others).

■Source Code The Arrays application is located under the Chapter 3 subdirectory.

Understanding C# Nullable Types

As you have seen, CLR data types have a fixed range. For example, the System.Boolean data type can be assigned a value from the set {true, false}. As of .NET 2.0, it is now possible to create *nullable* data types. Simply put, a nullable type can represent all the values of its underlying type, plus the value null. Thus, if we declare a nullable System.Boolean, it could be assigned a value from the set {true, false, null}. This is significant, as non-nullable value types *cannot* be assigned the value null:

```
static void Main(string[] args)
{
    // Compiler errors!
    // Value types cannot be set to null!
    bool myBool = null;
    int myInt = null;
}
```

To define a nullable variable type, the question mark symbol (?) is suffixed to the underlying data type. Do note that this syntax is only legal when applied to value types or an array of value types. If you attempt to create a nullable reference type (including strings), you are issued a compile-time error. Like a non-nullable variable, local nullable variables must be assigned an initial value:

```
static void Main(string[] args)
{
    // Define some local nullable types.
    int? nullableInt = 10;
    double? nullableDouble = 3.14;
    bool? nullableBool = null;
```

```
    char? nullableChar = 'a';
    int?[] arrayOfNullableInts = new int?[10];

    // Error!  Strings are reference types!
    string? s = "oops";
}
```

In C#, the ? suffix notation is a shorthand for creating a variable of the generic System.Nullable<T> structure type. Although we will not examine generics until Chapter 10, it is important to understand that the System.Nullable<T> type provides a set of members that all nullable types can make use of. For example, you are able to programmatically discover if the nullable variable indeed has been assigned a null value using the HasValue property or the != operator. The assigned value of a nullable type may be obtained directly or via the Value property.

Working with Nullable Types

Nullable data types can be particularly useful when you are interacting with databases, given that columns in a data table may be intentionally empty (e.g., undefined). To illustrate, assume the following class, which simulates the process of accessing a database that has a table containing two columns that may be null. Note that the GetIntFromDatabase() method is not assigning a value to the nullable integer member variable, while GetBoolFromDatabase() is assigning a valid value to the bool? member:

```
class DatabaseReader
{
    // Nullable data field.
    public int? numbericValue;
    public bool? boolValue = true;

    // Note the nullable return type.
    public int? GetIntFromDatabase()
    { return numbericValue; }

    // Note the nullable return type.
    public bool? GetBoolFromDatabase()
    { return boolValue; }
}
```

Now, assume the following Main() method, which invokes each member of the DatabaseReader class, and discovers the assigned values using the HasValue and Value members as well as a C#-specific syntax:

```
static void Main(string[] args)
{
    Console.WriteLine("***** Fun with Nullable Data *****\n");
    DatabaseReader dr = new DatabaseReader();

    // Get int from 'database'.
    int? i = dr.GetIntFromDatabase();
    if (i.HasValue)
        Console.WriteLine("Value of 'i' is: {0}", i);
    else
        Console.WriteLine("Value of 'i' is undefined.");
```

```
    // Get bool from 'database'.
    bool? b = dr.GetBoolFromDatabase();
    if (b != null)
        Console.WriteLine("Value of 'b' is: {0}", b);
    else
        Console.WriteLine("Value of 'b' is undefined.");
    Console.ReadLine();
}
```

The ?? Operator

The final aspect of nullable types to be aware of is that they can make use of the C# 2005–specific ??
operator. This operator allows you to assign a value to a nullable type if the retrieved value is in fact
null. For this example, assume you wish to assign a local nullable integer to 100 if the value returned
from GetIntFromDatabase() is null (of course, this method is programmed to *always* return null,
but I am sure you get the general idea):

```
static void Main(string[] args)
{
    Console.WriteLine("***** Fun with Nullable Data *****\n");
    DatabaseReader dr = new DatabaseReader();
...
    // If the value from GetIntFromDatabase() is null,
    // assign local variable to 100.
    int? myData = dr.GetIntFromDatabase() ?? 100;
    Console.WriteLine("Value of myData: {0}", myData);
    Console.ReadLine();
}
```

■**Source Code** The NullableType application is located under the Chapter 3 subdirectory.

Defining Custom Namespaces

Up to this point, you have been building small test programs leveraging existing namespaces in the
.NET universe (System in particular). When you build your own custom applications, it can be very
helpful to group your related types into custom namespaces. In C#, this is accomplished using the
namespace keyword.

Assume you are developing a collection of geometric classes named Square, Circle, and Hexagon.
Given their similarities, you would like to group them all together into a common custom namespace.
You have two basic approaches. First, you may choose to define each class within a single file (shapes-
lib.cs) as follows:

```
// shapeslib.cs
using System;

namespace MyShapes
{
    // Circle class.
    class Circle{  /* Interesting methods... */ }
    // Hexagon class.
    class Hexagon{ /* More interesting methods... */ }
    // Square class.
    class Square{  /* Even more interesting methods... */ }
}
```

Notice how the MyShapes namespace acts as the conceptual "container" of these types. Alternatively, you can split a single namespace into multiple C# files. To do so, simply wrap the given class definitions in the same namespace:

```
// circle.cs
using System;

namespace MyShapes
{
    // Circle class.
    class Circle{ }
}
```

```
// hexagon.cs
using System;

namespace MyShapes
{
    // Hexagon class.
    class Hexagon{ }
}
```

```
// square.cs
using System;

namespace MyShapes
{
    // Square class.
    class Square{ }
}
```

As you already know, when another namespace wishes to use objects within a distinct namespace, the using keyword can be used as follows:

```
// Make use of types defined the MyShape namespace.
using System;
using MyShapes;

namespace MyApp
{
    class ShapeTester
    {
        static void Main(string[] args)
        {
            Hexagon h = new Hexagon();
            Circle c = new Circle();
            Square s = new Square();
        }
    }
}
```

A Type's Fully Qualified Name

Technically speaking, you are not required to make use of the C# using keyword when declaring a type defined in an external namespace. You could make use of the fully qualified name of the type, which as you recall from Chapter 1 is the type's name prefixed with the defining namespace:

```
// Note we are not 'using' MyShapes anymore.
using System;

namespace MyApp
{
    class ShapeTester
    {
        static void Main(string[] args)
        {
            MyShapes.Hexagon h = new MyShapes.Hexagon();
            MyShapes.Circle c = new MyShapes.Circle();
            MyShapes.Square s = new MyShapes.Square();
        }
    }
}
```

Typically there is no need to use a fully qualified name. Not only does it require a greater number of keystrokes, but also it makes no difference whatsoever in terms of code size or execution speed. In fact, in CIL code, types are *always* defined with the fully qualified name. In this light, the C# using keyword is simply a typing time-saver.

However, fully qualified names can be very helpful (and sometimes necessary) to avoid name clashes that may occur when using multiple namespaces that contain identically named types. Assume a new namespace termed My3DShapes, which defines three classes capable of rendering a shape in stunning 3D:

```
// Another shapes namespace...
using System;

namespace My3DShapes
{
    // 3D Circle class.
    class Circle{ }
    // 3D Hexagon class
    class Hexagon{ }
    // 3D Square class
    class Square{ }
}
```

If you update ShapeTester as was done here, you are issued a number of compile-time errors, because both namespaces define identically named types:

```
// Ambiguities abound!
using System;
using MyShapes;
using My3DShapes;

namespace MyApp
{
    class ShapeTester
    {
        static void Main(string[] args)
        {
            // Which namespace do I reference?
            Hexagon h = new Hexagon();     // Compiler error!
            Circle c = new Circle();       // Compiler error!
            Square s = new Square();       // Compiler error!
        }
    }
}
```

The ambiguity can be resolved using the type's fully qualified name:

```
// We have now resolved the ambiguity.
static void Main(string[] args)
{
    My3DShapes.Hexagon h = new My3DShapes.Hexagon();
    My3DShapes.Circle c = new My3DShapes.Circle();
    MyShapes.Square s = new MyShapes.Square();
}
```

Defining using Aliases

The C# using keyword can also be used to create an *alias* to a type's fully qualified name. When you do so, you are able to define a token that is substituted with the type's full name at compile time, for example:

```
using System;
using MyShapes;
using My3DShapes;

// Resolve the ambiguity using a custom alias.
using The3DHexagon = My3DShapes.Hexagon;

namespace MyApp
{
    class ShapeTester
    {
        static void Main(string[] args)
        {
            // This is really creating a My3DShapes.Hexagon type.
            The3DHexagon h2 = new The3DHexagon();
...
        }
    }
}
```

This alternative using syntax can also be used to create an alias to a lengthy namespace. One of the longer namespaces in the base class library would have to be System.Runtime.Serialization. Formatters.Binary, which contains a member named BinaryFormatter. If you wish, you could create an instance of the BinaryFormatter as so:

```
using MyAlias = System.Runtime.Serialization.Formatters.Binary;

namespace MyApp
{
    class ShapeTester
    {
        static void Main(string[] args)
        {
            MyAlias.BinaryFormatter b = new MyAlias.BinaryFormatter();
        }
    }
}
```

as well with a traditional using directive:

```
using System.Runtime.Serialization.Formatters.Binary;
```

```
namespace MyApp
{
    class ShapeTester
    {
        static void Main(string[] args)
        {
            BinaryFormatter b = new BinaryFormatter();
        }
    }
}
```

■Note C# now provides a mechanism that can be used to resolve name clashes between identically named *namespaces* using the namespace alias qualifier (::) and "global" token. Thankfully, this type of name collision is rare. If you require more information regarding this topic, look up my article "Working with the C# 2.0 Command Line Compiler" from http://msdn.microsoft.com.

Creating Nested Namespaces

When organizing your types, you are free to define namespaces within other namespaces. The .NET base class libraries do so in numerous places to provide an even deeper level of type organization. For example, the Collections namespace is nested within System, to yield System.Collections. If you wish to create a root namespace that contains the existing My3DShapes namespace, you can update your code as follows:

```
// Nesting a namespace.
namespace Chapter3
{
    namespace My3DShapes
    {
        // 3D Circle class.
        class Circle{ }
        // 3D Hexagon class
        class Hexagon{ }
        // 3D Square class
        class Square{ }
    }
}
```

In many cases, the role of a root namespace is simply to provide a further level of scope, and therefore may not define any types directly within its scope (as in the case of the Chapter3 namespace). If this is the case, a nested namespace can be defined using the following compact form:

```
// Nesting a namespace (take two).
namespace Chapter3.My3DShapes
{
    // 3D Circle class.
    class Circle{ }
    // 3D Hexagon class
    class Hexagon{ }
    // 3D Square class
    class Square{ }
}
```

Given that you have now nested the My3DShapes namespace within the Chapter3 root namespace, you need to update any existing using directives and type aliases:

```
using Chapter3.My3DShapes;
using The3DHexagon = Chapter3.My3DShapes.Hexagon;
```

The "Default Namespace" of Visual Studio 2005

On a final namespace-related note, it is worth pointing out that by default, when you create a new C# project using Visual Studio 2005, the name of your application's default namespace will be identical to the project name. From this point on, when you insert new items using the Project ➤ Add New Item menu selection, types will automatically be wrapped within the default namespace. If you wish to change the name of the default namespace (e.g., to be your company name), simply access the Default namespace option using the Application tab of the project's Properties window (see Figure 3-24).

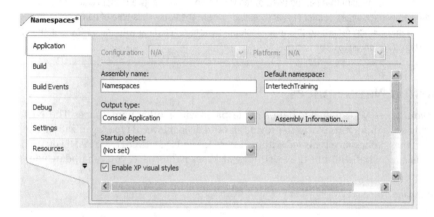

Figure 3-24. *Configuring the default namespace*

With this update, any new item inserted into the project will be wrapped within the Intertech-Training namespace (and, obviously, if another namespace wishes to use these types, the correct using directive must be applied).

■**Source Code**   The Namespaces project is located under the Chapter 3 subdirectory.

Summary

This (rather lengthy) chapter exposed you to the numerous core aspects of the C# programming language and the .NET platform. The focus was to examine the constructs that will be commonplace in any application you may be interested in building.

As you have seen, all intrinsic C# data types alias a corresponding type in the System namespace. Each system type has a number of members that provide a programmatic manner to obtain the range of the type. Furthermore, you learned the basic process of building C# class types and examined the various parameter-passing conventions, value types and reference types, and the role of the mighty System.Object.

You also examined various aspects of the CLR that place an OO spin on common programming constructs, such as arrays, strings, structures, and enumerations. In addition, this chapter illustrated the concept of boxing and unboxing. This simple mechanism allows you to easily move between value-based and reference-based data types. Finally, the chapter wrapped up by explaining the role of nullable data types and the construction of custom namespaces.

CHAPTER 4

■ ■ ■

Object-Oriented Programming with C# 2.0

In the previous chapter, you were introduced to a number of core constructs of the C# language and the .NET platform as well as select types within the System namespace. Here, you will spend your time digging deeper into the details of object-based development. I begin with a review of the famed "pillars of OOP" and then examine exactly how C# contends with the notions of encapsulation, inheritance, and polymorphism. This will equip you with the knowledge you need in order to build custom class hierarchies.

During this process, you examine some new constructs such as type properties, versioning type members, "sealed" classes, and XML code documentation syntax. Do be aware that the information presented here will serve as the foundation for more advanced class design techniques (such as overloaded operators, events, and custom conversion routines) examined in later chapters.

By way of a friendly invitation, even if you are currently comfortable with the constructs of object-oriented programming using other languages, I would encourage you to pound out the code examples found within this chapter. As you will see, C# does place a new spin on many common OO techniques.

Understanding the C# Class Type

If you have been "doing objects" in another programming language, you are no doubt aware of the role of class definitions. Formally, a class is nothing more than a custom user-defined type (UDT) that is composed of field data (sometimes termed *member variables*) and functions (often called *methods* in OO speak) that act on this data. The set of field data collectively represents the "state" of a class instance.

The power of object-oriented languages is that by grouping data and functionality in a single UDT, you are able to model your software types after real-world entities. For example, assume you are interested in modeling a generic employee for a payroll system. At minimum, you may wish to build a class that maintains the name, current pay, and employee ID for each worker. In addition, the Employee class defines one method, named GiveBonus(), which increases an individual's current pay by some amount, and another, named DisplayStats(), which prints out the state data for this individual. Figure 4-1 illustrates the Employee class type.

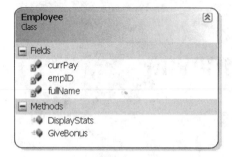

Figure 4-1. *The* Employee *class type*

As you recall from Chapter 3, C# classes can define any number of *constructors*. These special class methods provide a simple way for an object user to create an instance of a given class with an initial look and feel. Every C# class is initially provided with a *default constructor*, which by definition never takes arguments. In addition to the default constructor, you are also free to define as many custom constructors as you feel are necessary.

To get the ball rolling, here is our first crack at the Employee class (we will add more functionality throughout the chapter):

```
// The initial Employee class definition.
namespace Employees
{
    public class Employee
    {
        // Field data.
        private string fullName;
        private int empID;
        private float currPay;

        // Constructors.
        public Employee(){ }
        public Employee(string fullName, int empID, float currPay)
        {
            this.fullName = fullName;
            this.empID = empID;
            this.currPay = currPay;
        }

        // Bump the pay for this employee.
        public void GiveBonus(float amount)
        { currPay += amount; }

        // Show current state of this object.
        public void DisplayStats()
        {
            Console.WriteLine("Name: {0} ", fullName);
            Console.WriteLine("Pay: {0} ", currPay);
            Console.WriteLine("ID: {0} ", empID);
        }
    }
}
```

Notice the empty implementation of the default constructor for the Employee class:

```
public class Employee
{
...
    public Employee(){ }
...
}
```

Like C++ and Java, if you choose to define custom constructors in a class definition, the default constructor is *silently removed*. Therefore, if you wish to allow the object user to create an instance of your class as follows:

```
static void Main(string[] args)
{
    // Calls the default constructor.
    Employee e = new Employee();
}
```

you must explicitly redefine the default constructor for your class (as we have done here). If you do not, you will receive a compiler error when creating an instance of your class type using the default constructor. In any case, the following Main() method creates a few Employee objects using our custom three-argument constructor:

```
// Make some Employee objects.
static void Main(string[] args)
{
    Employee e = new Employee("Joe", 80, 30000);
    Employee e2;
    e2 = new Employee("Beth", 81, 50000);
    Console.ReadLine();
}
```

Understanding Method Overloading

Like other object-oriented languages, C# allows a type to *overload* various methods. Simply put, when a class has a set of identically named members that differ by the number (or type) of parameters, the member in question is said to be *overloaded*. In the Employee class, you have overloaded the class constructor, given that you have provided two definitions that differ only by the parameter set:

```
public class Employee
{
...
    // Overloaded constructors.
    public Employee(){ }
    public Employee(string fullName, int empID, float currPay){...}
...
}
```

Constructors, however, are not the only members that may be overloaded for a type. By way of example, assume you have a class named Triangle that supports an overloaded Draw() method. By doing so, you allow the object user to render the image using various input parameters:

```
public class Triangle
{
    // The overloaded Draw() method.
    public void Draw(int x, int y, int height, int width) {...}
    public void Draw(float x, float y, float height, float width) {...}
    public void Draw(Point upperLeft, Point bottomRight) {...}
    public void Draw(Rect r) {...}
}
```

If C# did not support method overloading, you would be forced to create four uniquely named members, which, as you can see, is far from ideal:

```
public class Triangle
{
    // Yuck...
    public void DrawWithInts(int x, int y, int height, int width) {...}
    public void DrawWIthFloats(float x, float y, float height, float width) {...}
    public void DrawWithPoints(Point upperLeft, Point bottomRight) {...}
    public void DrawWithRect(Rect r) {...}
}
```

Again, remember that when you are overloading a member, the return type alone is not unique enough. Thus, the following is illegal:

```
public class Triangle
{
    ...
    // Error! Cannot overload methods
    // based solely on return values!
    public float GetX() {...}
    public int GetX() {...}
}
```

Self-Reference in C# Using this

Next, note that the custom constructor of the Employee class makes use of the C# this keyword:

```
// Explicitly use "this" to resolve name-clash.
public Employee(string fullName, int empID, float currPay)
{
    // Assign the incoming params to my state data.
    this.fullName = fullName;
    this.empID = empID;
    this.currPay = currPay;
}
```

This particular C# keyword is used when you wish to explicitly reference the fields and members of the *current object*. The reason you made use of this in your custom constructor was to avoid clashes between the parameter names and names of your internal state variables. Of course, another approach would be to change the names for each parameter and avoid the name clash altogether:

```
// When there is no name clash, "this" is assumed.
public Employee(string name, int id, float pay)
{
    fullName = name;
    empID = id;
    currPay = pay;
}
```

In this case, we have no need to explicitly prefix the this keyword to the Employee's member variables, because we have removed the name clash. The compiler can resolve the scope of these member variables using what is known as an *implict* this. Simply put, when your class references its own field data and member variables (in an unambiguous manner), this is assumed. Therefore, the previous constructor logic is functionally identical to the following:

```
public Employee(string name, int id, float pay)
{
    this.fullName = name;
```

```
    this.empID = id;
    this.currPay = pay;
}
```

■**Note** Static members of a type cannot make use of the `this` keyword within its method scope. This fact should make some sense, as static member functions operate on the class (not object) level. At the class level, there is no `this`!

Forwarding Constructor Calls Using this

Another use of the `this` keyword is to force one constructor to call another in order to avoid redundant member initialization logic. Consider the following update to the `Employee` class:

```
public class Employee
{
...
    public Employee(string fullName, int empID, float currPay)
    {
        this.fullName = fullName;
        this.empID = empID;
        this.currPay = currPay;
    }

    // If the user calls this ctor, forward to the 3-arg version.
    public Employee(string fullName)
        : this(fullName, IDGenerator.GetNewEmpID(), 0.0F) { }
...
}
```

This iteration of the `Employee` class defines two custom constructors, the second of which requires a single parameter (the individual's name). However, to fully construct a new `Employee`, you want to ensure you have a proper ID and rate of pay. Assume you have created a custom class (`IDGenerator`) that defines a static method named `GetNewEmpID()`, which generates a new employee ID (in some way or another). Once you gather the correct set of startup parameters, you forward the creation request to the alternate three-argument constructor.

If you did not forward the call, you would need to add redundant code to each constructor:

```
// currPay automatically set to 0.0F via default values.
public Employee(string fullName)
{
    this.fullName = fullName;
    this.empID = IDGenerator.GetNewEmpID();
}
```

Understand that using the `this` keyword to forward constructor calls is not mandatory. However, when you make use of this technique, you do tend to end up with a more maintainable and concise class definition. In fact, using this technique you can simplify your programming tasks, as the real work is delegated to a single constructor (typically the constructor that has the most parameters), while the other constructors simply "pass the buck."

Defining the Public Interface of a Class

Once you have established a class's internal state data and constructor set, your next step is to flesh out the details of the *public interface* to the class. The term refers to the set of members that are directly accessible from an object variable via the dot operator.

From the class builder's point of view, the public interface is any item declared in a class using the public keyword. Beyond field data and constructors, the public interface of a class may be populated by numerous members, including the following:

- *Methods*: Named units of work that model some behavior of a class
- *Properties*: Traditional accessor and mutator functions in disguise
- *Constants/Read-only fields*: Field data that cannot be changed after assignment (see Chapter 3)

■**Note** As you will see later in this chapter, nested type definitions may also appear on a type's public interface. Furthermore, as you will see in Chapter 8, the public interface of a class may also be configured to support events.

Given that our Employee currently defines two public methods (GiveBonus() and DisplayStats()), we are able to interact with the public interface as follows:

```
// Interact with the public interface of the Employee class type.
static void Main(string[] args)
{
    Console.WriteLine("***** The Employee Type at Work *****\n");
    Employee e = new Employee("Joe", 80, 30000);
    e.GiveBonus(200);
    e.DisplayStats();

    Employee e2;
    e2 = new Employee("Beth", 81, 50000);
    e2.GiveBonus(1000);
    e2.DisplayStats();
    Console.ReadLine();
}
```

If you were to run the application as it now stands, you would find the output shown in Figure 4-2.

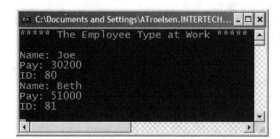

Figure 4-2. *The* Employee *class type at work*

At this point we have created a very simple class type with a minimal public interface. Before we move ahead with more complex examples, let's take a moment to review the cornerstones of object-oriented programming (we will return to the Employee type shortly).

Reviewing the Pillars of OOP

All object-oriented languages contend with three core principles of object-oriented programming, often called the famed "pillars of OOP."

- *Encapsulation*: How does this language hide an object's internal implementation?
- *Inheritance*: How does this language promote code reuse?
- *Polymorphism*: How does this language let you treat related objects in a similar way?

Before digging into the syntactic details of each pillar, it is important you understand the basic role of each. Therefore, here is a brisk, high-level rundown, just to clear off any cobwebs you may have acquired between project deadlines.

Encapsulation

The first pillar of OOP is called *encapsulation*. This trait boils down to the language's ability to hide unnecessary implementation details from the object user. For example, assume you are using a class named DatabaseReader that has two methods named Open() and Close():

```
// DatabaseReader encapsulates the details of database manipulation.
DatabaseReader dbObj = new DatabaseReader();

dbObj.Open(@"C:\Employees.mdf");
    // Do something with database...
dbObj.Close();
```

The fictitious DatabaseReader class has encapsulated the inner details of locating, loading, manipulating, and closing the data file. Object users love encapsulation, as this pillar of OOP keeps programming tasks simpler. There is no need to worry about the numerous lines of code that are working behind the scenes to carry out the work of the DatabaseReader class. All you do is create an instance and send the appropriate messages (e.g., "open the file named Employees.mdf located on my C drive").

Another aspect of encapsulation is the notion of data protection. Ideally, an object's state data should be defined as *private* rather than *public* (as was the case in previous chapters). In this way, the outside world must "ask politely" in order to change or obtain the underlying value.

Inheritance

The next pillar of OOP, inheritance, boils down to the language's ability to allow you to build new class definitions based on existing class definitions. In essence, inheritance allows you to extend the behavior of a base (or *parent*) class by enabling a subclass to inherit core functionality (also called a *derived class* or *child class*). Figure 4-3 illustrates the "is-a" relationship.

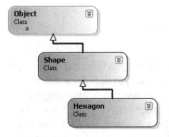

Figure 4-3. *The "is-a" relationship*

You can read this diagram as "A hexagon is-a shape that is-an object." When you have classes related by this form of inheritance, you establish "is-a" relationships between types. The "is-a" relationship is often termed *classical inheritance*.

Recall from Chapter 3 that System.Object is the ultimate base class in any .NET hierarchy. Here, the Shape class extends Object. You can assume that Shape defines some number of properties, fields, methods, and events that are common to all shapes. The Hexagon class extends Shape and inherits the functionality defined by Shape and Object, in addition to defining its own set of members (whatever they may be).

There is another form of code reuse in the world of OOP: the containment/delegation model (also known as the "has-a" relationship). This form of reuse is not used to establish base/subclass relationships. Rather, a given class can define a member variable of another class and expose part or all of its functionality to the outside world.

For example, if you are modeling an automobile, you might wish to express the idea that a car "has-a" radio. It would be illogical to attempt to derive the Car class from a Radio, or vice versa. (A Car "is-a" Radio? I think not!) Rather, you have two independent classes working together, where the containing class creates and exposes the contained class's functionality:

```
public class Radio
{
    public void Power(bool turnOn)
    { Console.WriteLine("Radio on: {0}", turnOn);}
}

public class Car
{
    // Car "has-a" Radio.
    private Radio myRadio = new Radio();

    public void TurnOnRadio(bool onOff)
    {
        // Delegate to inner object.
        myRadio.Power(onOff);
    }
}
```

Here, the containing type (Car) is responsible for creating the contained object (Radio). If the Car wishes to make the Radio's behavior accessible from a Car instance, it must extend its own public interface with some set of functions that operate on the contained type. Notice that the object user has no clue that the Car class is making use of an inner Radio object:

```
static void Main(string[] args)
{
    // Call is forward to Radio internally.
    Car viper = new Car();
    viper.TurnOnRadio(true);
}
```

Polymorphism

The final pillar of OOP is *polymorphism*. This trait captures a language's ability to treat related objects the same way. This tenet of an object-oriented language allows a base class to define a set of members (formally termed the *polymorphic interface*) to all descendents. A class type's polymorphic interface is constructed using any number of *virtual* or *abstract* members. In a nutshell, a virtual member *may* be changed (or more formally speaking, *overridden*) by a derived class, whereas an abstract method *must* be overriden by a derived type. When derived types override the members defined by a base class, they are essentially redefining how they respond to the same request.

To illustrate polymorphism, let's revisit the shapes hierarchy. Assume that the Shape class has defined a method named Draw(), taking no parameters and returning nothing. Given the fact that every shape needs to render itself in a unique manner, subclasses (such as Hexagon and Circle) are free to override this method to their own liking (see Figure 4-4).

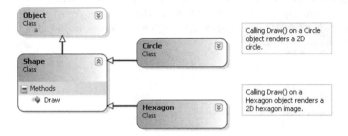

Figure 4-4. *Classical polymorphism*

Once a *polymorphic interface* has been designed, you can begin to make various assumptions in your code. For example, given that Hexagon and Circle derive from a common parent (Shape), an array of Shape types could contain any derived class. Furthermore, given that Shape defines a polymorphic interface to all derived types (the Draw() method in this example), we can assume each member in the array has this functionaltiy. Ponder the following Main() method, which instructs an array of Shape-derived types to render themselves using the Draw() method:

```
static void Main(string[] args)
{
    // Create an array of Shape derived items.
    Shape[] myShapes = new Shape[3];
    myShapes[0] = new Hexagon();
    myShapes[1] = new Circle();
    myShapes[2] = new Hexagon();

    // Iterate over the array and draw each item.
    foreach (Shape s in myShapes)
        s.Draw();
    Console.ReadLine();
}
```

This wraps up our basic (and brisk) review of the pillars of OOP. Now that you have the theory in your minds, the bulk of this chapter explores further details and exact C# syntax that represents each trait.

The First Pillar: C#'s Encapsulation Services

The concept of encapsulation revolves around the notion that an object's field data should not be directly accessible from the public interface. Rather, if an object user wishes to alter the state of an object, it does so indirectly using accessor (get) and mutator (set) methods. In C#, encapsulation is enforced at the syntactic level using the public, private, protected, and protected internal keywords, as described in Chapter 3. To illustrate the need for encapsulation, assume you have created the following class definition:

```
// A class with a single public field.
public class Book
{
    public int numberOfPages;
}
```

The problem with public field data is that the items have no ability to "understand" whether the current value to which they are assigned is valid with regard to the current business rules of the system. As you know, the upper range of a C# int is quite large (2,147,483,647). Therefore, the compiler allows the following assignment:

```
// Humm...
static void Main(string[] args)
{
    Book miniNovel = new Book();
    miniNovel.numberOfPages = 30000000;
}
```

Although you do not overflow the boundaries of an integer data type, it should be clear that a mini-novel with a page count of 30,000,000 pages is a bit unreasonable in the real world. As you can see, public fields do not provide a way to enforce data validation rules. If your system has a business rule that states a mini-novel must be between 1 and 200 pages, you are at a loss to enforce this programmatically. Because of this, public fields typically have no place in a production-level class definition (public read-only fields being the exception).

Encapsulation provides a way to preserve the integrity of state data. Rather than defining public fields (which can easily foster data corruption), you should get in the habit of defining *private data fields*, which are indirectly manipulated by the caller using one of two main techniques:

- Define a pair of traditional accessor and mutator methods.

- Define a named property.

Whichever technique you choose, the point is that a well-encapsulated class should hide its raw data and the details of how it operates from the prying eyes of the outside world. This is often termed *black box programming*. The beauty of this approach is that a class author is free to change how a given method is implemented under the hood, without breaking any existing code making use of it (provided that the signature of the method remains constant).

Enforcing Encapsulation Using Traditional Accessors and Mutators

Let's return to the existing Employee class. If you want the outside world to interact with your private fullName data field, tradition dictates defining an *accessor* (get method) and *mutator* (set method). For example:

```
// Traditional accessor and mutator for a point of private data.
public class Employee
{
    private string fullName;
...
    // Accessor.
    public string GetFullName() { return fullName; }

    // Mutator.
    public void SetFullName(string n)
    {
        // Remove any illegal characters (!, @, #, $, %),
        // check maximum length (or case rules) before making assignment.
```

```
        fullName = n;
    }
}
```

Understand, of course, that the compiler could not care less what you call your accessor and mutator methods. Given the fact that GetFullName() and SetFullName() encapsulate a private string named fullName, this choice of method names seems to fit the bill. The calling logic is as follows:

```
// Accessor/mutator usage.
static void Main(string[] args)
{
    Employee p = new Employee();
    p.SetFullName("Fred Flintstone");
    Console.WriteLine("Employee is named: {0}", p.GetFullName());
    Console.ReadLine();
}
```

Another Form of Encapsulation: Class Properties

In contrast to traditional accessor and mutator methods, .NET languages prefer to enforce encapsulation using *properties*, which simulate publicly accessible points of data. Rather than requiring the user to call two different methods to get and set the state data, the user is able to call what appears to be a public field. To illustrate, assume you have provided a property named ID that wraps the internal empID member variable of the Employee type. The calling syntax would look like this:

```
// Setting / getting a person's ID through property syntax.
static void Main(string[] args)
{
    Employee p = new Employee();

    // Set the value.
    p.ID = 81;

    // Get the value.
    Console.WriteLine("Person ID is: {0} ", p.ID);
    Console.ReadLine();
}
```

Type properties always map to "real" accessor and mutator methods under the hood. Therefore, as a class designer you are able to perform any internal logic necessary before making the value assignment (e.g., uppercase the value, scrub the value for illegal characters, check the bounds of a numerical value, and so on). Here is the C# syntax behind the ID property, another property (Pay) that encapsulates the currPay field, and a final property (Name) to encapsulate the fullName data point.

```
// Encapsulation with properties.
public class Employee
{
...
    private int empID;
    private float currPay;
    private string fullName;

    // Property for empID.
    public int ID
    {
        get { return empID;}
        set
```

```
        {
            // You are still free to investigate (and possibly transform)
            // the incoming value before making an assignment.
            empID = value;
        }
    }

    // Property for fullName.
    public string Name
    {
        get {return fullName;}
        set {fullName = value;}
    }

    // Property for currPay.
    public float Pay
    {
        get {return currPay;}
        set {currPay = value;}
    }
}
```

A C# property is composed using a get block (accessor) and set block (mutator). The C# "value" token represents the right-hand side of the assignment. The underlying data type of the value token depends on which sort of data it represents. In this example, the ID property is operating on a int data type, which, as you recall, maps to a System.Int32:

```
// 81 is a System.Int32, so "value" is a System.Int32.
Employee e = new Employee();
e.ID = 81;
```

To prove the point, assume you have updated the ID property's set logic as follows:

```
// Property for the empID.
public int ID
{
    get { return empID;}
    set
    {
        Console.WriteLine("value is an instance of: {0} ", value.GetType());
        Console.WriteLine("value's value: {0} ", value);

        empID = value;
    }
}
```

Once you run this application, you would see the output shown in Figure 4-5.

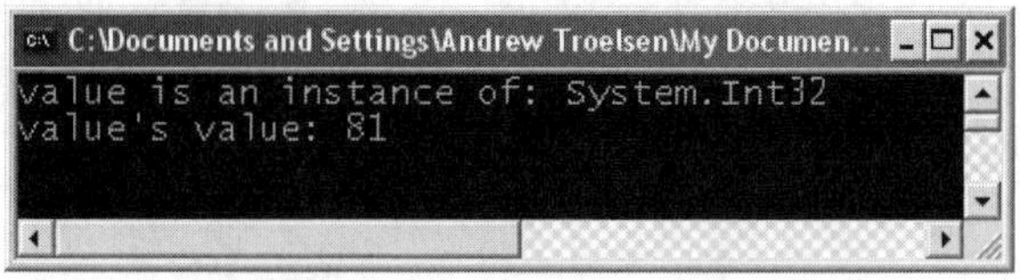

Figure 4-5. *The value of* value *when setting* ID *to 81*

■Note Strictly speaking, the C# value token is not a keyword, but rather a *contextual keyword* that represents the implicit parameter used during a property assignment when within the scope of a property set. Given this, you are free to have member variables and local data points named "value".

Understand that properties (as opposed to traditional accessors and mutators) also make your types easier to manipulate, in that properties are able to respond to the intrinsic operators of C#. To illustrate, assume that the Employee class type has an internal private member variable representing the age of the employee. Here is our update:

```csharp
public class Employee
{
...
    // Current age of employee.
    private int empAge;

    public Employee(string fullName, int age, int empID, float currPay)
    {
...
        this.empAge = age;
    }

    public int Age
    {
        get{return empAge;}
        set{empAge = value;}
    }

    public void DisplayStats()
    {
...
        Console.WriteLine("Age: {0} ", empAge);
    }
}
```

Now assume you have created an Employee object named joe. On his birthday, you wish to increment the age by one. Using traditional accessor and mutator methods, you would need to write code such as the following:

```csharp
Employee joe = new Employee();
joe.SetAge(joe.GetAge() + 1);
```

However, if you encapsulate empAge using property syntax, you are able to simply write

```csharp
Employee joe = new Employee();
joe.Age++;
```

Internal Representation of C# Properties

Many programmers (especially those of the C++ ilk) tend to design traditional accessor and mutator methods using "get_" and "set_" prefixes (e.g., get_FullName() and set_FullName()). This naming convention itself is not problematic. However, it is important to understand that under the hood, a C# property is represented in CIL code using these same prefixes. For example, if you open up the Employees.exe assembly using ildasm.exe, you see that each property actually resolves to hidden get_XXX()/set_XXX() methods (see Figure 4-6).

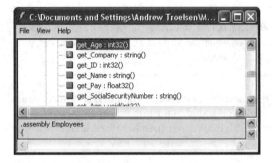

Figure 4-6. *Properties map to hidden* get_XXX() *and* set_XXX() *methods.*

Assume the Employee type now has a private member variable named empSSN to represent an individual's Social Security number, which is manipulated by a property named SocialSecurityNumber and set via constructor parameter.

```
// Add support for a new field representing the employee's SSN.
public class Employee
{
...
    // Social Security Number.
    private string empSSN;

    public Employee(string fullName, int age, int empID,
        float currPay, string ssn)
    {
...
        this.empSSN = ssn;
    }

    public string SocialSecurityNumber
    {
        get {  return empSSN; }
        set {  empSSN = value;}
    }

    public void DisplayStats()
    {
...
        Console.WriteLine("SSN: {0} ", empSSN);
    }
}
```

If you were to also define two methods named get_SocialSecurityNumber() and set_SocialSecurityNumber(), you would be issued compile-time errors:

```
// Remember, a C# property really maps to a get_/set_ pair.
public class Employee
{
...
    // ERROR! Already defined under the hood by the property!
    public string get_SocialSecurityNumber() {return empSSN;}
    public void set_SocialSecurityNumber (string val) {empSSN = val;}
}
```

Note The .NET base class libraries always favor type properties over traditional accessor and mutator methods. Therefore, if you wish to build custom types that integrate well with the .NET platform, avoid defining traditional get and set methods.

Controlling Visibility Levels of Property get/set Statements

Prior to C# 2005, the visibility of get and set logic was solely controlled by the access modifer of the property declaration:

```
// The get and set logic is both public,
// given the declaration of the property.
public string SocialSecurityNumber
{
    get {  return empSSN; }
    set {  empSSN = value;}
}
```

In some cases, it would be helpful to specify unique accessability levels for get and set logic. To do so, simply prefix an accessibility keyword to the appropriate get or set keyword (the unqualified scope takes the visibility of the property's declaration):

```
// Object users can only get the value, however
// derived types can set the value.
public string SocialSecurityNumber
{
    get {  return empSSN; }
    protected set {  empSSN = value;}
}
```

In this case, the set logic of SocialSecurityNumber can only be called by the current class and *derived* classes and therefore cannot be called from an object instance.

Read-Only and Write-Only Properties

When creating class types, you may wish to configure a read-only property. To do so, simply build a property without a corresponding set block. Likewise, if you wish to have a write-only property, omit the get block. We have no need to do so for this example; however, here is how the SocialSecurityNumber property could be retrofitted as read-only:

```
public class Employee
{
...
    // Now as a read-only property.
    public string SocialSecurityNumber { get {  return empSSN; }  }
}
```

Given this adjustment, the only manner in which an employee's US Social Security number can be set is through a constructor argument.

Static Properties

C# also supports *static properties*. Recall from Chapter 3 that static members are accessed at the class level, not from an instance (object) of that class. For example, assume that the Employee type defines a point of static data to represent the name of the organization employing these workers. You may define a static (e.g., class-level) property as follows:

```
// Static properties must operate on static data!
public class Employee
{
    private static string companyName;
    public static string Company
    {
        get {  return companyName; }
        set {  companyName = value;}
    }
...
}
```

Static properties are manipulated in the same manner as static methods, as seen here:

```
// Set and get the name of the company that employs these people...
public static int Main(string[] args)
{
    Employee.Company = "Intertech Training";
    Console.WriteLine("These folks work at {0} ", Employee.Company);
...
}
```

Also, recall from Chapter 3 that C# provides static constructors. Therefore, if you wish to ensure that the static companyName property is always set to Intertech Training, you could add the following member to the Employee class:

```
// A static ctor takes no access modifer or arguments.
public class Employee
{
...
    static Employee()
    {
        companyName = "Intertech Training";
    }
}
```

In this case, we did not gain too much by adding a static constructor, given that the same end result could have been achieved by simply assigning the companyName member variable as follows:

```
// Static properties must operate on static data!
public class Employee
{
    private static string companyName = "Intertech Training";
...
}
```

However, recall that if you need to perform runtime logic to obtain the value to a point of static data (such as reading a database), static constructors are very helpful indeed.

To wrap up our examination of encapsulation, understand that properties are used for the same purpose as a classical accessor/mutator pair. The benefit of properties is that the users of your objects are able to manipulate the internal data point using a single named item.

The Second Pillar: C#'s Inheritance Support

Now that you have seen various techniques that allow you to create a single well-encapsulated class, it is time to turn your attention to building a family of related classes. As mentioned, inheritance is the aspect of OOP that facilitates code reuse. Inheritance comes in two flavors: classical inheritance (the "is-a" relationship) and the containment/delegation model (the "has-a" relationship). Let's begin by examining the classical "is-a" model.

When you establish "is-a" relationships between classes, you are building a dependency between types. The basic idea behind classical inheritance is that new classes may leverage (and possibily extend) the functionality of other classes. To illustrate, assume that you wish to leverage the functionality of the Employee class to create two new classes (SalesPerson and Manager). The class hierarchy looks something like what you see in Figure 4-7.

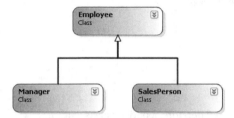

Figure 4-7. *The employee hierarchy*

As illustrated in Figure 4-7, you can see that a SalesPerson "is-a" Employee (as is a Manager). In the classical inheritance model, base classes (such as Employee) are used to define general characteristics that are common to all descendents. Subclasses (such as SalesPerson and Manager) extend this general functionality while adding more specific behaviors.

For our example, we will assume that the Manager class extends Employee by recording the number of stock options, while the SalesPerson class maintains the number of sales. In C#, extending a class is accomplished using the colon operator (:) on the class definition. This being said, here are the derived class types:

```
// Add two new subclasses to the Employees namespace.
namespace Employees
{
    public class Manager : Employee
    {
        // Managers need to know their number of stock options.
        private ulong numberOfOptions;
        public ulong NumbOpts
        {
            get { return numberOfOptions;}
            set { numberOfOptions = value; }
        }
    }

    public class SalesPerson : Employee
    {
        // Salespeople need to know their number of sales.
        private int numberOfSales;
        public int NumbSales
        {
            get { return numberOfSales;}
            set { numberOfSales = value; }
        }
    }
}
```

Now that you have established an "is-a" relationship, `SalesPerson` and `Manager` have automatically inherited all public (and protected) members of the `Employee` base class. To illustrate:

```
// Create a subclass and access base class functionality.
static void Main(string[] args)
{
    // Make a salesperson.
    SalesPerson stan = new SalesPerson();

    // These members are inherited from the Employee base class.
    stan.ID = 100;
    stan.Name = "Stan";

    // This is defined by the SalesPerson class.
    stan.NumbSales = 42;
    Console.ReadLine();
}
```

Do be aware that inheritance preserves encapsulation. Therefore, a derived class cannot directly access the private members defined by its base class.

Controlling Base Class Creation with base

Currently, `SalesPerson` and `Manager` can only be created using a default constructor. With this in mind, assume you have added a new six-argument constructor to the `Manager` type, which is invoked as follows:

```
static void Main(string[] args)
{
    // Assume we now have the following constructor.
    // (name, age, ID, pay, SSN, number of stock options).
    Manager chucky = new Manager("Chucky", 35, 92, 100000, "333-23-2322", 9000);
}
```

If you look at the argument list, you can clearly see that most of these parameters should be stored in the member variables defined by the `Employee` base class. To do so, you could implement this new constructor as follows:

```
// If you do not say otherwise, a subclass constructor automatically calls the
// default constructor of its base class.
public Manager(string fullName, int age, int empID,
            float currPay, string ssn, ulong numbOfOpts)
{
    // This point of data belongs with us!
    numberOfOptions = numbOfOpts;

    // Leverage the various members inherited from Employee
    // to assign the state data.
    ID = empID;
    Age = age;
    Name = fullName;
    SocialSecurityNumber = ssn;
    Pay = currPay;
}
```

Although this is technically permissible, it is not optimal. In C#, unless you say otherwise, the *default constructor* of a base class is called automatically before the logic of the custom `Manager` constructor is executed. After this point, the current implementation accesses numerous public properties of the Employee base class to establish its state. Thus, you have really made seven hits (five inherited properties and two constructor calls) during the creation of this derived object!

To help optimize the creation of a derived class, you will do well to implement your subclass constructors to *explicitly* call an appropriate custom base class constructor, rather than the default. In this way, you are able to reduce the number of calls to inherited initialization members (which saves time). Let's retrofit the custom constructor to do this very thing:

```
// This time, use the C# "base" keyword to call a custom
// constructor on the base class.
public Manager(string fullName, int age, int empID, float currPay,
            string ssn, ulong numbOfOpts)
    : base(fullName, age, empID, currPay, ssn)
{
    numberOfOptions = numbOfOpts;
}
```

Here, your constructor has been adorned with an odd bit of syntax. Directly after the closing parenthesis of the constructor's argument list, there is a single colon followed by the C# base keyword. In this situation, you are explicitly calling the five-argument constructor defined by Employee and saving yourself unnecessary calls during the creation of the child class.

The SalesPerson constructor looks almost identical:

```
// As a general rule, all subclasses should explicitly call an appropriate
// base class constructor.
public SalesPerson(string fullName, int age, int empID,
                float currPay, string ssn, int numbOfSales)
    : base(fullName, age, empID, currPay, ssn)
{
    numberOfSales = numbOfSales;
}
```

Also be aware that you may use the base keyword anytime a subclass wishes to access a public or protected member defined by a parent class. Use of this keyword is not limited to constructor logic. You will see examples using the base keyword in this manner during our examination of polymorphism.

Regarding Multiple Base Classes

Speaking of base classes, it is important to keep in mind that C# demands that a given class have *exactly one* direct base class. Therefore, it is not possible to have a single type with two or more base classes (this technique is known as *multiple inheritance*, or simply *MI*). As you will see in Chapter 7, C# does allow a given type to implement any number of discrete interfaces. In this way, a C# class can exhibit a number of behaviors while avoiding the problems associated with classic MI. On a related note, it is permissible to configure a single *interface* to derive from multiple *interfaces* (again, see Chapter 7).

Keeping Family Secrets: The protected Keyword

As you already know, public items are directly accessible from anywhere, while private items cannot be accessed from any object beyond the class that has defined it. C# takes the lead of many other modern object languages and provides an additional level of accessibility: protected.

When a base class defines protected data or protected members, it is able to create a set of items that can be accessed directly by any descendent. If you wish to allow the SalesPerson and Manager child classes to directly access the data sector defined by Employee, you can update the original Employee class definition as follows:

```
// Protected state data.
public class Employee
{
        // Child classes can directly access this information. Object users cannot.
        protected string fullName;
        protected int empID;
        protected float currPay;
        protected string empSSN;
        protected int empAge;
...
}
```

The benefit of defining protected members in a base class is that derived types no longer have to access the data using public methods or properties. The possible downfall, of course, is that when a derived type has direct access to its parent's internal data, it is very possible to accidentally bypass existing business rules found within public properties (such as the mini-novel that exceeds the page count). When you define protected members, you are creating a level of trust between the parent and child class, as the compiler will not catch any violation of your type's business rules.

Finally, understand that as far as the object user is concerned, protected data is regarded as private (as the user is "outside" of the family). Therefore, the following is illegal:

```
static void Main(string[] args)
{
        // Error! Can't access protected data from object instance.
        Employee emp = new Employee();
        emp.empSSN = "111-11-1111";
}
```

Preventing Inheritance: Sealed Classes

When you establish base class/subclass relationships, you are able to leverage the behavior of existing types. However, what if you wish to define a class that cannot be subclassed? For example, assume you have added yet another class to your employee namespaces that extends the existing SalesPerson type. Figure 4-8 shows the current update.

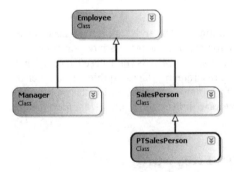

Figure 4-8. *The extended employee hierarchy*

PTSalesPerson is a class representing (of course) a part-time salesperson. For the sake of argument, let's say that you wish to ensure that no other developer is able to subclass from PTSalesPerson. (After all, how much more part-time can you get than "part-time"?) To prevent others from extending a class, make use of the C# sealed keyword:

```
// Ensure that PTSalesPerson cannot act as a base class to others.
public sealed class PTSalesPerson : SalesPerson
{
    public PTSalesPerson(string fullName, int age, int empID,
        float currPay, string ssn, int numbOfSales)
        : base(fullName, age, empID, currPay, ssn, numbOfSales)
    {
        // Interesting constructor logic...
    }
    // Other interesting members...
}
```

Because PTSalesPerson is sealed, it cannot serve as a base class to any other type. Thus, if you attempted to extend PTSalesPerson, you receive a compiler error:

```
// Compiler error!
public class ReallyPTSalesPerson : PTSalesPerson
{ ... }
```

The sealed keyword is most useful when creating stand-alone utility classes. As an example, the String class defined in the System namespace has been explicitly sealed:

```
public sealed class string : object,
    IComparable, ICloneable,
    IConvertible, IEnumerable {...}
```

Therefore, you cannot create some new class deriving from System.String:

```
// Another error!
public class MyString : string
{...}
```

If you wish to build a new class that leverages the functionality of a sealed class, your only option is to forego classical inheritance and make use of the containment/delegation model (aka the "has-a" relationship).

Programming for Containment/Delegation

As noted a bit earlier in this chapter, inheritance comes in two flavors. We have just explored the classical "is-a" relationship. To conclude the exploration of the second pillar of OOP, let's examine the "has-a" relationship (also known as the *containment/delegation* model). Assume you have created a new class that models an employee benefits package:

```
// This type will function as a contained class.
public class BenefitPackage
{
    // Assume we have other members that represent
    // 401K plans, dental / health benefits and so on.
    public double ComputePayDeduction()
    { return 125.0; }
}
```

Obviously, it would be rather odd to establish an "is-a" relationship between the BenefitPackage class and the employee types. (Manager "is-a" BenefitPackage? I don't think so) However, it should be clear that some sort of relationship between the two could be established. In short, you would like to express the idea that each employee "has-a" BenefitPackage. To do so, you can update the Employee class definition as follows:

```
// Employees now have benefits.
public class Employee
{
...
    // Contain a BenefitPackage object.
    protected BenefitPackage empBenefits = new BenefitPackage();
}
```

At this point, you have successfully contained another object. However, to expose the function-ality of the contained object to the outside world requires *delegation*. Delegation is simply the act of adding members to the containing class that make use of the contained object's functionality. For example, we could update the Employee class to expose the contained empBenefits object using a custom property as well as make use of its functionality internally using a new method named GetBenefitCost():

```
public class Employee
{
    protected BenefitPackage empBenefits = new BenefitPackage();

    // Expose certain benefit behaviors of object.
    public double GetBenefitCost()
    {
        return empBenefits.ComputePayDeduction();
    }

    // Expose object through a custom property.
    public BenefitPackage Benefits
    {
        get { return empBenefits; }
        set { empBenefits = value; }
    }
}
```

In the following updated Main() method, notice how we can interact with the internal BenefitsPackage type defined by the Employee type:

```
static void Main(string[] args)
{
    Manager mel;
    mel = new Manager();
    Console.WriteLine(mel.Benefits.ComputePayDeduction());
...
    Console.ReadLine();
}
```

Nested Type Definitions

Before examining the final pillar of OOP (polymorphism), let's explore a programming technique termed *nested types*. In C#, it is possible to define a type (enum, class, interface, struct, or delegate) directly within the scope of a class or structure. When you have done so, the nested (or "inner") type is considered a *member* of the nesting (or "outer") class, and in the eyes of the runtime can be manipulated like any other member (fields, properties, methods, events, etc.). The syntax used to nest a type is quite straightforward:

```
public class OuterClass
{
    // A public nested type can be used by anybody.
    public class PublicInnerClass {}
```

```
    // A private nested type can only be used by members
    // of the containing class.
    private class PrivateInnerClass {}
}
```

Although the syntax is clean, understanding *why* you might do this is not readily apparent. To understand this technique, ponder the following:

- Nesting types is similar to composition ("has-a"), except that you have complete control over the access level of the inner *type* instead of a contained *object*.

- Because a nested type is a member of the containing class, it can access private members of the containing class.

- Oftentimes, a nested type is only useful as helper for the outer class, and is not intended for use by the outside world.

When a type nests another class type, it can create member variables of the type, just as it would for any point of data. However, if you wish to make use of a nested type from outside of the containing type, you must qualify it by the scope of the nesting type. Ponder the following code:

```
static void Main(string[] args)
{
    // Create and use the public inner class. OK!
    OuterClass.PublicInnerClass inner;
    inner = new OuterClass.PublicInnerClass();

    // Compiler Error! Cannot access the private class.
    OuterClass.PrivateInnerClass inner2;
    inner2 = new OuterClass.PrivateInnerClass();
}
```

To make use of this concept within our employees example, assume we have now nested the BenefitPackage directly within the Employee class type:

```
// Nesting the BenefitPackage.
public class Employee
{
...
    public class BenefitPackage
    {
        public double ComputePayDeduction()
        { return 125.0; }
    }
}
```

The nesting process can be as "deep" as you require. For example, assume we wish to create an enumeration named BenefitPackageLevel, which documents the various benefit levels an employee may choose. To programmatically enforce the connection between Employee, BenefitPackage, and BenefitPackageLevel, we could nest the enumeration as follows:

```
// Employee nests BenefitPackage.
public class Employee
{
    // BenefitPackage nests BenefitPackageLevel.
    public class BenefitPackage
    {
        public double ComputePayDeduction()
        { return 125.0; }
```

```
        public enum BenefitPackageLevel
        {
            Standard, Gold, Platinum
        }
    }
}
```

Because of the nesting relationships, note how we are required to make use of this enumeration:

```
static void Main(string[] args)
{
    // Creating a BenefitPackageLevel variable.
    Employee.BenefitPackage.BenefitPackageLevel myBenefitLevel =
        Employee.BenefitPackage.BenefitPackageLevel.Platinum;
...
}
```

The Third Pillar: C#'s Polymorphic Support

Let's now examine the final pillar of OOP: polymorphism. Recall that the Employee base class defined a method named GiveBonus(), which was implemented as follows:

```
// Give bonus to employees.
public class Employee
{
...
    public void GiveBonus(float amount)
    { currPay += amount; }
}
```

Because this method has been defined as public, you can now give bonuses to salespeople and managers (as well as part-time salespeople):

```
static void Main(string[] args)
{
    // Give each employee a bonus.
    Manager chucky = new Manager("Chucky", 50, 92, 100000, "333-23-2322", 9000);
    chucky.GiveBonus(300);
    chucky.DisplayStats();

    SalesPerson fran = new SalesPerson("Fran", 43, 93, 3000, "932-32-3232", 31);
    fran.GiveBonus(200);
    fran.DisplayStats();
    Console.ReadLine();
}
```

The problem with the current design is that the inherited GiveBonus() method operates identically for all subclasses. Ideally, the bonus of a salesperson or part-time salesperson should take into account the number of sales. Perhaps managers should gain additional stock options in conjunction with a monetary bump in salary. Given this, you are suddenly faced with an interesting question: "How can related objects respond differently to the same request?"

The virtual and override Keywords

Polymorphism provides a way for a subclass to customize how it implements a method defined by its base class. To retrofit your current design, you need to understand the meaning of the C# virtual and override keywords. If a base class wishes to define a method that *may be* overridden by a subclass, it must specify the method as virtual:

```
public class Employee
{
    // GiveBonus() has a default implementation, however
    // child classes are free to override this behavior.
    public virtual void GiveBonus(float amount)
    { currPay += amount; }
...
}
```

When a subclass wishes to redefine a virtual method, it does so using the override keyword. For example, the SalesPerson and Manager could override GiveBonus() as follows (assume that PTSalesPerson overrides GiveBonus() in manner similar to SalesPerson):

```
public class SalesPerson : Employee
{
    // A salesperson's bonus is influenced by the number of sales.
    public override void GiveBonus(float amount)
    {
        int salesBonus = 0;
        if(numberOfSales >= 0 && numberOfSales <= 100)
            salesBonus = 10;
        else if(numberOfSales >= 101 && numberOfSales <= 200)
            salesBonus = 15;
        else
            salesBonus = 20;       // Anything greater than 200.
        base.GiveBonus (amount * salesBonus);
    }
...
}
```

```
public class Manager : Employee
{
    // Managers get some number of new stock options, in addition to raw cash.
    public override void GiveBonus(float amount)
    {
        // Increase salary.
        base.GiveBonus(amount);

        // And give some new stock options...
        Random r = new Random();
        numberOfOptions += (ulong)r.Next(500);
    }
...
}
```

Notice how each overridden method is free to leverage the default behavior using the base keyword. In this way, you have no need to completely reimplement the logic behind GiveBonus(), but can reuse (and possibly extend) the default behavior of the parent class.

Also assume that Employee.DisplayStats() has been declared virtual, and has been overridden by each subclass to account for displaying the number of sales (for salespeople) and current stock options (for managers). Now that each subclass can interpret what these virtual methods means to itself, each object instance behaves as a more independent entity:

```
static void Main(string[] args)
{
    // A better bonus system!
    Manager chucky = new Manager("Chucky", 50, 92, 100000, "333-23-2322", 9000);
```

```
    chucky.GiveBonus(300);
    chucky.DisplayStats();

    SalesPerson fran = new SalesPerson("Fran", 43, 93, 3000, "932-32-3232", 31);
    fran.GiveBonus(200);
    fran.DisplayStats();
}
```

Revisiting the sealed Keyword

The sealed keyword can also be applied to type members to prevent virtual members from being further overridden by derived types. This can be helpful when you do not wish to seal an entire class, just a few select methods or properties.

For the sake of illustration, if we (for some reason) did wish to allow the PTSalesPerson class to be extended by other classes but make sure those classes did *not* further override the virtual GiveBonus(), we could write the following:

```
// This class can be extended;
// however, GiveBonus() cannot be overriden by derived classes.
public class PTSalesPerson : SalesPerson
{
...
    public override sealed void GiveBonus(float amount)
    {
...
    }
}
```

Understanding Abstract Classes

Currently, the Employee base class has been designed to supply protected member variables for its descendents, as well as supply two virtual methods (GiveBonus() and DisplayStats()) that may be overridden by a given descendent. While this is all well and good, there is a rather odd byproduct of the current design: You can directly create instances of the Employee base class:

```
// What exactly does this mean?
Employee X = new Employee();
```

In this example, the only real purpose of the Employee base class is to define common fields and members for all subclasses. In all likelihood, you did not intend anyone to create a direct instance of this class, reason being that the Employee type itself is too general of a concept. For example, if I were to walk up to you and say, "I'm an employee!," I would bet your very first question to me would be, "What *kind* of employee are you?" (a consultant, trainer, admin assistant, copy editor, White House aide, etc.).

Given that many base classes tend to be rather nebulous entities, a far better design for our example is to *prevent* the ability to directly create a new Employee object in code. In C#, you can enforce this programmatically by using the abstract keyword:

```
// Update the Employee class as abstract to prevent direct instantiation.
abstract public class Employee
{ ...}
```

With this, if you now attempt to create an instance of the Employee class, you are issued a compile-time error:

```
// Error! Can't create an instance of an abstract class.
Employee X = new Employee();
```

Excellent! At this point you have constructed a fairly interesting employee hierarchy. We will add a bit more functionaltiy to this application later in this chapter when examining C# casting rules. Until then, Figure 4-9 illustrates the core design of our current types.

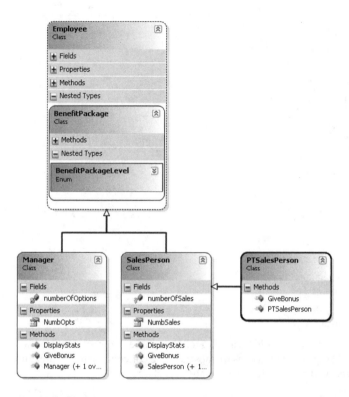

Figure 4-9. *The completed employee hierarchy*

■**Source Code** The Employees project is included under the Chapter 4 subdirectory.

Enforcing Polymorphic Activity: Abstract Methods

When a class has been defined as an abstract base class, it may define any number of *abstract members* (which is analogous to a C++ pure virtual function). Abstract methods can be used whenever you wish to define a method that *does not* supply a default implementation. By doing so, you enforce a polymorphic trait on each descendent, leaving them to contend with the task of providing the details behind your abstract methods.

The first logical question you might have is, "Why would I ever want to do this?" To understand the role of abstract methods, let's revisit the shapes hierarchy seen earlier in this chapter, extended as shown in Figure 4-10.

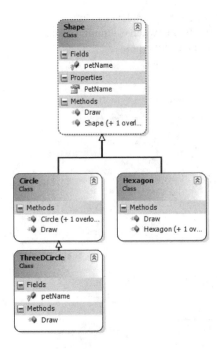

Figure 4-10. *The shapes hierarchy*

Much like the employee hierarchy, you should be able to tell that you don't want to allow the object user to create an instance of Shape directly, as it is too abstract of a concept. Again, to prevent the direct creation of the Shape type, you could define it as an abstract class:

```
namespace Shapes
{
    public abstract class Shape
    {
        // Shapes can be assigned a friendly pet name.
        protected string petName;

        // Constructors.
        public Shape(){ petName = "NoName"; }
        public Shape(string s) {  petName = s;}

        // Draw() is virtual and may be overridden.
        public virtual void Draw()
        {
            Console.WriteLine("Shape.Draw()");
        }

        public string PetName
        {
            get { return petName;}
            set {  petName = value;}
        }
    }
}
```

```
// Circle DOES NOT override Draw().
public class Circle : Shape
{
    public Circle() { }
    public Circle(string name): base(name) { }
}

// Hexagon DOES override Draw().
public class Hexagon : Shape
{
    public Hexagon(){ }
    public Hexagon(string name): base(name) { }
    public override void Draw()
    {
        Console.WriteLine("Drawing {0} the Hexagon", petName);
    }
}
}
```

Notice that the Shape class has defined a virtual method named Draw(). As you have just seen, subclasses are free to redefine the behavior of a virtual method using the override keyword (as in the case of the Hexagon class). The point of abstract methods becomes crystal clear when you understand that subclasses are not required to override virtual methods (as in the case of Circle). Therefore, if you create an instance of the Hexagon and Circle types, you'd find that the Hexagon understands how to draw itself correctly. The Circle, however, is more than a bit confused (see Figure 4-11 for output):

```
// The Circle object did not override the base class implementation of Draw().
static void Main(string[] args)
{
    Hexagon hex = new Hexagon("Beth");
    hex.Draw();
    Circle cir = new Circle("Cindy");

    // Humm. Using base class implementation.
    cir.Draw();
    Console.ReadLine();
}
```

Figure 4-11. *Virtual methods do not have to be overridden.*

Clearly this is not a very intelligent design for the shapes hierarchy. To enforce that each child class defines what Draw() means to itself, you can simply establish Draw() as an abstract method of the Shape class, which by definition means you provide no default implementation whatsoever. Note that abstract methods can only be defined in abstract classes. If you attempt to do otherwise, you will be issued a compiler error:

```
// Force all kids to figure out how to be rendered.
public abstract class Shape
{
    ...
    // Draw() is now completely abstract (note semicolon).
    public abstract void Draw();
...
}
```

Given this, you are now obligated to implement Draw() in your Circle class. If you do not, Circle is also assumed to be a noncreatable abstract type that must be adorned with the abstract keyword (which is obviously not very useful in this example):

```
// If we did not implement the abstract Draw() method, Circle would also be
// considered abstract, and could not be directly created!
public class Circle : Shape
{
    public Circle(){ }
    public Circle(string name): base(name) { }

    // Now Circle must decide how to render itself.
    public override void Draw()
    {
        Console.WriteLine("Drawing {0} the Circle", petName);
    }
}
```

To illustrate the full story of polymorphism, consider the following code:

```
// Create an array of various Shapes.
static void Main(string[] args)
{
    Console.WriteLine("***** Fun with Polymorphism *****\n");
    Shape[] myShapes = {new Hexagon(), new Circle(), new Hexagon("Mick"),
                new Circle("Beth"), new Hexagon("Linda")};

    // Loop over the array and ask each object to draw itself.
    for(int i = 0; i < myShapes.Length; i++)
        myShapes[i].Draw();
    Console.ReadLine();
}
```

Figure 4-12 shows the output.

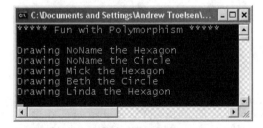

Figure 4-12. *Fun with polymorphism*

This Main() method illustrates polymorphism at its finest. Recall that when you mark a class as abstract, you are unable to create a *direct instance* of that type. However, you can freely store references to any subclass within an abstract base variable. As you iterate over the array of Shape references, it is at runtime that the correct type is determined. At this point, the correct method is invoked.

Member Hiding

C# provides a facility that is the logical opposite of method overriding: member hiding. Formally speaking, if a derived class redeclares an identical member inherited from a base class, the derived class has hidden (or *shadowed*) the parent's member. In the real world, this possibility is the greatest when you are subclassing from a class you (or your team) did not create yourselves (for example, if you purchase a third-party .NET software package).

For the sake of illustration, assume you receive a class named ThreeDCircle from a coworker (or classmate) that currently derives from System.Object:

```
public class ThreeDCircle
{
    public void Draw()
    {
        Console.WriteLine("Drawing a 3D Circle");
    }
}
```

You figure that a ThreeDCircle "is-a" Circle, so you derive from your existing Circle type:

```
public class ThreeDCircle : Circle
{
    public void Draw()
    {
        Console.WriteLine("Drawing a 3D Circle");
    }
}
```

Once you recompile, you find the following warning shown in Visual Studio 2005 (see Figure 4-13).

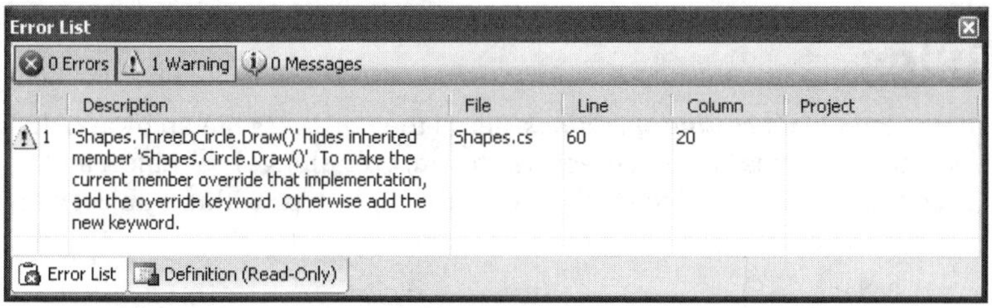

Figure 4-13. *Oops!* ThreeDCircle.Draw() *shadows* Circle.Draw.

To address this issue, you have two options. You could simply update the parent's version of Draw() using the override keyword. With this approach, the ThreeDCircle type is able to extend the parent's default behavior as required.

As an alternative, you can prefix the new keyword to the offending Draw() member of the ThreeDCircle type. Doing so explicitly states that the derived type's implemention is intentionally designed to hide the parent's version (again, in the real world, this can be helpful if external .NET software somehow conflicts with your current software).

```
// This class extends Circle and hides the inherited Draw() method.
public class ThreeDCircle : Circle
{
    // Hide any Draw() implementation above me.
    public new void Draw()
    {
        Console.WriteLine("Drawing a 3D Circle");
    }
}
```

You can also apply the new keyword to any member type inherited from a base class (field, constant, static member, property, etc.). As a further example, assume that ThreeDCircle wishes to hide the inherited petName field:

```
public class ThreeDCircle : Circle
{
    new protected string petName;
    new public void Draw()
    {
        Console.WriteLine("Drawing a 3D Circle");
    }
}
```

Finally, be aware that it is still possible to trigger the base class implementation of a shadowed member using an *explicit cast* (described in the next section). For example:

```
static void Main(string[] args)
{
    ThreeDCircle o = new ThreeDCircle();
    o.Draw();                // Calls ThreeDCircle.Draw()
    ((Circle)o).Draw();      // Calls Circle.Draw()
}
```

■**Source Code** The Shapes hierarchy can be found under the Chapter 4 subdirectory.

C# Casting Rules

Next up, you need to learn the laws of C# *casting operations*. Recall the Employees hierarchy and the fact that the topmost class in the system is System.Object. Therefore, everything "is-a" object and can be treated as such. Given this fact, it is legal to store an instance of any type within a object variable:

```
// A Manager "is-a" System.Object.
object frank = new Manager("Frank Zappa", 9, 40000, "111-11-1111", 5);
```

In the Employees system, Managers, SalesPerson, and PTSalesPerson types all extend Employee, so we can store any of these objects in a valid base class reference. Therefore, the following statements are also legal:

```
// A Manager "is-a" Employee too.
Employee moonUnit = new Manager("MoonUnit Zappa", 2, 20000, "101-11-1321", 1);
```

```
// A PTSalesPerson "is-a" SalesPerson.
SalesPerson jill = new PTSalesPerson("Jill", 834, 100000, "111-12-1119", 90);
```

The first law of casting between class types is that when two classes are related by an "is-a" relationship, it is always safe to store a derived type within a base class reference. Formally, this is called an *implicit cast*, as "it just works" given the laws of inheritance. This leads to some powerful programming constructs. For example, if you have a class named TheMachine that supports the following static method:

```
public class TheMachine
{
    public static void FireThisPerson(Employee e)
    {
        // Remove from database...
        // Get key and pencil sharpener from fired employee...
    }
}
```

you can effectively pass any descendent from the Employee class into this method directly, given the "is-a" relationship:

```
// Streamline the staff.
TheMachine.FireThisPerson(moonUnit);    // "moonUnit" was declared as an Employee.
TheMachine.FireThisPerson(jill);        // "jill" was declared as a SalesPerson.
```

The following code compiles given the implicit cast from the base class type (Employee) to the derived type. However, what if you also wanted to fire Frank Zappa (currently stored in a generic System.Object reference)? If you pass the frank object directly into TheMachine.FireThisPerson() as follows:

```
// A Manager "is-a" object, but...
object frank = new Manager("Frank Zappa", 9, 40000, "111-11-1111", 5);
...
TheMachine.FireThisPerson(frank);       // Error!
```

you are issued a compiler error. The reason is you cannot automatically treat a System.Object as a derived Employee directly, given that Object "is-not-a" Employee. As you can see, however, the object reference is pointing to an Employee-compatible object. You can satisfy the compiler by performing an *explicit cast*.

In C#, explicit casts are denoted by placing parentheses around the type you wish to cast to, followed by the object you are attempting to cast from. For example:

```
// Cast from the generic System.Object into a strongly
// typed Manager.
Manager mgr = (Manager)frank;
Console.WriteLine("Frank's options: {0}", mgr.NumbOpts);
```

If you would rather not declare a specific variable of "type to cast to," you are able to condense the previous code as follows:

```
// An "inline" explicit cast.
Console.WriteLine("Frank's options: {0}", ((Manager)frank).NumbOpts);
```

As far as passing the System.Object reference into the FireThisPerson() method, the problem can be rectified as follows:

```
// Explicitly cast System.Object into an Employee.
TheMachine.FireThisPerson((Employee)frank);
```

■**Note** If you attempt to cast an object into an incompatable type, you receive an invalid cast exception at runtime. Chapter 6 examines the details of structured exception handling.

Determining the "Type of" Employee

Given that the static `TheMachine.FireThisPerson()` method has been designed to take any possible type derived from `Employee`, one question on your mind may be how this method can determine which derived type was sent into the method. On a related note, given that the incoming parameter is of type `Employee`, how can you gain access to the specialized members of the `SalesPerson` and `Manager` types?

The C# language provides three ways to determine whether a given base class reference is actually referring to a derived type: explicit casting (previously examined), the `is` keyword, and the `as` keyword. The `is` keyword is helpful in that it will return a Boolean that signals whether the base class reference is compatible with a given derived type. Ponder the following updated `FireThisPerson()` method:

```
public class TheMachine
{
    public static void FireThisPerson(Employee e)
    {
        if(e is SalesPerson)
        {
            Console.WriteLine("Lost a sales person named {0}", e.GetFullName());
            Console.WriteLine("{0} made {1} sale(s)...",
                e.GetFullName(), ((SalesPerson)e).NumbSales);
        }
        if(e is Manager)
        {
            Console.WriteLine("Lost a suit named {0}", e.GetFullName());
            Console.WriteLine("{0} had {1} stock options...",
                e.GetFullName(), ((Manager)e).NumbOpts);
        }
    }
}
```

Here, you make use of the `is` keyword to dynamically determine the type of employee. To gain access to the `NumbSales` and `NumbOpts` properties, you make use of an explicit cast. As an alternative, you could make use of the `as` keyword to obtain a reference to the more derived type (if the types are incompatible, the reference is set to null):

```
SalesPerson p = e as SalesPerson;
if(p != null)
    Console.WriteLine("# of sales: {0}", p.NumbSales);
```

■**Note** As you will see in Chapter 7, these same techniques (explicit cast, `is`, and `as`) can be used to obtain an interface reference from an implementing type.

Numerical Casts

To wrap up our examination of C# casting operations, be aware that numerical conversions follow more or less the same rules. If you are attempting to place a "larger" numerical type to a "smaller" type (such as an integer into a byte), you must also make an explicit cast that informs the compiler you are willing to accept any possible data loss:

```
// If "x" were larger than a byte's upper limit, data loss is almost certain;
// however, in Chapter 9 you will learn about "checked exceptions," which
// can alter the outcome.
int x = 6;
byte b = (byte)x;
```

However, when you are storing a "smaller" numerical type into a "larger" type (such as a byte to an integer), the type is implicitly cast on your behalf, as there is no loss of data:

```
// No need to cast, as an int is big enough to store a byte.
byte b = 30;
int x = b;
```

Understanding C# Partial Types

C# 2005 introduces a new type modifer named `partial` that allows you to define a C# type across multiple *.cs files. Earlier versions of the C# programming language required all code for a given type be defined within a single *.cs file. Given the fact that a production-level C# class may be hundreds of lines of code (or more), this can end up being a mighty long file indeed.

In these cases, it would be ideal to partition a type's implementation across numerous C# files in order to separate code that is in some way more important for other details. For example, using the `partial` class modifer, you could place all public members in a file named `MyType_Public.cs`, while the private field data and private helper functions are defined within `MyType_Private.cs`:

```
// MyClass_Public.cs
namespace PartialTypes
{
    public partial class MyClass
    {
        // Constructors.
        public MyClass() { }

        // All public members.
        public void MemberA() { }
        public void MemberB() { }
    }
}

// MyClass_Private.cs
namespace PartialTypes
{
    public partial class MyClass
    {
        // Private field data.
        private string someStringData;

        // All private helper members.
        public static void SomeStaticHelper() { }
    }
}
```

As you might guess, this can be helpful to new team members who need to quickly learn about the public interface of the type. Rather than reading though a single (lengthy) C# file to find the members of interest, they can focus on the public members. Of course, once these files are compiled by `csc.exe`, the end result is a single unified type (see Figure 4-14).

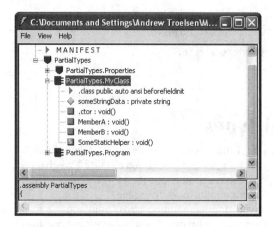

Figure 4-14. *Once compiled, partial types are no longer partial.*

■**Note** As you will see during our examination of Windows Forms and ASP .NET, Visual Studio 2005 makes use of the partial keyword to partition code generated by the IDE's designer tools. Using this approach, you can keep focused on your current solution, and be blissfully unaware of the designer-generated code.

■**Source Code** The PartialTypes project can be found under the Chapter 4 subdirectory.

Documenting C# Source Code via XML

To wrap this chapter up, the final task is to examine specific C# comment tokens that yield XML-based code documentation. If you have a background in Java, you are most likely familiar with the javadoc utility. Using javadoc, you are able to turn Java source code into a corresponding HTML representation. The C# documentation model is slightly different, in that the "code comments to XML" conversion process is the job of the C# compiler (via the /doc option) rather than a stand-alone utility.

So, why use XML to document our type definitions rather than HTML? The main reason is that XML is a very "enabling technology." Given that XML separates the definition of data from the presentation of that data, we can apply any number of XML transformations to the underlying XML to display the code documentation in a variety of formats (MSDN format, HTML, etc).

When you wish to document your C# types in XML, your first step is to make use of one of two notations, the triple forward slash (///) or a delimited comment that begins with a single forward slash and two stars (/**) and ends with a single star-slash combo (*/). Once a documentation comment has been declared, you are free to use any well-formed XML elements, including the recommended set shown in Table 4-1.

Table 4-1. *Recommended Code Comment XML Elements*

Predefined XML Documentation Element	Meaning in Life
<c>	Indicates that the following text should be displayed in a specific "code font"
<code>	Indicates multiple lines should be marked as code
<example>	Mocks up a code example for the item you are describing
<exception>	Documents which exceptions a given class may throw
<list>	Inserts a list or table into the documentation file
<param>	Describes a given parameter
<paramref>	Associates a given XML tag with a specific parameter
<permission>	Documents the security constraints for a given member
<remarks>	Builds a description for a given member
<returns>	Documents the return value of the member
<see>	Cross-references related items in the document
<seealso>	Builds an "also see" section within a description
<summary>	Documents the "executive summary" for a given member
<value>	Documents a given property

As a concrete example, here is a definition of a type named Car (note the use of the <summary> and <param> elements):

```
/// <summary>
/// This is a simple Car that illustrates
/// working with XML style documentation.
/// </summary>
public class Car
{
    /// <summary>
    /// Do you have a sunroof?
    /// </summary>
    private bool hasSunroof = false;

    /// <summary>
    /// The ctor lets you set the sunroofedness.
    /// </summary>
    /// <param name="hasSunroof"> </param>
    public Car(bool hasSunroof)
    {
        this.hasSunroof = hasSunroof;
    }

    /// <summary>
    /// This method allows you to open your sunroof.
    /// </summary>
    /// <param name="state"> </param>
    public void OpenSunroof(bool state)
    {
        if(state == true && hasSunroof == true)
            Console.WriteLine("Put sunscreen on that bald head!");
        else
```

```
        Console.WriteLine("Sorry...you don't have a sunroof.");
    }
}
```

The program's Main() method is also documented using select XML elements:

```
/// <summary>
/// Entry point to application.
/// </summary>
static void Main(string[] args)
{
    Car c = new Car(true);
    c.OpenSunroof(true);
}
```

If you are building your C# programs using csc.exe, the /doc flag is used to generate a specified *.xml file based on your XML code comments:

```
csc /doc:XmlCarDoc.xml *.cs
```

Visual Studio 2005 allows you to specify the name of an XML documentation file using the Build tab of the Properties window (see Figure 4-15).

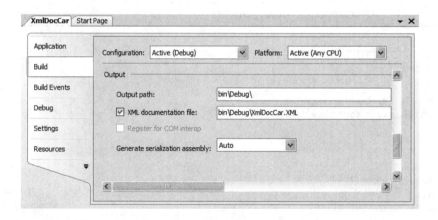

Figure 4-15. *Generating an XML documentation file using Visual Studio 2005*

XML Code Comment Format Characters

If you were now to open the generated XML file, you will notice that the elements are qualified by numerous characters such as "M", "T", "F", and so on. For example:

```
<member name="T:XmlDocCar.Car">
    <summary>
        This is a simple Car that illustrates
        working with XML style documentation.
    </summary>
</member>
```

Table 4-2 describes the meaning behind these tokens.

Table 4-2. *XML Format Characters*

Format Character	Meaning in Life
E	Item denotes an event.
F	Item represents a field.
M	Item represents a method (including constructors and overloaded operators).
N	Item denotes a namespace.
P	Item represents type properties (including indexes).
T	Item represents a type (e.g., class, interface, struct, enum, delegate).

Transforming XML Code Comments

Previous versions of Visual Studio 2005 (Visual Studio .NET 2003 in particular) included a very help-ful tool that would transform XML code documentation files into an HTML-based help system. Sadly, Visual Studio 2005 does not ship with this utility, leaving us with a raw XML document. If you are comfortable with the ins and outs of XML transformations, you are, of course, free to manually create your own style sheets.

A simpler alternative, however, are the numerous third-party tools that will translate an XML code file into various helpful formats. For example, recall from Chapter 2 that the NDoc application generates documentation in several different formats. Again, information regarding NDoc can be found at `http://ndoc.sourceforge.net`.

■**Source Code** The XmlDocCar project can be found under the Chapter 4 subdirectory.

Summary

If you already come to the universe of .NET from another object-oriented language, this chapter may have been more of a quick compare and contrast between your current language of choice and C#. On the other hand, if you are exploring OOP for the first time, you may have found many of the concepts presented here a bit confounding. Fear not; as you work through the remainder of this book, you will have have numerous opportunities to solidify the concepts presented here.

This chapter began with a review of the pillars of OOP: encapsulation, inheritance, and poly-morphism. Encapsulation services can be accounted for using traditional accessor/mutator methods, type properties, or read-only public fields. Inheritance under C# could not be any simpler, given that the language does not provide a specific keyword, but rather makes use of the simple colon operator. Last but not least, you have polymorphism, which is supported via the abstract, virtual, override, and new keywords.

CHAPTER 5

■ ■ ■

Understanding Object Lifetime

In the previous chapter, you learned a great deal about how to build custom class types using C#. Here, you will come to understand how the CLR is managing allocated objects via *garbage collection*. C# programmers never directly deallocate a managed object from memory (recall there is no "delete" keyword in the C# language). Rather, .NET objects are allocated onto a region of memory termed the *managed heap*, where they will be automatically destroyed by the garbage collector at "some time in the future."

Once you have examined the core details of the collection process, you will learn how to programmatically interact with the garbage collector using the System.GC class type. Next you examine how the virtual System.Object.Finalize() method and IDisposable interface can be used to build types that release internal *unmanaged resources* in a timely manner. By the time you have completed this chapter, you will have a solid understanding of how .NET objects are managed by the CLR.

Classes, Objects, and References

To frame the topics examined in this chapter, it is important to further clarify the distinction between classes, objects, and references. Recall from the previous chapter that a class is nothing more than a blueprint that describes how an instance of this type will look and feel in memory. Classes, of course, are defined within a code file (which in C# takes a *.cs extension by convention). Consider a simple Car class defined within Car.cs:

```
// Car.cs
public class Car
{
    private int currSp;
    private string petName;

    public Car(){}
    public Car(string name, int speed)
    {
        petName = name;
        currSp = speed;
    }
    public override string ToString()
    {
        return string.Format("{0} is going {1} MPH",
            petName, currSp);
    }
}
```

Once a class is defined, you can allocate any number of objects using the C# new keyword. Understand, however, that the new keyword returns a *reference* to the object on the heap, not the actual object itself. This reference variable is stored on the stack for further use in your application. When you wish to invoke members on the object, apply the C# dot operator to the stored reference:

```
class Program
{
    static void Main(string[] args)
    {
        // Create a new Car object on
        // the managed heap. We are
        // returned a reference to this
        // object ('refToMyCar').
        Car refToMyCar = new Car("Zippy", 50);

        // The C# dot operator (.) is used
        // to invoke members on the object
        // using our reference variable.
        Console.WriteLine(refToMyCar.ToString());
        Console.ReadLine();
    }
}
```

Figure 5-1 illustrates the class, object, and reference relationship.

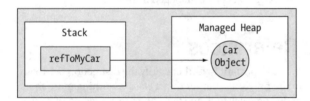

Figure 5-1. *References to objects on the managed heap*

The Basics of Object Lifetime

When you are building your C# applications, you are correct to assume that the managed heap will take care of itself without your direct intervention. In fact, the golden rule of .NET memory management is simple:

- **Rule:** Allocate an object onto the managed heap using the new keyword and forget about it.

Once "new-ed," the garbage collector will destroy the object when it is no longer needed. The next obvious question, of course, is, "How does the garbage collector determine when an object is no longer needed"? The short (i.e., incomplete) answer is that the garbage collector removes an object from the heap when it is *unreachable* by any part of your code base. Assume you have a method that allocates a local Car object:

```
public static void MakeACar()
{
    // If myCar is the only reference to the Car object,
    // it may be destroyed when the method returns.
    Car myCar = new Car();
    ...
}
```

Notice that the Car reference (myCar) has been created directly within the MakeACar() method and has not been passed outside of the defining scope (via a return value or ref/out parameters). Thus, once this method call completes, the myCar reference is no longer reachable, and the associated Car object is now a *candidate* for garbage collection. Understand, however, that you cannot guarantee that this object will be reclaimed from memory immediately after MakeACar() has completed. All you can assume at this point is that when the CLR performs the next garbage collection, the myCar object could be safely destroyed.

As you will most certainly discover, programming in a garbage-collected environment will greatly simplify your application development. In stark contrast, C++ programmers are painfully aware that if they fail to manually delete heap-allocated objects, memory leaks are never far behind. In fact, tracking down memory leaks is one of the most time-consuming (and tedious) aspects of programming with unmanaged languages. By allowing the garbage collector to be in charge of destroying objects, the burden of memory management has been taken from your shoulders and placed onto those of the CLR.

■**Note** If you happen to have a background in COM development, do know that .NET objects do not maintain an internal reference counter, and therefore managed objects do not expose methods such as AddRef() or Release().

The CIL of new

When the C# compiler encounters the new keyword, it will emit a CIL newobj instruction into the method implementation. If you were to compile the current example code and investigate the resulting assembly using ildasm.exe, you would find the following CIL statements within the MakeACar() method:

```
.method public hidebysig static void MakeACar() cil managed
{
  // Code size  7 (0x7)
  .maxstack  1
  .locals init ([0] class SimpleFinalize.Car c)
  IL_0000:  newobj instance void  SimpleFinalize.Car::.ctor()
  IL_0005:  stloc.0
  IL_0006:  ret
} // end of method Program::MakeACar
```

Before we examine the exact rules that determine when an object is removed from the managed heap, let's check out the role of the CIL newobj instruction in a bit more detail. First, understand that the managed heap is more than just a random chunk of memory accessed by the CLR. The .NET garbage collector is quite a tidy housekeeper of the heap, given that it will compact empty blocks of memory (when necessary) for purposes of optimization. To aid in this endeavor, the managed heap maintains a pointer (commonly referred to as the *next object pointer* or *new object pointer*) that identifies exactly where the next object will be located.

These things being said, the newobj instruction informs the CLR to perform the following core tasks:

- Calculate the total amount of memory required for the object to be allocated (including the necessary memory required by the type's member variables and the type's base classes).

- Examine the managed heap to ensure that there is indeed enough room to host the object to be allocated. If this is the case, the type's constructor is called, and the caller is ultimately returned a reference to the new object in memory, whose address just happens to be identical to the last position of the next object pointer.

- Finally, before returning the reference to the caller, advance the next object pointer to point to the next available slot on the managed heap.

The basic process is illustrated in Figure 5-2.

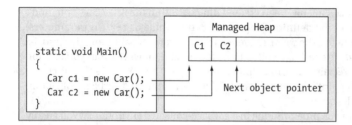

Figure 5-2. *The details of allocating objects onto the managed heap*

As you are busy allocating objects in your application, the space on the managed heap may eventually become full. When processing the newobj instruction, if the CLR determines that the managed heap does not have sufficient memory to allocate the requested type, it will perform a garbage collection in an attempt to free up memory. Thus, the next rule of garbage collection is also quite simple.

- **Rule:** If the managed heap does not have sufficient memory to allocate a requested object, a garbage collection will occur.

When a collection does take place, the garbage collector temporarily suspends all active *threads* within the current process to ensure that the application does not access the heap during the collection process. We will examine the topic of threads in Chapter 14; however, for the time being, simply regard a thread as a path of execution within a running executable. Once the garbage collection cycle has completed, the suspended threads are permitted to carry on their work. Thankfully, the .NET garbage collector is highly optimized; you will seldom (if ever) notice this brief interruption in your application.

The Role of Application Roots

Now, back to the topic of how the garbage collector determines when an object is "no longer needed." To understand the details, you need to be aware of the notion of *application roots*. Simply put, a *root* is a storage location containing a reference to an object on the heap. Strictly speaking, a root can fall into any of the following categories:

- References to global objects (while not allowed in C#, CIL code does permit allocation of global objects)
- References to currently used static objects/static fields
- References to local objects within a given method
- References to object parameters passed into a method
- References to objects waiting to be *finalized* (described later in this chapter)
- Any CPU register that references a local object

During a garbage collection process, the runtime will investigate objects on the managed heap to determine if they are still reachable (aka *rooted*) by the application. To do so, the CLR will build an *object graph*, which represents each reachable object on the heap. Object graphs will be seen again during our discussion of object serialization (Chapter 17). For now, just understand that object graphs are used to document all reachable objects. As well, be aware that the garbage collector will never graph the same object twice, thus avoiding the nasty circular reference count found in classic COM programming.

Assume the managed heap contains a set of objects named A, B, C, D, E, F, and G. During a garbage collection, these objects (as well as any internal object references they may contain) are examined for active roots. Once the graph has been constructed, unreachable objects (which we will assume are objects C and F) are marked as garbage. Figure 5-3 diagrams a possible object graph for the scenario just described (you can read the directional arrows using the phrase *depends on* or *requires*, for example, "E depends on G and indirectly B," "A depends on nothing," and so on).

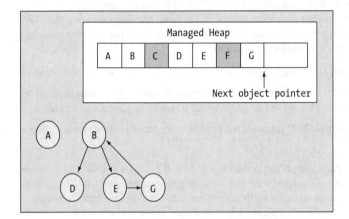

Figure 5-3. *Object graphs are constructed to determine which objects are reachable by application roots.*

Once an object has been marked for termination (C and F in this case—as they are not accounted for in the object graph), they are swept from memory. At this point, the remaining space on the heap is compacted, which in turn will cause the CLR to modify the set of active application roots to refer to the correct memory location (this is done automatically and transparently). Last but not least, the next object pointer is readjusted to point to the next available slot. Figure 5-4 illustrates the resulting readjustment.

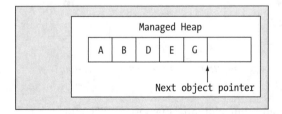

Figure 5-4. *A clean and compacted heap*

■**Note** Strictly speaking, the garbage collector makes use of *two* distinct heaps, one of which is specifically used to store very large objects. This heap is less frequently consulted during the collection cycle, given possible performance penalties involved with relocating large objects. Regardless of this fact, it is safe to consider the "managed heap" as a single region of memory.

Understanding Object Generations

When the CLR is attempting to locate unreachable objects, is does *not* literally examine each and every object placed on the managed heap. Obviously, doing so would involve considerable time, especially in larger (i.e., real-world) applications.

To help optimize the process, each object on the heap is assigned to a specific "generation." The idea behind generations is simple: The longer an object has existed on the heap, the more likely it is to stay there. For example, the object implementing Main() will be in memory until the program terminates. Conversely, objects that have been recently placed on the heap are likely to be unreachable rather quickly (such as an object created within a method scope). Given these assumptions, each object on the heap belongs to one of the following generations:

- *Generation 0*: Identifies a newly allocated object that has never been marked for collection
- *Generation 1*: Identifies an object that has survived a garbage collection (i.e., it was marked for collection, but was not removed due to the fact that the sufficient heap space was acquired)
- *Generation 2*: Identifies an object that has survived more than one sweep of the garbage collector

The garbage collector will investigate all generation 0 objects first. If marking and sweeping these objects results in the required amount of free memory, any surviving objects are promoted to generation 1. To illustrate how an object's generation affects the collection process, ponder Figure 5-5, which diagrams how a set of surviving generation 0 objects (A, B, and E) are promoted once the required memory has been reclaimed.

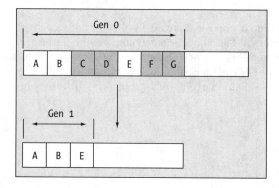

Figure 5-5. *Generation 0 objects that survive a garbage collection are promoted to generation 1.*

If all generation 0 objects have been evaluated, but additional memory is still required, generation 1 objects are then investigated for their "reachability" and collected accordingly. Surviving generation 1 objects are then promoted to generation 2. If the garbage collector *still* requires additional memory, generation 2 objects are then evaluated for their reachability. At this point, if a generation 2 object survives a garbage collection, it remains a generation 2 object given the predefined upper limit of object generations.

The bottom line is that by assigning a generational value to objects on the heap, newer objects (such as local variables) will be removed quickly, while older objects (such as a program's application object) are not "bothered" as often.

The System.GC Type

The base class libraries provide a class type named System.GC that allows you to programmatically interact with the garbage collector using a set of static members. Now, do be very aware that you will seldom (if ever) need to make use of this type directly in your code. Typically speaking, the only time you will make use of the members of System.GC is when you are creating types that make use of *unmanaged resources*. Table 5-1 provides a rundown of some of the more interesting members (consult the .NET Framework 2.0 SDK Documentation for complete details).

Table 5-1. *Select Members of the* System.GC *Type*

System.GC **Member**	**Meaning in Life**
AddMemoryPressure(), RemoveMemoryPressure()	Allow you to specify a numerical value that represents the calling object's "urgency level" regarding the garbage collection process. Be aware that these methods should alter pressure *in tandem* and thus never remove more pressure than the total amount you have added.
Collect()	Forces the GC to perform a garbage collection.
CollectionCount()	Returns a numerical value representing how many times a given generation has been swept.
GetGeneration()	Returns the generation to which an object currently belongs.
GetTotalMemory()	Returns the estimated amount of memory (in bytes) currently allocated on the managed heap. The Boolean parameter specifies whether the call should wait for garbage collection to occur before returning.
MaxGeneration	Returns the maximum of generations supported on the target system. Under Microsoft's .NET 2.0, there are three possible generations (0, 1, and 2).
SuppressFinalize()	Sets a flag indicating that the specified object should not have its Finalize() method called.
WaitForPendingFinalizers()	Suspends the current thread until all finalizable objects have been finalized. This method is typically called directly after invoking GC.Collect().

Ponder the following Main() method, which illustrates select members of System.GC:

```
static void Main(string[] args)
{
    // Print out estimated number of bytes on heap.
    Console.WriteLine("Estimated bytes on heap: {0}",
        GC.GetTotalMemory(false));

    // MaxGeneration is zero based, so add 1 for display purposes.
    Console.WriteLine("This OS has {0} object generations.\n",
        (GC.MaxGeneration + 1));

    Car refToMyCar = new Car("Zippy", 100);
    Console.WriteLine(refToMyCar.ToString());

    // Print out generation of refToMyCar object.
    Console.WriteLine("Generation of refToMyCar is: {0}",
        GC.GetGeneration(refToMyCar));

    Console.ReadLine();
}
```

Forcing a Garbage Collection

Again, the whole purpose of the .NET garbage collector is to manage memory on our behalf. However, under some very rare circumstances, it may be beneficial to programmatically force a garbage collection using GC.Collect(). Specifically:

- Your application is about to enter into a block of code that you do not wish to be interrupted by a possible garbage collection.

- Your application has just finished allocating an extremely large number of objects and you wish to remove as much of the acquired memory as possible.

If you determine it may be beneficial to have the garbage collector check for unreachable objects, you could explicitly trigger a garbage collection, as follows:

```
static void Main(string[] args)
{
...
    // Force a garbage collection and wait for
    // each object to be finalized.
    GC.Collect();
    GC.WaitForPendingFinalizers();
...
}
```

When you manually force a garbage collection, you should always make a call to GC.WaitForPendingFinalizers(). With this approach, you can rest assured that all *finalizable objects* have had a chance to perform any necessary cleanup before your program continues forward. Under the hood, GC.WaitForPendingFinalizers() will suspend the calling "thread" during the collection process. This is a good thing, as it ensures your code does not invoke methods on an object currently being destroyed!

The GC.Collect() method can also be supplied a numerical value that identifies the oldest generation on which a garbage collection will be performed. For example, if you wished to instruct the CLR to only investigate generation 0 objects, you would write the following:

```
static void Main(string[] args)
{
...
    // Only investigate generation 0 objects.
    GC.Collect(0);
    GC.WaitForPendingFinalizers();
...
}
```

Like any garbage collection, calling GC.Collect() will promote surviving generations. To illustrate, assume that our Main() method has been updated as follows:

```
static void Main(string[] args)
{
    Console.WriteLine("***** Fun with System.GC *****\n");

    // Print out estimated number of bytes on heap.
    Console.WriteLine("Estimated bytes on heap: {0}",
        GC.GetTotalMemory(false));

    // MaxGeneration is zero based.
    Console.WriteLine("This OS has {0} object generations.\n",
        (GC.MaxGeneration + 1));
```

```
Car refToMyCar = new Car("Zippy", 100);
Console.WriteLine(refToMyCar.ToString());

// Print out generation of refToMyCar.
Console.WriteLine("\nGeneration of refToMyCar is: {0}",
    GC.GetGeneration(refToMyCar));

// Make a ton of objects for testing purposes.
object[] tonsOfObjects = new object[50000];
for (int i = 0; i < 50000; i++)
    tonsOfObjects[i] = new object();

// Collect only gen 0 objects.
GC.Collect(0);
GC.WaitForPendingFinalizers();

// Print out generation of refToMyCar.
Console.WriteLine("Generation of refToMyCar is: {0}",
    GC.GetGeneration(refToMyCar));

// See if tonsOfObjects[9000] is still alive.
if (tonsOfObjects[9000] != null)
{
    Console.WriteLine("Generation of tonsOfObjects[9000] is: {0}",
        GC.GetGeneration(tonsOfObjects[9000]));
}
else
    Console.WriteLine("tonsOfObjects[9000] is no longer alive.");

// Print out how many times a generation has been swept.
Console.WriteLine("\nGen 0 has been swept {0} times",
    GC.CollectionCount(0));
Console.WriteLine("Gen 1 has been swept {0} times",
    GC.CollectionCount(1));
Console.WriteLine("Gen 2 has been swept {0} times",
    GC.CollectionCount(2));
Console.ReadLine();
}
```

Here, we have purposely created a very large array of objects for testing purposes. As you can see from the output shown in Figure 5-6, even though this Main() method only made one explicit request for a garbage collection, the CLR performed a number of them in the background.

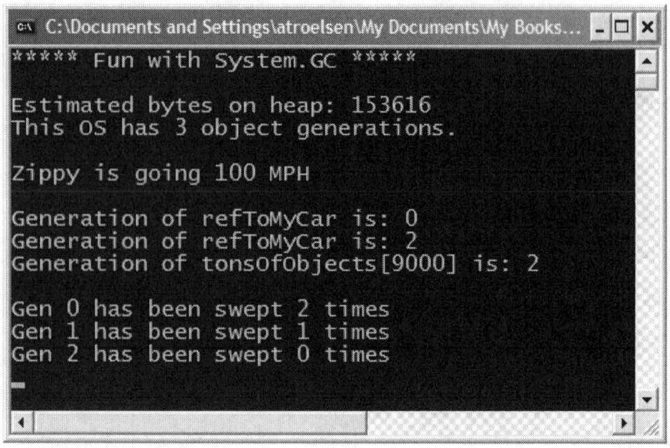

Figure 5-6. *Interacting with the CLR garbage collector via* System.GC

At this point in the chapter, I hope you feel more comfortable regarding the details of object lifetime. The remainder of this chapter examines the garbage collection process a bit further by addressing how you can build *finalizable objects* as well as *disposable objects*. Be very aware that the following techniques will only be useful if you are build managed classes that maintain internal unmanaged resources.

■**Source Code** The SimpleGC project is included under the Chapter 5 subdirectory.

Building Finalizable Objects

In Chapter 3, you learned that the supreme base class of .NET, System.Object, defines a virtual method named Finalize(). The default implementation of this method does nothing whatsoever:

```
// System.Object
public class Object
{
    ...
    protected virtual void Finalize() {}
}
```

When you override Finalize() for your custom classes, you establish a specific location to perform any necessary cleanup logic for your type. Given that this member is defined as protected, it is not possible to directly call an object's Finalize() method. Rather, the *garbage collector* will call an object's Finalize() method (if supported) before removing the object from memory.

Of course, a call to Finalize() will (eventually) occur during a "natural" garbage collection or when you programmatically force a collection via GC.Collect(). In addition, a type's finalizer method will automatically be called when the *application domain* hosting your application is unloaded from memory. Based on your current background in .NET, you may know that application domains (or simply AppDomains) are used to host an executable assembly and any necessary external code libraries. If you are not familiar with this .NET concept, you will be by the time you've finished Chapter 13. The short answer is that when your AppDomain is unloaded from memory, the CLR automatically invokes finalizers for every finalizable object created during its lifetime.

Now, despite what your developer instincts may tell you, a *vast majority* of your C# classes will not require any explicit cleanup logic. The reason is simple: If your types are simply making use of other managed objects, everything will eventually be garbage collected. The only time you would need to design a class that can clean up after itself is when you are making use of *unmanaged resources* (such as raw OS file handles, raw unmanaged database connections, or other unmanaged resources). As you may know, unmanaged resources are obtained by directly calling into the API of the operating system using PInvoke (platform invocation) services or due to some very elaborate COM interoperability scenarios. Given this, consider the next rule of garbage collection:

- **Rule:** The only reason to override `Finalize()` is if your C# class is making use of unmanaged resources via PInvoke or complex COM interoperability tasks (typically via the `System.Runtime.InteropServices.Marshal` type).

Note Recall from Chapter 3 that it is illegal to override `Finalize()` on structure types. This makes perfect sense given that structures are value types, which are never allocated on the heap to begin with.

Overriding System.Object.Finalize()

In the rare case that you do build a C# class that makes use of unmanaged resources, you will obviously wish to ensure that the underlying memory is released in a predictable manner. Assume you have created a class named `MyResourceWrapper` that makes use of an unmanaged resource (whatever that may be) and you wish to override `Finalize()`. The odd thing about doing so in C# is that you cannot do so using the expected `override` keyword:

```
public class MyResourceWrapper
{
    // Compile time error!
    protected override void Finalize(){ }
}
```

Rather, when you wish to configure your custom C# class types to override the `Finalize()` method, you make use of the following (C++-like) destructor syntax to achieve the same effect. The reason for this alternative form of overriding a virtual method is that when the C# compiler processes a destructor, it will automatically add a good deal of required infrastructure within the `Finalize()` method (shown in just a moment).

Here is a custom finalizer for `MyResourceWrapper` that will issue a system beep when invoked. Obviously this is only for instructional purposes. A real-world finalizer would do nothing more than free any unmanaged resources and would *not* interact with the members of other managed objects, as you cannot assume they are still alive at the point the garbage collector invokes your `Finalize()` method:

```
// Override System.Object.Finalize() via destructor syntax.
class MyResourceWrapper
{
    ~MyResourceWrapper()
    {
        // Clean up unmanaged resources here.

        // Beep when destroyed (testing purposes only!)
        Console.Beep();
    }
}
```

If you were to examine this C# destructor using ildasm.exe, you will see that the compiler inserts some necessary error checking code. First, the code statements within the scope of your Finalize() method are placed within a try block. This bit of syntax is used to hold code statements that may trigger a runtime error (formally termed an *exception*) during their execution. The related finally block ensures that your base classes' Finalize() method will always execute, regardless of any exceptions encountered within the try scope. You'll investigate the formalities of structured exception handling in the next chapter; however, ponder the following CIL representation of MyResourceWrapper's C# destructor:

```
.method family hidebysig virtual instance void
    Finalize() cil managed
{
    // Code size        13 (0xd)
    .maxstack  1
    .try
    {
        IL_0000:  ldc.i4      0x4e20
        IL_0005:  ldc.i4      0x3e8
        IL_000a:  call
            void [mscorlib]System.Console::Beep(int32, int32)
        IL_000f:  nop
        IL_0010:  nop
        IL_0011:  leave.s     IL_001b
    } // end .try
    finally
    {
        IL_0013:  ldarg.0
        IL_0014:
            call instance void [mscorlib]System.Object::Finalize()
        IL_0019:  nop
        IL_001a:  endfinally
    } // end handler
    IL_001b:  nop
    IL_001c:  ret
} // end of method MyResourceWrapper::Finalize
```

If you were to now test the MyResourceWrapper type, you would find that a system beep occurs when the application terminates, given that the CLR will automatically invoke finalizers upon AppDomain shutdown:

```
static void Main(string[] args)
{
    Console.WriteLine("***** Fun with Finalizers *****\n");
    Console.WriteLine("Hit the return key to shut down this app");
    Console.WriteLine("and force the GC to invoke Finalize()");
    Console.WriteLine("for finalizable objects created in this AppDomain.");
    Console.ReadLine();
    MyResourceWrapper rw = new MyResourceWrapper();
}
```

Source Code The SimpleFinalize project is included under the Chapter 5 subdirectory.

Detailing the Finalization Process

Not to beat a dead horse, but always remember that the role of the Finalize() method is to ensure that a .NET object can clean up unmanaged resources when garbage collected. Thus, if you are building a type that does not make use of unmanaged entities (by far the most common case), finalization is of little use. In fact, if at all possible, you should design your types to avoid supporting a Finalize() method for the very simple reason that finalization takes time.

When you allocate an object onto the managed heap, the runtime automatically determines whether your object supports a custom Finalize() method. If so, the object is marked as *finalizable*, and a pointer to this object is stored on an internal queue named the *finalization queue*. The finalization queue is a table maintained by the garbage collector that points to each and every object that must be finalized before it is removed from the heap.

When the garbage collector determines it is time to free an object from memory, it examines each entry on the finalization queue, and copies the object off the heap to yet another managed structure termed the *finalization reachable* table (often abbreviated as freachable, and pronounced "eff-reachable"). At this point, a separate thread is spawned to invoke the Finalize() method for each object on the freachable table *at the next garbage collection*. Given this, it will take at very least *two* garbage collections to truly finalize an object.

The bottom line is that while finalization of an object does ensure an object can clean up unmanaged resources, it is still nondeterministic in nature, and due to the extra behind-the-curtains processing, considerably slower.

Building Disposable Objects

Given that so many unmanaged resources are "precious items" that should be cleaned up ASAP, allow me to introduce you to another possible technique used to handle an object's cleanup. As an alternative to overriding Finalize(), your class could implement the IDisposable interface, which defines a single method named Dispose():

```
public interface IDisposable
{
    void Dispose();
}
```

If you are new to interface-based programming, Chapter 7 will take you through the details. In a nutshell, an interface as a collection of abstract members a class or structure may support. When you do support the IDisposable interface, the assumption is that when the *object user* is finished using the object, it manually calls Dispose() before allowing the object reference to drop out of scope. In this way, your objects can perform any necessary cleanup of unmanaged resources without incurring the hit of being placed on the finalization queue and without waiting for the garbage collector to trigger the class's finalization logic.

■**Note** Structures and class types can both support IDisposable (unlike overriding Finalize(), which is reserved for class types).

Here is an updated MyResourceWrapper class that now implements IDisposable, rather than overriding System.Object.Finalize():

```
// Implementing IDisposable.
public class MyResourceWrapper : IDisposable
{
```

```
// The object user should call this method
// when they finished with the object.
public void Dispose()
{
    // Clean up unmanaged resources here.

    // Dispose other contained disposable objects.
}
}
```

Notice that a `Dispose()` method is not only responsible for releasing the type's unmanaged resources, but should also call `Dispose()` on any other contained disposable methods. Unlike `Finalize()`, it is perfectly safe to communicate with other managed objects within a `Dispose()` method. The reason is simple: The garbage collector has no clue about the `IDisposable` interface and will never call `Dispose()`. Therefore, when the object user calls this method, the object is still living a productive life on the managed heap and has access to all other heap-allocated objects. The calling logic is straightforward:

```
public class Program
{
    static void Main()
    {
        MyResourceWrapper rw = new MyResourceWrapper();
        rw.Dispose();
        Console.ReadLine();
    }
}
```

Of course, before you attempt to call `Dispose()` on an object, you will want to ensure the type supports the `IDisposable` interface. While you will typically know which objects implement `IDisposable` by consulting the .NET Framework 2.0 SDK documentation, a programmatic check can be accomplished using the `is` or `as` keywords discussed in Chapter 4:

```
public class Program
{
    static void Main()
    {
        MyResourceWrapper rw = new MyResourceWrapper();
        if (rw is IDisposable)
            rw.Dispose();
        Console.ReadLine();
    }
}
```

This example exposes yet another rule of working with garbage-collected types.

- **Rule:** Always call `Dispose()` on any object you directly create if the object supports `IDisposable`. The assumption you should make is that if the class designer chose to support the `Dispose()` method, the type has some cleanup to perform.

Reusing the C# using Keyword

When you are handling a managed object that implements `IDisposable`, it will be quite common to make use of structured exception handling (again, see Chapter 6) to ensure the type's `Dispose()` method is called in the event of a runtime exception:

```
static void Main(string[] args)
{
    MyResourceWrapper rw = new MyResourceWrapper ();
    try
    {
        // Use the members of rw.
    }
    finally
    {
        // Always call Dispose(), error or not.
        rw.Dispose();
    }
}
```

While this is a fine example of defensive programming, the truth of the matter is that few developers are thrilled by the prospects of wrapping each and every disposable type within a try/catch/finally block just to ensure the Dispose() method is called. To achieve the same result in a much less obtrusive manner, C# supports a special bit of syntax that looks like this:

```
static void Main(string[] args)
{
    // Dispose() is called automatically when the
    // using scope exits.
    using(MyResourceWrapper rw = new MyResourceWrapper())
    {
        // Use rw object.
    }
}
```

If you were to look at the CIL code of the Main() method using ildasm.exe, you will find the using syntax does indeed expand to try/final logic, with the expected call to Dispose():

```
.method private hidebysig static void Main(string[] args) cil managed
{
...
    .try
    {
        ...
    } // end .try
    finally
    {
...
        IL_0012:  callvirt instance void
                SimpleFinalize.MyResourceWrapper::Dispose()
    } // end handler
...
} // end of method Program::Main
```

■Note If you attempt to "use" an object that does not implement IDisposable, you will receive a compiler error.

While this syntax does remove the need to manually wrap disposable objects within try/finally logic, the C# using keyword unfortunately now has a double meaning (specifying namespaces and invoking a Dispose() method). Nevertheless, when you are working with .NET types that support the IDisposable interface, this syntactical construct will ensure that the object "being used" will automatically have its Dispose() method called once the using block has exited.

Building Finalizable and Disposable Types

At this point, we have seen two different approaches to construct a class that cleans up internal unmanaged resources. On the one hand, we could override System.Object.Finalize(). Using this technique, we have the peace of mind that comes with knowing the object cleans itself up when garbage collected (whenever that may be) without the need for user interaction. On the other hand, we could implement IDisposable to provide a way for the object user to clean up the object as soon as it is finished. However, if the caller forgets to call Dispose(), the unmanaged resources may be held in memory indefinitely.

As you might suspect, it is possible to blend both techniques into a single class definition. By doing so, you gain the best of both models. If the object user *does* remember to call Dispose(), you can inform the garbage collector to bypass the finalization process by calling GC.SuppressFinalize(). If the object user *forgets* to call Dispose(), the object will eventually be finalized. The good news is that the object's internal unmanaged resources will be freed one way or another. Here is the next iteration of MyResourceWrapper, which is now finalizable and disposable:

```
// A sophisticated resource wrapper.
public class MyResourceWrapper : IDisposable
{
    // The garbage collector will call this method if the
    // object user forgets to call Dispose().
    ~ MyResourceWrapper()
    {
        // Clean up any internal unmanaged resources.
        // Do **not** call Dispose() on any managed objects.
    }

    // The object user will call this method to clean up
    // resources ASAP.
    public void Dispose()
    {
        // Clean up unmanaged resources here.
        // Call Dispose() on other contained disposable objects.

        // No need to finalize if user called Dispose(),
        // so suppress finalization.
        GC.SuppressFinalize(this);
    }
}
```

Notice that this Dispose() method has been updated to call GC.SuppressFinalize(), which informs the CLR that it is no longer necessary to call the destructor when this object is garbage collected, given that the unmanaged resources have already been freed via the Dispose() logic.

A Formalized Disposal Pattern

The current implementation of MyResourceWrapper does work fairly well; however, we are left with a few minor drawbacks. First, the Finalize() and Dispose() method each have to clean up the same unmanaged resources. This of course results in duplicate code, which can easily become a nightmare to maintain. Ideally, you would define a private helper function that is called by either method.

Next, you would like to make sure that the Finalize() method does not attempt to dispose of any managed objects, while the Dispose() method should do so. Finally, you would also like to make sure that the object user can safely call Dispose() multiple times without error. Currently our Dispose() method has no such safeguards.

To address these design issues, Microsoft has defined a formal, prim-and-proper disposal pattern that strikes a balance between robustness, maintainability, and performance. Here is the final (and annotated) version of MyResourceWrapper, which makes use of this official pattern:

```
public class MyResourceWrapper : IDisposable
{
    // Used to determine if Dispose()
    // has already been called.
    private bool disposed = false;

    public void Dispose()
    {
        // Call our helper method.
        // Specifying "true" signifies that
        // the object user triggered the clean up.
        CleanUp(true);

        // Now suppress finialization.
        GC.SuppressFinalize(this);
    }

    private void CleanUp(bool disposing)
    {
        // Be sure we have not already been disposed!
        if (!this.disposed)
        {
            // If disposing equals true, dispose all
            // managed resources.
            if (disposing)
            {
                // Dispose managed resources.
            }
            // Clean up unmanaged resources here.
        }
        disposed = true;
    }

    ~MyResourceWrapper()
    {
        // Call our helper method.
        // Specifying "false" signifies that
        // the GC triggered the clean up.
        CleanUp(false);
    }
}
```

Notice that MyResourceWrapper now defines a private helper method named CleanUp(). When specifying true as an argument, we are signifying that the object user has initiated the cleanup, therefore we should clean up all managed *and* unmanaged resources. However, when the garbage collector initiates the cleanup, we specify false when calling CleanUp() to ensure that internal disposable objects are *not* disposed (as we can't assume they are still in memory!). Last but not least, our Boolean member variable (disposed) is set to true before exiting CleanUp() to ensure that Dispose() can be called numerous times without error.

■Source Code The FinalizableDisposableClass project is included under the Chapter 5 subdirectory.

That wraps up our investigation of how the CLR is managing your objects via garbage collection. While there are additional details regarding the collection process I have not examined here (such as weak references and object resurrection), you are certainly in a perfect position for further exploration on your own terms.

Summary

The point of this chapter was to demystify the garbage collection process. As you have seen, the garbage collector will only run when it is unable to acquire the necessary memory from the managed heap (or when a given AppDomain unloads from memory). When a collection does occur, you can rest assured that Microsoft's collection algorithm as been optimized by the use of object generations, secondary threads for the purpose of object finalization, and a managed heap dedicated to host large objects.

This chapter also illustrated how to programmatically interact with the garbage collector using the System.GC class type. As mentioned, the only time when you will really need to do so is when you are building finalizable or disposable class types. Recall that finalizable types are classes that have overridden the virtual System.Object.Finalize() method to clean up unmanaged resources (at some time in the future). Disposable objects, on the other hand, are classes (or structures) that implement the IDisposable interface. Using this technique, you expose a public method to the object user that can be called to perform internal cleanup ASAP. Finally, you learned about an official "disposal" pattern that blends both approaches.

■ ■ ■

## CHAPTER 6

Understanding Structured Exception Handling

The point of this chapter is to understand how to handle runtime anomalies in your C# code base through the use of *structured exception handling*. Not only will you learn about the C# keywords that allow you to handle such matters (try, catch, throw, finally), but you will also come to understand the distinction between application-level and system-level exceptions. This discussion will also provide a lead-in to the topic of building custom exceptions, as well as how to leverage the exception-centric debugging tools of Visual Studio 2005.

Ode to Errors, Bugs, and Exceptions

Despite what our (sometimes inflated) egos may tell us, no programmer is perfect. Writing software is a complex undertaking, and given this complexity, it is quite common for even the best software to ship with various *problems*. Sometimes the problem is caused by "bad code" (such as overflowing the bounds of an array). Other times, a problem is caused by bogus user input that has not been accounted for in the application's code base (e.g., a phone number field assigned "Chucky"). Now, regardless of the cause of said problem, the end result is that your application does not work as expected. To help frame the upcoming discussion of structured exception handling, allow me to provide definitions for three commonly used anomaly-centric terms:

- *Bugs*: This is, simply put, an error on the part of the programmer. For example, assume you are programming with unmanaged C++. If you make calls on a NULL pointer or fail to delete allocated memory (resulting in a memory leak), you have a bug.

- *User errors*: Unlike bugs, user errors are typically caused by the individual running your application, rather than by those who created it. For example, an end user who enters a malformed string into a text box could very well generate an error *if* you fail to handle this faulty input in your code base.

- *Exceptions*: Exceptions are typically regarded as runtime anomalies that are difficult, if not impossible, to account for while programming your application. Possible exceptions include attempting to connect to a database that no longer exists, opening a corrupted file, or contacting a machine that is currently offline. In each of these cases, the programmer (and end user) has little control over these "exceptional" circumstances.

Given the previous definitions, it should be clear that .NET structured *exception* handling is a technique well suited to deal with runtime *exceptions*. However, as for the bugs and user errors that have escaped your view, the CLR will often generate a corresponding exception that identifies the problem at hand. The .NET base class libraries define numerous exceptions such as FormatException, IndexOutOfRangeException, FileNotFoundException, ArgumentOutOfRangeException, and so forth.

Before we get too far ahead of ourselves, let's formalize the role of structured exception handling and check out how it differs from traditional error handling techniques.

■**Note** To make the code examples used in this book as clean as possible, I will *not* catch every possible exception that may be thrown by a given method in the base class libraries. In your production-level projects, you should, of course, make liberal use of the techniques presented in this chapter.

The Role of .NET Exception Handling

Prior to .NET, error handling under the Windows operating system was a confused mishmash of techniques. Many programmers rolled their own error handling logic within the context of a given application. For example, a development team may define a set of numerical constants that represent known error conditions, and make use of them as method return values. By way of an example, ponder the following partial C code:

```c
/* A very C-style error trapping mechanism. */
#define E_FILENOTFOUND 1000

int SomeFunction()
{
    // Assume something happens in this f(x)
    // that causes the following return value.
    return E_FILENOTFOUND;
}

void main()
{
    int retVal = SomeFunction();
    if(retVal == E_FILENOTFOUND)
        printf("Cannot find file...");
}
```

This approach is less than ideal, given the fact that the constant E_FILENOTFOUND is little more than a numerical value, and is far from being a helpful agent regarding how to deal with the problem. Ideally, you would like to wrap the name, message, and other helpful information regarding this error condition into a single, well-defined package (which is exactly what happens under structured exception handling).

In addition to a developer's ad hoc techniques, the Windows API defines hundreds of error codes that come by way of #defines, HRESULTs, and far too many variations on the simple Boolean (bool, BOOL, VARIANT_BOOL, and so on). Also, many C++ COM developers (and indirectly, many VB6 COM developers) have made use of a small set of standard COM interfaces (e.g., ISupportErrorInfo, IErrorInfo, ICreateErrorInfo) to return meaningful error information to a COM client.

The obvious problem with these previous techniques is the tremendous lack of symmetry. Each approach is more or less tailored to a given technology, a given language, and perhaps even a given project. In order to put an end to this madness, the .NET platform provides a standard technique to send and trap runtime errors: structured exception handling (SEH).

The beauty of this approach is that developers now have a unified approach to error handling, which is common to all languages targeting the .NET universe. Therefore, the way in which a C# programmer handles errors is syntactically similar to that of a VB .NET programmer, and a C++ programmer using managed extensions. As an added bonus, the syntax used to throw and catch exceptions across assemblies and machine boundaries is identical.

Another bonus of .NET exceptions is the fact that rather than receiving a cryptic numerical value that identifies the problem at hand, exceptions are objects that contain a human-readable description of the problem, as well as a detailed snapshot of the call stack that triggered the exception in the first place. Furthermore, you are able to provide the end user with help link information that points the user to a URL that provides detailed information regarding the error at hand as well as custom user-defined data.

The Atoms of .NET Exception Handling

Programming with structured exception handling involves the use of four interrelated entities:

- A class type that represents the details of the exception that occurred

- A member that *throws* an instance of the exception class to the caller

- A block of code on the caller's side that invokes the exception-prone member

- A block of code on the caller's side that will process (or *catch*) the exception should it occur

The C# programming language offers four keywords (try, catch, throw, and finally) that allow you to throw and handle exceptions. The type that represents the problem at hand is a class derived from System.Exception (or a descendent thereof). Given this fact, let's check out the role of this exception-centric base class.

The System.Exception Base Class

All user- and system-defined exceptions ultimately derive from the System.Exception base class (which in turn derives from System.Object). Note that some of these members are virtual and may thus be overridden by derived types:

```
public class Exception : ISerializable, _Exception
{
    public virtual IDictionary Data { get; }
    protected Exception(SerializationInfo info, StreamingContext context);
    public Exception(string message, Exception innerException);
    public Exception(string message);
    public Exception();
    public virtual Exception GetBaseException();
    public virtual void GetObjectData(SerializationInfo info,
        StreamingContext context);
    public System.Type GetType();
    protected int HResult { get; set; }
    public virtual string HelpLink { get; set; }
    public System.Exception InnerException { get; }
    public virtual string Message { get; }
    public virtual string Source { get; set; }
    public virtual string StackTrace { get; }
    public MethodBase TargetSite { get; }
    public override string ToString();
}
```

As you can see, many of the properties defined by System.Exception are read-only in nature. This is due to the simple fact that derived types will typically supply default values for each property (for example, the default message of the IndexOutOfRangeException type is "Index was outside the bounds of the array").

■**Note** As of .NET 2.0, the _Exception interface is implemented by System.Exception to expose its functionality to unmanaged code.

Table 6-1 describes the details of some (but not all) of the members of System.Exception.

Table 6-1. *Core Members of the* System.Exception *Type*

System.Exception **Property**	**Meaning in Life**
Data	This property (which is new to .NET 2.0) retrieves a collection of key/value pairs (represented by an object implementing IDictionary) that provides additional, user-defined information about the exception. By default, this collection is empty.
HelpLink	This property returns a URL to a help file describing the error in full detail.
InnerException	This read-only property can be used to obtain information about the previous exception(s) that caused the current exception to occur. The previous exception(s) are recorded by passing them into the constructor of the most current exception.
Message	This read-only property returns the textual description of a given error. The error message itself is set as a constructor parameter.
Source	This property returns the name of the assembly that threw the exception.
StackTrace	This read-only property contains a string that identifies the sequence of calls that triggered the exception. As you might guess, this property is very useful during debugging.
TargetSite	This read-only property returns a MethodBase type, which describes numerous details about the method that threw the exception (ToString() will identify the method by name).

The Simplest Possible Example

To illustrate the usefulness of structured exception handling, we need to create a type that may throw an exception under the correct circumstances. Assume we have created a new console application project (named SimpleException) that defines two class types (Car and Radio) associated using the "has-a" relationship. The Radio type defines a single method that turns the radio's power on or off:

```
public class Radio
{
    public void TurnOn(bool on)
    {
        if(on)
            Console.WriteLine("Jamming...");
        else
            Console.WriteLine("Quiet time...");
    }
}
```

In addition to leveraging the Radio type via containment/delegation, the Car type is defined in such a way that if the user accelerates a Car object beyond a predefined maximum speed (specified using a constant member variable), its engine explodes, rendering the Car unusable (captured by a bool member variable named carIsDead). Beyond these points, the Car type has a few member variables to represent the current speed and a user supplied "pet name" as well as various constructors. Here is the complete definition (with code annotations):

```
public class Car
{
    // Constant for maximum speed.
    public const int maxSpeed = 100;

    // Internal state data.
    private int currSpeed;
    private string petName;

    // Is the car still operational?
    private bool carIsDead;

    // A car has-a radio.
    private Radio theMusicBox = new Radio();

    // Constructors.
    public Car() {}
    public Car(string name, int currSp)
    {
        currSpeed = currSp;
        petName = name;
    }

    public void CrankTunes(bool state)
    {
        // Delegate request to inner object.
        theMusicBox.TurnOn(state);
    }

    // See if Car has overheated.
    public void Accelerate(int delta)
    {
        if (carIsDead)
            Console.WriteLine("{0} is out of order...", petName);
        else
        {
            currSpeed += delta;
            if (currSpeed > maxSpeed)
            {
                Console.WriteLine("{0} has overheated!", petName);
                currSpeed = 0;
                carIsDead = true;
            }
            else
                Console.WriteLine("=> CurrSpeed = {0}", currSpeed);
        }
    }
}
```

Now, if we were to implement a Main() method that forces a Car object to exceed the predefined maximum speed (represented by the maxSpeed constant) as shown here:

```
static void Main(string[] args)
{
    Console.WriteLine("***** Creating a car and stepping on it *****");
    Car myCar = new Car("Zippy", 20);
    myCar.CrankTunes(true);

    for (int i = 0; i < 10; i++)
        myCar.Accelerate(10);
    Console.ReadLine();
}
```

we would see the output displayed in Figure 6-1.

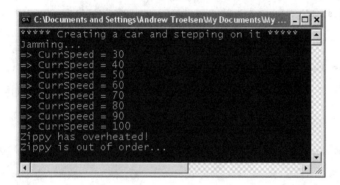

Figure 6-1. *The* Car *in action*

Throwing a Generic Exception

Now that we have a functional Car type, I'll illustrate the simplest way to throw an exception. The current implementation of Accelerate() displays an error message if the caller attempts to speed up the Car beyond its upper limit.

To retrofit this method to throw an exception if the user attempts to speed up the automobile after it has met its maker, you want to create and configure a new instance of the System.Exception class, setting the value of the read-only Message property via the class constructor. When you wish to send the error object back to the caller, make use of the C# throw keyword. Here is the relevant code update to the Accelerate() method:

```
// This time, throw an exception if the user speeds up beyond maxSpeed.
public void Accelerate(int delta)
{
    if (carIsDead)
        Console.WriteLine("{0} is out of order...", petName);
    else
    {
        currSpeed += delta;
        if (currSpeed >= maxSpeed)
        {
            carIsDead = true;
            currSpeed = 0;
```

```
            // Use "throw" keyword to raise an exception.
            throw new Exception(string.Format("{0} has overheated!", petName));
        }
        else
            Console.WriteLine("=> CurrSpeed = {0}", currSpeed);
    }
}
```

Before examining how a caller would catch this exception, a few points of interest. First of all, when you are throwing an exception, it is always up to you to decide exactly what constitutes the error in question, and when it should be thrown. Here, you are making the assumption that if the program attempts to increase the speed of a car that has expired, a System.Exception type should be thrown to indicate the Accelerate() method cannot continue (which may or may not be a valid assumption).

Alternatively, you could implement Accelerate() to recover automatically without needing to throw an exception in the first place. By and large, exceptions should be thrown only when a more terminal condition has been met (for example, not finding a necessary file, failing to connect to a database, and whatnot). Deciding exactly what constitutes throwing an exception is a design issue you must always contend with. For our current purposes, assume that asking a doomed automobile to increase its speed justifies a cause to throw an exception.

Catching Exceptions

Because the Accelerate() method now throws an exception, the caller needs to be ready to handle the exception should it occur. When you are invoking a method that may throw an exception, you make use of a try/catch block. Once you have caught the exception type, you are able to invoke the members of the System.Exception type to extract the details of the problem. What you do with this data is largely up to you. You may wish to log this information to a report file, write the data to the Windows event log, e-mail a system administrator, or display the problem to the end user. Here, you will simply dump the contents to the console window:

```
// Handle the thrown exception.
static void Main(string[] args)
{
    Console.WriteLine("***** Creating a car and stepping on it *****");
    Car myCar = new Car("Zippy", 20);
    myCar.CrankTunes(true);

    // Speed up past the car's max speed to
    // trigger the exception.
    try
    {
        for(int i = 0; i < 10; i++)
            myCar. Accelerate(10);
    }
    catch(Exception e)
    {
        Console.WriteLine("\n*** Error! ***");
        Console.WriteLine("Method: {0}", e.TargetSite);
        Console.WriteLine("Message: {0}", e.Message);
        Console.WriteLine("Source: {0}", e.Source);
    }

    // The error has been handled, processing continues with the next statement.
    Console.WriteLine("\n***** Out of exception logic *****");
    Console.ReadLine();
}
```

In essence, a `try` block is a section of statements that may throw an exception during execution. If an exception is detected, the flow of program execution is sent to the appropriate `catch` block. On the other hand, if the code within a `try` block does not trigger an exception, the `catch` block is skipped entirely, and all is right with the world. Figure 6-2 shows a test run of this program.

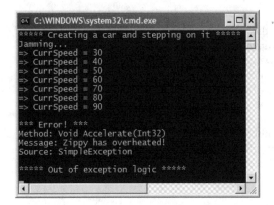

Figure 6-2. *Dealing with the error using structured exception handling*

As you can see, once an exception has been handled, the application is free to continue on from the point after the `catch` block. In some circumstances, a given exception may be critical enough to warrant the termination of the application. However, in a good number of cases, the logic within the exception handler will ensure the application will be able to continue on its merry way (although it may be slightly less functional, such as the case of not being able to connect to a remote data source).

Configuring the State of an Exception

Currently, the `System.Exception` object configured within the `Accelerate()` method simply establishes a value exposed to the `Message` property (via a constructor parameter). As shown in Table 6-1, however, the `Exception` class also supplies a number of additional members (`TargetSite`, `StackTrace`, `HelpLink`, and `Data`) that can be useful in further qualifying the nature of the problem. To spruce up our current example, let's examine further details of these members on a case-by-case basis.

The TargetSite Property

The `System.Exception.TargetSite` property allows you to determine various details about the method that threw a given exception. As shown in the previous `Main()` method, printing the value of `TargetSite` will display the return value, name, and parameters of the method that threw the exception. However, `TargetSite` does not simply return a vanilla-flavored string, but a strongly typed `System.Reflection.MethodBase` object. This type can be used to gather numerous details regarding the offending method as well as the class that defines the offending method. To illustrate, assume the previous `catch` logic has been updated as follows:

```
static void Main(string[] args)
{
...
```

```
    // TargetSite actually returns a MethodBase object.
    catch(Exception e)
    {
        Console.WriteLine("\n*** Error! ***");
        Console.WriteLine("Member name: {0}", e.TargetSite);
        Console.WriteLine("Class defining member: {0}",
            e.TargetSite.DeclaringType);
        Console.WriteLine("Member type: {0}", e.TargetSite.MemberType);
        Console.WriteLine("Message: {0}", e.Message);
        Console.WriteLine("Source: {0}", e.Source);
    }

        Console.WriteLine("\n***** Out of exception logic *****");
        myCar.Accelerate(10);  // Will not speed up car.
        Console.ReadLine();
}
```

This time, you make use of the `MethodBase.DeclaringType` property to determine the fully qualified name of the class that threw the error (`SimpleException.Car` in this case) as well as the `MemberType` property of the `MethodBase` object to identify the type of member (such as a property versus a method) where this exception originated. Figure 6-3 shows the updated output.

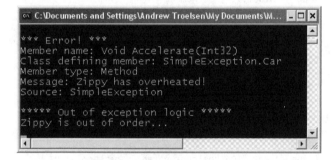

Figure 6-3. *Obtaining aspects of the target site*

The StackTrace Property

The `System.Exception.StackTrace` property allows you to identify the series of calls that resulted in the exception. Be aware that you never set the value of `StackTrace` as it is established automatically at the time the exception is created. To illustrate, assume you have once again updated your `catch` logic:

```
catch(Exception e)
{
    ...
    Console.WriteLine("Stack: {0}", e.StackTrace);
}
```

If you were to run the program, you would find the following stack trace is printed to the console (your line numbers and application folder may differ, of course):

```
Stack: at SimpleException.Car.Accelerate(Int32 delta)
in c:\myapps\exceptions\car.cs:line 65
at Exceptions.App.Main()
in c:\myapps\exceptions\app.cs:line 21
```

The string returned from StackTrace documents the sequence of calls that resulted in the throwing of this exception. Notice how the bottommost line number of this string identifies the first call in the sequence, while the topmost line number identifies the exact location of the offending member. Clearly, this information can be quite helpful during the debugging of a given application, as you are able to "follow the flow" of the error's origin.

The HelpLink Property

While the TargetSite and StackTrace properties allow programmers to gain an understanding of a given exception, this information is of little use to the end user. As you have already seen, the System.Exception.Message property can be used to obtain human-readable information that may be displayed to the current user. In addition, the HelpLink property can be set to point the user to a specific URL or standard Windows help file that contains more detailed information.

By default, the value managed by the HelpLink property is an empty string. If you wish to fill this property with an interesting value, you will need to do so before throwing the System.Exception type. Here are the relevant updates to the Car.Accelerate() method:

```
public void Accelerate(int delta)
{
    if (carIsDead)
        Console.WriteLine("{0} is out of order...", petName);
    else
    {
        currSpeed += delta;
        if (currSpeed >= maxSpeed)
        {
            carIsDead = true;
            currSpeed = 0;

            // We need to call the HelpLink property, thus we need to
            // create a local variable before throwing the Exception object.
            Exception ex =
                new Exception(string.Format("{0} has overheated!", petName));
            ex.HelpLink = "http://www.CarsRUs.com";
            throw ex;
        }
        else
            Console.WriteLine("=> CurrSpeed = {0}", currSpeed);
    }
}
```

The catch logic could now be updated to print out this help link information as follows:

```
catch(Exception e)
{
    ...
    Console.WriteLine("Help Link: {0}", e.HelpLink);
}
```

The Data Property

The Data property of System.Exception is new to .NET 2.0, and allows you to fill an exception object with relevant user-supplied information (such as a time stamp or what have you). The Data property returns an object implementing an interface named IDictionary, defined in the System.Collection namespace. The next chapter examines the role of interface-based programming as well as the System.Collections namespace. For the time being, just understand that dictionary collections allow you to create a set of values that are retrieved using a specific key value. Observe the next relevant update to the Car.Accelerate() method:

```
public void Accelerate(int delta)
{
    if (carIsDead)
        Console.WriteLine("{0} is out of order...", petName);
    else
    {
        currSpeed += delta;
        if (currSpeed >= maxSpeed)
        {
            carIsDead = true;
            currSpeed = 0;

            // We need to call the HelpLink property, thus we need
            // to create a local variable before throwing the Exception object.
            Exception ex =
                new Exception(string.Format("{0} has overheated!", petName));
            ex.HelpLink = "http://www.CarsRUs.com";

            // Stuff in custom data regarding the error.
            ex.Data.Add("TimeStamp",
                string.Format("The car exploded at {0}", DateTime.Now));
            ex.Data.Add("Cause", "You have a lead foot.");
            throw ex;
        }
        else
            Console.WriteLine("=> CurrSpeed = {0}", currSpeed);
    }
}
```

To successfully enumerate over the key/value pairs, you first must make sure to specify a using directive for the System.Collection namespace, given we will make use of a DictionaryEntry type in the file containing the class implementing your Main() method:

```
using System.Collections;
```

Next, we need to update the catch logic to test that the value returned from the Data property is not null (the default setting). After this point, we make use of the Key and Value properties of the DictionaryEntry type to print the custom user data to the console:

```
catch (Exception e)
{
...
    // By default, the data field is empty, so check for null.
    Console.WriteLine("\n-> Custom Data:");
    if (e.Data != null)
    {
        foreach (DictionaryEntry de in e.Data)
        Console.WriteLine("-> {0}: {1}", de.Key, de.Value);
    }
}
```

With this, we would now find the update shown in Figure 6-4.

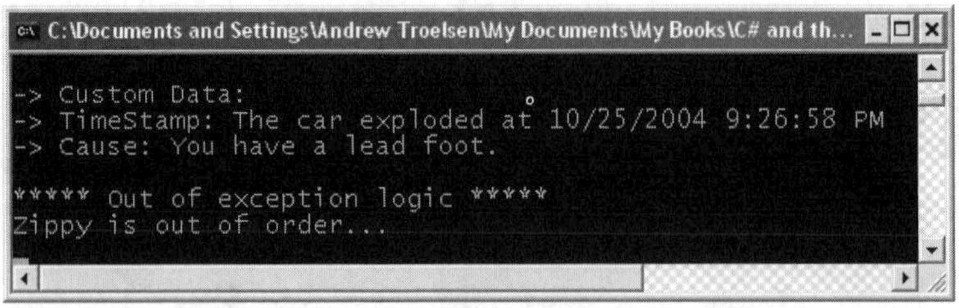

Figure 6-4. *Obtaining custom user-defined data*

Source Code The SimpleException project is included under the Chapter 5 subdirectory.

System-Level Exceptions (System. SystemException)

The .NET base class libraries define many classes derived from System.Exception. For example, the System namespace defines core error objects such as ArgumentOutOfRangeException, IndexOutOfRange-Exception, StackOverflowException, and so forth. Other namespaces define exceptions that reflect the behavior of that namespace (e.g., System.Drawing.Printing defines printing exceptions, System.IO defines IO-based exceptions, System.Data defines database-centric exceptions, and so forth).

Exceptions that are thrown by the CLR are (appropriately) called *system exceptions*. These exceptions are regarded as nonrecoverable, fatal errors. System exceptions derive directly from a base class named System.SystemException, which in turn derives from System.Exception (which derives from System.Object):

```
public class SystemException : Exception
{
    // Various constructors.
}
```

Given that the System.SystemException type does not add any additional functionality beyond a set of constructors, you might wonder why SystemException exists in the first place. Simply put, when an exception type derives from System.SystemException, you are able to determine that the .NET runtime is the entity that has thrown the exception, rather than the code base of the executing application.

Application-Level Exceptions (System. ApplicationException)

Given that all .NET exceptions are class types, you are free to create your own application-specific exceptions. However, due to the fact that the System.SystemException base class represents exceptions thrown from the CLR, you may naturally assume that you should derive your custom exceptions from the System.Exception type. While you could do so, best practice dictates that you instead derive from the System.ApplicationException type:

```
public class ApplicationException : Exception
{
    // Various constructors.
}
```

Like SystemException, ApplicationException does not define any additional members beyond a set of constructors. Functionally, the only purpose of System.ApplicationException is to identify the source of the (nonfatal) error. When you handle an exception deriving from System.ApplicationException, you can assume the exception was raised by the code base of the executing application, rather than by the .NET base class libraries.

Building Custom Exceptions, Take One

While you can always throw instances of System.Exception to signal a runtime error (as shown in our first example), it is sometimes advantageous to build a *strongly typed exception* that represents the unique details of your current problem. For example, assume you wish to build a custom exception (named CarIsDeadException) to represent the error of speeding up a doomed automobile. The first step is to derive a new class from System.ApplicationException (by convention, all exception classes end with the "Exception" suffix).

```
// This custom exception describes the details of the car-is-dead condition.
public class CarIsDeadException : ApplicationException
{}
```

Like any class, you are free to include any number of custom members that can be called within the catch block of the calling logic. You are also free to override any virtual members defined by your parent classes. For example, we could implement CarIsDeadException by overriding the virtual Message property:

```
public class CarIsDeadException : ApplicationException
{
    private string messageDetails;

    public CarIsDeadException(){ }
    public CarIsDeadException(string message)
    {
        messageDetails = message;
    }

    // Override the Exception.Message property.
    public override string Message
    {
        get
        {
            return string.Format("Car Error Message: {0}", messageDetails);
        }
    }
}
```

Here, the CarIsDeadException type maintains a private data member (messageDetails) that represents data regarding the current exception, which can be set using a custom constructor. Throwing this error from the Accelerate() is straightforward. Simply allocate, configure, and throw a CarIsDeadException type rather than a generic System.Exception:

```
// Throw the custom CarIsDeadException.
public void Accelerate(int delta)
{
...
    CarIsDeadException ex =
        new CarIsDeadException(string.Format("{0} has overheated!", petName));
    ex.HelpLink = "http://www.CarsRUs.com";
    ex.Data.Add("TimeStamp",
```

```
            string.Format("The car exploded at {0}", DateTime.Now));
        ex.Data.Add("Cause", "You have a lead foot.");
        throw ex;
...
}
```

To catch this incoming exception explicitly, your catch scope can now be updated to catch a specific CarIsDeadException type (however, given that CarIsDeadException "is-a" System.Exception, it is still permissible to catch a generic System.Exception as well):

```
static void Main(string[] args)
{
...
    catch(CarIsDeadException e)
    {
        // Process incoming exception.
    }
...
}
```

So, now that you understand the basic process of building a custom exception, you may wonder when you are required to do so. Typically, you only need to create custom exceptions when the error is tightly bound to the class issuing the error (for example, a custom File class that throws a number of file-related errors, a Car class that throws a number of car-related errors, and so forth). In doing so, you provide the caller with the ability to handle numerous exceptions on an error-by-error basis.

Building Custom Exceptions, Take Two

The current CarIsDeadException type has overridden the System.Exception.Message property in order to configure a custom error message. However, we can simplify our programming tasks if we set the parent's Message property via an incoming constructor parameter. By doing so, we have no need to write anything other than the following:

```
public class CarIsDeadException : ApplicationException
{
    public CarIsDeadException(){ }
    public CarIsDeadException(string message)
        : base(message){ }
}
```

Notice that this time you have *not* defined a string variable to represent the message, and have *not* overridden the Message property. Rather, you are simply passing the parameter to your base class constructor. With this design, a custom exception class is little more than a uniquely named class deriving from System.ApplicationException, devoid of any member variables (or base class overrides).

Don't be surprised if most (if not all) of your custom exception classes follow this simple pattern. Many times, the role of a custom exception is not necessarily to provide additional functionality beyond what is inherited from the base classes, but to provide a *strongly named type* that clearly identifies the nature of the error.

Building Custom Exceptions, Take Three

If you wish to build a truly prim-and-proper custom exception class, you would want to make sure your type adheres to the exception-centric .NET best practices. Specifically, this requires that your custom exception:

- Derives from Exception/ApplicationException

- Is marked with the [System.Serializable] attribute

- Defines a default constructor

- Defines a constructor that sets the inherited Message property

- Defines a constructor to handle "inner exceptions"

- Defines a constructor to handle the serialization of your type

Now, based on your current background with .NET, you may have no idea regarding the role of attributes or object serialization, which is just fine. I'll address these topics at this point later in the text. However, to finalize our examination of building custom exceptions, here is the final iteration of CarIsDeadException:

```
[Serializable]
public class CarIsDeadException : ApplicationException
{
    public CarIsDeadException() { }
    public CarIsDeadException(string message) : base( message ) { }
    public CarIsDeadException(string message,
        System.Exception inner) : base( message, inner ) { }
    protected CarIsDeadException(
        System.Runtime.Serialization.SerializationInfo info,
        System.Runtime.Serialization.StreamingContext context)
            : base( info, context ) { }
}
```

Given that building custom exceptions that adhere to .NET best practices really only differ by their name, you will be happy to know that Visual Studio 2005 provides a code snippet template named "Exception" (see Figure 6-5), which will autogenerate a new exception class that adheres to .NET best practices (see Chapter 2 for an explanation of code snippet templates).

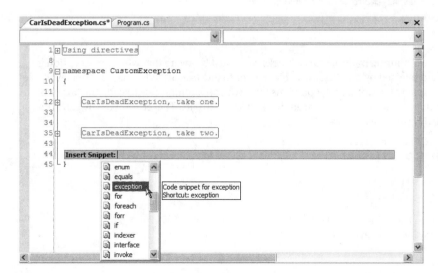

Figure 6-5. *The Exception code snippet template*

Processing Multiple Exceptions

In its simplest form, a try block has a single catch block. In reality, you often run into a situation where the statements within a try block could trigger *numerous* possible exceptions. For example, assume the car's Accelerate() method also throws a base-class-library predefined ArgumentOutOfRangeException if you pass an invalid parameter (which we will assume is any value less than zero):

```
// Test for invalid argument before proceeding.
public void Accelerate(int delta)
{
    if(delta < 0)
        throw new ArgumentOutOfRangeException("Speed must be greater than zero!");
    ...
}
```

The catch logic could now specifically respond to each type of exception:

```
static void Main(string[] args)
{
...
    // Here, we are on the lookout for multiple exceptions.
    try
    {
        for(int i = 0; i < 10; i++)
            myCar.Accelerate(10);
    }
    catch(CarIsDeadException e)
    {
        // Process CarIsDeadException.
    }
    catch(ArgumentOutOfRangeException e)
    {
        // Process ArgumentOutOfRangeException.
    }
...
}
```

When you are authoring multiple catch blocks, you must be aware that when an exception is thrown, it will be processed by the "first available" catch. To illustrate exactly what the "first available" catch means, assume you retrofitted the previous logic with an addition catch scope that attempts to handle all exceptions beyond CarIsDeadException and ArgumentOutOfRangeException by catching a generic System.Exception as follows:

```
// This code will not compile!
static void Main(string[] args)
{
...
    try
    {
        for(int i = 0; i < 10; i++)
            myCar.Accelerate(10);
    }
    catch(Exception e)
    {
        // Process all other exceptions?
    }
    catch(CarIsDeadException e)
    {
```

```
        // Process CarIsDeadException.
    }
    catch(ArgumentOutOfRangeException e)
    {
        // Process ArgumentOutOfRangeException.
    }
...
}
```

This exception handling logic generates compile-time errors. The problem is due to the fact that the first catch block can handle *anything* derived from System.Exception (given the "is-a" relationship), including the CarIsDeadException and ArgumentOutOfRangeException types. Therefore, the final two catch blocks are unreachable!

The rule of thumb to keep in mind is to make sure your catch blocks are structured such that the very first catch is the most specific exception (i.e., the most derived type in an exception type inheritance chain), leaving the final catch for the most general (i.e., the base class of a given exception inheritance chain, in this case System.Exception).

Thus, if you wish to define a catch statement that will handle any errors beyond CarIsDeadException and ArgumentOutOfRangeException, you would write the following:

```
// This code compiles just fine.
static void Main(string[] args)
{
...
    try
    {
        for(int i = 0; i < 10; i++)
            myCar.Accelerate(10);
    }
    catch(CarIsDeadException e)
    {
        // Process CarIsDeadException.
    }
    catch(ArgumentOutOfRangeException e)
    {
        // Process ArgumentOutOfRangeException.
    }
    catch(Exception e)
    {
        // This will now handle all other possible exceptions
        // thrown from statements within the try scope.
    }
...
}
```

Generic catch Statements

C# also supports a "generic" catch scope that does not explicitly receive the exception object thrown by a given member:

```
// A generic catch.
static void Main(string[] args)
{
...
    try
    {
```

```
        for(int i = 0; i < 10; i++)
            myCar.Accelerate(10);
    }
    catch
    {
        Console.WriteLine("Something bad happened...");
    }
    ...
}
```

Obviously, this is not the most informative way to handle exceptions, given that you have no way to obtain meaningful data about the error that occurred (such as the method name, call stack, or custom message). Nevertheless, C# does allow for such a construct.

Rethrowing Exceptions

Be aware that it is permissible for logic in a try block to *rethrow* an exception up the call stack to the previous caller. To do so, simply make use of the throw keyword within a catch block. This passes the exception up the chain of calling logic, which can be helpful if your catch block is only able to partially handle the error at hand:

```
// Passing the buck.
static void Main(string[] args)
{
    ...
    try
    {
        // Speed up car logic...
    }
    catch(CarIsDeadException e)
    {
        // Do any partial processing of this error and pass the buck.
        // Here, we are rethrowing the incoming CarIsDeadException object.
        // However, you are also free to throw a different exception if need be.
        throw e;
    }
    ...
}
```

Be aware that in this example code, the ultimate receiver of CarIsDeadException is the CLR, given that it is the Main() method rethrowing the exception. Given this point, your end user is presented with a system-supplied error dialog box. Typically, you would only rethrow a partial handled exception to a caller that has the ability to handle the incoming exception more gracefully.

Inner Exceptions

As you may suspect, it is entirely possible to trigger an exception at the time you are handling another exception. For example, assume that you are handing a CarIsDeadException within a particular catch scope, and during the process you attempt to record the stack trace to a file on your C drive named carErrors.txt:

```
catch(CarIsDeadException e)
{
    // Attempt to open a file named carErrors.txt on the C drive.
    FileStream fs = File.Open(@"C:\carErrors.txt", FileMode.Open);
    ...
}
```

Now, if the specified file is not located on your C drive, the call to File.Open() results in a FileNotFoundException! Later in this text, you will learn all about the System.IO namespace where you will discover how to programmatically determine if a file exists on the hard drive before attempting to open the file in the first place (thereby avoiding the exception altogether). However, to keep focused on the topic of exceptions, assume the exception has been raised.

When you encounter an exception while processing another exception, best practice states that you should record the new exception object as an "inner exception" within a new object of the same type as the initial exception (that was a mouthful). The reason we need to allocate a new object of the exception being handled is that the only way to document an inner exception is via a constructor parameter. Consider the following code:

```
catch (CarIsDeadException e)
{
    try
    {
        FileStream fs = File.Open(@"C:\carErrors.txt", FileMode.Open);
        ...
    }
    catch (Exception e2)
    {
        // Throw a exception that records the new exception,
        // as well as the message of the first exception.
        throw new CarIsDeadException(e.Message, e2);
    }
}
```

Notice in this case, we have passed in the FileNotFoundException object as the second parameter to the CarIsDeadException constructor. Once we have configured this new object, we throw it up the call stack to the next caller, which in this case would be the Main() method.

Given that there is no "next caller" after Main() to catch the exception, we would be again presented with an error dialog box. Much like the act of rethrowing an exception, recording inner exceptions is usually only useful when the caller has the ability to gracefully catch the exception in the first place. If this is the case, the caller's catch logic can make use of the InnerException property to extract the details of the inner exception object.

The Finally Block

A try/catch scope may also define an optional finally block. The motivation behind a finally block is to ensure that a set of code statements will *always* execute, exception (of any type) or not. To illustrate, assume you wish to always power down the car's radio before exiting Main(), regardless of any handled exception:

```
static void Main(string[] args)
{
    ...
    Car myCar = new Car("Zippy", 20);
    myCar.CrankTunes(true);

    try
    {
        // Speed up car logic.
    }
    catch(CarIsDeadException e)
    {
        // Process CarIsDeadException.
    }
```

```
        catch(ArgumentOutOfRangeException e)
        {
            // Process ArgumentOutOfRangeException.
        }
        catch(Exception e)
        {
            // Process any other Exception.
        }
        finally
        {
            // This will always occur. Exception or not.
            myCar.CrankTunes(false);
        }
...
}
```

If you did not include a `finally` block, the radio would not be turned off if an exception is encountered (which may or may not be problematic). In a more real-world scenario, when you need to dispose of objects, close a file, detach from a database (or whatever), a `finally` block ensures a location for proper cleanup.

Who Is Throwing What?

Given that a method in the .NET Framework could throw any number of exceptions (under various circumstances), a logical question would be "How do I know which exceptions may be thrown by a given base class library method?" The ultimate answer is simple: Consult the .NET Framework 2.0 SDK documentation. Each method in the help system documents the exceptions a given member may throw. As a quick alternative, Visual Studio 2005 allows you to view the list of all exceptions thrown by a base class library member (if any) simply by hovering your mouse cursor over the member name in the code window (see Figure 6-6).

Figure 6-6. *Identifying the exceptions thrown from a given method*

For those coming to .NET from a Java background, understand that type members are *not* prototyped with the set of exceptions it may throw (in other words, .NET does not support typed exceptions). Given this, you are *not* required to handle each and every exception thrown from a given member. In many cases, you can handle all possible errors thrown from a set scope by catching a single System.Exception:

```
static void Main(string[] args)
{
    try
    {
        File.Open("IDontExist.txt", FileMode.Open);
    }
    catch(Exception ex)
    {
        Console.WriteLine(ex.Message);
    }
}
```

However, if you do wish to handle specific exceptions uniquely, just make use of multiple catch blocks as shown throughout this chapter.

The Result of Unhandled Exception

At this point, you might be wondering what would happen if you do not handle an exception thrown your direction. Assume that the logic in Main() increases the speed of the Car object beyond the maximum speed, without the benefit of try/catch logic. The result of ignoring an exception would be highly obstructive to the end user of your application, as an "unhandled exception" dialog box is displayed. On a machine where .NET debugging tools are installed, you would see something similar to Figure 6-7 (a nondevelopment machine would display a similar intrusive dialog box).

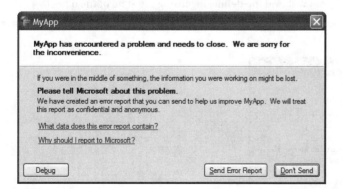

Figure 6-7. *The result of not dealing with exceptions*

Source Code The CustomException project is included under the Chapter 5 subdirectory.

Debugging Unhandled Exceptions Using Visual Studio 2005

To wrap things up, do be aware that Visual Studio 2005 provides a number of tools that help you debug unhandled custom exceptions. Again, assume you have increased the speed of a Car object beyond the maximum. If you were to start a debugging session (using the Debug ➤ Start menu selection), Visual Studio automatically breaks at the time the uncaught exception is thrown. Better yet, you are presented with a window (see Figure 6-8) displaying the value of the Message property.

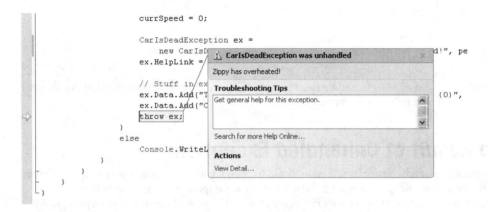

Figure 6-8. *Debugging unhandled custom exceptions with Visual Studio 2005*

If you click the View Detail link, you will find the details regarding the state of the object (see Figure 6-9).

Figure 6-9. *Debugging unhandled custom exceptions with Visual Studio 2005*

■**Note** If you fail to handle an exception thrown by a method in the .NET base class libraries, the Visual Studio 2005 debugger breaks at the statement that called the offending method.

Summary

In this chapter, you examined the role of structured exception handling. When a method needs to send an error object to the caller, it will allocate, configure, and throw a specific System.Exception derived type via the C# throw keyword. The caller is able to handle any possible incoming exceptions using the C# catch keyword and an optional finally scope.

When you are creating your own custom exceptions, you ultimately create a class type deriving from System.ApplicationException, which denotes an exception thrown from the currently executing application. In contrast, error objects deriving from System.SystemException represent critical (and fatal) errors thrown by the CLR. Last but not least, this chapter illustrated various tools within Visual Studio 2005 that can be used to create custom exceptions (according to .NET best practices) as well as debug exceptions.

CHAPTER 7

■ ■ ■

Interfaces and Collections

This chapter builds on your current understanding of object-oriented development by examining the topic of interface-based programming. Here you learn how to use C# to define and implement interfaces, and come to understand the benefits of building types that support "multiple behaviors." Along the way, a number of related topics are also discussed, such as obtaining interface references, explicit interface implementation, and the construction of interface hierarchies.

The remainder of this chapter is spent examining a number of interfaces defined within the .NET base class libraries. As you will see, your custom types are free to implement these predefined interfaces to support a number of advanced behaviors such as object cloning, object enumeration, and object sorting.

To showcase how interfaces are leveraged in the .NET base class libraries, this chapter will also examine numerous predefined interfaces implemented by various collection classes (ArrayList, Stack, etc.) defined by the System.Collections namespace. The information presented here will equip you to understand the topic of Chapter 10, .NET generics and the System.Collections.Generic namespace.

Defining Interfaces in C#

To begin this chapter, allow me to provide a formal definition of the "interface" type. An interface is nothing more than a named collection of semantically related *abstract members*. The specific members defined by an interface depend on the exact *behavior* it is modeling. Yes, it's true. An interface expresses a behavior that a given class or structure may choose to support.

At a syntactic level, an interface is defined using the C# interface keyword. Unlike other .NET types, interfaces never specify a base class (not even System.Object) and contain members that do *not* take an access modifier (as all interface members are implicitly public). To get the ball rolling, here is a custom interface defined in C#:

```
// This interface defines the behavior of "having points."
public interface IPointy
{
    // Implicitly public and abstract.
    byte GetNumberOfPoints();
}
```

■**Note** By convention, interfaces in the .NET base class libraries are prefixed with a capital letter "I." When you are creating your own custom interfaces, it is considered a best practice to do the same.

As you can see, the IPointy interface defines a single method. However, .NET interface types are also able to define any number of properties. For example, you could create the IPointy interface to use a read-only property rather than a traditional accessor method:

```
// The pointy behavior as a read-only property.
public interface IPointy
{
    byte Points{get;}
}
```

Do understand that interface types are quite useless on their own, as they are nothing more than a named collection of abstract members. Given this, you cannot allocate interface types as you would a class or structure:

```
// Ack! Illegal to "new" interface types.
static void Main(string[] args)
{
    IPointy p = new IPointy();   // Compiler error!
}
```

Interfaces do not bring much to the table until they are implemented by a class or structure. Here, IPointy is an interface that expresses the behavior of "having points." As you can tell, this behavior might be useful in the shapes hierarchy developed in Chapter 4. The idea is simple: Some classes in the Shapes hierarchy have points (such as the Hexagon), while others (such as the Circle) do not. If you configure Hexagon and Triangle to implement the IPointy interface, you can safely assume that each class now supports a common behavior, and therefore a common set of members.

Implementing an Interface in C#

When a class (or structure) chooses to extend its functionality by supporting interface types, it does so using a comma-delimited list in the type definition. Be aware that the direct base class must be the *first item* listed after the colon operator. When your class type derives directly from System.Object, you are free to simply list the interface(s) supported by the class, as the C# compiler will extend your types from System.Object if you do not say otherwise. On a related note, given that structures always derive from System.ValueType (see Chapter 3), simply list each interface directly after the structure definition. Ponder the following examples:

```
// This class derives from System.Object and
// implements a single interface.
public class SomeClass : ISomeInterface
{...}

// This class also derives from System.Object
// and implements a single interface.
public class MyClass : object, ISomeInterface
{...}

// This class derives from a custom base class
// and implements a single interface.
public class AnotherClass : MyBaseClass, ISomeInterface
{...}

// This struct derives from System.ValueType and
// implements two interfaces.
public struct SomeStruct : ISomeInterface, IPointy
{...}
```

Understand that implementing an interface is an all-or-nothing proposition. The supporting type is not able to selectively choose which members it will implement. Given that the IPointy interface defines a single property, this is not too much of a burden. However, if you are implementing an interface that defines ten members, the type is now responsible for fleshing out the details of the ten abstract entities.

In any case, here is the implementation of the updated shapes hierarchy (note the new Triangle class type):

```
// Hexagon now implements IPointy.
public class Hexagon : Shape, IPointy
{
    public Hexagon(){ }
    public Hexagon(string name) : base(name){ }
    public override void Draw()
    { Console.WriteLine("Drawing {0}  the Hexagon", PetName); }

    // IPointy Implementation.
    public byte Points
    {
        get { return 6; }
    }
}

// New Shape derived class named Triangle.
public class Triangle : Shape, IPointy
{
    public Triangle() { }
    public Triangle(string name) : base(name) { }
    public override void Draw()
    { Console.WriteLine("Drawing {0} the Triangle", PetName); }

    // IPointy Implementation.
    public byte Points
    {
        get { return 3; }
    }
}
```

Each class now returns its number of points to the caller when asked to do so. To sum up the story so far, the Visual Studio 2005 class diagram shown in Figure 7-1 illustrates IPointy-compatible classes using the popular "lollipop" notation.

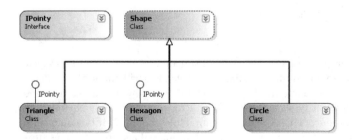

Figure 7-1. *The Shapes hierarchy (now with interfaces)*

Contrasting Interfaces to Abstract Base Classes

Given your work in Chapter 4, you may be wondering what the point of interface types are in the first place. After all, C# already allows you to build abstract class types containing abstract methods. Like an interface, when a class derives from an abstract base class, it is also under obligation to flesh out the details of the abstract methods (provided the derived class is not declared abstract as well). However, abstract base classes do far more than define a group of abstract methods. They are free to define public, private, and protected state data, as well as any number of concrete methods that can be accessed by the subclasses.

Interfaces, on the other hand, are pure protocol. Interfaces *never* define state data and *never* provide an implementation of the methods (if you try, you receive a compile-time error):

```
public interface IAmABadInterface
{
    // Error, interfaces can't define data!
    int myInt = 0;

    // Error, only abstract members allowed!
    void MyMethod()
    { Console.WriteLine("Eek!"); }
}
```

Interface types are also quite helpful given that C# (and .NET-aware languages in general) only support single inheritance; the interface-based protocol allows a given type to support numerous behaviors, while avoiding the issues that arise when deriving from extending multiple base classes.

Most importantly, interface-based programming provides yet another way to inject polymorphic behavior into a system. If multiple classes (or structures) implement the same interface in their unique ways, you have the power to treat each type in the same manner. As you will see a bit later in this chapter, interfaces are extremely polymorphic, given that types that are not related via classical inheritance can support identical behaviors.

Invoking Interface Members at the Object Level

Now that you have a set of types that support the IPointy interface, the next question is how you interact with the new functionality. The most straightforward way to interact with functionality supplied by a given interface is to invoke the methods directly from the object level. For example:

```
static void Main(string[] args)
{
    // Call new Points member defined by IPointy.
    Hexagon hex = new Hexagon();
    Console.WriteLine("Points: {0}", hex.Points);
    Console.ReadLine();
}
```

This approach works fine in this particular case, given that you are well aware that the Hexagon type has implemented the interface in question. Other times, however, you will not be able to determine at compile time which interfaces are supported by a given type. For example, assume you have an array containing 50 Shape-compatible types, only some of which support IPointy. Obviously, if you attempt to invoke the Points property on a type that has not implemented IPointy, you receive a compile-time error. Next question: How can we dynamically determine the set of interfaces supported by a type?

The first way you can determine at runtime if a type supports a specific interface is to make use of an explicit cast. If the type does not support the requested interface, you receive an InvalidCastException. To handle this possibility gracefully, make use of structured exception handling, for example:

```
static void Main(string[] args)
{
...
    // Catch a possible InvalidCastException.
    Circle c = new Circle("Lisa");
    IPointy itfPt;
    try
    {
        itfPt = (IPointy)c;
        Console.WriteLine(itfPt.Points);
    }
    catch (InvalidCastException e)
    { Console.WriteLine(e.Message); }
    Console.ReadLine();
}
```

While you could make use of try/catch logic and hope for the best, it would be ideal to determine which interfaces are supported before invoking the interface members in the first place. Let's see two ways of doing so.

Obtaining Interface References: The as Keyword

The second way you can determine whether a given type supports an interface is to make use of the as keyword, which was first introduced in Chapter 4. If the object can be treated as the specified interface, you are returned a reference to the interface in question. If not, you receive a null reference:

```
static void Main(string[] args)
{
...
    // Can we treat hex2 as IPointy?
    Hexagon hex2 = new Hexagon("Peter");
    IPointy itfPt2 = hex2 as IPointy;

    if(itfPt2 != null)
        Console.WriteLine("Points: {0}", itfPt2.Points);
    else
        Console.WriteLine("OOPS! Not pointy...");
}
```

Notice that when you make use of the as keyword, you have no need to make use of try/catch logic, given that if the reference is not null, you know you are calling on a valid interface reference.

Obtaining Interface References: The is Keyword

You may also check for an implemented interface using the is keyword. If the object in question is not compatible with the specified interface, you are returned the value false. On the other hand, if the type is compatible with the interface in question, you can safely call the members without needing to make use of try/catch logic.

To illustrate, assume we have updated the array of Shape types by including some members that implement IPointy. Notice how we are able to determine which item in the array supports this interface using the is keyword:

```
static void Main(string[] args)
{
...
    Shape[] s = { new Hexagon(), new Circle(), new Triangle("Joe"),
            new Circle("JoJo")} ;
```

```
    for(int i = 0; i < s.Length; i++)
    {
        // Recall the Shape base class defines an abstract Draw()
        // member, so all shapes know how to draw themselves.
        s[i].Draw();

        // Who's pointy?
        if(s[i] is IPointy)
            Console.WriteLine("-> Points: {0} ", ((IPointy)s[i]).Points);
        else
            Console.WriteLine("-> {0}\'s not pointy!", s[i].PetName);
    }
}
```

The output follows in Figure 7-2.

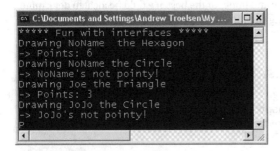

Figure 7-2. *Dynamically determining implemented interfaces*

Interfaces As Parameters

Given that interfaces are valid .NET types, you may construct methods that take interfaces as parameters. To illustrate, assume you have defined another interface named IDraw3D:

```
// Models the ability to render a type in stunning 3D.
public interface IDraw3D
{
    void Draw3D();
}
```

Next, assume that two of your three shapes (Circle and Hexagon) have been configured to support this new behavior:

```
// Circle supports IDraw3D.
public class Circle : Shape, IDraw3D
{
...
    public void Draw3D()
    { Console.WriteLine("Drawing Circle in 3D!"); }
}
```

```
// Hexagon supports IPointy and IDraw3D.
public class Hexagon : Shape, IPointy, IDraw3D
{
...
```

```
    public void Draw3D()
    { Console.WriteLine("Drawing Hexagon in 3D!"); }
}
```

Figure 7-3 presents the updated Visual Studio 2005 class diagram.

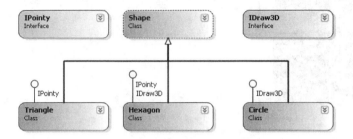

Figure 7-3. *The updated Shapes hierarchy*

If you now define a method taking an IDraw3D interface as a parameter, you are able to effectively send in *any* object implementing IDraw3D (if you attempt to pass in a type not supporting the necessary interface, you receive a compile-time error). Consider the following:

```
// Make some shapes. If they can be rendered in 3D, do it!
public class Program
{
    // I'll draw anyone supporting IDraw3D.
    public static void DrawIn3D(IDraw3D itf3d)
    {
        Console.WriteLine("-> Drawing IDraw3D compatible type");
        itf3d.Draw3D();
    }

    static void Main()
    {
        Shape[] s = { new Hexagon(), new Circle(),
                    new Triangle(), new Circle("JoJo")} ;

        for(int i = 0; i < s.Length; i++)
        {
            ...
            // Can I draw you in 3D?
            if(s[i] is IDraw3D)
                DrawIn3D((IDraw3D)s[i]);
        }
    }
}
```

Notice that the triangle is never drawn, as it is not IDraw3D-compatible (see Figure 7-4).

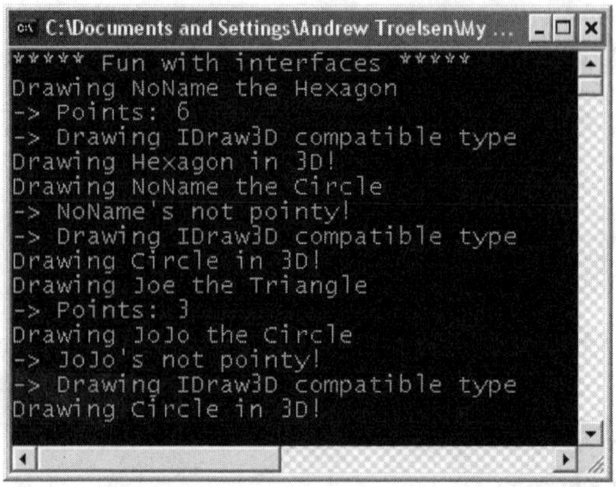

Figure 7-4. *Interfaces as parameters*

Interfaces As Return Values

Interfaces can also be used as method return values. For example, you could write a method that takes any System.Object, checks for IPointy compatibility, and returns a reference to the extracted interface:

```
// This method tests for IPointy-compatibility and,
// if able, returns an interface reference.
static IPointy ExtractPointyness(object o)
{
    if (o is IPointy)
        return (IPointy)o;
    else
        return null;
}
```

We could interact with this method as follows:

```
static void Main(string[] args)
{
    // Attempt to get IPointy from Car object.
    Car myCar = new Car();
    IPointy itfPt = ExtractPointyness(myCar);

    if(itfPt != null)
        Console.WriteLine("Object has {0} points.", itfPt.Points);
    else
        Console.WriteLine("This object does not implement IPointy");
}
```

Arrays of Interface Types

Understand that the same interface can be implemented by numerous types, even if they are not within the same class hierarchy. This can yield some very powerful programming constructs. For example, assume that you have developed a brand new class hierarchy modeling kitchen utensils and another modeling gardening equipment.

Although these hierarchies are completely unrelated from a classical inheritance point of view, you can treat them polymorphically using interface-based programming. To illustrate, assume you have an array of IPointy-compatible objects. Given that these members all support the same interface, you are able to iterate through the array and treat each object as an IPointy-compatible object, regardless of the overall diversity of the class hierarchies:

```
static void Main(string[] args)
{
    // This array can only contain types that
    // implement the IPointy interface.
    IPointy[] myPointyObjects = {new Hexagon(), new Knife(),
        new Triangle(), new Fork(), new PitchFork()};

    for (int i = 0; i < myPointyObjects.Length; i++)
        Console.WriteLine("Object has {0} points.", myPointyObjects[i].Points);
}
```

■Note Given the language-agonistic nature of .NET, understand that it is permissible to define an interface in one language (C#) and implement it in another (VB .NET). To understand how this is possible requires an understanding of .NET assemblies, which is the topic of Chapter 11.

Understanding Explicit Interface Implementation

In our current definition of IDraw3D, we were forced to name its sole method Draw3D() in order to avoid clashing with the abstract Draw() method defined in the Shape base class. While there is nothing horribly wrong with this interface definition, a more natural method name would simply be Draw():

```
// Refactor method name from "Draw3D" to "Draw".
public interface IDraw3D
{
    void Draw();
}
```

If we were to make such a change, this would require us to also update our implementation of DrawIn3D().

```
public static void DrawIn3D(IDraw3D itf3d)
{
    Console.WriteLine("-> Drawing IDraw3D compatible type");
    itf3d.Draw();
}
```

Now, assume you have defined a new class named Line that derives from the abstract Shape class and implements IDraw3D (both of which now define an identically named abstract Draw() method):

```
// Problems? It depends...
public class Line : Shape, IDraw3D
{
    public override void Draw()
    {
        Console.WriteLine("Drawing a line...");
    }
}
```

The Line class compiles without a hitch. But consider the following Main() logic:

```
static void Main(string[] args)
{
...
    // Calls Draw().
    Line myLine = new Line();
    myLine.Draw();

    // Calls same implementation of Draw()!
    IDraw3D itfDraw3d= (IDraw3D) myLine;
    itfDraw3d.Draw();
}
```

Given what you already know about the Shape base class and IDraw3D interface, it looks as if you have called *two* variations of the Draw() method (one from the object level, the other from an interface reference). Nevertheless, the compiler is happy to call the same implementation from an interface or object reference, given that the Shape abstract base class and IDraw3D interface have an identically named member. This would be problematic if you would like to have the IDraw3D.Draw() method render a type in stunning 3D, while the overridden Shape.Draw() method draws in boring 2D.

Now consider a related problem. What if you wish to ensure that the methods defined by a given interface are only accessible from an interface reference rather than an object reference? Currently, the members defined by the IPointy interface can be accessed using either an object reference or an IPointy reference.

The answer to both questions comes by way of *explicit interface implementation*. Using this technique, you are able to ensure that the object user can only access methods defined by a given interface using the correct interface reference, as well as circumvent possible name clashes. To illustrate, here is the updated Line class (assume you have updated Hexagon and Circle in a similar manner):

```
// Using explicit method implementation we are able
// to provide distinct Draw() implementations.
public class Line : Shape, IDraw3D
{
    // You can only call this method from an IDraw3D interface reference.
    void IDraw3D.Draw()
    { Console.WriteLine("Drawing a 3D line..."); }

    // You can only call this at the object level.
    public override void Draw()
    {  Console.WriteLine("Drawing a line..."); }
}
```

As you can see, when explicitly implementing an interface member, the general pattern breaks down to *returnValue InterfaceName.MethodName(args)*. There are a few odds and ends to be aware of when using explicit interface implementation. First and foremost, you cannot define the explicitly implemented members with an access modifier. For example, the following is illegal syntax:

```
// Nope! Illegal.
public class Line : Shape, IDraw3D
{
    public void IDraw3D.Draw()  // <= Error!
    {
        Console.WriteLine("Drawing a 3D line...");
    }
...
}
```

This should make sense. The whole reason to use explicit interface method implementation is to ensure that a given interface method is bound at the interface level. If you were to add the public keyword, this would suggest that the method is a member of the public sector of the class, which defeats the point! Given this design, the caller is only able to invoke the Draw() method defined by the Shape base class from the object level:

```
// This invokes the overridden Shape.Draw() method.
Line myLine = new Line();
myLine.Draw();
```

To invoke the Draw() method defined by IDraw3D, we must now explicitly obtain the interface reference using any of the techniques shown previously. For example:

```
// This triggers the IDraw3D.Draw() method.
Line myLine = new Line();
IDraw3D i3d = (IDraw3D)myLine;
i3d.Draw();
```

Resolving Name Clashes

Explicit interface implementation can also be very helpful whenever you are implementing a number of interfaces that happen to contain identical members. For example, assume you wish to create a class that implements all the following new interface types:

```
// Three interfaces each define identically named methods.
public interface IDraw
{
    void Draw();
}

public interface IDrawToPrinter
{
    void Draw();
}
```

If you wish to build a class named SuperImage that supports basic rendering (IDraw), 3D rendering (IDraw3D), as well as printing services (IDrawToPrinter), the only way to provide unique implementations for each method is to use explicit interface implementation:

```
// Not deriving from Shape, but still injecting a name clash.
public class SuperImage : IDraw, IDrawToPrinter, IDraw3D
{
    void IDraw.Draw()
    {  /* Basic drawing logic. */ }

    void IDrawToPrinter.Draw()
    {  /* Printer logic. */ }

    void IDraw3D.Draw()
    {  /* 3D rendering logic. */ }
}
```

■**Source Code** The CustomInterface project is located under the Chapter 7 subdirectory.

Building Interface Hierarchies

To continue our investigation of creating custom interfaces, let's examine the topic of *interface hierarchies*. Just as a class can serve as a base class to other classes (which can in turn function as base classes to yet another class), it is possible to build inheritance relationships among interfaces. As you might expect, the topmost interface defines a general behavior, while the most derived interface defines more specific behaviors. To illustrate, ponder the following interface hierarchy:

```
// The base interface.
public interface IDrawable
{   void Draw();}

public interface IPrintable : IDrawable
{   void Print(); }

public interface IMetaFileRender : IPrintable
{   void Render(); }
```

Figure 7-5 illustrates the chain of inheritance.

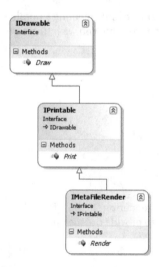

Figure 7-5. *An interface hierarchy*

Now, if a class wished to support each behavior expressed in this interface hierarchy, it would derive from the *nth-most* interface (IMetaFileRender in this case). Any methods defined by the base interface(s) are automatically carried into the definition. For example:

```
// This class supports IDrawable, IPrintable, and IMetaFileRender.
public class SuperImage : IMetaFileRender
{
    public void Draw()
    { Console.WriteLine("Basic drawing logic."); }

    public void Print()
    { Console.WriteLine("Draw to printer."); }

    public void Render()
    { Console.WriteLine("Render to metafile."); }
}
```

Here is some sample usage of exercising each interface from a SuperImage instance:

```
// Exercise the interfaces.
static void Main(string[] args)
{
    SuperImage si = new SuperImage();

    // Get IDrawable.
    IDrawable itfDraw = (IDrawable)si;
    itfDraw.Draw();

    // Now get ImetaFileRender, which exposes all methods up
    // the chain of inheritance.
    if (itfDraw is IMetaFileRender)
    {
        IMetaFileRender itfMF = (IMetaFileRender)itfDraw;
        itfMF.Render();
        itfMF.Print();
    }
    Console.ReadLine();
}
```

Interfaces with Multiple Base Interfaces

As you build interface hierarchies, be aware that it is completely permissible to create an interface that derives from *multiple* base interfaces. Recall, however, that it is *not* permissible to build a class that derives from multiple base classes. To illustrate, assume you are building a new set of interfaces that model the automobile behaviors for a particular English agent:

```
public interface ICar
{  void Drive(); }

public interface IUnderwaterCar
{  void Dive(); }

// Here we have an interface with TWO base interfaces.
public interface IJamesBondCar : ICar, IUnderwaterCar
{  void TurboBoost(); }
```

Figure 7-6 illustrates the chain of inheritance.

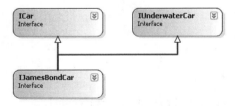

Figure 7-6. *Multiple inheritance of interface types is allowed by the CTS.*

If you were to build a class that implements IJamesBondCar, you would now be responsible for implementing TurboBoost(), Dive(), and Drive():

```
public class JamesBondCar : IJamesBondCar
{
    public void Drive(){ Console.WriteLine("Speeding up...");}
    public void Dive(){ Console.WriteLine("Submerging...");}
    public void TurboBoost(){ Console.WriteLine("Blast off!");}
}
```

This specialized automobile can now be manipulated as you would expect:

```
static void Main(string[] args)
{
...
    JamesBondCar j = new JamesBondCar();
    j.Drive();
    j.TurboBoost();
    j.Dive();
}
```

Implementing Interfaces Using Visual Studio 2005

Although interface-based programming is a very powerful programming technique, implementing interfaces may entail a healthy amount of typing. Given that interfaces are a named set of abstract members, you will be required to type in the stub code (and implementation) for *each* interface method on *each* class that supports the behavior.

As you would hope, Visual Studio 2005 does support various tools that make the task of implementing interfaces less burdensome. Assume you wish to implement the ICar interface on a new class named MiniVan. You will notice when you complete typing the interface's name (or when you position the mouse cursor on the interface name in the code window), the first letter is underlined (formally termed a "smart tag"). If you click the smart tag, you will be presented a drop-down list that allows you to implement the interface explicitly or implicitly (see Figure 7-7).

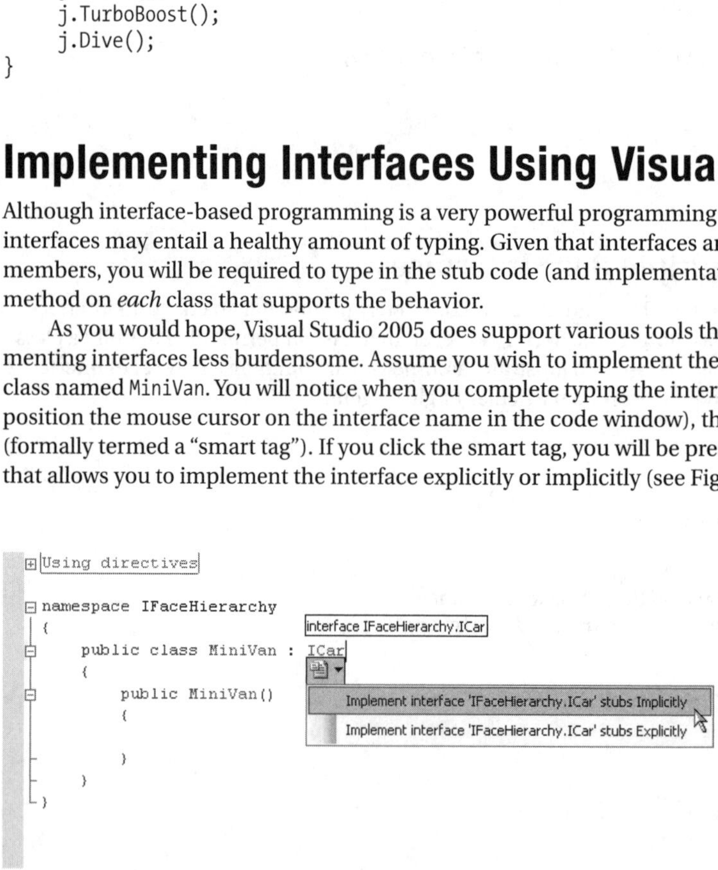

Figure 7-7. *Implementing interfaces using Visual Studio 2005*

Once you select options, you will see that Visual Studio 2005 has built generated stub code (within a named code region) for you to update (note that the default implementation throws a System.Exception).

```
namespace IFaceHierarchy
{
    public class MiniVan : ICar
    {
```

```
        public MiniVan()
        {
        }

        #region ICar Members
        public void Drive()
        {
            new Exception("The method or operation is not implemented.");
        }
        #endregion
    }
}
```

Now that you have drilled into the specifics of building and implementing custom interfaces, the remainder of the chapter examines a number of predefined interfaces contained within the .NET base class libraries.

■**Source Code** The IFaceHierarchy project is located under the Chapter 7 subdirectory.

Building Enumerable Types (IEnumerable and IEnumerator)

To illustrate the process of implementing existing .NET interfaces, let's first examine the role of IEnumerable and IEnumerator. Assume you have developed a class named Garage that contains a set of individual Car types (see Chapter 6) stored within a System.Array:

```
// Garage contains a set of Car objects.
public class Garage
{
    private Car[] carArray;

    // Fill with some Car objects upon startup.
    public Garage()
    {
        carArray = new Car[4];
        carArray[0] = new Car("Rusty", 30);
        carArray[1] = new Car("Clunker", 55);
        carArray[2] = new Car("Zippy", 30);
        carArray[3] = new Car("Fred", 30);
    }
}
```

Ideally, it would be convenient to iterate over the Garage object's subitems using the C# foreach construct:

```
// This seems reasonable...
public class Program
{
    static void Main(string[] args)
    {
        Garage carLot = new Garage();

        // Hand over each car in the collection?
        foreach (Car c in carLot)
        {
```

```
            Console.WriteLine("{0} is going {1} MPH",
                c.PetName, c.CurrSpeed);
        }
    }
}
```

Sadly, the compiler informs you that the Garage class does not implement a method named GetEnumerator(). This method is formalized by the IEnumerable interface, which is found lurking within the System.Collections namespace. Objects that support this behavior advertise that they are able to expose contained subitems to the caller:

```
// This interface informs the caller
// that the object's subitems can be enumerated.
public interface IEnumerable
{
    IEnumerator GetEnumerator();
}
```

As you can see, the GetEnumerator() method returns a reference to yet another interface named System.Collections.IEnumerator. This interface provides the infrastructure to allow the caller to traverse the internal objects contained by the IEnumerable-compatible container:

```
// This interface allows the caller to
// obtain a container's subitems.
public interface IEnumerator
{
    bool MoveNext ();          // Advance the internal position of the cursor.
    object Current { get;}     // Get the current item (read-only property).
    void Reset ();             // Reset the cursor before the first member.
}
```

If you wish to update the Garage type to support these interfaces, you could take the long road and implement each method manually. While you are certainly free to provide customized versions of GetEnumerator(), MoveNext(), Current, and Reset(), there is a simpler way. As the System.Array type (as well as many other types) already implements IEnumerable and IEnumerator, you can simply delegate the request to the System.Array as follows:

```
using System.Collections;
...
public class Garage : IEnumerable
{
    // System.Array already implements IEnumerator!
    private Car[] carArray;

    public Garage()
    {
        carArray = new Car[4];
        carArray[0] = new Car("FeeFee", 200, 0);
        carArray[1] = new Car("Clunker", 90, 0);
        carArray[2] = new Car("Zippy", 30, 0);
        carArray[3] = new Car("Fred", 30, 0);
    }

    public IEnumerator GetEnumerator()
    {
        // Return the array object's IEnumerator.
        return carArray.GetEnumerator();
    }
}
```

Once you have updated your Garage type, you can now safely use the type within the C# foreach construct. Furthermore, given that the GetEnumerator() method has been defined publicly, the object user could also interact with the IEnumerator type:

```
// Manually work with IEnumerator.
IEnumerator i = carLot.GetEnumerator();
i.MoveNext();
Car myCar = (Car)i.Current;
Console.WriteLine("{0} is going {1} MPH", myCar.PetName, myCar.CurrSpeed);
```

If you would prefer to hide the functionality of IEnumerable from the object level, simply make use of explicit interface implementation:

```
public IEnumerator IEnumerable.GetEnumerator()
{
    // Return the array object's IEnumerator.
    return carArray.GetEnumerator();
}
```

Source Code The CustomEnumerator project is located under the Chapter 7 subdirectory.

Understanding C# Iterator Methods

Under .NET 1.x, if you wished to have your custom collections (such as Garage) support foreach like enumeration, implementing the IEnumerable interface (and possibly the IEnumerator interface) was mandatory. However, C# 2005 offers an alternative way to build types that work with the foreach loop via *iterators*.

Simply put, an iterator is a member that specifies how a container's internal items should be returned when processed by foreach. While the iterator method must still be named GetEnumerator(), and the return value must still be of type IEnumerator, your custom class does *not* need to implement any of the expected interfaces:

```
public class Garage  // No longer implementing IEnumerable!
{
    private Car[] carArray;
    ...
    // Iterator method.
    public IEnumerator GetEnumerator()
    {
        foreach (Car c in carArray)
        {
            yield return c;
        }
    }
}
```

Notice that this implementation of GetEnumerator() iterates over the subitems using internal foreach logic and returns each Car to the caller using the new yield return syntax. The yield keyword is used to specify the value (or values) to be returned to the caller's foreach construct. When the yield return statement is reached, the current location is stored, and execution is restarted from this location the next time the iterator is called.

When the C# compiler encounters an iterator method, it will dynamically generate a nested class within the scope of the defining type (Garage in this case). The autogenerated class implements the GetEnumerator(), MoveNext() and Current members on your behalf (oddly, the Reset() method is not, and you will receive a runtime exception if you attempt to call it). If you were to load the current application into ildasm.exe, you would find that the Garage's implementation of GetEnumerator() is making use of this compiler-generated type (which happens to be named <GetEnumerator>d__0 in this example) internally:

```
.method public hidebysig instance class
    [mscorlib]System.Collections.IEnumerator
    GetEnumerator() cil managed
{
...
  newobj instance void
    CustomEnumeratorWithYield.Garage/'<GetEnumerator>d__0'::.ctor(int32)
  ...
} // end of method Garage::GetEnumerator
```

Now, understand that because our current Garage type originally implemented GetEnumerator() by delegating to the internal System.Array, we would not really gain much by defining an iterator method as shown here. However, if you are building a more exotic custom container (such as a binary tree) where you need to manually implement the IEnumerator and IEnumerable interfaces, the C# iterator syntax can be a massive time-saver. In any case, the caller's code is identical when interacting with a type's iterator method via foreach:

```
static void Main(string[] args)
{
    Console.WriteLine("***** Fun with Iterator Methods *****\n");
    Garage carLot = new Garage();
    foreach (Car c in carLot)
    {
        Console.WriteLine("{0} is going {1} MPH", c.PetName, c.CurrSpeed);
    }
    Console.ReadLine();
}
```

■**Source Code** The CustomEnumeratorWithYield project is located under the Chapter 7 subdirectory.

Building Cloneable Objects (ICloneable)

As you recall from Chapter 3, System.Object defines a member named MemberwiseClone(). This method is used to obtain a *shallow copy* of the current object. Object users do not call this method directly (as it is protected); however, a given object may call this method itself during the *cloning* process. To illustrate, assume you have a class named Point:

```
// A class named Point.
public class Point
{
    // Public for easy access.
    public int x, y;
    public Point(int x, int y) { this.x = x; this.y = y;}
    public Point(){}

    // Override Object.ToString().
    public override string ToString()
    { return string.Format("X = {0}; Y = {1}", x, y ); }
}
```

Given what you already know about reference types and value types (Chapter 3), you are aware that if you assign one reference variable to another, you have two references pointing to the same object in memory. Thus, the following assignment operation results in two references to the same Point object on the heap; modifications using either reference affect the same object on the heap:

```
static void Main(string[] args)
{
    // Two references to same object!
    Point p1 = new Point(50, 50);
    Point p2 = p1;
    p2.x = 0;
    Console.WriteLine(p1);
    Console.WriteLine(p2);
}
```

When you wish to equip your custom types to support the ability to return an identical copy of itself to the caller, you may implement the standard ICloneable interface. This type defines a single method named Clone():

```
public interface ICloneable
{
    object Clone();
}
```

Obviously, the implementation of the Clone() method varies between objects. However, the basic functionality tends to be the same: Copy the values of your member variables into a new object instance, and return it to the user. To illustrate, ponder the following update to the Point class:

```
// The Point now supports "clone-ability."
public class Point : ICloneable
{
    public int x, y;
    public Point(){ }
    public Point(int x, int y) { this.x = x; this.y = y;}

    // Return a copy of the current object.
    public object Clone()
    {   return new Point(this.x, this.y); }

    public override string ToString()
    {   return string.Format("X = {0}; Y = {1}", x, y ); }
}
```

In this way, you can create exact stand-alone copies of the Point type, as illustrated by the following code:

```
static void Main(string[] args)
{
    // Notice Clone() returns a generic object type.
    // You must perform an explicit cast to obtain the derived type.
    Point p3 = new Point(100, 100);
    Point p4 = (Point)p3.Clone();

    // Change p4.x (which will not change p3.x).
    p4.x = 0;

    // Print each object.
    Console.WriteLine(p3);
    Console.WriteLine(p4);
}
```

While the current implementation of Point fits the bill, you can streamline things just a bit. Because the Point type does not contain reference type variables, you could simplify the implementation of the Clone() method as follows:

```
public object Clone()
{
    // Copy each field of the Point member by member.
    return this.MemberwiseClone();
}
```

Be aware, however, that if the Point did contain any reference type member variables, Member-wiseClone() will copy the references to those objects (aka a *shallow copy*). If you wish to support a true deep copy, you will need to create a new instance of any reference type variables during the cloning process. Let's see an example.

A More Elaborate Cloning Example

Now assume the Point class contains a reference type member variable of type PointDescription. This class maintains a point's friendly name as well as an identification number expressed as a System.Guid (if you don't come from a COM background, know that a Globally Unique Identifier [GUID] is a statistically unique 128-bit number). Here is the implementation:

```
// This class describes a point.
public class PointDescription
{
    // Exposed publicly for simplicity.
    public string petName;
    public Guid pointID;

    public PointDescription()
    {
        this.petName = "No-name";
        pointID = Guid.NewGuid();
    }
}
```

The initial updates to the Point class itself included modifying ToString() to account for these new bits of state data, as well as defining and creating the PointDescription reference type. To allow the outside world to establish a pet name for the Point, you also update the arguments passed into the overloaded constructor:

```
public class Point : ICloneable
{
    public int x, y;
    public PointDescription desc = new PointDescription();

    public Point(){}
    public Point(int x, int y)
    {
        this.x = x; this.y = y;
    }
    public Point(int x, int y, string petname)
    {
        this.x = x;
        this.y = y;
        desc.petName = petname;
    }
```

```
    public object Clone()
    { return this.MemberwiseClone(); }

    public override string ToString()
    {
        return string.Format("X = {0}; Y = {1}; Name = {2};\nID = {3}\n",
            x, y, desc.petName, desc.pointID);
    }
}
```

Notice that you did not yet update your Clone() method. Therefore, when the object user asks for a clone using the current implementation, a shallow (member-by-member) copy is achieved. To illustrate, assume you have updated Main() as follows:

```
static void Main(string[] args)
{
    Console.WriteLine("Cloned p3 and stored new Point in p4");
    Point p3 = new Point(100, 100, "Jane");
    Point p4 = (Point)p3.Clone();

    Console.WriteLine("Before modification:");
    Console.WriteLine("p3: {0}", p3);
    Console.WriteLine("p4: {0}", p4);
    p4.desc.petName = "Mr. X";
    p4.x = 9;

    Console.WriteLine("\nChanged p4.desc.petName and p4.x");
    Console.WriteLine("After modification:");
    Console.WriteLine("p3: {0}", p3);
    Console.WriteLine("p4: {0}", p4);
}
```

Figure 7-8 shows the output.

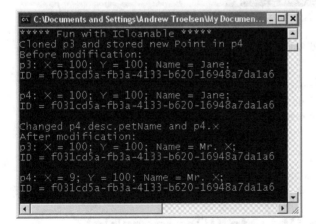

Figure 7-8. MemberwiseClone() *returns a shallow copy of the current object.*

In order for your Clone() method to make a complete deep copy of the internal reference types, you need to configure the object returned by MemberwiseClone() to account for the current point's name (the System.Guid type is in fact a structure, so the numerical data is indeed copied). Here is one possible implementation:

```
// Now we need to adjust for the PointDescription member.
public object Clone()
{
    Point newPoint = (Point)this.MemberwiseClone();
    PointDescription currentDesc = new PointDescription();
    currentDesc.petName = this.desc.petName;
    newPoint.desc = currentDesc;
    return newPoint;
}
```

If you rerun the application once again as shown in Figure 7-9, you see that the Point returned from Clone() does copy its internal reference type member variables (note the pet name is now unique for both p3 and p4).

Figure 7-9. *Now you have a true deep copy of the object.*

To summarize the cloning process, if you have a class or structure that contains nothing but value types, implement your Clone() method using MemberwiseClone(). However, if you have a custom type that maintains other reference types, you need to establish a new type that takes into account each reference type member variable.

■**Source Code** The CloneablePoint project is located under the Chapter 7 subdirectory.

Building Comparable Objects (IComparable)

The System.IComparable interface specifies a behavior that allows an object to be sorted based on some specified key. Here is the formal definition:

```
// This interface allows an object to specify its
// relationship between other like objects.
public interface IComparable
```

```
{
    int CompareTo(object o);
}
```

Let's assume you have updated the Car class to maintain an internal ID number (represented by a simple integer named carID) that can be set via a constructor parameter and manipulated using a new property named ID. Here are the relevant updates to the Car type:

```
public class Car
{
...
    private int carID;
    public int ID
    {
        get { return carID; }
        set { carID = value; }
    }
    public Car(string name, int currSp, int id)
    {
        currSpeed = currSp;
        petName = name;
        carID = id;
    }
...
}
```

Object users might create an array of Car types as follows:

```
static void Main(string[] args)
{
    // Make an array of Car types.
    Car[] myAutos = new Car[5];
    myAutos[0] = new Car("Rusty", 80, 1);
    myAutos[1] = new Car("Mary", 40, 234);
    myAutos[2] = new Car("Viper", 40, 34);
    myAutos[3] = new Car("Mel", 40, 4);
    myAutos[4] = new Car("Chucky", 40, 5);
}
```

As you recall, the System.Array class defines a static method named Sort(). When you invoke this method on an array of intrinsic types (int, short, string, etc.), you are able to sort the items in the array in numerical/alphabetic order as these intrinsic data types implement IComparable. However, what if you were to send an array of Car types into the Sort() method as follows?

```
// Sort my cars?
Array.Sort(myAutos);
```

If you run this test, you would find that an ArgumentException exception is thrown by the runtime, with the following message: "At least one object must implement IComparable." When you build custom types, you can implement IComparable to allow arrays of your types to be sorted. When you flesh out the details of CompareTo(), it will be up to you to decide what the baseline of the ordering operation will be. For the Car type, the internal carID seems to be the most logical candidate:

```
// The iteration of the Car can be ordered
// based on the CarID.
public class Car : IComparable
{
...
    // IComparable implementation.
    int IComparable.CompareTo(object obj)
```

```
    {
        Car temp = (Car)obj;
        if(this.carID > temp.carID)
            return 1;
        if(this.carID < temp.carID)
            return -1;
        else
            return 0;
    }
}
```

As you can see, the logic behind CompareTo() is to test the incoming type against the current instance based on a specific point of data. The return value of CompareTo() is used to discover if this type is less than, greater than, or equal to the object it is being compared with (see Table 7-1).

Table 7-1. CompareTo() *Return Values*

CompareTo() **Return Value**	**Meaning in Life**
Any number less than zero	This instance comes before the specified object in the sort order.
Zero	This instance is equal to the specified object.
Any number greater than zero	This instance comes after the specified object in the sort order.

Now that your Car type understands how to compare itself to like objects, you can write the following user code:

```
// Exercise the IComparable interface.
static void Main(string[] args)
{
    // Make an array of Car types.
    ...
    // Dump current array.
    Console.WriteLine("Here is the unordered set of cars:");
    foreach(Car c in myAutos)
        Console.WriteLine("{0} {1}", c.ID, c.PetName);

    // Now, sort them using IComparable!
    Array.Sort(myAutos);

    // Dump sorted array.
    Console.WriteLine("Here is the ordered set of cars:");
    foreach(Car c in myAutos)
        Console.WriteLine("{0} {1}", c.ID, c.PetName);
    Console.ReadLine();
}
```

Figure 7-10 illustrates a test run.

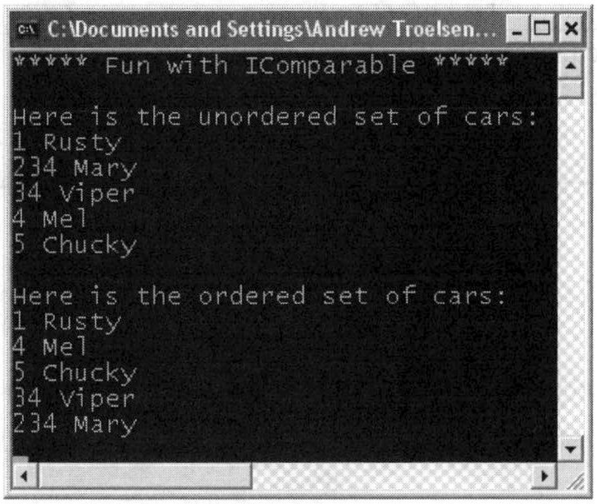

Figure 7-10. *Comparing automobiles based on car ID*

Specifying Multiple Sort Orders (IComparer)

In this version of the Car type, you made use of the car's ID to function as the baseline of the sort order. Another design might have used the pet name of the car as the basis of the sorting algorithm (to list cars alphabetically). Now, what if you wanted to build a Car that could be sorted by ID *as well as* by pet name? If this is the behavior you are interested in, you need to make friends with another standard interface named IComparer, defined within the System.Collections namespace as follows:

```
// A generic way to compare two objects.
interface IComparer
{
    int Compare(object o1, object o2);
}
```

Unlike the IComparable interface, IComparer is typically *not* implemented on the type you are trying to sort (i.e., the Car). Rather, you implement this interface on any number of helper classes, one for each sort order (pet name, car ID, etc.). Currently, the Car type already knows how to compare itself against other cars based on the internal car ID. Therefore, to allow the object user to sort an array of Car types by pet name will require an additional helper class that implements IComparer. Here's the code:

```
// This helper class is used to sort an array of Cars by pet name.
using System.Collections;

public class PetNameComparer : IComparer
{
    public PetNameComparer(){ }

    // Test the pet name of each object.
    int IComparer.Compare(object o1, object o2)
    {
        Car t1 = (Car)o1;
        Car t2 = (Car)o2;
        return String.Compare(t1.PetName, t2.PetName);
    }
}
```

The object user code is able to make use of this helper class. System.Array has a number of overloaded Sort() methods, one that just happens to take an object implementing IComparer (see Figure 7-11):

```
static void Main(string[] args)
{
...
    // Now sort by pet name.
    Array.Sort(myAutos, new PetNameComparer());

    // Dump sorted array.
    Console.WriteLine("Ordering by pet name:");
    foreach(Car c in myAutos)
        Console.WriteLine("{0} {1}", c.ID, c.PetName);
...
}
```

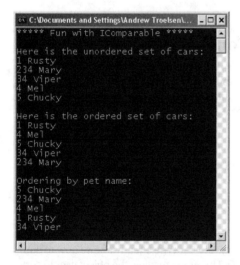

Figure 7-11. *Sorting automobiles by pet name*

Custom Properties, Custom Sort Types

It is worth pointing out that you can make use of a custom static property in order to help the object user along when sorting your Car types by a specific data point. Assume the Car class has added a static read-only property named SortByPetName that returns an instance of an object implementing the IComparer interface (PetNameComparer, in this case):

```
// We now support a custom property to return
// the correct IComparer interface.
public class Car : IComparable
{
    ...
    // Property to return the SortByPetName comparer.
    public static IComparer SortByPetName
    { get { return (IComparer)new PetNameComparer(); } }
}
```

The object user code can now sort by pet name using a strongly associated property, rather than just "having to know" to use the stand-alone PetNameComparer class type:

```
// Sorting by pet name made a bit cleaner.
Array.Sort(myAutos, Car.SortByPetName);
```

■**Source Code** The ComparableCar project is located under the Chapter 7 subdirectory.

Hopefully at this point, you not only understand how to define and implement interface types, but can understand their usefulness. To be sure, interfaces will be found within every major .NET namespace. To wrap up this chapter, let's check out the interfaces (and core classes) of the System.Collections namespace.

The Interfaces of the System.Collections Namespace

The most primitive container construct would have to be our good friend System.Array. As you have already seen in Chapter 3, this class provides a number of services (e.g., reversing, sorting, clearing, and enumerating). However, the simple Array class has a number of limitations, most notably it does not dynamically resize itself as you add or clear items. When you need to contain types in a more flexible container, you may wish to leverage the types defined within the System.Collections namespace (or as discussed in Chapter 10, the System.Collections.Generic namespace).

The System.Collections namespace defines a number of interfaces (some of which you have already implemented during the course of this chapter). As you can guess, a majority of the collection classes implement these interfaces to provide access to their contents. Table 7-2 gives a breakdown of the core collection-centric interfaces.

Table 7-2. *Interfaces of* System.Collections

System.Collections **Interface**	**Meaning in Life**
ICollection	Defines generic characteristics (e.g., count and thread safety) for a collection type.
IEqualityComparer	Defines methods to support the comparison of objects for equality.
IDictionary	Allows an object to represent its contents using name/value pairs.
IDictionaryEnumerator	Enumerates the contents of a type supporting IDictionary.
IEnumerable	Returns the IEnumerator interface for a given object.
IEnumerator	Generally supports foreach-style iteration of subtypes.
IHashCodeProvider	Returns the hash code for the implementing type using a customized hash algorithm.
IKeyComparer	(This interface is new to .NET 2.0.) Combines the functionality of IComparer and IHashCodeProvider to allow objects to be compared in a "hash-code-compatible manner" (e.g., if the objects are indeed equal, they must also return the same hash code value).
IList	Provides behavior to add, remove, and index items in a list of objects. Also, this interface defines members to determine whether the implementing collection type is read-only and/or a fixed-size container.

Many of these interfaces are related by an interface hierarchy, while others are stand-alone entities. Figure 7-12 illustrates the relationship between each type (recall that it is permissible for a single interface to derive from multiple interfaces).

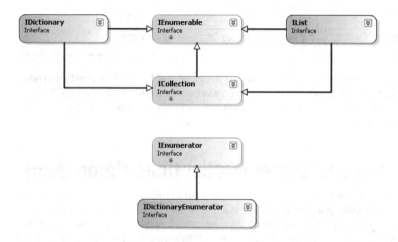

Figure 7-12. *The* System.Collections *interface hierarchy*

The Role of ICollection

The ICollection interface is the most primitive interface of the System.Collections namespace in that it defines a behavior supported by a collection type. In a nutshell, this interface provides a small set of properties that allow you to determine (a) the number of items in the container, (b) the thread safety of the container, as well as (c) the ability to copy the contents into a System.Array type. Formally, ICollection is defined as follows (note that ICollection extends IEnumerable):

```
public interface ICollection : IEnumerable
{
    // IEnumerable member...
    int Count { get; }
    bool IsSynchronized { get; }
    object SyncRoot { get; }
    void CopyTo(Array array, int index);
}
```

The Role of IDictionary

As you may already be aware, a *dictionary* is simply a collection that maintains a set of name/value pairs. For example, you could build a custom type that implements IDictionary such that you can store Car types (the values) that may be retrieved by ID or pet name (e.g., names). Given this functionality, you can see that the IDictionary interface defines a Keys and Values property as well as Add(), Remove(), and Contains() methods. The individual items may be obtained by the type indexer. Here is the formal definition:

```
public interface IDictionary :
    ICollection, IEnumerable
{
```

```
    bool IsFixedSize { get; }
    bool IsReadOnly { get; }
    object this[ object key ] { get; set; }
    ICollection Keys { get; }
    ICollection Values { get; }
    void Add(object key, object value);
    void Clear();
    bool Contains(object key);
    IDictionaryEnumerator GetEnumerator();
    void Remove(object key);
}
```

The Role of IDictionaryEnumerator

If you were paying attention, you may have noted that IDictionary.GetEnumerator() returns an instance of the IDictionaryEnumerator type. IDictionaryEnumerator is simply a strongly typed enumerator, given that it extends IEnumerator by adding the following functionality:

```
public interface IDictionaryEnumerator : IEnumerator
{
    // IEnumerator methods...
    DictionaryEntry Entry { get; }
    object Key { get; }
    object Value { get; }
}
```

Notice how IDictionaryEnumerator allows you to enumerate over items in the dictionary via the generic Entry property, which returns a System.Collections.DictionaryEntry class type. In addition, you are also able to traverse the name/value pairs using the Key/Value properties.

The Role of IList

The final key interface of System.Collections is IList, which provides the ability to insert, remove, and index items into (or out of) a container:

```
public interface IList :
    ICollection, IEnumerable
{
    bool IsFixedSize { get; }
    bool IsReadOnly { get; }
    object this[ int index ] { get; set; }
    int Add(object value);
    void Clear();
    bool Contains(object value);
    int IndexOf(object value);
    void Insert(int index, object value);
    void Remove(object value);
    void RemoveAt(int index);
}
```

The Class Types of System.Collections

As I hope you understand by this point in the chapter, interfaces by themselves are not very useful until they are implemented by a given class or structure. Table 7-3 provides a rundown of the core classes in the System.Collections namespace and the key interfaces they support.

Table 7-3. *Classes of* System.Collections

System.Collections **Class**	**Meaning in Life**	**Key Implemented Interfaces**
ArrayList	Represents a dynamically sized array of objects.	IList, ICollection, IEnumerable, and ICloneable
Hashtable	Represents a collection of objects identified by a numerical key. Custom types stored in a Hashtable should always override System.Object.GetHashCode().	IDictionary, ICollection, IEnumerable, and ICloneable
Queue	Represents a standard first-in, first-out (FIFO) queue.	ICollection, ICloneable, and IEnumerable
SortedList	Like a dictionary; however, the elements can also be accessed by ordinal position (e.g., index).	IDictionary, ICollection, IEnumerable, and ICloneable
Stack	A last-in, first-out (LIFO) queue providing push and pop (and peek) functionality.	ICollection, ICloneable, and IEnumerable

In addition to these key types, System.Collections defines some minor players (at least in terms of their day-to-day usefulness) such as BitArray, CaseInsensitiveComparer, and Case-InsensitiveHashCodeProvider. Furthermore, this namespace also defines a small set of abstract base classes (CollectionBase, ReadOnlyCollectionBase, and DictionaryBase) that can be used to build strongly typed containers.

As you begin to experiment with the System.Collections types, you will find they all tend to share common functionality (that's the point of interface-based programming). Thus, rather than listing out the members of each and every collection class, the next task of this chapter is to illustrate how to interact with three common collection types: ArrayList, Queue, and Stack. Once you understand the functionality of these types, gaining an understanding of the remaining collection classes should naturally follow (especially since each of the types is fully documented within online help).

Working with the ArrayList Type

The ArrayList type is bound to be your most frequently used type in the System.Collections namespace in that it allows you to dynamically resize the contents at your whim. To illustrate the basics of this type, ponder the following code, which leverages the ArrayList to manipulate a set of Car objects:

```
static void Main(string[] args)
{
    // Create ArrayList and fill with some initial values.
    ArrayList carArList = new ArrayList();
    carArList.AddRange(new Car[] { new Car("Fred", 90, 10),
        new Car("Mary", 100, 50), new Car("MB", 190, 11)});
    Console.WriteLine("Items in carArList: {0}", carArList.Count);

    // Print out current values.
    foreach(Car c in carArList)
        Console.WriteLine("Car pet name: {0}", c.PetName);

    // Insert a new item.
    Console.WriteLine("\n->Inserting new Car.");
    carArList.Insert(2, new Car("TheNewCar", 0, 12));
    Console.WriteLine("Items in carArList: {0}", carArList.Count);
```

```
// Get object array from ArrayList and print again.
object[] arrayOfCars = carArList.ToArray();
for(int i = 0; i < arrayOfCars.Length; i++)
{
    Console.WriteLine("Car pet name: {0}",
        ((Car)arrayOfCars[i]).PetName);
}
}
```

Here you are making use of the AddRange() method to populate your ArrayList with a set of Car types (as you can tell, this is basically a shorthand notation for calling Add() *n* number of times). Once you print out the number of items in the collection (as well as enumerate over each item to obtain the pet name), you invoke Insert(). As you can see, Insert() allows you to plug a new item into the ArrayList at a specified index. Finally, notice the call to the ToArray() method, which returns a generic array of System.Object types based on the contents of the original ArrayList. Figure 7-13 shows the output.

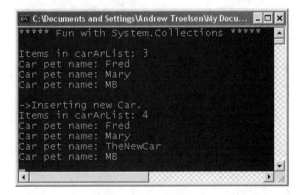

Figure 7-13. *Fun with* System.Collections.ArrayList

Working with the Queue Type

Queues are containers that ensure items are accessed using a first-in, first-out manner. Sadly, we humans are subject to queues all day long: lines at the bank, lines at the movie theater, and lines at the morning coffeehouse. When you are modeling a scenario in which items are handled on a first-come, first-served basis, System.Collections.Queue is your type of choice. In addition to the functionality provided by the supported interfaces, Queue defines the key members shown in Table 7-4.

Table 7-4. *Members of the* Queue *Type*

Member of System.Collection.Queue	Meaning in Life
Dequeue()	Removes and returns the object at the beginning of the Queue
Enqueue()	Adds an object to the end of the Queue
Peek()	Returns the object at the beginning of the Queue without removing it

To illustrate these methods, we will leverage our automobile theme once again and build a Queue object that simulates a line of cars waiting to enter a car wash. First, assume the following static helper method:

```
public static void WashCar(Car c)
{
    Console.WriteLine("Cleaning {0}", c.PetName);
}
```

Now, ponder the following code:

```
static void Main(string[] args)
{
...
    // Make a Q with three items.
    Queue carWashQ = new Queue();
    carWashQ.Enqueue(new Car("FirstCar", 0, 1));
    carWashQ.Enqueue(new Car("SecondCar", 0, 2));
    carWashQ.Enqueue(new Car("ThirdCar", 0, 3));

    // Peek at first car in Q.
    Console.WriteLine("First in Q is {0}",
        ((Car)carWashQ.Peek()).PetName);

    // Remove each item from Q.
    WashCar((Car)carWashQ.Dequeue());
    WashCar((Car)carWashQ.Dequeue());
    WashCar((Car)carWashQ.Dequeue());

    // Try to de-Q again?
    try
    { WashCar((Car)carWashQ.Dequeue()); }
    catch(Exception e)
    { Console.WriteLine("Error!! {0}", e.Message);}
}
```

Here, you insert three items into the Queue type via its Enqueue() method. The call to Peek() allows you to view (but not remove) the first item currently in the Queue, which in this case is the car named FirstCar. Finally, the call to Dequeue() removes the item from the line and sends it into the WashCar() helper function for processing. Do note that if you attempt to remove items from an empty queue, a runtime exception is thrown.

Working with the Stack Type

The System.Collections.Stack type represents a collection that maintains items using a last-in, first-out manner. As you would expect, Stack defines a member named Push() and Pop() (to place items onto or remove items from the stack). The following stack example makes use of the standard System.String:

```
static void Main(string[] args)
{
...
    Stack stringStack = new Stack();
    stringStack.Push("One");
    stringStack.Push("Two");
    stringStack.Push("Three");
```

```
// Now look at the top item, pop it, and look again.
Console.WriteLine("Top item is: {0}", stringStack.Peek());
Console.WriteLine("Popped off {0}", stringStack.Pop());
Console.WriteLine("Top item is: {0}", stringStack.Peek());
Console.WriteLine("Popped off {0}", stringStack.Pop());
Console.WriteLine("Top item is: {0}", stringStack.Peek());
Console.WriteLine("Popped off {0}", stringStack.Pop());

try
{
    Console.WriteLine("Top item is: {0}", stringStack.Peek());
    Console.WriteLine("Popped off {0}", stringStack.Pop());
}
catch(Exception e)
{ Console.WriteLine("Error!! {0}", e.Message);}
}
```

Here, you build a stack that contains three string types (named according to their order of insertion). As you peek onto the stack, you will always see the item at the very top, and therefore the first call to Peek() reveals the third string. After a series of Pop() and Peek() calls, the stack is eventually empty, at which time additional Peek()/Pop() calls raise a system exception.

■**Source Code** The CollectionTypes project can be found under the Chapter 7 subdirectory.

System.Collections.Specialized Namespace

In addition to the types defined within the System.Collections namespace, you should also be aware that the .NET base class libraries provide the System.Collections.Specialized namespace, which defines another set of types that are more (pardon the redundancy) specialized. For example, the StringDictionary and ListDictionary types each provide a stylized implementation of the IDictionary interface. Table 7-5 documents the key class types.

Table 7-5. *Types of the* System.Collections.Specialized *Namespace*

Member of System.Collections.Specialized	**Meaning in Life**
CollectionsUtil	Creates collections that ignore the case in strings.
HybridDictionary	Implements IDictionary by using a ListDictionary while the collection is small, and then switching to a Hashtable when the collection gets large.
ListDictionary	Implements IDictionary using a singly linked list. Recommended for collections that typically contain ten items or fewer.
NameValueCollection	Represents a sorted collection of associated String keys and String values that can be accessed either with the key or with the index.
StringCollection	Represents a collection of strings.
StringDictionary	Implements a hashtable with the key strongly typed to be a string rather than an object.
StringEnumerator	Supports a simple iteration over a StringCollection.

Summary

An interface can be defined as a named collection of *abstract members*. Because an interface does not provide any implementation details, it is common to regard an interface as a behavior that may be supported by a given type. When two or more classes implement the same interface, you are able to treat each type the same way (aka interface-based polymorphism).

C# provides the `interface` keyword to allow you to define a new interface. As you have seen, a type can support as many interfaces as necessary using a comma-delimited list. Furthermore, it is permissible to build interfaces that derive from multiple base interfaces.

In addition to building your custom interfaces, the .NET libraries define a number of standard (i.e., framework-supplied) interfaces. As you have seen, you are free to build custom types that implement these predefined interfaces to gain a number of desirable traits such as cloning, sorting, and enumerating. Finally, you spent some time investigating the stock collection classes defined within the `System.Collections` namespace and examining a number of common interfaces used by the collection-centric types.

CHAPTER 8

■ ■ ■

Callback Interfaces, Delegates, and Events

Up to this point in the text, every application you have developed added various bits of code to Main(), which, in some way or another, sent requests to a given object. However, you have not yet examined how an object can talk back to the entity that created it. In most programs, it is quite common for objects in a system to engage in a two-way conversation through the use of callback interfaces, events, and other programming constructs. To set the stage, this chapter begins by examining how interface types may be used to enable callback functionality.

Next, you learn about the .NET delegate type, which is a type-safe object that "points to" other method(s) that can be invoked at a later time. Unlike a traditional C++ function pointer, however, .NET delegates are objects that have built-in support for multicasting and asynchronous method invocation. We will examine the asynchronous behavior of delegate types later in this text during our examination of the System.Threading namespace (see Chapter 14).

Once you learn how to create and manipulate delegate types, you then investigate the C# event keyword, which simplifies and streamlines the process of working with delegate types. Finally, this chapter examines new delegate-and-event-centric language features of C#, including anonymous methods and method group conversions. As you will see, these techniques are shorthand notations for capturing the target of a given event.

Understanding Callback Interfaces

As you have seen in the previous chapter, interfaces define a behavior that may be supported by various types in your system. Beyond using interfaces to establish polymorphism, interfaces may also be used as a *callback mechanism*. This technique enables objects to engage in a two-way conversation using a common set of members.

To illustrate the use of callback interfaces, let's update the now familiar Car type in such a way that it is able to inform the caller when it is about to explode (the current speed is 10 miles below the maximum speed) and has exploded (the current speed is at or above the maximum speed). The ability to send and receive these events will be facilitated with a custom interface named IEngineEvents:

```
// The callback interface.
public interface IEngineEvents
{
    void AboutToBlow(string msg);
    void Exploded(string msg);
}
```

Event interfaces are not typically implemented directly by the object directly interested in receiving the events, but rather by a helper object called a *sink object*. The sender of the events (the Car type in this case) will make calls on the sink under the appropriate circumstances. Assume the sink class is called CarEventSink, which simply prints out the incoming messages to the console. Beyond this point, our sink will also maintain a string that identifies its friendly name:

```
// Car event sink.
public class CarEventSink : IEngineEvents
{
    private string name;
    public CarEventSink(){}
    public CarEventSink(string sinkName)
    { name = sinkName; }

    public void AboutToBlow(string msg)
    { Console.WriteLine("{0} reporting: {1}", name, msg); }
    public void Exploded(string msg)
    { Console.WriteLine("{0} reporting: {1}", name, msg); }
}
```

Now that you have a sink object that implements the event interface, your next task is to pass a reference to this sink into the Car type. The Car holds onto the reference and makes calls back on the sink when appropriate. In order to allow the Car to obtain a reference to the sink, we will need to add a public helper member to the Car type that we will call Advise(). Likewise, if the caller wishes to detach from the event source, it may call another helper method on the Car type named Unadvise(). Finally, in order to allow the caller to register multiple event sinks (for the purposes of multicasting), the Car now maintains an ArrayList to represent each outstanding connection:

```
// This Car and caller can now communicate
// using the IEngineEvents interface.
public class Car
{
    // The set of connected sinks.
    ArrayList clientSinks = new ArrayList();

    // Attach or disconnect from the source of events.
    public void Advise(IEngineEvents sink)
    {   clientSinks.Add(sink); }

    public void Unadvise(IEngineEvents sink)
    {   clientSinks.Remove(sink); }
...
}
```

To actually send the events, let's update the Car.Accelerate() method to iterate over the list of connections maintained by the ArrayList and fire the correct notification when appropriate (note the Car class now maintains a Boolean member variable named carIsDead to represent the engine's state):

```
// Interface-based event protocol!
class Car
{
...
    // Is the car alive or dead?
    bool carIsDead;

    public void Accelerate(int delta)
    {
```

```
        // If the car is 'dead', send Exploded event to each sink.
        if(carIsDead)
        {
            foreach(IEngineEvents e in clientSinks)
                e.Exploded("Sorry, this car is dead...");
        }
        else
        {
            currSpeed += delta;

            // Send AboutToBlow event.
            if(10 == maxSpeed - currSpeed)
            {
                foreach(IEngineEvents e in clientSinks)
                    e.AboutToBlow("Careful buddy!  Gonna blow!");
            }

            if(currSpeed >= maxSpeed)
                carIsDead = true;
            else
                Console.WriteLine("\tCurrSpeed = {0} ", currSpeed);
        }
}
```

Here is some client-side code, now making use of a callback interface to listen to the Car events:

```
// Make a car and listen to the events.
public class CarApp
{
    static void Main(string[] args)
    {
        Console.WriteLine("***** Interfaces as event enablers *****");
        Car c1 = new Car("SlugBug", 100, 10);

        // Make sink object.
        CarEventSink sink = new CarEventSink();

        // Pass the Car a reference to the sink.
        c1.Advise(sink);

        // Speed up (this will trigger the events).
        for(int i = 0; i < 10; i++)
            c1.Accelerate(20);

        // Detach from event source.
        c1.Unadvise(sink);
        Console.ReadLine();
    }
}
```

Figure 8-1 shows the end result of this interface-based event protocol.

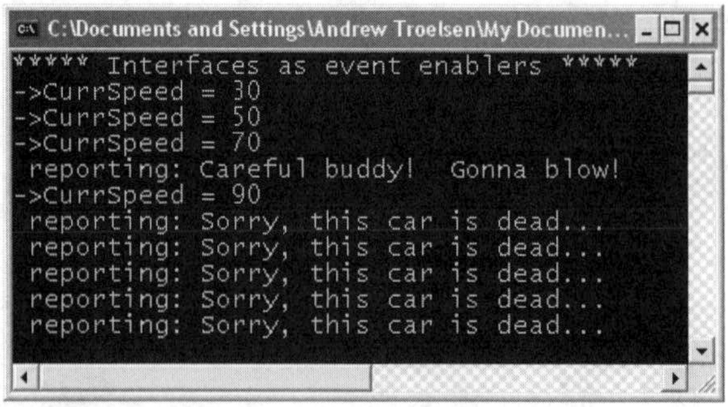

Figure 8-1. *An interface-based event protocol*

Do note that the Unadvise() method can be very helpful in that it allows the caller to selectively detach from an event source at will. Here, you call Unadvise() before exiting Main(), although this is not technically necessary. However, assume that the application now wishes to register two sinks, dynamically remove a particular sink during the flow of execution, and continue processing the program at large:

```
static void Main(string[] args)
{
    Console.WriteLine("***** Interfaces as event enablers *****");
    Car c1 = new Car("SlugBug", 100, 10);

    // Make 2 sink objects.
    Console.WriteLine("***** Creating sinks *****");
    CarEventSink sink = new CarEventSink("First sink");
    CarEventSink myOtherSink = new CarEventSink("Other sink");

    // Hand sinks to Car.
    Console.WriteLine("\n***** Sending 2 sinks into Car *****");
    c1.Advise(sink);
    c1.Advise(myOtherSink);

    // Speed up (this will generate the events).
    Console.WriteLine("\n***** Speeding up *****");
    for(int i = 0; i < 10; i++)
        c1.Accelerate(20);

    // Detach first sink from events.
    Console.WriteLine("\n***** Removing first sink *****");
    c1.Unadvise(sink);

    // Speed up again (only myOtherSink will be called).
    Console.WriteLine("\n***** Speeding up again *****");
    for(int i = 0; i < 10; i++)
        c1.Accelerate(20);

    // Detach other sink from events.
    Console.WriteLine("\n***** Removing second sink *****");
    c1.Unadvise(myOtherSink);
    Console.ReadLine();
}
```

Event interfaces can be helpful in that they can be used under any language or platform (.NET, J2EE, or otherwise) that supports interface-based programming. However, as you may be suspecting, the .NET platform defines an "official" event protocol. To understand this intrinsic event architecture, we begin by examining the role of the delegate type.

■**Source Code** The EventInterface project is located under the Chapter 8 subdirectory.

Understanding the .NET Delegate Type

Before formally defining .NET delegates, let's gain a bit of perspective. Historically speaking, the Windows API makes frequent use of C-style function pointers to create entities termed *callback functions* or simply *callbacks*. Using callbacks, programmers were able to configure one function to report back to (call back) another function in the application.

The problem with standard C-style callback functions is that they represent little more than a raw address in memory. Ideally, callbacks could be configured to include additional type-safe information such as the number of (and types of) parameters and the return value (if any) of the method pointed to. Sadly, this is not the case in traditional callback functions, and, as you may suspect, can therefore be a frequent source of bugs, hard crashes, and other runtime disasters.

Nevertheless, callbacks are useful entities. In the .NET Framework, callbacks are still possible, and their functionality is accomplished in a much safer and more object-oriented manner using *delegates*. In essence, a delegate is a type-safe object that points to another method (or possibly multiple methods) in the application, which can be invoked at a later time. Specifically speaking, a delegate type maintains three important pieces of information:

- The *name* of the method on which it makes calls
- The *arguments* (if any) of this method
- The *return value* (if any) of this method

■**Note** Unlike C(++) function pointers, .NET delegates can point to either static or instance methods.

Once a delegate has been created and provided the aforementioned information, it may dynamically invoke the method(s) it points to at runtime. As you will see, every delegate in the .NET Framework (including your custom delegates) is automatically endowed with the ability to call their methods *synchronously* or *asynchronously*. This fact greatly simplifies programming tasks, given that we can call a method on a secondary thread of execution without manually creating and managing a Thread object. We will examine the asynchronous behavior of delegate types during our investigation of the System. Threading namespace in Chapter 14.

Defining a Delegate in C#

When you want to create a delegate in C#, you make use of the delegate keyword. The name of your delegate can be whatever you desire. However, you must define the delegate to match the signature of the method it will point to. For example, assume you wish to build a delegate named BinaryOp that can point to any method that returns an integer and takes two integers as input parameters:

```
// This delegate can point to any method,
// taking two integers and returning an
// integer.
public delegate int BinaryOp(int x, int y);
```

When the C# compiler processes delegate types, it automatically generates a sealed class deriving from System.MulticastDelegate. This class (in conjunction with its base class, System.Delegate) provides the necessary infrastructure for the delegate to hold onto the list of methods to be invoked at a later time. For example, if you examine the BinaryOp delegate using ildasm.exe, you would find the items shown in Figure 8-2.

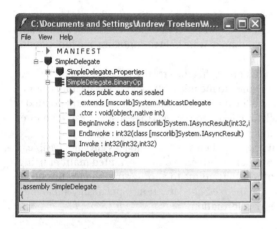

Figure 8-2. *The C# * delegate *keyword represents a sealed type deriving from* System.MulticastDelegate.

As you can see, the generated BinaryOp class defines three public methods. Invoke() is perhaps the core method, as it is used to invoke each method maintained by the delegate type in a *synchronous* manner, meaning the caller must wait for the call to complete before continuing on its way. Strangely enough, the synchronous Invoke() method is *not* directly callable from C#. As you will see in just a bit, Invoke() is called behind the scenes when you make use of the appropriate C# syntax.

BeginInvoke() and EndInvoke() provide the ability to call the current method *asynchronously* on a second thread of execution. If you have a background in multithreading, you are aware that one of the most common reason developers create secondary threads of execution is to invoke methods that require time to complete. Although the .NET base class libraries provide an entire namespace devoted to multithreaded programming (System.Threading), delegates provide this functionality out of the box.

Now, how exactly does the compiler know how to define the Invoke(), BeginInvoke(), and EndInvoke() methods? To understand the process, here is the crux of the generated BinaryOp class type (**bold** marks the items specified by the defined delegate type):

```
sealed class BinaryOp : System.MulticastDelegate
{
    public BinaryOp(object target, uint functionAddress);
    public int Invoke(int x, int y);
    public IAsyncResult BeginInvoke(int x, int y,
        AsyncCallback cb, object state);
    public int EndInvoke(IAsyncResult result);
}
```

First, notice that the parameters and return value defined for the Invoke() method exactly match the definition of the BinaryOp delegate. The initial parameters to BeginInvoke() members (two integers in our case) are also based on the BinaryOp delegate; however, BeginInvoke() will always provide two final parameters (of type AsyncCallback and object) that are used to facilitate asynchronous method invocations. Finally, the return value of EndInvoke() is identical to the original delegate declaration and will always take as a sole parameter an object implementing the IAsyncResult interface.

Let's see another example. Assume you have defined a delegate type that can point to any method returning a string and receiving three System.Boolean input parameters:

```
public delegate string MyDelegate(bool a, bool b, bool c);
```

This time, the auto-generated class breaks down as follows:

```
sealed class MyDelegate : System.MulticastDelegate
{
    public MyDelegate(object target, uint functionAddress);
    public string Invoke(bool a, bool b, bool c);
    public IAsyncResult BeginInvoke(bool a, bool b, bool c,
        AsyncCallback cb, object state);
    public string EndInvoke(IAsyncResult result);
}
```

Delegates can also "point to" methods that contain any number of out or ref parameters. For example, assume the following delegate type:

```
public delegate string MyOtherDelegate(out bool a, ref bool b, int c);
```

The signatures of the Invoke() and BeginInvoke() methods look as you would expect; however, check out the EndInvoke() method, which now includes the set of all out/ref arguments defined by the delegate type:

```
sealed class MyOtherDelegate : System.MulticastDelegate
{
    public MyOtherDelegate (object target, uint functionAddress);
    public string Invoke(out bool a, ref bool b, int c);
    public IAsyncResult BeginInvoke(out bool a, ref bool b, int c,
        AsyncCallback cb, object state);
    public string EndInvoke(out bool a, ref bool b, IAsyncResult result);
}
```

To summarize, a C# delegate definition results in a sealed class with three compiler-generated methods whose parameter and return types are based on the delegate's declaration. The following pseudo-code approximates the basic pattern:

```
// This is only pseudo-code!
public sealed class DelegateName : System.MulticastDelegate
{
    public DelegateName (object target, uint functionAddress);
    public delegateReturnValue Invoke(allDelegateInputRefAndOutParams);
    public IAsyncResult BeginInvoke(allDelegateInputRefAndOutParams,
        AsyncCallback cb, object state);
    public delegateReturnValue EndInvoke(allDelegateRefAndOutParams,
        IAsyncResult result);
}
```

The System.MulticastDelegate and System. Delegate Base Classes

So, when you build a type using the C# delegate keyword, you indirectly declare a class type that derives from System.MulticastDelegate. This class provides descendents with access to a list that contains the addresses of the methods maintained by the delegate type, as well as several additional methods (and a few overloaded operators) to interact with the invocation list. Here are some select members of System.MulticastDelegate:

```
[Serializable]
public abstract class MulticastDelegate : Delegate
{
    // Methods
    public sealed override Delegate[] GetInvocationList();

    // Overloaded operators
    public static bool operator ==(MulticastDelegate d1, MulticastDelegate d2);
    public static bool operator !=(MulticastDelegate d1, MulticastDelegate d2);

    // Fields
    private IntPtr _invocationCount;
    private object _invocationList;
}
```

System.MulticastDelegate obtains additional functionality from its parent class, System. Delegate. Here is a partial snapshot of the class definition:

```
[Serializable, ClassInterface(ClassInterfaceType.AutoDual)]
public abstract class Delegate : ICloneable, ISerializable
{
    // Methods
    public static Delegate Combine(params Delegate[] delegates);
    public static Delegate Combine(Delegate a, Delegate b);
    public virtual Delegate[] GetInvocationList();
    public static Delegate Remove(Delegate source, Delegate value);
    public static Delegate RemoveAll(Delegate source, Delegate value);

    // Overloaded operators
    public static bool operator ==(Delegate d1, Delegate d2);
    public static bool operator !=( Delegate d1, Delegate d2);

    // Properties
    public MethodInfo Method { get; }
    public object Target { get; }
}
```

Now, remember that you will never directly derive from these base classes and can typically concern yourself only with the members documented in Table 8-1.

Table 8-1. *Select Members of* System.MultcastDelegate/System.Delegate

Inherited Member	Meaning in Life
Method	This property returns a System.Reflection.MethodInfo type that represents details of a static method that is maintained by the delegate.
Target	If the method to be called is defined at the object level (rather than a static method), Target returns an object that represents the method maintained by the delegate. If the value returned from Target equals null, the method to be called is a static member.
Combine()	This static method adds a method to the list maintained by the delegate. In C#, you trigger this method using the overloaded += operator as a shorthand notation.
GetInvocationList()	This method returns an array of System.Delegate types, each representing a particular method that may be invoked.
Remove() RemoveAll()	These static methods removes a method (or all methods) from the invocation list. In C#, the Remove() method can be called indirectly using the overloaded -= operator.

The Simplest Possible Delegate Example

Delegates can tend to cause a great deal of confusion when encountered for the first time. Thus, to get the ball rolling, let's take a look at a very simple example that leverages our BinaryOp delegate type. Here is the complete code, with analysis to follow:

```
namespace SimpleDelegate
{
    // This delegate can point to any method,
    // taking two integers and returning an
    // integer.
    public delegate int BinaryOp(int x, int y);

    // This class contains methods BinaryOp will
    // point to.
    public class SimpleMath
    {
        public static int Add(int x, int y)
        { return x + y; }
        public static int Subtract(int x, int y)
        { return x - y; }
    }

    class Program
    {
        static void Main(string[] args)
        {
            Console.WriteLine("***** Simple Delegate Example *****\n");

            // Create a BinaryOp object that
            // "points to" SimpleMath.Add().
            BinaryOp b = new BinaryOp(SimpleMath.Add);
```

```
        // Invoke Add() method using delegate.
        Console.WriteLine("10 + 10 is {0}", b(10, 10));
        Console.ReadLine();
      }
    }
}
```

Again notice the format of the BinaryOp delegate, which can point to any method taking two integers and returning an integer. Given this, we have created a class named SimpleMath, which defines two static methods that (surprise, surprise) match the pattern defined by the BinaryOp delegate.

When you want to insert the target method to a given delegate, simply pass in the name of the method to the delegate's constructor. At this point, you are able to invoke the member pointed to using a syntax that looks like a direct function invocation:

```
// Invoke() is really called here!
Console.WriteLine("10 + 10 is {0}", b(10, 10));
```

Under the hood, the runtime actually calls the compiler-generated Invoke() method. You can verify this fact for yourself if you open your assembly in ildasm.exe and investigate the CIL code within the Main() method:

```
.method private hidebysig static void Main(string[] args) cil managed
{
...
    .locals init ([0] class SimpleDelegate.BinaryOp b)
    ldftn int32 SimpleDelegate.SimpleMath::Add(int32, int32)
...
    newobj instance void SimpleDelegate.BinaryOp::.ctor(object, native int)
    stloc.0
    ldstr "10 + 10 is {0}"
    ldloc.0
    ldc.i4.s 10
    ldc.i4.s 10
    callvirt instance int32 SimpleDelegate.BinaryOp::Invoke(int32, int32)
...
}
```

Recall that .NET delegates (unlike C-style function pointers) are *type safe*. Therefore, if you attempt to pass a delegate a method that does not "match the pattern," you receive a compile-time error. To illustrate, assume the SimpleMath class defines an additional method named SquareNumber():

```
public class SimpleMath
{
...
    public static int SquareNumber(int a)
    { return a * a; }
}
```

Given that the BinaryOp delegate can *only* point to methods that take two integers and return an integer, the following code is illegal and will not compile:

```
// Error! Method does not match delegate pattern!
BinaryOp b = new BinaryOp(SimpleMath.SquareNumber);
```

Investigating a Delegate Object

Let's spice up the current example by creating a helper function named DisplayDelegateInfo(). This method will print out names of the methods maintained by the incoming System.Delegate-derived type as well as the name of the class defining the method. To do so, we will iterate over the

System.Delegate array returned by GetInvocationList(), invoking each object's Target and Method properties:

```
static void DisplayDelegateInfo(Delegate delObj)
{
    // Print the names of each member in the
    // delegate's invocation list.
    foreach (Delegate d in delObj.GetInvocationList())
    {
        Console.WriteLine("Method Name: {0}", d.Method);
        Console.WriteLine("Type Name: {0}", d.Target);
    }
}
```

Assuming you have updated your Main() method to actually call this new helper method, you would find the output shown in Figure 8-3.

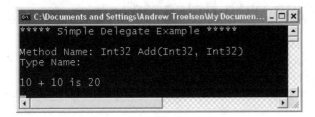

Figure 8-3. *Examining a delegate's invocation list*

Notice that the name of the type (SimpleMath) is currently not displayed by the Target property. The reason has to do with the fact that our BinaryOp delegate is pointing to *static* methods and therefore there is no object to reference! However, if we update the Add() and Subtract methods to be nonstatic, we could create an instance of the SimpleMath type and specify the methods to invoke as follows:

```
static void Main(string[] args)
{
    Console.WriteLine("***** Simple Delegate Example *****\n");

    // .NET delegates can also point to instance methods.
    SimpleMath m = new SimpleMath();
    BinaryOp b = new BinaryOp(m.Add);

    // Show information about this object.
    DisplayDelegateInfo(b);

    Console.WriteLine("\n10 + 10 is {0}", b(10, 10));
    Console.ReadLine();
}
```

In this case, we would find the output shown in Figure 8-4.

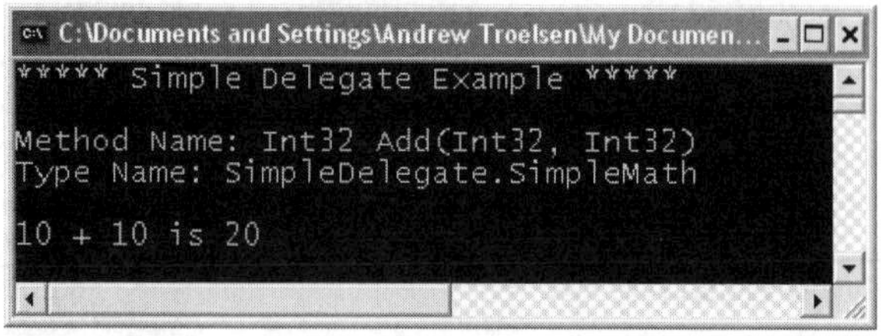

Figure 8-4. *Examining a delegate's invocation list (once again)*

■Source Code The SimpleDelegate project is located under the Chapter 8 subdirectory.

Retrofitting the Car Type with Delegates

Clearly, the previous SimpleDelegate example was intended to be purely illustrative in nature, given that there would be no reason to build a delegate simply to add two numbers. Hopefully, however, this example demystifies the process of working with delegate types. To provide a more realistic use of delegate types, let's retrofit our Car type to send the Exploded and AboutToBlow notifications using .NET delegates rather than a custom callback interface. Beyond no longer implementing IEngineEvents, here are the steps we will need to take:

- Define the AboutToBlow and Exploded delegates.

- Declare member variables of each delegate type in the Car class.

- Create helper functions on the Car that allow the caller to specify the methods maintained by the delegate member variables.

- Update the Accelerate() method to invoke the delegate's invocation list under the correct circumstances.

Ponder the following updated Car class, which addresses the first three points:

```
public class Car
{
    // Define the delegate types.
    public delegate void AboutToBlow(string msg);
    public delegate void Exploded (string msg);

    // Define member variables of each delegate type.
    private AboutToBlow almostDeadList;
    private Exploded explodedList;

    // Add members to the invocation lists using helper methods.
    public void OnAboutToBlow(AboutToBlow clientMethod)
    { almostDeadList = clientMethod; }
    public void OnExploded(Exploded clientMethod)
    { explodedList = clientMethod; }
...
}
```

Notice in this example that we define the delegate types directly within the scope of the Car type. As you explore the base class libraries, you will find it is quite common to define a delegate within the scope of the type it naturally works with. On a related note, given that the compiler transforms a delegate into a full class definition, what we have actually done is create two nested classes.

Next, note that we declare two member variables (one for each delegate type) and two helper functions (OnAboutToBlow() and OnExploded()) that allow the client to add a method to the delegates invocation list. In concept, these methods are similar to the Advise() and Unadvise() method we created during the EventInterface example. Of course, in this case, the incoming parameter is a client-allocated delegate object rather than a class implementing a specific interface.

At this point, we need to update the Accelerate() method to invoke each delegate, rather than iterate over an ArrayList of client-side sinks (as we did in the EventInterface example). Here is the update:

```
public void Accelerate(int delta)
{
    // If the car is dead, fire Exploded event.
    if (carIsDead)
    {
        if (explodedList != null)
            explodedList("Sorry, this car is dead...");
    }
    else
    {
        currSpeed += delta;

        // Almost dead?
        if (10 == maxSpeed - currSpeed
            && almostDeadList != null)
        {
            almostDeadList("Careful buddy!  Gonna blow!");
        }

        // Still OK!
        if (currSpeed >= maxSpeed)
            carIsDead = true;
        else
            Console.WriteLine("->CurrSpeed = {0}", currSpeed);
    }
}
```

Notice that before we invoke the methods maintained by the almostDeadList and explodedList member variables, we are checking them against a null value. The reason is that it will be the job of the caller to allocate these objects by calling the OnAboutToBlow() and OnExploded() helper methods. If the caller does not call these methods, and we attempt to invoke the delegate's invocation list, we will trigger a NullReferenceException and bomb at runtime (which would obviously be a bad thing!).

Now that we have the delegate infrastructure in place, observe the updates to the Program class:

```
class Program
{
    static void Main(string[] args)
    {
        Console.WriteLine("***** Delegates as event enablers *****");

        // Make a car as usual.
        Car c1 = new Car("SlugBug", 100, 10);

        // Register event handlers with Car type.
        c1.OnAboutToBlow(new Car.AboutToBlow(CarAboutToBlow));
        c1.OnExploded(new Car.Exploded(CarExploded));
```

```
        // Speed up (this will trigger the events).
        Console.WriteLine("\n***** Speeding up *****");
        for (int i = 0; i < 6; i++)
            c1.Accelerate(20);
        Console.ReadLine();
    }

    // The Car will call these methods.
    public static void CarAboutToBlow(string msg)
    { Console.WriteLine(msg); }

    public static void CarExploded(string msg)
    { Console.WriteLine(msg); }
}
```

The only major point to be made here is the fact that the caller is the entity that assigns the delegate member variables via the helper registration methods. Also, because the AboutToBlow and Exploded delegates are nested within the Car class, we must allocate them using their full name (e.g., Car.AboutToBlow). Like any delegate constructor, we pass in the name of the method to add to the invocation list, which in this case are two static members on the Program class (if you wanted to wrap these methods in a new class, it would look very similar to the CarEventSink type of the EventInterface example).

Enabling Multicasting

Recall that .NET delegates have the intrinsic ability to *multicast*. In other words, a delegate object can maintain a list of methods to call, rather than a single method. When you wish to add multiple methods to a delegate object, you simply make use of the overloaded += operator, rather than a direct assignment. To enable multicasting on the Car type, we could update the OnAboutToBlow() and OnExploded() methods as follows:

```
public class Car
{
    // Add member to the invocation lists.
    public void OnAboutToBlow(AboutToBlow clientMethod)
    { almostDeadList += clientMethod; }

    public void OnExploded(Exploded clientMethod)
    { explodedList += clientMethod; }
...
}
```

With this, the caller can now register multiple targets:

```
class Program
{
    static void Main(string[] args)
    {
        Car c1 = new Car("SlugBug", 100, 10);

        // Register multiple event handlers!
        c1.OnAboutToBlow(new Car.AboutToBlow(CarAboutToBlow));
        c1.OnAboutToBlow(new Car.AboutToBlow(CarIsAlmostDoomed));
        c1.OnExploded(new Car.Exploded(CarExploded));
...
    }
```

```
// Car will call these.
public static void CarAboutToBlow(string msg)
{ Console.WriteLine(msg); }
public static void CarIsAlmostDoomed(string msg)
{ Console.WriteLine("Critical Message from Car: {0}", msg); }
public static void CarExploded(string msg)
{ Console.WriteLine(msg); }
}
```

In terms of CIL code, the += operator resolves to a call to the static Delegate.Combine() method (you could call Delegate.Combine() directly, but the += operator offers a simpler alternative). Ponder the following CIL implementation of OnAboutToBlow():

```
.method public hidebysig instance void OnAboutToBlow
    (class CarDelegate.Car/AboutToBlow clientMethod) cil managed
{
    .maxstack  8
    ldarg.0
    dup
    ldfld class CarDelegate.Car/AboutToBlow CarDelegate.Car::almostDeadList
    ldarg.1
    call class [mscorlib]System.Delegate
        [mscorlib]System.Delegate::Combine(
            class [mscorlib]System.Delegate,
            class [mscorlib]System.Delegate)
    castclass  CarDelegate.Car/AboutToBlow
    stfld class CarDelegate.Car/AboutToBlow CarDelegate.Car::almostDeadList
    ret
}
```

The Delegate class also defines a static Remove() method that allows a caller to dynamically remove a member from the invocation list. As you may be suspecting, C# developers can leverage the overloaded -= operator as a shorthand notation. If you wish to allow the caller the option to detach from the AboutToBlow and Exploded notifications, you could add the following additional helper methods to the Car type (note the -= operators at work):

```
public class Car
{
    // Remove member from the invocation lists.
    public void RemoveAboutToBlow(AboutToBlow clientMethod)
    { almostDeadList -= clientMethod; }

    public void RemoveExploded(Exploded clientMethod)
    { explodedList -= clientMethod; }
...
}
```

Again, the -= syntax is simply a shorthand notation for manually calling the static Delegate.Remove() method, as illustrated by the following CIL code for the RemoveAboutToBlow() member of the Car type:

```
.method public hidebysig instance void  RemoveAboutToBlow(class
CarDelegate.Car/AboutToBlow clientMethod) cil managed
{
    .maxstack  8
    ldarg.0
    dup
    ldfld class CarDelegate.Car/AboutToBlow CarDelegate.Car::almostDeadList
    ldarg.1
    call class [mscorlib]System.Delegate
```

```
        [mscorlib]System.Delegate::Remove(
        class [mscorlib]System.Delegate,
        class [mscorlib]System.Delegate)
    castclass CarDelegate.Car/AboutToBlow
    stfld class CarDelegate.Car/AboutToBlow CarDelegate.Car::almostDeadList
    ret
}
```

If the caller does indeed wish to remove an item from a delegate's invocation list, you will need to supply the same delegate object you added previously. Thus, we could stop receiving the Exploded notification by updating Main() as follows:

```
static void Main(string[] args)
{
    Car c1 = new Car("SlugBug", 100, 10);

    // Hold onto Car.Exploded delegate object for later use.
    Car.Exploded d = new Car.Exploded(CarExploded);
    c1.OnExploded(d);
...
    // Remove CarExploded method
    // from invocation list.
    c1.RemoveExploded(d);
...
}
```

The output of our CarDelegate application can be seen in Figure 8-5.

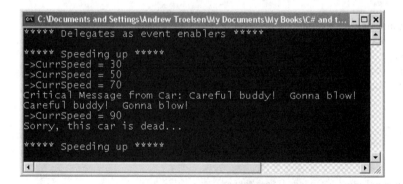

Figure 8-5. *The* CarDelegate *application at work*

■**Source Code** The CarDelegate project is located under the Chapter 8 subdirectory.

A More Elaborate Delegate Example

To illustrate a more advanced use of delegates, let's begin by updating the Car class to include two new Boolean member variables. The first is used to determine whether your automobile is due for a wash (isDirty); the other represents whether the car in question is in need of a tire rotation (shouldRotate). To enable the object user to interact with this new state data, Car also defines some additional properties and an updated constructor. Here is the story so far:

```
// Updated Car class.
public class Car
{
...
    // Are we in need of a wash? Need to rotate tires?
    private bool isDirty;
    private bool shouldRotate;

    // Extra params to set bools.
    public Car(string name, int max, int curr,
        bool washCar, bool rotateTires)
    {
        ...
        isDirty = washCar;
        shouldRotate = rotateTires;
    }
    public bool Dirty
    {
        get{  return isDirty; }
        set{  isDirty = value; }
    }
    public bool Rotate
    {
        get{  return shouldRotate; }
        set{  shouldRotate = value; }
    }
}
```

Now, also assume the Car type nests a new delegate, CarDelegate:

```
// Car defines yet another delegate.
public class Car
{
...
    // Can call any method taking a Car as
    // a parameter and returning nothing.
    public delegate void CarDelegate(Car c);
...
}
```

Here, you have created a delegate named CarDelegate. The CarDelegate type represents "some function" taking a Car as a parameter and returning void.

Delegates As Parameters

Now that you have a new delegate type that points to methods taking a Car parameter and returning nothing, you can create other functions that take this delegate as a parameter. To illustrate, assume you have a new class named Garage. This type maintains a collection of Car types contained in a System.Collections.ArrayList. Upon creation, the ArrayList is filled with some initial Car types:

```
// The Garage class maintains a list of Car types.
Using System.Collections;
...
public class Garage
{
    // A list of all cars in the garage.
    ArrayList theCars = new ArrayList();
```

```
    // Create the cars in the garage.
    public Garage()
    {
        // Recall, we updated the ctor to set isDirty and shouldRotate.
        theCars.Add(new Car("Viper", 100, 0, true, false));
        theCars.Add(new Car("Fred", 100, 0, false, false));
        theCars.Add(new Car("BillyBob", 100, 0, false, true));
    }
}
```

More importantly, the Garage class defines a public ProcessCars() method, which takes a single argument of our new delegate type (Car.CarDelegate). In the implementation of ProcessCars(), you pass each Car in your collection as a parameter to the "function pointed to" by the delegate. ProcessCars() also makes use of the Target and Method members of System.MulticastDelegate to determine exactly which function the delegate is currently pointing to:

```
// The Garage class has a method that makes use of the CarDelegate.
Using System.Collections;
...
public class Garage
{
...
    // This method takes a Car.CarDelegate as a parameter.
    public void ProcessCars(Car.CarDelegate proc)
    {
        // Where are we forwarding the call?
        Console.WriteLine("***** Calling: {0}  *****",
            proc.Method);

        // Are we calling an instance method or a static method?
        if(proc.Target != null)
            Console.WriteLine("->Target: {0} ", proc.Target);
        else
            Console.WriteLine("->Target is a static method");

        // Call the method "pointed to," passing in each car.
        foreach (Car c in theCars)
        {
            Console.WriteLine("\n-> Processing a Car");
            proc(c);
        }
    }
}
```

Like any delegate operation, when calling ProcessCars(), we send in the name of the method that should handle this request. Recall that these methods may be either static or instance level. For the sake of argument, assume these are instance members named WashCar() and RotateTires() that are defined by a new class named ServiceDepartment. Notice that these two methods are making use of the new Rotate and Dirty properties of the Car type.

```
// This class defines method to be invoked by
// the Car.CarDelegate type.
public class ServiceDepartment
{
    public void WashCar(Car c)
    {
```

```
        if(c.Dirty)
            Console.WriteLine("Cleaning a car");
        else
            Console.WriteLine("This car is already clean...");
    }

    public void RotateTires(Car c)
    {
        if(c.Rotate)
            Console.WriteLine("Tires have been rotated");
        else
            Console.WriteLine("Don't need to be rotated...");
    }
}
```

Now, to illustrate the interplay between the new Car.CarDelegate, Garage, and ServiceDepartment types, consider the following usage:

```
// The Garage delegates all work orders to the ServiceDepartment
// (finding a good mechanic is always a problem...)
public class Program
{
    static void Main(string[] args)
    {
        // Make the garage.
        Garage g = new Garage();

        // Make the service department.
        ServiceDepartment sd = new ServiceDepartment();

        // The Garage washes cars and rotates tires
        // by delegating to the ServiceDepartment.
        g.ProcessCars(new Car.CarDelegate(sd.WashCar));
        g.ProcessCars(new Car.CarDelegate(sd.RotateTires));
        Console.ReadLine();
    }
}
```

Figure 8-6 shows the current output.

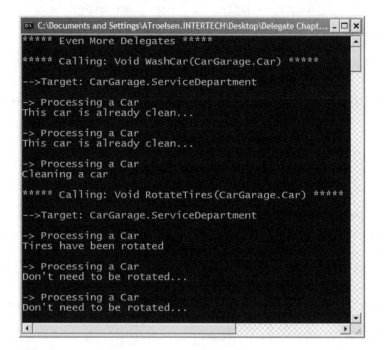

Figure 8-6. *Passing the buck*

Analyzing the Delegation Code

The Main() method begins by creating an instance of the Garage and ServiceDepartment types. Now, when you write the following:

```
// Wash all dirty cars.
g.ProcessCars(new Car.CarDelegate(sd.WashCar));
```

what you are effectively saying is "Add a pointer to the ServiceDepartment.WashCar() method to a Car.CarDelegate object, and pass this object to Garage.ProcessCars()." Like most real-world garages, the real work is delegated to the service department (which explains why a 30-minute oil change takes 2 hours). Given this, ProcessCars() can be understood as

```
// CarDelegate points to the ServiceDepartment.WashCar function.
public void ProcessCars(Car.CarDelegate proc)
{
...
    foreach(Car c in theCars)
        proc(c);      // proc(c) => ServiceDepartment.WashCar(c)
}
```

Likewise, if you say the following:

```
// Rotate the tires.
g.ProcessCars(new Car.CarDelegate(sd.RotateTires));
```

then ProcessCars() can be understood as

```
// CarDelegate points to the ServiceDepartment.RotateTires function:
public void ProcessCars(Car.CarDelegate proc)
{
```

```
    foreach(Car c in theCars)
        proc(c);      // proc(c) => ServiceDepartment.RotateTires(c)
...
}
```

Source Code The CarGarage project is located under the Chapter 8 subdirectory.

Understanding Delegate Covariance

Hopefully at this point in the game, you are more comfortable with the creation and use of delegate types. Before turning our attention to the C# event syntax, let's examine a new delegate-centric feature provided by .NET 2.0 termed *covariance*. As you may have noticed, each of the delegates created thus far point to methods returning simple numerical data types (or void). However, assume you are designing a delegate that can point to methods returning a custom class type:

```
// Define a delegate pointing to targets returning Car types.
public delegate Car ObtainCarDelegate();
```

Of course, you would be able to define a target for the delegate as expected:

```
class Program
{
    public delegate Car ObtainCarDelegate();

    public static Car GetBasicCar()
    { return new Car(); }

    static void Main(string[] args)
    {
        ObtainCarDelegate targetA = new ObtainCarDelegate(GetBasicCar);
        Car c = targetA();
        Console.ReadLine();
    }
}
```

So far, so good. However, what if you were to derive a new class from the Car type named SportsCar and wish to create a delegate type that can point to methods returning this class type? Prior to .NET 2.0, you would be required to define an entirely new delegate to do so:

```
// A new delegate pointing to targets returning SportsCar types.
public delegate SportsCar ObtainSportsCarDelegate();
```

As we now have two delegate types, we now must create an instance of each to obtain Car and SportsCar types:

```
class Program
{
    public delegate Car ObtainCarDelegate();
    public delegate SportsCar ObtainSportsCarDelegate();

    public static Car GetBasicCar()
    { return new Car(); }

    public static SportsCar GetSportsCar()
    { return new SportsCar(); }
```

```
      static void Main(string[] args)
      {
          ObtainCarDelegate targetA = new ObtainCarDelegate(GetBasicCar);
          Car c = targetA();

          ObtainSportsCarDelegate targetB =
              new ObtainSportsCarDelegate(GetSportsCar);
          SportsCar sc = targetB();
          Console.ReadLine();
      }
}
```

Given the laws of classic inheritance, it would be ideal to build a single delegate type that can point to methods returning *either* Car or SportsCar types (after all, a SportsCar "is-a" Car). *Covariance* allows for this very possibility. Simply put, covariance allows you to build a single delegate that can point to methods returning class types related by classical inheritance:

```
class Program
{
    // Define a single deletate that may return a Car
    // or SportsCar.
    public delegate Car ObtainVehicalDelegate();

    public static Car GetBasicCar()
    { return new Car(); }

    public static SportsCar GetSportsCar()
    { return new SportsCar(); }

    static void Main(string[] args)
    {
        Console.WriteLine("***** Delegate Covariance *****\n");
        ObtainVehicalDelegate targetA = new ObtainVehicalDelegate(GetBasicCar);
        Car c = targetA();

        // Covariance allows this target assignment.
        ObtainVehicalDelegate targetB = new ObtainVehicalDelegate(GetSportsCar);
        SportsCar sc = (SportsCar)targetB();
        Console.ReadLine();
    }
}
```

Notice that the ObtainVehicalDelegate delegate type has been defined to point to methods returning a strongly typed Car type. Given covariance, however, we can point to methods returning derived types as well. To obtain the derived type, simply perform an explicit cast.

■**Note** In a similar vein, *contravariance* allows you to create a single delegate that can point to numerous methods that receive objects related by classical inheritance. Consult the .NET Framework 2.0 SDK Documentation for further details.

■**Source Code** The DelegateCovariance project is located under the Chapter 8 subdirectory.

Understanding C# Events

Delegates are fairly interesting constructs in that they enable two objects in memory to engage in a two-way conversation. As you may agree, however, working with delegates in the raw does entail a good amount of boilerplate code (defining the delegate, declaring necessary member variables, and creating custom registration/unregistration methods).

Because the ability for one object to call back to another object is such a helpful construct, C# provides the event keyword to lessen the burden of using delegates in the raw. When the compiler processes the event keyword, you are automatically provided with registration and unregistration methods as well as any necessary member variable for your delegate types. In this light, the event keyword is little more than syntactic sugar, which can be used to save you some typing time.

■**Note** Even if you choose to leverage the C# event keyword, you are still required to manually define the related delegate types.

Defining an event is a two-step process. First, you need to define a delegate that contains the methods to be called when the event is fired. Next, you declare the events (using the C# event keyword) in terms of the related delegate. In a nutshell, defining a type that can send events entails the following pattern (shown in pseudo-code):

```
public class SenderOfEvents
{
    public delegate retval AssociatedDelegate(args);
    public event AssociatedDelegate NameOfEvent;
...
}
```

The events of the Car type will take the same name as the previous delegates (AboutToBlow and Exploded). The new delegate to which the events are associated will be called CarEventHandler. Here are the initial updates to the Car type:

```
public class Car
{
    // This delegate works in conjunction with the
    // Car's events.
    public delegate void CarEventHandler(string msg);

    // This car can send these events.
    public event CarEventHandler Exploded;
    public event CarEventHandler AboutToBlow;
...
}
```

Sending an event to the caller is as simple as specifying the event by name as well as any required parameters as defined by the associated delegate. To ensure that the caller has indeed registered with event, you will want to check the event against a null value before invoking the delegate's method set. These things being said, here is the new iteration of the Car's Accelerate() method:

```
public void Accelerate(int delta)
{
    // If the car is dead, fire Exploded event.
    if (carIsDead)
    {
```

```
            if (Exploded != null)
                Exploded("Sorry, this car is dead...");
        }

        else
        {
            currSpeed += delta;

            // Almost dead?
            if (10 == maxSpeed - currSpeed
                && AboutToBlow != null)
            {
                AboutToBlow("Careful buddy!  Gonna blow!");
            }

            // Still OK!
            if (currSpeed >= maxSpeed)
                carIsDead = true;
            else
                Console.WriteLine("->CurrSpeed = {0}", currSpeed);
        }
    }
}
```

With this, you have configured the car to send two custom events without the need to define custom registration functions. You will see the usage of this new automobile in just a moment, but first, let's check the event architecture in a bit more detail.

Events Under the Hood

A C# event actually expands into two hidden public methods, one having an add_ prefix; the other having a remove_ prefix. This prefix is followed by the name of the C# event. For example, the Exploded event results in two CIL methods named add_Exploded() and remove_Exploded(). In addition to the add_XXX() and remove_XXX() methods, the CIL-level event definition associates the correct delegate to a given event.

If you were to check out the CIL instructions behind add_AboutToBlow(), you would find code that looks just about identical to the OnAboutToBlow() helper method you wrote previously in the CarDelegate example (note the call to Delegate.Combine()):

```
.method public hidebysig specialname instance void
    add_AboutToBlow(class CarEvents.Car/CarEventHandler 'value')
    cil managed synchronized
{
    .maxstack  8
    ldarg.0
    ldarg.0
    ldfld class CarEvents.Car/CarEventHandler CarEvents.Car::AboutToBlow
    ldarg.1
    call class [mscorlib]System.Delegate
    [mscorlib]System.Delegate::Combine(
        class [mscorlib]System.Delegate, class [mscorlib]System.Delegate)
    castclass CarEvents.Car/CarEventHandler
    stfld class CarEvents.Car/CarEventHandler CarEvents.Car::AboutToBlow
    ret
}
```

As you would expect, remove_AboutToBlow() will indirectly call Delegate.Remove() and is more or less identical to the previous RemoveAboutToBlow() helper method:

```
.method public hidebysig specialname instance void
    remove_AboutToBlow(class CarEvents.Car/CarEventHandler 'value')
    cil managed synchronized
{
    .maxstack  8
    ldarg.0
    ldarg.0
    ldfld class CarEvents.Car/CarEventHandler CarEvents.Car::AboutToBlow
    ldarg.1
    call class [mscorlib]System.Delegate
        [mscorlib]System.Delegate::Remove(
        class [mscorlib]System.Delegate, class [mscorlib]System.Delegate)
    castclass CarEvents.Car/CarEventHandler
    stfld class CarEvents.Car/CarEventHandler CarEvents.Car::AboutToBlow
    ret
}
```

Finally, the CIL code representing the event itself makes use of the `.addon` and `.removeon` directives to map the names of the correct add_XXX() and remove_XXX() methods to invoke:

```
.event CarEvents.Car/EngineHandler AboutToBlow
{
    .addon void CarEvents.Car::add_AboutToBlow
        (class CarEvents.Car/CarEngineHandler)
    .removeon void CarEvents.Car::remove_AboutToBlow
        (class CarEvents.Car/CarEngineHandler)
}
```

Now that you understand how to build a class that can send C# events (and are aware that events are nothing more than a typing time-saver), the next big question is how to "listen to" the incoming events on the caller's side.

Listening to Incoming Events

C# events also simplify the act of registering the caller-side event handlers. Rather than having to specify custom helper methods, the caller simply makes use of the += and -= operators directly (which triggers the correct add_XXX() or remove_XXX() method in the background). When you wish to register with an event, follow the pattern shown here:

```
// ObjectVariable.EventName +=
// new AssociatedDelegate(functionToCall);
Car.EngineHandler d = new Car.CarEventHandler(CarExplodedEventHandler)
myCar.Exploded += d;
```

When you wish to detach from a source of events, use the -= operator:

```
// ObjectVariable.EventName -= delegateObject;
myCar.Exploded -= d;
```

Given these very predictable patterns, here is the refactored Main() method, now using the C# event registration syntax:

```
class Program
{
    static void Main(string[] args)
    {
        Console.WriteLine("***** Events *****");
        Car c1 = new Car("SlugBug", 100, 10);
```

```
        // Register event handlers.
        c1.AboutToBlow += new Car.CarEventHandler(CarIsAlmostDoomed);
        c1.AboutToBlow += new Car.CarEventHandler(CarAboutToBlow);

        Car.CarEventHandler d = new Car.CarEventHandler(CarExploded);
        c1.Exploded += d;

        Console.WriteLine("\n***** Speeding up *****");
        for (int i = 0; i < 6; i++)
            c1.Accelerate(20);

        // Remove CarExploded method
        // from invocation list.
        c1.Exploded -= d;

        Console.WriteLine("\n***** Speeding up *****");
        for (int i = 0; i < 6; i++)
            c1.Accelerate(20);
        Console.ReadLine();
    }

    public static void CarAboutToBlow(string msg)
    { Console.WriteLine(msg); }
    public static void CarIsAlmostDoomed(string msg)
    { Console.WriteLine("Critical Message from Car: {0}", msg); }
    public static void CarExploded(string msg)
    { Console.WriteLine(msg); }
}
```

Source Code   The CarEvents project is located under the Chapter 8 subdirectory.

Simplifying Event Registration Using Visual Studio 2005

Visual Studio .NET 2003 and Visual Studio 2005 each offer assistance with the process of registering event handlers. When you apply the += syntax during the act of event registration, you will find an IntelliSense window is displayed inviting you to hit the Tab key to auto-fill the associated delegate instance (see Figure 8-7).

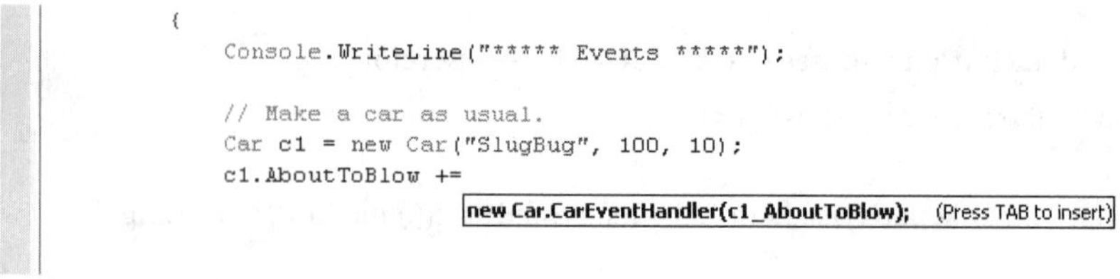

```
    {
        Console.WriteLine("***** Events *****");

        // Make a car as usual.
        Car c1 = new Car("SlugBug", 100, 10);
        c1.AboutToBlow +=
           ┌──────────────────────────────────────────────────────┐
           │ new Car.CarEventHandler(c1_AboutToBlow);  (Press TAB to insert) │
           └──────────────────────────────────────────────────────┘
```

Figure 8-7. *Delegate selection IntelliSense*

Once you do hit the Tab key, you are then invited to enter the name of the event handler to be generated (or simply accept the default name) as shown in Figure 8-8.

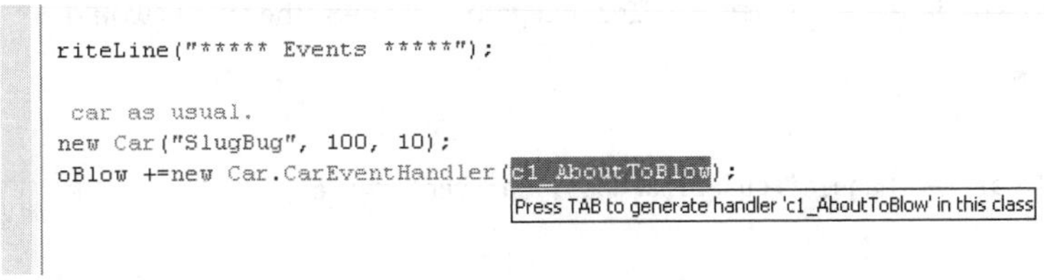

```
riteLine("***** Events *****");

 car as usual.
new Car("SlugBug", 100, 10);
oBlow +=new Car.CarEventHandler(c1_AboutToBlow);
                                └─ Press TAB to generate handler 'c1_AboutToBlow' in this class
```

Figure 8-8. *Delegate target format IntelliSense*

Once you hit the Tab key again, you will be provided with stub code in the correct format of the delegate target (note that this method has been declared static due to the fact that the event was registered within a static method):

```
static void c1_AboutToBlow(string msg)
{
    // Add your code!
}
```

This IntelliSense feature is available to all .NET events in the base class libraries. This IDE feature is a massive timesaver, given that this removes you from the act of needing to search the .NET help system to figure out the correct delegate to use with a particular event as well as the format of the delegate target.

A "Prim-and-Proper" Event

Truth be told, there is one final enhancement we could make to the CarEvents example that mirrors Microsoft's recommended event pattern. As you begin to explore the events sent by a given type in the base class libraries, you will find that the first parameter of the underlying delegate is a System.Object, while the second parameter is a type deriving from System.EventArgs.

The System.Object argument represents a reference to the object that sent the event (such as the Car), while the second parameter represents information regarding the event at hand. The System.EventArgs base class represents an event that is not sending any custom information:

```
public class EventArgs
{
    public static readonly System.EventArgs Empty;
    public EventArgs();
}
```

For simple events, you can pass an instance of EventArgs directly. However, when you wish to pass along custom data, you should build a suitable class deriving from EventArgs. For our example, assume we have a class named CarEventArgs, which maintains a string representing the message sent to the receiver:

```
public class CarEventArgs : EventArgs
{
    public readonly string msg;
    public CarEventArgs(string message)
    {
        msg = message;
    }
}
```

With this, we would now update the CarEventHandler delegate as follows (the events would be unchanged):

```
public class Car
{
    public delegate void CarEventHandler(object sender, CarEventArgs e);
...
}
```

When firing our events from within the Accelerate() method, we would now need to supply a reference to the current Car (via the this keyword) and an instance of our CarEventArgs type:

```
public void Accelerate(int delta)
{
    // If the car is dead, fire Exploded event.
    if (carIsDead)
    {
        if (Exploded != null)
            Exploded(this, new CarEventArgs("Sorry, this car is dead..."));
    }
    else
    {
...
            AboutToBlow(this, new CarEventArgs("Careful buddy!  Gonna blow!"));
    }
...
}
```

On the caller's side, all we would need to do is update our event handlers to receive the incoming parameters and obtain the message via our read-only field. For example:

```
public static void CarAboutToBlow(object sender, CarEventArgs e)
{ Console.WriteLine("{0} says: {1}", sender, e.msg); }
```

If the receiver wishes to interact with the object that sent the event, we can explicitly cast the System.Object. Thus, if we wish to power down the radio when the Car object is about to meet its maker, we could author an event handler looking something like the following:

```
public static void CarIsAlmostDoomed(object sender, CarEventArgs e)
{
    // Just to be safe, perform a
    // runtime check before casting.
    if (sender is Car)
    {
        Car c = (Car)sender;
        c.CrankTunes(false);
    }
        Console.WriteLine("Critical Message from {0}: {1}", sender, e.msg);
}
```

■**Source Code** The PrimAndProperCarEvents project is located under the Chapter 8 subdirectory.

Understanding C# Anonymous Methods

To wrap up this chapter, let's examine some final delegate-and-event-centric features of .NET 2.0 as seen through the eyes of C#. To begin, consider the fact that when a caller wishes to listen to incoming events, it must define a unique method that matches the signature of the associated delegate:

```
class SomeCaller
{
    static void Main(string[] args)
    {
        SomeType t = new SomeType();
        t.SomeEvent += new SomeDelegate(MyEventHandler);
    }

    // Typically only called by the SomeDelegate object.
    public static void MyEventHandler()
    { ...}
}
```

When you think about it, however, methods such as MyEventHandler() are seldom intended to be called by any part of the program other than the invoking delegate. As far as productivity is concerned, it is a bit of a bother (though in no way a showstopper) to manually define a separate method to be called by the delegate object.

To address this point, it is now possible to associate a delegate directly to a block of code statements at the time of event registration. Formally, such code is termed an *anonymous method*. To illustrate the basic syntax, check out the following Main() method, which handles the events sent from the Car type using anonymous methods, rather than specifically named event handlers:

```
class Program
{
    static void Main(string[] args)
    {
        Console.WriteLine("***** Anonymous Methods *****\n");
        Car c1 = new Car("SlugBug", 100, 10);

        // Register event handlers as anonymous methods.
        c1.AboutToBlow += delegate {
            Console.WriteLine("Eek! Going too fast!");
        };

        c1.AboutToBlow += delegate(object sender, CarEventArgs e) {
            Console.WriteLine("Message from Car: {0}", e.msg);
        };

        c1.Exploded += delegate(object sender, CarEventArgs e) {
            Console.WriteLine("Fatal Message from Car: {0}", e.msg);
        };
        ...
    }
}
```

Note The final curly bracket of an anonymous method must be terminated by a semicolon. If you fail to do so, you are issued a compilation error.

Again, notice that the Program type no longer defines specific static event handlers such as CarAboutToBlow() or CarExploded(). Rather, the unnamed (aka anonymous) methods are defined inline at the time the caller is handling the event using the += syntax.

The basic syntax of an anonymous method matches the following pseudo-code:

```
class SomeCaller
{
    static void Main(string[] args)
    {
        SomeType t = new SomeType();
        t.SomeEvent += delegate (optionallySpecifiedDelegateArgs)
            { /* statements */ };
    }
}
```

When handling the first AboutToBlow event within the previous Main() method, notice that you are not defining the arguments passed by the delegate:

```
c1.AboutToBlow += delegate {
    Console.WriteLine("Eek! Going too fast!");
};
```

Strictly speaking, you are not required to receive the incoming arguments sent by a specific event. However, if you wish to make use of the possible incoming arguments, you will need to specify the parameters prototyped by the delegate type (as seen in the second handling of the AboutToBlow and Exploded events). For example:

```
c1.AboutToBlow += delegate(object sender, CarEventArgs e) {
    Console.WriteLine("Critical Message from Car: {0}", e.msg);
};
```

Accessing "Outer" Variables

Anonymous methods are interesting in that they are able to access the local variables of the method that defines them. Formally speaking, such variables are termed "outer variables" of the anonymous method. To illustrate, assume our Main() method defined a local integer named aboutToBlowCounter. Within the anonymous methods that handle the AboutToBlow event, we will increment this counter by 1 and print out the tally before Main() completes:

```
static void Main(string[] args)
{
...
    int aboutToBlowCounter = 0;

    // Make a car as usual.
    Car c1 = new Car("SlugBug", 100, 10);

    // Register event handlers as anonymous methods.
    c1.AboutToBlow += delegate
    {
        aboutToBlowCounter++;
        Console.WriteLine("Eek!  Going too fast!");
    };

    c1.AboutToBlow += delegate(string msg)
    {
        aboutToBlowCounter++;
        Console.WriteLine("Critical Message from Car: {0}", msg);
    };
...
    Console.WriteLine("AboutToBlow event was fired {0} times.",
        aboutToBlowCounter);
    Console.ReadLine();
}
```

Once you run this updated `Main()` method, you will find the final `Console.WriteLine()` reports the `AboutToBlow` event was fired twice.

■Note An anonymous method cannot access `ref` or `out` parameters of the defining method.

C# Method Group Conversions

Another delegate-and-event-centric feature of C# is termed *method group conversion*. This feature allows you to register the "simple" name of an event handler. To illustrate, let's revisit the `SimpleMath` type examined earlier in this chapter, which is now updated with a new event named `ComputationFinished`:

```
public class SimpleMath
{
    // Not bothering to create a System.EventArgs
    // derived type here.
    public delegate void MathMessage(string msg);
    public event MathMessage ComputationFinished;

    public int Add(int x, int y)
    {
        ComputationFinished("Adding complete.");
        return x + y;
    }

    public int Subtract(int x, int y)
    {
        ComputationFinished("Subtracting complete.");
        return x - y;
    }
}
```

If we are not using anonymous method syntax, you know that the way we would handle the `ComputationComplete` event is as follows:

```
class Program
{
    static void Main(string[] args)
    {
        SimpleMath m = new SimpleMath();
        m.ComputationFinished +=
            new SimpleMath.MathMessage(ComputationFinishedHandler);
        Console.WriteLine("10 + 10 is {0}", m.Add(10, 10));
        Console.ReadLine();
    }

    static void ComputationFinishedHandler(string msg)
    { Console.WriteLine(msg); }
}
```

However, we can register the event handler with a specific event like this (the remainder of the code is identical):

```
m.ComputationFinished += ComputationFinishedHandler;
```

Notice that we are not directly "new-ing" the associated delegate type, but rather simply specifying a method that matches the delegate's expected signature (a method returning nothing and taking a single System.String in this case). Understand that the C# compiler is still ensuring type safety. Thus, if the ComputationFinishedHandler() method did not take a System.String and return void, we would be issued a compiler error.

It is also possible to explicitly convert an event hander into an instance of the delegate it relates to. This can be helpful if you need to obtain the underlying delegate using a predefined method. For example:

```
// .NET 2.0 allows event handlers to be converted into
// their underlying delegate.
SimpleMath.MathMessage mmDelegate =
    (SimpleMath.MathMessage)ComputationFinishedHandler;
Console.WriteLine(mmDelegate.Method);
```

If you executed this code, the final Console.WriteLine() prints out the signature of Computation FinishedHandler, as shown in Figure 8-9.

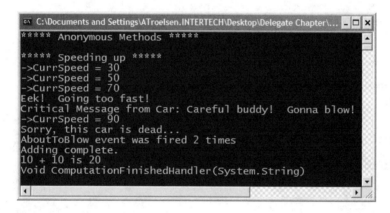

Figure 8-9. *You can extract a delegate from the related event handler.*

■Source Code The AnonymousMethods project is located under the Chapter 8 subdirectory.

Summary

In this chapter, you have examined a number of ways in which multiple objects can partake in a bidirectional conversation. First, you examined the use of *callback interfaces*, which provide a way to have object B make calls on object A through a common interface type. Do understand that this design pattern is not specific to .NET, but may be employed in any language or platform that honors the use of interface-based programming techniques.

Next, you examined the C# delegate keyword, which is used to indirectly construct a class derived from System.MulticastDelegate. As you have seen, a delegate is simply an object that maintains a list of methods to call when told to do so. These invocations may be made synchronously (using the Invoke() method) or asynchronously (via the BeginInvoke() and EndInvoke() methods). Again, the asynchronous nature of .NET delegate types will be examined at a later time.

You then examined the C# event keyword which, when used in conjunction with a delegate type, can simplify the process of sending your event notifications to awaiting callers. As shown via the resulting CIL, the .NET event model maps to hidden calls on the System.Delegate/System.Multicast-Delegate types. In this light, the C# event keyword is purely optional in that it simply saves you some typing time.

Finally, this chapter examined a new C# 2005 language feature termed *anonymous methods*. Using this syntactic construct, you are able to directly associate a block of code statements to a given event. As you have seen, anonymous methods are free to ignore the parameters sent by the event and have access to the "outer variables" of the defining method. Last but not least, you examined a simplified way to register events using *method group conversion*.

CHAPTER 9

■■■

Advanced C# Type Construction Techniques

In this chapter, you'll deepen your understanding of the C# programming language by examining a number of advanced (but still quite useful) syntactic constructs. To begin, you'll learn how to construct and use an indexer method. This C# mechanism enables you to build custom types that provide access to internal subtypes using an array-like syntax. Once you learn how to build an indexer method, you'll then examine how to overload various operators (+, -, <, >, and so forth), and create custom explicit and implicit conversion routines for your types (and you'll learn why you may wish to do so).

The later half of this chapter examines a small set of lesser used (but nonetheless interesting) C# keywords. For example, you'll learn how to programmatically account for overflow and underflow conditions using the checked and unchecked keywords, as well as how to create an "unsafe" code context in order to directly manipulate pointer types using C#. The chapter wraps up with an examination of the role of C# preprocessor directives.

Building a Custom Indexer

As programmers, we are very familiar with the process of accessing discrete items contained within a standard array using the index operator, for example:

```
// Declare an array of integers.
int[] myInts = { 10, 9, 100, 432, 9874};

// Use the [] operator to access each element.
for(int j = 0; j < myInts.Length; j++)
    Console.WriteLine("Index {0}  = {1} ", j,  myInts[j]);
```

The previous code is by no means a major newsflash. However, the C# language provides the capability to build custom classes and structures that may be indexed just like a standard array. It should be no big surprise that the method that provides the capability to access items in this manner is termed an *indexer*.

Before exploring how to create such a construct, let's begin by seeing one in action. Assume you have added support for an indexer method to the custom collection (Garage) developed in Chapter 8. Observe the following usage:

```
// Indexers allow you to access items in an arraylike fashion.
public class Program
{
    static void Main(string[] args)
    {
        Console.WriteLine("***** Fun with Indexers *****\n");

        // Assume the Garage type has an indexer method.
        Garage carLot = new Garage();

        // Add some cars to the garage using indexer.
        carLot[0] = new Car("FeeFee", 200);
        carLot[1] = new Car("Clunker", 90);
        carLot[2] = new Car("Zippy", 30);

        // Now obtain and display each item using indexer.
        for (int i = 0; i < 3; i++)
        {
            Console.WriteLine("Car number: {0}", i);
            Console.WriteLine("Name: {0}", carLot[i].PetName);
            Console.WriteLine("Max speed: {0}", carLot[i].CurrSpeed);
            Console.WriteLine();
        }
        Console.ReadLine();
    }
}
```

As you can see, indexers behave much like a custom collection supporting the IEnumerator and IEnumerable interfaces. The only major difference is that rather than accessing the contents using interface types, you are able to manipulate the internal collection of automobiles just like a standard array.

Now for the big question: How do you configure the Garage class (or any class/structure) to support this functionality? An indexer is represented as a slightly mangled C# property. In its simplest form, an indexer is created using the this[] syntax. Here is the relevant update to the Garage type:

```
// Add the indexer to the existing class definition.
public class Garage : IEnumerable // foreach iteration
{
...
    // Use ArrayList to contain the Car types.
    private ArrayList carArray = new ArrayList();

    // The indexer returns a Car based on a numerical index.
    public Car this[int pos]
    {
        // Note ArrayList has an indexer as well!
        get { return (Car)carArray[pos]; }
        set { carArray[pos] = value }
    }
}
```

Beyond the use of the this keyword, the indexer looks just like any other C# property declaration. Do be aware that indexers do not provide any array-like functionality beyond the use of the subscript operator. In other words, the object user cannot write code such as the following:

```
// Use ArrayList.Count property? Nope!
Console.WriteLine("Cars in stock: {0} ", carLot.Count);
```

To support this functionality, you would need to add your own Count property to the Garage type, and delegate accordingly:

```
public class Garage: IEnumerable
{
    ...
    // Containment/delegation in action once again.
    public int Count { get { return carArray.Count; } }
}
```

As you can gather, indexers are yet another form of syntactic sugar, given that this functionality can also be achieved using "normal" public methods. For example, if the Garage type did not support an indexer, you would be able to allow the outside world to interact with the internal array list using a named property or traditional accessor/mutator methods. Nevertheless, when you support indexers on your custom collection types, they integrate well into the fabric of the .NET base class libraries.

Source Code   The SimpleIndexer project is located under the Chapter 9 subdirectory.

A Variation of the Garage Indexer

The current Garage type defined an indexer that allowed the caller to identify subitems using a numerical value. Understand, however, that this is not a requirement of an indexer method. Assume you would rather contain the Car objects within a System.Collections.Specialized.ListDictionary rather than an ArrayList. Given that ListDictionary types allow access to the contained types using a key token (such as a string), you could configure the new Garage indexer as follows:

```
public class Garage : IEnumerable
{
    private ListDictionary carDictionary = new ListDictionary();

    // This indexer returns a Car based on a string index.
    public Car this[string name]
    {
        get { return (Car)carDictionary[name]; }
        set { carDictionary[name] = value; }
    }

    public int Length { get { return carDictionary.Count; } }

    public IEnumerator GetEnumerator()
    { return carDictionary.GetEnumerator(); }
}
```

The caller would now be able to interact with the internal cars as shown here:

```
public class Program
{
    static void Main(string[] args)
    {
        Console.WriteLine("***** Fun with Indexers *****\n");
        Garage carLot = new Garage();
```

```
// Add named cars to garage.
carLot["FeeFee"] = new Car("FeeFee", 200, 0);
carLot["Clunker"] = new Car("Clunker", 90, 0);
carLot["Zippy"] = new Car("Zippy", 30, 0);

// Now get Zippy.
Car zippy = carLot["Zippy"];
Console.WriteLine("{0} is going {1} MPH",
    zippy.PetName, zippy.CurrSpeed);
Console.ReadLine();
    }
}
```

Understand that indexers may be overloaded. Thus, if it made sense to allow the caller to access subitems using a numerical index *or* a string value, you might define multiple indexers for a single type.

■**Source Cone** The StringIndexer project is located under the Chapter 9 subdirectory.

Internal Representation of Type Indexers

Now that you have seen a few variations on the C# indexer method, you may be wondering how indexers are represented in terms of CIL. If you were to open up the numerical indexer of the Garage type, you would find that the C# compiler has created a property named Item, which maps to the correct getter/setter methods:

```
property instance class SimpleIndexer.Car Item(int32)
{
  .get instance class SimpleIndexer.Car SimpleIndexer.Garage::get_Item(int32)
  .set instance void SimpleIndexer.Garage::set_Item(int32,
    class SimpleIndexer.Car)
} // end of property Garage::Item
```

The get_Item() and set_Item() methods are implemented like any other .NET property, for example:

```
method public hidebysig specialname instance class SimpleIndexer.Car
  get_Item(int32 pos) cil managed
{
  Code size       22 (0x16)
  .maxstack  2
  .locals init ([0] class SimpleIndexer.Car CS$1$0000)
  IL_0000:  ldarg.0
  IL_0001:  ldfld class [mscorlib]System.Collections.ArrayList
    SimpleIndexer.Garage::carArray
  IL_0006:  ldarg.1
  IL_0007:  callvirt instance object [mscorlib]
    System.Collections.ArrayList::get_Item(int32)
  IL_000c:  castclass SimpleIndexer.Car
  IL_0011:  stloc.0
  IL_0012:  br.s IL_0014
  IL_0014:  ldloc.0
  IL_0015:  ret
} // end of method Garage::get_Item
```

Indexers: Final Details

If you want to get really exotic, you can also create an indexer that takes multiple parameters. Assume you have a custom collection that stores subitems in a 2D array. If this is the case, you may configure an indexer method as follows:

```
public class SomeContainer
{
    private int[,] my2DintArray = new int[10, 10];

    public int this[int row, int column]
    { /* get or set value from 2D array */  }
}
```

Finally, understand that indexers can be defined on a given .NET interface type to allow implementing types to provide a custom implementation. Such an interface is as follows:

```
public interface IEstablishSubObjects
{
    // This interface defines an indexer that returns
    // strings based on a numerical index.
    string this[int index] { get; set; }
}
```

So much for the topic of C# indexers. Next up, you'll examine a technique supported by some (but not all) .NET programming languages: operator overloading.

Understanding Operator Overloading

C#, like any programming language, has a canned set of tokens that are used to perform basic operations on intrinsic types. For example, you know that the + operator can be applied to two integers in order to yield a larger integer:

```
// The + operator with ints.
int a = 100;
int b = 240;
int c = a + b;   // c is now 340
```

Again, this is no major news flash, but have you ever stopped and noticed how the same + operator can be applied to most intrinsic C# data types? For example, consider this code:

```
// + operator with strings.
string s1 = "Hello";
string s2 = " world!";
string s3 = s1 + s2;   // s3 is now "Hello world!"
```

In essence, the + operator functions in unique ways based on the supplied data types (strings or integers in this case). When the + operator is applied to numerical types, the result is the summation of the operands. However, when the + operator is applied to string types, the result is string concatenation.

The C# language provides the capability for you to build custom classes and structures that also respond uniquely to the same set of basic tokens (such as the + operator). Be aware that you cannot overload each and every intrinsic C# operator. Table 9-1 outlines the "overloadability" of the core operators.

Table 9-1. *Valid Overloadable Operators*

C# Operator	Overloadability
+, -, !, ~, ++, --, true, false	This set of unary operators can be overloaded.
+, -, *, /, %, &, |, ^, <<, >>	These binary operators can be overloaded.
==, !=, <, >, <=, >=	The comparison operators can be overloaded. C# will demand that "like" operators (i.e., < and >, <= and >=, == and !=) are overloaded together.
[]	The [] operator cannot be overloaded. As you saw earlier in this chapter, however, the indexer construct provides the same functionality.
()	The () operator cannot be overloaded. As you will see later in this chapter, however, custom conversion methods provide the same functionality.
+=, -=, *=, /=, %=, &=, |=, ^=, <<=, >>=	Shorthand assignment operators cannot be overloaded; however, you receive them as a freebie when you overload the related binary operator.

Overloading Binary Operators

To illustrate the process of overloading binary operators, assume the following simple Point structure:

```
// Just a simple everyday C# struct.
public struct Point
{
    private int x, y;
    public Point(int xPos, int yPos)
    {
        x = xPos;
        y = yPos;
    }

    public override string ToString()
    {
        return string.Format("[{0}, {1}]", this.x, this.y);
    }
}
```

Now, logically speaking, it makes sense to add Points together. On a related note, it may be helpful to subtract one Point from another. For example, you would like to be able to author the following code:

```
// Adding and subtracting two points.
static void Main(string[] args)
{
    Console.WriteLine("***** Fun with Overloaded Operators *****\n");

    // Make two points.
    Point ptOne = new Point(100, 100);
    Point ptTwo = new Point(40, 40);
    Console.WriteLine("ptOne = {0}", ptOne);
    Console.WriteLine("ptTwo = {0}", ptTwo);

    // Add the points to make a bigger point?
    Console.WriteLine("ptOne + ptTwo: {0} ", ptOne + ptTwo);
```

```
    // Subtract the points to make a smaller point?
    Console.WriteLine("ptOne - ptTwo: {0} ", ptOne - ptTwo);
    Console.ReadLine();
}
```

To allow a custom type to respond uniquely to intrinsic operators, C# provides the operator keyword, which you can only use in conjunction with *static* methods. When you are overloading a binary operator (such as + and -), you will pass in two arguments that are the same type as the defining class (a Point in this example), as illustrated in the following code:

```
// A more intelligent Point type.
public struct Point
{
...
    // overloaded operator +
    public static Point operator + (Point p1, Point p2)
    { return new Point(p1.x + p2.x, p1.y + p2.y); }

    // overloaded operator -
    public static Point operator - (Point p1, Point p2)
    { return new Point(p1.x - p2.x, p1.y - p2.y); }
}
```

The logic behind operator + is simply to return a brand new Point based on the summation of the fields of the incoming Point parameters. Thus, when you write pt1 + pt2, under the hood you can envision the following hidden call to the static operator + method:

```
// p3 = Point.operator+ (p1, p2)
p3 = p1 + p2;
```

Likewise, p1 – p2 maps to the following:

```
// p3 = Point.operator- (p1, p2)
p3 = p1 - p2;
```

And What of the += and –+ Operators?

If you are coming to C# from a C++ background, you may lament the loss of overloading the shorthand assignment operators (+=, -=, and so forth). Fear not. In terms of C#, the shorthand assignment operators are automatically simulated if a type overloads the related binary operator. Thus, given that the Point structure has already overloaded the + and - operators, you are able to write the following:

```
// Overloading binary operators results in a freebie shorthand operator.
static void Main(string[] args)
{
...
    // Freebie +=
    Point ptThree = new Point(90, 5);
    Console.WriteLine("ptThree = {0}", ptThree);
    Console.WriteLine("ptThree += ptTwo: {0}", ptThree += ptTwo);

    // Freebie -=
    Point ptFour = new Point(0, 500);
    Console.WriteLine("ptFour = {0}", ptFour);
    Console.WriteLine("ptFour -= ptThree: {0}", ptFour -= ptThree);
}
```

Overloading Unary Operators

C# also allows you to overload various unary operators, such as ++ and --. When you overload a unary operator, you will also define a static method via the operator keyword; however in this case you will simply pass in a single parameter that is the same type as the defining class/structure. For example, if you were to update the Point with the following overloaded operators:

```
public struct Point
{
...
    // Add 1 to the incoming Point.
    public static Point operator ++(Point p1)
    { return new Point(p1.x+1, p1.y+1); }

    // Subtract 1 from the incoming Point.
    public static Point operator --(Point p1)
    { return new Point(p1.x-1, p1.y-1); }
}
```

you could increment and decrement Point's X and Y values as so:

```
static void Main(string[] args)
{
...
    // Applying the ++ and -- unary operators to a Point.
    Console.WriteLine("++ptFive = {0}", ++ptFive);
    Console.WriteLine("--ptFive = {0}", --ptFive);
}
```

Overloading Equality Operators

As you may recall from Chapter 3, System.Object.Equals() can be overridden to perform value-based (rather than referenced-based) comparisons between types. If you choose to override Equals() (and the often related System.Object.GetHashCode() method), it is trivial to overload the equality operators (== and !=). To illustrate, here is the updated Point type:

```
// This incarnation of Point also overloads the == and != operators.
public struct Point
{
...
    public override bool Equals(object o)
    {
        if(o is Point)
        {
            if( ((Point)o).x == this.x &&
                ((Point)o).y == this.y)
                    return true;
        }
        return false;
    }

    public override int GetHashCode()
    { return this.ToString().GetHashCode(); }

    // Now let's overload the == and != operators.
    public static bool operator ==(Point p1, Point p2)
    { return p1.Equals(p2); }
```

```
    public static bool operator !=(Point p1, Point p2)
    {   return !p1.Equals(p2); }
}
```

Notice how the implementation of operator == and operator != simply makes a call to the overridden Equals() method to get the bulk of the work done. Given this, you can now exercise your Point class as follows:

```
// Make use of the overloaded equality operators.
static void Main(string[] args)
{
...
    Console.WriteLine("ptOne == ptTwo : {0}", ptOne == ptTwo);
    Console.WriteLine("ptOne != ptTwo : {0}", ptOne != ptTwo);
}
```

As you can see, it is quite intuitive to compare two objects using the well-known == and != operators rather than making a call to Object.Equals(). If you do overload the equality operators for a given class, keep in mind that C# demands that if you override the == operator, you *must* also override the != operator (if you forget, the compiler will let you know).

Overloading Comparison Operators

In Chapter 7, you learned how to implement the IComparable interface in order to compare the relative relationship between two like objects. Additionally, you may also overload the comparison operators (<, >, <=, and >=) for the same class. Like the equality operators, C# demands that if you overload <, you must also overload >. The same holds true for the <= and >= operators. If the Point type overloaded these comparison operators, the object user could now compare Points as follows:

```
// Using the overloaded < and > operators.
static void Main(string[] args)
{
...
    Console.WriteLine("ptOne < ptTwo : {0}", ptOne < ptTwo);
    Console.WriteLine("ptOne > ptTwo : {0}", ptOne > ptTwo);
}
```

Assuming you have implemented the IComparable interface, overloading the comparison operators is trivial. Here is the updated class definition:

```
// Point is also comparable using the comparison operators.
public struct Point : IComparable
{
...
    public int CompareTo(object obj)
    {
        if (obj is Point)
        {
            Point p = (Point)obj;
            if (this.x > p.x && this.y > p.y)
                return 1;
            if (this.x < p.x && this.y < p.y)
                return -1;
            else
                return 0;
        }
```

```
        else
            throw new ArgumentException();
    }

    public static bool operator <(Point p1, Point p2)
    { return (p1.CompareTo(p2) < 0); }

    public static bool operator >(Point p1, Point p2)
    { return (p1.CompareTo(p2) > 0); }

    public static bool operator <=(Point p1, Point p2)
    { return (p1.CompareTo(p2) <= 0); }

    public static bool operator >=(Point p1, Point p2)
    { return (p1.CompareTo(p2) >= 0); }
}
```

The Internal Representation of Overloaded Operators

Like any C# programming element, overloaded operators are represented using specific CIL syntax. To begin examining what takes place behind the scenes, open the OverloadedOps.exe assembly using ildasm.exe. As you can see from Figure 9-1, the overloaded operators are internally expressed via hidden methods (e.g., op_Addition(), op_Subtraction(), op_Equality(), and so on).

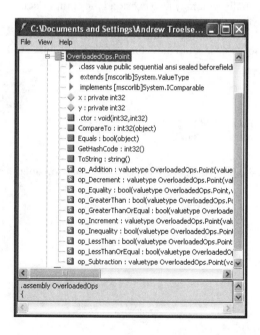

Figure 9-1. *In terms of CIL, overloaded operators map to hidden methods.*

Now, if you were to examine the specific CIL instructions for the op_Addition method, you would find that the specialname method decoration has also been inserted by csc.exe:

```
.method public hidebysig specialname static
        valuetype OverloadedOps.Point
            op_Addition(valuetype OverloadedsOps.Point p1,
                valuetype OverloadedOps.Point p2) cil managed
{
    ...
}
```

The truth of the matter is that any operator that you may overload equates to a specially named method in terms of CIL. Table 9-2 documents the C# operator-to-CIL mapping for the most common C# operators.

Table 9-2. *C# Operator-to-CIL Special Name Road Map*

Intrinsic C# Operator	CIL Representation
--	op_Decrement()
++	op_Increment()
+	op_Addition()
-	op_Subtraction()
*	op_Multiply()
/	op_Division()
==	op_Equality()
>	op_GreaterThan()
<	op_LessThan()
!=	op_Inequality()
>=	op_GreaterThanOrEqual()
<=	op_LessThanOrEqual()
-=	op_SubtractionAssignment()
+=	op_AdditionAssignment()

Interacting with Overloaded Operators from Overloaded Operator–Challenged Languages

Understanding how overloaded operators are represented in CIL code is not simply interesting from an academic point of view. To understand the practical reason for this knowledge, recall that the capability to overload operators is *not* supported by every .NET-aware language. Given this, what would happen if you wanted to add two Point types together in an overloaded operator–challenged language?

One approach is to provide "normal" public members that perform the same task as the overloaded operators. For example, you could update the Point type with Add() and Subtract() methods, which leverage the work performed by the custom + and - operators:

```
// Exposing overloaded operator semantics using simple
// member functions.
public struct Point
{
...
    // Operator + via Add()
    public static Point Add (Point p1, Point p2)
    { return p1 + p2; }
```

```
// Operator - via Subtract()
public static Point Subtract (Point p1, Point p2)
{ return p1 - p2; }
}
```

With this, the Point type is able to expose the same functionality using whichever technique a given language demands. C# users can apply the + and - operators and/or call Add()/Subtract():

```
// Use operator + or Add().
Console.WriteLine("ptOne + ptTwo: {0} ", ptOne + ptTwo);
Console.WriteLine("Point.Add(ptOne, ptTwo): {0} ", Point.Add(ptOne, ptTwo));
```

```
// Use operator - or Subtract().
Console.WriteLine("ptOne - ptTwo: {0} ", ptOne - ptTwo);
Console.WriteLine("Point.Subtract(ptOne, ptTwo): {0} ",
    Point.Subtract(ptOne, ptTwo));
```

Languages that cannot use overloaded operators can simply make due with the public static methods. As an alternative to providing duplicate functionality on the same type, understand that it is also possible to directly call the specially named methods from languages that lack overloaded operators.

Consider the initial release of the VB .NET programming language. If you were to build a VB .NET console application that references the Point type, you could add or subtract Point types using the CIL "special names," for example:

```
' Assume this VB .NET application has access to the Point type.
Module OverLoadedOpClient
    Sub Main()
        Dim p1 As Point
        p1.x = 200
        p1.y = 9

        Dim p2 As Point
        p2.x = 9
        p2.y = 983

        ' Not as clean as calling AddPoints(),
        ' but it gets the job done.
        Dim bigPoint = Point.op_Addition(p1, p2)
        Console.WriteLine("Big point is {0}", bigPoint)
    End Sub
End Module
```

As you can see, overloaded operator–challenged .NET programming languages are able to directly invoke the internal CIL methods as if they were "normal" methods. While it is not pretty, it works.

■**Note** Do be aware that the current version of VB .NET (Visual Basic .NET 2005) supports operator overloading. However, for the (many) managed languages that do not support operator overloading, knowledge of CIL "special names" can prove helpful.

Final Thoughts Regarding Operator Overloading

As you have seen, C# provides the capability to build types that can respond uniquely to various intrinsic, well-known operators. Now, before you go and retrofit all your classes to support such behavior, you must be sure that the operator(s) you are about to overload make some sort of logical sense in the world at large.

For example, let's say you overloaded the multiplication operator for the Engine class. What exactly would it mean to multiply two Engine objects? Not much. Overloading operators is generally only useful when you're building utility types. Strings, points, rectangles, fractions, and hexagons make good candidates for operator overloading. People, managers, cars, headphones, and baseball hats do not. As a rule of thumb, if an overloaded operator makes it *harder* for the user to understand a type's functionality, don't do it. Use this feature wisely.

■**Source Code** The OverloadedOps project is located under the Chapter 9 subdirectory.

Understanding Custom Type Conversions

Let's now examine a topic closely related to operator overloading: custom type conversions. To set the stage for the discussion to follow, let's quickly review the notion of explicit and implicit conversions between numerical data and related class types.

Recall: Numerical Conversions

In terms of the intrinsic numerical types (sbyte, int, float, etc.), an *explicit conversion* is required when you attempt to store a larger value in a smaller container, as this may result in a loss of data. Basically, this is your way to tell the compiler, "Leave me alone, I know what I am trying to do." Conversely, an *implicit conversion* happens automatically when you attempt to place a smaller type in a destination type that will not result in a loss of data:

```
static void Main()
{
    int a = 123;
    long b = a;          // Implicit conversion from int to long
    int c = (int) b;     // Explicit conversion from long to int
}
```

Recall: Conversions Among Related Class Types

As shown in Chapter 4, class types may be related by classical inheritance (the "is-a" relationship). In this case, the C# conversion process allows you to cast up and down the class hierarchy. For example, a derived class can always be implicitly cast into a given base type. However, if you wish to store a base class type in a derived variable, you must perform an explicit cast:

```
// Two related class types.
class Base{}
class Derived : Base{}

class Program
{
    static void Main()
    {
```

```
        // Implicit cast between derived to base.
        Base myBaseType;
        myBaseType = new Derived();

        // Must explicitly cast to store base reference
        // in derived type.
        Derived myDerivedType = (Derived)myBaseType;
    }
}
```

This explicit cast works due to the fact that the Base and Derived classes are related by classical inheritance. However, what if you have two class types in *different hierarchies* that require conversions? Given that they are not related by classical inheritance, explicit casting offers no help.

On a related note, consider value types. Assume you have two .NET structures named Square and Rectangle. Given that structures cannot leverage classic inheritance, you have no natural way to cast between these seemingly related types (assuming it made sense to do so).

While you could build helper methods in the structures (such as Rectangle.ToSquare()), C# allows you to build custom conversion routines that allow your types to respond to the () operator. Therefore, if you configured the Square type correctly, you would be able to use the following syntax to explicitly convert between these structure types:

```
// Convert a Rectangle to a Square.
Rectangle rect;
rect.Width = 3;
rect.Height = 10;
Square sq = (Square)rect;
```

Creating Custom Conversion Routines

C# provides two keywords, explicit and implicit, that you can use to control how your types respond during an attempted conversion. Assume you have the following structure definitions:

```
public struct Rectangle
{
    // Public for ease of use;
    // however, feel free to encapsulate with properties.
    public int Width, Height;

    public void Draw()
    { Console.WriteLine("Drawing a rect."); }

    public override string ToString()
    {
        return string.Format("[Width = {0}; Height = {1}]",
            Width, Height);
    }
}

public struct Square
{
    public int Length;

    public void Draw()
    { Console.WriteLine("Drawing a square."); }
```

```
public override string ToString()
{ return string.Format("[Length = {0}]", Length); }

// Rectangles can be explicitly converted
// into Squares.
public static explicit operator Square(Rectangle r)
{
    Square s;
    s.Length = r.Width;
    return s;
}
}
```

Notice that this iteration of the Rectangle type defines an explicit conversion operator. Like the process of overloading an operator, conversion routines make use of the C# operator keyword (in conjunction with the explicit or implicit keyword) and must be defined as static. The incoming parameter is the entity you are converting *from*, while the return value is the entity you are converting *to*:

```
public static explicit operator Square(Rectangle r)
{...}
```

In any case, the assumption is that a square (being a geometric pattern in which all sides are of equal length) can be obtained from the width of a rectangle. Thus, you are free to convert a Rectangle into a Square as so:

```
static void Main(string[] args)
{
    Console.WriteLine("***** Fun with Custom Conversions *****\n");

    // Create a 5 * 10 Rectangle.
    Rectangle rect;
    rect.Width = 10;
    rect.Height = 5;
    Console.WriteLine("rect = {0}", rect);

    // Convert Rectangle to a 10 * 10 Square.
    Square sq = (Square)rect;
    Console.WriteLine("sq = {0}", sq);
    Console.ReadLine();
}
```

While it may not be all that helpful to convert a Rectangle into a Square within the same scope, assume you have a function that has been prototyped to take Square types.

```
// This method requires a Square type.
private static void DrawSquare(Square sq)
{
    sq.Draw();
}
```

Using your explicit conversion operation, you can safely pass in Square types for processing:

```
static void Main(string[] args)
{
...
    // Convert Rectangle to Square to invoke method.
    DrawSquare((Square)rect);
}
```

Additional Explicit Conversions for the Square Type

Now that you can explicitly convert Rectangles into Squares, let's examine a few additional explicit conversions. Given that a square is symmetrical on each side, it might be helpful to provide an explicit conversion routine that allows the caller to cast from a System.Int32 type into a Square (which, of course, will have a side length equal to the incoming integer). Likewise, what if you were to update Square such that the caller can cast *from* a Square into a System.Int32? Here is the calling logic:

```
static void Main(string[] args)
{
...
    // Converting a System.Int32 to a Square.
    Square sq2 = (Square)90;
    Console.WriteLine("sq2 = {0}", sq2);

    // Converting a Square to a System.Int32.
    int side = (int)sq2;
    Console.WriteLine("Side length of sq2 = {0}", side);
}
```

And here is the update to the Square type:

```
public struct Square
{
...
    public static explicit operator Square(int sideLength)
    {
        Square newSq;
        newSq.Length = sideLength;
        return newSq;
    }

    public static explicit operator int (Square s)
    {return s.Length;}
}
```

Wild, huh? To be honest, converting from a Square into a System.Int32 may not be the most intuitive (or useful) operation. However, this does point out a very important fact regarding custom conversion routines: the compiler does not care what you convert to or from, as long as you have written syntactically correct code. Thus, as with overloading operators, just because you can create an explicit cast operation for a given type does not mean you should. Typically, this technique will be most helpful when you're creating .NET structure types, given that they are unable to participate in classical inheritance (where casting comes for free).

Defining Implicit Conversion Routines

Thus far, you have created various custom *explicit* conversion operations. However, what about the following *implicit* conversion?

```
static void Main(string[] args)
{
...
    // Attempt to make an implicit cast?
    Square s3;
    s3.Length = 83;
    Rectangle rect2 = s3;
}
```

As you might expect, this code will not compile, given that you have not provided an implicit conversion routine for the Rectangle type. Now here is the catch: it is illegal to define explicit and implicit conversion functions on the same type, if they do not differ by their return type or parameter set. This might seem like a limitation; however, the second catch is that when a type defines an *implicit* conversion routine, it is legal for the caller to make use of the *explicit* cast syntax!

Confused? To clear things up, let's add an implicit conversion routine to the Rectangle structure using the C# implicit keyword (note that the following code assumes the width of the resulting Rectangle is computed by multiplying the side of the Square by 2):

```
public struct Rectangle
{
...
    public static implicit operator Rectangle(Square s)
    {
        Rectangle r;
        r.Height = s.Length;

        // Assume the length of the new Rectangle with
        // (Length x 2)
        r.Width = s.Length * 2;
        return r;
    }
}
```

With this update, you are now able to convert between types as follows:

```
static void Main(string[] args)
{
...
    // Implicit cast OK!
    Square s3;
    s3.Length= 83;
    Rectangle rect2 = s3;
    Console.WriteLine("rect2 = {0}", rect2);
    DrawSquare(s3);

    // Explicit cast syntax still OK!
    Square s4;
    s4.Length = 3;
    Rectangle rect3 = (Rectangle)s4;
    Console.WriteLine("rect3 = {0}", rect3);
...
}
```

Again, be aware that it is permissible to define explicit and implicit conversion routines for the same type as long as their signatures differ. Thus, you could update the Square as follows:

```
public struct Square
{
...
    // Can call as:
    // Square sq2 = (Square)90;
    // or as:
    // Square sq2 = 90;
    public static implicit operator Square(int sideLength)
    {
```

```
            Square newSq;
            newSq.Length = sideLength;
            return newSq;
        }

        // Must call as:
        // int side = (int)mySquare;
        public static explicit operator int (Square s)
        { return s.Length; }
}
```

The Internal Representation of Custom Conversion Routines

Like overloaded operators, methods that are qualified with the implicit or explicit keywords have "special" names in terms of CIL: op_Implicit and op_Explicit, respectively (see Figure 9-2).

Figure 9-2. *CIL representation of user-defined conversion routines*

That wraps up our examination of defining custom conversion routines. As with overloaded operators, remember that this bit of syntax is simply a shorthand notation for "normal" member functions, and in this light it is always optional.

──

■**Source Code** The CustomConversions project is located under the Chapter 9 subdirectory.

──

The Advanced Keywords of C#

To close this chapter, you'll examine some of the more esoteric C# keywords:

- checked/unchecked
- unsafe/stackalloc/fixed/sizeof

To start, let's check out how C# provides automatic detection of arithmetic overflow and underflow conditions using the checked and unchecked keywords.

The checked Keyword

As you are no doubt well aware, each numerical data type has a fixed upper and lower limit (which may be obtained programmatically using the MaxValue and MinValue properties). Now, when you are performing arithmetic operations on a specific type, it is very possible that you may accidentally *overflow* the maximum storage of the type (i.e., assign a value that is greater than the maximum value) or *underflow* the minimum storage of the type (i.e., assign a value that is less than the minimum value). To keep in step with the CLR, I will refer to both of these possibilities collectively as "overflow." (As you will see, checked overflow and underflow conditions result in a System.OverflowException type. There is no System.UnderflowException type in the base class libraries.)

To illustrate the issue, assume you have created two System.Byte types (a C# byte), each of which has been assigned a value that is safely below the maximum (255). If you were to add the values of these types (casting the resulting integer as a byte), you would assume that the result would be the exact sum of each member:

```
namespace CheckedUnchecked
{
    class Program
    {
        static void Main(string[] args)
        {
            // Overflow the max value of a System.Byte.
            Console.WriteLine("Max value of byte is {0}.", byte.MaxValue);
            Console.WriteLine("Min value of byte is {0}.", byte.MinValue);
            byte b1 = 100;
            byte b2 = 250;
            byte sum = (byte)(b1 + b2);

            // sum should hold the value 350, however...
            Console.WriteLine("sum = {0}", sum);
            Console.ReadLine();
        }
    }
}
```

If you were to view the output of this application, you might be surprised to find that sum contains the value 94 (rather than the expected 350). The reason is simple. Given that a System.Byte can hold a value only between 0 and 255 (inclusive, for a grand total of 256 slots), sum now contains the overflow value (350 – 256 = 94). As you have just seen, if you take no corrective course of action, overflow occurs without exception. At times, this hidden overflow may cause no harm whatsoever in your project. Other times, this loss of data is completely unacceptable.

To handle overflow or underflow conditions in your application, you have two options. Your first choice is to leverage your wits and programming skills to handle all overflow conditions manually. Assuming you were indeed able to find each overflow condition in your program, you could resolve the previous overflow error as follows:

```
// Store sum in an integer to prevent overflow.
byte b1 = 100;
byte b2 = 250;
int sum = b1 + b2;
```

Of course, the problem with this technique is the simple fact that you *are* human, and even your best attempts may result in errors that have escaped your eyes. Given this, C# provides the checked keyword. When you wrap a statement (or a block of statements) within the scope of the checked keyword, the C# compiler emits specific CIL instructions that test for overflow conditions that may result when adding, multiplying, subtracting, or dividing two numerical data types. If an overflow has occurred, the runtime will throw a System.OverflowException type. Observe the following update:

```
class Program
{
    static void Main(string[] args)
    {
        // Overflow the max value of a System.Byte.
        Console.WriteLine("Max value of byte is {0}.", byte.MaxValue);
        byte b1 = 100;
        byte b2 = 250;

        try
        {
            byte sum = checked((byte)(b1 + b2));
            Console.WriteLine("sum = {0}", sum);
        }
        catch(OverflowException e)
        { Console.WriteLine(e.Message); }
    }
}
```

Here, you wrap the addition of b1 and b2 within the scope of the checked keyword. If you wish to force overflow checking to occur over a block of code, you can interact with the checked keyword as follows:

```
try
{
    checked
    {
        byte sum = (byte)(b1 + b2);
        Console.WriteLine("sum = {0}", sum);
    }
}
catch(OverflowException e)
{
    Console.WriteLine(e.Message);
}
```

In either case, the code in question will be evaluated for possible overflow conditions automatically, which will trigger an overflow exception if encountered.

Setting Projectwide Overflow Checking

Now, if you are creating an application that should never allow silent overflow to occur, you may find yourself in the annoying position of wrapping numerous lines of code within the scope of the checked keyword. As an alternative, the C# compiler supports the /checked flag. When enabled, *all* of your arithmetic will be evaluated for overflow without the need to make use of the C# checked keyword. If overflow has been discovered, you will still receive a runtime OverflowException.

To enable this flag using Visual Studio 2005, open your project's property page and click the Advanced button on the Build tab. From the resulting dialog box, select the "Check for arithmetic overflow/underflow" check box (see Figure 9-3).

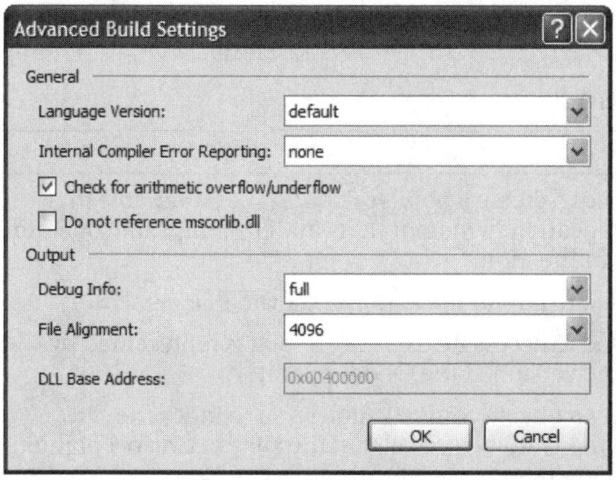

Figure 9-3. *Enabling Visual Studio 2005 overflow checking*

As you may guess, this setting can be very helpful when you're creating a debug build. Once all of the overflow exceptions have been squashed out of the code base, you're free to disable the /checked flag for subsequent builds (which will increase the runtime execution of your application).

The unchecked Keyword

Now, assuming you have enabled this projectwide setting, what are you to do if you have a block of code where silent overflow is acceptable? Given that the /checked flag will evaluate *all* arithmetic logic, the C# language provides the unchecked keyword to disable the throwing of System.OverflowException on a case-by-case basis. This keyword's use is identical to that of the checked keyword in that you can specify a single statement or a block of statements, for example:

```
// Assuming /checked is enabled,
// this block will not trigger
// a runtime exception.
unchecked
{
    byte sum = (byte)(b1 + b2);
    Console.WriteLine("sum = {0}", sum);
}
```

So, to summarize the C# checked and unchecked keywords, remember that the default behavior of the .NET runtime is to ignore arithmetic overflow. When you want to selectively handle discrete statements, make use of the checked keyword. If you wish to trap overflow errors throughout your application, enable the /checked flag. Finally, the unchecked keyword may be used if you have a block of code where overflow is acceptable (and thus should not trigger a runtime exception).

■**Source Code** The CheckedUnchecked project can be found under the Chapter 9 subdirectory.

Working with Pointer Types

In Chapter 3, you learned that the .NET platform defines two major categories of data: value types and reference types. Truth be told, however, there is a third category: *pointer types*. To work with pointer types, we are provided with specific operators and keywords that allow us to bypass the CLR's memory management scheme and take matters into our own hands (see Table 9-3).

Table 9-3. *Pointer-centric C# Operators and Keywords*

Operator/Keyword	Meaning in Life
*	This operator is used to create a *pointer variable* (i.e., a variable that represents a direct location in memory). As in C(++), this same operator is used for pointer indirection.
&	This operator is used to obtain the address of a variable in memory.
->	This operator is used to access fields of a type that is represented by a pointer (the unsafe version of the C# dot operator).
[]	The [ ] operator (in an unsafe context) allows you to index the slot pointed to by a pointer variable (recall the interplay between a pointer variable and the [ ] operator in C(++)!).
++, --	In an unsafe context, the increment and decrement operators can be applied to pointer types.
+, -	In an unsafe context, the addition and subtraction operators can be applied to pointer types.
==, !=, <, >, <=, =>	In an unsafe context, the comparison and equality operators can be applied to pointer types.
stackalloc	In an unsafe context, the stackalloc keyword can be used to allocate C# arrays directly on the stack.
fixed	In an unsafe context, the fixed keyword can be used to temporarily fix a variable so that its address may be found.

Now, before we dig into the details, let me point out the fact that you will *seldom if ever* need to make use of pointer types. Although C# does allow you to drop down to the level of pointer manipulations, understand that the .NET runtime has absolutely no clue of your intentions. Thus, if you mismanage a pointer, you are the one in charge of dealing with the consequences. Given these warnings, when exactly would you need to work with pointer types? There are two common situations:

- You are looking to optimize select parts of your application by directly manipulating memory outside the management of the CLR.
- You are calling methods of a C-based *.dll or COM server that demand pointer types as parameters.

In the event that you do decide to make use of this C# language feature, you will be required to inform csc.exe of your intentions by enabling your project to support "unsafe code." To do so using the C# command-line compiler (csc.exe), simply supply the /unsafe flag as an argument. From Visual Studio 2005, you will need to access your project's Properties page and enable the Allow Unsafe Code option from the Build tab (see Figure 9-4).

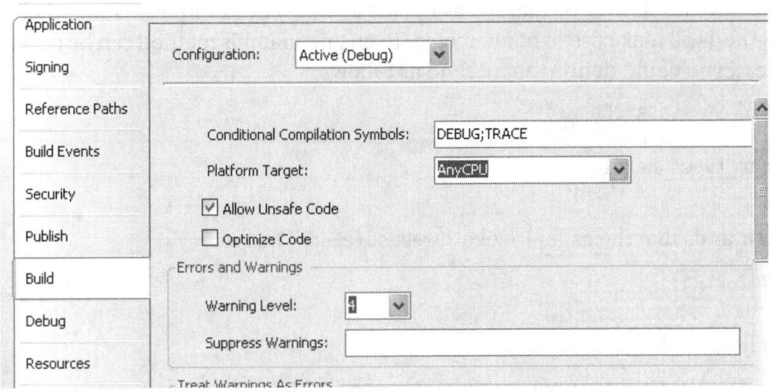

Figure 9-4. *Enabling unsafe code using Visual Studio 2005*

The unsafe Keyword

In the examples that follow, I'm assuming that you have some background in C(++) pointer manipulations. If this is not true in your case, don't sweat it. Again, writing unsafe code will not be a common task for a majority of .NET applications. When you wish to work with pointers in C#, you must specifically declare a block of "unsafe" code using the unsafe keyword (as you might guess, any code that is not marked with the unsafe keyword is considered "safe" automatically):

```
unsafe
{
    // Work with pointer types here!
}
```

In addition to declaring a scope of unsafe code, you are able to build structures, classes, type members, and parameters that are "unsafe." Here are a few examples to gnaw on:

```
// This entire structure is 'unsafe' and can
// be used only in an unsafe context.
public unsafe struct Node
{
    public int Value;
    public Node* Left;
    public Node* Right;
}


// This struct is safe, but the Node* members
// are not. Technically, you may access 'Value' from
// outside an unsafe context, but not 'Left' and 'Right'.
public struct Node
{
    public int Value;

    // These can be accessed only in an unsafe context!
    public unsafe Node* Left;
    public unsafe Node* Right;
}
```

Methods (static or instance level) may be marked as unsafe as well. For example, assume that you know a given static method will make use of pointer logic. To ensure that this method can be called only from an unsafe context, you could define the method as follows:

```
unsafe public static void SomeUnsafeCode()
{
    // Work with pointer types here!
}
```

This configuration demands that the caller invoke SomeUnsafeCode() as so:

```
static void Main(string[] args)
{
    unsafe
    {
        SomeUnsafeCode();
    }
}
```

Conversely, if you would rather not force the caller to wrap the invocation within an unsafe context, you could remove the unsafe keyword from the SomeUnsafeCode() method signature and opt for the following:

```
public static void SomeUnsafeCode()
{
    unsafe
    {
        // Work with pointers here!
    }
}
```

which would simplify the call to this:

```
static void Main(string[] args)
{
    SomeUnsafeCode();
}
```

Working with the * and & Operators

Once you have established an unsafe context, you are then free to build pointers to data types using the * operator and obtain the address of said pointer using the & operator. Using C#, the * operator is applied to the underlying type only, not as a prefix to each pointer variable name. For example, the following code declares two variables, both of type int* (a pointer to an integer):

```
// No! This is incorrect under C#!
int *pi, *pj;

// Yes! This is the way of C#.
int* pi, pj;
```

Consider the following example:

```
unsafe
{
    int myInt;

    // Define an int pointer, and
    // assign it the address of myInt.
    int* ptrToMyInt = &myInt;
```

```
    // Assign value of myInt using pointer indirection.
    *ptrToMyInt = 123;

    // Print some stats.
    Console.WriteLine("Value of myInt {0}", myInt);
    Console.WriteLine("Address of myInt {0:X}", (int)&ptrToMyInt);
}
```

An Unsafe (and Safe) Swap Function

Of course, declaring pointers to local variables simply to assign their value (as shown in the previous example) is never required and not altogether useful. To illustrate a more practical example of unsafe code, assume you wish to build a swap function using pointer arithmetic:

```
unsafe public static void UnsafeSwap(int* i, int* j)
{
    int temp = *i;
    *i = *j;
    *j = temp;
}
```

Very C-like, don't you think? However, given your work in Chapter 3, you should be aware that you could write the following safe version of your swap algorithm using the C# ref keyword:

```
public static void SafeSwap(ref int i, ref int j)
{
    int temp = i;
    i = j;
    j = temp;
}
```

The functionality of each method is identical, thus reinforcing the point that direct pointer manipulation is not a mandatory task under C#. Here is the calling logic:

```
static void Main(string[] args)
{
    Console.WriteLine("***** Calling method with unsafe code *****");

    // Values for swap.
    int i = 10, j = 20;

    // Swap values 'safely'.
    Console.WriteLine("\n***** Safe swap *****");
    Console.WriteLine("Values before safe swap: i = {0}, j = {1}", i, j);
    SafeSwap(ref i, ref j);
    Console.WriteLine("Values after safe swap: i = {0}, j = {1}", i, j);

    // Swap values 'unsafely'.
    Console.WriteLine("\n***** Unsafe swap *****");
    Console.WriteLine("Values before unsafe swap: i = {0}, j = {1}", i, j);
    unsafe { UnsafeSwap(&i, &j); }
    Console.WriteLine("Values after unsafe swap: i = {0}, j = {1}", i, j);
    Console.ReadLine();
}
```

Field Access via Pointers (the -> Operator)

Now assume that you have defined a Point structure and wish to declare a pointer to a Point type. Like C(++), when you wish to invoke methods or trigger fields of a pointer type, you will need to make use of the pointer-field access operator (->). As mentioned in Table 9-3, this is the unsafe version of the standard (safe) dot operator (.). In fact, using the pointer indirection operator (*), it is possible to dereference a pointer to (once again) apply the dot operator notation. Check out the following:

```
struct Point
{
    public int x;
    public int y;
    public override string ToString()
    { return string.Format("({0}, {1})", x, y);}
}

static void Main(string[] args)
{
    // Access members via pointer.
    unsafe
    {
        Point point;
        Point* p = &point;
        p->x = 100;
        p->y = 200;
        Console.WriteLine(p->ToString());
    }

    // Access members via pointer indirection.
    unsafe
    {
        Point point;
        Point* p = &point;
        (*p).x = 100;
        (*p).y = 200;
        Console.WriteLine((*p).ToString());
    }
}
```

The stackalloc Keyword

In an unsafe context, you may need to declare a local variable that allocates memory directly from the call stack (and is therefore not subject to .NET garbage collection). To do so, C# provides the stackalloc keyword, which is the C# equivalent to the _alloca function of the C runtime library. Here is a simple example:

```
unsafe
{
    char* p = stackalloc char[256];
    for (int k = 0; k < 256; k++)
        p[k] = (char)k;
}
```

Pinning a Type via the fixed Keyword

As you saw in the previous example, allocating a chunk of memory within an unsafe context may be facilitated via the stackalloc keyword. By the very nature of this operation, the allocated memory is cleaned up as soon as the allocating method has returned (as the memory is acquired from the stack). However, assume a more complex example. During our examination of the -> operator, you created a value type named Point. Like all value types, the allocated memory is popped off the stack once the executing scope has terminated. For the sake of argument, assume Point was instead defined as a *reference* type:

```csharp
class Point  // <= Now a class!
{
    public int x;
    public int y;
    public override string ToString()
    { return string.Format("({0}, {1})", x, y);}
}
```

As you are well aware, if the caller declares a variable of type Point, the memory is allocated on the garbage collected heap. The burning question then becomes, what if an unsafe context wishes to interact with this object (or any object on the heap)? Given that garbage collection can occur at any moment, imagine the pain of accessing the members of Point at the very point in time at which a sweep of the heap is under way. Theoretically, it is possible that the unsafe context is attempting to interact with a member that is no longer accessible or has been repositioned on the heap after surviving a generational sweep (which is an obvious problem).

To lock a reference type variable in memory from an unsafe context, C# provides the fixed keyword. The fixed statement sets a pointer to a managed type and "pins" that variable during the execution of statement. Without fixed, pointers to managed variables would be of little use, since garbage collection could relocate the variables unpredictably. (In fact, the C# compiler will not allow you to set a pointer to a managed variable except in a fixed statement.)

Thus, if you create a Point type (now redesigned as a class) and want to interact with its members, you must write the following code (or receive a compiler error):

```csharp
unsafe public static void Main()
{
    Point pt = new Point();
    pt.x = 5;
    pt.y = 6;

    // pin pt in place so it will not
    // be moved or GC-ed.
    fixed (int* p = &pt.x)
    {
        // Use int* variable here!
    }

    // pt is now unpinned, and ready to be GC-ed.
    Console.WriteLine ("Point is: {0}", pt);
}
```

In a nutshell, the fixed keyword allows you to build a statement that locks a reference variable in memory, such that its address remains constant for the duration of the statement. To be sure, any time you interact with a reference type from within the context of unsafe code, pinning the reference is a must.

The sizeof Keyword

The final unsafe-centric C# keyword to consider is sizeof. As in C(++), the C# sizeof keyword is used to obtain the size in bytes for a value type (never a reference type), and it may only be used within an unsafe context. As you may imagine, this ability may prove helpful when you're interacting with unmanaged C-based APIs. Its usage is straightforward:

```
unsafe
{
    Console.WriteLine("The size of short is {0}.", sizeof(short));
    Console.WriteLine("The size of int is {0}.", sizeof(int));
    Console.WriteLine("The size of long is {0}.", sizeof(long));
}
```

As sizeof will evaluate the number of bytes for any System.ValueType-derived entity, you are able to obtain the size of custom structures as well. Assume you have defined the following struct:

```
struct MyValueType
{
    public short s;
    public int i;
    public long l;
}
```

You can now obtain its size as follows:

```
unsafe
{
    Console.WriteLine("The size of short is {0}.", sizeof(short));
    Console.WriteLine("The size of int is {0}.", sizeof(int));
    Console.WriteLine("The size of long is {0}.", sizeof(long));
    Console.WriteLine("The size of MyValueType is {0}.",
        sizeof(MyValueType));
}
```

■**Source Code** The UnsafeCode project can be found under the Chapter 9 subdirectory.

C# Preprocessor Directives

Like many other languages in the C family, C# supports the use of various symbols that allow you to interact with the compilation process. Before examining various C# preprocessor directives, let's get our terminology correct. The term "C# preprocessor directive" is not entirely accurate. In reality, this term is used only for consistency with the C and C++ programming languages. In C#, there is no separate preprocessing step. Rather, preprocessing directives are processed as part of the lexical analysis phase of the compiler.

In any case, the syntax of the C# preprocessor directives is very similar to that of the other members of the C family, in that the directives are always prefixed with the pound sign (#). Table 9-4 defines some of the more commonly used directives (consult the .NET Framework 2.0 SDK documentation for complete details).

Table 9-4. *Common C# Preprocessor Directives*

Directives	Meaning in Life
#region, #endregion	Used to mark sections of collapsible source code
#define, #undef	Used to define and undefine conditional compilation symbols
#if, #elif, #else, #endif	Used to conditionally skip sections of source code (based on specified compilation symbols)

Specifying Code Regions

Perhaps some of the most useful of all preprocessor directives are #region and #endregion. Using these tags, you are able to specify a block of code that may be hidden from view and identified by a friendly textual marker. Use of regions can help keep lengthy *.cs files more manageable. For example, you could create one region for a type's constructors, another for type properties, and so forth:

```
class Car
{
    private string petName;
    private int currSp;

    #region Constructors
    public Car()
    { ... }
    public Car Car(int currSp, string petName)
    {...}
    #endregion

    #region Properties
    public int Speed
    { ... }
    public string Name
    {...}
    #endregion
}
```

When you place your mouse cursor over a collapsed region, you are provided with a snapshot of the code lurking behind (see Figure 9-5).

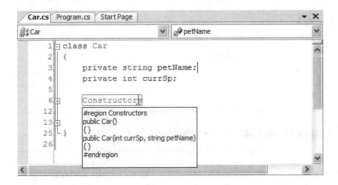

Figure 9-5. *Regions at work*

Conditional Code Compilation

The next batch of preprocessor directives (#if, #elif, #else, #endif) allows you to conditionally compile a block of code, based on predefined symbols. The classic use of these directives is to identify a block of code that is compiled only under a debug (rather than a release) build:

```
class Program
{
    static void Main(string[] args)
    {
        // This code will only execute if the project is
        // compiled as a Debug build.
        #if DEBUG
        Console.WriteLine("App directory: {0}",
            Environment.CurrentDirectory);
        Console.WriteLine("Box: {0}",
            Environment.MachineName);
        Console.WriteLine("OS: {0}",
            Environment.OSVersion);
        Console.WriteLine(".NET Version: {0}",
            Environment.Version);
        #endif
    }
}
```

Here, you are checking for a symbol named DEBUG. If it is present, you dump out a number of interesting statistics using some static members of the System.Environment class. If the DEBUG symbol is not defined, the code placed between #if and #endif will not be compiled into the resulting assembly, and it will be effectively ignored.

By default, Visual Studio 2005 always defines a DEBUG symbol; however, this can be prevented by deselecting the "Define DEBUG constant" check box located under the Build tab of your project's Properties page. Assuming you did disable this autogenerated DEBUG symbol, you could now define this symbol on a file-by-file basis using the #define preprocessor directive:

```
#define DEBUG
using System;

namespace Preprocessor
{
    class ProcessMe
    {
        static void Main(string[] args)
        {
            // Same code as before...
        }
    }
}
```

■**Note** #define directives must be listed before anything else in a C# code file.

You are also able to define your own custom preprocessor symbols. For example, assume you have authored a C# class that should be compiled a bit differently under the Mono distribution of .NET (see Chapter 1). Using #define, you can define a symbol named MONO_BUILD on a file-by-file basis:

```
#define DEBUG
#define MONO_BUILD

using System;

namespace Preprocessor
{
    class Program
    {
        static void Main(string[] args)
        {
            #if MONO_BUILD
                Console.WriteLine("Compiling under Mono!");
            #else
                Console.WriteLine("Compiling under Microsoft .NET");
            #endif
        }
    }
}
```

To create a project-wide symbol, make use of the "Conditional compilation symbols" text box located on the Build tab of your project's Properties page (see Figure 9-6).

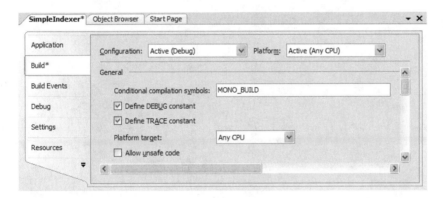

Figure 9-6. *Defining a projectwide preprocessor symbol*

Summary

The purpose of this chapter is to deepen your understanding of the C# programming language. You began by investigating various advanced type construction techniques (indexer methods, overloaded operators, and custom conversion routines). You spent the remainder of this chapter examining a small set of lesser-known keywords (e.g., sizeof, checked, unsafe, and so forth), and during the process came to learn how to work with raw pointer types. As stated throughout the chapter's examination of pointer types, a vast majority of your C# applications will *never* need to make use of them.

CHAPTER 10

■■■

Understanding Generics

With the release of .NET 2.0, the C# programming language has been enhanced to support a new feature of the CTS termed *generics*. Simply put, generics provide a way for programmers to define "placeholders" (formally termed *type parameters*) for method arguments and type definitions, which are specified at the time of invoking the generic method or creating the generic type.

To illustrate this new language feature, this chapter begins with an examination of the System.Collections.Generic namespace. Once you've seen generic support within the base class libraries, in the remainder of this chapter you'll examine how you can build your own generic members, classes, structures, interfaces, and delegates.

Revisiting the Boxing, Unboxing, and System.Object Relationship

To understand the benefits provided by generics, it is helpful to understand the "issues" programmers had without them. As you recall from Chapter 3, the .NET platform supports automatic conversion between stack-allocated and heap-allocated memory through *boxing* and *unboxing*. At first glance, this may seem like a rather uneventful language feature that is more academic than practical. In reality, the (un)boxing process is very helpful in that it allows us to assume everything can be treated as a System.Object, while the CLR takes care of the memory-related details on our behalf.

To review the boxing process, assume you have created a System.Collections.ArrayList to hold numeric (stack-allocated) data. Recall that the members of ArrayList are all prototyped to receive and return System.Object types. However, rather than forcing programmers to manually wrap the stack-based integer in a related object wrapper, the runtime will automatically do so via a boxing operation:

```
static void Main(string[] args)
{
    // Value types are automatically boxed when
    // passed to a member requesting an object.
    ArrayList myInts = new ArrayList();
    myInts.Add(10);
    Console.ReadLine();
}
```

If you wish to retrieve this value from the ArrayList object using the type indexer, you must unbox the heap-allocated object into a stack-allocated integer using a casting operation:

```
static void Main(string[] args)
{
...
    // Value is now unboxed...then reboxed!
```

```
        Console.WriteLine("Value of your int: {0}",
            (int)myInts[0]);
        Console.ReadLine();
}
```

When the C# compiler transforms a boxing operation into terms of CIL code, you find the box opcode is used internally. Likewise, the unboxing operation is transformed into a CIL unbox operation. Here is the relevant CIL code for the previous Main() method (which can be viewed using ildasm.exe):

```
.method private hidebysig static void  Main(string[] args) cil managed
{
...
    box    [mscorlib]System.Int32
    callvirt  instance int32 [mscorlib]System.Collections.ArrayList::Add(object)
    pop
    ldstr  "Value of your int: {0}"
    ldloc.0
    ldc.i4.0
    callvirt  instance object [mscorlib]
        System.Collections.ArrayList::get_Item(int32)
    unbox  [mscorlib]System.Int32
    ldind.i4
    box    [mscorlib]System.Int32
    call  void [mscorlib]System.Console::WriteLine(string, object)
...
}
```

Note that the stack-allocated System.Int32 is boxed prior to the call to ArrayList.Add() in order to pass in the required System.Object. Also note that the System.Object is unboxed back into a System.Int32 once retrieved from the ArrayList using the type indexer (which maps to the hidden get_Item() method), only to be *boxed again* when it is passed to the Console.WriteLine() method.

The Problem with (Un)Boxing Operations

Although boxing and unboxing are very convenient from a programmer's point of view, this simplified approach to stack/heap memory transfer comes with the baggage of performance issues and a lack of type safety. To understand the performance issues, ponder the steps that must occur to box and unbox a simple integer:

1. A new object must be allocated on the managed heap.

2. The value of the stack-based data must be transferred into that memory location.

3. When unboxed, the value stored on the heap-based object must be transferred back to the stack.

4. The now unused object on the heap will (eventually) be garbage collected.

Although the current Main() method won't cause a major bottleneck in terms of performance, you could certainly feel the impact if an ArrayList contained thousands of integers that are manipulated by your program on a somewhat regular basis.

Now consider the lack of type safety regarding unboxing operations. As you know, to unbox a value using the syntax of C#, you make use of the casting operator. However, the success or failure of a cast is not known until *runtime*. Therefore, if you attempt to unbox a value into the wrong data type, you receive an InvalidCastException:

```
static void Main(string[] args)
{
...
    // Ack!  Runtime exception!
    Console.WriteLine("Value of your int: {0}",
        (short)myInts[0]);
    Console.ReadLine();
}
```

In an ideal world, the C# compiler would be able to resolve illegal unboxing operations at compile time, rather than at runtime. On a related note, in a *really* ideal world, we could store sets of value types in a container that did not require boxing in the first place. .NET 2.0 generics are the solution to each of these issues. However, before we dive into the details of generics, let's see how programmers attempted to contend with these issues under .NET 1.x using strongly typed collections.

Type Safety and Strongly Typed Collections

In the world of .NET prior to version 2.0, programmers attempted to address type safety by building custom strongly typed collections. To illustrate, assume you wish to create a custom collection that can only contain objects of type Person:

```
public class Person
{
    // Made public for simplicity.
    public int currAge;
    public string fName, lName;

    public Person(){}
    public Person(string firstName, string lastName, int age)
    {
        currAge = age;
        fName = firstName;
        lName = lastName;
    }

    public override string ToString()
    {
        return string.Format("{0}, {1} is {2} years old",
            lName, fName, currAge);
    }
}
```

To build a person collection, you could define a System.Collections.ArrayList member variable within a class named PeopleCollection and configure all members to operate on strongly typed Person objects, rather than on generic System.Objects:

```
public class PeopleCollection : IEnumerable
{
    private ArrayList arPeople = new ArrayList();
    public PeopleCollection(){}

    // Cast for caller.
    public Person GetPerson(int pos)
    { return (Person)arPeople[pos]; }

    // Only insert Person types.
    public void AddPerson(Person p)
    { arPeople.Add(p); }
```

```
    public void ClearPeople()
    { arPeople.Clear(); }

    public int Count
    { get { return arPeople.Count; } }

    // Foreach enumeration support.
    IEnumerator IEnumerable.GetEnumerator()
    { return arPeople.GetEnumerator(); }
}
```

With these types defined, you are now assured of type safety, given that the C# compiler will be able to determine any attempt to insert an incompatible type:

```
static void Main(string[] args)
{
    Console.WriteLine("***** Custom Person Collection *****\n");
    PeopleCollection myPeople = new PeopleCollection();
    myPeople.AddPerson(new Person("Homer", "Simpson", 40));
    myPeople.AddPerson(new Person("Marge", "Simpson", 38));
    myPeople.AddPerson(new Person("Lisa", "Simpson", 9));
    myPeople.AddPerson(new Person("Bart", "Simpson", 7));
    myPeople.AddPerson(new Person("Maggie", "Simpson", 2));

    // This would be a compile-time error!
    myPeople.AddPerson(new Car());

    foreach (Person p in myPeople)
        Console.WriteLine(p);
    Console.ReadLine();
}
```

While custom collections do ensure type safety, this approach leaves you in a position where you must create a (almost identical) custom collection for each type you wish to contain. Thus, if you need a custom collection that will be able to operate only on classes deriving from the Car base class, you need to build a very similar type:

```
public class CarCollection : IEnumerable
{
    private ArrayList arCars = new ArrayList();
    public CarCollection(){}

    // Cast for caller.
    public Car GetCar(int pos)
    { return (Car) arCars[pos]; }

    // Only insert Car types.
    public void AddCar(Car c)
    { arCars.Add(c); }

    public void ClearCars()
    { arCars.Clear(); }

    public int Count
    { get { return arCars.Count; } }

    // Foreach enumeration support.
    IEnumerator IEnumerable.GetEnumerator()
    { return arCars.GetEnumerator(); }
}
```

As you may know from firsthand experience, the process of creating multiple strongly typed collections to account for various types is not only labor intensive, but also a nightmare to maintain. Generic collections allow us to delay the specification of the contained type until the time of creation. Don't fret about the syntactic details just yet, however. Consider the following code, which makes use of a generic class named System.Collections.Generic.List<> to create two type-safe container objects:

```
static void Main(string[] args)
{
    // Use the generic List type to hold only people.
    List<Person> morePeople = new List<Person>();
    morePeople.Add(new Person());

    // Use the generic List type to hold only cars.
    List<Car> moreCars = new List<Car>();

    // Compile-time error!
    moreCars.Add(new Person());
}
```

Boxing Issues and Strongly Typed Collections

Strongly typed collections are found throughout the .NET base class libraries and are very useful programming constructs. However, these custom containers do little to solve the issue of boxing penalties. Even if you were to create a custom collection named IntCollection that was constructed to operate only on System.Int32 data types, you must allocate some type of object to hold the data (System.Array, System.Collections.ArrayList, etc.):

```
public class IntCollection : IEnumerable
{
    private ArrayList arInts = new ArrayList();
    public IntCollection() { }

    // Unbox for caller.
    public int GetInt(int pos)
    { return (int)arInts[pos]; }

    // Boxing operation!
    public void AddInt(int i)
    { arInts.Add(i); }

    public void ClearInts()
    { arInts.Clear(); }

    public int Count
    { get { return arInts.Count; } }

    IEnumerator IEnumerable.GetEnumerator()
    { return arInts.GetEnumerator(); }
}
```

Regardless of which type you may choose to hold the integers (System.Array, System.Collections.ArrayList, etc.), you cannot escape the boxing dilemma using .NET 1.1. As you might guess, generics come to the rescue again. The following code leverages the System.Collections.Generic.List<> type to create a container of integers that does *not* incur any boxing or unboxing penalties when inserting or obtaining the value type:

```
static void Main(string[] args)
{
    // No boxing!
    List<int> myInts = new List<int>();
    myInts.Add(5);

    // No unboxing!
    int i = myInts[0];
}
```

Just to prove the point, the previous Main() method results in the following CIL code (note the lack of any box or unbox opcodes):

```
.method private hidebysig static void Main(string[] args) cil managed
{
    .entrypoint
    .maxstack  2
    .locals init ([0] class [mscorlib]System.Collections.Generic.'List`1'<int32>
        myInts, [1] int32 i)
    newobj instance void class
        [mscorlib]System.Collections.Generic.'List`1'<int32>::.ctor()
    stloc.0
    ldloc.0
    ldc.i4.5
    callvirt instance void class [mscorlib]
        System.Collections.Generic.'List`1'<int32>::Add(!0)
    nop
    ldloc.0
    ldc.i4.0
    callvirt instance !0 class [mscorlib]
        System.Collections.Generic.'List`1'<int32>::get_Item(int32)
    stloc.1
    ret
}
```

So now that you have a better feel for the role generics can play under .NET 2.0, you're ready to dig into the details. To begin, allow me to formally introduce the System.Collections.Generic namespace.

■**Source Code** The CustomNonGenericCollection project is located under the Chapter 10 directory.

The System.Collections.Generic Namespace

Generic types are found sprinkled throughout the .NET 2.0 base class libraries; however, the System.Collections.Generic namespace is chock full of them (as its name implies). Like its nongeneric counterpart (System.Collections), the System.Collections.Generic namespace contains numerous class and interface types that allow you to contain subitems in a variety of containers. Not surprisingly, the generic interfaces mimic the corresponding nongeneric types in the System.Collections namespace:

- ICollection<T>
- IComparer<T>
- IDictionary<K, V>
- IEnumerable<T>
- IEnumerator<T>
- IList<T>

■Note By convention, generic types specify their placeholders using uppercase letters. Although any letter (or word) will do, typically T is used to represent types, K is used for keys, and V is used for values.

The System.Collections.Generic namespace also defines a number of classes that implement many of these key interfaces. Table 10-1 describes the core class types of this namespace, the interfaces they implement, and any corresponding type in the System.Collections namespace.

Table 10-1. *Classes of* System.Collections.Generic

Generic Class	Nongeneric Counterpart in System.Collections	Meaning in Life
Collection<T>	CollectionBase	The basis for a generic collection
Comparer<T>	Comparer	Compares two generic objects for equality
Dictionary<K, V>	Hashtable	A generic collection of name/value pairs
List<T>	ArrayList	A dynamically resizable list of items
Queue<T>	Queue	A generic implementation of a first-in, first-out (FIFO) list
SortedDictionary<K, V>	SortedList	A generic implementation of a sorted set of name/value pairs
Stack<T>	Stack	A generic implementation of a last-in, first-out (LIFO) list
LinkedList<T>	N/A	A generic implementation of a doubly linked list
ReadOnlyCollection<T>	ReadOnlyCollectionBase	A generic implementation of a set of read-only items

The System.Collections.Generic namespace also defines a number of "helper" classes and structures that work in conjunction with a specific container. For example, the LinkedListNode<T> type represents a node within a generic LinkedList<T>, the KeyNotFoundException exception is raised when attempting to grab an item from a container using a nonexistent key, and so forth.

As you can see from Table 10-1, many of the generic collection classes have a nongeneric counterpart in the System.Collections namespace (some of which are identically named). Given that Chapter 7 illustrated how to work with these nongeneric types, I will not provide a detailed examination of each generic counterpart. Rather, I'll make use of List<T> to illustrate the process of working with generics. If you require details regarding other members of the System.Collections.Generic namespace, consult the .NET Framework 2.0 documentation.

Examining the List<T> Type

Like nongeneric classes, generic classes are heap-allocated objects, and therefore must be new-ed with any required constructor arguments. In addition, you are required to specify the type(s) to be substituted for the type parameter(s) defined by the generic type. For example, System.Collections.Generic.List<T> requires you to specify a single value that describes the type of item the List<T> will operate upon. Therefore, if you wish to create three List<> objects to contain integers and SportsCar and Person objects, you would write the following:

```
static void Main(string[] args)
{
    // Create a List containing integers.
    List<int> myInts = new List<int>();

    // Create a List containing SportsCar objects.
    List<SportsCar> myCars = new List<SportsCar>();

    // Create a List containing Person objects.
    List<Person> myPeople = new List<Person>();
}
```

At this point, you might wonder what exactly becomes of the specified placeholder value. If you were to make use of the Visual Studio 2005 Code Definition View window (see Chapter 2), you will find that the placeholder T is used throughout the definition of the List<T> type. Here is a partial listing (note the items in **bold**):

```
// A partial listing of the List<T> type.
namespace System.Collections.Generic
{
    public class List<T> :
        IList<T>, ICollection<T>, IEnumerable<T>,
        IList, ICollection, IEnumerable
    {
...
        public void Add(T item);
        public IList<T> AsReadOnly();
        public int BinarySearch(T item);
        public bool Contains(T item);
        public void CopyTo(T[] array);
        public int FindIndex(System.Predicate<T> match);
        public T FindLast(System.Predicate<T> match);
        public bool Remove(T item);
        public int RemoveAll(System.Predicate<T> match);
        public T[] ToArray();
        public bool TrueForAll(System.Predicate<T> match);
        public T this[int index] { get; set; }
..
    }
}
```

When you create a List<T> specifying SportsCar types, it is as if the List<T> type was really defined as so:

```
namespace System.Collections.Generic
{
    public class List<SportsCar> :
        IList<SportsCar>, ICollection<SportsCar>, IEnumerable<SportsCar>,
        IList, ICollection, IEnumerable
    {
...
        public void Add(SportsCar item);
        public IList<SportsCar> AsReadOnly();
        public int BinarySearch(SportsCar item);
        public bool Contains(SportsCar item);
        public void CopyTo(SportsCar[] array);
        public int FindIndex(System.Predicate<SportsCar> match);
        public SportsCar FindLast(System.Predicate<SportsCar> match);
        public bool Remove(SportsCar item);
```

```
    public int RemoveAll(System.Predicate<SportsCar> match);
    public SportsCar [] ToArray();
    public bool TrueForAll(System.Predicate<SportsCar> match);
    public SportsCar this[int index] { get; set; }
..
    }
}
```

Of course, when you create a generic List<T>, the compiler does not literally create a brand-new implementation of the List<T> type. Rather, it will address only the members of the generic type you actually invoke. To solidify this point, assume you exercise a List<T> of SportsCar objects as so:

```
static void Main(string[] args)
{
    // Exercise a List containing SportsCars
    List<SportsCar> myCars = new List<SportsCar>();
    myCars.Add(new SportsCar());
    Console.WriteLine("Your List contains {0} item(s).", myCars.Count);
}
```

If you examine the generated CIL code using ildasm.exe, you will find the following substitutions:

```
.method private hidebysig static void Main(string[] args) cil managed
{
    .entrypoint
    .maxstack  2
    .locals init ([0] class [mscorlib]System.Collections.Generic.'List`1'
        <class SportsCar> myCars)
    newobj instance void class [mscorlib]System.Collections.Generic.'List`1'
        <class SportsCar>::.ctor()
    stloc.0
    ldloc.0
    newobj instance void CollectionGenerics.SportsCar::.ctor()
    callvirt instance void class [mscorlib]System.Collections.Generic.'List`1'
        <class SportsCar>::Add(!0)
    nop
    ldstr "Your List contains {0} item(s)."
    ldloc.0
    callvirt  instance int32 class [mscorlib]System.Collections.Generic.'List`1'
        <class SportsCar>::get_Count()
    box [mscorlib]System.Int32
    call void [mscorlib]System.Console::WriteLine(string, object)
    nop
    ret
}
```

Now that you've looked at the process of working with generic types provided by the base class libraries, in the remainder of this chapter you'll examine how to create your own generic methods, types, and collections.

Creating Generic Methods

To learn how to incorporate generics into your own projects, you'll begin with a simple example of a generic swap routine. The goal of this example is to build a swap method that can operate on any possible data type (value-based or reference-based) using a single type parameter. Due to the nature of swapping algorithms, the incoming parameters will be sent by reference (via the C# ref keyword). Here is the full implementation:

```
// This method will swap any two items.
// as specified by the type parameter <T>.
static void Swap<T>(ref T a, ref T b)
{
    Console.WriteLine("You sent the Swap() method a {0}",
        typeof(T));
    T temp;
    temp = a;
    a = b;
    b = temp;
}
```

Notice how a generic method is defined by specifying the type parameter after the method name but before the parameter list. Here, you're stating that the Swap() method can operate on any two parameters of type <T>. Just to spice things up a bit, you're printing out the type name of the supplied placeholder to the console using the C# typeof() operator. Now ponder the following Main() method that swaps integer and string types:

```
static void Main(string[] args)
{
    Console.WriteLine("***** Fun with Generics *****\n");
    // Swap 2 ints.
    int a = 10, b = 90;
    Console.WriteLine("Before swap: {0}, {1}", a, b);
    Swap<int>(ref a, ref b);
    Console.WriteLine("After swap: {0}, {1}", a, b);
    Console.WriteLine();

    // Swap 2 strings.
    string s1 = "Hello", s2 = "There";
    Console.WriteLine("Before swap: {0} {1}!", s1, s2);
    Swap<string>(ref s1, ref s2);
    Console.WriteLine("After swap: {0} {1}!", s1, s2);
    Console.ReadLine();
}
```

Omission of Type Parameters

When you invoke generic methods such as Swap<T>, you can optionally omit the type parameter if (and only if) the generic method requires arguments, as the compiler can infer the type parameter based on the member parameters. For example, you could swap two System.Boolean types as so:

```
// Compiler will infer System.Boolean.
bool b1 = true, b2 = false;
Console.WriteLine("Before swap: {0}, {1}", b1, b2);
Swap(ref b1, ref b2);
Console.WriteLine("After swap: {0}, {1}", b1, b2);
```

However, if you had another generic method named DisplayBaseClass<T> that did not take any incoming parameters, as follows:

```
static void DisplayBaseClass<T>()
{
    Console.WriteLine("Base class of {0} is: {1}.",
        typeof(T), typeof(T).BaseType);
}
```

you are required to supply the type parameter upon invocation:

```
static void Main(string[] args)
{
...
    // Must supply type parameter if
    // the method does not take params.
    DisplayBaseClass<int>();
    DisplayBaseClass<string>();

    // Compiler error! No params?  Must supply placeholder!
    // DisplayBaseClass();
...
}
```

Figure 10-1 shows the current output of this application.

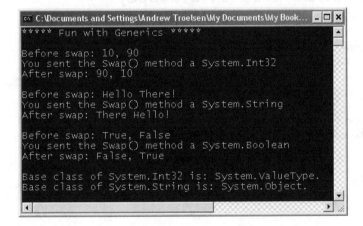

Figure 10-1. *Generic methods in action*

Currently, the generic Swap<T> and DisplayBaseClass<T> methods have been defined within the application object (i.e., the type defining the Main() method). If you would rather define these members in a new class type (MyHelperClass), you are free to do so:

```
public class MyHelperClass
{
    public static void Swap<T>(ref T a, ref T b)
    {
        Console.WriteLine("You sent the Swap() method a {0}",
            typeof(T));
        T temp;
        temp = a;
        a = b;
        b = temp;
    }

    public static void DisplayBaseClass<T>()
    {
        Console.WriteLine("Base class of {0} is: {1}.",
            typeof(T), typeof(T).BaseType);
    }
}
```

Notice that the `MyHelperClass` type is not in itself generic; rather, it defines two generic methods. In any case, now that the `Swap<T>` and `DisplayBaseClass<T>` methods have been scoped within a new class type, you will need to specify the type's name when invoking either member, for example:

```
MyHelperClass.Swap<int>(ref a, ref b);
```

Finally, generic methods do not need to be static. If `Swap<T>` and `DisplayBaseClass<T>` were instance level, you would simply make an instance of `MyHelperClass` and invoke them off the object variable:

```
MyHelperClass c = new MyHelperClass();
c.Swap<int>(ref a, ref b);
```

Creating Generic Structures (or Classes)

Now that you understand how to define and invoke generic methods, let's turn our attention to the construction of a generic structure (the process of building a generic class is identical). Assume you have built a flexible `Point` structure that supports a single type parameter representing the underlying storage for the (x, y) coordinates. The caller would then be able to create `Point<T>` types as so:

```
// Point using ints.
Point<int> p = new Point<int>(10, 10);

// Point using double.
Point<double> p2 = new Point<double>(5.4, 3.3);
```

Here is the complete definition of `Point<T>`, with analysis to follow:

```
// A generic Point structure.
public struct Point<T>
{
    // Generic state date.
    private T xPos;
    private T yPos;

    // Generic constructor.
    public Point(T xVal, T yVal)
    {
        xPos = xVal;
        yPos = yVal;
    }

    // Generic properties.
    public T X
    {
        get { return xPos; }
        set { xPos = value; }
    }

    public T Y
    {
        get { return yPos; }
        set { yPos = value; }
    }

    public override string ToString()
```

```
    {
        return string.Format("[{0}, {1}]", xPos, yPos);
    }

    // Reset fields to the default value of the
    // type parameter.
    public void ResetPoint()
    {
        xPos = default(T);
        yPos = default(T);
    }
}
```

The default Keyword in Generic Code

As you can see, Point<T> leverages its type parameter in the definition of the field data, constructor arguments, and property definitions. Notice that in addition to overriding ToString(), Point<T> defines a method named ResetPoint() that makes use of some new syntax:

```
// The 'default' keyword is overloaded in C# 2005.
// when used with generics, it represents the default
// value of a type parameter.
public void ResetPoint()
{
    xPos = default(T);
    yPos = default(T);
}
```

Under C# 2005, the default keyword has been given a dual identity. In addition to its use within a switch construct, it can be used to set a type parameter to its default value. This is clearly helpful given that a generic type does not know the actual placeholders up front and therefore cannot safely assume what the default value will be. The defaults for a type parameter are as follows:

- Numeric values have a default value of 0.
- Reference types have a default value of null.
- Fields of a structure are set to 0 (for value types) or null (for reference types).

For Point<T>, you could simply set xPos and yPos to 0 directly, given that it is safe to assume the caller will supply only numerical data. However, by using the default(T) syntax, you increase the overall flexibility of the generic type. In any case, you can now exercise the methods of Point<T> as so:

```
static void Main(string[] args)
{
    Console.WriteLine("***** Fun with Generics *****\n");

    // Point using ints.
    Point<int> p = new Point<int>(10, 10);
    Console.WriteLine("p.ToString()={0}", p.ToString());
    p.ResetPoint();
    Console.WriteLine("p.ToString()={0}", p.ToString());
    Console.WriteLine();

    // Point using double.
    Point<double> p2 = new Point<double>(5.4, 3.3);
    Console.WriteLine("p2.ToString()={0}", p2.ToString());
    p2.ResetPoint();
```

```
        Console.WriteLine("p2.ToString()={0}", p2.ToString());
        Console.WriteLine();

        // Swap 2 Points.
        Point<int> pointA = new Point<int>(50, 40);
        Point<int> pointB = new Point<int>(543, 1);
        Console.WriteLine("Before swap: {0}, {1}", pointA, pointB);
        Swap<Point<int>>(ref pointA, ref pointB);
        Console.WriteLine("After swap: {0}, {1}", pointA, pointB);
        Console.ReadLine();
    }
```

Figure 10-2 shows the output.

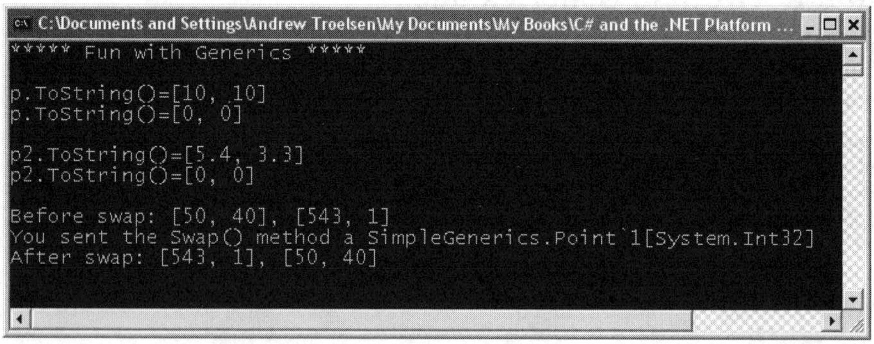

Figure 10-2. *Using the generic* Point *type*

■**Source Code**   The SimpleGenerics project is located under the Chapter 10 subdirectory.

Creating a Custom Generic Collection

As you have seen, the System.Collections.Generic namespace provides numerous types that allow you to create type-safe and efficient containers. Given the set of available choices, the chances are quite good that you will not need to build custom collection types when programming with .NET 2.0. Nevertheless, to illustrate how you could build a stylized generic container, the next task is to build a generic collection class named CarCollection<T>.

Like the nongeneric CarCollection created earlier in this chapter, this iteration will leverage an existing collection type to hold the subitems (a List<> in this case). As well, you will support foreach iteration by implementing the generic IEnumerable<> interface. Do note that IEnumerable<> extends the nongeneric IEnumerable interface; therefore, the compiler expects you to implement *two* versions of the GetEnumerator() method. Here is the update:

```
public class CarCollection<T> : IEnumerable<T>
{
    private List<T> arCars = new List<T>();

    public T GetCar(int pos)
    { return arCars[pos]; }
```

```
    public void AddCar(T c)
    { arCars.Add(c); }

    public void ClearCars()
    { arCars.Clear(); }

    public int Count
    { get { return arCars.Count; } }

    // IEnumerable<T> extends IEnumerable, therefore
    // we need to implement both versions of GetEnumerator().
    IEnumerator<T> IEnumerable<T>.GetEnumerator()
    { return arCars.GetEnumerator(); }
    IEnumerator IEnumerable.GetEnumerator()
    { return arCars.GetEnumerator(); }
}
```

You could make use of this updated CarCollection<T> as so:

```
static void Main(string[] args)
{
    Console.WriteLine("***** Custom Generic Collection *****\n");

    // Make a collection of Cars.
    CarCollection<Car> myCars = new CarCollection<Car>();
    myCars.AddCar(new Car("Rusty", 20));
    myCars.AddCar(new Car("Zippy", 90));

    foreach (Car c in myCars)
    {
        Console.WriteLine("PetName: {0}, Speed: {1}",
        c.PetName, c.Speed);
    }
    Console.ReadLine();
}
```

Here you are creating a CarCollection<T> type that contains only Car types. Again, you could achieve a similar end result if you make use of the List<T> type directly. The major benefit at this point is the fact that you are free to add unique methods to the CarCollection that delegate the request to the internal List<T>.

Constraining Type Parameters Using where

Currently, the CarCollection<T> class does not buy you much beyond uniquely named public methods. Furthermore, an object user could create an instance of CarCollection<T> and specify a completely unrelated type parameter:

```
// This is syntactically correct, but confusing at best...
CarCollection<int> myInts = new CarCollection<int>();
myInts.AddCar(5);
myInts.AddCar(11);
```

To illustrate another form of generic abuse, assume that you have now created two new classes (SportsCar and MiniVan) that derive from the Car type:

```
public class SportsCar : Car
{
    public SportsCar(string p, int s)
        : base(p, s){}
    // Assume additional SportsCar methods.
}

public class MiniVan : Car
{
    public MiniVan(string p, int s)
        : base(p, s){}
    // Assume additional MiniVan methods.
}
```

Given the laws of inheritance, it is permissible to add a MiniVan or SportsCar type directly into a CarCollection<T> created with a type parameter of Car:

```
// CarCollection<Car> can hold any type deriving from Car.
CarCollection<Car> myCars = new CarCollection<Car>();
myInts.AddCar(new MiniVan("Family Truckster", 55));
myInts.AddCar(new SportsCar("Crusher", 40));
```

Although this is syntactically correct, what if you wished to update CarCollection<T> with a new public method named PrintPetName()? This seems simple enough—just access the correct item in the List<T> and invoke the PetName property:

```
// Error! System.Object does not have a
// property named PetName.
public void PrintPetName(int pos)
{
    Console.WriteLine(arCars[pos].PetName);
}
```

However, this will not compile, given that the true identity of T is not yet known, and you cannot say for certain if the item in the List<T> type has a PetName property. When a type parameter is not constrained in any way (as is the case here), the generic type is said to be *unbound*. By design, unbound type parameters are assumed to have only the members of System.Object (which clearly does not provide a PetName property).

You may try to trick the compiler by casting the item returned from the List<T>'s indexer method into a strongly typed Car, and invoking PetName from the returned object:

```
// Error!
// Cannot convert type 'T' to 'Car'
public void PrintPetName(int pos)
{
    Console.WriteLine(((Car)arCars[pos]).PetName);
}
```

This again does not compile, given that the compiler does not yet know the value of the type parameter <T> and cannot guarantee the cast would be legal.

To address such issues, .NET generics may be defined with optional constraints using the where keyword. As of .NET 2.0, generics may be constrained in the ways listed in Table 10-2.

Table 10-2. *Possible Constraints for Generic Type Parameters*

Generic Constraint	Meaning in Life
where T : struct	The type parameter <T> must have System.ValueType in its chain of inheritance.
where T : class	The type parameter <T> must *not* have System.ValueType in its chain of inheritance (e.g., <T> must be a reference type).
where T : new()	The type parameter <T> must have a default constructor. This is very helpful if your generic type must create an instance of the type parameter, as you cannot assume the format of custom constructors. Note that this constraint must be listed last on a multiconstrained type.
where T : *NameOfBaseClass*	The type parameter <T> must be derived from the class specified by *NameOfBaseClass*.
where T : *NameOfInterface*	The type parameter <T> must implement the interface specified by *NameOfInterface*.

When constraints are applied using the where keyword, the constraint list is placed after the generic type's base class and interface list. By way of a few concrete examples, ponder the following constraints of a generic class named MyGenericClass:

```
// Contained items must have a default ctor.
public class MyGenericClass<T> where T : new()
{...}
```

```
// Contained items must be a class implementing IDrawable
// and support a default ctor.
public class MyGenericClass<T> where T : class, IDrawable, new()
{...}
```

```
// MyGenericClass derives from MyBase and implements ISomeInterface,
// while the contained items must be structures.
public class MyGenericClass<T> : MyBase, ISomeInterface where T : struct
{...}
```

On a related note, if you are building a generic type that specifies multiple type parameters, you can specify a unique set of constraints for each:

```
// <K> must have a default ctor, while <T> must
// implement the generic IComparable interface.
public class MyGenericClass<K, T> where K : new()
    where T : IComparable<T>
{...}
```

If you wish to update CarCollection<T> to ensure that only Car-derived types can be placed within it, you could write the following:

```
public class CarCollection<T> : IEnumerable<T> where T : Car
{
...
    public void PrintPetName(int pos)
    {
        // Because all subitems must be in the Car family,
        // we can now directly call the PetName property.
        Console.WriteLine(arCars[pos].PetName);
    }
}
```

Notice that once you constrain CarCollection<T> such that it can contain only Car-derived types, the implementation of PrintPetName() is straightforward, given that the compiler now assumes <T> is a Car-derived type. Furthermore, if the specified type parameter is not Car-compatible, you are issued a compiler error:

```
// Compiler error!
CarCollection<int> myInts = new CarCollection<int>();
```

Do be aware that generic methods can also leverage the where keyword. For example, if you wish to ensure that only System.ValueType-derived types are passed into the Swap() method created previously in this chapter, update the code accordingly:

```
// This method will swap any Value types.
static void Swap<T>(ref T a, ref T b) where T : struct
{
...
}
```

Understand that if you were to constrain the Swap() method in this manner, you would no longer be able to swap string types (as they are reference types).

The Lack of Operator Constraints

When you are creating generic methods, it may come as a surprise to you that it is a *compiler error* to apply any C# operators (+, -, *, ==, etc.) on the type parameters. As an example, I am sure you could imagine the usefulness of a class that can Add(), Subtract(), Multiply(), and Divide() generic types:

```
// Compiler error!  Cannot apply
// operators to type parameters!
public class BasicMath<T>
{
    public T Add(T arg1, T arg2)
    { return arg1 + arg2; }
    public T Subtract(T arg1, T arg2)
    { return arg1 - arg2; }
    public T Multiply(T arg1, T arg2)
    { return arg1 * arg2; }
    public T Divide(T arg1, T arg2)
    { return arg1 / arg2; }
}
```

Sadly, the preceding BasicMath<T> class will not compile. While this may seem like a major restriction, you need to remember that generics *are* generic. Of course, the System.Int32 type can work just fine with the binary operators of C#. However, for the sake of argument, if <T> were a custom class or structure type, the compiler cannot assume it has overloaded the +, -, *, and / operators. Ideally, C# would allow a generic type to be constrained by supported operators, for example:

```
// Illustrative code only!
// This is not legal code under C# 2.0.
public class BasicMath<T> where T : operator +, operator -,
    operator *, operator /
{
    public T Add(T arg1, T arg2)
    { return arg1 + arg2; }
    public T Subtract(T arg1, T arg2)
    { return arg1 - arg2; }
    public T Multiply(T arg1, T arg2)
```

```
{ return arg1 * arg2; }
public T Divide(T arg1, T arg2)
{ return arg1 / arg2; }
}
```

Alas, operator constraints are not supported under C# 2005.

■**Source Code** The CustomGenericCollection project is located under the Chapter 10 subdirectory.

Creating Generic Base Classes

Before we examine generic interfaces, it is worth pointing out that generic classes can be the base class to other classes, and can therefore define any number of virtual or abstract methods. However, the derived types must abide by a few rules to ensure that the nature of the generic abstraction flows through. First of all, if a nongeneric class extends a generic class, the derived class must specify a type parameter:

```
// Assume you have created a custom
// generic list class.
public class MyList<T>
{
    private List<T> listOfData = new List<T>();
}


// Concrete types must specify the type
// parameter when deriving from a
// generic base class.
public class MyStringList : MyList<string>
{}
```

Furthermore, if the generic base class defines generic virtual or abstract methods, the derived type must override the generic methods using the specified type parameter:

```
// A generic class with a virtual method.
public class MyList<T>
{
    private List<T> listOfData = new List<T>();
    public virtual void PrintList(T data) { }
}

public class MyStringList : MyList<string>
{
    // Must substitute the type parameter used in the
    // parent class in derived methods.
    public override void PrintList(string data) { }
}
```

If the derived type is generic as well, the child class can (optionally) reuse the type placeholder in its definition. Be aware, however, that any constraints placed on the base class must be honored by the derived type, for example:

```
// Note that we now have a default constructor constraint.
public class MyList<T> where T : new()
{
    private List<T> listOfData = new List<T>();
```

```
        public virtual void PrintList(T data) { }
}

// Derived type must honor constraints.
public class MyReadOnlyList<T> : MyList<T> where T : new()
{
        public override void PrintList(T data) { }
}
```

Now, unless you plan to build your own generics library, the chances that you will need to build generic class hierarchies are slim to none. Nevertheless, C# does support generic inheritance.

Creating Generic Interfaces

As you saw earlier in the chapter during the examination of the System.Collections.Generic namespace, generic interfaces are also permissible (e.g., IEnumerable<T>). You are, of course, free to define your own generic interfaces (with or without constraints). Assume you wish to define an interface that can perform binary operations on a generic type parameter:

```
public interface IBinaryOperations<T>
{
        T Add(T arg1, T arg2);
        T Subtract(T arg1, T arg2);
        T Multiply(T arg1, T arg2);
        T Divide(T arg1, T arg2);
}
```

Of course, interfaces are more or less useless until they are implemented by a class or structure. When you implement a generic interface, the supporting type specifies the placeholder type:

```
public class BasicMath : IBinaryOperations<int>
{
        public int Add(int arg1, int arg2)
        { return arg1 + arg2; }

        public int Subtract(int arg1, int arg2)
        { return arg1 - arg2; }

        public int Multiply(int arg1, int arg2)
        { return arg1 * arg2; }

        public int Divide(int arg1, int arg2)
        { return arg1 / arg2; }
}
```

At this point, you make use of BasicMath as you would expect:

```
static void Main(string[] args)
{
        Console.WriteLine("***** Generic Interfaces *****\n");
        BasicMath m = new BasicMath();
        Console.WriteLine("1 + 1 = {0}", m.Add(1, 1));
        Console.ReadLine();
}
```

If you would rather create a BasicMath class that operates on floating-point numbers, you could specify the type parameter as so:

```
public class BasicMath : IBinaryOperations<double>
{
    public double Add(double arg1, double arg2)
    { return arg1 + arg2; }
...
}
```

Source Code The GenericInterface project is located under the Chapter 10 subdirectory.

Creating Generic Delegates

Last but not least, .NET 2.0 does allow you to define generic delegate types. For example, assume you wish to define a delegate that can call any method returning void and receiving a single argument. If the argument in question may differ, you could model this using a type parameter. To illustrate, ponder the following code (notice the delegate targets are being registered using both "traditional" delegate syntax and method group conversion):

```
namespace GenericDelegate
{
    // This generic delegate can call any method
    // returning void and taking a single parameter.
    public delegate void MyGenericDelegate<T>(T arg);

    class Program
    {
        static void Main(string[] args)
        {
            Console.WriteLine("***** Generic Delegates *****\n");

            // Register target with 'traditional' delegate syntax.
            MyGenericDelegate<string> strTarget =
                new MyGenericDelegate<string>(StringTarget);
            strTarget("Some string data");

            // Register target using method group conversion.
            MyGenericDelegate<int> intTarget = IntTarget;
            intTarget(9);
            Console.ReadLine();
        }

        static void StringTarget(string arg)
        {
            Console.WriteLine("arg in uppercase is: {0}", arg.ToUpper());
        }

        static void IntTarget(int arg)
        {
            Console.WriteLine("++arg is: {0}", ++arg);
        }
    }
}
```

Notice that MyGenericDelegate<T> defines a single type parameter that represents the argument to pass to the delegate target. When creating an instance of this type, you are required to specify the value of the type parameter as well as the name of the method the delegate will invoke. Thus, if you specified a string type, you send a string value to the target method:

```
// Create an instance of MyGenericDelegate<T>
// with string as the type parameter.
MyGenericDelegate<string> strTarget =
    new MyGenericDelegate<string>(StringTarget);
strTarget("Some string data");
```

Given the format of the strTarget object, the StringTarget() method must now take a single string as a parameter:

```
static void StringTarget(string arg)
{
    Console.WriteLine("arg in uppercase is: {0}", arg.ToUpper());
}
```

Simulating Generic Delegates Under .NET 1.1

As you can see, generic delegates offer a more flexible way to specify the method to be invoked. Under .NET 1.1, you could achieve a similar end result using a generic System.Object:

```
public delegate void MyDelegate(object arg);
```

Although this allows you to send any type of data to a delegate target, you do so without type safety and with possible boxing penalties. For instance, assume you have created two instances of MyDelegate, both of which point to the same method, MyTarget. Note the boxing/unboxing penalties as well as the inherent lack of type safety:

```
class Program
{
    static void Main(string[] args)
    {
...

        // Register target with 'traditional' delegate syntax.
        MyDelegate d = new MyDelegate(MyTarget);
        d("More string data");

        // Register target using method group conversion.
        MyDelegate d2 = MyTarget;
        d2(9);  // Boxing penalty.
...
    }

    // Due to a lack of type safety, we must
    // determine the underlying type before casting.
    static void MyTarget(object arg)
    {
        if(arg is int)
        {
            int i = (int)arg;  // Unboxing penalty.
            Console.WriteLine("++arg is: {0}", ++i);
        }
        if(arg is string)
```

```
        {
            string s = (string)arg;
            Console.WriteLine("arg in uppercase is: {0}", s.ToUpper());
        }
    }
}
```

When you send out a value type to the target site, the value is (of course) boxed and unboxed once received by the target method. As well, given that the incoming parameter could be anything at all, you must dynamically check the underlying type before casting. Using generic delegates, you can still obtain the desired flexibility without the "issues."

A Brief Word Regarding Nested Delegates

I'll wrap up this chapter by covering one final aspect regarding generic delegates. As you know, delegates may be nested within a class type to denote a tight association between the two reference types. If the nesting type is a generic, the nested delegate may leverage any type parameters in its definition:

```
// Nested generic delegates may access
// the type parameters of the nesting generic type.
public class MyList<T>
{
    private List<T> listOfData = new List<T>();
    public delegate void ListDelegate(T arg);
}
```

■**Source Code** The GenericDelegate project is located under the Chapter 10 directory.

Summary

Generics can arguably be viewed as the major enhancement provided by C# 2005. As you have seen, a generic item allows you to specify "placeholders" (i.e., type parameters) that are specified at the time of creation (or invocation, in the case of generic methods). Essentially, generics provide a solution to the boxing and type-safety issues that plagued .NET 1.1 development.

While you will most often simply make use of the generic types provided in the .NET base class libraries, you are also able to create your own generic types. When you do so, you have the option of specifying any number of constraints to increase the level of type safety and ensure that you are performing operations on types of a "known quantity."

PART 3

■■■

Programming with .NET Assemblies

■ ■ ■

## CHAPTER 11

Introducing .NET Assemblies

Each of the applications developed in this book's first ten chapters were along the lines of traditional "stand-alone" applications, given that all of your custom programming logic was contained within a single executable file (*.exe). However, one major aspect of the .NET platform is the notion of *binary reuse*, where applications make use of the types contained within various external assemblies (aka code libraries). The point of this chapter is to examine the core details of creating, deploying, and configuring .NET assemblies.

In this chapter, you'll first learn the distinction between single-file and multifile assemblies, as well as "private" and "shared" assemblies. Next, you'll examine exactly how the .NET runtime resolves the location of an assembly and come to understand the role of the Global Assembly Cache (GAC), application configuration files (*.config files), publisher policy assemblies, and the System.Configuration namespace.

The Role of .NET Assemblies

.NET applications are constructed by piecing together any number of *assemblies*. Simply put, an assembly is a versioned, self-describing binary file hosted by the CLR. Now, despite the fact that .NET assemblies have exactly the same file extensions (*.exe or *.dll) as previous Win32 binaries (including legacy COM servers), they have very little in common under the hood. Thus, to set the stage for the information to come, let's ponder some of the benefits provided by the assembly format.

Assemblies Promote Code Reuse

As you have been building your console applications over the previous chapters, it may have seemed that *all* of the applications' functionality was contained within the executable assembly you were constructing. In reality, your applications were leveraging numerous types contained within the always accessible .NET code library, mscorlib.dll (recall that the C# compiler references mscorlib.dll automatically), as well as System.Windows.Forms.dll.

As you may know, a *code library* (also termed a *class library*) is a *.dll that contains types intended to be used by external applications. When you are creating executable assemblies, you will no doubt be leveraging numerous system-supplied and custom code libraries as you create the application at hand. Do be aware, however, that a code library need not take a *.dll file extension. It is perfectly possible for an executable assembly to make use of types defined within an external executable file. In this light, a referenced *.exe can also be considered a "code library."

■**Note** Before the release of Visual Studio 2005, the only way to reference an executable code library was using the `/reference` flag of the C# compiler. However, the Add Reference dialog box of Visual Studio 2005 now allows you to reference `*.exe` assemblies.

Regardless of how a code library is packaged, the .NET platform allows you to reuse types in a language-independent manner. For example, you could create a code library in C# and reuse that library in any other .NET programming language. It is possible to not only allocate types across languages, but derive from them as well. A base class defined in C# could be extended by a class authored in Visual Basic .NET. Interfaces defined in Pascal .NET can be implemented by structures defined in C#, and so forth. The point is that when you begin to break apart a single monolithic executable into numerous .NET assemblies, you achieve a *language-neutral* form of code reuse.

Assemblies Establish a Type Boundary

In Chapter 3, you learned about the formalities behind .NET namespaces. Recall that a type's *fully qualified name* is composed by prefixing the type's namespace (e.g., `System`) to its name (e.g., `Console`). Strictly speaking however, the assembly in which a type resides further establishes a type's identity. For example, if you have two uniquely named assemblies (say, `MyCars.dll` and `YourCars.dll`) that both define a namespace (`CarLibrary`) containing a class named `SportsCar`, they are considered unique types in the .NET universe.

Assemblies Are Versionable Units

.NET assemblies are assigned a four-part numerical version number of the form *<major>.<minor>. <build>.<revision>* (if you do not explicitly provide a version number using the [`AssemblyVersion`] attribute, the assembly is automatically assigned a version of 0.0.0.0). This number, in conjunction with an optional *public key value*, allows multiple versions of the same assembly to coexist in harmony on a single machine. Formally speaking, assemblies that provide public key information are termed *strongly named*. As you will see in this chapter, using a strong name, the CLR is able to ensure that the correct version of an assembly is loaded on behalf of the calling client.

Assemblies Are Self-Describing

Assemblies are regarded as *self-describing* in part because they record every external assembly it must have access to in order to function correctly. Thus, if your assembly requires `System.Windows. Forms.dll` and `System.Drawing.dll`, they will be documented in the assembly's *manifest*. Recall from Chapter 1 that a manifest is a blob of metadata that describes the assembly itself (name, version, external assemblies, etc.).

In addition to manifest data, an assembly contains metadata that describes the composition (member names, implemented interfaces, base classes, constructors and so forth) of every contained type. Given that an assembly is documented in such vivid detail, the CLR does *not* consult the Win32 system registry to resolve its location (quite the radical departure from Microsoft's legacy COM programming model). As you will discover during this chapter, the CLR makes use of an entirely new scheme to resolve the location of external code libraries.

Assemblies Are Configurable

Assemblies can be deployed as "private" or "shared." Private assemblies reside in the same directory (or possibly a subdirectory) as the client application making use of them. Shared assemblies, on the other hand, are libraries intended to be consumed by numerous applications on a single machine and are deployed to a specific directory termed the *Global Assembly Cache* (*GAC*).

Regardless of how you deploy your assemblies, you are free to author XML-based configuration files. Using these configuration files, the CLR can be instructed to "probe" for assemblies under a specific location, load a specific version of a referenced assembly for a particular client, or consult an arbitrary directory on your local machine, your network location, or a web-based URL. You'll learn a good deal more about XML configuration files throughout this chapter.

Understanding the Format of a .NET Assembly

Now that you've learned about several benefits provided by the .NET assembly, let's shift gears and get a better idea of how an assembly is composed under the hood. Structurally speaking, a .NET assembly (*.dll or *.exe) consists of the following elements:

- A Win32 file header
- A CLR file header
- CIL code
- Type metadata
- An assembly manifest
- Optional embedded resources

While the first two elements (the Win32 and CLR headers) are blocks of data that you can typically ignore, they do deserve some brief consideration. This being said, an overview of each element follows.

The Win32 File Header

The Win32 file header establishes the fact that the assembly can be loaded and manipulated by the Windows family of operating systems. This header data also identifies the kind of application (console-based, GUI-based, or *.dll code library) to be hosted by the Windows operating system. If you open a .NET assembly using the dumpbin.exe utility (via a .NET Framework 2.0 SDK command prompt) and specify the /headers flag, you can view an assembly's Win32 header information. Figure 11-1 shows (partial) Win32 header information for the CarLibrary.dll assembly you will build a bit later in this chapter.

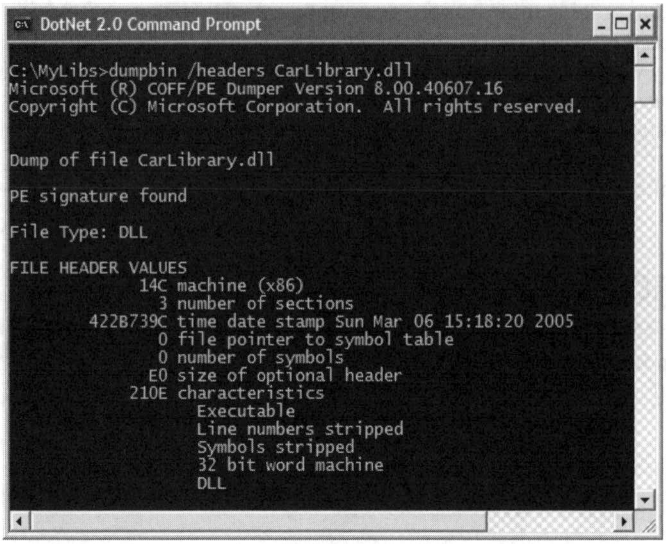

```
DotNet 2.0 Command Prompt                                    _ □ ×

C:\MyLibs>dumpbin /headers CarLibrary.dll
Microsoft (R) COFF/PE Dumper Version 8.00.40607.16
Copyright (C) Microsoft Corporation.  All rights reserved.


Dump of file CarLibrary.dll

PE signature found

File Type: DLL

FILE HEADER VALUES
            14C machine (x86)
              3 number of sections
       422B739C time date stamp Sun Mar 06 15:18:20 2005
              0 file pointer to symbol table
              0 number of symbols
             E0 size of optional header
           210E characteristics
                  Executable
                  Line numbers stripped
                  Symbols stripped
                  32 bit word machine
                  DLL
```

Figure 11-1. *An assembly's Win32 file header information*

The CLR File Header

The CLR header is a block of data that all .NET files must support (and do support, courtesy of the C# compiler) in order to be hosted by the CLR. In a nutshell, this header defines numerous flags that enable the runtime to understand the layout of the managed file. For example, flags exist that identify the location of the metadata and resources within the file, the version of the runtime the assembly was built against, the value of the (optional) public key, and so forth. If you supply the /clrheader flag to dumpbin.exe, you are presented with the internal CLR header information for a given .NET assembly, as shown in Figure 11-2.

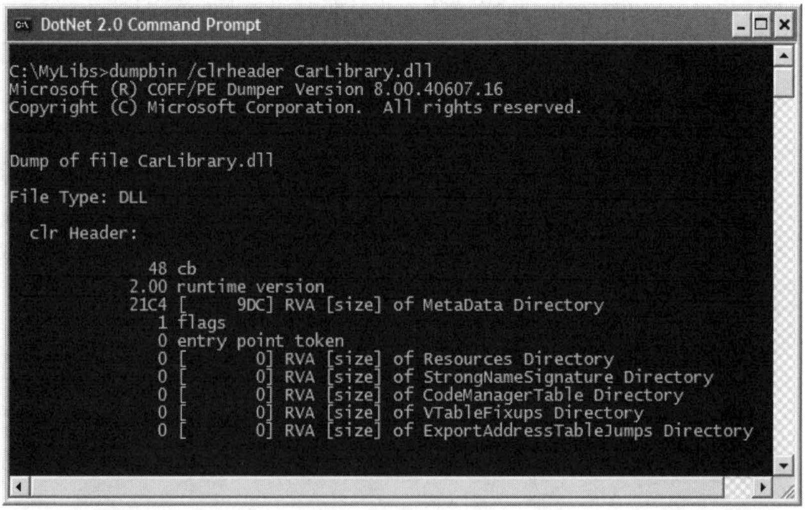

```
DotNet 2.0 Command Prompt                                    _ □ ×

C:\MyLibs>dumpbin /clrheader CarLibrary.dll
Microsoft (R) COFF/PE Dumper Version 8.00.40607.16
Copyright (C) Microsoft Corporation.  All rights reserved.


Dump of file CarLibrary.dll

File Type: DLL

  clr Header:

            48 cb
          2.00 runtime version
          21C4 [     9DC] RVA [size] of MetaData Directory
             1 flags
             0 entry point token
             0 [       0] RVA [size] of Resources Directory
             0 [       0] RVA [size] of StrongNameSignature Directory
             0 [       0] RVA [size] of CodeManagerTable Directory
             0 [       0] RVA [size] of VTableFixups Directory
             0 [       0] RVA [size] of ExportAddressTableJumps Directory
```

Figure 11-2. *An assembly's CLR file header information*

CLR header data is represented by an unmanaged C-style structure (IMAGE_COR20_HEADER) defined in the C-based header file, corhdr.h. For those who are interested, here is the layout of the structure in question:

```
// CLR 2.0 header structure.
typedef struct IMAGE_COR20_HEADER
{
    // Header versioning
    ULONG   cb;
    USHORT  MajorRuntimeVersion;
    USHORT  MinorRuntimeVersion;

    // Symbol table and startup information
    IMAGE_DATA_DIRECTORY    MetaData;
    ULONG   Flags;
    ULONG   EntryPointToken;

    // Binding information
    IMAGE_DATA_DIRECTORY    Resources;
    IMAGE_DATA_DIRECTORY    StrongNameSignature;

    // Regular fixup and binding information
    IMAGE_DATA_DIRECTORY    CodeManagerTable;
    IMAGE_DATA_DIRECTORY    VTableFixups;
    IMAGE_DATA_DIRECTORY    ExportAddressTableJumps;

    // Precompiled image info (internal use only - set to zero)
    IMAGE_DATA_DIRECTORY    ManagedNativeHeader;
} IMAGE_COR20_HEADER;
```

Again, as a .NET developer you will not need to concern yourself with the gory details of Win32 or CLR header information (unless perhaps you are building a new managed compiler!). Just understand that every .NET assembly contains this data, which is used behind the scenes by the .NET runtime and Win32 operating system.

CIL Code, Type Metadata, and the Assembly Manifest

At its core, an assembly contains CIL code, which as you recall is a platform- and CPU-agnostic intermediate language. At runtime, the internal CIL is compiled on the fly (using a just-in-time [JIT] compiler) to platform- and CPU-specific instructions. Given this architecture, .NET assemblies can indeed execute on a variety of architectures, devices, and operating systems. Although you can live a happy and productive life without understanding the details of the CIL programming language, Chapter 15 offers an introduction to the syntax and semantics of CIL.

An assembly also contains metadata that completely describes the format of the contained types as well as the format of external types referenced by this assembly. The .NET runtime uses this metadata to resolve the location of types (and their members) within the binary, lay out types in memory, and facilitate remote method invocations. You'll check out the details of the .NET metadata format in Chapter 12 during our examination of reflection services.

An assembly must also contain an associated *manifest* (also referred to as *assembly metadata*). The manifest documents each module within the assembly, establishes the version of the assembly, and also documents any *external* assemblies referenced by the current assembly (unlike legacy COM type libraries, which did not provide a way to document external dependencies). As you will see over the course of this chapter, the CLR makes extensive use of an assembly's manifest during the process of locating external assembly references.

Note Needless to say by this point in the book, when you wish to view an assembly's CIL code, type metadata, or manifest, `ildasm.exe` is the tool of choice. I will assume you will make extensive use of `ildasm.exe` as you work through the code examples in this chapter.

Optional Assembly Resources

Finally, a .NET assembly may contain any number of embedded resources such as application icons, image files, sound clips, or string tables. In fact, the .NET platform supports *satellite assemblies* that contain nothing but localized resources. This can be useful if you wish to partition your resources based on a specific culture (English, German, etc.) for the purposes of building international software. The topic of building satellite assemblies is outside the scope of this text; however, you *will* learn how to embed application resources into an assembly during our examination of GDI+ in Chapter 20.

Single-File and Multifile Assemblies

Technically speaking, an assembly can be composed of multiple *modules*. A module is really nothing more than a generic term for a valid .NET binary file. In most situations, an assembly is in fact composed of a single module. In this case, there is a one-to-one correspondence between the (logical) assembly and the underlying (physical) binary (hence the term *single-file assembly*).

Single-file assemblies contain all of the necessary elements (header information, CIL code, type metadata, manifest, and required resources) in a single *.exe or *.dll package. Figure 11-3 illustrates the composition of a single-file assembly.

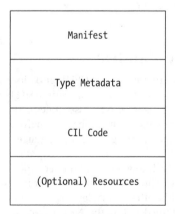

Figure 11-3. *A single-file assembly*

A multifile assembly, on the other hand, is a set of .NET *.dlls that are deployed and versioned as a single logic unit. Formally speaking, one of these *.dlls is termed the *primary module* and contains the assembly-level manifest (as well as any necessary CIL code, metadata, header information, and optional resources). The manifest of the primary module records each of the related *.dll files it is dependent upon.

As a naming convention, the secondary modules in a multifile assembly take a `*.netmodule` file extension; however, this is not a requirement of the CLR. Secondary `*.netmodules` also contain CIL code and type metadata, as well as a *module-level manifest*, which simply records the externally required assemblies of that specific module.

The major benefit of constructing multifile assemblies is that they provide a very efficient way to download content. For example, assume you have a machine that is referencing a remote multifile assembly composed of three modules, where the primary module is installed on the client. If the client requires a type within a secondary remote `*.netmodule`, the CLR will download the binary to the local machine on demand to a specific location termed the *download cache*. If each `*.netmodule` is 1MB, I'm sure you can see the benefit.

Another benefit of multifile assemblies is that they enable modules to be authored using multiple .NET programming languages (which is very helpful in larger corporations, where individual departments tend to favor a specific .NET language). Once each of the individual modules has been compiled, the modules can be logically "connected" into a logical assembly using tools such as the assembly linker (`al.exe`).

In any case, do understand that the modules that compose a multifile assembly are *not* literally linked together into a single (larger) file. Rather, multifile assemblies are only logically related by information contained in the primary module's manifest. Figure 11-4 illustrates a multifile assembly composed of three modules, each authored using a unique .NET programming language.

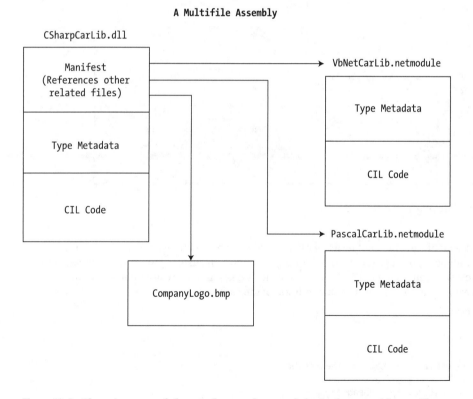

Figure 11-4. *The primary module records secondary modules in the assembly manifest*

At this point you (hopefully) have a better understanding about the internal composition of a .NET binary file. With this necessary preamble out of the way, we are ready to dig into the details of building and configuring a variety of code libraries.

Building and Consuming a Single-File Assembly

To begin the process of comprehending the world of .NET assemblies, you'll first create a single-file *.dll assembly (named CarLibrary) that contains a small set of public types. To build a code library using Visual Studio 2005, simply select the Class Library project workspace (see Figure 11-5).

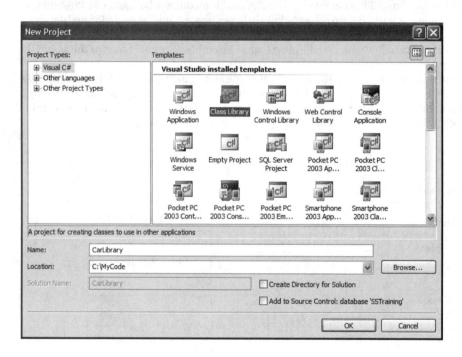

Figure 11-5. *Creating a C# code library*

The design of your automobile library begins with an abstract base class named Car that defines a number of protected data members exposed through custom properties. This class has a single abstract method named TurboBoost(), which makes use of a custom enumeration (EngineState) representing the current condition of the car's engine:

```
using System;

namespace CarLibrary
{
    // Represents the state of the engine.
    public enum EngineState
    { engineAlive, engineDead }

// The abstract base class in the hierarchy.
public abstract class Car
{
```

```
protected string petName;
protected short currSpeed;
protected short maxSpeed;
protected EngineState egnState = EngineState.engineAlive;

public abstract void TurboBoost();

public Car(){}
public Car(string name, short max, short curr)
{
    petName = name; maxSpeed = max; currSpeed = curr;
}

public string PetName
{
    get {  return petName; }
    set {  petName = value; }
}
public short CurrSpeed
{
    get {  return currSpeed; }
    set {  currSpeed = value; }
}
public short MaxSpeed
{ get {  return maxSpeed; }  }
public EngineState EngineState
{ get {  return egnState; }  }
}
}
```

Now assume that you have two direct descendents of the Car type named MiniVan and SportsCar. Each overrides the abstract TurboBoost() method in an appropriate manner.

```
using System;
using System.Windows.Forms;

namespace CarLibrary
{
    public class SportsCar : Car
    {
        public SportsCar(){ }
        public SportsCar(string name, short max, short curr)
            : base (name, max, curr){ }

        public override void TurboBoost()
        {
            MessageBox.Show("Ramming speed!", "Faster is better...");
        }
    }


    public class MiniVan : Car
    {
        public MiniVan(){ }
        public MiniVan(string name, short max, short curr)
            : base (name, max, curr){ }
```

```
        public override void TurboBoost()
        {
            // Minivans have poor turbo capabilities!
            egnState = EngineState.engineDead;
            MessageBox.Show("Time to call AAA", "Your car is dead");
        }
    }
}
```

Notice how each subclass implements TurboBoost() using the MessageBox class, which is defined in the System.Windows.Forms.dll assembly. For your assembly to make use of the types defined within this external assembly, the CarLibrary project must set a reference to this binary via the Add Reference dialog box (see Figure 11-6), which you can access through the Visual Studio 2005 Project ➤ Add Reference menu selection.

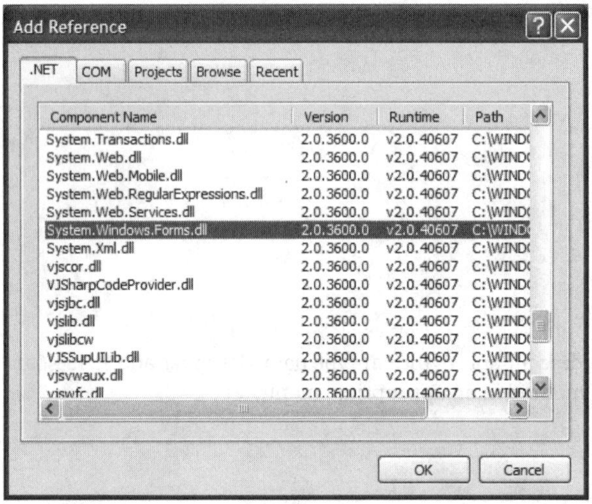

Figure 11-6. *Referencing external .NET assemblies begins here.*

It is *really* important to understand that the assemblies displayed in the .NET tab of the Add Reference dialog box do not represent each and every assembly on your machine. The Add Reference dialog box will *not* display your custom assemblies, and it does *not* display all assemblies located in the GAC. Rather, this dialog box simply presents a list of common assemblies that Visual Studio 2005 is preprogrammed to display. When you are building applications that require the use of an assembly not listed within the Add Reference dialog box, you need to click the Browse tab to manually navigate to the *.dll or *.exe in question.

■**Note** Although it is technically possible to have your custom assemblies appear in the Add Reference dialog box's list by deploying a copy to C:\Program Files\Microsoft Visual Studio 8\Common7\IDE\PublicAssemblies, there is little benefit in doing so. The Recent tab keeps a running list of previously referenced assemblies.

Exploring the Manifest

Before making use of CarLibrary.dll from a client application, let's check out how the code library is composed under the hood. Assuming you have compiled this project, load CarLibrary.dll into ildasm.exe (see Figure 11-7).

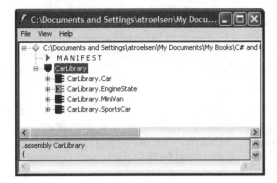

Figure 11-7. CarLibrary.dll *loaded into* ildasm.exe

Now, open the manifest of CarLibrary.dll by double-clicking the MANIFEST icon. The first code block encountered in a manifest is used to specify all external assemblies that are required by the current assembly to function correctly. As you recall, CarLibrary.dll made use of types within mscorlib.dll and System.Windows.Forms.dll, both of which are listed in the manifest using the .assembly extern token:

```
.assembly extern mscorlib
{
  .publickeytoken = (B7 7A 5C 56 19 34 E0 89 )
  .ver 2:0:0:0
}
.assembly extern System.Windows.Forms
{
  .publickeytoken = (B7 7A 5C 56 19 34 E0 89 )
  .ver 2:0:0:0
}
```

Here, each .assembly extern block is qualified by the .publickeytoken and .ver directives. The .publickeytoken instruction is present only if the assembly has been configured with a *strong name* (more details later in this chapter). The .ver token marks (of course) the numerical version identifier.

After cataloging each of the external references, you will find a number of .custom tokens that identify assembly-level attributes. If you examine the AssemblyInfo.cs file created by Visual Studio 2005, you will find these attributes represent basic characteristics about the assembly such as company name, trademark, and so forth (all of which are currently empty). Chapter 14 examines attributes in detail, so don't sweat the details at this point. Do be aware, however, that the attributes defined in AssemblyInfo.cs update the manifest with various .custom tokens, such as [AssemblyTitle]:

```
.assembly CarLibrary
{
...
  .custom instance void [mscorlib]
```

```
   System.Reflection.AssemblyTitleAttribute::.ctor(string) = ( 01 00 00 00 00 )
   .hash algorithm 0x00008004
  .ver 1:0:454:30104
}
.module CarLibrary.dll
```

Finally, you can also see that the .assembly token is used to mark the friendly name of your assembly (CarLibrary), while the .module token specifies the name of the module itself (CarLibrary.dll). The .ver token defines the version number assigned to this assembly, as specified by the [AssemblyVersion] attribute within AssemblyInfo.cs. More details on assembly versioning later in this chapter, but note that the * wildcard character within the [AssemblyVersion] attribute informs Visual Studio 2005 to increment the build and revision numbers during compilation.

Exploring the CIL

Recall that an assembly does not contain platform-specific instructions; rather, it contains platform-agnostic CIL. When the .NET runtime loads an assembly into memory, the underlying CIL is compiled (using the JIT compiler) into instructions that can be understood by the target platform. If you double-click the TurboBoost() method of the SportsCar class, ildasm.exe will open a new window showing the CIL instructions:

```
.method public hidebysig virtual instance void
        TurboBoost() cil managed
{
  // Code size        17 (0x11)
  .maxstack  2
  IL_0000:  ldstr      "Ramming speed!"
  IL_0005:  ldstr      "Faster is better..."
  IL_000a:  call       valuetype [System.Windows.Forms]
     System.Windows.Forms.DialogResult [System.Windows.Forms]
     System.Windows.Forms.MessageBox::Show(string, string)
  IL_000f:  pop
  IL_0010:  ret
} // end of method SportsCar::TurboBoost
```

Notice that the .method tag is used to identify a method defined by the SportsCar type. Member variables defined by a type are marked with the .field tag. Recall that the Car class defined a set of protected data, such as currSpeed:

```
.field family int16 currSpeed
```

Properties are marked with the .property tag. Here is the CIL describing the public CurrSpeed property (note that the read/write nature of a property is marked by .get and .set tags):

```
.property instance int16 CurrSpeed()
{
  .get instance int16 CarLibrary.Car::get_CurrSpeed()
  .set instance void CarLibrary.Car::set_CurrSpeed(int16)
} // end of property Car::CurrSpeed
```

Exploring the Type Metadata

Finally, if you now press Ctrl+M, ildasm.exe displays the metadata for each type within the CarLibrary.dll assembly (see Figure 11-8).

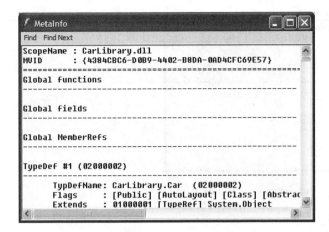

Figure 11-8. *Type metadata for the types within* `CarLibrary.dll`

Now that you have looked inside the `CarLibrary.dll` assembly, you can build some client applications.

■**Source Code** The CarLibrary project is located under the Chapter 11 subdirectory.

Building a C# Client Application

Because each of the CarLibrary types has been declared using the `public` keyword, other assemblies are able to make use of them. Recall that you may also define types using the C# `internal` keyword (in fact, this is the default C# access mode if you do not specifically define a type as `public`). Internal types can be used only by the assembly in which they are defined. External clients can neither see nor create internal types.

■**Note** .NET 2.0 now provides a way to specify "friend assemblies" that allow internal types to be consumed by specific assemblies. Look up the `InternalsVisibleToAttribute` class in the .NET Framework 2.0 SDK documentation for details.

To consume these types, create a new C# console application project (CSharpCarClient). Once you have done so, set a reference to `CarLibrary.dll` using the Browse tab of the Add Reference dialog box (if you compiled `CarLibrary.dll` using Visual Studio 2005, your assembly is located under the \Bin\Debug subdirectory of the CarLibrary project folder). Once you click the OK button, Visual Studio 2005 responds by placing a copy of `CarLibrary.dll` into the \Bin\Debug folder of the CSharpCarClient project folder (see Figure 11-9).

Figure 11-9. *Visual Studio 2005 copies private assemblies to the client's directory.*

At this point you can build your client application to make use of the external types. Update your initial C# file as so:

```
using System;

// Don't forget to 'use' the CarLibrary namespace!
using CarLibrary;

namespace CSharpCarClient
{
    public class CarClient
    {
        static void Main(string[] args)
        {
            // Make a sports car.
            SportsCar viper = new SportsCar("Viper", 240, 40);
            viper.TurboBoost();

            // Make a minivan.
            MiniVan mv = new MiniVan();
            mv.TurboBoost();
            Console.ReadLine();
        }
    }
}
```

This code looks just like the other applications developed thus far. The only point of interest is that the C# client application is now making use of types defined within a separate custom assembly. Go ahead and run your program. As you would expect, the execution of this program results in the display of various message boxes.

■Source Code   The CSharpCarClient project is located under the Chapter 11 subdirectory.

Building a Visual Basic .NET Client Application

To illustrate the language-agnostic attitude of the .NET platform, let's create another console application (VbNetCarClient), this time using Visual Basic .NET (see Figure 11-10). Once you have created the project, set a reference to CarLibrary.dll using the Add Reference dialog box.

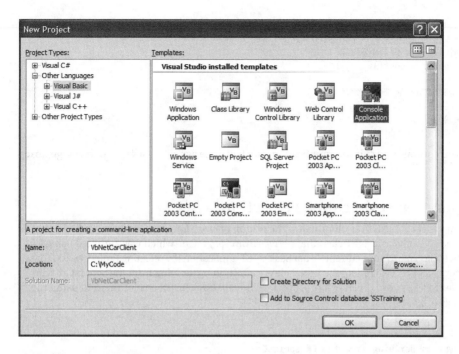

Figure 11-10. *Creating a Visual Basic .NET console application*

Like C#, Visual Basic .NET requires you to list each namespace used within the current file. However, Visual Basic .NET offers the Imports keyword rather than the C# using keyword. Given this, add the following Imports statement within the Module1.vb code file:

```
Imports CarLibrary

Module Module1

    Sub Main()
    End Sub

End Module
```

Notice that the Main() method is defined within a Visual Basic .NET Module type (which has nothing to do with a *.netmodule file for a multifile assembly). Modules are simply a Visual Basic .NET shorthand notation for defining a sealed class that can contain only static methods. To drive this point home, here would be the same construct in C#:

```
// A VB .NET 'Module' is simply a sealed class
// containing static methods.
public sealed class Module1
{
    public static void Main()
    {
    }
}
```

In any case, to exercise the MiniVan and SportsCar types using the syntax of Visual Basic .NET, update your Main() method as so:

```
Sub Main()
    Console.WriteLine("***** Fun with Visual Basic .NET *****")
    Dim myMiniVan As New MiniVan()
    myMiniVan.TurboBoost()

    Dim mySportsCar As New SportsCar()
    mySportsCar.TurboBoost()
    Console.ReadLine()
End Sub
```

When you compile and run your application, you will once again find a series of message boxes displayed.

Cross-Language Inheritance in Action

A very enticing aspect of .NET development is the notion of *cross-language inheritance*. To illustrate, let's create a new Visual Basic .NET class that derives from SportsCar (which was authored using C#). First, add a new class file to your current Visual Basic .NET application (by selecting Project ➤ Add Class) named PerformanceCar.vb. Update the initial class definition by deriving from the SportsCar type using the Inherits keyword. Furthermore, override the abstract TurboBoost() method using the Overrides keyword:

```
Imports CarLibrary

' This VB type is deriving from the C# SportsCar.
Public Class PerformanceCar
    Inherits SportsCar
        Public Overrides Sub TurboBoost()
            Console.WriteLine("Zero to 60 in a cool 4.8 seconds...")
        End Sub
End Class
```

To test this new class type, update the Module's Main() method as so:

```
Sub Main()
...
    Dim dreamCar As New PerformanceCar()

    ' Inherited property.
    dreamCar.PetName = "Hank"
    dreamCar.TurboBoost()
    Console.ReadLine()
End Sub
```

Notice that the dreamCar object is able to invoke any public member (such as the PetName property) found up the chain of inheritance, regardless of the fact that the base class has been defined in a completely different language and is defined in a completely different code library.

■Source Code The VbNetCarClient project is located under the Chapter 11 subdirectory.

Building and Consuming a Multifile Assembly

Now that you have constructed and consumed a single-file assembly, let's examine the process of building a multifile assembly. Recall that a multifile assembly is simply a collection of related modules that is deployed and versioned as a single unit. At the time of this writing, Visual Studio 2005 does not support a C# multifile assembly project template. Therefore, you will need to make use of the command-line compiler (csc.exe) if you wish to build such a beast.

To illustrate the process, you will build a multifile assembly named AirVehicles. The primary module (airvehicles.dll) will contain a single class type named Helicopter. The related manifest (also contained in airvehicles.dll) catalogues an additional *.netmodule file named ufo.netmodule, which contains another class type named (of course) Ufo. Although both class types are physically contained in separate binaries, you will group them into a single namespace named AirVehicles. Finally, both classes are created using C# (although you could certainly mix and match languages if you desire).

To begin, open a simple text editor (such as Notepad) and create the following Ufo class definition saved to a file named ufo.cs:

```
using System;

namespace AirVehicles
{
    public class Ufo
    {
        public void AbductHuman()
        {
            Console.WriteLine("Resistance is futile");
        }
    }
}
```

To compile this class into a .NET module, navigate to the folder containing ufo.cs and issue the following command to the C# compiler (the module option of the /target flag instructs csc.exe to produce a *.netmodule as opposed to a *.dll or *.exe file):

```
csc.exe /t:module ufo.cs
```

If you now look in the folder that contains the ufo.cs file, you should see a new file named ufo.netmodule (take a peek). Next, create a new file named helicopter.cs that contains the following class definition:

```
using System;

namespace AirVehicles
{
    public class Helicopter
    {
        public void TakeOff()
        {
            Console.WriteLine("Helicopter taking off!");
        }
    }
}
```

Given that airvehicles.dll is the intended name of the primary module of this multifile assembly, you will need to compile helicopter.cs using the /t:library and /out: options. To enlist the ufo.netmodule binary into the assembly manifest, you must also specify the /addmodule flag. The following command does the trick:

```
csc /t:library /addmodule:ufo.netmodule /out:airvehicles.dll helicopter.cs
```

At this point, your directory should contain the primary airvehicles.dll module as well as the secondary ufo.netmodule binaries.

Exploring the ufo.netmodule File

Now, using ildasm.exe, open ufo.netmodule. As you can see, *.netmodules contain a *module-level manifest*; however, its sole purpose is to list each external assembly referenced by the code base. Given that the Ufo class did little more than make a call to Console.WriteLine(), you find the following:

```
.assembly extern mscorlib
{
  .publickeytoken = (B7 7A 5C 56 19 34 E0 89 )
  .ver 2:0:0:0
}
.module ufo.netmodule
```

Exploring the airvehicles.dll File

Next, using ildasm.exe, open the primary airvehicles.dll module and investigate the assembly-level manifest. Notice that the .file token documents the associated modules in the multifile assembly (ufo.netmodule in this case). The .class extern tokens are used to document the names of the external types referenced for use from the secondary module (Ufo):

```
.assembly extern mscorlib
{
  .publickeytoken = (B7 7A 5C 56 19 34 E0 89 )
  .ver 2:0:0:0
}
.assembly airvehicles
{
...
  .hash algorithm 0x00008004
  .ver 0:0:0:0
}
.file ufo.netmodule
...
.class extern public AirVehicles.Ufo
{
  .file ufo.netmodule
  .class 0x02000002
}
.module airvehicles.dll
```

Again, realize that the only entity that links together airvehicles.dll and ufo.netmodule is the assembly manifest. These two binary files have not been merged into a single, larger *.dll.

Consuming a Multifile Assembly

The consumers of a multifile assembly couldn't care less that the assembly they are referencing is composed of numerous modules. To keep things simple, let's create a new Visual Basic .NET client application at the command line. Create a new file named Client.vb with the following Module definition. When you are done, save it in the same location as your multifile assembly.

```
Imports AirVehicles

Module Module1
    Sub Main()
        Dim h As New AirVehicles.Helicopter()
        h.TakeOff()
```

```vb
      ' This will load the *.netmodule on demand.
      Dim u As New UFO()
      u.AbductHuman()
   End Sub
End Module
```

To compile this executable assembly at the command line, you will make use of the Visual Basic .NET command-line compiler, vbc.exe, with the following command set:

```
vbc /r:airvehicles.dll *.vb
```

Notice that when you are referencing a multifile assembly, the compiler needs to be supplied only with the name of the primary module (the *.netmodules are loaded on demand when used by the client's code base). In and of themselves, *.netmodules do not have an individual version number and cannot be directly loaded by the CLR. Individual *.netmodules can be loaded only by the primary module (e.g., the file that contains the assembly manifest).

■**Note** Visual Studio 2005 also allows you to reference a multifile assembly. Simply use the Add References dialog box and select the primary module. Any related *.netmodules are copied during the process.

At this point, you should feel comfortable with the process of building both single-file and multifile assemblies. To be completely honest, chances are that 99.99 percent of your assemblies will be single-file entities. Nevertheless, multifile assemblies can prove helpful when you wish to break a large physical binary into more modular units (and they are quite useful for remote download scenarios). Next up, let's formalize the concept of a private assembly.

■**Source Code** The MultifileAssembly project is included under the Chapter 11 subdirectory.

Understanding Private Assemblies

Technically speaking, the assemblies you've created thus far in this chapter have been deployed as *private assemblies*. Private assemblies are required to be located within the same directory as the client application (termed the *application directory*) or a subdirectory thereof. Recall that when you set a reference to CarLibrary.dll while building the CSharpCarClient.exe and VbNetCarClient.exe applications, Visual Studio 2005 responded by placing a copy of CarLibrary.dll within the client's application directory.

When a client program uses the types defined within this external assembly, the CLR simply loads the local copy of CarLibrary.dll. Because the .NET runtime does not consult the system registry when searching for referenced assemblies, you can relocate the CSharpCarClient.exe (or VbNetCarClient.exe) and CarLibrary.dll assemblies to location on your machine and run the application (this is often termed *Xcopy deployment*).

Uninstalling (or replicating) an application that makes exclusive use of private assemblies is a no-brainer: simply delete (or copy) the application folder. Unlike with COM applications, you do not need to worry about dozens of orphaned registry settings. More important, you do not need to worry that the removal of private assemblies will break any other applications on the machine.

The Identity of a Private Assembly

The full identity of a private assembly consists of the friendly name and numerical version, both of which are recorded in the assembly manifest. The *friendly name* simply is the name of the module that contains the assembly's manifest minus the file extension. For example, if you examine the manifest of the `CarLibrary.dll` assembly, you find the following (your version will no doubt differ):

```
.assembly CarLibrary
{
...
    .ver 1:0:454:30104
}
```

Given the isolated nature of a private assembly, it should make sense that the CLR does not bother to make use of the version number when resolving its location. The assumption is that private assemblies do not need to have any elaborate version checking, as the client application is the only entity that "knows" of its existence. Given this, it is (very) possible for a single machine to have multiple copies of the same private assembly in various application directories.

Understanding the Probing Process

The .NET runtime resolves the location of a private assembly using a technique termed *probing*, which is much less invasive than it sounds. Probing is the process of mapping an external assembly request to the location of the requested binary file. Strictly speaking, a request to load an assembly may be either *implicit* or *explicit*. An implicit load request occurs when the CLR consults the manifest in order to resolve the location of an assembly defined using the `.assembly` extern tokens:

```
// An implicit load request.
.assembly extern CarLibrary
{ ...}
```

An explicit load request occurs programmatically using the `Load()` or `LoadFrom()` method of the `System.Reflection.Assembly` class type, typically for the purposes of late binding and dynamic invocation of type members. You'll examine these topics further in Chapter 12, but for now you can see an example of an explicit load request in the following code:

```
// An explicit load request.
Assembly asm = Assembly.Load("CarLibrary");
```

In either case, the CLR extracts the friendly name of the assembly and begins probing the client's application directory for a file named `CarLibrary.dll`. If this file cannot be located, an attempt is made to locate an executable assembly based on the same friendly name (`CarLibrary.exe`). If neither of these files can be located in the application directory, the runtime gives up and throws a `FileNotFound` exception at runtime.

Note Technically speaking, if a copy of the requested assembly cannot be found within the client's application directory, the CLR will also attempt to locate a client subdirectory with the exact same name as the assembly's friendly name (e.g., C:\MyClient\CarLibrary). If the requested assembly resides within this subdirectory, the CLR will load the assembly into memory.

Configuring Private Assemblies

While it is possible to deploy a .NET application by simply copying all required assemblies to a single folder on the user's hard drive, you will most likely wish to define a number of subdirectories to group related content. For example, assume you have an application directory named C:\MyApp that contains `CSharpCarClient.exe`. Under this folder might be a subfolder named MyLibraries that contains `CarLibrary.dll`.

Regardless of the intended relationship between these two directories, the CLR will *not* probe the MyLibraries subdirectory unless you supply a configuration file. Configuration files contain various XML elements that allow you to influence the probing process. By "law," configuration files must have the same name as the launching application and take a `*.config` file extension, and they must be deployed in the client's application directory. Thus, if you wish to create a configuration file for `CSharpCarClient.exe`, it must be named `CSharpCarClient.exe.config`.

To illustrate the process, create a new directory on your C drive named MyApp using Windows Explorer. Next, copy `CSharpCarClient.exe` and `CarLibrary.dll` to this new folder, and run the program by double-clicking the executable. Your program should run successfully at this point (remember, the assemblies are not registered!). Next, create a new subdirectory under C:\MyApp named MyLibraries (see Figure 11-11), and move `CarLibrary.dll` to this location.

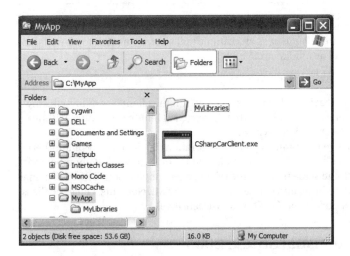

Figure 11-11. `CarLibrary.dll` *now resides under the MyLibraries subdirectory.*

Try to run your client program again. Because the CLR could not locate "CarLibrary" directly within the application directory, you are presented with a rather nasty unhandled `FileNotFound` exception.

To rectify the situation, create a new configuration file named `CSharpCarClient.exe.config` and save it in the *same* folder containing the `CSharpCarClient.exe` application, which in this example would be C:\MyApp. Open this file and enter the following content exactly as shown (be aware that XML is case sensitive!):

```
<configuration>
    <runtime>
        <assemblyBinding xmlns="urn:schemas-microsoft-com:asm.v1">
            <probing privatePath="MyLibraries"/>
        </assemblyBinding>
    </runtime>
</configuration>
```

.NET `*.config` files always open with a root element named `<configuration>`. The nested `<runtime>` element may specify an `<assemblyBinding>` element, which nests a further element named `<probing>`. The `privatePath` attribute is the key point in this example, as it is used to specify the subdirectories relative to the application directory where the CLR should probe.

Do note that the `<probing>` element does not specify *which* assembly is located under a given subdirectory. In other words, you cannot say, "CarLibrary is located under the MyLibraries subdirectory, but MathUtils is located under Bin subdirectory." The `<probing>` element simply instructs the CLR to investigate all specified subdirectories for the requested assembly until the first match is encountered.

■**Note** Be very aware that the `privatePath` attribute *cannot be used* to specify an absolute (C:\SomeFolder\ SomeSubFolder) or relative (..\\SomeFolder\\AnotherFolder) path! If you wish to specify a directory outside the client's application directory, you will need to make use of a completely different XML element named `<codeBase>` (more details on this element later in the chapter).

Multiple subdirectories can be assigned to the `privatePath` attribute using a semicolon-delimited list. You have no need to do so at this time, but here is an example that informs the CLR to consult the MyLibraries and MyLibraries\Tests client subdirectories:

```
<probing privatePath="MyLibraries; MyLibraries\Tests"/>
```

Once you've finished creating `CSharpCarClient.exe.config`, run the client by double-clicking the executable in Windows Explorer. You should find that `CSharpCarClient.exe` executes without a hitch (if this is not the case, double-check it for typos).

Next, for testing purposes, change the name of your configuration file (in one way or another) and attempt to run the program once again. The client application should now fail. Remember that `*.config` files must be prefixed with the same name as the related client application. By way of a final test, open your configuration file for editing and capitalize any of the XML elements. Once the file is saved, your client should fail to run once again (as XML is case sensitive).

Configuration Files and Visual Studio 2005

While you are always able to create XML configuration files by hand using your text editor of choice, Visual Studio 2005 allows you create a configuration file during the development of the client program. To illustrate, load the CSharpCarClient solution into Visual Studio 2005 and insert a new Application Configuration File item using the Project ➤ Add New Item menu selection. Before you click the OK button, take note that the file is named `App.config` (don't rename it!). If you look in the Solution Explorer window, you will now find `App.config` has been inserted into your current project (see Figure 11-12).

Figure 11-12. *The Visual Studio 2005* `App.config` *file*

At this point, you are free to enter the necessary XML elements for the client you happen to be creating. Now, here is the cool thing. Each time you compile your project, Visual Studio 2005 will automatically copy the data in App.config to the \Bin\Debug directory using the proper naming convention (such as CSharpCarClient.exe.config). However, this behavior will happen only if your configuration file is indeed named App.config.

Using this approach, all you need to do is maintain App.config, and Visual Studio 2005 will ensure your application directory contains the latest and greatest content (even if you happen to rename your project).

Introducing the .NET Framework 2.0 Configuration Utility

Although authoring a *.config file by hand is not too traumatic, the .NET Framework 2.0 SDK does ship with a tool that allows you to build XML configuration files using a friendly GUI. You can find the .NET Framework 2.0 Configuration utility under the Administrative folder of your Control Panel. Once you launch this tool, you will find a number of configuration options (see Figure 11-13).

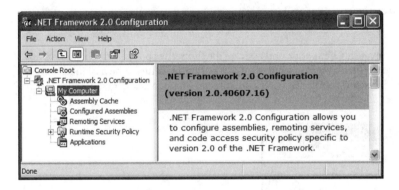

Figure 11-13. *The .NET Framework 2.0 Configuration utility*

To build a client *.config file using this utility, your first step is to add the application to configure by right-clicking the Applications node and selecting Add. In the resulting dialog box, you *may* find the application you wish to configure, provided that you have executed it using Windows Explorer. If this is not the case, click the Other button and navigate to the location of the client program you wish to configure. For this example, select the VbNetCarClient.exe application created earlier in this chapter (look under the Bin folder). Once you have done so, you will now find a new subnode, as shown in Figure 11-14.

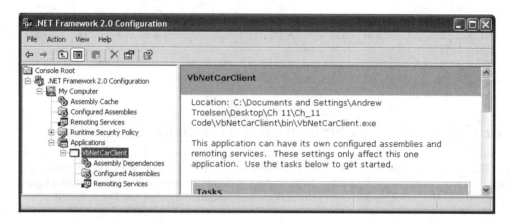

Figure 11-14. *Preparing to configure* VbNetCarClient.exe

If you right-click the VbNetCarClient node and activate the Properties page, you will notice a text field located at the bottom of the dialog box where you can enter the values to be assigned to the privatePath attribute. Just for testing purposes, enter a subdirectory named **TestDir** (see Figure 11-15).

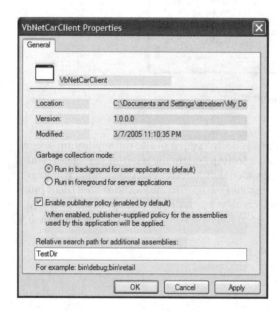

Figure 11-15. *Configuring a private probing path graphically*

Once you click the OK button, you can examine the VbNetCarClient\Debug directory and find that the default *.config file (which Visual Studio 2005 provides for most VB .NET programs) has been updated with the correct <probing> element.

■**Note** As you may guess, you can copy the XML content generated by the .NET Framework 2.0 Configuration utility into a Visual Studio 2005 `App.config` file for further editing. Using this approach, you can certainly decrease your typing burden by allowing the tool to generate the initial content.

Understanding Shared Assemblies

Now that you understand how to deploy and configure a private assembly, you can begin to examine the role of a *shared assembly*. Like a private assembly, a shared assembly is a collection of types and (optional) resources. The most obvious difference between shared and private assemblies is the fact that a single copy of a shared assembly can be used by several applications on a single machine.

Consider all the applications created in this text that required you to set a reference to `System. Windows.Forms.dll`. If you were to look in the application directory of each of these clients, you would *not* find a private copy of this .NET assembly. The reason is that `System.Windows.Forms.dll` has been deployed as a shared assembly. Clearly, if you need to create a machine-wide class library, this is the way to go.

As suggested in the previous paragraph, a shared assembly is not deployed within the same directory as the application making use of it. Rather, shared assemblies are installed into the Global Assembly Cache (GAC). The GAC is located under a subdirectory of your Windows directory named Assembly (e.g., C:\Windows\Assembly), as shown in Figure 11-16.

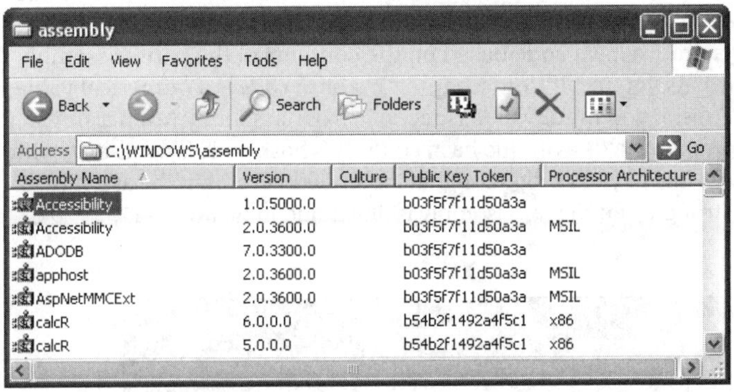

Figure 11-16. *The GAC*

■**Note** You cannot install executable assemblies (`*.exe`) into the GAC. Only assemblies that take the `*.dll` file extension can be deployed as a shared assembly.

Understanding Strong Names

Before you can deploy an assembly to the GAC, you must assign it a *strong name*, which is used to uniquely identify the publisher of a given .NET binary. Understand that a "publisher" could be an individual programmer, a department within a given company, or an entire company at large.

In some ways, a strong name is the modern day .NET equivalent of the COM globally unique identifier (GUID) identification scheme. If you have a COM background, you may recall that AppIDs are GUIDs that identify a particular COM application. Unlike COM GUID values (which are nothing more than 128-bit numbers), strong names are based (in part) on two cryptographically related keys (termed the *public key* and the *private key*), which are much more unique and resistant to tampering than a simple GUID.

Formally, a strong name is composed of a set of related data, much of which is specified using assembly-level attributes:

- The friendly name of the assembly (which you recall is the name of the assembly minus the file extension)

- The version number of the assembly (assigned using the [AssemblyVersion] attribute)

- The public key value (assigned using the [AssemblyKeyFile] attribute)

- An optional culture identity value for localization purposes (assigned using the [AssemblyCulture] attribute)

- An embedded *digital signature* created using a hash of the assembly's contents and the private key value

To provide a strong name for an assembly, your first step is to generate public/private key data using the .NET Framework 2.0 SDK's sn.exe utility (which you'll do momentarily). The sn.exe utility responds by generating a file (typically ending with the *.snk [Strong Name Key] file extension) that contains data for two distinct but mathematically related keys, the "public" key and the "private" key. Once the C# compiler is made aware of the location for your *.snk file, it will record the full public key value in the assembly manifest using the .publickey token at the time of compilation.

The C# compiler will also generate a hash code based on the contents of the entire assembly (CIL code, metadata, and so forth). As you recall from Chapter 3, a *hash code* is a numerical value that is unique for a fixed input. Thus, if you modify any aspect of a .NET assembly (even a single character in a string literal) the compiler yields a unique hash code. This hash code is combined with the private key data within the *.snk file to yield a digital signature embedded within the assembly's CLR header data. The process of strongly naming an assembly is illustrated in Figure 11-17.

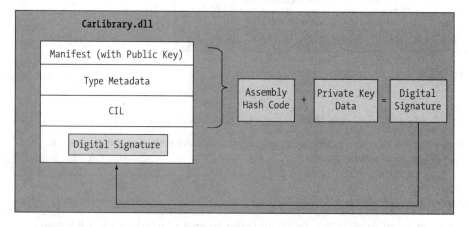

Figure 11-17. *At compile time, a digital signature is generated and embedded into the assembly based in part on public and private key data.*

Understand that the actual *private* key data is not listed anywhere within the manifest, but is used only to digitally sign the contents of the assembly (in conjunction with the generated hash code). Again, the whole idea of making use of public/private key cryptography is to ensure that no two companies, departments, or individuals have the same identity in the .NET universe. In any case, once the process of assigning a strong name is complete, the assembly may be installed into the GAC.

■**Note** Strong names also provide a level of protection against potential evildoers tampering with your assembly's contents. Given this point, it considered a .NET best practice to strongly name every assembly regardless if it is deployed to the GAC.

Strongly Naming CarLibrary.dll

Let's walk through the process of assigning a strong name to the CarLibrary assembly created earlier in this chapter (go ahead and open up that project using your IDE of choice). The first order of business is to generate the required key data using the sn.exe utility. Although this tool has numerous command-line options, all you need to concern yourself with for the moment is the -k flag, which instructs the tool to generate a new file containing the public/private key information. Create a new folder on your C drive named MyTestKeyPair and change to that directory using the .NET Command Prompt. Now, issue the following command to generate a file named MyTestKeyPair.snk:

```
sn -k MyTestKeyPair.snk
```

Now that you have your key data, you need to inform the C# compiler exactly where MyTestKeyPair.snk is located. When you create any new C# project workspace using Visual Studio 2005, you will notice that one of your initial project files (located under the Properties node of Solution Explorer) is named AssemblyInfo.cs. This file contains a number of attributes that describe the assembly itself. The AssemblyKeyFile assembly-level attribute can be used to inform the compiler of the location of a valid *.snk file. Simply specify the path as a string parameter, for example:

```
[assembly: AssemblyKeyFile(@"C:\MyTestKeyPair\MyTestKeyPair.snk")]
```

Given that the version of a shared assembly is one aspect of a strong name, let's also specify a specific version number for CarLibrary.dll. In the AssemblyInfo.cs file, you will find another attribute named AssemblyVersion. Initially the value is set to 1.0.*:

```
[assembly: AssemblyVersion("1.0.*")]
```

Recall that a .NET version number is composed of the four parts (*<major>.<minor>.<build>. <revision>*). Until you say otherwise, Visual Studio 2005 automatically increments the build and revision numbers (as marked by the * wildcard token) as part of each compilation. To enforce a fixed value for the assembly's build version, replace the wildcard token with a specific build and revision value:

```
// Format: <Major version>.<Minor version>.<Build number>.<Revision>
// Valid values for each part of the version number are between 0 and 65535.
[assembly: AssemblyVersion("1.0.0.0")]
```

At this point, the C# compiler has all the information needed to generate strong name data (as you are not specifying a unique culture value via the [AssemblyCulture] attribute, you "inherit" the culture of your current machine). Compile your CarLibrary code library and open the manifest using ildasm.exe. You will now see a new .publickey tag is used to document the full public key information, while the .ver token records the version specified via the [AssemblyVersion] attribute (see Figure 11-18).

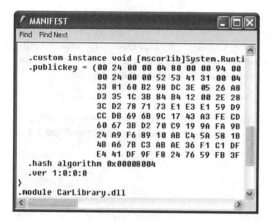

```
/ MANIFEST                          [_][□][X]
Find  Find Next

  .custom instance void [mscorlib]System.Runti
  .publickey = (00 24 00 00 04 80 00 00 94 00
                00 24 00 00 52 53 41 31 00 04
                33 81 60 B2 98 DC 3E 05 26 A8
                D3 35 1C 3B 84 B4 12 00 2E 28
                3C D2 78 71 73 E1 E3 E1 59 D9
                CC DB 69 6B 9C 17 43 A3 FE CD
                60 67 3B D2 70 C9 19 9A FA 9B
                24 A9 F6 89 10 AB C4 5A 58 1B
                4B A6 7B C3 AB AE 36 F1 C1 DF
                E4 41 DF 9F F8 24 76 59 FB 3F
  .hash algorithm 0x00008004
  .ver 1:0:0:0
}
.module CarLibrary.dll
```

Figure 11-18. *A strongly named assembly records the public key in the manifest.*

Assigning Strong Names Using Visual Studio 2005

Before you deploy CarLibrary.dll to the GAC, let me point out that Visual Studio 2005 allows you to specify the location of your *.snk file using the project's Properties page (in fact, this is now considered the preferred approach; using the [AssemblyKeyFile] attribute generates a compiler warning under Visual Studio 2005). To do so, select the Signing node, supply the path to the *.snk file, and select the "Sign the assembly" check box (see Figure 11-19).

Figure 11-19. *Specifying a* *.snk *file via the Properties page*

Installing/Removing Shared Assemblies to/from the GAC

The final step is to install the (now strongly named) CarLibrary.dll into the GAC. The simplest way to install a shared assembly into the GAC is to drag and drop the assembly to C:\Windows\Assembly using Windows Explorer (which is ideal for a quick test).

In addition, the .NET Framework 2.0 SDK provides a command-line utility named gacutil.exe that allows you to examine and modify the contents of the GAC. Table 11-1 documents some relevant options of gacutil.exe (specify the /? flag to see each option).

Table 11-1. *Various Options of* gacutil.exe

Option	Meaning in Life
/i	Installs a strongly named assembly into the GAC
/u	Uninstalls an assembly form the GAC
/l	Displays the assemblies (or a specific assembly) in the GAC

Using either technique, deploy CarLibrary.dll to the GAC. Once you've finished, you should see your library present and accounted for (see Figure 11-20).

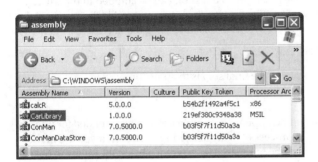

Figure 11-20. *The strongly named, shared CarLibrary (version 1.0.0.0)*

■**Note** You may right-click any assembly icon to pull up its Properties page, and you may also uninstall a specific version of an assembly altogether from the right-click context menu (the GUI equivalent of supplying the /u flag to gacutil.exe).

The Role of Delayed Signing

When you are building your own custom .NET assemblies, you are able to assign a strong name using your own personal *.snk file. However, given the sensitive nature of a public/private key file, don't be too surprised if your company/department refuses to give you access to the master *.snk file. This is an obvious problem, given that we (as developers) will often need to install an assembly into the GAC for testing purposes. To allow this sort of testing (while not distributing the true *.snk file), you are able to make use of *delayed signing*. We have no need to do so for the current CarLibrary.dll; however, here is an overview of the process.

Delayed signing begins by the trusted individual holding the *.snk file extracting the public key value from the public/private *.snk file using the -p command-line flag of sn.exe, to produce a new file that only contains the public key value:

```
sn -p myKey.snk testPublicKey.snk
```

At this point, the testPublicKey.snk file can be distributed to individual developers for the creation and testing of strongly named assemblies. To inform the C# compiler that the assembly in question is making use of delayed signing, the developer must make sure to set the value of the AssemblyDelaySign attribute to true in addition to specifying the pseudo-key file as the parameter to the AssemblyKeyFile attribute. Here are the relevant updates to the project's AssemblyInfo.cs file:

```
[assembly: AssemblyDelaySign(true)]
[assembly: AssemblyKeyFile(@"C:\MyKey\testPublicKey.snk")]
```

> **■Note** If you are using Visual Studio 2005, these same attributes can be established visually using the Properties page of your project.

Once an assembly has enabled delayed signing, the next step is to disable the signature verification process that happens automatically when an assembly is deployed to the GAC. To do so, specify the -vr flag (using sn.exe) to skip the verification process on the current machine:

```
sn.exe -vr MyAssembly.dll
```

Once all testing has been performed, the assembly in question can be shipped to the trusted individual who holds the "true" public/private key file to resign the binary to provide the correct digital signature. Again, sn.exe provides the necessary behavior, this time using the -r flag:

```
sn.exe -r MyAssembly.dll C:\MyKey\myKey.snk
```

To enable the signature verification process, the final step is to apply the -vu flag:

```
sn.exe -vu MyAssembly.dll
```

Understand, of course, that if you (or your company) only build assemblies intended for internal use, you may never need to bother with the process of delayed signing. However, if you are in the business of building .NET assemblies that may be purchased by external parties, the ability to delay signing keeps things safe and sane for all involved.

Consuming a Shared Assembly

When you are building applications that make use of a shared assembly, the only difference from consuming a private assembly is in how you reference the library using Visual Studio 2005. In reality, there is no difference as far as the tool is concerned (you still make use of the Add Reference dialog box). What you must understand is that this dialog box will *not* allow you to reference the assembly by browsing to the Assembly folder. Any efforts to do so will be in vain, as you cannot reference the assembly you have highlighted (see Figure 11-21).

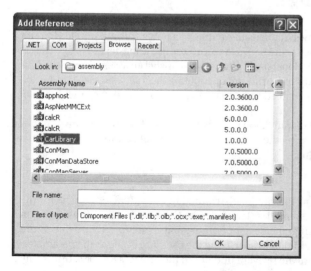

Figure 11-21. *Nope! You can't reference shared assemblies by navigating to the Assembly folder using Visual Studio 2005.*

Rather, you will need to browse to the \Bin\Debug directory of the *original* project via the Browse tab (see Figure 11-22).

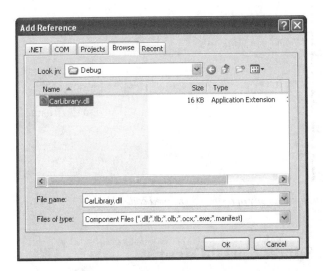

Figure 11-22. *Correct! You must reference shared assemblies by navigating to the project's \Bin\Debug directory using Visual Studio 2005.*

This (somewhat annoying) fact aside, create a new C# console application named SharedCarLibClient and exercise your types as you wish:

```csharp
using CarLibrary;

namespace SharedCarLibClient
{
    class Program
    {
        static void Main(string[] args)
        {
            SportsCar c = new SportsCar();
            c.TurboBoost();
            Console.ReadLine();
        }
    }
}
```

Once you have compiled your client application, navigate to the directory that contains SharedCarLibClient.exe using Windows Explorer and notice that Visual Studio 2005 has *not* copied CarLibrary.dll to the client's application directory. When you reference an assembly whose manifest contains a .publickey value, Visual Studio 2005 assumes the strongly named assembly will most likely be deployed in the GAC, and therefore does not bother to copy the binary.

As a quick side note, if you wish to have Visual Studio 2005 copy a shared assembly to the client directory, you can select an assembly from the References node of Solution Explorer and set the Copy Local property to True using the Properties window (see Figure 11-23).

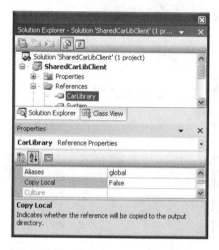

Figure 11-23. *The Copy Local property can force a copy of a strongly named code library.*

Exploring the Manifest of SharedCarLibClient

Recall that when you generate a strong name for an assembly, the entire public key is recorded in the assembly manifest. On a related note, when a client references a strongly named assembly, its manifest records a condensed hash-value of the full public key, denoted by the .publickeytoken tag. If you were to open the manifest of SharedCarLibClient.exe using ildasm.exe, you would find the following:

```
.assembly extern CarLibrary
{
  .publickeytoken = (21 9E F3 80 C9 34 8A 38)
  .ver 1:0:0:0
}
```

If you compare the value of the public key token recorded in the client manifest with the public key token value shown in the GAC, you will find a dead-on match. Recall that a public key represents one aspect of the strongly named assembly's identity. Given this, the CLR will only load version 1.0.0.0 of an assembly named CarLibrary that has a public key that can be hashed down to the value 219EF380C9348A38. If the CLR does not find an assembly meeting this description in the GAC (and cannot find a private assembly named CarLibrary in the client's directory), a FileNotFound exception is thrown.

■**Source Code** The SharedCarLibClient application can be found under the Chapter 11 subdirectory.

Configuring Shared Assemblies

Like a private assembly, shared assemblies can be configured using a client *.config file. Of course, because shared assemblies are found in a well-known location (the GAC), you will not specify a <privatePath> element as you did for private assemblies (although if the client is using both shared and private assemblies, the <privatePath> element may still exist in the *.config file).

You can use application configuration files in conjunction with shared assemblies whenever you wish to instruct the CLR to bind to a *different* version of a specific assembly, effectively bypassing the value recorded in the client's manifest. This can be useful for a number of reasons. For example, imagine that you have shipped version 1.0.0.0 of an assembly and discover a major bug some time after the fact. One corrective action would be to rebuild the client application to reference the correct version of the bug-free assembly (say, 1.1.0.0) and redistribute the updated client and new library to each and every target machine.

Another option is to ship the new code library and a *.config file that automatically instructs the runtime to bind to the new (bug-free) version. As long as the new version has been installed into the GAC, the original client runs without recompilation, redistribution, or fear of having to update your resume.

Here's another example: you have shipped the first version of a bug-free assembly (1.0.0.0), and after a month or two, you add new functionality to the assembly in question to yield version 2.0.0.0. Obviously, existing client applications that were compiled against version 1.0.0.0 have no clue about these new types, given that their code base makes no reference to them.

New client applications, however, wish to make reference to the new functionality found in version 2.0.0.0. Under .NET, you are free to ship version 2.0.0.0 to the target machines, and have version 2.0.0.0 run alongside the older version 1.0.0.0. If necessary, existing clients can be dynamically redirected to load version 2.0.0.0 (to gain access to the implementation refinements), using an application configuration file without needing to recompile and redeploy the client application.

Freezing the Current Shared Assembly

To illustrate how to dynamically bind to a specific version of a shared assembly, open Windows Explorer and copy the current version of CarLibrary (1.0.0.0) into a distinct subdirectory (I called mine "Version 1") off the project root to symbolize the freezing of this version (see Figure 11-24).

Figure 11-24. *Freezing the current version of* CarLibrary.dll

Building Shared Assembly Version 2.0.0.0

Now, update your CarLibrary project to define a new enum named MusicMedia that defines four possible musical devices:

```
// Holds source of music.
public enum MusicMedia
{
    musicCd,
    musicTape,
    musicRadio,
    musicMp3
}
```

As well, add a new public method to the Car type that allows the caller to turn on one of the given media players:

```
public abstract class Car
{
...
    public void TurnOnRadio(bool musicOn, MusicMedia mm)
    {
        if(musicOn)
            MessageBox.Show(string.Format("Jamming {0}", mm));
        else
            MessageBox.Show("Quiet time...");
    }
...
}
```

Update the constructors of the Car class to display a MessageBox that verifies you are indeed using CarLibrary 2.0.0.0:

```
public abstract class Car
{
...
    public Car()
    {
        MessageBox.Show("Car 2.0.0.0");
    }
    public Car(string name, short max, short curr)
    {
        MessageBox.Show("Car 2.0.0.0");
        petName = name; maxSpeed = max; currSpeed = curr;
    }
...
}
```

Finally, before you recompile, be sure to update this version of this assembly to 2.0.0.0 by updating the value passed to the [AssemblyVersion] attribute:

```
// CarLibrary version 2.0.0.0 (now with music!)
[assembly: AssemblyVersion("2.0.0.0")]
```

If you look in your project's \Bin\Debug folder, you'll see that you have a new version of this assembly (2.0.0.0), while version 1.0.0.0 is safe in storage under the Version 1 subdirectory. Install this new assembly into the GAC as described earlier in this chapter. Notice that you now have two versions of the same assembly (see Figure 11-25).

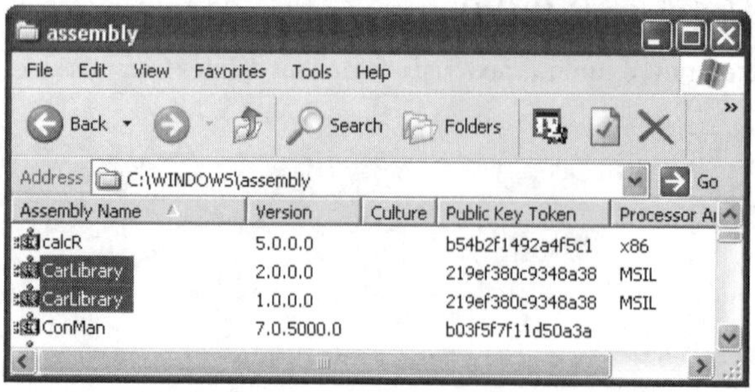

Figure 11-25. *Side-by-side execution*

If you were to run the current `SharedCarLibClient.exe` program by double-clicking the icon using Windows Explorer, you should *not* see the "Car 2.0.0.0" message box appear, as the manifest is specifically requesting version 1.0.0.0. How then can you instruct the CLR to bind to version 2.0.0.0? Glad you asked.

Dynamically Redirecting to Specific Versions of a Shared Assembly

When you wish to inform the CLR to load a version of a shared assembly other than the version listed in its manifest, you may build a `*.config` file that contains a `<dependentAssembly>` element. When doing so, you will need to create an `<assemblyIdentity>` subelement that specifies the friendly name of the assembly listed in the client manifest (CarLibrary, for this example) and an optional culture attribute (which can be assigned an empty string or omitted altogether if you wish to specify the default culture for the machine). Moreover, the `<dependentAssembly>` element will define a `<bindingRedirect>` subelement to define the version *currently* in the manifest (via the `oldVersion` attribute) and the version in the GAC to load instead (via the `newVersion` attribute).

Create a new configuration file in the application directory of SharedCarLibClient named `SharedCarLibClient.exe.config` that contains the following XML data. Of course, the value of your public key token will be different from what you see in the following code, and it can be obtained either by examining the client manifest using `ildasm.exe` or via the GAC.

```
<configuration>
    <runtime>
        <assemblyBinding xmlns="urn:schemas-microsoft-com:asm.v1">
            <dependentAssembly>
                <assemblyIdentity name="CarLibrary"
                        publicKeyToken="219ef380c9348a38"
                        culture="neutral"/>
                <bindingRedirect oldVersion= "1.0.0.0"
                    newVersion= "2.0.0.0"/>
            </dependentAssembly>
        </assemblyBinding>
    </runtime>
</configuration>
```

Now run the `SharedCarLibClient.exe` program. You should see the message that displays version 2.0.0.0 has loaded. If you set the `newVersion` attribute to 1.0.0.0 (or if you simply deleted the `*.config` file), you now see the message that version 1.0.0.0 has loaded, as the CLR found version 1.0.0.0 listed in the client's manifest.

Multiple `<dependentAssembly>` elements can appear within a client's configuration file. Although you have no need to do so, assume that the manifest of `SharedCarLibClient.exe` also referenced version 2.5.0.0 of an assembly named MathLibrary. If you wished to redirect to version 3.0.0.0 of MathLibrary (in addition to version 2.0.0.0 of CarLibrary), the `SharedCarLibClient.exe.config` file would look like the following:

```
<configuration>
    <runtime>
        <assemblyBinding xmlns="urn:schemas-microsoft-com:asm.v1">
            <dependentAssembly>
                <assemblyIdentity name="CarLibrary"
                        publicKeyToken="219ef380c9348a38"
                        culture=""/>
                <bindingRedirect oldVersion= "1.0.0.0"
                    newVersion= "2.0.0.0"/>
            </dependentAssembly>
```

```
            <dependentAssembly>
                <assemblyIdentity name="MathLibrary"
                        publicKeyToken="219ef380c9348a38"
                        culture=""/>
                <bindingRedirect oldVersion= "2.5.0.0"
                    newVersion= "3.0.0.0"/>
            </dependentAssembly>
        </assemblyBinding>
    </runtime>
</configuration>
```

Revisiting the .NET Framework 2.0 Configuration Utility

As you would hope, you can generate shared assembly–centric `*.config` files using the graphical .NET Framework 2.0 Configuration utility. Like the process of building a `*.config` file for private assemblies, the first step is to reference the `*.exe` to configure. To illustrate, delete the `SharedCarLibClient.exe.config` you just authored. Now, add a reference to `SharedCarLibClient.exe` by right-clicking the Applications node. Once you do, expand the plus sign (+) icon and select the Configured Assemblies subnode. From here, click the Configure an Assembly link on the right side of the utility.

At this point, you are presented with a dialog box that allows you to establish a `<dependentAssembly>` element using a number of friendly UI elements. First, select the "Choose an assembly from the list of assemblies this application uses" radio button (which simply means, "Show me the manifest!") and click the Choose Assembly button.

A dialog box now displays that shows you not only the assemblies specifically listed in the client manifest, but also the assemblies referenced by these assemblies. For this example's purposes, select CarLibrary. When you click the Finish button, you will be shown a Properties page for this one small aspect of the client's manifest. Here, you can generate the `<dependentAssembly>` using the Binding Policy tab.

Once you select the Binding Policy tab, you can set the `oldVersion` attribute (1.0.0.0) via the Requested Version text field and the `newVersion` attribute (2.0.0.0) using the New Version text field. Once you have committed the settings, you will find the following configuration file is generated for you:

```
<?xml version="1.0"?>
<configuration>
    <runtime>
        <assemblyBinding xmlns="urn:schemas-microsoft-com:asm.v1">
            <dependentAssembly>
                <assemblyIdentity name="CarLibrary"
                    publicKeyToken="219ef380c9348a38" />
                <publisherPolicy apply="yes" />
                <bindingRedirect oldVersion="1.0.0.0" newVersion="2.0.0.0" />
            </dependentAssembly>
        </assemblyBinding>
    </runtime>
</configuration>
```

Investigating the Internal Composition of the GAC

So far, so good. Now, let's dig into the internal composition of the GAC itself. When you view the GAC using Windows Explorer, you find a number of icons representing each version of a shared assembly. This graphical shell is provided courtesy of a COM server named `shfusion.dll`. As you may suspect, however, beneath these icons is an elaborate (but predictable) directory structure.

To understand what the GAC really boils down to, open a command prompt and change to the Assembly directory:

```
cd c:\windows\assembly
```

Issue a dir command from the command line. Here you will find a folder named GAC_MISL
(see Figure 11-26).

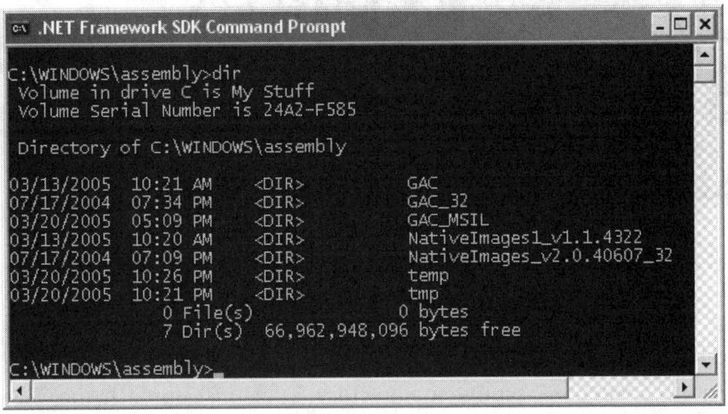

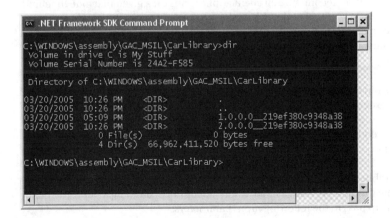

Figure 11-26. *The hidden GAC_MSIL subdirectory*

Change to the GAC_MSIL directory and issue a dir command once more. You will now be
presented with a list of a number of subdirectories that happen to have the same exact name as the
icons displayed by shfusion.dll. Change to the CarLibrary subdirectory and again issue a dir command (see Figure 11-27).

Figure 11-27. *Inside the hidden CarLibrary subdirectory*

As you can see, the GAC maintains a subdirectory for each version of a shared assembly, which
follows the naming convention <versionOfAssembly>_PublicKeyToken. If you were again to change
the current directory to version 1.0.0.0 of CarLibrary, you would indeed find a copy of the code library
(see Figure 11-28).

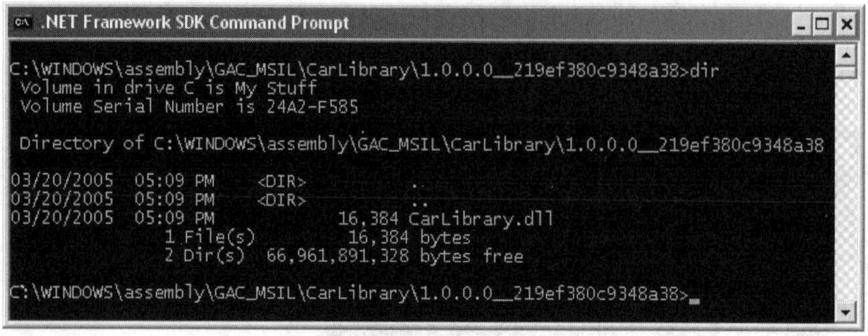

Figure 11-28. *Behold! The GAC's internal copy of* CarLibrary.dll.

When you install a strongly named assembly into the GAC, the operating system responds by extending the directory structure beneath the Assembly subdirectory. Using this approach, the CLR is able to manipulate multiple versions of a specific assembly while avoiding the expected name clashes resulting from identically named *.dlls.

Understanding Publisher Policy Assemblies

The next configuration issue you'll examine is the role of *publisher policy assemblies*. As you've just seen, *.config files can be constructed to bind to a specific version of a shared assembly, thereby bypassing the version recorded in the client manifest. While this is all well and good, imagine you're an administrator who now needs to reconfigure all client applications on a given machine to rebind to version 2.0.0.0 of the CarLibrary.dll assembly. Given the strict naming convention of a configuration file, you would need to duplicate the same XML content in numerous locations (assuming you are, in fact, aware of the locations of the executables using CarLibrary!). Clearly this would be a maintenance nightmare.

Publisher policy allows the publisher of a given assembly (you, your department, your company, or what have you) to ship a binary version of a *.config file that is installed into the GAC along with the newest version of the associated assembly. The benefit of this approach is that client application directories do *not* need to contain specific *.config files. Rather, the CLR will read the current manifest and attempt to find the requested version in the GAC. However, if the CLR finds a publisher policy assembly, it will read the embedded XML data and perform the requested redirection *at the level of the GAC*.

Publisher policy assemblies are created at the command line using a .NET utility named al.exe (the assembly linker). While this tool provides a large number of options, building a publisher policy assembly requires you only to pass in the following input parameters:

- The location of the *.config or *.xml file containing the redirecting instructions

- The name of the resulting publisher policy assembly

- The location of the *.snk file used to sign the publisher policy assembly

- The version numbers to assign the publisher policy assembly being constructed

If you wish to build a publisher policy assembly that controls CarLibrary.dll, the command set is as follows:

```
al /link: CarLibraryPolicy.xml /out:policy.1.0.CarLibrary.dll
/keyf:C:\MyKey\myKey.snk /v:1.0.0.0
```

Here, the XML content is contained within a file named CarLibraryPolicy.xml. The name of the output file (which must be in the format *policy.<major>.<minor>.assemblyToConfigure*) is specified using the obvious /out flag. In addition, note that the name of the file containing the public/private key pair will also need to be supplied via the /keyf option. (Remember, publisher policy files are shared, and therefore must have a strong name!)

Once the al.exe tool has executed, the result is a new assembly that can be placed into the GAC to force all clients to bind to version 2.0.0.0 of CarLibrary.dll, without the use of a specific client application configuration file.

Disabling Publisher Policy

Now, assume you (as a system administrator) have deployed a publisher policy assembly (and the latest version of the related assembly) to a client machine. As luck would have it, nine of the ten affected applications rebind to version 2.0.0.0 without error. However, the remaining client application (for whatever reason) blows up when accessing CarLibrary.dll 2.0.0.0 (as we all know, it is next to impossible to build backward-compatible software that works 100 percent of the time).

In such a case, it is possible to build a configuration file for a specific troubled client that instructs the CLR to *ignore* the presence of any publisher policy files installed in the GAC. The remaining client applications that are happy to consume the newest .NET assembly will simply be redirected via the installed publisher policy assembly. To disable publisher policy on a client-by-client basis, author a (properly named) *.config file that makes use of the <publisherPolicy> element and set the apply attribute to no. When you do so, the CLR will load the version of the assembly originally listed in the client's manifest.

```
<configuration>
  <runtime>
    <assemblyBinding xmlns="urn:schemas-microsoft-com:asm.v1">
      <publisherPolicy apply="no" />
    </assemblyBinding>
  </runtime>
</configuration>
```

Understanding the <codeBase> Element

Application configuration files can also specify *code bases*. The <codeBase> element can be used to instruct the CLR to probe for dependent assemblies located at arbitrary locations (such as network share points, or simply a local directory outside a client's application directory).

■**Note** If the value assigned to a <codeBase> element is located on a remote machine, the assembly will be downloaded on demand to a specific directory in the GAC termed the *download cache*. You can view the content of your machine's download cache by supplying the /ldl option to gacutil.exe.

Given what you have learned about deploying assemblies to the GAC, it should make sense that assemblies loaded from a <codeBase> element will need to be assigned a strong name (after all, how else could the CLR install remote assemblies to the GAC?).

■**Note** Technically speaking, the <codeBase> element can be used to probe for assemblies that do not have a strong name. However, the assembly's location must be relative to the client's application directory (and thus is little more than an alternative to the <privatePath> element).

Create a console application named CodeBaseClient, set a reference to CarLibrary.dll version 2.0.0.0, and update the initial file as so:

```
using CarLibrary;

namespace CodeBaseClient
{
    class Program
    {
        static void Main(string[] args)
        {
            Console.WriteLine("***** Fun with CodeBases *****");
            SportsCar c = new SportsCar();
            Console.WriteLine("Sports car has been allocated.");
            Console.ReadLine();
        }
    }
}
```

Given that CarLibrary.dll has been deployed to the GAC, you are able to run the program as is. However, to illustrate the use of the <codeBase> element, create a new folder under your C drive (perhaps C:\MyAsms) and place a copy of CarLibrary.dll version 2.0.0.0 into this directory.

Now, add an App.config file to the CodeBaseClient project (as explained earlier in this chapter) and author the following XML content (remember that your .publickeytoken value will differ; consult your GAC as required):

```
<configuration>
  <runtime>
    <assemblyBinding xmlns="urn:schemas-microsoft-com:asm.v1">
      <dependentAssembly>
        <assemblyIdentity name=" CarLibrary" publicKeyToken="219ef380c9348a38" />
        <codeBase version="2.0.0.0" href="file:///C:\MyAsms\CarLibrary.dll" />
      </dependentAssembly>
    </assemblyBinding>
  </runtime>
</configuration>
```

As you can see, the <codeBase> element is nested within the <assemblyIdentity> element, which makes use of the name and publicKeyToken attributes to specify the friendly name as associated publicKeyToken values. The <codeBase> element itself specifies the version and location (via the href property) of the assembly to load. If you were to delete version 2.0.0.0 of CarLibrary.dll from the GAC, this client would still run successfully, as the CLR is able to resolve locate the external assembly under C:\MyAsms.

However, if you were to delete the MyAsms directory from your machine, the client would now fail. Clearly the <codeBase> elements (if present) take precedence over the investigation of the GAC.

■Note If you place assemblies at random locations on your development machine, you are in effect re-creating the system registry (and the related DLL hell), given that if you move or rename the folder containing your binaries, the current bind will fail. Given this point, use <codeBase> with caution.

The <codeBase> element can also be helpful when referencing assemblies located on a remote networked machine. Assume you have permission to access a folder located at http://www.IntertechTraining.com. To download the remote *.dll to the GAC's download cache on your location machine, you could update the <codeBase> element as so:

```
<codeBase version="2.0.0.0"
href="http://www.IntertechTraining.com/Assemblies/CarLibrary.dll" />
```

■**Source Code** The CodeBaseClient application can be found under the Chapter 11 subdirectory.

The System.Configuration Namespace

Currently, all of the *.config files shown in this chapter have made use of well-known XML elements that are read by the CLR to resolve the location of external assemblies. In addition to these recognized elements, it is perfectly permissible for a client configuration file to contain application-specific data that has nothing to do with binding heuristics. Given this, it should come as no surprise that the .NET Framework provides a namespace that allows you to programmatically read the data within a client configuration file.

The System.Configuration namespace provides a small set of types you may use to read custom data from a client's *.config file. These custom settings must be contained within the scope of an <appSettings> element. The <appSettings> element contains any number of <add> elements that define a key/value pair to be obtained programmatically.

For example, assume you have a *.config file for a console application named AppConfigReaderApp that defines a database connection string and a point of data named timesToSayHello:

```
<configuration>
    <appSettings>
        <add key="appConStr"
            value="server=localhost;uid='sa';pwd='';database=Cars" />
        <add key="timesToSayHello" value="8" />
    </appSettings>
</configuration>
```

Reading these values for use by the client application is as simple as calling the instance-level GetValue() method of the System.Configuration.AppSettingsReader type. As shown in the following code, the first parameter to GetValue() is the name of the key in the *.config file, whereas the second parameter is the underlying type of the key (obtained via the C# typeof operator):

```
class Program
{
    static void Main(string[] args)
    {
        // Create a reader and get the connection string value.
        AppSettingsReader ar = new AppSettingsReader();
        Console.WriteLine(ar.GetValue("appConStr", typeof(string)));

        // Now get the number of times to say hello, and then do it!
        int numbOfTimes = (int)ar.GetValue("timesToSayHello", typeof(int));
        for(int i = 0; i < numbOfTimes; i++)
            Console.WriteLine("Yo!");
        Console.ReadLine();
    }
}
```

The AppSettingsReader class type does *not* provide a way to write application-specific data to a *.config file. While this may seem like a limitation at first encounter, it actually makes good sense. The whole idea of a *.config file is that it contains read-only data that is consulted by the CLR (or possibly the AppSettingsReader type) after an application has already been deployed to a target machine.

> **Note** During our examination of ADO.NET (Chapter 22) you will learn about the new `<connectionStrings>` configuration element and new types within the `System.Configuration` namespace. These .NET 2.0–specific items provide a standard manner to handle connection string data.

> **Source Code** The AppConfigReaderApp application can be found under the Chapter 11 subdirectory.

The Machine Configuration File

The configuration files you've examined in this chapter have a common theme: they apply only to a specific application (that is why they have the same name as the launching application). In addition, each .NET-aware machine has a file named `machine.config` that contains a vast number of configuration details (many of which have nothing to do with resolving external assemblies) that control how the .NET platform operates.

The .NET platform maintains a separate `*.config` file for each version of the framework installed on the local machine. The `machine.config` file for .NET 2.0 can be found under the C:\WINDOWS\Microsoft.NET\Framework\v2.0.50215\CONFIG directory (your version may differ). If you were to open this file, you would find numerous XML elements that control ASP.NET settings, various security details, debugging support, and so forth. However, if you wish to update the `machine.config` file with machinewide application settings (via an `<appSettings>` element), you are free to do so.

Although this file can be directly edited using Notepad, be warned that if you alter this file incorrectly, you may cripple the ability of the runtime to function correctly. This scenario can be far more painful than a malformed application `*.config` file, given that XML errors in an application configuration file affect only a single application, but erroneous XML in the `machine.config` file can break a specific version of the .NET platform.

The Assembly Binding "Big Picture"

Now that you have drilled down into the details regarding how the CLR resolves the location of requested external assemblies, remember that the simple case is, indeed, simple. Many (if not most) of your .NET applications will consist of nothing more than a group of private assemblies deployed to a single directory. In this case, simply copy the folder to a location of your choosing and run the client executable.

As you have seen, however, the CLR will check for client configuration files and publisher policy assemblies during the resolution process. To summarize the path taken by the CLR to resolve an external assembly reference, ponder Figure 11-29.

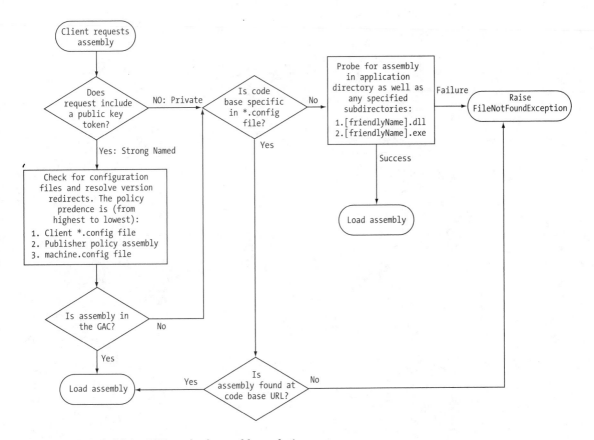

Figure 11-29. *Behold the CLR's path of assembly resolution.*

Summary

This chapter drilled down into the details of how the CLR resolves the location of externally referenced assemblies. You began by examining the content within an assembly: headers, metadata, manifests, and CIL. Then you constructed single-file and multifile assemblies and a handful of client applications (written in a language-agnostic manner).

As you have seen, assemblies may be private or shared. Private assemblies are copied to the client's subdirectory, whereas shared assemblies are deployed to the Global Assembly Cache (GAC), provided they have been assigned a strong name. Finally, has you have seen, private and shared assemblies can be configured using a client-side XML configuration file or, alternatively, via a publisher policy assembly.

■ ■ ■

## CHAPTER 12

Type Reflection, Late Binding, and Attribute-Based Programming

As shown in the previous chapter, assemblies are the basic unit of deployment in the .NET universe. Using the integrated object browsers of Visual Studio 2005, you are able to examine the public types within a project's referenced set of assemblies. Furthermore, external tools such as ildasm.exe allow you to peek into the underlying CIL code, type metadata, and assembly manifest for a given .NET binary. In addition to this design-time investigation of .NET assemblies, you are also able to *programmatically* obtain this same information using the System.Reflection namespace. To this end, the first task of this chapter is to define the role of reflection and the necessity of .NET metadata.

The remainder of the chapter examines a number of closely related topics, all of which hinge upon reflection services. For example, you'll learn how a .NET client may employ dynamic loading and late binding to activate types it has no compile-time knowledge of. You'll also learn how to insert custom metadata into your .NET assemblies through the use of system-supplied and custom attributes. To put all of these (seemingly esoteric) topics into perspective, the chapter closes by demonstrating how to build several "snap-in objects" that you can plug into an extendable Windows Forms application.

The Necessity of Type Metadata

The ability to fully describe types (classes, interfaces, structures, enumerations, and delegates) using metadata is a key element of the .NET platform. Numerous .NET technologies, such as object serialization, .NET remoting, and XML web services, require the ability to discover the format of types at runtime. Furthermore, cross-language interoperability, compiler support, and an IDE's IntelliSense capabilities all rely on a concrete description of *type*.

Regardless of (or perhaps due to) its importance, metadata is not a new idea supplied by the .NET Framework. Java, CORBA, and COM all have similar concepts. For example, COM type libraries (which are little more than compiled IDL code) are used to describe the types contained within a COM server. Like COM, .NET code libraries also support type metadata. Of course, .NET metadata has no syntactic similarities to COM IDL. Recall that the ildasm.exe utility allows you to view an assembly's type metadata using the Ctrl+M keyboard option (see Chapter 1). Thus, if you were to open any of the *.dll or *.exe assemblies created over the course of this book (such as CarLibrary.dll) using ildasm.exe and press Ctrl+M, you would find the relevant type metadata (see Figure 12-1).

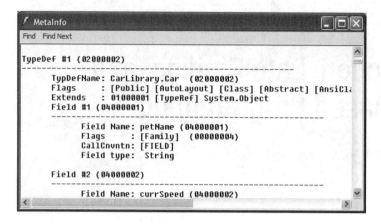

Figure 12-1. *Viewing an assembly's metadata*

As you can see, ildasm.exe's display of .NET type metadata is very verbose (the actual binary format is much more compact). In fact, if I were to list the entire metadata description representing the CarLibrary.dll assembly, it would span several pages. Given that this act would be a woeful waste of your time (and paper), let's just glimpse into some key types of the CarLibrary.dll assembly.

Viewing (Partial) Metadata for the EngineState Enumeration

Each type defined within the current assembly is documented using a "TypeDef #*n*" token (where TypeDef is short for *type definition*). If the type being described uses a type defined within a separate .NET assembly, the referenced type is documented using a "TypeRef #*n*" token (where TypeRef is short for *type reference*). A TypeRef token is a pointer (if you will) to the referenced type's full metadata definition. In a nutshell, .NET metadata is a set of tables that clearly mark all type definitions (TypeDefs) and referenced entities (TypeRefs), all of which can be viewed using ildasm.exe's metadata window.

As far as CarLibrary.dll goes, one TypeDef we encounter is the metadata description of the CarLibrary.EngineState enumeration (your number may differ; TypeDef numbering is based on the order in which the C# compiler processes the file):

TypeDef #1
```
------------------------------------------------------------
    TypDefName: CarLibrary.EngineState  (02000002)
    Flags     : [Public] [AutoLayout] [Class] [Sealed] [AnsiClass]  (00000101)
    Extends   : 01000001 [TypeRef] System.Enum
...
    Field #2
    ------------------------------------------------------------
    Field Name: engineAlive (04000002)
    Flags      : [Public] [Static] [Literal] [HasDefault]  (00008056)
    DefltValue: (I4) 0
    CallCnvntn: [FIELD]
    Field type:  ValueClass CarLibrary.EngineState
...
```

Here, the TypDefName token is used to establish the name of the given type. The Extends metadata token is used to document the base class of a given .NET type (in this case, the referenced type, System.Enum). Each field of an enumeration is marked using the "Field #*n*" token. For brevity, I have simply listed the metadata for EngineState.engineAlive.

Viewing (Partial) Metadata for the Car Type

Here is a partial dump of the Car type that illustrates the following:

- How fields are defined in terms of .NET metadata
- How methods are documented via .NET metadata
- How a single type property is mapped to two discrete member functions

```
TypeDef #3
-----------------------------------------------------------
    TypDefName: CarLibrary.Car  (02000004)
    Flags     : [Public] [AutoLayout] [Class] [Abstract] [AnsiClass]  (00100081)
    Extends   : 01000002 [TypeRef] System.Object
    Field #1
    ------------------------------------------------------------
        Field Name: petName (04000008)
        Flags     : [Family]  (00000004)
        CallCnvntn: [FIELD]
        Field type:  String
...
    Method #1
    ------------------------------------------------------------
        MethodName: .ctor (06000001)
        Flags     : [Public] [HideBySig] [ReuseSlot] [SpecialName]
        [RTSpecialName] [.ctor]  (00001886)
        RVA       : 0x00002050
        ImplFlags : [IL] [Managed]  (00000000)
        CallCnvntn: [DEFAULT]
        hasThis
        ReturnType: Void
        No arguments.
...
    Property #1
    ------------------------------------------------------------
        Prop.Name : PetName (17000001)
        Flags     : [none] (00000000)
        CallCnvntn: [PROPERTY]
        hasThis
        ReturnType: String
        No arguments.
        DefltValue:
        Setter    : (06000004) set_PetName
        Getter    : (06000003) get_PetName
        0 Others
...
```

First, note that the Car class metadata marks the type's base class and includes various flags that describe how this type was constructed (e.g., [public], [abstract], and whatnot). Methods (such as our Car's constructor) are described in regard to their parameters, return value, and name. Finally, note how properties are mapped to their internal get/set methods using the .NET metadata Setter/Getter tokens. As you would expect, the derived Car types (SportsCar and MiniVan) are described in a similar manner.

Examining a TypeRef

Recall that an assembly's metadata will describe not only the set of internal types (Car, EngineState, etc.), but also any external types the internal types reference. For example, given that CarLibrary.dll has defined two enumerations, you find a TypeRef block for the System.Enum type:

```
TypeRef #1 (01000001)
--------------------------------------------------------
Token:              0x01000001
ResolutionScope:    0x23000001
TypeRefName:        System.Enum
    MemberRef #1
    --------------------------------------------------------
    Member: (0a00000f) ToString:
    CallCnvntn: [DEFAULT]
    hasThis
    ReturnType: String
     No arguments.
```

Documenting the Defining Assembly

The ildasm.exe metadata window also allows you to view the .NET metadata that describes the assembly itself using the Assembly token. As you can see from the following (partial) listing, information documented within the Assembly table is (surprise, surprise!) the same information that can be viewable via the MANIFEST icon. Here is a partial dump of the manifest of CarLibrary.dll (version 2.0.0.0):

```
Assembly
--------------------------------------------------------
      Token: 0x20000001
      Name : CarLibrary
      Public Key    : 00 24 00 00 04 80 00 00  // Etc...

      Hash Algorithm : 0x00008004
      Major Version: 0x00000002
      Minor Version: 0x00000000
      Build Number: 0x00000000
      Revision Number: 0x00000000
      Locale: <null>
      Flags : [SideBySideCompatible]  (00000000)
```

Documenting Referenced Assemblies

In addition to the Assembly token and the set of TypeDef and TypeRef blocks, .NET metadata also makes use of "AssemblyRef #n" tokens to document each external assembly. Given that the CarLibrary.dll makes use of the MessageBox type, you find an AssemblyRef for System.Windows.Forms, for example:

```
AssemblyRef #2
--------------------------------------------------------
      Token: 0x23000002
      Public Key or Token: b7 7a 5c 56 19 34 e0 89
      Name: System.Windows.Forms
      Version: 2.0.3600.0
      Major Version: 0x00000002
      Minor Version: 0x00000000
```

```
Build Number: 0x00000e10
Revision Number: 0x00000000
Locale: <null>
HashValue Blob:
Flags: [none] (00000000)
```

Documenting String Literals

The final point of interest regarding .NET metadata is the fact that each and every string literal in your code base is documented under the User Strings token, for example:

```
User Strings
-------------------------------------------------------
70000001 : (11) L"Car 2.0.0.0"
70000019 : (11) L"Jamming {0}"
70000031 : (13) L"Quiet time..."
7000004d : (14) L"Ramming speed!"
7000006b : (19) L"Faster is better..."
70000093 : (16) L"Time to call AAA"
700000b5 : (16) L"Your car is dead"
700000d7 : ( 9) L"Be quiet "
700000eb : ( 2) L"!!"
```

Now, don't be too concerned with the exact syntax of each and every piece of .NET metadata. The bigger point to absorb is that .NET metadata is very descriptive and lists each internally defined (and externally referenced) type found within a given code base.

The next question on your mind may be (in the best-case scenario) "How can I leverage this information in my applications?" or (in the worst-case scenario) "Why should I care about metadata?" To address both points of view, allow me to introduce .NET reflection services. Be aware that the usefulness of the topics presented over the pages that follow may be a bit of a head-scratcher until this chapter's endgame. So hang tight.

■**Note** You will also find a number of CustomAttribute tokens displayed by the MetaInfo window, which documents the attributes applied within the code base. You'll learn about the role of .NET attributes later in this chapter.

Understanding Reflection

In the .NET universe, *reflection* is the process of runtime type discovery. Using reflection services, you are able to programmatically obtain the same metadata information displayed by ildasm.exe using a friendly object model. For example, through reflection, you can obtain a list of all types contained within a given assembly (or *.netmodule), including the methods, fields, properties, and events defined by a given type. You can also dynamically discover the set of interfaces supported by a given class (or structure), the parameters of a method, and other related details (base classes, namespace information, manifest data, and so forth).

Like any namespace, System.Reflection contains a number of related types. Table 12-1 lists some of the core items you should be familiar with.

Table 12-1. *A Sampling of Members of the* System.Reflection *Namespace*

Type	Meaning in Life
Assembly	This class (in addition to numerous related types) contains a number of methods that allow you to load, investigate, and manipulate an assembly.
AssemblyName	This class allows you to discover numerous details behind an assembly's identity (version information, culture information, and so forth).
EventInfo	This class holds information for a given event.
FieldInfo	This class holds information for a given field.
MemberInfo	This is the abstract base class that defines common behaviors for the EventInfo, FieldInfo, MethodInfo, and PropertyInfo types.
MethodInfo	This class contains information for a given method.
Module	This class allows you to access a given module within a multifile assembly.
ParameterInfo	This class holds information for a given parameter.
PropertyInfo	This class holds information for a given property.

To understand how to leverage the System.Reflection namespace to programmatically read .NET metadata, you need to first come to terms with the System.Type class.

The System.Type Class

The System.Type class defines a number of members that can be used to examine a type's metadata, a great number of which return types from the System.Reflection namespace. For example, Type.GetMethods() returns an array of MethodInfo types, Type.GetFields() returns an array of FieldInfo types, and so on. The complete set of members exposed by System.Type is quite expansive; however, Table 12-2 offers a partial snapshot of the members supported by System.Type (see the .NET Framework 2.0 SDK documentation for full details).

Table 12-2. *Select Members of* System.Type

Type	Meaning in Life
IsAbstract IsArray IsClass IsCOMObject IsEnum IsGenericTypeDefinition IsGenericParameter IsInterface IsPrimitive IsNestedPrivate IsNestedPublic IsSealed IsValueType	These properties (among others) allow you to discover a number of basic traits about the Type you are referring to (e.g., if it is an abstract method, an array, a nested class, and so forth).
GetConstructors() GetEvents() GetFields() GetInterfaces() GetMembers() GetMethods() GetNestedTypes() GetProperties()	These methods (among others) allow you to obtain an array representing the items (interface, method, property, etc.) you are interested in. Each method returns a related array (e.g., GetFields() returns a FieldInfo array, GetMethods() returns a MethodInfo array, etc.). Be aware that each of these methods has a singular form (e.g., GetMethod(), GetProperty(), etc.) that allows you to retrieve a specific item by name, rather than an array of all related items.

Type	Meaning in Life
FindMembers()	This method returns an array of MemberInfo types based on search criteria.
GetType()	This static method returns a Type instance given a string name.
InvokeMember()	This method allows late binding to a given item.

Obtaining a Type Reference Using System.Object.GetType()

You can obtain an instance of the Type class in a variety of ways. However, the one thing you cannot do is directly create a Type object using the new keyword, as Type is an abstract class. Regarding your first choice, recall that System.Object defines a method named GetType(), which returns an instance of the Type class that represents the metadata for the current object:

```
// Obtain type information using a SportsCar instance.
SportsCar sc = new SportsCar();
Type t = sc.GetType();
```

Obviously, this approach will only work if you have compile-time knowledge of the type (SportsCar in this case). Given this restriction, it should make sense that tools such as ildasm.exe do not obtain type information by directly calling System.Object.GetType() for each type, given the ildasm.exe was not compiled against your custom assemblies!

Obtaining a Type Reference Using System.Type.GetType()

To obtain type information in a more flexible manner, you may call the static GetType() member of the System.Type class and specify the fully qualified string name of the type you are interested in examining. Using this approach, you do *not* need to have compile-time knowledge of the type you are extracting metadata from, given that Type.GetType() takes an instance of the omnipresent System.String.

The Type.GetType() method has been overloaded to allow you to specify two Boolean parameters, one of which controls whether an exception should be thrown if the type cannot be found, and the other of which establishes the case sensitivity of the string. To illustrate, ponder the following:

```
// Obtain type information using the static Type.GetType() method.
// (don't throw an exception if SportsCar cannot be found and ignore case).
Type t = Type.GetType("CarLibrary.SportsCar", false, true);
```

In the previous example, notice that the string you are passing into GetType() makes no mention of the assembly containing the type. In this case, the assumption is that the type is defined within the currently executing assembly. However, when you wish to obtain metadata for a type within an external private assembly, the string parameter is formatted using the type's fully qualified name, followed by the friendly name of the assembly containing the type (each of which is separated by a comma):

```
// Obtain type information for a type within an external assembly.
Type t = null;
t = Type.GetType("CarLibrary.SportsCar, CarLibrary");
```

As well, do know that the string passed into Type.GetType() may specify a plus token (+) to denote a *nested type*. Assume you wish to obtain type information for an enumeration (SpyOptions) nested within a class named JamesBondCar. To do so, you would write the following:

```
// Obtain type information for a nested enumeration
// within the current assembly.
Type t =
    Type.GetType("CarLibrary.JamesBondCar+SpyOptions");
```

Obtaining a Type Reference Using typeof()

The final way to obtain type information is using the C# typeof operator:

```
// Get the Type using typeof.
Type t = typeof(SportsCar);
```

Like Type.GetType(), the typeof operator is helpful in that you do not need to first create an object instance to extract type information. However, your code base must still have compile-time knowledge of the type you are interested in examining.

Building a Custom Metadata Viewer

To illustrate the basic process of reflection (and the usefulness of System.Type), let's create a console application named MyTypeViewer. This program will display details of the methods, properties, fields, and supported interfaces (in addition to some other points of interest) for any type within mscorlib.dll (recall all .NET applications have automatic access to this core framework class library) or a type within MyTypeViewer itself.

Reflecting on Methods

The Program class will be updated to define a number of static methods, each of which takes a single System.Type parameter and returns void. First you have ListMethods(), which (as you might guess) prints the name of each method defined by the incoming type. Notice how Type.GetMethods() returns an array of System.Reflection.MethodInfo types:

```
// Display method names of type.
public static void ListMethods(Type t)
{
    Console.WriteLine("***** Methods *****");
    MethodInfo[] mi = t.GetMethods();
    foreach(MethodInfo m in mi)
        Console.WriteLine("->{0}", m.Name);
    Console.WriteLine("");
}
```

Here, you are simply printing the name of the method using the MethodInfo.Name property. As you might guess, MethodInfo has many additional members that allow you to determine if the method is static, virtual, or abstract. As well, the MethodInfo type allows you to obtain the method's return value and parameter set. You'll spruce up the implementation of ListMethods() in just a bit.

Reflecting on Fields and Properties

The implementation of ListFields() is similar. The only notable difference is the call to Type.GetFields() and the resulting FieldInfo array. Again, to keep things simple, you are printing out only the name of each field.

```
// Display field names of type.
public static void ListFields(Type t)
{
    Console.WriteLine("***** Fields *****");
    FieldInfo[] fi = t.GetFields();
    foreach(FieldInfo field in fi)
        Console.WriteLine("->{0}", field.Name);
    Console.WriteLine("");
}
```

The logic to display a type's properties is similar:

```
// Display property names of type.
public static void ListProps(Type t)
{
    Console.WriteLine("***** Properties *****");
    PropertyInfo[] pi = t.GetProperties();
    foreach(PropertyInfo prop in pi)
        Console.WriteLine("->{0}", prop.Name);
    Console.WriteLine("");
}
```

Reflecting on Implemented Interfaces

Next, you will author a method named ListInterfaces() that will print out the names of any interfaces supported on the incoming type. The only point of interest here is that the call to GetInterfaces() returns an array of System.Types! This should make sense given that interfaces are, indeed, types:

```
// Display implemented interfaces.
public static void ListInterfaces(Type t)
{
    Console.WriteLine("***** Interfaces *****");
    Type[] ifaces = t.GetInterfaces();
    foreach(Type i in ifaces)
        Console.WriteLine("->{0}", i.Name);
}
```

Displaying Various Odds and Ends

Last but not least, you have one final helper method that will simply display various statistics (indicating whether the type is generic, what the base class is, whether the type is sealed, and so forth) regarding the incoming type:

```
// Just for good measure.
public static void ListVariousStats(Type t)
{
    Console.WriteLine("***** Various Statistics *****");
    Console.WriteLine("Base class is: {0}", t.BaseType);
    Console.WriteLine("Is type abstract? {0}", t.IsAbstract);
    Console.WriteLine("Is type sealed? {0}", t.IsSealed);
    Console.WriteLine("Is type generic? {0}", t.IsGenericTypeDefinition);
    Console.WriteLine("Is type a class type? {0}", t.IsClass);
    Console.WriteLine("");
}
```

Implementing Main()

The Main() method of the Program class prompts the user for the fully qualified name of a type. Once you obtain this string data, you pass it into the Type.GetType() method and send the extracted System.Type into each of your helper methods. This process repeats until the user enters **Q** to terminate the application:

```
// Need to make use of the reflection namespace.
using System;
using System.Reflection;
...
static void Main(string[] args)
```

```
{
    Console.WriteLine("***** Welcome to MyTypeViewer *****");
    string typeName = "";
    bool userIsDone = false;

    do
    {
        Console.WriteLine("\nEnter a type name to evaluate");
        Console.Write("or enter Q to quit: ");

        // Get name of type.
        typeName = Console.ReadLine();

        // Does user want to quit?
        if (typeName.ToUpper() == "Q")
        {
            userIsDone = true;
            break;
        }

        // Try to display type.
        try
        {
            Type t = Type.GetType(typeName);
            Console.WriteLine("");
            ListVariousStats(t);
            ListFields(t);
            ListProps(t);
            ListMethods(t);
            ListInterfaces(t);
        }
        catch
        {
            Console.WriteLine("Sorry, can't find type");
        }
    } while (!userIsDone);
}
```

At this point, MyTypeViewer.exe is ready to take out for a test drive. For example, run your application and enter the following fully qualified names (be aware that the manner in which you invoked Type.GetType() requires case-sensitive string names):

- System.Int32
- System.Collections.ArrayList
- System.Threading.Thread
- System.Void
- System.IO.BinaryWriter
- System.Math
- System.Console
- MyTypeViewer.Program

Figure 12-2 shows the partial output when specifying System.Math.

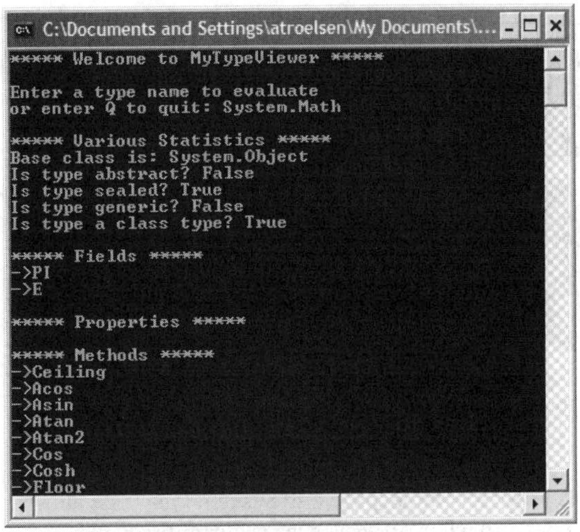

Figure 12-2. *Reflecting on* System.Math

Reflecting on Method Parameters and Return Values

So far, so good! Let's make one minor enhancement to the current application. Specifically, you will update the ListMethods() helper function to list not only the name of a given method, but also the return value and incoming parameters. The MethodInfo type provides the ReturnType property and GetParameters() method for these very tasks. In the following code, notice that you are building a string type that contains the type and name of each parameter using a nested foreach loop:

```
public static void ListMethods(Type t)
{
    Console.WriteLine("***** Methods *****");
    MethodInfo[] mi = t.GetMethods();
    foreach (MethodInfo m in mi)
    {
        // Get return value.
        string retVal = m.ReturnType.FullName;
        string paramInfo = "(";

        // Get params.
        foreach (ParameterInfo pi in m.GetParameters())
        {
            paramInfo += string.Format("{0} {1} ", pi.ParameterType, pi.Name);
        }
        paramInfo += ")";

        // Now display the basic method sig.
        Console.WriteLine("->{0} {1} {2}", retVal, m.Name, paramInfo);
    }
    Console.WriteLine("");
}
```

If you now run this updated application, you will find that the methods of a given type are much more detailed. Figure 12-3 shows the method metadata of the System.Globalization. GregorianCalendar type.

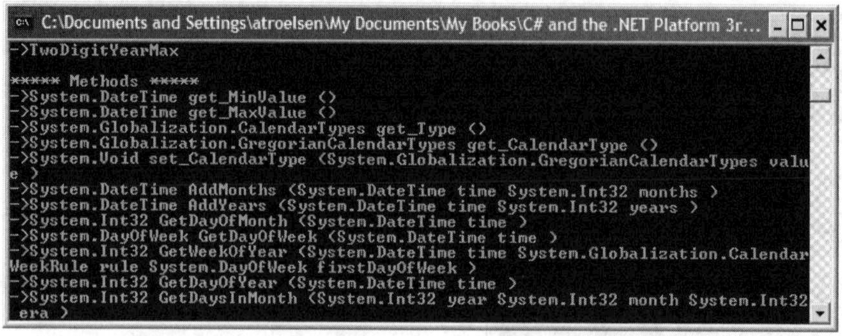

Figure 12-3. *Method details of* `System.Globalization.GregorianCalendar`

Interesting stuff, huh? Clearly the `System.Reflection` namespace and `System.Type` class allow you to reflect over many other aspects of a type beyond what `MyTypeViewer` is currently displaying. As you would hope, you can obtain a type's events, discover which interfaces have been implemented explicitly, get the list of any generic parameters for a given member, and glean dozens of other details.

Nevertheless, at this point you have created an (somewhat capable) object browser. The major limitation, of course, is that you have no way to reflect beyond the current assembly (`MyTypeViewer`) or the always accessible `mscorlib.dll`. This begs the question, "How can I build applications that can load (and reflect over) assemblies not known at compile time?"

■**Source Code** The MyTypeViewer project can be found under the Chapter 12 subdirectory.

Dynamically Loading Assemblies

In the previous chapter, you learned all about how the CLR consults the assembly manifest when probing for an externally referenced assembly. While this is all well and good, there will be many times when you need to load assemblies on the fly programmatically, even if there is no record of said assembly in the manifest. Formally speaking, the act of loading external assemblies on demand is known as a *dynamic load*.

`System.Reflection` defines a class named `Assembly`. Using this type, you are able to dynamically load an assembly as well as discover properties about the assembly itself. Using the `Assembly` type, you are able to dynamically load private or shared assemblies, as well as load an assembly located at an arbitrary location. In essence, the `Assembly` class provides methods (`Load()` and `LoadFrom()` in particular) that allow you to programmatically supply the same sort of information found in a client-side *.config file.

To illustrate dynamic loading, create a brand-new console application named `ExternalAssemblyReflector`. Your task is to construct a `Main()` method that prompts for the friendly name of an assembly to load dynamically. You will pass the `Assembly` reference into a helper method named `DisplayTypes()`, which will simply print the names of each class, interface, structure, enumeration, and delegate it contains. The code is refreshingly simple:

```
using System;
using System.Reflection;
using System.IO;  // For FileNotFoundException definition.
```

```
namespace ExternalAssemblyReflector
{
    class Program
    {
        static void DisplayTypesInAsm(Assembly asm)
        {
            Console.WriteLine("\n***** Types in Assembly *****");
            Console.WriteLine("->{0}", asm.FullName);
            Type[] types = asm.GetTypes();
            foreach (Type t in types)
                Console.WriteLine("Type: {0}", t);
            Console.WriteLine("");
        }

        static void Main(string[] args)
        {
            Console.WriteLine("***** External Assembly Viewer *****");

            string asmName = "";
            bool userIsDone = false;
            Assembly asm = null;

            do
            {
                Console.WriteLine("\nEnter an assembly to evaluate");
                Console.Write("or enter Q to quit: ");

                // Get name of assembly.
                asmName = Console.ReadLine();

                // Does user want to quit?
                if (asmName.ToUpper() == "Q")
                {
                    userIsDone = true;
                    break;
                }

                // Try to load assembly.
                try
                {
                    asm = Assembly.Load(asmName);
                    DisplayTypesInAsm(asm);
                }
                catch
                {
                    Console.WriteLine("Sorry, can't find assembly.");
                }
            } while (!userIsDone);
        }
    }
}
```

Notice that the static Assembly.Load() method has been passed only the friendly name of the assembly you are interested in loading into memory. Thus, if you wish to reflect over CarLibrary.dll, you will need to copy the CarLibrary.dll binary to the \Bin\Debug directory of the ExternalAssemblyReflector application to run this program. Once you do, you will find output similar to Figure 12-4.

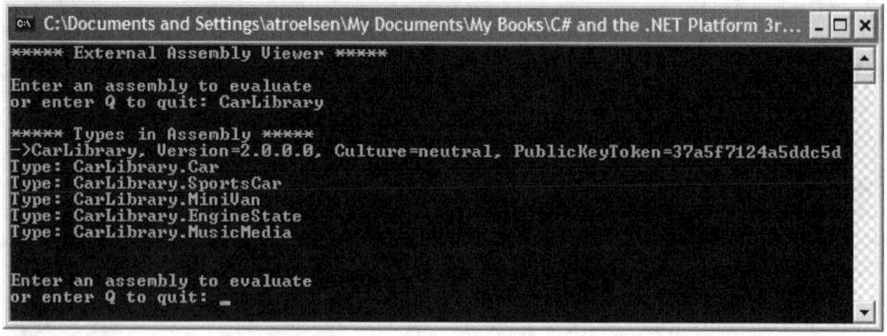

Figure 12-4. *Reflecting on the external CarLibrary assembly*

■**Note** If you wish to make ExternalAssemblyReflector more flexible, load the external assembly using Assembly.LoadFrom() rather than Assembly.Load(). By doing so, you can enter an absolute path to the assembly you wish to view (e.g., C:\MyApp\MyAsm.dll).

■**Source Code** The ExternalAssemblyReflector project is included in the Chapter 12 subdirectory.

Reflecting on Shared Assemblies

As you may suspect, Assembly.Load() has been overloaded a number of times. One variation of the Assembly.Load() method allows you to specify a culture value (for localized assemblies) as well as a version number and public key token value (for shared assemblies).

Collectively speaking, the set of items identifying an assembly is termed the *display name*. The format of a display name is a comma-delimited string of name/value pairs that begins with the friendly name of the assembly, followed by optional qualifiers (that may appear in any order). Here is the template to follow (optional items appear in parentheses):

Name (,**Culture** = culture token) (,**Version** = major.minor.build.revision)
(,**PublicKeyToken**= public key token)

When you're crafting a display name, the convention PublicKeyToken=null indicates that binding and matching against a non–strongly-named assembly is required. Additionally, Culture="" indicates matching against the default culture of the target machine, for example:

```
// Load version 1.0.982.23972 of CarLibrary using the default culture.
Assembly a = Assembly.Load(
  @"CarLibrary, Version=1.0.982.23972, PublicKeyToken=null, Culture=""");
```

Also be aware that the System.Reflection namespace supplies the AssemblyName type, which allows you to represent the preceding string information in a handy object variable. Typically, this class is used in conjunction with System.Version, which is an OO wrapper around an assembly's version number. Once you have established the display name, it can then be passed into the overloaded Assembly.Load() method:

```
// Make use of AssemblyName to define the display name.
AssemblyName asmName;
```

```
asmName = new AssemblyName();
asmName.Name = "CarLibrary";
Version v = new Version("1.0.982.23972");
asmName.Version = v;
Assembly a = Assembly.Load(asmName);
```

To load a shared assembly from the GAC, the Assembly.Load() parameter must specify
a publickeytoken value. For example, assume you wish to load version 2.0.0.0 of the System.Windows.
Forms.dll assembly provided by the .NET base class libraries. Given that the number of types in this
assembly is quite large, the following application simply prints out the names of the first 20 types:

```
using System;
using System.Reflection;
using System.IO;

namespace SharedAsmReflector
{
    public class SharedAsmReflector
    {
        private static void DisplayInfo(Assembly a)
        {
            Console.WriteLine("***** Info about Assembly *****");
            Console.WriteLine("Loaded from GAC? {0}", a.GlobalAssemblyCache);
            Console.WriteLine("Asm Name: {0}", a.GetName().Name);
            Console.WriteLine("Asm Version: {0}", a.GetName().Version);
            Console.WriteLine("Asm Culture: {0}",
                a.GetName().CultureInfo.DisplayName);

            Type[] types = a.GetTypes();
            for(int i = 0; i < 20; i++)
                Console.WriteLine("Type: {0}", types[i]);
        }

        static void Main(string[] args)
        {
            Console.WriteLine("***** The Shared Asm Reflector App *****\n");

            // Load System.Windows.Forms.dll from GAC.
            string displayName = null;
            displayName = "System.Windows.Forms," +
                "Version=2.0.0.0," +
                "PublicKeyToken=b77a5c561934e089," +
                @"Culture=""";
                Assembly asm = Assembly.Load(displayName);
            DisplayInfo(asm);
            Console.ReadLine();
        }
    }
}
```

■**Source Code** The SharedAsmReflector project is included in the Chapter 12 subdirectory.

Sweet! At this point you should understand how to use some of the core items defined within
the System.Reflection namespace to discover metadata at runtime. Of course, I realize despite the

"cool factor," you likely will not need to build custom object browsers at your place of employment. Do recall, however, that reflection services are the foundation for a number of very common programming activities, including *late binding*.

Understanding Late Binding

Simply put, *late binding* is a technique in which you are able to create an instance of a given type and invoke its members at runtime without having compile-time knowledge of its existence. When you are building an application that binds late to a type in an external assembly, you have no reason to set a reference to the assembly; therefore, the caller's manifest has no direct listing of the assembly.

At first glance, you may not understand the value of late binding. It is true that if you can "bind early" to a type (e.g., set an assembly reference and allocate the type using the C# new keyword), you should opt to do so. For one reason, early binding allows you to determine errors at compile time, rather than at runtime. Nevertheless, late binding does have a critical role in any extendable application you may be building.

The System.Activator Class

The System.Activator class is the key to .NET late binding process. Beyond the methods inherited from System.Object, Activator defines only a small set of members, many of which have to do with .NET remoting (see Chapter 18). For our current example, we are only interested in the Activator. CreateInstance() method, which is used to create an instance of a type à la late binding.

This method has been overloaded numerous times to provide a good deal of flexibility. The simplest variation of the CreateInstance() member takes a valid Type object that describes the entity you wish to allocate on the fly. Create a new application named LateBinding, and update the Main() method as so (be sure to place a copy of CarLibrary.dll in the project's \Bin\Debug directory):

```
// Create a type dynamically.
public class Program
{
    static void Main(string[] args)
    {
        // Try to load a local copy of CarLibrary.
        Assembly a = null;
        try
        {
            a = Assembly.Load("CarLibrary");
        }
        catch(FileNotFoundException e)
        {
            Console.WriteLine(e.Message);
            Console.ReadLine();
            return;
        }

        // Get metadata for the Minivan type.
        Type miniVan = a.GetType("CarLibrary.MiniVan");

        // Create the Minivan on the fly.
        object obj = Activator.CreateInstance(miniVan);
    }
}
```

Notice that the `Activator.CreateInstance()` method returns a generic `System.Object` rather than a strongly typed `MiniVan`. Therefore, if you apply the dot operator on the `obj` variable, you will fail to see any members of the `MiniVan` type. At first glance, you may assume you can remedy this problem with an explicit cast; however, this program has no clue what a `MiniVan` is in the first place!

Remember that the whole point of late binding is to create instances of objects for which there is no compile-time knowledge. Given this, how can you invoke the underlying methods of the `MiniVan` object stored in the `System.Object` variable? The answer, of course, is by using reflection.

Invoking Methods with No Parameters

Assume you wish to invoke the `TurboBoost()` method of the `MiniVan`. As you recall, this method will set the state of the engine to "dead" and display an informational message box. The first step is to obtain a `MethodInfo` type for the `TurboBoost()` method using `Type.GetMethod()`. From the resulting `MethodInfo`, you are then able to call `MiniVan.TurboBoost` using `Invoke()`. `MethodInfo.Invoke()` requires you to send in all parameters that are to be given to the method represented by `MethodInfo`. These parameters are represented by an array of `System.Object` types (as the parameters for a given method could be any number of various entities).

Given that `TurboBoost()` does not require any parameters, you can simply pass `null` (meaning "this method has no parameters"). Update your `Main()` method as so:

```
static void Main(string[] args)
{
    // Try to load a local copy of CarLibrary.
    ...

    // Get the MiniVan type.
    Type miniVan = a.GetType("CarLibrary.MiniVan");

    // Create the MiniVan on the fly.
    object obj = Activator.CreateInstance(miniVan);

    // Get info for TurboBoost.
    MethodInfo mi = miniVan.GetMethod("TurboBoost");

    // Invoke method ('null' for no parameters).
    mi.Invoke(obj, null);
}
```

At this point you are happy to see the message box in Figure 12-5.

Figure 12-5. *Late-bound method invocation*

Invoking Methods with Parameters

To illustrate how to dynamically invoke a method that does take some number of parameters, assume the `MiniVan` type defines a method named `TellChildToBeQuiet()`:

```
// Quiet down the troops...
public void TellChildToBeQuiet(string kidName, int shameIntensity)
{
    for(int i = 0 ; i < shameIntensity; i++)
        MessageBox.Show("Be quiet {0} !!", kidName);
}
```

TellChildToBeQuiet() takes two parameters: a string representing the child's name and an integer representing your current level of frustration. When using late binding, parameters are packaged as an array of System.Objects. To invoke the new method, add the following code to your Main() method:

```
// Bind late to a method taking params.
object[] paramArray = new object[2];
paramArray[0] = "Fred";  // Child name.
paramArray[1] = 4;        // Shame Intensity.
mi = miniVan.GetMethod("TellChildToBeQuiet");
mi.Invoke(obj, paramArray);
```

If you run this program, you will see four message boxes pop up, shaming young Fred. Hopefully at this point you can see the relationships among reflection, dynamic loading, and late binding. Again, you still may wonder exactly *when* you might make use of these techniques in your own applications. The conclusion of this chapter should shed light on this question; however, the next topic under investigation is the role of .NET attributes.

■**Source Code** The LateBinding project is included in the Chapter 12 subdirectory.

Understanding Attributed Programming

As illustrated at beginning of this chapter, one role of a .NET compiler is to generate metadata descriptions for all defined and referenced types. In addition to this standard metadata contained within any assembly, the .NET platform provides a way for programmers to embed additional metadata into an assembly using *attributes*. In a nutshell, attributes are nothing more than code annotations that can be applied to a given type (class, interface, structure, etc.), member (property, method, etc.), assembly, or module.

The idea of annotating code using attributes is not new. COM IDL provided numerous predefined attributes that allowed developers to describe the types contained within a given COM server. However, COM attributes were little more than a set of keywords. If a COM developer needed to create a custom attribute, they could do so, but it was referenced in code by a 128-bit number (GUID), which was cumbersome at best.

Unlike COM IDL attributes (which again were simply keywords), .NET attributes are class types that extend the abstract System.Attribute base class. As you explore the .NET namespaces, you will find many predefined attributes that you are able to make use of in your applications. Furthermore, you are free to build custom attributes to further qualify the behavior of your types by creating a new type deriving from Attribute.

Understand that when you apply attributes in your code, the embedded metadata is essentially useless until another piece of software explicitly reflects over the information. If this is not the case, the blurb of metadata embedded within the assembly is ignored and completely harmless.

Attribute Consumers

As you would guess, the .NET Framework 2.0 SDK ships with numerous utilities that are indeed on the lookout for various attributes. The C# compiler (csc.exe) itself has been preprogrammed to discover the presence of various attributes during the compilation cycle. For example, if the C# compiler encounters the [CLSCompilant] attribute, it will automatically check the attributed item to ensure it is exposing only CLS-compliant constructs. By way of another example, if the C# compiler discovers an item attributed with the [Obsolete] attribute, it will display a compiler warning in the Visual Studio 2005 Error List window.

In addition to development tools, numerous methods in the .NET base class libraries are pre-programmed to reflect over specific attributes. For example, if you wish to persist the state of an object to file, all you are required to do is annotate your class with the [Serializable] attribute. If the Serialize() method of the BinaryFormatter class encounters this attribute, the object is auto-matically persisted to file in a compact binary format.

The .NET CLR is also on the prowl for the presence of certain attributes. Perhaps the most famous .NET attribute is [WebMethod]. If you wish to expose a method via HTTP requests and automatically encode the method return value as XML, simply apply [WebMethod] to the method and the CLR handles the details. Beyond web service development, attributes are critical to the operation of the .NET security system, .NET remoting layer, and COM/.NET interoperability (and so on).

Finally, you are free to build applications that are programmed to reflect over your own custom attributes as well as any attribute in the .NET base class libraries. By doing so, you are essentially able to create a set of "keywords" that are understood by a specific set of assemblies.

Applying Predefined Attributes in C#

As previously mentioned, the .NET base class library provides a number of attributes in various namespaces. Table 12-3 gives a snapshot of some—but by *absolutely* no means all—predefined attributes.

Table 12-3. *A Tiny Sampling of Predefined Attributes*

Attribute	Meaning in Life
[CLSCompliant]	Enforces the annotated item to conform to the rules of the Common Language Specification (CLS). Recall that CLS-compliant types are guaranteed to be used seamlessly across all .NET programming languages.
[DllImport]	Allows .NET code to make calls to any unmanaged C- or C++-based code library, including the API of the underlying operating system. Do note that [DllImport] is not used when communicating with COM-based software.
[Obsolete]	Marks a deprecated type or member. If other programmers attempt to use such an item, they will receive a compiler warning describing the error of their ways.
[Serializable]	Marks a class or structure as being "serializable."
[NonSerialized]	Specifies that a given field in a class or structure should not be persisted during the serialization process.
[WebMethod]	Marks a method as being invokable via HTTP requests and instructs the CLR to serialize the method return value as XML (see Chapter 25 for complete details).

To illustrate the process of applying attributes in C#, assume you wish build a class named Motorcycle that can be persisted in a binary format. To do so, simply apply the [Serializable] attribute to the class definition. If you have a field that should not be persisted, you may apply the [NonSerialized] attribute:

```
// This class can be saved to disk.
[Serializable]
public class Motorcycle
{
    // However this field will not be persisted.
    [NonSerialized]
    float weightOfCurrentPassengers;

    // These fields are still serializable.
    bool hasRadioSystem;
    bool hasHeadSet;
    bool hasSissyBar;
}
```

Note An attribute only applies to the "very next" item. For example, the only nonserialized field of the `Motorcycle` class is `weightOfCurrentPassengers`. The remaining fields are serializable given that the entire class has been annotated with `[Serializable]`.

At this point, don't concern yourself with the actual process of object serialization (Chapter 17 examines the details). Just notice that when you wish to apply an attribute, the name of the attribute is sandwiched between square brackets.

Once this class has been compiled, you can view the extra metadata using `ildasm.exe`. Notice that these attributes are recorded using the `serializable` and `notserialized` tokens (see Figure 12-6).

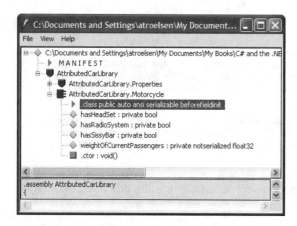

Figure 12-6. *Attributes shown in* `ildasm.exe`

As you might guess, a single item can be attributed with multiple attributes. Assume you have a legacy C# class type (`HorseAndBuggy`) that was marked as serializable, but is now considered obsolete for current development. To apply multiple attributes to a single item, simply use a comma-delimited list:

```
[Serializable,
Obsolete("This class is obsolete, use another vehicle!")]
public class HorseAndBuggy
{
    // ...
}
```

As an alternative, you can also apply multiple attributes on a single item by stacking each attribute as so (the end result is identical):

```
[Serializable]
[Obsolete("This class is obsolete, use another vehicle!")]
public class HorseAndBuggy
{
    // ...
}
```

Specifying Constructor Parameters for Attributes

Notice that the [Obsolete] attribute is able to accept what appears to be a constructor parameter. If you view the formal definition of the [Obsolete] attribute using the Code Definition window of Visual Studio 2005, you will find that this class indeed provides a constructor receiving a System.String:

```
public sealed class ObsoleteAttribute : System.Attribute
{
    public bool IsError { get; }
    public string Message { get; }
    public ObsoleteAttribute(string message, bool error);
    public ObsoleteAttribute(string message);
    public ObsoleteAttribute();
}
```

Understand that when you supply constructor parameters to an attribute, the attribute is *not* allocated into memory until they parameters are reflected upon by another type or an external tool. The string data defined at the attribute level is simply stored within the assembly as a blurb of metadata.

The Obsolete Attribute in Action

Now that HorseAndBuggy has been marked as obsolete, if you were to allocate an instance of this type, you would find that the supplied string data is extracted and displayed within the Error List window of Visual Studio 2005 (see Figure 12-7).

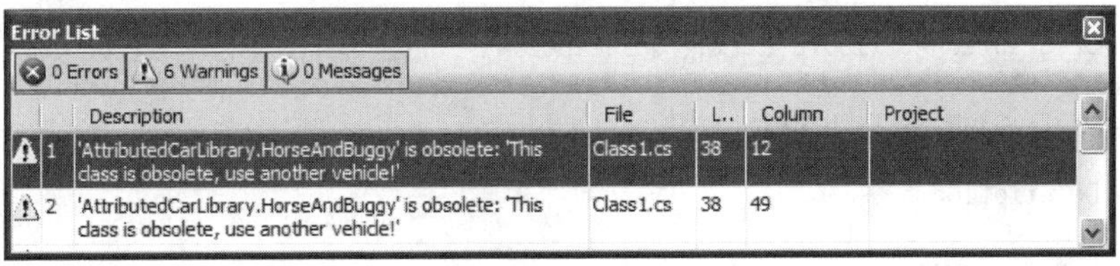

	Description	File	L..	Column	Project	
⚠ 1	'AttributedCarLibrary.HorseAndBuggy' is obsolete: 'This class is obsolete, use another vehicle!'	Class1.cs	38	12		
⚠ 2	'AttributedCarLibrary.HorseAndBuggy' is obsolete: 'This class is obsolete, use another vehicle!'	Class1.cs	38	49		

Figure 12-7. *Attributes in action*

In this case, the "other piece of software" that is reflecting on the [Obsolete] attribute is the C# compiler.

C# Attribute Shorthand Notation

If you were reading closely, you may have noticed that the actual class name of the [Obsolete] attribute is ObsoleteAttribute, not Obsolete. As a naming convention, all .NET attributes (including custom attributes you may create yourself) are suffixed with the "Attribute" token. However, to simplify the process of applying attributes, the C# language does not require you to type in the Attribute suffix. Given this, the following iteration of the HorseAndBuggy type is identical to the previous (it just involves a few more keystrokes):

```
[SerializableAttribute]
[ObsoleteAttribute("This class is obsolete, use another vehicle!")]
public class HorseAndBuggy
{
    // ...
}
```

Be aware that this is a courtesy provided by C#. Not all .NET-enabled languages support this feature. In any case, at this point you should hopefully understand the following key points regarding .NET attributes:

- Attributes are classes that derive from System.Attribute.

- Attributes result in embedded metadata.

- Attributes are basically useless until another agent reflects upon them.

- Attributes are applied in C# using square brackets.

Next up, let's examine how you can build your own custom attributes and a piece of custom software that reflects over the embedded metadata.

Building Custom Attributes

The first step in building a custom attribute is to create a new class deriving from System.Attribute. Keeping in step with the automobile theme used throughout this book, assume you have created a brand new C# class library named AttributedCarLibrary. This assembly will define a handful of vehicles (some of which you have already seen in this text), each of which is described using a custom attribute named VehicleDescriptionAttribute:

```
// A custom attribute.
public sealed class VehicleDescriptionAttribute : System.Attribute
{
    private string msgData;

    public VehicleDescriptionAttribute(string description)
    { msgData = description;}
    public VehicleDescriptionAttribute(){ }

    public string Description
    {
        get { return msgData; }
        set { msgData = value; }
    }
}
```

As you can see, VehicleDescriptionAttribute maintains a private internal string (msgData) that can be set using a custom constructor and manipulated using a type property (Description). Beyond the fact that this class derived from System.Attribute, there is nothing unique to this class definition.

■**Note** For security reasons, it is considered a .NET best practice to design all custom attributes as sealed.

Applying Custom Attributes

Given that VehicleDescriptionAttribute is derived from System.Attribute, you are now able to annotate your vehicles as you see fit:

```
// Assign description using a 'named property'.
[Serializable,
VehicleDescription(Description = "My rocking Harley")]
public class Motorcycle
{
    // ...
}

[SerializableAttribute]
[ObsoleteAttribute("This class is obsolete, use another vehicle!"),
VehicleDescription("The old gray mare, she ain't what she used to be...")]
public class HorseAndBuggy
{
    // ...
}

[VehicleDescription("A very long, slow, but feature-rich auto")]
public class Winnebago
{
    // ...
}
```

Notice that the description of the Motorcycle is assigned a description using a new bit of attribute-centric syntax termed a *named property*. In the constructor of the first [VehicleDescription] attribute, you set the underlying System.String using a name/value pair. If this attribute is reflected upon by an external agent, the value is fed into the Description property (named property syntax is legal only if the attribute supplies a writable .NET property). In contrast, the HorseAndBuggy and Winnebago types are not making use of named property syntax and are simply passing the string data via the custom constructor.

Once you compile the AttributedCarLibrary assembly, you can make use of ildasm.exe to view the injected metadata descriptions for your type. For example, here is an embedded description of the Winnebago type (see Figure 12-8).

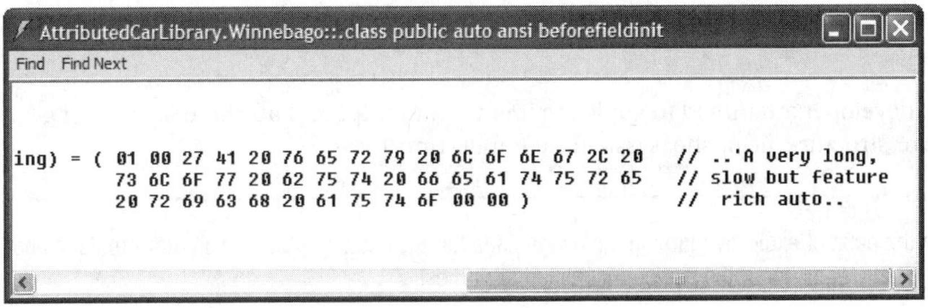

```
AttributedCarLibrary.Winnebago::.class public auto ansi beforefieldinit
Find   Find Next

ing) = (  01 00 27 41 20 76 65 72 79 20 6C 6F 6E 67 2C 20   // ..'A very long,
          73 6C 6F 77 20 62 75 74 20 66 65 61 74 75 72 65   // slow but feature
          20 72 69 63 68 20 61 75 74 6F 00 00 )             //  rich auto..
```

Figure 12-8. *Embedded vehicle description data*

Restricting Attribute Usage

By default, custom attributes can be applied to just about any aspect of your code (methods, classes, properties, and so on). Thus, if it made sense to do so, you could use VehicleDescription to qualify methods, properties, or fields (among other things):

```
[VehicleDescription("A very long, slow, but feature-rich auto")]
public class Winnebago
{
    [VehicleDescription("My rocking CD player")]
    public void PlayMusic(bool On)
    {
        ...
    }
}
```

In some cases, this is exactly the behavior you require. Other times, however, you may want to build a custom attribute that can be applied only to select code elements. If you wish to constrain the scope of a custom attribute, you will need to apply the [AttributeUsage] attribute on the definition of your custom attribute. The [AttributeUsage] attribute allows you to supply any combination of values (via an OR operation) from the AttributeTargets enumeration:

```
// This enumeration defines the possible targets of an attribute.
public enum AttributeTargets
{
    All, Assembly, Class, Constructor,
    Delegate, Enum, Event, Field,
    Interface, Method, Module, Parameter,
    Property, ReturnValue, Struct
}
```

Furthermore, [AttributeUsage] also allows you to optionally set a named property (AllowMultiple) that specifies whether the attribute can be applied more than once on the same item. As well, [AttributeUsage] allows you to establish whether the attribute should be inherited by derived classes using the Inherited named property.

To establish that the [VehicleDescription] attribute can be applied only once on a class or structure (and the value is not inherited by derived types), you can update the VehicleDescriptionAttribute definition as so:

```
// This time, we are using the AttributeUsage attribute
// to annotate our custom attribute.
[AttributeUsage(AttributeTargets.Class | AttributeTargets.Struct,
    AllowMultiple = false, Inherited = false)]
public class VehicleDescriptionAttribute : System.Attribute
{
...
}
```

With this, if a developer attempted to apply the [VehicleDescription] attribute on anything other than a class or structure, he or she is issued a compile-time error.

Tip Always get in the habit of explicitly marking the usage flags for any custom attribute you may create, as not all .NET programming languages honor the use of unqualified attributes!

Assembly-Level (and Module-Level) Attributes

It is also possible to apply attributes on all types within a given module or all modules within a given assembly using the [module:] and [assembly:] tags, respectively. For example, assume you wish to ensure that every public type defined within your assembly is CLS-compliant. To do so, simply add the following line in any one of your C# source code files (do note that assembly-level attributes must be outside the scope of a namespace definition):

```
// Enforce CLS compliance for all public types in this assembly.
[assembly:System.CLSCompliantAttribute(true)]
```

If you now add a bit of code that falls outside the CLS specification (such as an exposed point of unsigned data)

```
// Ulong types don't jive with the CLS.
public class Winnebago
{
    public ulong notCompliant;
}
```

you are issued a compiler error.

The Visual Studio 2005 AssemblyInfo.cs File

By default, Visual Studio 2005 generates a file named AssemblyInfo.cs (see Figure 12-9).

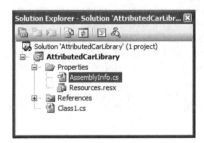

Figure 12-9. *The* AssemblyInfo.cs *file*

This file is a handy place to put attributes that are to be applied at the assembly level. Table 12-4 lists some assembly-level attributes to be aware of.

Table 12-4. *Select Assembly-Level Attributes*

Attribute	Meaning in Life
AssemblyCompanyAttribute	Holds basic company information
AssemblyCopyrightAttribute	Holds any copyright information for the product or assembly
AssemblyCultureAttribute	Provides information on what cultures or languages the assembly supports
AssemblyDescriptionAttribute	Holds a friendly description of the product or modules that make up the assembly

Continued

Table 12-4. *(Continued)*

Attribute	Meaning in Life
AssemblyKeyFileAttribute	Specifies the name of the file containing the key pair used to sign the assembly (i.e., establish a shared name)
AssemblyOperatingSystemAttribute	Provides information on which operating system the assembly was built to support
AssemblyProcessorAttribute	Provides information on which processors the assembly was built to support
AssemblyProductAttribute	Provides product information
AssemblyTrademarkAttribute	Provides trademark information
AssemblyVersionAttribute	Specifies the assembly's version information, in the format *<major.minor.build.revision>*

■**Source Code** The AttributedCarLibrary project is included in the Chapter 12 subdirectory.

Reflecting on Attributes Using Early Binding

As mentioned in this chapter, an attribute is quite useless until some piece of software reflects over its values. Once a given attribute has been discovered, that piece of software can take whatever course of action necessary. Now, like an application, this "other piece of software" could discover the presence of a custom attribute using either early binding or late binding. If you wish to make use of early binding, you'll require the client application to have a compile-time definition of the attribute in question (VehicleDescriptionAttribute in this case). Given that the AttributedCarLibrary assembly has defined this custom attribute as a public class, early binding is the best option.

To illustrate the process of reflecting on custom attributes, create a new C# console application named VehicleDescriptionAttributeReader. Next, set a reference to the AttributedCarLibrary assembly. Finally, update your initial *.cs file with the following code:

```
// Reflecting on custom attributes using early binding.
using System;
using AttributedCarLibrary;

public class Program
{
    static void Main(string[] args)
    {
        // Get a Type representing the Winnebago.
        Type t = typeof(Winnebago);

        // Get all attributes on the Winnebago.
        object[] customAtts = t.GetCustomAttributes(false);

        // Print the description.
        Console.WriteLine("***** Value of VehicleDescriptionAttribute *****\n");
        foreach(VehicleDescriptionAttribute v in customAtts)
            Console.WriteLine("-> {0}\n", v.Description);
        Console.ReadLine();
    }
}
```

As the name implies, `Type.GetCustomAttributes()` returns an object array that represents all the attributes applied to the member represented by the `Type` (the Boolean parameter controls whether the search should extend up the inheritance chain). Once you have obtained the list of attributes, iterate over each `VehicleDescriptionAttribute` class and print out the value obtained by the `Description` property.

■**Source Code** The VehicleDescriptionAttributeReader application is included under the Chapter 12 subdirectory.

Reflecting on Attributes Using Late Binding

The previous example made use of early binding to print out the vehicle description data for the Winnebago type. This was possible due to the fact that the `VehicleDescriptionAttribute` class type was defined as a public member in the AttributedCarLibrary assembly. It is also possible to make use of dynamic loading and late binding to reflect over attributes.

Create a new project called VehicleDescriptionAttributeReaderLateBinding and copy AttributedCarLibrary.dll to the project's \Bin\Debug directory. Now, update your `Main()` method as so:

```
using System.Reflection;

namespace VehicleDescriptionAttributeReaderLateBinding
{
    class Program
    {
        static void Main(string[] args)
        {
            Console.WriteLine("***** Descriptions of Your Vehicles *****\n");

            // Load the local copy of AttributedCarLibrary.
            Assembly asm = Assembly.Load("AttributedCarLibrary");

            // Get type info of VehicleDescriptionAttribute.
            Type vehicleDesc =
                asm.GetType("AttributedCarLibrary.VehicleDescriptionAttribute");

            // Get type info of the Description property.
            PropertyInfo propDesc = vehicleDesc.GetProperty("Description");

            // Get all types in the assembly.
            Type[] types = asm.GetTypes();

            // Iterate over each type and obtain any VehicleDescriptionAttributes.
            foreach (Type t in types)
            {
                object[] objs = t.GetCustomAttributes(vehicleDesc, false);

                // Iterate over each VehicleDescriptionAttribute and print
                // the description using late binding.
                foreach (object o in objs)
                {
                    Console.WriteLine("-> {0}: {1}\n",
                        t.Name, propDesc.GetValue(o, null));
                }
            }
        }
    }
```

```
        Console.ReadLine();
      }
   }
}
```

If you were able to follow along with the examples in this chapter, this Main() method should be (more or less) self-explanatory. The only point of interest is the use of the PropertyInfo.GetValue() method, which is used to trigger the property's accessor. Figure 12-10 shows the output.

■**Source Code** The VehicleDescriptionAttributeReaderLateBinding application is included under the Chapter 12 subdirectory.

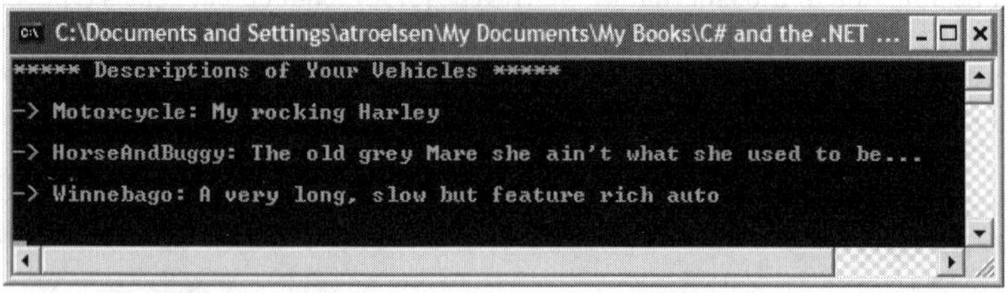

Figure 12-10. *Reflecting on attributes using late binding*

Putting Reflection, Late Binding, and Custom Attributes in Perspective

Even though you have seen numerous examples of these techniques in action, you may still be wondering when to make use of reflection, dynamic loading, late binding, and custom attributes in your programs. To be sure, these topics (while fascinating) can seem a bit on the academic side of programming (which may or may not be a bad thing, depending on your point of view). To help map these topics to a real-world situation, you need a solid example. Assume for the moment that you are on a programming team that is building an application with the following requirement:

- The product must be extendible by the use of additional third-party tools.

So, what exactly is meant by *extendable*? Consider Visual Studio 2005. When this application was developed, various "hooks" were inserted to allow other software vendors to snap custom modules into the IDE. Obviously, the Visual Studio 2005 team had no way to set references to external .NET assemblies it had not programmed (thus, no early binding), so how exactly would an application provide the required hooks?

- First, an extendable application must provide some input vehicle to allow the user to specify the module to plug in (such as a dialog box or command-line flag). This requires *dynamic loading*.

- Second, an extendable application must be able to determine if the module supports the correct functionality (such as a set of required interfaces) in order to be plugged into the environment. This requires *reflection*.

- Finally, an extendable application must obtain a reference to the required infrastructure (e.g., the interface types) and invoke the members to trigger the underlying functionality. This often requires *late binding*.

Simply put, if the extendible application has been preprogrammed to query for specific interfaces, it is able to determine at runtime if the type can be activated. Once this verification test has been passed, the type in question may support additional interfaces that provide a polymorphic fabric to their functionality. This is the exact approach taken by the Visual Studio 2005 team, and despite what you may be thinking, is not at all difficult.

Building an Extendable Application

In the sections that follow, I will take you through a complete example that illustrates the process of building an extendible Windows Forms application that can be augmented by the functionality of external assemblies. What I will not do at this point is comment on the process of programming Windows Forms applications (Chapters 19, 20, and 21 will tend to that chore). So, if you are not familiar with the process of building Windows Forms applications, feel free to simply open up the supplied sample code and follow along (or build a console-based alternative). To serve as a road map, our extendible application entails the following assemblies:

- CommonSnappableTypes.dll: This assembly contains type definitions that will be implemented by each snap-in as well as referenced by the extendible Windows Forms application.

- CSharpSnapIn.dll: A snap-in written in C#, which leverages the types of CommonSnappableTypes.dll.

- VbNetSnapIn.dll: A snap-in written in Visual Basic .NET, which leverages the types of CommonSnappableTypes.dll.

- MyPluggableApp.exe: This Windows Forms application will be the entity that may be extended by the functionality of each snap-in. Again, this application will make use of dynamic loading, reflection, and late binding to dynamically gain the functionality of assemblies it has no prior knowledge of.

Building CommonSnappableTypes.dll

The first order of business is to create an assembly that contains the types that a given snap-in must leverage to be plugged into your expandable Windows Forms application. The CommonSnappableTypes class library project defines two types:

```
namespace CommonSnappableTypes
{
    public interface IAppFunctionality
    {
        void DoIt();
    }

    [AttributeUsage(AttributeTargets.Class)]
    public sealed class CompanyInfoAttribute : System.Attribute
    {
        private string companyName;
        private string companyUrl;
        public CompanyInfoAttribute(){}

        public string Name
        {
            get { return companyName; }
            set { companyName = value; }
        }
```

```
        public string Url
        {
          get { return companyUrl; }
          set { companyUrl = value; }
        }
    }
}
```

The IAppFunctionality interface provides a polymorphic interface for all snap-ins that can be consumed by the extendible Windows Forms application. Of course, as this example is purely illustrative in nature, you supply a single method named DoIt(). To map this to a real-world example, imagine an interface (or a set of interfaces) that allows the snapper to generate scripting code, render an image onto the application's toolbox, or integrate into the main menu of the hosting application.

The CompanyInfoAttribute type is a custom attribute that will be applied on any class type that wishes to be snapped in to the container. As you can tell by the definition of this class, [CompanyInfo] allows the developer of the snap-in to provide some basic details about the component's point of origin.

Building the C# Snap-In

Next up, you need to create a type that implements the IAppFunctionality interface. Again, to focus on the overall design of an extendible application, a trivial type is in order. Assume a new C# code library named CSharpSnapIn that defines a class type named CSharpModule. Given that this class must make use of the types defined in CommonSnappableTypes, be sure to set a reference to this binary (as well as System.Windows.Forms.dll to display a noteworthy message). This being said, here is the code:

```
using System;
using CommonSnappableTypes;
using System.Windows.Forms;

namespace CSharpSnapIn
{
    [CompanyInfo(Name = "Intertech Training",
         Url = "www.intertechtraining.com")]
    public class TheCSharpModule : IAppFunctionality
    {
        void IAppFunctionality.DoIt()
        {
            MessageBox.Show("You have just used the C# snap in!");
        }
    }
}
```

Notice that I choose to make use of explicit interface implementation when supporting the IAppFunctionality interface. This is not required; however, the idea is that the only part of the system that needs to directly interact with this interface type is the hosting Windows application.

Building the Visual Basic .NET Snap-In

Now, to simulate the role of a third-party vendor who prefers Visual Basic .NET over C#, create a new Visual Basic .NET code library (VbNetSnapIn) that references the same external assemblies as the previous CSharpSnapIn project. The code is (again) intentionally simple:

```
Imports System.Windows.Forms
Imports CommonSnappableTypes
```

```
<CompanyInfo(Name:="Chucky's Software", Url:="www.ChuckySoft.com")> _
Public Class VbNetSnapIn
    Implements IAppFunctionality

    Public Sub DoIt() Implements CommonSnappableTypes.IAppFunctionality.DoIt
        MessageBox.Show("You have just used the VB .NET snap in!")
    End Sub
End Class
```

Not too much to say here! Do notice, however, that applying attributes in the syntax of Visual Basic .NET requires angle brackets (< >) rather than square brackets ([ ]).

Building an Extendable Windows Forms Application

The final step is to create a new Windows Forms application (MyExtendableApp) that allows the user to select a snap-in using a standard Windows Open dialog box. Next, set a reference to the CommonSnappableTypes.dll assembly, but *not* the CSharpSnapIn.dll or VbNetSnapIn.dll code libraries. Remember that the whole goal of this application is to make use of late binding and reflection to determine the "snapability" of independent binaries created by third-party vendors.

Again, I won't bother to examine all the details of Windows Forms development at this point in the text. However, assuming you have placed a MenuStrip component onto the Form template, define a topmost menu item named Tools that provides a single submenu named Snap In Module (see Figure 12-11).

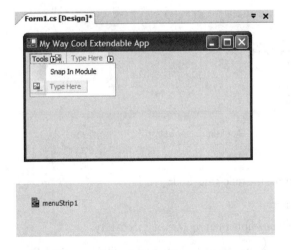

Figure 12-11. *Initial GUI for MyExtendableApp*

This Windows Form will also contain a ListBox type (which I renamed as lstLoadedSnapIns) that will be used to display the names of each snap-in loaded by the user. Figure 12-12 shows the final GUI.

Figure 12-12. *Final GUI for MyExtendableApp*

The code that handles the Tools ➤ Snap In Module menu item (which may be created simply by double-clicking the menu item from the design-time editor) displays a File Open dialog box and extracts the path to the selected file. This path is then sent into a helper function named LoadExternalModule() for processing. This method will return false when it is unable to find a class implementing IAppFunctionality:

```
private void snapInModuleToolStripMenuItem_Click(object sender,
  EventArgs e)
{
    // Allow user to select an assembly to load.
    OpenFileDialog dlg = new OpenFileDialog();

    if (dlg.ShowDialog() == DialogResult.OK)
    {
        if (LoadExternalModule(dlg.FileName) == false)
            MessageBox.Show("Nothing implements IAppFunctionality!");
    }
}
```

The LoadExternalModule() method performs the following tasks:

- Dynamically loads the assembly into memory

- Determines if the assembly contains a type implementing IAppFunctionality

If a type implementing IAppFunctionality is found, the DoIt() method is called, and the fully qualified name of the type is added to the ListBox (note that the for loop will iterate over all types in the assembly to account for the possibility that a single assembly has multiple snap-ins):

```
private bool LoadExternalModule(string path)
{
    bool foundSnapIn = false;
    IAppFunctionality itfAppFx;

    // Dynamically load the selected assembly.
    Assembly theSnapInAsm = Assembly.LoadFrom(path);

    // Get all types in assembly.
    Type[] theTypes = theSnapInAsm.GetTypes();
```

```
// See if a type implement IAppFunctionality.
for (int i = 0; i < theTypes.Length; i++)
{
    Type t = theTypes[i].GetInterface("IAppFunctionality");
    if (t != null)
    {
        foundSnapIn = true;

        // Use late binding to create the type.
        object o =
            theSnapInAsm.CreateInstance(theTypes[i].FullName);

        // Call DoIt() off the interface.
        itfAppFx = o as IAppFunctionality;
        itfAppFx.DoIt();
        lstLoadedSnapIns.Items.Add(theTypes[i].FullName);
    }
}
return foundSnapIn;
}
```

At this point, you can run your application. When you select the CSharpSnapIn.dll or VbNetSnapIn.dll assemblies, you should see the correct message displayed. Figure 12-13 shows one possible run.

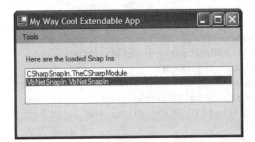

Figure 12-13. *Snapping in external assemblies*

The final task is to display the metadata provided by the [CompanyInfo]. To do so, simply update LoadExternalModule() to call a new helper function named DisplayCompanyData() before exiting the if scope. Notice this method takes a single System.Type parameter.

```
private bool LoadExternalModule(string path)
{
...
    if (t != null)
    {
...
        // Show company info.
        DisplayCompanyData(theTypes[i]);
    }
}
return foundSnapIn;
}
```

Using the incoming type, simply reflect over the [CompanyInfo] attribute:

```
private void DisplayCompanyData(Type t)
{
    // Get [CompanyInfo] data.
    object[] customAtts = t.GetCustomAttributes(false);

    // Show data.
    foreach (CompanyInfoAttribute c in customAtts)
    {
        MessageBox.Show(c.Url,
            string.Format("More info about {0} can be found at", c.Name));
    }
}
```

Excellent! That wraps up the example application. I hope at this point you can see that the topics presented in this chapter can be quite helpful in the real world and are not limited to the tool builders of the world.

Source Code The CommonSnappableTypes, CSharpSnapIn, VbNetSnapIn, and MyExtendableApp applications are included under the Chapter 12 subdirectory.

Summary

Reflection is a very interesting aspect of a robust OO environment. In the world of .NET, the keys to reflection services revolve around the System.Type class and the System.Reflection namespace. As you have seen, reflection is the process of placing a type under the magnifying glass at runtime to understand the who, what, where, when, why, and how of a given item.

Late binding is the process of creating a type and invoking its members without prior knowledge of the specific names of said members. As shown during this chapter's extendible application example, this is a very powerful technique used by tool builders as well as tool consumers. This chapter also examined the role of attribute-based programming. When you adorn your types with attributes, the result is the augmentation of the underlying assembly metadata.

CHAPTER 13

■ ■ ■

Processes, AppDomains, Contexts, and CLR Hosts

In the previous two chapters, you examined the steps taken by the CLR to resolve the location of an externally referenced assembly as well as the role of .NET metadata. In this chapter, you'll drill deeper into the details of how an assembly is hosted by the CLR and come to understand the relationship between processes, application domains, and object contexts.

In a nutshell, *application domains* (or, simply, *AppDomains*) are logical subdivisions within a given process that host a set of related .NET assemblies. As you will see, an AppDomain is further subdivided into contextual boundaries, which are used to group together like-minded .NET objects. Using the notion of context, the CLR is able to ensure that objects with special runtime requirements are handled appropriately.

Once you have come to understand how an assembly is hosted by the CLR, it's time to address the next obvious question: what is hosting the CLR? As you recall from Chapter 1, the CLR itself is represented (in part) by mscoree.dll. When you launch an executable assembly, mscoree.dll is loaded automatically; however, as you will see, there are actually a number of transparent steps happening in the background.

Reviewing Traditional Win32 Processes

The concept of a "process" has existed within Windows-based operating systems well before the release of the .NET platform. Simply put, *process* is the term used to describe the set of resources (such as external code libraries and the primary thread) and the necessary memory allocations used by a running application. For each *.exe loaded into memory, the OS creates a separate and isolated process for use during its lifetime. Using this approach to application isolation, the result is a much more robust and stable runtime environment, given that the failure of one process does not affect the functioning of another.

Now, every Win32 process is assigned a unique process identifier (PID) and may be independently loaded and unloaded by the OS as necessary (as well as programmatically using Win32 API calls). As you may be aware, the Processes tab of the Windows Task Manager utility (activated via the Ctrl+Shift+Esc keystroke combination) allows you to view various statistics regarding the processes running on a given machine, including its PID and image name (see Figure 13-1).

■Note If you do not see a PID column listed in Task Manager, simply select View ➤ Select Columns and check
the PID box.

Figure 13-1. *Windows Task Manager*

An Overview of Threads

Every Win32 process has exactly one main "thread" that functions as the entry point for the application.
The next chapter examines how to create additional threads and thread-safe code using the System.
Threading namespace; however, to facilitate the topics presented here, we need a few working definitions. First of all, a *thread* is a path of execution within a process. Formally speaking, the first thread
created by a process's entry point is termed the *primary thread*. Win32 GUI desktop applications
define the WinMain() method as the application's entry point. On the other hand, a console application provides the Main() method for the same purpose.

Processes that contain a single primary thread of execution are intrinsically *thread-safe*, given
the fact that there is only one thread that can access the data in the application at a given time.
However, a single-threaded process (especially one that is GUI-based) will often appear a bit unresponsive to the user if this single thread is performing a complex operation (such as printing out
a lengthy text file, performing an exotic calculation, or attempting to connect to a remote server
located thousands of miles away).

Given this potential drawback of single-threaded applications, the Win32 API makes it is possible
for the primary thread to spawn additional secondary threads (also termed *worker threads*) using
a handful of Win32 API functions such as CreateThread(). Each thread (primary or secondary) becomes
a unique path of execution in the process and has concurrent access to all shared points of data.

As you may have guessed, developers typically create additional threads to help improve the
program's overall responsiveness. Multithreaded processes provide the illusion that numerous
activities are happening at more or less the same time. For example, an application may spawn

a worker thread to perform a labor-intensive unit of work (again, such as printing a large text file). As this secondary thread is churning away, the main thread is still responsive to user input, which gives the entire process the potential of delivering greater performance. However, this may not actually be the case: using too many threads in a single process can actually *degrade* performance, as the CPU must switch between the active threads in the process (which takes time).

In reality, it is always worth keeping in mind that multithreading is most commonly an illusion provided by the OS. Machines that host a single CPU do not have the ability to literally handle multiple threads at the same exact time. Rather, a single CPU will execute one thread for a unit of time (called a *time slice*) based on the thread's priority level. When a thread's time slice is up, the existing thread is suspended to allow another thread to perform its business. For a thread to remember what was happening before it was kicked out of the way, each thread is given the ability to write to Thread Local Storage (TLS) and is provided with a separate call stack, as illustrated in Figure 13-2.

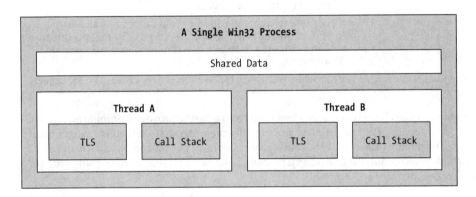

Figure 13-2. *The Win32 process/thread relationship*

If the subject of threads is new to you, don't sweat the details. At this point, just remember that a thread is a unique path of execution within a Win32 process. Every process has a primary thread (created via the executable's entry point) and may contain additional threads that have been programmatically created.

■**Note** Newer Intel CPUs have a feature called *Hyper-Threading Technology* that allows a single CPU to handle multiple threads simultaneously under certain circumstances. See http://www.intel.com/info/hyperthreading for more details.

Interacting with Processes Under the .NET Platform

Although processes and threads are nothing new, the manner in which we interact with these primitives under the .NET platform has changed quite a bit (for the better). To pave the way to understanding the world of building multithreaded assemblies (see Chapter 14), let's begin by checking out how to interact with processes using the .NET base class libraries.

The System.Diagnostics namespace defines a number of types that allow you to programmatically interact with processes and various diagnostic-related types such as the system event log and performance counters. In this chapter, we are only concerned with the process-centric types defined in Table 13-1.

Table 13-1. *Select Members of the* System.Diagnostics *Namespace*

Process-Centric Types of the System.Diagnostics **Namespace**	Meaning in Life
Process	The Process class provides access to local and remote processes and also allows you to programmatically start and stop processes.
ProcessModule	This type represents a module (*.dll or *.exe) that is loaded into a particular process. Understand that the ProcessModule type can represent *any* module—COM-based, .NET-based, or traditional C-based binaries.
ProcessModuleCollection	Provides a strongly typed collection of ProcessModule objects.
ProcessStartInfo	Specifies a set of values used when starting a process via the Process.Start() method.
ProcessThread	Represents a thread within a given process. Be aware that ProcessThread is a type used to diagnose a process's thread set and is not used to spawn new threads of execution within a process.
ProcessThreadCollection	Provides a strongly typed collection of ProcessThread objects.

The System.Diagnostics.Process type allows you to analyze the processes running on a given machine (local or remote). The Process class also provides members that allow you to programmatically start and terminate processes, establish a process's priority level, and obtain a list of active threads and/or loaded modules within a given process. Table 13-2 lists some (but not all) of the key members of System.Diagnostics.Process.

Table 13-2. *Select Members of the* Process *Type*

Members	Meaning in Life
ExitCode	This property gets the value that the associated process specified when it terminated. Do note that you will be required to handle the Exited event (for asynchronous notification) or call the WaitForExit() method (for synchronous notification) to obtain this value.
ExitTime	This property gets the timestamp associated with the process that has terminated (represented with a DateTime type).
Handle	This property returns the handle associated to the process by the OS.
HandleCount	This property returns the number of handles opened by the process.
Id	This property gets the process ID (PID) for the associated process.
MachineName	This property gets the name of the computer the associated process is running on.
MainModule	This property gets the ProcessModule type that represents the main module for a given process.
MainWindowTitle MainWindowHandle	MainWindowTitle gets the caption of the main window of the process (if the process does not have a main window, you receive an empty string). MainWindowHandle gets the underlying handle (represented via a System.IntPtr type) of the associated window. If the process does not have a main window, the IntPtr type is assigned the value System.IntPtr.Zero.
Modules	This property provides access to the strongly typed ProcessModuleCollection type, which represents the set of modules (*.dll or *.exe) loaded within the current process.

Members	Meaning in Life
PriorityBoostEnabled	This property determines if the OS should temporarily boost the process if the main window has the focus.
PriorityClass	This property allows you to read or change the overall priority for the associated process.
ProcessName	This property gets the name of the process (which, as you would assume, is the name of the application itself).
Responding	This property gets a value indicating whether the user interface of the process is responding (or not).
StartTime	This property gets the time that the associated process was started (via a DateTime type).
Threads	This property gets the set of threads that are running in the associated process (represented via an array of ProcessThread types).
CloseMainWindow()	This method closes a process that has a user interface by sending a close message to its main window.
GetCurrentProcess()	This static method returns a new Process type that represents the currently active process.
GetProcesses()	This static method returns an array of new Process components running on a given machine.
Kill()	This method immediately stops the associated process.
Start()	This method starts a process.

Enumerating Running Processes

To illustrate the process of manipulating Process types (pardon the redundancy), assume you have a C# console application named ProcessManipulator, which defines the following static helper method:

```
public static void ListAllRunningProcesses()
{
    // Get all the processes on the local machine.
    Process[] runningProcs = Process.GetProcesses(".");

    // Print out PID and name of each process.
    foreach(Process p in runningProcs)
    {
        string info = string.Format("-> PID: {0}\tName: {1}",
            p.Id, p.ProcessName);
        Console.WriteLine(info);
    }
    Console.WriteLine("*********************************\n");
}
```

Notice how the static Process.GetProcesses() method returns an array of Process types that represent the running processes on the target machine (the dot notation shown here represents the local computer).

Once you have obtained the array of Process types, you are able to trigger any of the members seen in Table 13-2. Here, you are simply displaying the PID and the name of each process. Assuming the Main() method has been updated to call ListAllRunningProcesses(), you will see something like the output shown in Figure 13-3.

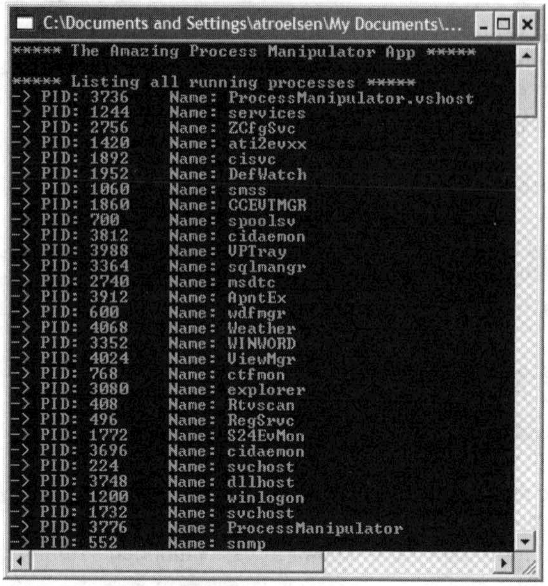

Figure 13-3. *Enumerating running processes*

Investigating a Specific Process

In addition to obtaining a full and complete list of all running processes on a given machine, the static Process.GetProcessById() method allows you to obtain a single Process type via the associated PID. If you request access to a nonexistent process ID, an ArgumentException exception is thrown. Therefore, if you were interested in obtaining a Process object representing a process with the PID of 987, you could write the following:

```
// If there is no process with the PID of 987, a
// runtime exception will be thrown.
static void Main(string[] args)
{
    Process theProc;
    try
    {
        theProc = Process.GetProcessById(987);
    }
    catch  // Generic catch for used simplicity.
    {
        Console.WriteLine("-> Sorry...bad PID!");
    }
}
```

Investigating a Process's Thread Set

The Process class type also provides a manner to programmatically investigate the set of all threads currently used by a specific process. The set of threads is represented by the strongly typed ProcessThreadCollection collection, which contains some number of individual ProcessThread types. To illustrate, assume the following additional static helper function has been added to your current application:

```
public static void EnumThreadsForPid(int pID)
{
    Process theProc;
    try
    {
        theProc = Process.GetProcessById(pID);
    }
    catch
    {
        Console.WriteLine("-> Sorry...bad PID!");
        Console.WriteLine("*********************************\n");
        return;
    }

    // List out stats for each thread in the specified process.
    Console.WriteLine("Here are the threads used by: {0}",
        theProc.ProcessName);
    ProcessThreadCollection theThreads = theProc.Threads;
    foreach(ProcessThread pt in theThreads)
    {
        string info =
            string.Format("-> Thread ID: {0}\tStart Time {1}\tPriority {2}",
                pt.Id , pt.StartTime.ToShortTimeString(), pt.PriorityLevel);
        Console.WriteLine(info);
    }
    Console.WriteLine("*********************************\n");
}
```

As you can see, the Threads property of the System.Diagnostics.Process type provides access to the ProcessThreadCollection class. Here, you are printing out the assigned thread ID, start time, and priority level of each thread in the process specified by the client. Thus, if you update your program's Main() method to prompt the user for a PID to investigate, as follows:

```
static void Main(string[] args)
{
...
    // Prompt user for a PID and print out the set of active threads.
    Console.WriteLine("***** Enter PID of process to investigate *****");
    Console.Write("PID: ");
    string pID = Console.ReadLine();
    int theProcID = int.Parse(pID);

    EnumThreadsForPid(theProcID);
    Console.ReadLine();
}
```

you would find output along the lines of that shown in Figure 13-4.

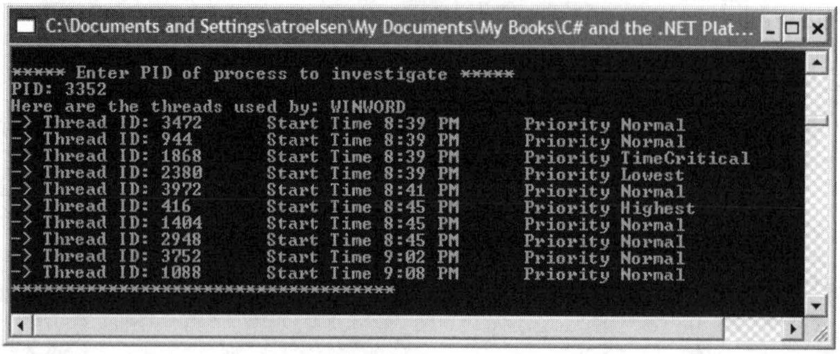

Figure 13-4. *Enumerating the threads within a running process*

The `ProcessThread` type has additional members of interest beyond `Id`, `StartTime`, and `PriorityLevel`. Table 13-3 documents some members of interest.

Table 13-3. *Select Members of the* `ProcessThread` *Type*

Member	Meaning in Life
BasePriority	Gets the base priority of the thread
CurrentPriority	Gets the current priority of the thread
Id	Gets the unique identifier of the thread
IdealProcessor	Sets the preferred processor for this thread to run on
PriorityLevel	Gets or sets the priority level of the thread
ProcessorAffinity	Sets the processors on which the associated thread can run
StartAddress	Gets the memory address of the function that the operating system called that started this thread
StartTime	Gets the time that the operating system started the thread
ThreadState	Gets the current state of this thread
TotalProcessorTime	Gets the total amount of time that this thread has spent using the processor
WaitReason	Gets the reason that the thread is waiting

Before you read any further, be very aware that the `ProcessThread` type is *not* the entity used to create, suspend, or kill threads under the .NET platform. Rather, `ProcessThread` is a vehicle used to obtain diagnostic information for the active Win32 threads within a running process. You will investigate how to build multithreaded applications using the `System.Threading` namespace in Chapter 14.

Investigating a Process's Module Set

Next up, let's check out how to iterate over the number of loaded modules that are hosted within a given process. Recall that a *module* is a generic name used to describe a given `*.dll` (or the `*.exe` itself) that is hosted by a specific process. When you access the `ProcessModuleCollection` via the `Process.Module` property, you are able to enumerate over *all modules* hosted within a process: .NET-based, COM-based, or traditional C-based libraries. Ponder the following additional helper function that will enumerate the modules in a specific process based on the PID:

```csharp
public static void EnumModsForPid(int pID)
{
    Process theProc;
    try
    {
        theProc = Process.GetProcessById(pID);
    }
    catch
    {
        Console.WriteLine("-> Sorry...bad PID!");
        Console.WriteLine("********************************\n");
        return;
    }
    Console.WriteLine("Here are the loaded modules for: {0}",
        theProc.ProcessName);
    try
    {
        ProcessModuleCollection theMods = theProc.Modules;
        foreach(ProcessModule pm in theMods)
        {
            string info = string.Format("-> Mod Name: {0}", pm.ModuleName);
            Console.WriteLine(info);
        }
        Console.WriteLine("********************************\n");
    }
    catch
    {
        Console.WriteLine("No mods!");
    }
}
```

To see some possible output, let's check out the loaded modules for the process hosting the current console application (ProcessManipulator). To do so, run the application, identify the PID assigned to ProcessManipulator.exe, and pass this value to the EnumModsForPid() method (be sure to update your Main() method accordingly). Once you do, you may be surprised to see the list of *.dlls used for a simple console application (atl.dll, mfc42u.dll, oleaut32.dll, and so forth). Figure 13-5 shows a test run.

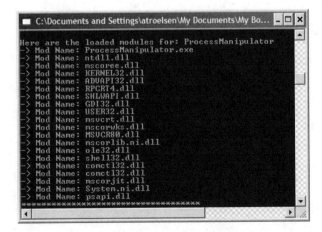

Figure 13-5. *Enumerating the loaded modules within a running process*

Starting and Stopping Processes Programmatically

The final aspects of the System.Diagnostics.Process type examined here are the Start() and Kill() methods. As you can gather by their names, these members provide a way to programmatically launch and terminate a process, respectively. For example, ponder the static StartAndKillProcess() helper method:

```
public static void StartAndKillProcess()
{
    // Launch Internet Explorer.
    Process ieProc = Process.Start("IExplore.exe",
        "www.intertechtraining.com");

    Console.Write("--> Hit enter to kill {0}...", ieProc.ProcessName);
    Console.ReadLine();

    // Kill the iexplorer.exe process.
    try
    {
        ieProc.Kill();
    }
    catch{}    // In case the user already killed it...
}
```

The static Process.Start() method has been overloaded a few times, however. At minimum, you will need to specify the friendly name of the process you wish to launch (such as Microsoft Internet Explorer). This example makes use of a variation of the Start() method that allows you to specify any additional arguments to pass into the program's entry point (i.e., the Main() method).

The Start() method also allows you to pass in a System.Diagnostics.ProcessStartInfo type to specify additional bits of information regarding how a given process should come to life. Here is the formal definition of ProcessStartInfo (see the .NET Framework 2.0 SDK documentation for full details):

```
public sealed class System.Diagnostics.ProcessStartInfo :
    object
{
    public ProcessStartInfo();
    public ProcessStartInfo(string fileName);
    public ProcessStartInfo(string fileName, string arguments);
    public string Arguments { get; set; }
    public bool CreateNoWindow { get; set; }
    public StringDictionary EnvironmentVariables { get; }
    public bool ErrorDialog { get; set; }
    public IntPtr ErrorDialogParentHandle { get; set; }
    public string FileName { get; set; }
    public bool RedirectStandardError { get; set; }
    public bool RedirectStandardInput { get; set; }
    public bool RedirectStandardOutput { get; set; }
    public bool UseShellExecute { get; set; }
    public string Verb { get; set; }
    public string[] Verbs { get; }
    public ProcessWindowStyle WindowStyle { get; set; }
    public string WorkingDirectory { get; set; }
    public virtual bool Equals(object obj);
    public virtual int GetHashCode();
    public Type GetType();
    public virtual string ToString();
}
```

Regardless of which version of the `Process.Start()` method you invoke, do note that you are returned a reference to the newly activated process. When you wish to terminate the process, simply call the instance-level `Kill()` method.

Source Code The ProcessManipulator application is included under the Chapter 13 subdirectory.

Understanding .NET Application Domains

Now that you understand the role of Win32 processes and how to interact with them from managed code, we need to investigate the concept of a .NET application domain. Under the .NET platform, assemblies are not hosted directly within a process (as is the case in traditional Win32 applications). Rather, a .NET executable is hosted by a logical partition within a process termed an *application domain* (aka AppDomain). As you will see, a single process may contain multiple application domains, each of which is hosting a .NET executable. This additional subdivision of a traditional Win32 process offers several benefits, some of which are as follows:

- AppDomains are a key aspect of the OS-neutral nature of the .NET platform, given that this logical division abstracts away the differences in how an underlying OS represents a loaded executable.

- AppDomains are far less expensive in terms of processing power and memory than a full-blown process. Thus, the CLR is able to load and unload application domains much quicker than a formal process.

- AppDomains provide a deeper level of isolation for hosting a loaded application. If one App-Domain within a process fails, the remaining AppDomains remain functional.

As suggested in the previous hit list, a single process can host any number of AppDomains, each of which is fully and completely isolated from other AppDomains within this process (or any other process). Given this factoid, be very aware that an application running in one AppDomain is unable to obtain data of any kind (global variables or static fields) within another AppDomain unless they make use of the .NET remoting protocol (which you'll examine in Chapter 18).

While a single process *may* host multiple AppDomains, this is not always the case. At the very least, an OS process will host what is termed the *default application domain*. This specific application domain is automatically created by the CLR at the time the process launches.

After this point, the CLR creates additional application domains on an as-needed basis. If the need should arise (which it most likely *will not* for the majority of your .NET endeavors), you are also able to programmatically create application domains at runtime within a given process using static methods of the `System.AppDomain` class. This class is also useful for low-level control of application domains. Key members of this class are shown in Table 13-4.

Table 13-4. *Select Members of* `AppDomain`

Member	Meaning in Life
`CreateDomain()`	This static method creates a new AppDomain in the current process. Understand that the CLR will create new application domains as necessary, and thus the chance of you absolutely needing to call this member is slim to none.
`GetCurrentThreadId()`	This static method returns the ID of the active thread in the current application domain.

Continued

Table 13-4. (*Continued*)

Member	Meaning in Life
Unload()	This is another static method that allows you to unload a specified AppDomain within a given process.
BaseDirectory	This property returns the base directory used to probe for dependent assemblies.
CreateInstance()	This method creates an instance of a specified type defined in a specified assembly file.
ExecuteAssembly()	This method executes an assembly within an application domain, given its file name.
GetAssemblies()	This method gets the set of .NET assemblies that have been loaded into this application domain (COM-based or C-based binaries are ignored).
Load()	This method is used to dynamically load an assembly into the current application domain.

In addition, the AppDomain type also defines a small set of events that correspond to various aspects of an application domain's life cycle, as shown in Table 13-5.

Table 13-5. *Events of the* AppDomain *Type*

Event	Meaning in Life
AssemblyLoad	Occurs when an assembly is loaded
AssemblyResolve	Occurs when the resolution of an assembly fails
DomainUnload	Occurs when an AppDomain is about to be unloaded
ProcessExit	Occurs on the default application domain when the default application domain's parent process exits
ResourceResolve	Occurs when the resolution of a resource fails
TypeResolve	Occurs when the resolution of a type fails
UnhandledException	Occurs when an exception is not caught by an event handler

Enumerating a Process's AppDomains

To illustrate how to interact with .NET application domains programmatically, assume you have a new C# console application named AppDomainManipulator that defines a static method named PrintAllAssembliesInAppDomain(). This helper method makes use of AppDomain.GetAssemblies() to obtain a list of all .NET binaries hosted within the application domain in question.

This list is represented by an array of System.Reflection.Assembly types, and thus you are required to use the System.Reflection namespace (see Chapter 12). Once you acquire the assembly array, you iterate over the array and print out the friendly name and version of each module:

```
public static void PrintAllAssembliesInAppDomain(AppDomain ad)
{
    Assembly[] loadedAssemblies = ad.GetAssemblies();
    Console.WriteLine("***** Here are the assemblies loaded in {0} *****\n",
        ad.FriendlyName);
    foreach(Assembly a in loadedAssemblies)
    {
        Console.WriteLine("-> Name: {0}", a.GetName().Name);
        Console.WriteLine("-> Version: {0}\n", a.GetName().Version);
    }
}
```

Now let's update the Main() method to obtain a reference to the current application domain before invoking PrintAllAssembliesInAppDomain(), using the AppDomain.CurrentDomain property.

To make things a bit more interesting, notice that the Main() method launches a Windows Forms message box to force the CLR to load the System.Windows.Forms.dll, System.Drawing.dll, and System.dll assemblies (so be sure to set a reference to these assemblies and update your using statements appropriately):

```
static void Main(string[] args)
{
    Console.WriteLine("***** The Amazing AppDomain app *****\n");

    // Get info for current AppDomain.
    AppDomain defaultAD= AppDomain.CurrentDomain;
    MessageBox.Show("Hello");
    PrintAllAssembliesInAppDomain(defaultAD);

    Console.ReadLine();
}
```

Figure 13-6 shows the output (your version numbers may differ).

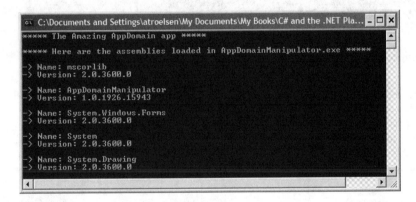

Figure 13-6. *Enumerating assemblies within the current application domain*

Programmatically Creating New AppDomains

Recall that a single process is capable of hosting multiple AppDomains. While it is true that you will seldom (if ever) need to manually create AppDomains in code, you are able to do so via the static CreateDomain() method. As you would guess, AppDomain.CreateDomain() has been overloaded a number of times. At minimum, you will specify the friendly name of the new application domain, as shown here:

```
static void Main(string[] args)
{
...
    // Make a new AppDomain in the current process.
    AppDomain anotherAD = AppDomain.CreateDomain("SecondAppDomain");
    PrintAllAssembliesInAppDomain(anotherAD);

    Console.ReadLine();
}
```

Now, if you run the application again (see Figure 13-7), notice that the System.Windows.Forms.dll, System.Drawing.dll, and System.dll assemblies are only loaded within the default application domain. This may seem counterintuitive if you have a background in traditional Win32 (as you might suspect, both application domains have access to the same assembly set). Recall, however, that an assembly loads into an *application domain*, not directly into the process itself.

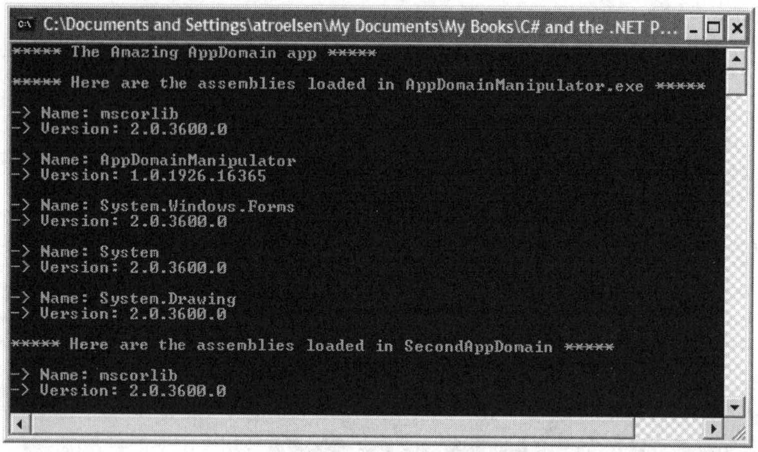

Figure 13-7. *A single process with two application domains*

Next, notice how the SecondAppDomain application domain automatically contains its own copy of mscorlib.dll, as this key assembly is automatically loaded by the CLR for each and every application domain. This begs the question, "How can I programmatically load an assembly into an application domain?" Answer: with the AppDomain.Load() method (or, alternatively, AppDomain.ExecuteAssembly()). Assuming you have copied CarLibrary.dll to the application directory of AppDomainManipulator.exe, you may load CarLibrary.dll into the SecondAppDomain AppDomain as so:

```
static void Main(string[] args)
{
    Console.WriteLine("***** The Amazing AppDomain app *****\n");
    ...
    // Load CarLibrary.dll into the new AppDomain.
    AppDomain anotherAD = AppDomain.CreateDomain("SecondAppDomain");
    anotherAD.Load("CarLibrary");
    PrintAllAssembliesInAppDomain(anotherAD);
    Console.ReadLine();
}
```

To solidify the relationship between processes, application domains, and assemblies, Figure 13-8 diagrams the internal composition of the AppDomainManipulator.exe process just constructed.

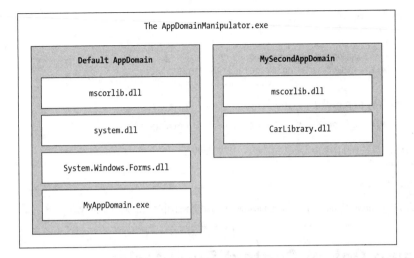

Figure 13-8. *The* AppDomainManipulator.exe *process under the hood*

Programmatically Unloading AppDomains

It is important to point out that the CLR does not permit unloading individual .NET assemblies. However, using the AppDomain.Unload() method, you are able to selectively unload a given application domain from its hosting process. When you do so, the application domain will unload each assembly in turn.

Recall that the AppDomain type defines a small set of events, one of which is DomainUnload. This event is fired when a (nondefault) AppDomain is unloaded from the containing process. Another event of interest is the ProcessExit event, which is fired when the default application domain is unloaded from the process (which obviously entails the termination of the process itself). Thus, if you wish to programmatically unload anotherAD from the AppDomainManipulator.exe process and be notified when the associated application domain is torn down, you are able to write the following event logic:

```
static void Main(string[] args)
{
...
    // Hook into DomainUnload event.
    anotherAD.DomainUnload +=
        new EventHandler(anotherAD_DomainUnload);
    // Now unload anotherAD.
    AppDomain.Unload(anotherAD);
}
```

Notice that the DomainUnload event works in conjunction with the System.EventHandler delegate, and therefore the format of anotherAD_DomainUnload() takes the following arguments:

```
public static void anotherAD_DomainUnload(object sender, EventArgs e)
{
    Console.WriteLine("***** Unloaded anotherAD! *****\n");
}
```

If you wish to be notified when the default AppDomain is unloaded, modify your Main() method to handle the ProcessEvent event of the default application domain:

```
static void Main(string[] args)
{
...
    AppDomain defaultAD = AppDomain.CurrentDomain;
    defaultAD.ProcessExit +=new EventHandler(defaultAD_ProcessExit);
}
```

and define an appropriate event handler:

```
private static void defaultAD_ProcessExit(object sender, EventArgs e)
{
    Console.WriteLine("***** Unloaded defaultAD! *****\n");
}
```

■Source Code The AppDomainManipulator project is included under the Chapter 13 subdirectory.

Understanding Object Context Boundaries

As you have just seen, AppDomains are logical partitions within a process used to host .NET assemblies. On a related note, a given application domain may be further subdivided into numerous context boundaries. In a nutshell, a .NET context provides a way for a single AppDomain to establish a "specific home" for a given object.

Using context, the CLR is able to ensure that objects that have special runtime requirements are handled in an appropriate and consistent manner by intercepting method invocations into and out of a given context. This layer of interception allows the CLR to adjust the current method invocation to conform to the contextual settings of a given object. For example, if you define a C# class type that requires automatic thread safety (using the [Synchronization] attribute), the CLR will create a "synchronized context" during allocation.

Just as a process defines a default AppDomain, every application domain has a default context. This default context (sometimes referred to as *context 0*, given that it is always the first context created within an application domain) is used to group together .NET objects that have no specific or unique contextual needs. As you may expect, a vast majority of .NET objects are loaded into context 0. If the CLR determines a newly created object has special needs, a new context boundary is created within the hosting application domain. Figure 13-9 illustrates the process/AppDomain/context relationship.

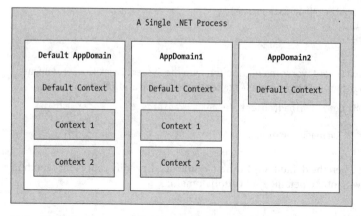

Figure 13-9. *Processes, application domains, and context boundaries*

Context-Agile and Context-Bound Types

.NET types that do not demand any special contextual treatment are termed *context-agile* objects. These objects can be accessed from anywhere within the hosting AppDomain without interfering with the object's runtime requirements. Building context-agile objects is a no-brainer, given that you simply do nothing (specifically, you do not adorn the type with any contextual attributes and do not derive from the System.ContextBoundObject base class):

```
// A context-agile object is loaded into context 0.
public class SportsCar{}
```

On the other hand, objects that do demand contextual allocation are termed *context-bound* objects, and they *must* derive from the System.ContextBoundObject base class. This base class solidifies the fact that the object in question can function appropriately only within the context in which it was created. Given the role of .NET context, it should stand to reason that if a context-bound object were to somehow end up in an incompatible context, bad things would be guaranteed to occur at the most inopportune times.

In addition to deriving from System.ContextBoundObject, a context-sensitive type will also be adorned by a special category of .NET attributes termed (not surprisingly) *context attributes*. All context attributes derive from the System.Runtime.Remoting.Contexts.ContextAttribute base class:

```
public class System.Runtime.Remoting.Contexts.ContextAttribute :
    Attribute, IContextAttribute, IContextProperty
{
    public ContextAttribute(string name);
    public string Name { virtual get; }
    public object TypeId { virtual get; }
    public virtual bool Equals(object o);
    public virtual void Freeze(System.Runtime.Remoting.Contexts.Context newContext);
    public virtual int GetHashCode();
    public virtual void GetPropertiesForNewContext(
        System.Runtime.Remoting.Activation.IConstructionCallMessage ctorMsg);
    public Type GetType();
    public virtual bool IsContextOK(
      System.Runtime.Remoting.Contexts.Context ctx,
      System.Runtime.Remoting.Activation.IConstructionCallMessage ctorMsg);
    public virtual bool IsDefaultAttribute();
    public virtual bool IsNewContextOK(
        System.Runtime.Remoting.Contexts.Context newCtx);
    public virtual bool Match(object obj);
    public virtual string ToString();
}
```

Given that the ContextAttribute class is not sealed, it is possible for you to build your own custom contextual attribute (simply derive from ContextAttribute and override the necessary virtual methods). Once you have done so, you are able to build a custom piece of software that can respond to the contextual settings.

■**Note** This book doesn't dive into the details of building custom object contexts; however, if you are interested in learning more, check out *Applied .NET Attributes* (Apress, 2003).

Defining a Context-Bound Object

Assume that you wish to define a class (SportsCarTS) that is automatically thread-safe in nature, even though you have not hard-coded thread synchronization logic within the member implementations. To do so, derive from ContextBoundObject and apply the [Synchronization] attribute as follows:

```
using System.Runtime.Remoting.Contexts;

// This context-bound type will only be loaded into a
// synchronized (hence thread-safe) context.
[Synchronization]
public class SportsCarTS : ContextBoundObject
{}
```

Types that are attributed with the [Synchronization] attribute are loaded into a thread-safe context. Given the special contextual needs of the MyThreadSafeObject class type, imagine the problems that would occur if an allocated object were moved from a synchronized context into a nonsynchronized context. The object is suddenly no longer thread-safe and thus becomes a candidate for massive data corruption, as numerous threads are attempting to interact with the (now thread-volatile) reference object. To ensure the CLR does not move SportsCarTS objects outside of a synchronized context, simply derive from ContextBoundObject.

Inspecting an Object's Context

Although very few of the applications you will write will need to programmatically interact with context, here is an illustrative example. Create a new console application named ContextManipulator. This application defines one context-agile class (SportsCar) and a single context-bound type (SportsCarTS):

```
using System.Runtime.Remoting.Contexts;   // For Context type.
using System.Threading;   // For Thread type.

// SportsCar has no special contextual
// needs and will be loaded into the
// default context of the app domain.
public class SportsCar
{
    public SportsCar()
    {
        // Get context information and print out context ID.
        Context ctx = Thread.CurrentContext;
        Console.WriteLine("{0} object in context {1}",
            this.ToString(), ctx.ContextID);
        foreach(IContextProperty itfCtxProp in ctx.ContextProperties)
            Console.WriteLine("-> Ctx Prop: {0}", itfCtxProp.Name);
    }
}

// SportsCarTS demands to be loaded in
// a synchronization context.
[Synchronization]
public class SportsCarTS : ContextBoundObject
{
    public SportsCarTS()
    {
```

```
        // Get context information and print out context ID.
        Context ctx = Thread.CurrentContext;
        Console.WriteLine("{0} object in context {1}",
            this.ToString(), ctx.ContextID);
        foreach(IContextProperty itfCtxProp in ctx.ContextProperties)
            Console.WriteLine("-> Ctx Prop: {0}", itfCtxProp.Name);
    }
}
```

Notice that each constructor obtains a Context type from the current thread of execution, via the static Thread.CurrentContext property. Using the Context object, you are able to print out statistics about the contextual boundary, such as its assigned ID, as well as a set of descriptors obtained via Context.ContextProperties. This property returns an object implementing the IContextProperty interface, which exposes each descriptor through the Name property. Now, update Main() to allocate an instance of each class type:

```
static void Main(string[] args)
{
    Console.WriteLine("***** The Amazing Context Application *****\n");

    // Objects will display contextual info upon creation.
    SportsCar sport = new SportsCar();
    Console.WriteLine();

    SportsCar sport2 = new SportsCar();
    Console.WriteLine();

    SportsCarTS synchroSport = new SportsCarTS();
    Console.ReadLine();
}
```

As the objects come to life, the class constructors will dump out various bits of context-centric information (see Figure 13-10).

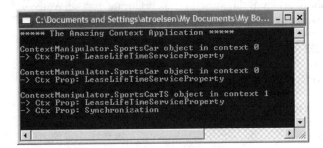

Figure 13-10. *Investigating an object's context*

Given that the SportsCar class has not been qualified with a context attribute, the CLR has allocated sport and sport2 into context 0 (i.e., the default context). However, the SportsCarTS object is loaded into a unique contextual boundary (which has been assigned a context ID of 1), given the fact that this context-bound type was adorned with the [Synchronization] attribute.

■**Source Code** The ContextManipulator project is included under the Chapter 13 subdirectory

---

Summarizing Processes, AppDomains, and Context

At this point, you hopefully have a much better idea about how a .NET assembly is hosted by the CLR. To summarize the key points,

- A .NET process hosts one to many application domains. Each AppDomain is able to host any number of related .NET assemblies and may be independently loaded and unloaded by the CLR (or programmatically via the System.AppDomain type).

- A given AppDomain consists of one to many contexts. Using a context, the CLR is able to place a "special needs" object into a logical container, to ensure that its runtime requirements are honored.

If the previous pages have seemed to be a bit too low level for your liking, fear not. For the most part, the .NET runtime automatically deals with the details of processes, application domains, and contexts on your behalf. The good news, however, is that this information provides a solid foundation for understanding multithreaded programming under the .NET platform. Before we turn our attention to the System.Threading namespace, though, we'll examine how the CLR itself is hosted by the Win32 OS.

Hosting the Common Language Runtime

To the end user, running a .NET executable is achieved simply by double-clicking the *.exe in Windows Explorer (or activating an associated shortcut). As you recall from Chapter 1, however, the .NET Framework is not (currently) incorporated directly into the Windows OS, but sits on top of the OS itself. When you install Visual Studio 2005 (or the .NET Framework 2.0 SDK) on your development machine, the .NET runtime environment (including the necessary base class libraries) is installed as well. Also recall that Microsoft provides a freely distributable .NET runtime setup program (dotnetfx.exe) to configure end user machines to host .NET assemblies.

Given that the Windows OS does not natively understand the format of a .NET assembly, it should be clear that various steps occur in the background when an executable assembly is activated. Under the Windows XP OS, the basic steps are as follows (do recall from Chapter 11 that all .NET assemblies contain Win32 header information):

1. The Windows OS loads the executable binary file into memory.

2. The Windows OS reads the embedded WinNT header to determine if the binary file is a .NET assembly (via the IMAGE_DIRECTORY_ENTRY_COM_DESCRIPTOR flag).

3. If the image is a .NET assembly, mscoree.dll is loaded.

4. mscoree.dll then loads *one of two* implementations of the CLR (mscorwks.dll or mscorsvr.dll).

5. At this point, the CLR takes over the show, performing all .NET-centric details (finding external assemblies, performing security checks, processing CIL code, performing garbage collections, etc.).

As suggested by the previous list, `mscoree.dll` is *not* the CLR itself (as I have suggested in previous chapters). Although it is safe to regard `mscoree.dll` as the actual CLR, in reality this binary file is a shim to one of two possible CLR implementations. If the host machine makes use of a single CPU, `mscorwks.dll` is loaded. If the machine supports multiple CPUs, `mscorsvr.dll` is loaded into memory (which is a version of the CLR optimized to execute on multiple-processor machines).

Side-by-Side Execution of the CLR

To dig just a bit deeper, realize that the .NET platform supports side-by-side execution, meaning that multiple versions of the .NET platform can be installed on a single machine (1.0, 1.1, and 2.0 at the time of this writing). `mscoree.dll` itself resides in the machine's System32 subdirectory of the registered Windows installation directory. On my machine, `mscoree.dll` lives under C:\WINDOWS\ system32 (see Figure 13-11).

Figure 13-11. `mscoree.dll` *lives under the System32 directory*

Once `mscoree.dll` has been loaded, the Win32 system registry (yes, *that* system registry) is consulted to determine the latest installed version and installation path of the .NET Framework via HKEY_LOCAL_MACHINE\Software\Microsoft\.NETFramework (see Figure 13-12).

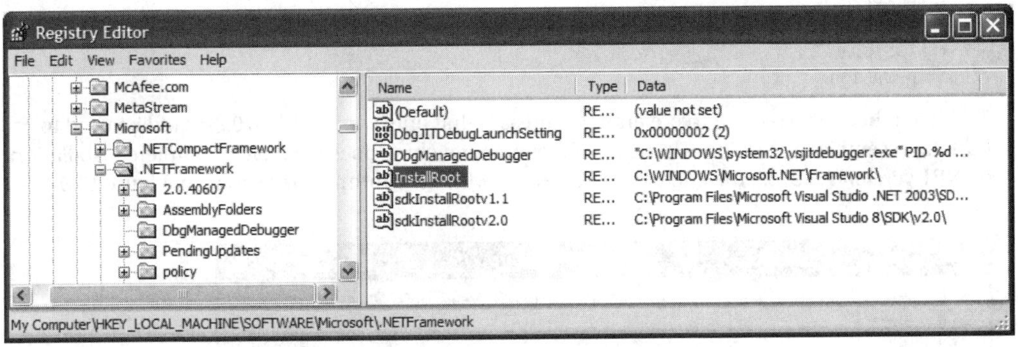

Figure 13-12. *Resolving the version and installation path of the .NET platform*

Once the version and installation path of the .NET platform have been determined, the correct version of `mscorwks.dll/mscorsvr.dll` is loaded into memory. Again, on my machine, the root installation path of the .NET platform is C:\WINDOWS\Microsoft.NET\Framework. Under this directory are specific subdirectories for .NET version 1.0, 1.1, and (at the time of this writing) the current build of 2.0 (see Figure 13-13; your version numbers may differ).

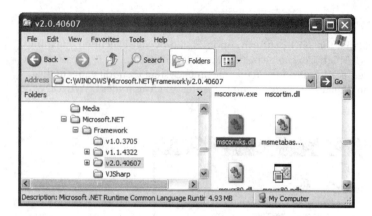

Figure 13-13. `mscorwks.dll` *version 2.0*

Loading a Specific Version of the CLR

When `mscoree.dll` determines which version of `mscorwks.dll/mscorsrv.dll` to load (by consulting the system registry), it will also read a subfolder under HKEY_LOCAL_MACHINE\Software\Microsoft\ .NET\Framework named "policy." This subfolder records the CLR upgrades that may be safely performed. For example, if you execute an assembly that was built using .NET version 1.0.3705, `mscoree.dll` learns from the policy file that it can safely load version 1.1.4322.

This promotion occurs silently in the background and only when the upgrade is known to produce compatible execution. In the rare case that you wish to instruct `mscoree.dll` to load a *specific* version of the CLR, you may do so using a client-side *.config file:

```xml
<?xml version="1.0" encoding="utf-8" ?>
<configuration>
    <startup>
        <requiredRuntime version ="1.0.3705"/>
    </startup>
</configuration>
```

Here, the `<requiredRuntime>` element expresses that only version 1.0.3705 should be used to host the assembly in question. Therefore, if the target machine does not have a complete installation of .NET version 1.0.3705, the end user is presented with the runtime error shown in Figure 13-14.

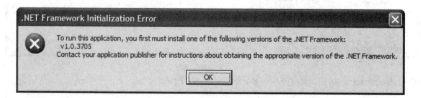

Figure 13-14. `<requiredRuntime>` *results in a runtime error if the specified version of the CLR is not installed.*

Additional CLR Hosts

The process just defined qualifies the basic steps taken by the Windows OS to host the CLR when an executable assembly is activated. However, Microsoft provides many applications that bypass this out-of-the-box behavior in favor of loading the CLR *programmatically*. For example, Microsoft Internet Explorer can natively host custom Windows Forms controls (the managed equivalent of the now legacy ActiveX controls). The latest version of Microsoft SQL Server (code-named Yukon and officially called SQL Server 2005) also has the ability to directly host the CLR internally.

As a final note, Microsoft has defined a set of interfaces that allow developers to build their own custom CLR host. This may be done using straight C/C++ code or via a COM type library (`mscoree.tlb`). While the process of building a custom CLR host is surprisingly simple (especially using the COM type library), this topic is outside the scope of this text. If you require further information, you can find numerous articles online (just do a search for "CLR hosts").

Summary

The point of this chapter was to examine exactly how a .NET executable image is hosted by the .NET platform. As you have seen, the long-standing notion of a Win32 process has been altered under the hood to accommodate the needs of the CLR. A single process (which can be programmatically manipulated via the `System.Diagnostics.Process` type) is now composed of multiple application domains, which represent isolated and independent boundaries within a process. As you have seen, a single process can host multiple application domains, each of which is capable of hosting and executing any number of related assemblies.

Furthermore, a single application domain can contain any number of contextual boundaries. Using this additional level of type isolation, the CLR can ensure that special-need objects are handled correctly. The chapter concluded by examining the details regarding how the CLR is hosted by the Win32 OS.

CHAPTER 14

■ ■ ■

Building Multithreaded Applications

In the previous chapter, you examined the relationship between processes, application domains, and contexts. This chapter builds on your newfound knowledge by examining how the .NET platform allows you to build multithreaded applications and how to keep shared resources thread-safe.

You'll begin by revisiting the .NET delegate type and come to understand its intrinsic support for asynchronous method invocations. As you'll see, this technique allows you to invoke a method on a secondary thread of execution automatically. Next, you'll investigate the types within the `System.Threading` namespace. Here you'll examine numerous types (Thread, ThreadStart, etc.) that allow you to easily create additional threads of execution. Of course, the complexity of multithreaded development isn't in the creation of threads, but in ensuring that your code base is well equipped to handle concurrent access to shared resources. Given this, the chapter closes by examining various synchronization primitives that the .NET Framework provides.

The Process/AppDomain/Context/Thread Relationship

In the previous chapter, a *thread* was defined as a path of execution within an executable application. While many .NET applications can live happy and productive single-threaded lives, an assembly's primary thread (spawned by the CLR when `Main()` executes) may create secondary threads of execution to perform additional units of work. By implementing additional threads, you can build more responsive (but not necessarily faster executing) applications.

The `System.Threading` namespace contains various types that allow you to create multithreaded applications. The `Thread` class is perhaps the core type, as it represents a given thread. If you wish to programmatically obtain a reference to the thread currently executing a given member, simply call the static `Thread.CurrentThread` property:

```
private static void ExtractExecutingThread()
{
    // Get the thread currently
    // executing this method.
    Thread currThread = Thread.CurrentThread;
}
```

Under the .NET platform, there is *not* a direct one-to-one correspondence between application domains and threads. In fact, a given AppDomain can have numerous threads executing within it at any given time. Furthermore, a particular thread is not confined to a single application domain during its lifetime. Threads are free to cross application domain boundaries as the Win32 thread scheduler and CLR see fit.

Although active threads can be moved between AppDomain boundaries, a given thread can execute within only a single application domain at any point in time (in other words, it is impossible for a single thread to be doing work in more than one AppDomain). When you wish to programmatically gain access to the AppDomain that is hosting the current thread, call the static `Thread.GetDomain()` method:

```
private static void ExtractAppDomainHostingThread()
{
    // Obtain the AppDomain hosting the current thread.
    AppDomain ad = Thread.GetDomain();
}
```

A single thread may also be moved into a particular context at any given time, and it may be relocated within a new context at the whim of the CLR. When you wish to obtain the current context a thread happens to be executing in, make use of the static `Thread.CurrentContext` property:

```
private static void ExtractCurrentThreadContext()
{
    // Obtain the Context under which the
    // current thread is operating.
    Context ctx = Thread.CurrentContext;
}
```

Again, the CLR is the entity that is in charge of moving threads into (and out of) application domains and contexts. As a .NET developer, you can usually remain blissfully unaware where a given thread ends up (or exactly when it is placed into its new boundary). Nevertheless, you should be aware of the various ways of obtaining the underlying primitives.

The Problem of Concurrency and the Role of Thread Synchronization

One of the many "joys" (read: painful aspects) of multithreaded programming is that you have little control over how the underlying operating system or the CLR makes use of its threads. For example, if you craft a block of code that creates a new thread of execution, you cannot guarantee that the thread executes immediately. Rather, such code only instructs the OS to execute the thread as soon as possible (which is typically when the thread scheduler gets around to it).

Furthermore, given that threads can be moved between application and contextual boundaries as required by the CLR, you must be mindful of which aspects of your application are *thread-volatile* (e.g., subject to multithreaded access) and which operations are *atomic* (thread-volatile operations are the dangerous ones!). To illustrate, assume a thread is invoking a method of a specific object. Now assume that this thread is instructed by the thread scheduler to suspend its activity, in order to allow another thread to access the same method of the same object.

If the original thread was not completely finished with the current operation, the second incoming thread may be viewing an object in a partially modified state. At this point, the second thread is basically reading bogus data, which is sure to give way to extremely odd (and very hard to find) bugs, which are even harder to replicate and debug.

Atomic operations, on the other hand, are always safe in a multithreaded environment. Sadly, there are very few operations in the .NET base class libraries that are guaranteed to be atomic. Even the act of assigning a value to a member variable is not atomic! Unless the .NET Framework 2.0 SDK documentation specifically says an operation is atomic, you must assume it is thread-volatile and take precautions.

At this point, it should be clear that multithreaded application domains are in themselves quite volatile, as numerous threads can operate on the shared functionality at (more or less) the same time. To protect an application's resources from possible corruption, .NET developers must make use of any number of threading primitives (such as locks, monitors, and the [Synchronization] attribute) to control access among the executing threads.

Although the .NET platform cannot make the difficulties of building robust multithreaded applications completely disappear, the process has been simplified considerably. Using types defined within the System.Threading namespace, you are able to spawn additional threads with minimal fuss and bother. Likewise, when it is time to lock down shared points of data, you will find additional types that provide the same functionality as the Win32 API threading primitives (using a much cleaner object model).

However, the System.Threading namespace is not the only way to build multithread .NET programs. During our examination of the .NET delegate (see Chapter 8), it was mentioned that all delegates have the ability to invoke members asynchronously. This is a *major* benefit of the .NET platform, given that one of the most common reasons a developer creates threads is for the purpose of invoking methods in a nonblocking (aka asynchronous) manner. Although you could make use of the System.Threading namespace to achieve a similar result, delegates make the whole process much easier.

A Brief Review of the .NET Delegate

Recall that the .NET delegate type is a type-safe object-oriented function pointer. When you declare a .NET delegate, the C# compiler responds by building a sealed class that derives from System.MulticastDelegate (which in turn derives from System.Delegate). These base classes provide every delegate with the ability to maintain a list of method addresses, all of which may be invoked at a later time. Consider the BinaryOp delegate first defined in Chapter 8:

```
// A C# delegate type.
public delegate int BinaryOp(int x, int y);
```

Based on its definition, BinaryOp can point to any method taking two integers as arguments and returning an integer. Once compiled, the defining assembly now contains a full-blown class definition that is dynamically generated based on the delegate declaration. In the case of BinaryOp, this class looks more or less like the following (shown in pseudo-code):

```
sealed class BinaryOp : System.MulticastDelegate
{
    public BinaryOp(object target, uint functionAddress);
    public void Invoke(int x, int y);
    public IAsyncResult BeginInvoke(int x, int y,
        AsyncCallback cb, object state);
    public int EndInvoke(IAsyncResult result);
}
```

Recall that the generated Invoke() method is used to invoke the methods maintained by a delegate object in a synchronous manner. Therefore, the calling thread (such as the primary thread of the application) is forced to wait until the delegate invocation completes. Also recall that in C#, the Invoke() method is not directly called in code, but is triggered under the hood when applying "normal" method invocation syntax. Consider the following program, which invokes the static Add() method in a synchronous (aka blocking) manner:

```
// Need this for the Thread.Sleep() call.
using System.Threading;
using System;

namespace SyncDelegate
{
    public delegate int BinaryOp(int x, int y);
```

```
class Program
{
    static void Main(string[] args)
    {
        Console.WriteLine("***** Synch Delegate Review *****");

        // Print out the ID of the executing thread.
        Console.WriteLine("Main() invoked on thread {0}.",
            Thread.CurrentThread.GetHashCode());

        // Invoke Add() in a synchronous manner.
        BinaryOp b = new BinaryOp(Add);
        int answer = b(10, 10);

        // These lines will not execute until
        // the Add() method has completed.
        Console.WriteLine("Doing more work in Main()!");
        Console.WriteLine("10 + 10 is {0}.", answer);
        Console.ReadLine();
    }

    static int Add(int x, int y)
    {
        // Print out the ID of the executing thread.
        Console.WriteLine("Add() invoked on thread {0}.",
            Thread.CurrentThread.GetHashCode());

        // Pause to simulate a lengthy operation.
        Thread.Sleep(5000);
        return x + y;
    }
}
```

Notice first of all that this program is making use of the System.Threading namespace. Within the Add() method, you are invoking the static Thread.Sleep() method to suspend the calling thread for (more or less) five seconds to simulate a lengthy task. Given that you are invoking the Add() method in a *synchronous* manner, the Main() method will not print out the result of the operation until the Add() method has completed.

Next, note that the Main() method is obtaining access to the current thread (via Thread.CurrentThread) and printing out its hash code. Given that a hash code represents an object in a specific state, this value can be used to as a quick-and-dirty thread ID. This same logic is repeated in the static Add() method. As you might suspect, given that all the work in this application is performed exclusively by the primary thread, you find the same hash code value displayed to the console (see Figure 14-1).

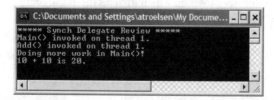

Figure 14-1. *Synchronous method invocations are "blocking" calls.*

When you run this program, you should notice that a five-second delay takes place before you see the `Console.WriteLine()` logic execute. Although many (if not most) methods may be called synchronously without ill effect, .NET delegates can be instructed to call their methods asynchronously if necessary.

■Source Code The SyncDelegate project is located under the Chapter 14 subdirectory.

The Asynchronous Nature of Delegates

If you are new to the topic of multithreading, you may wonder what exactly an *asynchronous* method invocation is all about. As you are no doubt fully aware, some programming operations take time. Although the previous `Add()` was purely illustrative in nature, imagine that you built a single-threaded application that is invoking a method on a remote object, performing a long-running database query, or writing 500 lines of text to an external file. While performing these operations, the application will appear to hang for quite some time. Until the task at hand has been processed, all other aspects of this program (such as menu activation, toolbar clicking, or console output) are unresponsive.

The question therefore is, how can you tell a delegate to invoke a method on a separate thread of execution to simulate numerous tasks performing "at the same time"? The good news is that every .NET delegate type is automatically equipped with this capability. The even better news is that you are *not* required to directly dive into the details of the System.Threading namespace to do so (although these entities can quite naturally work hand in hand).

The BeginInvoke() and EndInvoke() Methods

When the C# compiler processes the `delegate` keyword, the dynamically generated class defines two methods named `BeginInvoke()` and `EndInvoke()`. Given our definition of the `BinaryOp` delegate, these methods are prototyped as so:

```
sealed class BinaryOp : System.MulticastDelegate
{
...
    // Used to invoke a method asynchronously.
    public IAsyncResult BeginInvoke(int x, int y,
        AsyncCallback cb, object state);

    // Used to fetch the return value
    // of the invoked method.
    public int EndInvoke(IAsyncResult result);
}
```

The first stack of parameters passed into `BeginInvoke()` will be based on the format of the C# delegate (two integers in the case of `BinaryOp`). The final two arguments will always be `System.AsyncCallback` and `System.Object`. We'll examine the role of these parameters shortly; for the time being, though, we'll supply `null` for each.

The System.IAsyncResult Interface

Also note that the `BeginInvoke()` method always returns an object implementing the `IAsyncResult` interface, while `EndInvoke()` requires an `IAsyncResult`-compatible type as its sole parameter. The `IAsyncResult`-compatible object returned from `BeginInvoke()` is basically a coupling mechanism that allows the calling thread to obtain the result of the asynchronous method invocation at a later time via `EndInvoke()`. The `IAsyncResult` interface (defined in the `System` namespace) is defined as follows:

```
public interface IAsyncResult
{
    object AsyncState { get; }
    WaitHandle AsyncWaitHandle { get; }
    bool CompletedSynchronously { get; }
    bool IsCompleted { get; }
}
```

In the simplest case, you are able to avoid directly invoking these members. All you have to do is cache the IAsyncResult-compatible object returned by BeginInvoke() and pass it to EndInvoke() when you are ready to obtain the result of the method invocation. As you will see, you are able to invoke the members of an IAsyncResult-compatible object when you wish to become "more involved" with the process of fetching the method's return value.

■**Note** If you asynchronously invoke a method that does not provide a return value, you can simply "fire and for-get." In such cases, you will never need to cache the IAsyncResult-compatible object or call EndInvoke() in the first place (as there is no return value to retrieve).

Invoking a Method Asynchronously

To instruct the BinaryOp delegate to invoke Add() asynchronously, you can update the previous Main() method as follows:

```
static void Main(string[] args)
{
    Console.WriteLine("***** Async Delegate Invocation *****");

    // Print out the ID of the executing thread.
    Console.WriteLine("Main() invoked on thread {0}.",
        Thread.CurrentThread.GetHashCode());

    // Invoke Add() on a secondary thread.
    BinaryOp b = new BinaryOp(Add);
    IAsyncResult iftAR = b.BeginInvoke(10, 10, null, null);

    // Do other work on primary thread...
    Console.WriteLine("Doing more work in Main()!");

    // Obtain the result of the Add()
    // method when ready.
    int answer = b.EndInvoke(iftAR);
    Console.WriteLine("10 + 10 is {0}.", answer);
    Console.ReadLine();
}
```

If you run this application, you will find that two unique hash codes are displayed, given that there are in fact two threads working within the current AppDomain (see Figure 14-2).

In addition to the unique hash code values, you will also notice upon running the application that the Doing more work in Main()! message displays immediately, while the secondary thread is occupied attending to its business.

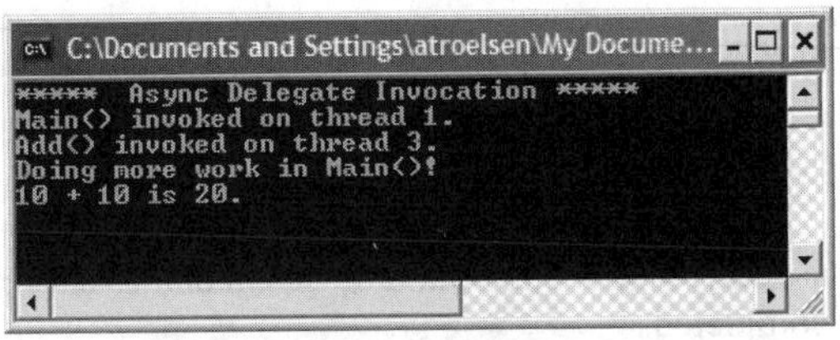

Figure 14-2. *Methods invoked asynchronously are done so on a unique thread.*

Synchronizing the Calling Thread

If you ponder the current implementation of Main(), you might have realized that the time span between calling BeginInvoke() and EndInvoke() is clearly less than five seconds. Therefore, once Doing more work in Main()! prints to the console, the calling thread is now blocked and waiting for the secondary thread to complete before being able to obtain the result of the Add() method. Therefore, you are effectively making yet another *synchronous call*:

```
static void Main(string[] args)
{
...
    BinaryOp b = new BinaryOp(Add);
    IAsyncResult iftAR = b.BeginInvoke(10, 10, null, null);

    // This call takes far less than 5 seconds!
    Console.WriteLine("Doing more work in Main()!");

    // The calling thread is now blocked until
    // EndInvoke() completes.
    int answer = b.EndInvoke(iftAR);
...
}
```

Obviously, asynchronous delegates would lose their appeal if the calling thread had the potential of being blocked under various circumstances. To allow the calling thread to discover if the asynchronously invoked method has completed its work, the IAsyncResult interface provides the IsCompleted property. Using this member, the calling thread is able to determine if the asynchronous call has indeed completed before calling EndInvoke(). If the method has not completed, IsCompleted returns false, and the calling thread is free to carry on its work. If IsCompleted returns true, the calling thread is able to obtain the result in the "least blocking manner" possible. Ponder the following update to the Main() method:

```
static void Main(string[] args)
{
...
    BinaryOp b = new BinaryOp(Add);
    IAsyncResult iftAR = b.BeginInvoke(10, 10, null, null);

    // This message will keep printing until
    // the Add() method is finished.
    while(!iftAR.IsCompleted)
    {
        Console.WriteLine("Doing more work in Main()!");
    }
```

```
    // Now we know the Add() method is complete.
    int answer = b.EndInvoke(iftAR);
...
}
```

Here, you enter a loop that will continue processing the Console.WriteLine() statement until the secondary thread has completed. Once this has occurred, you can obtain the result of the Add() method knowing full well the method has indeed completed.

In addition to the IsCompleted property, the IAsyncResult interface provides the AsyncWaitHandle property for more flexible waiting logic. This property returns an instance of the WaitHandle type, which exposes a method named WaitOne(). The benefit of WaitHandle.WaitOne() is that you can specify the maximum wait time. If the specified amount of time is exceeded, WaitOne() returns false. Ponder the following updated while loop:

```
while (!iftAR.AsyncWaitHandle.WaitOne(2000, true))
{
    Console.WriteLine("Doing more work in Main()!");
}
```

While these properties of IAsyncResult do provide a way to synchronize the calling thread, they are not the most efficient approach. In many ways, the IsCompleted property is much like a really annoying manager (or classmate) who is constantly asking, "Are you done yet?" Thankfully, delegates provide a number of additional (and more effective) techniques to obtain the result of a method that has been called asynchronously.

■Source Code The AsyncDelegate project is located under the Chapter 14 subdirectory.

The Role of the AsyncCallback Delegate

Rather than polling a delegate to determine if an asynchronously invoked method has completed, it would be ideal to have the delegate inform the calling thread when the task is finished. When you wish to enable this behavior, you will need to supply an instance of the System.AsyncCallback delegate as a parameter to BeginInvoke(), which up until this point has been null. However, when you do supply an AsyncCallback object, the delegate will call the specified method automatically when the asynchronous call has completed.

Like any delegate, AsyncCallback can only invoke methods that match a specific pattern, which in this case is a method taking IAsyncResult as the sole parameter and returning nothing:

```
void MyAsyncCallbackMethod(IAsyncResult itfAR)
```

Assume you have another application making use of the BinaryOp delegate. This time, however, you will not poll the delegate to determine if the Add() method has completed. Rather, you will define a static method named AddComplete() to receive the notification that the asynchronous invocation is finished:

```
namespace AsyncCallbackDelegate
{
    public delegate int BinaryOp(int x, int y);

    class Program
    {
        static void Main(string[] args)
        {
            Console.WriteLine("***** AsyncCallbackDelegate Example *****");
```

```
            Console.WriteLine("Main() invoked on thread {0}.",
                Thread.CurrentThread.GetHashCode());

            BinaryOp b = new BinaryOp(Add);
            IAsyncResult iftAR = b.BeginInvoke(10, 10,
                new AsyncCallback(AddComplete), null);

            // Other work performed here...

            Console.ReadLine();
        }

        static void AddComplete(IAsyncResult itfAR)
        {
            Console.WriteLine("AddComplete() invoked on thread {0}.",
                Thread.CurrentThread.GetHashCode());
            Console.WriteLine("Your addition is complete");
        }

        static int Add(int x, int y)
        {
            Console.WriteLine("Add() invoked on thread {0}.",
                Thread.CurrentThread.GetHashCode());
            Thread.Sleep(5000);
            return x + y;
        }
    }
}
```

Again, the static AddComplete() method will be invoked by the AsyncCallback delegate when the Add() method has completed. If you run this program, you can confirm that the secondary thread is the thread invoking the AddComplete() callback (see Figure 14-3).

Figure 14-3. *The* AsyncCallback *delegate in action*

The Role of the AsyncResult Class

You may have noticed in the current example that the Main() method is not caching the IAsyncResult type returned from BeginInvoke() and is no longer calling EndInvoke(). The reason is that the target of the AsyncCallback delegate (AddComplete() in this example) does not have access to the original BinaryOp delegate created in the scope of Main(). While you could simply declare the BinaryOp variable as a static class member to allow both methods to access the same object, a more elegant solution is to use the incoming IAsyncResult parameter.

The incoming IAsyncResult parameter passed into the target of the AsyncCallback delegate is actually an instance of the AsyncResult class (note the lack of an I prefix) defined in the System. Runtime.Remoting.Messaging namespace. The static AsyncDelegate property returns a reference to

the original asynchronous delegate that was created elsewhere. Therefore, if you wish to obtain
a reference to the BinaryOp delegate object allocated within Main(), simply cast the System.Object
returned by the AsyncDelegate property into type BinaryOp. At this point, you can trigger EndInvoke()
as expected:

```
// Don't forget to add a 'using' directive for
// System.Runtime.Remoting.Messaging!
static void AddComplete(IAsyncResult itfAR)
{
    Console.WriteLine("AddComplete() invoked on thread {0}.",
        Thread.CurrentThread.GetHashCode());
    Console.WriteLine("Your addition is complete");

    // Now get the result.
    AsyncResult ar = (AsyncResult)itfAR;
    BinaryOp b = (BinaryOp)ar.AsyncDelegate;
    Console.WriteLine("10 + 10 is {0}.", b.EndInvoke(itfAR));
}
```

Passing and Receiving Custom State Data

The final aspect of asynchronous delegates we need to address is the final argument to the BeginInvoke()
method (which has been null up to this point). This parameter allows you to pass additional state
information to the callback method from the primary thread. Because this argument is prototyped
as a System.Object, you can pass in any type of data whatsoever, as long as the callback method
knows what to expect. Assume for the sake of demonstration that the primary thread wishes to pass
in a custom text message to the AddComplete() method:

```
static void Main(string[] args)
{
...
    IAsyncResult iftAR = b.BeginInvoke(10, 10,
        new AsyncCallback(AddComplete),
        "Main() thanks you for adding these numbers.");
...
}
```

To obtain this data within the scope of AddComplete(), make use of the AsyncState property of
the incoming IAsyncResult parameter:

```
static void AddComplete(IAsyncResult itfAR)
{
...
    // Retrieve the informational object and cast it to string
    string msg = (string)itfAR.AsyncState;
    Console.WriteLine(msg);
}
```

Figure 14-4 shows the output of the current application.

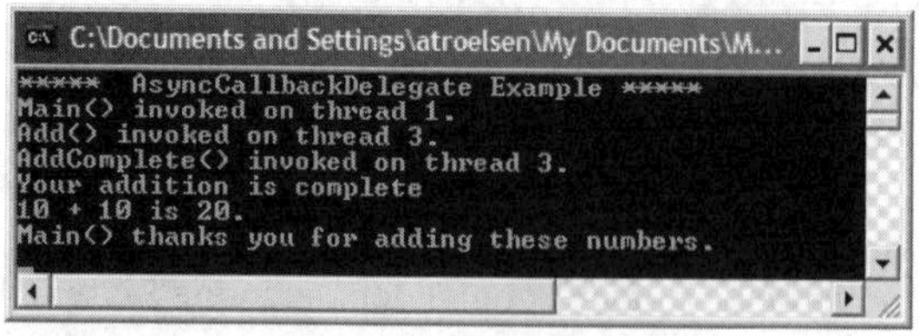

Figure 14-4. *Passing and receiving custom state data*

Cool! Now that you understand how a .NET delegate can be used to automatically spin off a secondary thread of execution to handle an asynchronous method invocation, let's turn our attention to directly interacting with threads using the System.Threading namespace.

■Source Code The AsyncCallbackDelegate project is located under the Chapter 14 subdirectory.

The System.Threading Namespace

Under the .NET platform, the System.Threading namespace provides a number of types that enable the construction of multithreaded applications. In addition to providing types that allow you to interact with a particular CLR thread, this namespace defines types that allow access to the CLR maintained thread pool, a simple (non–GUI-based) Timer class, and numerous types used to provide synchronized access to shared resources. Table 14-1 lists some of the core members of this namespace. (Be sure to consult the .NET Framework 2.0 SDK documentation for full details.)

Table 14-1. *Select Types of the* System.Threading *Namespace*

Type	Meaning in Life
Interlocked	This type provides atomic operations for types that are shared by multiple threads.
Monitor	This type provides the synchronization of threading objects using locks and wait/signals. The C# lock keyword makes use of a Monitor type under the hood.
Mutex	This synchronization primitive can be used for synchronization between application domain boundaries.
ParameterizedThreadStart	This delegate (which is new to .NET 2.0) allows a thread to call methods that take any number of arguments.
Semaphore	This type allows you to limit the number of threads that can access a resource, or a particular type of resource, concurrently.
Thread	This type represents a thread that executes within the CLR. Using this type, you are able to spawn additional threads in the originating AppDomain.
ThreadPool	This type allows you to interact with the CLR-maintained thread pool within a given process.
ThreadPriority	This enum represents a thread's priority level (Highest, Normal, etc.).
ThreadStart	This delegate is used to specify the method to call for a given thread. Unlike the ParameterizedThreadStart delegate, targets of ThreadStart must match a fixed prototype.
ThreadState	This enum specifies the valid states a thread may take (Running, Aborted, etc.).
Timer	This type provides a mechanism for executing a method at specified intervals.
TimerCallback	This delegate type is used in conjunction with Timer types.

The System.Threading.Thread Class

The most primitive of all types in the System.Threading namespace is Thread. This class represents an object-oriented wrapper around a given path of execution within a particular AppDomain. This type also defines a number of methods (both static and shared) that allow you to create new threads within the current AppDomain, as well as to suspend, stop, and destroy a particular thread. Consider the list of core static members in Table 14-2.

Table 14-2. *Key Static Members of the* Thread *Type*

Static Member	Meaning in Life
CurrentContext	This read-only property returns the context in which the thread is currently running.
CurrentThread	This read-only property returns a reference to the currently running thread.
GetDomain() GetDomainID()	These methods return a reference to the current AppDomain or the ID of this domain in which the current thread is running.
Sleep()	This method suspends the current thread for a specified time.

The Thread class also supports several instance-level members, some of which are shown in Table 14-3.

Table 14-3. *Select Instance-Level Members of the* Thread *Type*

Instance-Level Member	Meaning in Life
IsAlive	Returns a Boolean that indicates whether this thread has been started.
IsBackground	Gets or sets a value indicating whether or not this thread is a "background thread" (more details in just a moment).
Name	Allows you to establish a friendly text name of the thread.
Priority	Gets or sets the priority of a thread, which may be assigned a value from the ThreadPriority enumeration.
ThreadState	Gets the state of this thread, which may be assigned a value from the ThreadState enumeration.
Abort()	Instructs the CLR to terminate the thread as soon as possible.
Interrupt()	Interrupts (e.g., wakes) the current thread from a suitable wait period.
Join()	Blocks the calling thread until the specified thread (the one on which Join() is called) exits.
Resume()	Resumes a thread that has been previously suspended.
Start()	Instructs the CLR to execute the thread ASAP.
Suspend()	Suspends the thread. If the thread is already suspended, a call to Suspend() has no effect.

Obtaining Statistics About the Current Thread

Recall that the entry point of an executable assembly (i.e., the Main() method) runs on the primary thread of execution. To illustrate the basic use of the Thread type, assume you have a new console application named ThreadStats. As you know, the static Thread.CurrentThread property retrieves a Thread type that represents the currently executing thread. Once you have obtained the current thread, you are able to print out various statistics:

```
// Be sure to 'use' the System.Threading namespace.
static void Main(string[] args)
{
    Console.WriteLine("***** Primary Thread stats *****\n");

    // Obtain and name the current thread.
    Thread primaryThread = Thread.CurrentThread;
    primaryThread.Name = "ThePrimaryThread";

    // Show details of hosting AppDomain/Context.
    Console.WriteLine("Name of current AppDomain: {0}",
        Thread.GetDomain().FriendlyName);
    Console.WriteLine("ID of current Context: {0}",
        Thread.CurrentContext.ContextID);

    // Print out some stats about this thread.
    Console.WriteLine("Thread Name: {0}",
        primaryThread.Name);
    Console.WriteLine("Has thread started?: {0}",
        primaryThread.IsAlive);
    Console.WriteLine("Priority Level: {0}",
        primaryThread.Priority);
    Console.WriteLine("Thread State: {0}",
        primaryThread.ThreadState);
    Console.ReadLine();
}
```

Figure 14-5 shows the output for the current application.

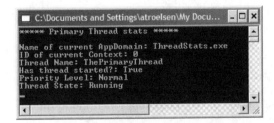

Figure 14-5. *Gathering thread statistics*

The Name Property

While this code is more or less self-explanatory, do notice that the Thread class supports a property called Name. If you do not set this value, Name will return an empty string. However, once you assign a friendly string moniker to a given Thread object, you can greatly simplify your debugging endeavors. If you are making use of Visual Studio 2005, you may access the Threads window during a debugging session (select Debug ➤ Windows ➤ Threads). As you can see from Figure 14-6, you can quickly identify the thread you wish to diagnose.

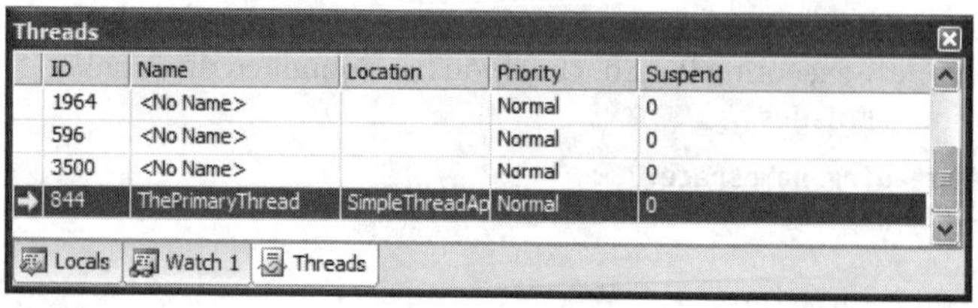

Figure 14-6. *Debugging a thread with Visual Studio 2005*

The Priority Property

Next, notice that the Thread type defines a property named Priority. By default, all threads have a priority level of Normal. However, you can change this at any point in the thread's lifetime using the ThreadPriority property and the related System.Threading.ThreadPriority enumeration:

```
public enum ThreadPriority
{
    AboveNormal,
    BelowNormal,
    Highest,
    Idle,
    Lowest,
    Normal,     // Default value.
    TimeCritical
}
```

If you were to assign a thread's priority level to a value other than the default (ThreadPriority.Normal), understand that you would have little control over when the thread scheduler switches between threads. In reality, a thread's priority level offers a hint to the CLR regarding the importance of the thread's activity. Thus, a thread with the value ThreadPriority.Highest is not necessarily guaranteed to given the highest precedence.

Again, if the thread scheduler is preoccupied with a given task (e.g., synchronizing an object, switching threads, or moving threads), the priority level will most likely be altered accordingly. However, all things being equal, the CLR will read these values and instruct the thread scheduler how to best allocate time slices. All things still being equal, threads with an identical thread priority should each receive the same amount of time to perform their work.

In most cases, you will seldom (if ever) need to directly alter a thread's priority level. In theory, it is possible to jack up the priority level on a set of threads, thereby preventing lower-priority threads from executing at their required levels (so use caution).

■**Source Code** The ThreadStats project is included under the Chapter 14 subdirectory.

Programmatically Creating Secondary Threads

When you wish to programmatically create additional threads to carry on some unit of work, you will follow a very predictable process:

1. Create a type method to be the entry point for the new thread.

2. Create a new ParameterizedThreadStart (or legacy ThreadStart) delegate, passing the address of the method defined in step 1 to the constructor.

3. Create a Thread object, passing the ParameterizedThreadStart/ThreadStart delegate as a constructor argument.

4. Establish any initial thread characteristics (name, priority, etc.).

5. Call the Thread.Start() method. This starts the thread at the method referenced by the delegate created in step 2 as soon as possible.

As stated in step 2, you may make use of two distinct delegate types to "point to" the method that the secondary thread will execute. The ThreadStart delegate has been part of the System.Threading namespace since .NET 1.0, and it can point to any method that takes no arguments and returns nothing. This delegate can be helpful when the method is designed to simply run in the background without further interaction.

The obvious limitation of ThreadStart is that you are unable to pass in parameters for processing. As of .NET 2.0, you are provided with the ParameterizedThreadStart delegate type, which allows a single parameter of type System.Object. Given that anything can be represented as a System.Object, you can pass in any number of parameters via a custom class or structure. Do note, however, that the ParameterizedThreadStart delegate can only point to methods that return void.

Working with the ThreadStart Delegate

To illustrate the process of building a multithreaded application (as well as to demonstrate the usefulness of doing so), assume you have a console application (SimpleMultiThreadApp) that allows the end user to choose whether the application will perform its duties using the single primary thread or split its workload using two separate threads of execution.

Assuming you have "used" the System.Threading namespace via the C# using keyword, your first step is to define a type method to perform the work of the (possible) secondary thread. To keep focused on the mechanics of building multithreaded programs, this method will simply print out a sequence of numbers to the console window, pausing for approximately two seconds with each pass. Here is the full definition of the Printer class:

```
public class Printer
{
    public void PrintNumbers()
    {
        // Display Thread info.
        Console.WriteLine("-> {0} is executing PrintNumbers()",
            Thread.CurrentThread.Name);

        // Print out numbers.
        Console.Write("Your numbers: ");
        for(int i = 0; i < 10; i++)
        {
            Console.Write(i + ", ");
            Thread.Sleep(2000);
        }
        Console.WriteLine();
    }
}
```

Now, within Main(), you will first prompt the user to determine if one or two threads will be used to perform the application's work. If the user requests a single thread, you will simply invoke the PrintNumbers() method within the primary thread. However, if the user specifies two threads, you will create a ThreadStart delegate that points to PrintNumbers(), pass this delegate object into the constructor of a new Thread object, and call Start() to inform the CLR this thread is ready for processing.

To begin, set a reference to the System.Windows.Forms.dll assembly and display a message within Main() using MessageBox.Show() (you'll see the point of doing so once you run the program). Here is the complete implementation of Main():

```
static void Main(string[] args)
{
    Console.WriteLine("***** The Amazing Thread App *****\n");
    Console.Write("Do you want [1] or [2] threads? ");
    string threadCount = Console.ReadLine();

    // Name the current thread.
    Thread primaryThread = Thread.CurrentThread;
    primaryThread.Name = "Primary";

    // Display Thread info.
    Console.WriteLine("-> {0} is executing Main()",
    Thread.CurrentThread.Name);

    // Make worker class.
    Printer p = new Printer();

    switch(threadCount)
    {
        case "2":
            // Now make the thread.
            Thread backgroundThread =
                new Thread(new ThreadStart(p.PrintNumbers));
            backgroundThread.Name = "Secondary";
            backgroundThread.Start();
        break;
        case "1":
            p.PrintNumbers();
        break;
        default:
            Console.WriteLine("I don't know what you want...you get 1 thread.");
            goto case "1";
    }

    // Do some additional work.
    MessageBox.Show("I'm busy!", "Work on main thread...");
    Console.ReadLine();
}
```

Now, if you run this program with a single thread, you will find that the final message box will not display the message until the entire sequence of numbers has printed to the console. As you are explicitly pausing for approximately two seconds after each number is printed, this will result in a less-than-stellar end user experience. However, if you select two threads, the message box displays instantly, given that a unique Thread object is responsible for printing out the numbers to the console (see Figure 14-7).

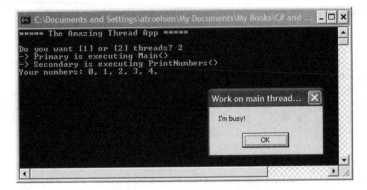

Figure 14-7. *Multithreaded applications provide results in more responsive applications.*

Before we move on, it is important to note that when you build multithreaded applications (which includes the use of asynchronous delegates) on single CPU machines, you do not end up with an application that *runs* any faster, as that is a function of a machine's CPU. When running this application using either one or two threads, the numbers are still displaying at the same pace. In reality, multithreaded applications result in *more responsive* applications. To the end user, it may appear that the program is "faster," but this is not the case. Threads have no power to make foreach loops execute quicker, to make paper print faster, or to force numbers to be added together at rocket speed. Multithreaded applications simply allow multiple threads to share the workload.

■**Source Code** The SimpleMultiThreadApp project is included under the Chapter 14 subdirectory.

Working with the ParameterizedThreadStart Delegate

Recall that the ThreadStart delegate can point only to methods that return void and take no arguments. While this may fit the bill in many cases, if you wish to pass data to the method executing on the secondary thread, you will need to make use of the ParameterizedThreadStart delegate type. To illustrate, let's re-create the logic of the AsyncCallbackDelegate project created earlier in this chapter, this time making use of the ParameterizedThreadStart delegate type.

To begin, create a new console application named AddWithThreads and "use" the System.Threading namespace. Now, given that ParameterizedThreadStart can point to any method taking a System.Object parameter, you will create a custom type containing the numbers to be added:

```
class AddParams
{
    public int a;
    public int b;

    public AddParams(int numb1, int numb2)
    {
        a = numb1;
        b = numb2;
    }
}
```

Next, create a static method in the Program class that will take an AddParams type and print out the summation of each value:

```
public static void Add(object data)
{
    if (data is AddParams)
    {
        Console.WriteLine("ID of thread in Main(): {0}",
            Thread.CurrentThread.GetHashCode());

        AddParams ap = (AddParams)data;
        Console.WriteLine("{0} + {1} is {2}",
            ap.a, ap.b, ap.a + ap.b);
    }
}
```

The code within `Main()` is straightforward. Simply use `ParameterizedThreadStart` rather than `ThreadStart`:

```
static void Main(string[] args)
{
    Console.WriteLine("***** Adding with Thread objects *****");
    Console.WriteLine("ID of thread in Main(): {0}",
        Thread.CurrentThread.GetHashCode());

    AddParams ap = new AddParams(10, 10);
    Thread t = new Thread(new ParameterizedThreadStart(Add));
    t.Start(ap);
...
}
```

■**Source Code** The AddWithThreads project is included under the Chapter 14 subdirectory.

Foreground Threads and Background Threads

Now that you have seen how to programmatically create new threads of execution using the `System.Threading` namespace, let's formalize the distinction between foreground threads and background threads:

- *Foreground threads* have the ability to prevent the current application from terminating. The CLR will not shut down an application (which is to say, unload the hosting AppDomain) until all foreground threads have ended.

- *Background threads* (sometimes called *daemon threads*) are viewed by the CLR as expendable paths of execution that can be ignored at any point in time (even if they are currently laboring over some unit of work). Thus, if all foreground threads have terminated, any and all background threads are automatically killed when the application domain unloads.

It is important to note that foreground and background threads are *not* synonymous with primary and worker threads. By default, every thread you create via the `Thread.Start()` method is automatically a *foreground* thread. Again, this means that the AppDomain will not unload until all threads of execution have completed their units of work. In most cases, this is exactly the behavior you require.

For the sake of argument, however, assume that you wish to invoke `Printer.PrintNumbers()` on a secondary thread that should behave as a background thread. Again, this means that the method pointed to by the `Thread` type (via the `ThreadStart` or `ParameterizedThreadStart` delegate) should be able to halt safely as soon as all foreground threads are done with their work. Configuring such a thread is as simple as setting the `IsBackground` property to true:

```
static void Main(string[] args)
{
    Printer p = new Printer();
    Thread bgroundThread =
        new Thread(new ThreadStart(p.PrintNumbers));
    bgroundThread.IsBackground = true;
    bgroundThread.Start();
}
```

Notice that this Main() method is *not* making a call to Console.ReadLine() to force the console to remain visible until you press the Enter key. Thus, when you run the application, it will shut down immediately because the Thread object has been configured as a background thread. Given that the Main() method triggers the creation of the primary *foreground* thread, as soon as the logic in Main() completes, the AppDomain unloads before the secondary thread is able to complete its work. However, if you comment out the line that sets the IsBackground property, you will find that each number prints to the console, as all foreground threads must finish their work before the AppDomain is unloaded from the hosting process.

For the most part, configuring a thread to run as a background type can be helpful when the worker thread in question is performing a noncritical task that is no longer needed when the main task of the program is finished.

■**Source Code** The BackgroundThread project is included under the Chapter 14 subdirectory.

The Issue of Concurrency

All the multithreaded sample applications you have written over the course of this chapter have been thread-safe, given that only a single Thread object was executing the method in question. While some of your applications may be this simplistic in nature, a good deal of your multithreaded applications may contain numerous secondary threads. Given that all threads in an AppDomain have concurrent access to the shared data of the application, imagine what might happen if multiple threads were accessing the same point of data. As the thread scheduler will force threads to suspend their work at random, what if thread A is kicked out of the way before it has fully completed its work? Thread B is now reading unstable data.

To illustrate the problem of concurrency, let's build another C# console application named MultiThreadedPrinting. This application will once again make use of the Printer class created previously, but this time the PrintNumbers() method will force the current thread to pause for a randomly generated amount of time:

```
public class Printer
{
    public void PrintNumbers()
    {
...
        for (int i = 0; i < 10; i++)
        {
            Random r = new Random();
            Thread.Sleep(1000 * r.Next(5));
            Console.Write(i + ", ");
        }
        Console.WriteLine();
    }
}
```

The Main() method is responsible for creating an array of ten (uniquely named) Thread objects, each of which is making calls on the same instance of the Printer object:

```
class Program
{
    static void Main(string[] args)
    {
        Console.WriteLine("*****Synchronizing Threads *****\n");

        Printer p = new Printer();

        // Make 10 threads that are all pointing to the same
        // method on the same object.
        Thread[] threads = new Thread[10];
        for (int i = 0; i < 10; i++)
        {
            threads[i] =
                new Thread(new ThreadStart(p.PrintNumbers));
            threads[i].Name = string.Format("Worker thread #{0}", i);
        }

        // Now start each one.
        foreach (Thread t in threads)
            t.Start();
        Console.ReadLine();
    }
}
```

Before looking at some test runs, let's recap the problem. The primary thread within this App-Domain begins life by spawning ten secondary worker threads. Each worker thread is told to make calls on the PrintNumbers() method on the same Printer instance. Given that you have taken no precautions to lock down this object's shared resources (the console), there is a good chance that the current thread will be kicked out of the way before the PrintNumbers() method is able to print out the complete results. Because you don't know exactly when (or if) this might happen, you are bound to get unpredictable results. For example, you might find the output shown in Figure 14-8.

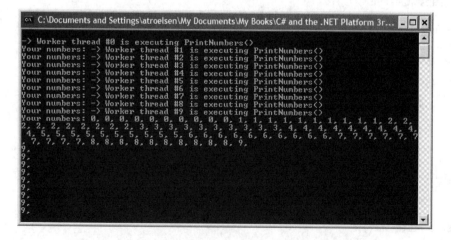

Figure 14-8. *Concurrency in action, take one*

Now run the application a few more times. Figure 14-9 shows another possibility (your results will obviously differ).

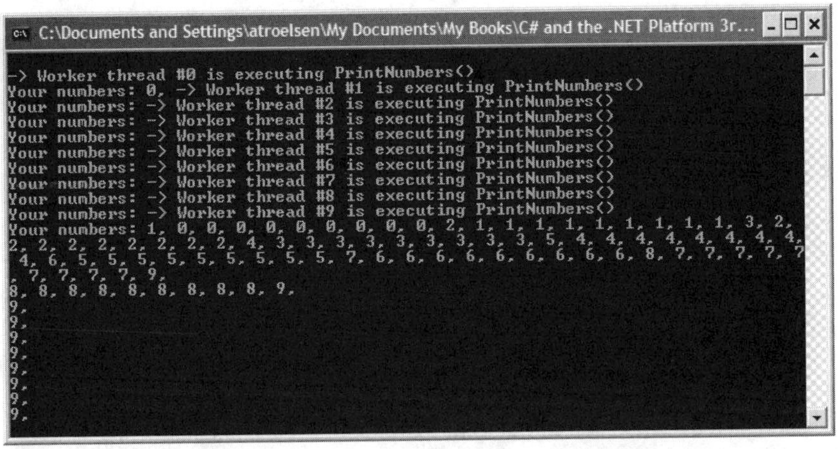

Figure 14-9. *Concurrency in action, take two*

There are clearly some problems here. As each thread is telling the Printer to print out the numerical data, the thread scheduler is happily swapping threads in the background. The result is inconsistent output. What we need is a way to programmatically enforce synchronized access to the shared resources. As you would guess, the System.Threading namespace provides a number of synchronization-centric types. The C# programming language also provides a particular keyword for the very task of synchronizing shared data in multithreaded applications.

■**Note** If you are unable to generate unpredictable outputs, increase the number of threads from 10 to 100 (for example) or introduce a call to Thread.Sleep() within your program. Eventually, you will encounter the concurrency issue.

Synchronization Using the C# lock Keyword

The first technique you can use to synchronize access to shared resources is the C# lock keyword. This keyword allows you to define a scope of statements that must be synchronized between threads. By doing so, incoming threads cannot interrupt the current thread, preventing it from finishing its work. The lock keyword requires you to specify a *token* (an object reference) that must be acquired by a thread to enter within the lock scope. When you are attempting to lock down an instance-level method, you can simply pass in a reference to the current type:

```
// Use the current object as the thread token.
lock(this)
{
    // All code within this scope is thread-safe.
}
```

If you examine the PrintNumbers() method, you can see that the shared resource the threads are competing to gain access to is the console window. Therefore, if you scope all interactions with the Console type within a lock scope as so:

```
public void PrintNumbers()
{
    lock (this)
    {
        // Display Thread info.
        Console.WriteLine("-> {0} is executing PrintNumbers()",
            Thread.CurrentThread.Name);

        // Print out numbers.
        Console.Write("Your numbers: ");
        for (int i = 0; i < 10; i++)
        {
            Random r = new Random();
            Thread.Sleep(1000 * r.Next(5));
            Console.Write(i + ", ");
        }
        Console.WriteLine();
    }
}
```

you have effectively designed a method that will allow the current thread to complete its task. Once a thread enters into a lock scope, the lock token (in this case, a reference to the current object) is inaccessible by other threads until the lock is released once the lock scope has exited. Thus, if thread A has obtained the lock token, other threads are unable to enter the scope until thread A relinquishes the lock token.

■**Note** If you are attempting to lock down code in a static method, you obviously cannot use the this keyword. If this is the case, you can simply pass in the System.Type of the respective class using the C# typeof operator.

If you now run the application, you can see that each thread has ample opportunity to finish its business (see Figure 14-10).

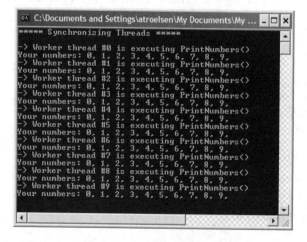

Figure 14-10. *Concurrency in action, take three*

Source Code The MultiThreadedPrinting application is included under the Chapter 14 subdirectory.

Synchronization Using the System.Threading.Monitor Type

The C# lock statement is really just a shorthand notation for working with the System.Threading.Monitor class type. Once processed by the C# compiler, a lock scope actually resolves to the following (which you can verify using ildasm.exe):

```
public void PrintNumbers()
{
    Monitor.Enter(this);
    try
    {
        // Display Thread info.
        Console.WriteLine("-> {0} is executing PrintNumbers()",
            Thread.CurrentThread.Name);

        // Print out numbers.
        Console.Write("Your numbers: ");
        for (int i = 0; i < 10; i++)
        {
            Random r = new Random();
            Thread.Sleep(1000 * r.Next(5));
            Console.Write(i + ", ");
        }
        Console.WriteLine();
    }
    finally
    {
        Monitor.Exit(this);
    }
}
```

First, notice that the Monitor.Enter() method is the ultimate recipient of the thread token you specified as the argument to the lock keyword. Next, all code within a lock scope is wrapped within a try block. The corresponding finally clause ensures that the thread token is released (via the Monitor.Exit() method), regardless of any possible runtime exception. If you were to modify the MultiThreadSharedData program to make direct use of the Monitor type (as just shown), you will find the output is identical.

Now, given that the lock keyword seems to require less code than making explicit use of the System.Threading.Monitor type, you may wonder about the benefits of using the Monitor type directly. The short answer is control. If you make use of the Monitor type, you are able to instruct the active thread to wait for some duration of time (via the Wait() method), inform waiting threads when the current thread is completed (via the Pulse() and PulseAll() methods), and so on.

As you would expect, in a great number of cases, the C# lock keyword will fit the bill. However, if you are interested in checking out additional members of the Monitor class, consult the .NET Framework 2.0 SDK documentation.

Synchronization Using the System.Threading.Interlocked Type

Although it always is hard to believe until you look at the underlying CIL code, assignments and simple arithmetic operations are *not atomic*. For this reason, the System.Threading namespace provides a type that allows you to operate on a single point of data atomically with less overhead than with the Monitor type. The Interlocked class type defines the static members shown in Table 14-4.

Table 14-4. *Members of the* System.Threading.Interlocked *Type*

Member	Meaning in Life
CompareExchange()	Safely tests two values for equality and, if equal, changes one of the values with a third
Decrement()	Safely decrements a value by 1
Exchange()	Safely swaps two values
Increment()	Safely increments a value by 1

Although it might not seem like it from the onset, the process of atomically altering a single value is quite common in a multithreaded environment. Assume you have a method named AddOne() that increments an integer member variable named intVal. Rather than writing synchronization code such as the following:

```
public void AddOne()
{
    lock(this)
    {
        intVal++;
    }
}
```

you can simplify your code via the static Interlocked.Increment() method. Simply pass in the variable to increment by reference. Do note that the Increment() method not only adjusts the value of the incoming parameter, but also returns the new value:

```
public void AddOne()
{
    int newVal = Interlocked.Increment(ref intVal);
}
```

In addition to Increment() and Decrement(), the Interlocked type allows you to atomically assign numerical and object data. For example, if you wish to assign the value of a member variable to the value 83, you can avoid the need to use an explicit lock statement (or explicit Monitor logic) and make use of the Interlocked.Exchange() method:

```
public void SafeAssignment()
{
    Interlocked.Exchange(ref myInt, 83);
}
```

Finally, if you wish to test two values for equality to change the point of comparison in a thread-safe manner, you are able to leverage the Interlocked.CompareExchange() method as follows:

```
public void CompareAndExchange()
{
    // If the value of i is currently 83, change i to 99.
    Interlocked.CompareExchange(ref i, 99, 83);
}
```

Synchronization Using the [Synchronization] Attribute

The final synchronization primitive examined here is the [Synchronization] attribute, which is a member of the System.Runtime.Remoting.Contexts namespace. In essence, this class-level attribute effectively locks down *all* instance member code of the object for thread safety. When the CLR allocates objects attributed with [Synchronization], it will place the object within a synchronized context. As you may recall from Chapter 13, objects that should not be removed from a contextual boundary should derive from ContextBoundObject. Therefore, if you wish to make the Printer class type thread-safe (without explicitly writing thread-safe code within the class members), you could update the definition as so:

```
using System.Runtime.Remoting.Contexts;
...

// All methods of Printer are now thread-safe!
[Synchronization]
public class Printer : ContextBoundObject
{
    public void PrintNumbers()
    {
        ...
    }
}
```

In some ways, this approach can be seen as the lazy way to write thread-safe code, given that you are not required to dive into the details about which aspects of the type are truly manipulating thread-sensitive data. The major downfall of this approach, however, is that even if a given method is not making use of thread-sensitive data, the CLR will *still* lock invocations to the method. Obviously, this could degrade the overall functionality of the type, so use this technique with care.

At this point, you have seen a number of ways you are able to provide synchronized access to shared blocks of data. To be sure, additional types are available under the System.Threading namespace, which I will encourage you to explore at your leisure. To wrap up our examination of thread programming, allow me to introduce three additional types: TimerCallback, Timer, and ThreadPool.

Programming with Timer Callbacks

Many applications have the need to call a specific method during regular intervals of time. For example, you may have an application that needs to display the current time on a status bar via a given helper function. As another example, you may wish to have your application call a helper function every so often to perform noncritical background tasks such as checking for new e-mail messages. For situations such as these, you can use the System.Threading.Timer type in conjunction with a related delegate named TimerCallback.

To illustrate, assume you have a console application that will print the current time every second until the user presses a key to terminate the application. The first obvious step is to write the method that will be called by the Timer type:

```
class TimePrinter
{
    static void PrintTime(object state)
    {
        Console.WriteLine("Time is: {0}",
            DateTime.Now.ToLongTimeString());
    }
}
```

Notice how this method has a single parameter of type System.Object and returns void. This is not optional, given that the TimerCallback delegate can only call methods that match this signature. The value passed into the target of your TimerCallback delegate can be any bit of information whatsoever (in the case of the e-mail example, this parameter might represent the name of the Microsoft Exchange server to interact with during the process). Also note that given that this parameter is indeed a System.Object, you are able to pass in multiple arguments using a System.Array or custom class/structure.

The next step is to configure an instance of the TimerCallback delegate and pass it into the Timer object. In addition to configuring a TimerCallback delegate, the Timer constructor allows you to specify the optional parameter information to pass into the delegate target (defined as a System.Object), the interval to poll the method, and the amount of time to wait (in milliseconds) before making the first call, for example:

```
static void Main(string[] args)
{
    Console.WriteLine("***** Working with Timer type *****\n");

    // Create the delegate for the Timer type.
    TimerCallback timeCB = new TimerCallback(PrintTime);

    // Establish timer settings.
    Timer t = new Timer(
        timeCB,     // The TimerCallback delegate type.
        "Hi",       // Any info to pass into the called method (null for no info).
        0,          // Amount of time to wait before starting.
        1000);      // Interval of time between calls (in milliseconds).

    Console.WriteLine("Hit key to terminate...");
    Console.ReadLine();
}
```

In this case, the PrintTime() method will be called roughly every second and will pass in no additional information to said method. If you did wish to send in some information for use by the delegate target, simply substitute the null value of the second constructor parameter with the appropriate information. For example, ponder the following updates:

```
static void PrintTime(object state)
{
    Console.WriteLine("Time is: {0}, Param is: {1}",
        DateTime.Now.ToLongTimeString(), state.ToString());
}
```

Figure 14-11 shows the output.

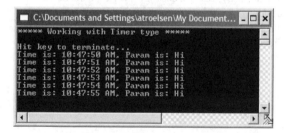

Figure 14-11. *Timers at work*

■**Source Code** The TimerApp application is included under the Chapter 14 subdirectory.

Understanding the CLR ThreadPool

The final thread-centric topic we will examine in this chapter is the CLR thread pool. When you invoke a method asynchronously using delegate types (via the `BeginInvoke()` method), the CLR does not literally create a brand-new thread. For purposes of efficiency, a delegate's `BeginInvoke()` method leverages a pool of worker threads that is maintained by the runtime. To allow you to interact with this pool of waiting threads, the `System.Threading` namespace provides the `ThreadPool` class type.

If you wish to queue a method call for processing by a worker thread in the pool, you can make use of the `ThreadPool.QueueUserWorkItem()` method. This method has been overloaded to allow you to specify an optional `System.Object` for custom state data in addition to an instance of the `WaitCallback` delegate:

```
public sealed class ThreadPool
{
    ...
    public static bool QueueUserWorkItem(WaitCallback callBack);
    public static bool QueueUserWorkItem(WaitCallback callBack,
        object state);
}
```

The `WaitCallback` delegate can point to any method that takes a `System.Object` as its sole parameter (which represents the optional state data) and returns nothing. Do note that if you do not provide a `System.Object` when calling `QueueUserWorkItem()`, the CLR automatically passes a null value. To illustrate queuing methods for use by the CLR thread pool, ponder the following program, which makes use of the `Printer` type once again. In this case, however, you are not manually creating an array of `Thread` types; rather, you are assigning members of the pool to the `PrintNumbers()` method:

```
class Program
{
    static void Main(string[] args)
    {
        Console.WriteLine("Main thread started. ThreadID = {0}",
            Thread.CurrentThread.GetHashCode());

        Printer p = new Printer();

        WaitCallback workItem = new WaitCallback(PrintTheNumbers);

        // Queue the method 10 times
        for (int i = 0; i < 10; i++)
        {
            ThreadPool.QueueUserWorkItem(workItem, p);
        }

        Console.WriteLine("All tasks queued");
        Console.ReadLine();
    }

    static void PrintTheNumbers(object state)
    {
        Printer task = (Printer)state;
        task.PrintNumbers();
    }
}
```

At this point, you may be wondering if it would be advantageous to make use of the CLR-maintained thread pool rather than explicitly creating Thread objects. Consider these major benefits of leveraging the thread pool:

- The thread pool manages threads efficiently by minimizing the number of threads that must be created, started, and stopped.

- By using the thread pool, you can focus on your business problem rather than the application's threading infrastructure.

However, using manual thread management is preferred in some cases, for example:

- If you require foreground threads or must set the thread priority. Pooled threads are *always* background threads with default priority (ThreadPriority.Normal).

- If you require a thread with a fixed identity in order to abort it, suspend it, or discover it by name.

Source Code The ThreadPoolApp application is included under the Chapter 14 subdirectory.

That wraps up our examination of multithreaded programming under .NET. To be sure, the System.Threading namespace defines numerous types beyond what I had the space to cover in this chapter. Nevertheless, at this point you should have a solid foundation to build on.

Summary

This chapter began by examining how .NET delegate types can be configured to execute a method in an asynchronous manner. As you have seen, the BeginInvoke() and EndInvoke() methods allow you to indirectly manipulate a background thread with minimum fuss and bother. During this discussion, you were also introduced to the IAsyncResult interface and AsyncResult class type. As you learned, these types provide various ways to synchronize the calling thread and obtain possible method return values.

The remainder of this chapter examined the role of the System.Threading namespace. As you learned, when an application creates additional threads of execution, the result is that the program in question is able to carry out numerous tasks at (what appears to be) the same time. You also examined several manners in which you can protect thread-sensitive blocks of code to ensure that shared resources do not become unusable units of bogus data. Last but not least, you learned that the CLR maintains an internal pool of threads for the purposes of performance and convenience.

CHAPTER 15

■■■

Understanding CIL and the Role of Dynamic Assemblies

The goal of this chapter is twofold. In the first half (more or less), you will have a chance to examine the syntax and semantics of the common intermediate language (CIL) in much greater detail than in previous chapters. Now, to be perfectly honest, you are able to live a happy and productive life as a .NET programmer without concerning yourself with the details of CIL code. However, once you learn the basics of CIL, you will gain a much deeper understanding of how some of the "magical" aspects of .NET (such as cross-language inheritance) actually work.

In the remainder of this chapter, you will examine the role of the `System.Reflection.Emit` namespace. Using these types, you are able to build software that is capable of generating .NET assemblies in memory at runtime. Formally speaking, assemblies defined and executed in memory are termed *dynamic assemblies*. As you might guess, this particular aspect of .NET development requires you to speak the language of CIL, given that you will be required to specify the CIL instruction set that will be used during the assembly's construction.

Reflecting on the Nature of CIL Programming

CIL is the true mother tongue of the .NET platform. When you build a .NET assembly using your managed language of choice, the associated compiler translates your source code into terms of CIL. Like any programming language, CIL provides numerous structural and implementation tokens. Given that CIL is just another .NET programming language, it should come as no surprise that it is possible to build your .NET assemblies directly using CIL and the CIL compiler (`ilasm.exe`) that ships with the .NET Framework 2.0 SDK.

Now while it is true that few programmers would choose to build an entire .NET application directly with CIL, CIL is still an extremely interesting intellectual pursuit. Simply put, the more you understand the grammar of CIL, the better able you are to move into the realm of advanced .NET development. By way of some concrete examples, individuals who possess an understanding of CIL are capable of the following:

- Talking intelligently about how different .NET programming languages map their respective keywords to CIL tokens.

- Disassembling an existing .NET assembly, editing the CIL code, and recompiling the updated code base into a modified .NET binary.

- Building dynamic assemblies using the `System.Reflection.Emit` namespace.

- Leveraging aspects of the CTS that are not supported by higher-level managed languages, but do exist at the level of CIL. To be sure, CIL is the only .NET language that allows you to access each and every aspect of the CTS. For example, using raw CIL, you are able to define global-level members and fields (which are not permissible in C#).

Again, to be perfectly clear, if you choose *not* to concern yourself with the details of CIL code, you are absolutely able to gain mastery of the .NET base class libraries. In many ways, knowledge of CIL is analogous to a C(++) programmer's understanding of assembly language. Those who know the ins and outs of the low-level "goo" are able to create rather advanced solutions for the task at hand and gain a deeper understanding of the underlying programming (and runtime) environment. So, if you are up for the challenge, let's begin to examine the details of CIL.

■**Note** Understand that this chapter is not intended to be a comprehensive treatment of the syntax and semantics of CIL. If you require a full examination of CIL, check out *CIL Programming: Under the Hood of .NET* by Jason Bock (Apress, 2002).

Examining CIL Directives, Attributes, and Opcodes

When you begin to investigate low-level languages such as CIL, you are guaranteed to find new (and often intimidating-sounding) names for very familiar concepts. For example, at this point in the text, if you were shown the following set of items:

```
{new, public, this, base, get, set, explicit, unsafe, enum, operator, partial}
```

you would most certainly understand them to be keywords of the C# language (which is correct). However, if you look more closely at the members of this set, you may be able to see that while each item is indeed a C# keyword, it has radically different semantics. For example, the enum keyword defines a System.Enum-derived type, while the this and base keywords allow you to reference the current object or the object's parent class, respectively. The unsafe keyword is used to establish a block of code that cannot be directly monitored by the CLR, while the operator keyword allows you to build a hidden (specially named) method that will be called when you apply a specific C# operator (such as the plus sign).

In stark contrast to a higher-level language such as C#, CIL does not just simply define a generic set of keywords, per se. Rather, the token set understood by the CIL compiler is subdivided into three broad categories based on semantic connotation:

- CIL directives
- CIL attributes
- CIL operation codes (opcodes)

Each category of CIL token is expressed using a particular syntax, and the tokens are combined to build a valid .NET assembly.

The Role of CIL Directives

First up, we have a set of well-known CIL tokens that are used to describe the overall structure of a .NET assembly. These tokens are called *directives*. CIL directives are used to inform the CIL compiler how to define the namespaces(s), type(s), and member(s) that will populate the assembly.

Directives are represented syntactically using a single dot (.) prefix (e.g., .namespace, .class, .publickeytoken, .override, .method, .assembly, etc.). Thus, if your *.il file (the conventional extension for a file containing CIL code) has a single .namespace directive and three .class directives, the CIL compiler will generate an assembly that defines a single .NET namespace containing three .NET class types.

The Role of CIL Attributes

In many cases, CIL directives in and of themselves are not descriptive enough to fully express the definition of a given .NET type or type member. Given this fact, many CIL directives can be further specified with various CIL *attributes* to qualify how a directive should be processed. For example, the .class directive can be adorned with the public attribute (to establish the type visibility), the extends attribute (to explicitly specify the type's base class), and the implements attribute (to list the set of interfaces supported by the type).

The Role of CIL Opcodes

Once a .NET assembly, namespace, and type set has been defined in terms of CIL using various directives and related attributes, the final remaining task is to provide the type's implementation logic. This is a job for *operation codes*, or simply *opcodes*. In the tradition of other low-level languages, CIL opcodes tend to be completely unpronounceable by us mere humans. For example, if you need to define a string variable, you don't use a friendly opcode named LoadString, but rather ldstr.

Now, to be fair, some CIL opcodes do map quite naturally to their C# counterparts (e.g., box, unbox, throw, and sizeof). As you will see, the opcodes of CIL are always used within the scope of a member's implementation, and unlike CIL directives, they are never written with a dot prefix.

The CIL Opcode/CIL Mnemonic Distinction

As just explained, opcodes such as ldstr are used to implement the members of a given type. In reality, however, tokens such as ldstr are *CIL mnemonics* for the actual *binary CIL opcodes*. To clarify the distinction, assume you have authored the following method in C#:

```
static int Add(int x, int y)
{
    return x + y;
}
```

The act of adding two numbers is expressed in terms of the CIL opcode 0X58. In a similar vein, subtracting two numbers is expressed using the opcode 0X59, and the act of allocating a new object on the managed heap is achieved using the 0X73 opcode. Given this reality, understand that the "CIL code" processed by a JIT compiler is actually nothing more than blobs of binary data.

Thankfully, for each binary opcode of CIL, there is a corresponding mnemonic. For example, the add mnemonic can be used rather than 0X58, sub rather than 0X59, and newobj rather than 0X73. Given this opcode/mnemonic distinction, realize that CIL decompilers such as ildasm.exe translate an assembly's binary opcodes into their corresponding CIL mnemonics:

```
.method public hidebysig static int32 Add(int32 x,
    int32 y) cil managed
{
...
    // The 'add' token is a friendly mnemonic
    // for the 0X58 CIL opcode.
    add
...
}
```

Unless you're building some extremely low-level .NET software (such as a custom managed compiler), you'll never need to concern yourself with the literal numeric opcodes of CIL. For all practical purposes, when .NET programmers speak about "CIL opcodes" they're referring to the set of friendly string token mnemonics (as I've done within this text) rather than the underlying binary values.

Pushing and Popping: The Stack-Based Nature of CIL

Higher-level .NET languages (such as C#) attempt to hide low-level grunge from view as much as possible. One aspect of .NET development that is particularly well hidden is the fact that CIL is a completely stack-based programming language. Recall from our examination of the System. Collections namespace (see Chapter 7) that the Stack type can be used to push a value onto a stack as well as pop the topmost value off of the stack for use. Of course, CIL developers do not literally use an object of type System.Collections.Stack to load and unload the values to be evaluated; however, the same pushing and popping mind-set still applies.

Formally speaking, the entity used to hold a set of values is termed the *virtual execution stack*. As you will see, CIL provides a number of opcodes that are used to push a value onto the stack; this process is termed *loading*. As well, CIL defines a number of additional opcodes that transfer the topmost value on the stack into memory (such as a local variable) using a process termed *storing*.

In the world of CIL, it is impossible to access a point of data directly, including locally defined variables, incoming method arguments, or field data of a type. Rather, you are required to explicitly load the item onto the stack, only to then pop it off for later use (keep this point in mind, as it will help explain why a given block of CIL code can look a bit redundant).

To understand how CIL leverages a stack-based model, consider a simple C# method, PrintMessage(), which takes no arguments and returns nothing. Within the implementation of this method, you will simply print out the value of a local string variable to the standard output stream:

```csharp
public void PrintMessage()
{
    string myMessage = "Hello.";
    Console.WriteLine(myMessage);
}
```

If you were to examine how the C# compiler translates this method in terms of CIL, you would first find that the PrintMessage() method defines a storage slot for a local variable using the .locals directive. The local string is then loaded and stored in this local variable using the ldstr (load string) and stloc.0 opcodes (which can be read as "store the current value in a local variable at index zero").

The value (again, at index 0) is then loaded into memory using the ldloc.0 ("load the local argument at index 0") opcode for use by the System.Console.WriteLine() method invocation (specified using the call opcode). Finally, the function returns via the ret opcode:

```
.method public hidebysig instance void PrintMessage() cil managed
{
    .maxstack  1
    // Define a local string variable (at index 0).
    .locals init ([0] string myMessage)
    // Load a string with the value "Hello."
    ldstr  " Hello."
    // Store string value on the stack in the local variable.
    stloc.0
    // Load the value at index 0.
    ldloc.0
    // Call method with current value.
    call  void [mscorlib]System.Console::WriteLine(string)
    ret
}
```

■**Note** As you can see, CIL supports code comments using the double-slash syntax (as well as the /*...*/ syntax, for that matter). As in C#, code comments are completely ignored by the CIL compiler.

Understanding Round-Trip Engineering

You are aware of how to use ildasm.exe to view the CIL code generated by the C# compiler. What you may not know, however, is that ildasm.exe allows you to dump the CIL contained within a loaded assembly to an external file. Once you have the CIL code at your disposal, you are free to edit and recompile the code base using the CIL compiler, ilasm.exe.

Formally speaking, this technique is termed *round-trip engineering*, and it can be useful under a number of circumstances:

- You need to modify an assembly for which you no longer have the source code.

- You are working with a less-than-perfect .NET language compiler that has emitted ineffective CIL code, and you wish to modify the code base.

- You are building COM interoperability assemblies and wish to account for some IDL attributes that have been lost during the conversion process (such as the COM [helpstring] attribute).

To illustrate the process of round-tripping, begin by creating a new C# code file (HelloProgram.cs) using a simple text editor, and define the following class type (you are free to use Visual Studio 2005 as well; however, be sure to delete the AssemblyInfo.cs file to decrease the amount of generated CIL code):

```csharp
// A simple C# console app.
using System;

class Program
{
    static void Main(string[] args)
    {
        Console.WriteLine("Hello CIL code!");
        Console.ReadLine();
    }
}
```

Save your file to a convenient location and compile your program using csc.exe:

```
csc HelloProgram.cs
```

Now, open HelloProgram.exe with ildasm.exe and, using the File ➤ Dump menu option, save the raw CIL code to a new *.il file (HelloProgram.il) in a convenient location on your hard drive (the default values of the resulting dialog box are fine as is). Now you are able to view this file using your text editor of choice. Here is the (slightly reformatted and annotated) result:

```
// Referenced Assemblies.
.assembly extern mscorlib
{
  .publickeytoken = (B7 7A 5C 56 19 34 E0 89 )
  .ver 2:0:0:0
}

// Our assembly.
.assembly HelloProgram
{
  .hash algorithm 0x00008004
  .ver 0:0:0:0
}
.module HelloProgram.exe
.imagebase 0x00400000
.file alignment 0x00000200
```

```
.stackreserve 0x00100000
.subsystem 0x0003
.corflags 0x00000001

// Definition of Program class.
.class private auto ansi beforefieldinit Program
       extends [mscorlib]System.Object
{
  .method private hidebysig static void  Main(string[] args) cil managed
  {
    // Marks this method as the entry point of the
    // executable.
    .entrypoint
    .maxstack  8
    IL_0000:  nop
    IL_0001:  ldstr    "Hello CIL code!"
    IL_0006:  call void [mscorlib]System.Console::WriteLine(string)
    IL_000b:  nop
    IL_000c:  call string [mscorlib]System.Console::ReadLine()
    IL_0011:  pop
    IL_0012:  ret
  }

  // The default constructor.
  .method public hidebysig specialname rtspecialname
          instance void  .ctor() cil managed
  {
    .maxstack  8
    IL_0000:  ldarg.0
    IL_0001:  call instance void [mscorlib]System.Object::.ctor()
    IL_0006:  ret
  }
}
```

First, notice that the *.il file opens by declaring each externally referenced assembly the current assembly is compiled against. Here, you can see a single .assembly extern token set for the always present mscorlib.dll. Of course, if your class library made use of types within other referenced assemblies, you would find additional .assembly extern directives.

Next, you find the formal definition of your HelloProgram.exe assembly, which has been assigned a default version of 0.0.0.0 (given that you did not specify a value using the [AssemblyVersion] attribute). The assembly is further described using various CIL directives (such as .module, .imagebase, and so forth).

After documenting the externally referenced assemblies and defining the current assembly, you find a definition of the Program type. Note that the .class directive has various attributes (many of which are optional) such as extends, which marks the base class of the type:

```
.class private auto ansi beforefieldinit Program
       extends [mscorlib]System.Object
{ ... }
```

The bulk of the CIL code implements the class's default constructor and the Main() method, both of which are defined (in part) with the .method directive. Once the members have been defined using the correct directives and attributes, they are implemented using various opcodes.

It is critical to understand that when interacting with .NET types (such as System.Console) in CIL, you will *always* need to use the type's fully qualified name. Furthermore, the type's fully qualified name must *always* be prefixed with the friendly name of the defining assembly (in square brackets). Consider the CIL implementation of Main():

```
.method private hidebysig static void  Main(string[] args) cil managed
{
    .entrypoint
    .maxstack  8
    IL_0000:  nop
    IL_0001:  ldstr  "Hello CIL code!"
    IL_0006:  call void [mscorlib]System.Console::WriteLine(string)
    IL_000b:  nop
    IL_000c:  call string [mscorlib]System.Console::ReadLine()
    IL_0011:  pop
    IL_0012:  ret
}
```

The implementation of the default constructor in terms of CIL code makes use of yet another "load-centric" instruction (ldarg.0). In this case, the value is loaded onto the stack is not a custom variable specified by us, but the current object reference (more details on this later). Also note that the default constructor explicitly makes a call to the base class constructor:

```
.method public hidebysig specialname rtspecialname
    instance void  .ctor() cil managed
{
    .maxstack  8
    IL_0000:  ldarg.0
    IL_0001:  call instance void [mscorlib]System.Object::.ctor()
    IL_0006:  ret
}
```

The Role of CIL Code Labels

One thing you certainly have noticed is that each line of implementation code is prefixed with a token of the form IL_XXX: (e.g., IL_0000:, IL_0001:, and so on). These tokens are called *code labels* and may be named in any manner you choose (provided they are not duplicated within the same scope). When you dump an assembly to file using ildasm.exe, it will automatically generate code labels that follow an IL_XXX: naming convention. However, you may change them to reflect a more descriptive marker:

```
.method private hidebysig static void  Main(string[] args) cil managed
{
    .entrypoint
    .maxstack  8
    Nothing_1:  nop
    Load_String:  ldstr  "Hello CIL code!"
    PrintToConsole: call void [mscorlib]System.Console::WriteLine(string)
    Nothing_2:  nop
    WaitFor_KeyPress: call string [mscorlib]System.Console::ReadLine()
    RemoveValueFromStack:  pop
    Leave_Function:  ret
}
```

The truth of the matter is that most code labels are completely optional. The only time code labels are truly useful (and mandatory) is when you are authoring CIL code that makes use of various branching or looping constructs. Given this, you can remove these autogenerated labels altogether with no ill effect:

```
.method private hidebysig static void  Main(string[] args) cil managed
{
    .entrypoint
    .maxstack  8
```

```
    nop
    ldstr  "Hello CIL code!"
    call void [mscorlib]System.Console::WriteLine(string)
    nop
    call string [mscorlib]System.Console::ReadLine()
    pop
    ret
}
```

Interacting with CIL: Modifying an *.il File

Now that you have a better understanding of how a basic CIL file is composed, let's complete our round-tripping experiment. The goal here is to update the CIL within the existing *.il file as so:

- Add a reference to the System.Windows.Forms.dll assembly.

- Load a local string within Main().

- Call the System.Windows.Forms.MessageBox.Show() method using the local string variable as an argument.

The first step is to add a new .assembly directive (qualified with the extern attribute) that specifies you are using System.Windows.Forms.dll. To do so, simply update the *.il file with the following logic after the external reference to mscorlib:

```
.assembly extern System.Windows.Forms
{
  .publickeytoken = (B7 7A 5C 56 19 34 E0 89)
  .ver 2:0:0:0
}
```

Be aware that the value assigned to the .ver directive may differ depending on which version of the .NET platform you have installed on your development machine. Here, you see that System.Windows.Forms.dll version 2.0.0.0 is used and has the public key token of B77A5C561934E089. If you open the GAC (see Chapter 11) and locate your version of the System.Windows.Forms.dll assembly, you can simply copy the correct version and public key token value via the assembly's Properties page.

Next, you need to alter the current implementation of the Main() method. Locate this method within the *.il file and remove the current implementation code (the .maxstack and .entrypoint directives should remain intact; I'll describe them later):

```
.method private hidebysig static void  Main(string[] args) cil managed
{
    .entrypoint
    .maxstack  8
    // ToDo: Write new CIL code!
}
```

Again, the goal is to push a new string onto the stack and call the MessageBox.Show() method (rather than the Console.WriteLine() method). Recall that when you specify the name of an external type, you must make use of the type's fully qualified name (in conjunction with the friendly name of the assembly). Keeping this in mind, update the Main() method as follows:

```
.method private hidebysig static void  Main(string[] args) cil managed
{
    .entrypoint
    .maxstack  8
    ldstr   "CIL is way cool"
    call    valuetype [System.Windows.Forms]
            System.Windows.Forms.DialogResult
            [System.Windows.Forms]
            System.Windows.Forms.MessageBox::Show(string)
    pop
    ret
}
```

In effect, you have just updated the CIL code to correspond to the following C# class definition:

```
public class Program
{
    static void Main(string[] args)
    {
        System.Windows.Forms.MessageBox.Show("CIL is way cool");
    }
}
```

Compiling CIL Code Using ilasm.exe

Assuming you have saved this modified *.il file, you can compile a new .NET assembly using the ilasm.exe (CIL compiler) utility. Perhaps surprisingly, the CIL compiler has far fewer command-line flags than the C# compiler. Table 15-1 shows the core flags of interest.

Table 15-1. *Common* ilasm.exe *Command-Line Flags*

Flag	Meaning in Life
/debug	Includes debug information (such as local variable and argument names, as well as line numbers).
/dll	Produces a *.dll file as output.
/exe	Produces an *.exe file as output. This is the default setting and may be omitted.
/key	Compiles the assembly with a strong name using a given *.snk file.
/noautoinherit	Prevents class types from automatically inheriting from System.Object when a specific base class is not defined.
/output	Specifies the output file name and extension. If you do not make use of the /output flag, the resulting file name is the same as the name of the first source file.

To compile your updated simplehelloclass.il file into a .NET *.exe, you can issue the following command within a Visual Studio 2005 command prompt:

```
ilasm /exe HelloProgram.il
```

Assuming things have worked successfully, you will see the report shown in Figure 15-1.

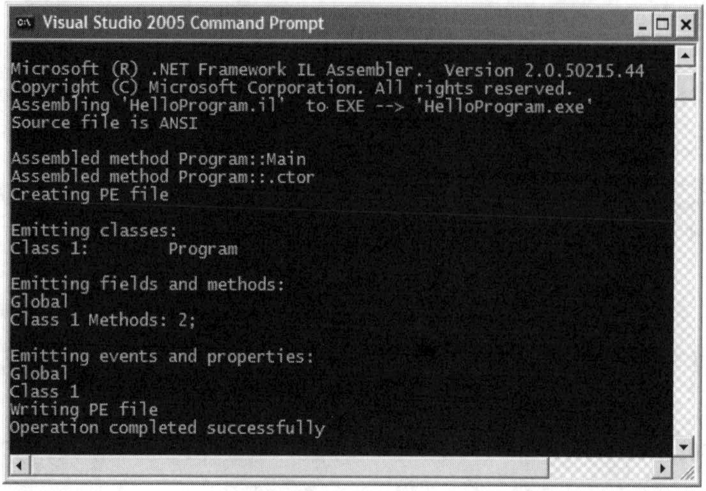

```
Visual Studio 2005 Command Prompt                              _ □ ×

Microsoft (R) .NET Framework IL Assembler.  Version 2.0.50215.44
Copyright (C) Microsoft Corporation. All rights reserved.
Assembling 'HelloProgram.il'  to EXE --> 'HelloProgram.exe'
Source file is ANSI

Assembled method Program::Main
Assembled method Program::.ctor
Creating PE file

Emitting classes:
Class 1:        Program

Emitting fields and methods:
Global
Class 1 Methods: 2;

Emitting events and properties:
Global
Class 1
Writing PE file
Operation completed successfully
```

Figure 15-1. *Compiling* *.il *files using* ilasm.exe

At this point, you can run your new application. Sure enough, rather than pumping a message to the Console window, you will now see a message box displaying your message (see Figure 15-2).

Figure 15-2. *The result of the round-trip*

Compiling CIL Code Using SharpDevelop

When working with *.il files, you may wish to make use of the freely available SharpDevelop IDE (see Chapter 2). When you create a new combine (via the File ➤ New Combine menu option), one of your choices is to create a CIL project workspace. While SharpDevelop does not have IntelliSense support for CIL projects, CIL tokens are color-coded, and you are able to compile and run your application directly within the IDE (rather than running ilasm.exe from a command prompt).

Compiling CIL Code Using ILIDE#

If you're truly interested in experimenting with the CIL programming language, I also recommend downloading the latest version of a free open source CIL editor named ILIDE#. This tool, like SharpDevelop, provides color-coding, ilasm.exe integration, and various related tools. Unlike SharpDevelop, the latest version of ILIDE# now supports CIL IntelliSense! You can download ILIDE# from http://ilide.aspfreeserver.com/default-en.aspx (of course, this URL is subject to change). Figure 15-3 shows ILIDE# in action.

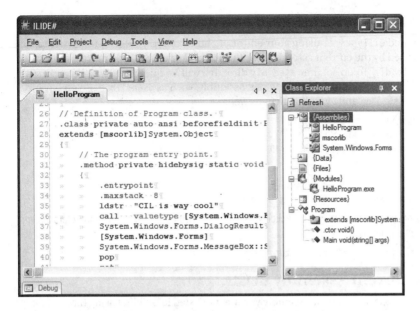

Figure 15-3. *ILIDE# is a free CIL IDE.*

The Role of peverify.exe

When you are building or modifying assemblies using CIL code, it is always advisable to verify that the compiled binary image is a well-formed .NET image using the peverify.exe command-line tool:

```
peverify HelloProgram.exe
```

This tool will examine all opcodes within the specified assembly for valid CIL code. For example, in terms of CIL code, the evaluation stack must always be empty before exiting a function. If you forget to pop off any remaining values, the ilasm.exe compiler will still generate a valid assembly (given that compilers are concerned only with *syntax*). peverify.exe, on the other hand, is concerned with *semantics*. If you did forget to clear the stack before exiting a given function, peverify.exe will let you know.

■**Source Code** The HelloProgram.il file is included under the Chapter 15 subdirectory.

Understanding CIL Directives and Attributes

Now that you have seen how ildasm.exe and ilasm.exe can be used to perform a round-trip, we can get down to the business of checking out the syntax and semantics of CIL itself. The next sections will walk you through the process of authoring a custom namespace containing a set of types. However, to keep things simple, these types will not contain any implementation logic for their members. Once you understand how to create empty types, you can then turn your attention to the process of providing "real" members using CIL opcodes.

Specifying Externally Referenced Assemblies in CIL

Create a new file named CilTypes.il using your editor of choice. First, you need to list the set of external assemblies used by the current assembly. For this example, you will only make use of types found within mscorlib.dll. To do so, the .assembly directive will be qualified using the external attribute. When you are referencing a strongly named assembly, such as mscorlib.dll, you'll want to specify the .publickeytoken and .ver directives as well:

```
.assembly extern mscorlib
{
  .publickeytoken = (B7 7A 5C 56 19 34 E0 89 )
  .ver 2:0:0:0
}
```

■**Note** Strictly speaking, you are not required to explicitly reference mscorlib.dll as an external reference, as ilasm.exe will do so automatically.

Defining the Current Assembly in CIL

The next order of business is to define the assembly you are interested in building using the .assembly directive. At the simplest level, an assembly can be defined by specifying the friendly name of the binary:

```
// Our assembly.
.assembly CILTypes { }
```

While this indeed defines a new .NET assembly, you will typically place additional directives within the scope of the assembly declaration. For this example, update your assembly definition to include a version number of 1.0.0.0 using the .ver directive (note that each numerical identifier is separated by *colons*, not the C#-centric dot notation):

```
// Our assembly.
.assembly CILTypes
{
    .ver 1:0:0:0
}
```

Given that the CILTypes assembly is a single-file assembly, you will finish up the assembly definition using a single .module directive, which marks the official name of your .NET binary, CILTypes.dll:

```
.assembly CILTypes
{
    .ver 1:0:0:0
}
// The module of our single-file assembly.
.module CILTypes.dll
```

In addition to .assembly and .module are CIL directives that further qualify the overall structure of the .NET binary you are composing. Table 15-2 lists a few of the more common assembly-level directives.

Table 15-2. *Additional Assembly-Centric Directives*

Directive	Meaning in Life
.mresources	If your assembly makes use of internal resource (such as bitmaps or string tables), this directive is used to identify the name of the file that contains the resources to be embedded. Chapter 20 examines .NET resources in detail.
.subsystem	This CIL directive is used to establish the preferred UI that the assembly wishes to execute within. For example, a value of 2 signifies that the assembly should run within a Forms-based GUI, whereas a value of 3 denotes a console application.

Defining Namespaces in CIL

Now that you have defined the look and feel of your assembly (and the required external references), you can create a .NET namespace (MyNamespace) using the .namespace directive:

```
// Our assembly has a single namespace.
.namespace MyNamespace {}
```

Like C#, CIL namespace definitions can be nested within an outer namespace. For the sake of argument, assume you wish to create a root namespace named IntertechTraining:

```
.namespace IntertechTraining
{
    .namespace MyNamespace {}
}
```

Like C#, CIL allows you to define a nested namespace as so:

```
// Defining a nested namespace.
.namespace IntertechTraining.MyNamespace{}
```

Defining Class Types in CIL

Empty namespaces are not very interesting, so let's now check out the process of defining a class type using CIL. Not surprisingly, the .class directive is used to define a new class type. However, this simple directive can be adorned with numerous additional attributes, to further qualify the nature of the type. To illustrate, add a simple public class named MyBaseClass. As in C#, if you do not specify an explicit base class, your type will automatically be derived from System.Object:

```
.namespace MyNamespace
{
    // System.Object base class assumed.
    .class public MyBaseClass {}
}
```

When you are building a class type that derives from any class other than System.Object, you make use of the extends attribute. Whenever you need to reference a type defined within the same assembly, CIL demands that you also make use of the fully qualified name (however, if the base type is within the same assembly, you can omit the assembly's friendly name prefix). Therefore, the following attempt to extend MyBaseClass results in a compiler error:

```
// This will not compile!
.namespace MyNamespace
{
    .class public MyBaseClass {}
    .class public MyDerivedClass
        extends MyBaseClass {}
}
```

To correctly define the parent class of MyDerivedClass, you must specify the full name of MyBaseClass as so:

```
// Better!
.namespace MyNamespace
{
    .class public MyBaseClass {}
    .class public MyDerivedClass
        extends MyNamespace.MyBaseClass {}
}
```

In addition to the public and extends attributes, a CIL class definition may take numerous additional qualifiers that control the type's visibility, field layout, and so on. Table 15-3 illustrates some (but not all) of the attributes that may be used in conjunction with the .class directive.

Table 15-3. *Various Attributes Used in Conjunction with the* .class *Directive*

Attributes	Meaning in Life
public, private, nested assembly, nested famandassem, nested family, nested famorassem, nested public, nested private	CIL defines various attributes that are used to specify the visibility of a given type. As you can see, raw CIL offers numerous possibilities other than those offered by C#.
abstract sealed	These two attributes may be tacked onto a .class directive to define an abstract class or sealed class, respectively.
auto sequential explicit	These attributes are used to instruct the CLR how to lay out field data in memory. For class types, the default layout flag (auto) is appropriate.
extends implements	These attributes allow you to define the base class of a type (via extends) or implement an interface on a type (via implements).

Defining and Implementing Interfaces in CIL

As odd as it may seem, interface types are defined in CIL using the .class directive. However, when the .class directive is adorned with the interface attribute, the type is realized as a CTS interface type. Once an interface has been defined, it may be bound to a class or structure type using the CIL implements attribute:

```
.namespace MyNamespace
{
    // An interface definition.
    .class public interface IMyInterface {}
    .class public MyBaseClass {}

    // DerivedTestClass now implements IAmAnInterface.
    .class public MyDerivedClass
        extends MyNamespace.MyBaseClass
        implements MyNamespace.IMyInterface {}
}
```

As you recall from Chapter 7, interfaces can function as the base interface to other interface types in order to build interface hierarchies. However, contrary to what you might be thinking, the extends attribute cannot be used to derive interface A from interface B. The extends attribute is used only to qualify a type's base class. When you wish to extend an interface, you will make use of the implements attribute yet again:

```
// Extending interfaces in terms of CIL.
.class public interface IMyInterface {}
.class public interface IMyOtherInterface
      implements MyNamespace.IMyInterface {}
```

Defining Structures in CIL

The .class directive can be used to define a CTS structure if the type extends System.ValueType. As well, the .class directive is qualified with the sealed attribute (given that structures can never be a base structure to other value types). If you attempt to do otherwise, ilasm.exe will issue a compiler error.

```
// A structure definition is always sealed.
.class public sealed MyStruct
      extends [mscorlib]System.ValueType{}
```

Do be aware that CIL provides a shorthand notation to define a structure type. If you use the value attribute, the new type will derive the type from [mscorlib]System.ValueType and be marked as sealed automatically. Therefore, you could define MyStruct as so:

```
// Shorthand notation for declaring a structure.
.class public value MyStruct{}
```

Defining Enums in CIL

.NET enumerations (as you recall) derive from System.Enum, which is a System.ValueType (and therefore must also be sealed). When you wish to define an enum in terms of CIL, simply extend [mscorlib]System.Enum:

```
// An enum.
.class public sealed MyEnum
      extends [mscorlib]System.Enum{}
```

Like a structure definition, enumerations can be defined with a shorthand notation using the enum attribute:

```
// Enum shorthand.
.class public enum MyEnum{}
```

■**Note** The other fundamental .NET type, the delegate, also has a specific CIL representation. See Chapter 8 for full details.

Compiling the CILTypes.il file

Even though you have not yet added any members or implementation code to the types you have defined, you are able to compile this *.il file into a .NET DLL assembly (which you must do, as you have not specified a Main() method). Open up a command prompt and enter the following command to ilasm.exe:

```
ilasm /dll CilTypes.il
```

Once you have done so, you are able to open your binary into ildasm.exe (see Figure 15-4).

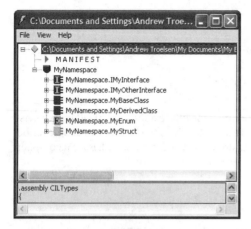

Figure 15-4. *The* CILTypes.dll *assembly*

Once you have confirmed the contents of your assembly, run peverify.exe against it. Notice that you are issued a number of errors, given that all your types are completely empty. To understand how to populate a type with content, you first need to examine the fundamental data types of CIL.

■**Source Code** The CilTypes.il file is included under the Chapter 15 subdirectory.

.NET Base Class Library, C#, and CIL Data Type Mappings

Table 15-4 illustrates how a .NET base class type maps to the corresponding C# keyword, and how each C# keyword maps into raw CIL. As well, Table 15-4 documents the shorthand constant notations used for each CIL type. As you will see in just a moment, these constants are often referenced by numerous CIL opcodes.

Table 15-4. *Mapping .NET Base Class Types to C# Keywords, and C# Keywords to CIL*

.NET Base Class Type	C# Keyword	CIL Representation	CIL Constant Notation
System.SByte	sbyte	int8	I1
System.Byte	byte	unsigned int8	U1
System.Int16	short	int16	I2
System.UInt16	ushort	unsigned int16	U2
System.Int32	int	int32	I4
System.UInt32	uint	unsigned int32	U4
System.Int64	long	int64	I8
System.UInt64	ulong	unsigned int64	U8
System.Char	char	char	CHAR
System.Single	float	float32	R4
System.Double	double	float64	R8

.NET Base Class Type	C# Keyword	CIL Representation	CIL Constant Notation
System.Boolean	bool	bool	BOOLEAN
System.String	string	string	N/A
System.Object	object	object	N/A
System.Void	void	void	VOID

Defining Type Members in CIL

As you are already aware, .NET types may support various members. Enumerations have some set of name/value pairs. Structures and classes may have constructors, fields, methods, properties, static members, and so on. Over the course of this book's first 14 chapters, you have already seen partial CIL definitions for the items previously mentioned, but nevertheless, here is a quick recap of how various members map to CIL primitives.

Defining Field Data in CIL

Enumerations, structures, and classes can all support field data. In each case, the .field directive will be used. For example, let's breathe some life into the skeleton MyEnum enumeration and define three name/value pairs (note the values are specified using a parentheses syntax):

```
.class public auto ansi sealed MyEnum
    extends [mscorlib]System.Enum
{
    .field public static literal valuetype
        MyNamespace.MyEnum NameOne = int32(0)
    .field public static literal valuetype
        MyNamespace.MyEnum NameTwo = int32(1)
    .field public static literal valuetype
        MyNamespace.MyEnum NameThree = int32(2)
}
```

Fields that reside within the scope of a .NET System.Enum-derived type are qualified using the static and literal attributes. As you would guess, these attributes set up the field data to be a fixed value accessible from the type itself (e.g., MyEnum.NameOne).

■**Note** The values assigned to an enum value may also be in hexadecimal.

Of course, when you wish to define a point of field data within a class or structure, you are not limited to a point of public static literal data. For example, you could update MyBaseClass to support two points of private, instance-level field data:

```
.class public MyBaseClass
{
    .field private string stringField
    .field private int32 intField
}
```

As in C#, class field data will automatically be assigned to the correct default value. If you wish to allow the object user to supply custom values at the time of creation for each of these points of private field data, you (of course) need to create custom constructors.

Defining Type Constructors in CIL

The CTS supports both instance-level and class-level (static) constructors. In terms of CIL, instance-level constructors are represented using the .ctor token, while a static-level constructor is expressed via .cctor (class constructor). Both of these CIL tokens must be qualified using the rtspecialname (return type special name) and specialname attributes. Simply put, these attributes are used to identify a specific CIL token that can be treated in unique ways by a given .NET language. For example, in C#, constructors do not define a return type; however, in terms of CIL, the return value of a constructor is indeed void:

```
.class public MyBaseClass
{
    .field private string stringField
    .field private int32 intField

    .method public hidebysig specialname rtspecialname
      instance void .ctor(string s, int32 i) cil managed
    {
        // TODO: Add implementation code...
    }
}
```

Note that the .ctor directive has been qualified with the instance attribute (as it is not a static constructor). The cil managed attributes denote that the scope of this method contains CIL code, rather than unmanaged code, which may be used during platform invocation requests.

Defining Properties in CIL

Properties and methods also have specific CIL representations. By way of an example, if MyBaseClass were updated to support a public property named TheString, you would author the following CIL (note again the use of the specialname attribute):

```
.class public MyBaseClass
{
...
    .method public hidebysig specialname
        instance string  get_TheString() cil managed
    {
        // TODO: Add implementation code...
    }

    .method public hidebysig specialname
        instance void  set_TheString(string 'value') cil managed
    {
        // TODO: Add implementation code...
    }

    .property instance string TheString()
    {
        .get instance string
            MyNamespace.MyBaseClass::get_TheString()
        .set instance void
            MyNamespace. MyBaseClass::set_TheString(string)
    }
}
```

Recall that in terms of CIL, a property maps to a pair of methods that take get_ and set_ prefixes. The .property directive makes use of the related .get and .set directives to map property syntax to the correct "specially named" methods.

■Note The previous property definitions will fail to compile, given that you have not yet implemented the mutator logic.

Defining Member Parameters

Now assume that you wish to define methods that take some number of arguments. In a nutshell, specifying arguments in CIL is (more or less) identical to doing so in C#. For example, each argument is defined by specifying its data type followed by the parameter name. Furthermore, like C#, CIL provides a way to define input, output, and pass-by-reference parameters. As well, CIL allows you to define a parameter array argument (aka the C# params keyword) as well as optional parameters (which are not supported in C#, but are used in VB .NET).

To illustrate the process of defining parameters in raw CIL, assume you wish to build a method that takes an int32 (by value), int32 (by reference), a [mscorlib]System.Collection.ArrayList, and a single output parameter (of type int32). In terms of C#, this method would look something like the following:

```
public static void MyMethod(int inputInt,
     ref int refInt, ArrayList ar, out int outputInt)
{
     outputInt = 0;  // Just to satisfy the C# compiler...
}
```

If you were to map this method into CIL terms, you would find that C# reference parameters are marked with an ampersand (&) suffixed to the parameter's underlying data type (int32&). Output parameters also make use of the & suffix, but they are further qualified using the CIL [out] token. Also notice that if the parameter is a reference type (in this case, the [mscorlib]System.Collections.ArrayList type), the class token is prefixed to the data type (not to be confused with the .class directive!):

```
.method public hidebysig static void  MyMethod(int32 inputInt,
     int32& refInt,
     class [mscorlib]System.Collections.ArrayList ar,
     [out] int32& outputInt) cil managed
{
...
}
```

Examining CIL Opcodes

The final aspect of CIL code you'll examine in this chapter has to do with the role of various operational codes (opcodes). Recall that an opcode is simply a CIL token used to build the implementation logic for a given member. The complete set of CIL opcodes (which is fairly large) can be grouped into the following broad categories:

- Opcodes that control program flow
- Opcodes that evaluate expressions
- Opcodes that access values in memory (via parameters, local variables, etc.)

To provide some insight to the world of member implementation via CIL, Table 15-5 defines some of the more useful opcodes that are directly related to member implementation logic, grouped by related functionality.

Table 15-5. *Various Implementation-Specific CIL Opcodes*

Opcodes	Meaning in Life
add, sub, mul, div, rem	These CIL opcodes allow you to add, subtract, multiply, and divide two values (rem returns the remainder of a division operation).
and, or, not, xor	These CIL opcodes allow you to perform binary operations on two values.
ceq, cgt, clt	These CIL opcodes allow you to compare two values on the stack in various manners, for example: ceq: Compare for equality cgt: Compare for greater than clt: Compare for less than
box, unbox	These CIL opcodes are used to convert between reference types and value types.
ret	This CIL opcode is used to exit a method and return a value to the caller (if necessary).
beq, bgt, ble, blt, switch	These CIL opcodes (in addition to many other related opcodes) are used to control branching logic within a method, for example: beq: Break to code label if equal bgt: Break to code label if greater than ble: Break to code label if less than or equal to blt: Break to code label if less than All of the branch-centric opcodes require that you specify a CIL code label to jump to if the result of the test is true.
call	This CIL opcode is used to call a member on a given type.
newarr, newobj	These CIL opcodes allow you to allocate a new array or new object type into memory (respectively).

The next broad category of CIL opcodes (a subset of which is shown in Table 15-6) are used to load (push) arguments onto the virtual execution stack. Note how these load-specific opcodes take an ld (load) prefix.

Table 15-6. *The Primary Stack-Centric Opcodes of CIL*

Opcode	Meaning in Life
ldarg (with numerous variations)	Loads a method's argument onto the stack. In addition to the generic ldarg (which works in conjunction with a given index that identifies the argument), there are numerous other variations. For example, ldarg opcodes that have a numerical suffix (ldarg_0) hard-code which argument to load. As well, variations of the ldarg opcode allow you to hard-code the data type using the CIL constant notation shown in Table 15-4 (ldarg_I4, for an int32) as well as the data type and value (ldarg_I4_5, to load an int32 with the value of 5).
ldc (with numerous variations)	Loads a constant value onto the stack.
ldfld (with numerous variations)	Loads the value of an instance-level field onto the stack.
ldloc (with numerous variations)	Loads the value of a local variable onto the stack.

Opcode	Meaning in Life
ldobj	Obtains all the values gathered by a heap-based object and places them on the stack.
ldstr	Loads a string value onto the stack.

In addition to the set of load-specific opcodes, CIL provides numerous opcodes that *explicitly* pop the topmost value off the stack. As shown over the first few examples in this chapter, popping a value off the stack typically involves storing the value into temporary local storage for further use (such as a parameter for an upcoming method invocation). Given this, note how many opcodes that pop the current value off the virtual execution stack take an st (store) prefix. Table 15-7 hits the highlights.

Table 15-7. *Various Pop-Centric Opcodes*

Opcode	Meaning in Life
pop	Removes the value currently on top of the evaluation stack, but does not bother to store the value
starg	Stores the value on top of the stack into the method argument at a specified index
stloc (with numerous variations)	Pops the current value from the top of the evaluation stack and stores it in a local variable list at a specified index
stobj	Copies a value of a specified type from the evaluation stack into a supplied memory address
stsfld	Replaces the value of a static field with a value from the evaluation stack

Do be aware that various CIL opcodes will *implicitly* pop values off the stack to perform the task at hand. For example, if you are attempting to subtract two numbers using the sub opcode, it should be clear that sub will have to pop off the next two available values before it can perform the calculation. Once the calculation is complete, the result of the value (surprise, surprise) is pushed onto the stack once again.

Considering the .maxstack Directive

When you write method implementations using raw CIL, you need to be mindful of a special directive named .maxstack. As its name suggests, .maxstack establishes the maximum number of variables that may be pushed onto the stack at any given time during the execution of the method. The good news is that the .maxstack directive has a default value (8), which should be safe for a vast majority of methods you may be authoring. However, if you wish to be very explicit, you are able to manually calculate the number of local variables on the stack and define this value explicitly:

```
.method public hidebysig instance void
    Speak() cil managed
{
    // During the scope of this method, exactly
    // 1 value (the string literal) is on the stack.
    .maxstack  1
    ldstr "Hello there..."
    call void [mscorlib]System.Console::WriteLine(string)
    ret
}
```

Declaring Local Variables in CIL

Let's first check out how to declare a local variable. Assume you wish to build a method in CIL named MyLocalVariables() that takes no arguments and returns void. Within the method, you wish to define three local variables of type System.String, System.Int32, and System.Object. In C#, this member would appear as so (recall that locally scoped variables do not receive a default value and should be set to an initial state before further use):

```
public static void MyLocalVariables()
{
    string myStr = "CIL me dude...";
    int myInt = 33;
    object myObj = new object();
}
```

If you were to construct MyLocalVariables() directly in CIL, you could author the following:

```
.method public hidebysig static void
    MyLocalVariables() cil managed
{
    .maxstack  8
    // Define three local variables.
    .locals init ([0] string myStr, [1] int32 myInt, [2] object myObj)

    // Load a string onto the virtual execution stack.
    ldstr "CIL me dude..."
    // Pop off current value and store in local variable [0].
    stloc.0

    // Load a constant of type 'i4'
    // (shorthand for int32) set to the value 33.
    ldc.i4 33
    // Pop off current value and store in local variable [1].
    stloc.1

    // Create a new object and place on stack.
    newobj     instance void [mscorlib]System.Object::.ctor()
    // Pop off current value and store in local variable [2].
    stloc.2
    ret
}
```

As you can see, the first step taken to allocate local variables in raw CIL is to make use of the .locals directive, which is paired with the init attribute. Within the scope of the related parentheses, your goal is to associate a given numerical index to each variable (seen here as [0], [1], and [2]). As you can see, each index is identified by its data type and an optional variable name. Once the local variables have been defined, you load a value onto the stack (using the various load-centric opcodes) and store the value within the local variable (using the various storage-centric opcodes).

Mapping Parameters to Local Variables in CIL

You have already seen how to declare local variables in raw CIL using the .local init directive; however, you have yet to see exactly how to map incoming parameters to local methods. Consider the following static C# method:

```
public static int Add(int a, int b)
{
    return a + b;
}
```

This innocent-looking method has a lot to say in terms of CIL. First, the incoming arguments (a and b) must be pushed onto the virtual execution stack using the ldarg (load argument) opcode. Next, the add opcode will be used to pop the next two values off the stack and find the summation, and store the value on the stack yet again. Finally, this sum is popped off the stack and returned to the caller via the ret opcode. If you were to disassemble this C# method using ildasm.exe, you would find numerous additional tokens injected by csc.exe, but the crux of the CIL code is quite simple:

```
.method public hidebysig static int32  Add(int32 a,
    int32 b) cil managed
{
  .maxstack  2
  ldarg.0    // Load 'a' onto the stack.
  ldarg.1    // Load 'b' onto the stack.
  add        // Add both values.
  ret
}
```

The Hidden this Reference

Notice that the two incoming arguments (a and b) are referenced within the CIL code using their indexed position (index 0 and index 1), given that the virtual execution stack begins indexing at position 0.

One thing to be very mindful of when you are examining or authoring raw CIL code is that every (nonstatic) method that takes incoming arguments automatically receives an implicit additional parameter, which is a reference to the current object (think the C# this keyword). Given this, if the Add() method were defined as *non*static

```
// No longer static!
public int Add(int a, int b)
{
    return a + b;
}
```

the incoming a and b arguments are loaded using ldarg.1 and ldarg.2 (rather than the expected ldarg.0 and ldarg.1 opcodes). Again, the reason is that slot 0 actually contains the implicit this reference. Consider the following pseudo-code:

```
// This is JUST pseudo-code!
.method public hidebysig static int32  AddTwoIntParams(
    MyClass_HiddenThisPointer this, int32 a, int32 b) cil managed
{
  ldarg.0    // Load MyClass_HiddenThisPointer onto the stack.
  ldarg.1    // Load 'a' onto the stack.
  ldarg.2    // Load 'b' onto the stack.
...
}
```

Representing Iteration Constructs in CIL

Iteration constructs in the C# programming language are represented using the for, foreach, while, and do keywords, each of which has a specific representation in CIL. Consider the classic for loop:

```
public static void CountToTen()
{
    for(int i = 0; i < 10; i++)
        ;
}
```

Now, as you may recall, the br opcodes (br, blt, and so on) are used to control a break in flow when some condition has been met. In this example, you have set up a condition in which the for loop should break out of its cycle when the local variable i is equal to the value of 10. With each pass, the value of 1 is added to i, at which point the test condition is yet again evaluated.

Also recall that when you make use of any of the CIL branching opcodes, you will need to define a specific code label (or two) that marks the location to jump to when the condition is indeed true. Given these points, ponder the following (augmented) CIL code generated via ildasm.exe (including the autogenerated code labels):

```
.method public hidebysig static void  CountToTen() cil managed
{
  .maxstack  2
  .locals init ([0] int32 i)  // Init the local integer 'i'.
  IL_0000:  ldc.i4.0         // Load this value onto the stack.
  IL_0001:  stloc.0          // Store this value at index '0'.
  IL_0002:  br.s IL_0008     // Jump to IL_0008.
  IL_0004:  ldloc.0          // Load value of variable at index 0.
  IL_0005:  ldc.i4.1         // Load the value '1' on the stack.
  IL_0006:  add              // Add current value on the stack at index 0.
  IL_0007:  stloc.0
  IL_0008:  ldloc.0          // Load value at index '0'.
  IL_0009:  ldc.i4.s   10    // Load value of '10' onto the stack.
  IL_000b:  blt.s IL_0004    // Less than?  If so, jump back to IL_0004
  IL_000d:  ret
}
```

In a nutshell, this CIL code begins by defining the local int32 and loading it onto the stack. At this point, you jump back and forth between code label IL_0008 and IL_0004, each time bumping the value of i by 1 and testing to see whether i is still less than the value 10. If so, you exit the method.

Building a .NET Assembly with CIL

Now that you've taken a tour of the syntax and semantics of raw CIL, it's time to solidify your current understanding by building a .NET application using nothing but CIL and your text editor of choice. Specifically, your application will consist of a privately deployed, single-file *.dll that contains two class type definitions, and a console-based *.exe that interacts with these types.

Building CILCars.dll

The first order of business is to build the *.dll to be consumed by the client. Open a text editor and create a new *.il file named CILCars.il. This single-file assembly will make use of two external .NET binaries, and you can begin creating your CIL code file as so:

```
// Reference mscorlib.dll and
// System.Windows.Forms.dll
.assembly extern mscorlib
{
  .publickeytoken = (B7 7A 5C 56 19 34 E0 89 )
  .ver 2:0:0:0
}
.assembly extern System.Windows.Forms
{
  .publickeytoken = (B7 7A 5C 56 19 34 E0 89 )
  .ver 2:0:0:0
}
```

```
// Define the single-file assembly.
.assembly CILCars
{
  .hash algorithm 0x00008004
  .ver 1:0:0:0
}
.module CILCars.dll
```

As mentioned, this assembly will contain two class types. The first type, CILCar, defines two points of field data and a custom constructor. The second type, CarInfoHelper, defines a single static method named DisplayCarInfo(), which takes CILCar as a parameter and returns void. Both types are in the CILCars namespace. In terms of CIL, CILCar can be implemented as so:

```
// Implementation of CILCars.CILCar type.
.namespace CILCars
{
  .class public auto ansi beforefieldinit CILCar
      extends [mscorlib]System.Object
  {
    // The field data of the CILCar.
    .field public string petName
    .field public int32 currSpeed

    // The custom constructor simply allows the caller
    // to assign the field data.
    .method public hidebysig specialname rtspecialname
        instance void  .ctor(int32 c, string p) cil managed
    {
      .maxstack  8

      // Load first arg onto the stack and call base class ctor.
      ldarg.0  // 'this' object, not the int32!
      call instance void [mscorlib]System.Object::.ctor()

      // Now load first and second args onto the stack.
      ldarg.0  // 'this' object
      ldarg.1  // int32 arg

      // Store topmost stack (int 32) member in currSpeed field.
      stfld int32 CILCars.CILCar::currSpeed

      // Load string arg and store in petName field.
      ldarg.0  // 'this' object
      ldarg.2  // string arg
      stfld string CILCars.CILCar::petName
      ret
    }
  }
}
```

Keeping in mind that the real first argument for any nonstatic member is the current object reference, the first block of CIL simply loads the object reference and calls the base class constructor. Next, you push the incoming constructor arguments onto the stack and store them into the type's field data using the stfld (store in field) opcode.

Next, you need to implement the second type in this namespace: CILCarInfo. The meat of the type is found within the static Display() method. In a nutshell, the role of this method is to take the incoming CILCar parameter, extract the values of its field data, and display it in a Windows Forms message box. Here is the complete implementation of CILCarInfo, with analysis to follow:

```
.class public auto ansi beforefieldinit CILCarInfo
       extends [mscorlib]System.Object
{
    .method public hidebysig static void
          Display(class CILCars.CILCar c) cil managed
    {
      .maxstack  8

      // We need a local string variable.
      .locals init ([0] string caption)

      // Load string and the incoming CILCar onto the stack.
      ldstr      "{0}'s speed is:"
      ldarg.0

      // Now place the value of the CILCar's petName on the
      // stack and call the static String.Format() method.
      ldfld       string CILCars.CILCar::petName
      call        string [mscorlib]System.String::Format(string, object)
      stloc.0

      // Now load the value of the currSpeed field and get its string
      // representation (note call to ToString() ).
      ldarg.0
      ldflda      int32 CILCars.CILCar::currSpeed
      call        instance string [mscorlib]System.Int32::ToString()
      ldloc.0

      // Now call the MessageBox.Show() method with loaded values.
      call        valuetype [System.Windows.Forms]
                    System.Windows.Forms.DialogResult
                    [System.Windows.Forms]
                    System.Windows.Forms.MessageBox::Show(string, string)
      pop
      ret
    }
}
```

Although the amount of CIL code is a bit more than you see in the implementation of CILCar, things are still rather straightforward. First, given that you are defining a static method, you don't have to be concerned with the hidden object reference (thus, the ldarg.0 opcode really does load the incoming CILCar argument).

The method begins by loading a string ("{0}'s speed is") onto the stack, followed by the CILCar argument. Once these two values are in place, you load the value of the petName field and call the static System.String.Format() method to substitute the curly bracket placeholder with the CILCar's pet name.

The same general procedure takes place when processing the currSpeed field, but note that you use the ldflda opcode, which loads the argument address onto the stack. At this point, you call System.Int32.ToString() to transform the value at said address into a string type. Finally, once both strings have been formatted as necessary, you call the MessageBox.Show() method.

At this point, you are able to compile your new *.dll using ilasm.exe with the following command:

```
ilasm /dll CILCars.il
```

and verify the contained CIL using peverify.exe:

```
peverify CILCars.dll
```

Building CILCarClient.exe

Now you can build a simple *.exe assembly that will

- Make a CILCar type.
- Pass the type into the static CILCarInfo.Display() method.

Create a new *.il file and define external references to mscorlib.dll and CILCars.dll (don't forget to place a copy of this .NET assembly in the client's application directory!). Next, define a single type (Program) that manipulates the CILCars.dll assembly. Here's the complete code:

```
// External assembly refs.
.assembly extern mscorlib
{
  .publickeytoken = (B7 7A 5C 56 19 34 E0 89 )
  .ver 2:0:0:0
}
.assembly extern CILCars
{
  .ver 1:0:0:0
}

// Our executable assembly.
.assembly CILCarClient
{
  .hash algorithm 0x00008004
  .ver 0:0:0:0
}
.module CILCarClient.exe

// Implementation of Program type
.namespace CILCarClient
{
  .class private auto ansi beforefieldinit Program
  extends [mscorlib]System.Object
  {
    .method private hidebysig static void
    Main(string[] args) cil managed
    {
      // Marks the entry point of the *.exe.
      .entrypoint
      .maxstack  8

      // Declare a local CILCar type and push
      // values on the stack for ctor call.
      .locals init ([0] class
      [CILCars]CILCars.CILCar myCilCar)
      ldc.i4 55
      ldstr "Junior"

      // Make new CilCar; store and load reference.
      newobj instance void
        [CILCars]CILCars.CILCar::.ctor(int32, string)
      stloc.0
      ldloc.0
```

```
        // Call Display() and pass in topmost value on stack.
        call void [CILCars]
            CILCars.CILCarInfo::Display(
                class [CILCars]CILCars.CILCar)
        ret
      }
    }
}
```

The one opcode that is important to point out is .entrypoint. Recall from the discussion earlier in this chapter that this opcode is used to mark which method of an *.exe functions as the entry point of the module. In fact, given that .entrypoint is how the CLR identifies the initial method to execute, this method can be called anything at all *other* than Main(). The remainder of the CIL code found in the Main() method is your basic pushing and popping of stack-based values.

Do note, however, that the creation of CILCar involves the use of the .newobj opcode. On a related note, recall that when you wish to invoke a member of a type using raw CIL, you make use of the double-colon syntax and, as always, make use of the fully qualified name of the type. With this, you can compile your new file with ilasm.exe, verify your assembly with peverify.exe, and execute your program:

```
ilasm CilCarClient.il
peverify CilCarClient.exe
CilCarClient.exe
```

Figure 15-5 shows the end result.

Figure 15-4. *Your* CILCar *in action*

That wraps up the CIL primer and the first goal of this chapter. At this point, I hope you feel confident that you can open a particular .NET assembly using ildasm.exe and gain a better understanding of what exactly is occurring behind the scenes.

Understanding Dynamic Assemblies

As you may have gathered, the process of building a complex .NET application in CIL would be quite the labor of love. On the one hand, CIL is an extremely expressive programming language that allows you to interact with all of the programming constructs allowed by the CTS. On the other hand, authoring raw CIL is tedious, error-prone, and painful. While it is true that knowledge is power, you may indeed wonder just how important it is to commit the laws of CIL syntax to memory. The answer is, "It depends." To be sure, most of your .NET programming endeavors will not require you to view, edit, or author raw CIL code. However, with the CIL primer behind you, you are now ready investigate the world of dynamic assemblies (as opposed to static assemblies) and the role of the System.Reflection.Emit namespace.

The first question you may have is, "What exactly is the difference between static and dynamic assemblies?" By definition, *static assemblies* are .NET binaries loaded directly from disk storage, meaning they are located somewhere on your hard drive in a physical file (or possibly a set of files in the case of a multifile assembly) at the time the CLR requests them. As you might guess, every time you compile your C# source code, you end up with a static assembly.

A *dynamic assembly*, on the other hand, is created in memory on the fly using the types provided by the System.Reflection.Emit namespace. The System.Reflection.Emit namespace makes it possible to create an assembly and its modules, type definitions, and CIL implementation logic at *runtime*. Once you have done so, you are then free to save your in-memory binary to disk. This, of course, results in a new static assembly. To be sure, the process of building a dynamic assembly using the System.Reflection.Emit namespace does require some level of understanding regarding the nature of CIL opcodes.

Although creating dynamic assemblies is a fairly advanced (and uncommon) programming task, they can be useful under various circumstances:

- You are building a .NET programming tool that needs to generate assemblies on demand based on user input.

- You are building a program that needs to generate proxies to remote types on the fly based on the obtained metadata.

- You wish to load a static assembly and dynamically insert new types into the binary image.

This being said, let's check out the types within System.Reflection.Emit.

Exploring the System.Reflection.Emit Namespace

Creating a dynamic assembly requires you to have some familiarity with CIL opcodes, but the types of the System.Reflection.Emit namespace hide the complexity of CIL as much as possible. For example, rather than directly specifying the necessary CIL directives and attributes to define a class type, you can simply make use of the TypeBuilder class. Likewise, if you wish to define a new instance-level constructor, you have no need to emit the specialname, rtspecialname, or .ctor tokens; rather, you can make use of the ConstructorBuilder. Table 15-8 documents the key members of the System.Reflection.Emit namespace.

Table 15-8. *Select Members of the* System.Reflection.Emit *Namespace*

Members	Meaning in Life
AssemblyBuilder	Used to create an assembly (*.dll or *.exe) at runtime. *.exes must call the ModuleBuilder.SetEntryPoint() method to set the method that is the entry point to the module. If no entry point is specified, a *.dll will be generated.
ModuleBuilder	Used to define the set of modules within the current assembly.
EnumBuilder	Used to create a .NET enumeration type.
TypeBuilder	May be used to create classes, interfaces, structures, and delegates within a module at runtime.
MethodBuilder EventBuilder LocalBuilder PropertyBuilder FieldBuilder ConstructorBuilder CustomAttributeBuilder ParameterBuilder	Used to create type members (such as methods, local variables, properties, constructors, and attributes) at runtime.
ILGenerator	Emits CIL opcodes into a given type member.
OpCodes	Provides numerous fields that map to CIL opcodes. This type is used in conjunction with the various members of System.Reflection.Emit.ILGenerator.

In general, the types of the `System.Reflection.Emit` namespace allow you represent raw CIL tokens programmatically during the construction of your dynamic binary. You will see many of these members in the example that follows; however, the `ILGenerator` type is worth checking out straightaway.

The Role of the System.Reflection.Emit.ILGenerator

As its name implies, the `ILGenerator` type's role is to inject CIL opcodes into a given type member. Typically, you will not need to directly create `ILGenerator` objects, but rather receive a valid reference to the `ILGenerator` type using the builder-centric types (such as the `MethodBuilder` and `ConstructorBuilder` types), for example:

```
// Obtain an ILGenerator from a ConstructorBuilder
// object named 'myCtorBuilder'.
ConstructorBuilder myCtorBuilder =
  new ConstructorBuilder(/* ...various args... */);
ILGenerator myCILGen = myCtorBuilder.GetILGenerator();
```

Once you have an `ILGenerator` in your hands, you are then able to emit the raw CIL opcodes using any number of methods. Table 15-9 documents some (but not all) methods of `ILGenerator`.

Table 15-9. *Select Methods of* `ILGenerator`

Method	Meaning in Life
`BeginCatchBlock()`	Begins a `catch` block
`BeginExceptionBlock()`	Begins an exception block for a nonfiltered exception
`BeginFinallyBlock()`	Begins a `finally` block
`BeginScope()`	Begins a lexical scope
`DeclareLocal()`	Declares a local variable
`DefineLabel()`	Declares a new label
`Emit()`	Is overloaded numerous times to allow you to emit CIL opcodes
`EmitCall()`	Pushes a `call` or `callvirt` opcode into the CIL stream
`EmitWriteLine()`	Emits a call to `Console.WriteLine()` with different types of values
`EndExceptionBlock()`	Ends an exception block
`EndScope()`	Ends a lexical scope
`ThrowException()`	Emits an instruction to throw an exception
`UsingNamespace()`	Specifies the namespace to be used in evaluating locals and watches for the current active lexical scope

The key method of `ILGenerator` is `Emit()`, which works in conjunction with the `System.Reflection.Emit.OpCodes` class type. As mentioned earlier in this chapter, this type exposes a good number of read-only fields that map to raw CIL opcodes. The full set of these members are all documented within online help, and you will see various examples in the pages that follow.

Emitting a Dynamic Assembly

To illustrate the process of defining a .NET assembly at runtime, let's walk through the process of creating a single-file dynamic assembly named `MyAssembly.dll`. Within this module is a class named `HelloWorld`. The `HelloWorld` type supports a default constructor and a custom constructor that is used to assign the value of a private member variable (`theMessage`) of type `string`. In addition,

HelloWorld supports a public instance method named SayHello(), which prints a greeting to the standard I/O stream, and another instance method named GetMsg(), which returns the internal private string. In effect, you are going to programmatically generate the following class type:

```
// This class will be created at runtime
// using System.Reflection.Emit.
public class HelloWorld
{
    private string theMessage;
    HelloWorld() {}
    HelloWorld(string s) {  theMessage = s;}
    public string GetMsg() {  return theMessage;}
    public void SayHello()
    {
        System.Console.WriteLine("Hello from the HelloWorld class!");
    }
}
```

Assume you have created a new Visual Studio 2005 console application project workspace named DynAsmBuilder. Rename your initial class as MyAsmBuilder and define a static method named CreateMyAsm(). This single method is in charge of the following:

- Defining the characteristics of the dynamic assembly (name, version, etc.)
- Implementing the HelloClass type
- Saving the in-memory assembly to a physical file

Also note that the CreateMyAsm() method takes as a single parameter a System.AppDomain type, which will be used to obtain access to the AssemblyBuilder type associated with the current application domain (see Chapter 13 for a discussion of .NET application domains). Here is the complete code, with analysis to follow:

```
// The caller sends in an AppDomain type.
public static void CreateMyAsm(AppDomain curAppDomain)
{
    // Establish general assembly characteristics.
    AssemblyName assemblyName = new AssemblyName();
    assemblyName.Name = "MyAssembly";
    assemblyName.Version = new Version("1.0.0.0");

    // Create new assembly within the current AppDomain.
    AssemblyBuilder assembly =
        curAppDomain.DefineDynamicAssembly(assemblyName,
        AssemblyBuilderAccess.Save);

    // Given that we are building a single-file
    // assembly, the name of the module is the same as the assembly.
    ModuleBuilder module =
        assembly.DefineDynamicModule("MyAssembly", "MyAssembly.dll");

    // Define a public class named "HelloWorld".
    TypeBuilder helloWorldClass = module.DefineType("MyAssembly.HelloWorld",
        TypeAttributes.Public);

    // Define a private String member variable named "theMessage".
    FieldBuilder msgField =
        helloWorldClass.DefineField("theMessage", Type.GetType("System.String"),
        FieldAttributes.Private);
```

```
    // Create the custom ctor.
    Type[] constructorArgs = new Type[1];
    constructorArgs[0] = typeof(string);
    ConstructorBuilder constructor =
        helloWorldClass.DefineConstructor(MethodAttributes.Public,
        CallingConventions.Standard,
        constructorArgs);
    ILGenerator constructorIL = constructor.GetILGenerator();
    constructorIL.Emit(OpCodes.Ldarg_0);
    Type objectClass = typeof(object);
    ConstructorInfo superConstructor =
        objectClass.GetConstructor(new Type[0]);
    constructorIL.Emit(OpCodes.Call, superConstructor);
    constructorIL.Emit(OpCodes.Ldarg_0);
    constructorIL.Emit(OpCodes.Ldarg_1);
    constructorIL.Emit(OpCodes.Stfld, msgField);
    constructorIL.Emit(OpCodes.Ret);

    // Create the default ctor.
    helloWorldClass.DefineDefaultConstructor(MethodAttributes.Public);

    // Now create the GetMsg() method.
    MethodBuilder getMsgMethod =
        helloWorldClass.DefineMethod("GetMsg", MethodAttributes.Public,
        typeof(string), null);
    ILGenerator methodIL = getMsgMethod.GetILGenerator();
    methodIL.Emit(OpCodes.Ldarg_0);
    methodIL.Emit(OpCodes.Ldfld, msgField);
    methodIL.Emit(OpCodes.Ret);

    // Create the SayHello method.
    MethodBuilder sayHiMethod =
        helloWorldClass.DefineMethod("SayHello",
        MethodAttributes.Public, null, null);
    methodIL = sayHiMethod.GetILGenerator();
    methodIL.EmitWriteLine("Hello from the HelloWorld class!");
    methodIL.Emit(OpCodes.Ret);

    // 'Bake' the class HelloWorld.
    // (Baking is the formal term for emitting the type)
    helloWorldClass.CreateType();

    // (Optionally) save the assembly to file.
    assembly.Save("MyAssembly.dll");
}
```

Emitting the Assembly and Module Set

The method body begins by establishing the minimal set of characteristics about your assembly, using the AssemblyName and Version types (defined in the System.Reflection namespace). Next, you obtain an AssemblyBuilder type via the instance-level AppDomain.DefineDynamicAssembly() method (recall the caller will pass in an AppDomain reference into the CreateMyAsm() method):

```
// Establish general assembly characteristics.
// and gain access to the AssemblyBuilder type
public static void CreateMyAsm(AppDomain curAppDomain)
{
    AssemblyName assemblyName = new AssemblyName();
    assemblyName.Name = "MyAssembly";
    assemblyName.Version = new Version("1.0.0.0");

    // Create new assembly within the current AppDomain.
    AssemblyBuilder assembly =
        curAppDomain.DefineDynamicAssembly(assemblyName,
            AssemblyBuilderAccess.Save);
...
}
```

As you can see, when calling `AppDomain.DefineDynamicAssembly()`, you must specify the access mode of the assembly you wish to define, which can be any of the values shown in Table 15-10.

Table 15-10. *Values of the* `AssemblyBuilderAccess` *Enumeration*

Value	Meaning in Life
ReflectionOnly	Represents that a dynamic assembly that can only be reflected over
Run	Represents that a dynamic assembly can be executed in memory but not saved to disk
RunAndSave	Represents that a dynamic assembly can be executed in memory and saved to disk
Save	Represents that a dynamic assembly can be saved to disk but not executed in memory

The next task is to define the module set for your new assembly. Given that the assembly is a single file unit, you need to define only a single module. If you were to build a multifile assembly using the `DefineDynamicModule()` method, you would specify an optional second parameter that represents the name of a given module (e.g., `myMod.dotnetmodule`). However, when creating a single-file assembly, the name of the module will be identical to the name of the assembly itself. In any case, once the `DefineDynamicModule()` method has returned, you are provided with a reference to a valid `ModuleBuilder` type:

```
// The single-file assembly.
ModuleBuilder module =
    assembly.DefineDynamicModule("MyAssembly", "MyAssembly.dll");
```

The Role of the ModuleBuilder Type

`ModuleBuilder` is key type used during the development of dynamic assemblies. As you would expect, `ModuleBuilder` supports a number of members that allow you to define the set of types contained within a given module (classes, interfaces, structures, etc.) as well as the set of embedded resources (string tables, images, etc.) contained within (the .NET resource format will be examined in Chapter 15). Table 15-11 describes a few of the creation-centric methods. (Do note that each method will return to you a related type that represents the type you wish to construct.)

Table 15-11. *Select Members of the* ModuleBuilder *Type*

Method	Meaning in Life
DefineEnum()	Used to emit a .NET enum definition
DefineResource()	Defines a managed embedded resource to be stored in this module
DefineType()	Constructs a TypeBuilder, which allows you to define value types, interfaces, and class types (including delegates)

The key member of the ModuleBuilder class to be aware of is DefineType(). In addition to specifying the name of the type (via a simple string), you will also make use of the System.Reflection. TypeAttributes enum to describe the format of the type itself. Table 15-12 lists some (but not all) of the key members the TypeAttributes enumeration.

Table 15-12. *Select Members of the* TypeAttributes *Enumeration*

Member	Meaning in Life
Abstract	Specifies that the type is abstract
Class	Specifies that the type is a class
Interface	Specifies that the type is an interface
NestedAssembly	Specifies that the class is nested with assembly visibility and is thus accessible only by methods within its assembly
NestedFamAndAssem	Specifies that the class is nested with assembly and family visibility, and is thus accessible only by methods lying in the intersection of its family and assembly
NestedFamily	Specifies that the class is nested with family visibility and is thus accessible only by methods within its own type and any subtypes
NestedFamORAssem	Specifies that the class is nested with family or assembly visibility, and is thus accessible only by methods lying in the union of its family and assembly
NestedPrivate	Specifies that the class is nested with private visibility
NestedPublic	Specifies that the class is nested with public visibility
NotPublic	Specifies that the class is not public
Public	Specifies that the class is public
Sealed	Specifies that the class is concrete and cannot be extended
Serializable	Specifies that the class can be serialized

Emitting the HelloClass Type and the String Member Variable

Now that you have a better understanding of the role of the ModuleBuilder.CreateType() method, let's examine how you can emit the public HelloWorld class type and the private string variable:

```
// Define a public class named "MyAssembly.HelloWorld".
TypeBuilder helloWorldClass = module.DefineType("MyAssembly.HelloWorld",
    TypeAttributes.Public);

// Define a private String member variable named "theMessage".
FieldBuilder msgField =
    helloWorldClass.DefineField("theMessage",
        typeof(string),
        FieldAttributes.Private);
```

Notice how the `TypeBuilder.DefineField()` method provides access to a `FieldBuilder` type. The `TypeBuilder` class also defines other methods that provide access to other "builder" types. For example, `DefineConstructor()` returns a `ConstructorBuilder`, `DefineProperty()` returns a `PropertyBuilder`, and so forth.

Emitting the Constructors

As mentioned earlier, the `TypeBuilder.DefineConstructor()` method can be used to define a constructor for the current type. However, when it comes to implementing the constructor of `HelloClass`, you need to inject raw CIL code into the constructor body, which is responsible for assigning the incoming parameter to the internal private string. To obtain an `ILGenerator` type, you call the `GetILGenerator()` method from the respective "builder" type you have reference to (in this case, the `ConstructorBuilder` type).

The `Emit()` method of the `ILGenerator` class is the entity in charge of placing CIL into a member implementation. `Emit()` itself makes frequent use of the `OpCodes` class type, which exposes the opcode set of CIL using read-only fields. For example, `OpCodes.Ret` signals the return of a method call. `OpCodes.Stfld` makes an assignment to a member variable. `OpCodes.Call` is used to call a given method (in this case, the base class constructor). That said, ponder the following constructor logic:

```
// Create the custom constructor taking
// a single System.String argument.
Type[] constructorArgs = new Type[1];
constructorArgs[0] = typeof(string);
ConstructorBuilder constructor =
    helloWorldClass.DefineConstructor(MethodAttributes.Public,
        CallingConventions.Standard, constructorArgs);

// Now emit the necessary CIL into the ctor.
ILGenerator constructorIL = constructor.GetILGenerator();
constructorIL.Emit(OpCodes.Ldarg_0);
Type objectClass = typeof(object);
ConstructorInfo superConstructor = objectClass.GetConstructor(new Type[0]);
constructorIL.Emit(OpCodes.Call, superConstructor);    // Call base class ctor.

// Load the object's 'this' pointer on the stack.
constructorIL.Emit(OpCodes.Ldarg_0);

// load incoming argument on virtual stack and store in msgField.
constructorIL.Emit(OpCodes.Ldarg_1);
constructorIL.Emit(OpCodes.Stfld, msgField);           // Assign msgField.
constructorIL.Emit(OpCodes.Ret);                       // Return.
```

Now, as you are well aware, as soon as you define a custom constructor for a type, the default constructor is silently removed. To redefine the no-argument constructor, simply call the `DefineDefaultConstructor()` method of the `TypeBuilder` type as so:

```
// Reinsert the default ctor.
helloWorldClass.DefineDefaultConstructor(MethodAttributes.Public);
```

This single call emits the standard CIL code used to define a default constructor:

```
.method public hidebysig specialname rtspecialname
        instance void  .ctor() cil managed
{
    .maxstack  1
    ldarg.0
```

```
        call instance void [mscorlib]System.Object::.ctor()
        ret
}
```

Emitting the HelloWorld() Method

Last but not least, let's examine the process of emitting the SayHello() method. The first task is to obtain a MethodBuilder type from the helloWorldClass variable. Once you do this, you define the method and obtain the underlying ILGenerator to inject the CIL instructions:

```
// Create the SayHello method.
MethodBuilder sayHiMethod =
    helloWorldClass.DefineMethod("SayHello",
    MethodAttributes.Public, null, null);
methodIL = sayHiMethod.GetILGenerator();

// Write a line to the Console.
methodIL.EmitWriteLine("Hello there!");
methodIL.Emit(OpCodes.Ret);
```

Here you have established a public method (MethodAttributes.Public) that takes no parameters and returns nothing (marked by the null entries contained in the DefineMethod() call). Also note the EmitWriteLine() call. This helper member of the ILGenerator class automatically writes a line to the standard output with minimal fuss and bother.

Using the Dynamically Generated Assembly

Now that you have the logic in place to create and save your assembly, all that's needed is a class to trigger the logic. To come full circle, assume your current project defines a second class named AsmReader. The logic in Main() obtains the current AppDomain via the Thread.GetDoMain() method that will be used to host the assembly you will dynamically create. Once you have a reference, you are able to call the CreateMyAsm() method.

To make things a bit more interesting, once the call to CreateMyAsm() returns, you will exercise some late binding (see Chapter 12) to load your newly created assembly into memory and interact with the members of the HelloWorld class:

```
using System;
using System.Reflection.Emit;
using System.Reflection;
using System.Threading;
...
public class Program
{
    static void Main(string[] args)
    {
        Console.WriteLine("***** The Amazing Dynamic Assembly Builder App *****");
        // Get the application domain for the current thread.
        AppDomain curAppDomain = Thread.GetDomain();

        // Create the dynamic assembly using our helper f(x).
        CreateMyAsm(curAppDomain);
        Console.WriteLine("-> Finished creating MyAssembly.dll.");
```

```
            // Now load the new assembly from file.
            Console.WriteLine("-> Loading MyAssembly.dll from file.");
            Assembly a = Assembly.Load("MyAssembly");

            // Get the HelloWorld type.
            Type hello = a.GetType("MyAssembly.HelloWorld");

            // Create HelloWorld object and call the correct ctor.
            Console.Write("-> Enter message to pass HelloWorld class: ");
            string msg = Console.ReadLine();
            object[] ctorArgs = new object[1];
            ctorArgs[0] = msg;
            object obj = Activator.CreateInstance(hello, ctorArgs);

            // Call SayHello and show returned string.
            Console.WriteLine("-> Calling SayHello() via late binding.");
            MethodInfo mi = hello.GetMethod("SayHello");
            mi.Invoke(obj, null);

            // Trigger GetMsg(). Invoke() returns an object that
            // holds the method's return value.
            mi = hello.GetMethod("GetMsg");
            Console.WriteLine(mi.Invoke(obj, null));
        }
}
```

In effect, you have just created a .NET assembly that is able to create .NET assemblies at runtime.

That wraps up our examination of CIL and the role of dynamic assemblies. I hope this chapter has deepened your understanding of the .NET type system and the syntax and semantics of CIL.

■**Note** Be sure to load your dynamically created assembly into `ildasm.exe` to connect the dots between raw CIL code and the functionality within the `System.Reflection.Emit` namespace.

■**Source Code** The DynAsmBuilder application is included under the Chapter 15 subdirectory.

A Brief Word Regarding System.CodeDOM

Now that you have seen how to build dynamic assemblies using `System.Reflection.Emit` and various CIL tokens, I must confess there is another (often easier) alternative. The .NET platform provides a technology termed *code DOM* that allows you to represent the structure of a .NET type in *language-agnostic* terms via a related object graph. Once this graph has been established using members of the `System.CodeDOM` namespace, you are able to dynamically persist its contents in *language-specific* code files (C#, Visual Basic .NET, or any third-party language that supports a code DOM provider). As well, the `System.CodeDOM.Compiler` namespace (and related namespaces) can be used to compile an in-memory (or persisted) object graph into a valid static .NET assembly.

Alas, I don't have the space to include information regarding code DOM technology in this edition of the text. If you require more information, look up the topic "CodeDOM, quick reference" within the .NET Framework 2.0 SDK documentation.

Summary

This chapter provided an overview of the syntax and semantics of CIL. Unlike higher-level managed languages such as C#, CIL does not simply define a set of keywords, but provides directives (used to define the structure of an assembly and its types), attributes (which further qualify a given directive), and opcodes (which are used to implementation type members). You were introduced to the CIL compiler (ilasm.exe) and learned how to alter the contents of a .NET assembly with new CIL code and also the basic process of building a .NET assembly using raw CIL.

The latter half of this chapter introduced you to the System.Reflection.Emit namespace. Using these types, you are able to emit a .NET assembly on the fly to memory. As well, if you so choose, you may persist this in-memory image to a physical file. Recall that many types of System.Reflection.Emit will automatically generate the correct CIL directives and attributes using friendly types such as ConstructorBuilder, TypeBuilder, and so forth. The ILGenerator type can be used to inject the necessary CIL opcodes into a given member. While we do have a number of helper types that attempt to make the process of programming with the CIL opcode set more palatable, you must have an understanding of CIL when programming with dynamic assemblies.

PART 4

■ ■ ■

Programming with the .NET Libraries

■ ■ ■

## CHAPTER 16

The System.IO Namespace

When you are creating full-blown desktop applications, the ability to save information between user sessions is imperative. This chapter examines a number of I/O-related topics as seen through the eyes of the .NET Framework. The first order of business is to explore the core types defined in the System.IO namespace and come to understand how to programmatically modify a machine's directory and file structure. Once you can do so, the next task is to explore various ways to read from and write to character-based, binary-based, string-based, and memory-based data stores.

Exploring the System.IO Namespace

In the framework of .NET, the System.IO namespace is the region of the base class libraries devoted to file-based (and memory-based) input and output (I/O) services. Like any namespace, System.IO defines a set of classes, interfaces, enumerations, structures, and delegates, most of which are contained in mscorlib.dll. In addition to the types contained within mscorlib.dll, the System.dll assembly defines additional members of the System.IO namespace (given that all Visual Studio 2005 projects automatically set a reference to both assemblies, you should be ready to go).

Many of the types within the System.IO namespace focus on the programmatic manipulation of physical directories and files. However, additional types provide support to read data from and write data to string buffers as well as raw memory locations. To give you a road map of the functionality in System.IO, Table 16-1 outlines the core (nonabstract) classes.

Table 16-1. *Key Members of the* System.IO *Namespace*

Nonabstract I/O Class Type	Meaning in Life
BinaryReader BinaryWriter	These types allow you to store and retrieve primitive data types (integers, Booleans, strings, and whatnot) as a binary value.
BufferedStream	This type provides temporary storage for a stream of bytes that may be committed to storage at a later time.
Directory DirectoryInfo	These types are used to manipulate a machine's directory structure. The Directory type exposes functionality primarily as *static methods*. The DirectoryInfo type exposes similar functionality from a valid *object variable*.
DriveInfo	This type (new to .NET 2.0) provides detailed information regarding the drives on a given machine.

Continued

Table 16-1. (*Continued*)

Nonabstract I/O Class Type	Meaning in Life
File FileInfo	These types are used to manipulate a machine's set of files. The File type exposes functionality primarily as *static methods*. The FileInfo type exposes similar functionality from a valid *object variable*.
FileStream	This type allows for random file access (e.g., seeking capabilities) with data represented as a stream of bytes.
FileSystemWatcher	This type allows you to monitor the modification of a given external file.
MemoryStream	This type provides random access to streamed data stored in memory rather than a physical file.
Path	This type performs operations on System.String types that contain file or directory path information in a platform-neutral manner.
StreamWriter StreamReader	These types are used to store (and retrieve) textual information to (or from) a file. These types do not support random file access.
StringWriter StringReader	Like the StreamReader/StreamWriter types, these classes also work with textual information. However, the underlying storage is a string buffer rather than a physical file.

In addition to these creatable class types, System.IO defines a number of enumerations, as well as a set of abstract classes (Stream, TextReader, TextWriter, and so forth), that define a shared polymorphic interface to all descendents. You will read about many of these types in this chapter.

The Directory(Info) and File(Info) Types

System.IO provides four types that allow you to manipulate individual files, as well as interact with a machine's directory structure. The first two types, Directory and File, expose creation, deletion, copying, and moving operations using various static members. The closely related FileInfo and DirectoryInfo types expose similar functionality as instance-level methods (and therefore must be "new-ed"). In Figure 16-1, notice that the Directory and File types directly extend System.Object, while DirectoryInfo and FileInfo derive from the abstract FileSystemInfo type.

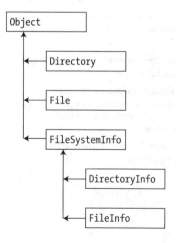

Figure 16-1. *The File- and Directory-centric types*

Generally speaking, `FileInfo` and `DirectoryInfo` are better choices for recursive operations (such as enumerating all subdirectories under a given root), as the `Directory` and `File` class members tend to return string values rather than strongly typed objects.

The Abstract FileSystemInfo Base Class

The `DirectoryInfo` and `FileInfo` types receive many behaviors from the abstract `FileSystemInfo` base class. For the most part, the members of the `FileSystemInfo` class are used to discover general characteristics (such as time of creation, various attributes, and so forth) about a given file or directory. Table 16-2 lists some core properties of interest.

Table 16-2. `FileSystemInfo` *Properties*

Property	Meaning in Life
Attributes	Gets or sets the attributes associated with the current file that are represented by the `FileAttributes` enumeration.
CreationTime	Gets or sets the time of creation for the current file or directory.
Exists	Can be used to determine if a given file or directory exists.
Extension	Retrieves a file's extension.
FullName	Gets the full path of the directory or file.
LastAccessTime	Gets or sets the time the current file or directory was last accessed.
LastWriteTime	Gets or sets the time when the current file or directory was last written to.
Name	For files, gets the name of the file. For directories, gets the name of the last directory in the hierarchy if a hierarchy exists. Otherwise, the `Name` property gets the name of the directory.

The `FileSystemInfo` type also defines the `Delete()` method. This is implemented by derived types to delete a given file or directory from the hard drive. As well, `Refresh()` can be called prior to obtaining attribute information to ensure that the statistics regarding the current file (or directory) are not outdated.

Working with the DirectoryInfo Type

The first creatable I/O-centric type you will examine is the `DirectoryInfo` class. This class contains a set of members used for creating, moving, deleting, and enumerating over directories and subdirectories. In addition to the functionality provided by its base class (`FileSystemInfo`), `DirectoryInfo` offers the key members in Table 16-3.

Table 16-3. *Key Members of the* `DirectoryInfo` *Type*

Members	Meaning in Life
Create() CreateSubdirectory()	Create a directory (or set of subdirectories), given a path name
Delete()	Deletes a directory and all its contents
GetDirectories()	Returns an array of strings that represent all subdirectories in the current directory

Continued

Table 16-3. (*Continued*)

Members	Meaning in Life
GetFiles()	Retrieves an array of FileInfo types that represent a set of files in the given directory
MoveTo()	Moves a directory and its contents to a new path
Parent	Retrieves the parent directory of the specified path
Root	Gets the root portion of a path

You begin working with the DirectoryInfo type by specifying a particular directory path as a constructor parameter. If you want to obtain access to the current application directory (i.e., the directory of the executing application), use the "." notation. Here are some examples:

```
// Bind to the current application directory.
DirectoryInfo dir1 = new DirectoryInfo(".");
```

```
// Bind to C:\Windows,
// using a verbatim string.
DirectoryInfo dir2 = new DirectoryInfo(@"C:\Windows");
```

In the second example, you are making the assumption that the path passed into the constructor (C:\Windows) already exists on the physical machine. However, if you attempt to interact with a nonexistent directory, a System.IO.DirectoryNotFoundException is thrown. Thus, if you specify a directory that is not yet created, you will need to call the Create() method before proceeding:

```
// Bind to a nonexistent directory, then create it.
DirectoryInfo dir3 = new DirectoryInfo(@"C:\Windows\Testing");
dir3.Create();
```

Once you have created a DirectoryInfo object, you can investigate the underlying directory contents using any of the properties inherited from FileSystemInfo. To illustrate, the following class creates a new DirectoryInfo object mapped to C:\Windows (adjust your path if need be) and displays a number of interesting statistics (see Figure 16-2 for output):

```
class Program
{
    static void Main(string[] args)
    {
        Console.WriteLine("***** Fun with Directory(Info) *****\n");
        DirectoryInfo dir = new DirectoryInfo(@"C:\Windows");

        // Dump directory information.
        Console.WriteLine("***** Directory Info *****");
        Console.WriteLine("FullName: {0} ", dir.FullName);
        Console.WriteLine("Name: {0} ", dir.Name);
        Console.WriteLine("Parent: {0} ", dir.Parent);
        Console.WriteLine("Creation: {0} ", dir.CreationTime);
        Console.WriteLine("Attributes: {0} ", dir.Attributes);
        Console.WriteLine("Root: {0} ", dir.Root);
        Console.WriteLine("*************************\n");
    }
}
```

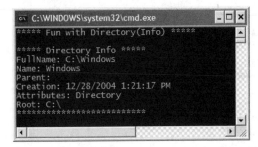

Figure 16-2. *Information about your Windows directory*

The FileAttributes Enumeration

The Attributes property exposed by FileSystemInfo provides various traits for the current directory or file, all of which are represented by the FileAttributes enumeration (enum). While the names of this enum are fairly self-describing, some of the less obvious names are documented here (consult the .NET Framework 2.0 SDK documentation for full details):

```
public enum FileAttributes
{
    ReadOnly,
    Hidden,
    // The file is part of the operating system or is used
    // exclusively by the operating system
    System,
    Directory,
    Archive,
    // This name is reserved for future use.
    Device,
    // The file is 'normal' as it has no other attributes set.
    Normal,
    Temporary,
    // Sparse files are typically large files whose data are mostly zeros.
    SparseFile,
    // A block of user-defined data associated with a file or a directory
    ReparsePoint,
    Compressed,
    Offline,
    // The file will not be indexed by the operating system's
    // content indexing service.
    NotContentIndexed,
    Encrypted
}
```

Enumerating Files with the DirectoryInfo Type

In addition to obtaining basic details of an existing directory, you can extend the current example to use some methods of the DirectoryInfo type. First, let's leverage the GetFiles() method to obtain information about all *.bmp files located under the C:\Windows directory. This method returns an array of FileInfo types, each of which exposes details of a particular file (full details of the FileInfo type are explored later in this chapter):

```
class Program
{
    static void Main(string[] args)
    {
        Console.WriteLine("***** Fun with Directory(Info) *****\n");
        DirectoryInfo dir = new DirectoryInfo(@"C:\Windows");
        ...
        // Get all files with a *.bmp extension.
        FileInfo[] bitmapFiles = dir.GetFiles("*.bmp");

        // How many were found?
        Console.WriteLine("Found {0}  *.bmp files\n", bitmapFiles.Length);

            // Now print out info for each file.
            foreach (FileInfo f in bitmapFiles)
            {
                Console.WriteLine("*************************\n");
                Console.WriteLine("File name: {0} ", f.Name);
                Console.WriteLine("File size: {0} ", f.Length);
                Console.WriteLine("Creation: {0} ", f.CreationTime);
                Console.WriteLine("Attributes: {0} ", f.Attributes);
                Console.WriteLine("*************************\n");
            }
    }
}
```

Once you run the application, you see a listing something like that shown in Figure 16-3. (Your bitmaps may vary!)

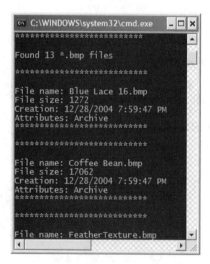

Figure 16-3. *Bitmap file information*

Creating Subdirectories with the DirectoryInfo Type

You can programmatically extend a directory structure using the DirectoryInfo.CreateSubdirectory() method. This method can create a single subdirectory, as well as multiple nested subdirectories, in a single function call. To illustrate, here is a block of code that extends the directory structure of C:\Windows with some custom subdirectories:

```
class Program
{
    static void Main(string[] args)
    {
        Console.WriteLine("***** Fun with Directory(Info) *****\n");
        DirectoryInfo dir = new DirectoryInfo(@"C:\Windows");
        ...
        // Create \MyFoo off initial directory.
        dir.CreateSubdirectory("MyFoo");

        // Create \MyBar\MyQaaz off initial directory.
        dir.CreateSubdirectory(@"MyBar\MyQaaz");
    }
}
```

If you examine your Windows directory using Windows Explorer, you will see that the new subdirectories are present and accounted for (see Figure 16-4).

Figure 16-4. *Creating subdirectories*

Although you are not required to capture the return value of the CreateSubdirectory() method, be aware that a DirectoryInfo type representing the newly created item is passed back on successful execution:

```
// CreateSubdirectory() returns a DirectoryInfo item representing the new item.
DirectoryInfo d = dir.CreateSubdirectory("MyFoo");
Console.WriteLine("Created: {0} ", d.FullName);

d = dir. CreateSubdirectory(@"MyBar\MyQaaz");
Console.WriteLine("Created: {0} ", d.FullName);
```

Working with the Directory Type

Now that you have seen the DirectoryInfo type in action, you can learn about the Directory type. For the most part, the members of Directory mimic the functionality provided by the instance-level members defined by DirectoryInfo. Recall, however, that the members of Directory typically return string types rather than strongly typed FileInfo/DirectoryInfo types.

To illustrate some functionality of the Directory type, the final iteration of this example displays the names of all drives mapped to the current computer (via the Directory.GetLogicalDrives() method) and uses the static Directory.Delete() method to remove the \MyFoo and \MyBar\MyQaaz subdirectories previously created:

```
class Program
{
    static void Main(string[] args)
    {
...
        // List all drives on current computer.
        string[] drives = Directory.GetLogicalDrives();
        Console.WriteLine("Here are your drives:");
        foreach(string s in drives)
            Console.WriteLine("->{0} ", s);

        // Delete what was created.
        Console.WriteLine("Press Enter to delete directories");
        Console.ReadLine();
        try
        {
            Directory.Delete(@"C:\Windows\MyFoo");

            // The second parameter specifies if you
            // wish to destroy any subdirectories.
            Directory.Delete(@"C:\Windows\MyBar", true);
        }
        catch(IOException e)
        {
            Console.WriteLine(e.Message);
        }
    }
}
```

■**Source Code** The MyDirectoryApp project is located under the Chapter 16 subdirectory.

Working with the DriveInfo Class Type

As of .NET 2.0, the System.IO namespace provides a class named DriveInfo. Like Directory.
GetLogicalDrives(), the static DriveInfo.GetDrives() method allows you to discover the names of
a machine's drives. Unlike Directory.GetLogicalDrives(), however, DriveInfo provides numerous
other details (such as the drive type, available free space, volume label, and whatnot). Consider the
following sample code:

```
class Program
{
    static void Main(string[] args)
    {
        Console.WriteLine("***** Fun with DriveInfo *****\n");

        // Get info regarding all drives.
        DriveInfo[] myDrives = DriveInfo.GetDrives();

        // Now print drive stats.
        foreach(DriveInfo d in myDrives)
        {
            Console.WriteLine("Name: {0}", d.Name);
            Console.WriteLine("Type: {0}", d.DriveType);
```

```
        // Check to see if the drive is mounted.
        if (d.IsReady)
        {
            Console.WriteLine("Free space: {0}", d.TotalFreeSpace);
            Console.WriteLine("Format: {0}", d.DriveFormat);
            Console.WriteLine("Label: {0}\n", d.VolumeLabel);
        }
    }
    Console.ReadLine();
    }
}
```

Figure 16-5 shows the output based on my current machine.

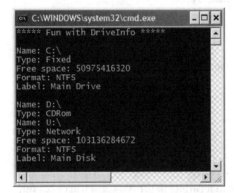

Figure 16-5. *Gather drive details via* DriveInfo

At this point, you have investigated some core behaviors of the Directory, DirectoryInfo, and DriveInfo classes. Next, you'll learn how to create, open, close, and destroy the files that populate a given directory.

■**Source Code** The DriveTypeApp project is located under the Chapter 16 subdirectory.

Working with the FileInfo Class

As shown in the MyDirectoryApp example, the FileInfo class allows you to obtain details regarding existing files on your hard drive (time created, size, file attributes, and so forth) and aids in the creation, copying, moving, and destruction of files. In addition to the set of functionality inherited by FileSystemInfo are some core members unique to the FileInfo class, which are described in Table 16-4.

Table 16-4. FileInfo *Core Members*

Member	Meaning in Life
AppendText()	Creates a StreamWriter type (described later) that appends text to a file
CopyTo()	Copies an existing file to a new file
Create()	Creates a new file and returns a FileStream type (described later) to interact with the newly created file
CreateText()	Creates a StreamWriter type that writes a new text file
Delete()	Deletes the file to which a FileInfo instance is bound
Directory	Gets an instance of the parent directory
DirectoryName	Gets the full path to the parent directory
Length	Gets the size of the current file or directory
MoveTo()	Moves a specified file to a new location, providing the option to specify a new filename
Name	Gets the name of the file
Open()	Opens a file with various read/write and sharing privileges
OpenRead()	Creates a read-only FileStream
OpenText()	Creates a StreamReader type (described later) that reads from an existing text file
OpenWrite()	Creates a write-only FileStream type

It is important to understand that a majority of the members of the FileInfo class return a specific I/O-centric object (FileStream, StreamWriter, and so forth) that allows you to begin reading and writing data to (or reading from) the associated file in a variety of formats. You will check out these types in just a moment, but until then, let's examine various ways to obtain a file handle using the FileInfo class type.

The FileInfo.Create() Method

The first way you can create a file handle is to make use of the FileInfo.Create() method:

```
public class Program
{
    static void Main(string[] args)
    {
        // Make a new file on the C drive.
        FileInfo f = new FileInfo(@"C:\Test.dat");
        FileStream fs = f.Create();

        // Use the FileStream object...

        // Close down file stream.
        fs.Close();
    }
}
```

Notice that the FileInfo.Create() method returns a FileStream type, which exposes synchronous and asynchronous write/read operations to/from the underlying file. Do know that the FileStream object returned by FileInfo.Create() grants full read/write access to all users.

The FileInfo.Open() Method

You can use the FileInfo.Open() method to open existing files as well as create new files with far more precision than FileInfo.Create(). Once the call to Open() completes, you are returned a FileStream object. Ponder the following logic:

```
static void Main(string[] args)
{
...
    // Make a new file via FileInfo.Open().
    FileInfo f2 = new FileInfo(@"C:\Test2.dat");
    FileStream fs2 = f2.Open( FileMode.OpenOrCreate,
        FileAccess.ReadWrite, FileShare.None);

    // Use the FileStream object...

    // Close down file stream.
    fs2.Close();
}
```

This version of the overloaded Open() method requires three parameters. The first parameter specifies the general flavor of the I/O request (e.g., make a new file, open an existing file, append to a file, etc.), which is specified using the FileMode enumeration:

```
public enum FileMode
{
    // Specifies that the operating system should create a new file.
    // If the file already exists, a System.IO.IOException is thrown.
    CreateNew,
    // Specifies that the operating system should create a new file.
    // If the file already exists, it will be overwritten.
    Create,
    Open,
    // Specifies that the operating system should open a file if it exists;
    // otherwise, a new file should be created.
    OpenOrCreate,
    Truncate,
    Append
}
```

The second parameter, a value from the FileAccess enumeration, is used to determine the read/write behavior of the underlying stream:

```
public enum FileAccess
{
    Read,
    Write,
    ReadWrite
}
```

Finally, you have the third parameter, FileShare, which specifies how the file is to be shared among other file handlers. Here are the core names:

```
public enum FileShare
{
    None,
    Read,
    Write,
    ReadWrite
}
```

The FileInfo.OpenRead() and FileInfo.OpenWrite() Methods

While the FileInfo.Open() method allows you to obtain a file handle in a very flexible manner, the FileInfo class also provides members named OpenRead() and OpenWrite(). As you might imagine, these methods return a properly configured read-only or write-only FileStream type, without the need to supply various enumeration values. Like FileInfo.Create() and FileInfo.Open(), OpenRead() and OpenWrite() return a FileStream object:

```
static void Main(string[] args)
{
...
    // Get a FileStream object with read-only permissions.
    FileInfo f3 = new FileInfo(@"C:\Test3.dat");
    FileStream readOnlyStream = f3.OpenRead();

    // Use the FileStream object...

    readOnlyStream.Close();

    // Now get a FileStream object with write-only permissions.
    FileInfo f4 = new FileInfo(@"C:\ Test4.dat");
    FileStream writeOnlyStream = f4.OpenWrite();

    // Use the FileStream object...

    writeOnlyStream.Close();
}
```

The FileInfo.OpenText() Method

Another open-centric member of the FileInfo type is OpenText(). Unlike Create(), Open(), OpenRead(), and OpenWrite(), the OpenText() method returns an instance of the StreamReader type, rather than a FileStream type:

```
static void Main(string[] args)
{
...
    // Get a StreamReader object.
    FileInfo f5 = new FileInfo(@"C:\boot.ini");
    StreamReader sreader = f5.OpenText();

    // Use the StreamReader object...

    sreader.Close();
}
```

As you will see shortly, the StreamReader type provides a way to read character data from the underlying file.

The FileInfo.CreateText() and FileInfo.AppendText() Methods

The final two methods of interest at this point are CreateText() and AppendText(), both of which return a StreamWriter reference, as shown here:

```
static void Main(string[] args)
{
...
    FileInfo f6 = new FileInfo(@"C:\Test5.txt");
    StreamWriter swriter = f6.CreateText();

    // Use the StreamWriter object...

    swriter.Close();

    FileInfo f7 = new FileInfo(@"C:\FinalTest.txt");
    StreamWriter swriterAppend = f7.AppendText();

    // Use the StreamWriter object...

    swriterAppend.Close();
}
```

As you would guess, the StreamWriter type provides a way to write character data to the underlying file.

Working with the File Type

The File type provides functionality almost identical to that of the FileInfo type, using a number of static members. Like FileInfo, File supplies AppendText(), Create(), CreateText(), Open(), OpenRead(), OpenWrite(), and OpenText() methods. In fact, in many cases, the File and FileInfo types may be used interchangeably. To illustrate, each of the previous FileStream examples can be simplified by using the File type instead:

```
static void Main(string[] args)
{
    // Obtain FileStream object via File.Create().
    FileStream fs = File.Create(@"C:\Test.dat");
    fs.Close();

    // Obtain FileStream object via File.Open().
    FileStream fs2 = File.Open(@"C:\Test2.dat",
        FileMode.OpenOrCreate,
        FileAccess.ReadWrite, FileShare.None);
    fs2.Close();

    // Get a FileStream object with read-only permissions.
    FileStream readOnlyStream = File.OpenRead(@"Test3.dat");
    readOnlyStream.Close();

    // Get a FileStream object with write-only permissions.
    FileStream writeOnlyStream = File.OpenWrite(@"Test4.dat");
    writeOnlyStream.Close();

    // Get a StreamReader object.
    StreamReader sreader = File.OpenText(@"C:\boot.ini");
    sreader.Close();
```

```
// Get some StreamWriters.
StreamWriter swriter = File.CreateText(@"C:\Test3.txt");
swriter.Close();
StreamWriter swriterAppend = File.AppendText(@"C:\FinalTest.txt");
swriterAppend.Close();
}
```

New .NET 2.0 File Members

Unlike FileInfo, the File type supports a few unique members (as of .NET 2.0) shown in Table 16-5, which can greatly simplify the processes of reading and writing textual data.

Table 16-5. *Methods of the* File *Type*

Method	Meaning in Life
ReadAllBytes()	Opens the specified file, returns the binary data as an array of bytes, and then closes the file
ReadAllLines()	Opens a specified file, returns the character data as an array of strings, and then closes the file
ReadAllText()	Opens a specified file, returns the character data as a System.String, and then closes the file
WriteAllBytes()	Opens the specified file, writes out the byte array, and then closes the file
WriteAllLines()	Opens a specified file, writes out an array of strings, and then closes the file
WriteAllText()	Opens a specified file, writes the character data, and then closes the file

Using these new methods of the File type, you are able to read and write batches of data in just a few lines of code. Even better, each of these new members automatically closes down the underlying file handle, for example:

```
class Program
{
    static void Main(string[] args)
    {
        string[] myTasks = {
            "Fix bathroom sink",
            "Call Dave",
            "Call Mom and Dad",
            "Play XBox"};

        // Write out all data to file on C drive.
        File.WriteAllLines(@"C:\tasks.txt", myTasks);

        // Read it all back and print out.
        foreach (string task in File.ReadAllLines(@"C:\tasks.txt"))
        {
            Console.WriteLine("TODO: {0}", task);
        }
    }
}
```

Clearly, when you wish to quickly obtain a file handle, the File type will save you some keystrokes. However, one benefit of first creating a FileInfo object is that you are able to investigate the file using the members of the abstract FileSystemInfo base class:

```
static void Main(string[] args)
{
    // Display info about boot.ini and then open
    // for read-only access.
    FileInfo bootFile = new FileInfo(@"C:\boot.ini");
    Console.WriteLine(bootFile.CreationTime);
    Console.WriteLine(bootFile.LastAccessTime);
    FileStream readOnlyStream = bootFile.OpenRead();
    readOnlyStream.Close();
}
```

The Abstract Stream Class

At this point, you have seen numerous ways to obtain FileStream, StreamReader, and StreamWriter objects, but you have yet to read data from, or written data to, a file using these types. To understand how to do so, you'll need to become familiar with the concept of a stream. In the world of I/O manipulation, a *stream* represents a chunk of data. Streams provide a common way to interact with *a sequence of bytes*, regardless of what kind of device (file, network connection, printer, etc.) is storing or displaying the bytes in question.

The abstract System.IO.Stream class defines a number of members that provide support for synchronous and asynchronous interactions with the storage medium (e.g., an underlying file or memory location). Figure 16-6 shows a few descendents of the Stream type.

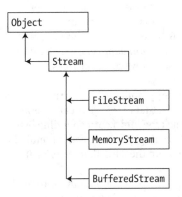

Figure 16-6. Stream-*derived types*

■**Note** Be aware that the concept of a stream is not limited to files or memory locations. To be sure, the .NET libraries provide stream access to networks and other stream-centric abstractions.

Again, Stream descendents represent data as a raw stream of bytes; therefore, working with raw streams can be quite cryptic. Some Stream-derived types support *seeking*, which refers to the process of obtaining and adjusting the current position in the stream. To begin understanding the functionality provided by the Stream class, take note of the core members described in Table 16-6.

Table 16-6. *Abstract* Stream *Members*

Members	Meaning in Life
CanRead CanSeek CanWrite	Determine whether the current stream supports reading, seeking, and/or writing.
Close()	Closes the current stream and releases any resources (such as sockets and file handles) associated with the current stream.
Flush()	Updates the underlying data source or repository with the current state of the buffer and then clears the buffer. If a stream does not implement a buffer, this method does nothing.
Length	Returns the length of the stream, in bytes.
Position	Determines the position in the current stream.
Read() ReadByte()	Read a sequence of bytes (or a single byte) from the current stream and advance the current position in the stream by the number of bytes read.
Seek()	Sets the position in the current stream.
SetLength()	Sets the length of the current stream.
Write() WriteByte()	Write a sequence of bytes (or a single byte) to the current stream and advance the current position in this stream by the number of bytes written.

Working with FileStreams

The FileStream class provides an implementation for the abstract Stream members in a manner appropriate for file-based streaming. It is a fairly primitive stream; it can read or write only a single byte or an array of bytes. In reality, you will not often need to directly interact with the members of the FileStream type. Rather, you will most likely make use of various *stream wrappers*, which make it easier to work with textual data or .NET types. Nevertheless, for illustrative purposes, let's experiment with the synchronous read/write capabilities of the FileStream type.

Assume you have a new console application named FileStreamApp. Your goal is to write a simple text message to a new file named myMessage.dat. However, given that FileStream can operate only on raw bytes, you will be required to encode the System.String type into a corresponding byte array. Luckily, the System.Text namespace defines a type named Encoding, which provides members that encode and decode strings to (or from) an array of bytes (check out the .NET Framework 2.0 SDK documentation for full details of the Encoding type).

Once encoded, the byte array is persisted to file using the FileStream.Write() method. To read the bytes back into memory, you must reset the internal position of the stream (via the Position property) and call the ReadByte() method. Finally, you display the raw byte array and the decoded string to the console. Here is the complete Main() method:

```
// Don't forget to 'use' System.Text.
static void Main(string[] args)
{
    Console.WriteLine("***** Fun with FileStreams *****\n");

    // Obtain a FileStream object.
    FileStream fStream = File.Open(@"C:\myMessage.dat",
        FileMode.Create);
```

```
// Encode a string as an array of bytes.
string msg = "Hello!";
byte[] msgAsByteArray = Encoding.Default.GetBytes(msg);

// Write byte[] to file.
fStream.Write(msgAsByteArray, 0, msgAsByteArray.Length);

// Reset internal position of stream.
fStream.Position = 0;

// Read the types from file and display to console.
Console.Write("Your message as an array of bytes: ");
byte[] bytesFromFile = new byte[msgAsByteArray.Length];
for (int i = 0; i < msgAsByteArray.Length; i++)
{
    bytesFromFile[i] = (byte)fStream.ReadByte();
    Console.Write(bytesFromFile[i]);
}

// Display decoded messages.
Console.Write("\nDecoded Message: ");
Console.WriteLine(Encoding.Default.GetString(bytesFromFile));

// Close stream.
fStream.Close();
}
```

While this example does indeed populate the file with data, it punctuates the major downfall of working directly with the FileStream type: it demands to operate on raw bytes. Other Stream-derived types operate in a similar manner. For example, if you wish to write a sequence of bytes to a region of memory, you can allocate a MemoryStream. Likewise, if you wish to push an array of bytes through a network connection, you can make use of the NetworkStream type.

Thankfully, the System.IO namespace provides a number of "reader" and "writer" types that encapsulate the details of working with Stream-derived types.

■**Source Code** The FileStreamApp project is included under the Chapter 16 subdirectory.

Working with StreamWriters and StreamReaders

The StreamWriter and StreamReader classes are useful whenever you need to read or write character-based data (e.g., strings). Both of these types work by default with Unicode characters; however, you can change this by supplying a properly configured System.Text.Encoding object reference. To keep things simple, let's assume that the default Unicode encoding fits the bill.

StreamReader derives from an abstract type named TextReader, as does the related StringReader type (discussed later in this chapter). The TextReader base class provides a very limited set of functionality to each of these descendents, specifically the ability to read and peek into a character stream.

The StreamWriter type (as well as StringWriter, also examined later in this chapter) derives from an abstract base class named TextWriter. This class defines members that allow derived types to write textual data to a given character stream. The relationship between each of these new I/O-centric types is shown in Figure 16-7.

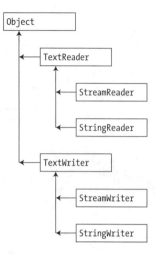

Figure 16-7. *Readers and writers*

To aid in your understanding of the core writing capabilities of the StreamWriter and StringWriter classes, Table 16-7 describes the core members of the abstract TextWriter base class.

Table 16-7. *Core Members of* TextWriter

Member	Meaning in Life
Close()	Closes the writer and frees any associated resources. In the process, the buffer is automatically flushed.
Flush()	Clears all buffers for the current writer and causes any buffered data to be written to the underlying device, but does not close the writer.
NewLine	Indicates the newline constant for the derived writer class. The default line terminator is a carriage return followed by a line feed (\r\n).
Write()	Writes a line to the text stream without a newline constant.
WriteLine()	Writes a line to the text stream with a newline constant.

■Note The last two members of the TextWriter class probably look familiar to you. If you recall, the System. Console type has Write() and WriteLine() members that push textual data to the standard output device. In fact, the Console.In property wraps a TextWriter, and the Console.Out property wraps a TextReader.

The derived StreamWriter class provides an appropriate implementation for the Write(), Close(), and Flush() methods, and it defines the additional AutoFlush property. This property, when set to true, forces StreamWriter to flush all data every time you perform a write operation. Be aware that you can gain better performance by setting AutoFlush to false, provided you always call Close() when you are done writing with a StreamWriter.

Writing to a Text File

Now for an example of working with the StreamWriter type. The following class creates a new file named reminders.txt using the File.CreateText() method. Using the obtained StreamWriter object, you add some textual data to the new file, as shown here:

```
static void Main(string[] args)
{
    Console.WriteLine("***** Fun with StreamWriter / StreamReader *****\n");

    // Get a StreamWriter and write string data.
    StreamWriter writer = File.CreateText("reminders.txt");
    writer.WriteLine("Don't forget Mother's Day this year...");
    writer.WriteLine("Don't forget Father's Day this year...");
    writer.WriteLine("Don't forget these numbers:");
    for(int i = 0; i < 10; i++)
        writer.Write(i + " ");

    // Insert a new line.
    writer.Write(writer.NewLine);

    // Closing automatically flushes!
    writer.Close();
    Console.WriteLine("Created file and wrote some thoughts...");
}
```

Once you run this program, you can examine the contents of this new file (see Figure 16-8).

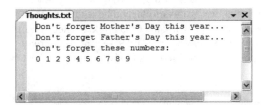

Figure 16-8. *The contents of your* *.txt *file*

Reading from a Text File

Now you need to understand how to programmatically read data from a file using the corresponding StreamReader type. As you recall, this class derives from TextReader, which offers the functionality described in Table 16-8.

Table 16-8. TextReader *Core Members*

Member	Meaning in Life
Peek()	Returns the next available character without actually changing the position of the reader. A value of –1 indicates you are at the end of the stream.
Read()	Reads data from an input stream.
ReadBlock()	Reads a maximum of count characters from the current stream and writes the data to a buffer, beginning at index.
ReadLine()	Reads a line of characters from the current stream and returns the data as a string (a null string indicates EOF).
ReadToEnd()	Reads all characters from the current position to the end of the stream and returns them as a single string.

If you now extend the current MyStreamWriterReader class to use a StreamReader, you can read in the textual data from the reminders.txt file as shown here:

```
static void Main(string[] args)
{
    Console.WriteLine("***** Fun with StreamWriter / StreamReader *****\n");
...

    // Now read data from file.
    Console.WriteLine("Here are your thoughts:\n");
    StreamReader sr = File.OpenText("reminders.txt");

    string input = null;
    while ((input = sr.ReadLine()) != null)
    {
        Console.WriteLine (input);
    }
}
```

Once you run the program, you will see the character data within Thoughts.txt displayed to the console.

Directly Creating StreamWriter/StreamReader Types

One of the slightly confusing aspects of working with the types within System.IO is that you can often achieve an identical result using numerous approaches. For example, you have already seen that you can obtain a StreamWriter via the File or FileInfo type using the CreateText() method. In reality, there is yet another way in which you can work with StreamWriters and StreamReaders: create them directly. For example, the current application could be retrofitted as so:

```
static void Main(string[] args)
{
    Console.WriteLine("***** Fun with StreamWriter / StreamReader *****\n");

    // Get a StreamWriter and write string data.
    StreamWriter writer = new StreamWriter("reminders.txt");
...

    // Now read data from file.
    StreamReader sr = new StreamReader("reminders.txt");
...
}
```

Although it can be a bit confusing to see so many seemingly identical approaches to file I/O, keep in mind that the end result is greater flexibility. In any case, now that you have seen how to move character data to and from a given file using the StreamWriter and StreamReader types, you will next examine the role of the StringWriter and StringReader classes.

■**Source Code**   The StreamWriterReaderApp project is included under the Chapter 16 subdirectory.

Working with StringWriters and StringReaders

Using the StringWriter and StringReader types, you can treat textual information as a stream of in-memory characters. This can prove helpful when you wish to append character-based information to an underlying buffer. To illustrate, the following example writes a block of string data to a StringWriter object rather than a file on the local hard drive:

```
static void Main(string[] args)
{
    Console.WriteLine("***** Fun with StringWriter / StringReader *****\n");

    // Create a StringWriter and emit character data to memory.
    StringWriter strWriter = new StringWriter();
    strWriter.WriteLine("Don't forget Mother's Day this year...");
    strWriter.Close();

    // Get a copy of the contents (stored in a string) and pump
    // to console.
    Console.WriteLine("Contents of StringWriter:\n{0}", strWriter);
}
```

Because StringWriter and StreamWriter both derive from the same base class (TextWriter), the writing logic is more or less identical. However, given that nature of StringWriter, be aware that this class allows you to extract a System.Text.StringBuilder object via the GetStringBuilder() method:

```
static void Main(string[] args)
{
    Console.WriteLine("***** Fun with StringWriter / StringReader *****\n");

    // Create a StringWriter and emit character data to memory.
    StringWriter strWriter = new StringWriter();
...
    // Get the internal StringBuilder.
    StringBuilder sb = strWriter.GetStringBuilder();
    sb.Insert(0, "Hey!! ");
    Console.WriteLine("-> {0}", sb.ToString());
    sb.Remove(0, "Hey!! ".Length);
    Console.WriteLine("-> {0}", sb.ToString());
}
```

When you wish to read from a stream of character data, make use of the corresponding StringReader type, which (as you would expect) functions identically to the related StreamReader class. In fact, the StringReader class does nothing more than override the inherited members to read from a block of character data, rather than a file, as shown here:

```
static void Main(string[] args)
{
    Console.WriteLine("***** Fun with StringWriter / StringReader *****\n");

    // Create a StringWriter and emit character data to memory.
    StringWriter strWriter = new StringWriter();
...
    // Read data from the StringWriter.
    StringReader strReader = new StringReader(writer.ToString());
    string input = null;
    while ((input = strReader.ReadLine()) != null)
    {
        Console.WriteLine (input);
    }
    strReader.Close();
}
```

■**Source Code**   The StringReaderWriterApp is included under the Chapter 16 subdirectory.

Working with BinaryWriters and BinaryReaders

The final writer/reader sets you will examine here are BinaryReader and BinaryWriter, both of which derive directly from System.Object. These types allow you to read and write discrete *data types* to an underlying stream in a compact binary format. The BinaryWriter class defines a highly overloaded Write() method to place a data type in the underlying stream. In addition to Write(), BinaryWriter provides additional members that allow you to get or set the Stream-derived type and offers support for random access to the data (see Table 16-9).

Table 16-9. BinaryWriter *Core Members*

Member	Meaning in Life
BaseStream	This read-only property provides access to the underlying stream used with the BinaryWriter object.
Close()	This method closes the binary stream.
Flush()	This method flushes the binary stream.
Seek()	This method sets the position in the current stream.
Write()	This method writes a value to the current stream.

The BinaryReader class complements the functionality offered by BinaryWriter with the members described in Table 16-10.

Table 16-10. BinaryReader *Core Members*

Member	Meaning in Life
BaseStream	This read-only property provides access to the underlying stream used with the BinaryReader object.
Close()	This method closes the binary reader.
PeekChar()	This method returns the next available character without actually advancing the position in the stream.
Read()	This method reads a given set of bytes or characters and stores them in the incoming array.
ReadXXXX()	The BinaryReader class defines numerous ReadXXXX() methods that grab the next type from the stream (ReadBoolean(), ReadByte(), ReadInt32(), and so forth).

The following example writes a number of data types to a new *.dat file:

```
static void Main(string[] args)
{
    // Open a binary writer for a file.
    FileInfo f = new FileInfo("BinFile.dat");
    BinaryWriter bw = new BinaryWriter(f.OpenWrite());

    // Print out the type of BaseStream.
    // (System.IO.FileStream in this case).
    Console.WriteLine("Base stream is: {0}", bw.BaseStream);

    // Create some data to save in the file
    double aDouble = 1234.67;
    int anInt = 34567;
    char[] aCharArray = { 'A', 'B', 'C' };
```

```
    // Write the data
    bw.Write(aDouble);
    bw.Write(anInt);
    bw.Write(aCharArray);
    bw.Close();
}
```

Notice how the FileStream object returned from FileInfo.OpenWrite() is passed to the constructor of the BinaryWriter type. Using this technique, it is very simple to "layer in" a stream before writing out the data. Do understand that the constructor of BinaryWriter takes any Stream-derived type (e.g., FileStream, MemoryStream, or BufferedStream). Thus, if you would rather write binary data to memory, simply supply a valid MemoryStream object.

To read the data out of the BinFile.dat file, the BinaryReader type provides a number of options. Here, you will make use of PeekChar() to determine if the stream still has data to provide and, if so, use ReadByte() to obtain the value. Note that you are formatting the bytes in hexadecimal and inserting seven spaces between each:

```
static void Main(string[] args)
{
    // Open a binary writer for a file.
    FileInfo f = new FileInfo("BinFile.dat");
...
    // Read the data as raw bytes
    BinaryReader br = new BinaryReader(f.OpenRead());
    int temp = 0;
    while (br.PeekChar() != -1)
    {
        Console.Write("{0,7:x} ", br.ReadByte());
        if (++temp == 4)
        {
            // Write a new line every 4 bytes
            Console.WriteLine();
            temp = 0;
        }
    }
    Console.WriteLine();
}
```

The output of this program appears in Figure 16-9.

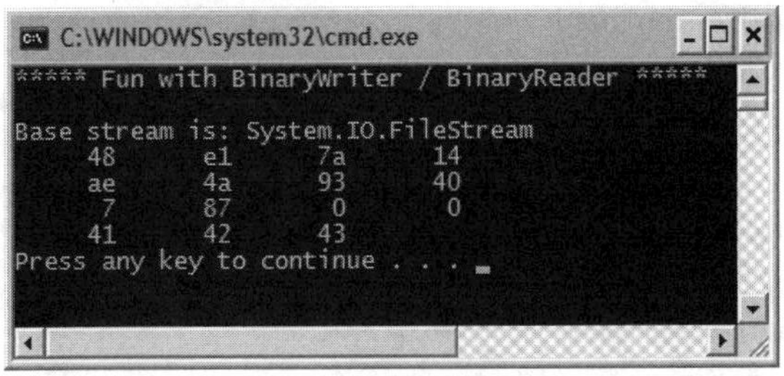

Figure 16-9. *Reading bytes from a binary file*

■**Source Code** The BinaryWriterReader application is included under the Chapter 16 subdirectory.

Programmatically "Watching" Files

Now that you have a better handle on the use of various readers and writers, next you'll look at the role of the FileSystemWatcher class. This type can be quite helpful when you wish to programmatically monitor (or "watch") files on your system. Specifically, the FileSystemWatcher type can be instructed to monitor files for any of the actions specified by the NotifyFilters enumeration (while many of these members are self-explanatory, check the online help for further details):

```
public enum System.IO.NotifyFilters
{
    Attributes, CreationTime,
    DirectoryName, FileName,
    LastAccess, LastWrite,
    Security, Size,
}
```

The first step you will need to take to work with the FileSystemWatcher type is to set the Path property to specify the name (and location) of the directory that contains the files to be monitored, as well as the Filter property that defines the file extensions of the files to be monitored.

At this point, you may choose to handle the Changed, Created, and Deleted events, all of which work in conjunction with the FileSystemEventHandler delegate. This delegate can call any method matching the following pattern:

```
// The FileSystemEventHandler delegate must point
// to methods matching the following signature.
void MyNotificationHandler(object source, FileSystemEventArgs e)
```

As well, the Renamed event may also be handled via the RenamedEventHandler delegate type, which can call methods matching the following signature:

```
// The RenamedEventHandler delegate must point
// to methods matching the following signature.
void MyNotificationHandler(object source, RenamedEventArgs e)
```

To illustrate the process of watching a file, assume you have created a new directory on your C drive named MyFolder that contains various *.txt files (named whatever you wish). The following console application will monitor the *.txt files within the MyFolder and print out messages in the event that the files are created, deleted, modified, or renamed:

```
static void Main(string[] args)
{
    Console.WriteLine("***** The Amazing File Watcher App *****\n");

    // Establish the path to the directory to watch.
    FileSystemWatcher watcher = new FileSystemWatcher();
    try{
        watcher.Path = @"C:\MyFolder";
    }
    catch(ArgumentException ex) {
        Console.WriteLine(ex.Message);
        return;
    }
```

```
    // Set up the things to be on the
    // lookout for.
    watcher.NotifyFilter = NotifyFilters.LastAccess
          | NotifyFilters.LastWrite
          | NotifyFilters.FileName
          | NotifyFilters.DirectoryName;

    // Only watch text files.
    watcher.Filter = "*.txt";

    // Add event handlers.
    watcher.Changed += new FileSystemEventHandler(OnChanged);
    watcher.Created += new FileSystemEventHandler(OnChanged);
    watcher.Deleted += new FileSystemEventHandler(OnChanged);
    watcher.Renamed += new RenamedEventHandler(OnRenamed);

    // Begin watching the directory.
    watcher.EnableRaisingEvents = true;

    // Wait for the user to quit the program.
    Console.WriteLine(@"Press 'q' to quit app.");
    while(Console.Read()!='q');
}
```

The two event handlers simply print out the current file modification:

```
static void OnChanged(object source, FileSystemEventArgs e)
{
    // Specify what is done when a file is changed, created, or deleted.
    Console.WriteLine("File: {0} {1}!", e.FullPath, e.ChangeType);
}

static void OnRenamed(object source, RenamedEventArgs e)
{
    // Specify what is done when a file is renamed.
    Console.WriteLine("File: {0} renamed to\n{1}", e.OldFullPath, e.FullPath);
}
```

To test this program, run the application and open Windows Explorer. Try renaming your files, creating a *.txt file, deleting a *.txt file, or whatnot. You will see the console application print out various bits of information regarding the state of the text files within MyFolder (see Figure 16-10).

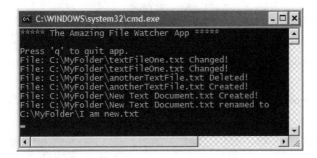

Figure 16-10. *Watching some text files*

Performing Asynchronous File I/O

To conclude our examination of the System.IO namespace, let's see how to interact with FileStream types asynchronously. You have already seen the asynchronous support provided by the .NET Framework during the examination of multithreading (see Chapter 14). Because I/O can be a lengthy task, all types deriving from System.IO.Stream inherit a set of methods that enable asynchronous processing of the data. As you would expect, these methods work in conjunction with the IAsyncResult type:

```
public abstract class System.IO.Stream :
    MarshalByRefObject,
    IDisposable
{
...
    public virtual IAsyncResult BeginRead(byte[] buffer, int offset,
        int count, AsyncCallback callback, object state);
    public virtual IAsyncResult BeginWrite(byte[] buffer, int offset,
        int count, AsyncCallback callback, object state);

    public virtual int EndRead(IAsyncResult asyncResult);
    public virtual void EndWrite(IAsyncResult asyncResult);
}
```

The process of working with the asynchronous behavior of Stream-derived types is identical to working with asynchronous delegates and asynchronous remote method invocations. While it's unlikely that asynchronous behaviors will greatly improve file access, other streams (e.g., socket based) are much more likely to benefit from asynchronous handling. In any case, the following example illustrates one manner in which you can asynchronously interact with a FileStream type:

```
class Program
{
    static void Main(string[] args)
    {
        Console.WriteLine("Main thread started. ThreadID = {0}",
            Thread.CurrentThread.GetHashCode());

        // Must use this ctor to get a FileStream with asynchronous
        // read or write access.
        FileStream fs = new FileStream("logfile.txt", FileMode.Append,
            FileAccess.Write, FileShare.None, 4096, true);

        string msg = "this is a test";
        byte[] buffer = Encoding.ASCII.GetBytes(msg);

        // Start the asynchronous write. WriteDone invoked when finished.
        // Note that the FileStream object is passed as state info to the
        // callback method.
        fs.BeginWrite(buffer, 0, buffer.Length,
            new AsyncCallback(WriteDone), fs);
    }
```

```
    private static void WriteDone(IAsyncResult ar)
    {
        Console.WriteLine("AsyncCallback method on ThreadID = {0}",
            Thread.CurrentThread.GetHashCode());

        Stream s = (Stream)ar.AsyncState;
        s.EndWrite(ar);
        s.Close();
    }
}
```

The only point of interest in this example (assuming you recall the process of working with delegates!) is that in order to enable the asynchronous behavior of the FileStream type, you must make use of a specific constructor (shown here). The final System.Boolean parameter (when set to true) informs the FileStream object to perform its work on a secondary thread of execution.

■**Source Code**   The AsyncFileStream application is included under the Chapter 16 subdirectory.

Summary

This chapter began by examining the use of the Directory(Info) and File(Info) types (including several new members of the File type brought about with .NET 2.0). As you learned, these classes allow you to manipulate a physical file or directory on your hard drive. Next, you examined a number of types derived from the abstract Stream class, specifically FileStream. Given that Stream-derived types operate on a raw stream of bytes, the System.IO namespace provides numerous reader/writer types (StreamWriter, StringWriter, BinaryWriter, etc.) that simplify the process.

Along the way, you also checked out a new I/O-centric type provided by .NET 2.0 (DriveType), and you learned how to monitor files using the FileSystemWatcher type and how to interact with streams in an asynchronous manner.

■ ■ ■

## CHAPTER 17

Understanding Object Serialization

In Chapter 16, you learned about the functionality provided by the System.IO namespace. As shown, this namespace provides numerous reader/writer types that can be used to persist data to a given location (in a given format). This chapter examines the related topic of *object serialization*. Using object serialization, you are able to persist and retrieve the state of an object to (or from) any System.IO.Stream-derived type.

As you might imagine, the ability to serialize types is critical when attempting to copy an object to a remote machine (the subject of the next chapter). Understand, however, that serialization is quite useful in its own right and will likely play a role in many of your .NET applications (distributed or not). Over the course of this chapter, you will be exposed to numerous aspects of the .NET serialization scheme, including a set of new attributes introduced with .NET 2.0 that allow you to customize the process.

Understanding Object Serialization

The term *serialization* describes the process of persisting (and possibly transferring) the state of an object to a stream. The persisted data sequence contains all necessary information needed to reconstruct (or *deserialize*) the state of the object for use later. Using this technology, it is trivial to save vast amounts of data (in various formats) with minimal fuss and bother. In fact, in many cases, saving application data using serialization services is much less cumbersome than making direct use of the readers/writers found within the System.IO namespace.

For example, assume you have created a GUI-based desktop application and wish to provide a way for end users to save their preferences. To do so, you might define a class named UserPrefs that encapsulates 20 or so pieces of field data. If you were to make use of a System.IO.BinaryWriter type, you would need to *manually* save each field of the UserPrefs object. Likewise, when you wish to load the data from file back into memory, you would need to make use of a System.IO.BinaryReader and (once again) *manually* read in each value to reconfigure a new UserPrefs object.

While this is certainly doable, you would save yourself a good amount of time simply by marking the UserPrefs class with the [Serializable] attribute. In this case, the entire state of the object can be persisted out using a few lines of code:

```
static void Main(string[] args)
{
    // Assume UserPrefs has been marked [Serializable].
    UserPrefs userData= new UserPrefs();
    userData.WindowColor = "Yellow";
    userData.FontSize = "50";
    userData.IsPowerUser = false;
```

```
    // Now save object to a file named user.dat.
    BinaryFormatter binFormat = new BinaryFormatter();
    Stream fStream = new FileStream("user.dat",
        FileMode.Create, FileAccess.Write, FileShare.None);
    binFormat.Serialize(fStream, userData);
    fStream.Close();
    Console.ReadLine();
}
```

While it is quite simple to persist objects using .NET object serialization, the processes used behind the scenes are quite sophisticated. For example, when an object is persisted to a stream, all associated data (base classes, contained objects, etc.) are automatically serialized as well. Therefore, if you are attempting to persist a derived class, all data up the chain of inheritance comes along for the ride. As you will see, a set of interrelated objects is represented using an object graph.

.NET serialization services also allow you to persist an object graph in a variety of formats. The previous code example made use of the BinaryFormatter type; therefore, the state of the UserPrefs object was persisted as a compact binary format. You are also able to persist an object graph into a Simple Object Access Protocol (SOAP) or XML format using other types. These formats can be quite helpful when you wish to ensure that your persisted objects travel well across operating systems, languages, and architectures.

Finally, understand that an object graph can be persisted into *any* System.IO.Stream-derived type. In the previous example, you persisted a UserPrefs object into a local file via the FileStream type. However, if you would rather persist an object to memory, you could make use of a MemoryStream type instead. All that matters is the fact that the sequence of data correctly represents the state of objects within the graph.

The Role of Object Graphs

As mentioned, when an object is serialized, the CLR will account for all related objects. The set of related objects is collectively referred to as an *object graph*. Object graphs provide a simple way to document how a set of objects refer to each other and do not necessarily map to classic OO relationships (such as the "is-a" or "has-a" relationship), although they model this paradigm quite well.

Each object in an object graph is assigned a unique numerical value. Keep in mind that the numbers assigned to the members in an object graph are arbitrary and have no real meaning to the outside world. Once all objects have been assigned a numerical value, the object graph can record each object's set of dependencies.

As a simple example, assume you have created a set of classes that model some automobiles (of course). You have a base class named Car, which "has-a" Radio. Another class named JamesBondCar extends the Car base type. Figure 17-1 shows a possible object graph that models these relationships.

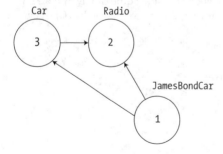

Figure 17-1. *A simple object graph*

When reading object graphs, you can use the phrase "depends on" or "refers to" when connecting the arrows. Thus, in Figure 17-1 you can see that the Car class refers to the Radio class (given the "has-a" relationship). JamesBondCar refers to Car (given the "is-a" relationship) as well as Radio (as it inherits this protected member variable).

Of course, the CLR does not paint pictures in memory to represent a graph of related objects. Rather, the relationship documented in the previous diagram is represented by a more mathematical formula that looks something like this:

```
[Car 3, ref 2], [Radio 2], [JamesBondCar 1, ref 3, ref 2]
```

If you parse this formula, you can again see that object 3 (the Car) has a dependency on object 2 (the Radio). Object 2, the Radio, is a lone wolf and requires nobody. Finally, object 1 (the JamesBondCar) has a dependency on object 3 as well as object 2. In any case, when you serialize or deserialize an instance of JamesBondCar, the object graph ensures that the Radio and Car types also participate in the process.

The beautiful thing about the serialization process is that the graph representing the relationships among your objects is established automatically behind the scenes. As you will see later in this chapter, however, if you do wish to become more involved in the construction of a given object graph, it is possible to do so.

Configuring Objects for Serialization

To make an object available to .NET serialization services, all you need to do is decorate each related class with the [Serializable] attribute. That's it (really). If you determine that a given class has some member data that should not (or perhaps cannot) participate in the serialization scheme, you can mark such fields with the [NonSerialized] attribute. This can be helpful if you have member variables in a serializable class that do not need to be "remembered" (e.g., fixed values, random values, transient data, etc.) and you wish to reduce the size of the persisted graph.

To get the ball rolling, here is the Radio class, which has been marked [Serializable], excluding a single member variable (radioID) that has been marked [NonSerialized] and will therefore not be persisted into the specified data stream:

```
[Serializable]
public class Radio
{
    public bool hasTweeters;
    public bool hasSubWoofers;
    public double[] stationPresets;

    [NonSerialized]
    public string radioID = "XF-552RR6";
}
```

The JamesBondCar class and Car base class are also marked [Serializable] and define the following pieces of field data:

```
[Serializable]
public class Car
{
    public Radio theRadio = new Radio();
    public bool isHatchBack;
}
```

```
[Serializable]
public class JamesBondCar : Car
{
    public bool canFly;
    public bool canSubmerge;
}
```

Be aware that the [Serializable] attribute cannot be inherited. Therefore, if you derive a class from a type marked [Serializable], the child class must be marked [Serializable] as well, or it cannot be persisted. In fact, all objects in an object graph must be marked with the [Serializable] attribute. If you attempt to serialize a nonserializable object using the BinaryFormatter or SoapFormatter, you will receive a SerializationException at runtime.

Public Fields, Private Fields, and Public Properties

Notice that in each of these classes, I have defined the field data as public, just to simplify the example. Of course, private data exposed using public properties would be preferable from an OO point of view. Also, for the sake of simplicity, I have not defined any custom constructors on these types, and therefore all unassigned field data will receive the expected default values.

OO design principles aside, you may wonder how the various formatters expect a type's field data to be defined in order to be serialized into a stream. The answer is, it depends. If you are persisting an object using the BinaryFormatter, it makes absolutely no difference. This type is programmed to serialize *all* serializable fields of a type, regardless of whether they are public fields, private fields, or private fields exposed through type properties. The situation is quite different if you make use of the XmlSerializer or SoapFormatter type, however. These types will *only* serialize public pieces of field data or private data exposed through public properties.

Do recall, however, that if you have points of data that you do not want to be persisted into the object graph, you can selectively mark public or private fields as [NonSerialized], as done with the string field of the Radio type.

Choosing a Serialization Formatter

Once you have configured your types to participate in the .NET serialization scheme, your next step is to choose which format should be used when persisting your object graph. As of .NET 2.0, you have three choices out of the box:

- BinaryFormatter
- SoapFormatter
- XmlSerializer

The BinaryFormatter type serializes your object graph to a stream using a compact binary format. This type is defined within the System.Runtime.Serialization.Formatters.Binary namespace that is part of mscorlib.dll. Therefore, to serialize your objects using a binary format, all you need to do is specify the following C# using directive:

```
// Gain access to the BinaryFormatter in mscorlib.dll.
using System.Runtime.Serialization.Formatters.Binary;
```

The SoapFormatter type represents your graph as a SOAP message. This type is defined within the System.Runtime.Serialization.Formatters.Soap namespace that is defined within a *separate assembly*. Thus, to format your object graph into a SOAP message, you must set a reference to System.Runtime. Serialization.Formatters.Soap.dll and specify the following C# using directive:

```
// Must reference System.Runtime.Serialization.Formatters.Soap.dll!
using System.Runtime.Serialization.Formatters.Soap;
```

Finally, if you wish to persist an object graph as an XML document, you will need to specify that you are using the System.Xml.Serialization namespace, which is also defined in a separate assembly: System.Xml.dll. As luck would have it, all Visual Studio 2005 project templates automatically reference System.Xml.dll, therefore you will simply need to use the following namespace:

```
// Defined within System.Xml.dll.
using System.Xml.Serialization;
```

The IFormatter and IRemotingFormatting Interfaces

Regardless of which formatter you choose to make use of, be aware that each of them derives directly from System.Object, and therefore they do not share a common set of members from a serialization-centric base class. However, the BinaryFormatter and SoapFormatter types do support common members through the implementation of the IFormatter and IRemotingFormatter interfaces (of which XmlSerializer implements neither).

System.Runtime.Serialization.IFormatter defines the core Serialize() and Deserialize() methods, which do the grunt work to move your object graphs into and out of a specific stream. Beyond these members, IFormatter defines a few properties that are used behind the scenes by the implementing type:

```
public interface IFormatter
{
    SerializationBinder Binder { get; set; }
    StreamingContext Context { get; set; }
    ISurrogateSelector SurrogateSelector { get; set; }
    object Deserialize(System.IO.Stream serializationStream);
    void Serialize(System.IO.Stream serializationStream, object graph);
}
```

The System.Runtime.Remoting.Messaging.IRemotingFormatter interface (which is leveraged internally by the .NET remoting layer) overloads the Serialize() and Deserialize() members into a manner more appropriate for distributed persistence. Note that IRemotingFormatter derives from the more general IFormatter interface:

```
public interface IRemotingFormatter : IFormatter
{
    object Deserialize(Stream serializationStream,
        HeaderHandler handler);
    void Serialize(Stream serializationStream, object graph,
        Header[] headers);
}
```

Although you may not need to directly interact with these interfaces for most of your serialization endeavors, recall that interface-based polymorphism allows you to hold an instance of BinaryFormatter or SoapFormatter using an IFormatter reference. Therefore, if you wish to build a method that can serialize an object graph using either of these classes, you could write the following:

```
static void SerializeObjectGraph(IFormatter itfFormat,
    Stream destStream, object graph)
{
    itfFormat.Serialize(destStream, graph);
}
```

Type Fidelity Among the Formatters

The most obvious difference among the three formatters is how the object graph is persisted to stream (binary, SOAP, or pure XML). You should be aware of a few more subtle points of distinction, specifically how the formatters contend with *type fidelity*. When you make use of the BinaryFormatter type, it will not only persist the field data of the objects in the object graph, but also each type's fully qualified name and the full name of the defining assembly. These extra points of data make the BinaryFormatter an ideal choice when you wish to transport objects by value (e.g., as a full copy) across machine boundaries (see Chapter 18). As noted, to achieve this level of type fidelity, the BinaryFormatter will account for all field data of a type (public or private).

The SoapFormatter and XmlSerializer, on the other hand, do *not* attempt to preserve full type fidelity and therefore do not record the type's fully qualified name or assembly of origin, and only persist public field data/public properties. While this may seem like a limitation at first glance, the reason has to do with the open-ended nature of XML data representation. If you wish to persist object graphs that can be used by any operating system (Windows XP, Mac OS X, and *nix distributions), application framework (.NET, J2EE, COM, etc.), or programming language, you do not want to maintain full type fidelity, as you cannot assume all possible recipients can understand .NET-specific data types. Given this, SoapFormatter and XmlSerializer are ideal choices when you wish to ensure as broad a reach as possible for the persisted object graph.

Serializing Objects Using the BinaryFormatter

To illustrate how easy it is to persist an instance of the JamesBondCar to a physical file, let's make use of the BinaryFormatter type. Again, the two key methods of the BinaryFormatter type to be aware of are Serialize() and Deserialize():

- Serialize(): Persists an object graph to a specified stream as a sequence of bytes

- Deserialize(): Converts a persisted sequence of bytes to an object graph

Assume you have created an instance of JamesBondCar, modified some state data, and want to persist your spymobile into a *.dat file. The first task is to create the *.dat file itself. This can be achieved by creating an instance of the System.IO.FileStream type (see Chapter 16). At this point, simply create an instance of the BinaryFormatter and pass in the FileStream and object graph to persist:

```
using System.Runtime.Serialization.Formatters.Binary;
using System.IO;
...
static void Main(string[] args)
{
    Console.WriteLine("***** Fun with Object Serialization *****\n");

    // Make a JamesBondCar and set state.
    JamesBondCar jbc = new JamesBondCar();
    jbc.canFly = true;
    jbc.canSubmerge = false;
    jbc.theRadio.stationPresets = new double[]{89.3, 105.1, 97.1};
    jbc.theRadio.hasTweeters = true;

    // Save object to a file named CarData.dat in binary.
    BinaryFormatter binFormat = new BinaryFormatter();
    Stream fStream = new FileStream("CarData.dat",
            FileMode.Create, FileAccess.Write, FileShare.None);
```

```
    binFormat.Serialize(fStream, jbc);
    fStream.Close();
    Console.ReadLine();
}
```

As you can see, the BinaryFormatter.Serialize() method is the member responsible for composing the object graph and moving the byte sequence to some Stream-derived type. In this case, the stream happens to be a physical file. However, you could also serialize your object types to any Stream-derived type such as a memory location, given that MemoryStream is a descendent of the Stream type.

Deserializing Objects Using the BinaryFormatter

Now suppose you want to read the persisted JamesBondCar from the binary file back into an object variable. Once you have programmatically opened CarData.dat (via the File.OpenRead() method), simply call the Deserialize() method of the BinaryFormatter. Be aware that Deserialize() returns a generic System.Object type, so you need to impose an explicit cast, as shown here:

```
static void Main(string[] args)
{
...
    // Read the JamesBondCar from the binary file.
    fStream = File.OpenRead("CarData.dat");
    JamesBondCar carFromDisk =
        (JamesBondCar)binFormat.Deserialize(fStream);
    Console.WriteLine("Can this car fly? : {0}", carFromDisk.canFly);
    fStream.Close();
    Console.ReadLine();
}
```

Notice that when you call Deserialize(), you pass the Stream-derived type that represents the location of the persisted object graph (again, a file stream in this case). Now if that is not painfully simple, I'm not sure what is. In a nutshell, mark each class you wish to persist to a stream with the [Serializable] attribute. After this point, use the BinaryFormatter type to move your object graph to and from a binary stream. At this point, you can view the binary image that represents this instance of the JamesBondCar (see Figure 17-2).

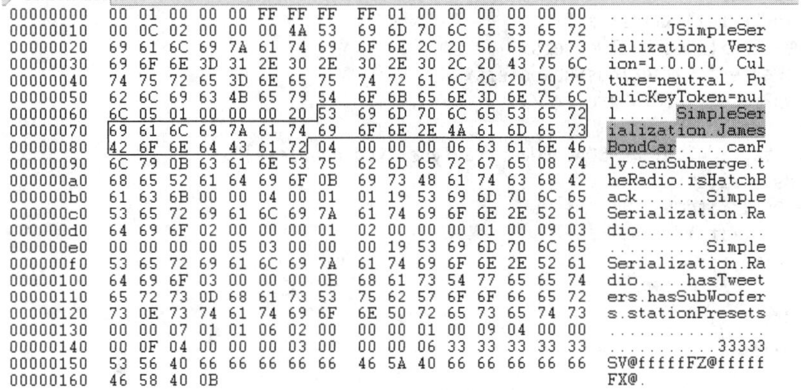

Figure 17-2. JamesBondCar *serialized using a* BinaryFormatter

Serializing Objects Using the SoapFormatter

Your next choice of formatter is the SoapFormatter type. The SoapFormatter will persist an object graph into a SOAP message, which makes this formatter a solid choice when you wish to distribute objects remotely using the HTTP protocol. If you are unfamiliar with the SOAP specification, don't sweat the details right now. In a nutshell, SOAP defines a standard process in which methods may be invoked in a platform- and OS-neutral manner (we'll examine SOAP in a bit more detail in the final chapter of this book during a discussion of XML web services).

Assuming you have set a reference to the System.Runtime.Serialization.Formatters.Soap.dll assembly, you could persist and retrieve a JamesBondCar as a SOAP message simply by replacing each occurrence of BinaryFormatter with SoapFormatter. Consider the following code, which serializes an object to a local file named CarData.soap:

```
using System.Runtime.Serialization.Formatters.Soap;
...
static void Main(string[] args)
{
...
    // Save object to a file named CarData.soap in SOAP format.
    SoapFormatter soapFormat = new SoapFormatter();
    fStream = new FileStream("CarData.soap",
    FileMode.Create, FileAccess.Write, FileShare.None);
        soapFormat.Serialize(fStream, jbc);
    fStream.Close();
    Console.ReadLine();
}
```

As before, simply use Serialize() and Deserialize() to move the object graph in and out of the stream. If you open the resulting *.soap file, you can locate the XML elements that mark the stateful values of the current JamesBondCar as well as the relationship between the objects in the graph via the #ref tokens. Consider the following end result (XML namespaces snipped for brevity):

```
<SOAP-ENV:Envelope xmlns:xsi="...">
    <SOAP-ENV:Body>
        <a1:JamesBondCar id="ref-1" xmlns:a1="...">
            <canFly>true</canFly>
            <canSubmerge>false</canSubmerge>
            <theRadio href="#ref-3"/>
            <isHatchBack>false</isHatchBack>
        </a1:JamesBondCar>
        <a1:Radio id="ref-3" xmlns:a1="...">
            <hasTweeters>true</hasTweeters>
            <hasSubWoofers>false</hasSubWoofers>
            <stationPresets href="#ref-4"/>
        </a1:Radio>
        <SOAP-ENC:Array id="ref-4" SOAP-ENC:arrayType="xsd:double[3]">
            <item>89.3</item>
            <item>105.1</item>
            <item>97.1</item>
        </SOAP-ENC:Array>
    </SOAP-ENV:Body>
</SOAP-ENV:Envelope>
```

Serializing Objects Using the XmlSerializer

In addition to the SOAP and binary formatters, the System.Xml.dll assembly provides a third format-ter, System.Xml.Serialization.XmlSerializer, which can be used to persist the state of a given object as pure XML, as opposed to XML data wrapped within a SOAP message. Working with this type is a bit different from working with the SoapFormatter or BinaryFormatter type. Consider the following code:

```
using System.Xml.Serialization;
...
static void Main(string[] args)
{
...
    // Save object to a file named CarData.xml in XML format.
    XmlSerializer xmlFormat = new XmlSerializer(typeof(JamesBondCar),
        new Type[] { typeof(Radio), typeof(Car) });

    fStream = new FileStream("CarData.xml",
        FileMode.Create, FileAccess.Write, FileShare.None);
    xmlFormat.Serialize(fStream, jbc);
    fStream.Close();
...
}
```

The key difference is that the XmlSerializer type requires you to specify type information that represents the items in the object graph. Notice that the first constructor argument of the XmlSerializer defines the root element of the XML file, while the second argument is an array of System.Type types that hold metadata regarding the subelements. If you were to look within the newly generated CarData.xml file, you would find the following (abbreviated) XML data:

```
<?xml version="1.0" encoding="utf-8"?>
<JamesBondCar xmlns:xsi="...">
  <theRadio>
    <hasTweeters>true</hasTweeters>
    <hasSubWoofers>false</hasSubWoofers>
    <stationPresets>
      <double>89.3</double>
      <double>105.1</double>
      <double>97.1</double>
    </stationPresets>
  </theRadio>
  <isHatchBack>false</isHatchBack>
  <canFly>true</canFly>
  <canSubmerge>false</canSubmerge>
</JamesBondCar>
```

■**Note** The XmlSerializer demands that all serialized types in the object graph support a default construc-tor (so be sure to add it back if you define custom constructors). If this is not the case, you will receive an InvalidOperationException at runtime.

Controlling the Generated XML Data

If you have a background in XML technologies, you are well aware that it is often critical to ensure the elements within an XML document conform to a set of rules that establish the "validity" of the data. Understand that a "valid" XML document does not have to do with the syntactic well-being of the XML elements (e.g., all opening elements must have a closing element). Rather, valid documents conform to agreed-upon formatting rules (e.g., field X must be an expressed as an attribute and not a subelement), which are typically defined by an XML schema or document-type definition (DTD) file.

By default, all field data of a [Serializable] type is formatted as elements rather than XML attributes. If you wish to control how the XmlSerializer generates the resulting XML document, you may decorate your [Serializable] types with any number of additional attributes from the System.Xml.Serialization namespace. Table 17-1 documents some (but not all) of the attributes that influence how XML data is encoded to a stream.

Table 17-1. *Serialization-centric Attributes of the* System.Xml.Serialization *Namespace*

Attribute	Meaning in Life
XmlAttributeAttribute	The member will be serialized as an XML attribute.
XmlElementAttribute	The field or property will be serialized as an XML element.
XmlEnumAttribute	The element name of an enumeration member.
XmlRootAttribute	This attribute controls how the root element will be constructed (namespace and element name).
XmlTextAttribute	The property or field should be serialized as XML text.
XmlTypeAttribute	The name and namespace of the XML type.

By way of a simple example, first consider how the field data of JamesBondCar is currently persisted as XML:

```
<?xml version="1.0" encoding="utf-8"?>
<JamesBondCar xmlns:xsi="http://www.w3.org/2001/XMLSchema-instance"
  xmlns:xsd="http://www.w3.org/2001/XMLSchema">
...
  <canFly>true</canFly>
  <canSubmerge>false</canSubmerge>
</JamesBondCar>
```

If you wished to specify a custom XML namespace that qualifies the JamesBondCar as well as encodes the canFly and canSubmerge values as XML attributes, you can do so by modifying the C# definition of JamesBondCar as so:

```
[Serializable,
XmlRoot(Namespace = "http://www.intertechtraining.com")]
public class JamesBondCar : Car
{
...
    [XmlAttribute]
    public bool canFly;
    [XmlAttribute]
    public bool canSubmerge;
}
```

This would yield the following XML document (note the opening <JamesBondCar> element):

```
<?xml version="1.0" encoding="utf-8"?>
<JamesBondCar xmlns:xsi="http://www.w3.org/2001/XMLSchema-instance"
    xmlns:xsd="http://www.w3.org/2001/XMLSchema"
    canFly="true" canSubmerge="false"
    xmlns="http://www.intertechtraining.com">
...
</JamesBondCar>
```

Of course, there are numerous other attributes that can be used to control how the XmlSerializer generates the resulting XML document. If you wish to see all of your options, look up the System.Xml. Serialization namespace using the .NET Framework 2.0 SDK documentation.

Persisting Collections of Objects

Now that you have seen how to persist a single object to a stream, let's examine how to save a set of objects. As you may have noticed, the Serialize() method of the IFormatter interface does not provide a way to specify an arbitrary number of objects (only a single System.Object). On a related note, the return value of Deserialize() is, again, a single System.Object:

```
public interface IFormatter
{
...
    object Deserialize(System.IO.Stream serializationStream);
    void Serialize(System.IO.Stream serializationStream, object graph);
}
```

Recall that the System.Object in fact represents a complete object graph. Given this, if you pass in an object that has been marked as [Serializable] and contains other [Serializable] objects, the entire set of objects is persisted right away. As luck would have it, most of the types found within the System.Collections and System.Collections.Generic namespaces have already been marked as [Serializable]. Therefore, if you wish to persist a set of objects, simply add the set to the container (such as an ArrayList or List<>) and serialize the object to your stream of choice.

Assume you have updated the JamesBondCar class with a two-argument constructor to set a few pieces of state data (note that you add back the default constructor as required by the XmlSerializer):

```
[Serializable,
XmlRoot(Namespace = "http://www.intertechtraining.com")]
public class JamesBondCar : Car
{
    public JamesBondCar(bool skyWorthy, bool seaWorthy)
    {
        canFly = skyWorthy;
        canSubmerge = seaWorthy;
    }
    // The XmlSerializer demands a default constructor!
    public JamesBondCar(){}
...
}
```

With this, you are now able to persist any number of JamesBondCars as so:

```
static void Main(string[] args)
{
...
    // Now persist a List<> of JamesBondCars.
    List<JamesBondCar> myCars = new List<JamesBondCar>();
    myCars.Add(new JamesBondCar(true, true));
    myCars.Add(new JamesBondCar(true, false));
    myCars.Add(new JamesBondCar(false, true));
    myCars.Add(new JamesBondCar(false, false));

    fStream = new FileStream("CarCollection.xml",
        FileMode.Create, FileAccess.Write, FileShare.None);
```

```
    xmlFormat = new XmlSerializer(typeof(List<JamesBondCar>),
        new Type[] { typeof(JamesBondCar), typeof(Car), typeof(Radio) });
    xmlFormat.Serialize(fStream, myCars);
    fStream.Close();
    Console.ReadLine();
}
```

Again, because you made use of the XmlSerializer, you are required to specify type information for each of the subobjects within the root object (which in this case is the ArrayList). Had you
made use of the BinaryFormatter or SoapFormatter type, the logic would be even more straightforward,
for example:

```
static void Main(string[] args)
{
    ...
    // Save ArrayList object (myCars) as binary.
    List<JamesBondCar> myCars = new List<JamesBondCar>();

    ...
    BinaryFormatter binFormat = new BinaryFormatter();
    Stream fStream = new FileStream("AllMyCars.dat",
        FileMode.Create, FileAccess.Write, FileShare.None);
    binFormat.Serialize(fStream, myCars);
    fStream.Close();
    Console.ReadLine();
}
```

Excellent! At this point, you should see how you can use object serialization services to simplify
the process of persisting and resurrecting your application's data. Next up, allow me to illustrate how
you can customize the default serialization process.

■**Source Code** The SimpleSerialize application is located under the Chapter 17 subdirectory.

Customizing the Serialization Process

In a vast majority of cases, the default serialization scheme provided by the .NET platform will be
exactly what you require. Simply apply the [Serializable] attribute and pass the object graph to
your formatter of choice. In some cases, however, you may wish to become more involved with how
an object graph is handled during the serialization process. For example, maybe you have a business
rule that says all field data must be persisted in uppercase format, or perhaps you wish to add additional bits of data to the stream that do not directly map to fields in the object being persisted (time
stamps, unique identifiers, or whatnot).

When you wish to become more involved with the process of object serialization, the System.
Runtime.Serialization namespace provides several types that allow you to do so. Table 17-2 describes
some of the core types to be aware of.

Table 17-2. `System.Runtime.Serialization` *Namespace Core Types*

Type	Meaning in Life
ISerializable	As of .NET 1.1, implementing this interface was the preferred way to perform custom serialization. As of .NET 2.0, the preferred way to customize the serialization process is to apply a new set of attributes (described in just a bit).
ObjectIDGenerator	This type generates IDs for members in an object graph.
OnDeserializedAttribute	This .NET 2.0 attribute allows you to specify a method that will be called immediately after the object has been deserialized.
OnDeserializingAttribute	This .NET 2.0 attribute allows you to specify a method that will be called during the deserialization process.
OnSerializedAttribute	This .NET 2.0 attribute allows you to specify a method that will be called immediately after the object has been serialized.
OnSerializingAttribute	This .NET 2.0 attribute allows you to specify a method that will be called during the serialization process.
OptionalFieldAttribute	This .NET 2.0 attribute allows you to define a field on a type that can be missing from the specified stream.
SerializationInfo	In essence, this class is a "property bag" that maintains name/value pairs representing the state of an object during the serialization process.

A Deeper Look at Object Serialization

Before we examine various ways in which you can customize the serialization process, it will be helpful to take a deeper look at what takes place behind the scenes. When the `BinaryFormatter` serializes an object graph, it is in charge of transmitting the following information into the specified stream:

- The fully qualified name of the objects in the graph (e.g., `MyApp.JamesBondCar`)

- The name of the assembly defining the object graph (e.g., `MyApp.exe`)

- An instance of the `SerializationInfo` class that contains all stateful data maintained by the members in the object graph

During the deserialization process, the `BinaryFormatter` uses this same information to build an identical copy of the object, using the information extracted from the underlying stream.

■**Note** Recall that the `SoapFormatter` and `XmlSerializer` do not persist a type's fully qualified name or the name of the defining assembly. These types are concerned only with persisting exposed field data.

The big picture can be visualized as shown in Figure 17-3.

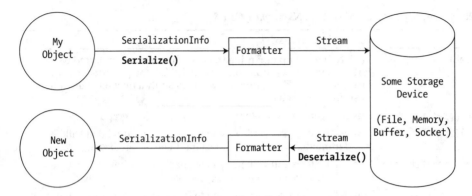

Figure 17-3. *The serialization process*

Beyond moving the required data into and out of a stream, formatters also analyze the members in the object graph for the following pieces of infrastructure:

- A check is made to determine whether the object is marked with the [Serializable] attribute. If the object is not, a SerializationException is thrown.

- If the object is marked [Serializable], a check is made to determine if the object implements the ISerializable interface. If this is the case, GetObjectData() is called on the object.

- If the object does not implement ISerializable, the default serialization process is used, serializing all fields not marked as [NonSerialized].

In addition to determining if the type supports ISerializable, formatters (as of .NET 2.0) are also responsible for discovering if the types in question support members that have been adorned with the [OnSerializing], [OnSerialized], [OnDeserializing], or [OnDeserialized] attribute. We'll examine the role of these attributes in just a bit, but first let's look at the role of ISerializable.

Customizing Serialization Using ISerializable

Objects that are marked [Serializable] have the option of implementing the ISerializable interface. By doing so, you are able to "get involved" with the serialization process and perform any pre- or post-data formatting. This interface is quite simple, given that it defines only a single method, GetObjectData():

```
// When you wish to tweak the serialization process,
// implement ISerializable.
public interface ISerializable
{
    void GetObjectData(SerializationInfo info,
        StreamingContext context);
}
```

The GetObjectData() method is called automatically by a given formatter during the serialization process. The implementation of this method populates the incoming SerializationInfo parameter with a series of name/value pairs that (typically) map to the field data of the object being persisted. SerializationInfo defines numerous variations on the overloaded AddValue() method, in addition to a small set of properties that allow the type to get and set the type's name, defining assembly, and member count. Here is a partial snapshot:

```
public sealed class SerializationInfo : object
{
    public SerializationInfo(Type type, IFormatterConverter converter);
    public string AssemblyName { get; set; }
    public string FullTypeName { get; set; }
    public int MemberCount { get; }
    public void AddValue(string name, short value);
    public void AddValue(string name, UInt16 value);
    public void AddValue(string name, int value);
...
}
```

Types that implement the `ISerializable` interface must also define a special constructor taking the following signature:

```
// You must supply a custom constructor with this signature
// to allow the runtime engine to set the state of your object.
[Serializable]
class SomeClass : ISerializable
{
    private SomeClass (SerializationInfo si, StreamingContext ctx) {...}
...
}
```

Notice that the visibility of this constructor is set as *private*. This is permissible given that the formatter will have access to this member regardless of its visibility. These special constructors tend to be marked as private to ensure that the casual object user would never create an object in this manner. As you can see, the first parameter of this constructor is an instance of the `SerializationInfo` type (seen previously).

The second parameter of this special constructor is a `StreamingContext` type, which contains information regarding the source or destination of the bits. The most informative member of this type is the `State` property, which represents a value from the `StreamingContextStates` enumeration. The values of this enumeration represent the basic composition of the current stream.

To be honest, unless you are implementing some low-level custom remoting services, you will seldom need to deal with this enumeration directly. Nevertheless, here are the possible names of the `StreamingContextStates` enum (consult the .NET Framework 2.0 SDK documentation for full details):

```
public enum StreamingContextStates
{
    CrossProcess,
    CrossMachine,
    File,
    Persistence,
    Remoting,
    Other,
    Clone,
    CrossAppDomain,
    All
}
```

To illustrate customizing the serialization process using `ISerializable`, assume you have a class type that defines two points of string data. Furthermore, assume that you must ensure the string values are serialized to the stream in all uppercase and deserialized from the stream in all lowercase. To account for such rules, you could implement `ISerializable` as so (be sure to "use" the `System.Runtime.Serialization` namespace):

```
[Serializable]
class MyStringData : ISerializable
{
    public string dataItemOne, dataItemTwo;

    public MyStringData(){}
    private MyStringData(SerializationInfo si, StreamingContext ctx)
    {
        // Rehydrate member variables from stream.
        dataItemOne = si.GetString("First_Item").ToLower();
        dataItemTwo = si.GetString("dataItemTwo").ToLower();
    }

    void ISerializable.GetObjectData(SerializationInfo info, StreamingContext ctx)
    {
        // Fill up the SerializationInfo object with the formatted data.
        info.AddValue("First_Item", dataItemOne.ToUpper());
        info.AddValue("dataItemTwo", dataItemTwo.ToUpper());
    }
}
```

Notice that when you are filling the SerializationInfo type from within the GetObjectData() method, you are *not* required to name the data points identically to the type's internal member variables. This can obviously be helpful if you need to further decouple the type's data from the persisted format. Do be aware, however, that you will need to obtain the values from within the private constructor using the same names assigned within GetObjectData().

To test your customization, assume you have persisted an instance of MyStringData using a SoapFormatter. When you view the resulting *.soap file, you will note that the string fields have indeed been persisted in uppercase:

```
<SOAP-ENV:Envelope xmlns:xsi="...">
    <SOAP-ENV:Body>
        <a1:MyStringData id="ref-1" xmlns:a1="...">
            <First_Item id="ref-3">THIS IS SOME DATA.</First_Item>
            <dataItemTwo id="ref-4">HERE IS SOME MORE DATA</dataItemTwo>
        </a1:MyStringData>
    </SOAP-ENV:Body>
</SOAP-ENV:Envelope>
```

Customizing Serialization Using Attributes

Although implementing the ISerializable interface is still possible under .NET 2.0, the preferred manner to customize the serialization process is to define methods that are attributed with any of the new serialization-centric attributes ([OnSerializing], [OnSerialized], [OnDeserializing], or [OnDeserialized]). Using these attributes is less cumbersome than implementing ISerializable, given that you do not need to manually interact with an incoming SerializationInfo parameter. Instead, you are able to directly modify your state data while the formatter is operating on the type.

When applying these attributes, the methods must be defined to receive a StreamingContext parameter and return nothing (otherwise, you will receive a runtime exception). Do note that you are not required to account for each of the serialization-centric attributes, and you can simply contend with the stages of serialization you are interested in intercepting. To illustrate, here is a new [Serializable] type that has the same requirements as MyStringData, this time accounted for using the [OnSerializing] and [OnDeserialized] attributes:

```
[Serializable]
class MoreData
{
    public string dataItemOne, dataItemTwo;

    [OnSerializing]
    internal void OnSerializing(StreamingContext context)
    {
        // Called during the serialization process.
        dataItemOne = dataItemOne.ToUpper();
        dataItemTwo = dataItemTwo.ToUpper();
    }

    [OnDeserialized]
    internal void OnDeserialized(StreamingContext context)
    {
        // Called once the deserialization process is complete.
        dataItemOne = dataItemOne.ToLower();
        dataItemTwo = dataItemTwo.ToLower();
    }
}
```

If you were to serialize this new type, you would again find that the data has been persisted as uppercase and deserialized as lowercase.

■**Source Code** The CustomSerialization project is included under the Chapter 17 subdirectory.

Versioning Serializable Objects

To wrap up this chapter, the final topic to address is the process of versioning serializable objects. To understand why this may be necessary, consider the following scenario. Assume you have created the UserPrefs class (mentioned at the beginning of the chapter) as so:

```
[Serializable]
class UserPrefs
{
    public string objVersion = "1.0";
    public ConsoleColor BackgroundColor;
    public ConsoleColor ForegroundColor;

    public UserPrefs()
    {
        BackgroundColor = ConsoleColor.Black;
        ForegroundColor = ConsoleColor.Red;
    }
}
```

Now, assume you have an application that serializes an instance of this class using a BinaryFormatter:

```
static void Main(string[] args)
{
    UserPrefs up = new UserPrefs();
    up.BackgroundColor = ConsoleColor.DarkBlue;
    up.ForegroundColor = ConsoleColor.White;
```

```
    // Save an instance of UserPrefs to file.
    BinaryFormatter binFormat = new BinaryFormatter();
    Stream fStream = new FileStream(@"C:\user.dat",
            FileMode.Create, FileAccess.Write, FileShare.None);
    binFormat.Serialize(fStream, up);
    fStream.Close();
    Console.ReadLine();
}
```

At this point, an instance of UserPrefs (version 1.0) has been persisted to C:\user.dat. Now, what if you updated the definition of UserPrefs class with two new fields:

```
[Serializable]
class UserPrefs
{
    public string objVersion = "2.0";
    public ConsoleColor BackgroundColor;
    public ConsoleColor ForegroundColor;

    // New!
    public int BeepFreq;
    public string ConsoleTitle;

    public UserPrefs()
    {
        BeepFreq = 1000;
        ConsoleTitle = "My Console";
        BackgroundColor = ConsoleColor.Black;
        ForegroundColor = ConsoleColor.Red;
    }
}
```

Imagine this same application now attempts to deserialize the instance of the persisted UserPrefs object version 1.0 as so (note the previous serialization logic has been removed in order for this example to work):

```
static void Main(string[] args)
{
    // Load an instance of UserPrefs (1.0) to memory?
    UserPrefs up = null;
    BinaryFormatter binFormat = new BinaryFormatter();
    Stream fStream = new FileStream(@"C:\user.dat",
        FileMode.Open, FileAccess.Read, FileShare.None);
    up = (UserPrefs)binFormat.Deserialize(fStream);
    fStream.Close();
    Console.ReadLine();
}
```

You will find a runtime exception is thrown:

```
Unhandled Exception: System.Runtime.Serialization.SerializationException:
Member 'BeepFreq' in class ' VersionedObject.UserPrefs' is not present in the
serialized stream and is not marked with
System.Runtime.Serialization.OptionalFieldAttribute.
```

The problem is that the original UserPrefs object persisted to C:\user.dat did *not* have storage for the two new fields found in your updated class definition (BeepFreq and ConsoleTitle). Clearly, this is problematic, as it is quite natural for a serialized object to evolve over its lifetime.

Prior to .NET 2.0, the only way to account for the possibility that previously persisted objects may not have each and every field of the latest and greatest version of the class was to implement

ISerializable and take matters into your own hands. However, as of .NET 2.0, new fields can now be explicitly marked with the [OptionalField] attribute (found within the System.Runtime.Serialization namespace):

```
[Serializable]
class UserPrefs
{
    public ConsoleColor BackgroundColor;
    public ConsoleColor ForegroundColor;

    // New!
    [OptionalField]
    public int BeepFreq;
    [OptionalField]
    public string ConsoleTitle;

    public UserPrefs()
    {
        BeepFreq = 1000;
        ConsoleTitle = "My Console";
        BackgroundColor = ConsoleColor.Black;
        ForegroundColor = ConsoleColor.Red;
    }
}
```

When a formatter deserializes an object that does not contain fields such optional fields, it will no longer throw a runtime exception. Rather, the data that is preserved is mapped back into the existing fields (BackgroundColor and ForegroundColor, in this case), while the remaining fields are simply assigned their default values.

■Note Understand that the use of [OptionalField] does not completely solve the process of versioning persisted objects. However, this attribute does provide a workaround for the most common headache of the versioning process (adding new field data). More elaborate versioning tasks may still require implementing the ISerializable interface.

■Source Code The VersionedObject project is included under the Chapter 17 subdirectory.

Summary

This chapter introduced the topic of object serialization services. As you have seen, the .NET platform makes use of an object graph to correctly account for the full set of related objects that are to be persisted to a stream. As long as each member in the object graph has been marked with the [Serializable] attribute, the data is persisted using your format of choice (binary, SOAP, or XML).

You also learned that it is possible to customize the out-of-the-box serialization process using two possible approaches. First, you learned how to implement the ISerializable interface (and support a special private constructor) to become more involved with how formatters persist the supplied data. Next, you came to know a set of new attributes introduced with .NET 2.0, which simplifies the process of custom serialization. Just apply the [OnSerializing], [OnSerialized], [OnDeserializing], or [OnDeserialized] attribute on members taking a StreamingContext parameter, and the formatters will invoke them accordingly. The chapter wrapped up with an examination of a final attribute, [OptionalField], which can be used to gracefully version a serializable type.

The .NET Remoting Layer

Developers who are new to the .NET platform often assume that .NET is all about building Internet-centric applications (given that the term ".NET" often conjures the notion of "interNET" software). As you have already seen, however, this is simply not the case. In fact, the construction of web-centric programs is simply one tiny (but quite well-touted) aspect of the .NET platform. In this same vein of misinformation, many new .NET developers tend to assume that XML web services are the only way to interact with remote objects. Again, this is not true. Using the .NET remoting layer, you are able to build peer-to-peer distributed applications that have nothing to do with HTTP or XML (if you so choose).

The first goal of this chapter is to examine the low-level grunge used by the CLR to move information between application boundaries. Along the way, you will come to understand the numerous terms used when discussing .NET remoting, such as proxies, channels, marshaling by reference (as opposed to by value), server-activated (versus client-activated) objects, and so forth. After these background elements are covered, the remainder of the chapter offers numerous code examples that illustrate the process of building distributed systems using the .NET platform.

Defining .NET Remoting

As you recall from your reading in Chapter 13, an *application domain* (*AppDomain*) is a logical boundary for a .NET assembly, which is itself housed within a Win32 process. Understanding this concept is critical when discussing distributed computing under .NET, given that *remoting* is nothing more than the act of two objects communicating across application domains. The two application domains in question could be physically configured in any of the following manners:

- Two application domains in the same process (and thus on the same machine)
- Two application domains in separate processes on the same machine
- Two application domains in separate processes on different machines

Given these three possibilities, you can see that remoting does not necessarily need to involve two networked computers. In fact, each of the examples presented in this chapter can be successfully run on a single, stand-alone machine. Regardless of the distance between two objects, it is common to refer to each agent using the terms "client" and "server." Simply put, the *client* is the entity that attempts to interact with remote objects. The *server* is the software agent that houses the remote objects.

The .NET Remoting Namespaces

Before we dive too deep into the details of the .NET remoting layer, we need to check out the functionality provided by the remoting-centric namespaces. The .NET base class libraries provide numerous namespaces that allow you to build distributed applications. The bulk of the types found within these namespaces are contained within `mscorlib.dll`, but the `System.Runtime.Remoting.dll` assembly does complement and extend the core namespaces. Table 18-1 briefly describes the role of the remoting-centric namespaces as of .NET 2.0.

Table 18-1. *.NET Remoting-centric Namespaces*

Namespace	Meaning in Life
System.Runtime.Remoting	This is the core namespace you must use when building any sort of distributed .NET application.
System.Runtime.Remoting.Activation	This relatively small namespace defines a handful of types that allow you to fine-tune the process of activating a remote object.
System.Runtime.Remoting.Channels	This namespace contains types that represent channels and channel sinks.
System.Runtime.Remoting.Channels.Http	This namespace contains types that use the HTTP protocol to transport messages and objects to and from remote locations.
System.Runtime.Remoting.Channels.Ipc	This namespace (which is new to .NET 2.0) contains types that leverage the Win32 interprocess communication (IPC) architecture. As you may know, IPC proves fast communications between AppDomains on the *same* physical machine.
System.Runtime.Remoting.Channels.Tcp	This namespace contains types that use the TCP protocol to transport messages and objects to and from remote locations.
System.Runtime.Remoting.Contexts	This namespace allows you to configure the details of an object's context.
System.Runtime.Remoting.Lifetime	This namespace contains types that manage the lifetime of remote objects.
System.Runtime.Remoting.Messaging	This namespace contains types used to create and transmit message objects.
System.Runtime.Remoting.Metadata	This namespace contains types that can be used to customize the generation and processing of SOAP formatting.
System.Runtime.Remoting.Metadata.W3cXsd2001	Closely related to the previous namespace, this namespace contains types that represent the XML Schema Definition (XSD) defined by the World Wide Web Consortium (W3C) in 2001.
System.Runtime.Remoting.MetadataServices	This namespace contains the types used by the soapsuds.exe command-line tool to convert .NET metadata to and from an XML schema for the remoting infrastructure.

Namespace	Meaning in Life
System.Runtime.Remoting.Proxies	This namespace contains types that provide functionality for proxy objects.
System.Runtime.Remoting.Services	This namespace defines a number of common base classes (and interfaces) that are typically only leveraged by other intrinsic remoting agents.

Understanding the .NET Remoting Framework

When clients and servers exchange information across application boundaries, the CLR makes use of several low-level primitives to ensure the entities in question are able to communicate with each other as transparently as possible. This means that as a .NET programmer, you are *not* required to provide reams and reams of grungy networking code to invoke a method on a remote object. Likewise, the server process is *not* required to manually pluck a network packet out of the queue and reformat the message into terms the remote object can understand. As you would hope, the CLR takes care of such details automatically using a default set of remoting primitives (although you are certainly able to get involved with the process if you so choose).

In a nutshell, the .NET remoting layer revolves around a careful orchestration that takes place between four key players:

- Proxies
- Messages
- Channels
- Formatters

Let's check out each entity in turn and see how their combined functionality facilitates remote method invocations.

Understanding Proxies and Messages

Clients and server objects do not communicate via a direct connection, but rather through the use of an intermediary termed a *proxy*. The role of a .NET proxy is to fool the client into believing it is communicating with the requested remote object in the *same application domain*. To facilitate this illusion, a proxy has the identical interface (i.e., members, properties, fields, and whatnot) as the remote type it represents. As far as the client is concerned, a given proxy *is* the remote object. Under the hood, however, the proxy is forwarding calls to the remote object.

Formally speaking, the proxy invoked directly by the client is termed the *transparent proxy*. This CLR autogenerated entity is in charge of ensuring that the client has provided the correct number of (and type of) parameters to invoke the remote method. Given this, you can regard the transparent proxy as a fixed interception layer that *cannot* be modified or extended programmatically.

Assuming the transparent proxy is able to verify the incoming arguments, this information is packaged up into another CLR-generated type termed the *message object*. By definition, all message objects implement the System.Runtime.Remoting.Messaging.IMessage interface:

```
public interface IMessage
{
    IDictionary Properties { get; }
}
```

As you can see, the IMessage interface defines a single property (named Properties) that provides access to a collection used to hold the client-supplied arguments. Once this message object has been populated by the CLR, it is then passed into a closely related type termed the *real proxy*.

The real proxy is the entity that actually passes the message object into the channel (described momentarily). Unlike the transparent proxy, the real proxy *can* be extended by the programmer and is represented by a base class type named (of course) RealProxy. Again, it is worth pointing out that the CLR will always generate a default implementation of the client-side real proxy, which will serve your needs most (if not all) of the time. Nevertheless, to gain some insight into the functionality provided by the abstract RealProxy base class, ponder the formal definition type:

```
public abstract class RealProxy : object
{
    public virtual ObjRef CreateObjRef(Type requestedType);
    public virtual bool Equals(object obj);
    public virtual IntPtr GetCOMIUnknown(bool fIsMarshalled);
    public virtual int GetHashCode();
    public virtual void GetObjectData(SerializationInfo info,
        StreamingContext context);
    public Type GetProxiedType();
    public static object GetStubData(RealProxy rp);
    public virtual object GetTransparentProxy();
    public Type GetType();
    public IConstructionReturnMessage InitializeServerObject(
        IConstructionCallMessage ctorMsg);
    public virtual IMessage Invoke(IMessage msg);
    public virtual void SetCOMIUnknown(IntPtr i);
    public static void SetStubData(RealProxy rp, object stubData);
    public virtual IntPtr SupportsInterface(ref Guid iid);
    public virtual string ToString();
}
```

Unless you are interested in building a custom implementation of the client-side real proxy, the only member of interest is RealProxy.Invoke(). Under the hood, the CLR-generated transparent proxy passes the formatted message object into the RealProxy type via its Invoke() method.

Understanding Channels

Once the proxies have validated and formatted the client-supplied arguments into a message object, this IMessage-compatible type is passed from the real proxy into a channel object. *Channels* are the entities in charge of transporting a message to the remote object and, if necessary, ensuring that any member return value is passed from the remote object back to the client. The .NET 2.0 base class libraries provide three channel implementations out of the box:

- TCP channel
- HTTP channel
- IPC channel

The *TCP channel* is represented by the TcpChannel class type and is used to pass messages using the TCP/IP network protocol. TcpChannel is helpful in that the formatted packets are quite lightweight, given that the messages are converted into a tight binary format using a related BinaryFormatter (yes, the same BinaryFormatter you saw in Chapter 17). Use of the TcpChannel type tends to result in faster remote access. The downside is that TCP channels are not firewall-friendly and may require the services of a system administrator to allow messages to pass across machine boundaries.

In contrast, the *HTTP channel* is represented by the HttpChannel class type, which converts message objects into a SOAP format using a related SOAP formatter. As you have seen, SOAP is XML-based and thus tends to result in beefier payloads than the payloads used by the TcpChannel type. Given this, using the HttpChannel can result in slightly slower remote access. On the plus side, HTTP is far more firewall-friendly, given that most firewalls allow textual packets to be passed over port 80.

Finally, as of .NET 2.0, we have access to the *IPC channel*, represented by the IpcChannel type, which defines a communication channel for remoting using the IPC system of the Windows operating system. Because IpcChannel bypasses traditional network communication to cross AppDomains, the IpcChannel is much faster than the HTTP and TCP channels; however, it can be used only for communication between application domains *on the same physical computer*. Given this, you could never use IpcChannel to build a distributed application that spans multiple physical computers. IpcChannel can be an ideal option, however, when you wish to have two local programs share information in the fastest possible manner.

Regardless of which channel type you choose to use, understand that the HttpChannel, TcpChannel, and IpcChannel types all implement the IChannel, IChannelSender, and IChannelReceiver interfaces. The IChannel interface (as you will see in just a bit) defines a small set of members that provide common functionality to all channel types. The role of IChannelSender is to define a common set of members for channels that are able to send information *to* a specific receiver. On the other hand, IChannelReceiver defines a set of members that allow a channel to receive information *from* a given sender.

To allow the client and server applications to register their channel of choice, you will make use of the ChannelServices.RegisterChannel() method, which takes a type implementing IChannel. Just to preview things to come, the following code snippet illustrates how a server-side application domain can register an HTTP channel on port 32469 (you'll see the client's role shortly):

```
// Create and register a server-side HttpChannel on port 32469.
HttpChannel c = new HttpChannel(32469);
ChannelServices.RegisterChannel(c);
```

Revisiting the Role of .NET Formatters

The final piece of the .NET remoting puzzle is the role of *formatter* objects. The TcpChannel and HttpChannel types both leverage an internal formatter, whose job it is to translate the message object into protocol-specific terms. As mentioned, the TcpChannel type makes use of the BinaryFormatter type, while the HttpChannel type uses the functionality provided by the SoapFormatter type. Given your work in the previous chapter, you should already have some insights as to how a given channel will format the incoming messages.

Once the formatted message has been generated, it is passed into the channel, where it will eventually reach its destination application domain, at which time the message is formatted from protocol-specific terms back to .NET-specific terms, at which point an entity termed the *dispatcher* invokes the correct method on the remote object.

All Together Now!

If your head is spinning from reading the previous sections, fear not! The transparent proxy, real proxy, message object, and dispatcher can typically be completely ignored, provided you are happy with the default remoting plumbing. To help solidify the sequence of events, ponder Figure 18-1, which illustrates the basic process of two objects communicating across distinct application domains.

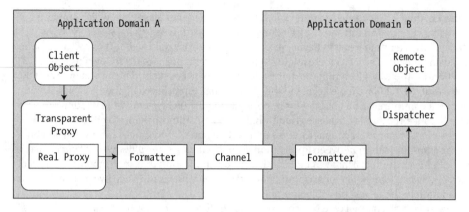

Figure 18-1. *A high-level view of the default .NET remoting architecture*

A Brief Word Regarding Extending the Default Plumbing

A key aspect of the .NET remoting layer is the fact that most of the default remoting layers can be extended or completely replaced at the whim of the developer. Thus, if you truly want (or possibly need) to build a custom message dispatcher, custom formatter, or custom real proxy, you are free to do so. You are also able to inject *additional* levels of indirection by plugging in custom types that stand between a given layer (e.g., a custom sink used to perform preprocessing or postprocessing of a given message). Now, to be sure, you may never need to retrofit the core .NET remoting layer in such ways. However, the fact remains that the .NET platform does provide the namespaces to allow you to do so.

■**Note** This chapter does not address the topic of extending the default .NET remoting layer. If you wish to learn how to do so, check out *Advanced .NET Remoting* by Ingo Rammer (Apress, 2002).

Terms of the .NET Remoting Trade

Like any new paradigm, .NET remoting brings a number of TLAs (three-letter acronyms) into the mix. Thus, before you see your first code example, we do need to define a few terms used when describing the composition of a .NET remoting application. As you would guess, this terminology is used to describe a number of details regarding common questions that arise during the construction of a distributed application: How do we pass a type across application domain boundaries? When exactly is a remote type activated? How do we manage the lifetime of a remote object (and so forth)? Once you have an understanding of the related terminology, the act of building a distributed .NET application will be far less perplexing.

Object Marshaling Choices: MBR or MBV?

Under the .NET platform, you have two options regarding how a remote object is marshaled to the client. Simply put, *marshaling* describes how a remote object is passed between application domains. When you are designing a remotable object, you may choose to employ *marshal-by-reference* (*MBR*) or *marshal-by-value* (*MBV*) semantics. The distinction is as follows:

- *MBR objects*: The caller receives a proxy to the remote object.

- *MBV objects*: The caller receives a full copy of the object in its own application domain.

If you configure an MBR object type, the CLR ensures that the transparent and real proxies are created in the client's application domain, while the MBR object itself remains in the server's application domain. As the client invokes methods on the remote type, the .NET remoting plumbing (examined previously) takes over the show and will package, pass, and return information between application domain boundaries. To be sure, MBR objects have a number of traits above and beyond their physical location. As you will see, MBR objects have various configuration options regarding their activation options and lifetime management.

MBV objects, on the other hand, are *local copies* of remote objects (which leverage the .NET serialization protocol examined in Chapter 17). MBV objects have far fewer configuration settings, given that their lifetime is directly controlled by the client. Like any .NET object, once a client has released all references to an MBV type, it is a candidate for garbage collection. Given that MBV types are local copies of remote objects, as a client invokes members on the type, no network activity occurs during the process.

Now, understand that it will be quite common for a single server to provide access to numerous MBR and MBV types. As you may also suspect, MBR types tend to support methods that return various MBV types, which gives way to the familiar factory pattern (e.g., an object that creates and returns other related objects). The next question is, how do you configure your custom class types as MBR or MBV entities?

Configuring an MBV Object

The process of configuring an object as an MBV type is identical to the process of configuring an object for serialization. Simply annotate the type with the [Serializable] attribute:

```
[Serializable]
public class SportsCar
{...}
```

Configuring an MBR Object

MBR objects are not marked as such using a .NET attribute, but rather by deriving (directly or indirectly) from the System.MarshalByRefObject base class:

```
public class SportsCarFactory : MarshalByRefObject
{...}
```

Formally, the MarshalByRefObject type is defined as follows:

```
public abstract class MarshalByRefObject : object
{
    public virtual ObjRef CreateObjRef(Type requestedType);
    public virtual bool Equals(object obj);
    public virtual int GetHashCode();
    public virtual object GetLifetimeService();
    public Type GetType();
    public virtual object InitializeLifetimeService();
    public virtual string ToString();
}
```

Beyond the expected functionality provided by System.Object, Table 18-2 describes the role of the remaining members.

Table 18-2. *Key Members of* `System.MarshalByRefObject`

Member	Meaning in Life
`CreateObjRef()`	Creates an object that contains all the relevant information required to generate a proxy used to communicate with a remote object
`GetLifetimeServices()`	Retrieves the current lifetime service object that controls the lifetime policy for this instance
`InitializeLifetimeServices()`	Obtains a lifetime service object to control the lifetime policy for this instance

As you can tell, the gist of `MarshalByRefObject` is to define members that can be overridden to programmatically control the lifetime of the MBR object (more on lifetime management later in this chapter).

■**Note** Just because you have configured a type as an MBV or MBR entity does not mean it is only usable within a remoting application, just that it *may* be used in a remoting application. For example, the `System.Windows.Forms.Form` type is a descendent of `MarshalByRefObject`; thus, if accessed remotely it is realized as an MBR type. If not, it is just another local object in the client's application domain.

■**Note** As a corollary to the previous note, understand that if a .NET type is not serializable and does not include `MarshalByRefObject` in its inheritance chain, the type in question can only be activated and used in the originating application domain (meaning, the type is *context bound*; see Chapter 13 for more details).

Now that you understand the distinct traits of MBR and MBV types, let's check out some issues that are specific to MBR types (MBV types need not apply).

Activation Choices for MBR Types: WKO or CAO?

Another remoting-centric choice you face as a .NET programmer has to do with exactly *when* an MBR object is activated and *when* it should be a candidate for garbage collection on the server. This might seem like a strange choice to make, as you might naturally assume that MBR objects are created when the client requests them and die when the client is done with them. While it is true that the client is the entity in charge of instructing the remoting layer it wishes to communicate with a remote type, the server application domain may (or may not) create the type at the exact moment the client's code base requests it.

The reason for this seemingly strange behavior has to do with the optimization. Specifically, every MBR type may be configured to be activated using one of two techniques:

- As a well-known object (WKO)
- As a client-activated object (CAO)

■**Note** A potential point of confusion is that fact that the acronym WKO is also called a *server-activated object* (*SAO*) in the .NET literature. In fact, you may see the SAO acronym in various .NET-centric articles and books. In keeping with the current terminology, I will use WKO throughout this chapter.

WKO objects are MBR types whose lifetimes are directly controlled by the server's application domain. The client-side application activates the remote type using a friendly, well-known string name (hence the term WKO). The server's application domain allocates WKO types when the client makes the first method call on the object (via the transparent proxy), *not* when the client's code base makes use of the new keyword or via the static `Activator.GetObject()` method, for example:

```
// Get a proxy to remote object. This line does NOT create the WKO type!
object remoteObj = Activator.GetObject( /* params seen later... */ );

// Invoke a method on remote WKO type. This WILL create the WKO object
// and invoke the ReturnMessage() method.
RemoteMessageObject simple = (RemoteMessageObject)remoteObj;
Console.WriteLine("Server says: {0}", simple.ReturnMessage());
```

The rationale for this behavior? This approach saves a network round-trip solely for the purpose of creating the object. As another interesting corollary, WKO types can *be created only via the type's default constructor*. This should make sense, given that the remote type's constructor is triggered only when the client makes the initial member invocation. Thus, the runtime has no other option than to invoke the type's default constructor.

Note Always remember: All WKO types must support a default constructor!

If you wish to allow the client to create a remote MBR object using a custom constructor, the server must configure the object as a CAO. CAO objects are entities whose lifetime is controlled by the client's application domain. When accessing a CAO type, a round-trip to the server occurs at the time the client makes use of the new keyword (using any of the type's constructors) or via the `Activator` type.

Stateful Configuration of WKO Types: Singleton or Single Call?

The final .NET design choice to consider with regard to MBR types has to do with how the server should handle multiple requests to a WKO type. CAO types need not apply, given that there is always a one-to-one correspondence between a client and a remote CAO type (because they are stateful).

Your first option is to configure a WKO type to function as a *singleton type*. The CLR will create a single instance of the remote type that will take requests from any number of clients, and it is a natural choice if you need to maintain stateful information among multiple remote callers. Given the fact that multiple clients could invoke the same method at the same time, the CLR places each client invocation on a new thread. It is *your* responsibility, however, to ensure that your objects are thread-safe using the same techniques described in Chapter 14.

In contrast, a *single call* object is a WKO type that exists only during the context of a single method invocation. Thus, if there are 20 clients making use of a WKO type configured with single call semantics, the server will create 20 distinct objects (one for each client), all of which are candidates for garbage collection directly after the method invocation. As you can guess, single call objects are far more scalable than singleton types, given that they are invariably stateless entities.

The server is the entity in charge of determining the stateful configuration of a given WKO type. Programmatically, these options are expressed via the `System.Runtime.Remoting.WellKnownObjectMode` enumeration:

```
public enum WellKnownObjectMode
{
    SingleCall,
    Singleton
}
```

Summarizing the Traits of MBR Object Types

As you have seen, configuring an MBV object is a no-brainer: Apply the [Serializable] attribute to allow copies of the type to be returned to the client's application domain. At this point, all interaction with the MBV type takes place in the client's locale. When the client is finished using the MBV type, it is a candidate for garbage collection, and all is well with the world.

With MBR types, however, you have a number of possible configuration choices. As you have seen, a given MBR type can be configured with regard to its time of activation, statefulness, and lifetime management. To summarize the array of possibilities, Table 18-3 documents how WKO and CAO types stack up against the traits you have just examined.

Table 18-3. *Configuration Options for MBR Types*

MBR Object Trait	WKO Behavior	CAO Behavior
Instantiation options	WKO types can only be activated using the default constructor of the type, which is triggered when the client makes the first method invocation.	CAO types can be activated using any constructor of the type. The remote object is created at the point the caller makes use of constructor semantics (or via the Activator type).
State management	WKO types can be configured as singleton or single call entities. Singleton types can service multiple clients and are therefore stateful. Single call types are alive only during a specific client-side invocation and are therefore stateless.	The lifetime of a CAO type is dictated by the caller; therefore, CAO types are stateful entities.
Lifetime management	Singleton WKO types make use of a lease-based management scheme (described later in this chapter). Single call WKO types are candidates for garbage collection after the current method invocation.	CAO types make use of a lease-based management scheme (described later in this chapter).

Basic Deployment of a .NET Remoting Project

Enough acronyms! At this point you are almost ready to build your first .NET remoting application. Before you do, however, I need to discuss one final detail: deployment. When you are building a .NET remoting application, you are almost certain to end up with three (yes, three, not two) distinct .NET assemblies that will constitute the entirety of your remote application. I am sure you can already account for the first two assemblies:

- *The client*: This assembly is the entity that is interested in obtaining access to a remote object (such as a Windows Forms or console application).

- *The server*: This assembly is the entity that receives channel requests from the remote client and hosts the remote objects.

So then, where does the third assembly fit in? In many cases, the server application is typically a host to a third assembly that defines and implements the remote objects. For convenience, I'll call this assembly the *general assembly*. This decoupling of the assembly containing the remote objects and server host is quite important, in that both the client and the server assemblies typically set a reference to the general assembly to obtain the metadata definitions of the remotable types.

In the simplest case, the general assembly is placed into the application directory of the client and server. The only possible drawback to this approach is the fact that the client has a reference to an assembly that contains CIL code that is never used (which may be a problem if you wish to ensure that the end user cannot view proprietary code). Specifically, the only reason the client requires a reference to the general assembly is to obtain the metadata descriptions of the remotable types. You can overcome this glitch in several ways, for example:

- Construct your remote objects to make use of interface-based programming techniques. Given this, the client is able to set a reference to a .NET binary that contains nothing but interface definitions.

- Make use of the soapsuds.exe command-line application. Using this tool, you are able to generate an assembly that contains nothing but metadata descriptions of the remote types.

- Manually build an assembly that contains nothing but metadata descriptions of the remote types.

To keep things simple over the course of this chapter, you will build and deploy general assemblies that contain the required metadata as well as the CIL implementation.

> **Note** If you wish to examine how to implement general assemblies using each of these alternatives, check out *Distributed .NET Programming in C#* by Tom Barnaby (Apress, 2002).

Building Your First Distributed Application

There is nothing more satisfying than building a distributed application using a new platform. To illustrate how quickly you're able to get up and running with the .NET remoting layer, let's build a simple example. As mentioned, the entirety of this example consists of three .NET assemblies:

- A general assembly named SimpleRemotingAsm.dll
- A client assembly named SimpleRemoteObjectClient.exe
- A server assembly named SimpleRemoteObjectServer.exe

Building the General Assembly

First, let's create the general assembly, SimpleRemotingAsm.dll, which will be referenced by both the server and client applications. SimpleRemotingAsm.dll defines a single MBR type named RemoteMessageObject, which supports two public members. The DisplayMessage() method prints a client-supplied message on the server's console window, while ReturnMessage() returns a message to the client. Here is the complete code of this new C# class library:

```
namespace SimpleRemotingAsm
{
    // This is a type that will be
    // marshaled by reference (MBR) if accessed remotely.
    public class RemoteMessageObject: MarshalByRefObject
    {
        public RemoteMessageObject()
        { Console.WriteLine("Constructing RemoteMessageObject!"); }
```

```
// This method takes an input string
// from the caller.
public void DisplayMessage(string msg)
{ Console.WriteLine("Message is: {0}", msg);}

// This method returns a value to the caller.
public string ReturnMessage()
{ return "Hello from the server!"; }
    }
}
```

The major point of interest is the fact that the type derives from the System.MarshalByRefObject base class, which ensures that the derived class will be accessible via a client-side proxy. Also note the custom default constructor that will print out a message when an instance of the type comes to life. That's it. Go ahead and build your new SimpleRemotingAsm.dll assembly.

Building the Server Assembly

Recall that server assemblies are essentially hosts for general assemblies that contain the remotable objects. Create a console program named SimpleRemoteObjectServer. The role of this assembly is to open a channel for the incoming requests and register RemoteMessageObject as a WKO. To begin, reference the System.Runtime.Remoting.dll and SimpleRemotingAsm.dll assemblies, and update Main() as follows:

```
using System;
using System.Runtime.Remoting;
using System.Runtime.Remoting.Channels;
using System.Runtime.Remoting.Channels.Http;
using SimpleRemotingAsm;

namespace SimpleRemoteObjectServer
{
    class SimpleObjServer
    {
        static void Main(string[] args)
        {
            Console.WriteLine("***** SimpleRemoteObjectServer started! *****");
            Console.WriteLine("Hit enter to end.");

            // Register a new HttpChannel
            HttpChannel c = new HttpChannel(32469);
            ChannelServices.RegisterChannel(c);

            // Register a WKO type, using singleton activation.
            RemotingConfiguration.RegisterWellKnownServiceType(
                typeof(SimpleRemotingAsm.RemoteMessageObject),
                "RemoteMsgObj.soap",
                WellKnownObjectMode.Singleton);
            Console.ReadLine();
        }
    }
}
```

Main() begins by creating a new HttpChannel type using an arbitrary port ID. This port is opened on registering the channel via the static ChannelServices.RegisterChannel() method. Once the channel as been registered, the remote server assembly is now equipped to process incoming messages via port number 32469.

> **Note** The number you assign to a port is typically up to you (or your system administrator). Do be aware, however, that port IDs below 1024 are reserved for system use.

Next, to register the `SimpleRemotingAsm.RemoteMessageObject` type as a WKO requires the use of the `RemotingConfiguration.RegisterWellKnownServiceType()` method. The first argument to this method is the type information of the type to be registered. The second parameter to `RegisterWellKnownServiceType()` is a simple string (of your choosing) that will be used to identify the object across application domain boundaries. Here, you are informing the CLR that this object is to be realized by the client using the name `RemoteMsgObj.soap`.

The final parameter is a member of the `WellKnownObjectMode` enumeration, which you have specified as `WellKnownObjectMode.Singleton`. Recall that singleton WKO types ensure that a single instance of the `RemoteMessageObject` will service all incoming requests. Build your server assembly and let's move on to the client-side code.

Building the SimpleRemoteObjectClient.exe Assembly

Now that you have a listener that is hosting your remotable object, the final step is to build an assembly that will request access to its services. Again, let's use a simple console application. Set a reference to `System.Runtime.Remoting.dll` and `SimpleRemotingAsm.dll`. Implement `Main()` as follows:

```
using System;
using System.Runtime.Remoting;
using System.Runtime.Remoting.Channels;
using System.Runtime.Remoting.Channels.Http;
using SimpleRemotingAsm;

namespace SimpleRemoteObjectClient
{
    class SimpleObjClient
    {
        static void Main(string[] args)
        {
            Console.WriteLine("***** SimpleRemoteObjectClient started! *****");
            Console.WriteLine("Hit enter to end.");

            // Create a new HttpChannel.
            HttpChannel c = new HttpChannel();
            ChannelServices.RegisterChannel(c);

            // Get a proxy to remote WKO type.
            object remoteObj = Activator.GetObject(
                typeof(SimpleRemotingAsm.RemoteMessageObject),
                "http://localhost:32469/RemoteMsgObj.soap");

            // Now use the remote object.
            RemoteMessageObject simple = (RemoteMessageObject)remoteObj;
            simple.DisplayMessage("Hello from the client!");
            Console.WriteLine("Server says: {0}", simple.ReturnMessage());
            Console.ReadLine();
        }
    }
}
```

A few notes about this client application. First, notice that the client is also required to register an HTTP channel, but the client does not specify a port ID, as the end point is specified by the client-supplied activation URL. Given that the client is interacting with a registered WKO type, you are limited to triggering the type's default constructor. To do so, make use of the `Activator.GetObject()` method, specifying two parameters. The first is the type information that describes the remote object you are interested in interacting with. Read that last sentence again. Given that the `Activator.GetObject()` method requires the object's metadata description, it should make more sense as to why the client is *also* required to reference the general assembly! Again, at the end of the chapter you'll examine various ways to clean up this aspect of your client-side assembly.

The second parameter to `Activator.GetObject()` is termed the *activation URL*. Activation URLs that describe a WKO type can be generalized into the following format:

```
ProtocolScheme://ComputerName:Port/ObjectUri
```

Finally, note that the `Activator.GetObject()` method returns a generic `System.Object` type, and thus you must make use of an explicit cast to gain access to the members of the `RemoteMessageObject`.

Testing the Remoting Application

To test your application, begin by launching the server application, which will open an HTTP channel and register `RemoteMessageObject` for remote for access. Next, launch an instance of the client application. If all is well, your server window should appear as shown in Figure 18-2, while the client application displays what you see in Figure 18-3.

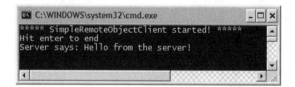

Figure 18-2. *The server's output*

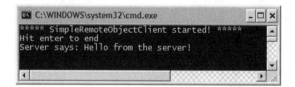

Figure 18-3. *The client's output*

Understanding the ChannelServices Type

As you have seen, when a server application wishes to advertise the existence of a remote type, it makes use of the `System.Runtime.Remoting.Channels.ChannelServices` type. `ChannelServices` provides a small set of static methods that aid in the process of remoting channel registration, resolution, and URL discovery. Table 18-4 documents some of the core members.

Table 18-4. *Select Members of the* ChannelServices *Type*

Member	Meaning in Life
RegisteredChannels	This property gets or sets a list of currently registered channels, each of which is represented by the IChannel interface.
DispatchMessage()	This method dispatches incoming remote calls.
GetChannel()	This method returns a registered channel with the specified name.
GetUrlsForObject()	This method returns an array of all the URLs that can be used to reach the specified object.
RegisterChannel()	This method registers a channel with the channel services.
UnregisterChannel()	This method unregisters a particular channel from the registered channels list.

In addition to the aptly named RegisterChannel() and UnregisterChannel() methods, ChannelServices defines the RegisteredChannels property. This member returns an array of IChannel interfaces, each representing a handle to each channel registered in a given application domain. The definition of the IChannel interface is quite straightforward:

```
public interface IChannel
{
    string ChannelName { get; }
    int ChannelPriority { get; }
    string Parse(string url, ref String objectURI);
}
```

As you can see, each channel is given a friendly string name as well as a priority level. To illustrate, if you were to update the Main() method of the SimpleRemoteObjectClient application with the following logic:

```
// List all registered channels.
IChannel[] channelObjs = ChannelServices.RegisteredChannels;
foreach(IChannel i in channelObjs)
{
    Console.WriteLine("Channel name: {0}", i.ChannelName);
    Console.WriteLine("Channel Priority: {0}", i.ChannelPriority);
}
```

you would find the client-side console now looks like Figure 18-4.

Figure 18-4. *Enumerating client-side channels*

Understanding the RemotingConfiguration Type

Another key remoting-centric type is RemotingConfiguration, which as its name suggests is used to configure various aspects of a remoting application. Currently, you have seen this type in use on the server side (via the call to the RegisterWellKnownServiceType() method). Table 18-5 lists additional static members of interest, some of which you'll see in action over the remainder of this chapter.

Table 18-5. *Members of the* RemotingConfiguration *Type*

Member	Meaning in Life
ApplicationId	Gets the ID of the currently executing application
ApplicationName	Gets or sets the name of a remoting application
ProcessId	Gets the ID of the currently executing process
Configure()	Reads the configuration file and configures the remoting infrastructure
GetRegisteredActivatedClientTypes()	Retrieves an array of object types registered on the client as types that will be activated remotely
GetRegisteredActivatedServiceTypes()	Retrieves an array of object types registered on the service end that can be activated on request from a client
GetRegisteredWellKnownClientTypes()	Retrieves an array of object types registered on the client end as well-known types
GetRegisteredWellKnownServiceTypes()	Retrieves an array of object types registered on the service end as well-known types
IsWellKnownClientType()	Checks whether the specified object type is registered as a well-known client type
RegisterActivatedClientType()	Registers an object on the client end as a type that can be activated on the server
RegisterWellKnownClientType()	Registers an object on the client end as a well-known type (single call or singleton)
RegisterWellKnownServiceType()	Registers an object on the service end as a well-known type (single call or singleton)

Recall that the .NET remoting layer distinguishes between two types of MBR objects: WKO (server-activated) and CAO (client-activated). Furthermore, WKO types can be configured to make use of singleton or single call activations. Using the functionality of the RemotingConfiguration type, you are able to dynamically obtain such information at runtime. For example, if you update the Main() method of your SimpleRemoteObjectServer application with the following:

```
static void Main(string[] args)
{
...
    // Set a friendly name for this server app.
    RemotingConfiguration.ApplicationName = "First server app!";
    Console.WriteLine("App Name: {0}",
        RemotingConfiguration.ApplicationName);

    // Get an array of WellKnownServiceTypeEntry types
    // that represent all the registered WKOs.
    WellKnownServiceTypeEntry[] WKOs =
        RemotingConfiguration.GetRegisteredWellKnownServiceTypes();
    // Now print their statistics.
```

```
    foreach(WellKnownServiceTypeEntry wko in WKOs)
    {
        Console.WriteLine("Asm name containing WKO: {0}", wko.AssemblyName);
        Console.WriteLine("URL to WKO: {0}", wko.ObjectUri);
        Console.WriteLine("Type of WKO: {0}", wko.ObjectType);
        Console.WriteLine("Mode of WKO: {0}", wko.Mode);
    }
}
```

you would find a list of all WKO types registered by this server application domain. As you iterate over the array of WellKnownServiceTypeEntry types, you are able to print out various points of interest regarding each WKO. Given that your server's application registered only a single type (SimpleRemotingAsm.RemoteMessageObject), you'll receive the output shown in Figure 18-5.

Figure 18-5. *Server-side statistics*

The other major method of the RemotingConfiguration type is Configure(). As you'll see in just a bit, this static member allows the client- and server-side application domains to make use of remoting configuration files.

Revisiting the Activation Mode of WKO Types

Recall that WKO types can be configured to function under singleton or single call activation. Currently, your server application has registered your WKO to employ singleton activation semantics:

```
// Singletons can service multiple clients.
RemotingConfiguration.RegisterWellKnownServiceType(
    typeof(SimpleRemotingAsm.RemoteMessageObject),
    "RemoteMsgObj.soap",
    WellKnownObjectMode.Singleton);
```

Again, singleton WKOs are capable of receiving requests from multiple clients. Thus, singleton objects maintain a one-to-many relationship between themselves and the remote clients. To test this behavior for yourself, run the server application (if it is not currently running) and launch three separate client applications. If you look at the output for the server, you will find a single call to the RemoteMessageObject's default constructor.

Now to test the behavior of single call objects, modify the server to register the WKO to support single call activation:

```
// Single call types maintain a 1-to-1 relationship
// between client and WKO.
RemotingConfiguration.RegisterWellKnownServiceType(
    typeof(SimpleRemotingAsm.RemoteMessageObject),
    "RemoteMsgObj.soap",
    WellKnownObjectMode.SingleCall);
```

Once you have recompiled and run the server application, again launch three clients. This time you can see that a new RemoteMessageObject is created for each client request. As you might be able to gather, if you wish to share stateful data between multiple remote clients, singleton activation provides one possible alternative, as all clients are communicating with a single instance of the remote object.

■**Source Code** The SimpleRemotingAsm, SimpleRemoteObjectServer, and SimpleRemoteObjectClient projects are located under the Chapter 18 directory.

Deploying the Server to a Remote Machine

At this point, you have just crossed an application and process boundary on a single machine. If you're connected to an additional machine, let's extend this example to allow the client to interact with the RemoteMessageObject type across a machine boundary. To do so, follow these steps:

1. On your server machine, create and share a folder to hold your server-side assemblies.

2. Copy the SimpleRemoteObjectServer.exe and SimpleRemotingAsm.dll assemblies to this server-side share point.

3. Open your SimpleRemoteObjectClient project workspace and retrofit the activation URL to specify the name of the remote machine, for example:

```
// Get a proxy to remote object.
object remoteObj = Activator.GetObject(
    typeof(SimpleRemotingAsm.RemoteMessageObject),
    "http://YourRemoteBoxName:32469/RemoteMsgObj.soap");
```

4. Execute the SimpleRemoteObjectServer.exe application on the server machine.

5. Execute the SimpleRemoteObjectClient.exe application on the client machine.

6. Sit back and grin.

■**Note** Activation URLs may specify a machine's IP address in place of its friendly name.

Leveraging the TCP Channel

Currently, your remote object is accessible via the HTTP network protocol. As mentioned, this protocol is quite firewall-friendly, but the resulting SOAP packets are a bit on the bloated side (given the nature of XML data representation). To lighten the payload, you can update the client and server assemblies to make use of the TCP channel, and therefore make use of the BinaryFormatter type behind the scenes. Here are the relevant updates to the server assembly:

■**Note** When you are defining an object to be URI-accessible via a TCP endpoint, it is common (but not required) to make use of the *.rem (i.e., remote) extension.

```
// Server adjustments!
using System.Runtime.Remoting.Channels.Tcp;
...
static void Main(string[] args)
```

```
{
...
    // Create a new TcpChannel
    TcpChannel c = new  TcpChannel(32469);
    ChannelServices.RegisterChannel(c);

    // Register a 'well-known' object in single call mode.
    RemotingConfiguration.RegisterWellKnownServiceType(
        typeof(SimpleRemotingAsm.RemoteMessageObject),
        "RemoteMsgObj.rem",
        WellKnownObjectMode.SingleCall);
    Console.ReadLine();
}
```

Notice that you are now registering a System.Runtime.Remoting.Channels.Tcp.TcpChannel type to the .NET remoting layer. Also note that the object URI has been altered to support a more generic name (RemoteMsgObj.rem) rather than the SOAP-centric *.soap extension. The client-side updates are equally as simple:

```
// Client adjustments!
using System.Runtime.Remoting.Channels.Tcp;
...
static void Main(string[] args)
{
...
    // Create a new TcpChannel
    TcpChannel c = new TcpChannel();
    ChannelServices.RegisterChannel(c);
    // Get a proxy to remote object.
    object remoteObj = Activator.GetObject(
        typeof(SimpleRemotingAsm.RemoteMessageObject),
        "tcp://localhost:32469/RemoteMsgObj.rem");

    // Use object.
    RemoteMessageObject simple = (RemoteMessageObject)remoteObj;
    simple.DisplayMessage("Hello from the client!");
    Console.WriteLine("Server says: {0}", simple.ReturnMessage());
    Console.ReadLine();
}
```

The only point to be aware of here is that the client's activation URL now must specify the tcp:// channel qualifier rather than http://. Beyond that, the bulk of the code base is identical to the previous HttpChannel logic.

■**Source Code** The TCPSimpleRemoteObjectServer and TCPSimpleRemoteObjectClient projects are located under the Chapter 18 directory (both projects use the SimpleRemotingAsm.dll created previously).

A Brief Word Regarding the IpcChannel

Before moving on to an examination of remoting configuration files, recall that .NET 2.0 also provides the IpcChannel type, which provides the fastest possible manner in which two applications *on the same machine* can exchange information. Given that this chapter is geared toward covering distributed programs that involve two or more computers, interested readers should look up IpcChannel in the .NET Framework 2.0 SDK documentation (as you might guess, the code is just about identical to working with HttpChannel and TcpChannel).

Remoting Configuration Files

At this point you have successfully built a distributed application using the .NET remoting layer. One issue you may have noticed in these first examples is the fact that the client and the server applications have a good deal of hard-coded logic within their respective binaries. For example, the server specifies a fixed port ID, fixed activation mode, and fixed channel type. The client, on the other hand, hard-codes the name of the remote object it is attempting to interact with.

As you might agree, it is wishful thinking to assume that initial design notes remain unchanged once an application is deployed. Ideally, details such as port ID and object activation mode (and whatnot) could be altered on the fly without needing to recompile and redistribute the client or server code bases. Under the .NET remoting scheme, all the aforementioned issues can be circumvented using the remoting configuration file.

As you will recall from Chapter 11, *.config can be used to provide hints to the CLR regarding the loading of externally referenced assemblies. The same *.config files can be used to inform the CLR of a number of remoting-related details, on both the client side and the server side.

When you build a remoting *.config file, the <system.runtime.remoting> element is used to hold various remoting-centric details. Do be aware that if you're building an application that already has a *.config file that specifies assembly resolution details, you're free to add remoting elements within the same file. Thus, a single *.config file that contains remoting and binding information would look something like this:

```
<configuration>
    <system.runtime.remoting>
        <! -- configure client/server remoting settings here -- >
    </system.runtime.remoting>
    <runtime>
        <! -- binding assembly settings here -- >
    </runtime>
</configuration>
```

If your configuration file has no need to specify assembly binding logic, you can omit the <runtime> element and make use of the following skeleton *.config file:

```
<configuration>
    <system.runtime.remoting>
        <! -- configure client/server remoting settings here -- >
    </system.runtime.remoting>
</configuration>
```

Building Server-Side *.config Files

Server-side configuration files allow you to declare the objects that are to be reached via remote invocations as well as channel and port information. Basically, using the <service>, <wellknown>, and <channels> elements, you are able to replace the following server-side logic:

```
// Hard-coded HTTP server logic.
HttpChannel c = new HttpChannel(32469);
ChannelServices.RegisterChannel(c);
RemotingConfiguration.RegisterWellKnownServiceType(
    typeof(SimpleRemotingAsm.RemoteMessageObject),
    "RemoteMsgObj.soap",
    WellKnownObjectMode.Singleton);
```

with the following *.config file:

```
<configuration>
  <system.runtime.remoting>
    <application>
      <service>
        <wellknown
          mode="Singleton"
          type="SimpleRemotingAsm.RemoteMessageObject, SimpleRemotingAsm"
          objectUri="RemoteMsgObj.soap"/>
      </service>
      <channels>
          <channel ref="http" port="32469"/>
      </channels>
    </application>
  </system.runtime.remoting>
</configuration>
```

Notice that much of the relevant server-side remoting information is wrapped within the scope of the <service> (not *server*) element. The child <wellknown> element makes use of three attributes (mode, type, and objectUri) to specify the well-known object to register with the .NET remoting layer. The child <channels> element contains any number of <channel> elements that allow you to define the type of channel (in this case, HTTP) to open on the server. TCP channels would simply make use of the tcp string token in place of http.

As the SimpleRemoteObjectServer.exe.config file contains all the necessary information, the server-side Main() method cleans up considerably. All you are required to do is make a single call to RemotingConfiguration.Configure() and specify the name of your configuration file.

```
static void Main(string[] args)
{
    // Register a 'well-known' object using a *.config file.
    RemotingConfiguration.Configure("SimpleRemoteObjectServer.exe.config");
    Console.WriteLine("Server started!  Hit enter to end");
    Console.ReadLine();
}
```

Building Client-Side *.config Files

Clients are also able to leverage remoting-centric *.config files. Unlike a server-side configuration file, client-side configuration files make use of the <client> element to identify the name of the well-known object the caller wishes to interact with. In addition to providing the ability to dynamically change the remoting information without the need to recompile the code base, client-side *.config files allow you to create the proxy type directly using the C# new keyword, rather than the Activator.GetObject() method. Thus, if you have the following client-side *.config file:

```
<configuration>
  <system.runtime.remoting>
    <application>
      <client displayName = "SimpleRemoteObjectClient">
        <wellknown
          type="SimpleRemotingAsm.RemoteMessageObject, SimpleRemotingAsm"
          url="http://localhost:32469/RemoteMsgObj.soap"/>
      </client>
      <channels>
          <channel ref="http"/>
      </channels>
    </application>
  </system.runtime.remoting>
</configuration>
```

you are able to update the client's Main() method as follows:

```
static void Main(string[] args)
{
    RemotingConfiguration.Configure("SimpleRemoteObjectClient.exe.config");
    // Using *.config file, the client is able to directly 'new' the type.
    RemoteMessageObject simple = new RemoteMessageObject();
    simple.DisplayMessage("Hello from the client!");
    Console.WriteLine("Server says: {0}", simple.ReturnMessage());
    Console.WriteLine("Client started!  Hit enter to end");
    Console.ReadLine();
}
```

Of course, when you run the application, the output is identical. If the client wishes to make use of the TCP channel, the url property of the <wellknown> element and <channel> ref property must make use of the tcp token in place of http.

■**Source Code** The SimpleRemoteObjectServerWithConfig and SimpleRemoteObjectClientWithConfig projects are located under the Chapter 18 subdirectory (both of which make use of the SimpleRemotingAsm.dll created previously).

Working with MBV Objects

Our first remoting applications allowed client-side access to a single WKO type. Recall that WKO types are (by definition) MBR types, and therefore client access takes place via an intervening proxy. In contrast, MBV types are local copies of a server-side object, which are typically returned from a public member of an MBR type. Although you already know how to configure an MBV type (mark a class with the [Serializable] attribute), you have not yet seen an example of MBV types in action (beyond passing string data between the two parties). To illustrate the interplay of MBR and MBV types, let's see another example involving three assemblies:

- The general assembly named CarGeneralAsm.dll

- The client assembly named CarProviderClient.exe

- The server assembly named CarProviderServer.exe

As you might assume, the code behind the client and server applications is more or less identical to the previous example, especially since these applications will again make use of *.config files. Nevertheless, let's step through the process of building each assembly one at a time.

Building the General Assembly

During our examination of object serialization in Chapter 17, you created a type named JamesBondCar (in addition to the dependent Radio and Car classes). The CarGeneralAsm.dll code library will reuse these types, so begin by using the Project ➤ Add Existing Item menu command and include these *.cs files into this new Class Library project (the automatically provided Class1.cs file can be deleted). Given that each of these types has already been marked with the [Serializable] attribute, they are ready to be marshaled by value to a remote client.

All you need now is an MBR type that provides access to the JamesBondCar type. To make things a bit more interesting, however, your MBR object (CarProvider) will maintain a generic List<> of JamesBondCar types. CarProvider will also define two members that allow the caller to obtain a specific JamesBondCar as well as receive the entire List<> of types. Here is the complete code for the new class type:

```
namespace CarGeneralAsm
{
    // This type is an MBR object that provides
    // access to related MBV types.
    public class CarProvider : MarshalByRefObject
    {
        private List<JamesBondCar> theJBCars =
            new List<JamesBondCar>();

        // Add some cars to the list.
        public CarProvider()
        {
            Console.WriteLine("Car provider created");
            theJBCars.Add(new JamesBondCar("QMobile", 140, true, true));
            theJBCars.Add(new JamesBondCar("Flyer", 140, true, false));
            theJBCars.Add(new JamesBondCar("Swimmer", 140, false, true));
            theJBCars.Add(new JamesBondCar("BasicJBC", 140, false, false));
        }
        // Get all the JamesBondCars.
        public List<JamesBondCar>  GetAllAutos()
        { return theJBCars; }
        // Get one JamesBondCar.
        public JamesBondCar GetJBCByIndex(int i)
        { return (JamesBondCar)theJBCars[i]; }
    }
}
```

Notice that the GetAllAutos() method returns the internal List<> type. The obvious question is how this member of the System.Collections.Generic namespace is marshaled back to the caller. If you look up this type using the .NET Framework 2.0 SDK documentation, you will find that List<> has been decorated with the [Serializable] attribute:

```
[SerializableAttribute()]
public class List<T> : IList, ICollection, IEnumerable
```

Therefore, the entire contents of the List<> type will be marshaled by value to the caller (provided the contained types are also serializable)! This brings up a very good point regarding .NET remoting and members of the base class libraries. In addition to the custom MBV and MBR types you may create yourself, understand that any type in the base class libraries that is decorated with the [Serializable] attribute is able to function as an MBV type in the .NET remoting architecture. Likewise, any type that derives (directly or indirectly) from MarshalByRefObject will function as an MBR type.

▓**Note** Be aware that the SoapFormatter does not support serialization of generic types. If you build methods that receive or return generic types (such as the List<>), you must make use of the BinaryFormatter and the TcpChannel object.

Building the Server Assembly

The server host assembly (CarProviderServer.exe) has the following logic within Main():

```
using System;
using System.Runtime.Remoting;
using System.Runtime.Remoting.Channels;
using System.Runtime.Remoting.Channels.Http;
using CarGeneralAsm;
```

```
namespace CarProviderServer
{
    class CarServer
    {
        static void Main(string[] args)
        {
            RemotingConfiguration.Configure("CarProviderServer.exe.config");
            Console.WriteLine("Car server started!  Hit enter to end");
            Console.ReadLine();
        }
    }
}
```

The related *.config file is just about identical to the server-side *.config file you created in the previous example. The only point of interest is to define an object URI value that makes sense for the CarProvider type:

```
<configuration>
    <system.runtime.remoting>
        <application>
            <service>
                <wellknown mode="Singleton"
                    type="CarGeneralAsm.CarProvider, CarGeneralAsm"
                    objectUri="carprovider.rem" />
            </service>
            <channels>
                <channel ref="tcp" port="32469" />
            </channels>
        </application>
    </system.runtime.remoting>
</configuration>
```

Building the Client Assembly

Last but not least, we have the client application that will make use of the MBR CarProvider type in order to obtain discrete JamesBondCars types as well as the List<> type. Once you obtain a type from the CarProvider, you'll send it into the UseCar() helper function from processing:

```
using System;
using System.Runtime.Remoting;
using System.Runtime.Remoting.Channels;
using System.Runtime.Remoting.Channels.Http;
using CarGeneralAsm;
using System.Collections.Generic;

namespace CarProviderClient
{
    class CarClient
    {
        private static void UseCar(JamesBondCar c)
        {
            Console.WriteLine("-> Name: {0}", c.PetName);
            Console.WriteLine("-> Max speed: {0}", c.MaxSpeed);
            Console.WriteLine("-> Seaworthy? : {0}", c.isSeaWorthy);
            Console.WriteLine("-> Flight worthy? : {0}", c.isFlightWorthy);
            Console.WriteLine();
        }
```

```
static void Main(string[] args)
{
    RemotingConfiguration.Configure("CarProviderClient.exe.config");
    // Make the car provider.
    CarProvider cp = new CarProvider();
    // Get first JBC.
    JamesBondCar qCar = cp.GetJBCByIndex(0);
    // Get all JBCs.
    List<JamesBondCar> allJBCs = cp.GetAllAutos();
    // Use first car.
    UseCar(qCar);
    // Use all cars in List<>.
    foreach(JamesBondCar j in allJBCs)
        UseCar(j);
    Console.WriteLine("Client started!  Hit enter to end");
    Console.ReadLine();
}
}
}
```

The client side *.config file is also what you would expect. Simply update the activation URL:

```
<configuration>
    <system.runtime.remoting>
        <application>
            <client displayName = "CarClient">
                <wellknown
                    type="CarGeneralAsm.CarProvider, CarGeneralAsm"
                    url="tcp://localhost:32469/carprovider.rem"/>
            </client>
            <channels>
                <channel ref="tcp"/>
            </channels>
        </application>
    </system.runtime.remoting>
</configuration>
```

Now, run your server and client applications (in that order, of course) and observe the output. Your client-side console window will whirl through the JamesBondCars and print out the statistics of each type. Recall that as you interact with the List<> and JamesBondCar types, you are operating on their members within the client's application domain, as they have both been marked with the [Serializable] attribute.

To prove that point, update the UseCar() helper function to call the TurnOnRadio() method on the incoming JamesBondCar. Now, run the server and client applications once again. Notice that the message box appears on the client machine! Had the Car, Radio, and JamesBondCar types been configured as MBR types, the server would be the machine displaying the message box prompts. If you wish to verify this, derive each type from MarshalByRefObject and recompile all three assemblies (to ensure Visual Studio 2005 copies the latest CarGeneralAsm.dll into the client's and server's application directory). When you run the application once again, the message boxes appear on the remote machine.

■**Source Code** The CarGeneralAsm, CarProviderServer, and CarProviderClient projects are located under the Chapter 18 subdirectory.

Understanding Client-Activated Objects

All of these current remoting examples have made use of WKOs. Recall that WKOs have the following characteristics:

- WKOs can be configured either as singleton or single call.
- WKOs can only be activated using the type's default constructor.
- WKOs are instantiated on the server on the first client-side member invocation.

CAO types on the other hand, can be instantiated using any constructor on the type and are created at the point the client makes use of the C# new keyword or Activator type. Furthermore, the lifetime of CAO types is monitored by the .NET leasing mechanism. Do be aware that when you configure a CAO type, the .NET remoting layer will generate a specific CAO remote object to service each client. Again, the big distinction is the fact that CAOs are always alive (and therefore stateful) beyond a single method invocation.

To illustrate the construction, hosting, and consumption of CAO types, let's retrofit the previous automobile-centric general assembly. Assume that your MBR CarProvider class has defined an additional constructor that allows the client to pass in an array of JamesBondCar types that will be used to populate the generic List<>:

```
public class CarProvider : MarshalByRefObject
{
    private List<JamesBondCar> theJBCars
        = new List<JamesBondCar>();

    public CarProvider(JamesBondCar[] theCars)
    {
        Console.WriteLine("Car provider created with custom ctor");
        theJBCars.AddRange(theCars);
    }
...
}
```

To allow the caller to activate the CarProvider using your new constructor syntax, you need to build a server application that registers CarProvider as a CAO type rather than a WKO type. This may be done programmatically (à la the RemotingConfiguration.RegisterActivatedServiceType() method) or using a server-side *.config file. If you wish to hard-code the name of the CAO object within the host server's code base, all you need to do is pass in the type information of the type(s) (after creating and registering a channel) as follows:

```
// Hard-code the fact that CarProvider is a CAO type.
RemotingConfiguration.RegisterActivatedServiceType(
    typeof(CAOCarGeneralAsm.CarProvider));
```

If you would rather leverage the *.config file, replace the <wellknown> element with the <activated> element as follows:

```
<configuration>
    <system.runtime.remoting>
        <application>
            <service>
                <activated type = "CAOCarGeneralAsm.CarProvider,
                    CAOCarGeneralAsm"/>
            </service>
            <channels>
                <channel ref="tcp" port="32469" />
            </channels>
```

```
        </application>
    </system.runtime.remoting>
</configuration>
```

Finally, you need to update the client application, not only by way of the *.config file (or pro-grammatically in the code base) to request access to the remote CAO, but also to indeed trigger the custom constructor of the CarProvider type. Here are the relevant updates to the client-side Main() method:

```
static void Main(string[] args)
{
    // Read updated *.config file.
    RemotingConfiguration.Configure("CAOCarProviderClient.exe.config");
    // Create array of types to pass to provider.
    JamesBondCar[] cars =
    {
        new JamesBondCar("Viper", 100, true, false),
        new JamesBondCar("Shaken", 100, false, true),
        new JamesBondCar("Stirred", 100, true, true)
    };
    // Now trigger the custom ctor.
    CarProvider cp = new CarProvider(cars);
...
}
```

The updated client-side *.config file also makes use of the <activated> element, as opposed to <wellknown>. In addition, the <client> element now requires the url property to define the location of the registered CAO. Recall that when the server registered the CarProvider as a WKO, the client specified such information within the <wellknown> element.

```
<configuration>
    <system.runtime.remoting>
        <application>
            <client displayName = "CarClient"
                    url = "tcp://localhost:32469">
                <activated type = "CAOCarGeneralAsm.CarProvider, CAOCarGeneralAsm" />
            </client>
            <channels>
                <channel ref="tcp"/>
            </channels>
        </application>
    </system.runtime.remoting>
</configuration>
```

If you would rather hard-code the client's request to the CAO type, you can make use of the RegistrationServices.RegisterActivatedClientType() method as follows:

```
static void Main(string[] args)
{
    // Use hard-coded values.
    RemotingConfiguration.RegisterActivatedClientType(
        typeof(CAOCarGeneralAsm.CarProvider),
        "tcp://localhost:32469");
...
}
```

If you now execute the updated server and client assemblies, you will be pleased to find that you are able to pass your custom array of JamesBondCar types to the remote CarProvider via the overloaded constructor.

The Lease-Based Lifetime of CAO/WKO-Singleton Objects

As you have seen, WKO types configured with single call activation are alive only for the duration of the current method call. Given this fact, WKO single call types are stateless entities. As soon as the current invocation has completed, the WKO single call type is a candidate for garbage collection.

On the other hand, CAO types and WKO types that have been configured to use singleton activation are both, by their nature, stateful entities. Given these two object configuration settings, the question that must be asked is, how does the server process know when to destroy these MBR objects? Clearly, it would be a huge problem if the server machine garbage-collected MBR objects that were currently in use by a remote client. If the server machine waits too long to release its set of MBR types, this may place undo stress on the system, especially if the MBR object(s) in question maintain valuable system resources (database connections, unmanaged types, and whatnot).

The lifetime of a CAO or WKO-singleton MBR type is governed by a "lease time" that is tightly integrated with the .NET garbage collector. If the lease time of a CAO or WKO-singleton MBR type expires, the object is ready to be garbage-collected on the next collection cycle. Like any .NET type, if the remote object has overridden System.Object.Finalize() (via the C# destructor syntax), the .NET runtime will indeed trigger the finalization logic.

The Default Leasing Behavior

CAO and WKO-singleton MBR types have what is known as a *default lease*, which lasts for five minutes. If the runtime detects five minutes of inactivity have passed for a CAO or WKO-singleton MBR type, the assumption is that the client is no longer making use of the object and therefore the remote object may be garbage-collected. However, when the default lease expires, this does not imply that the object is *immediately* marked for garbage collection. In reality, there are many ways to influence the behavior of the default lease.

First and foremost, anytime the remote client invokes a member of the remote CAO or WKO-singleton MBR type, the lease is renewed back to its five-minute limit. In addition to the automatic client-invocation-centric renew policy, the .NET runtime provides three additional alternatives:

- *.config files can be authored that override the default lease settings for remote objects.
- Server-side lease sponsors can be used to act on behalf of a remote object whose lease time has expired.
- Client-side lease sponsors can be used to act on behalf of a remote object whose lease time has expired.

We will check out these options over the next several sections, but for the time being let's examine the default lease settings of a remote type. Recall that the MarshalByRefObject base class defines a member named GetLifetimeService(). This method returns a reference to an internally implemented object that supports the System.Runtime.Remoting.Lifetime.ILease interface. As you would guess, the ILease interface can be used to interact with the leasing behavior of a given CAO or WKO-singleton type. Here is the formal definition:

```
public interface ILease
{
    TimeSpan CurrentLeaseTime { get; }
```

```
        LeaseState CurrentState { get; }
        TimeSpan InitialLeaseTime { get; set; }
        TimeSpan RenewOnCallTime { get; set; }
        TimeSpan SponsorshipTimeout { get; set; }
        void Register(System.Runtime.Remoting.Lifetime.ISponsor obj);
        void Register(System.Runtime.Remoting.Lifetime.ISponsor obj,
            TimeSpan renewalTime);
        TimeSpan Renew(TimeSpan renewalTime);
        void Unregister(System.Runtime.Remoting.Lifetime.ISponsor obj);
}
```

The ILease interface not only allows you to obtain information regarding the current lease (via CurrentLeaseTime, CurrentState, and InitialLeaseTime), but also provides the ability to build lease "sponsors" (more details on this later). Table 18-6 documents role of each ILease member.

Table 18-6. *Members of the* ILease *Interface*

Member	Meaning in Life
CurrentLeaseTime	Gets the amount of time remaining before the object deactivates, if it does not receive further method invocations.
CurrentState	Gets the current state of the lease, represented by the LeaseState enumeration.
InitialLeaseTime	Gets or sets the initial amount of time for a given lease. The initial lease time of an object is the amount of time following the initial activation before the lease expires if no other method calls occur.
RenewOnCallTime	Gets or sets the amount of time by which a call to the remote object increases the CurrentLeaseTime.
SponsorshipTimeout	Gets or sets the amount of time to wait for a sponsor to return with a lease renewal time.
Register()	Overloaded. Registers a sponsor for the lease.
Renew()	Renews a lease for the specified time.
Unregister()	Removes a sponsor from the sponsor list.

To illustrate the characteristics of the default lease of a CAO or WKO-singleton remote object, assume that your current CAOCarGeneralAsm project has defined a new internal class named LeaseInfo. LeaseInfo supports a static member named LeaseStats(), which dumps select statistics regarding the current lease for the CarProvider type to the server-side console window (be sure to specify a using directive for the System.Runtime.Remoting.Lifetime namespace to inform the compiler where the ILease type is defined):

```
internal class LeaseInfo
{
    public static void LeaseStats(ILease itfLease)
    {
        Console.WriteLine("***** Lease Stats *****");
        Console.WriteLine("Lease state: {0}", itfLease.CurrentState);
        Console.WriteLine("Initial lease time: {0}:{1}",
            itfLease.InitialLeaseTime.Minutes,
            itfLease.InitialLeaseTime.Seconds);
        Console.WriteLine("Current lease time: {0}:{1}",
            itfLease.CurrentLeaseTime.Minutes,
            itfLease.CurrentLeaseTime.Seconds);
        Console.WriteLine("Renew on call time: {0}:{1}",
            itfLease.RenewOnCallTime.Minutes,
```

```
            itfLease.RenewOnCallTime.Seconds);
        Console.WriteLine();
    }
}
```

Now that you have this helper type in place, assume LeaseInfo.LeaseStats() is called within the GetJBCByIndex() and GetAllAutos() methods of the CarProvider type. Once you recompile the server and client assemblies (again, simply to ensure Visual Studio 2005 copies the latest and greatest version of the CarGeneralAsm.dll to the client and server application directories), run the application once again. Your server's console window should now look something like Figure 18-6.

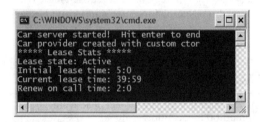

Figure 18-6. *The default lease information for* CarProvider

Altering the Default Lease Characteristics

Obviously, the default lease characteristics of a CAO/WKO-singleton type may not be appropriate for each and every CAO or WKO-singleton remote object. If you wish to alter these default settings, you have two approaches:

- You can adjust the default lease settings using a server-side *.config file.

- You can programmatically alter the settings of a type's default lease by overriding members of the MarshalByRefObject base class.

While each of these options will indeed alter the default lease settings, there is a key difference. When you make use of a server-side *.config file, the lease settings affect *all* objects hosted by the server process. In contrast, when you override select members of the MarshalByRefObject type, you are able to change lease settings on an object-by-object basis.

To illustrate changing the default lease settings via a remoting *.config file, assume you have updated the server-side XML data with the following additional <lifetime> element:

```
<configuration>
    <system.runtime.remoting>
        <application>
            <lifetime leaseTime = "15M" renewOnCallTime = "5M"/>
            <service>
                <activated type = "CarGeneralAsm.CarProvider, CarGeneralAsm"/>
            </service>
            <channels>
                <channel ref="tcp" port="32469" />
            </channels>
        </application>
    </system.runtime.remoting>
</configuration>
```

Notice how the leaseTime and renewOnCallTime properties have been marked with the M suffix, which as you might guess stands for the number of minutes to set for each lease-centric unit of time. If you wish, your <lifetime> element may also suffix the numerical values with MS (milliseconds), S (seconds), H (hours), or even D (days).

Now recall that when you update the server's *.config file, you have effectively changed the leasing characteristics for each CAO/WKO-singleton object hosted by the server. As an alternative, you may choose to programmatically override the InitializeLifetime() method in a specific remote type:

```
public class CarProvider : MarshalByRefObject
{
    public override object InitializeLifetimeService()
    {
        // Obtain the current lease info.
        ILease itfLeaseInfo =
            (ILease) base.InitializeLifetimeService();
        // Adjust settings.
        itfLeaseInfo.InitialLeaseTime = TimeSpan.FromMinutes(50);
        itfLeaseInfo.RenewOnCallTime = TimeSpan.FromMinutes(10);
        return itfLeaseInfo;
    }
...
}
```

Here, the CarProvider has altered its InitialLeaseTime value to 50 minutes and its RenewOn-CallTime value to 10. Again, the benefit of overriding InitializeLifetimeServices() is the fact that you can configure each remote type individually.

Finally, on an odd note, if you wish to disable lease-based lifetime for a given CAO/WKO-singleton object type, you may override InitializeLifetimeServices() and simply return null. If you do so, you have basically configured an MBR type that will *never* die as long as the hosting server application is alive and kicking.

Server-Side Lease Adjustment

As you have just seen, when an MBR type overrides InitializeLifetimeServices(), it is able to change its default leasing behavior at the time of activation. However, for the sake of argument, what if a remote type desires to change its current lease *after* its activation cycle? For example, assume the CarProvider has a new method whose implementation requires a lengthy operation (such as connecting to a remote database and reading a large set of records). Before beginning the task, you may programmatically adjust your lease such that if you have less than one minute, you renew the lease time to ten minutes. To do so, you can make use of the inherited MarshalByRefObject.GetLifetimeService() and ILease.Renew() methods as follows:

```
// Server-side lease adjustment.
// Assume this new method is of the CarProvider type.
public void DoLengthyOperation()
{
    ILease itfLeaseInfo = (ILease)this.GetLifetimeService();
    if(itfLeaseInfo.CurrentLeaseTime.TotalMinutes < 1.0)
        itfLeaseInfo.Renew(TimeSpan.FromMinutes(10));

    // Do lengthy task...
}
```

Client-Side Lease Adjustment

On an additional ILease-related note, it is possible for the client's application domain to adjust the current lease properties for a CAO/WKO-singleton type it is communicating with across the wire. To do so, the client makes use of the static RemotingServices.GetLifetimeService() method. As a parameter to this member, the client passes in the reference to the remote type as follows:

```
// Client-side lease adjustment.
CarProvider cp = new CarProvider(cars);
ILease itfLeaseInfo = (ILease)RemotingServices.GetLifetimeService(cp);
if(itfLeaseInfo.CurrentLeaseTime.TotalMinutes < 10.0)
    itfLeaseInfo.Renew(TimeSpan.FromMinutes(1000));
```

This approach can be helpful if the client's application domain is about to enter a lengthy process on the same thread of execution that is using the remote type. For example, if a single-threaded application is about to print out a 100-page document, the chances are quite good that a remote CAO/WKO-singleton type may time out during the process. The other (more elegant) solution, of course, is to spawn a secondary thread of execution, but I think you get the general idea.

Server-Side (and Client-Side) Lease Sponsorship

The final topic regarding the lease-based lifetime of a CAO/WKO-singleton object to consider is the notion of *lease sponsorship*. As you have just seen, every CAO/WKO-singleton entity has a default lease, which may be altered in a number of ways on both the server side as well as the client side. Now, regardless of the type's lease configuration, eventually an MBR object's time will be up. At this point, the runtime will garbage-collect the entity . . . well, almost.

The truth of the matter is that before an expired type is truly marked for garbage collection, the runtime will check to see if the MBR object in question has any registered lease sponsors. Simply put, a sponsor is a type that implements the ISponsor interface, which is defined as follows:

```
public interface System.Runtime.Remoting.Lifetime.ISponsor
{
    TimeSpan Renewal(ILease lease);
}
```

If the runtime detects that an MBR object has a sponsor, it will *not* garbage-collect the type, but rather call the Renewal() method of the sponsor object to (once again) add time to the current lease. On the other hand, if the MBR has no sponsor, the object's time is truly up.

Assuming that you have created a custom class that implements ISponsor, and thus implements Renewal() to return a specific unit of time (via the TimeSpan type), the next question is how exactly to associate the type to a given remote object. Again, this operation may be performed by either the server's application domain or the client's application domain.

To do so, the interested party obtains an ILease reference (via the inherited GetLifetimeService() method on the server or using the static RemotingServices.GetLifetimeService() method on the client) and calls Register():

```
// Server-side sponsor registration.
CarSponsor mySponsor = new CarSponsor();
ILease itfLeaseInfo = (ILease)this.GetLifetimeService();
itfLeaseInfo.Register(mySponsor);
```

```
// Client-side sponsor registration.
CarSponsor mySponsor = new CarSponsor();
CarProvider cp = new CarProvider(cars);
ILease itfLeaseInfo = (ILease)RemotingServices.GetLifetimeService(cp);
itfLeaseInfo.Register(mySponsor);
```

In either case, if a client or server wishes to revoke sponsorship, it may do so using the `ILease`. `Unregister()` method, for example:

```
// Remove the sponsor for a given object.
itfLeaseInfo.Unregister(mySponsor);
```

■**Note** Client-side sponsored objects, in addition to implementing `ISponsor`, must also derive from `MarshalByRefObject`, given that the client must pass the sponsor to the remote application domain!

So, as you can see, the lifetime management of stateful MBR types is a bit more complex than a standard garbage collection. On the plus side, you have a *ton* of control regarding when a remote type is destined to meet its maker. However, as you may have gathered, there is the chance that a remote type may be removed from memory without the client's knowledge. Should a client attempt to invoke members on a type that has already been removed from memory, the runtime will throw a `System.Runtime.Remoting.RemotingException`, at which point the client may create a brand-new instance of the remote type or simply take an alternative course of action.

■**Source Code** The CAOCarGeneralAsmLease, CAOCarProviderServerLease, and CAOCarProviderClientLease projects are located under the Chapter 18 subdirectory.

Alternative Hosts for Remote Objects

Over the course of this chapter, you have constructed numerous console-based server hosts, which provide access to some set of remote objects. If you have a background in the classic Distributed Component Object Model (DCOM), this step may have seemed a bit odd. In the world of DCOM, it was not unusual to build a single server-side COM server that contained the remote objects and was also in charge of receiving incoming requests from some remote client. This single `*.exe` DCOM application would quietly load in the background without presenting a looming command window.

When you are building a .NET server assembly, the chances are quite good that the remote machine does not need to display any sort of UI. Rather, all you really wish to do is build a server-side entity that opens the correct channel(s) and registers the remote object(s) for client-side access. Moreover, when you build a simple console host, you (or someone) is required to manually run the server-side `*.exe` assembly, due to the fact that .NET remoting will not automatically run a server-side `*.exe` when called by a remote client.

Given these two issues, the question then becomes, how can you build an invisible listener that loads automatically? .NET programmers have two major choices at their disposal when they wish to build a transparent host for various remote objects:

- Build a .NET Windows service application to host the remote objects.
- Allow IIS to host the remote objects.

Hosting Remote Objects Using a Windows Service

Perhaps the ideal host for remote objects is a Windows service, given that it

- Can be configured to load automatically on system startup
- Runs as an invisible background process
- Can be run under specific user accounts

As luck would have it, building a custom Windows service using the .NET platform is extremely simple when contrasted to the raw Win32 API. To illustrate, let's create a Windows Service project named CarWinService (see Figure 18-7) that will be in charge of hosting the remote types contained within the CarGeneralAsm.dll.

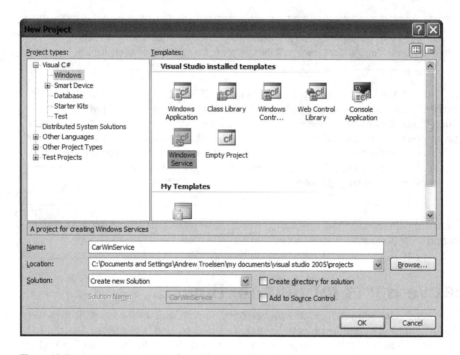

Figure 18-7. *Creating a new Windows Service project workspace*

Visual Studio 2005 responds by generating a partial class (named Service1 by default), which derives from System.ServiceProcess.ServiceBase, and another class (Program), which implements the service's Main() method. Given that Service1 is a rather nondescript name for your custom service, the first order of business is to change the values of the (Name) and ServiceName properties to CarService using the IDE's Properties window. The distinction between these two settings is that the (Name) value is used to define the name used to refer to your type in the code base, while the ServiceName property marks the name to display to Windows service–centric configuration tools.

Before moving on, be sure you set a reference to the CarGeneralAsm.dll and System.Remoting.dll assemblies, and specify the following additional using directives to the file containing the CarService class definition:

```
using System.Runtime.Remoting;
using System.Runtime.Remoting.Channels.Http;
using System.Runtime.Remoting.Channels;
using System.Diagnostics;
```

Implementing the Main() Method

The Main() method of the Program class is in charge of running each service defined in the project by passing an array of ServiceBase types into the static Service.Run() method. Given that you have renamed your custom service from Service1 to CarService, you should find the following class definition (comments deleted for clarity):

```
static class Program
{
    static void Main()
    {
        ServiceBase[] ServicesToRun;
        ServicesToRun = new ServiceBase[] { new CarService() };
        ServiceBase.Run(ServicesToRun);
    }
}
```

Implementing CarService.OnStart()

You can likely already assume what sort of logic should happen when your custom service is started on a given machine. Recall that the role of CarService is to perform the same tasks as your custom console-based service. Thus, if you wish to register CarService as a WKO-singleton type that is available via HTTP, you could add the following code to the OnStart() method (as you would hope, you may make use of the RemotingConfiguration type to load up a server-side remoting *.config file, rather than hard-coding your implementation, when hosting remote objects using a Windows service):

```
protected override void OnStart(string[] args)
{
    // Create a new HttpChannel.
    HttpChannel c = new HttpChannel(32469);
    ChannelServices.RegisterChannel(c);
    // Register as single call WKO.
    RemotingConfiguration.RegisterWellKnownServiceType(
        typeof(CarGeneralAsm.CarProvider),
        "CarProvider.soap",
        WellKnownObjectMode.SingleCall);

    // Log successful startup.
    EventLog.WriteEntry("CarWinService",
        "CarWinService started successfully!",
        EventLogEntryType.Information);
}
```

Note that once the type has been registered, you log a custom message to the Windows event log (via the System.Diagnostics.EventLog type) to document that the host machine successfully started your service.

Implementing OnStop()

Technically speaking, the CarService does not demand any sort of shutdown logic. For illustrative purposes, let's post another event to the EventLog to log the termination of the custom Windows service:

```
protected override void OnStop()
{
    EventLog.WriteEntry("CarWinService",
        "CarWinService stopped",
        EventLogEntryType.Information);
}
```

Now that the service is complete, the next task is to install this service on the remote machine.

Adding a Service Installer

Before you can install your service on a given machine, you need to add an additional type into your current CarWinService project. Specifically, any Windows service (written using .NET or the Win32 API) requires a number of registry entries to be made to allow the OS to interact with the service itself. Rather than making these entries manually, you can simply add an Installer type to a Windows service project, which will configure your ServiceBase-derived type correctly when installed on the target machine.

To add an installer for the CarService, open the design-time service editor (by double-clicking the CarService.cs file from Solution Explorer), right-click anywhere within the designer, and select Add Installer (see Figure 18-8).

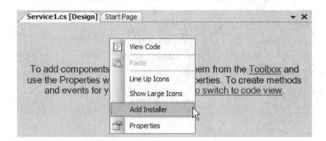

Figure 18-8. *Including an installer for the custom Windows service*

This selection will add a new component that derives from the System.Configuration.Install. Installer base class. On your designer will be two components. The serviceInstaller1 type represents a specific service installer for a specific service in your project. If you select this icon and view the Properties window, you will find that the ServiceName property has been set to the CarService class type.

The second component (serviceProcessInstaller1) allows you to establish the identity under which the installed service will execute. By default, the Account property is set to User. Using the Properties window of Visual Studio 2005, change this value to **LocalService** (see Figure 18-9).

Figure 18-9. *Establishing the identity of the* CarService

That's it! Now compile your project.

Installing the CarWinService

Installing `CarService.exe` on a given machine (local or remote) requires two steps:

1. Move the compiled service assembly (and any necessary external assemblies; `CarGeneralAsm.dll` in this example) to the remote machine.

2. Run the `installutil.exe` command-line tool, specifying your service as an argument.

Assuming step 1 is complete, open a Visual Studio 2005 command window, navigate to the location of the `CarWinService.exe` assembly, and issue the following command (note that this same tool can be used to uninstall a service as well):

```
installutil carwinservice.exe
```

Once this Windows service has been properly installed, you are now able to start and configure it using the Services applet, which is located under the Administrative Tools folder of your system's Control Panel. Once you have located your `CarService` (see Figure 18-10), click the Start link to load and run the binary.

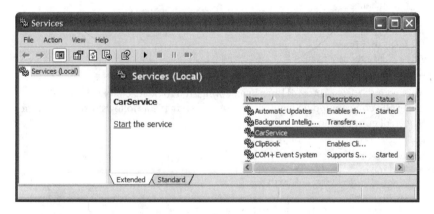

Figure 18-10. *The Windows Services applet*

■Source Code The CarWinService project is located under the Chapter 18 subdirectory.

Hosting Remote Objects Using IIS

Hosting a remote assembly under IIS is even simpler than building a Windows service, as IIS is preprogrammed to allow incoming HTTP requests via port 80. Now, given the fact that IIS is a *web* server, it should stand to reason that IIS is only able to host remote objects using the `HttpChannel` type (unlike a Windows service, which can also leverage the `TcpChannel` type). Assuming this is not perceived as a limitation, follow these steps to leverage the remoting support of IIS:

1. On your hard drive, create a new folder to hold your CarGeneralAsm.dll. Within this folder, create a subdirectory named \Bin. Now, copy the CarGeneralAsm.dll to this subdirectory (e.g., C:\IISCarService\Bin).

2. Open the Internet Information Services applet on the host machine (located under the Administrative Tools folder in your system's Control Panel).

3. Right-click the Default Web Site node and select New ➤ Virtual Directory.

4. Create a virtual directory that maps to the root folder you just created (C:\IISCarService). The remaining default settings presented by the New Virtual Directory Wizard are fine.

5. Finally, create a new configuration file named web.config to control how this virtual directory should register the remote type (see the following code). Make sure this file is saved under the root folder (in this example, C:\IISCarService).

```
<configuration>
    <system.runtime.remoting>
        <application>
            <service>
                <wellknown mode="Singleton"
                        type="CarGeneralAsm.CarProvider, CarGeneralAsm"
                        objectUri="carprovider.soap" />
            </service>
            <channels>
                <channel ref="http"/>
            </channels>
        </application>
    </system.runtime.remoting>
</configuration>
```

Now that your CarGeneralAsm.dll has been configured to be reachable via HTTP requests under IIS, you can update your client-side *.config file as follows (using the name of your IIS host, of course):

```
<configuration>
    <system.runtime.remoting>
        <application>
            <client displayName = "CarClient">
                <wellknown
                    type="CarGeneralAsm.CarProvider, CarGeneralAsm"
                    url="http://NameTheRemoteIISHost/IISCarHost/carprovider.soap"/>
            </client>
            <channels>
                <channel ref="http"/>
            </channels>
        </application>
    </system.runtime.remoting>
</configuration>
```

At this point, you are able to run your client application as before.

Asynchronous Remoting

To wrap things up, let's examine how to invoke members of a remote type asynchronously. In Chapter 14, you were first introduced to the topic of asynchronous method invocations using delegate types. As you would expect, if a client assembly wishes to call a remote object asynchronously, the first step is to define a custom delegate to represent the remote method in question. At this point, the caller can make use of any of the techniques seen in Chapter 14 to invoke and receive the method return value.

By way of a simple illustration, create a new console application (AsyncWKOCarProviderClient) and set a reference to the first iteration of the CarGeneralAsm.dll assembly. Now, update the Program class as so:

```
class Program
{
    // The delegate for the GetAllAutos() method.
    internal delegate List<JamesBondCar> GetAllAutosDelegate();

    static void Main(string[] args)
    {
        Console.WriteLine("Client started!  Hit enter to end");
        RemotingConfiguration.Configure
            ("AsyncWKOCarProviderClient.exe.config");
        // Make the car provider.
        CarProvider cp = new CarProvider();

        // Make the delegate.
        GetAllAutosDelegate getCarsDel =
            new GetAllAutosDelegate(cp.GetAllAutos);
        // Call GetAllAutos() asynchronously.
        IAsyncResult ar = getCarsDel.BeginInvoke(null, null);

        // Simulate client-side activity.
        while(!ar.IsCompleted)
        { Console.WriteLine("Client working..."); }

        // All done!  Get return value from delegate.
        List<JamesBondCar> allJBCs = getCarsDel.EndInvoke(ar);

        // Use all cars in List.
        foreach(JamesBondCar j in allJBCs)
            UseCar(j);
        Console.ReadLine();
    }
}
```

Notice how the client application first declares a delegate that matches the signature of the GetAllAutos() method of the remote CarProvider type. When the delegate is created, you pass in the name of the method to call (GetAllAutos), as always. Next, you trigger the BeginInvoke() method, cache the resulting IAsyncResult interface, and simulate some work on the client side (recall that the IAsyncResult.IsCompleted property allows you to monitor if the associated method has completed processing). Finally, once the client's work has completed, you obtain the List<> returned from the CarProvider.GetAllAutos() method by invoking the EndInvoke() member, and pass each JamesBondCar into a static helper function named UseCar():

```
public static void UseCar(JamesBondCar j)
{
    Console.WriteLine("Can car fly? {0}", j.isFlightWorthy);
    Console.WriteLine("Can car swim? {0}", j.isSeaWorthy);
}
```

Again, the beauty of the .NET delegate type is the fact that the logic used to invoke remote methods asynchronously is identical to the process of local method invocations.

■**Source Code** The AsyncWKOCarProviderClient project is located under the Chapter 18 subdirectory.

The Role of the [OneWay] Attribute

Imagine that your `CarProvider` has a new method named `AddCar()`, which takes a `JamesBondCar` input parameter and returns nothing. The key point is that it returns *nothing.* As you might assume given the name of the `System.Runtime.Remoting.Messaging.OneWayAttribute` class, the .NET remoting layer passes the call to the remote one-way method, but does *not* bother to set up the infrastructure used to return a given value (hence the name *one-way*). Here is the update:

```
// Home of the [OneWay] attribute.
using System.Runtime.Remoting.Messaging;
...
namespace CarGeneralAsm
{
    public class CarProvider : MarshalByRefObject
    {
...
        // The client can 'fire and forget' when calling this method.
        [OneWay]
        public void AddCar(JamesBondCar newJBC)
        { theJBCars.Add(newJBC);}
    }
}
```

Callers would invoke this method directly as always:

```
// Make the car provider.
CarProvider cp = new CarProvider();
// Add a new car.
cp.AddCar(new JamesBondCar("Zippy", 200, false, false));
```

From the client's point of view, the call to `AddCar()` is completely asynchronous, as the CLR will ensure that a background thread is used to remotely trigger the method. Given that `AddCar()` has been decorated with the `[OneWay]` attribute, the client is unable to obtain any return value from the call. Because `AddCar()` returns `void`, this is not an issue.

In addition to this restriction, also be aware that if you have a `[OneWay]` method that defines output or reference parameters (via the `out` or `ref` keyword), the caller will *not* be able to obtain the callee's modification(s). Furthermore, if the `[OneWay]` method happens to throw an exception (of any type), the caller is completely oblivious of this fact. In a nutshell, remote objects can mark select methods as `[OneWay]` to allow the caller to employ a fire-and-forget mentality.

Summary

In this chapter, you examined how to configure distinct .NET assemblies to share types between application boundaries. As you have seen, a remote object may be configured as an MBV or MBR type. This choice ultimately controls how a remote type is realized in the client's application domain (a copy or transparent proxy).

If you have configured a type to function as an MBR entity, you are suddenly faced with a number of related choices (WKO versus CAO, single call versus singleton, and so forth), each of which was addressed during this chapter. As well, you examined the process of tracking the lifetime of a remote object via the use of leases and lease sponsorship. Finally, you revisited of the role of the .NET delegate type to understand how to asynchronously invoke a remote method (which, as luck would have it, is identical to the process of asynchronously invoking a local type).

■ ■ ■

## CHAPTER 19

Building a Better Window with System.Windows.Forms

If you have read through the previous 18 chapters, you should have a solid handle on the C# programming language as well as the foundation of the .NET architecture. While you could take your newfound knowledge and begin building the next generation of console applications (boring!), you are more likely to be interested in building an attractive graphical user interface (GUI) to allow users to interact with your system.

This chapter is the first of three aimed at introducing you to the process of building traditional form-based desktop applications. Here, you'll learn how to build a highly stylized main window using the Form and Application classes. This chapter also illustrates how to capture and respond to user input (i.e., handle mouse and keyboard events) within the context of a GUI desktop environment. Finally, you will learn to construct menu systems, toolbars, status bars, and multiple-document interface (MDI) applications, both by hand and using the designers incorporated into Visual Studio 2005.

Overview of the System.Windows.Forms Namespace

Like any namespace, System.Windows.Forms is composed of various classes, structures, delegates, interfaces, and enumerations. Although the difference in appearance between a console UI (CUI) and graphical UI (GUI) seems at first glance like night and day, in reality the process of building a Windows Forms application involves nothing more than learning how to manipulate a new set of types using the C# syntax you already know. From a high level, the hundreds of types within the System.Windows.Forms namespace can be grouped into the following broad categories:

- *Core infrastructure*: These are types that represent the core operations of a .NET Forms program (Form, Application, etc.) and various types to facilitate interoperability with legacy ActiveX controls.

- *Controls*: These are types used to create rich UIs (Button, MenuStrip, ProgressBar, DataGridView, etc.), all of which derive from the Control base class. Controls are configurable at design time and are visible (by default) at runtime.

- *Components*: These are types that do not derive from the Control base class but still provide visual features to a .NET Forms program (ToolTip, ErrorProvider, etc.). Many components (such as the Timer) are not visible at runtime, but can be configured visually at design time.

- *Common dialog boxes*: Windows Forms provides a number of canned dialog boxes for common operations (OpenFileDialog, PrintDialog, etc.). As you would hope, you can certainly build your own custom dialog boxes if the standard dialog boxes do not suit your needs.

Given that the total number of types within System.Windows.Forms is well over 100 strong, it would be redundant (not to mention a terrible waste of paper) to list every member of the Windows Forms family. To set the stage for the next several chapters, however, Table 19-1 lists some of the core .NET 2.0 System.Windows.Forms types (consult the .NET Framework 2.0 SDK documentation for full details).

Table 19-1. *Core Types of the* System.Windows.Forms *Namespace*

Classes	Meaning in Life
Application	This class encapsulates the runtime operation of a Windows Forms application.
Button, CheckBox, ComboBox, DateTimePicker, ListBox, LinkLabel, MaskedTextBox, MonthCalendar, PictureBox, TreeView	These classes (in addition to many others) correspond to various GUI widgets. You'll examine many of these items in detail in Chapter 21.
FlowLayoutPanel, TableLayoutPanel	.NET 2.0 now supplies various "layout managers" that automatically arrange a Form's controls during resizing.
Form	This type represents a main window, dialog box, or MDI child window of a Windows Forms application.
ColorDialog, OpenFileDialog, SaveFileDialog, FontDialog, PrintPreviewDialog, FolderBrowserDialog	These are various standard dialog boxes for common GUI operations.
Menu, MainMenu, MenuItem, ContextMenu, MenuStrip, ContextMenuStrip,	These types are used to build topmost and context-sensitive menu systems. The new (.NET 2.0) MenuStrip and ContextMenuStrip controls allow you to build menus that may contain traditional drop-down menu items as well as other controls (text boxes, combo boxes, and so forth).
StatusBar, Splitter, ToolBar, ScrollBar, StatusStrip, ToolStrip	These types are used to adorn a Form with common child controls.

Note In addition to System.Windows.Forms, the System.Windows.Forms.dll assembly defines additional GUI-centric namespaces. For the most part, these additional types are used internally by the Forms engine and/or the designer tools of Visual Studio 2005. Given this fact, we will keep focused on the core System.Windows.Forms namespace.

Working with the Windows Forms Types

When you build a Windows Forms application, you may choose to write all the relevant code by hand (using Notepad or TextPad, perhaps) and feed the resulting *.cs files into the C# compiler using the /target:winexe flag. Taking time to build some Windows Forms applications by hand not only is a great learning experience, but also helps you understand the code generated by the various graphics designers found within various .NET IDEs.

To make sure you truly understand the basic process of building a Windows Forms application, the initial examples in this chapter will avoid the use of graphics designers. Once you feel comfortable with the process of building a Windows Forms application "wizard-free," you will then leverage the various designer tools provided by Visual Studio 2005.

Building a Main Window by Hand

To begin learning about Windows Forms programming, you'll build a minimal main window from scratch. Create a new folder on your hard drive (e.g., C:\MyFirstWindow) and create a new file within this directory named MainWindow.cs using your editor of choice.

In the world of Windows Forms, the Form class is used to represent any window in your application. This includes a topmost main window in a single-document interface (SDI) application, modeless and modal dialog boxes, and the parent and child windows of a multiple-document interface (MDI) application. When you are interested in creating and displaying the main window in your program, you have two mandatory steps:

1. Derive a new class from System.Windows.Forms.Form.

2. Configure your application's Main() method to invoke Application.Run(), passing an instance of your Form-derived type as an argument.

Given this, update your MainWindow.cs file with the following class definition:

```
using System;
using System.Windows.Forms;

namespace MyWindowsApp
{
    public class MainWindow : Form
    {
        // Run this application and identify the main window.
        static void Main(string[] args)
        {
            Application.Run(new MainWindow());
        }
    }
}
```

In addition to the always present mscorlib.dll, a Windows Forms application needs to reference the System.dll and System.Windows.Forms.dll assemblies. As you may recall from Chapter 2, the default C# response file (csc.rsp) instructs csc.exe to automatically include these assemblies during the compilation process, so you are good to go. Also recall that the /target:winexe option of csc.exe instructs the compiler to generate a Windows executable.

■**Note** Technically speaking, you can build a Windows application at the command line using the /target:exe option; however, if you do, you will find that a command window will be looming in the background (and it will stay there until you shut down the main window). When you specify /target:winexe, your executable runs as a native Windows Forms application (without the looming command window).

To compile your C# code file, open a Visual Studio 2005 command prompt and issue the following command:

```
csc /target:winexe *.cs
```

Figure 19-1 shows a test run.

Figure 19-1. *A simple main window à la Windows Forms*

Granted, the Form is not altogether that interesting at this point. But simply by deriving from Form, you have a minimizable, maximizable, resizable, and closable main window (with a default system-supplied icon to boot!). Unlike other Microsoft GUI frameworks you may have used in the past (Microsoft Foundation Classes, in particular), there is no need to bolt in hundreds of lines of coding infrastructure (frames, documents, views, applications, or message maps). Unlike a C-based Win32 API Windows application, there is no need to manually implement WinProc() or WinMain() procedures. Under the .NET platform, those dirty details have been encapsulated within the Form and Application types.

Honoring the Separation of Concerns

Currently, the MainWindow class defines the Main() method directly within its scope. If you prefer, you may create a second static class (I named mine Program) that is responsible for the task of launching the main window, leaving the Form-derived class responsible for representing the window itself:

```
namespace MyWindowsApp
{
    // The main window.
    public class MainWindow : Form { }

    // The application object.
    public static class Program
    {
        static void Main(string[] args)
        {
            // Don't forget to 'use' System.Windows.Forms!
            Application.Run(new MainWindow());
        }
    }
}
```

By doing so, you are abiding by an OO principal termed *the separation of concerns*. Simply put, this rule of OO design states that a class should be in charge of doing the least amount of work possible. Given that you have refactored the initial class into two unique classes, you have decoupled the Form from the class that creates it. The end result is a more portable window, as it can be dropped into any project without carrying the extra baggage of a project-specific Main() method.

■**Source Code**　The MyFirstWindow project can be found under the Chapter 19 subdirectory.

The Role of the Application Class

The `Application` class defines numerous static members that allow you to control various low-level behaviors of a Windows Forms application. For example, the `Application` class defines a set of events that allow you to respond to events such as application shutdown and idle-time processing. In addition to the `Run()` method, here are some other methods to be aware of:

- `DoEvents()`: Provides the ability for an application to process messages currently in the message queue during a lengthy operation.

- `Exit()`: Terminates the Windows application and unloads the hosting AppDomain.

- `EnableVisualStyles()`: Configures your application to support Windows XP visual styles. Do note that if you enable XP styles, this method must be called before loading your main window via `Application.Run()`.

The `Application` class also defines a number of properties, many of which are read-only in nature. As you examine Table 19-2, note that most of these properties represent an "application-level" trait such as company name, version number, and so forth. In fact, given what you already know about assembly-level attributes (see Chapter 12), many of these properties should look vaguely familiar.

Table 19-2. *Core Properties of the* `Application` *Type*

Property	Meaning in Life
CompanyName	Retrieves the value of the assembly-level [AssemblyCompany] attribute
ExecutablePath	Gets the path for the executable file
ProductName	Retrieves the value of the assembly-level [AssemblyProduct] attribute
ProductVersion	Retrieves the value of the assembly-level [AssemblyVersion] attribute
StartupPath	Retrieves the path for the executable file that started the application

Finally, the `Application` class defines various static events, some of which are as follows:

- `ApplicationExit`: Occurs when the application is just about to shut down

- `Idle`: Occurs when the application's message loop has finished processing the current batch of messages and is about to enter an idle state (as there are no messages to process at the current time)

- `ThreadExit`: Occurs when a thread in the application is about to terminate

Fun with the Application Class

To illustrate some of the functionality of the `Application` class, let's enhance your current `MainWindow` to perform the following:

- Reflect over select assembly-level attributes.

- Handle the static `ApplicationExit` event.

The first task is to make use of select properties in the `Application` class to reflect over some assembly-level attributes. To begin, add the following attributes to your `MainWindow.cs` file (note you are now using the `System.Reflection` namespace):

```
using System;
using System.Windows.Forms;
using System.Reflection;
```

```
// Some attributes regarding this assembly.
[assembly:AssemblyCompany("Intertech Training")]
[assembly:AssemblyProduct("A Better Window")]
[assembly:AssemblyVersion("1.1.0.0")]

namespace MyWindowsApp
{
    ...
}
```

Rather than manually reflecting over the [AssemblyCompany] and [AssemblyProduct] attributes using the techniques illustrated in Chapter 12, the Application class will do so automatically using various static properties. To illustrate, implement the default constructor of MainForm as so:

```
public class MainWindow : Form
{
    public MainWindow()
    {
        MessageBox.Show(Application.ProductName,
            string.Format("This app brought to you by {0}",
            Application.CompanyName));
    }
}
```

When you run this application, you'll see a message box that displays various bits of information (see Figure 19-2).

Figure 19-2. *Reading attributes via the* Application *type*

Now, let's equip this Form to respond to the ApplicationExit event. When you wish to respond to events from within a Windows Forms application, you will be happy to find that the same event syntax detailed in Chapter 8 is used to handle GUI-based events. Therefore, if you wish to intercept the static ApplicationExit event, simply register an event handler using the += operator:

```
public class MainForm : Form
{
    public MainForm()
    {
        ...
        // Intercept the ApplicationExit event.
        Application.ApplicationExit += new EventHandler(MainWindow_OnExit);
    }
    private void MainWindow_OnExit(object sender, EventArgs evArgs)
    {
        MessageBox.Show(string.Format("Form version {0} has terminated.",
            Application.ProductVersion));
    }
}
```

The System.EventHandler Delegate

Notice that the ApplicationExit event works in conjunction with the System.EventHandler delegate. This delegate must point to methods that conform to the following signature:

```
delegate void EventHandler(object sender, EventArgs e);
```

System.EventHandler is the most primitive delegate used to handle events within Windows Forms, but many variations do exist for other events. As far as EventHandler is concerned, the first parameter of the assigned method is of type System.Object, which represents the object sending the event. The second EventArgs parameter (or a descendent thereof) contains any relevant information regarding the current event.

■**Note** EventArgs is the base class to numerous derived types that contain information for a family of related events. For example, mouse events work with the MouseEventArgs parameter, which contains details such as the (*x*, *y*) position of the cursor. Many keyboard events work with the KeyEventArgs type, which contains details regarding the current keypress, and so forth.

In any case, if you now recompile and run the application, you will find your message box appear upon the termination of the application.

■**Source Code** The AppClassExample project can be found under the Chapter 19 subdirectory.

The Anatomy of a Form

Now that you understand the role of the Application type, the next task is to examine the functionality of the Form class itself. Not surprisingly, the Form class inherits a great deal of functionality from its parent classes. Figure 19-3 shows the inheritance chain (including the set of implemented interfaces) of a Form-derived type using the Visual Studio 2005 Object Browser.

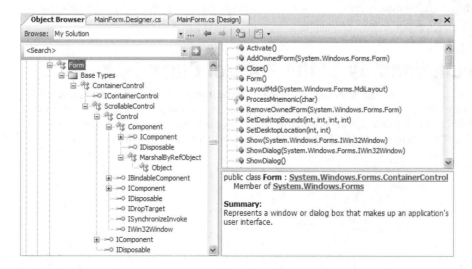

Figure 19-3. *The derivation of the* Form *type*

Although the complete derivation of a Form type involves numerous base classes and interfaces, do understand that you are *not* required to learn the role of each and every member from each and every parent class or implemented interface to be a proficient Windows Forms developer. In fact, the majority of the members (properties and events in particular) you will use on a daily basis are easily set using the Visual Studio 2005 IDE Properties window. Before we move on to examine some specific members inherited from these parent classes, Table 19-3 outlines the basic role of each base class.

Table 19-3. *Base Classes in the* Form *Inheritance Chain*

Parent Class	Meaning in Life
System.Object	Like any class in .NET, a Form "is-a" object.
System.MarshalByRefObject	Recall during our examination of .NET remoting (see Chapter 18) that types deriving from this class are accessed remotely via a *reference* (not a copy) of the remote type.
System.ComponentModel.Component	This class provides a default implementation of the IComponent interface. In the .NET universe, a component is a type that supports design-time editing, but is not necessarily visible at runtime.
System.Windows.Forms.Control	This class defines common UI members for all Windows Forms UI controls, including the Form type itself.
System.Windows.Forms.ScrollableControl	This class defines support for auto-scrolling behaviors.
System.Windows.Forms.ContainerControl	This class provides focus-management functionality for controls that can function as a container for other controls.
System.Windows.Forms.Form	This class represents any custom Form, MDI child, or dialog box.

As you might guess, detailing each and every member of each class in the Form's inheritance chain would require a large book in itself. However, it is important to understand the behavior supplied by the Control and Form types. I'll assume that you will spend time examining the full details behind each class at your leisure using the .NET Framework 2.0 SDK documentation.

The Functionality of the Control Class

The System.Windows.Forms.Control class establishes the common behaviors required by any GUI type. The core members of Control allow you to configure the size and position of a control, capture keyboard and mouse input, get or set the focus/visibility of a member, and so forth. Table 19-4 defines some (but not all) properties of interest, grouped by related functionality.

Table 19-4. *Core Properties of the* Control *Type*

Properties	Meaning in Life
BackColor, ForeColor, BackgroundImage, Font, Cursor	These properties define the core UI of the control (colors, font for text, mouse cursor to display when the mouse is over the widget, etc.).
Anchor, Dock, AutoSize	These properties control how the control should be positioned within the container.
Top, Left, Bottom, Right, Bounds, ClientRectangle, Height, Width	These properties specify the current dimensions of the control.
Enabled, Focused, Visible	These properties each return a Boolean that specifies the state of the current control.
ModifierKeys	This static property checks the current state of the modifier keys (Shift, Ctrl, and Alt) and returns the state in a Keys type.
MouseButtons	This static property checks the current state of the mouse buttons (left, right, and middle mouse buttons) and returns this state in a MouseButtons type.
TabIndex, TabStop	These properties are used to configure the tab order of the control.
Opacity	This property determines the opacity of the control, in fractions (0.0 is completely transparent; 1.0 is completely opaque).
Text	This property indicates the string data associated with this control.
Controls	This property allows you to access a strongly typed collection (ControlsCollection) that contains any child controls within the current control.

As you would guess, the Control class also defines a number of events that allow you to intercept mouse, keyboard, painting, and drag-and-drop activities (among other things). Table 19-5 lists some (but not all) events of interest, grouped by related functionality.

Table 19-5. *Events of the* Control *Type*

Events	Meaning in Life
Click, DoubleClick, MouseEnter, MouseLeave, MouseDown, MouseUp, MouseMove, MouseHover, MouseWheel	Various events that allow you to interact with the mouse
KeyPress, KeyUp, KeyDown	Various events that allow you to interact with the keyboard
DragDrop, DragEnter, DragLeave, DragOver	Various events used to monitor drag-and-drop activity
Paint	This event allows you to interact with GDI+ (see Chapter 20)

Finally, the Control base class also defines a number of methods that allow you to interact with any Control-derived type. As you examine the methods of the Control type, you will notice that a good number of them have an On prefix followed by the name of a specific event (OnMouseMove, OnKeyUp, OnPaint, etc.). Each of these On-prefixed virtual methods is the default event handler for its respective event. If you override any of these virtual members, you gain the ability to perform any necessary pre- or postprocessing of the event before (or after) invoking your parent's default implementation:

```
public class MainWindow : Form
{
    protected override void OnMouseDown(MouseEventArgs e)
    {
        // Add code for MouseDown event.

        // Call parent implementation when finished.
        base.OnMouseDown(e);
    }
}
```

While this can be helpful in some circumstances (especially if you are building a custom control that derives from a standard control; see Chapter 21), you will often handle events using the standard C# event syntax (in fact, this is the default behavior of the Visual Studio 2005 designers). When you do so, the framework will call your custom event handler once the parent's implementation has completed:

```
public class MainWindow : Form
{
    public MainWindow()
    {
        MouseDown += new MouseEventHandler(MainWindow_MouseDown);
    }

    void MainWindow_MouseDown(object sender, MouseEventArgs e)
    {
        // Add code for MouseDown event.
    }
}
```

Beyond these OnXXX() methods, here are a few other methods to be aware of:

- Hide(): Hides the control and sets the Visible property to false
- Show(): Shows the control and sets the Visible property to true
- Invalidate(): Forces the control to redraw itself by sending a Paint event

To be sure, the Control class does define additional properties, methods, and events beyond the subset you've just examined. You should, however, now have a solid understanding regarding the overall functionality of this base class. Let's see it in action.

Fun with the Control Class

To illustrate the usefulness of some members from the Control class, let's build a new Form that is capable of handling the following events:

- Respond to the MouseMove and MouseDown events.
- Capture and process keyboard input via the KeyUp event.

To begin, create a new class derived from Form. In the default constructor, you'll make use of various inherited properties to establish the initial look and feel. Note you're now using the System. Drawing namespace to gain access to the Color structure (you'll examine this namespace in detail in the next chapter):

```
using System;
using System.Windows.Forms;
using System.Drawing;
```

```
namespace MyWindowsApp
{
    public class MainWindow : Form
    {
        public MainWindow()
        {
            // Use inherited properties to set basic UI.
            Text = "My Fantastic Form";
            Height = 300;
            Width = 500;
            BackColor = Color.LemonChiffon;
            Cursor = Cursors.Hand;
        }
    }

    public static class Program
    {
        static void Main(string[] args)
        {
            Application.Run(new MainWindow());
        }
    }
}
```

Compile your application at this point, just to make sure you have not injected any typing errors:

```
csc /target:winexe *.cs
```

Responding to the MouseMove Event

Next, you need to handle the MouseMove event. The goal is to display the current (x, y) location within the Form's caption area. All mouse-centric events (MouseMove, MouseUp, etc.) work in conjunction with the MouseEventHandler delegate, which can call any method matching the following signature:

```
void MyMouseHandler(object sender, MouseEventArgs e);
```

The incoming MouseEventArgs structure extends the general EventArgs base class by adding a number of members particular to the processing of mouse activity (see Table 19-6).

Table 19-6. *Properties of the* MouseEventArgs *Type*

Property	Meaning in Life
Button	Gets which mouse button was pressed, as defined by the MouseButtons enumeration
Clicks	Gets the number of times the mouse button was pressed and released
Delta	Gets a signed count of the number of detents the mouse wheel has rotated
X	Gets the x-coordinate of a mouse click
Y	Gets the y-coordinate of a mouse click

Here, then, is the updated MainForm class that handles the MouseMove event as intended:

```
public class MainForm : Form
{
    public MainForm()
    {
```

```
        ...
        // Handle the MouseMove event
        MouseMove += new MouseEventHandler(MainForm_MouseMove);
    }
    // MouseMove event handler.
    public void MainForm_MouseMove(object sender, MouseEventArgs e)
    {
        Text = string.Format("Current Pos: ({0}, {1})", e.X, e.Y);
    }
}
```

If you now run your program and move the mouse over your Form, you will find the current (*x, y*) value display on the caption area (see Figure 19-4).

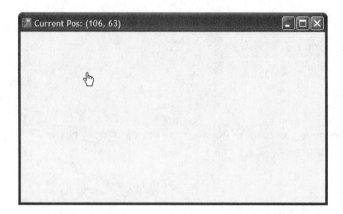

Figure 19-4. *Monitoring mouse movement*

Determining Which Mouse Button Was Clicked

One thing to be aware of is that the MouseUp (or MouseDown) event is sent whenever *any* mouse button is clicked. If you wish to determine exactly *which* button was clicked (such as left, right, or middle), you need to examine the Button property of the MouseEventArgs class. The value of the Button property is constrained by the related MouseButtons enumeration. Assume you have updated your default constructor to handle the MouseUp event as so:

```
public MainWindow()
{
...
    // Handle the MouseUp event.
    MouseUp += new MouseEventHandler(MainForm_MouseUp);
}
```

The following MouseUp event handler displays which mouse button was clicked inside a message box:

```
public void MainForm_MouseUp (object sender, MouseEventArgs e)
{
    // Which mouse button was clicked?
    if(e.Button == MouseButtons.Left)
        MessageBox.Show("Left click!");
    if(e.Button == MouseButtons.Right)
```

most of the mundane code on your behalf. Given this, let's say good-bye to the command-line compiler for the time being and turn our attention to the process of building Windows Forms applications using Visual Studio 2005.

■Source Code The FormLifeTime project can be found under the Chapter 19 subdirectory.

Building Windows Applications with Visual Studio 2005

Visual Studio 2005 has a specific project type dedicated to the creation of Windows Forms applications. When you select the Windows Application project type, you not only receive an application object with a proper `Main()` method, but also are provided with an initial `Form`-derived type. Better yet, the IDE provides a number of graphical designers that make the process of building a UI child's play. Just to learn the lay of the land, create a new Windows Application project workspace (see Figure 19-6). You are not going to build a working example just yet, so name this project whatever you desire.

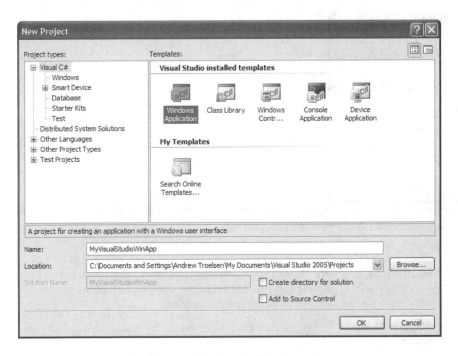

Figure 19-6. *The Visual Studio 2005 Windows Application project*

Once the project has loaded, you will no doubt notice the Forms designer, which allows you to build a UI by dragging controls/components from the Toolbox (see Figure 19-7) and configuring their properties and events using the Properties window (see Figure 19-8).

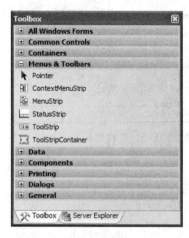

Figure 19-7. *The Visual Studio 2005 Toolbox*

Figure 19-8. *The Visual Studio 2005 Properties window*

As you can see, the Toolbox groups UI controls by various categories. While most are self-explanatory (e.g., Printing contains printing controls, Menus & Toolbars contains recommended menu/toolbar controls, etc.), a few categories deserve special mention:

- *Common Controls*: Members in this category are considered the "recommended set" of common UI controls.

- *All Windows Forms*: Here you will find the full set of Windows Forms controls, including various .NET 1.*x* controls that are considered depreciated.

The second bullet point is worth reiterating. If you have worked with Windows Forms using .NET 1.*x*, be aware that many of your old friends (such as the DataGrid control) have been placed under the All Windows Forms category. Furthermore, the common UI controls you may have used under .NET 1.*x* (such as MainMenu, ToolBar, and StatusBar) are *not* shown in the Toolbox by default.

Enabling the Deprecated Controls

The first bit of good news is that these (deprecated) UI elements are still completely usable under .NET 2.0. The second bit of good news is that if you still wish to program with them, you can add them back to the Toolbox by right-clicking anywhere in the Toolbox and selecting Choose Items. From the resulting dialog box, check off the items of interest (see Figure 19-9).

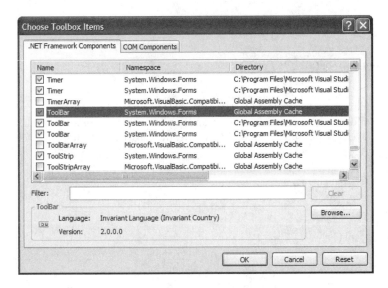

Figure 19-9. *Adding additional controls to the Toolbox*

Note At first glance, it might appear that there are redundant listings for a given control (such as the `ToolBar`). In reality, each listing is unique, as a control may be versioned (1.0 versus 2.0) and/or may be a member of the .NET Compact Framework. Be sure to examine the directory path to select the correct item.

At this point, I am sure you are wondering why many of these old standbys have been hidden from view. The reason is that .NET 2.0 provides a set of new menu, toolbar, and status bar–centric controls that are now favored. For example, rather than using the legacy `MainMenu` control to build a menu, you can use the `MenuStrip` control, which provides a number of new bells and whistles in addition to the functionality found within `MainMenu`.

Note In this chapter, I will favor the use of this new recommend set of UI elements. If you wish to work with the legacy `MainMenu`, `StatusBar`, or `ToolBar` types, consult the .NET Framework 2.0 SDK documentation.

Dissecting a Visual Studio 2005 Windows Forms Project

Each `Form` in a Visual Studio 2005 Windows Application project is composed of two related C# files, which can be verified using Solution Explorer (see Figure 19-10).

Figure 19-10. *Each Form is composed of two* *.cs *files.*

Right-click the Form1.cs icon and select View Code. Here you will see a partial class that contains all of the Form's event handlers, constructors, overrides, and any member you author yourself (note that I renamed this initial class from Form1 to MainWindow using the Rename refactoring):

```
namespace MyVisualStudioWinApp
{
    public partial class MainWindow : Form
    {
        public MainWindow()
        {
            InitializeComponent();
        }
    }
}
```

The default constructor of your Form makes a call to a method named InitializeComponent(), which is defined within the related *.Designer.cs file. This method is maintained on your behalf by Visual Studio 2005, and it contains all of the code representing your design-time modifications.

To illustrate, switch back to the Forms designer and locate the Text property in the Properties window. Change this value to something like **My Test Window**. Now open your Form1.Designer.cs file and notice that InitializeComponent() has been updated accordingly:

```
private void InitializeComponent()
{
...
    this.Text = "My Test Window";
}
```

In addition to maintaining InitializeComponent(), the *.Designer.cs file will define the member variables that represent each control placed on the designer. Again, to illustrate, drag a Button control onto the Forms designer. Now, using the Properties window, rename your member variable from button1 to btnTestButton via the Name property.

Note It is always a good idea to rename the controls you place on the designer before handling events. If you fail to do so, you will most likely end up with a number of nondescript event handlers, such as button27_Click, given that the default names simply suffix a numerical value to the variable name.

Handling Events at Design Time

Notice that the Properties window has a button depicting a lightning bolt. Although you are always free to handle Form-level events by authoring the necessary logic by hand (as done in the previous examples), this event button allows you to visually handle an event for a given control. Simply select the control you wish to interact with from the drop-down list box (mounted at the top of the Properties window), locate the event you are interested in handling, and type in the name to be used as an event handler (or simply double-click the event to generate a default name of the form ControlName_EventName).

Assuming you have handled the Click event for the Button control, you will find that the Form1.cs file contains the following event handler:

```
public partial class MainWindow : Form
{
    public MainWindow()
    {
        InitializeComponent();
    }
    private void btnButtonTest_Click(object sender, EventArgs e)
    {
    }
}
```

As well, the Form1.Designer.cs file contains the necessary infrastructure and member variable declaration:

```
partial class MainWindow
{
...
    private void InitializeComponent()
    {
...
        this.btnButtonTest.Click +=
            new System.EventHandler(this.btnButtonTest_Click);
    }
    private System.Windows.Forms.Button btnButtonTest;
}
```

■**Note** Every control has a *default event*, which refers to the event that will be handled if you double-click the item on the control using the Forms designer. For example, a Form's default event is Load, and if you double-click anywhere on a Form type, the IDE will automatically write code to handle this event.

The Program Class

Beyond the Form-centric files, a Visual Studio 2005 Windows application defines a second class that represents the application object (e.g., the type defining the Main() method). Notice that the Main() method has been configured to call Application.EnableVisualStyles() as well as Application.Run():

```
static class Program
{
    [STAThread]
    static void Main()
    {
        Application.EnableVisualStyles();
```

```
        Application.Run(new MainWindow());
    }
}
```

■**Note** The [STAThread] attribute instructs the CLR to host any legacy COM objects (including ActiveX controls) in a *single-threaded apartment* (*STA*). If you have a background in COM, you may recall that the STA was used to ensure access to a COM type occurred in a synchronous (hence, thread-safe) manner.

Autoreferenced Assemblies

Finally, if you examine Solution Explorer, you will notice that a Windows Forms project automatically references a number of assemblies, including System.Windows.Forms.dll and System.Drawing.dll. Again, the details of System.Drawing.dll will be examined in the next chapter.

Working with MenuStrips and ContextMenuStrips

As of .NET 2.0, the recommended control for building a menu system is MenuStrip. This control allows you to create "normal" menu items such as File ➤ Exit, and you may also configure it to contain any number of relevant controls within the menu area. Here are some common UI elements that may be contained within a MenuStrip:

- ToolStripMenuItem: A traditional menu item
- ToolStripComboBox: An embedded ComboBox
- ToolStripSeparator: A simple line that separates content
- ToolStripTextBox: An embedded TextBox

Programmatically speaking, the MenuStrip control contains a strongly typed collection named ToolStripItemCollection. Like other collection types, this object supports members such as Add(), AddRange(), Remove(), and the Count property. While this collection is typically populated indirectly using various design-time tools, you are able to manually manipulate this collection if you so choose.

To illustrate the process of working with the MenuStrip control, create a new Windows Forms application named MenuStripApp. Using the Forms designer, place a MenuStrip control named mainMenuStrip onto your Form. When you do so, your *.Designer.cs file is updated with a new MenuStrip member variable:

```
private System.Windows.Forms.MenuStrip mainMenuStrip;
```

MenuStrips can be highly customized using the Visual Studio 2005 Forms designer. For example, if you look at the extreme upper-left of the control, you will notice a small arrow icon. After you select this icon, you are presented with a context-sensitive "inline editor," as shown in Figure 19-11.

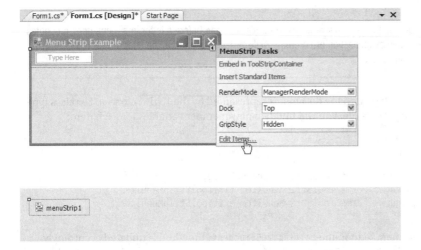

Figure 19-11. *The inline* MenuStrip *editor*

Many Windows Forms controls support such context-sensitive inline editors. As far as MenuStrip is concerned, the editor allows you to quickly do the following:

- Insert a "standard" menu system (File, Save, Tools, Help, etc.) using the Insert Standard Items link.

- Change the docking and gripping behaviors of the MenuStrip.

- Edit each item in the MenuStrip (this is simply a shortcut to selecting a specific item in the Properties window).

For this example, you'll ignore the options of the inline editor and stay focused on the design of the menu system. To begin, select the MenuStrip control on the designer and define a standard File ➤ Exit menu by typing in the names within the Type Here prompts (see Figure 19-12).

Figure 19-12. *Designing a menu system*

■**Note** As you may know, when the ampersand character (&) is placed before a letter in a menu item, it denotes the item's shortcut key. In this example, you are creating &File ➤ E&xit; therefore, the user may activate the Exit menu by pressing Alt+f, and then x.

Each menu item you type into the designer is represented by the `ToolStripMenuItem` class type. If you open your `*.Designer.cs` file, you will find two new member variables for each item:

```
partial class MainWindow
{
...
    private System.Windows.Forms.MenuStrip mainMenuStrip;
    private System.Windows.Forms.ToolStripMenuItem fileToolStripMenuItem;
    private System.Windows.Forms.ToolStripMenuItem exitToolStripMenuItem;
}
```

When you use the menu editor, the `InitializeComponent()` method is updated accordingly. Notice that the `MenuStrip`'s internal `ToolStripItemCollection` has been updated to contain the new topmost menu item (`fileToolStripMenuItem`). In a similar fashion, the `fileToolStripMenuItem` variable has been updated to insert the `exitToolStripMenuItem` variable into its `ToolStripItemCollection` collection via the `DropDownItems` property:

```
private void InitializeComponent()
{
...
    //
    // menuStrip1
    //
    this.menuStrip1.Items.AddRange(new System.Windows.Forms.ToolStripItem[] {
      this.fileToolStripMenuItem});
    ...
    //
    // fileToolStripMenuItem
    //
    this.fileToolStripMenuItem.DropDownItems.AddRange(new
      System.Windows.Forms.ToolStripItem[] {
        this.exitToolStripMenuItem});
...
    //
    // MainWindow
    //
    this.Controls.Add(this.menuStrip1);
}
```

Last but not least, notice that the `MenuStrip` control is inserted to the Form's controls collection. This collection will be examined in greater detail in Chapter 21, but for the time being, just know that in order for a control to be visible at runtime, it must be a member of this collection.

To finish the initial code of this example, return to the designer and handle the `Click` event for the Exit menu item using the events button of the Properties window. Within the generated event handler, make a call to `Application.Exit`:

```
private void exitToolStripMenuItem_Click(object sender, EventArgs e)
{
    Application.Exit();
}
```

At this point, you should be able to compile and run your program. Verify that you can terminate the application via File ➤ Exit as well as pressing Alt+f and then x on the keyboard.

Adding a TextBox to the MenuStrip

Now, let's create a new topmost menu item named Change Background Color. The subitem in this case will not be a menu item, but a ToolStripTextBox (see Figure 19-13). Once you have added the new control, rename this control to toolStripTextBoxColor using the Properties window.

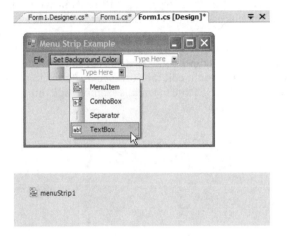

Figure 19-13. *Adding* TextBox*es to a* MenuStrip

The goal here is to allow the user to enter the name of a color (red, green, pink, etc.) that will be used to set the BackColor property of the Form. First, handle the LostFocus event on the new ToolStripTextBox member variable within the Form's constructor (as you would guess, this event fires when the TextBox within the ToolStrip is no longer the active UI element):

```
public MainWindow()
{
...
    toolStripTextBoxColor.LostFocus
        += new EventHandler(toolStripTextBoxColor_LostFocus);
}
```

Within the generated event handler, you will extract the string data entered within the ToolStripTextBox (via the Text property) and make use of the System.Drawing.Color.FromName() method. This static method will return a Color type based on a known string value. To account for the possibility that the user enters an unknown color (or types bogus data), you will make use of some simple try/catch logic:

```
void toolStripTextBoxColor_LostFocus(object sender, EventArgs e)
{
    try
    {
        BackColor = Color.FromName(toolStripTextBoxColor.Text);
    } catch { } // Just do nothing if the user provides bad data.
}
```

Go ahead and take your updated application out for another test drive and try entering in the names of various colors. Once you do, you should see your Form's background color change. If you are interested in checking out some valid color names, look up the System.Drawing.Color type using the Visual Studio 2005 Object Browser or the .NET Framework 2.0 SDK documentation.

Creating a Context Menu

Let's now examine the process of building a context-sensitive pop-up (i.e., right-click) menu. Under .NET 1.1, the ContextMenu type was the class of choice for building context menus, but under .NET 2.0 the preferred type is ContextMenuStrip. Like the MenuStrip type, ContextMenuStrip maintains a ToolStripItemCollection to represent the possible subitems (such as ToolStripMenuItem, ToolStripComboBox, ToolStripSeperator, ToolStripTextBox, etc.).

Drag a new ContextMenuStrip control from the Toolbox onto the Forms designer and rename the control to fontSizeContextStrip using the Properties window. Notice that you are able to populate the subitems graphically in much the same way you would edit the Form's main MenuStrip (a welcome change from the method used in Visual Studio .NET 2003). For this example, add three ToolStripMenuItems named Huge, Normal, and Tiny (see Figure 19-14).

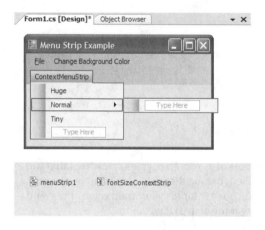

Figure 19-14. *Designing a* ContextMenuStrip

This context menu will be used to allow the user to select the size to render a message within the Form's client area. To facilitate this endeavor, create an enum type named TextFontSize within the MenuStripApp namespace and declare a new member variable of this type within your Form type (set to TextFontSize.FontSizeNormal):

```
namespace MainForm
{
    // Helper enum for font size.
    enum TextFontSize
    {
        FontSizeHuge = 30,
        FontSizeNormal = 20,
        FontSizeTiny = 8
    }

    public class MainForm : Form
    {
```

```
        // Current size of font.
        private TextFontSize currFontSize
            = TextFontSize.FontSizeNormal;
...
    }
}
```

The next step is to handle the Form's Paint event using the Properties window. As described in greater detail in the next chapter, the Paint event allows you to render graphical data (including stylized text) onto a Form's client area. Here, you are going to draw a textual message using a font of user-specified size. Don't sweat the details at this point, but do update your Paint event handler as so:

```
private void MainWindow_Paint(object sender, PaintEventArgs e)
{
    Graphics g = e.Graphics;
    g.DrawString("Right click on me...",
            new Font("Times New Roman", (float)currFontSize),
            new SolidBrush(Color.Black), 50, 50);
}
```

Last but not least, you need to handle the Click events for each of the ToolStripMenuItem types maintained by the ContextMenuStrip. While you could have a separate Click event handler for each, you will simply specify a single event handler that will be called when any of the three ToolStripMenuItems have been clicked. Using the Properties window, specify the name of the Click event handler as ContextMenuItemSelection_Clicked for each of the three ToolStripMenuItems and implement this method as so:

```
private void ContextMenuItemSelection_Clicked(object sender, EventArgs e)
{
    // Obtain the currently clicked ToolStripMenuItem.
    ToolStripMenuItem miClicked =
        (ToolStripMenuItem)sender;

    // Figure out which item was clicked using its Name.
    if (miClicked.Name == "hugeToolStripMenuItem")
        currFontSize = TextFontSize.FontSizeHuge;
    if (miClicked.Name == "normalToolStripMenuItem")
        currFontSize = TextFontSize.FontSizeNormal;
    if (miClicked.Name == "tinyToolStripMenuItem")
        currFontSize = TextFontSize.FontSizeTiny;

    // Tell the Form to repaint itself.
    Invalidate();
}
```

Notice that using the "sender" argument, you are able to determine the name of the ToolStripMenuItem member variable in order to set the current text size. Once you have done so, the call to Invalidate() fires the Paint event, which will cause your Paint event handler to execute.

The final step is to inform the Form which ContextMenuStrip it should display when the right mouse button is clicked in its client area. To do so, simply use the Properties window to set the ContextMenuStrip property equal to the name of your context menu item. Once you have done so, you will find the following line within InitializeComponent():

```
    this.ContextMenuStrip = this.fontSizeContextStrip;
```

■**Note** Be aware that *any* control can be assigned a context menu via the `ContextMenuStrip` property. For example, you could create a `Button` object on a dialog box that responds to a particular context menu. In this way, the menu would be displayed only if the mouse button were right-clicked within the bounding rectangle of the button.

If you now run the application, you should be able to change the size of the rendered text message via a right-click of your mouse.

Checking Menu Items

`ToolStripMenuItem` defines a number of members that allow you to check, enable, and hide a given item. Table 19-11 gives a rundown of some (but not all) of the interesting properties.

Table 19-11. *Members of the* `ToolStripMenuItem` *Type*

Member	Meaning in Life
Checked	Gets or sets a value indicating whether a check mark appears beside the text of the `ToolStripMenuItem`
CheckOnClick	Gets or sets a value indicating whether the `ToolStripMenuItem` should automatically appear checked/unchecked when clicked
Enabled	Gets or sets a value indicating whether the `ToolStripMenuItem` is enabled

Let's extend the previous pop-up menu to display a check mark next to the currently selected menu item. Setting a check mark on a given menu item is not at all difficult (just set the `Checked` property to true). However, tracking which menu item should be checked does require some additional logic. One possible approach is to define a distinct `ToolStripMenuItem` member variable that represents the currently checked item:

```
public class MainWindow : Form
{
...
    // Marks the item checked.
    private ToolStripMenuItem currentCheckedItem;
}
```

Recall that the default text size is `TextFontSize.FontSizeNormal`. Given this, the initial item to be checked is the `normalToolStripMenuItem` `ToolStripMenuItem` member variable. Update your Form's constructor as so:

```
public MainWindow()
{
    // Inherited method to center the Form.
    CenterToScreen();
    InitializeComponent();

    // Now check the 'Normal' menu item.
    currentCheckedItem = normalToolStripMenuItem;
    currentCheckedItem.Checked = true;
}
```

Now that you have a way to programmatically identify the currently checked item, the last step is to update the `ContextMenuItemSelection_Clicked()` event handler to uncheck the previous item and check the new current `ToolStripMenuItem` object in response to the user selection:

```
private void ContextMenuItemSelection_Clicked(object sender, EventArgs e)
{
    // Uncheck the currently checked item.
    currentCheckedItem.Checked = false;
...
    if (miClicked.Name == "hugeToolStripMenuItem")
    {
        currFontSize = TextFontSize.FontSizeHuge;
        currentCheckedItem = hugeToolStripMenuItem;
    }
    if (miClicked.Name == "normalToolStripMenuItem")
    {
        currFontSize = TextFontSize.FontSizeNormal;
        currentCheckedItem = normalToolStripMenuItem;
    }
    if (miClicked.Name == "tinyToolStripMenuItem")
    {
        currFontSize = TextFontSize.FontSizeTiny;
        currentCheckedItem = tinyToolStripMenuItem;
    }
    // Check new item.
    currentCheckedItem.Checked = true;
...
}
```

Figure 19-15 shows the completed MenuStripApp project in action.

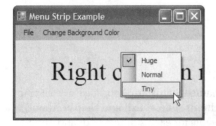

Figure 19-15. *Checking/unchecking* ToolStripMenuItems

■**Source Code** The MenuStripApp application is located under the Chapter 19 subdirectory.

Working with StatusStrips

In addition to a menu system, many Forms also maintain a *status bar* that is typically mounted at the bottom of the Form. A status bar may be divided into any number of "panes" that hold some textual (or graphical) information such as menu help strings, the current time, or other application-specific information.

Although status bars have been supported since the release of the .NET platform (via the System. Windows.Forms.StatusBar type), as of .NET 2.0 the simple StatusBar has been ousted by the new StatusStrip type. Like a status bar, a StatusStrip can consist of any number of panes to hold textual/graphical data using a ToolStripStatusLabel type. However, status strips have the ability to contain additional tool strip items such as the following:

- `ToolStripProgressBar`: An embedded progress bar.

- `ToolStripDropDownButton`: An embedded button that displays a drop-down list of choices when clicked.

- `ToolStripSplitButton`: This is similar to the `ToolStripDropDownButton`, but the items of the drop-down list are displayed only if the user clicks directly on the drop-down area of the control. The `ToolStripSplitButton` also has normal buttonlike behavior and can thus support the `Click` event.

In this example, you will build a new `MainWindow` that supports a simple menu (File ➤ Exit and Help ➤ About) as well as a `StatusStrip`. The leftmost pane of the status strip will be used to display help string data regarding the currently selected menu subitem (e.g., if the user selects the Exit menu, the pane will display "Exits the app").

The far right pane will display one of two dynamically created strings that will show either the current time or the current date. Finally, the middle pane will be a `ToolStripDropDownButton` type that allows the user to toggle the date/time display (with a happy face icon to boot!). Figure 19-16 shows the application in its completed form.

Figure 19-16. *The* `StatusStrip` *application*

Designing the Menu System

To begin, create a new Windows Forms application project named StatusStripApp. Place a `MenuStrip` control onto the Forms designer and build the two menu items (File ➤ Exit and Help ➤ About). Once you have done so, handle the `Click` and `MouseHover` events for each subitem (Exit and About) using the Properties window.

The implementation of the File ➤ Exit `Click` event handler will simply terminate the application, while the Help ➤ About `Click` event handler shows a friendly `MessageBox`.

```
private void exitToolStripMenuItem_Click(object sender, EventArgs e)
{ Application.Exit(); }

private void aboutToolStripMenuItem_Click(object sender, EventArgs e)
{ MessageBox.Show("My StatusStripApp!"); }
```

You will update the `MouseHover` event handler to display the correct prompt in the leftmost pane of the `StatusStrip` in just a bit, so leave them empty for the time being.

Designing the StatusStrip

Next, place a `StatusStrip` control onto the designer and rename this control to `mainStatusStrip`. Understand that by default a `StatusStrip` contains no panes whatsoever. To add the three panes, you may take various approaches:

- Author the code by hand without designer support (perhaps using a helper method named CreateStatusStrip() that is called in the Form's constructor).

- Add the items via a dialog box activated using the Edit Items link using the StatusStrip context-sensitive inline editor (see Figure 19-17).

- Add the items one by one via the new item drop-down editor mounted on the StatusStrip (see Figure 19-18).

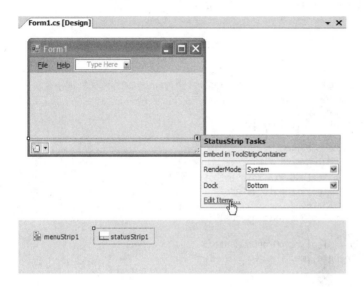

Figure 19-17. *The* StatusStrip *context editor*

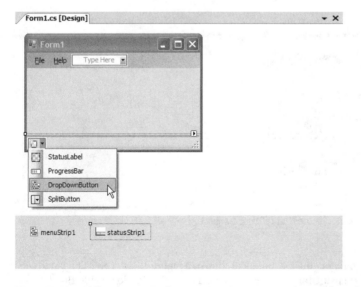

Figure 19-18. *Adding items via the* StatusStrip *new item drop-down editor*

For this example, you will leverage the new item drop-down editor. Add two new ToolStripStatusLabel types named toolStripStatusLabelMenuState and toolStripStatusLabelClock, and a ToolStripDropDownButton named toolStripDropDownButtonDateTime. As you would expect, this will add new member variables in the *.Designer.cs file and update InitializeComponent() accordingly. Note that the StatusStrip maintains an internal collection to hold each of the panes:

```
partial class MainForm
{
    private void InitializeComponent()
    {
...
        //
        // mainStatusStrip
        //
        this.mainStatusStrip.Items.AddRange(new System.Windows.Forms.ToolStripItem[] {
            this.toolStripStatusLabelMenuState,
            this.toolStripStatusLabelClock,
            this.toolStripDropDownButtonDateTime});
...
    }

    private System.Windows.Forms.StatusStrip mainStatusStrip;
    private System.Windows.Forms.ToolStripStatusLabel
        toolStripStatusLabelMenuState;
    private System.Windows.Forms.ToolStripStatusLabel
        toolStripStatusLabelClock;
    private System.Windows.Forms.ToolStripDropDownButton
        toolStripDropDownButtonDateTime;
...
}
```

Now, select the ToolStripDropDownButton on the designer and add two new menu items named currentTimeToolStripMenuItem and dayoftheWeekToolStripMenuItem (see Figure 19-19).

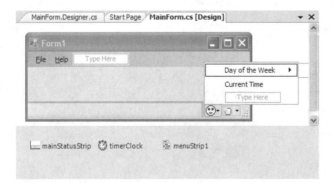

Figure 19-19. *Adding menu items to the* ToolStripDropDownButton

To configure your panes to reflect the look and feel shown in Figure 19-19, you will need to set several properties, which you do using the Visual Studio 2005 Properties window. Table 19-12 documents the necessary properties to set and events to handle for each item on your StatusStrip (of course, feel free to stylize the panes with additional settings as you see fit).

Table 19-12. StatusStrip *Pane Configuration*

Pane Member Variable	Properties to Set	Events to Handle
toolStripStatusLabelMenuState	Spring = true Text = (empty) TextAlign = TopLeft	None
toolStripStatusLabelClock	BorderSides = All Text = (empty)	None
toolStripDropDownButtonDateTime	Image = (see text that follows)	None
dayoftheWeekToolStripMenuItem	Text = "Day of the Week"	MouseHover Click
currentTimeToolStripMenuItem	Text = "Current Time"	MouseHover Click

The Image property of the toolStripDropDownButtonDateTime member can be set to any image file on your machine (of course, extremely large image files will be quite skewed). For this example, you may wish to use the happyDude.bmp file included with this book's downloadable source code (please visit the Downloads section of the Apress website, http://www.apress.com).

So at this point, the GUI design is complete! Before you implement the remaining event handlers, you need to get to know the role of the Timer component.

Working with the Timer Type

Recall that the second pane should display the current time or current date based on user preference. The first step to take to achieve this design goal is to add a Timer member variable to the Form. A Timer is a component that calls some method (specified using the Tick event) at a given interval (specified by the Interval property).

Drag a Timer component onto your Forms designer and rename it to timerDateTimeUpdate. Using the Properties window, set the Interval property to 1,000 (the value in milliseconds) and set the Enabled property to true. Finally, handle the Tick event. Before implementing the Tick event handler, define a new enum type in your project named DateTimeFormat. This enum will be used to determine whether the second ToolStripStatusLabel should display the current time or the current day of the week:

```
enum DateTimeFormat
{
    ShowClock,
    ShowDay
}
```

With this enum in place, update your MainWindow with the following code:

```
public partial class MainWindow : Form
{
    // Which format to display?
    DateTimeFormat dtFormat = DateTimeFormat.ShowClock;
...
    private void timerDateTimeUpdate_Tick(object sender, EventArgs e)
    {
        string panelInfo = "";

        // Create current format.
        if (dtFormat == DateTimeFormat.ShowClock)
            panelInfo = DateTime.Now.ToLongTimeString();
```

```
        else
            panelInfo = DateTime.Now.ToLongDateString();

        // Set text on pane.
        toolStripStatusLabelClock.Text = panelInfo;
    }
}
```

Notice that the Timer event handler makes use of the DateTime type. Here, you simply find the current system time or date using the Now property and use it to set the Text property of the toolStripStatusLabelClock member variable.

Toggling the Display

At this point, the Tick event handler should be displaying the current time within the toolStripStatusLabelClock pane, given that the default value of your DateTimeFormat member variable as been set to DateTimeFormat.ShowClock. To allow the user to toggle between the date and time display, update your MainWindow as so (note you are also toggling which of the two menu items in the ToolStripDropDownButton should be checked):

```
public partial class MainWindow : Form
{
    // Which format to display?
    DateTimeFormat dtFormat = DateTimeFormat.ShowClock;

    // Marks the item checked.
    private ToolStripMenuItem currentCheckedItem;

    public MainWindow()
    {
        InitializeComponent();

        // These properties can also be set
        // with the Properties window.
        Text = "Status Strip Example";
        CenterToScreen();
        BackColor = Color.CadetBlue;
        currentCheckedItem = currentTimeToolStripMenuItem;
        currentCheckedItem.Checked = true;
    }
...
    private void currentTimeToolStripMenuItem_Click(object sender, EventArgs e)
    {
        // Toggle check mark and set pane format to time.
        currentCheckedItem.Checked = false;
        dtFormat = DateTimeFormat.ShowClock;
        currentCheckedItem = currentTimeToolStripMenuItem;
        currentCheckedItem.Checked = true;
    }
    private void dayoftheWeekToolStripMenuItem_Click(object sender, EventArgs e)
    {
        // Toggle check mark and set pane format to date.
        currentCheckedItem.Checked = false;
        dtFormat = DateTimeFormat.ShowDay;
        currentCheckedItem = dayoftheWeekToolStripMenuItem;
        currentCheckedItem.Checked = true;
    }
}
```

Displaying the Menu Selection Prompts

Finally, you need to configure the first pane to hold menu help strings. As you know, most applications send a small bit of text information to the first pane of a status bar whenever the end user selects a menu item (e.g., "This terminates the application"). Given that you have already handled the MouseHover events for each submenu on the MenuStrip and TooStripDropDownButton, all you need to do is assign a proper value to the Text property for the toolStripStatusLabelMenuState member variable, for example:

```
private void exitToolStripMenuItem_MouseHover(object sender, EventArgs e)
{ toolStripStatusLabelMenuState.Text = "Exits the app."; }

private void aboutToolStripMenuItem_MouseHover(object sender, EventArgs e)
{ toolStripStatusLabelMenuState.Text = "Shows about box."; }

private void dayoftheWeekToolStripMenuItem_MouseHover(object sender, EventArgs e)
{ toolStripStatusLabelMenuState.Text = "Shows the day of the week."; }

private void currentTimeToolStripMenuItem_MouseHover(object sender, EventArgs e)
{ toolStripStatusLabelMenuState.Text = "Shows the current time."; }
```

Take your updated project out for a test drive. You should now be able to find these informational help strings in the first pane of your StatusStrip as you select each menu item.

Establishing a "Ready" State

The final thing to do for this example is ensure that when the user deselects a menu item, the first text pane is set to a default message (e.g., "Ready"). With the current design, the previously selected menu prompt remains on the leftmost text pane, which is confusing at best. To rectify this issue, handle the MouseLeave event for the Exit, About, Day of the Week, and Current Time menu items. *However*, rather than generating a new event handler for each item, have them all call a method named SetReadyPrompt():

```
private void SetReadyPrompt(object sender, EventArgs e)
{   toolStripStatusLabelMenuState.Text = "Ready."; }
```

With this, you should find that the first pane resets to this default message as soon as the mouse cursor leaves any of your four menu items.

■**Source Code** The StatusBarApp project is included under the Chapter 19 subdirectory.

Working with ToolStrips

The next Form-level GUI item to examine in this chapter is the .NET 2.0 ToolStrip type, which overshadows the functionality found within the depreciated .NET 1.*x* ToolBar class. As you know, toolbars typically provide an alternate means to activate a given menu item. Thus, if the user clicks a Save button, this has the same effect as selecting File ➤ Save. Much like MenuStrip and StatusStrip, the ToolStrip type can contain numerous toolbar items, some of which you have already encountered in previous examples:

- ToolStripButton
- ToolStripLabel
- ToolStripSplitButton

- ToolStripDropDownButton
- ToolStripSeparator
- ToolStripComboBox
- ToolStripTextBox
- ToolStripProgressBar

Like other Windows Forms controls, the ToolStrip supports an inline editor that allows you to quickly add standard button types (File, Exit, Help, Copy, Paste, etc.) to a ToolStrip, change the docking position, and embed the ToolStrip in a ToolStripContainer (more details in just a bit). Figure 19-20 illustrates the designer support for ToolStrips.

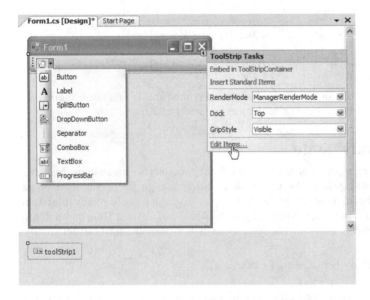

Figure 19-20. *Designing* ToolStrips

Like MenuStrips and StatusStrips, individual ToolStrip controls are added to the ToolStrip's internal collection via the Items property. If you click the Insert Standard Items link on the inline ToolStrip editor, your InitializeComponent() method is updated to insert an array of ToolStripItem-derived types that represent each item:

```
private void InitializeComponent()
{
...
    // Autogenerated code to prep a ToolStrip.
    this.toolStrip1.Items.AddRange(new System.Windows.Forms.ToolStripItem[] {
        this.newToolStripButton, this.openToolStripButton,
        this.saveToolStripButton, this.printToolStripButton,
        this.toolStripSeparator, this.cutToolStripButton,
        this.copyToolStripButton, this.pasteToolStripButton,
        this.toolStripSeparator1, this.helpToolStripButton});
...
}
```

To illustrate working with ToolStrips, the following Windows Forms application creates a ToolStrip containing two ToolStripButton types (named toolStripButtonGrowFont and toolStripButtonShrinkFont), a ToolBarSeparator, and a ToolBarTextBox (named toolStripTextBoxMessage).

The end user is able to enter a message to be rendered on the Form via the ToolBarTextBox, and the two ToolBarButton types will be used to increase or decrease the font size. Figure 19-21 shows the end result of the project you will construct.

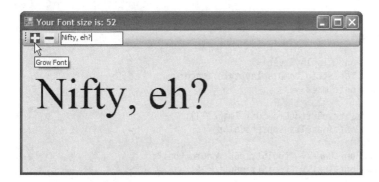

Figure 19-21. *ToolStripApp in action*

By now I'd guess you have a handle on working with the Visual Studio 2005 Forms designer, so I won't belabor the point of building the ToolStrip. Do note, however, that each ToolStripButton has a custom (albeit poorly drawn by yours truly) icon that was created using the Visual Studio 2005 image editor. If you wish to create image files for your project, simply select the Project ➤ Add New Item menu option, and from the resulting dialog box add a new icon file (see Figure 19-22).

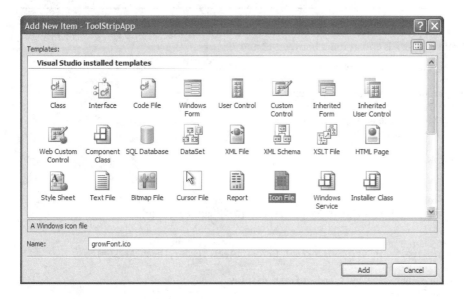

Figure 19-22. *Inserting new image files*

Once you have done so, you are able to edit your images using the Colors tab on the Toolbox and the Image Editor toolbox. In any case, once you have designed your icons, you are able to associate them with the ToolStripButton types via the Image property in the Properties window. Once you are happy with the ToolStrip's look and feel, handle the Click event for each ToolStripButton.

Here is the relevant code in the InitializeComponent() method for the first ToolStripButton type (the second ToolStripButton will look just about the same):

```
private void InitializeComponent()
{
...
    // toolStripButtonGrowFont
    //
    this.toolStripButtonGrowFont.DisplayStyle =
        System.Windows.Forms.ToolStripItemDisplayStyle.Image;
    this.toolStripButtonGrowFont.Image =
    ((System.Drawing.Image)
    (resources.GetObject("toolStripButtonGrowFont.Image")));
    this.toolStripButtonGrowFont.ImageTransparentColor =
        System.Drawing.Color.Magenta;
    this.toolStripButtonGrowFont.Name = "toolStripButtonGrowFont";
    this.toolStripButtonGrowFont.Text = "toolStripButton2";
    this.toolStripButtonGrowFont.ToolTipText = "Grow Font";
    this.toolStripButtonGrowFont.Click += new
        System.EventHandler(this.toolStripButtonGrowFont_Click);
...
}
```

■**Note** Notice that the value assigned to the Image of a ToolStripButton is obtained using a method named GetObject(). As explained in the next chapter, this method is used to extract embedded resources used by your assembly.

The remaining code is extremely straightforward. In the following updated MainWindow, notice that the current font size is constrained between 12 and 70:

```
public partial class MainWindow : Form
{
    // The current, max and min font sizes.
    int currFontSize = 12;
    const int MinFontSize = 12;
    const int MaxFontSize = 70;

    public MainWindow()
    {
        InitializeComponent();
        CenterToScreen();
        Text = string.Format("Your Font size is: {0}", currFontSize);
    }

    private void toolStripButtonShrinkFont_Click(object sender, EventArgs e)
    {
        // Reduce font size by 5 and refresh display.
        currFontSize -= 5;
        if (currFontSize <= MinFontSize)
            currFontSize = MinFontSize;
```

```
        Text = string.Format("Your Font size is: {0}", currFontSize);
        Invalidate();
    }

    private void toolStripButtonGrowFont_Click(object sender, EventArgs e)
    {
        // Increase font size by 5 and refresh display.
        currFontSize += 5;
        if (currFontSize >= MaxFontSize)
            currFontSize = MaxFontSize;
        Text = string.Format("Your Font size is: {0}", currFontSize);
        Invalidate();
    }

    private void MainWindow_Paint(object sender, PaintEventArgs e)
    {
        // Paint the user-defined message.
        Graphics g = e.Graphics;
        g.DrawString(toolStripTextBoxMessage.Text,
            new Font("Times New Roman", currFontSize),
            Brushes.Black, 10, 60);
    }
}
```

As a final enhancement, if you wish to ensure that the user message is updated as soon as the ToolStripTextBox loses focus, you can handle the LostFocus event and Invalidate() your Form within the generated event handler:

```
public partial class MainWindow : Form
{
...
    public MainWindow()
    {
...
        this.toolStripTextBoxMessage.LostFocus
            += new EventHandler(toolStripTextBoxMessage_LostFocus);
    }
    void toolStripTextBoxMessage_LostFocus(object sender, EventArgs e)
    {
        Invalidate();
    }
...
}
```

Working with ToolStripContainers

ToolStrips, if required, can be configured to be "dockable" against any or all sides of the Form that contains it. To illustrate how you can accomplish this, right-click your current ToolStrip using the designer and select the Embed in ToolStripContainer menu option. Once you have done so, you will find that the ToolStrip has been contained within a ToolStripContainer. For this example, select the Dock Fill in Form option (see Figure 19-23).

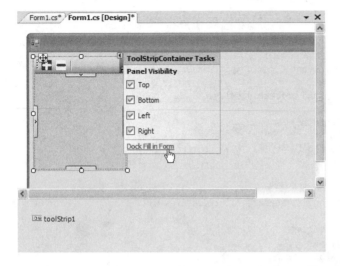

Figure 19-23. *Docking the* `ToolStripContainer` *within the entire Form*

If you run your current update, you will find that the `ToolStrip` can be moved and docked to each side of the container. However, your custom message has now vanished. The reason for this is that `ToolStripContainers` are actually *child controls* of the Form. Therefore, the graphical render is still taking place, but the output is being hidden by the container that now sits on top of the Form's client area.

To fix this problem, you will need to handle the `Paint` event on the `ToolStripContainer` rather than on the Form. First, locate the Form's `Paint` event within the Properties window and right-click the current event handler. From the context menu, select Reset (see Figure 19-24).

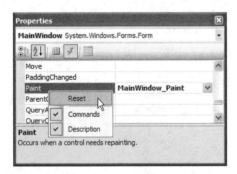

Figure 19-24. *Resetting an event*

This will remove the event handling logic in `InitializeComponent()`, but it will leave the event handler in place (just to ensure you don't lose code you would like to maintain).

Now, handle the `Paint` event for the `ToolStripContainer` and move the rendering code from the existing Form's `Paint` event handler into the container's `Paint` event handler. Once you have done so, you can delete the (now empty) `MainWindow_Paint()` method. Finally, you will need to replace each occurrence of the call to the Form's `Invalidate()` method to the container's `Invalidate()` method. Here are the relevant code updates:

```
public partial class MainWindow : Form
{
...
    void toolStripTextBoxMessage_LostFocus(object sender, EventArgs e)
    {
        toolStripContainer1.Invalidate(true);
    }

    private void toolStripButtonShrinkFont_Click(object sender, EventArgs e)
    {
...
        toolStripContainer1.Invalidate(true);
    }
    private void toolStripButtonGrowFont_Click(object sender, EventArgs e)
    {
...
        toolStripContainer1.Invalidate(true);
    }
    // We are now painting on the container, not the form!
    private void ContentPanel_Paint(object sender, PaintEventArgs e)
    {
        Graphics g = e.Graphics;
        g.DrawString(toolStripTextBoxMessage.Text,
            new Font("Times New Roman", currFontSize),
            Brushes.Black, 10, 60);
    }
}
```

Of course, the ToolStripContainer can be configured in various ways to tweak how it operates. I leave it to you to check out the .NET Framework 2.0 SDK documentation for complete details. Figure 19-25 shows the completed project.

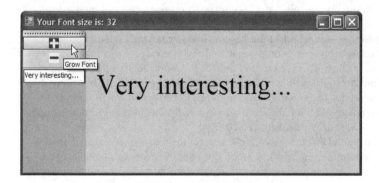

Figure 19-25. *ToolStripApp, now with a dockable* ToolStrip

■**Source Code** The ToolStripApp project is included under the Chapter 19 subdirectory.

Building an MDI Application

To wrap up our initial look at Windows Forms, I'll close this chapter by discussing how to configure a Form to function as a parent to any number of child windows (i.e., an MDI container). MDI applications allow users to have multiple child windows open at the same time within the same topmost window. In the world of MDIs, each window represents a given "document" of the application. For example, Visual Studio 2005 is an MDI application in that you are able to have multiple documents open from within an instance of the application.

When you are building MDI applications using Windows Forms, your first task is to (of course) create a brand-new Windows application. The initial Form of the application typically hosts a menu system that allows you to create new documents (such as File ➤ New) as well as arrange existing open windows (cascade, vertical tile, and horizontal tile).

Creating the child windows is interesting, as you typically define a prototypical Form that functions as a basis for each child window. Given that Forms are class types, any private data defined in the child Form will be unique to a particular instance. For example, if you were to create an MDI word processing application, you might create a child Form that maintains a StringBuilder to represent the text. If a user created five new child windows, each Form would maintain its own StringBuilder instance, which could be individually manipulated.

Additionally, MDI applications allow you to "merge menus." As mentioned previously, parent windows typically have a menu system that allows the user to spawn and organize additional child windows. However, what if the child window also maintains a menuing system? If the user maximizes a particular child window, you need to merge the child's menu system within the parent Form to allow the user to activate items from each menu system. The Windows Forms namespace defines a number of properties, methods, and events that allow you to programmatically merge menu systems. In addition, there is a "default merge" system, which works in a good number of cases.

Building the Parent Form

To illustrate the basics of building an MDI application, begin by creating a brand-new Windows application named SimpleMdiApp. Almost all of the MDI infrastructure can be assigned to your initial Form using various design-time tools. To begin, locate the IsMdiContainer property in the Properties window and set it to true. If you look at the design-time Form, you'll see that the client area has been modified to visually represent a container of child windows.

Next, place a new MenuStrip control on your main Form. This menu specifies three topmost items named File, Window, and Arrange Windows. The File menu contains two subitems named New and Exit. The Window menu does not contain any subitems, because you will programmatically add new items as the user creates additional child windows. Finally, the Arrange Window menu defines three subitems named Cascade, Vertical, and Horizontal.

Once you have created the menu UI, handle the Click event for the Exit, New, Cascade, Vertical, and Horizontal menu items (remember, the Window menu does not have any subitems just yet). You'll implement the File ➤ New handler in the next section, but for now here is the code behind the remaining menu selections:

```
// Handle File | Exit event and arrange all child windows.
private void cascadeToolStripMenuItem_Click(object sender, EventArgs e)
{
    LayoutMdi(MdiLayout.Cascade);
}
private void verticalToolStripMenuItem_Click(object sender, EventArgs e)
{
    LayoutMdi(MdiLayout.TileVertical);
}
private void horizontalToolStripMenuItem_Click(object sender, EventArgs e)
```

```
{
    LayoutMdi(MdiLayout.TileHorizontal);
}
private void exitToolStripMenuItem_Click(object sender, EventArgs e)
{
    Application.Exit();
}
```

The main point of interest here is the use of the LayoutMdi() method and the corresponding MdiLayout enumeration. The code behind each menu select handler should be quite clear. When the user selects a given arrangement, you tell the parent Form to automatically reposition any and all child windows.

Before you move on to the construction of the child Form, you need to set one additional property of the MenuStrip. The MdiWindowListItem property is used to establish which topmost menu item should be used to automatically list the name of each child window as a possible menu selection. Set this property to the windowToolStripMenuItem member variable. By default, this list is the value of the child's Text property followed by a numerical suffix (i.e., Form1, Form2, Form3, etc.).

Building the Child Form

Now that you have the shell of an MDI container, you need to create an additional Form that functions as the prototype for a given child window. Begin by inserting a new Form type into your current project (using Project ➤ Add Windows Form) named ChildPrototypeForm and handle the Click event for this Form. In the generated event handler, randomly set the background color of the client area. In addition, print out the "stringified" value of the new Color object into the child's caption bar. The following logic should do the trick:

```
private void ChildPrototypeForm_Click(object sender, EventArgs e)
{
    // Get three random numbers
    int r, g, b;
    Random ran = new Random();
    r = ran.Next(0, 255);
    g = ran.Next(0, 255);
    b = ran.Next(0, 255);

    // Now create a color for the background.
    Color currColor = Color.FromArgb(r, g, b);
    this.BackColor = currColor;
    this.Text = currColor.ToString();
}
```

Spawning Child Windows

Your final order of business is to flesh out the details behind the parent Form's File ➤ New event handler. Now that you have defined a child Form, the logic is simple: create and show a new instance of the ChildPrototypeForm type. As well, you need to set the value of the child Form's MdiParent property to point to the containing Form (in this case, your main window). Here is the update:

```
private void newToolStripMenuItem_Click(object sender, EventArgs e)
{
    // Make a new child window.
    ChildPrototypeForm newChild = new ChildPrototypeForm();

    // Set the Parent Form of the Child window.
    newChild.MdiParent = this;
```

```
    // Display the new form.
    newChild.Show();
}
```

Note A child Form may access the MdiParent property directly whenever it needs to manipulate (or communicate with) its parent window.

To take this application out for a test drive, begin by creating a set of new child windows and click each one to establish a unique background color. If you examine the subitems under the Windows menu, you should see each child Form present and accounted for. As well, if you access the Arrange Window menu items, you can instruct the parent Form to vertically tile, horizontally tile, or cascade the child Forms. Figure 19-26 shows the completed application.

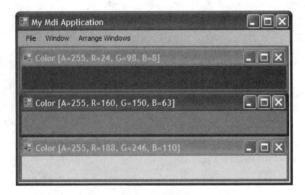

Figure 19-26. *An MDI application*

Source Code The SimpleMdiApp project can be found under the Chapter 19 subdirectory.

Summary

This chapter introduced the fine art of building a UI with the types contained in the System.Windows. Forms namespace. You began by building a number of applications by hand, and you learned along the way that at a minimum, a GUI application needs a class that derives from Form and a Main() method that invokes Application.Run().

During the course of this chapter, you learned how to build topmost menus (and pop-up menus) and how to respond to a number of menu events. You also came to understand how to further enhance your Form types using toolbars and status bars. As you have seen, .NET 2.0 prefers to build such UI elements using MenuStrips, ToolStrips, and StatusStrips rather than the older .NET 1.x MainMenu, ToolBar, and StatusBar types (although these deprecated types are still supported). Finally, this chapter wrapped up by illustrating how to construct MDI applications using Windows Forms.

■ ■ ■

## CHAPTER 20

Rendering Graphical Data with GDI+

The previous chapter introduced you to the process of building a GUI-based desktop application using System.Windows.Forms. The point of this chapter is to examine the details of rendering graphics (including stylized text and image data) onto a Form's surface area. We'll begin by taking a high-level look at the numerous drawing-related namespaces, and we'll examine the role of the Paint event, and the almighty Graphics object.

The remainder of this chapter covers how to manipulate colors, fonts, geometric shapes, and graphical images. This chapter also explores a number of rendering-centric programming techniques, such as nonrectangular hit testing, drag-and-drop logic, and the .NET resource format. While *technically* not part of GDI+ proper, resources often involve the manipulation of graphical data (which, in my opinion, is "GDI+-enough" to be presented here).

█Note If you are a web programmer by trade, you may think that GDI+ is of no use to you. However, GDI+ is not limited to traditional desktop applications and is extremely relevant for web applications.

A Survey of the GDI+ Namespaces

The .NET platform provides a number of namespaces devoted to two-dimensional graphical rendering. In addition to the basic functionality you would expect to find in a graphics toolkit (colors, fonts, pens, brushes, etc.), you also find types that enable geometric transformations, antialiasing, palette blending, and document printing support. Collectively speaking, these namespaces make up the .NET facility we call *GDI+*, which is a managed alternative to the Win32 Graphical Device Interface (GDI) API. Table 20-1 gives a high-level view of the core GDI+ namespaces.

Table 20-1. *Core GDI+ Namespaces*

Namespace	Meaning in Life
System.Drawing	This is the core GDI+ namespace that defines numerous types for basic rendering (fonts, pens, basic brushes, etc.) as well as the almighty Graphics type.
System.Drawing.Drawing2D	This namespace provides types used for more advanced two-dimensional/vector graphics functionality (e.g., gradient brushes, pen caps, geometric transforms, etc.).
System.Drawing.Imaging	This namespace defines types that allow you to manipulate graphical images (e.g., change the palette, extract image metadata, manipulate metafiles, etc.).
System.Drawing.Printing	This namespace defines types that allow you to render images to the printed page, interact with the printer itself, and format the overall appearance of a given print job.
System.Drawing.Text	This namespace allows you to manipulate collections of fonts.

■**Note** All of the GDI+ namespaces are defined within the System.Drawing.dll assembly. While many Visual Studio 2005 project types automatically set a reference to this code library, you can manually reference System.Drawing.dll using the Add References dialog box if necessary.

An Overview of the System.Drawing Namespace

The vast majority of the types you'll use when programming GDI+ applications are found within the System.Drawing namespace. As you would expect, there are classes that represent images, brushes, pens, and fonts. Furthermore, System.Drawing defines a number of related utility types such as Color, Point, and Rectangle. Table 20-2 lists some (but not all) of the core types.

Table 20-2. *Core Types of the* System.Drawing *Namespace*

Type	Meaning in Life
Bitmap	This type encapsulates image data (*.bmp or otherwise).
Brush Brushes SolidBrush SystemBrushes TextureBrush	Brush objects are used to fill the interiors of graphical shapes such as rectangles, ellipses, and polygons.
BufferedGraphics	This new .NET 2.0 type provides a graphics buffer for double buffering, which is used to reduce or eliminate flicker caused by redrawing a display surface.
Color SystemColors	The Color and SystemColors types define a number of static read-only properties used to obtain specific colors for the construction of various pens/brushes.
Font FontFamily	The Font type encapsulates the characteristics of a given font (i.e., type name, bold, italic, point size, etc.). FontFamily provides an abstraction for a group of fonts having a similar design but with certain variations in style.
Graphics	This core class represents a valid drawing surface, as well as a number of methods to render text, images, and geometric patterns.

Type	Meaning in Life
Icon SystemIcons	These classes represent custom icons, as well as the set of standard system-supplied icons.
Image ImageAnimator	Image is an abstract base class that provides functionality for the Bitmap, Icon, and Cursor types. ImageAnimator provides a way to iterate over a number of Image-derived types at some specified interval.
Pen Pens SystemPens	Pens are objects used to draw lines and curves. The Pens type defines a number of static properties that return a new Pen of a given color.
Point PointF	These structures represent an (*x*, *y*) coordinate mapping to an underlying integer or float, respectively.
Rectangle RectangleF	These structures represent a rectangular dimension (again mapping to an underlying integer or float).
Size SizeF	These structures represent a given height/width (again mapping to an underlying integer or float).
StringFormat	This type is used to encapsulate various features of textual layout (i.e., alignment, line spacing, etc.).
Region	This type describes the interior of a geometric image composed of rectangles and paths.

The System.Drawing Utility Types

Many of the drawing methods defined by the System.Drawing.Graphics object require you to specify the position or area in which you wish to render a given item. For example, the DrawString() method requires you to specify the location to render the text string on the Control-derived type. Given that DrawString() has been overloaded a number of times, this positional parameter may be specified using an (*x*, *y*) coordinate or the dimensions of a "box" to draw within. Other GDI+ type methods may require you to specify the width and height of a given item, or the internal bounds of a geometric image.

To specify such information, the System.Drawing namespace defines the Point, Rectangle, Region, and Size types. Obviously, a Point represents an (*x*, *y*) coordinate. Rectangle types capture a pair of points representing the upper-left and bottom-right bounds of a rectangular region. Size types are similar to Rectangles, but this structure represent a particular dimension using a given length and width. Finally, Regions provide a way to represent and qualify nonrectangular surfaces.

The member variables used by the Point, Rectangle, and Size types are internally represented as an integer data type. If you need a finer level of granularity, you are free to make use of the corresponding PointF, RectangleF, and SizeF types, which (as you might guess) map to an underlying float. Regardless of the underlying data representation, each type has an identical set of members, including a number of overloaded operators.

The Point(F) Type

The first utility type you should be aware of is System.Drawing.Point(F). Unlike the illustrative Point types created in previous chapters, the GDI+ Point(F) type supports a number of helpful members, including

- +, -, ==, !=: The Point type overloads various C# operators.
- X, Y: These members provide access to the underlying (*x*, *y*) values of the Point.
- IsEmpty: This member returns true if *x* and *y* are both set to 0.

To illustrate working with the GDI+ utility types, here is a console application (named UtilTypes) that makes use of the System.Drawing.Point type (be sure to set a reference to System.Drawing.dll).

```
using System;
using System.Drawing;

namespace UtilTypes
{
    public class Program
    {
        static void Main(string[] args)
        {
            // Create and offset a point.
            Point pt = new Point(100, 72);
            Console.WriteLine(pt);
            pt.Offset(20, 20);
            Console.WriteLine(pt);

            // Overloaded Point operators.
            Point pt2 = pt;
            if(pt == pt2)
                WriteLine("Points are the same");
            else
                WriteLine("Different points");

            // Change pt2's X value.
            pt2.X = 4000;

            // Now show each X value:
            Console.WriteLine("First point: {0} ", pt);
            Console.WriteLine("Second point: {0} ", pt2);
            Console.ReadLine();
        }
    }
}
```

The Rectangle(F) Type

Rectangles, like Points, are useful in many applications (GUI-based or otherwise). One of the more useful methods of the Rectangle type is Contains(). This method allows you to determine if a given Point or Rectangle is within the current bounds of another object. Later in this chapter, you'll see how to make use of this method to perform hit testing of GDI+ images. Until then, here is a simple example:

```
static void Main(string[] args)
{
    ...
    // Point is initially outside of rectangle's bounds.
    Rectangle r1 = new Rectangle(0, 0, 100, 100);
    Point pt3 = new Point(101, 101);
    if(r1.Contains(pt3))
        Console.WriteLine("Point is within the rect!");
    else
        Console.WriteLine("Point is not within the rect!");

    // Now place point in rectangle's area.
    pt3.X = 50;
    pt3.Y = 30;
```

```
    if(r1.Contains(pt3))
        Console.WriteLine("Point is within the rect!");
    else
        Console.WriteLine("Point is not within the rect!");
    Console.ReadLine();
}
```

The Region Class

The Region type represents the interior of a geometric shape. Given this last statement, it should make sense that the constructors of the Region class require you to send an instance of some existing geometric pattern. For example, assume you have created a 100×100 pixel rectangle. If you wish to gain access to the rectangle's interior region, you could write the following:

```
// Get the interior of this rectangle.
Rectangle r = new Rectangle(0, 0, 100, 100);
Region rgn = new Region(r);
```

Once you have the interior dimensions of a given shape, you may manipulate it using various members such as the following:

- Complement(): Updates this Region to the portion of the specified graphics object that does not intersect with this Region

- Exclude(): Updates this Region to the portion of its interior that does not intersect with the specified graphics object

- GetBounds(): Returns a Rectangle(F) that represents a rectangular region that bounds this Region

- Intersect(): Updates this Region to the intersection of itself with the specified graphics object

- Transform(): Transforms a Region by the specified Matrix object

- Union(): Updates this Region to the union of itself and the specified graphics object

- Translate(): Offsets the coordinates of this Region by a specified amount

I'm sure you get the general idea behind these coordinate primitives; please consult the .NET Framework 2.0 SDK documentation if you require further details.

■**Note** The Size and SizeF types require little comment. These types each define Height and Width properties and a handful of overloaded operators.

■**Source Code** The UtilTypes project is included under the Chapter 20 subdirectory.

Understanding the Graphics Class

The System.Drawing.Graphics class is the gateway to GDI+ rendering functionality. This class not only represents the surface you wish to draw upon (such as a Form's surface, a control's surface, or region of memory), but also defines dozens of members that allow you to render text, images (icons, bitmaps, etc.), and numerous geometric patterns. Table 20-3 gives a partial list of members.

Table 20-3. *Members of the* Graphics *Class*

Methods	Meaning in Life
FromHdc() FromHwnd() FromImage()	These static methods provide a way to obtain a valid Graphics object from a given image (e.g., icon, bitmap, etc.) or GUI widget.
Clear()	Fills a Graphics object with a specified color, erasing the current drawing surface in the process.
DrawArc() DrawBezier() DrawBeziers() DrawCurve() DrawEllipse() DrawIcon() DrawLine() DrawLines() DrawPie() DrawPath() DrawRectangle() DrawRectangles() DrawString()	These methods are used to render a given image or geometric pattern. As you will see, DrawXXX() methods require the use of GDI+ Pen objects.
FillEllipse() FillPath() FillPie() FillPolygon() FillRectangle()	These methods are used to fill the interior of a given geometric shape. As you will see, FillXXX() methods require the use of GDI+ Brush objects.

As well as providing a number of rendering methods, the Graphics class defines additional members that allow you to configure the "state" of the Graphics object. By assigning values to the properties shown in Table 20-4, you are able to alter the current rendering operation.

Table 20-4. *Stateful Properties of the* Graphics *Class*

Properties	Meaning in Life
Clip ClipBounds VisibleClipBounds IsClipEmpty IsVisibleClipEmpty	These properties allow you to set the clipping options used with the current Graphics object.
Transform	This property allows you to transform "world coordinates" (more details on this later).
PageUnit PageScale DpiX DpiY	These properties allow you to configure the point of origin for your rendering operations, as well as the unit of measurement.
SmoothingMode PixelOffsetMode TextRenderingHint	These properties allow you to configure the smoothness of geometric objects and text.
CompositingMode CompositingQuality	The CompositingMode property determines whether drawing overwrites the background or is blended with the background.
InterpolationMode	This property specifies how data is interpolated between endpoints.

■**Note** As of .NET 2.0, the `System.Drawing` namespace provides a `BufferedGraphics` type that allows you to render graphics using a double-buffering system to minimize or eliminate the flickering that can occur during a rendering operation. Consult the .NET Framework 2.0 SDK documentation for full details.

Now, despite what you may be thinking, the `Graphics` class is not directly creatable via the `new` keyword, as there are no publicly defined constructors. How, then, do you obtain a valid `Graphics` object? Glad you asked.

Understanding Paint Sessions

The most common way to obtain a `Graphics` object is to interact with the `Paint` event. Recall from the previous chapter that the `Control` class defines a virtual method named `OnPaint()`. When you want a Form to render graphical data to its surface, you may override this method and extract a `Graphics` object from the incoming `PaintEventArgs` parameter. To illustrate, create a new Windows Forms application named BasicPaintForm, and update the `Form`-derived class as so:

```
public partial class MainForm : Form
{
    public MainForm()
    {
        InitializeComponent();
        CenterToScreen();
        this.Text = "Basic Paint Form";
    }

    protected override void OnPaint(PaintEventArgs e)
    {
        // If overriding OnPaint(), be sure to call base class implementation.
        base.OnPaint(e);

        // Obtain a Graphics object from the incoming
        // PaintEventArgs.
        Graphics g = e.Graphics;

        // Render a textual message in a given font and color.
        g.DrawString("Hello GDI+", new Font("Times New Roman", 20),
                        Brushes.Green, 0, 0);
    }
}
```

While overriding `OnPaint()` is permissible, it is more common to handle the `Paint` event using the associated `PaintEventHandler` delegate (in fact, this is the default behavior taken by Visual Studio 2005 when handling events with the Properties window). This delegate can point to any method taking a `System.Object` as the first parameter and a `PaintEventArgs` as the second. Assuming you have handled the `Paint` event (via the Visual Studio 2005 designers or manually in code), you are once again able to extract a `Graphics` object from the incoming `PaintEventArgs`. Here is the update:

```
public partial class MainForm : Form
{
    public MainForm()
    {
        InitializeComponent();
        CenterToScreen();
```

```
        this.Text = "Basic Paint Form";

        // Visual Studio 2005 places this
        // code within InitializeComponent().
        this.Paint += new PaintEventHandler(MainForm_Paint);
    }

    private void MainForm_Paint(object sender, PaintEventArgs e)
    {
        Graphics g = e.Graphics;
        g.DrawString("Hello GDI+", new Font("Times New Roman", 20),
            Brushes.Green, 0, 0);
    }
}
```

Regardless of how you respond to the Paint event, be aware that whenever a window becomes "dirty," the Paint event will fire. As you may be aware, a window is considered "dirty" whenever it is resized, uncovered by another window (partially or completely), or minimized and then restored. In all these cases, the .NET platform ensures that when your Form needs to be redrawn, the Paint event handler (or overridden OnPaint() method) is called automatically.

Invalidating the Form's Client Area

During the flow of a GDI+ application, you may need to explicitly fire the Paint event, rather than waiting for the window to become "naturally dirty." For example, you may be building a program that allows the user to select from a number of bitmap images using a custom dialog box. Once the dialog box is dismissed, you need to draw the newly selected image onto the Form's client area. Obviously, if you waited for the window to become "naturally dirty," the user would not see the change take place until the window was resized or uncovered by another window. To force a window to repaint itself programmatically, simply call the inherited Invalidate() method:

```
public partial class MainForm: Form
{
...
    private void MainForm_Paint(object sender, PaintEventArgs e)
    {
        Graphics g = e.Graphics;
        // Render a bitmap here.
    }

    private void GetNewBitmap()
    {
        // Show dialog box and get new image.
        // Repaint the entire client area.
        Invalidate();
    }
}
```

The Invalidate() method has been overloaded a number of times to allow you to specify a specific rectangular region to repaint, rather than repainting the entire client area (which is the default). If you wish to only update the extreme upper-left rectangle of the client area, you could write the following:

```
// Repaint a given rectangular area of the Form.
private void UpdateUpperArea()
{
```

```
    Rectangle myRect = new Rectangle(0, 0, 75, 150);
    Invalidate(myRect);
}
```

Obtaining a Graphics Object Outside of a Paint Event Handler

In some rare cases, you may need to access a Graphics object *outside* the scope of a Paint event handler. For example, assume you wish to draw a small circle at the (*x, y*) position where the mouse has been clicked. To obtain a valid Graphics object from within the scope of a MouseDown event handler, one approach is to call the static Graphics.FromHwnd() method. Based on your background in Win32 development, you may know that an HWND is a data structure that represents a given Win32 window. Under the .NET platform, the inherited Handle property extracts the underlying HWND, which can be used as a parameter to Graphics.FromHwnd():

```
private void MainForm_MouseDown(object sender, MouseEventArgs e)
{
    // Grab a Graphics object via Hwnd.
    Graphics g = Graphics.FromHwnd(this.Handle);

    // Now draw a 10*10 circle at mouse click.
    g.FillEllipse(Brushes.Firebrick, e.X, e.Y, 10, 10);

    // Dispose of all Graphics objects you create directly.
    g.Dispose();
}
```

While this logic renders a circle outside an OnPaint() event handler, it is very important to understand that when the form is invalidated (and thus redrawn), each of the circles is erased! This should make sense, given that this rendering happens only within the context of a MouseDown event. A far better approach is to have the MouseDown event handler create a new Point type, which is then added to an internal collection (such as a List<T>), followed by a call to Invalidate(). At this point, the Paint event handler can simply iterate over the collection and draw each Point:

```
public partial class MainForm : Form
{
    // Used to hold all the points.
    private List<Point> myPts = new List<Point>();

    public MainForm()
    {
...
        this.MouseDown += new MouseEventHandler(MainForm_MouseDown);
    }

    private void MainForm_MouseDown(object sender, MouseEventArgs e)
    {
        // Add to points collection.
        myPts.Add(new Point(e.X, e.Y));
        Invalidate();
    }

    private void MainForm_Paint(object sender, PaintEventArgs e)
    {
        Graphics g = e.Graphics;
        g.DrawString("Hello GDI+", new Font("Times New Roman", 20),
                new SolidBrush(Color.Black), 0, 0);
        foreach(Point p in myPts)
```

```
                g.FillEllipse(Brushes.Firebrick, p.X, p.Y, 10, 10);
        }
}
```

Using this approach, the rendered circles are always present and accounted for, as the graphical rendering has been handled within the Paint event. Figure 20-1 shows a test run of this initial GDI+ application.

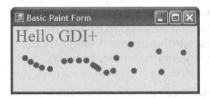

Figure 20-1. *A simple painting application*

■**Source Code** The BasicPaintForm project is included under the Chapter 20 subdirectory.

Regarding the Disposal of a Graphics Object

If you were reading closely over the last several pages, you may have noticed that *some* of the sample code directly called the Dispose() method of the Graphics object, while other sample code did not. Given that a Graphics type is manipulating various underlying unmanaged resources, it should make sense that it would be advantageous to release said resources via Dispose() as soon as possible (rather than via the garbage collector in the finalization process). The same can be said for any type that supports the IDisposable interface. When working with GDI+ Graphics objects, remember the following rules of thumb:

- If you directly create a Graphics object, dispose of it when you are finished.

- If you reference an existing Graphics object, do *not* dispose of it.

To clarify, consider the following Paint event handler:

```
private void MainForm_Paint(object sender, PaintEventArgs e)
{
    // Load a local *.jpg file.
    Image myImageFile = Image.FromFile("landscape.jpg");

    // Create new Graphics object based on the image.
    Graphics imgGraphics = Graphics.FromImage(myImageFile);

    // Render new data onto the image.
    imgGraphics.FillEllipse(Brushes.DarkOrange, 50, 50, 150, 150);

    // Draw image to Form.
    Graphics g = e.Graphics;
    g.DrawImage(myImageFile, new PointF(0.0F, 0.0F));

    // Release Graphics object we created.
    imgGraphics.Dispose();
}
```

Now at this point in the chapter, don't become concerned if some of this GDI+ logic looks a bit foreign. However, notice that you are obtaining a Graphics object from a *.jpg file loaded from the local application directory (via the static Graphics.FromImage() method). Because you have explicitly created this Graphics object, best practice states that you should Dispose() of the object when you have finished making use of it, to free up the internal resources for use by other parts of the system.

However, notice that you did not explicitly call Dispose() on the Graphics object you obtained from the incoming PaintEventArgs. This is due to the fact that you did not directly create the object and cannot ensure other parts of the program are making use of it. Clearly, it would be a problem if you released a Graphics object used elsewhere!

On a related note, recall from our examination of the .NET garbage collector in Chapter 5 that if you do forget to call Dispose() on a method implementing IDisposable, the internal resources will eventually be freed when the object is garbage-collected at a later time. In this light, the manual disposal of the imgGraphics object is not technically necessary. Although explicitly disposing of GDI+ objects you directly created is smart programming, in order to keep the code examples in this chapter crisp, I will not manually dispose of each GDI+ type.

The GDI+ Coordinate Systems

Our next task is to examine the underlying coordinate system. GDI+ defines three distinct coordinate systems, which are used by the runtime to determine the location and size of the content to be rendered. First we have what are known as *world coordinates*. World coordinates represent an abstraction of the size of a given GDI+ type, irrespective of the unit of measurement. For example, if you draw a rectangle using the dimensions (0, 0, 100, 100), you have specified a rectangle 100×100 "things" in size. As you may guess, the default "thing" is a pixel; however, it can be configured to be another unit of measure (inch, centimeter, etc.).

Next, we have *page coordinates*. Page coordinates represent an offset applied to the original world coordinates. This is helpful in that you are not the one in charge of manually applying offsets in your code (should you need them). For example, if you have a Form that needs to maintain a 100×100 pixel border, you can specify a (100*100) page coordinate to allow all rendering to begin at point (100*100). In your code base, however, you are able to specify simple world coordinates (thereby avoiding the need to manually calculate the offset).

Finally, we have *device coordinates*. Device coordinates represent the result of applying page coordinates to the original world coordinates. This coordinate system is used to determine exactly where the GDI+ type will be rendered. When you are programming with GDI+, you will typically think in terms of world coordinates, which are the baseline used to determine the size and location of a GDI+ type. To render in world coordinates requires no special coding actions—simply pass in the dimensions for the current rendering operation:

```
void MainForm_Paint(object sender, PaintEventArgs e)
{
    // Render a rectangle in world coordinates.
    Graphics g = e.Graphics;
    g.DrawRectangle(Pens.Black, 10, 10, 100, 100);
}
```

Under the hood, your world coordinates are automatically mapped in terms of page coordinates, which are then mapped into device coordinates. In many cases, you will never directly make use of page or device coordinates unless you wish to apply some sort of graphical transformation. Given that the previous code did not specify any transformational logic, the world, page, and device coordinates are identical.

If you do wish to apply various transformations before rendering your GDI+ logic, you will make use of various members of the Graphics type (such as the TranslateTransform() method) to specify various "page coordinates" to your existing world coordinate system before the rendering operation. The result is the set of device coordinates that will be used to render the GDI+ type to the target device:

```
private void MainForm_Paint(object sender, PaintEventArgs e)
{
    // Specify page coordinate offsets (10 * 10).
    Graphics g = e.Graphics;
    g.TranslateTransform(10, 10);
    g.DrawRectangle(10, 10, 100, 100);
}
```

In this case, the rectangle is actually rendered with a top-left point of (20, 20), given that the world coordinates have been offset by the call to TranslateTransform().

The Default Unit of Measure

Under GDI+, the default unit of measure is pixel-based. The origin begins in the upper-left corner with the *x*-axis increasing to the right and the *y*-axis increasing downward (see Figure 20-2).

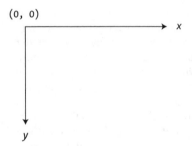

Figure 20-2. *The default coordinate system of GDI+*

Thus, if you render a Rectangle using a 5-pixel thick red pen as follows:

```
void MainForm_Paint(object sender, PaintEventArgs e)
{
    // Set up world coordinates using the default unit of measure.
    Graphics g = e.Graphics;
    g.DrawRectangle(new Pen(Color.Red, 5), 10, 10, 100, 100);
}
```

you would see a square rendered 10 pixels down and in from the top-left client edge of the Form, as shown in Figure 20-3.

Figure 20-3. *Rendering via pixel units*

Specifying an Alternative Unit of Measure

If you do not wish to render images using a pixel-based unit of measure, you are able to change this default setting by setting the PageUnit property of the Graphics object to alter the units used by the page coordinate system. The PageUnit property can be assigned any member of the GraphicsUnit enumeration:

```
public enum GraphicsUnit
{
    // Specifies world coordinates.
    World,
    // Pixels for video displays and 1/100 inch for printers.
    Display,
    // Specifies a pixel.
    Pixel,
    // Specifies a printer's point (1/72 inch).
    Point,
    // Specifies an inch.
    Inch,
    // Specifies a document unit (1/300 inch).
    Document,
    // Specifies a millimeter.
    Millimeter
}
```

To illustrate how to change the underlying GraphicsUnit, update the previous rendering code as follows:

```
private void MainForm_Paint(object sender, PaintEventArgs e)
{
    // Draw a rectangle in inches...not pixels.
    Graphics g = e.Graphics;
    g.PageUnit = GraphicsUnit.Inch;
    g.DrawRectangle(new Pen(Color.Red, 5), 0, 0, 100, 100);
}
```

You would find a *radically* different rectangle, as shown in Figure 20-4.

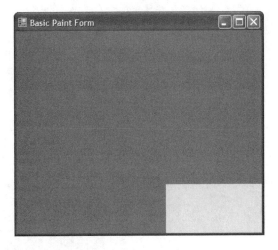

Figure 20-4. *Rendering using inch units*

The reason that 95 percent (or so) of the Form's client area is now filled with red is because you have configured a Pen with a 5-*inch* nib! The rectangle itself is 100×100 *inches* in size. In fact, the small gray box you see located in the lower-right corner is the upper-left interior of the rectangle.

Specifying an Alternative Point of Origin

Recall that when you make use of the default coordinate and measurement system, point (0, 0) is at the extreme upper left of the surface area. While this is often what you desire, what if you wish to alter the location where rendering begins? For example, let's assume that your application always needs to reserve a 100-pixel boundary around the Form's client area (for whatever reason). You need to ensure that all GDI+ operations take place somewhere within this internal region.

One approach you could take is to offset all your rendering code manually. This, of course, would be bothersome, as you would need to constantly apply some offset value to each and every rendering operation. It would be far better (and simpler) if you could set a property that says in effect, "Although *I* might say render a rectangle with a point of origin at (0, 0), make sure *you* begin at point (100, 100)." This would simplify your life a great deal, as you could continue to specify your plotting points without modification.

In GDI+, you can adjust the point of origin by setting the transformation value using the TranslateTransform() method of the Graphics class, which allows you to specify a page coordinate system that will be applied to your original world coordinate specifications, for example:

```
void MainForm_Paint(object sender, PaintEventArgs e)
{
    Graphics g = e.Graphics;
    // Set page coordinate to (100, 100).
    g.TranslateTransform(100, 100);

    // World origin is still (0, 0, 100, 100),
    // however, device origin is now (100, 100, 200, 200).
    g.DrawRectangle(new Pen(Color.Red, 5), 0, 0, 100, 100);
}
```

Here, you have set the world coordinate values (0, 0, 100, 100). However, the page coordinate values have specified an offset of (100, 100). Given this, the device coordinates map to (100, 100, 200, 200). Thus, although the call to DrawRectangle() looks as if you are rendering a rectangle on the upper left of the Form, the rendering shown in Figure 20-5 has taken place.

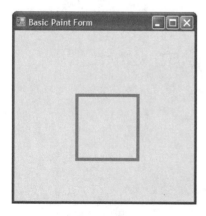

Figure 20-5. *The result of applying page offsets*

To help you experiment with some of the ways to alter the GDI+ coordinate system, this book's downloadable source code (visit the Downloads section of the Apress website at www.apress.com) provides a sample application named CoorSystem. Using two menu items, you are able to alter the point of origin as well as the unit of measurement (see Figure 20-6).

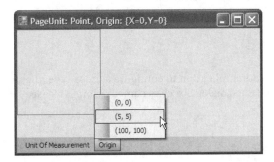

Figure 20-6. *Altering coordinate and measurement modes*

Now that you have a better understanding of the underlying transformations used to determine where to render a given GDI+ type onto a target device, the next order of business is to examine details of color manipulation.

■Source Code The CoorSystem project is included under the Chapter 20 subdirectory.

Defining a Color Value

Many of the rendering methods defined by the Graphics class require you to specify the color that should be used during the drawing process. The System.Drawing.Color structure represents an alpha-red-green-blue (ARGB) color constant. Most of the Color type's functionality comes by way of a number of static read-only properties, which return a specific Color type:

```
// One of many predefined colors...
Color c = Color.PapayaWhip;
```

If the default color values do not fit the bill, you are also able to create a new Color type and specify the A, R, G, and B values using the FromArgb() method:

```
// Specify ARGB manually.
Color myColor = Color.FromArgb(0, 255, 128, 64);
```

As well, using the FromName() method, you are able to generate a Color type given a string value. The characters in the string parameter must match one of the members in the KnownColor enumeration (which includes values for various Windows color elements such as KnownColor.WindowFrame and KnownColor.WindowText):

```
// Get Color from a known name.
Color myColor = Color.FromName("Red");
```

Regardless of the method you use, the Color type can be interacted with using a variety of members:

- GetBrightness(): Returns the brightness of the Color type based on hue-saturation-brightness (HSB) measurements

- GetSaturation(): Returns the saturation of the Color type based on HSB measurements

- GetHue(): Returns the hue of the Color type based on HSB measurements

- IsSystemColor: Determines if the Color type is a registered system color

- A, R, G, B: Returns the value assigned to the alpha, red, green, and blue aspects of a Color type

The ColorDialog Class

If you wish to provide a way for the end user of your application to configure a Color type, the System.Windows.Forms namespace provides a predefined dialog box class named ColorDialog (see Figure 20-7).

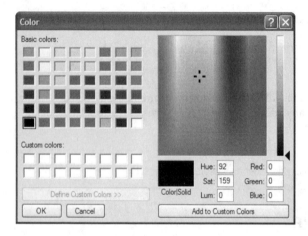

Figure 20-7. *The Windows Forms color dialog box*

Working with this dialog box is quite simple. Using a valid instance of the ColorDialog type, call ShowDialog() to display the dialog box modally. Once the user has closed the dialog box, you can extract the corresponding Color object using the ColorDialog.Color property.

Assume you wish to allow the user to configure the background color of the Form's client area using the ColorDialog. To keep things simple, you will display the ColorDialog when the user clicks anywhere on the client area:

```
public partial class MainForm : Form
{
    private ColorDialog colorDlg;
    private Color currColor = Color.DimGray;

    public MainForm()
    {
        InitializeComponent();
        colorDlg = new ColorDialog();
        Text = "Click on me to change the color";
        this.MouseDown += new MouseEventHandler(MainForm_MouseDown);
    }
```

```
private void MainForm_MouseDown(object sender, MouseEventArgs e)
{
    if (colorDlg.ShowDialog() != DialogResult.Cancel)
    {
        currColor = colorDlg.Color;
        this.BackColor = currColor;
        string strARGB = colorDlg.Color.ToString();
        MessageBox.Show(strARGB, "Color is:");
    }
}
}
```

■**Source Code** The ColorDlg application is included under the Chapter 20 subdirectory.

Manipulating Fonts

Next, let's examine how to programmatically manipulate fonts. The System.Drawing.Font type represents a given font installed on the user's machine. Font types can be defined using any number of overloaded constructors. Here are a few examples:

```
// Create a Font of a given type name and size.
Font f = new Font("Times New Roman", 12);
```

```
// Create a Font with a given name, size, and style set.
Font f2 = new Font("WingDings", 50, FontStyle.Bold | FontStyle.Underline);
```

Here, f2 has been created by OR-ing together a set of values from the FontStyle enumeration:

```
public enum FontStyle
{
    Regular, Bold,
    Italic, Underline, Strikeout
}
```

Once you have configured the look and feel of your Font object, the next task is to pass it as a parameter to the Graphics.DrawString() method. Although DrawString() has also been overloaded a number of times, each variation typically requires the same basic information: the text to draw, the font to draw it in, a brush used for rendering, and a location in which to place it.

```
private void MainForm_Paint(object sender, PaintEventArgs e)
{
    Graphics g = e.Graphics;

    // Specify (String, Font, Brush, Point) as args.
    g.DrawString("My string", new Font("WingDings", 25),
        Brushes.Black, new Point(0,0));

    // Specify (String, Font, Brush, int, int)
    g .DrawString("Another string", new Font("Times New Roman", 16),
        Brushes.Red, 40, 40);
}
```

Working with Font Families

The System.Drawing namespace also defines the FontFamily type, which abstracts a group of typefaces having a similar basic design but with certain style variations. A family of fonts, such as Verdana, can include several fonts that differ in style and size. For example, Verdana 12-point bold and Verdana 24-point italic are different fonts within the Verdana font family.

The constructor of the FontFamily type takes a string representing the name of the font family you are attempting to capture. Once you create the "generic family," you are then able to create a more specific Font object:

```
private void MainForm_Paint(object sender, PaintEventArgs e)
{
    Graphics g = e.Graphics;

    // Make a family of fonts.
    FontFamily myFamily = new FontFamily("Verdana");

    // Pass family into ctor of Font.
    Font myFont = new Font(myFamily, 12);
    g.DrawString("Hello!", myFont, Brushes.Blue, 10, 10);
}
```

Of greater interest is the ability to gather statistics regarding a given family of fonts. For example, say you are building a text-processing application and wish to determine the average width of a character in a particular FontFamily. What if you wish to know the ascending and descending values for a given character? To answer such questions, the FontFamily type defines the key members shown in Table 20-5.

Table 20-5. *Members of the* FontFamily *Type*

Member	Meaning in Life
GetCellAscent()	Returns the ascender metric for the members in this family
GetCellDescent()	Returns the descender metric for members in this family
GetLineSpacing()	Returns the distance between two consecutive lines of text for this FontFamily with the specified FontStyle
GetName()	Returns the name of this FontFamily in the specified language
IsStyleAvailable()	Indicates whether the specified FontStyle is available

To illustrate, here is a Paint event handler that prints a number of characteristics of the Verdana font family:

```
private void MainForm_Paint(object sender, PaintEventArgs e)
{
    Graphics g = e.Graphics;
    FontFamily myFamily = new FontFamily("Verdana");
    Font myFont = new Font(myFamily, 12);
    int y = 0;
    int fontHeight = myFont.Height;

    // Show units of measurement for FontFamily members.
    this.Text = "Measurements are in GraphicsUnit." + myFont.Unit;
    g.DrawString("The Verdana family.", myFont, Brushes.Blue, 10, y);
    y += 20;
```

```
    // Print our family ties...
    g.DrawString("Ascent for bold Verdana: " +
                myFamily.GetCellAscent(FontStyle.Bold),
                myFont, Brushes.Black, 10, y + fontHeight);
    y += 20;
    g.DrawString("Descent for bold Verdana: " +
                myFamily.GetCellDescent(FontStyle.Bold),
                myFont, Brushes.Black, 10, y + fontHeight);
    y += 20;
    g.DrawString("Line spacing for bold Verdana: " +
                myFamily.GetLineSpacing(FontStyle.Bold),
                myFont, Brushes.Black, 10, y + fontHeight);
    y += 20;
    g.DrawString("Height for bold Verdana: " +
                myFamily.GetEmHeight(FontStyle.Bold),
                myFont, Brushes.Black, 10, y + fontHeight);
    y += 20;
}
```

Figure 20-8 shows the result.

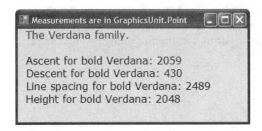

Figure 20-8. *Gathering statistics of the Verdana font family*

Note that these members of the FontFamily type return values using GraphicsUnit.Point (not Pixel) as the unit of measure, which corresponds to 1/72 inch. You are free to transform these values to other units of measure as you see fit.

■**Source Code** The FontFamilyApp application is included under the Chapter 20 subdirectory.

Working with Font Faces and Font Sizes

Next, you'll build a more complex application that allows the user to manipulate a Font object maintained by a Form. The application will allow the user to select the current font face from a predefined set using the Configure ➤ Font Face menu selection. You'll also allow the user to indirectly control the size of the Font object using a Windows Forms Timer object. If the user activates the Timer using the Configure ➤ Swell? menu item, the size of the Font object increases at a regular interval (to a maximum upper limit). In this way, the text appears to swell and thus provides an animation of "breathing" text. Finally, you'll use a final menu item under the Configure menu named List All Fonts, which will be used to list all fonts installed on the end user's machine. Figure 20-9 shows the menu UI logic.

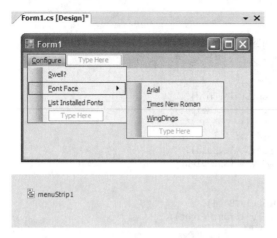

Figure 20-9. *Menu layout of the FontApp project*

To begin implementing the application, update the Form with a Timer member variable (named swellTimer), a string (strFontFace) to represent the current font face, and an integer (swellValue) to represent the amount to adjust the font size. Within the Form's constructor, configure the Timer to emit a Tick event every 100 milliseconds:

```
public partial class MainForm : Form
{
    private Timer swellTimer = new Timer();
    private int swellValue;
    private string strFontFace = "WingDings";

    public MainForm()
    {
        InitializeComponent();
        BackColor = Color.Honeydew;
        CenterToScreen();

        // Configure the Timer.
        swellTimer.Enabled = true;
        swellTimer.Interval = 100;
        swellTimer.Tick += new EventHandler(swellTimer_Tick);
    }
}
```

In the Tick event handler, increase the value of the swellValue data member by 5. Recall that the swellValue integer will be added to the current font size to provide a simple animation (assume swellValue has a maximum upper limit of 50). To help reduce the flicker that can occur when redrawing the entire client area, notice how the call to Invalidate() is only refreshing the upper rectangular area of the Form:

```
private void swellTimer_Tick(object sender, EventArgs e)
{
    // Increase current swellValue by 5.
    swellValue += 5;
    // If this value is greater than or equal to 50, reset to zero.
    if(swellValue >= 50)
        swellValue = 0;
```

```
    // Just invalidate the minimal dirty rectangle to help reduce flicker.
    Invalidate(new Rectangle(0, 0, ClientRectangle.Width, 100));
}
```

Now that the upper 100 pixels of your client area are refreshed with each tick of the Timer, you had better have something to render! In the Form's Paint handler, create a Font object based on the user-defined font face (as selected from the appropriate menu item) and current swellValue (as dictated by the Timer). Once you have your Font object fully configured, render a message into the center of the dirty rectangle:

```
private void MainForm_Paint(object sender, PaintEventArgs e)
{
    Graphics g = e.Graphics;
    // Our font size can be between 12 and 62,
    // based on the current swellValue.
    Font theFont = new Font(strFontFace, 12 + swellValue);
    string message = "Hello GDI+";

    // Display message in the center of the rect.
    float windowCenter = this.DisplayRectangle.Width/2;
    SizeF stringSize = g.MeasureString(message, theFont);
    float startPos = windowCenter - (stringSize.Width/2);
    g.DrawString(message, theFont, new SolidBrush(Color.Blue), startPos, 10);
}
```

As you would guess, if a user selects a specific font face, the Clicked handler for each menu selection is in charge of updating the fontFace string variable and invalidating the client area, for example:

```
private void arialToolStripMenuItem_Click(object sender, EventArgs e)
{
    strFontFace = "Arial";
    Invalidate();
}
```

The Click menu handler for the Swell menu item will be used to allow the user to stop or start the swelling of the text (i.e., enable or disable the animation). To do so, toggle the Enabled property of the Timer as follows:

```
private void swellToolStripMenuItem_Click(object sender, EventArgs e)
{
    swellTimer.Enabled = !swellTimer.Enabled;
}
```

Enumerating Installed Fonts

Next, let's expand this program to display the set of installed fonts on the target machine using types within System.Drawing.Text. This namespace contains a handful of types that can be used to discover and manipulate the set of fonts installed on the target machine. For our purposes, we are only concerned with the InstalledFontCollection class.

When the user selects the Configure ➤ List Installed Fonts menu item, the corresponding Clicked handler creates an instance of the InstalledFontCollection class. This class maintains an array named FontFamily, which represents the set of all fonts on the target machine and may be obtained using the InstalledFontCollection.Families property. Using the FontFamily.Name property, you are able to extract the font face (e.g., Times New Roman, Arial, etc.) for each font.

Add a private string data member to your Form named installedFonts to hold each font face. The logic in the List Installed Fonts menu handler creates an instance of the InstalledFontCollection type, reads the name of each string, and adds the new font face to the private installedFonts data member:

```csharp
public partial class MainForm : Form
{
    // Holds the list of fonts.
    private string installedFonts;

    // Menu handler to get the list of installed fonts.
    private void mnuConfigShowFonts_Clicked(object sender, EventArgs e)
    {
        InstalledFontCollection fonts = new InstalledFontCollection();
        for(int i = 0; i < fonts.Families.Length; i++)
            installedFonts += fonts.Families[i].Name + "  ";

        // This time, we need to invalidate the entire client area,
        // as we will paint the installedFonts string on the lower half
        // of the client rectangle.
        Invalidate();
    }
...
}
```

The final task is to render the `installedFonts` string to the client area, directly below the screen real estate that is used for your swelling text:

```csharp
private void MainForm_Paint(object sender, PaintEventArgs e)
{
    Graphics g = e.Graphics;
    Font theFont = new Font(strFontFace, 12 + swellValue);
    string message = "Hello GDI+";

    // Display message in the center of the window!
    float windowCenter = this.DisplayRectangle.Width/2;
    SizeF stringSize = e.Graphics.MeasureString(message, theFont);
    float startPos = windowCenter - (stringSize.Width/2);
    g.DrawString(message, theFont, Brushes.Blue, startPos, 10);

    // Show installed fonts in the rectangle below the swell area.
    Rectangle myRect = new Rectangle(0, 100,
        ClientRectangle.Width, ClientRectangle.Height);

    // Paint this area of the Form black.
    g.FillRectangle(new SolidBrush(Color.Black), myRect);
    g.DrawString(installedFonts, new Font("Arial", 12),
        Brushes.White, myRect);
}
```

Recall that the size of the "dirty rectangle" has been mapped to the upper 100 pixels of the client rectangle. Because your `Tick` handler invalidates only a portion of the Form, the remaining area is not redrawn when the `Tick` event has been sent (to help optimize the rendering of the client area).

As a final touch to ensure proper redrawing, let's handle the Form's `Resize` event to ensure that if the user resizes the Form, the lower part of client rectangle is redrawn correctly:

```csharp
private void MainForm_Resize(object sender, System.EventArgs e)
{
    Rectangle myRect = new Rectangle(0, 100,
        ClientRectangle.Width, ClientRectangle.Height);
    Invalidate(myRect);
}
```

Figure 20-10 shows the result (with the text rendered in Wingdings!).

Figure 20-10. *The FontApp application in action*

■**Source Code** The SwellingFontApp project is included under the Chapter 20 subdirectory.

The FontDialog Class

As you might assume, there is an existing font dialog box (FontDialog), as shown in Figure 20-11.

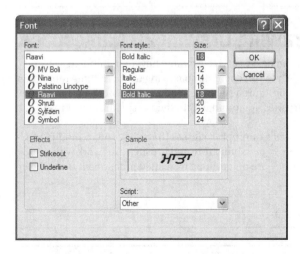

Figure 20-11. *The Windows Forms Font dialog box*

Like the ColorDialog type examined earlier in this chapter, when you wish to work with the FontDialog, simply call the ShowDialog() method. Using the Font property, you may extract the characteristics of the current selection for use in the application. To illustrate, here is a Form that mimics the logic of the previous ColorDlg project. When the user clicks anywhere on the Form, the Font dialog box displays and renders a message with the current selection:

```
public partial class MainForm : Form
{
    private FontDialog fontDlg = new FontDialog();
    private Font currFont = new Font("Times New Roman", 12);
    public MainForm()
    {
        InitializeComponent();
        CenterToScreen();
    }
    private void MainForm_MouseDown(object sender, MouseEventArgs e)
    {
        if (fontDlg.ShowDialog() != DialogResult.Cancel)
        {
            currFont = fontDlg.Font;
            this.Text = string.Format("Selected Font: {0}", currFont);
            Invalidate();
        }
    }
    private void MainForm_Paint(object sender, PaintEventArgs e)
    {
        Graphics g = e.Graphics;
        g.DrawString("Testing...", currFont, Brushes.Black, 0, 0);
    }
}
```

■**Source Code** The FontDlgForm application is included under the Chapter 20 subdirectory.

Survey of the System.Drawing.Drawing2D Namespace

Now that you have manipulated Font types, the next task is to examine how to manipulate Pen and Brush objects to render geometric patterns. While you could do so making use of nothing more than Brushes and Pens helper types to obtain preconfigured types in a solid color, you should be aware that many of the more "exotic" pens and brushes are found within the System.Drawing.Drawing2D namespace.

This additional GDI+ namespace provides a number of classes that allow you to modify the end cap (triangle, diamond, etc.) used for a given pen, build textured brushes, and work with vector graphic manipulations. Some core types to be aware of (grouped by related functionality) are shown in Table 20-6.

Table 20-6. *Classes of* System.Drawing.Drawing2D

Classes	Meaning in Life
AdjustableArrowCap CustomLineCap	Pen caps are used to paint the beginning and end points of a given line. These types represent an adjustable arrow-shaped and user-defined cap.
Blend ColorBlend	These classes are used to define a blend pattern (and colors) used in conjunction with a LinearGradientBrush.

Classes	Meaning in Life
GraphicsPath GraphicsPathIterator PathData	A GraphicsPath object represents a series of lines and curves. This class allows you to insert just about any type of geometrical pattern (arcs, rectangles, lines, strings, polygons, etc.) into the path. PathData holds the graphical data that makes up a path.
HatchBrush LinearGradientBrush PathGradientBrush	These are exotic brush types.

Also be aware that the System.Drawing.Drawing2D namespace defines another set of enumerations (DashStyle, FillMode, HatchStyle, LineCap, and so forth) that are used in conjunction with these core types.

Working with Pens

GDI+ Pen types are used to draw lines between two end points. However, a Pen in and of itself is of little value. When you need to render a geometric shape onto a Control-derived type, you send a valid Pen type to any number of render methods defined by the Graphics class. In general, the DrawXXX() methods are used to render some set of lines to a graphics surface and are typically used with Pen objects.

The Pen type defines a small set of constructors that allow you to determine the initial color and width of the pen nib. Most of a Pen's functionality comes by way of its supported properties. Table 20-7 gives a partial list.

Table 20-7. Pen *Properties*

Properties	Meaning in Life
Brush	Determines the Brush used by this Pen.
Color	Determines the Color type used by this Pen.
CustomStartCap CustomEndCap	Gets or sets a custom cap style to use at the beginning or end of lines drawn with this Pen. *Cap style* is simply the term used to describe how the initial and final stroke of the Pen should look and feel. These properties allow you to build custom caps for your Pen types.
DashCap	Gets or sets the cap style used at the beginning or end of dashed lines drawn with this Pen.
DashPattern	Gets or sets an array of custom dashes and spaces. The dashes are made up of line segments.
DashStyle	Gets or sets the style used for dashed lines drawn with this Pen.
StartCap EndCap	Gets or sets the predefined cap style used at the beginning or end of lines drawn with this Pen. Set the cap of your Pen using the LineCap enumeration defined in the System.Drawing.Drawing2D namespace.
Width	Gets or sets the width of this Pen.
DashOffset	Gets or sets the distance from the start of a line to the beginning of a dash pattern.

Remember that in addition to the Pen type, GDI+ provides a Pens collection. Using a number of static properties, you are able to retrieve a Pen (or a given color) on the fly, rather than creating a custom Pen by hand. Be aware, however, that the Pen types returned will always have a width of 1.

If you require a more exotic pen, you will need to build a Pen type by hand. This being said, let's render some geometric images using simple Pen types. Assume you have a main Form object that is capable of responding to paint requests. The implementation is as follows:

```
private void MainForm_Paint(object sender, PaintEventArgs e)
{
    Graphics g = e.Graphics;
    // Make a big blue pen.
    Pen bluePen = new Pen(Color.Blue, 20);

    // Get a stock pen from the Pens type.
    Pen pen2 = Pens.Firebrick;

    // Render some shapes with the pens.
    g.DrawEllipse(bluePen, 10, 10, 100, 100);
    g.DrawLine(pen2, 10, 130, 110, 130);
    g.DrawPie(Pens.Black, 150, 10, 120, 150, 90, 80);

    // Draw a purple dashed polygon as well...
    Pen pen3 = new Pen(Color.Purple, 5);
    pen3.DashStyle = DashStyle.DashDotDot;
    g.DrawPolygon(pen3, new Point[]{new Point(30, 140),
        new Point(265, 200), new Point(100, 225),
        new Point(190, 190), new Point(50, 330),
        new Point(20, 180)});

    // And a rectangle containing some text...
    Rectangle r = new Rectangle(150, 10, 130, 60);
    g.DrawRectangle(Pens.Blue, r);
    g.DrawString("Hello out there...How are ya?",
                new Font("Arial", 12), Brushes.Black, r);
}
```

Notice that the Pen used to render your polygon makes use of the DashStyle enumeration (defined in System.Drawing.Drawing2D):

```
public enum DashStyle
{
    Solid, Dash, Dot,
    DashDot, DashDotDot, Custom
}
```

In addition to the preconfigured DashStyles, you are able to define custom patterns using the DashPattern property of the Pen type:

```
private void MainForm_Paint(object sender, PaintEventArgs e)
{
    Graphics g = e.Graphics;
...
    // Draw custom dash pattern all around the border of the form.
    Pen customDashPen = new Pen(Color.BlueViolet, 10);
    float[] myDashes = { 5.0f, 2.0f, 1.0f, 3.0f };
    customDashPen.DashPattern = myDashes;
    g.DrawRectangle(customDashPen, ClientRectangle);
}
```

Figure 20-12 shows the final output of this Paint event handler.

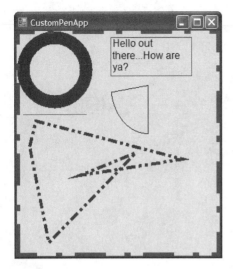

Figure 20-12. *Working with* Pen *types*

■**Source Code** The CustomPenApp project is included under the Chapter 20 subdirectory.

Working with Pen Caps

If you examine the output of the previous pen example, you should notice that the beginning and end of each line was rendered using a standard pen protocol (an end cap composed of 90 degree angles). Using the LineCap enumeration, however, you are able to build Pens that exhibit a bit more flair:

```
public enum LineCap
{
    Flat, Square, Round,
    Triangle, NoAnchor,
    SquareAnchor, RoundAnchor,
    DiamondAnchor, ArrowAnchor,
    AnchorMask, Custom
}
```

To illustrate, the following Pens application draws a series of lines using each of the LineCap styles. The end result can be seen in Figure 20-13.

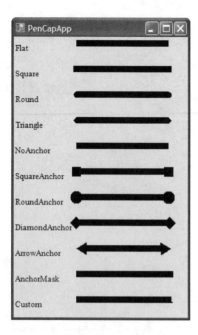

Figure 20-13. *Working with pen caps*

The code simply loops through each member of the LineCap enumeration and prints out the name of the item (e.g., ArrowAnchor). It then configures and draws a line with the current cap:

```
private void MainForm_Paint(object sender, PaintEventArgs e)
{
    Graphics g = e.Graphics;
    Pen thePen = new Pen(Color.Black, 10);
    int yOffSet = 10;
    // Get all members of the LineCap enum.
    Array obj = Enum.GetValues(typeof(LineCap));

    // Draw a line with a LineCap member.
    for(int x = 0; x < obj.Length; x++)
    {
        // Get next cap and configure pen.
        LineCap temp = (LineCap)obj.GetValue(x);
        thePen.StartCap = temp;
        thePen.EndCap = temp;

        // Print name of LineCap enum.
        g.DrawString(temp.ToString(), new Font("Times New Roman", 10),
                new SolidBrush(Color.Black), 0, yOffSet);

        // Draw a line with the correct cap.
        g.DrawLine(thePen, 100, yOffSet, Width - 50, yOffSet);
        yOffSet += 40;
    }
}
```

Working with Brushes

System.Drawing.Brush-derived types are used to fill a region with a given color, pattern, or image. The Brush class itself is an abstract type and cannot be directly created. However, Brush serves as a base class to the other related brush types (e.g., SolidBrush, HatchBrush, LinearGradientBrush, and so forth). In addition to specific Brush-derived types, the System.Drawing namespace also defines two helper classes that return a configured brush using a number of static properties: Brushes and SystemBrushes. In any case, once you obtain a brush, you are able to call any number of the FillXXX() methods of the Graphics type.

Interestingly enough, you are also able to build a custom Pen type based on a given brush. In this way, you are able to build some brush of interest (e.g., a brush that paints a bitmap image) and render geometric patterns with configured Pen. To illustrate, here is a small sample program that makes use of various Brushes:

```
private void MainForm_Paint(object sender, PaintEventArgs e)
{
    Graphics g = e.Graphics;

    // Make a blue SolidBrush.
    SolidBrush blueBrush = new SolidBrush(Color.Blue);
    // Get a stock brush from the Brushes type.
    SolidBrush pen2 = (SolidBrush)Brushes.Firebrick;
    // Render some shapes with the brushes.
    g.FillEllipse(blueBrush, 10, 10, 100, 100);
    g.FillPie(Brushes.Black, 150, 10, 120, 150, 90, 80);
    // Draw a purple polygon as well...
    SolidBrush brush3= new SolidBrush(Color.Purple);
    g.FillPolygon(brush3, new Point[]{ new Point(30, 140),
        new Point(265, 200), new Point(100, 225),
        new Point(190, 190), new Point(50, 330),
        new Point(20, 180)} );
    // And a rectangle with some text...
    Rectangle r = new Rectangle(150, 10, 130, 60);
    g.FillRectangle(Brushes.Blue, r);
    g.DrawString("Hello out there...How are ya?",
                new Font("Arial", 12), Brushes.White, r);
}
```

If you can't tell, this application is little more than the CustomPenApp program, this time making use of the FillXXX() methods and SolidBrush types, rather than pens and the related DrawXXX() methods. Figure 20-14 shows the output.

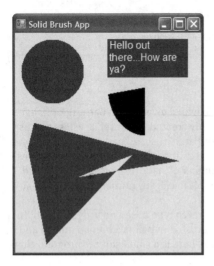

Figure 20-14. *Working with* Brush *types*

Working with HatchBrushes

The System.Drawing.Drawing2D namespace defines a Brush-derived type named HatchBrush. This type allows you to fill a region using a (very large) number of predefined patterns, represented by the HatchStyle enumeration. Here is a partial list of names:

```
public enum HatchStyle
{
    Horizontal, Vertical, ForwardDiagonal,
    BackwardDiagonal, Cross, DiagonalCross,
    LightUpwardDiagonal, DarkDownwardDiagonal,
    DarkUpwardDiagonal, LightVertical,
    NarrowHorizontal, DashedDownwardDiagonal,
    SmallConfetti, LargeConfetti, ZigZag,
    Wave, DiagonalBrick, Divot, DottedGrid, Sphere,
    OutlinedDiamond, SolidDiamond,
...
}
```

When constructing a HatchBrush, you need to specify the foreground and background colors to use during the fill operation. To illustrate, let's rework the logic seen previously in the PenCapApp example:

```
private void MainForm_Paint(object sender, PaintEventArgs e)
{
    Graphics g = e.Graphics;
    int yOffSet = 10;
```

```
// Get all members of the HatchStyle enum.
Array obj = Enum.GetValues(typeof(HatchStyle));
// Draw an oval with first 5 HatchStyle values.
for (int x = 0; x < 5; x++)
{
    // Configure Brush.
    HatchStyle temp = (HatchStyle)obj.GetValue(x);
    HatchBrush theBrush = new HatchBrush(temp,
        Color.White, Color.Black);
    // Print name of HatchStyle enum.
    g.DrawString(temp.ToString(), new Font("Times New Roman", 10),
        Brushes.Black, 0, yOffSet);
    // Fill a rectangle with the correct brush.
    g.FillEllipse(theBrush, 150, yOffSet, 200, 25);
    yOffSet += 40;
}
}
```

The output renders a filled oval for the first five hatch values (see Figure 20-15).

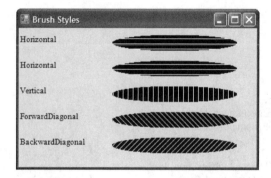

Figure 20-15. *Select hatch styles*

■**Source Code**   The BrushStyles application is included under the Chapter 20 subdirectory.

Working with TextureBrushes

The TextureBrush type allows you to attach a bitmap image to a brush, which can then be used in conjunction with a fill operation. In just a few pages, you will learn about the details of the GDI+ Image class. For the time being, understand that a TextureBrush is assigned an Image reference for use during its lifetime. The image itself is typically found stored in some local file (*.bmp, *.gif, *.jpg) or embedded into a .NET assembly.

Let's build a sample application that makes use of the TextureBrush type. One brush is used to paint the entire client area with the image found in a file named clouds.bmp, while the other brush is used to paint text with the image found within soap bubbles.bmp. The output is shown in Figure 20-16.

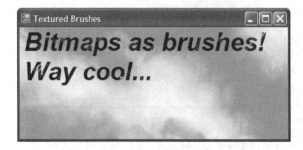

Figure 20-16. *Bitmaps as brushes*

To begin, your Form-derived class maintains two Brush member variables, which are assigned to a new TextureBrush in the constructor. Notice that the constructor of the TextureBrush type requires a type derived from Image:

```
public partial class MainForm : Form
{
    // Data for the image brush.
    private Brush texturedTextBrush;
    private Brush texturedBGroundBrush;

    public MainForm()
    {
        ...
        // Load image for background brush.
        Image bGroundBrushImage = new Bitmap("Clouds.bmp");
        texturedBGroundBrush = new TextureBrush(bGroundBrushImage);

        // Now load image for text brush.
        Image textBrushImage = new Bitmap("Soap Bubbles.bmp");
        texturedTextBrush = new TextureBrush(textBrushImage);
    }
}
```

■**Note** The *.bmp files used in this example must be in the same folder as the application (or specified using hard-coded paths). We'll address this limitation later in this chapter.

Now that you have two TextureBrush types to render with, the Paint event handler is quite straightforward:

```
private void MainForm_Paint(object sender, PaintEventArgs e)
{
    Graphics g = e.Graphics;
    Rectangle r = ClientRectangle;
    // Paint the clouds on the client area.
    g.FillRectangle(texturedBGroundBrush, r);
    // Some big bold text with a textured brush.
    g.DrawString("Bitmaps as brushes!  Way cool...",
        new Font("Arial", 30,
        FontStyle.Bold | FontStyle.Italic),  texturedTextBrush, r);
}
```

■**Source Code** The TexturedBrushes application is included under the Chapter 20 subdirectory.

Working with LinearGradientBrushes

Last but not least is the LinearGradientBrush type, which you can use whenever you want to blend two colors together in a gradient pattern. Working with this type is just as simple as working with the other brush types. The only point of interest is that when you build a LinearGradientBrush, you need to specify a pair of Color types and the direction of the blend via the LinearGradientMode enumeration:

```
public enum LinearGradientMode
{
    Horizontal, Vertical,
    ForwardDiagonal, BackwardDiagonal
}
```

To test each value, let's render a series of rectangles using a LinearGradientBrush:

```
private void MainForm_Paint(object sender, PaintEventArgs e)
{
    Graphics g = e.Graphics;
    Rectangle r = new Rectangle(10, 10, 100, 100);
    // A gradient brush.
    LinearGradientBrush theBrush = null;
    int yOffSet = 10;
    // Get all members of the LinearGradientMode enum.
    Array obj = Enum.GetValues(typeof(LinearGradientMode));
    // Draw an oval with a LinearGradientMode member.
    for(int x = 0; x < obj.Length; x++)
    {
        // Configure Brush.
        LinearGradientMode temp = (LinearGradientMode)obj.GetValue(x);
        theBrush = new LinearGradientBrush(r, Color.GreenYellow,
                                    Color.Blue, temp);
        // Print name of LinearGradientMode enum.
        g.DrawString(temp.ToString(), new Font("Times New Roman", 10),
                    new SolidBrush(Color.Black), 0, yOffSet);
        // Fill a rectangle with the correct brush.
        g. FillRectangle(theBrush, 150, yOffSet, 200, 50);
        yOffSet += 80;
    }
}
```

Figure 20-17 shows the end result.

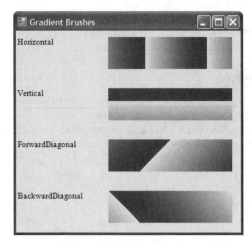

Figure 20-17. *Gradient brushes at work*

■**Source Code** The GradientBrushes application is included under the Chapter 20 subdirectory.

Rendering Images

At this point, you have examined how to manipulate three of the four major GDI+ types: fonts, pens, and brushes. The final type you'll examine in this chapter is the Image class and related subtypes. The abstract System.Drawing.Image type defines a number of methods and properties that hold various bits of information regarding the underlying image data it represents. For example, the Image class supplies the Width, Height, and Size properties to retrieve the dimensions of the image. Other properties allow you to gain access to the underlying palette. The Image class defines the core members shown in Table 20-8.

Table 20-8. *Members of the* Image *Type*

Members	Meaning in Life
FromFile()	This static method creates an Image from the specified file.
FromStream()	This static method creates an Image from the specified data stream.
Height Width Size HorizontalResolution VerticalResolution	These properties return information regarding the dimensions of this Image.
Palette	This property returns a ColorPalette data type that represents the underlying palette used for this Image.
GetBounds()	This method returns a Rectangle that represents the current size of this Image.
Save()	This method saves the data held in an Image-derived type to file.

Given that the abstract Image class cannot be directly created, you typically make a direct instance of the Bitmap type. Assume you have some Form-derived class that renders three bitmaps into the client area. Once you fill the `Bitmap` types with the correct image file, simply render each one within your `Paint` event handler using the `Graphics.DrawImage()` method:

```
public partial class MainForm : Form
{
    private Bitmap[] myImages = new Bitmap[3];
    public MainForm()
    {
        // Load some local images.
        myImages[0] = new Bitmap("imageA.bmp");
        myImages[1] = new Bitmap("imageB.bmp");
        myImages[2] = new Bitmap("imageC.bmp");
        CenterToScreen();
        InitializeComponent();
    }

    private void MainForm_Paint(object sender, PaintEventArgs e)
    {
        Graphics g = e.Graphics;
        // Render all three images.
        int yOffset = 10;
        foreach (Bitmap b in myImages)
        {
            g.DrawImage(b, 10, yOffset, 90, 90);
            yOffset += 100;
        }
    }
}
```

■Note The `*.bmp` files used in this example must be in the same folder as the application (or specified using hard-coded paths). We'll resolve this limitation later in this chapter.

Figure 20-18 shows the output.

Figure 20-18. *Rendering images*

Finally, be aware that regardless of its name, the `Bitmap` class can contain image data stored in any number of file formats (*.tif, *.gif, *.bmp, etc.).

■**Source Code** The BasicImages application is included under the Chapter 20 subdirectory.

Dragging and Hit Testing the PictureBox Control

While you are free to render `Bitmap` images directly onto any `Control`-derived class, you will find that you gain far greater control and functionality if you instead choose to make use of a `PictureBox` type to contain your image. For example, because the `PictureBox` type "is-a" `Control`, you inherit a great deal of functionality, such as the ability to handle various events, assign a tool tip or context menu, and so forth. While you could achieve similar behaviors using a raw `Bitmap`, you would be required to author a fair amount of boilerplate code.

To showcase the usefulness of the `PictureBox` type, let's create a simple "game" that illustrates the ability to capture mouse activity over a graphical image. If the user clicks the mouse somewhere within the bounds of the image, he is in "dragging" mode and can move the image around the Form. To make things more interesting, let's monitor where the user releases the image. If it is within the bounds of a GDI+-rendered rectangle, you'll take some additional course of action (seen shortly). As you may know, the process of testing for mouse click events within a specific region is termed *hit testing*.

The `PictureBox` type gains most of its functionality from the `Control` base class. You've already explored a number of `Control`'s members in the previous chapter, so let's quickly turn your attention to the process of assigning an image to the `PictureBox` member variable using the `Image` property (again, the `happyDude.bmp` file must be in the application directory):

```
public partial class MainForm : Form
{
    // This holds an image of a smiley face.
    private PictureBox happyBox = new PictureBox();

    public MainForm()
    {
        // Configure the PictureBox.
        happyBox.SizeMode = PictureBoxSizeMode.StretchImage;
        happyBox.Location = new System.Drawing.Point(64, 32);
        happyBox.Size = new System.Drawing.Size(50, 50);
        happyBox.Cursor = Cursors.Hand;
        happyBox.Image = new Bitmap("happyDude.bmp");

        // Now add to the Form's Controls collection.
        Controls.Add(happyBox);
    }
}
```

Beyond the `Image` property, the only other property of interest is `SizeMode`, which makes use of the `PictureBoxSizeMode` enumeration. This type is used to control how the associated image should be rendered within the bounding rectangle of the `PictureBox`. Here, you assigned `PictureBoxSize-Mode.StretchImage`, indicating that you wish to skew the image over the entire area of the `PictureBox` type (which is set to 50×50 pixels).

The next task is to handle the `MouseMove`, `MouseUp`, and `MouseDown` events for the `PictureBox` member variable using the expected C# event syntax:

```
public MainForm()
{
    ...
    // Add handlers for the following events.
    happyBox.MouseDown += new MouseEventHandler(happyBox_MouseDown);
    happyBox.MouseUp += new MouseEventHandler(happyBox_MouseUp);
    happyBox.MouseMove += new MouseEventHandler(happyBox_MouseMove);
    Controls.Add(happyBox);
    InitializeComponent();
}
```

The MouseDown event handler is in charge of storing the incoming (x, y) location of the cursor within two System.Int32 member variables (oldX and oldY) for later use, as well as setting a System.Boolean member variable (isDragging) to true, to indicate that a drag operation is in process. Add these member variables to your Form and implement the MouseDown event handler as so:

```
private void happyBox_MouseDown(object sender, MouseEventArgs e)
{
    isDragging = true;
    oldX = e.X;
    oldY = e.Y;
}
```

The MouseMove event handler simply relocates the position of the PictureBox (using the Top and Left properties) by offsetting the current cursor location with the integer data captured during the MouseDown event:

```
private void happyBox_MouseMove(object sender, MouseEventArgs e)
{
    if (isDragging)
    {
        // Need to figure new Y value based on where the mouse
        // down click happened.
        happyBox.Top = happyBox.Top + (e.Y - oldY);
        // Same process for X (use oldX as a baseline).
        happyBox.Left = happyBox.Left + (e.X - oldX);
    }
}
```

The MouseUp event handler sets the isDragging Boolean to false, to signal the end of the drag operation. As well, if the MouseUp event occurs when the PictureBox is contained within our GDI+-rendered Rectangle image, you can assume the user has won the (albeit rather simplistic) game. First, add a Rectangle member variable (named dropRect) to your Form class set to a given size:

```
public partial class MainForm : Form
{
    private PictureBox happyBox = new PictureBox();
    private int oldX, oldY;
    private bool isDragging;
    private Rectangle dropRect = new Rectangle(100, 100, 140, 170);
    ...
}
```

The MouseUp event handler can now be implemented as so:

```
private void happyBox_MouseUp(object sender, MouseEventArgs e)
{
    isDragging = false;

    // Is the mouse within the area of the drop rect?
```

```
        if(dropRect.Contains(happyBox.Bounds))
            MessageBox.Show("You win!", "What an amazing test of skill...");
}
```

Finally, you need to render the rectangular area (maintained by the dropRect member variable) on the Form within a Paint event handler:

```
private void MainForm_Paint(object sender, PaintEventArgs e)
{
    // Draw the drop box.
    Graphics g = e.Graphics;
    g.FillRectangle(Brushes.AntiqueWhite, dropRect);
    // Display instructions.
    g.DrawString("Drag the happy guy in here...",
        new Font("Times New Roman", 25), Brushes.Red, dropRect);
}
```

When you run the application, you are presented with what appears in Figure 20-19.

Figure 20-19. *The amazing happy-dude game*

If you have what it takes to win the game, you are rewarded with the kudos shown in Figure 20-20.

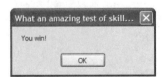

Figure 20-20. *You have nerves of steel!*

■**Source Code** The DraggingImages application is included under the Chapter 20 subdirectory.

Hit Testing Rendered Images

Validating a hit test against a Control-derived type (such as the PictureBox) is very simple, as it can respond directly to mouse events. However, what if you wish to perform a hit test on a geometric shape rendered directly on the surface of a Form?

To illustrate the process, let's revisit the previous BasicImages application and add some new functionality. The goal is to determine when the user clicks one of the three images. Once you discover which image was clicked, you'll adjust the Text property of the Form and highlight the image with a 5-pixel outline.

The first step is to define a new set of member variables in the Form type that represents the Rectangles you will be testing against in the MouseDown event. When this event occurs, you need to programmatically figure out if the incoming (*x*, *y*) coordinate is somewhere within the bounds of the Rectangles used to represent the dimension of each Image. If the user does click a given image, you set a private Boolean member variable (isImageClicked) to true and indicate which image was selected via another member variable of a custom enumeration named ClickedImage, defined as so:

```
enum ClickedImage
{
    ImageA, ImageB, ImageC
}
```

With this, here is the initial update to the Form-derived class:

```
public partial class MainForm : Form
{
    private Bitmap[] myImages = new Bitmap[3];
    private Rectangle[] imageRects = new Rectangle[3];
    private bool isImageClicked = false;
    ClickedImage imageClicked = ClickedImage.ImageA;

    public MainForm()
    {
...
        // Set up the rectangles.
        imageRects[0] = new Rectangle(10, 10, 90, 90);
        imageRects[1] = new Rectangle(10, 110, 90, 90);
        imageRects[2] = new Rectangle(10, 210, 90, 90);
    }

    private void MainForm_MouseDown(object sender, MouseEventArgs e)
    {
        // Get (x, y) of mouse click.
        Point mousePt = new Point(e.X, e.Y);

        // See if the mouse is anywhere in the 3 Rectangles.
        if (imageRects[0].Contains(mousePt))
        {
            isImageClicked = true;
            imageClicked = ClickedImage.ImageA;
            this.Text = "You clicked image A";
        }
        else if (imageRects[1].Contains(mousePt))
        {
            isImageClicked = true;
            imageClicked = ClickedImage.ImageB;
            this.Text = "You clicked image B";
        }
        else if (imageRects[2].Contains(mousePt))
```

```
    {
        isImageClicked = true;
        imageClicked = ClickedImage.ImageC;
        this.Text = "You clicked image C";
    }
    else      // Not in any shape, set defaults.
    {
        isImageClicked = false;
        this.Text = "Hit Testing Images";
    }
    // Redraw the client area.
    Invalidate();
    }
}
```

Notice that the final conditional check sets the isImageClicked member variable to false, indicating that the user did not click one of the three images. This is important, as you want to erase the outline of the previously selected image. Once all items have been checked, invalidate the client area. Here is the updated Paint handler:

```
private void MainForm_Paint(object sender, PaintEventArgs e)
{
    Graphics g = e.Graphics;

    // Render all three images.
...
    // Draw outline (if clicked)
    if (isImageClicked == true)
    {
        Pen outline = new Pen(Color.Tomato, 5);
        switch (imageClicked)
        {
            case ClickedImage.ImageA:
                g.DrawRectangle(outline, imageRects[0]);
                break;
            case ClickedImage.ImageB:
                g.DrawRectangle(outline, imageRects[1]);
                break;
            case ClickedImage.ImageC:
                g.DrawRectangle(outline, imageRects[2]);
                break;
            default:
                break;
        }
    }
}
```

At this point, you should be able to run your application and validate that an outline appears around each image that has been clicked (and that no outline is present when you click outside the bounds of said images).

Hit Testing Nonrectangular Images

Now, what if you wish to perform a hit test in a nonrectangular region, rather than a simple square? Assume you updated your application to render an oddball geometric shape that will also sport an outline when clicked (see Figure 20-21).

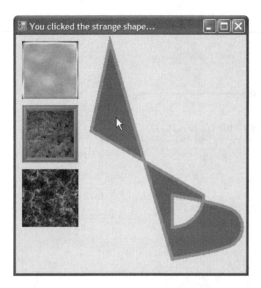

Figure 20-21. *Hit-testing polygons*

This geometric image was rendered on the Form using the FillPath() method of the Graphics type. This method takes an instance of a GraphicsPath object, which encapsulates a series of connected lines, curves, and strings. Adding new items to a GraphicsPath instance is achieved using a number of related Add methods, as described in Table 20-9.

Table 20-9. Add-*Centric Methods of the* GraphicsPath *Class*

Methods	Meaning in Life
AddArc()	Appends an elliptical arc to the current figure
AddBezier() AddBeziers()	Adds a cubic Bezier curve (or set of Bezier curves) to the current figure
AddClosedCurve()	Adds a closed curve to the current figure
AddCurve()	Adds a curve to the current figure
AddEllipse()	Adds an ellipse to the current figure
AddLine() AddLines()	Appends a line segment to the current figure
AddPath()	Appends the specified GraphicsPath to the current figure
AddPie()	Adds the outline of a pie shape to the current figure
AddPolygon()	Adds a polygon to the current figure
AddRectangle() AddRectangles()	Adds one (or more) rectangle to the current figure
AddString()	Adds a text string to the current figure

Specify that you are "using" System.Drawing.Drawing2D and add a new GraphicsPath member variable to your Form-derived class. In the Form's constructor, build the set of items that represent your path as follows:

```
public partial class MainForm : Form
{
    GraphicsPath myPath = new GraphicsPath();
...
    public MainForm()
    {
        // Create an interesting path.
        myPath.StartFigure();
        myPath.AddLine(new Point(150, 10), new Point(120, 150));
        myPath.AddArc(200, 200, 100, 100, 0, 90);
        Point point1 = new Point(250, 250);
        Point point2 = new Point(350, 275);
        Point point3 = new Point(350, 325);
        Point point4 = new Point(250, 350);
        Point[] points = { point1, point2, point3, point4} ;
        myPath.AddCurve(points);
        myPath.CloseFigure();
...
    }
}
```

Notice the calls to StartFigure() and CloseFigure(). When you call StartFigure(), you are able to insert a new item into the current path you are building. A call to CloseFigure() closes the current figure and begins a new figure (if you require one). Also know that if the figure contains a sequence of connected lines and curves (as in the case of the myPath instance), the loop is closed by connecting a line from the endpoint to the starting point. First, add an additional name to the ImageClicked enumeration named StrangePath:

```
enum ClickedImage
{
    ImageA, ImageB,
    ImageC, StrangePath
}
```

Next, update your existing MouseDown event handler to test for the presence of the cursor's (x, y) position within the bounds of the GraphicsPath. Like a Region type, this can be discovered using the IsVisible() member:

```
protected void OnMouseDown (object sender, MouseEventArgs e)
{
    // Get (x, y) of mouse click.
    Point mousePt = new Point(e.X, e.Y);
...
    else if(myPath.IsVisible(mousePt))
    {
        isImageClicked = true;
        imageClicked = ClickedImage.StrangePath;
        this.Text = "You clicked the strange shape...";
    }
...
}
```

Finally, update the Paint handler as follows:

```
private void MainForm_Paint(object sender, PaintEventArgs e)
{
    Graphics g = e.Graphics;
...
    // Draw the graphics path.
    g.FillPath(Brushes.Sienna, myPath);
```

```
    // Draw outline (if clicked)
    if(isImageClicked == true)
    {
        Pen outline = new Pen(Color.Red, 5);
        switch(imageClicked)
        {
            ...
            case ClickedImage.StrangePath:
                g.DrawPath(outline, myPath);
                break;
            default:
                break;
        }
    }
}
```

■**Source Code** The HitTestingImages project is included under the Chapter 20 subdirectory.

Understanding the .NET Resource Format

Up to this point in the chapter, each application that made use of external resources (such as bitmap files) demanded that the image files be within the client's application directory. Given this, you loaded your *.bmp files using an absolute name:

```
// Fill the images with bitmaps.
bMapImageA = new Bitmap("imageA.bmp");
bMapImageB = new Bitmap("imageB.bmp");
bMapImageC = new Bitmap("imageC.bmp");
```

This logic, of course, demands that the application directory does indeed contain three files named imageA.bmp, imageB.bmp, and imageC.bmp; otherwise, you will receive a runtime exception.

As you may recall from Chapter 11, an assembly is a collection of types and *optional resources*. Given this, your final task of the chapter is to learn how to bundle external resources (such as image files and strings) into the assembly itself. In this way, your .NET binary is truly self-contained. At the lowest level, bundling external resources into a .NET assembly involves the following steps:

1. Create an *.resx file that establishes name/value pairs for each resource in your application via XML data representation.

2. Use the resgen.exe command-line utility to convert your XML-based *.resx file into a binary equivalent (a *.resources file).

3. Using the /resource flag of the C# compiler, embed the binary *.resources file into your assembly.

As you might suspect, these steps are automated when using Visual Studio 2005. You'll examine how this IDE can assist you in just a moment. For the time being, let's check out how to generate and embed .NET resources at the command line.

The System.Resources Namespace

The key to understanding the .NET resource format is to know the types defined within the System.Resources namespace. This set of types provides the programmatic means to read and write *.resx (XML-based) and *.resources (binary) files, as well as obtain resources embedded in a given assembly. Table 20-10 provides a rundown of the core types.

Table 20-10. *Members of the* System.Resources *Namespace*

Members	Meaning in Life
ResourceReader ResourceWriter	These types allow you to read from and write to binary *.resources files.
ResXResourceReader ResXResourceWriter	These types allow you to read from and write to XML-based *.resx files.
ResourceManager	This type allows you to programmatically obtain embedded resources from a given assembly.

Programmatically Creating an *.resx File

As mentioned, an *.resx file is a block of XML data that assigns name/value pairs for each resource in your application. The ResXResourceWriter class provides a set of members that allow you to create the *.resx file, add binary and string-based resources, and commit them to storage. To illustrate, let's create a simple application (ResXWriter) that will generate an *.resx file containing an entry for the happyDude.bmp file (first seen in the DraggingImages example) and a single string resource. The GUI consists of a single Button type (see Figure 20-22).

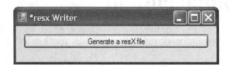

Figure 20-22. *The ResX application*

The Click event handler for the Button adds the happyDude.bmp and string resource to the *.resx file, which is saved on the local C drive:

```csharp
private void btnGenResX_Click(object sender, EventArgs e)
{
    // Make an resx writer and specify the file to write to.
    ResXResourceWriter w =
        new ResXResourceWriter(@"C:\ResXForm.resx");
    // Add happy dude and string.
    Image i = new Bitmap("happyDude.bmp");
    w.AddResource("happyDude", i);
    w.AddResource("welcomeString", "Hello new resource format!");
    // Commit file.
    w.Generate();
    w.Close();
}
```

The member of interest is ResXResourceWriter.AddResource(). This method has been overloaded a few times to allow you to insert binary data (as you did with the happyDude.bmp image), as well as textual data (as you have done for your test string). Notice that each version takes two parameters: the name of a given resource in the *.resx file and the data itself. The Generate() method commits the information to file. At this point, you have an XML description of the image and string resources. To verify, open the new ResXForm.resx file using a text editor (see Figure 20-23).

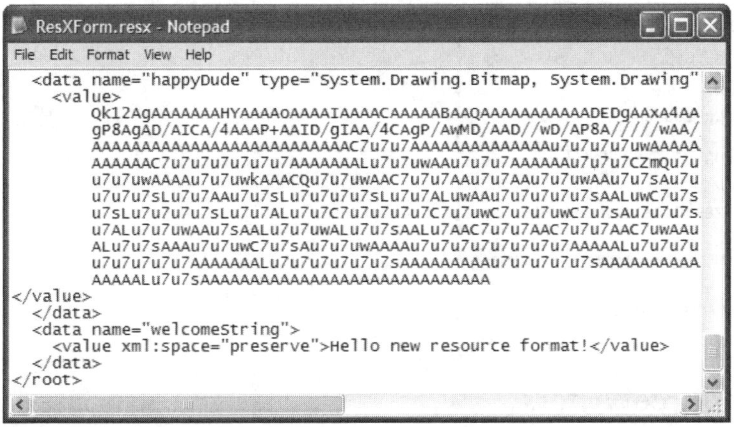

Figure 20-23. *.resx expressed as XML*

Building the *.resources File

Now that you have an *.resx file, you can make use of the resgen.exe utility to produce the binary equivalent. To do so, open a Visual Studio 2005 command prompt, navigate to your C drive, and issue the following command:

```
resgen resxform.resx resxform.resources
```

You can now open the new *.resources file using Visual Studio 2005 and view the binary format (see Figure 20-24).

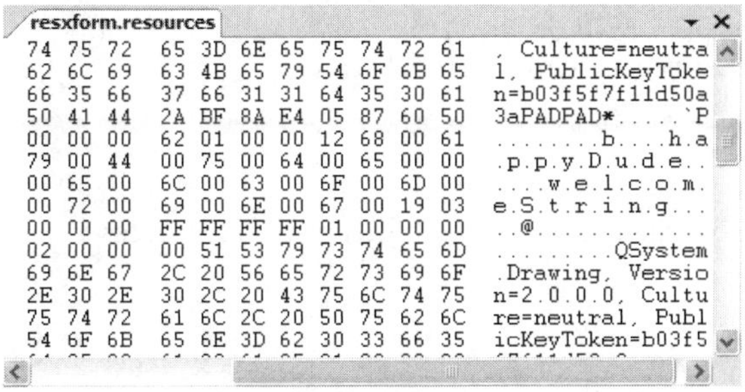

Figure 20-24. *The binary *.resources file*

Binding the *.resources File into a .NET Assembly

At this point, you are able to embed the *.resources file into a .NET assembly using the /resources command-line argument of the C# compiler. To illustrate, copy the Program.cs, Form1.cs, and Form1.Designer.cs files to your C drive, open a Visual Studio 2005 command prompt, and issue the following command:

```
csc /resource:resxform.resources /r:System.Drawing.dll *.cs
```

If you were to now open your new assembly using ildasm.exe, you would find the manifest has been updated as shown in Figure 20-25.

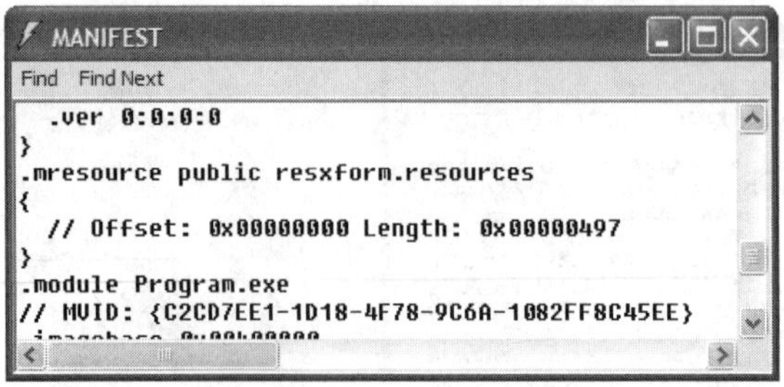

Figure 20-25. *The embedded resources*

Working with ResourceWriters

The previous example made use of the ResXResourceWriter types to generate an XML file that contains name/value pairs for each application resource. The resulting *.resx file was then run through the resgen.exe utility. Finally, the *.resources file was embedded into the assembly using the /resource flag of the C# compiler. The truth of the matter is that you do not need to build an *.resx file (although having an XML representation of your resources can come in handy and is readable). If you do not require an *.resx file, you can make use of the ResourceWriter type to directly create a binary *.resources file:

```
private void GenerateResourceFile()
{
    // Make a new *.resources file.
    ResourceWriter rw;
    rw = new ResourceWriter(@"C:\myResources.resources");

    // Add 1 image and 1 string.
    rw.AddResource("happyDude", new Bitmap("happyDude.bmp"));
    rw.AddResource("welcomeString", "Hello new resource format!");
    rw.Generate();
    rw.Close();
}
```

At this point, the *.resources file can be bundled into an assembly using the /resources option:

```
csc /resource:myresources.resources *.cs
```

■**Source Code** The ResXWriter project is included under the Chapter 20 subdirectory.

Generating Resources Using Visual Studio 2005

Although it is possible to work with *.resx/*.resources files manually at the command line, the good news is that Visual Studio 2005 automates the creation and embedding of your project's resources. To illustrate, create a new Windows Forms application named MyResourcesWinApp. Now, if you open Solution Explorer, you will notice that each Form in your application has an associated *.resx file in place automatically (see Figure 20-26).

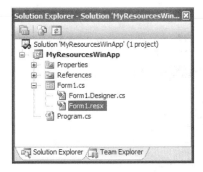

Figure 20-26. *The autogenerated* *.resx *files of Visual Studio 2005*

This *.resx file will be maintained automatically while you naturally add resources (such as an image in a PictureBox widget) using the visual designers. Now, despite what you may be thinking, you should *not* manually update this file to specify your custom resources as Visual Studio 2005 regenerates this file with each compilation. To be sure, you will do well if you allow the IDE to manage a Form's *.resx file on your behalf.

When you want to maintain a custom set of resources that are not directly mapped to a given Form, simply insert a new *.resx file (named MyCustomResources.resx in this example) using the Project ➤ Add New Item menu item (see Figure 20-27).

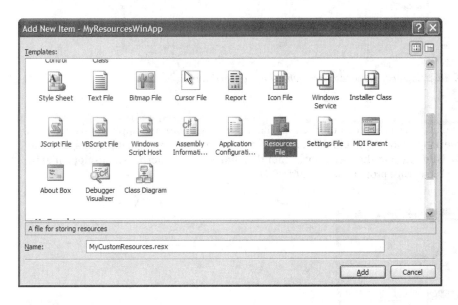

Figure 20-27. *Inserting a new* *.resx *file*

If you open your new *.resx file, a friendly GUI editor appears that allows you to insert string data, image files, sound clips, and other resources. The leftmost drop-down menu item allows you to select the type of resource you wish to add. First, add a new string resource named WelcomeString that is set to a message of your liking (see Figure 20-28).

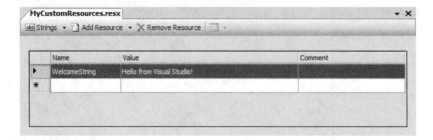

Figure 20-28. *Inserting new string resources with the* `*.resx` *editor*

Next, add the `happyDude.bmp` image file by selecting Images from the leftmost drop-down, choosing the Add Existing File option (see Figure 20-29), and navigating to the `happyDude.bmp` file.

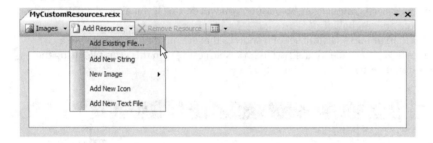

Figure 20-29. *Inserting new* `*.bmp` *resources with the* `*.resx` *editor*

At this point, you will find that the `*.bmp` file has been copied into your application directory. If you select the happyDude icon from the `*.resx` editor, you can now specify that this image should be embedded directly into the assembly (rather than linked as an external stand-alone file) by adjusting the Persistence property (see Figure 20-30).

Figure 20-30. *Embedding specified resources*

Furthermore, Solution Explorer now has a new folder named Resources that contains each item to be embedded into the assembly. As you would guess, if you open a given resource, Visual Studio 2005 launches an associated editor. In any case, if you were to now compile your application, the string and image data will be embedded within your assembly.

Programmatically Reading Resources

Now that you understand the process of embedding resources into your assembly (using csc.exe or Visual Studio 2005), you'll need to learn how to programmatically read them for use in your program using the ResourceManager type. To illustrate, add a Button and PictureBox widget on your Form type (see Figure 20-31).

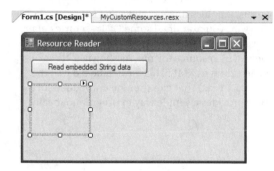

Figure 20-31. *The updated UI*

Next, handle the Button's Click event. Update the event handler with the following code:

```
// Be sure to 'use' System.Resources and System.Reflection!
private void btnGetStringData_Click(object sender, EventArgs e)
{
    // Make a resource manager.
    ResourceManager rm =
        new ResourceManager("MyResourcesWinApp.MyCustomResources",
        Assembly.GetExecutingAssembly());
    // Get the embedded string (case sensitive!)
    MessageBox.Show(rm.GetString("WelcomeString"));
    // Get the embedded bitmap (case sensitive!)
    myPictureBox.Image = (Bitmap)rm.GetObject("HappyDude");
    // Clean up.
    rm.ReleaseAllResources();
}
```

Notice that the first constructor argument to the ResourceManager is the fully qualified name of your *.resx file (minus the file extension). The second parameter is a reference to the assembly that contains the embedded resource (which is the current assembly in this case). Once you have created the ResourceManager, you can call GetString() or GetObject() to extract the embedded data. If you were to run the application and click the button, you would find that the string data is displayed in the MessageBox and the image data has been extracted from the assembly and placed into the PictureBox.

Source Code The MyResourcesWinApp project is included under the Chapter 20 subdirectory.

Well, that wraps up our examination of GDI+ and the System.Drawing namespaces. If you are interested in exploring GDI+ further (including printing support), be sure to check out *GDI+ Programming in C# and VB .NET* by Nick Symmonds (Apress, 2002).

Summary

GDI+ is the name given to a number of related .NET namespaces, each of which is used to render graphic images to a Control-derived type. The bulk of this chapter was spent examining how to work with core GDI+ object types such as colors, fonts, graphics images, pens, and brushes in conjunction with the almighty Graphics type. Along the way, you examined some GDI+-centric details such as hit testing and how to drag and drop images.

This chapter wrapped up by examining the new .NET resource format. As shown, a *.resx denotes resources using a set of name/value pairs describes as XML. This file can be fed into the resgen.exe utility, resulting in a binary format (*.resources) that can then be embedded into a related assembly. Finally, the ResourceManager type provides a simple way to programmatically retrieve embedded resources at runtime.

■ ■ ■

## CHAPTER 21

Programming with Windows Forms Controls

This chapter is concerned with providing a road map of the controls defined in the System.Windows.
Forms namespace. Chapter 19 already gave you a chance to work with some controls mounted onto
a main Form such as MenuStrip, ToolStrip, and StatusStrip. In this chapter, however, you will
examine various types that tend to exist within the boundaries of a Form's client area (e.g., Button,
MaskedTextBox, WebBrowser, MonthCalendar, TreeView, and the like). Once you look at the core UI
widgets, you will then cover the process of building custom Windows Forms controls that integrate
into the Visual Studio 2005 IDE.

The chapter then investigates the process of building custom dialog boxes and the role of *form
inheritance*, which allows you to build hierarchies of related Form types. The chapter wraps up with
a discussion of how to establish the *docking* and *anchoring* behaviors for your family of GUI types,
and the role of the FlowControlPanel and TableControlPanel types supplied by .NET 2.0.

The World of Windows Forms Controls

The System.Windows.Forms namespace contains a number of types that represent common GUI
widgets typically used to allow you to respond to user input in a Windows Forms application. Many
of the controls you will work with on a day-to-day basis (such as Button, TextBox, and Label) are quite
intuitive to work with. Other, more exotic controls and components (such as TreeView, ErrorProvider,
and TabControl) require a bit more explanation.

As you learned in Chapter 19, the System.Windows.Forms.Control type is the base class for all
derived widgets. Recall that Control provides the ability to process mouse and keyboard events,
establish the physical dimensions and position of the widget using various properties (Height,
Width, Left, Right, Location, etc.), manipulate background and foreground colors, establish the
active font/cursor, and so forth. As well, the Control base type defines members that control a widget's anchoring and docking behaviors (explained at the conclusion of this chapter).

As you read through this chapter, remember that the widgets you examine here gain a good
deal of their functionality from the Control base class. Thus, we'll focus (more or less) on the unique
members of a given widget. Do understand that this chapter does not attempt to fully describe each
and every member of each and every control (that is a task for the .NET Framework 2.0 SDK documentation). Rest assured, though, that once you complete this chapter, you will have no problem
understanding the widgets I have not directly described.

■**Note** Windows Forms provide a number of controls that allow you to display relational data (DataGridView, BindingSource, etc.). Some of these data-centric controls are examined in Chapter 22 during our discussion of ADO.NET.

Adding Controls to Forms by Hand

Regardless of which type of control you choose to place on a Form, you will follow an identical set of steps to do so. First of all, you must define member variables that represent the controls themselves. Next, inside the Form's constructor (or within a helper method called by the constructor), you'll configure the look and feel of each control using the exposed properties, methods, and events. Finally (and most important), once you've set the control to its initial state, you must add it into the Form's internal controls collection using the inherited Controls property. If you forget this final step, your widgets will *not* be visible at runtime.

To illustrate the process of adding controls to a Form, let's begin by building a Form type "wizard-free" using your text editor of choice and the C# command-line compiler. Create a new C# file named ControlsByHand.cs and code a new MainWindow class as so:

```csharp
using System;
using System.Drawing;
using System.Windows.Forms;

namespace ControlsByHand
{
    class MainWindow : Form
    {
        // Form widget member variables.
        private TextBox firstNameBox = new TextBox();
        private Button btnShowControls = new Button();

        public MainWindow()
        {
            // Configure Form.
            this.Text = "Simple Controls";
            this.Width = 300;
            this.Height = 200;
            CenterToScreen();

            // Add a new textbox to the Form.
            firstNameBox.Text = "Hello";
            firstNameBox.Size = new Size(150, 50);
            firstNameBox.Location = new Point(10, 10);
            this.Controls.Add(firstNameBox);

            // Add a new button to the Form.
            btnShowControls.Text = "Click Me";
            btnShowControls.Size = new Size(90, 30);
            btnShowControls.Location = new Point(10, 70);
            btnShowControls.BackColor = Color.DodgerBlue;
            btnShowControls.Click +=
                new EventHandler(btnShowControls_Clicked);
            this.Controls.Add(btnShowControls);
        }
```

```
    // Handle Button's Click event.
    private void btnShowControls_Clicked(object sender, EventArgs e)
    {
        // Call ToString() on each control in the
        // Form's Controls collection
        string ctrlInfo= "";
        foreach (Control c in this.Controls)
        {
            ctrlInfo += string.Format("Control: {0}\n",
                c.ToString());
        }
        MessageBox.Show(ctrlInfo, "Controls on Form");
    }
  }
}
```

Now, add a second class to the ControlsByHand namespace that implements the program's Main() method:

```
class Program
{
    public static void Main(string[] args)
    {
        Application.Run(new MainWindow());
    }
}
```

At this point, compile your C# file at the command line using the following command:

```
csc /target:winexe *.cs
```

When you run your program and click the Form's button, you will find a message box that lists each item on the Form (see Figure 21-1).

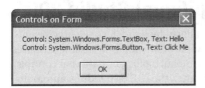

Figure 21-1. *Interacting with the Form's controls collection*

The Control.ControlCollection Type

While the process of adding a new widget to a Form is quite simple, I'd like to discuss the Controls property in a bit more detail. This property returns a reference to a nested class named ControlCollection defined within the Control class. The nested ControlCollection type maintains an entry for each widget placed on the Form. You can obtain a reference to this collection anytime you wish to "walk the list" of child widgets:

```
// Get access to the nested ControlCollection for this Form.
Control.ControlCollection coll = this.Controls;
```

Once you have a reference to this collection, you can manipulate its contents using the members shown in Table 21-1.

Table 21-1. ControlCollection *Members*

Member	Meaning in Life
Add() AddRange()	Used to insert a new Control-derived type (or array of types) in the collection
Clear()	Removes all entries in the collection
Count	Returns the number of items in the collection
GetEnumerator()	Returns the IEnumerator interface for this collection
Remove() RemoveAt()	Used to remove a control from the collection

Given that a Form maintains a collection of its controls, it is very simple under Windows Forms to dynamically create, remove, or otherwise manipulate visual elements. For example, assume you wish to disable all Button types on a given Form (or some such similar operation, such as change the background color of all TextBoxes). To do so, you can leverage the C# is keyword to determine who's who and change the state of the widgets accordingly:

```
private void DisableAllButtons()
{
    foreach (Control c in this.Controls)
    {
        if (c is Button)
            ((Button)c).Enabled = false;
    }
}
```

■**Source Code** The ControlsByHand project is included under the Chapter 21 subdirectory.

Adding Controls to Forms Using Visual Studio 2005

Now that you understand the process of adding controls to a Form by hand, let's see how Visual Studio 2005 can automate the process. Create a new Windows Application project for testing purposes named whatever you choose. Similar to the process of designing menu, toolbar, or status bar controls, when you drop a control from the Toolbox onto the Forms designer, the IDE responds by automatically adding the correct member variable to the *.Designer.cs file. As well, when you design the look and feel of the widget using the IDE's Properties window, the related code changes are added to the InitializeComponent() member function (also located within the *.Designer.cs file).

■**Note** Recall that the Properties window also allows you handle events for a given control when you click the lightning bolt icon. Simply select the widget from the drop-down list and type in the name of the method to be called for the events you are interested in responding to (or just double-click the event to generate a default event handler name).

Assume you have added a TextBox and Button type to the Forms designer. Notice that when you reposition a control on the designer, the Visual Studio 2005 IDE provides visual hints regarding the spacing and alignment of the current widget (see Figure 21-2).

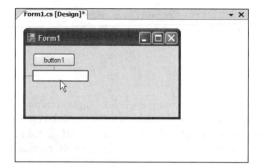

Figure 21-2. *Alignment and spacing hints*

Once you have placed the `Button` and `TextBox` on the designer, examine the code generated in the `InitializeComponent()` method. Here you will find that the types have been new-ed and inserted into the Form's `ControlCollection` automatically (in addition to any settings you may have made using the Properties window):

```
private void InitializeComponent()
{
    this.btnMyButton = new System.Windows.Forms.Button();
    this.txtMyTextBox = new System.Windows.Forms.TextBox();
...
    // MainWindow
    //
    ...
    this.Controls.Add(this.txtMyTextBox);
    this.Controls.Add(this.btnMyButton);
...
}
```

As you can see, a tool such as Visual Studio 2005 simply saves you some typing time (and helps you avoid hand cramps). Although `InitializeComponent()` is maintained on your behalf, do understand that you are free to configure a given control directly in code anywhere you see necessary (constructors, event handlers, helper functions, etc.). The role of `InitializeComponent()` is simply to establish the initial state of your UI elements. If you want to keep your life simple, I suggest allowing Visual Studio 2005 to maintain `InitializeComponent()` on your behalf, given that the designers may ignore or overwrite edits you make within this method.

Working with the Basic Controls

The `System.Windows.Forms` namespace defines numerous "basic controls" that are commonplace to any windowing framework (buttons, labels, text boxes, check boxes, etc.). Although I would guess you are familiar with the basic operations of such types, let's examine some of the more interesting aspects of the following basic UI elements:

- `Label`, `TextBox`, and `MaskedTextBox`
- `Button`
- `CheckBox`, `RadioButton`, and `GroupBox`
- `CheckedListBox`, `ListBox`, and `ComboBox`

Once you have become comfortable with these basic Control-derived types, we will turn our attention to more exotic widgets such as MonthCalendar, TabControl, TrackBar, WebBrowser, and so forth.

Fun with Labels

The Label control is capable of holding read-only information (text or image based) that explains the role of the other controls to help the user along. Assume you have created a new Visual Studio 2005 Windows Forms project named LabelsAndTextBoxes. Define a method called CreateLabelControl in your Form-derived type that creates and configures a Label type, and then adds it to the Form's controls collection:

```
private void CreateLabelControl()
{
    // Create and configure a Label.
    Label lblInstructions = new Label();
    lblInstructions.Name = "lblInstructions";
    lblInstructions.Text = "Please enter values in all the text boxes";
    lblInstructions.Font = new Font("Times New Roman", 9.75F, FontStyle.Bold);
    lblInstructions.AutoSize = true;
    lblInstructions.Location = new System.Drawing.Point(16, 13);
    lblInstructions.Size = new System.Drawing.Size(240, 16);

    // Add to Form's controls collection.
    Controls.Add(lblInstructions);
}
```

If you were to call this helper function within your Form's constructor, you would find your prompt displayed in the upper portion of the main window:

```
public MainWindow()
{
    InitializeComponent();
    CreateLabelControl();
    CenterToScreen();
}
```

Unlike most other widgets, Label controls cannot receive focus via a Tab keypress. However, under .NET 2.0, it is now possible to create *mnemonic keys* for any Label by setting the UseMnemonic property to true (which happens to be the default setting). Once you have done so, a Label's Text property can define a shortcut key (via the ampersand symbol, &), which is used to tab to the control that follows it in the tab order.

▪**Note**   You'll learn more about configuring tab order later in this chapter, but for the time being, understand that a control's tab order is established via the TabIndex property. By default, a control's TabIndex is set based on the order in which it was added to the Forms designer. Thus, if you add a Label followed by a TextBox, the Label is set to TabIndex 0 while the TextBox is set to TabIndex 1.

To illustrate, let's now leverage the Forms designer to build a UI containing a set of three Labels and three TextBoxes (be sure to leave room on the upper part of the Form to display the Label dynamically created in the CreateLabelControl() method). In Figure 21-3, note that each label has an underlined letter that was identified using the & character in the value assigned to the Text property (as you might know, &-specified characters allow the user to activate an item using the Alt+*<some key>* keystroke).

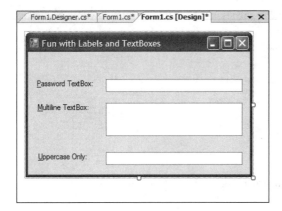

Figure 21-3. *Assigning mnemonics to* Label *controls*

If you now run your project, you will be able to tab between each TextBox using the Alt+p, Alt+m, or Alt+u keystrokes.

Fun with TextBoxes

Unlike the Label control, the TextBox control is typically not read-only (although it could be if you set the ReadOnly property to true), and it is commonly used to allow the user to enter textual data for processing. The TextBox type can be configured to hold a single line or multiple lines of text, it can be configured with a *password character* (such as an asterisk, *), and it may support scroll bars in the case of multiline text boxes. In addition to the behavior inherited by its base classes, TextBox defines a few particular properties of interest (see Table 21-2).

Table 21-2. TextBox *Properties*

Property	Meaning in Life
AcceptsReturn	Gets or sets a value indicating whether pressing Enter in a multiline TextBox control creates a new line of text in the control or activates the "default button" for the Form
CharacterCasing	Gets or sets whether the TextBox control modifies the case of characters as they are typed
PasswordChar	Gets or sets the character used to mask characters in a single-line TextBox control used to enter passwords
ScrollBars	Gets or sets which scroll bars should appear in a multiline TextBox control
TextAlign	Gets or sets how text is aligned in a TextBox control, using the HorizontalAlignment enumeration

To illustrate some aspects of the TextBox, let's configure the three TextBox controls on the current Form. The first TextBox (named txtPassword) should be configured as a password text box, meaning the characters typed into the TextBox should not be directly visible, but are instead masked with a predefined password character via the PasswordChar property.

The second TextBox (named txtMultiline) will be a multiline text area that has been configured to accept return key processing and displays a vertical scroll bar when the text entered exceeds the space of the TextBox area. Finally, the third TextBox (named txtUppercase) will be configured to translate the entered character data into uppercase.

Configure each TextBox accordingly via the Properties window and use the following (partial) InitializeComponent() implementation as a guide:

```
private void InitializeComponent()
{
...
    // txtPassword
    //
    this.txtPassword.PasswordChar = '*';
...
    // txtMultiline
    //
    this.txtMultiline.Multiline = true;
    this.txtMultiline.ScrollBars = System.Windows.Forms.ScrollBars.Vertical;
...
    // txtUpperCase
    //
    this.txtUpperCase.CharacterCasing =
        System.Windows.Forms.CharacterCasing.Upper;
...
}
```

Notice that the ScrollBars property is assigned a value from the ScrollBars enumeration, which defines the following values:

```
public enum System.Windows.Forms.ScrollBars
{
    Both, Horizontal, None, Vertical
}
```

The CharacterCasing property works in conjunction with the CharacterCasing enum, which is defined as so:

```
public enum System.Windows.Forms.CharacterCasing
{
    Normal, Upper, Lower
}
```

Now assume you have placed a Button on the Form (named btnDisplayData) and added an event handler for the Button's Click event. The implementation of this method simply displays the value in each TextBox within a message box:

```
private void btnDisplayData_Click(object sender, EventArgs e)
{
    // Get data from all the text boxes.
    string textBoxData = "";
    textBoxData += string.Format("MultiLine:  {0}\n", txtMultiline.Text);
    textBoxData += string.Format("\nPassword:  {0}\n", txtPassword.Text);
    textBoxData += string.Format("\nUppercase:  {0}\n", txtUpperCase.Text);

    // Display all the data.
    MessageBox.Show(textBoxData, "Here is the data in your TextBoxes");
}
```

Figure 21-4 shows one possible input session (note that you need to hold down the Alt key to see the label mnemonics).

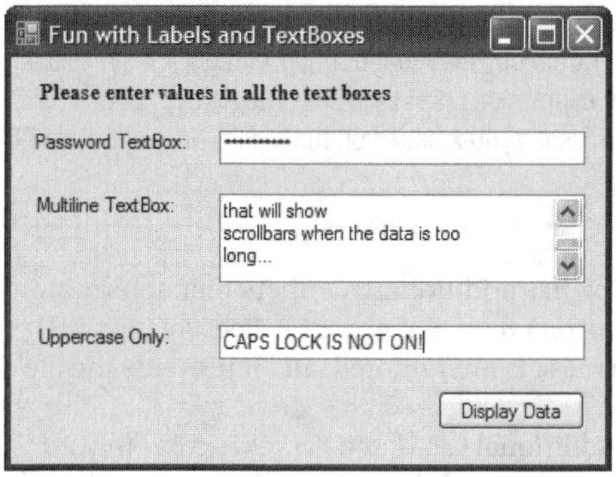

Figure 21-4. *The many faces of the* TextBox *type*

Figure 21-5 shows the result of clicking the Button type.

Figure 21-5. *Extracting values from* TextBox *types*

Fun with MaskedTextBoxes

As of .NET 2.0, we now have a *masked* text box that allows us to specify a valid sequence of characters that will be accepted by the input area (Social Security number, phone number with area code, zip code, or whatnot). The mask to test against (termed a *mask expression*) is established using specific tokens embedded into a string literal. Once you have created a mask expression, this value is assigned to the Mask property. Table 21-3 documents some (but not all) valid masking tokens.

Table 21-3. *Mask Tokens of* MaskedTextBox

Mask Token	Meaning in Life
0	Represents a mandatory digit with the value 0–9
9	Represents an optional digit or a space
L	Required letter (in uppercase or lowercase), A–Z
?	Optional letter (in uppercase or lowercase), A–Z
,	Represents a thousands separator placeholder
:	Represents a time placeholder
/	Represents a date placeholder
$	Represents a currency symbol

■**Note** The characters understood by the MaskedTextBox *do not* directly map to the syntax of regular expressions. Although .NET provides namespaces to work with proper regular expressions (System.Text.RegularExpressions and System.Web.RegularExpressions), the MaskedTextBox uses syntax based on the legacy MaskedEdit VB6 COM control.

In addition to the Mask property, the MaskedTextBox has additional members that determine how this control should respond if the user enters incorrect data. For example, BeepOnError will cause the control to (obviously) issue a beep when the mask is not honored, and it prevents the illegal character from being processed.

To illustrate the use of the MaskedTextBox, add an additional Label and MaskedTextBox to your current Form. Although you are free to build a mask pattern directly in code, the Properties window provides an ellipsis button for the Mask property that will launch a dialog box with a number of predefined masks (see Figure 21-6).

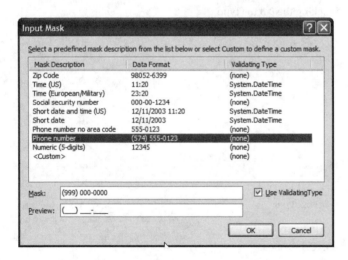

Figure 21-6. *Predefined mask values of the* Mask *property*

Find a masking pattern (such as Phone number), enable the BeepOnError property, and take your program out for another test run. You should find that you are unable to enter any alphabetic characters (in the case of the Phone number mask).

As you would expect, the MaskedTextBox will send out various events during its lifetime, one of which is MaskInputRejected, which is fired when the end user enters erroneous input. Handle this event using the Properties window and notice that the second incoming argument of the generated event handler is of type MaskInputRejectedEventArgs. This type has a property named RejectionHint that contains a brief description of the input error. For testing purposes, simply display the error on the Form's caption.

```
private void txtMaskedTextBox_MaskInputRejected(object sender,
    MaskInputRejectedEventArgs e)
{
    this.Text = string.Format("Error: {0}", e.RejectionHint);
}
```

To ensure that this error is not displayed when the user enters valid data, handle the KeyDown event on the MaskedTextBox and implement the event handler to reset the Form's caption to a default value:

```
private void txtMaskedTextBox_KeyDown(object sender, KeyEventArgs e)
{
    this.Text = "Fun with Labels and TextBoxes";
}
```

■Source Code The LabelsAndTextBoxes project is included under the Chapter 21 subdirectory.

Fun with Buttons

The role of the System.Windows.Forms.Button type is to provide a vehicle for user confirmation, typically in response to a mouse click or keypress. The Button class immediately derives from an abstract type named ButtonBase, which provides a number of key behaviors for all derived types (such as CheckBox, RadioButton, and Button). Table 21-4 describes some (but by no means all) of the core properties of ButtonBase.

Table 21-4. ButtonBase *Properties*

Property	Meaning in Life
FlatStyle	Gets or sets the flat style appearance of the Button control, using members of the FlatStyle enumeration.
Image	Configures which (optional) image is displayed somewhere within the bounds of a ButtonBase-derived type. Recall that the Control class also defines a BackgroundImage property, which is used to render an image over the entire surface area of a widget.
ImageAlign	Sets the alignment of the image on the Button control, using the ContentAlignment enumeration.
TextAlign	Gets or sets the alignment of the text on the Button control, using the ContentAlignment enumeration.

The TextAlign property of ButtonBase makes it extremely simple to position text at just about any location. To set the position of your Button's caption, use the ContentAlignment enumeration (defined in the System.Drawing namespace). As you will see, this same enumeration can be used to place an optional image on the Button type:

```
public enum System.Drawing.ContentAlignment
{
    BottomCenter, BottomLeft, BottomRight,
    MiddleCenter, MiddleLeft, MiddleRight,
    TopCenter, TopLeft, TopRight
}
```

FlatStyle is another property of interest. It is used to control the general look and feel of the Button control, and it can be assigned any value from the FlatStyle enumeration (defined in the System.Windows.Forms namespace):

```
public enum System.Windows.Forms.FlatStyle
{
    Flat, Popup, Standard, System
}
```

To illustrate working with the Button type, create a new Windows Forms application named Buttons. On the Forms designer, add three Button types (named btnFlat, btnPopup, and btnStandard) and set each Button's FlatStyle property value accordingly (e.g., FlatStyle.Flat, FlatStyle.Popup, or FlatStyle.Standard). As well, set the Text value of each Button to a fitting value and handle the Click event for the btnStandard Button. As you will see in just a moment, when the user clicks this button, you will reposition the button's text using the TextAlign property.

Now, add a final fourth Button (named btnImage) that supports a background image (set via the BackgroundImage property) and a small bull's-eye icon (set via the Image property), which will also be dynamically relocated when the btnStandard Button is clicked. Feel free to use any image files to assign to the BackgroundImage and Image properties, but do note that the downloadable source code contains the images used here.

Given that the designer has authored all the necessary UI prep code within InitializeComponent(), the remaining code makes use of the ContentAlignment enumeration to reposition the location of the text on btnStandard and the icon on btnImage. In the following code, notice that you are calling the static Enum.GetValues() method to obtain the list of names from the ContentAlignment enumeration:

```
partial class MainWindow : Form
{
    // Used to hold the current text alignment value.
    ContentAlignment currAlignment = ContentAlignment.MiddleCenter;
    int currEnumPos = 0;

    public MainWindow()
    {
        InitializeComponent();
        CenterToScreen();
    }

    private void btnStandard_Click (object sender, EventArgs e)
    {
        // Get all possible values of the ContentAlignment enum.
        Array values = Enum.GetValues(currAlignment.GetType());

        // Bump the current position in the enum.
        // and check for wraparound.
        currEnumPos++;
        if(currEnumPos >= values.Length)
            currEnumPos = 0;

        // Bump the current enum value.
        currAlignment = (ContentAlignment)Enum.Parse(currAlignment.GetType(),
            values.GetValue(currEnumPos).ToString());

        // Paint enum value and align text on btnStandard.
        btnStandard.TextAlign = currAlignment;
            btnStandard.Text = currAlignment.ToString();

        // Now assign the location of the icon on btnImage
        btnImage.ImageAlign = currAlignment;
    }
}
```

Now run your program. As you click the middle button, you will see its text is set to the current name and position of the currAlignment member variable. As well, the icon within the btnImage is repositioned based on the same value. Figure 21-7 shows the output.

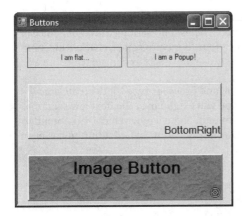

Figure 21-7. *The many faces of the* Button *type*

■**Source Code** The Buttons project is included under the Chapter 21 directory.

Fun with CheckBoxes, RadioButtons, and GroupBoxes

The System.Windows.Forms namespace defines a number of other types that extend ButtonBase, specifically CheckBox (which can support up to three possible states) and RadioButton (which can be either selected or not selected). Like the Button, these types also receive most of their functionality from the Control base class. However, each class defines some additional functionality. First, consider the core properties of the CheckBox widget described in Table 21-5.

Table 21-5. CheckBox *Properties*

Property	Meaning in Life
Appearance	Configures the appearance of a CheckBox control, using the Appearance enumeration.
AutoCheck	Gets or sets a value indicating if the Checked or CheckState value and the CheckBox's appearance are automatically changed when it is clicked.
CheckAlign	Gets or sets the horizontal and vertical alignment of a CheckBox on a CheckBox control, using the ContentAlignment enumeration (much like the Button type).
Checked	Returns a Boolean value representing the state of the CheckBox (checked or unchecked). If the ThreeState property is set to true, the Checked property returns true for either checked or indeterminately checked values.
CheckState	Gets or sets a value indicating whether the CheckBox is checked, using a CheckState enumeration rather than a Boolean value.
ThreeState	Configures whether the CheckBox supports three states of selection (as specified by the CheckState enumeration) rather than two.

The RadioButton type requires little comment, given that it is (more or less) just a slightly redesigned CheckBox. In fact, the members of a RadioButton are almost identical to those of the CheckBox type. The only notable difference is the CheckedChanged event, which (not surprisingly) is fired when the Checked value changes. Also, the RadioButton type does not support the ThreeState property, as a RadioButton must be on or off.

Typically, multiple RadioButton objects are logically and physically grouped together to function as a whole. For example, if you have a set of four RadioButton types representing the color choice of a given automobile, you may wish to ensure that only one of the four types can be checked at a time. Rather than writing code programmatically to do so, simply use the GroupBox control to ensure all RadioButtons are mutually exclusive.

To illustrate working with the CheckBox, RadioButton, and GroupBox types, let's create a new Windows Forms application named CarConfig, which you will extend over the next few sections. The main Form allows users to enter (and confirm) information about a new vehicle they intend to purchase. The order summary is displayed in a Label type once the Confirm Order button has been clicked. Figure 21-8 shows the initial UI.

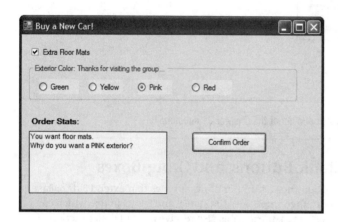

Figure 21-8. *The initial UI of the CarConfig Form*

Assuming you have leveraged the Forms designer to build your UI, you will now have numerous member variables representing each GUI widget. As well, the InitializeComponent() method will be updated accordingly. The first point of interest is the construction of the CheckBox type. As with any Control-derived type, once the look and feel has been established, it must be inserted into the Form's internal collection of controls:

```
private void InitializeComponent()
{
...
    // checkFloorMats
    //
    this.checkFloorMats.Name = "checkFloorMats";
    this.checkFloorMats.TabIndex = 0;
    this.checkFloorMats.Text = "Extra Floor Mats";
...
    this.Controls.Add(this.checkFloorMats);
}
```

Next, you have the configuration of the GroupBox and its contained RadioButton types. When you wish to place a control under the ownership of a GroupBox, you want to add each item to the GroupBox's Controls collection (in the same way you add widgets to the Form's Controls collection). To make things a bit more interesting, use the Properties window to handle the Enter and Leave events sent by the GroupBox object, as shown here:

```
private void InitializeComponent()
{
...
    // radioRed
    //
    this.radioRed.Name = "radioRed";
    this.radioRed.Size = new System.Drawing.Size(64, 23);
    this.radioRed.Text = "Red";
    //
    // groupBoxColor
    //
...
    this.groupBoxColor.Controls.Add(this.radioRed);
    this.groupBoxColor.Text = "Exterior Color";
    this.groupBoxColor.Enter += new System.EventHandler(this.groupBoxColor_Enter);
    this.groupBoxColor.Leave += new System.EventHandler(this.groupBoxColor_Leave);
...
}
```

Understand, of course, that you do not need to capture the Enter or Leave event for a GroupBox. However, to illustrate, the event handlers update the caption text of the GroupBox as shown here:

```
// Figure out when the focus is in your group.
private void groupBoxColor_Leave(object sender, EventArgs e)
{
    groupBoxColor.Text = "Exterior Color: Thanks for visiting the group...";
}

private void groupBoxColor_Enter(object sender, EventArgs e)
{
    groupBoxColor.Text = "Exterior Color: You are in the group...";
}
```

The final GUI widgets on this Form (the Label and Button types) will also be configured and inserted in the Form's Controls collection via InitializeComponent(). The Label is used to display the order confirmation, which is formatted in the Click event handler of the order Button, as shown here:

```
private void btnOrder_Click (object sender, System.EventArgs e)
{
    // Build a string to display information.
    string orderInfo = "";
    if(checkFloorMats.Checked)
        orderInfo += "You want floor mats.\n";
    if(radioRed.Checked)
        orderInfo += "You want a red exterior.\n";
    if(radioYellow.Checked)
        orderInfo += "You want a yellow exterior.\n";
    if(radioGreen.Checked)
        orderInfo += "You want a green exterior.\n";
    if(radioPink.Checked)
        orderInfo += "Why do you want a PINK exterior?\n";
    // Send this string to the Label.
    infoLabel.Text = orderInfo;
}
```

Notice that both the CheckBox and RadioButton support the Checked property, which allows you to investigate the state of the widget. Finally, recall that if you have configured a tri-state CheckBox, you will need to check the state of the widget using the CheckState property.

Fun with CheckedListBoxes

Now that you have explored the basic Button-centric widgets, let's move on to the set of list selection–centric types, specifically CheckedListBox, ListBox, and ComboBox. The CheckedListBox widget allows you to group related CheckBox options in a scrollable list control. Assume you have added such a control to your CarConfig Form that allows users to configure a number of options regarding an automobile's sound system (see Figure 21-9).

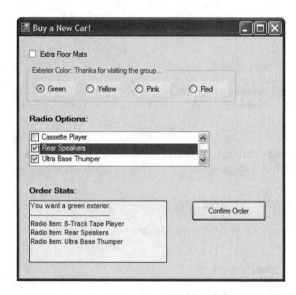

Figure 21-9. *The* CheckedListBox *type*

To insert new items in a CheckedListBox, call Add() for each item, or use the AddRange() method and send in an array of objects (strings, to be exact) that represent the full set of checkable items. Be aware that you can fill any of the list types at design time using the Items property located on the Properties window (just click the ellipsis button and type the string values). Here is the relevant code within InitializeComponent() that configures the CheckedListBox:

```
private void InitializeComponent()
{
...
    // checkedBoxRadioOptions
    //
    this.checkedBoxRadioOptions.Items.AddRange(new object[] {
        "Front Speakers", "8-Track Tape Player",
        "CD Player", "Cassette Player",
        "Rear Speakers", "Ultra Base Thumper"});
...
    this.Controls.Add (this.checkedBoxRadioOptions);
}
```

Now update the logic behind the Click event for the Confirm Order button. Ask the CheckedListBox which of its items are currently selected and add them to the orderInfo string. Here are the relevant code updates:

```
private void btnOrder_Click (object sender, EventArgs e)
{
    // Build a string to display information.
```

```
string orderInfo = "";
...
orderInfo += "-------------------------------\n";

// For each item in the CheckedListBox:
for(int i = 0; i < checkedBoxRadioOptions.Items.Count; i++)
{
    // Is the current item checked?
    if(checkedBoxRadioOptions.GetItemChecked(i))
    {
        // Get text of checked item and append to orderinfo string.
        orderInfo += "Radio Item: ";
        orderInfo += checkedBoxRadioOptions.Items[i].ToString();
        orderInfo += "\n";
    }
}
...
}
```

The final note regarding the CheckedListBox type is that it supports the use of multiple columns through the inherited MultiColumn property. Thus, if you make the following update:

```
checkedBoxRadioOptions.MultiColumn = true;
```

you see the multicolumn CheckedListBox shown in Figure 21-10.

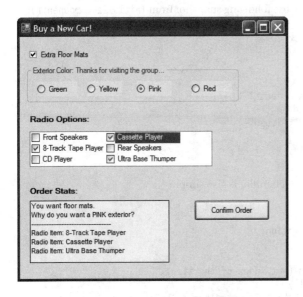

Figure 21-10. *Multicolumn* CheckedListBox *type*

Fun with ListBoxes

As mentioned earlier, the CheckedListBox type inherits most of its functionality from the ListBox type. To illustrate using the ListBox type, let's add another feature to the current CarConfig application: the ability to select the make (BMW, Yugo, etc.) of the automobile. Figure 21-11 shows the desired UI.

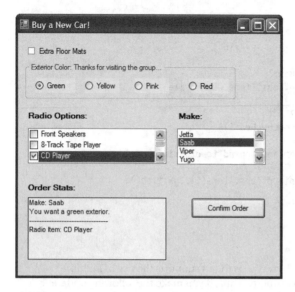

Figure 21-11. *The* ListBox *type*

As always, begin by creating a member variable to manipulate your type (in this case, a ListBox type). Next, configure the look and feel using the following snapshot from InitializeComponent():

```
private void InitializeComponent()
{
...
    // carMakeList
    //
    this.carMakeList.Items.AddRange(new object[] {
        "BMW", "Caravan", "Ford", "Grand Am",
        "Jeep", "Jetta", "Saab", "Viper", "Yugo"});
...
    this.Controls.Add (this.carMakeList);
}
```

The update to the btnOrder_Click() event handler is also simple:

```
private void btnOrder_Click (object sender, EventArgs e)
{
    // Build a string to display information.
    string orderInfo = "";
    ...
    // Get the currently selected item (not index of the item).
    if(carMakeList.SelectedItem != null)
        orderInfo += "Make: " + carMakeList.SelectedItem + "\n";
    ...
}
```

Fun with ComboBoxes

Like a ListBox, a ComboBox allows users to make a selection from a well-defined set of possibilities. However, the ComboBox type is unique in that users can also insert additional items. Recall that ComboBox derives from ListBox (which then derives from Control). To illustrate its use, add yet another GUI widget to the CarConfig Form that allows a user to enter the name of a preferred salesperson. If the salesperson in question is not on the list, the user can enter a custom name. One possible UI update is shown in Figure 21-12 (feel free to add your own salesperson monikers).

Figure 21-12. *The* ComboBox *type*

This modification begins with configuring the ComboBox itself. As you can see here, the logic looks identical to that for the ListBox:

```
private void InitializeComponent()
{
...
    // comboSalesPerson
    //
    this.comboSalesPerson.Items.AddRange(new object[] {
        "Baby Ry-Ry", "Dan \'the Machine\'",
        "Danny Boy", "Tommy Boy"});
...
    this.Controls.Add (this.comboSalesPerson);
}
```

The update to the btnOrder_Click() event handler is again simple, as shown here:

```
private void btnOrder_Click (object sender, EventArgs e)
{
    // Build a string to display information.
    string orderInfo = "";
    ...
    // Use the Text property to figure out the user's salesperson.
    if(comboSalesPerson.Text != "")
        orderInfo += "Sales Person: " + comboSalesPerson.Text + "\n";
    else
        orderInfo += "You did not select a sales person!" + "\n";
    ...
}
```

Configuring the Tab Order

Now that you have created a somewhat interesting Form, let's formalize the issue of tab order. As you may know, when a Form contains multiple GUI widgets, users expect to be able to shift focus using the Tab key. Configuring the tab order for your set of controls requires that you understand two key properties: TabStop and TabIndex.

The TabStop property can be set to true or false, based on whether or not you wish this GUI item to be reachable using the Tab key. Assuming the TabStop property has been set to true for a given widget, the TabOrder property is then set to establish its order of activation in the tabbing sequence (which is zero based). Consider this example:

```
// Configure tabbing properties.
radioRed.TabIndex = 2;
radioRed.TabStop = true;
```

The Tab Order Wizard

The Visual Studio 2005 IDE supplies a Tab Order Wizard, which you access by choosing View ➤ Tab Order (be aware that you will not find this menu option unless the Forms designer is active). Once activated, your design-time Form displays the current TabIndex value for each widget. To change these values, click each item in the order you choose (see Figure 21-13).

To exit the Tab Order Wizard, simply press the Esc key.

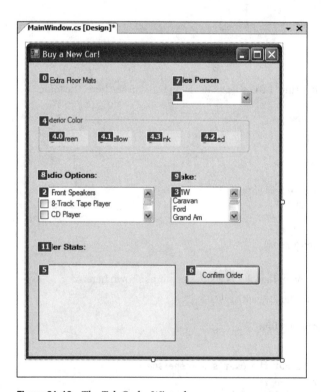

Figure 21-13. *The Tab Order Wizard*

Setting the Form's Default Input Button

Many user-input forms (especially dialog boxes) have a particular Button that will automatically respond to the user pressing the Enter key. For the current Form, if you wish to ensure that when the user presses the Enter key, the Click event handler for btnOrder is invoked, simply set the Form's AcceptButton property as so:

```
// When the Enter key is pressed, it is as if
// the user clicked the btnOrder button.
this.AcceptButton = btnOrder;
```

■**Note** Some Forms require the ability to simulate clicking the Form's Cancel button when the user presses the Esc key. This can be done by assigning the CancelButton property to the Button object representing the Cancel button.

Working with More Exotic Controls

At this point, you have seen how to work most of the basic Windows Forms controls (Labels, TextBoxes, and the like). The next task is to examine some GUI widgets, which are a bit more high-powered in their functionality. Thankfully, just because a control may seem "more exotic" does not mean it is hard to work with, only that it requires a bit more elaboration from the outset. Over the next several pages, we will examine the following GUI elements:

- MonthCalendar
- ToolTip
- TabControl
- TrackBar
- Panel
- UpDown controls
- ErrorProvider
- TreeView
- WebBrower

To begin, let's wrap up the CarConfig project by examining the MonthCalendar and ToolTip controls.

Fun with MonthCalendars

The System.Windows.Forms namespace provides an extremely useful widget, the MonthCalendar control, that allows the user to select a date (or range of dates) using a friendly UI. To showcase this new control, update the existing CarConfig application to allow the user to enter in the new vehicle's delivery date. Figure 21-14 shows the updated (and slightly rearranged) Form.

Figure 21-14. *The* MonthCalendar *type*

Although the MonthCalendar control offers a fair bit of functionality, it is very simple to programmatically capture the range of dates selected by the user. The default behavior of this type is to always select (and mark) today's date automatically. To obtain the currently selected date programmatically, you can update the Click event handler for the order Button, as shown here:

```
private void btnOrder_Click (object sender, EventArgs e)
{
    // Build a string to display information.
    string orderInfo = "";
    ...
    // Get ship date.
    DateTime d = monthCalendar.SelectionStart;
    string dateStr = string.Format("{0}/{1}/{2}", d.Month, d.Day, d.Year);
    orderInfo += "Car will be sent: " + dateStr;
    ...
}
```

Notice that you can ask the MonthCalendar control for the currently selected date by using the SelectionStart property. This property returns a DateTime reference, which you store in a local variable. Using a handful of properties of the DateTime type, you can extract the information you need in a custom format.

At this point, I assume the user will specify exactly one day on which to deliver the new automobile. However, what if you want to allow the user to select a range of possible shipping dates? In that case, all the user needs to do is drag the cursor across the range of possible shipping dates. You already have seen that you can obtain the start of the selection using the SelectionStart property. The end of the selection can be determined using the SelectionEnd property. Here is the code update:

```
private void btnOrder_Click (object sender, EventArgs e)
{
    // Build a string to display information.
    string orderInfo = "";
    ...
    // Get ship date range....
    DateTime startD = monthCalendar.SelectionStart;
    DateTime endD = monthCalendar.SelectionEnd;
    string dateStartStr =
        string.Format("{0}/{1}/{2}", startD.Month, startD.Day, startD.Year);
    string dateEndStr =
        string.Format("{0}/{1}/{2}", endD.Month, endD.Day, endD.Year);

    // The DateTime type supports overloaded operators!
    if(dateStartStr != dateEndStr)
    {
        orderInfo += "Car will be sent between "
        + dateStartStr + " and\ n" + dateEndStr;
    }
    else    // They picked a single date.
        orderInfo += "Car will be sent on "  + dateStartStr;
    ...
}
```

■Note The Windows Forms toolkit also provides the DateTimePicker control, which exposes a MonthCalendar from a DropDown control.

Fun with ToolTips

As far as the CarConfig Form is concerned, we have one final point of interest. Most modern UIs support *tool tips*. In the System.Windows.Forms namespace, the ToolTip type represents this functionality. These widgets are simply small floating windows that display a helpful message when the cursor hovers over a given item.

To illustrate, add a tool tip to the CarConfig's Calendar type. Begin by dragging a new ToolTip control from the Toolbox onto your Forms designer, and rename it to calendarTip. Using the Properties window, you are able to establish the overall look and feel of the ToolTip widget, for example:

```
private void InitializeComponent()
{
...
    // calendarTip
    //
    this.calendarTip.IsBalloon = true;
    this.calendarTip.ShowAlways = true;
    this.calendarTip.ToolTipIcon = System.Windows.Forms.ToolTipIcon.Info;
...
}
```

To associate a ToolTip with a given control, select the control that should activate the ToolTip and set the "ToolTip on" property (see Figure 21-15).

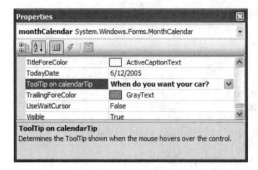

Figure 21-15. *Associating a* ToolTip *to a given widget*

At this point, the CarConfig project is complete. Figure 21-16 shows the ToolTip in action.

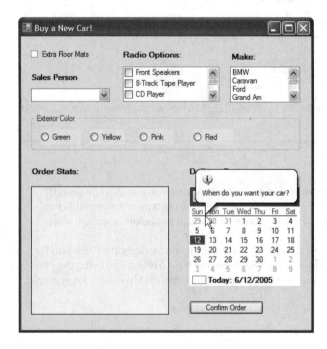

Figure 21-16. *The* ToolTip *in action*

■**Source Code** The CarConfig project is included under the Chapter 21 directory.

Fun with TabControls

To illustrate the remaining "exotic" controls, you will build a new Form that maintains a TabControl. As you may know, TabControls allow you to selectively hide or show pages of related GUI content via clicking a given tab. To begin, create a new Windows Forms application named ExoticControls and rename your initial Form to MainWindow.

Next, add a TabControl onto the Forms designer and, using the Properties window, open the page editor via the TabPages collection (just click the ellipsis button on the Properties window). A dialog configuration tool displays. Add a total of six pages, setting each page's Text and Name properties based on the completed TabControl shown in Figure 21-17.

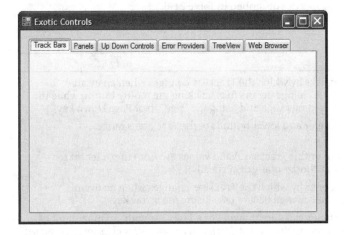

Figure 21-17. *A multipage* TabControl

As you are designing your TabControl, be aware that each page is represented by a TabPage object, which is inserted into the TabControl's internal collection of pages. Once the TabControl has been configured, this object (like any other GUI widget within a Form) is inserted into the Form's Controls collection. Consider the following partial InitializeComponent() method:

```
private void InitializeComponent()
{
...
    // tabControlExoticControls
    //
    this.tabControlExoticControls.Controls.Add(this.pageTrackBars);
    this.tabControlExoticControls.Controls.Add(this.pagePanels);
    this.tabControlExoticControls.Controls.Add(this.pageUpDown);
    this.tabControlExoticControls.Controls.Add(this.pageErrorProvider);
    this.tabControlExoticControls.Controls.Add(this.pageTreeView);
    this.tabControlExoticControls.Controls.Add(this.pageWebBrowser);
    this.tabControlExoticControls.Location = new System.Drawing.Point(13, 13);
    this.tabControlExoticControls.Name = "tabControlExoticControls";
    this.tabControlExoticControls.SelectedIndex = 0;
    this.tabControlExoticControls.Size = new System.Drawing.Size(463, 274);
    this.tabControlExoticControls.TabIndex = 0;
...
    this.Controls.Add(this.tabControlExoticControls);
}
```

Now that you have a basic Form supporting multiple tabs, you can build each page to illustrate the remaining exotic controls. First up, let's check out the role of the TrackBar.

■**Note** The TabControl widget supports Selected, Selecting, Deselected, and Deselecting events. These can prove helpful when you need to dynamically generate the elements within a given page.

Fun with TrackBars

The TrackBar control allows users to select from a range of values, using a scroll bar–like input mechanism. When working with this type, you need to set the minimum and maximum range, the minimum and maximum change increments, and the starting location of the slider's thumb. Each of these aspects can be set using the properties described in Table 21-6.

Table 21-6. TrackBar *Properties*

Properties	Meaning in Life
LargeChange	The number of ticks by which the TrackBar changes when an event considered a large change occurs (e.g., clicking the mouse button while the cursor is on the sliding range and using the Page Up or Page Down key).
Maximum Minimum	Configure the upper and lower bounds of the TrackBar's range.
Orientation	The orientation for this TrackBar. Valid values are from the Orientation enumeration (i.e., horizontally or vertically).
SmallChange	The number of ticks by which the TrackBar changes when an event considered a small change occurs (e.g., using the arrow keys).
TickFrequency	Indicates how many ticks are drawn. For a TrackBar with an upper limit of 200, it is impractical to draw all 200 ticks on a control 2 inches long. If you set the TickFrequency property to 5, the TrackBar draws 20 total ticks (each tick represents 5 units).
TickStyle	Indicates how the TrackBar control draws itself. This affects both where the ticks are drawn in relation to the movable thumb and how the thumb itself is drawn (using the TickStyle enumeration).
Value	Gets or sets the current location of the TrackBar. Use this property to obtain the numeric value contained by the TrackBar for use in your application.

To illustrate, you'll update the first tab of your TabControl with three TrackBars, each of which has an upper range of 255 and a lower range of 0. As the user slides each thumb, the application intercepts the Scroll event and dynamically builds a new System.Drawing.Color type based on the value of each slider. This Color type will be used to display the color within a PictureBox widget (named colorBox) and the RGB values within a Label type (named lblCurrColor). Figure 21-18 shows the (completed) first page in action.

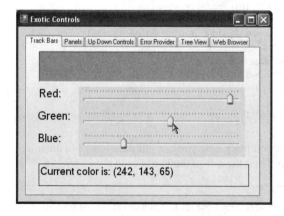

Figure 21-18. *The* TrackBar *page*

First, place three TrackBars onto the first tab using the Forms designer and rename your member variables with an appropriate value (redTrackBar, greenTrackBar, and blueTrackBar). Next, handle the Scroll event for each of your TrackBar controls. Here is the relevant code within InitializeComponent() for blueTrackBar (the remaining bars look almost identical, with the exception of the name of the Scroll event handler):

```
private void InitializeComponent()
{
...
    //
    // blueTrackBar
    //
    this.blueTrackBar.Maximum = 255;
    this.blueTrackBar.Name = "blueTrackBar";
    this.blueTrackBar.TickFrequency = 5;
    this.blueTrackBar.TickStyle = System.Windows.Forms.TickStyle.TopLeft;
    this.blueTrackBar.Scroll += new System.EventHandler(this.blueTrackBar_Scroll);
...
}
```

Note that the default minimum value of the TrackBar is 0 and thus does not need to be explicitly set. In the Scroll event handlers for each TrackBar, you make a call to a yet-to-be-written helper function named UpdateColor():

```
private void blueTrackBar_Scroll (object sender, EventArgs e)
{
    UpdateColor();
}
```

UpdateColor() is responsible for two major tasks. First, you read the current value of each TrackBar and use this data to build a new Color variable using Color.FromArgb(). Once you have the newly configured color, update the PictureBox member variable (again, named colorBox) with the current background color. Finally, UpdateColor() formats the thumb values in a string placed on the Label (lblCurrColor), as shown here:

```
private void UpdateColor()
{
    // Get the new color based on track bars.
    Color c = Color.FromArgb(redTrackBar.Value,
        greenTrackBar.Value, blueTrackBar.Value);
    // Change the color in the PictureBox.
    colorBox.BackColor = c;
    // Set color label.
    lblCurrColor.Text =
        string.Format("Current color is: (R:{0}, G:{1}, B:{2})",
        redTrackBar.Value, greenTrackBar.Value,
        blueTrackBar.Value);
}
```

The final detail is to set the initial values of each slider when the Form comes to life and render the current color, as shown here:

```
public MainWindow()
{
    InitializeComponent();
    CenterToScreen();
    // Set initial position of each slider.
    redTrackBar.Value = 100;
    greenTrackBar.Value = 255;
```

```
    blueTrackBar.Value = 0;
    UpdateColor();
}
```

Fun with Panels

As you saw earlier in this chapter, the GroupBox control can be used to logically bind a number of controls (such as RadioButtons) to function as a collective. Closely related to the GroupBox is the Panel control. Panels are also used to group related controls in a logical unit. One difference is that the Panel type derives from the ScrollableControl class, thus it can support scroll bars, which is not possible with a GroupBox.

Panels can also be used to conserve screen real estate. For example, if you have a group of controls that takes up the entire bottom half of a Form, you can contain the group in a Panel that is half the size and set the AutoScroll property to true. In this way, the user can use the scroll bar(s) to view the full set of items. Furthermore, if a Panel's BorderStyle property is set to None, you can use this type to simply group a set of elements that can be easily shown or hidden from view in a manner transparent to the end user.

To illustrate, let's update the second page of the TabControl with two Button types (btnShowPanel and btnHidePanel) and a single Panel that contains a pair of text boxes (txtNormalText and txtUpperText) and an instructional Label. (Mind you, the widgets on the Panel are not terribly important for this example.) Figure 21-19 shows the final GUI.

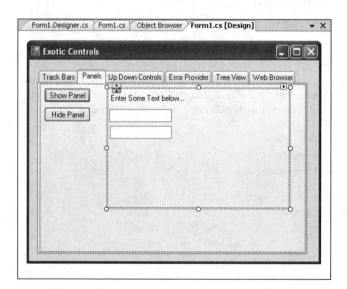

Figure 21-19. *The* TrackBar *page*

Using the Properties window, handle the TextChanged event for the first TextBox, and within the generated event handler, place an uppercase version of the text entered within txtNormalText into txtUpperText:

```
private void txtNormalText_TextChanged(object sender, EventArgs e)
{
    txtUpperText.Text = txtNormalText.Text.ToUpper();
}
```

Now, handle the Click event for each button. As you might suspect, you will simply hide or show the Panel (and all of its contained UI elements):

```
private void btnShowPanel_Click(object sender, EventArgs e)
{
    panelTextBoxes.Visible = true;
}
private void btnHidePanel_Click(object sender, EventArgs e)
{
    panelTextBoxes.Visible = false;
}
```

If you now run your program and click either button, you will find that the Panel's contents are shown and hidden accordingly. While this example is hardly fascinating, I am sure you can see the possibilities. For example, you may have a menu option (or security setting) that allows the user to see a "simple" or "complex" view. Rather than having to manually set the Visible property to false for multiple widgets, you can group them all within a Panel and set its Visible property accordingly.

Fun with the UpDown Controls

Windows Forms provide two widgets that function as *spin controls* (also known as *up/down controls*). Like the ComboBox and ListBox types, these new items also allow the user to choose an item from a range of possible selections. The difference is that when you're using a DomainUpDown or NumericUpDown control, the information is selected using a pair of small up and down arrows. For example, check out Figure 21-20.

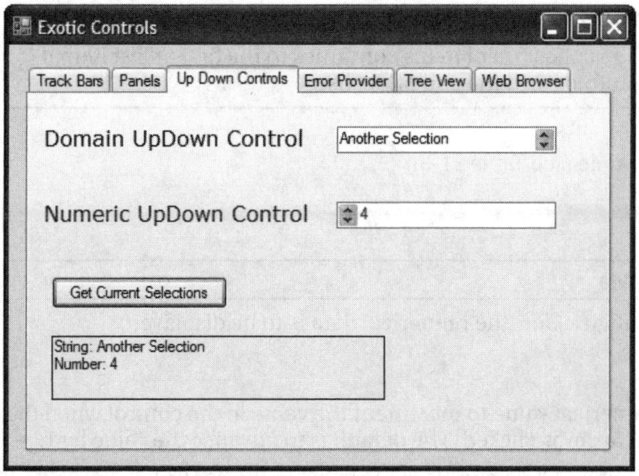

Figure 21-20. *Working with* UpDown *types*

Given your work with similar types, you should find working with the UpDown widgets painless. The DomainUpDown widget allows the user to select from a set of string data. NumericUpDown allows selections from a range of numeric data points. Each widget derives from a common direct base class, UpDownBase. Table 21-7 describes some important properties of this class.

Table 21-7. UpDownBase *Properties*

Property	Meaning in Life
InterceptArrowKeys	Gets or sets a value indicating whether the user can use the up arrow and down arrow keys to select values
ReadOnly	Gets or sets a value indicating whether the text can only be changed by the use of the up and down arrows and not by typing in the control to locate a given string
Text	Gets or sets the current text displayed in the spin control
TextAlign	Gets or sets the alignment of the text in the spin control
UpDownAlign	Gets or sets the alignment of the up and down arrows on the spin control, using the LeftRightAlignment enumeration

The DomainUpDown control adds a small set of properties (see Table 21-8) that allow you to configure and manipulate the textual data in the widget.

Table 21-8. DomainUpDown *Properties*

Property	Meaning in Life
Items	Allows you to gain access to the set of items stored in the widget
SelectedIndex	Returns the zero-based index of the currently selected item (a value of –1 indicates no selection)
SelectedItem	Returns the selected item itself (not its index)
Sorted	Configures whether or not the strings should be alphabetized
Wrap	Controls if the collection of items continues to the first or last item if the user continues past the end of the list

The NumericUpDown type is just as simple (see Table 21-9).

Table 21-9. NumericUpDown *Properties*

Property	Meaning in Life
DecimalPlaces ThousandsSeparator Hexadecimal	Used to configure how the numerical data is to be displayed.
Increment	Sets the numerical value to increment the value in the control when the up or down arrow is clicked. The default is to advance the value by 1.
Minimum Maximum	Sets the upper and lower limits of the value in the control.
Value	Returns the current value in the control.

Here is a partial InitializeComponent() that configures this page's NumericUpDown and DomainUpDown widgets:

```
private void InitializeComponent()
{
...
    //
    // numericUpDown
    //
```

```
...
    this.numericUpDown.Maximum = new decimal(new int[] {
        5000, 0, 0, 0});
    this.numericUpDown.Name = "numericUpDown";
    this.numericUpDown.ThousandsSeparator = true;
    //
    // domainUpDown
    //
    this.domainUpDown.Items.Add("Another Selection");
    this.domainUpDown.Items.Add("Final Selection");
    this.domainUpDown.Items.Add("Selection One");
    this.domainUpDown.Items.Add("Third Selection");
    this.domainUpDown.Name = "domainUpDown";
    this.domainUpDown.Sorted = true;
...
}
```

The Click event handler for this page's Button type simply asks each type for its current value
and places it in the appropriate Label (lblCurrSel) as a formatted string, as shown here:

```
private void btnGetSelections_Click (object sender, EventArgs e)
{
    // Get info from updowns...
    lblCurrSel.Text =
        string.Format("String: {0}\nNumber: {1}",
        domainUpDown.Text, numericUpDown.Value);
}
```

Fun with ErrorProviders

Most Windows Forms applications will need to validate user input in one way or another. This is
especially true with dialog boxes, as you should inform users if they make a processing error before
continuing forward. The ErrorProvider type can be used to provide a visual cue of user input error.
For example, assume you have a Form containing a TextBox and Button widget. If the user enters
more than five characters in the TextBox and the TextBox loses focus, the error information shown
in Figure 21-21 could be displayed.

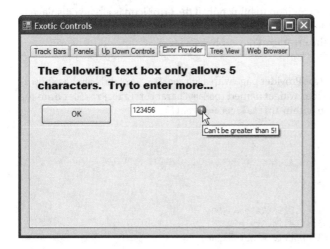

Figure 21-21. *The* ErrorProvider *in action*

Here, you have detected that the user entered more than five characters and responded by placing a small error icon (!) next to the TextBox object. When the user places his cursor over this icon, the descriptive error text appears as a pop-up. Also, this ErrorProvider is configured to cause the icon to blink a number of times to strengthen the visual cue (which, of course, you can't see without running the application).

If you wish to support this type of input validation, the first step is to understand the properties of the Control class shown in Table 21-10.

Table 21-10. Control *Properties*

Property	Meaning in Life
CausesValidation	Indicates whether selecting this control causes validation on the controls requiring validation
Validated	Occurs when the control is finished performing its validation logic
Validating	Occurs when the control is validating user input (e.g., when the control loses focus)

Every GUI widget can set the CausesValidation property to true or false (the default is true). If you set this bit of state data to true, the control forces the other controls on the Form to validate themselves when it receives focus. Once a validating control has received focus, the Validating and Validated events are fired for each control. In the scope of the Validating event handler, you configure a corresponding ErrorProvider. Optionally, the Validated event can be handled to determine when the control has finished its validation cycle.

The ErrorProvider type has a small set of members. The most important item for your purposes is the BlinkStyle property, which can be set t any of the values of the ErrorBlinkStyle enumeration described in Table 21-11.

Table 21-11. ErrorBlinkStyle *Properties*

Property	Meaning in Life
AlwaysBlink	Causes the error icon to blink when the error is first displayed or when a new error description string is set for the control and the error icon is already displayed
BlinkIfDifferentError	Causes the error icon to blink only if the error icon is already displayed, but a new error string is set for the control
NeverBlink	Indicates the error icon never blinks

To illustrate, update the UI of the Error Provider page with a Button, TextBox, and Label as shown in Figure 20-21. Next, drag an ErrorProvider widget named tooManyCharactersErrorProvider onto the designer. Here is the configuration code within InitializeComponent():

```
private void InitializeComponent()
{
...
    //
    // tooManyCharactersErrorProvider
    //
    this.tooManyCharactersErrorProvider.BlinkRate = 500;
    this.tooManyCharactersErrorProvider.BlinkStyle =
        System.Windows.Forms.ErrorBlinkStyle.AlwaysBlink;
```

```
    this.tooManyCharactersErrorProvider.ContainerControl = this;
...
}
```

Once you have configured how the `ErrorProvider` looks and feels, you bind the error to the `TextBox` within the scope of its `Validating` event handler, as shown here:

```
private void txtInput_Validating (object sender, CancelEventArgs e)
{
    // Check if the text length is greater than 5.
    if(txtInput.Text.Length > 5)
    {
        errorProvider1.SetError( txtInput, "Can't be greater than 5!");
    }
    else // Things are OK, don't show anything.
        errorProvider1.SetError(txtInput, "");
}
```

Fun with TreeViews

`TreeView` controls are very helpful types in that they allow you to visually display hierarchical data (such as a directory structure or any other type of parent/child relationship). As you would expect, the Window Forms `TreeView` control can be highly customized. If you wish, you can add custom images, node colors, node subcontrols, and other visual enhancements. (I'll assume interested readers will consult the .NET Framework 2.0 SDK documentation for full details of this widget.)

To illustrate the basic use of the `TreeView`, the next page of your `TabControl` will programmatically construct a `TreeView` defining a series of topmost nodes that represent a set of `Car` types. Each Car node has two subnodes that represent the selected car's current speed and favorite radio station. In Figure 21-22, notice that the selected item will be highlighted. Also note that if the selected node has a parent (or sibling), its name is presented in a `Label` widget.

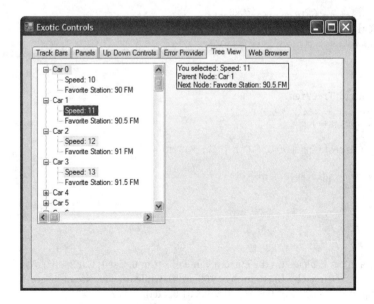

Figure 21-22. *The* `TreeView` *in action*

Assuming your Tree View UI is composed of a `TreeView` control (named `treeViewCars`) and a `Label` (named `lblNodeInfo`), insert a new C# file into your ExoticControls project that models a trivial `Car` that has-a `Radio`:

```
namespace ExoticControls
{
    class Car
    {
        public Car(string pn, int cs)
        {
            petName = pn;
            currSp = cs;
        }
        public string petName;
        public int currSp;
        public Radio r;
    }

    class Radio
    {
        public double favoriteStation;
        public Radio(double station)
        { favoriteStation = station; }
    }
}
```

The `Form`-derived type will maintain a generic `List<>` (named `listCars`) of 100 `Car` types, which will be populated in the default constructor of the `MainForm` type. As well, the constructor will call a new helper method named `BuildCarTreeView()`, which takes no arguments and returns void. Here is the initial update:

```
public partial class MainWindow : Form
{
    // Create a new generic List to hold the Car objects.
    private List<Car> listCars = new List<Car>();

    public MainWindow()
    {
...
        // Fill List<> and build TreeView.
        double offset = 0.5;
        for (int x = 0; x < 100; x++)
        {
            listCars.Add(new Car(string.Format("Car {0}", x), 10 + x));
            offset += 0.5;
            listCars[x].r = new Radio(89.0 + offset);
        }
        BuildCarTreeView();
    }
...
}
```

Note that the `petName` of each car is based on the current value of x (Car 0, Car 1, Car 2, etc.). As well, the current speed is set by offsetting x by 10 (10 mph to 109 mph), while the favorite radio station is established by offsetting the value 89.0 by 0.5 (90, 90.5, 91, 91.5, etc.).

Now that you have a list of Cars, you need to map these values to nodes of the TreeView control. The most important aspect to understand when working with the TreeView widget is that each topmost node and subnode is represented by a System.Windows.Forms.TreeNode object, derived directly from MarshalByRefObject. Here are some of the interesting properties of TreeNode:

```csharp
public class TreeNode : MarshalByRefObject,
  ICloneable, ISerializable
{
...
    public Color BackColor { get; set; }
    public bool Checked { get; set; }
    public virtual ContextMenu ContextMenu { get; set; }
    public virtual ContextMenuStrip ContextMenuStrip { get; set; }
    public Color ForeColor { get; set; }
    public int ImageIndex { get; set; }
    public bool IsExpanded { get; }
    public bool IsSelected { get; }
    public bool IsVisible { get; }
    public string Name { get; set; }
    public TreeNode NextNode { get; }
    public Font NodeFont { get; set; }
    public TreeNodeCollection Nodes { get; }
    public TreeNode PrevNode { get; }
    public string Text { get; set; }
    public string ToolTipText { get; set; }
...
}
```

As you can see, each node of a TreeView can be assigned images, colors, fonts, tool tips, and context menus. As well, the TreeNode provides members to navigate to the next (or previous) TreeNode. Given this, consider the initial implementation of BuildCarTreeView():

```csharp
private void BuildCarTreeView()
{
    // Don't paint the TreeView until all the nodes have been created.
    treeViewCars.BeginUpdate();

    // Clear the TreeView of any current nodes.
    treeViewCars.Nodes.Clear();

    // Add a TreeNode for each Car object in the List<>.
    foreach (Car c in listCars)
    {
        // Add the current Car as a topmost node.
        treeViewCars.Nodes.Add(new TreeNode(c.petName));

        // Now, get the Car you just added to build
        // two subnodes based on the speed and
        // internal Radio object.
        treeViewCars.Nodes[listCars.IndexOf(c)].Nodes.Add(
            new TreeNode(string.Format("Speed: {0}",
            c.currSp.ToString())));
        treeViewCars.Nodes[listCars.IndexOf(c)].Nodes.Add(
            new TreeNode(string.Format("Favorite Station: {0} FM",
            c.r.favoriteStation)));
    }
```

```
    // Now paint the TreeView.
    treeViewCars.EndUpdate();
}
```

As you can see, the construction of the TreeView nodes are sandwiched between a call to BeginUpdate() and EndUpdate(). This can be helpful when you are populating a massive TreeView with a great many nodes, given that the widget will wait to display the items until you have finished filling the Nodes collection. In this way, the end user does not see the gradual rendering of the TreeView's elements.

The topmost nodes are added to the TreeView simply by iterating over the generic List<> type and inserting a new TreeNode object into the TreeView's Nodes collection. Once a topmost node has been added, you pluck it from the Nodes collection (via the type indexer) to add its subnodes (which are also represented by TreeNode objects). As you might guess, if you wish to add subnodes to a current subnode, simply populate its internal collection of nodes via the Nodes property.

The next task for this page of the TabControl is to highlight the currently selected node (via the BackColor property) and display the selected item (as well as any parent or subnodes) within the Label widget. All of this can be accomplished by handling the TreeView control's AfterSelect event via the Properties window. This event fires after the user has selected a node via a mouse click or keyboard navigation. Here is the complete implementation of the AfterSelect event handler:

```
private void treeViewCars_AfterSelect(object sender, TreeViewEventArgs e)
{
    string nodeInfo = "";

    // Build info about selected node.
    nodeInfo = string.Format("You selected: {0}\n", e.Node.Text);
    if (e.Node.Parent != null)
        nodeInfo += string.Format("Parent Node: {0}\n", e.Node.Parent.Text);
    if (e.Node.NextNode != null)
        nodeInfo += string.Format("Next Node: {0}", e.Node.NextNode.Text);

    // Show info and highlight node.
    lblNodeInfo.Text = nodeInfo;
    e.Node.BackColor = Color.AliceBlue;
}
```

The incoming TreeViewEventArgs object contains a property named Node, which returns a TreeNode object representing the current selection. From here, you are able to extract the node's name (via the Text property) as well as the parent and next node (via the Parent/NextNode properties). Note you are explicitly checking the TreeNode objects returned from Parent/NextNode for null, in case the user has selected the first topmost node or the very last subnode (if you did not do this, you might trigger a NullReferenceException).

Adding Node Images

To wrap up our examination of the TreeView type, let's spruce up the current example by defining three new *.bmp images that will be assigned to each node type. To do so, add a new ImageList component (named imageListTreeView) to the designer of the MainForm type. Next, add three new bitmap images to your project via the Project ➤ Add New Item menu selection (or make use of the supplied *.bmp files within this book's downloadable code) that represent (or at least closely approximate) a car, radio, and "speed" image. Do note that each of these *.bmp files is 16×16 pixels (set via the Properties window) so that they have a decent appearance within the TreeView.

Once you have created these image files, select the ImageList on your designer and populate the Images property with each of these three images, ordered as shown in Figure 21-23, to ensure you can assign the correct ImageIndex (0, 1, or 2) to each node.

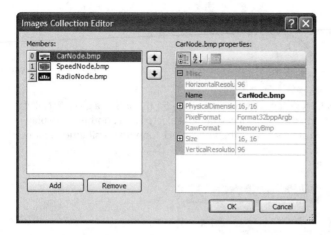

Figure 21-23. *Populating the* ImageList

As you recall from Chapter 20, when you incorporate resources (such as bitmaps) into your Visual Studio 2005 solutions, the underlying *.resx file is automatically updated. Therefore, these images will be embedded into your assembly with no extra work on your part. Now, using the Properties window, set the TreeView control's ImageList property to your ImageList member variable (see Figure 21-24).

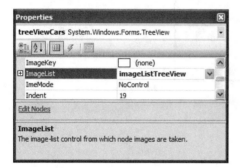

Figure 21-24. *Associating the* ImageList *to the* TreeView

Last but not least, update your BuildCarTreeView() method to specify the correct ImageIndex (via constructor arguments) when creating each TreeNode:

```
private void BuildCarTreeView()
{
...
    foreach (Car c in listCars)
    {
        treeViewCars.Nodes.Add(new TreeNode(c.petName, 0, 0));

        treeViewCars.Nodes[listCars.IndexOf(c)].Nodes.Add(
            new TreeNode(string.Format("Speed: {0}",
            c.currSp.ToString()), 1, 1));
```

```
        treeViewCars.Nodes[listCars.IndexOf(c)].Nodes.Add(
            new TreeNode(string.Format("Favorite Station: {0} FM",
            c.r.favoriteStation), 2, 2));
    }
...
}
```

Notice that you are specifying each ImageIndex twice. The reason for this is that a given TreeNode can have two unique images assigned to it: one to display when unselected and another to display when selected. To keep things simple, you are specifying the same image for both possibilities. In any case, Figure 21-25 shows the updated TreeView type.

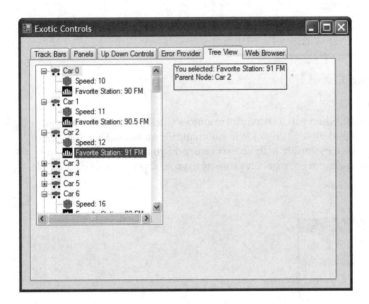

Figure 21-25. *The* TreeView *with images*

Fun with WebBrowsers

The final page of this example will make use of the System.Windows.Forms.WebBrowser widget, which is new to .NET 2.0. This widget is a highly configurable mini web browser that may be embedded into any Form-derived type. As you would expect, this control defines a Url property that can be set to any valid URI, formally represented by the System.Uri type. On the Web Browser page, add a WebBrowser (configured to your liking), a TextBox (to enter the URL), and a Button (to perform the HTTP request). Figure 21-26 shows the runtime behavior of assigning the Url property to http://www.intertechtraining.com (yes, a shameless promotion for the company I am employed with).

Figure 21-26. *The* WebBrowser *showing the home page of Intertech Training*

The only necessary code to instruct the WebBrowser to display the incoming HTTP request form data is to assign the Url property, as shown in the following Button Click event handler:

```
private void btnGO_Click(object sender, EventArgs e)
{
    // Set URL based on value within page's TextBox control.
    myWebBrowser.Url = new System.Uri(txtUrl.Text);
}
```

That wraps up our examination of the widgets of the System.Windows.Forms namespace. Although I have not commented on each possible UI element, you should have no problem investigating the others further on your own time. Next up, let's look at the process of building *custom* Windows Forms controls.

■**Source Code** The ExoticControls project is included under the Chapter 21 directory.

Building Custom Windows Forms Controls

The .NET platform provides a very simple way for developers to build custom UI elements. Unlike (the now legacy) ActiveX controls, Windows Forms controls do not require vast amounts of COM infrastructure or complex memory management. Rather, .NET developers simply build a new class deriving from UserControl and populate the type with any number of properties, methods, and events. To demonstrate this process, during the next several pages you'll construct a custom control named CarControl using Visual Studio 2005.

> **Note** As with any .NET application, you are always free to build a custom Windows Forms control using nothing more than the command-line compiler and a simple text editor. As you will see, custom controls reside in a *.dll assembly; therefore, you may specify the /target:dll option of csc.exe.

To begin, fire up Visual Studio 2005 and select a new Windows Control Library workspace named CarControlLibrary (see Figure 21-27).

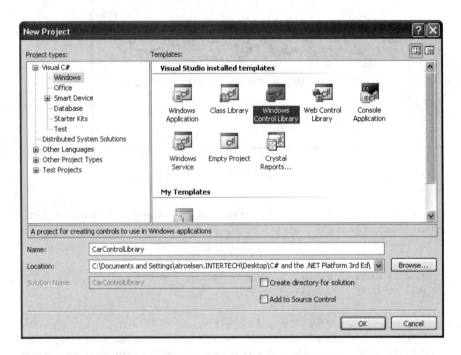

Figure 21-27. *Creating a new Windows Control Library workspace*

When you are finished, rename the initial C# class to CarControl. Like a Windows Application project workspace, your custom control is composed of two partial classes. The *.Designer.cs file contains all of the designer-generated code, while your primary partial class definition defines a type deriving from System.Windows.Forms.UserControl:

```
namespace CarControlLibrary
{
    public partial class CarControl : UserControl
    {
        public CarControl()
        {
            InitializeComponent();
        }
    }
}
```

Before we get too far along, let's establish the big picture of where you are going with this example. The CarControl type is responsible for animating through a series of bitmaps that will change based on the internal state of the automobile. If the car's current speed is safely under the car's maximum speed limit, the CarControl loops through three bitmap images that render an automobile driving safely along. If the current speed is 10 mph below the maximum speed, the CarControl loops through four images, with the fourth image showing the car slowly breaking down. Finally, if the car has surpassed its maximum speed, the CarControl loops over five images, where the fifth image represents a doomed automobile.

Creating the Images

Given the preceding design notes, the first order of business is to create a set of five *.bmp files for use by the animation loop. If you wish to create custom images, begin by activating the Project ➤ Add New Item menu selection and insert five new bitmap files. If you would rather not showcase your artistic abilities, feel free to use the images that accompany this sample application (keep in mind that I in *no way* consider myself a graphic artist!). The first of these three images (Lemon1.bmp, Lemon2.bmp, and Lemon3.bmp) illustrates a car navigating down the road in a safe and orderly fashion. The final two bitmap images (AboutToBlow.bmp and EngineBlown.bmp) represent a car approaching its maximum upper limit and its ultimate demise.

Building the Design-Time UI

The next step is to leverage the design-time editor for the CarControl type. As you can see, you are presented with a Form-like designer that represents the client area of the control under construction. Using the Toolbox window, add an ImageList type to hold each of the bitmaps (named carImages), a Timer type to control the animation cycle (named imageTimer), and a PictureBox to hold the current image (named currentImage). Don't worry about configuring the size or location of the PictureBox type, as you will programmatically position this widget within the bounds of the CarControl. However, be sure to set the SizeMode property of the PictureBox to StretchImage via the Properties window. Figure 21-28 shows the story thus far.

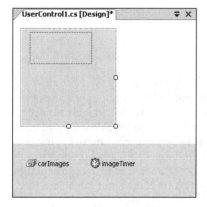

Figure 21-28. *Creating the design-time GUI*

Now, using the Properties window, configure the ImageList's Images collection by adding each bitmap to the list. Be aware that you will want to add these items sequentially (Lemon1.bmp, Lemon2.bmp, Lemon3.bmp, AboutToBlow.bmp, and EngineBlown.bmp) to ensure a linear animation cycle. Also be aware that the default width and height of *.bmp files inserted by Visual Studio 2005 is 47×47 pixels. Thus, the ImageSize of the ImageList should also be set to 47×47 (or else you will have with some skewed rendering). Finally, configure the state of your Timer type such that the Interval property is set to 200 and is initially disabled.

Implementing the Core CarControl

With this UI prep work out of the way, you can now turn to implementation of the type members. To begin, create a new public enumeration named AnimFrames, which has a member representing each item maintained by the ImageList. You will make use of this enumeration to determine the current frame to render into the PictureBox:

```
// Helper enum for images.
public enum AnimFrames
{
    Lemon1, Lemon2, Lemon3,
    AboutToBlow, EngineBlown
}
```

The CarControl type maintains a good number of private data points to represent the animation logic. Here is the rundown of each member:

```
public partial class CarControl : UserControl
{
    // State data.
    private AnimFrames currFrame = AnimFrames.Lemon1;
    private AnimFrames currMaxFrame = AnimFrames.Lemon3;
    private bool IsAnim;
    private int currSp = 50;
    private int maxSp = 100;
    private string carPetName= "Lemon";
    private Rectangle bottomRect = new Rectangle();

    public CarControl()
    {
        InitializeComponent();
    }
}
```

As you can see, you have data points that represent the current and maximum speed, the pet name of the automobile, and two members of type AnimFrames. The currFrame variable is used to specify which member of the ImageList is to be rendered. The currMaxFrame variable is used to mark the current upper limit in the ImageList (recall that the CarControl loops through three to five images based on the current speed). The IsAnim data point is used to determine if the car is currently in animation mode. Finally, you have a Rectangle member (bottomRect), which is used to represent the bottom region of the CarControl type. Later, you render the pet name of the automobile into this piece of control real estate.

To divide the CarControl into two rectangular regions, create a private helper function named StretchBox(). The role of this member is to calculate the correct size of the bottomRect member and to ensure that the PictureBox widget is stretched out over the upper two-thirds (or so) of the CarControl type.

```
private void StretchBox()
{
    // Configure picture box.
    currentImage.Top = 0;
    currentImage.Left = 0;
    currentImage.Height = this.Height - 50;
    currentImage.Width = this.Width;
    currentImage.Image =
        carImages.Images[(int)AnimFrames.Lemon1];
    // Figure out size of bottom rect.
    bottomRect.X = 0;
    bottomRect.Y = this.Height - 50;
    bottomRect.Height = this.Height - currentImage.Height;
    bottomRect.Width = this.Width;
}
```

Once you have carved out the dimensions of each rectangle, call StretchBox() from the default constructor:

```
public CarControl()
{
    InitializeComponent();
    StretchBox();
}
```

Defining the Custom Events

The CarControl type supports two events that are fired back to the host Form based on the current speed of the automobile. The first event, AboutToBlow, is sent out when the CarControl's speed approaches the upper limit. BlewUp is sent to the container when the current speed is greater than the allowed maximum. Each of these events leverages a custom delegate (CarEventHandler) that can hold the address of any method returning void and taking a single System.String as its parameter. You'll fire these events in just a moment, but for the time being, add the following members to the public sector of the CarControl:

```
// Car events/custom delegate.
public delegate void CarEventHandler(string msg);
public event CarEventHandler AboutToBlow;
public event CarEventHandler BlewUp;
```

Note Recall that a "prim and proper" delegate (see Chapter 8) would specify two arguments, the first of which is a System.Object (to represent the sender), and the second of which is a System.EventArgs-derived type. For this example, however, your delegate fits the bill.

Defining the Custom Properties

Like any class type, custom controls may define a set of properties to allow the outside world to interact with the state of the widget. For your current purposes, you are interested only in defining three properties. First, you have Animate. This property enables or disables the Timer type:

```
// Used to configure the internal Timer type.
public bool Animate
{
    get {return IsAnim;}
```

```
    set
    {
        IsAnim = value;
        imageTimer.Enabled = IsAnim;
    }
}
```

The PetName property is what you would expect and requires little comment. Do notice, however, that when the user sets the pet name, you make a call to Invalidate() to render the name of the CarControl into the bottom rectangular area of the widget (you'll do this step in just a moment):

```
// Configure pet name.
public string PetName
{
    get{return carPetName;}
    set
    {
        carPetName = value;
        Invalidate();
    }
}
```

Next, you have the Speed property. In addition to simply modifying the currSp data member, Speed is the entity that fires the AboutToBlow and BlewUp events based on the current speed of the CarControl. Here is the complete logic:

```
// Adjust currSp and currMaxFrame, and fire our events.
public int Speed
{
    get { return currSp; }
    set
    {
        // Within safe speed?
        if (currSp <= maxSp)
        {
            currSp = value;
            currMaxFrame = AnimFrames.Lemon3;
        }
        // About to explode?
        if ((maxSp - currSp) <= 10)
        {
            if (AboutToBlow != null)
            {
                AboutToBlow("Slow down dude!");
                currMaxFrame = AnimFrames.AboutToBlow;
            }
        }
        // Maxed out?
        if (currSp >= maxSp)
        {
            currSp = maxSp;
            if (BlewUp != null)
            {
                BlewUp("Ug...you're toast...");
                currMaxFrame = AnimFrames.EngineBlown;
            }
        }
    }
}
```

As you can see, if the current speed is 10 mph below the maximum upper speed, you fire the AboutToBlow event and adjust the upper frame limit to AnimFrames.AboutToBlow. If the user has pushed the limits of your automobile, you fire the BlewUp event and set the upper frame limit to AnimFrames.EngineBlown. If the speed is below the maximum speed, the upper frame limit remains as AnimFrames.Lemon3.

Controlling the Animation

The next detail to attend to is ensuring that the Timer type advances the current frame to render within the PictureBox. Again, recall that the number of frames to loop through depends on the current speed of the automobile. You only want to bother adjusting the image in the PictureBox if the Animate property has been set to true. Begin by handling the Tick event for the Timer type, and flesh out the details as follows:

```
private void imageTimer_Tick(object sender, EventArgs e)
{
    if(IsAnim)
        currentImage.Image = carImages.Images[(int)currFrame];
    // Bump frame.
    int nextFrame = ((int)currFrame) + 1;
    currFrame = (AnimFrames)nextFrame;
    if (currFrame > currMaxFrame)
        currFrame = AnimFrames.Lemon1;
}
```

Rendering the Pet Name

Before you can take your control out for a spin, you have one final detail to attend to: rendering the car's moniker. To do this, handle the Paint event for your CarControl, and within the handler, render the CarControl's pet name into the bottom rectangular region of the client area:

```
private void CarControl_Paint(object sender, PaintEventArgs e)
{
    // Render the pet name on the bottom of the control.
    Graphics g = e.Graphics;
    g.FillRectangle(Brushes.GreenYellow, bottomRect);
    g.DrawString(PetName, new Font("Times New Roman", 15),
        Brushes.Black, bottomRect);
}
```

At this point, your initial crack at the CarControl is complete. Go ahead and build your project.

Testing the CarControl Type

When you run or debug a Windows Control Library project within Visual Studio 2005, the UserControl Test Container (a managed replacement for the now legacy ActiveX Control Test Container) automatically loads your control into its designer test bed. As you can see from Figure 21-29, this tool allows you to set each custom property (as well as all inherited properties) for testing purposes.

Figure 21-29. *Testing the* `CarControl` *with the UserControl Test Container*

If you set the `Animate` property to true, you should see the `CarControl` cycle through the first three *.bmp files. What you are unable to do with this testing utility, however, is handle events. To test this aspect of your UI widget, you need to build a custom Form.

Building a Custom CarControl Form Host

As with all .NET types, you are now able to make use of your custom control from any language targeting the CLR. Begin by closing down the current workspace and creating a new C# Windows Application project named `CarControlTestForm`. To reference your custom controls from within the Visual Studio 2005 IDE, right-click anywhere within the Toolbox window and select the Choose Item menu selection. Using the Browse button on the .NET Framework Components tab, navigate to your `CarControlLibrary.dll` library. Once you click OK, you will find a new icon on the Toolbox named, of course, `CarControl`.

Next, place a new `CarControl` widget onto the Forms designer. Notice that the `Animate`, `PetName`, and `Speed` properties are all exposed through the Properties window. Again, like the UserControl Test Container, the control is "alive" at design time. Thus, if you set the `Animate` property to true, you will find your car is animating on the Forms designer.

Once you have configured the initial state of your `CarControl`, add additional GUI widgets that allow the user to increase and decrease the speed of the automobile, and view the string data sent by the incoming events as well as the car's current speed (`Label` controls will do nicely for these purposes). One possible GUI design is shown in Figure 21-30.

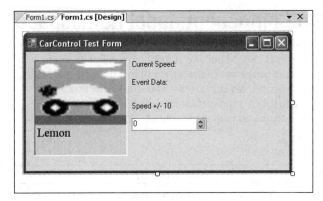

Figure 21-30. *The client-side GUI*

Provided you have created a GUI identical to mine, the code within the Form-derived type is quite straightforward (here I am assuming you have handled each of the CarControl events using the Properties window):

```
public partial class MainForm : Form
{
    public MainForm()
    {
        InitializeComponent();
        lblCurrentSpeed.Text = string.Format("Current Speed: {0}",
            this.myCarControl.Speed.ToString());
        numericUpDownCarSpeed.Value = myCarControl.Speed;
    }
    private void numericUpDownCarSpeed_ValueChanged(object sender, EventArgs e)
    {
        // Assume the min of this NumericUpDown is 0 and max is 300.
        this.myCarControl.Speed = (int)numericUpDownCarSpeed.Value;
        lblCurrentSpeed.Text = string.Format("Current Speed: {0}",
            this.myCarControl.Speed.ToString());
    }
    private void myCarControl_AboutToBlow(string msg)
    { lblEventData.Text = string.Format("Event Data: {0}", msg); }

    private void myCarControl_BlewUp(string msg)
    { lblEventData.Text = string.Format("Event Data: {0}", msg); }
}
```

At this point, you are able to run your client application and interact with the CarControl. As you can see, building and using custom controls is a fairly straightforward task, given what you already know about OOP, the .NET type system, GDI+ (aka System.Drawing.dll), and Windows Forms.

While you now have enough information to continue exploring the process of .NET Windows controls development, there is one additional programmatic aspect you have to contend with: design-time functionality. Before I describe exactly what this boils down to, you'll need to understand the role of the System.ComponentModel namespace.

The Role of the System.ComponentModel Namespace

The System.ComponentModel namespace defines a number of attributes (among other types) that allow you to describe how your custom controls should behave at design time. For example, you can opt to supply a textual description of each property, define a default event, or group related properties or events into a custom category for display purposes within the Visual Studio 2005 Properties window. When you are interested in making the sorts of modifications previously mentioned, you will want to make use of the core attributes shown in Table 21-12.

Table 21-12. *Select Members of* System.ComponentModel

Attribute	Applied To	Meaning in Life
BrowsableAttribute	Properties and events	Specifies whether a property or an event should be displayed in the property browser. By default, all custom properties and events can be browsed.
CategoryAttribute	Properties and events	Specifies the name of the category in which to group a property or event.
DescriptionAttribute	Properties and events	Defines a small block of text to be displayed at the bottom of the property browser when the user selects a property or event.
DefaultPropertyAttribute	Properties	Specifies the default property for the component. This property is selected in the property browser when a user selects the control.
DefaultValueAttribute	Properties	Defines a default value for a property that will be applied when the control is "reset" within the IDE.
DefaultEventAttribute	Events	Specifies the default event for the component. When a programmer double-clicks the control, stub code is automatically written for the default event.

Enhancing the Design-Time Appearance of CarControl

To illustrate the use of some of these new attributes, close down the CarControlTestForm project and reopen your CarControlLibrary project. Let's create a custom category called "Car Configuration" to which each property and event of the CarControl belongs. Also, let's supply a friendly description for each member and default value for each property. To do so, simply update each of the properties and events of the CarControl type to support the [Category], [DefaultValue], and [Description] attributes as required:

```
public partial class CarControl : UserControl
{
    ...
    [Category("Car Configuration"),
    Description("Sent when the car is approaching terminal speed.")]
    public event CarEventHandler AboutToBlow;
    ...
    [Category("Car Configuration"),
    Description("Name your car!"),
    DefaultValue("Lemon")]
```

```
    public string PetName {...}
...
}
```

Now, let me make a comment on what it means to assign a *default value* to a property, because I can guarantee you it is not what you would (naturally) assume. Simply put, the [DefaultValue] attribute does *not* ensure that the underlying value of the data point wrapped by a given property will be automatically initialized to the default value. Thus, although you specified a default value of "No Name" for the PetName property, the carPetName member variable will not be set to "Lemon" unless you do so via the type's constructor or via member initialization syntax (as you have already done):

```
private string carPetName= "Lemon";
```

Rather, the [DefaultValue] attribute comes into play when the programmer "resets" the value of a given property using the Properties window. To reset a property using Visual Studio 2005, select the property of interest, right-click it, and select Reset. In Figure 21-31, notice that the [Description] value appears in the bottom pane of the Properties window.

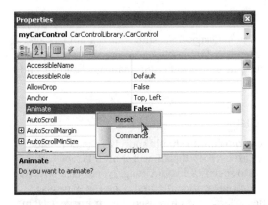

Figure 21-31. *Resetting a property to the default value*

The [Category] attribute will be realized only if the programmer selects the categorized view of the Properties window (as opposed to the default alphabetical view) as shown in Figure 21-32.

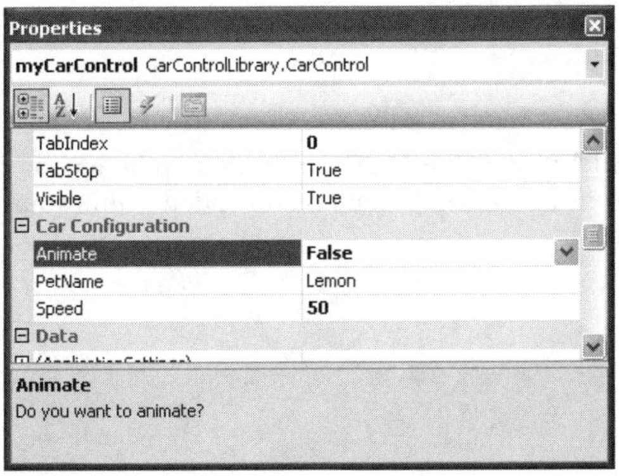

Figure 21-32. *The custom category*

Defining a Default Property and Default Event

In addition to describing and grouping like members into a common category, you may want to configure your controls to support default behaviors. A given control may support a default property. When you define the default property for a class using the [DefaultProperty] attribute as follows:

```
//Mark the default property for this control.
[DefaultProperty("Animate")]
public partial class CarControl : UserControl
{...}
```

you ensure that when the user selects this control at design time, the Animate property is automatically highlighted in the Properties window. Likewise, if you configure your control to have a default event as follows:

```
// Mark the default event and property for this control.
[DefaultEvent("AboutToBlow"),
DefaultProperty("Animate")]
public partial class CarControl : UserControl
{...}
```

you ensure that when the user double-clicks the widget at design time, stub code is automatically written for the default event (which explains why when you double-click a Button, the Click event is automatically handled; when you double-click a Form, the Load event is automatically handled; and so on).

Specifying a Custom Toolbox Bitmap

A final design-time bell-and-whistle any polished custom control should sport is a custom toolbox bitmap image. Currently, when the user selects the CarControl, the IDE will show this type within the Toolbox using the default "gear" icon. If you wish to specify a custom image, your first step is to insert a new *.bmp file into your project (CarControl.bmp) that is configured to be 16×16 pixels in size (established via the Width and Height properties). Here, I simply reused the Car image used in the TreeView example.

Once you have created the image as you see fit, use the [ToolboxBitmap] attribute (which is applied at the type level) to assign this image to your control. The first argument to the attribute's constructor is the type information for the control itself, while the second argument is the friendly name of the *.bmp file.

```
[DefaultEvent("AboutToBlow"),
DefaultProperty("Animate"),
ToolboxBitmap(typeof(CarControl), "CarControl")]
public partial class CarControl : UserControl
{...}
```

The final step is to make sure you set the Build Action value of the control's icon image to Embedded Resource (via the Properties window) to ensure the image data is embedded within your assembly (see Figure 21-33).

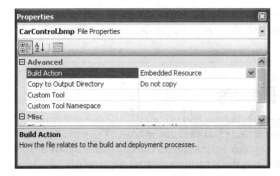

Figure 21-33. *Embedding the image resource*

■**Note** The reason you are manually embedding the *.bmp file (in contrast to when you make use of the ImageList type) is that you are not assigning the CarControl.bmp file to a UI element at design time, therefore the underlying *.resx file will not automatically update.

Once you recompile your Windows Controls library, you can now load your previous CarControlTest-Form project. Right-click the current CarControl icon within the Toolbox and select Delete. Next, re-add the CarControl widget to the Toolbox (by right-clicking and selecting Choose Items). This time, you should see your custom toolbox bitmap (see Figure 21-34).

Figure 21-34. *The custom toolbox bitmap*

So, that wraps up our examination of the process of building custom Windows Forms controls. I hope this example sparked your interest in custom control development. Here, I stuck with the book's automobile theme. Imagine, though, the usefulness of a custom control that will render a pie chart based on the current inventory of a given table in a given database, or a control that extends the functionality of standard UI widgets.

■**Note** If you are interested in learning more about developing custom Windows Forms controls, pick up a copy of *User Interfaces in C#: Windows Forms and Custom Controls,* by Matthew MacDonald (Apress, 2002).

■**Source Code** The CarControlLibrary and CarControlTestForm projects are included under the Chapter 21 directory.

Building Custom Dialog Boxes

Now that you have a solid understanding of the core Windows Forms controls and the process of building custom controls, let's examine the construction of custom dialog boxes. The good news is that everything you have already learned about Windows Forms applies directly to dialog box programming. By and large, creating (and showing) a dialog box is no more difficult than inserting a new Form into your current project.

There is no "Dialog" base class in the System.Windows.Forms namespace. Rather, a dialog box is simply a stylized Form. For example, many dialog boxes are intended to be nonsizable, therefore you will typically want to set the FormBorderStyle property to FormBorderStyle.FixedDialog. As well, dialog boxes typically set the MinimizeBox and MaximizeBox properties to false. In this way, the dialog box is configured to be a fixed constant. Finally, if you set the ShowInTaskbar property to false, you will prevent the Form from being visible in the Windows XP task bar.

To illustrate the process of working with dialog boxes, create a new Windows application named SimpleModalDialog. The main Form type supports a MenuStrip that contains a File ➤ Exit menu item as well as Tools ➤ Configure. Build this UI now, and handle the Click event for the Exit and Enter Message menu items. As well, define a string member variable in your main Form type (named userMessage), and render this data within a Paint event handler of your main Form. Here is the current code within the MainForm.cs file:

```
public partial class MainWindow : Form
{
    private string userMessage = "Default Message";

    public MainWindow()
    {
        InitializeComponent();
    }

    private void exitToolStripMenuItem_Click(object sender, EventArgs e)
    {
        Application.Exit();
    }

    private void configureToolStripMenuItem_Click(object sender, EventArgs e)
    {
        // We will implement this method in just a bit...
    }

    private void MainWindow_Paint(object sender, PaintEventArgs e)
    {
        Graphics g = e.Graphics;
        g.DrawString(userMessage, new Font("Times New Roman", 24), Brushes.DarkBlue,
            50, 50);
    }
}
```

Now add a new Form to your current project using the Project ➤ Add Windows Form menu item named UserMessageDialog.cs. Set the ShowInTaskbar, MinimizeBox, and MaximizeBox properties to false. Next, build a UI that consists of two Button types (for the OK and Cancel buttons), a single

TextBox (to allow the user to enter her message), and an instructive Label. Figure 21-35 shows one possible UI.

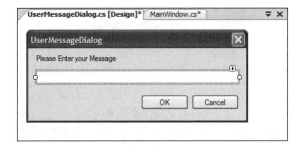

Figure 21-35. *A custom dialog box*

Finally, expose the Text value of the Form's TextBox using a custom property named Message:

```
public partial class UserMessageDialog : Form
{
    public UserMessageDialog()
    {
        InitializeComponent();
    }

    public string Message
    {
        set { txtUserInput.Text = value; }
        get { return txtUserInput.Text; }
    }
}
```

The DialogResult Property

As a final UI task, select the OK button on the Forms designer and find the DialogResult property. Assign DialogResult.OK to your OK button and DialogResult.Cancel to your Cancel button. Formally, you can assign the DialogResult property to any value from the DialogResult enumeration:

```
public enum System.Windows.Forms.DialogResult
{
    Abort, Cancel, Ignore, No,
    None, OK, Retry, Yes
}
```

So, what exactly does it mean to assign a Button's DialogResult value? This property can be assigned to any Button type (as well as the Form itself) and allows the parent Form to determine which button the end user selected. To illustrate, update the Tools ➤ Configure menu handler on the MainForm type as so:

```
private void configureToolStripMenuItem_Click(object sender, EventArgs e)
{
    // Create an instance of UserMessageDialog.
    UserMessageDialog dlg = new UserMessageDialog();

    // Place the current message in the TextBox.
    dlg.Message = userMessage;
```

```
    // If user clicked OK button, render his message.
    if (DialogResult.OK == dlg.ShowDialog())
    {
        userMessage = dlg.Message;
        Invalidate();
    }

    // Have dialog clean up internal widgets now, rather
    // than when the GC destroys the object.
    dlg.Dispose();
}
```

Here, you are showing the UserMessageDialog via a call to ShowDialog(). This method will launch the Form as a *modal* dialog box which, as you may know, means the user is unable to activate the main form until she dismisses the dialog box. Once the user does dismiss the dialog box (by clicking the OK or Cancel button), the Form is no longer visible, but it is still in memory. Therefore, you are able to ask the UserMessageDialog instance (dlg) for its new Message value in the event the user has clicked the OK button. If so, you render the new message. If not, you do nothing.

■**Note** If you wish to show a modeless dialog box (which allows the user to navigate between the parent and dialog Forms), call Show() rather than ShowDialog().

Understanding Form Inheritance

One very appealing aspect of building dialog boxes under Windows Forms is *form inheritance*. As you are no doubt aware, inheritance is the pillar of OOP that allows one class to extend the functionality of another class. Typically, when you speak of inheritance, you envision one non-GUI type (e.g., SportsCar) deriving from another non-GUI type (e.g., Car). However, in the world of Windows Forms, it is possible for one Form to derive from another Form and in the process inherit the base class's widgets and implementation.

Form-level inheritance is a very powerful technique, as it allows you to build a base Form that provides core-level functionality for a family of related dialog boxes. If you were to bundle these base-level Forms into a .NET assembly, other members of your team could extend these types using the .NET language of their choice.

For the sake of illustration, assume you wish to subclass the UserMessageDialog to build a new dialog box that also allows the user to specify if the message should be rendered in italics. To do so, active the Project ➤ Add Windows Form menu item, but this time add a new Inherited Form named ItalicUserMessageDialog.cs (see Figure 21-36).

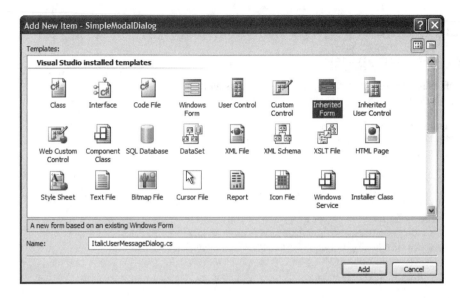

Figure 21-36. *A derived Form*

Once you select Add, you will be shown the *inheritance picker* utility, which allows you to choose from a Form in your current project or select a Form in an external assembly via the Browse button. For this example, select your existing UserMessageDialog type. You will find that your new Form type extends your current dialog type rather than directly from Form. At this point, you are free to extend this derived Form any way you choose. For test purposes, simply add a new CheckBox control (named checkBoxItalic) that is exposed through a property named Italic:

```
public partial class ItalicUserMessageDialog :
    SimpleModalDialog.UserMessageDialog
{
    public ItalicUserMessageDialog()
    {
        InitializeComponent();
    }
    public bool Italic
    {
        set { checkBoxItalic.Checked = value; }
        get { return checkBoxItalic.Checked; }
    }
}
```

Now that you have subclassed the basic UserMessageDialog type, update your MainForm to leverage the new Italic property. Simply add a new Boolean member variable that will be used to build an italic Font object, and update your Tools ➤ Configure Click menu handler to make use of ItalicUserMessageDialog. Here is the complete update:

```
public partial class MainWindow : Form
{
    private string userMessage = "Default Message";
    private bool textIsItalic = false;
...
    private void configureToolStripMenuItem_Click(object sender, EventArgs e)
```

```
    {
        ItalicUserMessageDialog dlg = new ItalicUserMessageDialog();
        dlg.Message = userMessage;
        dlg.Italic = textIsItalic;

        // If user clicked OK button, render his message.
        if (DialogResult.OK == dlg.ShowDialog())
        {
            userMessage = dlg.Message;
            textIsItalic = dlg.Italic;
            Invalidate();
        }
        // Have dialog clean up internal widgets now, rather
        // than when the GC destroys the object.
        dlg.Dispose();
    }

    private void MainWindow_Paint(object sender, PaintEventArgs e)
    {
        Graphics g = e.Graphics;
        Font f = null;
        if(textIsItalic)
            f = new Font("Times New Roman", 24, FontStyle.Italic);
        else
            f = new Font("Times New Roman", 24);
        g.DrawString(userMessage, f, Brushes.DarkBlue,
            50, 50);
    }
}
```

■**Source Code** The SimpleModalDialog application is included under the Chapter 21 directory.

Dynamically Positioning Windows Forms Controls

To wrap up this chapter, let's examine a few techniques you can use to control the layout of widgets on a Form. By and large, when you build a Form type, the assumption is that the controls are rendered using *absolute position*, meaning that if you placed a Button on your Forms designer 10 pixels down and 10 pixels over from the upper left portion of the Form, you expect the Button to stay put during its lifetime.

On a related note, when you are creating a Form that contains UI controls, you need to decide whether the Form should be resizable. Typically speaking, main windows are resizable, whereas dialog boxes are not. Recall that the resizability of a Form is controlled by the FormBorderStyle property, which can be set to any value of the FormBorderStyle enum.

```
public enum System.Windows.Forms.FormBorderStyle
{
    None, FixedSingle, Fixed3D,
    FixedDialog, Sizable,
    FixedToolWindow, SizableToolWindow
}
```

Assume that you have allowed your Form to be resizable. This brings up some interesting questions regarding the contained controls. For example, if the user makes the Form smaller than the rectangle needed to display each control, should the controls adjust their size (and possibly location) to morph correctly with the Form?

The Anchor Property

In Windows Forms, the Anchor property is used to define a relative fixed position in which the control should always be rendered. Every Control-derived type has an Anchor property, which can be set to any of the values from the AnchorStyles enumeration described in Table 21-13.

Table 21-13. AnchorStyles *Values*

Value	Meaning in Life
Bottom	The control's bottom edge is anchored to the bottom edge of its container.
Left	The control's left edge is anchored to the left edge of its container.
None	The control is not anchored to any edges of its container.
Right	The control's right edge is anchored to the right edge of its container.
Top	The control's top edge is anchored to the top edge of its container.

To anchor a widget at the upper-left corner, you are free to OR styles together (e.g., AnchorStyles.Top ➤ AnchorStyles.Left). Again, the idea behind the Anchor property is to configure which edges of the control are anchored to the edges of its container. For example, if you configure a Button with the following Anchor value:

```
// Anchor this widget relative to the right position.
myButton.Anchor = AnchorStyles.Right;
```

you are ensured that as the Form is resized, this Button maintains its position relative to the right side of the Form.

The Dock Property

Another aspect of Windows Forms programming is establishing the *docking behavior* of your controls. If you so choose, you can set a widget's Dock property to configure which side (or sides) of a Form the widget should be attached to. The value you assign to a control's Dock property is honored, regardless of the Form's current dimensions. Table 21-14 describes possible options.

Table 21-14. DockStyle *Values*

Value	Meaning in Life
Bottom	The control's bottom edge is docked to the bottom of its containing control.
Fill	All the control's edges are docked to all the edges of its containing control and sized appropriately.
Left	The control's left edge is docked to the left edge of its containing control.
None	The control is not docked.
Right	The control's right edge is docked to the right edge of its containing control.
Top	The control's top edge is docked to the top of its containing control.

So, for example, if you want to ensure that a given widget is always docked on the left side of a Form, you would write the following:

```
// This item is always located on the left of the Form, regardless
// of the Form's current size.
myButton.Dock = DockStyle.Left;
```

To help you understand the implications of setting the Anchor and Dock properties, the downloadable code for this book contains a project named AnchoringControls. Once you build and run this application, you can make use of the Form's menu system to set various AnchorStyles and DockStyle values and observe the change in behavior of the Button type (see Figure 21-37).

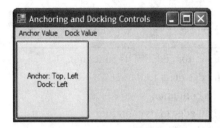

Figure 21-37. *The AnchoringControls application*

Be sure to resize the Form when changing the Anchor property to observe how the Button responds.

■**Source Code** The AnchoringControls application is included under the Chapter 21 directory.

Table and Flow Layout

.NET 2.0 offers an additional way to control the layout of a Form's widgets using one of two layout managers. The TableLayoutPanel and FlowLayoutPanel types can be docked into a Form's client area to arrange the internal controls. For example, assume you place a new FlowLayoutPanel widget onto the Forms designer and configure it to dock fully within the parent Form (see Figure 21-38).

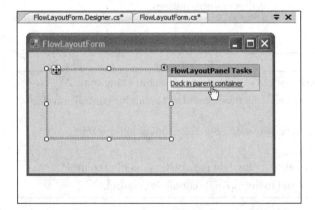

Figure 21-38. *Docking a* FlowLayoutPanel *into a Form*

Now, add ten new Button types within the FlowLayoutPanel using the Forms designer. If you now run your application, you will notice that the ten Buttons automatically rearrange themselves in a manner very close to standard HTML.

On the other hand, if you create a Form that contains a TableLayoutPanel, you are able to build a UI that is partitioned into various "cells" (see Figure 21-39).

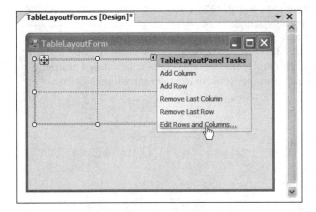

Figure 21-39. *The* TableLayoutPanel *type*

If you select the Edit Rows and Columns inline menu option using the Forms designer (as shown in Figure 21-39), you are able to control the overall format of the TableLayoutPanel on a cell-by-cell basis (see Figure 21-40).

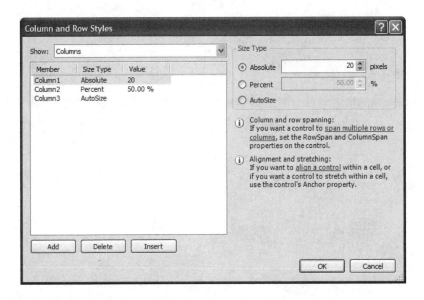

Figure 21-40. *Configuring the cells of the* TableLayoutPanel *type*

Truth be told, the only way to see the effects of the TableLayoutPanel type is to do so in a hands-on manner. I'll let interested readers handle that task.

Summary

This chapter rounded off your understanding of the Windows Forms namespace by examining the programming of numerous GUI widgets, from the simple (e.g., Label) to the more exotic (e.g., TreeView). After examining numerous control types, you moved on to cover the construction of custom controls, including the topic of design-time integration.

In the latter half of this chapter, you learned how to build custom dialog boxes and how to derive a new Form from an existing Form type using form inheritance. This chapter concluded by briefly exploring the various anchoring and docking behaviors you can use to enforce a specific layout of your GUI types, as well as the new .NET 2.0 layout managers.

CHAPTER 22

■■■

Database Access with ADO.NET

Unless you are a video game developer by trade, you are probably interested in the topic of database access. As you would expect, the .NET platform defines a number of namespaces that allow you to interact with local and remote data stores. Collectively speaking, these namespaces are known as *ADO.NET*.

In this chapter, once I frame the overall role of ADO.NET (in the next section), I'll move on to discuss the topic of ADO.NET data providers. The .NET platform supports numerous data providers, each of which is optimized to communicate with a specific database management system (Microsoft SQL Server, Oracle, MySQL, etc.). After you understand how to manipulate a specific data provider, you will then examine the new data provider factory pattern offered by .NET 2.0. Using types within the System.Data.Common namespace (and a related app.config file), you are able to build a single code base that can dynamically pick and choose the underlying data provider without the need to recompile or redeploy the application's code base.

The remaining part of this chapter examines how to programmatically interact with relational databases using your data provider of choice. As you will see, ADO.NET provides two distinct ways to interface with a data source, often termed the *connected layer* and *disconnected layer*. You will come to know the role of connection objects, command objects, data readers, data adapters, and numerous types within the System.Data namespace (specifically, DataSet, DataTable, DataRow, DataColumn, DataView, and DataRelation).

A High-Level Definition of ADO.NET

If you have a background in Microsoft's previous COM-based data access model (Active Data Objects, or ADO), understand that ADO.NET has very little to do with ADO beyond the letters "A," "D," and "O." While it is true that there is some relationship between the two systems (e.g., each has the concept of connection and command objects), some familiar ADO types (e.g., the Recordset) no longer exist. Furthermore, there are a number of new ADO.NET types that have no direct equivalent under classic ADO (e.g., the data adapter).

Unlike classic ADO, which was primarily designed for tightly coupled client/server systems, ADO.NET was built with the disconnected world in mind, using DataSets. This type represents a local copy of any number of related tables. Using the DataSet, the client tier is able to manipulate and update its contents while disconnected from the data source, and it can submit the modified data back for processing using a related data adapter.

Another major difference between classic ADO and ADO.NET is that ADO.NET has deep support for XML data representation. In fact, the data obtained from a data store is serialized (by default) as XML. Given that XML is often transported between layers using standard HTTP, ADO.NET is not limited by firewall constraints.

■**Note** As of .NET 2.0, DataSets (and DataTables) can now be serialized in a binary format via the RemotingFormat property. This can be helpful when building distributed systems using the .NET remoting layer (see Chapter 18), as binary data is much more compact than XML data.

Perhaps the most fundamental difference between classic ADO and ADO.NET is that ADO.NET is a managed library of code, therefore it plays by the same rules as any managed library. The types that make up ADO.NET use the CLR memory management protocol, adhere to the same type system (classes, interfaces, enums, structures, and delegates), and can be accessed by any .NET language.

The Two Faces of ADO.NET

The ADO.NET libraries can be used in two conceptually unique manners: connected or disconnected. When you are making use of the *connected layer*, your code base will explicitly connect to and disconnect from the underlying data store. When you are using ADO.NET in this manner, you typically interact with the data store using connection objects, command objects, and data reader objects. As you will see later in this chapter, data readers provide a way to pull records from a data store using a forward-only, read-only approach (much like a fire-hose cursor).

The disconnected layer, on the other hand, allows you to obtain a set of DataTable objects (contained within a DataSet) that functions as a client-side copy of the external data. When you obtain a DataSet using a related data adapter object, the connection is automatically opened and closed on your behalf. As you would guess, this approach helps quickly free up connections for other callers. Once the client receives a DataSet, it is able to traverse and manipulate the contents without incurring the cost of network traffic. As well, if the client wishes to submit the changes back to the data store, the data adapter (in conjunction with a set of SQL statements) is used once again to update the data source, at which point the connection is closed immediately.

Understanding ADO.NET Data Providers

ADO.NET does not provide a single set of types that communicate with multiple database management systems (DBMSs). Rather, ADO.NET supports multiple *data providers*, each of which is optimized to interact with a specific DBMS. The first benefit of this approach is that a specific data provider can be programmed to access any unique features of the DBMS. Another benefit is that a specific data provider is able to directly connect to the underlying engine of the DBMS without an intermediate mapping layer standing between the tiers.

Simply put, a *data provider* is a set of types defined in a given namespace that understand how to communicate with a specific data source. Regardless of which data provider you make use of, each defines a set of class types that provide core functionality. Table 22-1 documents some (but not all) of the core common objects, their base class (all defined in the System.Data.Common namespace), and their implemented data-centric interfaces (each defined in the System.Data namespace).

Table 22-1. *Core Objects of an ADO.NET Data Provider*

Object	Base Class	Implemented Interfaces	Meaning in Life
Connection	DbConnection	IDbConnection	Provides the ability to connect to and disconnect from the data store. Connection objects also provide access to a related transaction object.
Command	DbCommand	IDbCommand	Represents a SQL query or name of a stored procedure. Command objects also provide access to the provider's data reader object.
DataReader	DbDataReader	IDataReader, IDataRecord	Provides forward-only, read-only access to data.
DataAdapter	DbDataAdapter	IDataAdapter, IDbDataAdapter	Transfers DataSets between the caller and the data store. Data adapters contain a set of four internal command objects used to select, insert, update, and delete information from the data store.
Parameter	DbParameter	IDataParameter, IDbDataParameter	Represents a named parameter within a parameterized query.
Transaction	DbTransaction	IDbTransaction	Performs a database transaction.

Although the names of these types will differ among data providers (e.g., SqlConnection versus OracleConnection versus OdbcConnection versus MySqlConnection), each object derives from the same base class that implements identical interfaces. Given this, you are correct to assume that once you learn how to work with one data provider, the remaining providers are quite straightforward.

■**Note** As a naming convention, the objects in a specific data provider are prefixed with the name of the related DBMS.

Figure 22-1 illustrates the big picture behind ADO.NET data providers. Note that in the diagram, the "Client Assembly" can literally be any type of .NET application: console program, Windows Forms application, ASP.NET web page, XML web service, .NET code library, and so on.

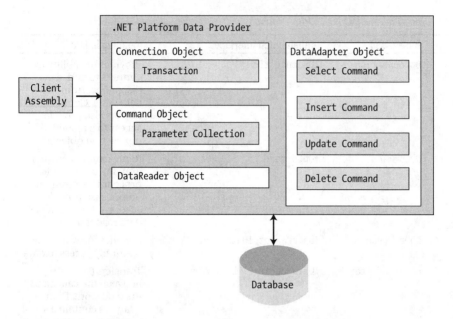

Figure 22-1. *ADO.NET data providers provide access to a given DBMS.*

Now, to be sure, a data provider will supply you with other types beyond the objects shown in Figure 22-1. However, these core objects define a common baseline across all data providers.

Microsoft-Supplied Data Providers

As of version 2.0, Microsoft's .NET distribution ships with numerous data providers, including a provider for Oracle, SQL Server, and ODBC-style connectivity. Table 22-2 documents the namespace and containing assembly for each Microsoft ADO.NET data provider.

Table 22-2. *Microsoft ADO.NET Data Providers*

Data Provider	Namespace	Assembly
OLE DB	System.Data.OleDb	System.Data.dll
Microsoft SQL Server	System.Data.SqlClient	System.Data.dll
Microsoft SQL Server Mobile	System.Data.SqlServerCe	System.Data.SqlServerCe.dll
ODBC	System.Data.Odbc	System.Data.dll
Oracle	System.Data.OracleClient	System.Data.OracleClient.dll

■**Note** There is no specific data provider that maps directly to the Jet engine (and therefore Microsoft Access). If you wish to interact with an Access data file, you can do so using the OLE DB or ODBC data provider.

The OLE DB data provider, which is composed of the types defined in the `System.Data.OleDb` namespace, allows you to access data located in any data store that supports the classic COM-based OLE DB protocol. Using this provider, you may communicate with any OLE DB–compliant database simply by tweaking the "Provider" segment of your connection string. Be aware, however, that the OLE DB provider interacts with various COM objects behind the scenes, which can affect the performance of your application. By and large, the OLE DB data provider is only useful if you are interacting with a DBMS that does not define a specific .NET data provider.

The Microsoft SQL Server data provider offers direct access to Microsoft SQL Server data stores, and *only* SQL Server data stores (version 7.0 and greater). The `System.Data.SqlClient` namespace contains the types used by the SQL Server provider and offers the same basic functionality as the OLE DB provider. The key difference is that the SQL Server provider bypasses the OLE DB layer and thus gives numerous performance benefits. As well, the Microsoft SQL Server data provider allows you to gain access to the unique features of this particular DBMS.

■**Note** If you are interested in making use of the `System.Data.SqlServerCe`, `System.Data.Odbc`, or `System.Data.Oracle` namespaces, check out the details as you see fit using the .NET Framework 2.0 SDK documentation.

Select Third-Party Data Providers

In addition to the data providers that ship from Microsoft, numerous third-party data providers exist for various open source and commercial databases. Table 22-3 documents where to obtain managed providers for several databases that do not directly ship with Microsoft .NET 2.0 (please note that the provided URLs are subject to change).

Table 22-3. *Third-Party ADO.NET Data Providers*

Data Provider	Website
Firebird Interbase	`http://www.mono-project.com/Firebird_Interbase`
IBM DB2 Universal Database	`http://www-306.ibm.com/software/data/db2`
MySQL	`http://dev.mysql.com/downloads/connector/net/1.0.html`
PostgreSQL	`http://www.mono-project.com/PostgreSQL`
Sybase	`http://www.mono-project.com/Sybase`

■**Note** Given the large number of ADO.NET data providers, the examples in this chapter will make use of the Microsoft SQL Server data provider (`System.Data.SqlClient`). If you intend to use ADO.NET to interact with another DBMS, you should have no problem doing so once you understand the material presented in the pages that follow.

Additional ADO.NET Namespaces

In addition to the .NET namespaces that define the types of a specific data provider, the base class libraries provide a number of additional ADO.NET-centric namespaces, as shown in Table 22-4.

Table 22-4. *Additional ADO.NET-centric Namespaces*

Namespace	Meaning in Life
Microsoft.SqlServer.Server	This new .NET 2.0 namespace provides types that allow you to author stored procedures via managed languages for SQL Server 2005.
System.Data	This namespace defines the core ADO.NET types used by all data providers.
System.Data.Common	This namespace contains types shared between data providers, including the .NET 2.0 data provider factory types.
System.Data.Design	This new .NET 2.0 namespace contains various types used to construct a design-time appearance for custom data components.
System.Data.Sql	This new .NET 2.0 namespace contains types that allow you to discover Microsoft SQL Server instances installed on the current local network.
System.Data.SqlTypes	This namespace contains native data types used by Microsoft SQL Server. Although you are always free to use the corresponding CLR data types, the SqlTypes are optimized to work with SQL Server.

Do understand that this chapter will not examine each and every type within each and every ADO.NET namespace (that task would require a large book in and of itself). However, it is quite important for you to understand the types within the System.Data namespace.

The System.Data Types

Of all the ADO.NET namespaces, System.Data is the lowest common denominator. You simply cannot build ADO.NET applications without specifying this namespace in your data access applications. This namespace contains types that are shared among all ADO.NET data providers, regardless of the underlying data store. In addition to a number of database-centric exceptions (NoNullAllowedException, RowNotInTableException, MissingPrimaryKeyException, and the like), System.Data contains types that represent various database primitives (tables, rows, columns, constraints, etc.), as well as the common interfaces implemented by data provider objects. Table 22-5 lists some of the core types to be aware of.

Table 22-5. *Core Members of the* System.Data *Namespace*

Type	Meaning in Life
Constraint	Represents a constraint for a given DataColumn object
DataColumn	Represents a single column within a DataTable object
DataRelation	Represents a parent/child relationship between two DataTable objects
DataRow	Represents a single row within a DataTable object
DataSet	Represents an in-memory cache of data consisting of any number of interrelated DataTable objects
DataTable	Represents a tabular block of in-memory data
DataTableReader	Allows you to treat a DataTable as a fire-hose cursor (forward only, read-only data access); new in .NET 2.0

Type	Meaning in Life
DataView	Represents a customized view of a DataTable for sorting, filtering, searching, editing, and navigation
IDataAdapter	Defines the core behavior of a data adapter object
IDataParameter	Defines the core behavior of a parameter object
IDataReader	Defines the core behavior of a data reader object
IDbCommand	Defines the core behavior of a command object
IDbDataAdapter	Extends IDataAdapter to provide additional functionality of a data adapter object
IDbTransaction	Defines the core behavior of a transaction object

Later in this chapter, you will get to know the role of the DataSet and its related cohorts (DataTable, DataRelation, DataRow, etc.). However, your next task is to examine the core interfaces of System.Data at a high level, to better understand the common functionality offered by any data provider. You will learn specific details throughout this chapter, so for the time being let's simply focus on the overall behavior of each interface type.

The Role of the IDbConnection Interface

First up is the IDbConnection type, which is implemented by a data provider's *connection object*. This interface defines a set of members used to configure a connection to a specific data store, and it also allows you to obtain the data provider's transactional object. Here is the formal definition of IDbConnection:

```
public interface IDbConnection : IDisposable
{
    string ConnectionString { get; set; }
    int ConnectionTimeout { get; }
    string Database { get; }
    ConnectionState State { get; }
    IDbTransaction BeginTransaction();
    IDbTransaction BeginTransaction(IsolationLevel il);
    void ChangeDatabase(string databaseName);
    void Close();
    IDbCommand CreateCommand();
    void Open();
}
```

The Role of the IDbTransaction Interface

As you can see, the overloaded BeginTransaction() method defined by IDbConnection provides access to the provider's *transaction object*. Using the members defined by IDbTransaction, you are able to programmatically interact with a transactional session and the underlying data store:

```
public interface IDbTransaction : IDisposable
{
    IDbConnection Connection { get; }
    IsolationLevel IsolationLevel { get; }
    void Commit();
    void Rollback();
}
```

The Role of the IDbCommand Interface

Next, we have the IDbCommand interface, which will be implemented by a data provider's *command object*. Like other data access object models, command objects allow programmatic manipulation of SQL statements, stored procedures, and parameterized queries. In addition, command objects provide access to the data provider's data reader type via the overloaded ExecuteReader() method:

```
public interface IDbCommand :  IDisposable
{
    string CommandText { get; set; }
    int CommandTimeout { get; set; }
    CommandType CommandType { get; set; }
    IDbConnection Connection { get; set; }
    IDataParameterCollection Parameters { get; }
    IDbTransaction Transaction { get; set; }
    UpdateRowSource UpdatedRowSource { get; set; }
    void Cancel();
    IDbDataParameter CreateParameter();
    int ExecuteNonQuery();
    IDataReader ExecuteReader();
    IDataReader ExecuteReader(CommandBehavior behavior);
    object ExecuteScalar();
    void Prepare();
}
```

The Role of the IDbDataParameter and IDataParameter Interfaces

Notice that the Parameters property of IDbCommand returns a strongly typed collection that implements IDataParameterCollection. This interface provides access to a set of IDbDataParameter-compliant class types (e.g., parameter objects):

```
public interface IDbDataParameter : IDataParameter
{
    byte Precision { get; set; }
    byte Scale { get; set; }
    int Size { get; set; }
}
```

IDbDataParameter extends the IDataParameter interface to obtain the following additional behaviors:

```
public interface IDataParameter
{
    DbType DbType { get; set; }
    ParameterDirection Direction { get; set; }
    bool IsNullable { get; }
    string ParameterName { get; set; }
    string SourceColumn { get; set; }
    DataRowVersion SourceVersion { get; set; }
    object Value { get; set; }
}
```

As you will see, the functionality of the IDbDataParameter and IDataParameter interfaces allows you to represent parameters within a SQL command (including stored procedures) via specific ADO.NET parameter objects rather than hard-coded string literals.

The Role of the IDbDataAdapter and IDataAdapter Interfaces

Data adapters are used to push and pull DataSets to and from a given data store. Given this, the IDbDataAdapter interface defines a set of properties that are used to maintain the SQL statements for the related select, insert, update, and delete operations:

```
public interface IDbDataAdapter : IDataAdapter
{
    IDbCommand DeleteCommand { get; set; }
    IDbCommand InsertCommand { get; set; }
    IDbCommand SelectCommand { get; set; }
    IDbCommand UpdateCommand { get; set; }
}
```

In addition to these four properties, an ADO.NET data adapter also picks up the behavior defined in the base interface, IDataAdapter. This interface defines the key function of a data adapter type: the ability to transfer DataSets between the caller and underlying data store using the Fill() and Update() methods.

As well, the IDataAdapter interface allows you to map database column names to more user-friendly display names via the TableMappings property:

```
public interface IDataAdapter
{
    MissingMappingAction MissingMappingAction { get; set; }
    MissingSchemaAction MissingSchemaAction { get; set; }
    ITableMappingCollection TableMappings { get; }
    int Fill(System.Data.DataSet dataSet);
    DataTable[] FillSchema(DataSet dataSet, SchemaType schemaType);
    IDataParameter[] GetFillParameters();
    int Update(DataSet dataSet);
}
```

The Role of the IDataReader and IDataRecord Interfaces

The next key interface to be aware of is IDataReader, which represents the common behaviors supported by a given data reader object. When you obtain an IDataReader-compatible type from an ADO.NET data provider, you are able to iterate over the result set in a forward-only, read-only manner.

```
public interface IDataReader : IDisposable, IDataRecord
{
    int Depth { get; }
    bool IsClosed { get; }
    int RecordsAffected { get; }
    void Close();
    DataTable GetSchemaTable();
    bool NextResult();
    bool Read();
}
```

Finally, as you can see, IDataReader extends IDataRecord, which defines a good number of members that allow you to extract a strongly typed value from the stream, rather than casting the generic System.Object retrieved from the data reader's overloaded indexer method. Here is a partial listing of the various GetXXX() methods defined by IDataRecord (see the .NET Framework 2.0 SDK documentation for a complete listing):

```
public interface IDataRecord
{
    int FieldCount { get; }
    object this[ string name ] { get; }
    object this[ int i ] { get; }
    bool GetBoolean(int i);
    byte GetByte(int i);
    char GetChar(int i);
    DateTime GetDateTime(int i);
    Decimal GetDecimal(int i);
    float GetFloat(int i);
    short GetInt16(int i);
    int GetInt32(int i);
    long GetInt64(int i);
...
    bool IsDBNull(int i);
}
```

■**Note** The IDataReader.IsDBNull() method can be used to programmatically discover if a specified field is set to null before obtaining a value from the data reader (to avoid triggering a runtime exception).

Abstracting Data Providers Using Interfaces

At this point, you should have a better idea of the common functionality found among all .NET data providers. Recall that even though the exact names of the implementing types will differ among data providers, you are able to program against these types in a similar manner—that's the beauty of interface-based polymorphism. Therefore, if you define a method that takes an IDbConnection parameter, you can pass in any ADO.NET connection object:

```
public static void OpenConnection(IDbConnection cn)
{
    // Open the incoming connection for the caller.
    cn.Open();
}
```

The same holds true for a member return value. For example, consider the following simple C# program, which allows the caller to obtain a specific connection object using the value of a custom enumeration (assume you have "used" System.Data):

```
namespace ConnectionApp
{
    enum DataProvider
    { SqlServer, OleDb, Odbc, Oracle }

    class Program
    {
        static void Main(string[] args)
        {
            // Get a specific connection.
            IDbConnection myCn = GetConnection(DataProvider.SqlServer);

            // Assume we wish to connect to the SQL Server Pubs database.
            myCn.ConnectionString =
                "Data Source=localhost;uid=sa;pwd=;Initial Catalog=Pubs";
```

```
        // Now open connection via our helper function.
        OpenConnection(myCn);

        // Use connection and close when finished.
        ...
        myCn.Close();
    }

    static IDbConnection GetConnection(DataProvider dp)
    {
        IDbConnection conn = null;
        switch (dp)
        {
            case DataProvider.SqlServer:
                conn = new SqlConnection();
                break;
            case DataProvider.OleDb:
                conn = new OleDbConnection();
                break;
            case DataProvider.Odbc:
                conn = new OdbcConnection();
                break;
            case DataProvider.Oracle:
                conn = new OracleConnection();
                break;
        }
        return conn;
    }
}
```

The benefit of working with the general interfaces of System.Data is that you have a much better chance of building a flexible code base that can evolve over time. For example, perhaps today you are building an application targeting Microsoft SQL Server, but what if your company switches to Oracle months down the road? If you hard-code the types of System.Data.SqlClient, you will obviously need to edit, recompile, and redeploy the assembly.

Increasing Flexibility Using Application Configuration Files

To further increase the flexibility of your ADO.NET applications, you could incorporate a client-side *.config file that makes use of custom key/value pairs within the <appSettings> element. Recall from Chapter 11 that custom data can be programmatically obtained using types within the System.Configuration namespace. For example, assume you have specified the connection string and data provider values within a configuration file as so:

```
<configuration>
  <appSettings>
    <add key="provider" value="SqlServer" />
    <add key="cnStr" value=
      "Data Source=localhost;uid=sa;pwd=;Initial Catalog=Pubs"/>
  </appSettings>
</configuration>
```

With this, you could update `Main()` to programmatically read these values. By doing so, you essentially build a *data provider factory*. Here are the relevant updates:

```
static void Main(string[] args)
{
    // Read the provider key.
    string dpStr = ConfigurationManager.AppSettings["provider"];
    DataProvider dp = (DataProvider)Enum.Parse(typeof(DataProvider), dpStr);

    // Read the cnStr.
    string cnStr = ConfigurationManager.AppSettings["cnStr"];

    // Get a specific connection.
    IDbConnection myCn = GetConnection(dp);
    myCn.ConnectionString = cnStr;
...
}
```

■ **Note** The `ConfigurationManager` type is new to .NET 2.0. Be sure to set a reference to the `System.Config-uration.dll` assembly and "use" the `System.Configuration` namespace.

If the previous example were reworked into a .NET code library (rather than a console application), you would be able to build any number of clients that could obtain specific connections using various layers of abstraction. However, to make a worthwhile data provider factory library, you would also have to account for command objects, data readers, data adapters, and other data-centric types. While building such a code library would not necessarily be difficult, it would require a good amount of code. Thankfully, as of .NET 2.0, the kind folks in Redmond have built this very thing into the base class libraries.

■ **Source Code** The MyConnectionFactory project is included under the Chapter 22 subdirectory.

The .NET 2.0 Provider Factory Model

Under .NET 2.0, we are now offered a data provider factory pattern that allows us to build a single code base using generalized data access types. Furthermore, using application configuration files (and the spiffy new `<connectionStrings>` section), we are able to obtain providers and connection strings declaratively without the need to recompile or redeploy the client software.

To understand the data provider factory implementation, recall from Table 22-1 that the objects within a data provider each derive from the same base classes defined within the `System.Data.Common` namespace:

- `DbCommand`: Abstract base class for all command objects
- `DbConnection`: Abstract base class for all connection objects
- `DbDataAdapter`: Abstract base class for all data adapter objects
- `DbDataReader`: Abstract base class for all data reader objects
- `DbParameter`: Abstract base class for all parameter objects
- `DbTransaction`: Abstract base class for all transaction objects

In addition, as of .NET 2.0, each of the Microsoft-supplied data providers now provides a specific class deriving from System.Data.Common.DbProviderFactory. This base class defines a number of methods that retrieve provider-specific data objects. Here is a snapshot of the relevant members of DbProviderFactory:

```
public abstract class DbProviderFactory
{
...
    public virtual DbCommand CreateCommand();
    public virtual DbCommandBuilder CreateCommandBuilder();
    public virtual DbConnection CreateConnection();
    public virtual DbConnectionStringBuilder CreateConnectionStringBuilder();
    public virtual DbDataAdapter CreateDataAdapter();
    public virtual DbDataSourceEnumerator CreateDataSourceEnumerator();
    public virtual DbParameter CreateParameter();
}
```

To obtain the DbProviderFactory-derived type for your data provider, the System.Data.Common namespace provides a class type named DbProviderFactories (note the plural in this type's name). Using the static GetFactory() method, you are able to obtain the specific (which is to say, singular) DbProviderFactory of the specified data provider, for example:

```
static void Main(string[] args)
{
    // Get the factory for the SQL data provider.
    DbProviderFactory sqlFactory =
        DbProviderFactories.GetFactory("System.Data.SqlClient");
...
    // Get the factory for the Oracle data provider.
    DbProviderFactory oracleFactory =
        DbProviderFactories.GetFactory("System.Data.OracleClient");
...
}
```

As you might be thinking, rather than obtaining a factory using a hard-coded string literal, you could read in this information from a client-side *.config file (much like the previous MyConnectionFactory example). You will do so in just a bit. However, in any case, once you have obtained the factory for your data provider, you are able to obtain the associated provider-specific data objects (connections, commands, etc.).

Registered Data Provider Factories

Before you look at a full example of working with ADO.NET data provider factories, it is important to point out that the DbProviderFactories type (as of .NET 2.0) is able to fetch factories for only a subset of all possible data providers. The list of valid provider factories is recorded within the <DbProviderFactories> element within the machine.config file for your .NET 2.0 installation (note that the value of the invariant attribute is identical to the value passed into the DbProviderFactories. GetFactory() method):

```
<system.data>
  <DbProviderFactories>
    <add name="Odbc Data Provider" invariant="System.Data.Odbc"
      description=".Net Framework Data Provider for Odbc"
      type="System.Data.Odbc.OdbcFactory,
      System.Data, Version=2.0.0.0, Culture=neutral,
      PublicKeyToken=b77a5c561934e089" />
    <add name="OleDb Data Provider" invariant="System.Data.OleDb"
```

```
        description=".Net Framework Data Provider for OleDb"
        type="System.Data.OleDb.OleDbFactory,
        System.Data, Version=2.0.0.0, Culture=neutral,
        PublicKeyToken=b77a5c561934e089" />
    <add name="OracleClient Data Provider" invariant="System.Data.OracleClient"
        description=".Net Framework Data Provider for Oracle"
        type="System.Data.OracleClient.OracleClientFactory, System.Data.OracleClient,
        Version=2.0.0.0, Culture=neutral, PublicKeyToken=b77a5c561934e089" />
    <add name="SqlClient Data Provider" invariant="System.Data.SqlClient"
        description=".Net Framework Data Provider for SqlServer"
        type="System.Data.SqlClient.SqlClientFactory, System.Data,
        Version=2.0.0.0, Culture=neutral, PublicKeyToken=b77a5c561934e089" />
  </DbProviderFactories>
</system.data>
```

■**Note** If you wish to leverage a similar data provider factory pattern for DMBSs not accounted for in the machine.config file, note that the Mono distribution of .NET (see Chapter 1) provides a similar data factory that accounts for numerous open source and commercial data providers.

A Complete Data Provider Factory Example

For a complete example, let's build a console application (named DataProviderFactory) that prints out the first and last names of individuals in the Authors table of a database named Pubs residing within Microsoft SQL Server (as you may know, Pubs is a sample database modeling a fictitious book publishing company).

First, add a reference to the System.Configuration.dll assembly and insert an app.config file to the current project and define an <appSettings> element. Remember that the format of the "official" provider value is the full namespace name for the data provider, rather than the string name of the ad hoc DataProvider enumeration used in the MyConnectionFactory example:

```
<configuration>
  <appSettings>
    <!-- Which provider? -->
    <add key="provider" value="System.Data.SqlClient" />
    <!-- Which connection string? -->
    <add key="cnStr" value=
    "Data Source=localhost;uid=sa;pwd=;Initial Catalog=Pubs"/>
  </appSettings>
</configuration>
```

Now that you have a proper *.config file, you can read in the provider and cnStr values using the ConfigurationManager.AppSettings() method. The provider value will be passed to DbProviderFactories.GetFactory() to obtain the data provider–specific factory type. The cnStr value will be used to set the ConnectionString property of the DbConnection-derived type. Assuming you have "used" the System.Data and System.Data.Common namespaces, update your Main() method as follows:

```
static void Main(string[] args)
{
    Console.WriteLine("***** Fun with Data Provider Factories *****\n");

    // Get Connection string/provider from *.config.
    string dp =
        ConfigurationManager.AppSettings["provider"];
    string cnStr =
```

```
    ConfigurationManager.AppSettings["cnStr"];

    // Make the factory provider.
    DbProviderFactory df = DbProviderFactories.GetFactory(dp);

    // Now make connection object.
    DbConnection cn = df.CreateConnection();
    Console.WriteLine("Your connection object is a: {0}", cn.GetType().FullName);
    cn.ConnectionString = cnStr;
    cn.Open();

    // Make command object.
    DbCommand cmd = df.CreateCommand();
    Console.WriteLine("Your command object is a: {0}", cmd.GetType().FullName);
    cmd.Connection = cn;
    cmd.CommandText = "Select * From Authors";

    // Print out data with data reader.
    DbDataReader dr =
        cmd.ExecuteReader(CommandBehavior.CloseConnection);
    Console.WriteLine("Your data reader object is a: {0}", dr.GetType().FullName);

    Console.WriteLine("\n***** Authors in Pubs *****");
    while (dr.Read())
        Console.WriteLine("-> {0}, {1}", dr["au_lname"], dr["au_fname"]);
    dr.Close();
}
```

Notice that for diagnostic purposes, you are printing out the fully qualified name of the underlying connection, command, and data reader using reflection services. If you run this application, you will find that the Microsoft SQL Server provider has been used to read data from the Authors table of the Pubs database (see Figure 22-2).

Figure 22-2. *Obtaining the SQL Server data provider via the .NET 2.0 data provider factory*

Now, if you change the *.config file to specify System.Data.OleDb as the data provider (and update your connection string) as follows:

```
<configuration>
  <appSettings>
    <!-- Which provider? -->
    <add key="provider" value="System.Data.OleDb" />
    <!-- Which connection string? -->
    <add key="cnStr" value=
```

```
    "Provider=SQLOLEDB.1;Data Source=localhost;uid=sa;pwd=;Initial Catalog=Pubs"/>
  </appSettings>
</configuration>
```

you will find the System.Data.OleDb types are used behind the scenes (see Figure 22-3).

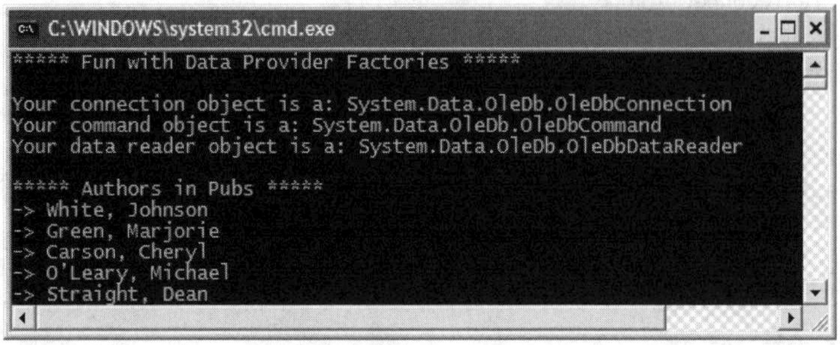

Figure 22-3. *Obtaining the OLE DB data provider via the .NET 2.0 data provider factory*

Of course, based on your experience with ADO.NET, you may be a bit unsure exactly what the connection, command, and data reader objects are actually doing. Don't sweat the details for the time being (quite a few pages remain in this chapter, after all!). At this point, just understand that under .NET 2.0, it is possible to build a single code base that can consume various data providers in a declarative manner.

Although this is a very powerful model, you must make sure that the code base does indeed make use only of types and methods that are common to all providers. Therefore, when authoring your code base, you will be limited to the members exposed by DbConnection, DbCommand, and the other types of the System.Data.Common namespace. Given this, you may find that this "generalized" approach will prevent you from directly accessing some of the bells and whistles of a particular DBMS (so be sure to test your code!).

The <connectionStrings> Element

As of .NET 2.0, application configuration files may define a new element named <connectionStrings>. Within this element, you are able to define any number of name/value pairs that can be programmatically read into memory using the ConfigurationManager.ConnectionStrings indexer. The chief advantage of this approach (rather than using the <appSettings> element and the ConfigurationManager.AppSettings indexer) is that you can define multiple connection strings for a single application in a consistent manner.

To illustrate, update your current app.config file as follows (note that each connection string is documented using the name and connectionString attributes rather than the key and value attributes as found in <appSettings>):

```
<configuration>
  <appSettings>
  <!-- Which provider? -->
    <add key="provider" value="System.Data.SqlClient" />
  </appSettings>
  <connectionStrings>
    <add name ="SqlProviderPubs"  connectionString =
    "Data Source=localhost;uid=sa;pwd=;Initial Catalog=Pubs"/>
```

```
    <add name ="OleDbProviderPubs"  connectionString =
    " Provider=SQLOLEDB.1;Data Source=localhost;uid=sa;pwd=;Initial Catalog=Pubs"/>
    </connectionStrings>
</configuration>
```

With this, you can now update your `Main()` method as so:

```
static void Main(string[] args)
{
    Console.WriteLine("***** Fun with Data Provider Factories *****\n");
    string dp =
        ConfigurationManager.AppSettings["provider"];
    string cnStr =
        ConfigurationManager.ConnectionStrings["SqlProviderPubs"].ConnectionString;
...
}
```

At this point, you should be clear on how to interact with the .NET 2.0 data provider factory (and the new `<connectionStrings>` element).

■**Note** Now that you understand the role of ADO.NET data provider factories, the remaining examples in this chapter will make explicit use of the types within `System.Data.SqlClient` and hard-coded connection strings, just to keep focused on the task at hand.

■**Source Code** The DataProviderFactory project is included under the Chapter 22 subdirectory.

Installing the Cars Database

Now that you understand the basic properties of a .NET data provider, you can begin to dive into the specifics of coding with ADO.NET. As mentioned earlier, the examples in this chapter will make use of Microsoft SQL Server. In keeping with the automotive theme used throughout this text, I have included a sample Cars database that contains three interrelated tables named Inventory, Orders, and Customers.

■**Note** If you do not have a copy of Microsoft SQL Server, you can download a (free) copy of Microsoft SQL Server 2005 Express Edition (`http://lab.msdn.microsoft.com/express`). While this tool does not have all the bells and whistles of the full version of Microsoft SQL Server, it will allow you to host the provided Cars database. Do be aware, however, that this chapter was written with Microsoft SQL Server in mind, so be sure to consult the provided SQL Server 2005 Express Edition documentation.

To install the Cars database on your machine, begin by opening the Query Analyzer utility that ships with SQL Server. Next, connect to your machine and open the provided `Cars.sql` file. Before you run the script, make sure that the path listed in the SQL file points to your installation of Microsoft SQL Server. Edit the following lines (in bold) as necessary:

```
CREATE DATABASE [Cars]  ON (NAME = N'Cars_Data', FILENAME
=N' C:\Program Files\Microsoft SQL Server\MSSQL\Data\Cars_Data.MDF' ,
SIZE = 2, FILEGROWTH = 10%)
```

```
LOG ON (NAME = N'Cars_Log', FILENAME
= N' C:\Program Files\Microsoft SQL Server\MSSQL\Data\Cars_Log.LDF' ,
SIZE = 1, FILEGROWTH = 10%)
GO
```

Now run the script. Once you do, open up SQL Server Enterprise Manager. You should see three interrelated tables (with some sample data to boot) and a single stored procedure. Figure 22-4 shows the tables that populate the Cars database.

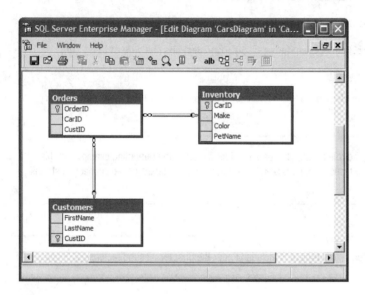

Figure 22-4. *The sample Cars database*

Connecting to the Cars Database from Visual Studio 2005

Now that you have the Cars database installed, you may wish to create a data connection to the database from within Visual Studio 2005. This will allow you to view and edit the various database objects from within the IDE. To do so, open the Server Explorer window using the View menu. Next, right-click the Data Connections node and select Add Connection from the context menu. From the resulting dialog box, select Microsoft SQL Server as the data source. In the next dialog box, select your machine name (or simply *localhost*) from the "Server name" drop-down list and specify the correct logon information. Finally, choose the Cars database from the "Select or enter a database name" drop-down list (see Figure 22-5).

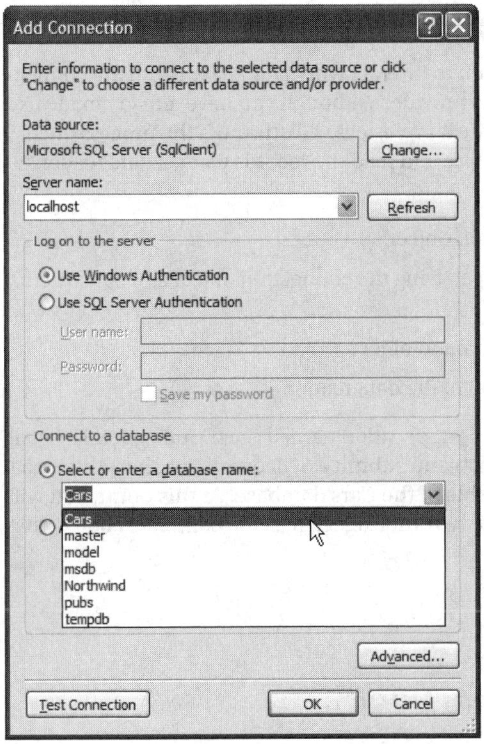

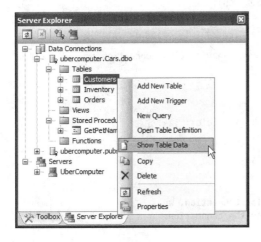

Figure 22-5. *Connecting to the Cars database from Visual Studio 2005*

Once you've finished, you should now see a node for Cars under Data Connections. Notice that you can pull up the records for a given data table simply by right-clicking and selecting Show Table Data (see Figure 22-6).

Figure 22-6. *Viewing table data*

Understanding the Connected Layer of ADO.NET

Recall that the *connected layer* of ADO.NET allows you to interact with a database using the connection, command, and data reader objects of your data provider. Although you have already made use of these objects in the previous DataProviderFactory example, let's walk through the process once again in detail. When you wish to connect to a database and read the records using a data reader object, you need to perform the following steps:

1. Allocate, configure, and open your connection object.

2. Allocate and configure a command object, specifying the connection object as a constructor argument or via the Connection property.

3. Call ExecuteReader() on the configured command object.

4. Process each record using the Read() method of the data reader.

To get the ball rolling, create a brand-new console application named CarsDataReader. The goal is to open a connection (via the SqlConnection object) and submit a SQL query (via the SqlCommand object) to obtain all records within the Inventory table of the Cars database. At this point, you will use a SqlDataReader to print out the results using the type indexer. Here is the complete code within Main(), with analysis to follow:

```
class Program
{
  static void Main(string[] args)
  {
    Console.WriteLine("***** Fun with Data Readers *****\n");

    // Create an open a connection.
    SqlConnection cn = new SqlConnection();
    cn.ConnectionString =
      "uid=sa;pwd=;Initial Catalog=Cars; Data Source=(local)";
    cn.Open();

    // Create a SQL command object.
    string strSQL = "Select * From Inventory";
    SqlCommand myCommand = new SqlCommand(strSQL, cn);

    // Obtain a data reader a la ExecuteReader().
    SqlDataReader myDataReader;
    myDataReader = myCommand.ExecuteReader(CommandBehavior.CloseConnection);

    // Loop over the results.
    while (myDataReader.Read())
    {
      Console.WriteLine("-> Make: {0}, PetName: {1}, Color: {2}.",
        myDataReader["Make"].ToString().Trim(),
        myDataReader["PetName"].ToString().Trim(),
        myDataReader["Color"].ToString().Trim());
    }

    // Because we specified CommandBehavior.CloseConnection, we
    // don't need to explicitly call Close() on the connection.
    myDataReader.Close();
  }
}
```

Working with Connection Objects

The first step to take when working with a data provider is to establish a session with the data source using the connection object (which, as you recall, derives from DbConnection). .NET connection types are provided with a formatted *connection string*, which contains a number of name/value pairs separated by semicolons. This information is used to identify the name of the machine you wish to connect to, required security settings, the name of the database on that machine, and other data provider–specific information.

As you can infer from the preceding code, the Initial Catalog name refers to the database you are attempting to establish a session with (Pubs, Northwind, Cars, etc.). The Data Source name identifies the name of the machine that maintains the database (for simplicity, I have assumed no specific password is required for local system administrators).

■Note Look up the ConnectionString property of your data provider's connection object in the .NET Framework 2.0 SDK documentation to learn about each name/value pair for your specific DBMS.

Once your construction string has been established, a call to Open() establishes your connection with the DBMS. In addition to the ConnectionString, Open(), and Close() members, a connection object provides a number of members that let you configure attritional settings regarding your connection, such as timeout settings and transactional information. Table 22-6 lists some (but not all) members of the DbConnection base class.

Table 22-6. *Members of the* DbConnection *Type*

Member	Meaning in Life
BeginTransaction()	This method is used to begin a database transaction.
ChangeDatabase()	This method changes the database on an open connection.
ConnectionTimeout	This read-only property returns the amount of time to wait while establishing a connection before terminating and generating an error (the default value is 15 seconds). If you wish to change the default, specify a "Connect Timeout" segment in the connection string (e.g., Connect Timeout=30).
Database	This property gets the name of the database maintained by the connection object.
DataSource	This property gets the location of the database maintained by the connection object.
GetSchema()	This method returns a DataSet that contains schema information from the data source.
State	This property sets the current state of the connection, represented by the ConnectionState enumeration.

As you can see, the properties of the DbConnection type are typically read-only in nature and are only useful when you wish to obtain the characteristics of a connection at runtime. When you wish to override default settings, you must alter the construction string itself. For example, the connection string sets the connection timeout setting from 15 seconds to 30 seconds (via the Connect Timeout segment of the connection string):

```
static void Main(string[] args)
{
    SqlConnection cn = new SqlConnection();
```

```
    cn.ConnectionString =
        "uid=sa;pwd=;Initial Catalog=Cars;" +
        "Data Source=(local);Connect Timeout=30";
    cn.Open();

    // New helper function (see below).
    ShowConnectionStatus(cn);
...
}
```

In the preceding code, notice you have now passed your connection object as a parameter to a new static helper method in the Program class named ShowConnectionStatus(), implemented as so:

```
static void ShowConnectionStatus(DbConnection cn)
{
    // Show various stats about current connection object.
    Console.WriteLine("***** Info about your connection *****");
    Console.WriteLine("Database location: {0}", cn.DataSource);
    Console.WriteLine("Database name: {0}", cn.Database);
    Console.WriteLine("Timeout: {0}", cn.ConnectionTimeout);
    Console.WriteLine("Connection state: {0}\n", cn.State.ToString());
}
```

While most of these properties are self-explanatory, the State property is worth special mention. Although this property may be assigned any value of the ConnectionState enumeration

```
public enum System.Data.ConnectionState
{
    Broken, Closed,
    Connecting, Executing,
    Fetching, Open
}
```

the only valid ConnectionState values are ConnectionState.Open and ConnectionState.Closed (the remaining members of this enum are reserved for future use). Also, understand that it is always safe to close a connection whose connection state is currently ConnectionState.Closed.

Working with .NET 2.0 ConnectionStringBuilders

Working with connection strings programmatically can be a bit clunky, given that they are often represented as string literals, which are difficult to maintain and error-prone at best. Under .NET 2.0, the Microsoft-supplied ADO.NET data providers now support *connection string builder objects*, which allow you to establish the name/value pairs using strongly typed properties. Consider the following update to the current Main() method:

```
static void Main(string[] args)
{
    // Create a connection string via the builder object.
    SqlConnectionStringBuilder cnStrBuilder =
        new SqlConnectionStringBuilder();
    cnStrBuilder.UserID = "sa";
    cnStrBuilder.Password = "";
    cnStrBuilder.InitialCatalog = "Cars";
    cnStrBuilder.DataSource = "(local)";
    cnStrBuilder.ConnectTimeout = 30;

    SqlConnection cn = new SqlConnection();
    cn.ConnectionString = cnStrBuilder.ConnectionString;
    cn.Open();
```

```
    ShowConnectionStatus(cn);
...
}
```

In this iteration, you create an instance of SqlConnectionStringBuilder, set the properties accordingly, and obtain the internal string via the ConnectionString property. Also note that you make use of the default constructor of the type. If you so choose, you can also create an instance of your data provider's connection string builder object by passing in an existing connection string as a starting point (which can be helpful when you are reading these values dynamically from an app.config file). Once you have hydrated the object with the initial string data, you can change specific name/value pairs using the related properties, for example:

```
static void Main(string[] args)
{
    Console.WriteLine("***** Fun with Data Readers *****\n");

    // Assume you really obtained cnStr from a *.config file.
    string cnStr = "uid=sa;pwd=;Initial Catalog=Cars;" +
        "Data Source=(local);Connect Timeout=30";

    SqlConnectionStringBuilder cnStrBuilder =
        new SqlConnectionStringBuilder(cnStr);
    cnStrBuilder.UserID = "sa";
    cnStrBuilder.Password = "";
    cnStrBuilder.InitialCatalog = "Cars";
    cnStrBuilder.DataSource = "(local)";

    // Change timeout value.
    cnStrBuilder.ConnectTimeout = 5;
...
}
```

Working with Command Objects

Now that you better understand the role of the connection object, the next order of business is to check out how to submit SQL queries to the database in question. The SqlCommand type (which derives from DbCommand) is an OO representation of a SQL query, table name, or stored procedure. The type of command is specified using the CommandType property, which may take any value from the CommandType enum:

```
public enum System.Data.CommandType
{
    StoredProcedure,
    TableDirect,
    Text    // Default value.
}
```

When creating a command object, you may establish the SQL query as a constructor parameter or directly via the CommandText property. Also when you are creating command object, you need to specify the connection to be used. Again, you may do so as a constructor parameter or via the Connection property:

```
static void Main(string[] args)
{
    SqlConnection cn = new SqlConnection();
...
    // Create command object via ctor args.
```

```
    string strSQL = "Select * From Inventory";
    SqlCommand myCommand = new SqlCommand(strSQL, cn);

    // Create another command object via properties.
    SqlCommand testCommand = new SqlCommand();
    testCommand.Connection = cn;
    testCommand.CommandText = strSQL;
...
}
```

Realize that at this point, you have not literally submitted the SQL query to the Cars database, but rather prepped the state of the command type for future use. Table 22-7 highlights some additional members of the DbCommand type.

Table 22-7. *Members of the* DbCommand *Type*

Member	Meaning in Life
CommandTimeout	Gets or sets the time to wait while executing the command before terminating the attempt and generating an error. The default is 30 seconds.
Connection	Gets or sets the DbConnection used by this instance of the DbCommand.
Parameters	Gets the collection of DbParameter types used for a parameterized query.
Cancel()	Cancels the execution of a command.
ExecuteReader()	Returns the data provider's DbDataReader object, which provides forward-only, read-only access to the underlying data.
ExecuteNonQuery()	Issues the command text to the data store.
ExecuteScalar()	A lightweight version of the ExecuteNonQuery() method, designed specifically for singleton queries (such as obtaining a record count).
ExecuteXmlReader()	Microsoft SQL Server (2000 and higher) is capable of returning result sets as XML. As you might suspect, this method returns a System.Xml.XmlReader that allows you to process the incoming stream of XML.
Prepare()	Creates a prepared (or compiled) version of the command on the data source. As you may know, a *prepared query* executes slightly faster and is useful when you wish to execute the same query multiple times.

Note As illustrated later in this chapter, as of .NET 2.0, the SqlCommand object has been updated with additional members that facilitate asynchronous database interactions.

Working with Data Readers

Once you have established the active connection and SQL command, the next step is to submit the query to the data source. As you might guess, you have a number of ways to do so. The DbDataReader type (which implements IDataReader) is the simplest and fastest way to obtain information from a data store. Recall that data readers represent a read-only, forward-only stream of data returned one record at a time. Given this, it should stand to reason that data readers are useful only when submitting SQL selection statements to the underlying data store.

Data readers are useful when you need to iterate over large amounts of data very quickly and have no need to maintain an in-memory representation. For example, if you request 20,000 records from a table to store in a text file, it would be rather memory-intensive to hold this information in a DataSet. A better approach is to create a data reader that spins over each record as rapidly as possible. Be aware, however, that data reader objects (unlike data adapter objects, which you'll examine later) maintain an open connection to their data source until you explicitly close the session.

Data reader objects are obtained from the command object via a call to ExecuteReader(). When invoking this method, you may optionally instruct the reader to automatically close down the related connection object by specifying CommandBehavior.CloseConnection.

The following use of the data reader leverages the Read() method to determine when you have reached the end of your records (via a false return value). For each incoming record, you are making use of the type indexer to print out the make, pet name, and color of each automobile. Also note that you call Close() as soon as you are finished processing the records, to free up the connection object:

```
static void Main(string[] args)
{
...
    // Obtain a data reader a la ExecuteReader().
    SqlDataReader myDataReader;
    myDataReader = myCommand.ExecuteReader(CommandBehavior.CloseConnection);

    // Loop over the results.
    while (myDataReader.Read())
    {
        Console.WriteLine("-> Make: {0}, PetName: {1}, Color: {2}.",
            myDataReader["Make"].ToString().Trim(),
            myDataReader["PetName"].ToString().Trim(),
            myDataReader["Color"].ToString().Trim());
    }
    myDataReader.Close();
    ShowConnectionStatus(cn);
}
```

■Note The trimming of the string data shown here is only used to remove trailing blank spaces in the database entries; it is not directly related to ADO.NET!

The indexer of a data reader object has been overloaded to take either a string (representing the name of the column) or an integer (representing the column's ordinal position). Thus, you could clean up the current reader logic (and avoid hard-coded string names) with the following update (note the use of the FieldCount property):

```
while (myDataReader.Read())
{
    Console.WriteLine("***** Record *****");
    for (int i = 0; i < myDataReader.FieldCount; i++)
    {
        Console.WriteLine("{0} = {1} ",
            myDataReader.GetName(i),
            myDataReader.GetValue(i).ToString().Trim());
    }
    Console.WriteLine();
}
```

If you compile and run your project, you should be presented with a list of all automobiles in the Inventory table of the Cars database (see Figure 22-7).

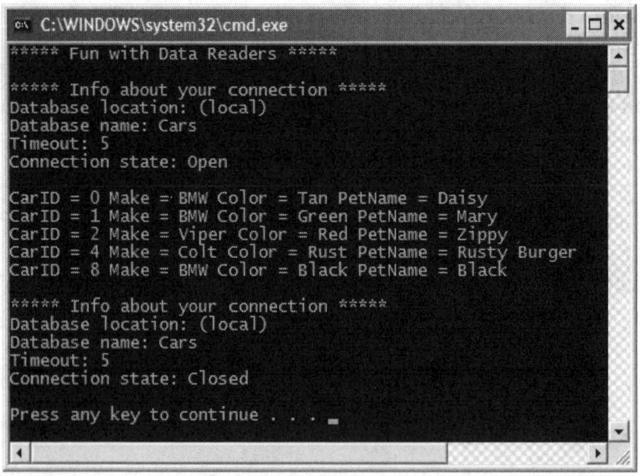

Figure 22-7. *Fun with data reader objects*

Obtaining Multiple Result Sets Using a Data Reader

Data reader objects are able to obtain multiple result sets from a single command object. For example, if you are interested in obtaining all rows from the Inventory table as well as all rows from the Customers table, you are able to specify both SQL select statements using a semicolon delimiter:

```
string theSQL = "Select * From Inventory;Select * from Customers";
```

Once you obtain the data reader, you are able to iterate over each result set via the NextResult() method. Do be aware that you are always returned the first result set automatically. Thus, if you wish to read over the rows of each table, you will be able to build the following iteration construct:

```
do
{
    while(myDataReader.Read())
    {
        // Read the info of the current result set.
    }
}while(myDataReader.NextResult());
```

So, at this point, you should be more aware of the functionality data reader objects bring to the table. While these objects provide additional bits of functionality than I have shown here (such as the ability to execute scalars and single-row queries), I'll leave it to interested readers to consult the .NET Framework 2.0 SDK documentation for complete details.

■**Source Code** The CarsDataReader project is included under the Chapter 22 subdirectory.

Modifying Tables Using Command Objects

As you have just seen, the ExecuteReader() method extracts a data reader object that allows you to examine the results of a SQL Select statement using a forward-only, read-only flow of information. However, when you wish to submit SQL commands that result in the modification of a given table, you will call the ExecuteNonQuery() method of your command object. This single method will perform inserts, updates, and deletes based on the format of your command text.

To illustrate how to modify an existing database using nothing more than a call to ExecuteNonQuery(), you will now build a new console application (CarsInventoryUpdater) that allows the caller to modify the Inventory table of the Cars database. Like in other examples in this text, the Main() method is responsible for prompting the user for a specific course of action and executing that request via a switch statement. This program will allow the user to enter the following commands:

- **I**: Inserts a new record into the Inventory table
- **U**: Updates an existing record in the Inventory table
- **D**: Deletes an existing record from the Inventory table
- **L**: Displays the current inventory using a data reader
- **S**: Shows these options to the user
- **Q**: Quits the program

Each possible option is handled by a unique static method within the Program class. For the purpose of completion, here is the implementation of Main(), which I assume requires no further comment:

```
static void Main(string[] args)
{
    Console.WriteLine("***** Car Inventory Updater *****");
    bool userDone = false;
    string userCommand = "";

    SqlConnection cn = new SqlConnection();
    cn.ConnectionString =
        "uid=sa;pwd=;Initial Catalog=Cars;" +
        "Data Source=(local);Connect Timeout=30";
    cn.Open();

    ShowInstructions();
    do
    {
        Console.Write("Please enter your command: ");
        userCommand = Console.ReadLine();
        Console.WriteLine();
        switch (userCommand.ToUpper())
        {
            case "I":
                InsertNewCar(cn);
                break;
            case "U":
                UpdateCarPetName(cn);
                break;
            case "D":
                DeleteCar(cn);
                break;
            case "L":
                ListInventory(cn);
                break;
            case "S":
                ShowInstructions();
                break;
            case "Q":
                userDone = true;
                break;
```

```
            default:
                Console.WriteLine("Bad data!  Try again");
                break;
        }
    } while (!userDone);
    cn.Close();
}
```

The ShowInstructions() method does what you would expect:

```
private static void ShowInstructions()
{
    Console.WriteLine();
    Console.WriteLine("I: Inserts a new car.");
    Console.WriteLine("U: Updated an existing car.");
    Console.WriteLine("D: Deletes an existing car.");
    Console.WriteLine("L: List current inventory.");
    Console.WriteLine("S: Show these instructions.");
    Console.WriteLine("Q: Quits program.");
}
```

As mentioned, ListInventory() prints out the current rows of the Inventory table using a data reader object (the code is identical to the previous CarsDataReader example):

```
private static void ListInventory(SqlConnection cn)
{
    string strSQL = "Select * From Inventory";
    SqlCommand myCommand = new SqlCommand(strSQL, cn);
    SqlDataReader myDataReader;
    myDataReader = myCommand.ExecuteReader();
    while (myDataReader.Read())
    {
        for (int i = 0; i < myDataReader.FieldCount; i++)
        {
            Console.Write("{0} = {1} ",
                myDataReader.GetName(i),
                myDataReader.GetValue(i).ToString().Trim());
        }
        Console.WriteLine();
    }
    myDataReader.Close();
}
```

Now that the CUI is in place, let's move on to the good stuff.

Inserting New Records

Inserting a new record into the Inventory table is as simple as formatting the SQL insert statement (based on user input) and calling ExecuteNonQuery(). To keep the code crisp, I have deleted the necessary try/catch logic that is present in the code download for this text:

```
private static void InsertNewCar(SqlConnection cn)
{
    // Gather info about new car.
    Console.Write("Enter CarID: ");
    int newCarID =  int.Parse(Console.ReadLine());
    Console.Write("Enter Make: ");
    string newCarMake = Console.ReadLine();
    Console.Write("Enter Color: ");
```

```
    string newCarColor = Console.ReadLine();
    Console.Write("Enter PetName: ");
    string newCarPetName = Console.ReadLine();

    // Format and execute SQL statement.
    string sql = string.Format("Insert Into Inventory" +
        "(CarID, Make, Color, PetName) Values" +
        "('{0}', '{1}', '{2}', '{3}')", newCarID, newCarMake,
        newCarColor, newCarPetName);
    SqlCommand cmd = new SqlCommand(sql, cn);
    cmd.ExecuteNonQuery();
}
```

■**Note** As you may know, building a SQL statement using string concatenation can be risky from a security point of view (think: SQL injection attacks). While I use this approach during this chapter for purposes of brevity, the preferred way to build command text is using a parameterized query, which I describe shortly.

Deleting Existing Records

Deleting an existing record is just as simple as inserting a new record. Unlike the code listing for InsertNewCar(), I will show one important try/catch scope that handles the possibility of attempting to delete a car that is currently on order for an individual in the Customers table (which will be used later in this chapter):

```
private static void DeleteCar(SqlConnection cn)
{
    // Get ID of car to delete, then do so.
    Console.Write("Enter CarID of car to delete: ");
    int carToDelete = int.Parse(Console.ReadLine());
    string sql = string.Format("Delete from Inventory where CarID = '{0}'",
        carToDelete);
    SqlCommand cmd = new SqlCommand(sql, cn);
    try { cmd.ExecuteNonQuery(); }
    catch { Console.WriteLine("Sorry!  That car is on order!"); }
}
```

Updating Existing Records

If you followed the code behind DeleteCar() and InsertNewCar(), then UpdateCarPetName() is a no-brainer (again, try/catch logic has been removed for clarity):

```
private static void UpdateCarPetName(SqlConnection cn)
{
    // Get ID of car to modify and new pet name.
    Console.Write("Enter CarID of car to modify: ");
    string newPetName = "";
    int carToUpdate = carToUpdate = int.Parse(Console.ReadLine());
    Console.Write("Enter new pet name: ");
    newPetName = Console.ReadLine();

    // Now update record.
    string sql =
        string.Format("Update Inventory Set PetName = '{0}' Where CarID = '{1}'",
```

```
            newPetName, carToUpdate);
    SqlCommand cmd = new SqlCommand(sql, cn);
    cmd.ExecuteNonQuery();
}
```

With this, our application is finished. Figure 22-8 shows a test run.

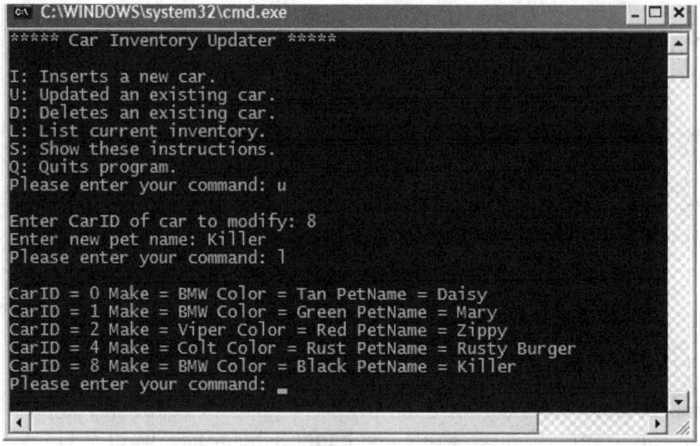

Figure 22-8. *Inserting, updating, and deleting records via command objects*

Working with Parameterized Command Objects

The previous insert, update, and delete logic works as expected; however, note that each of your SQL queries is represented using hard-coded string literals. As you may know, a *parameterized query* can be used to treat SQL parameters as objects, rather than a simple blob of text. Typically, parameterized queries execute much faster than a literal SQL string, in that they are parsed exactly once (rather than each time the SQL string is assigned to the CommandText property). As well, parameterized queries also help protect against SQL injection attacks (a well-known data access security issue).

ADO.NET command objects maintain a collection of discrete parameter types. By default this collection is empty, but you are free to insert any number of parameter objects that map to a "placeholder parameter" in the SQL query. When you wish to associate a parameter within a SQL query to a member in the command object's parameters collection, prefix the SQL text parameter with an at (@) symbol (at least when using Microsoft SQL Server; not all DBMSs support this notation).

Specifying Parameters Using the DbParameter Type

Before you build a parameterized query, let's get to know the DbParameter type (which is the base class to a provider's specific parameter object). This class maintains a number of properties that allow you to configure the name, size, and data type of the parameter, as well as other characteristics such as the parameter's direction of travel. Table 22-8 describes some key properties of the DbParameter type.

Table 22-8. *Key Members of the* DbParameter *Type*

Property	Meaning in Life
DbType	Gets or sets the native data type from the data source, represented as a CLR data type
Direction	Gets or sets whether the parameter is input-only, output-only, bidirectional, or a return value parameter
IsNullable	Gets or sets whether the parameter accepts null values
ParameterName	Gets or sets the name of the DbParameter
Size	Gets or sets the maximum parameter size of the data
Value	Gets or sets the value of the parameter

To illustrate, let's rework the previous InsertNewCar() method to make use of parameter objects. Here is the relevant code:

```
private static void InsertNewCar(SqlConnection cn)
{
...
    // Note the 'placeholders' in the SQL query.
    string sql = string.Format("Insert Into Inventory" +
        "(CarID, Make, Color, PetName) Values" +
        "(@CarID, @Make, @Color, @PetName)");

    // Fill params collection.
    SqlCommand cmd = new SqlCommand(sql, cn);
    SqlParameter param = new SqlParameter();
    param.ParameterName = "@CarID";
    param.Value = newCarID;
    param.SqlDbType = SqlDbType.Int;
    cmd.Parameters.Add(param);

    param = new SqlParameter();
    param.ParameterName = "@Make";
    param.Value = newCarMake;
    param.SqlDbType = SqlDbType.Char;
    param.Size = 20;
    cmd.Parameters.Add(param);

    param = new SqlParameter();
    param.ParameterName = "@Color";
    param.Value = newCarColor;
    param.SqlDbType = SqlDbType.Char;
    param.Size = 20;
    cmd.Parameters.Add(param);

    param = new SqlParameter();
    param.ParameterName = "@PetName";
    param.Value = newCarPetName;
    param.SqlDbType = SqlDbType.Char;
    param.Size = 20;
    cmd.Parameters.Add(param);
    cmd.ExecuteNonQuery();
}
```

While building a parameterized query requires a larger amount of code, the end result is a more convenient way to tweak SQL statements programmatically as well as better overall performance. While you are free to make use of this technique whenever a SQL query is involved, parameterized queries are most helpful when you wish to trigger a stored procedure.

■**Note** Here, I made use of various properties to establish a parameter object. Do know, however, that parameter objects support a number of overloaded constructors that allow you to set the values of various properties (which will result in a more compact code base).

Executing a Stored Procedure Using DbCommand

A *stored procedure* is a named block of SQL code stored in the database. Stored procedures can be constructed to return a set of rows or scalar data types and may take any number of optional parameters. The end result is a unit of work that behaves like a typical function, with the obvious difference of being located on a data store rather than a binary business object.

■**Note** Although I don't cover this topic in this chapter, it is worth pointing out that the newest version of Microsoft SQL Server (2005) is a CLR host! Therefore, stored procedures (and other database atoms) can be authored using managed languages (such as C#) rather than traditional SQL. Consult http://www.microsoft.com/sql/2005 for further details.

To illustrate the process, let's add a new option to the CarInventoryUpdate program that allows the caller to look up a car's pet name via the GetPetName stored procedure. This database object was established when you installed the Cars database and looks like this:

```
CREATE PROCEDURE GetPetName
@carID int,
@petName char(20) output
AS
SELECT @petName = PetName from Inventory where CarID = @carID
```

First, update the current switch statement in Main() to handle a new case for "P" that calls a new helper function named LookUpPetName() that takes a SqlConnection parameter and returns void. Update your ShowInstructions() method to account for this new option.

When you wish to execute a stored procedure, you begin as always by creating a new connection object, configuring your connection string, and opening the session. However, when you create your command object, the CommandText property is set to the name of the stored procedure (rather than a SQL query). As well, you must be sure to set the CommandType property to CommandType.StoredProcedure (the default is CommandType.Text).

Given that this stored procedure has one input and one output parameter, your goal is to build a command object that contains two SqlParameter objects within its parameter collection:

```
private static void LookUpPetName(SqlConnection cn)
{
    // Get the CarID.
    Console.Write("Enter CarID: ");
    int carID = int.Parse(Console.ReadLine());

    // Establish name of stored proc.
    SqlCommand cmd = new SqlCommand("GetPetName", cn);
    cmd.CommandType = CommandType.StoredProcedure;
```

```
// Input param.
SqlParameter param = new SqlParameter();
param.ParameterName = "@carID";
param.SqlDbType = SqlDbType.Int;
param.Value = carID;
param.Direction = ParameterDirection.Input;
cmd.Parameters.Add(param);

// Output param.
param = new SqlParameter();
param.ParameterName = "@petName";
param.SqlDbType = SqlDbType.Char;
param.Size = 20;
param.Direction = ParameterDirection.Output;
cmd.Parameters.Add(param);

// Execute the stored proc.
cmd.ExecuteNonQuery();

// Print output param.
Console.WriteLine("Pet name for car {0} is {1}",
    carID, cmd.Parameters["@petName"].Value);
}
```

Notice that the Direction property of the parameter object allows you to specify input and output parameters. Once the stored procedure completes via a call to ExecuteNonQuery(), you are able to obtain the value of the output parameter by investigating the command object's parameter collection. Figure 22-9 shows one possible test run.

Figure 22-9. *Triggering a stored proceedure*

Source Code The CarsInventoryUpdater application is included under the Chapter 22 subdirectory.

Asynchronous Data Access Under .NET 2.0

As of .NET 2.0, the SQL data provider (represented by the System.Data.SqlClient namespace) has been enhanced to support asynchronous database interactions via the following new members of SqlCommand:

- BeginExecuteReader()/EndExecuteReader()
- BeginExecuteNonQuery()/EndExecuteNonQuery()
- BeginExecuteXmlReader()/EndExecuteXmlReader()

Given your work in Chapter 14, the naming convention of these method pairs may ring a bell. Recall that the .NET asynchronous delegate pattern makes use of a "begin" method to execute a task on a secondary thread, whereas the "end" method can be used to obtain the result of the asynchronous invocation using the members of IAsyncResult and the optional AsyncCallback delegate. Because the process of working with asynchronous commands is modeled after the standard delegate patterns, a simple example should suffice (so be sure to consult Chapter 14 for full details of asynchronous delegates).

Assume you wish to select the records from the Inventory table on a secondary thread of execution using a data reader object. Here is the complete Main() method, with analysis to follow:

```
static void Main(string[] args)
{
    Console.WriteLine("***** Fun with ASNYC Data Readers *****\n");

    // Create an open a connection that is async-aware.
    SqlConnection cn = new SqlConnection();
    cn.ConnectionString =
        "uid=sa;pwd=;Initial Catalog=Cars;" +
        "Asynchronous Processing=true;Data Source=(local)";
    cn.Open();

    // Create a SQL command object that waits for approx 2 seconds.
    string strSQL = "WaitFor Delay '00:00:02';Select * From Inventory";
    SqlCommand myCommand = new SqlCommand(strSQL, cn);

    // Execute the reader on a second thread.
    IAsyncResult itfAsynch;
    itfAsynch = myCommand.BeginExecuteReader(CommandBehavior.CloseConnection);

    // Do something while other thread works.
    while (!itfAsynch.IsCompleted)
    {
        Console.WriteLine("Working on main thread...");
        Thread.Sleep(1000);
    }
    Console.WriteLine();

    // All done!  Get reader and loop over results.
    SqlDataReader myDataReader = myCommand.EndExecuteReader(itfAsynch);
    while (myDataReader.Read())
    {
        Console.WriteLine("-> Make: {0}, PetName: {1}, Color: {2}.",
            myDataReader["Make"].ToString().Trim(),
            myDataReader["PetName"].ToString().Trim(),
            myDataReader["Color"].ToString().Trim());
```

```
    }
    myDataReader.Close();
}
```

The first point of interest is the fact that you need to enable asynchronous activity using the new Asynchronous Processing segment of the connection string. Also note that you have padded into the command text of your SqlCommand object a new WaitFor Delay segment simply to simulate a long-running database interaction.

Beyond these points, notice that the call to BeginExecuteDataReader() returns the expected IasyncResult-compatible type, which is used to synchronize the calling thread (via the IsCompleted property) as well as obtain the SqlDataReader once the query has finished executing.

■**Source Code** The AsyncCmdObject application is included under the Chapter 22 subdirectory.

Understanding the Disconnected Layer of ADO.NET

As you have seen, working with the connected layer allows you to interact with a database using connection, command, and data reader objects. With this small handful of types, you are able to select, insert, update, and delete records to your heart's content (as well as trigger stored procedures). In reality, however, you have seen only half of the ADO.NET story. Recall that the ADO.NET object model can be used in a *disconnected* manner.

When you work with the disconnected layer of ADO.NET, you will still make use of connection and command objects. In addition, you will leverage a specific object named a *data adapter* (which extends the abstract DbDataAdapter) to fetch and update data. Unlike the connected layer, data obtained via a data adapter is not processed using data reader objects. Rather, data adapter objects make use of DataSet objects to move data between the caller and data source. The DataSet type is a container for any number of DataTable objects, each of which contains a collection of DataRow and DataColumn objects.

The data adapter object of your data provider handles the database connection automatically. In an attempt to increase scalability, data adapters keep the connection open for the shortest possible amount of time. Once the caller receives the DataSet object, he is completely disconnected from the DBMS and left with a local copy of the remote data. The caller is free to insert, delete, or update rows from a given DataTable, but the physical database is not updated until the caller explicitly passes the DataSet to the data adapter for updating. In a nutshell, DataSets allow the clients to pretend they are indeed always connected, when in fact they are operating on an in-memory database (see Figure 22-10).

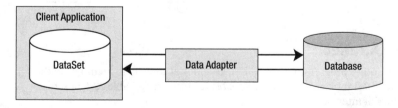

Figure 22-10. *Data adapter objects move* DataSets *to and from the client tier.*

Given that the centerpiece of the disconnected layer is the DataSet type, your next task is to learn how to manipulate a DataSet manually. Once you understand how to do so, you will have no problem manipulating the contents of a DataSet retrieved from a data adapter object.

Understanding the Role of the DataSet

Simply put, a DataSet is an in-memory representation of external data. More specifically, a DataSet is a class type that maintains three internal strongly typed collections (see Figure 22-11).

Figure 22-11. *The anatomy of a* DataSet

The Tables property of the DataSet allows you to access the DataTableCollection that contains the individual DataTables. Another important collection used by the DataSet is the DataRelationCollection. Given that a DataSet is a disconnected version of a database schema, it can programmatically represent the parent/child relationships between its tables. For example, a relation can be created between two tables to model a foreign key constraint using the DataRelation type. This object can then be added to the DataRelationCollection through the Relations property. At this point, you can navigate between the connected tables as you search for data. You will see how this is done a bit later in the chapter.

The ExtendedProperties property provides access to the PropertyCollection object, which allows you to associate any extra information to the DataSet as name/value pairs. This information can literally be anything at all, even if it has no bearing on the data itself. For example, you can associate your company's name to a DataSet, which can then function as in-memory metadata. Other examples of extended properties might include timestamps, an encrypted password that must be supplied to access the contents of the DataSet, a number representing a data refresh rate, and so forth.

■**Note** The DataTable class also supports extended properties via the ExtendedProperties property.

Members of the DataSet

Before exploring too many other programmatic details, take a look at some core members of the DataSet. Beyond the Tables, Relations, and ExtendedProperties properties, Table 22-9 describes some additional properties of interest.

Table 22-9. *Properties of the Mighty* DataSet

Property	Meaning in Life
CaseSensitive	Indicates whether string comparisons in DataTable objects are case sensitive (or not).
DataSetName	Represents the friendly name of this DataSet. Typically this value is established as a constructor parameter.
EnforceConstraints	Gets or sets a value indicating whether constraint rules are followed when attempting any update operation.
HasErrors	Gets a value indicating whether there are errors in any of the rows in any of the DataTables of the DataSet.
RemotingFormat	This new .NET 2.0 property allows you to define how the DataSet should serialize its content (binary or XML) for the .NET remoting layer.

The methods of the DataSet mimic some of the functionality provided by the aforementioned properties. In addition to interacting with XML streams, the DataSet provides methods that allow you to copy/clone the contents of your DataSet, as well as establish the beginning and ending points of a batch of updates. Table 22-10 describes some core methods.

Table 22-10. *Methods of the Mighty* DataSet

Methods	Meaning in Life
AcceptChanges()	Commits all the changes made to this DataSet since it was loaded or the last time AcceptChanges() was called.
Clear()	Completely clears the DataSet data by removing every row in each DataTable.
Clone()	Clones the structure of the DataSet, including all DataTables, as well as all relations and any constraints.
Copy()	Copies both the structure and data for this DataSet.
GetChanges()	Returns a copy of the DataSet containing all changes made to it since it was last loaded or since AcceptChanges() was called.
GetChildRelations()	Returns the collection of child relations that belong to a specified table.
GetParentRelations()	Gets the collection of parent relations that belong to a specified table.
HasChanges()	Overloaded. Gets a value indicating whether the DataSet has changes, including new, deleted, or modified rows.
Merge()	Overloaded. Merges this DataSet with a specified DataSet.
ReadXml() ReadXmlSchema()	Allow you to read XML data from a valid stream (file based, memory based, or network based) into the DataSet.
RejectChanges()	Rolls back all the changes made to this DataSet since it was created or the last time DataSet.AcceptChanges was called.
WriteXml() WriteXmlSchema()	Allow you to write out the contents of a DataSet into a valid stream.

Now that you have a better understanding of the role of the DataSet (and some idea of what you can do with one), create a new console application named SimpleDataSet. Within the Main() method, define a new DataSet object that contains two extended properties representing your company name and timestamp (don't forget to "use" System.Data):

```
class Program
{
    static void Main(string[] args)
    {
        Console.WriteLine("***** Fun with DataSets *****\n");

        // Create the DataSet object.
        DataSet carsInventoryDS = new DataSet("Car Inventory");
        carsInventoryDS.ExtendedProperties["TimeStamp"] = DateTime.Now;
        carsInventoryDS.ExtendedProperties["Company"] = "Intertech Training";
    }
}
```

A DataSet without DataTables is a bit like a workweek without a weekend. Therefore, the next task is to examine the internal composition of the DataTable, beginning with the DataColumn type.

Working with DataColumns

The DataColumn type represents a single column within a DataTable. Collectively speaking, the set of all DataColumn types bound to a given DataTable represents the foundation of a table's schema information. For example, if you were to model the Inventory table of the Cars database, you would create four DataColumns, one for each column (CarID, Make, Color, and PetName). Once you have created your DataColumn objects, they are typically added into the columns collection of the DataTable type (via the Columns property).

If you have a background in relational database theory, you know that a given column in a data table can be assigned a set of constraints (e.g., configured as a primary key, assigned a default value, configured to contain read-only information, etc.). Also, every column in a table must map to an underlying data type. For example, the Inventory table's schema requires that the CarID column map to an integer, while Make, Color, and PetName map to an array of characters. The DataColumn class has numerous properties that allow you to configure these very things. Table 22-11 provides a rundown of some core properties.

Table 22-11. *Properties of the* DataColumn

Properties	Meaning in Life
AllowDBNull	This property is used to indicate if a row can specify null values in this column. The default value is true.
AutoIncrement AutoIncrementSeed AutoIncrementStep	These properties are used to configure the autoincrement behavior for a given column. This can be helpful when you wish to ensure unique values in a given DataColumn (such as a primary key). By default, a DataColumn does not support autoincrement behavior
Caption	This property gets or sets the caption to be displayed for this column (e.g., what the end user sees in a DataGridView).
ColumnMapping	This property determines how a DataColumn is represented when a DataSet is saved as an XML document using the DataSet.WriteXml() method.
ColumnName	This property gets or sets the name of the column in the Columns collection (meaning how it is represented internally by the DataTable). If you do not set the ColumnName explicitly, the default values are Column with ($n+1$) numerical suffixes (i.e., Column1, Column2, Column3, etc.).
DataType	This property defines the data type (Boolean, string, float, etc.) stored in the column.
DefaultValue	This property gets or sets the default value assigned to this column when inserting new rows. This is used if not otherwise specified.

Properties	Meaning in Life
Expression	This property gets or sets the expression used to filter rows, calculate a column's value, or create an aggregate column.
Ordinal	This property gets the numerical position of the column in the Columns collection maintained by the DataTable.
ReadOnly	This property determines if this column can be modified once a row has been added to the table. The default is false.
Table	This property gets the DataTable that contains this DataColumn.
Unique	This property gets or sets a value indicating whether the values in each row of the column must be unique or if repeating values are permissible. If a column is assigned a primary key constraint, the Unique property should be set to true.

Building a DataColumn

To continue with the SimpleDataSet project (and illustrate the use of the DataColumn), assume you wish to model the columns of the Inventory table. Given that the CarID column will be the table's primary key, you will configure the DataColumn object as read-only, unique, and non-null (using the ReadOnly, Unique, and AllowDBNull properties). Update the Main() method to build four DataColumn objects:

```
static void Main(string[] args)
{
...
    // Create data columns that map to the
    // 'real' columns in the Inventory table
    // of the Cars database.
    DataColumn carIDColumn = new DataColumn("CarID", typeof(int));
    carIDColumn.Caption = "Car ID";
    carIDColumn.ReadOnly = true;
    carIDColumn.AllowDBNull = false;
    carIDColumn.Unique = true;

    DataColumn carMakeColumn = new DataColumn("Make", typeof(string));
    DataColumn carColorColumn = new DataColumn("Color", typeof(string));
    DataColumn carPetNameColumn = new DataColumn("PetName", typeof(string));
    carPetNameColumn.Caption = "Pet Name";
}
```

Enabling Autoincrementing Fields

One aspect of the DataColumn you may choose to configure is its ability to *autoincrement*. Simply put, autoincrementing columns are used to ensure that when a new row is added to a given table, the value of this column is assigned automatically, based on the current step of the incrementation. This can be helpful when you wish to ensure that a column has no repeating values (such as a primary key).

This behavior is controlled using the AutoIncrement, AutoIncrementSeed, and AutoIncrementStep properties. The seed value is used to mark the starting value of the column, whereas the step value identifies the number to add to the seed when incrementing. Consider the following update to the construction of the carIDColumn DataColumn:

```
static void Main(string[] args)
{
...
    DataColumn carIDColumn = new DataColumn("CarID", typeof(int));
```

```
    carIDColumn.ReadOnly = true;
    carIDColumn.Caption = "Car ID";
    carIDColumn.AllowDBNull = false;
    carIDColumn.Unique = true;
    carIDColumn.AutoIncrement = true;
    carIDColumn.AutoIncrementSeed = 0;
    carIDColumn.AutoIncrementStep = 1;
}
```

Here, the carIDColumn object has been configured to ensure that as rows are added to the respective table, the value for this column is incremented by 1. Because the seed has been set at 0, this column would be numbered 0, 1, 2, 3, and so forth.

Adding a DataColumn to a DataTable

The DataColumn type does not typically exist as a stand-alone entity, but is instead inserted into a related DataTable. To illustrate, create a new DataTable type (fully detailed in just a moment) and insert each DataColumn object in the columns collection using the Columns property:

```
static void Main(string[] args)
{
...
    // Now add DataColumns to a DataTable.
    DataTable inventoryTable = new DataTable("Inventory");
    inventoryTable.Columns.AddRange(new DataColumn[]
        { carIDColumn, carMakeColumn, carColorColumn, carPetNameColumn });
}
```

Working with DataRows

As you have seen, a collection of DataColumn objects represents the schema of a DataTable. In contrast, a collection of DataRow types represents the actual data in the table. Thus, if you have 20 listings in the Inventory table of the Cars database, you can represent these records using 20 DataRow types. Using the members of the DataRow class, you are able to insert, remove, evaluate, and manipulate the values in the table. Table 22-12 documents some (but not all) of the members of the DataRow type.

Table 22-12. *Key Members of the* DataRow *Type*

Members	Meaning in Life
HasErrors GetColumnsInError() GetColumnError() ClearErrors() RowError	The HasErrors property returns a Boolean value indicating if there are errors. If so, the GetColumnsInError() method can be used to obtain the offending members, and GetColumnError() can be used to obtain the error description, while the ClearErrors() method removes each error listing for the row. The RowError property allows you to configure a textual description of the error for a given row.
ItemArray	This property gets or sets all of the values for this row using an array of objects.
RowState	This property is used to pinpoint the current "state" of the DataRow using values of the RowState enumeration.
Table	This property is used to obtain a reference to the DataTable containing this DataRow.
AcceptChanges() RejectChanges()	These methods commit or reject all changes made to this row since the last time AcceptChanges() was called.

Members	Meaning in Life
BeginEdit() EndEdit() CancelEdit()	These methods begin, end, or cancel an edit operation on a DataRow object.
Delete()	This method marks this row to be removed when the AcceptChanges() method is called.
IsNull()	This method gets a value indicating whether the specified column contains a null value.

Working with a DataRow is a bit different from working with a DataColumn, because you cannot create a direct instance of this type; rather, you obtain a reference from a given DataTable. For example, assume you wish to insert two rows in the Inventory table. The DataTable.NewRow() method allows you to obtain the next slot in the table, at which point you can fill each column with new data via the type indexer, as shown here:

```
static void Main(string[] args)
{
...
    // Now add some rows to the Inventory Table.
    DataRow carRow = inventoryTable.NewRow();
    carRow["Make"] = "BMW";
    carRow["Color"] = "Black";
    carRow["PetName"] = "Hamlet";
    inventoryTable.Rows.Add(carRow);

    carRow = inventoryTable.NewRow();
    carRow["Make"] = "Saab";
    carRow["Color"] = "Red";
    carRow["PetName"] = "Sea Breeze";
    inventoryTable.Rows.Add(carRow);
}
```

Notice how the DataRow class defines an indexer that can be used to gain access to a given DataColumn by numerical position as well as column name. At this point, you have a single DataTable containing two rows.

Understanding the DataRow.RowState Property

The RowState property is useful when you need to programmatically identify the set of all rows in a table that have changed, have been newly inserted, and so forth. This property may be assigned any value from the DataRowState enumeration, as shown in Table 22-13.

Table 22-13. *Values of the* DataRowState *Enumeration*

Value	Meaning in Life
Added	The row has been added to a DataRowCollection, and AcceptChanges() has not been called.
Deleted	The row has been deleted via the Delete() method of the DataRow.
Detached	The row has been created but is not part of any DataRowCollection. A DataRow is in this state immediately after it has been created and before it is added to a collection, or if it has been removed from a collection.
Modified	The row has been modified, and AcceptChanges() has not been called.
Unchanged	The row has not changed since AcceptChanges() was last called.

While you are programmatically manipulating the rows of a given `DataTable`, the `RowState` property is set automatically:

```
static void Main(string[] args)
{
...
    DataRow carRow = inventoryTable.NewRow();
    // Prints out: Row State is: Detatched.
    Console.WriteLine("Row State is: {0}.", carRow.RowState);
    carRow["Make"] = "BMW";
    carRow["Color"] = "Black";
    carRow["PetName"] = "Hamlet";
    inventoryTable.Rows.Add(carRow);

    // Prints out: Row State is: Added.
    Console.WriteLine("Row State is: {0}.", inventoryTable.Rows[0].RowState);
...
}
```

As you can see, the ADO.NET `DataRow` is smart enough to remember its current state of affairs. Given this, the owning `DataTable` is able to identify which rows have been modified. This is a key feature of the `DataSet`, as when it comes time to send updated information to the data store, only the modified data is submitted.

Working with DataTables

The `DataTable` defines a good number of members, many of which are identical in name and functionality to those of the `DataSet`. Table 22-14 describes some core properties of the `DataTable` type beyond `Rows` and `Columns`.

Table 22-14. *Key Members of the* `DataTable` *Type*

Property	Meaning in Life
CaseSensitive	Indicates whether string comparisons within the table are case sensitive (or not). The default value is false.
ChildRelations	Returns the collection of child relations for this `DataTable` (if any).
Constraints	Gets the collection of constraints maintained by the table.
DataSet	Gets the `DataSet` that contains this table (if any).
DefaultView	Gets a customized view of the table that may include a filtered view or a cursor position.
MinimumCapacity	Gets or sets the initial number of rows in this table (the default is 25).
ParentRelations	Gets the collection of parent relations for this `DataTable`.
PrimaryKey	Gets or sets an array of columns that function as primary keys for the data table.
RemotingFormat	Allows you to define how the `DataSet` should serialize its content (binary or XML) for the .NET remoting layer. This property is new in .NET 2.0.
TableName	Gets or sets the name of the table. This same property may also be specified as a constructor parameter.

For the current example, let's set the PrimaryKey property of the DataTable to the carIDColumn DataColumn object:

```
static void Main(string[] args)
{
...
    // Mark the primary key of this table.
    inventoryTable.PrimaryKey = new DataColumn[] { inventoryTable.Columns[0] };
}
```

Once you do this, the DataTable example is complete. The final step is to insert your DataTable into the carsInventoryDS DataSet object. Then you'll pass your DataSet to a (yet to be written) helper method named PrintDataSet():

```
static void Main(string[] args)
{
...
    // Finally, add our table to the DataSet.
    carsInventoryDS.Tables.Add(inventoryTable);
    // Now print the DataSet.
    PrintDataSet(carsInventoryDS);
}
```

The PrintDataSet() method simply iterates over each DataTable in the DataSet, printing out the column names and row values using the type indexers:

```
static void PrintDataSet(DataSet ds)
{
    Console.WriteLine("Tables in '{0}' DataSet.\n", ds.DataSetName);
    foreach (DataTable dt in ds.Tables)
    {
        Console.WriteLine("{0} Table.\n", dt.TableName);

        // Print out the column names.
        for (int curCol = 0; curCol < dt.Columns.Count; curCol++)
        {
            Console.Write(dt.Columns[curCol].ColumnName.Trim() + "\t");
        }
        Console.WriteLine("\n----------------------------------");

        // Print the DataTable.
        for (int curRow = 0; curRow < dt.Rows.Count; curRow++)
        {
            for (int curCol = 0; curCol < dt.Columns.Count; curCol++)
            {
                Console.Write(dt.Rows[curRow][curCol].ToString() + "\t");
            }
            Console.WriteLine();
        }
    }
}
```

Figure 22-12 shows the program's output.

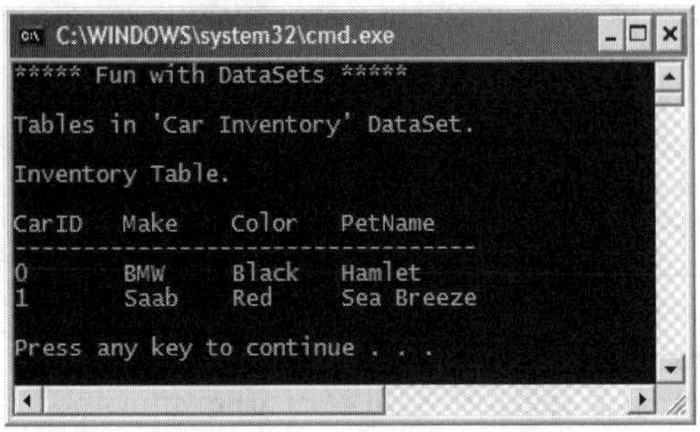

Figure 22-12. *Contents of the example's* DataSet *object*

Working with .NET 2.0 DataTableReaders

DataTables provide a number of methods beyond what we've examined thus far. For example, like DataSets, DataTables support AcceptChanges(), GetChanges(), Copy(), and ReadXml()/WriteXml() methods. As of .NET 2.0, DataTables also now support a method named CreateDataReader(). This method allows you to obtain the data within a DataTable using a data reader–like navigation scheme (forward-only, read-only). To illustrate, create a new helper function named PrintTable(), implemented as so:

```
private static void PrintTable(DataTable dt)
{
    Console.WriteLine("\n***** Rows in DataTable *****");

    // Get the new .NET 2.0 DataTableReader type.
    DataTableReader dtReader = dt.CreateDataReader();

    // The DataTableReader works just like the DataReader.
    while (dtReader.Read())
    {
        for (int i = 0; i < dtReader.FieldCount; i++)
        {
            Console.Write("{0} = {1} ",
                dtReader.GetName(i),
                dtReader.GetValue(i).ToString().Trim());
        }
        Console.WriteLine();
    }
    dtReader.Close();
}
```

Notice that the DataTableReader works identically to the data reader object of your data provider. Using a DataTableReader can be an ideal choice when you wish to quickly pump out the data within a DataTable without needing to traverse the internal row and column collections. To call this method, simply pass in the correct table:

```
static void Main(string[] args)
{
...
    // Print out the DataTable via 'table reader'.
    PrintTable(carsInventoryDS.Tables["Inventory"]);
}
```

Persisting DataSets (and DataTables) As XML

To wrap up the current example, recall that DataSets and DataTables both support WriteXml() and ReadXml() methods. WriteXml() allows you to persist the object's content to a local file (as well as into any System.IO.Stream-derived type) as an XML document. ReadXml() allows you to hydrate the state of a DataSet (or DataTable) from a given XML document. In addition, DataSets and DataTables both support WriteXmlSchema() and ReadXmlSchema() to save or load an *.xsd file. To test this out for yourself, update your Main() method with the final set of code statements:

```
static void Main(string[] args)
{
...
    // Save this DataSet as XML.
    carsInventoryDS.WriteXml("carsDataSet.xml");
    carsInventoryDS.WriteXmlSchema("carsDataSet.xsd");

    // Clear out DataSet and print contents (which are empty).
    carsInventoryDS.Clear();
    PrintDataSet(carsInventoryDS);

    // Load and print the DataSet.
    carsInventoryDS.ReadXml("carsDataSet.xml");
    PrintDataSet(carsInventoryDS);
}
```

If you open the carsDataSet.xml file, you will find that each column in the table has been encoded as an XML element:

```
<?xml version="1.0" standalone="yes"?>
<Car_x0020_Inventory>
  <Inventory>
    <CarID>0</CarID>
    <Make>BMW</Make>
    <Color>Black</Color>
    <PetName>Hamlet</PetName>
  </Inventory>
  <Inventory>
    <CarID>1</CarID>
    <Make>Saab</Make>
    <Color>Red</Color>
    <PetName>Sea Breeze</PetName>
  </Inventory>
</Car_x0020_Inventory>
```

Finally, recall that the DataColumn type supports a property named ColumnMapping, which can be used to control how a column should be represented in XML. The default setting is MappingType.Element. However, if you establish the CarID column as an XML attribute as follows by updating your existing carIDColumn DataColumn object

```
static void Main(string[] args)
{
    ...
    DataColumn carIDColumn = new DataColumn("CarID", typeof(int));
    ...
    carIDColumn.ColumnMapping = MappingType.Attribute;
}
```

you will find the following XML:

```xml
<?xml version="1.0" standalone="yes"?>
<Car_x0020_Inventory>
  <Inventory CarID="0">
    <Make>BMW</Make>
    <Color>Black</Color>
    <PetName>Hamlet</PetName>
  </Inventory>
  <Inventory CarID="1">
    <Make>Saab</Make>
    <Color>Red</Color>
    <PetName>Sea Breeze</PetName>
  </Inventory>
</Car_x0020_Inventory>
```

■**Source Code** The SimpleDataSet application is included under the Chapter 22 subdirectory.

Binding DataTables to User Interfaces

Now that you have been exposed to the process of interacting with DataSets in the raw, let's see a Windows Forms example. Your goal is to build a Form that displays the contents of a DataTable within a DataGridView widget. Figure 22-13 shows the initial UI design.

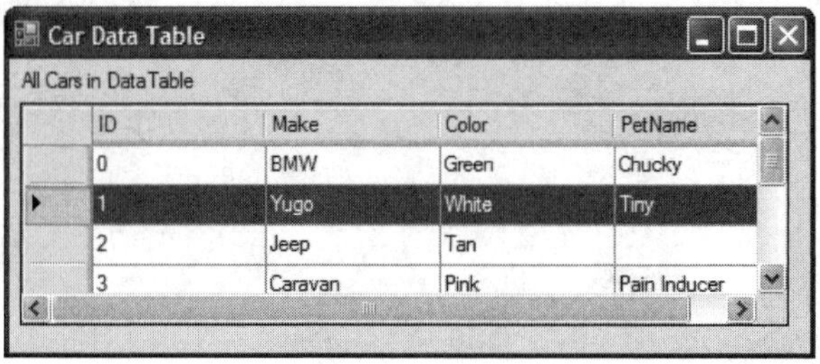

Figure 22-13. *Binding a* DataTable *to a* DataGridView

■**Note** As of .NET 2.0, the DataGridView widget is the preferred UI control used to bind relational data. Do be aware, however, that the legacy .NET 1.*x* DataGrid control is still available.

To begin, create a new Windows Forms application named CarDataTableViewer. Add a Data-GridView widget (named carInventoryGridView) and descriptive Label to your designer. Next, insert a new C# class into your project (named Car), which is defined as follows:

```csharp
public class Car
{
    // Made public for ease of use.
    public string carPetName, carMake, carColor;

    public Car(string petName, string make, string color)
    {
        carPetName = petName;
```

```
        carColor = color;
        carMake = make;
    }
}
```

Now, within the Form's default constructor, populate a List<> member variable with a set of new Car objects:

```
public partial class MainForm : System.Windows.Forms.Form
{
    // Our list of Cars.
    private List<Car> arTheCars = new List<Car>();

    public MainForm()
    {
        InitializeComponent();
        CenterToScreen();

        // Fill the list with some cars.
        arTheCars.Add(new Car("Chucky", "BMW", "Green"));
        arTheCars.Add(new Car("Tiny", "Yugo", "White"));
        arTheCars.Add(new Car("", "Jeep", "Tan"));
        arTheCars.Add(new Car("Pain Inducer", "Caravan", "Pink"));
        arTheCars.Add(new Car("Fred", "BMW", "Pea Soup Green"));
        arTheCars.Add(new Car("Buddha", "BMW", "Black"));
        arTheCars.Add(new Car("Mel", "Firebird", "Red"));
        arTheCars.Add(new Car("Sarah", "Colt", "Black"));
    }
}
```

Like the previous SimpleDataSet example, the CarDataTableViewer application will construct a DataTable that contains four DataColumns to represent the columns of the Inventory table within the Cars database. As well, this DataTable will contain a set of DataRows to represent a list of automobiles. This time, however, you will fill the rows using your generic List<> member variable.

First, add a new member variable named inventoryTable of type DataTable to your Form. Next, add a new helper function to your Form class named CreateDataTable(), and call this method within the Form's default constructor. The code required to add the DataColumns to the DataTable object is identical to that in the previous example, so I'll omit it here (consult this book's code download for complete details). Do note, though, that you are iterating over each member of the List<> to build your row set:

```
private void CreateDataTable()
{
    // Create DataColumns and add to DataTable.
...
    // Iterate over the array list to make rows.
    foreach(Car c in arTheCars)
    {
        DataRow newRow = inventoryTable.NewRow();
        newRow["Make"] = c.carMake;
        newRow["Color"] = c.carColor;
        newRow["PetName"] = c.carPetName;
        inventoryTable.Rows.Add(newRow);
    }

    // Bind the DataTable to the carInventoryGridView.
    carInventoryGridView.DataSource = inventoryTable;
}
```

Notice that the final line of code within the CreateDataTable() method assigns the inventoryTable to the DataSource property. This single property is all you need to set to bind a DataTable to a DataGridView object. As you might guess, this GUI widget is reading the rows and column collections internally to establish the UI. At this point, you should be able to run your application and see the DataTable within the DataGridView control.

Programmatically Deleting Rows

Now, what if you wish to remove a row from a DataTable? One approach is to call the Delete() method of the DataRow object that represents the row to terminate. Simply specify the index (or DataRow object) representing the row to remove. Assume you update your GUI as shown in Figure 22-14.

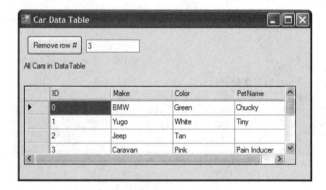

Figure 22-14. *Removing rows from the* DataTable

The following logic behind the new Button's Click event handler removes the specified row from your in-memory DataTable:

```
// Remove this row from the DataRowCollection.
private void btnRemoveRow_Click (object sender, EventArgs e)
{
    try
    {
        inventoryTable.Rows[(int.Parse(txtRowToRemove.Text))].Delete();
        inventoryTable.AcceptChanges();
    }
    catch(Exception ex)
    {
        MessageBox.Show(ex.Message);
    }
}
```

The Delete() method might have been better named MarkedAsDeletable(), as the row is not literally removed until the DataTable.AcceptChanges() method is called. In effect, the Delete() method simply sets a flag that says, "I am ready to die when my table tells me to." Also understand that if a row has been marked for deletion, a DataTable may reject the delete operation via RejectChanges(), as shown here:

```
// Mark a row as deleted, but reject the changes.
private void btnRemoveRow_Click (object sender, EventArgs e)
{
```

```
        inventoryTable.Rows[(int.Parse(txtRemove.Text))].Delete();
        // Do more work
        ...
        inventoryTable.RejectChanges();        // Restore previous RowState value.
}
```

Applying Filters and Sort Orders

You may wish to see a small subset of a DataTable's data, as specified by some sort of filtering criteria. For example, what if you wish to see only a certain make of automobile from the in-memory
Inventory table? The Select() method of the DataTable class provides this very functionality. Update
your GUI once again, this time allowing users to specify a string that represents the make of the
automobile they are interested in viewing (see Figure 22-15). The result will be placed into a Windows
Forms message box.

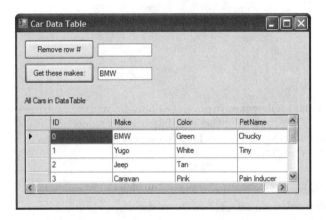

Figure 22-15. *Specifying a filter*

The Select() method has been overloaded a number of times to provide different selection
semantics. At its most basic level, the parameter sent to Select() is a string that contains some conditional operation. To begin, observe the following logic for the Click event handler of your new
button:

```
private void btnGetMakes_Click (object sender, EventArgs e)
{
    // Build a filter based on user input.
    string filterStr = string.Format("Make= '{0}' ", txtMakeToGet.Text);

    // Find all rows matching the filter.
    DataRow[] makes = inventoryTable.Select(filterStr);

    // Show what we got!
    if(makes.Length == 0)
        MessageBox.Show("Sorry, no cars...", "Selection error!");
    else
    {
        string strMake = null;
        for(int i = 0; i < makes.Length; i++)
```

```
        {
            DataRow temp = makes[i];
            strMake += temp["PetName"] + "\n";
        }
        MessageBox.Show(strMake, txtMakeToGet.Text + " type(s):");
    }
}
```

Here, you first build a simple filter based on the value in the associated TextBox. If you specify BMW, your filter is Make = 'BMW'. When you send this filter to the Select() method, you get back an array of DataRow types that represent each row that matches the filter (see Figure 22-16).

Figure 22-16. *Displaying filtered data*

As you can see, filtering logic is standard SQL syntax. To prove the point, assume you wish to obtain the results of the previous Select() invocation alphabetically based on pet name. In terms of SQL, this translates into a sort based on the PetName column. Luckily, the Select() method has been overloaded to send in a sort criterion, as shown here:

```
// Sort by PetName.
makes = inventoryTable.Select(filterStr, "PetName");
```

If you want the results in descending order, call Select(), as shown here:

```
// Return results in descending order.
makes = inventoryTable.Select(filterStr, "PetName DESC");
```

In general, the sort string contains the column name followed by "ASC" (ascending, which is the default) or "DESC" (descending). If need be, multiple columns can be separated by commas. Finally, understand that a filter string can be composed of any number of relational operators. For example, what if you want to find all cars with an ID greater than 5? Here is a helper function that does this very thing:

```
private void ShowCarsWithIdLessThanFive()
{
    // Now show the pet names of all cars with ID greater than 5.
    DataRow[] properIDs;
    string newFilterStr = "ID > 5";
    properIDs = inventoryTable.Select(newFilterStr);
    string strIDs = null;
    for(int i = 0; i < properIDs.Length; i++)
    {
        DataRow temp = properIDs[i];
        strIDs += temp["PetName"]
            + " is ID " + temp["ID"] + "\n";
    }
    MessageBox.Show(strIDs, "Pet names of cars where ID > 5");
}
```

Updating Rows

The final aspect of the DataTable you should be aware of is the process of updating an existing row with new values. One approach is to first obtain the row(s) that match a given filter criterion using the Select() method. Once you have the DataRow(s) in question, modify them accordingly. For example, assume you have a new Button that (when clicked) searches the DataTable for all rows where Make is equal to BMW. Once you identify these items, you change the Make from BMW to Colt:

```
// Find the rows you want to edit with a filter.
private void btnChangeBeemersToColts_Click(object sender, EventArgs e)
{
    // Make sure user has not lost his mind.
    if (DialogResult.Yes ==
        MessageBox.Show("Are you sure?? BMWs are much nicer than Colts!",
        "Please Confirm!", MessageBoxButtons.YesNo))
    {
        // Build a filter.
        string filterStr = "Make='BMW'";
        string strMake = null;

        // Find all rows matching the filter.
        DataRow[] makes = inventoryTable.Select(filterStr);

        // Change all Beemers to Colts!
        for (int i = 0; i < makes.Length; i++)
        {
            DataRow temp = makes[i];
            strMake += temp["Make"] = "Colt";
            makes[i] = temp;
        }
    }
}
```

The DataRow class also provides the BeginEdit(), EndEdit(), and CancelEdit() methods, which allow you to edit the content of a row while temporarily suspending any associated validation rules. In the previous logic, each row was validated with each assignment. (Also, if you capture any events from the DataRow, they fire with each modification.) When you call BeginEdit() on a given DataRow, the row is placed in edit mode. At this point you can make your changes as necessary and call either EndEdit() to commit these changes or CancelEdit() to roll back the changes to the original version, for example:

```
private void UpdateSomeRow()
{
    // Assume you have obtained a row to edit.
    // Now place this row in edit mode.
    rowToUpdate.BeginEdit();

    // Send the row to a helper function, which returns a Boolean.
    if( ChangeValuesForThisRow( rowToUpdate) )
        rowToUpdate.EndEdit();      // OK!
    else
        rowToUpdate.CancelEdit();  // Forget it.
}
```

Although you are free to manually call these methods on a given DataRow, these members are automatically called when you edit a DataGridView widget that has been bound to a DataTable. For example, when you select a row to edit from a DataGridView, that row is automatically placed in edit mode. When you shift focus to a new row, EndEdit() is called automatically.

Working with the DataView Type

In database nomenclature, a *view object* is a stylized representation of a table (or set of tables). For example, using Microsoft SQL Server, you could create a view for your current Inventory table that returns a new table containing automobiles only of a given color. In ADO.NET, the DataView type allows you to programmatically extract a subset of data from the DataTable into a stand-alone object.

One great advantage of holding multiple views of the same table is that you can bind these views to various GUI widgets (such as the DataGridView). For example, one DataGridView might be bound to a DataView showing all autos in the Inventory, while another might be configured to display only green automobiles.

To illustrate, update the current UI with an additional DataGridView type named dataGridColtsView and a descriptive Label. Next, define a member variable named coltsOnlyView of type DataView:

```
public partial class MainForm : Form
{
    // View of the DataTable.
    DataView coltsOnlyView;        // I only show red colts.
...
}
```

Now, create a new helper function named CreateDataView(), and call this method within the Form's default constructor directly after the DataTable has been fully constructed, as shown here:

```
public MainForm()
{
...
    // Make a data table.
    CreateDataTable();
    // Make Views.
    CreateDataView();
}
```

Here is the implementation of this new helper function. Notice that the constructor of each DataView has been passed the DataTable that will be used to build the custom set of data rows.

```
private void CreateDataView()
{
    // Set the table that is used to construct this view.
    coltsOnlyView = new DataView(inventoryTable);

    // Now configure the views using a filter.
    coltsOnlyView.RowFilter = "Make = 'Colt'";

    // Bind to grid.
    dataGridColtsView.DataSource = coltsOnlyView;
}
```

As you can see, the DataView class supports a property named RowFilter, which contains the string representing the filtering criteria used to extract matching rows. Once you have your view established, set the grid's DataSource property accordingly. Figure 22-17 shows the completed application in action.

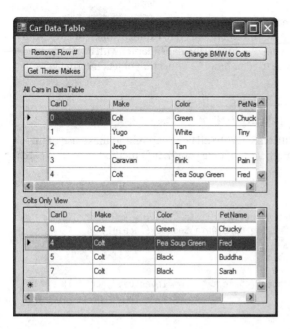

Figure 22-17. *Displaying filtered data*

■**Source Code** The CarDataTableViewer project is included under the Chapter 22 subdirectory.

Working with Data Adapters

Now that you understand the ins and outs of manipulating ADO.NET DataSets, let's turn our attention to the topic of data adapters. Recall that data adapter objects are used to fill a DataSet with
DataTable objects and send modified DataTables back to the database for processing. Table 22-15
documents the core members of the DbDataAdapter base class.

Table 22-15. *Core Members of the* DbDataAdapter *Class*

Members	Meaning in Life
SelectCommand InsertCommand UpdateCommand DeleteCommand	Establish SQL commands that will be issued to the data store when the Fill() and Update() methods are called.
Fill()	Fills a given table in the DataSet with some number of records based on the command object–specified SelectCommand.
Update()	Updates a DataTable using command objects within the InsertCommand, UpdateCommand, or DeleteCommand property. The exact command that is executed is based on the RowState value for a given DataRow in a given DataTable (of a given DataSet).

In the examples that follow, remember that data adapter objects manage the underlying connection to the database on your behalf; therefore, you will not need to explicitly open or close your session with the DBMS. However, you will still need to supply the data adapter with a valid connection object or a connection string (which will be used to build a connection object internally) as a constructor argument.

Filling a DataSet Using a Data Adapter

Create a new console application named FillDataSetWithSqlDataAdapter and make use of the System.Data and System.Data.SqlClient namespaces. Update your Main() method as so (try/catch logic has been omitted here for simplicity):

```
static void Main(string[] args)
{
    Console.WriteLine("***** Fun with Data Adapters *****\n");
    string cnStr = "uid=sa;pwd=;Initial Catalog=Cars;Data Source=(local)";

    // Fill the DataSet with a new DataTable.
    DataSet myDS = new DataSet("Cars");
    SqlDataAdapter dAdapt = new SqlDataAdapter("Select * From Inventory", cnStr);
    dAdapt.Fill(myDS, "Inventory");

    // Display contents.
    PrintDataSet(myDS);
}
```

Notice that the data adapter has been constructed by specifying a SQL Select statement. This value will be used to build a command object internally, which can be later obtained via the Select-Command property. Next, notice that the Fill() method takes an instance of the DataSet type and optionally a string name that will be used to set the TableName property of the new DataTable (if you do not specify a table name, the data adapter will simply name the table "Table").

Note The Fill() method returns an integer that represents the number of rows affected by the SQL query.

As you would expect, when you pass the DataSet to the PrintDataSet() method (implemented earlier in this chapter), you are presented with a list of all rows in the Inventory table of the Cars database (see Figure 22-18).

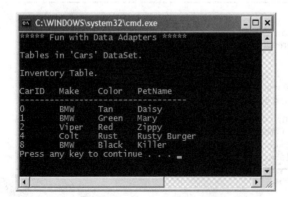

Figure 22-18. *Filling a* DataSet *with a data adapter object*

Mapping Database Names to Friendly Names

As you most certainly know, database administrators (DBAs) tend to create table and column names that can be less than friendly to end users. The good news is that data adapter objects maintain an internal strongly named collection (DataTableMappingCollection) of System.Data.Common. DataTableMapping types, accessed via the TableMappings property.

If you so choose, you may manipulate this collection to inform a DataTable about which "display names" it should use when asked to print its contents. For example, assume that you wish to map the DBMS table name "Inventory" to "Current Inventory" for display purposes. Furthermore, say you wish to display the CarID column name as "Car ID" (note the extra space) and the PetName column name as "Name of Car." To do so, add the following code before calling the Fill() method of your data adapter object (and be sure to "use" the System.Data.Common namespace):

```
static void Main(string[] args)
{
...
    // Now map DB column names to user-friendly names.
    DataTableMapping custMap =
        dAdapt.TableMappings.Add("Inventory", "Current Inventory");
    custMap.ColumnMappings.Add("CarID", "Car ID");
    custMap.ColumnMappings.Add("PetName", "Name of Car");
    dAdapt.Fill(myDS, "Inventory");
...
}
```

If you were to run this program once again, you would find that the PrintDataSet() method now displays the "friendly names" of the DataTable and DataRow objects, rather than the names established by the database schema.

■**Source Code** The FillDataSetWithSqlDataAdapter project is included under the Chapter 22 subdirectory.

Updating a Database Using Data Adapter Objects

Not only do data adapters fill the tables of a DataSet on your behalf, but they are also in charge of maintaining a set of core SQL command objects used to push updates back to the data store. When you call the Update() method of a given data adapter, it will examine the RowState property for each row in the DataTable and use the correct SQL commands assigned to the DeleteCommand, InsertCommand, and UpdateCommand properties to push the changes within a given DataTable back to the data source.

To illustrate the process of using a data adapter to push back modifications in a DataTable, the next example will re-engineer the CarsInventoryUpdater example developed earlier in the chapter to now make use of DataSet and data adapter objects. Given that you already created a bulk of the application, let's focus on the changes to the DeleteCar(), UpdateCarPetName(), and InsertNewCar() methods (check out the downloadable code for full details).

The first basic adjustment to make to the application is to define two new static member variables of the Program class to represent your DataSet and connection object. As well, the Main() method will be modified to fill the DataSet with the initial data upon startup:

```
class Program
{
    // The applicationwide DataSet.
    public static DataSet dsCarInventory = new DataSet("CarsDatabase");
```

```
    // The applicationwide connection object.
    public static SqlConnection cnObj = new
        SqlConnection("uid=sa;pwd=;Initial Catalog=Cars;Data Source=(local)");

    static void Main(string[] args)
    {
...
        // Create the adapter and fill DataSet.
        SqlDataAdapter dAdapter =
            new SqlDataAdapter("Select * From Inventory", cnObj);
        dAdapter.Fill(dsCarInventory, "Inventory");
        ShowInstructions();

        // Logic to get user command...
    }
...
}
```

Also note in the code that follows that the ListInventory(), DeleteCar(), UpdateCarPetName(), and InsertNewCar() methods have all been updated to take a SqlDataAdapter as the sole parameter.

Setting the InsertCommand Property

When you are using a data adapter to update a DataSet, the first order of business is to assign the UpdateCommand, DeleteCommand, and InsertCommand properties with valid command objects (until you do so, these properties return null!). By "valid" command objects, I am referring to the fact that the set of command objects you plug into a data adapter will change based on the table you are attempting to update. In this example, the table in question is Inventory. Here is the modified InsertNewCar() method:

```
private static void InsertNewCar(SqlDataAdapter dAdpater)
{
    // Gather info about new car.
...
    // Format SQL Insert and plug into DataAdapter.
    string sql = string.Format("Insert Into Inventory" +
        "(CarID, Make, Color, PetName) Values" +
        "('{0}', '{1}', '{2}', '{3}')",
        newCarID, newCarMake, newCarColor, newCarPetName);
    dAdpater.InsertCommand = new SqlCommand(sql);
    dAdpater.InsertCommand.Connection = cnObj;

    // Update Inventory Table with new row.
    DataRow newCar = dsCarInventory.Tables["Inventory"].NewRow();
    newCar["CarID"] = newCarID;
    newCar["Make"] = newCarMake;
    newCar["Color"] = newCarColor;
    newCar["PetName"] = newCarPetName;
    dsCarInventory.Tables["Inventory"].Rows.Add(newCar);
    dAdpater.Update(dsCarInventory.Tables["Inventory"]);
}
```

Once you have created your command object, you plug it into the adapter via the InsertCommand property. Next, you add a new row to the Inventory DataTable maintained by the dsCarInventory object. Once you have added this DataRow back into the DataTable, the adapter will execute the SQL found within the InsertCommand property, given that the RowState of this new row is DataRowState.Added.

Setting the UpdateCommand Property

The modification of the UpdateCarPetName() method is more or less identical. Simply build a new command object and plug it into the UpdateCommand property.

```
private static void UpdateCarPetName(SqlDataAdapter dAdpater)
{
    // Gather info about car to update.
...

    // Format SQL Insert and plug into DataAdapter.
    string sql = string.Format
    ("Update Inventory Set PetName = '{0}' Where CarID = '{1}'",
        newPetName, carToUpdate);
    SqlCommand cmd = new SqlCommand(sql, cnObj);
    dAdpater.UpdateCommand = cmd;

    DataRow[] carRowToUpdate =
        dsCarInventory.Tables["Inventory"].Select(
            string.Format("CarID = '{0}'", carToUpdate));
    carRowToUpdate[0]["PetName"] = newPetName;
    dAdpater.Update(dsCarInventory.Tables["Inventory"]);
}
```

In this case, when you select a specific row (via the Select() method), the RowState value of said row is automatically set to DataRowState.Modified. The only other point of interest here is that the Select() method returns an array of DataRow objects; therefore, you must specify the exact row you wish to modify.

Setting the DeleteCommand Property

Last but not least, you have the following update to the DeleteCar() method:

```
private static void DeleteCar(SqlDataAdapter dAdpater)
{
    // Get ID of car to delete.
,,,
    string sql = string.Format("Delete from Inventory where CarID = '{0}'",
        carToDelete);
    SqlCommand cmd = new SqlCommand(sql, cnObj);
    dAdpater.DeleteCommand = cmd;

    DataRow[] carRowToDelete =
        dsCarInventory.Tables["Inventory"].Select(string.Format("CarID = '{0}'",
        carToDelete));
    carRowToDelete[0].Delete();
    dAdpater.Update(dsCarInventory.Tables["Inventory"]);
}
```

In this case, you find the row you wish to delete (again using the Select() method) and then set the RowState property to DataRowState.Deleted by calling Delete().

■**Source Code** The CarsInvertoryUpdaterDS project is included under the Chapter 22 subdirectory.

Autogenerating SQL Commands Using Command-Builder Types

You might agree that working with data adapters can entail a fair amount of code, given the need to build each of the four command objects and the associated connection string (or DbConnection-derived object). To help simplify matters, each of the ADO.NET data providers that ships with .NET 2.0 provides a *command builder* type. Using this type, you are able to automatically obtain command objects that contain the correct Insert, Delete, and Update command types based on the initial Select statement.

The SqlCommandBuilder automatically generates the values contained within the SqlDataAdapter's InsertCommand, UpdateCommand, and DeleteCommand properties based on the initial SelectCommand. Clearly, the benefit is that you have no need to build all the SqlCommand and SqlParameter types by hand.

An obvious question at this point is how a command builder is able to build these SQL command objects on the fly. The short answer is metadata. At runtime, when you call the Update() method of a data adapter, the related command builder will read the database's schema data to autogenerate the underlying insert, delete, and update command objects.

Consider the following example, which deletes a row in a DataSet using the autogenerated SQL statements. Furthermore, this application will print out the underlying command text of each command object:

```
static void Main(string[] args)
{
    DataSet theCarsInventory = new DataSet();

    // Make connection.
    SqlConnection cn = new
        SqlConnection("server=(local);User ID=sa;Pwd=;database=Cars");

    // Autogenerate Insert, Update, and Delete commands
    // based on existing Select command.
    SqlDataAdapter da = new SqlDataAdapter("SELECT * FROM Inventory", cn);
    SqlCommandBuilder invBuilder = new SqlCommandBuilder(da);

    // Fill data set.
    da.Fill(theCarsInventory, "Inventory");
    PrintDataSet(theCarsInventory);

    // Delete row based on user input and update database.
    try
    {
        Console.Write("Row # to delete: ");
        int rowToDelete = int.Parse(Console.ReadLine());
        theCarsInventory.Tables["Inventory"].Rows[rowToDelete].Delete();
        da.Update(theCarsInventory, "Inventory");
    }
    catch (Exception e)
    {
        Console.WriteLine(e.Message);
    }

    // Refill and reprint Inventory table.
    theCarsInventory = new DataSet();
    da.Fill(theCarsInventory, "Inventory");
    PrintDataSet(theCarsInventory);
}
```

In the previous code, notice that you made no use of the command builder object (SqlCommandBuilder in this case) beyond passing in the data adapter object as a constructor parameter. As odd as this may seem, this is all you are required to do (at a minimum). Under the hood, this type will configure the data adapter with the remaining command objects.

Now, while you may love the idea of getting something for nothing, do understand that command builders come with some critical restrictions. Specifically, a command builder is only able to autogenerate SQL commands for use by a data adapter if all of the following conditions are true:

- The Select command interacts with only a single table (e.g., no joins).
- The single table has been attributed with a primary key.
- The column(s) representing the primary key is accounted for in your SQL Select statement.

In any case, Figure 22-19 verifies that the specified row has been deleted from the physical database (don't confuse the CarID value with the ordinal row number value when you run this example code!).

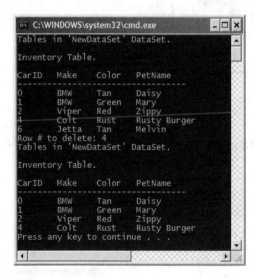

Figure 22-19. *Leveraging autogenerated SQL commands*

■**Source Code** The MySqlCommandBuilder project is found under the Chapter 22 subdirectory.

Multitabled DataSets and DataRelation Objects

Currently, all of this chapter's examples involved DataSets that contained a single DataTable object. However, the power of the disconnected layer really comes to light when a DataSet object contains numerous interrelated DataTables. In this case, you are able to insert any number of DataRelation objects into the DataSet's DataRelation collection to account for the interdependencies of the tables. Using these objects, the client tier is able to navigate between the table data without incurring network round-trips.

To illustrate the use of data relation objects, create a new Windows Forms project called MultitabledDataSet. The GUI is simple enough. In Figure 22-20 you can see three DataGridView widgets that hold the data retrieved from the Inventory, Orders, and Customers tables of the Cars database. In addition, the single Button pushes any and all changes back to the data store.

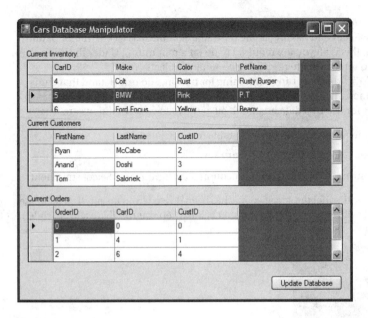

Figure 22-20. *Viewing related* DataTables

To keep things simple, the MainForm will make use of command builders to autogenerate the SQL commands for each of the three SqlDataAdapters (one for each table). Here is the initial update to the Form-derived type:

```
public partial class MainForm : Form
{
    // Formwide DataSet.
    private DataSet carsDS = new DataSet("CarsDataSet");

    // Make use of command builders to simplify data adapter configuration.
    private SqlCommandBuilder sqlCBInventory;
    private SqlCommandBuilder sqlCBCustomers;
    private SqlCommandBuilder sqlCBOrders;

    // Our data adapters (for each table).
    private SqlDataAdapter invTableAdapter;
    private SqlDataAdapter custTableAdapter;
    private SqlDataAdapter ordersTableAdapter;

    // Formwide connection object.
    private SqlConnection cn =
        new SqlConnection("server=(local);uid=sa;pwd=;database=Cars");
...
}
```

The Form's constructor does the grunge work of creating your data-centric member variables and filling the DataSet. Also note that there is a call to a private helper function, BuildTableRelationship(), as shown here:

```
public MainForm()
{
    InitializeComponent();

    // Create adapters.
    invTableAdapter = new SqlDataAdapter("Select * from Inventory", cn);
    custTableAdapter = new SqlDataAdapter("Select * from Customers", cn);
    ordersTableAdapter = new SqlDataAdapter("Select * from Orders", cn);

    // Autogenerate commands.
    sqlCBInventory = new SqlCommandBuilder(invTableAdapter);
    sqlCBOrders = new SqlCommandBuilder(ordersTableAdapter);
    sqlCBCustomers = new SqlCommandBuilder(custTableAdapter);

    // Add tables to DS.
    invTableAdapter.Fill(carsDS, "Inventory");
    custTableAdapter.Fill(carsDS, "Customers");
    ordersTableAdapter.Fill(carsDS, "Orders");

    // Build relations between tables.
    BuildTableRelationship();

    // Bind to grids.
    dataGridViewInventory.DataSource = carsDS.Tables["Inventory"];
    dataGridViewCustomers.DataSource = carsDS.Tables["Customers"];
    dataGridViewOrders.DataSource = carsDS.Tables["Orders"];
}
```

The BuildTableRelationship() helper function does just what you would expect. Recall that the Cars database expresses a number of parent/child relationships, accounted for with the following code:

```
private void BuildTableRelationship()
{
    // Create CustomerOrder data relation object.
    DataRelation dr = new DataRelation("CustomerOrder",
            carsDS.Tables["Customers"].Columns["CustID"],
            carsDS.Tables["Orders"].Columns["CustID"]);
    carsDS.Relations.Add(dr);

    // Create InventoryOrder data relation object.
    dr = new DataRelation("InventoryOrder",
            carsDS.Tables["Inventory"].Columns["CarID"],
            carsDS.Tables["Orders"].Columns["CarID"]);
    carsDS.Relations.Add(dr);
}
```

Now that the DataSet has been filled and disconnected from the data source, you can manipulate each table locally. To do so, simply insert, update, or delete values from any of the three DataGridViews. When you are ready to submit the data back for processing, click the Form's Update button. The code behind the Click event should be clear at this point:

```
private void btnUpdate_Click(object sender, EventArgs e)
{
    try
    {
        invTableAdapter.Update(carsDS, "Inventory");
        custTableAdapter.Update(carsDS, "Customers");
```

```
        ordersTableAdapter.Update(carsDS, "Orders");
    }
    catch (Exception ex)
    {
        MessageBox.Show(ex.Message);
    }
}
```

Once you update, you will find that each table in the Cars database has been correctly altered.

Navigating Between Related Tables

To illustrate how a DataRelation allows you to move between related tables programmatically, extend your GUI to include a new Button type and a related TextBox. The end user is able to enter the ID of a customer and obtain all the information about that customer's order, which is placed in a simple message box. The Button's Click event handler is implemented as so:

```
private void btnGetInfo_Click(object sender, System.EventArgs e)
{
    string strInfo = "";
    DataRow drCust = null;
    DataRow[] drsOrder = null;

    // Get the specified CustID from the TextBox.
    int theCust = int.Parse(this.txtCustID.Text);

    // Now based on CustID, get the correct row in Customers table.
    drCust = carsDS.Tables["Customers"].Rows[theCust];
    strInfo += "Cust #" + drCust["CustID"].ToString() + "\n";

    // Navigate from customer table to order table.
    drsOrder = drCust.GetChildRows(carsDS.Relations["CustomerOrder"]);

    // Get order number.
    foreach (DataRow r in drsOrder)
        strInfo += "Order Number: " + r["OrderID"] + "\n";

    // Now navigate from order table to inventory table.
    DataRow[] drsInv =
        drsOrder[0].GetParentRows(carsDS.Relations["InventoryOrder"]);

    // Get Car info.
    foreach (DataRow r in drsInv)
    {
        strInfo += "Make: " + r["Make"] + "\n";
        strInfo += "Color: " + r["Color"] + "\n";
        strInfo += "Pet Name: " + r["PetName"] + "\n";
    }
    MessageBox.Show(strInfo, "Info based on cust ID");
}
```

As you can see, the key to moving between data tables is to use a handful of methods defined by the DataRow type. Let's break this code down step by step. First, you obtain the correct customer ID from the text box and use it to grab the correct row in the Customers table (using the Rows property, of course), as shown here:

```
// Get the specified CustID from the TextBox.
int theCust = int.Parse(this.txtCustID.Text);
// Now based on CustID, get the correct row in the Customers table.
DataRow drCust = null;
drCust = carsDS.Tables["Customers"].Rows[theCust];
strInfo += "Cust #" + drCust["CustID"].ToString() + "\n";
```

Next, you navigate from the Customers table to the Orders table, using the CustomerOrder data relation. Notice that the DataRow.GetChildRows() method allows you to grab rows from your child table. Once you do, you can read information out of the table:

```
// Navigate from customer table to order table.
DataRow[] drsOrder = null;
drsOrder =   drCust.GetChildRows(carsDS.Relations["CustomerOrder"]);
// Get order number.
foreach(DataRow r in drsOrder)
strInfo += "Order Number: " + r["OrderID"] + "\n";
```

Your final step is to navigate from the Orders table to its parent table (Inventory), using the GetParentRows() method. At this point, you can read information from the Inventory table using the Make, PetName, and Color columns, as shown here:

```
// Now navigate from order table to inventory table.
DataRow[] drsInv =
    drsOrder[0].GetParentRows(carsDS.Relations["InventoryOrder"]);
foreach(DataRow r in drsInv)
{
    strInfo += "Make: " + r["Make"] + "\n";
    strInfo += "Color: " + r["Color"] + "\n";
    strInfo += "Pet Name: " + r["PetName"] + "\n";
}
```

Figure 22-21 shows one possible output.

Figure 22-21. *Navigating data relations*

Hopefully, this last example has you convinced of the usefulness of the DataSet type. Given that a DataSet is completely disconnected from the underlying data source, you can work with an in-memory copy of data and navigate around each table to make any necessary updates, deletes, or inserts. Once you've finished, you can then submit your changes to the data store for processing.

■**Source Code** The MultitabledDataSetApp project is included under the Chapter 22 subdirectory.

We're Off to See the (Data) Wizard

At this point in the chapter, you have seen numerous ways to interact with the types of ADO.NET in a "wizard-free" manner. While it is (most definitely) true that understanding the ins and outs of working with your data provider is quite important, it is also true that this can lead to hand cramps from typing the large amount of boilerplate code. To wrap things up, therefore, I'd like to point out a few data-centric wizards you may wish to make use of.

Be aware that I have *no* intention of commenting on all of the UI-centric data wizards provided by Visual Studio 2005, but to illustrate the basics, let's examine some additional configuration options of the DataGridView widget. Assume you have created a new Windows Forms application that has a single Form containing a DataGridView control named inventoryDataGridView. Using the designer, activate the inline editor for this widget, and from the Choose Data Source drop-down listbox, click the Add Project Data Source link (see Figure 22-22).

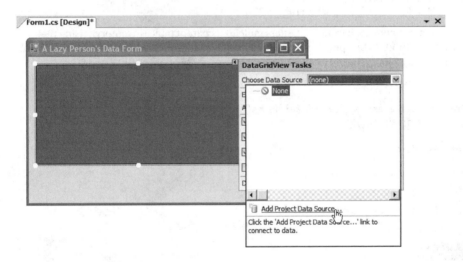

Figure 22-22. *Adding a data source*

This will launch the Data Source Configuration Wizard. On the first step, simply select the Database icon and click Next. On the second step, click New Connection and establish a connection to the Cars database (using the same set of steps described earlier in this chapter within the "Connecting to the Cars Database from Visual Studio 2005" section). The third step allows you to inform the wizard to store the connection string within an external App.config file (which is generally a good idea) within a properly configured <connectionStrings> element. As the final step, you are able to select which database objects you wish to account for within the generated DataSet, which for your purposes here will simply be the Inventory table (see Figure 22-23).

Figure 22-23. *Selecting the Inventory table*

Once you complete the wizard, you will notice that the DataGridView automatically displays the column names within the designer. In fact, if you run your application as is, you will find the contents of the Inventory table displayed within the grid's UI. If you were to examine the code placed in your Form's Load event, you would find that the grid is populated with the line of code highlighted in bold:

```csharp
public partial class MainForm : Form
{
    public MainForm()
    {
        InitializeComponent();
    }

    private void MainForm_Load(object sender, EventArgs e)
    {
        // TODO: This line of code loads data into
        // the 'carsDataSet.Inventory' table.
        // You can move, or remove it, as needed.
        this.inventoryTableAdapter.Fill(this.carsDataSet.Inventory);
    }
}
```

To understand what this line of code is in fact doing, you need to first understand the role of strongly typed DataSet objects.

Strongly Typed DataSets

Strongly typed DataSets (as the name implies) allow you to interact with a DataSet's internal tables using database-specific properties, methods, and events, rather than via the generalized Tables property. If you activate the View ➤ Class View menu option of Visual Studio 2005, you will find that the wizard has created a new type deriving from `DataSet` named `CarsDataSet`. As you can see in Figure 22-24, this class type defines a number of members that allow you select, modify, and update its contents.

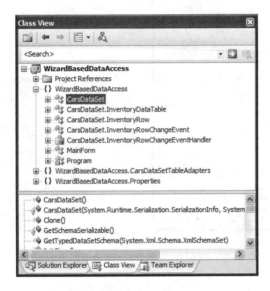

Figure 22-24. *The strongly typed* `DataSet`

Once the wizard completes its task, it places a member variable of type `CarDataSet` within your Form's `*.Designer.cs` file (which is the same member variable manipulated in the `Load` event of your Form):

```
partial class MainForm
{
...
    private CarsDataSet carsDataSet;
}
```

The Autogenerated Data Component

In addition to the strongly typed `DataSet`, the wizard generated a data component (named `InventoryTableAdapter` in this case) that encapsulates the underlying data connection, data adapter, and command objects used to interact with the Inventory table:

```
public partial class InventoryTableAdapter : System.ComponentModel.Component
{
    // field data for data access.
    private System.Data.SqlClient.SqlDataAdapter m_adapter;
    private System.Data.SqlClient.SqlConnection m_connection;
    private System.Data.SqlClient.SqlCommand[] m_commandCollection;
...
}
```

As well, this component defines custom `Fill()` and `Update()` methods that are tailor-made to operate on your `CarsDataSet`, in addition to a set of members used to insert, update, or delete row data from the internal Inventory table. I'll leave it up to interested readers to dive into the implementation details of each member. The good news is that after all your work in this chapter, the code behind each member should look quite familiar.

■**Note** If you are interested in taking a deeper look at the ADO.NET object model, including the numerous Visual Studio 2005 designers, check out *Pro ADO.NET 2.0* by Sahil Malik (Apress, 2005).

Summary

ADO.NET is a new data access technology developed with the disconnected *n*-tier application firmly in mind. The System.Data namespace contains most of the core types you need to programmatically interact with rows, columns, tables, and views. As you have seen, the .NET platform ships with numerous data providers that allow you to leverage the connected and disconnected layers of ADO.NET.

Using connection objects, command objects, and data reader objects of the connected layer, you are able to select, update, insert, and delete records. As you have seen, command objects support an internal parameter collection, which can be used to add some type safety to your SQL queries and are quite helpful when triggering stored procedures.

The centerpiece of the disconnected layer is the DataSet. This type is an in-memory representation of any number of tables and any number of optional interrelationships, constraints, and expressions. The beauty of establishing relations on your local tables is that you are able to programmatically navigate between them while disconnected from the remote data store.

You also examined the role of the data adapter in this chapter. Using this type (and the related SelectCommand, InsertCommand, UpdateCommand, and DeleteCommand properties), the adapter can resolve changes in the DataSet with the original data store. Also, you learned about the connected layer of ADO.NET and came to understand the role of data reader types.

PART 5

Web Applications and XML Web Services

■ ■ ■

## CHAPTER 23

ASP.NET 2.0 Web Pages and Web Controls

Until now, all of the example applications in this text have focused on console-based and Windows Forms front ends. In this chapter and the next, you'll explore how the .NET platform facilitates the construction of browser-based presentation layers. To begin, you'll quickly review a number of key web-centric concepts (HTTP, HTML, client-side, and server-side script) and the role of the web server (including the ASP.NET development server, WebDev.WebServer.exe).

With this web primer out of the way, the remainder of this chapter concentrates on the composition of ASP.NET (including the enhanced code-behind model) and how to work with ASP.NET web controls. As you will see, ASP.NET 2.0 provides a number of new web controls, a new "master page" model, and various customization techniques.

The Role of HTTP

Web applications are very different animals from traditional desktop applications (to say the least). The first obvious difference is that a production-level web application will always involve at least two networked machines (of course, during development it is entirely possible to have a single machine play the role of both client and server). Given this fact, the machines in question must agree upon a particular wire protocol to determine how to send and receive data. The wire protocol that connects the computers in question is the *Hypertext Transfer Protocol* (*HTTP*).

When a client machine launches a web browser (such as Netscape Navigator, Mozilla Firefox, or Microsoft Internet Explorer), an HTTP request is made to access a particular resource (such as an *.aspx or *.htm file) on the remote server machine. HTTP is a text-based protocol that is built upon a standard request/response paradigm. For example, if you navigate to http://www.IntertechTraining.com, the browser software leverages a web technology termed *Domain Name Service* (*DNS*) that converts the registered URL into a four-part, 32-bit numerical value (aka an IP address). At this point, the browser opens a socket connection (typically via port 80) and sends the HTTP request for the default page at the http://www.IntertechTraining.com website.

Once the hosting web server receives the incoming HTTP request, the specified resource may contain logic that scrapes out any client-supplied input values (such as values within a text box) in order to format a proper HTTP response. Web programmers may leverage any number of technologies (CGI, ASP, ASP.NET, Java servlets, etc.) to dynamically generate the content to be emitted into the HTTP response. At this point, the client-side browser renders the HTML emitted from the web server. Figure 23-1 illustrates the basic HTTP request/response cycle.

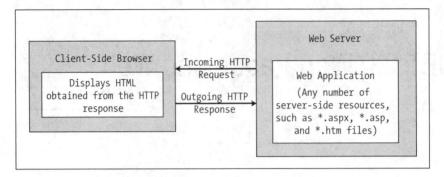

Figure 23-1. *The HTTP request and response cycle*

Another aspect of web development that is markedly different from traditional desktop programming is the fact that HTTP is an essentially *stateless* wire protocol. As soon as the web server emits a response to the client, everything about the previous interaction is forgotten. Therefore, as a web developer, it is up to you take specific steps to "remember" information (such as items in a shopping cart) about the clients who are currently logged on to your site. As you will see in the next chapter, ASP.NET provides numerous ways to handle state, many of which are commonplace to any web platform (session variables, cookies, and application variables) as well as some new techniques (view state, control state, and the cache).

Understanding Web Applications and Web Servers

A *web application* can be understood as a collection of files (*.htm, *.asp, *.aspx, image files, etc.) and related components (such as a .NET code library) stored within a particular set of directories on a given web server. As shown in Chapter 24, web applications have a specific life cycle and provide numerous events (such as initial startup or final shutdown) that you can hook into.

A *web server* is a software product in charge of hosting your web applications, and it typically provides a number of related services such as integrated security, File Transfer Protocol (FTP) support, mail exchange services, and so forth. Internet Information Server (IIS) is Microsoft's enterprise-level web server product, and as you would guess, it has intrinsic support for classic ASP as well as ASP.NET web applications.

When you build ASP.NET web applications, you will often need to interact with IIS. Be aware, however, that IIS is *not* automatically selected when you install the Windows Server 2003 or Windows XP Professional Edition (you can't install IIS on the Home editions of Windows). Therefore, depending on the configuration of your development machine, you may be required to manually install IIS before proceeding through this chapter. To do so, simply access the Add/Remove Program applet from the Control Panel folder and select Add/Remove Windows Components.

■**Note** Ideally, your development machine will have IIS installed *before* you install the .NET Framework. If you install IIS *after* you install the .NET Framework, none of your ASP.NET web applications will execute correctly (you will simply get back a blank page). Luckily, you can reconfigure IIS to host .NET applications by running the aspnet_regiis.exe command-line tool (using the /i flag).

Assuming you have IIS properly installed on your workstation, you can interact with IIS from the Administrative Tools folder (located in the Control Panel folder). For the purposes of this chapter, you are concerned only with the Default Web Site node (see Figure 23-2).

Figure 23-2. *The IIS applet*

Working with IIS Virtual Directories

A single IIS installation is able to host numerous web applications, each of which resides in a *virtual directory*. Each virtual directory is mapped to a physical directory on the local hard drive. Therefore, if you create a new virtual directory named CarsRUs, the outside world can navigate to this site using a URL such as http://www.CarsRUs.com (assuming your site's IP address has been registered with the world at large). Under the hood, the virtual directory maps to a physical root directory such as C:\inetpub\wwwroot\AspNetCarsSite, which contains the content of the web application.

When you create ASP.NET web applications using Visual Studio 2005, you have the option of generating a new virtual directory for the current website. However, you are also able to manually create a virtual directory by hand. For the sake of illustration, assume you wish to create a simple web application named Cars. The first step is to create a new folder on your machine to hold the collection of files that constitute this new site (e.g., C:\CodeTests\CarsWebSite).

Next, you need to create a new virtual directory to host the Cars site. Simply right-click the Default Web Site node of IIS and select New ➤ Virtual Directory from the context menu. This menu selection launches an integrated wizard. Skip past the welcome screen and give your website a name (Cars). Next, you are asked to specify the physical folder on your hard drive that contains the various files and images that represent this site (in this case, C:\CodeTests\CarsWebSite).

The final step of the wizard prompts you for some basic traits about your new virtual directory (such as read/write access to the files it contains, the ability to view these files from a web browser, the ability to launch executables [e.g., CGI applications], etc.). For this example, the default selections are just fine (be aware that you can always modify your selections after running this tool using various right-click Property dialog boxes integrated within IIS). When you are finished, you will see that your new virtual directory has been registered with IIS (see Figure 23-3).

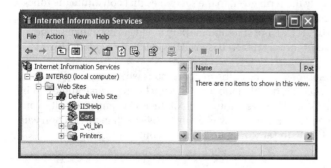

Figure 23-3. *The Cars virtual directory*

The ASP.NET 2.0 Development Server

ASP.NET 2.0 ships with a lightweight web server named WebDev.WebServer.exe. This utility allows developers host an ASP.NET 2.0 web application outside the bounds of IIS. Using this tool, you can build and test your web pages from any directory on your machine (which is quite helpful for team development scenarios and for building ASP.NET 2.0 web programs on Windows XP Home Edition, which does not support IIS).

■**Note** WebDev.WebServer.exe cannot be used to test classic ASP web applications.

When building a website with Visual Studio 2005, you have the option of using WebDev.WebServer.exe to host your pages. However, you are also able to manually interact with this tool from a .NET command prompt. If you enter the following command:

```
WebDev.WebServer.exe -?
```

you will be presented with a message box that describes the valid command-line options. In a nutshell, you will need to specify an unused port (via the /port: option), the root directory of the web application (via the /path: option), and an optional virtual path using the /vpath: option (if you do not supply a /vpath: option, the default is simply /). Consider the following usage:

```
WebDev.WebServer.exe /port:12345 /path:"C:\CodeTests\CarsWebSite"
```

Once you have entered this command, you can launch your web browser of choice to request pages. Thus, if the CarsWebSite folder had a file named MyPage.aspx, you could enter the following URL:

```
http://localhost:12345/CarsWebSite/MyPage.aspx
```

Many of the examples in this chapter and the next will make use of WebDev.WebServer.exe via Visual Studio 2005. Be aware that this web server is *not* intended to host production-level web applications. It is purely intended for development and testing purposes.

■**Note** The Mono project (see Chapter 1) provides a free ASP.NET plug-in for the Apache web server. Check out http://www.mono-project.com/ASP.NET for details.

The Role of HTML

Once you have configured a directory to host your web application, you need to create the content itself. Recall that *web application* is simply the term given to the set of files that constitute the functionality of the site. To be sure, a vast number of these files will contain syntactic tokens defined by the Hypertext Markup Language (HTML). HTML is a standard markup language used to describe how literal text, images, external links, and various HTML-based GUI widgets are rendered by the client-side browser.

This particular aspect of web development is one of the major reasons why many programmers dislike building web-based programs. While it is true that modern IDEs (including Visual Studio 2005) and web development platforms (such as ASP.NET) generate much of the HTML automatically, you will do well to have a working knowledge of HTML as you work with ASP.NET. While this section will most certainly not cover all aspects of HTML (by any means), let's check out some basics.

HTML Document Structure

An HTML file consists of a set of tags that describe the look and feel of a given web page. As you would expect, the basic structure of an HTML document tends to remain the same. For example, *.htm files (or, alternatively, *.html files) open and close with <html> and </html> tags, typically define a <body> section, and so forth. Keep in mind that HTML is *not* case sensitive. Therefore, in the eyes of the hosting browser, <HTML>, <html>, and <Html> are identical.

To illustrate some HTML basics, open Visual Studio 2005, insert an empty HTML file using the File ➤ New ➤ File menu selection, and save this file under your C:\CodeTests\CarsWebSite directory as default.htm. As you can see, the initial markup is uneventful:

```
<html>
<body>
</body>
</html>
```

The <html> and </html> tags are used to mark the beginning and end of your document. As you may guess, web browsers use these tags to understand where to begin applying the rendering formats specified in the body of the document. The <body> scope is where the vast majority of the actual content is defined. To spruce things up just a bit, define a title for your page as so:

```
<html>
<head>
  <title>This Is the Cars Website</title>
</head>
<body>
</body>
</html>
```

As you would guess, the <title> tags are used to specify the text string that should be placed in the title bar of the calling web browser.

HTML Form Development

The real action of an *.htm file occurs within the scope of the <form> elements. An *HTML form* is simply a named group of related UI elements used to gather user input, which is then transmitted to the web application via HTTP. Do not confuse an HTML form with the entire display area shown by a given browser. In reality, an HTML form is more of a *logical grouping* of widgets placed in the <form> and </form> tag set:

```
<html>
<head>
  <title>This Is the Cars Web Site</title>
</head>
<body>
  <form id="defaultPage" name="defaultPage">
    <!-- Insert web content here ->
  </form>
</body>
</html>
```

This form has been assigned the ID and name of "defaultPage". Typically, the opening <form> tag supplies an action attribute that specifies the URL to which to submit the form data, as well as the method of transmitting that data itself (POST or GET). You will examine this aspect of the <form>

tag in just a bit. For the time being, let's look at the sorts of items that can be placed in an HTML form. Visual Studio 2005 provides an HTML tab on the Toolbox that allows you to select each HTML-based UI widget (see Figure 23-4).

Figure 23-4. *The HTML controls tab of the Toolbox*

Building an HTML-Based User Interface

Before you add the HTML widgets to the HTML <form>, it is worth pointing out that Visual Studio 2005 allows you to edit the overall look and feel of the *.htm file itself using the integrated HTML designer and the Properties window. If you select DOCUMENT from the Properties window (see Figure 23-5), you are able to configure various aspects of the HTML page, such as the background color.

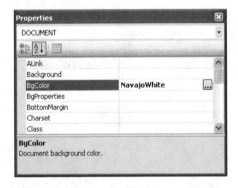

Figure 23-5. *Editing an HTML document via VS .NET*

Now, update the <body> of the default.htm file to display some literal text that prompts the user to enter a user name and password, and choose a background color of your liking (be aware that you can enter and format textual content by typing directly on the HTML designer):

```
<html>
<head>
    <title>This Is the Cars Website</title>
```

```
</head>
<body bgcolor="NavajoWhite">
    <!-- Prompt for user input-->
    <h1 align="center">
      The Cars Login Page</h1>
    <p align="center"> <br>
      Please enter your <i>user name</i> and <i>password</i>.</p>
  <form id="defaultPage" name="defaultPage">
  </form>
</body>
</html>
```

Now let's build the HTML form itself. In general, each HTML widget is described using a name attribute (used to identify the item programmatically) and a type attribute (used to specify which UI element you are interested in placing in the <form> declaration). Depending on which UI widget you manipulate, you will find additional attributes specific to that particular item that can be modified using the Properties window.

The UI you will build here will contain two text fields (one of which is a Password widget) and two button types (one to submit the form data and the other to reset the form data to the default values):

```
<!-- Build a form to get user info -->
<form name="defaultPage" id="defaultPage">
  <P align="center">User Name:
  <input id="txtUserName" type="text" NAME="txtUserName"></P>
  <P align="center">Password:
    <input name="txtPassword" type="password" ID="txtPassword"></P>
  <P align="center">
   <input name="btnSubmit" type="submit" value="Submit" ID="btnSubmit">
   <input name="btnReset" type="reset" value="Reset" ID="btnReset">
  </P>
</form>
```

Notice that you have assigned relevant names and IDs to each widget (txtUserName, txtPassword, btnSubmit, and btnReset). Of greater importance, note that each input item has an extra attribute named type that marks these buttons as UI items that automatically clear all fields to their initial values (type = "reset"), mask the input as a password (type="password"), or send the form data to the recipient (type = "submit"). Figure 23-6 displays the page thus far.

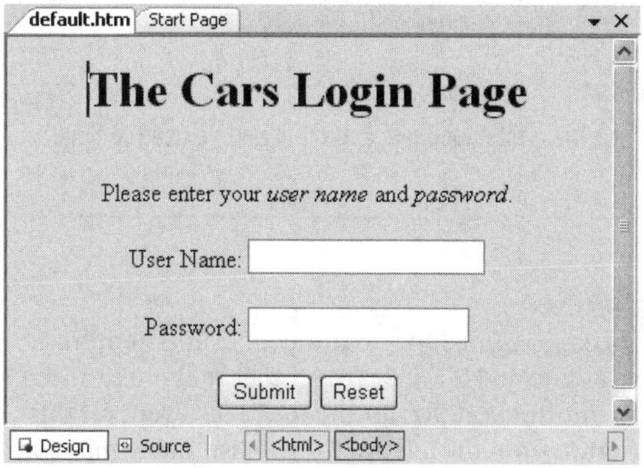

Figure 23-6. *The initial crack at the* default.htm *page*

The Role of Client-Side Scripting

A given *.htm file may contain blocks of script code that will be emitted in the response stream and processed by the requesting browser. There are two major reasons why client-side scripting is used:

- To validate user input before posting back to the web server
- To interact with the Document Object Model (DOM) of the target browser

Regarding the first point, understand that the inherent evil of a web application is the need to make frequent round-trips (aka postbacks) to the server machine to update the HTML rendered into the browser. While postbacks are unavoidable, you should always be mindful of ways to minimize travel across the wire. One technique that saves round-trips is to use client-side scripting to validate user input before submitting the form data to the web server. If an error is found (such as not specifying data within a required field), you can prompt the user of the error without incurring the cost of posting back to the web server. (After all, nothing is more annoying to users than posting back on a slow connection, only to receive instructions to address input errors!)

In addition to validating user input, client-side scripts can also be used to interact with the underlying object model (the DOM) of the browser itself. Most commercial browsers expose a set of objects that can be leveraged to control how the browser should behave. One major annoyance is the fact that different browsers tend to expose similar, but not identical, object models. Thus, if you emit a block of client-side script code that interacts with the DOM, it may not work identically on all browsers.

■**Note** ASP.NET provides the HttpRequest.Browser property, which allows you to determine at runtime the capacities of the browser that sent the current request.

There are many scripting languages that can be used to author client-side script code. Two of the more popular are VBScript and JavaScript. VBScript is a subset of the Visual Basic 6.0 programming language. Be aware that Microsoft Internet Explorer (IE) is the only web browser that has built-in support for client-side VBScript support. Thus, if you wish your HTML pages to work correctly in any commercial web browser, do *not* use VBScript for your client-side scripting logic.

The other popular scripting language is JavaScript. Be very aware that JavaScript is in no way, shape, or form a subset of the Java language. While JavaScript and Java have a somewhat similar syntax, JavaScript is not a full-fledged OOP language, and thus is far less powerful than Java. The good news is that all modern-day web browsers support JavaScript, which makes it a natural candidate for client-side scripting logic.

■**Note** To further confuse the issue, recall that JScript .NET is a managed language that can be used to build valid .NET assemblies using a scripting like syntax.

A Client-Side Scripting Example

To illustrate the role of client-side scripting, let's first examine how to intercept events sent from client-side HTML GUI widgets. Assume you have added an HTML Button (btnHelp) type to your default.htm page that allows the user to view help information. To capture the Click event for this button, activate the HTML view and select your button from the left drop-down list. Using the right drop-down list, select the onclick event. This will add an onclick attribute to the definition of the new Button type:

```
<input id="btnHelp" type="button" value="Help" language="javascript"
onclick="return btnHelp_onclick()" />
```

Visual Studio 2005 will also create an empty JavaScript function that will be called when the user clicks the button. Within this stub, simply make use of the alert() method to display a client-side message box:

```
<script language="javascript" type="text/javascript">
<!--
function btnHelp_onclick() {
    alert("Dude, it is not that hard.  Click the darn Submit button!");
}
// -->
</script>
```

Note that the scripting block has been wrapped within HTML comments (<!-- -->). The reason is simple. If your page ends up on a browser that does not support JavaScript, the code will be treated as a comment block and ignored. Of course, your page may be less functional, but the upside is that your page will not blow up when rendered by the browser.

Validating the default.htm Form Data

Now, let's update the default.htm page to support some client-side validation logic. The goal is to ensure that when the user clicks the Submit button, you call a JavaScript function that checks each text box for empty values. If this is the case, you pop up an alert that instructs the user to enter the required data. First, handle an onclick event for the Submit button:

```
<input name="btnSubmit" type="submit" value="Submit" id="btnSubmit"
language="javascript" onclick="return btnSubmit_onclick()">
```

Implement this handler as so:

```
function btnSubmit_onclick(){
    // If they forget either item, pop up a message box.
    if((defaultPage.txtUserName.value == "") ||
    (defaultPage.txtPassword.value == ""))
    {
        alert("You must supply a user name and password!");
        return false;
    }
    return true;
}
```

At this point, you can open your browser of choice and navigate to the default.htm page hosted by your Cars virtual directory and test out your client-side script logic:

```
http://localhost/Cars/default.htm
```

Submitting the Form Data (GET and POST)

Now that you have a simple HTML page, you need to examine how to transmit the form data back to the web server for processing. When you build an HTML form, you typically supply an action attribute on the opening <form> tag to specify the recipient of the incoming form data. Possible receivers include mail servers, other HTML files, an Active Server Pages (ASP; classic or .NET) file, and so forth. For this example, you'll use a classic ASP file named ClassicAspPage.asp. Update your default.htm file by specifying the following attribute in the opening <form> tag:

```
<form name="defaultPage" id="defaultPage"
  action="http://localhost/Cars/ClassicAspPage.asp" method = "GET">
    ...
</form>
```

These extra attributes ensure that when the Submit button for this form is clicked, the form data should be sent to the ClassicAspPage.asp at the specified URL. When you specify method = "GET" as the mode of transmission, the form data is appended to the query string as a set of name/value pairs separated by ampersands:

http://localhost/Cars/ClassicAspPage.asp?**txtUserName=
Andrew&txtPassword=abcd123$**&btnSubmit=Submit

The other method of transmitting form data to the web server is to specify method = "POST":

```
< form name="defaultPage" id="defaultPage"
  action="http://localhost/Cars/ClassicAspPage.asp" method = "POST">
    ...
</form>
```

In this case, the form data is not appended to the query string, but instead is written to a separate line within the HTTP header. Using POST, the form data is not directly visible to the outside world. More important, POST data does not have a character-length limitation (many browsers have a limit for GET queries). For the time being, make use of HTTP GET to send the form data to the receiving *.asp page.

Building a Classic ASP Page

A classic ASP page is a hodgepodge of HTML and server-side script code. If you have never worked with classic ASP, understand that the goal of ASP is to dynamically build HTML on the fly using *server-side* script and a small set of classic COM objects. For example, you may have a server-side VBScript (or JavaScript) block that reads a table from a data source using classic ADO and returns the rows as a generic HTML table.

For this example, the ASP page uses the intrinsic ASP Request COM object to read the values of the incoming form data (appended to the query string) and echo them back to the caller (not terribly exciting, but it makes the point). The server-side script logic will make use of VBScript (as denoted by the language directive).

To do so, create a new HTML file using Visual Studio .NET and save this file under the name ClassicAspPage.asp into the folder to which your virtual directory has been mapped (e.g., C:\CodeTests\CarsWebSite). Implement this page as so:

```
<%@ language="VBScript" %>
<html>
<head>
    <title>The Cars Page</title>
</head>
 <body>
    <h1 align="center">Here is what you sent me:</h1>
    <P align="center"> <b>User Name: </b>
    <%= Request.QueryString("txtUserName") %> <br>
    <b>Password: </b>
    <%= Request.QueryString("txtPassword") %> <br>
    </P>
</body>
</html>
```

Here, you use the classic ASP Request COM object to call the QueryString() method to examine the values contained in each HTML widget submitted via method = "GET". The <%= ...%> notation is a shorthand way of saying, "Insert the following directly into the outbound HTTP response." To gain a finer level of flexibility, you could interact with the ASP Response COM object within a full script block (denoted by the <%, %> notation). You have no need to do so here; however, the following is a simple example:

```
<%
  Dim pwd
  pwd = Request.QueryString("txtPassword")
  Response.Write(pwd)
%>
```

Obviously, the Request and Response objects of classic ASP provide a number of additional members beyond those shown here. Furthermore, classic ASP also defines a small number of additional COM objects (Session, Server, Application, and so on) that you can use while constructing your web application.

■**Note** Under ASP.NET, these COM objects are officially dead. However, you will see that the System.Web.UI.Page base class defines identically named properties that expose objects with similar functionality.

To test the ASP logic, simply load the default.htm page from a browser and submit the form data. Once the script is processed on the web server, you are returned a brand new (dynamically generated) HTML display (see Figure 23-7).

Figure 23-7. *The dynamically generated HTML*

Responding to POST Submissions

Currently, your default.htm file specifies HTTP GET as the method of sending the form data to the target *.asp file. Using this approach, the values contained in the various GUI widgets are appended to the end of the query string. It is important to note that the ASP Request.QueryString() method is *only* able to extract data submitted via the GET method.

If you would rather submit form data to the web resource using HTTP POST, you can use the Request.Form collection to read the values on the server, for example:

```
<body>
    <h1 align="center">Here is what you sent me:</h1>
    <P align="center">
        <b>User Name: </b>
        <%= Request.Form("txtUserName") %> <br>
        <b>Password: </b>
        <%= Request.Form("txtPassword") %> <br>
    </P>
</body>
```

That wraps up our web development primer. Hopefully, if you're new to web development you now have a better understanding of the basic building blocks. Before we check out how the .NET platform improves upon the current state of affairs, let's take a brief moment to bash (which is to say, "critique") classic ASP.

■**Source Code** The ClassicAspCars example is included under the Chapter 23 subdirectory.

Problems with Classic ASP

While many successful websites have been created using classic ASP, this architecture is not without its downsides. Perhaps the biggest downfall of classic ASP is the same thing that makes it a powerful platform: server-side scripting languages. Scripting languages such as VBScript and JavaScript are interpreted, typeless entities that do not lend themselves to robust OO programming techniques.

Another problem with classic ASP is the fact that an *.asp page does not yield very modularized code. Given that ASP is a blend of HTML and script in a *single* page, most ASP web applications are a confused mix of two very different programming techniques. While it is true that classic ASP allows you to partition reusable code into distinct include files, the underlying object model does not support true separation of concerns. In an ideal world, a web framework would allow the presentation logic (i.e., HTML tags) to exist independently from the business logic (i.e., functional code).

A final issue to consider here is the fact that classic ASP demands a good deal of boilerplate, redundant script code that tends to repeat between projects. Almost all web applications need to validate user input, repopulate the state of HTML widgets before emitting the HTTP response, generate an HTML table of data, and so forth.

Major Benefits of ASP.NET 1.x

The first major release of ASP.NET (version 1.x) did a fantastic job of addressing each of the limitations found with classic ASP. In a nutshell, the .NET platform brought about the following techniques:

- ASP.NET 1.x provides a model termed *code-behind*, which allows you to separate presentation logic from business logic.

- ASP.NET 1.x pages are compiled .NET assemblies, not interpreted scripting languages, which translates into much faster execution.

- Web controls allow programmers to build the GUI of a web application in a manner similar to building a Windows Forms application.

- ASP.NET web controls automatically maintain their state during postbacks using a hidden form field named __VIEWSTATE.

- ASP.NET web applications are completely object-oriented and make use of the CTS.

- ASP.NET web applications can be easily configured using standard IIS settings *or* using a web application configuration file (`Web.config`).

While ASP.NET 1.*x* was a major step in the right direction, ASP.NET 2.0 provides even more bells and whistles.

Major Enhancements of ASP.NET 2.0

ASP.NET 2.0 provides a number of new namespaces, types, utilities, and technologies to the .NET web development landscape. Consider this partial list:

- ASP.NET 2.0 no longer requires websites to be hosted under IIS during the testing and development of your site. You are now able to host your site from any directory on the hard drive.

- ASP.NET 2.0 ships with a large number of new web controls (security controls, new data controls, new UI controls, etc.) that complement the existing ASP.NET 1.*x* control set.

- ASP.NET 2.0 supports the use of *master pages*, which allow you to attach a common UI frame to a set of related pages.

- ASP.NET 2.0 supports *themes*, which offer a declarative manner to change the look and feel of the entire web application.

- ASP.NET 2.0 supports *web parts*, which can be used to allow end users to customize the look and feel of a web page.

- ASP.NET 2.0 supports a web-based configuration and management utility that maintains your `Web.config` files.

The truth of the matter is that if I were to truly do justice to every aspect of ASP.NET 2.0, this book would double in size. Given that this book is not focused exclusively on web development, be sure to consult the .NET Framework 2.0 documentation for details of topics not covered here.

The ASP.NET 2.0 Namespaces

As of .NET 2.0, there are no fewer than *34* web-centric namespaces in the base class libraries. From a high level, these namespaces can be grouped into four major categories:

- Core functionality (e.g., types that allow you to interact with the HTTP request and response, Web Form infrastructure, theme and profiling support, web parts, etc.)

- Web Form and HTML controls

- Mobile web development

- XML web services

This text will not examine the topic of mobile .NET development (web-based or otherwise); however, the role of XML web services will be examined in Chapter 25. Table 23-1 describes several of the core ASP.NET 2.0 namespaces.

Table 23-1. *ASP.NET Web-centric Namespaces*

Namespaces	Meaning in Life
System.Web	Defines types that enable browser/web server communication (such as request and response capabilities, cookie manipulation, and file transfer)
System.Web.Caching	Defines types that facilitate caching support for a web application
System.Web.Hosting	Defines types that allow you to build custom hosts for the ASP.NET runtime
System.Web.Management	Defines types for managing and monitoring the health of an ASP.NET web application
System.Web.Profile	Defines types that are used to implement ASP.NET user profiles
System.Web.Security	Defines types that allow you to programmatically secure your site
System.Web.SessionState	Defines types that allow you to maintain stateful information on a per-user basis (e.g., session state variables)
System.Web.UI System.Web.UI.WebControls System.Web.UI.HtmlControls	Define a number of types that allow you to build a GUI front end for your web application

The ASP.NET Web Page Code Model

ASP.NET web pages can be constructed using one of two approaches. You are free to create a single *.aspx file that contains a blend of server-side code and HTML (much like classic ASP). Using the single-file page model, server-side code is placed within a <script> scope, but the code itself is *not* script code proper (e.g., VBScript/JavaScript). Rather, the code statements within a <script> block are written in your managed language of choice (C#, Visual Basic .NET, etc).

If you are building a page that contains very little code (but a good deal of HTML), a single-file page model may be easier to work with, as you can see the code and the markup in one unified *.aspx file. In addition, crunching your code and HTML into a single *.aspx file provides a few other advantages:

- Pages written using the single-file model are slightly easier to deploy or to send to another developer.

- Because there is no dependency between files, a single-file page is easier to rename.

- Managing files in a source code control system is slightly easier, as all the action is taking place in a single file.

The default approach taken by Visual Studio 2005 (when creating a new website solution) is to make use of a technique termed *code-behind*, which allows you to separate your programming code from your HTML presentation logic using two distinct files. This model works quite well when your pages contain significant amounts of code or when multiple developers are working on the same website. The code-behind model offers a few additional benefits as well:

- Because code-behind pages offer a clean separation of HTML markup and code, it is possible to have designers working on the markup while programmers author the C# code.

- Code is not exposed to page designers or others who are working only with the page markup (as you might guess, HTML folks are not always interested in viewing reams of C# code).

- Code files can be used across multiple *.aspx files.

Regardless of which approach you take, do know that there is *no* difference in terms of per-formance. Also be aware that the single-file *.aspx model is no longer considered *evil* as proclaimed in .NET 1.*x*. In fact, many ASP.NET 2.0 web applications will benefit by building sites that make use of both approaches.

Working with the Single-File Page Model

First up, let's examine the single-file page model. Our goal is to build an *.aspx file (named Default.aspx) that displays the Inventory table of the Cars database (created in Chapter 22). While you could build this page using nothing but Notepad, Visual Studio 2005 can simplify matters via IntelliSense, code completion, and a visual page designer.

To begin, open Visual Studio 2005 and create a new Web Form using the File ➤ New ➤ File menu option (see Figure 23-8).

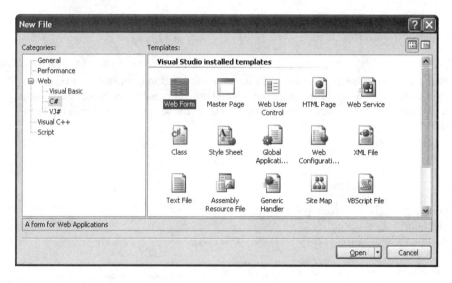

Figure 23-8. *Creating a new* *.aspx *file*

Once the page loads into the IDE, notice that the bottom area of the page designer allows you to view the *.aspx file in two distinct manners. If you select the Design button, you are shown a visual designer surface that allows you to build the UI of your page much like you would build a Windows Form (drag widgets to the surface, configure them via the Properties Window, etc.). If you select the Source button, you can view the HTML and <script> blocks that compose the *.aspx file itself.

■**Note** Unlike earlier versions of Visual Studio, the Source view of Visual Studio 2005 has full-blown IntelliSense and allows you to drag and drop UI elements directly onto the HTML.

Using the Visual Studio 2005 Toolbox, select the Standard tab and drag and drop a Button, Label, and GridView control onto the page designer (the GridView widget can be found under the Data tab of the Toolbox). Feel free to make use of the Properties window (or the HTML IntelliSense) to set various UI properties and give each web widget a proper name via the ID property. Figure 23-9 shows one possible design (I kept my look and feel intentionally bland to minimize the amount of generated control markup).

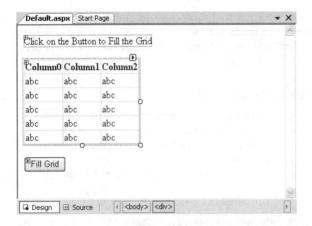

Figure 23-9. *The* Default.aspx *UI*

Now, click the Source button at the bottom of your code window and locate the <form> section of your page. Notice how each web control has been defined using an <asp:> tag. Before the closing tag, you will find a series of name/value pairs that correspond to the settings you made in the Properties window:

```
<form id="form1" runat="server">
<div>
    <asp:Label ID="lblInfo" runat="server"
        Text="Click on the Button to Fill the Grid">
    </asp:Label>
    <asp:GridView ID="carsGridView" runat="server">
    </asp:GridView>
    <asp:Button ID="btnFillData" runat="server" Text="Fill Grid" />
</div>
</form>
```

You will dig into the full details of ASP.NET web controls later in this chapter. Until then, understand that web controls are classes processed on the web server, and they emit back their HTML representation into the outgoing HTTP response automatically (that's right—you don't author the HTML!).

Beyond this major benefit, ASP.NET web controls support a Windows Forms–like programming model, given that the names of the properties, methods, and events mimic their Windows Forms equivalents. To illustrate, handle the Click event for the Button type using either the Visual Studio Properties window (via the lightning-bolt icon) or using the drop-down boxes mounted at the top of the Source view window. Once you do, you will find your Button's definition has been updated with an OnClick attribute that is assigned to the name of your Click event handler:

```
<asp:Button ID="btnFillData" runat="server"
Text="Fill Grid" OnClick="btnFillData_Click" />
```

As well, your <script> block has been updated with a server-side Click event handler (notice that the incoming parameters are a dead-on match for the target of the System.EventHandler delegate):

```
<script runat="server">
protected void btnFillData_Click(object sender, EventArgs e)
{
}
</script>
```

Implement your server-side event handler to make use of an ADO.NET data reader to fill the GridView. Also add an import directive (more details on this in just a moment) that specifies you are using the System.Data.SqlClient namespace. Here is the remaining relevant page logic of the Default.aspx file:

```
<%@ Page Language="C#" %>
<%@ Import Namespace = "System.Data.SqlClient" %>
...
<script runat="server">
protected void btnFillData_Click(object sender, EventArgs e)
{
  SqlConnection sqlConn =
    new SqlConnection("Data Source=.;Initial Catalog=Cars;UID=sa;PWD=");
  sqlConn.Open();
  SqlCommand cmd =
    new SqlCommand("Select * From Inventory", sqlConn);
  carsGridView.DataSource = cmd.ExecuteReader();
  carsGridView.DataBind();
  sqlConn.Close();
}
</script>
<html xmlns="http://www.w3.org/1999/xhtml" >
...
</html>
```

Before we dive into the details behind the format of this *.aspx file, let's try a test run. Open a Visual Studio 2005 command prompt and run the WebDev.WebServer.exe utility, making sure you specify the path where you saved your Default.aspx file:

```
webdev.webserver.exe /port:12345 /path:"C:\CodeTests\SinglePageModel"
```

Now, using your browser of choice, enter the following URL:

```
http://localhost:12345/
```

When the page is served, you will initially see your Label and Button types. However, when you click the Button, a postback occurs to the web server, at which point the web controls render back their corresponding HTML tags. Figure 23-10 shows the page hosted within Mozilla Firefox.

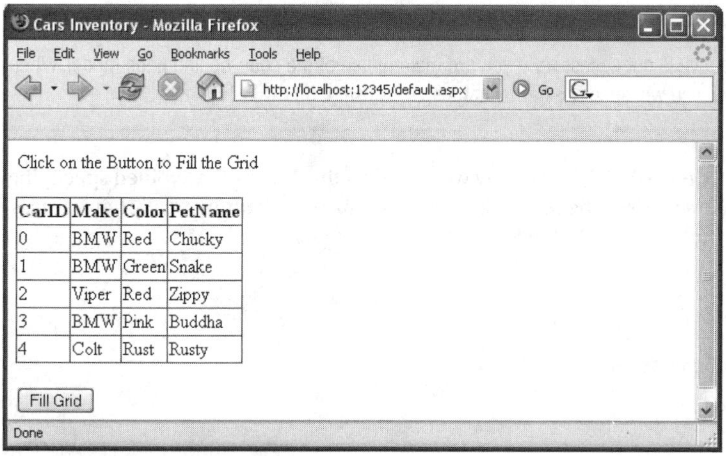

Figure 23-10. *Web-based data access*

That was simple, yes? Of course, as they say, the devil is in the details, so let's dig a bit deeper into the composition of this *.aspx file.

The <%@Page%> Directive

The first thing to be aware of is that a given *.aspx file will typically open with a set of directives. ASP.NET directives are always denoted with <%@ XXX %> markers and may be qualified with various attributes to inform the ASP.NET runtime how to process the attribute in question.

Every *.aspx file must have at minimum a <%@Page%> directive that is used to define the managed language used within the page (via the language attribute). Also, the <%@Page%> directive may define the name of the related code-behind file (if any), enable tracing support, and so forth. Table 23-2 documents some of the more interesting <%@Page%>-centric attributes.

Table 23-2. *Select Attributes of the* <%@Page%> *Directive*

Attribute	Meaning in Life
CompilerOptions	Allows you to define any command-line flags (represented as a single string) passed into the compiler when this page is processed.
CodeFile	Specifies the name of the related code-behind file.
EnableTheming	Establishes if the controls on the *.aspx page support ASP.NET 2.0 themes
EnableViewState	Indicates whether view state is maintained across page requests (more details on this in Chapter 24)
Inherits	Defines a class in the code-behind page the *.aspx file derives from, which can be any class derived from System.Web.UI.Page
MasterPageFile	Sets the master page used in conjunction with the current *.aspx page
Trace	Indicates whether tracing is enabled

The <%@Import%> Directive

In addition to the <%@Page%> directive, a given *.aspx file may specify various <%@Import%> directives to explicitly state the namespaces required by the current page. Here, you specified you were making use of the types within the System.Data.SqlClient namespace. As you would guess, if you need to make use of additional .NET namespaces, you simply specify multiple <%@Import%> directives.

■**Note** The <%@Import%> directive is not necessary if you are making use of the code-behind page model. When you do make use of code-behind, you will specify external namespaces using the C# using keyword.

Given your current knowledge of .NET, you may wonder how this *.aspx file avoided specifying the System.Data or System namespaces. The reason is that all *.aspx pages automatically have access to a set of key namespaces, including the following:

- System
- System.Collections
- System.Collections.Generic
- System.Configuration
- System.IO

- System.Text
- System.Text.RegularExpressions
- All of the System.Web-centric namespaces

ASP.NET does define a number of other directives that may appear in an *.aspx file above and beyond <%@Page%> and <%@Import%>; however, I'll reserve commenting on those for the time being.

The "Script" Block

Under the single-file page model, an *.aspx file may contain server-side scripting logic that executes on the web server. Given this it is *critical* that all of your server-side code blocks are defined to execute at the server, using the runat="server" attribute. If the runat="server" attribute is not supplied, the runtime assumes you have authored a block of *client-side* script to be emitted into the outgoing HTTP response:

```
<script runat="server">
protected void btnFillData_Click(object sender, EventArgs e)
{
}
</script>
```

The signature of this helper method should look strangely familiar. Recall from our examination of Windows Forms that a given event handler must match the pattern defined by a related .NET delegate. And, just like Windows Forms, when you wish to handle a server-side button click, the delegate in question is System.EventHandler which, as you recall, can only call methods that take a System.Object as the first parameter and a System.EventArgs as the second.

The ASP.NET Widget Declarations

The final point of interest is the declaration of the Button, Label, and GridView Web Form controls. Like classic ASP and raw HTML, ASP.NET web widgets are scoped within <form> elements. This time, however, the opening <form> element is marked with the runat="server" attribute. This again is critical, as this tag informs the ASP.NET runtime that before the HTML is emitted into the response stream, the contained ASP.NET widgets have a chance to render their HTML appearance:

```
<form id="form1" runat="server">
...
</form>
```

ASP.NET web controls are declared with <asp> and </asp> tags, and they are also marked with the runat="server" attribute. Within the opening tag, you will specify the name of the Web Form control and any number of name/value pairs that will be used at runtime to render the correct HTML.

■**Source Code** The SinglePageModel example is included under the Chapter 23 subdirectory.

Working with the Code-Behind Page Model

To illustrate the code-behind page model, let's re-create the previous example using the Visual Studio 2005 Web Site template (do know that Visual Studio 2005 is not required to build pages using code-behind). Activate the File ➤ New ➤ Web Site menu option, and select the ASP.NET Web Site template (see Figure 23-11).

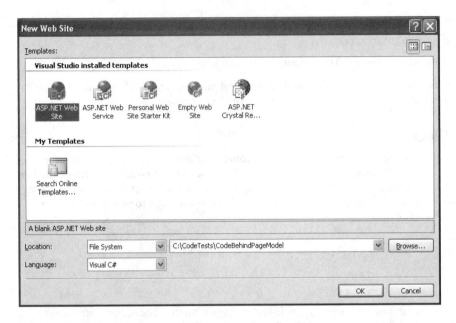

Figure 23-11. *The Visual Studio 2005 ASP.NET Web Site template*

Notice in Figure 23-11 that you are able to select the location of your new site. If you select File System, your content files will be placed within a local directory and pages will be served via WebDev. WebServer.exe. If you select FTP or HTTP, your site will be hosted within a virtual directory maintained by IIS. For this example, it makes no difference which option you select, but for simplicity I'd suggest the File System option.

■**Note** When you create an ASP.NET website, Visual Studio 2005 will place the solution file (*.sln) under the My Documents\Visual Studio 2005\Projects directory. Your site's content files (such as the *.aspx files) will be located under the specified local directory or (if using IIS) within the physical file mapped to the virtual directory.

Once again, make use of the designer to build a UI consisting of a Label, Button, and GridView, and make use of the Properties window to build a UI of your liking. Now, click the Source button at the bottom of your code window, and you will see the expected <asp> and </asp> tags. Also note that the <%@Page%> directive has been updated with two new attributes:

```
<%@ Page Language="C#" AutoEventWireup="true"
CodeFile="Default.aspx.cs" Inherits="_Default" %>
```

The CodeFile attribute is used to specify the related external file that contains this page's coding logic. By default, these code-behind files are named by suffixing .cs to the name of the *.aspx file (Default.aspx.cs in this example). If you examine Solution Explorer, you will see this code-behind file is visible via a subnode on the Web Form icon (see Figure 23-12).

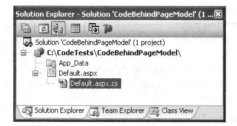

Figure 23-12. *The associated code-behind file for a given* `*.aspx` *file*

■Note The ASP.NET 1.*x* `Codebehind` attribute is no longer supported within the `<%@Page%>` directive.

Beyond a number of `using` statements to specify several web-centric namespaces, your code-behind file defines a partial class deriving from `System.Web.UI.Page`. Notice that the name of this class (`_Default`) is identical to the `Inherits` attribute within the `<%@Page%>` directive (more details on `Page_Load()` a bit later in this chapter):

```
public partial class _Default : System.Web.UI.Page
{
    protected void Page_Load(object sender, EventArgs e)
    {
    }
}
```

Handle the `Click` event for the `Button` type (again, just like you would for a Windows Forms application). As before, the `Button` definition has been updated with an `OnClick` attribute. However, the server-side event handler is no longer placed within a `<script>` scope of the `*.aspx` file, but as a method of the `_Default` class type. To complete this example, add a `using` statement for `System.Data.SqlClient` inside your code-behind file and implement the handler using the previous ADO.NET logic:

```
protected void btnFillGrid_Click(object sender, EventArgs e)
{
    SqlConnection sqlConn =
      new SqlConnection("Data Source=.;Initial Catalog=Cars;UID=sa;PWD=");
    sqlConn.Open();
    SqlCommand cmd =
      new SqlCommand("Select * From Inventory", sqlConn);
    carsGridView.DataSource = cmd.ExecuteReader();
    carsGridView.DataBind();
    sqlConn.Close();
}
```

If you selected the File System option, `WebDev.WebServer.exe` starts up automatically when you run your web application (if you selected IIS, this obviously does not occur). In either case, the default browser should now display the page's content.

Debugging and Tracing ASP.NET Pages

By and large, when you are building ASP.NET web projects, you can use the same debugging techniques as you would with any other sort of Visual Studio 2005 project type. Thus, you can set breakpoints in your code-behind file (as well as embedded "script" blocks in an *.aspx file), start a debug session (the F5 key by default), and step through your code.

However, to debug your ASP.NET web applications, your site must contain a property-constructed Web.config file. Chapter 24 will examine various details behind Web.config files, but in a nutshell these XML files provide the same general purpose as an executable assembly's app.config file. Visual Studio 2005 will detect if your project does not currently have a Web.config file and insert such a file into your project. The relevant element is <compilation>:

```
<configuration xmlns="http://schemas.microsoft.com/.NetConfiguration/v2.0">
...
  <system.web>
    <compilation debug="true"/>
  </system.web>
</configuration>
```

You are also able to enable tracing support for an *.aspx file by setting the Trace attribute to true within the <%@Page%> directive:

```
<%@ Page Language="C#" AutoEventWireup="true"
CodeFile="Default.aspx.cs" Inherits="_Default" Trace="true" %>
```

Once you do, the emitted HTML now contains numerous details regarding the previous HTTP request/response (server variables, session and application variables, request/response, etc.). To insert your own trace messages into the mix, you can use the Trace property of the System.Web.UI.Page type. Any time you wish to log a custom message (from a script block or C# source code file), simply call the Write() method:

```
protected void btnFillGrid_Click(object sender, EventArgs e)
{
    // Emit a custom trace message.
    Trace.Write("My Category", "Filling the grid!");
...
}
```

If you run your project once again and post back to the web server, you will find your custom category and custom message are present and accounted for. In Figure 23-13, take note of the final message before the "Control Tree" section.

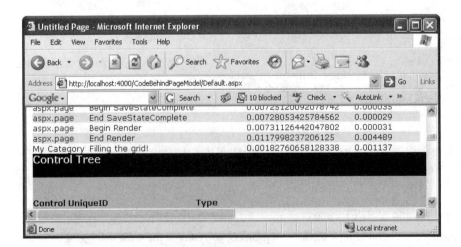

Figure 23-13. *Logging custom trace messages*

■**Source Code** The CodeBehindPageModel example is included under the Chapter 23 subdirectory.

Details of an ASP.NET Website Directory Structure

If you have created web applications using ASP.NET 1.*x*, you may be quite surprised to see that many familiar files (Web.config, Global.asax, AssemblyInfo.cs, and so on) are not included when creating a new website. As well, the Web Site template contains a folder named App_Data and does not appear to have References folder within Solution Explorer.

First of all, do know that Web.config and Global.asax files are most certainly supported under ASP.NET 2.0, but you will need to explicitly add them to your project using the WebSite ➤ Add New Item menu option. Chapter 24 will examine the role of both of these file types, so don't sweat the details for now. Next, be aware that your websites are still able to add references to any number of external .NET assemblies via the WebSite ➤ Add Reference menu option (the end result is a bit different, however, as you will soon see).

Another significant difference is that under Visual Studio 2005, websites may contain any number of specifically named subdirectories, each of which has a special meaning to the ASP.NET runtime. Table 23-3 documents these "special subdirectories."

Table 23-3. *Special ASP.NET 2.0 Subdirectories*

Subfolder	Meaning in Life
App_Browsers	Folder for browser definition files that are used to identify individual browsers and determine their capabilities.
App_Code	Folder for source code for components or classes that you want to compile as part of your application. ASP.NET compiles the code in this folder when pages are requested. Code in the App_Code folder is automatically accessible by your application.
App_Data	Folder for storing Access *.mdb files, SQL Express *.mdf files, XML files, or other data stores.
App_GlobalResources	Folder for *.resx files that are accessed programmatically from application code.
App_LocalResources	Folder for *.resx files that are bound to a specific page.
App_Themes	Folder that contains a collection of files that define the appearance of ASP.NET web pages and controls.
App_WebReferences	Folder for proxy classes, schemas, and other files associated with using a web service in your application.
Bin	Folder for compiled private assemblies (*.dll files). Assemblies in the Bin folder are automatically referenced by your application.

If you are interested in adding any of these known subfolders to your current web application, you may do so explicitly using the WebSite ➤ Add Folder menu option. However, in many cases, the IDE will automatically do so as you "naturally" insert related files into your site (e.g., adding a new C# file will automatically add an App_Code folder to your directory structure if one does not currently exist).

The Role of the Bin Folder

As described in a few pages, ASP.NET web pages are eventually compiled into a .NET assembly. Given this, it should come as no surprise that your websites can reference any number of private or shared assemblies. Under ASP.NET 2.0, the manner in which your site's externally required assemblies are recorded is quite different from ASP.NET 1.*x*. The reason for this fundamental shift is that Visual Studio 2005 now treats websites in a *projectless manner*.

Although the Web Site template does generate a *.sln file to load your *.aspx files into the IDE, there is no longer a related *.csproj file. As you may know, ASP.NET 1.*x* Web Application projects recorded all external assemblies within *.csproj. This fact brings up the obvious question, where are the external assemblies recorded under ASP.NET 2.0?

When you reference a private assembly, Visual Studio 2005 will automatically create a Bin directory within your directory structure to store a local copy of the binary. When your code base makes use of types within these code libraries, they are automatically loaded on demand. By way of a simple test, if you activate the WebSite ➤ Add Reference menu option and select any of the previous (non–strongly named) *.dlls you created over the course of this text, you will find a Bin folder is displayed within Solution Explorer (see Figure 23-14).

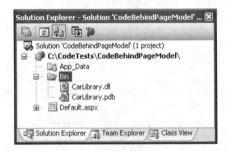

Figure 23-14. *The Bin folder contains copies of all referenced private assemblies.*

If you reference a shared assembly, Visual Studio 2005 automatically inserts a Web.config file into your current web solution (if one is not currently in place) and records the external reference within the ‹assemblies› element. For example, if you again activate the WebSite ➤ Add Reference menu option and this time select a shared assembly (such as System.Drawing.dll), you will find that your Web.config file has been updated as so:

```
<?xml version="1.0"?>
<configuration xmlns="http://schemas.microsoft.com/.NetConfiguration/v2.0">
  <appSettings/>
  <connectionStrings/>
  <system.web>
    <compilation debug="false">
      <assemblies>
        <add assembly="System.Drawing, Version=2.0.0.0,
        Culture=neutral, PublicKeyToken=B03F5F7F11D50A3A"/>
      </assemblies>
    </compilation>
    <authentication mode="Windows"/>
  </system.web>
</configuration>
```

As you can see, each assembly is described using the same information required for a dynamic load via the Assembly.Load() method (see Chapter 12).

The Role of the App_Code Folder

The App_Code folder is used to place source code files that are not directly tied to a specific web page (such as a code-behind file) but are to be compiled for use by your website. Code within the App_Code folder will be automatically compiled on the fly on an as-needed basis. After this point, the assembly is accessible to any other code in the website. To this end, the App_Code folder is much like the Bin folder, except that you can store source code in it instead of compiled code. The major benefit of this approach is that it is possible to define custom types for your web application without having to compile them independently.

A single App_Code folder can contain code files from multiple languages. At runtime, the appropriate compiler kicks in to generate the assembly in question. If you would rather partition your code, however, you can define multiple subdirectories that are used to hold any number of managed code files (*.cs, *.vb, etc.).

For example, assume you have added an App_Code folder to the root directory of a website application that contains two subfolders (MyCSharpCode and MyVbNetCode) that contain language-specific files. Once you do, you are able to author a Web.config file that specifies these subdirectories using a <codeSubDirectories> element:

```xml
<?xml version="1.0"?>
<configuration xmlns="http://schemas.microsoft.com/.NetConfiguration/v2.0">
  <appSettings/>
  <connectionStrings/>
  <system.web>
    <compilation debug="false">
      <assemblies>
        <add assembly="System.Drawing, Version=2.0.0.0,
        Culture=neutral, PublicKeyToken=B03F5F7F11D50A3A"/>
      </assemblies>
      <codeSubDirectories>
        <add directoryName="MyCSharpCode" />
        <add directoryName="MyVbNetCode" />
      </codeSubDirectories>
    </compilation>
    <authentication mode="Windows"/>
  </system.web>
</configuration>
```

■**Note** The App_Code directory will also be used to contain files that are not language files, but are useful nonetheless (*.xsd files, *.wsdl files, etc.).

The ASP.NET 2.0 Page Compilation Cycle

Regardless of which page model you make use of (single-file or code-behind), your *.aspx files (and any related code-behind file) are compiled on the fly into a valid .NET assembly. This assembly is then hosted by the ASP.NET worker process (aspnet_wp.exe) within its own application domain boundary (see Chapter 13 for details on AppDomains). The manner in which your website's assembly is compiled under ASP.NET 2.0, however, is quite different.

Compilation Cycle for Single-File Pages

If you are making use of the single-file page model, the HTML markup, <script> blocks, and web control definitions are dynamically compiled into a class type deriving from System.Web.UI.Page.

This name of this class is based on the name of the *.aspx file and takes an _aspx suffix (e.g., a page named MyPage.aspx becomes a class type named MyPage_aspx). Figure 23-15 illustrates the basic process.

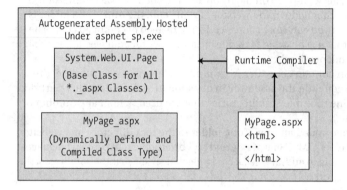

Figure 23-15. *The compilation model for single-file pages*

This dynamically compiled assembly is deployed to a runtime-defined subdirectory under the <%windir%>Microsoft.NET\Framework\v2.0.50215\Temporary ASP.NET Files\root directory. The path beneath \root will differ based on a number of factors (hash codes, etc.), but eventually you will find the *.dll (and supporting files) in question. Figure 23-16 shows one such assembly.

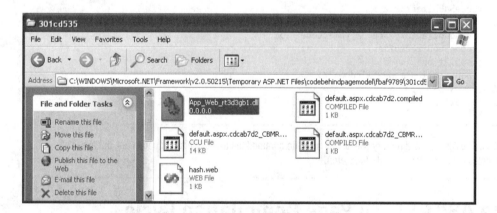

Figure 23-16. *The ASP.NET autogenerated assembly*

Compilation Cycle for Multifile Pages

The compilation process of a page making use of the code-behind model is similar to that of the single-file model. However, the type deriving from System.Web.UI.Page is composed from three (yes, *three*) files rather than the expected *two*.

Looking back at the previous CodeBehindPageModel example, recall that the Default.aspx file was connected to a partial class named _Default within the code-behind file. If you have a background in ASP.NET 1.*x*, you may wonder what happened to the member variable declarations for the various web controls as well as the code within InitializeComponent(), such as event handling logic. Under ASP.NET 2.0, these details are accounted for by a third "file" generated in memory. In reality, of course, this is not a literal file, but an in-memory representation of the partial class. Consider Figure 23-17.

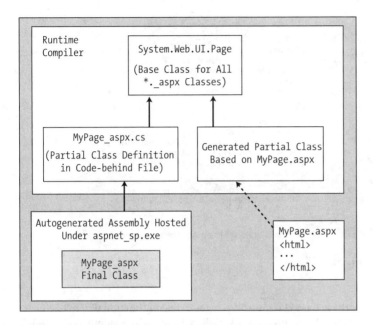

Figure 23-17. *The compilation model for multifile pages*

In this model, the web controls declared in the *.aspx file are used to build the additional partial class that defines each UI member variable and the configuration logic that used to be found within the InitializeComponent() method of ASP.NET 1.*x* (we just never directly see it). This partial class is combined at compile time with the code-behind file to result in the *base class* of the generated _aspx class type (in the single-file page compilation model, the generated _aspx file derived directly from System.Web.UI.Page).

In either case, once the assembly has been created upon the initial HTTP request, it will be reused for all subsequent requests, and thus will not have to be recompiled. Understanding this factoid should help explain why the first request of an *.aspx page takes the longest, and subsequent hits to the same page are extremely efficient.

■Note Under ASP.NET 2.0, it is now possible to precompile all pages (or a subset of pages) of a website using a command-line tool named aspnet_compiler.exe. Check out the .NET Framework 2.0 SDK documentation for details.

The Inheritance Chain of the Page Type

As you have just seen, the final generated class that represents your *.aspx file eventually derives from System.Web.UI.Page. Like any base class, this type provides a polymorphic interface to all derived types. However, the Page type is not the only member in your inheritance hierarchy. If you were to locate the Page type (within the System.Web.dll assembly) using the Visual Studio 2005 object browser, you would find that Page "is-a" TemplateControl, which "is-a" Control, which "is-a" Object (see Figure 23-18).

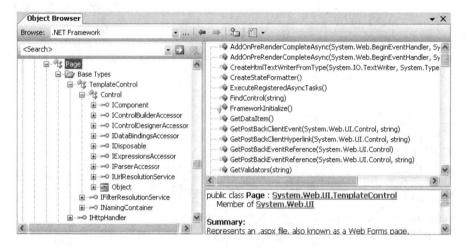

Figure 23-18. *The derivation of an ASP.NET page*

As you would guess, each of these base classes brings a good deal of functionality to each and every *.aspx file. For the majority of your projects, you will make use of the members defined within the Page and Control parent classes. By and large, the functionality gained from the System. Web.UI.TemplateControl class is only of interest to you if you are building custom Web Form controls or interacting with the rendering process. This being said, let's get to know the role of the Page type.

The System.Web.UI.Page Type

The first parent class of interest is Page itself. Here you will find numerous properties that enable you to interact with various web primitives such as application and session variables, the HTTP request/response, theme support, and so forth. Table 23-4 describes some (but by no means all) of the core properties.

Table 23-4. *Properties of the* Page *Type*

Property	Meaning in Life
Application	Allows you to interact with application variables for the current website
Cache	Allows you to interact with the cache object for the current website
ClientTarget	Allows you to specify how this page should render itself based on the requesting browser
IsPostBack	Gets a value indicating if the page is being loaded in response to a client postback or if it is being loaded and accessed for the first time
MasterPageFile	Establishes the master page for the current page
Request	Provides access to the current HTTP request
Response	Allows you to interact with the outgoing HTTP response

Property	Meaning in Life
Server	Provides access to the HttpServerUtility object, which contains various server-side helper functions
Session	Allows you to interact with the session data for the current caller
Theme	Gets or sets the name of the theme used for the current page
Trace	Provides access to a TraceContext object, which allows you to log custom messages during debugging sessions

Interacting with the Incoming HTTP Request

As you saw earlier in this chapter, the basic flow of a web session begins with a client logging on to a site, filling in user information, and clicking a Submit button to post back the HTML form data to a given web page for processing. In most cases, the opening tag of the form statement specifies an action attribute and a method attribute that indicates the file on the web server that will be sent the data in the various HTML widgets, as well as the method of sending this data (GET or POST):

```
<form name="defaultPage" id="defaultPage"
  action="http://localhost/Cars/ClassicAspPage.asp" method = "GET">
  ...
</form>
```

Unlike classic ASP, ASP.NET does not support an object named Request. However, all ASP.NET pages do inherit the System.Web.UI.Page.Request *property*, which provides access to an instance of the HttpRequest class type. Table 23-5 lists some core members that, not surprisingly, mimic the same members found within the legacy classic ASP Request object.

Table 23-5. *Members of the* HttpRequest *Type*

Member	Meaning in Life
ApplicationPath	Gets the ASP.NET application's virtual application root path on the server
Browser	Provides information about the capabilities of the client browser
Cookies	Gets a collection of cookies sent by the client browser
FilePath	Indicates the virtual path of the current request
Form	Gets a collection of Form variables
Headers	Gets a collection of HTTP headers
HttpMethod	Indicates the HTTP data transfer method used by the client (GET, POST)
IsSecureConnection	Indicates whether the HTTP connection is secure (i.e., HTTPS)
QueryString	Gets the collection of HTTP query string variables
RawUrl	Gets the current request's raw URL
RequestType	Indicates the HTTP data transfer method used by the client (GET, POST)
ServerVariables	Gets a collection of web server variables
UserHostAddress	Gets the IP host address of the remote client
UserHostName	Gets the DNS name of the remote client

In addition to these properties, the HttpRequest type has a number of useful methods, including the following:

- MapPath(): Maps the virtual path in the requested URL to a physical path on the server for the current request.

- SaveAs(): Saves details of the current HTTP request to a file on the web server (which can prove helpful for debugging purposes).

- ValidateInput(): If the validation feature is enabled via the Validate attribute of the page directive, this method can be called to check all user input data (including cookie data) against a predefined list of potentially dangerous input data.

Obtaining Brower Statistics

The first interesting aspect of the HttpRequest type is the Browser property, which provides access to an underlying HttpBrowserCapabilities object. HttpBrowserCapabilities in turn exposes numerous members that allow you to programmatically investigate statistics regarding the browser that sent the incoming HTTP request.

Create a new ASP.NET website named FunWithPageMembers. Your first task is to build a UI that allows users to click a Button web control to view various statistics about the calling browser. These statistics will be generated dynamically and attached to a Label type (named lblOutput). The Button Click event handler is as follows:

```
protected void btnGetBrowserStats_Click(object sender, System.EventArgs e)
{
    string theInfo = "";
    theInfo += String.Format("<li>Is the client AOL? {0}",
        Request.Browser.AOL);
    theInfo +=
        String.Format("<li>Does the client support ActiveX? {0}",
        Request.Browser.ActiveXControls);
    theInfo += String.Format("<li>Is the client a Beta? {0}",
        Request.Browser.Beta);
    theInfo +=
        String.Format("<li>Dose the client support Java Applets? {0}",
        Request.Browser.JavaApplets);
    theInfo +=
        String.Format("<li>Does the client support Cookies? {0}",
        Request.Browser.Cookies);
    theInfo +=
        String.Format("<li>Does the client support VBScript? {0}",
        Request.Browser.VBScript);
    lblOutput.Text = theInfo;
}
```

Here you are testing for a number of browser capabilities. As you would guess, it is (very) helpful to discover a browser's support for ActiveX controls, Java applets, and client-side VBScript code. If the calling browser does not support a given web technology, your *.aspx page would be able to take an alternative course of action.

Access to Incoming Form Data

Other aspects of the HttpResponse type are the Form and QueryString properties. These two properties allow you to examine the incoming form data using name/value pairs, and they function identically to classic ASP. Recall from our earlier discussion of classic ASP that if the data is submitted using HTTP GET, the form data is accessed using the QueryString property, whereas data submitted via HTTP POST is obtained using the Form property.

While you could most certainly make use of the HttpRequest.Form and HttpRequest.QueryString properties to access client-supplied form data on the web server, these old-school techniques are (for the most part) unnecessary. Given that ASP.NET supplies you with server-side web controls, you are able to treat HTML UI elements as true objects. Therefore, rather than obtaining the value within a text box as follows:

```
protected void btnGetFormData_Click(object sender, EventArgs e)
{
    // Get value for a widget with ID txtFirstName.
    string firstName = Request.Form["txtFirstName"];
}
```

you can simply ask the server-side widget directly via the Text property:

```
protected void btnGetFormData_Click(object sender, EventArgs e)
{
    // Get value for a widget with ID txtFirstName.
    string firstName = txtFirstName.Text;
}
```

Not only does this approach lend itself to solid OO principles, but also you do not need to concern yourself with how the form data was submitted (GET or POST) before obtaining the values. Furthermore, working with the widget directly is much more type-safe, given that typing errors are discovered at compile time rather than runtime. Of course, this is not to say that you will *never* need to make use of the Form or QueryString property in ASP.NET; rather, the need to do so has greatly diminished.

The IsPostBack Property

Another very important member of HttpRequest is the IsPostBack property. Recall that "postback" refers to the act of returning to a particular web page while still in session with the server. Given this definition, understand that the IsPostBack property will return true if the current HTTP request has been sent by a currently logged on user and false if this is the user's first interaction with the page.

Typically, the need to determine whether the current HTTP request is indeed a postback is most helpful when you wish to perform a block of code only the first time the user accesses a given page. For example, you may wish to populate an ADO.NET DataSet when the user first accesses an *.aspx file and cache the object for later use. When the caller returns to the page, you can avoid the need to hit the database unnecessarily (of course, some pages may require that the DataSet is always updated upon each request, but that is another issue):

```
protected void Page_Load(object sender, EventArgs e)
{
    // Only fill DataSet the very first time
    // the user comes to this page.
    if(!IsPostBack)
    {
        // Populate DataSet and cache it!
    }
    // Use cached DataSet.
}
```

Interacting with the Outgoing HTTP Response

Now that you have a better understanding how the Page type allows you to interact with the incoming HTTP request, the next step is to see how to interact with the outgoing HTTP response. In ASP.NET, the Response property of the Page class provides access to an instance of the HttpResponse type. This type defines a number of properties that allow you to format the HTTP response sent back to the client browser. Table 23-6 lists some core properties.

Table 23-6. *Properties of the* HttpResponse *Type*

Property	Meaning in Life
Cache	Returns the caching semantics of the web page (e.g., expiration time, privacy, vary clauses)
ContentEncoding	Gets or sets the HTTP character set of the output stream
ContentType	Gets or sets the HTTP MIME type of the output stream
Cookies	Gets the HttpCookie collection sent by the current request
IsClientConnected	Gets a value indicating whether the client is still connected to the server
Output	Enables custom output to the outgoing HTTP content body
OutputStream	Enables binary output to the outgoing HTTP content body
StatusCode	Gets or sets the HTTP status code of output returned to the client
StatusDescription	Gets or sets the HTTP status string of output returned to the client
SuppressContent	Gets or sets a value indicating that HTTP content will not be sent to the client

Also, consider the partial list of methods supported by the HttpResponse type described in Table 23-7.

Table 23-7. *Methods of the* HttpResponse *Type*

Method	Meaning in Life
AddCacheDependency()	Adds an object to the application catch (see Chapter 24)
Clear()	Clears all headers and content output from the buffer stream
End()	Sends all currently buffered output to the client, and then closes the socket connection
Flush()	Sends all currently buffered output to the client
Redirect()	Redirects a client to a new URL
Write()	Writes values to an HTTP output content stream
WriteFile()	Writes a file directly to an HTTP content output stream

Emitting HTML Content

Perhaps the most well-known aspect of the HttpResponse type is the ability to write content directly to the HTTP output stream. The HttpResponse.Write() method allows you to pass in any HTML tags and/or text literals. The HttpResponse.WriteFile() method takes this functionality one step further, in that you can specify the name of a physical file on the web server whose contents should be rendered to the output stream (this is quite helpful to quickly emit the contents of an existing *.htm file).

To illustrate, assume you have added another Button type to your current *.aspx file that implements the server-side Click event handler as so:

```
protected void btnHttpResponse_Click(object sender, EventArgs e)
{
  Response.Write("<b>My name is:</b><br>");
  Response.Write(this.ToString());
```

```
Response.Write("<br><br><b>Here was your last request:</b><br>");
Response.WriteFile("MyHTMLPage.htm");
}
```

The role of this helper function (which you can assume is called by some server-side event handler) is quite simple. The only point of interest is the fact that the `HttpResponse.WriteFile()` method is now emitting the contents of a server-side *.htm file within the root directory of the website.

Again, while you can always take this old-school approach and render HTML tags and content using the `Write()` method, this approach is far less common under ASP.NET than with classic ASP. The reason is (once again) due to the advent of server-side web controls. Thus, if you wish to render a block of textual data to the browser, your task is as simple as assigning a string to the `Text` property of a `Label` widget.

Redirecting Users

Another aspect of the `HttpResponse` type is the ability to redirect the user to a new URL:

```
protected void btnSomeTraining_Click(object sender, EventArgs e)
{
    Response.Redirect("http://www.IntertechTraining.com");
}
```

If this event handler was invoked via a client-side postback, the user will automatically be redirected to the specified URL.

■**Note** The `HttpResponse.Redirect()` method will always entail a trip back to the client browser. If you simply wish to transfer control to a *.aspx file in the same virtual directory, the `HttpServerUtility.Transfer()` method (accessed via the inherited `Server` property) will be more efficient.

So much for investigating the functionality of `System.Web.UI.Page`. We will examine the role of the `System.Web.UI.Control` base class in just a bit; however, the next task is to examine the life and times of a `Page`-derived object.

■**Source Code** The FunWithPageMembers files are included under the Chapter 23 subdirectory.

The Life Cycle of an ASP.NET Web Page

Every ASP.NET web page has a fixed life cycle. When the ASP.NET runtime receives an incoming request for a given *.aspx file, the associated `System.Web.UI.Page`-derived type is allocated into memory using the type's default constructor. After this point, the framework will automatically fire a series of events.

By default, a Visual Studio 2005–generated code-behind page defines an event handler for the page's `Load` event:

```
public partial class _Default : System.Web.UI.Page
{
    protected void Page_Load(object sender, EventArgs e)
    {
    }
}
```

Beyond the `Load` event, a given `Page` is able to intercept any of the core events in Table 23-8, which are listed in the order in which they are encountered.

Table 23-8. *Events of the* Page *Type*

Event	Meaning in Life
PreInit	The framework uses this event to allocate any web controls, apply themes, establish the master page, and set user profiles. You may intercept this event to customize the process.
Init	The framework uses this event to set the properties of web controls to their previous values via postback or view state data (more details on this in Chapter 24).
Load	When this event fires, the page and its controls are fully initialized, and their previous values are restored. At this point, it is safe to interact with each web widget.
"Event that triggered the postback"	There is of course, no event of this name. This "event" simply refers to whichever event caused the browser to perform the postback to the web server (such as a Button click).
PreRender	All control data binding and UI configuration has occurred and the controls are ready to render their data into the outbound HTTP response.
Unload	The page and its controls have finished the rendering process, and the page object is about to be destroyed. At this point, it is a runtime error to interact with the outgoing HTTP response. You may, however, capture this event to perform any page-level cleanup (close file or database connections, perform any form of logging activity, dispose of objects, etc.).

■**Note** Each event of the Page type works in conjunction with the System.EventHandler delegate.

The Role of the AutoEventWireUp Attribute

When you wish to handle events for your page, you will need to update your <script> block or code-behind file with an appropriate event handler. Unlike in ASP.NET 1.*x*, you are not required to rig up the event logic by hand. All you need to do is define a method using the following pattern:

```
protected Page_nameOfTheEvent(object sender, EventArgs e)
{
}
```

For example, the Unload event can be handle this event simply by writing the following:

```
public partial class _Default : System.Web.UI.Page
{
    protected void Page_Load(object sender, EventArgs e)
    {
    }
    protected void Page_Unload(object sender, EventArgs e)
    {
    }
}
```

The reason this method is magically called when the page unloads (despite the fact that you have not applied the expected C# event syntax) is due to the AutoEventWireUp attribute set to true by default in the <%@Page%> directive of your *.aspx file:

```
<%@ Page Language="C#" AutoEventWireup="true"
CodeFile="Default.aspx.cs" Inherits="_Default" %>
```

As its name suggests, this attribute (when enabled) will generate the necessary event riggings within the autogenerated partial class described in earlier in this chapter. If you were to set this attribute to false, neither the Load nor Unload event handlers of the _Default page will be called by the framework (you can verify this for yourself by setting breakpoints within the Page_Load() and Page_Unload() event handlers).

However, if you were to make use of the standard C# event syntax to hook into the Load and Unload events as shown here:

```csharp
public partial class _Default : System.Web.UI.Page
{
    public _Default()
    {
        // Explicitly hook into the Load and Unload events.
        this.Load +=new EventHandler(Page_Load);
        this.Unload += new EventHandler(Page_Unload);
    }
    protected void Page_Load(object sender, EventArgs e)
    {
        Response.Write("Load event fired!");
    }
    protected void Page_Unload(object sender, EventArgs e)
    {
        // No longer possible to emit data to the HTTP
        // response at this point, so we will write to a local file.
        System.IO.File.WriteAllText(@"C:\MyLog.txt", "Page unloading!");
    }
    protected void btnPostback_Click(object sender, EventArgs e)
    {
        // Nothing happens here; this is just to ensure a
        // postback to the page.
    }
}
```

these events will be captured in your page regardless of the value assigned to AutoEventWireup.

As a final note, remember that once the Unload event fires, you are no longer able to interact with the outbound HTTP response (if you attempt to call members of the HttpResponse object, you will receive a runtime exception). Given this, your Unload event handler is simply emitting a line of text to a file on the local C drive.

The Error Event

Another event that may occur during your page's life cycle is Error, which also works in conjunction with the System.EventHandler delegate. This event will be fired if a method on the Page-derived type triggered an exception that was not explicitly handled. Assume that you have handled the Click event for a given Button on your page, and within the event handler (which I named btnGetFile_Click), you attempt to write out the contents of a local file to the HTTP response.

Also assume you have *failed* to test for the presence of this file via standard structured exception handling. If you have rigged up the page's Error event, you have one final chance to deal with the problem before the end user finds an ugly error. Ponder the following code:

```csharp
public partial class _Default : System.Web.UI.Page
{
    public _Default()
    {
...
```

```
        // Rig up the Error event.
        this.Error += new EventHandler(_Default_Error);
    }
    void _Default_Error(object sender, EventArgs e)
    {
        // Gut the current response, issue an error,
        // and tell the runtime the error has been processed.
        Response.Clear();
        Response.Write("I am sorry...I can't find a required file.");
        Server.ClearError();
    }
    protected void btnGetFile_Click(object sender, EventArgs e)
    {
        // Try to open a nonexistent file.
        // This will fire the Error event for this page.
        System.IO.File.ReadAllText(@"C:\IDontExist.txt");
    }
...
}
```

Notice that your `Error` event handler begins by clearing out any content currently within the HTTP response and emits a generic error message. If you wish to gain access to the specific `System.Exception` object, you may do so using the `HttpServerUtility.GetLastError()` method exposed by the inherited `Server` property:

```
void _Default_Error(object sender, EventArgs e)
{
    Response.Clear();
    Response.Write("I am sorry...I can't find a required file.<br>");
    Response.Write(string.Format("The error was: <b>{0}</b>",
        Server.GetLastError().Message));
    Server.ClearError();
}
```

Finally, note that before exiting this generic error handler, you are explicitly calling the `HttpServerUtility.ClearError()` method via the `Server` property. This is required, as it informs the runtime that you have dealt with the issue at hand and require no further processing. If you forget to do so, you the end user will be presented with the runtime's error page. Figure 23-19 shows the result of this error-trapping logic.

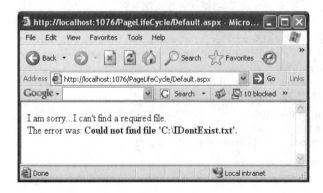

Figure 23-19. *Page-level error handling*

At this point, you should feel quite confident with your knowledge of the architecture of an ASP.NET Page type. Now that you have such a foundation, you can turn your attention to the role of ASP.NET web controls.

■Source Code The PageLifeCycle files are included under the Chapter 23 subdirectory.

Understanding the Nature of Web Controls

Perhaps the major benefit of ASP.NET is the ability to assemble the UI of your pages using the types defined in the System.Web.UI.WebControls namespace. As you have seen, these controls (which go by the names *server controls*, *web controls*, or *web form controls*) are *extremely* helpful in that they automatically generate the necessary HTML for the requesting browser and expose a set of events that may be processed on the web server. Furthermore, because each ASP.NET control has a corresponding class in the System.Web.UI.WebControls namespace, it can be manipulated in an OO manner from your *.aspx file (within a <script> block) as well as within the associated class defined in the code-behind file.

As you have seen, when you configure the properties of a web control using the Visual Studio 2005 Properties window, your edits are recorded in the open declaration of a given widget in the *.aspx file as a series of name/value pairs. Thus, if you add a new TextBox to the designer of a given *.aspx file and change the BorderStyle, BorderWidth, BackColor, Text, and BorderColor properties using the IDE, the opening <asp:TextBox> tag is modified as follows:

```
<asp:TextBox id=myTextBox runat="server" BorderStyle="Ridge" BorderWidth="5px"
BackColor="PaleGreen" BorderColor="DarkOliveGreen" Text = "Yo dude" >
</asp:TextBox>
```

Given that the HTML declaration of a web control eventually becomes a member variable from the System.Web.UI.WebControls namespace (via the dynamic compilation cycle), you are able to interact with the members of this type within a server-side <script> block or the page's code-behind file, for example:

```
public partial class _Default : System.Web.UI.Page
{
...
    protected void btnChangeTextBoxColor_Click(object sender, EventArgs e)
    {
        // Modify the HTTP response data for this widget.
        this.myTextBox.BackColor = System.Drawing.Color.Red;
    }
}
```

All ASP.NET web controls ultimately derive from a common base class named System.Web.UI. WebControls.WebControl. WebControl in turn derives from System.Web.UI.Control (which derives from System.Object). Control and WebControl each define a number of properties common to all server-side controls. Before we examine the inherited functionality, let's formalize what it means to handle a server-side event.

Qualifying Server-Side Event Handling

Given the current state of the World Wide Web, it is impossible to avoid the fundamental nature of browser/web server interaction. Whenever these two entities communicate, there is always an underlying, stateless, HTTP request-and-response cycle. While ASP.NET server controls do a great deal to shield you from the details of the raw HTTP protocol, always remember that treating the

Web as an event-driven entity is just a magnificent smoke-and-mirrors show provided by the CLR, and it is not identical to the event-driven model of a Windows-based UI.

Thus, although the System.Windows.Forms and System.Web.UI.WebControls namespaces define types with the same simple names (Button, TextBox, GridView, Label, and so on), they do not expose an identical set of events. For example, there is no way to handle a server-side MouseMove event when the user moves the cursor over a Web Form Button type. Obviously, this is a good thing. (Who wants to post back to the server each time the mouse moves?)

The bottom line is that a given ASP.NET web control will expose a limited set of events, all of which ultimately result in a postback to the web server. Any necessary client-side event processing will require you to author blurbs of *client-side* JavaScript/VBScript script code to be processed by the requesting browser's scripting engine.

The AutoPostBack Property

It is also worth pointing out that many of the ASP.NET web controls support a property named AutoPostBack (most notably, the CheckBox, RadioButton, and TextBox controls, as well as any widget that derives from the abstract ListControl type). By default, this property is set to false, which disables the automatic posting of server-side events (even if you have indeed rigged up the event in the code-behind file). In many cases, this is the exact behavior you require.

However, if you wish to cause any of these widgets to post back to a server-side event handler, simply set the value of AutoPostBack to true. This technique can be helpful if you wish to have the state of one widget automatically populate another value within another widget on the same page.

To illustrate, create a website that contains a single TextBox (named txtAutoPostback) and a single ListBox control (named lstTextBoxData). Now, handle the TextChanged event of the TextBox, and within the server-side event handler, populate the ListBox with the current value in the TextBox (got all that?):

```
protected void txtAutoPostback_TextChanged(object sender, EventArgs e)
{
    lstTextBoxData.Items.Add(txtAutoPostback.Text);
}
```

If you run the application as is, you will find that as you type in the TextBox, nothing happens. Furthermore, if you type in the TextBox and tab to the next control, nothing happens. The reason is that the AutoPostBack property of the TextBox is set to false by default. However, if you set this property to true as follows:

```
<asp:TextBox ID="txtAutoPostback" runat="server" AutoPostBack="True"
OnTextChanged="txtAutoPostback_TextChanged">
</asp:TextBox>
```

you will find that when you tab off the TextBox (or press the Enter key), the ListBox is automatically populated with the current value in the TextBox. To be sure, beyond the need to populate the items of one widget based on the value of another widget, you will typically not need to alter the state of a widget's AutoPostBack property.

The System.Web.UI.Control Type

The System.Web.UI.Control base class defines various properties, methods, and events that allow the ability to interact with core (typically non-GUI) aspects of a web control. Table 23-9 documents some, not all, members of interest.

Table 23-9. *Select Members of* System.Web.UI.Control

Member	Meaning in Life
Controls	This property gets a ControlCollection object that represents the child controls within the current control.
DataBind()	This method binds a data source to the invoked server control and all its child controls.
EnableThemeing	This property establishes if the control supports theme functionality.
HasControls()	This method determines if the server control contains any child controls.
ID	This property gets or sets the programmatic identifier assigned to the server control.
Page	This property gets a reference to the Page instance that contains the server control.
Parent	This property gets a reference to the server control's parent control in the page control hierarchy.
SkinID	This property gets or sets the "skin" to apply to the control. Under ASP.NET 2.0, it is now possible to establish a control's overall look and feel on the fly via skins.
Visible	This property gets or sets a value that indicates whether a server control is rendered as UI element on the page.

Enumerating Contained Controls

The first aspect of System.Web.UI.Control we will examine is the fact that all web controls (including Page itself) inherit a custom controls collection (accessed via the Controls property). Much like in a Windows Forms application, the Controls property provides access to a strongly typed collection of WebControl-derived types. Like any .NET collection, you have the ability to add, insert, and remove items dynamically at runtime.

While it is technically possible to directly add web controls directly to a Page-derived type, it is easier (and a wee bit safer) to make use of a Panel widget. The System.Web.UI.WebControls.Panel class represents a container of widgets that may or may not be visible to the end user (based on the value of its Visible and BorderStype properties).

To illustrate, create a new website named DynamicCtrls. Using the Visual Studio 2005 page designer, add a Panel type (named myPanel) that contains a TextBox, Button, and HyperLink widget named whatever you choose (be aware that the designer requires that you drag internal items within the UI of the Panel type). Once you have done so, the <form> element of your *.aspx file has been updated as so:

```
<asp:Panel ID="myPanel" runat="server" Height="50px" Width="125px">
  <asp:TextBox ID="TextBox1" runat="server"></asp:TextBox><br />
  <asp:Button ID="Button1" runat="server" Text="Button" /><br />
  <asp:HyperLink ID="HyperLink1" runat="server">HyperLink
  </asp:HyperLink>
</asp:Panel>
```

Next, place a Label widget outside the scope of the Panel (named lblControlInfo) to hold the rendered output. Assume in the Page_Load() event you wish to obtain a list of all the controls contained within the Panel and assign the results to the Label type:

```
public partial class _Default : System.Web.UI.Page
{
    protected void Page_Load(object sender, EventArgs e)
    {
        ListControlsInPanel();
    }
    private void ListControlsInPanel()
    {
        string theInfo;
        theInfo = String.Format("Has controls? {0}<br>",
            myPanel.HasControls());
        foreach (Control c in myPanel.Controls)
        {
            if (c.GetType() != typeof(System.Web.UI.LiteralControl))
            {
                theInfo += "***************************<br>";
                theInfo += String.Format("Control Name? {0}<br>",
                    c.ToString());
                theInfo += String.Format("ID? {0}<br>", c.ID);
                theInfo += String.Format("Control Visible? {0}<br>",
                    c.Visible);
                theInfo += String.Format("ViewState? {0}<br>",
                    c.EnableViewState);
            }
        }
        lblControlInfo.Text = theInfo;
    }
}
```

Here, you iterate over each WebControl maintained on the Panel and perform a check to see if the current type is of type System.Web.UI.LiteralControl. This type is used to represent literal HTML tags and content (such as <br>, text literals, etc.). If you do not do this sanity check, you might be surprised to find a total of seven types in the scope of the Panel (given the *.aspx declaration seen previously). Assuming the type is not literal HTML content, you then print out some various statistics about the widget. Figure 23-20 shows the output.

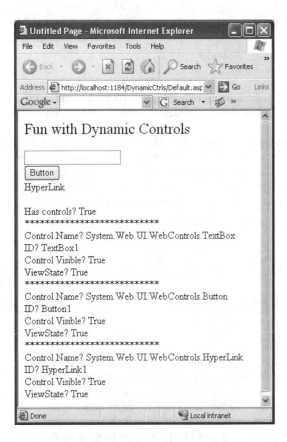

Figure 23-20. *Enumerating contained widgets*

Dynamically Adding (and Removing) Controls

Now, what if you wish to modify the contents of a Panel at runtime? The process should look very familiar to you, given your work with Windows Forms earlier in this text. Let's update the current page to support an additional Button (named btnAddWidgets) that dynamically adds five new TextBox types to the Panel, and another Button that clears the Panel widget of all controls. The Click event handlers for each are shown here:

```
protected void btnAddWidgets_Click(object sender, EventArgs e)
{
    for (int i = 0; i < 5; i++)
    {
        // Assign a name so we can get
        // the text value out later
        // using the HttpRequest.QueryString()
        // method.
        TextBox t = new TextBox();
        t.ID = string.Format("newTextBox{0}", i);
        myPanel.Controls.Add(t);
        ListControlsInPanel();
    }
}
```

```
protected void btnRemovePanelItems_Click(object sender, EventArgs e)
{
    myPanel.Controls.Clear();
    ListControlsInPanel();
}
```

Notice that you assign a unique ID to each TextBox (e.g., newTextBox1, newTextBox2, and so on) to obtain its contained text programmatically using the HttpRequest.Form collection (shown momentarily).

To obtain the values within these dynamically generated TextBoxes, update your UI with one additional Button and Label type. Within the Click event handler for the Button, loop over each item contained within the HttpRequest.NameValueCollection type (accessed via HttpRequest.Form) and concatenate the textual information to a locally scoped System.String. Once you have exhausted the collection, assign this string to the Text property of the new Label widget named lblTextBoxText:

```
protected void btnGetTextBoxValues_Click(object sender, System.EventArgs e)
{
    string textBoxValues = "";
    for(int i = 0; i < Request.Form.Count; i++)
    {
        textBoxValues +=
            string.Format("<li>{0}</li><br>", Request.Form[i]);
    }
    lblTextBoxText.Text = textBoxValues;
}
```

When you run the application, you will find that you are able to view the content of each text box, including a rather long (unreadable) string. This string contains the *view state* for each widget on the page and will be examined later in the next chapter. Also, you will notice that once the request has been processed, the ten new text boxes disappear. Again, the reason has to do with the stateless nature of HTTP. If you wish to maintain these dynamically created TextBoxes between postbacks, you need to persist these objects using ASP.NET state programming techniques (also examined in the next chapter).

■**Source Code** The DynamicCtrls files are included under the Chapter 23 subdirectory.

Key Members of the System.Web.UI.WebControls.WebControl Type

As you can tell, the Control type provides a number of non-GUI-related behaviors. On the other hand, the WebControl base class provides a graphical polymorphic interface to all web widgets, as suggested in Table 23-10.

Table 23-10. *Properties of the* WebControl *Base Class*

Properties	Meaning in Life
BackColor	Gets or sets the background color of the web control
BorderColor	Gets or sets the border color of the web control
BorderStyle	Gets or sets the border style of the web control
BorderWidth	Gets or sets the border width of the web control

Properties	Meaning in Life
Enabled	Gets or sets a value indicating whether the web control is enabled
CssClass	Allows you to assign a class defined within a Cascading Style Sheet to a web widget
Font	Gets font information for the web control
ForeColor	Gets or sets the foreground color (typically the color of the text) of the web control
Height Width	Get or set the height and width of the web control
TabIndex	Gets or sets the tab index of the web control
ToolTip	Gets or sets the tool tip for the web control to be displayed when the cursor is over the control

I'd bet that almost all of these properties are self-explanatory, so rather than drill through the use of all these properties, let's shift gears a bit and check out a number of ASP.NET Web Form controls in action.

Categories of ASP.NET Web Controls

The types in System.Web.UI.WebControls can be broken down into several broad categories:

- Simple controls
- (Feature) Rich controls
- Data-centric controls
- Input validation controls
- Login controls

The *simple controls* are so named because they are ASP.NET web controls that map to standard HTML widgets (buttons, lists, hyperlinks, image holders, tables, etc.). Next, we have a small set of controls named the *rich controls* for which there is no direct HTML equivalent (such as the Calendar, TreeView, Wizard, etc.). The *data-centric controls* are widgets that are typically populated via a given data connection. The best (and most exotic) example of such a control would be the ASP.NET GridView. Other members of this category include "repeater" controls and the lightweight DataList. The *validation controls* are server-side widgets that automatically emit client-side JavaScript, for the purpose of form field validation. Finally, as of ASP.NET 2.0, the base class libraries ship with a number of security-centric controls. These UI elements completely encapsulate the details of logging into a site, providing password-retrieval services and managing user roles.

■Note Given that this text does not cover the details of the .NET security system, I will not comment on the new security controls here. If you require a detailed treatment of ASP.NET 2.0 security, check out *Expert ASP.NET 2.0 Advanced Application Design* by Dominic Selly, Andrew Troelsen, and Tom Barnaby (Apress, 2006).

A Brief Word Regarding System.Web.UI.HtmlControls

Truth be told, there are two distinct web control toolkits that ship with ASP.NET 2.0. In addition to the ASP.NET web controls (within the System.Web.UI.WebControls namespace), the base class libraries also provide the System.Web.UI.HtmlControls widgets.

The HTML controls are a collection of types that allow you to make use of traditional HTML controls on a Web Forms page. However, unlike raw HTML tags, HTML controls are OO entities that can be configured to run on the server and thus support server-side event handling. Unlike ASP.NET web controls, HTML controls are quite simplistic in nature and offer little functionality beyond standard HTML tags (HtmlButton, HtmlInputControl, HtmlTable, etc.).

The HTML controls provide a public interface that mimics standard HTML attributes. For example, to obtain the information within an input area, you make use of the Value property, rather than the web control–centric Text property. Given that the HTML controls are not as feature-rich as the ASP.NET web controls, I won't make further mention of them in this text. If you wish to investigate these types, consult the .NET Framework 2.0 SDK documentation for further details.

Building a Simple ASP.NET 2.0 Website

Space does not permit me to walk through the details of each and every web control that ships with ASP.NET 2.0 (that would require a sizable book in and of itself). However, to illustrate the process of working with various ASP.NET web controls, the next task of this chapter is to construct a website that will demonstrate the use of the following techniques:

- Working with master pages
- Working with the Menu control
- Working with the GridView control
- Working with the Wizard control

As you work through this example, remember that Web Form controls encapsulate the process of generating corresponding HTML tags and follow a Windows Forms model. To begin, create a new ASP.NET web application named AspNetCarsSite.

Working with Master Pages

As I am sure you are aware, many websites provide a consistent look and feel across multiple pages (a common menu navigation system, common header and footer content, company logo, etc.). Under ASP.NET 1.*x*, developers made extensive use of UserControls and custom web controls to define web content that was to be used across multiple pages. While UserControls and custom web controls are still a very valid option under ASP.NET 2.0, we are now provided with the concept of *master pages* to address the same issue.

Simply put, a master page is little more than an ASP.NET page that takes a *.master file extension. On their own, master pages are not viewable from a client-side browser (in fact, the ASP.NET runtime will not server this flavor of web content). Rather, master pages define a common UI frame shared by all pages (or a subset of pages) in your site. As well, a *.master page defines various placeholder tags that contain additional content within an *.aspx file. The end result is a single, unified UI.

Insert a new master page into your website (via the WebSite ➤ Add New Item menu selection) and observe the initial definition:

```
<%@ Master Language="C#" AutoEventWireup="true"
CodeFile="MasterPage.master.cs" Inherits="MasterPage" %>

<!DOCTYPE html PUBLIC "-//W3C//DTD XHTML 1.1//EN"
"http://www.w3.org/TR/xhtml11/DTD/xhtml11.dtd">

<html xmlns="http://www.w3.org/1999/xhtml" >
<head runat="server">
```

```
    <title>Untitled Page</title>
</head>
<body>
    <form id="form1" runat="server">
    <div>
        <asp:contentplaceholder id="ContentPlaceHolder1" runat="server">
        </asp:contentplaceholder>
    </div>
    </form>
</body>
</html>
```

The first point of interest is the new `<%@Master%>` directive. For the most part, this directive supports the same attributes as `<%@Page%>`. For example, notice how by default a master page makes use of a code-behind file (which is technically optional). Like `Page` types, a master page derives from a specific base class, which in this case is `MasterPage`:

```
public partial class MasterPage : System.Web.UI.MasterPage
{
    protected void Page_Load(object sender, EventArgs e)
    {
    }
}
```

It is important to know that the attributes defined within the `<%@Master%>` directive do not "flow through" to the related `*.aspx` files. Thus, if you wish to make use of C# within your master page but author an associated `*.aspx` file in Visual Basic .NET, you may do so.

The other point of interest is the `<asp:contentplaceholder>` type. This region of a master page represents the UI widgets of the related `*.aspx` file, not the content of the master page itself. If you do intend to blend an `*.aspx` file within this region, the scope within the `<asp:contentplaceholder>` and `</asp:contentplaceholder>` tags will be empty. However, if you so choose, you are able to populate this area with various web controls that function as a default UI to use in the event that a given `*.aspx` file in the site does not supply specific content. For this example, assume that each `*.aspx` page in your site will indeed supply custom content.

■Note A `*.master` page may define as many content place holders as necessary. As well, a single `*.master` page may nest additional `*.master` pages.

As you would hope, you are able to build a common UI of a `*.master` file using the same Visual Studio 2005 designers used to build `*.aspx` files. For your site, you will add a descriptive `Label` (to serve as a common welcome message), an `AdRotator` control (which will randomly display one of two images), and a `Menu` control (to allow the user to navigate to other areas of the site).

Working with the Menu Control

ASP.NET 2.0 ships with several new web controls that allow you to handle site navigation: `SiteMapPath`, `TreeView`, and `Menu`. As you would expect, these web widgets can be configured in multiple ways. For example, each of these controls can dynamically generate its nodes via an external XML file or data source. For your `Menu` type, you will simply hard-code three values.

Using the page designer, select the `Menu` control, activate the inline editor (located at the upper left of the widget), and select the Edit Menu Items option. Add three root items named Home, Build a Car, and View Inventory. Before dismissing the dialog box, set the `NavigateUrl` property for each node to the following (yet to be constructed) pages:

- *Home*: Default.aspx

- *Build a Car*: BuildCar.aspx

- *View Inventory*: Inventory.aspx

This is all you need to do to configure your Menu widget to navigate to the additional pages on your site. If you wish to perform additional processing when the user selects a given menu item, you may do so by handling the MenuItemClick event. There is no need to do so for this example, but be aware that you are able to determine which menu item was selected using the incoming MenuEventArgs parameter.

Working with the AdRotator

The role of the ASP.NET AdRotator widget is to randomly display a given image at some position in the browser. When you first place an AdRotator widget on the designer, it is displayed as an empty placeholder. Functionally, this control cannot do its magic until you assign the AdvertisementFile property to point to the source file that describes each image. For this example, the data source will be a simple XML file named Ads.xml.

Once you have inserted this new XML file to your site, specify a unique <Ad> element for each image you wish to display. At minimum, each <Ad> element specifies the image to display (ImageUrl), the URL to navigate to if the image is selected (TargetUrl), mouseover text (AlternateText), and the weight of the ad (Impressions):

```
<Advertisements>
    <Ad>
        <ImageUrl>SlugBug.jpg</ImageUrl>
        <TargetUrl>http://www.Cars.com</TargetUrl>
        <AlternateText>Your new Car?</AlternateText>
        <Impressions>80</Impressions>
    </Ad>
    <Ad>
        <ImageUrl>car.gif</ImageUrl>
        <TargetUrl>http://www.CarSuperSite.com</TargetUrl>
        <AlternateText>Like this Car?</AlternateText>
        <Impressions>80</Impressions>
    </Ad>
</Advertisements>
```

At this point, you can associate your XML file to the AdRotator controls via the AdvertisementFile property (in the Properties window):

```
<asp:AdRotator ID="myAdRotator" runat="server"
AdvertisementFile="~/Ads.xml"/>
```

Later when you run this application and post back to the page, you will be randomly presented with one of two image files. Figure 23-21 illustrates the initial UI of the master page.

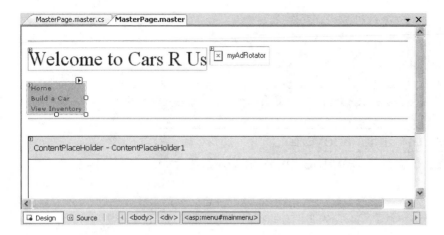

Figure 23-21. *The master page*

Defining the Default.aspx Content Page

Now that you have a master page established, you can begin designing the individual *.aspx pages that will define the UI content to merge within the <asp:contentplaceholder> tag of the master page. When you created this new website, Visual Studio 2005 automatically provided you with an initial *.aspx file, but as the file now stands, it cannot be merged within the master page.

The reason is that it is the *.master file that defines the <form> section of the final HTML page. Therefore, the existing <form> area within the *.aspx file will need to be replaced with an <asp:content> scope. Flip to the Source view of Default.aspx and replace the existing markup with the following:

```
<%@ Page Language="C#" MasterPageFile="~/MasterPage.master"
AutoEventWireup="true" CodeFile="Default.aspx.cs"
Inherits="_Default" Title="Untitled Page" %>

<asp:Content ID="Content1"
  ContentPlaceHolderID="ContentPlaceHolder1" Runat="Server">
</asp:Content>
```

First, notice that the <%@Page%> directive has been updated with a new MasterPageFile attribute that is assigned to your *.master file. Also note that the ContentPlaceHolderID value is identical to the <asp:contentplaceholder> widget in the master file.

Given these associations, you will now find that when you switch back to the Design view, the master's UI is now visible. The content area is visible as well, although it is currently empty. There is no need to build a complex UI for your Default.aspx content area, so for this example, simply add a few Labels to hold some basic site instructions (see Figure 23-22).

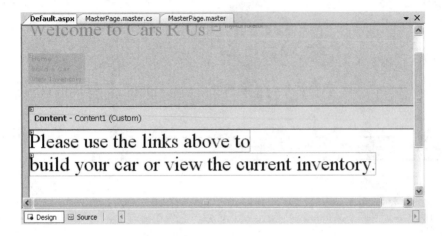

Figure 23-22. *The* Default.aspx *content page*

Now, if you run your project, you will find that the UI content of the *.master and Default.aspx files have been merged into a single stream of HTML. As you can see from Figure 23-23, the end user is unaware that the master page even exists.

Figure 23-23. *The default page of Cars R Us*

Designing the Inventory Content Page

To insert the Inventory.aspx content page into your current project, open the *.master page in the IDE and select WebSite ➤ Add Content Page (if a *.master file is not the active item in the designer, this menu option is not present). The role of the Inventory content page is to display the contents of the Inventory table of the Cars database within a GridView control.

As you may know, the GridView control is not limited to read-only data display. This widget can be configured to support sorting, paging, and in-place editing. If you wish, you can handle a series of server-side events and author ADO.NET code to do so; this ASP.NET 2.0 widget supersedes the ASP.NET 1.x control with a "zero-code" mentality.

With a few simple mouse clicks you can configure the GridView to automatically select, update, and delete records of the underlying data store. While this zero-code mind-set greatly simplifies the amount of boilerplate code, understand that this simplicity comes with a loss of control and may not be the best approach for an enterprise-level application.

Nevertheless, to illustrate how to work with the GridView in this declarative manner, insert a new content page (Inventory.aspx) and update the content area with a descriptive label and a GridView. Using the inline editor, select New Data Source from the Choose Data Source drop-down box. This will activate a wizard that walks you through a series of steps to connect this component to the required data source. Here are the steps to take for the current example:

1. Select the Database icon and change the name of the data source ID to CarsDataSource.

2. Select the Cars database (create a new connection if required).

3. If you wish, save the connection string data to a Web.config file. Recall from Chapter 22 that ADO.NET now supports the <connectionStrings> element.

4. Configure your SQL Select statement to select all records from the Inventory table (Figure 23-24 shows the settings I chose).

5. Test your query and click the Finish button.

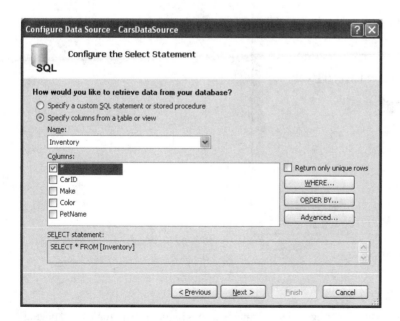

Figure 23-24. *Selecting the Inventory table*

Now, if you examine the opening declaration of the GridView control, you will see that the DataSourceID property has been set to the SqlDataSource you just defined:

```
<asp:GridView ID="GridView1" runat="server" AutoGenerateColumns="False"
  CellPadding="4" DataKeyNames="CarID" DataSourceID="CarsDataSource"
  ForeColor="#333333" GridLines="None">
...
</asp:GridView>
```

The SqlDataSource type (new to .NET 2.0) is a component that encapsulates the details of a given data store. Given your work in Chapter 23, the following attributes should be straightforward:

```
<asp:SqlDataSource ID="CarsDataSource" runat="server"
ConnectionString=
    "Data Source=localhost;Initial Catalog=Cars;Integrated Security=True"
ProviderName="System.Data.SqlClient"
SelectCommand="SELECT * FROM [Inventory]">
</asp:SqlDataSource>
```

At this point, you are able to run your web program, click the View Inventory menu item, and view your data (see Figure 23-25).

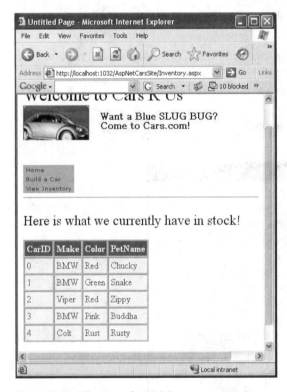

Figure 23-25. *The no-code* GridView

Enabling Sorting and Paging

The GridView control can easily be configured for sorting (via column name hyperlinks) and paging (via numeric or next/previous hyperlinks). To do so, activate the inline editor and check the appropriate options (see Figure 23-26).

Figure 23-26. *Enabling paging and sorting*

When you run your page again, you will be able to sort your data by clicking the column names and scrolling through your data via the paging links (provided you have enough records in the Inventory table!).

Enabling In-Place Editing

The final detail of this page is to enable the `GridView` control's support for in-place activation. To do so, open the inline editor for the `SqlDataSource` and select Configure Data Source. Skip past the first two steps of this wizard, but on Step 3, click the Advanced button and check the first option (see Figure 23-27).

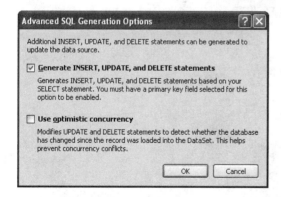

Figure 23-27. *Generating the remaining SQL statements*

If you examine the HTML definition of the control, you will now find the following that the `SqlDataSource` has been equipped with a `DeleteCommand`, `InsertCommand`, and `UpdateCommand` (each of which is making use of parameterized queries):

```
<asp:SqlDataSource ID="CarsDataSource" runat="server"
ConnectionString=
  "Data Source=localhost;Initial Catalog=Cars;Integrated Security=True"
```

```
ProviderName="System.Data.SqlClient"
SelectCommand="SELECT * FROM [Inventory]"
DeleteCommand="DELETE FROM [Inventory] WHERE [CarID] = @original_CarID"
InsertCommand="INSERT INTO [Inventory] ([CarID], [Make], [Color], [PetName]) VALUES
(@CarID, @Make, @Color, @PetName)"
UpdateCommand="UPDATE [Inventory] SET
[Make] = @Make, [Color] = @Color, [PetName] = @PetName WHERE [CarID] =
@original_CarID">
...
</asp:SqlDataSource>
```

As well, you are provided with a `SqlDataSource` component giving additional markup that defines the parameter objects for the parameterized queries:

```
<DeleteParameters>
    <asp:Parameter Name="original_CarID" Type="Int32" />
</DeleteParameters>
<UpdateParameters>
    <asp:Parameter Name="Make" Type="String" />
    <asp:Parameter Name="Color" Type="String" />
    <asp:Parameter Name="PetName" Type="String" />
    <asp:Parameter Name="original_CarID" Type="Int32" />
</UpdateParameters>
<InsertParameters>
    <asp:Parameter Name="CarID" Type="Int32" />
    <asp:Parameter Name="Make" Type="String" />
    <asp:Parameter Name="Color" Type="String" />
    <asp:Parameter Name="PetName" Type="String" />
</InsertParameters>
```

The final step is to enable editing and deleting support via the inline editor of the `GridView` (see Figure 23-28).

Figure 23-28. *Enabling editing and deleting support*

Sure enough, when you navigate back to the Inventory.aspx page, you are able to edit and delete records (see Figure 23-29).

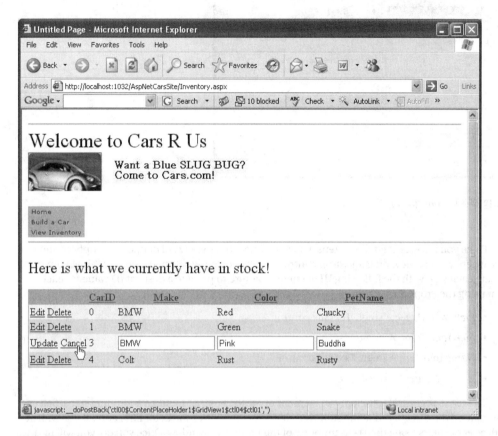

Figure 23-29. *The grids of all grids*

Designing the Build a Car Content Page

The final task for this example is to design the BuildCar.aspx content page. Insert this current project (via the WebSite ➤ Add Content Page menu option). This new page will make use of the ASP.NET 2.0 Wizard web control, which provides a simple way to walk the end user through a series of related steps. Here, the steps in question will simulate the act of building an automobile for purchase.

Place a descriptive Label and Wizard control onto the content area. Next, activate the inline editor for the Wizard and click the Add/Remove WizardSteps link. Add a total of four steps, as shown in Figure 23-30.

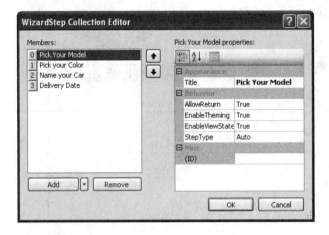

Figure 23-30. *Configuring* Wizard *steps*

Once you have defined these steps, you will notice that the Wizard defines an empty content area where you can now drag and drop controls for the currently selected step. For this example, update each step with the following UI elements (be sure to provide a descent ID value for each item using the Properties window):

- *Pick Your Model*: A single TextBox control
- *Pick Your Color*: A single ListBox control
- *Name Your Car*: A single TextBox control
- *Delivery Date*: A Calendar control

The ListBox control is the only UI element of the Wizard that requires additional steps. Select this item on the designer (making sure your first select the Pick Your Color link) and fill this widget with a set of colors using the Items property of the Properties window. Once you do, you will find markup much like the following within the scope of the Wizard definition:

```
<asp:ListBox ID="ListBoxColors" runat="server" Width="237px">
  <asp:ListItem>Purple</asp:ListItem>
  <asp:ListItem>Green</asp:ListItem>
  <asp:ListItem>Red</asp:ListItem>
  <asp:ListItem>Yellow</asp:ListItem>
  <asp:ListItem>Pea Soup Green</asp:ListItem>
  <asp:ListItem>Black</asp:ListItem>
  <asp:ListItem>Lime Green</asp:ListItem>
</asp:ListBox>
```

Now that you have defined each of the steps, you can handle the FinishButtonClick event for the autogenerated Finish button. Within the server-side event handler, obtain the selections from each UI element and build a description string that is assigned to the Text property of an additional Label type named lblOrder:

```
protected void carWizard_FinishButtonClick(object sender,
  WizardNavigationEventArgs e)
{
    // Get each value.
    string order = string.Format("{0}, your {1} {2} will arrive on {3}.",
```

```
      txtCarPetName.Text, ListBoxColors.SelectedValue,
      txtCarModel.Text, carCalendar.SelectedDate.ToShortDateString());
  // Assign to label
  lblOrder.Text = order;
}
```

At this point your AspNetCarSite is complete. Figure 23-31 shows the Wizard in action.

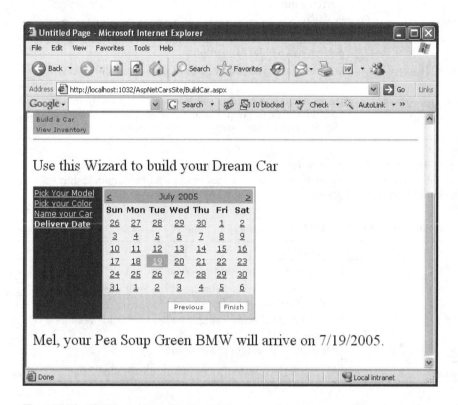

Figure 23-31. *The* Wizard *in action*

That wraps up our examination of various UI web controls. To be sure, there are many other widgets we haven't covered here. You should feel comfortable, though, with the basic programming model. To wrap things up for this chapter, let's look at the validation controls.

───

■**Source Code** The AspNetCarsSite files are included under the Chapter 23 subdirectory.

───

The Role of the Validation Controls

The final group of Web Form controls we will examine is termed *validation controls*. Unlike the other Web Form controls we've examined, validator controls are not used to emit HTML, but are used to emit client-side JavaScript (and possibly server-side operations) for the purpose of form validation. As illustrated at the beginning of this chapter, client-side form validation is quite useful in that you can ensure that various constraints are in place before posting back to the web server, thereby avoiding expensive round-trips. Table 23-11 gives a rundown of the ASP.NET validation controls.

Table 23-11. *ASP.NET Validation Controls*

Control	Meaning in Life
CompareValidator	Validates that the value of an input control is equal to a given value of another input control or a fixed constant.
CustomValidator	Allows you to build a custom validation function that validates a given control.
RangeValidator	Determines that a given value is in a predetermined range.
RegularExpressionValidator	Checks if the value of the associated input control matches the pattern of a regular expression.
RequiredFieldValidator	Ensures that a given input control contains a value (i.e., is not empty).
ValidationSummary	Displays a summary of all validation errors of a page in a list, bulleted list, or single-paragraph format. The errors can be displayed inline and/or in a pop-up message box.

All of the validator controls ultimately derive from a common base class named
System.Web.UI.WebControls.BaseValidator, and therefore they have a set of common features.
Table 23-12 documents the key members.

Table 23-12. *Common Properties of the ASP.NET Validators*

Member	Meaning in Life
ControlToValidate	Gets or sets the input control to validate
Display	Gets or sets the display behavior of the error message in a validation control
EnableClientScript	Gets or sets a value indicating whether client-side validation is enabled
ErrorMessage	Gets or sets the text for the error message
ForeColor	Gets or sets the color of the message displayed when validation fails

To illustrate the basics of working with validation controls, let's create a new Web Site project named
ValidatorCtrls. To begin, place four TextBox types (with four corresponding and descriptive Labels)
onto your page. Next, place a RequiredFieldValidator, RangeValidator, RegularExpressionValidator,
and CompareValidator type adjacent to each respective field. Finally, add a single Button and final
Label (see Figure 23-32).

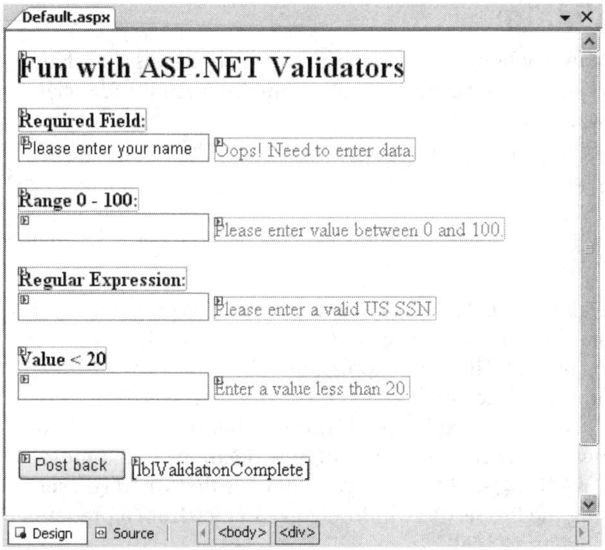

Figure 23-32. *The items to be validated*

Now that you have a UI, let's walk though the process of configuring each member.

The RequiredFieldValidator

Configuring the RequiredFieldValidator is straightforward. Simply set the ErrorMessage and ControlToValidate properties accordingly using the Visual Studio 2005 Properties window. The resulting *.aspx definition is as follows:

```
<asp:RequiredFieldValidator ID="RequiredFieldValidator1"
runat="server" ControlToValidate="txtRequiredField"
ErrorMessage="Oops!  Need to enter data.">
</asp:RequiredFieldValidator>
```

One nice thing about the RequiredFieldValidator is that it supports an InitialValue property. You can use this property to ensure that the user enters any value other than the initial value in the related TextBox. For example, when the user first posts to a page, you may wish to configure a TextBox to contain the value "Please enter your name". Now, if you did not set the InitialValue property of the RequiredFieldValidator, the runtime would assume that the string "Please enter your name" is valid. Thus, to ensure a required TextBox is valid only when the user enters anything other than "Please enter your name", configure your widgets as follows:

```
<asp:RequiredFieldValidator ID="RequiredFieldValidator1"
runat="server" ControlToValidate="txtRequiredField"
ErrorMessage="Oops!  Need to enter data."
InitialValue="Please enter your name">
</asp:RequiredFieldValidator>
```

The RegularExpressionValidator

The RegularExpressionValidator can be used when you wish to apply a pattern against the characters entered within a given input field. To ensure that a given TextBox contains a valid U.S. Social Security number, you could define the widget as follows:

```
<asp:RegularExpressionValidator ID="RegularExpressionValidator1"
runat="server" ControlToValidate="txtRegExp"
ErrorMessage="Please enter a valid US SSN."
ValidationExpression="\d{3}-\d{2}-\d{4}">
</asp:RegularExpressionValidator>
```

Notice how the RegularExpressionValidator defines a ValidationExpression property. If you have never worked with regular expressions before, all you need to be aware of for this example is that they are used to match a given string pattern. Here, the expression "\d{3}-\d{2}\d{4}" is capturing a standard U.S. Social Security number of the form xxx-xx-xxxx (where x is any digit).

This particular regular expression is fairly self-explanatory; however, assume you wish to test for a valid Japanese phone number. The correct expression now becomes much more complex: "(0\d{1,4}-|\(0\d{1,4}\) ?)?\d{1,4}-\d{4}". The good news is that when you select the ValidationExpression property using the Properties window, you can pick from a predefined set of common regular expressions (see Figure 23-33).

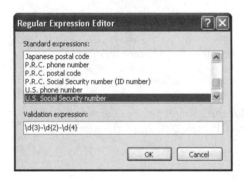

Figure 23-33. *Creating a regular expression via Visual Studio 2005*

■Note If you are really into regular expressions, you will be happy to know that the .NET platform supplies two namespaces (System.Text.RegularExpressions and System.Web.RegularExpressions) devoted to the programmatic manipulation of such patterns.

The RangeValidator

In addition to a MinimumValue and MaximumValue property, RangeValidators have a property named Type. Because you are interested in testing the user-supplied input against a range of whole numbers, you need to specify Integer (which is *not* the default!):

```
 <asp:RangeValidator ID="RangeValidator1"
runat="server" ControlToValidate="txtRange"
ErrorMessage="Please enter value between 0 and 100."
MaximumValue="100" MinimumValue="0" Type="Integer">
</asp:RangeValidator>
```

The RangeValidator can also be used to test if a given value is between a currency value, date, floating-point number, or string data (the default setting).

The CompareValidator

Finally, notice that the CompareValidator supports an Operator property:

```
<asp:CompareValidator ID="CompareValidator1" runat="server"
ControlToValidate="txtComparison"
ErrorMessage="Enter a value less than 20." Operator="LessThan"
ValueToCompare="20">
</asp:CompareValidator>
```

Given that the role of this validator is to compare the value in the text box against another value using a binary operator, it should be no surprise that the Operator property may be set to values such as LessThan, GreaterThan, Equal, and NotEqual. Also note that the ValueToCompare is used to establish a value to compare against.

Note The CompareValidator can also be configured to compare a value within another Web Form control (rather than a hard-coded value) using the ControlToValidate property.

To finish up the code for this page, handle the Click event for the Button type and inform the user he has succeeded in the validation logic:

```
protected void btnPostback_Click(object sender, EventArgs e)
{
    lblValidationComplete.Text = "You passed validation!";
}
```

Now, navigate to this page using your browser of choice. At this point, you should not see any noticeable changes. However, when you attempt to click the Submit button after entering bogus data, your error message is suddenly visible. Once you enter valid data, the error messages are removed and postback occurs.

If you look at the HTML rendered by the browser, you see that the validator controls generate a client-side JavaScript function that makes use of a specific library of JavaScript functions (contained in the WebUIValidation.js file) that is automatically downloaded to the user's machine. Once the validation has occurred, the form data is posted back to the server, where the ASP.NET runtime will perform the *same* validation tests on the web server (just to ensure that no along-the-wire tampering has taken place).

On a related note, if the HTTP request was sent by a browser that does not support client-side JavaScript, all validation will occur on the server. In this way, you can program against the validator controls without being concerned with the target browser; the returned HTML page redirects the error processing back to the web server.

Creating Validation Summaries

The final validation-centric topic we will examine here is the use of the ValidationSummary widget. Currently, each of your validators displays its error message at the exact place in which it was positioned at design time. In many cases, this may be exactly what you are looking for. However, on a complex form with numerous input widgets, you may not want to have random blobs of red text pop up. Using the ValidationSummary type, you can instruct all of your validation types to display their error messages at a specific location on the page.

The first step is to simply place a ValidationSummary on your *.aspx file. You may optionally set the HeaderText property of this type as well as the DisplayMode, which by default will list all error messages as a bulleted list.

```
<asp:ValidationSummary id="ValidationSummary1"
style="Z-INDEX: 123; LEFT: 152px; POSITION: absolute; TOP: 320px"
runat="server" Width="353px"
HeaderText="Here are the things you must correct.">
</asp:ValidationSummary>
```

Next, you need to set the Display property to None for each of the individual validators (e.g., RequiredFieldValidator, RangeValidator, etc.) on the page. This will ensure that you do not see duplicate error messages for a given validation failure (one in the summary pane and another at the validator's location).

Last but not least, if you would rather have the error messages displayed using a client-side MessageBox, set the ShowMessageBox property to true and the ShowSummary property to false.

■**Source Code** The ValidatorCtrls project is included under the Chapter 23 subdirectory.

Summary

Building web applications requires a different frame of mind than is used to assemble traditional desktop applications. In this chapter, you began with a quick and painless review of some core web atoms, including HTML, HTTP, the role of client-side scripting, and server-side scripts using classic ASP.

The bulk of this chapter was spent examining the architecture of an ASP.NET page. As you have seen, each *.aspx file in your project has an associated System.Web.UI.Page-derived class. Using this OO approach, ASP.NET allows you to build more reusable and OO-aware systems. This chapter examined the use of master pages and various Web Form controls (including the new GridView and Wizard types). As you have seen, these GUI widgets are in charge of emitting HTML tags to the client side. The validation controls are server-side widgets that are responsible for rendering client-side JavaScript to perform form validation, without incurring a round-trip to the server.

## CHAPTER 24

ASP.NET 2.0 Web Applications

The previous chapter concentrated on the composition and behavior of ASP.NET pages and the web controls they contain. This chapter builds on these basics by examining the role of the `HttpApplication` type. As you will see, the functionality of `HttpApplication` allows you to intercept numerous events that enable you to treat your web applications as a cohesive unit, rather than a set of stand-alone `*.aspx` files.

In addition to investigating the `HttpApplication` type, this chapter also addresses the all-important topic of state management. Here you will learn the role of view state, control state, and session- and application-level variables, as well as a state-centric entity provided by ASP.NET termed the *application cache*. Once you have a solid understanding of the state management techniques offered by the .NET platform, the chapter wraps up with a discussion of the role of the `Web.config` file and shows various configuration-centric techniques.

The Issue of State

At the beginning of the last chapter, I pointed out that HTTP is a *stateless* wire protocol. This very fact makes web development extremely different from the process of building an executable assembly. For example, when you are building a Windows Forms application, you can rest assured that any member variables defined in the `Form`-derived class will typically exist in memory until the user explicitly shuts down the executable:

```
public partial class MainWindow : Form
{
    // State data!
    private string userFavoriteCar;
...
}
```

In the world of the World Wide Web, however, you are not afforded the same luxurious assumption. To prove the point, create a new ASP.NET website (named SimpleStateExample) that has a single `*.aspx` file. Within the code-behind file, define a page-level string variable named `userFavoriteCar`:

```
public partial class _Default : Page
{
    // State data?
    private string userFavoriteCar;
    ...
}
```

Next, construct the web UI as shown in Figure 24-1.

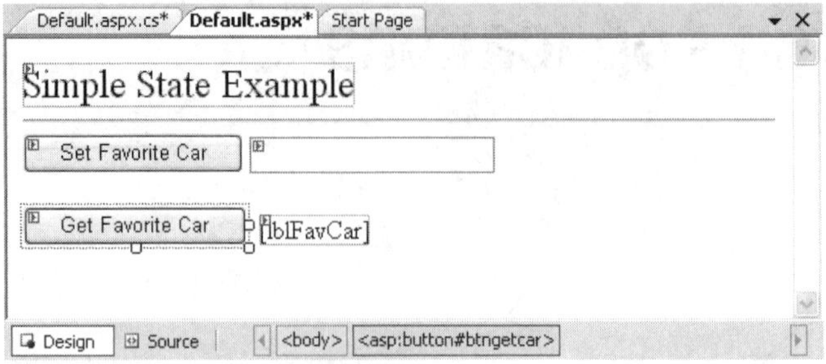

Figure 24-1. *The UI for the simple state page*

The server-side `Click` event handler for the Set button will allow the user to assign the string variable using the value within the `TextBox`:

```
protected void btnSetCar_Click(object sender, EventArgs e)
{
    // Store favorite car in member variable.
    userFavoriteCar = txtFavCar.Text;
}
```

while the `Click` event handler for the Get button will display the current value of the member variable within the page's `Label` widget:

```
protected void btnGetCar_Click(object sender, EventArgs e)
{
    // Set label text to value of member variable.
    lblFavCar.Text = userFavoriteCar;
}
```

Now, if you were building a Windows Forms application, you would be right to assume that once the user sets the initial value, it would be remembered throughout the life of the desktop application. Sadly, when you run this web application, you will find that each time you post back to the web server, the value of the `userFavoriteCar` string variable is set back to the initial empty value; therefore, the `Label`'s text is continuously empty.

Again, given that HTTP has no clue how to automatically remember data once the HTTP response has been sent, it stands to reason that the `Page` object is destroyed instantly. Therefore, when the client posts back to the *.aspx file, a *new* `Page` object is constructed that will reset any page-level member variables. This is clearly a major dilemma. Imagine how painful online shopping would be if every time you posted back to the web server, any and all information you previously entered (such as the items you wish to purchase) were discarded. When you wish to remember information regarding the users who are logged on to your site, you need to make use of various state management techniques.

Note This issue is in no way limited to ASP.NET. Java servlets, CGI applications, classic ASP, and PHP applications all must contend with the thorny issue of state management.

To remember the value of the `userFavoriteCar` string type between postbacks, you are required to store the value of this string type within a session variable. You will examine the exact details of session state in the pages that follow. For the sake of completion, however, here are the necessary updates for the current page (note that you are no longer using the private string member variable, therefore feel free to comment out or remove the definition altogether):

```
protected void btnSetCar_Click(object sender, EventArgs e)
{
    Session["UserFavCar"] = txtFavCar.Text;
}
protected void btnGetCar_Click(object sender, EventArgs e)
{
    lblFavCar.Text = (string)Session["UserFavCar"];
}
```

If you now run the application, the value of your favorite automobile will be preserved across postbacks, thanks to the HttpSessionState object manipulated with the inherited Session property.

■**Source Code** The SimpleStateExample files are included under the Chapter 24 subdirectory.

ASP.NET State Management Techniques

ASP.NET provides several mechanisms that you can use to maintain stateful information in your web applications. Specifically, you have the following options:

- Make use of ASP.NET view state.
- Make use of ASP.NET control state.
- Define application-level variables.
- Make use of the cache object.
- Define session-level variables.
- Interact with cookie data.

We'll examine the details of each approach in turn, beginning with the topic of ASP.NET view state.

Understanding the Role of ASP.NET View State

The term *view state* has been thrown out numerous times here and in the previous chapter without a formal definition, so let's demystify this term once and for all. Under classic ASP, web developers were required to manually repopulate the values of the incoming form widgets during the process of constructing the outgoing HTTP response. For example, if the incoming HTTP request contained five text boxes with specific values, the *.asp file needed to extract the current values (via the Form or QueryString collections of the Request object) and manually place them back into the HTTP response stream (needless to say, this was a drag). If the developer failed to do so, the caller was presented with a set of five empty text boxes!

Under ASP.NET, we are no longer required to manually scrape out and repopulate the values contained within the HTML widgets because the ASP.NET runtime will automatically embed a hidden form field (named __VIEWSTATE), which will flow between the browser and a specific page. The data assigned to this field is a Base64-encoded string that contains a set of name/value pairs that represent the values of each GUI widget on the page at hand.

The System.Web.UI.Page base class's Init event handler is the entity in charge of reading the incoming values found within the __VIEWSTATE field to populate the appropriate member variables in the derived class (which is why it is risky at best to access the state of a web widget within the scope of a page's Init event handler).

Also, just before the outgoing response is emitted back to the requesting browser, the __VIEWSTATE data is used to repopulate the form's widgets, to ensure that the current values of the HTML widgets appear as they did prior to the previous postback.

Clearly, the best thing about this aspect of ASP.NET is that it just happens without any work on your part. Of course, you are always able to interact with, alter, or disable this default functionality if you so choose. To understand how to do this, let's see a concrete view state example.

Demonstrating View State

First, create a new ASP.NET web application called ViewStateApp. On your initial *.aspx page, add a single ASP.NET ListBox web control and a single Button type. Handle the Click event for the Button to provide a way for the user to post back to the web server:

```
protected void btnDoPostBack_Click(object sender, EventArgs e)
{
    // This is just here to allow a postback.
}
```

Now, using the Visual Studio 2005 Properties window, access the Items property and add four ListItems to the ListBox. The result looks like this:

```
<asp:ListBox ID="myListBox" runat="server">
    <asp:ListItem>Item One</asp:ListItem>
    <asp:ListItem>Item Two</asp:ListItem>
    <asp:ListItem>Item Three</asp:ListItem>
    <asp:ListItem>Item Four</asp:ListItem>
</asp:ListBox>
```

Note that you are hard-coding the items in the ListBox directly within the *.aspx file. As you already know, all <asp:> definitions found within an HTML form will automatically render back their HTML representation before the final HTTP response (provided they have the runat="server" attribute).

The <%@Page%> directive has an optional attribute called enableViewState that by default is set to true. To disable this behavior, simply update the <%@Page%> directive as follows:

```
<%@ Page EnableViewState ="false"
Language="C#" AutoEventWireup="true"
CodeFile="Default.aspx.cs" Inherits="_Default" %>
```

So, what exactly does it mean to disable view state? The answer is, it depends. Given the previous definition of the term, you would think that if you disable view state for an *.aspx file, the values within your ListBox would not be remembered between postbacks to the web server. However, if you were to run this application as is, you might be surprised to find that the information in the ListBox is retained regardless of how many times you post back to the page. In fact, if you examine the source HTML returned to the browser, you may be further surprised to see that the hidden __VIEWSTATE field is *still present*:

```
<input type="hidden" name="__VIEWSTATE" id="__VIEWSTATE"
value="/wEPDwUKMTY1MjcxNTcxNmRkOXbNzW5+R2VDhNWtEtHMM+yhxvU=" />
```

The reason why the view state string is still visible is the fact that the *.aspx file has explicitly defined the ListBox items within the scope of the HTML <form> tags. Thus, the ListBox items will be autogenerated each time the web server responds to the client.

However, assume that your ListBox is dynamically populated within the code-behind file rather than within the HTML <form> definition. First, remove the <asp:ListItem> declarations from the current *.aspx file:

```
<asp:ListBox ID="myListBox" runat="server">
</asp:ListBox>
```

Next, fill the list items within the Load event handler of within your code-behind file:

```
protected void Page_Load(object sender, EventArgs e)
{
    if(!IsPostBack)
    {
        // Fill ListBox dynamically!
        myListBox.Items.Add("Item One");
        myListBox.Items.Add("Item Two");
        myListBox.Items.Add("Item Three");
        myListBox.Items.Add("Item Four");
    }
}
```

If you post to this updated page, you will find that the first time the browser requests the page, the values in the ListBox are present and accounted for. However, on postback, the ListBox is suddenly *empty*. The first rule of ASP.NET view state is that its effect is only realized when you have widgets whose values are dynamically generated through code. If you hard-code values within the *.aspx file's <form> tags, the state of these items is always remembered across postbacks (even when you set enableViewState to false for a given page).

Furthermore, view state is most useful when you have a dynamically populated web widget that always needs to be repopulated for each and every postback (such as an ASP.NET GridView, which is always filled using a database hit). If you did not disable view state for pages that contain such widgets, the entire state of the grid is represented within the hidden __VIEWSTATE field. Given that complex pages may contain numerous ASP.NET web controls, you can imagine how large this string would become. As the payload of the HTTP request/response cycle could become quite heavy, this may become a problem for the dial-up web surfers of the world. In cases such as these, you may find faster throughput if you disable view state for the page.

If the idea of disabling view state for the entire *.aspx file seems a bit too aggressive, recall that every descendent of the System.Web.UI.Control base class inherits the EnableViewState property, which makes it very simple to disable view state on a control-by-control basis:

```
<asp:GridView id="myHugeDynamicallyFilledDataGrid" runat="server"
 EnableViewState="false">
</asp:GridView>
```

■**Note** Be aware that ASP.NET pages reserve a small part of the __VIEWSTATE string for internal use. Given this, you will find that the __VIEWSTATE field will still appear in the client-side browser even when the entire page (and all the controls) have disabled view state.

Adding Custom View State Data

In addition to the EnableViewState property, the System.Web.UI.Control base class also provides an inherited property named ViewState. Under the hood, this property provides access to a System.Web.UI.StateBag type, which represents all the data contained within the __VIEWSTATE field. Using the indexer of the StateBag type, you can embed custom information within the hidden __VIEWSTATE form field using a set of name/value pairs. Here's a simple example:

```
protected void btnAddToVS_Click(object sender, EventArgs e)
{
    ViewState["CustomViewStateItem"] = "Some user data";
    lblVSValue.Text = (string)ViewState["CustomViewStateItem"];
}
```

Because the System.Web.UI.StateBag type has been designed to operate on any type-derived System.Object, when you wish to access the value of a given key, you will need to explicitly cast it into the correct underlying data type (in this case, a System.String). Be aware, however, that values placed within the __VIEWSTATE field cannot literally be *any* object. Specifically, the only valid types are strings, integers, Booleans, ArrayLists, Hashtables, or an array of these types.

So, given that *.aspx pages may insert custom bits of information into the __VIEWSTATE string, the next logical question is when you would want to do so. Most of the time, custom view state data is best suited for user-specific preferences. For example, you may establish a point of view-state data that specifies how a user wishes to view the UI of a GridView (such as a sort order). View state data is not well suited for full-blown user data, such as items in a shopping cart, cached DataSets, or whatnot. When you need to store this sort of complex information, you are required to work with session data. Before we get to that point, you need to understand the role of the Global.asax file.

■**Source Code** The ViewStateApp files are included under the Chapter 24 subdirectory.

A Brief Word Regarding Control State

As of ASP.NET 2.0, a control's state data can now be persisted via *control state* rather than view state. This technique is most helpful if you have written a custom ASP.NET web control that must remember data between round-trips. While the ViewState property can be used for this purpose, if view state is disabled at a page level, the custom control is effectively broken. For this very reason, web controls now support a ControlState property.

Control state works identically to view state; however, it will not be disabled if view state is disabled at the page level. As mentioned, this feature is most useful for those who are developing custom web controls (a topic not covered in this text). Consult the .NET Framework 2.0 SDK documentation for further details.

The Role of the Global.asax File

At this point, an ASP.NET application may seem to be little more than a set of *.aspx files and their respective web controls. While you could build a web application by simply linking a set of related web pages, you will most likely need a way to interact with the web application as a whole. To this end, your ASP.NET web applications may choose to include an optional Global.asax file via the WebSite ➤ Add New Item menu option (see Figure 24-2).

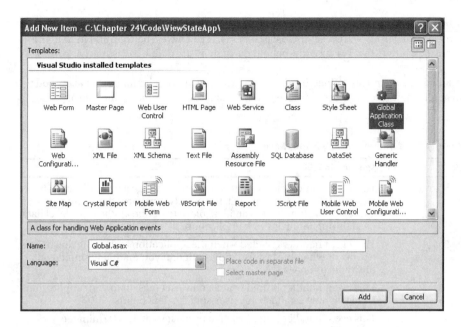

Figure 24-2. *The* Global.asax *file*

Simply put, Global.asax is just about as close to a traditional double-clickable *.exe that we can get in the world of ASP.NET, meaning this type represents the runtime behavior of the website itself. Once you insert a Global.asax file into a web project, you will notice it is little more than a <script> block containing a set of event handlers:

```
<%@ Application Language="C#" %>
<script runat="server">
    void Application_Start(Object sender, EventArgs e)
    {
        // Code that runs on application startup
    }
    void Application_End(Object sender, EventArgs e)
    {
        //  Code that runs on application shutdown
    }
    void Application_Error(Object sender, EventArgs e)
    {
        // Code that runs when an unhandled error occurs
    }
    void Session_Start(Object sender, EventArgs e)
    {
        // Code that runs when a new session is started
    }
    void Session_End(Object sender, EventArgs e)
    {
        // Code that runs when a session ends
    }
</script>
```

Looks can be deceiving, however. At runtime, the code within this <script> block is assembled into a class type deriving from System.Web.HttpApplication. If you have a background in ASP.NET 1.*x*, you may recall that the Global.asax code-behind file literally *did* define a class deriving from HttpApplication.

As mentioned, the members defined inside Global.asax are in event handlers that allow you to interact with application-level (and session-level) events. Table 24-1 documents the role of each member.

Table 24-1. *Core Types of the* System.Web *Namespace*

Event Handler	Meaning in Life
Application_Start()	This event handler is called the very first time the web application is launched. Thus, this event will fire exactly once over the lifetime of a web application. This is an ideal place to define application-level data used throughout your web application.
Application_End()	This event handler is called when the application is shutting down. This will occur when the last user times out or if you manually shut down the application via IIS.
Session_Start()	This event handler is fired when a new user logs on to your application. Here you may establish any user-specific data points.
Session_End()	This event handler is fired when a user's session has terminated (typically through a predefined timeout).
Application_Error()	This is a global error handler that will be called when an unhandled exception is thrown by the web application.

The Global Last Chance Exception Event Handler

First, let me point out the role of the Application_Error() event handler. Recall that a specific page may handle the Error event to process any unhandled exception that occurred within the scope of the page itself. In a similar light, the Application_Error() event handler is the final place to handle an exception that was not handled by a specific page. As with the page-level Error event, you are able to access the specific System.Exception using the inherited Server property:

```
void Application_Error(Object sender, EventArgs e)
{
    Exception ex = Server.GetLastError();
    Response.Write(ex.Message);
    Server.ClearError();
}
```

Given that the Application_Error() event handler is the last chance exception handler for your web application, odds are that you would rather not report the error to the user, but you would like to log this information to the web server's event log, for example:

```
<%@ Import Namespace = "System.Diagnostics"%>
...
void Application_Error(Object sender, EventArgs e)
{
    // Log last error to event log.
    Exception ex = Server.GetLastError();
    EventLog ev = new EventLog("Application");
    ev.WriteEntry(ex.Message, EventLogEntryType.Error);
    Server.ClearError();
    Response.Write("This app has bombed. Sorry!");
}
```

The HttpApplication Base Class

As mentioned, the Global.asax script is dynamically generated into a class deriving from the System.Web.HttpApplication base class, which supplies the same sort of functionality as the System.Web.UI.Page type. Table 24-2 documents the key members of interest.

Table 24-2. *Key Members Defined by the* System.Web.HttpApplication *Type*

Property	Meaning in Life
Application	This property allows you to interact with application-level variables, using the exposed HttpApplicationState type.
Request	This property allows you to interact with the incoming HTTP request (via HttpRequest).
Response	This property allows you to interact with the incoming HTTP response (via HttpResponse).
Server	This property gets the intrinsic server object for the current request (via HttpServerUtility).
Session	This property allows you to interact with session-level variables, using the exposed HttpSessionState type.

Understanding the Application/Session Distinction

Under ASP.NET, application state is maintained by an instance of the HttpApplicationState type. This class enables you to share global information across all users (and all pages) who are logged on to your ASP.NET application. Not only can application data be shared by all users on your site, but also if one user changes the value of an application-level data point, the change is seen by all others on their next postback.

On the other hand, session state is used to remember information for a specific user (again, such as items in a shopping cart). Physically, a user's session state is represented by the HttpSessionState class type. When a new user logs on to an ASP.NET web application, the runtime will automatically assign that user a new session ID, which by default will expire after 20 minutes of inactivity. Thus, if 20,000 users are logged on to your site, you have 20,000 distinct HttpSessionState objects, each of which is assigned a unique session ID. The relationship between a web application and web sessions is shown in Figure 24-3.

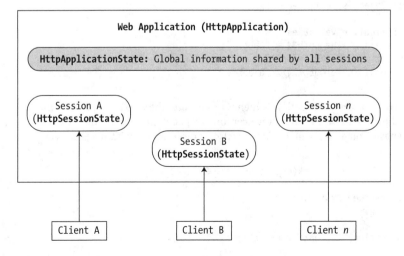

Figure 24-3. *The application/session state distinction*

As you may know, under classic ASP, application- and session-state data is represented using distinct COM objects (e.g., Application and Session). Under ASP.NET, Page-derived types as well as the HttpApplication type make use of identically named *properties* (i.e., Application and Session), which expose the underlying HttpApplicationState and HttpSessionState types.

Maintaining Application-Level State Data

The HttpApplicationState type enables developers to share global information across multiple sessions in an ASP.NET application. For example, you may wish to maintain an applicationwide connection string that can be used by all pages, a common DataSet used by multiple pages, or any other piece of data that needs to be accessed on an applicationwide scale. Table 24-3 describes some core members of this type.

Table 24-3. *Members of the* HttpApplicationState *Type*

Members	Meaning in Life
AllKeys	This property returns an array of System.String types that represent all the names in the HttpApplicationState type.
Count	This property gets the number of item objects in the HttpApplicationState type.
Add()	This method allows you to add a new name/value pair into the HttpApplicationState type. Do note that this method is typically *not* used in favor of the indexer of the HttpApplicationState class.
Clear()	This method deletes all items in the HttpApplicationState type. This is functionally equivalent to the RemoveAll() method.
Lock() Unlock()	These two methods are used when you wish to alter a set of application variables in a thread-safe manner.
RemoveAll() Remove() RemoveAt()	These methods remove a specific item (by string name) within the HttpApplicationState type. RemoveAt() removes the item via a numerical indexer.

When you create data members that can be shared among all active sessions, you need to establish a set of name/value pairs. In most cases, the most natural place to do so is within the Application_Start() event handler of the HttpApplication-derived type, for example:

```
void Application_Start(Object sender, EventArgs e)
{
    // Set up some application variables.
    Application["SalesPersonOfTheMonth"] = "Chucky";
    Application["CurrentCarOnSale"] = "Colt";
    Application["MostPopularColorOnLot"] = "Black";
}
```

During the lifetime of your web application (which is to say, until the web application is manually shut down or until the final user times out), any user (on any page) may access these values as necessary. Assume you have a page that will display the current discount car within a Label via a button click:

```
protected void btnShowCarDiscount_Click(object sender, EventArgs e)
{
    // Must cast the returned System.Object
    // to a System.String!
    lblCurrCarOnSale.Text =
        (string)Application["CurrentCarOnSale"];
}
```

Like the ViewState property, notice how you must cast the value returned from the HttpApplicationState type into the correct underlying type. Now, given that the HttpApplicationState type can hold *any* type, it should stand to reason that you can place custom types (or any .NET type) within your site's application state.

To illustrate this technique, create a new ASP.NET web application named AppState. Assume you would rather maintain the three current application variables within a strongly typed object named CarLotInfo:

```
public class CarLotInfo
{
    public CarLotInfo(string s, string c, string m)
    {
        salesPersonOfTheMonth = s;
        currentCarOnSale = c;
        mostPopularColorOnLot = m;
    }
    // Public for easy access.
    public string salesPersonOfTheMonth;
    public string currentCarOnSale;
    public string mostPopularColorOnLot;
}
```

With this helper class in place, you could modify the Application_Start() event handler as follows:

```
protected void Application_Start(Object sender, EventArgs e)
{
    // Place a custom object in the application data sector.
    Application["CarSiteInfo"] =
        new CarLotInfo("Chucky", "Colt", "Black");
}
```

and then access the information using the public field data within a server-side event handler:

```
protected void btnShowAppVariables_Click(object sender, EventArgs e)
{
    CarLotInfo appVars =
        ((CarLotInfo)Application["CarSiteInfo"]);
    string appState =
        string.Format("<li>Car on sale: {0}</li>",
        appVars.currentCarOnSale);
    appState +=
        string.Format("<li>Most popular color: {0}</li>",
        appVars.mostPopularColorOnLot);
    appState +=
        string.Format("<li>Big shot SalesPerson: {0}</li>",
        appVars.salesPersonOfTheMonth);
    lblAppVariables.Text = appState;
}
```

If you were now to run this page, you would find that a list of each application variable is displayed on the page's Label type.

Modifying Application Data

You may programmatically update or delete any or all members using members of the HttpApplicationState type during the execution of your web application. For example, to delete a specific item, simply call the Remove() method. If you wish to destroy all application-level data, call RemoveAll():

```
private void CleanAppData()
{
    // Remove a single item via string name.
    Application.Remove("SomeItemIDontNeed");

    // Destroy all application data!
    Application.RemoveAll();
}
```

If you wish to simply change the value of an existing application-level variable, you only need to make a new assignment to the data item in question. Assume your page now supports a new Button type that allows your user to change the current hotshot salesperson. The Click event handler is as you would expect:

```
protected void btnSetNewSP_Click(object sender, EventArgs e)
{
    // Set the new Salesperson.
    ((CarLotInfo)Application["CarSiteInfo"]).salesPersonOfTheMonth
        = txtNewSP.Text;
}
```

If you run the web application, you will find that the application-level variable has been updated. Furthermore, given that application variables are accessible from all user sessions, if you were to launch three or four instances of your web browser, you would find that if one instance changes the current hotshot salesperson, each of the other browsers displays the new value on postback.

Understand that if you have a situation where a set of application-level variables must be updated as a unit, you risk the possibility of data corruption (given that it is technically possible that an application-level data point may be changed while another user is attempting to access it!). While you could take the long road and manually lock down the logic using threading primitives of the System.Threading namespace, the HttpApplicationState type has two methods, Lock() and Unlock(), that automatically ensure thread safety:

```
// Safely access related application data.
Application.Lock();
    Application["SalesPersonOfTheMonth"] = "Maxine";
    Application["CurrentBonusedEmployee"] = Application["SalesPersonOfTheMonth"];
Application.Unlock();
```

■**Note** Much like the C# lock statement, if an exception occurs after the call to Lock() but before the call to Unlock(), the lock will automatically be released.

Handling Web Application Shutdown

The HttpApplicationState type is designed to maintain the values of the items it contains until one of two situations occurs: the last user on your site times out (or manually logs out) or someone manually shuts down the website via IIS. In each case, the Application_Exit() method of the HttpApplication-derived type will automatically be called. Within this event handler, you are able to perform whatever sort of cleanup code is necessary:

```
protected void Application_End(Object sender, EventArgs e)
{
    // Write current application variables
    // to a database or whatever else you need to do...
}
```

Working with the Application Cache

ASP.NET provides a second and more flexible manner to handle applicationwide data. As you recall, the values within the HttpApplicationState object remain in memory as long as your web application is alive and kicking. Sometimes, however, you may wish to maintain a piece of application data only for a specific period of time. For example, you may wish to obtain an ADO.NET DataSet that is valid for only five minutes. After that time, you may want to obtain a fresh DataSet to account for possible user modifications. While it is technically possible to build this infrastructure using HttpApplicationState and some sort of handcrafted monitor, your task is greatly simplified using the ASP.NET application cache.

As suggested by its name, the ASP.NET System.Web.Caching.Cache object (which is accessible via the Context.Cache property) allows you to define an object that is accessible by all users (from all pages) for a fixed amount of time. In its simplest form, interacting with the cache looks identical to interacting with the HttpApplicationState type:

```
// Add an item to the cache.
// This item will *not* expire.
Context.Cache["SomeStringItem"] = "This is the string item";
string s = (string)Context.Cache["SomeStringItem"];
```

■**Note** If you wish to access the Cache from within Global.asax, you are required to use the Context property. However, if you are within the scope of a System.Web.UI.Page-derived type, you can make use of the Cache object directly.

Now, understand that if you have no interest in automatically updating (or removing) an application-level data point (as seen here), the Cache object is of little benefit, as you can directly use the HttpApplicationState type. However, when you do wish to have a data point destroyed after a fixed point of time—and optionally be informed when this occurs—the Cache type is extremely helpful.

The System.Web.Caching.Cache class defines only a small number of members beyond the type's indexer. For example, the Add() method can be used to insert a new item into the cache that is not currently defined (if the specified item is already present, Add() does nothing). The Insert() method will also place a member into the cache. If, however, the item is currently defined, Insert() will replace the current item with the new type. Given that this is most often the behavior you will desire, I'll focus on the Insert() method exclusively.

Fun with Data Caching

Let's see an example. To begin, create a new ASP.NET web application named CacheState and insert a Global.asax file. Like an application-level variable maintained by the HttpApplicationState type, the Cache may hold any System.Object-derived type and is often populated within the Application_Start() event handler. For this example, the goal is to automatically update the contents of a DataSet every 15 seconds. The DataSet in question will contain the current set of records from the Inventory table of the Cars database created during our discussion of ADO.NET. Given these stats, update your Global class type as so (code analysis to follow):

```
<%@ Application Language="C#" %>
<%@ Import Namespace = "System.Data.SqlClient" %>
<%@ Import Namespace = "System.Data" %>

<script runat="server">
    // Define a static-level Cache member variable.
    static Cache theCache;

    void Application_Start(Object sender, EventArgs e)
    {
        // First assign the static 'theCache' variable.
        theCache = Context.Cache;

        // When the application starts up,
        // read the current records in the
        // Inventory table of the Cars DB.
        SqlConnection cn = new SqlConnection
          ("data source=localhost;initial catalog=Cars; user id ='sa';pwd=''");
        SqlDataAdapter dAdapt =
            new SqlDataAdapter("Select * From Inventory", cn);
        DataSet theCars = new DataSet();
        dAdapt.Fill(theCars, "Inventory");

        // Now store DataSet in the cache.
        theCache.Insert("AppDataSet",
            theCars, null,
            DateTime.Now.AddSeconds(15),
            Cache.NoSlidingExpiration,
            CacheItemPriority.Default,
            new CacheItemRemovedCallback(UpdateCarInventory));
    }

    // The target for the CacheItemRemovedCallback delegate.
    static void UpdateCarInventory(string key, object item,
        CacheItemRemovedReason reason)
    {
        // Populate the DataSet.
        SqlConnection cn = new SqlConnection
        ("data source=localhost;initial catalog=Cars; user id ='sa';pwd=''");
        SqlDataAdapter dAdapt =
            new SqlDataAdapter("Select * From Inventory", cn);
        DataSet theCars = new DataSet();
        dAdapt.Fill(theCars, "Inventory");

        // Now store in the cache.
        theCache.Insert("AppDataSet",
            theCars, null,
            DateTime.Now.AddSeconds(15),
            Cache.NoSlidingExpiration,
            CacheItemPriority.Default,
            new CacheItemRemovedCallback(UpdateCarInventory));
    }
...
</script>
```

First, notice that the Global type has defined a static-level Cache member variable. The reason is that you have also defined a static-level function (UpdateCarInventory()) that needs to access the Cache (recall that static members do not have access to inherited members, therefore you can't use the Context property!).

Inside the Application_Start() event handler, you fill a DataSet and place the object within the application cache. As you would guess, the Context.Cache.Insert() method has been overloaded a number of times. Here, you supply a value for each possible parameter:

```
// Now store in the cache.
theCache.Add("AppDataSet",          // Name used to identify item in the cache.
    theCars,                        // Object to put In the cache.
    null,                           // Any dependencies for this object?
    DateTime.Now. AddSeconds(15),   // How long item will be in cache.
    Cache.NoSlidingExpiration,      // Fixed or sliding time?
    CacheItemPriority.Default,      // Priority level of cache item.
    // Delegate for CacheItemRemove event
    new CacheItemRemovedCallback(UpdateCarInventory));
```

The first two parameters simply make up the name/value pair of the item. The third parameter allows you to define a CacheDependency type (which is null in this case, as you do not have any other entities in the cache that are dependent on the DataSet).

■Note The ability to define a CacheDependency type is quite interesting. For example, you could establish a dependency between a member and an external file. If the contents of the file were to change, the type can be automatically updated. Check out the .NET Framework 2.0 documentation for further details.

The next three parameters are used to define the amount of time the item will be allowed to remain in the application cache and its level of priority. Here, you specify the read-only Cache. NoSlidingExpiration field, which informs the cache that the specified time limit (15 seconds) is absolute. Finally, and most important for this example, you create a new CacheItemRemovedCallback delegate type, and pass in the name of the method to call when the DataSet is purged. As you can see from the signature of the UpdateCarInventory() method, the CacheItemRemovedCallback delegate can only call methods that match the following signature:

```
static void UpdateCarInventory(string key, object item,
    CacheItemRemovedReason reason)
{ ... }
```

So, at this point, when the application starts up, the DataSet is populated and cached. Every 15 seconds, the DataSet is purged, updated, and reinserted into the cache. To see the effects of doing this, you need to create a Page that allows for some degree of user interaction.

Modifying the *.aspx File

Update the UI of your initial *.aspx file as shown in Figure 24-4.

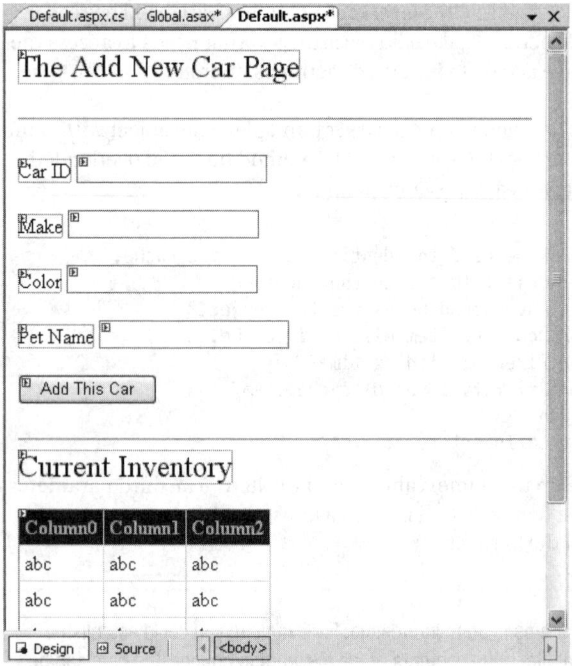

Figure 24-4. *The cache application GUI*

In the page's Load event handler, configure your GridView to display the current contents of the cached DataSet the first time the user posts to the page:

```
protected void Page_Load(object sender, EventArgs e)
{
    if(!IsPostBack)
    {
        carsGridView.DataSource =  (DataSet)Cache["AppDataSet"];
        carsGridView.DataBind();
    }
}
```

In the Click event handler of the Add this Car button, insert the new record into the Cars database using an ADO.NET SqlCommand object. Once the record has been inserted, call a helper function named RefreshGrid(), which will update the UI via an ADO.NET SqlDataReader (so don't forget to "use" the System.Data.SqlClient namespace). Here are the methods in question:

```
protected void btnAddCar_Click(object sender, EventArgs e)
{
    // Update the Inventory table
    // and call RefreshGrid().
    SqlConnection cn = new SqlConnection();
    cn.ConnectionString =
        "User ID=sa;Pwd=;Initial Catalog=Cars;" +
        "Data Source=(local)";
    cn.Open();
    string sql;
    SqlCommand cmd;
```

```
    // Insert new Car.
    sql = string.Format
        ("INSERT INTO Inventory(CarID, Make, Color, PetName) VALUES" +
        "('{0}', '{1}', '{2}', '{3}')",
        txtCarID.Text, txtCarMake.Text,
        txtCarColor.Text, txtCarPetName.Text);
    cmd = new SqlCommand(sql, cn);
    cmd.ExecuteNonQuery();
    cn.Close();
    RefreshGrid();
}
private void RefreshGrid()
{
    // Populate grid.
    SqlConnection cn = new SqlConnection();
    cn.ConnectionString =
        "User ID=sa;Pwd=;Initial Catalog=Cars;Data Source=(local)";
    cn.Open();
    SqlCommand cmd = new SqlCommand("Select * from Inventory", cn);
    carsGridView.DataSource = cmd.ExecuteReader();
    carsGridView.DataBind();
    cn.Close();
}
```

Now, to test the use of the cache, launch two instances of your web browser and navigate to this *.aspx page. At this point, you should see that both DataGrids display identical information. From one instance of the browser, add a new Car. Obviously, this results in an updated GridView viewable from the browser that initiated the postback.

In the second browser instance, click the Refresh button. You should *not* see the new item, given that the Page_Load event handler is reading directly from the cache. (If you did see the value, the 15 seconds had already expired. Either type faster or increase the amount of time the DataSet will remain in the cache.) Wait a few seconds and click the Refresh button from the second browser instance one more time. Now you *should* see the new item, given that the DataSet in the cache has expired and the CacheItemRemovedCallback delegate target method has automatically updated the cached DataSet.

As you can see, the major benefit of the Cache type is that you can ensure that when a member is removed, you have a chance to respond. In this example, you certainly could avoid using the Cache and simply have the Page_Load() event handler always read directly from the Cars database. Nevertheless, the point should be clear: the cache allows you to automatically refresh data using .NET delegates.

Note Unlike the HttpApplicationState type, the Cache class does not support Lock() and Unlock() methods. If you need to update interrelated items, you will need to directly make use of the types within the System.Threading namespace or the C# lock keyword.

Source Code The CacheState files are included under the Chapter 24 subdirectory.

Maintaining Session Data

So much for our examination of application-level state data. Next, let's check out the role of per-user data stores. As mentioned earlier, a *session* is little more than a given user's interaction with a web application, which is represented via the HttpSessionState type. To maintain stateful information for a particular user, the HttpApplication-derived type and any System.Web.UI.Page-derived types may access the Session property. The classic example of the need to maintain per-user data would be an online shopping cart. Again, if ten people all log on to an online store, each individual will maintain a unique set of items that she (may) intend to purchase.

When a new user logs on to your web application, the .NET runtime will automatically assign the user a unique session ID, which is used to identify the user in question. Each session ID is assigned a custom instance of the HttpSessionState type to hold on to user-specific data. Inserting or retrieving session data is syntactically identical to manipulating application data, for example:

```
// Add/retrieve a session variable for current user.
Session["DesiredCarColor"] = "Green";
string color = (string) Session["DesiredCarColor"];
```

The HttpApplication-derived type allows you to intercept the beginning and end of a session via the Session_Start() and Session_End() event handlers. Within Session_Start(), you can freely create any per-user data items, while Session_End() allows you to perform any work you may need to do when the user's session has terminated:

```
<%@ Application Language="C#" %>
<script runat="server">
...
    void Session_Start(Object sender, EventArgs e)
    {
    }
    void Session_End(Object sender, EventArgs e)
    {
    }
</script>
```

Like the HttpApplicationState type, the HttpSessionState may hold any System.Object-derived type, including your custom classes. For example, assume you have a new web application (SessionState) that defines a helper class named UserShoppingCart:

```
public class UserShoppingCart
{
  public string desiredCar;
  public string desiredCarColor;
  public float downPayment;
  public bool isLeasing;
  public DateTime dateOfPickUp;

  public override string ToString()
  {
    return string.Format
    ("Car: {0}<br>Color: {1}<br>$ Down: {2}<br>Lease: {3}<br>Pick-up Date: {4}",
     desiredCar, desiredCarColor, downPayment, isLeasing,
     dateOfPickUp.ToShortDateString());
  }
}
```

Within the Session_Start() event handler, you can now assign each user a new instance of the UserShoppingCart class:

```
void Session_Start(Object sender, EventArgs e)
{
    Session["UserShoppingCartInfo"]
        = new UserShoppingCart();
}
```

As the user traverses your web pages, you are able to pluck out the UserShoppingCart instance and fill the fields with user-specific data. For example, assume you have a simple *.aspx page that defines a set of input widgets that correspond to each field of the UserShoppingCart type and a Button used to set the values (see Figure 24-5).

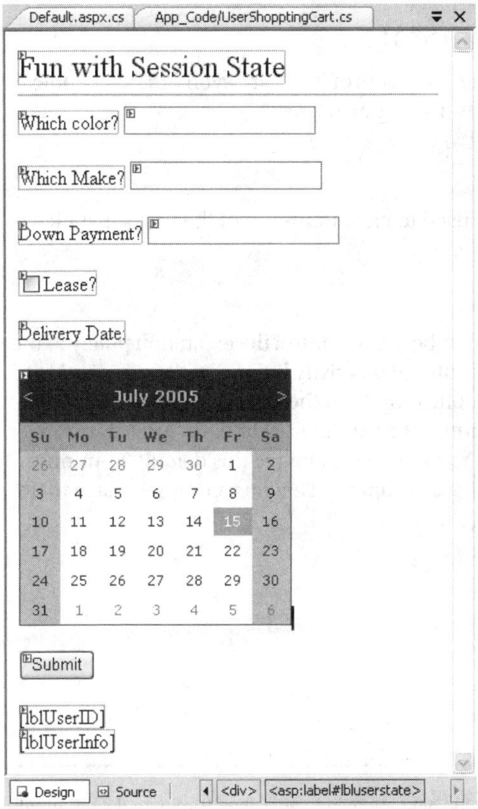

Figure 24-5. *The session application GUI*

The server-side Click event handler is straightforward (scrape out values from TextBoxes and display the shopping cart data on a Label type):

```
protected void btnSubmit_Click(object sender, EventArgs e)
{
    // Set current user prefs.
    UserShoppingCart u =
        (UserShoppingCart)Session["UserShoppingCartInfo"];
    u.dateOfPickUp = myCalendar.SelectedDate;
    u.desiredCar = txtCarMake.Text;
    u.desiredCarColor = txtCarColor.Text;
```

```
    u.downPayment = float.Parse(txtDownPayment.Text);
    u.isLeasing = chkIsLeasing.Checked;
    lblUserInfo.Text = u.ToString();

    Session["UserShoppingCartInfo"] = u;
}
```

Within Session_End(), you may wish to persist the fields of the UserShoppingCart to a database or whatnot. In any case, if you were to launch two or three instances of your browser of choice, you would find that each user is able to build a custom shopping cart that maps to his unique instance of HttpSessionState.

Additional Members of HttpSessionState

The HttpSessionState class defines a number of other members of interest beyond the type indexer. First, the SessionID property will return the current user's unique ID:

```
lblUserID.Text = string.Format("Here is your ID: {0}",
    Session.SessionID);
```

The Remove() and RemoveAll() methods may be used to clear items out of the user's instance of HttpSessionState:

```
Session.Remove["SomeItemWeDontNeedAnymore"];
```

The HttpSessionState type also defines a set of members that control the expiration policy of the current session. Again, by default each user has 20 minutes of inactivity before the HttpSessionState object is destroyed. Thus, if a user enters your web application (and therefore obtains a unique session ID), but does not return to the site within 20 minutes, the runtime assumes the user is no longer interested and destroys all session data for that user. You are free to change this default 20-minute expiration value on a user-by-user basis using the Timeout property. The most common place to do so is within the scope of your Global.Session_Start() method:

```
protected void Session_Start(Object sender, EventArgs e)
{
    // Each user has 5 minutes of inactivity.
    Session.Timeout = 5;
    Session["UserShoppingCartInfo"]
        = new UserShoppingCart();
}
```

■**Note** If you do not need to tweak each user's Timeout value, you are able to alter the 20-minute default for all users via the Timeout attribute of the <sessionState> element within the Web.config file (examined at the end of this chapter).

The benefit of the Timeout property is that you have the ability to assign specific timeout values discretely for each user. For example, imagine you have created a web application that allows users to pay cash for a given membership level. You may say that Gold members should time out within one hour, while Wood members should get only 30 seconds. This possibility begs the question, how can you remember user-specific information (such as the current membership level) across web visits? One possible answer is through the user of the HttpCookie type. (And speaking of cookies . . .)

■**Source Code** The SessionState files are included under the Chapter 24 subdirectory.

Understanding Cookies

The final state management technique examined here is the act of persisting data within *cookie*, which is often realized as a text file (or set of files) on the user's machine. When a user logs on to a given site, the browser checks to see if the user's machine has a cookie file for the URL in question and, if so, appends this data to the HTTP request.

The receiving server-side web page could then read the cookie data to create a GUI that may be based on the current user preferences. I am sure you've noticed that when you visit one of your favorite websites, it somehow just knows the sort of content you wish to see. For example, when I log on to `http://www.ministryofsound.com`, I am automatically shown content that reflects my musical tastes. The reason (in part) has to do with a cookie stored on my computer that contains information regarding the type of music I tend to play.

The exact location of your cookie files will depend on which browser you happen to be using. For those using Microsoft Internet Explorer, cookies are stored by default under C:\Documents and Settings\<loggedOnUser>\Cookies (see Figure 24-6).

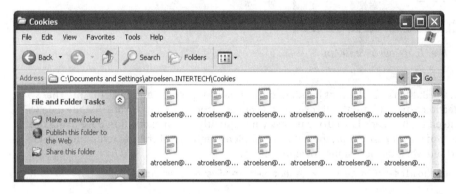

Figure 24-6. *Cookie data as persisted under Microsoft Internet Explorer*

The contents of a given cookie file will obviously vary among URLs, but keep in mind that they are ultimately text files. Thus, cookies are a horrible choice when you wish to maintain sensitive information about the current user (such as a credit card number, password, or whatnot). Even if you take the time to encrypt the data, a crafty hacker could decrypt the value and use it for purely evil pursuits. In any case, cookies do play a role in the development of web applications, so let's check out how ASP.NET handles this particular state management technique.

Creating Cookies

First of all, understand that ASP.NET cookies can be configured to be either persistent or temporary. A *persistent* cookie is typically regarded as the classic definition of cookie data, in that the set of name/value pairs is physically saved to the user's hard drive. *Temporary* cookies (also termed *session cookies*) contain the same data as a persistent cookie, but the name/value pairs are never saved to the user's machine; rather, they exist *only* within the HTTP header. Once the user logs off your site, all data contained within the session cookie is destroyed.

■Note Most browsers support cookies of up to 4,096 bytes. Because of this size limit, cookies are best used to store small amounts of data, such as a user ID that can be used to identify the user and pull details from a database.

The System.Web.HttpCookie type is the class that represents the server side of the cookie data (persistent or temporary). When you wish to create a new cookie, you access the Response.Cookies property. Once the new HttpCookie is inserted into the internal collection, the name/value pairs flow back to the browser within the HTTP header.

To check out cookie behavior firsthand, create a new ASP.NET web application (CookieStateApp) and create the UI displayed in Figure 24-7.

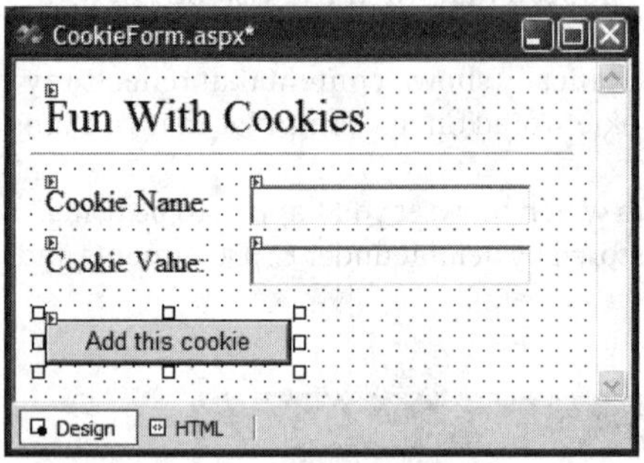

Figure 24-7. *The UI of CookiesStateApp*

Within the Button's Click event handler, build a new HttpCookie and insert it into the Cookie collection exposed from the HttpRequest.Cookies property. Be very aware that the data will *not* persist itself to the user's hard drive unless you explicitly set an expiration date using the HttpCookie.Expires property. Thus, the following implementation will create a temporary cookie that is destroyed when the user shuts down the browser:

```
protected void btnInsertCookie_Click(object sender, System.EventArgs e)
{
    // Make a new (temp) cookie.
    HttpCookie theCookie =
        new HttpCookie(txtCookieName.Text,
        txtCookieValue.Text);
    Response.Cookies.Add(theCookie);
}
```

However, the following generates a persistent cookie that will expire on March 24, 2009:

```
private void btnInsertCookie_Click(object sender, EventArgs e)
{
    // Make a new (persistent) cookie.
    HttpCookie theCookie =
        new HttpCookie(txtCookieName.Text,
        txtCookieValue.Text);
    theCookie.Expires = DateTime.Parse("03/24/2009");
    Response.Cookies.Add(theCookie);
}
```

If you were to run this application and insert some cookie data, the browser automatically persists this data to disk. When you open this text file, you will see something similar to Figure 24-8.

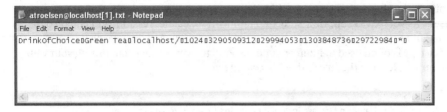

Figure 24-8. *The persistent cookie data*

Reading Incoming Cookie Data

Recall that the browser is the entity in charge of accessing persisted cookies when navigating to a previously visited page. To interact with the incoming cookie data under ASP.NET, access the HttpRequest.Cookies property. To illustrate, if you were to update your current UI with the means to obtain current cookie data via a Button widget, you could iterate over each name/value pair and present the information within a Label widget:

```
protected void btnShowCookies_Click(object sender, EventArgs e)
{
    string cookieData = "";
    foreach(string s in Request.Cookies)
    {
        cookieData +=
            string.Format("<li><b>Name</b>: {0}, <b>Value</b>: {1}</li>",
                s, Request.Cookies[s].Value);
    }
    lblCookieData.Text = cookieData;
}
```

If you now run the application and click your new button, you will find that the cookie data has indeed been sent by your browser (see Figure 24-9).

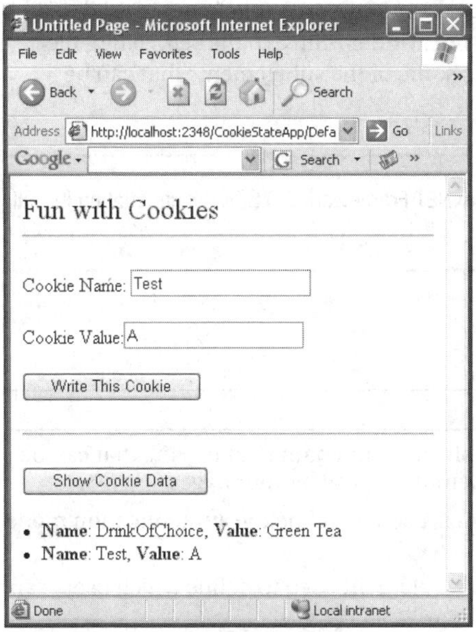

Figure 24-9. *Viewing cookie data*

At this point in the chapter, you have examined numerous ways to remember information about your users. As you have seen, view state and application, cache, session, and cookie data are manipulated in more or less the same way (via a class indexer). As you have also seen, the HttpApplication type is often used to intercept and respond to events that occur during your web application's lifetime. Next up: the role of the Web.config file.

■**Source Code** The CookieStateApp files are included under the Chapter 24 subdirectory.

Configuring Your ASP.NET Web Application Using Web.config

During your examination of .NET assemblies, you learned that client applications can leverage an XML-based configuration file to instruct the CLR how it should handle binding requests, assembly probing, and other runtime details. The same holds true for ASP.NET web applications, with the notable exception that web-centric configuration files (introduced in Chapter 23) are *always* named Web.config (unlike *.exe configuration files, which are named based on the related client executable).

When you insert a Web.config file to your site using the WebSite ➤ Add New Item menu option, the default structure looks something like the following (comments removed for clarity):

```
<?xml version="1.0"?>
<configuration xmlns="http://schemas.microsoft.com/.NetConfiguration/v2.0">
    <appSettings/>
    <connectionStrings/>
    <system.web>
        <compilation debug="false"/>
        <authentication mode="Windows"/>
    </system.web>
</configuration>
```

Like any *.config file, Web.config defines the root-level <configuration> element. Nested within the root is the <system.web> element, which can contain numerous subelements used to control how your web application should behave at runtime. Under ASP.NET, the Web.config file can be modified using any text editor. Table 24-4 outlines some of the subelements that can be found within a Web.config file.

■**Note** Look up the topic "ASP.NET Settings Schema" within the .NET Framework 2.0 SDK documentation for full details on the format of Web.config.

Table 24-4. *Select Elements of a* Web.config *File*

Element	Meaning in Life
<appSettings>	This element is used to establish custom name/value pairs that can be programmatically read in memory for use by your pages.
<authentication>	This security-related element is used to define the authentication mode for this web application.
<authorization>	This is another security-centric element used to define which users can access which resources on the web server.

Element	Meaning in Life
`<compilation>`	This element is used to enable (or disable) debugging and define the default .NET language used by this web application, and it may optionally define the set of external .NET assemblies that should be automatically referenced.
`<connectionStrings>`	This element is used to hold external connection strings used within this website.
`<customErrors>`	This element is used to tell the runtime exactly how to display errors that occur during the functioning of the web application.
`<globalization>`	This element is used to configure the globalization settings for this web application.
`<sessionState>`	This element is used to control how and where session state data will be stored by the .NET runtime.
`<trace>`	This element is used to enable (or disable) tracing support for this web application.

A `Web.config` file may contain additional subelements above and beyond the set presented in Table 24-4. The vast majority of these items are security-related, while the remaining items are useful only during advanced ASP.NET scenarios such as creating custom HTTP headers or custom HTTP modules (not covered here). If you wish to see the complete set of elements that can appear in a `Web.config` file, look up the topic "ASP.NET Settings Schema" using the online help.

Enabling Tracing via <trace>

The first aspect of the `Web.config` file you'll examine is the `<trace>` subelement. This XML entity may take any number of attributes to further qualify its behavior, as shown in the following skeleton:

```
<trace enabled="true|false"
      localOnly="true|false"
      pageOutput="true|false"
      requestLimit="integer"
      traceMode="SortByTime|SortByCategory"/>
```

Table 24-5 hits the highlights of each attribute.

Table 24-5. *Attributes of the* `<trace>` *Element*

Attribute	Meaning in Life
`Enabled`	Specifies whether tracing is enabled for an application as a whole (the default is false). As you saw in the previous chapter, you can selectively enable tracing for a given `*.aspx` file using the `@Page` directive.
`localOnly`	Indicates that the trace information is viewable only on the host web server and not by remote clients (the default is true).
`pageOutput`	Specifies how trace output should be viewed.
`requestLimit`	Specifies the number of trace requests to store on the server. The default is 10. If the limit is reached, trace is automatically disabled.
`traceMode`	Indicates that trace information is displayed in the order it is processed. The default is `SortByTime`, but it can also be configured to sort by category.

Recall from the previous chapter that individual pages may enable tracing using the `<%@Page%>` directive. However, if you wish to enable tracing for all pages in your web application, simply update `<trace>` as follows:

```
<trace
    enabled="true"
    requestLimit="10"
    pageOutput="false"
    traceMode="SortByTime"
    localOnly="true"
/>
```

Customizing Error Output via <customErrors>

The <customErrors> element can be used to automatically redirect all errors to a custom set of *.htm files. This can be helpful if you wish to build a more user-friendly error page than the default supplied by the CLR. In its skeletal form, the <customErrors> element looks like the following:

```
<customErrors defaultRedirect="url" mode="On|Off|RemoteOnly">
    <error statusCode="statuscode" redirect="url"/>
</customErrors>
```

To illustrate the usefulness of the <customErrors> element, assume your ASP.NET web application has two *.htm files. The first file (genericError.htm) functions as a catchall error page. Perhaps this page contains an image of your company logo, a link to e-mail the system administrator, and some sort of apologetic verbiage. The second file (Error404.htm) is a custom error page that should only occur when the runtime detects error number 404 (the dreaded "resource not found" error). Now, if you want to ensure that all errors are handled by these custom pages, you can update your Web.config file as follows:

```
<?xml version="1.0"?>
<configuration xmlns="http://schemas.microsoft.com/.NetConfiguration/v2.0">
    <appSettings/>
    <connectionStrings/>
    <system.web>
        <compilation debug="false"/>
        <authentication mode="Windows"/>
        <customErrors defaultRedirect = "genericError.htm" mode="On">
            <error statusCode="404" redirect="Error404.htm"/>
        </customErrors>
    </system.web>
</configuration>
```

Note how the root <customErrors> element is used to specify the name of the generic page for all unhandled errors. One attribute that may appear in the opening tag is mode. The default setting is RemoteOnly, which instructs the runtime *not* to display custom error pages if the HTTP request came from the same machine as the web server (this is quite helpful for developers, who would like to see the details). When you set the mode attribute to "on," this will cause custom errors to be seen from all machines (including your development box). Also note that the <customErrors> element may support any number of nested <error> elements to specify which page will be used to handle specific error codes.

To test these custom error redirects, build an *.aspx page that defines two Button widgets, and handle their Click events as follows:

```
private void btnGeneralError_Click(object sender, EventArgs e)
{
    // This will trigger a general error.
    throw new Exception("General error...");
}
private void btn404Error_Click(object sender, EventArgs e)
{
```

```
// This will trigger 404 (assuming there is no file named MyPage.aspx!)
Response.Redirect("MyPage.aspx");
}
```

Options for Storing State via <sessionState>

Far and away the most powerful aspect of a Web.config file is the <sessionState> element. By default, ASP.NET will store session state using an in-process *.dll hosted by the ASP.NET worker process (aspnet_wp.exe). Like any *.dll, the plus side is that access to the information is as fast as possible. However, the downside is that if this AppDomain crashes (for whatever reason), all of the user's state data is destroyed. Furthermore, when you store state data as an in-process *.dll, you cannot interact with a networked web farm. By default, the <sessionState> element of your Web.config file looks like this:

```
<sessionState
        mode="InProc"
        stateConnectionString="tcpip=127.0.0.1:42424"
        sqlConnectionString="data source=127.0.0.1;Trusted_Connection=yes"
        cookieless="false"
        timeout="20"
/>
```

This default mode of storage works just fine if your web application is hosted by a single web server. However, under ASP.NET, you can instruct the runtime to host the session state *.dll in a surrogate process named the ASP.NET session state server (aspnet_state.exe). When you do so, you are able to offload the *.dll from aspnet_wp.exe into a unique *.exe. The first step in doing so is to start the aspnet_state.exe Windows service. To do so at the command line, simply type

```
net start aspnet_state
```

Alternatively, you can start aspnet_state.exe using the Services applet accessed from the Administrative Tools folder of the Control Panel (see Figure 24-10).

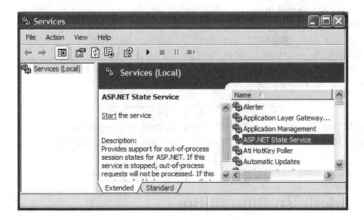

Figure 24-10. *The Services applet*

The key benefit of this approach is that you can configure aspnet_state.exe to start automatically when the machine boots up using the Properties window. In any case, once the session state server is running, alter the <sessionState> element of your Web.config file as follows:

```
<sessionState
        mode="StateServer"
        stateConnectionString="tcpip=127.0.0.1:42424"
        sqlConnectionString="data source=127.0.0.1;Trusted_Connection=yes"
        cookieless="false"
        timeout="20"
/>
```

Here, the mode attribute has been set to StateServer. That's it! At this point, the CLR will host session-centric data within aspnet_state.exe. In this way, if the AppDomain hosting the web application crashes, the session data is preserved. Also notice that the <sessionState> element can also support a stateConnectionString attribute. The default TCP/IP address value (127.0.0.1) points to the local machine. If you would rather have the .NET runtime use the aspnet_state.exe service located on another networked machine (again, think web farms), you are free to update this value.

Finally, if you require the highest degree of isolation and durability for your web application, you may choose to have the runtime store all your session state data within Microsoft SQL Server. The appropriate update to the Web.config file is simple:

```
<sessionState
        mode="SQLServer"
        stateConnectionString="tcpip=127.0.0.1:42424"
        sqlConnectionString="data source=127.0.0.1;Trusted_Connection=yes"
        cookieless="false"
        timeout="20"
/>
```

However, before you attempt to run the associated web application, you need to ensure that the target machine (specified by the sqlConnectionString attribute) has been properly configured. When you install the .NET Framework 2.0 SDK (or Visual Studio 2005), you will be provided with two files named InstallSqlState.sql and UninstallSqlState.sql, located by default under <%windir%>\Microsoft.NET\Framework\<version>. On the target machine, you must run the InstallSqlState.sql file using a tool such as the SQL Server Query Analyzer (which ships with Microsoft SQL Server).

Once this SQL script has executed, you will find a new SQL Server database has been created (ASPState) and that contains a number of stored procedures called by the ASP.NET runtime and a set of tables used to store the session data itself (also, the tempdb database has been updated with a set of tables for swapping purposes). As you would guess, configuring your web application to store session data within SQL Server is the slowest of all possible options. The benefit is that user data is as durable as possible (even if the web server is rebooted).

■**Note** If you make use of the ASP.NET session state server or SQL Server to store your session data, you must make sure that any custom types placed in the HttpSessionState object have been marked with the [Serializable] attribute.

The ASP.NET 2.0 Site Administration Utility

To finish up this section of the chapter, I'd like to mention the fact that ASP.NET 2.0 now provides a web-based configuration utility that will manage many settings within your site's Web.config file. To activate this utility (see Figure 24-11), select the WebSite ➤ ASP.NET Configuration menu option of Visual Studio 2005.

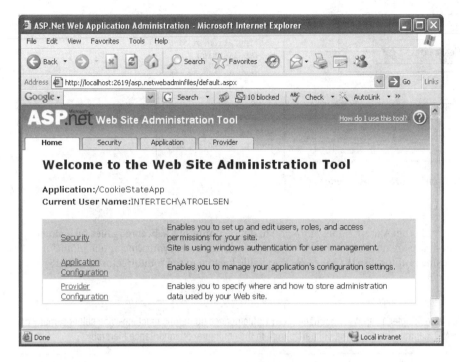

Figure 24-11. *The ASP.NET 2.0 site administration utility*

Most of this tool's functionality is used to establish security-centric details of your site (authentication mode, user roles, security providers, etc.). In addition, however, this tool allows you to establish application settings, debugging details, and error pages.

Configuration Inheritance

Last but not least is *configuration inheritance*. As you learned in the previous chapter, a web application can be defined as the set of all files contained within a root directory *and any optional subdirectories*. All the example applications in this and the previous chapter have existed on a single root directory managed by IIS (with the optional Bin folder). However, large-scale web applications tend to define numerous subdirectories off the root, each of which contains some set of related files. Like a traditional desktop application, this is typically done for the benefit of us mere humans, as a hierarchal structure can make a massive set of files more understandable.

When you have an ASP.NET web application that consists of optional subdirectories off the root, you may be surprised to discover that *each* subdirectory may have its own Web.config file! By doing so, you allow each subdirectory to override the settings of a parent directory. If the subdirectory in question does not supply a custom Web.config file, it will inherit the settings of the next available Web.config file up the directory structure. Thus, as bizarre as it sounds, it is possible to inject an OO look and feel to a raw directory structure. Figure 24-12 illustrates the concept.

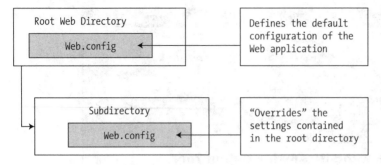

Figure 24-12. *Configuration inheritance*

Of course, although ASP.NET does allow you to define numerous Web.config files for a single web application, you are not required to do so. In a great many cases, your web applications function just fine using nothing else than the Web.config file located in the root directory of the IIS virtual directory.

■**Note** Recall from Chapter 11 that the machine.config file defines numerous machine-wide settings, many of which are ASP.NET-centric. This file is the ultimate parent in the configuration inheritance hierarchy.

That wraps up our examination of ASP.NET. As mentioned in Chapter 23, complete and total coverage of ASP.NET 2.0 would require an entire book on its own. In any case, I do hope you feel comfortable with the basics of the programming model.

■**Note** If you require an advanced treatment of ASP.NET 2.0, check out *Expert ASP.NET 2.0 Advanced Application Development* by Dominic Selly et al. (Apress, 2005).

To wrap up our voyage, the final chapter examines the topic of building XML web services under .NET 2.0.

Summary

In this chapter, you rounded out your knowledge of ASP.NET by examining how to leverage the HttpApplication type. As you have seen, this type provides a number of default event handlers that allow you to intercept various application- and session-level events.

The bulk of this chapter was spent examining a number of state management techniques. Recall that view state is used to automatically repopulate the values of HTML widgets between postbacks to a specific page. Next, you checked out the distinction of application- and session-level data, cookie management, and the ASP.NET application cache. Finally, you examined a number of elements that may be contained in the Web.config file.

■ ■ ■

## CHAPTER 25

Understanding XML Web Services

Chapter 18 introduced you to the .NET remoting layer. As you have seen, this technology allows any number of .NET-savvy computers to exchange information across machine boundaries. While this is all well and good, one possible limitation of the .NET remoting layer is the fact that each machine involved in the exchange must have the .NET Framework installed, must understand the CTS, and must speak the same wire format (such as TCP).

XML web services offer a more flexible alternative to distributed application development. Simply put, an *XML web service* is a unit of code hosted by a web server that can be accessed using industry standards such as HTTP and XML. As you would guess, using neutral technologies, XML web services offer an unprecedented level of operating system, platform, and language interoperability.

In this final chapter, you will learn how to build XML web services using the .NET platform. Along the way, you will examine a number of related topics, such as discovery services (UDDI and DISCO), the Web Service Description Language (WSDL), and the Simple Object Access Protocol (SOAP). Once you understand how to build an XML web service, you will examine various approaches to generate client-side proxies that are capable of invoking "web methods" in a synchronous and asynchronous fashion.

The Role of XML Web Services

From the highest level, you can define an XML web service as a unit of code that can be invoked via HTTP requests. Unlike a traditional web application, however, XML web services are not (necessarily) used to emit HTML back to a browser for display purposes. Rather, an XML web service often exposes the same sort of functionality found in a standard .NET code library (e.g., crunch some numbers, fetch a DataSet, return stock quotes, etc.).

Benefits of XML Web Services

At first glance, an XML web services may seem to be little more than just another remoting technology. While this is true, there is more to the story. Historically speaking, accessing remote objects required platform-specific (and often language-specific) protocols (DCOM, Java RMI, etc.). The problem with this approach is not the underlying technology, but the fact that each is locked into a specific (often proprietary) wire format. Thus, if you are attempting to build a distributed system that involves numerous operating systems, each machine must agree upon the packet format, transmission protocol, and so forth. To simplify matters, XML web services allow you to invoke methods and properties of a remote object using standard HTTP requests. To be sure, of all the protocols in existence today, HTTP is the one specific wire protocol that all platforms can agree on (after all, HTTP is the backbone of the World Wide Web).

Another fundamental problem with proprietary remoting architectures is that they require the sender and receiver to understand the same underlying type system. However, as I am sure you can agree, a Java `arrayList` has little to do with a .NET `ArrayList`, which has nothing to do with a C++ array. XML web services provide a way for unrelated platforms, operating systems, and programming languages to exchange information in harmony. Rather than forcing the caller to understand a specific type system, information is passed between systems via XML data representation (which is little more than a well-formatted string). The short answer is, if your operating system can go online and parse character data, it can interact with an XML web service.

■**Note** A production-level Microsoft .NET XML web service is hosted under IIS using a unique virtual directory. As explained in Chapter 23, however, as of .NET 2.0 it is now possible to load web content from a local directory (for development and testing purposes) using `WebDev.WebServer.exe`.

Defining an XML Web Service Client

One aspect of XML web services that might not be readily understood from the onset is the fact that an XML web service consumer is not limited to a web page. Console-based and Windows Forms–based clients can use a web service just as easily. In each case, the XML web service consumer indirectly interacts with the distant XML web service through an intervening proxy type.

An XML web service proxy looks and feels like the actual remote object and exposes the same set of members. Under the hood, however, the proxy's implementation code forwards requests to the XML web service using standard HTTP. The proxy also maps the incoming stream of XML back into .NET-specific data types (or whatever type system is required by the consumer application). Figure 25-1 illustrates the fundamental nature of XML web services.

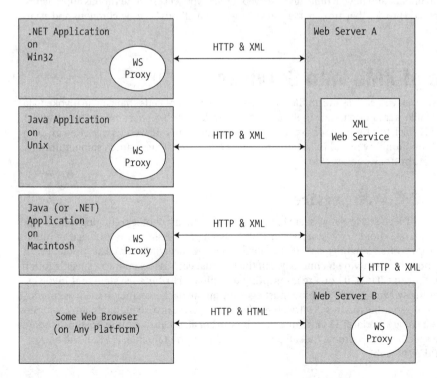

Figure 25-1. *XML web services in action*

The Building Blocks of an XML Web Service

In addition to the managed code library that constitutes the exposed functionality, an XML web service requires some supporting infrastructure. Specifically, an XML web service involves the following core technologies:

- A discovery service (so clients can resolve the location of the XML web service)
- A description service (so clients know what the XML web service can do)
- A transport protocol (to pass the information between the client and the XML web service)

We'll examine details behind each piece of infrastructure throughout this chapter. However, to get into the proper frame of mind, here is a brief overview of each supporting technology.

Previewing XML Web Service Discovery

Before a client can invoke the functionality of a web service, it must first know of its existence and location. Now, if you are the individual (or company) who is building the client and XML web service, the discovery phase is quite simple given that you already know the location of the web service in question. However, what if you wish to share the functionality of your web service with the world at large?

To do this, you have the option of registering your XML web service with a Universal Description, Discovery, and Integration (UDDI) server. Clients may submit request to a UDDI catalog to find a list of all web services that match some search criteria (e.g., "Find me all web services having to do real time weather updates"). Once you have identified a specific web server from the list returned via the UDDI query, you are then able to investigate its overall functionality. If you like, consider UDDI to be the white pages for XML web services.

In addition to UDDI discovery, an XML web service built using .NET can be located using DISCO, which is a somewhat forced acronym standing for *Discovery of Web Services*. Using static discovery (via a *.disco file) or dynamic discovery (via a *.vsdisco file), you are able to advertise the set of XML web services that are located at a specific URL. Potential web service clients can navigate to a web server's *.disco file to see links to all the published XML web services.

Understand, however, that dynamic discovery is disabled by default, given the potential security risk of allowing IIS to expose the set of all XML web services to any interested individual. Given this, I will not comment on DISCO services for the remainder of this text.

■**Note** If you wish to activate dynamic discovery support for a given web server, look up the Microsoft Knowledge Base article Q307303 on http://support.microsoft.com.

Previewing XML Web Service Description

Once a client knows the location of a given XML web service, the client in question must fully understand the exposed functionality. For example, the client must know that there is a method named GetWeatherReport() that takes some set of parameters and sends back a given return value before the client can invoke the method. As you may be thinking, this is a job for a platform-, language-, and operating system–neutral metalanguage. Specifically speaking, the XML-based metadata used to describe a XML web service is termed the *Web Service Description Language* (*WSDL*).

In a good number of cases, the WSDL description of an XML web service will be automatically generated by Microsoft IIS when the incoming request has a ?wsdl suffix. As you will see, the primary consumers of WSDL contracts are proxy generation tools. For example, the wsdl.exe command-line utility (explained in detail later in this chapter) will generate a client-side C# proxy class from a WSDL document.

For more complex cases (typically for the purposes of interoperability), many developers take a "WSDL first" approach and begin building their web services by defining the WSDL document manually. As luck would have it, the wsdl.exe command-line tool is also able to generate interface descriptions for an XML web service based on a WSDL definition.

Previewing the Transport Protocol

Once the client has created a proxy type to communicate with the XML web service, it is able to invoke the exposed web methods. As mentioned, HTTP is the wire protocol that transmits this data. Specifically, however, you can use HTTP GET, HTTP POST, or SOAP to move information between consumers and web services.

By and large, SOAP will be your first choice, for as you will see, SOAP messages can contain XML descriptions of complex types (including your custom types as well as types within the .NET base class libraries). On the other hand, if you make use of the HTTP GET or HTTP POST protocols, you are restricted to a more limited set of core data XML schema types.

The .NET XML Web Service Namespaces

Now that you have a basic understanding of XML web services, we can get down to the business of building such a creature using the .NET platform. As you would imagine, the base class libraries define a number of namespaces that allow you to interact with each web service technology (see Table 25-1).

Table 25-1. *XML Web Service–centric Namespaces*

Namespace	Meaning in Life
System.Web.Services	This namespace contains the core types needed to build an XML web service (including the all-important [WebMethod] attribute).
System.Web.Services.Configuration	These types allow you configure the runtime behavior of an ASP.NET XML web service.
System.Web.Services.Description	These types allow you to programmatically interact with the WSDL document that describes a given web service.
System.Web.Services.Discovery	These types allow a web consumer to programmatically discover the web services installed on a given machine.
System.Web.Services.Protocols	This namespace defines a number of types that represent the atoms of the various XML web service wire protocols (HTTP GET, HTTP POST, and SOAP).

■**Note** All XML web service–centric namespaces are contained within the System.Web.Services.dll assembly.

Examining the System.Web.Services Namespace

Despite the rich functionality provided by the .NET XML web service namespaces, the vast majority of your applications will only require you to directly interact with the types defined in System.Web.Services. As you can see from Table 25-2, the number of types is quite small (which is a good thing).

Table 25-2. *Members of the* System.Web.Services *Namespace*

Type	Meaning in Life
WebMethodAttribute	Adding the [WebMethod] attribute to a method or property in a web service class type marks the member as invokable via HTTP and serializable as XML.
WebService	This is an optional base class for XML web services built using .NET. If you choose to derive from this base type, your XML web service will have the ability to retain stateful information (e.g., session and application variables).
WebServiceAttribute	The [WebService] attribute may be used to add information to a web service, such as a string describing its functionality and underlying XML namespace.
WebServiceBindingAttribute	This attribute (new .NET 2.0) declares the binding protocol a given web service method is implementing (HTTP GET, HTTP POST, or SOAP) and advertises the level of web services interoperability (WSI) conformity.
WsiProfiles	This enumeration (new to .NET 2.0) is used to describe the web services interoperability (WSI) specification to which a web service claims to conform.

The remaining namespaces shown in Table 25-1 are typically only of direct interest to you if you are interested in manually interacting with a WSDL document, discovery services, or the underlying wire protocols. Consult the .NET Framework 2.0 SDK documentation for further details.

Building an XML Web Service by Hand

Like any .NET application, XML web services can be developed manually, without the use of an IDE such as Visual Studio 2005. In an effort to demystify XML web services, let's build a simple XML web service by hand. Using your text editor of choice, create a new file named HelloWorldWebService.asmx (by convention, *.asmx is the extension used to mark .NET web service files). Save it to a convenient location on your hard drive (e.g., C:\HelloWebService) and enter the following type definition:

```
<%@ WebService Language="C#" Class="HelloWebService.HelloService" %>
using System;
using System.Web.Services;

namespace HelloWebService
{
    public class HelloService
    {
        [WebMethod]
        public string HelloWorld()
        {
            return "Hello!";
        }
    }
}
```

For the most part, this *.asmx file looks like any other C# namespace definition. The first noticeable difference is the use of the <%@WebService%> directive, which at minimum must specify the name of the managed language used to build the contained class definition and the fully qualified name of the class. In addition to the Language and Class attributes, the <%@WebService%> directive may also take a Debug attribute (to inform the ASP.NET compiler to emit debugging symbols) and an optional CodeBehind value that identifies the associated code file within the optional App_Code directory (see Chapter 23). In this example, you have avoided the use of a code-behind file and embedded all required logic directly within a single *.asmx file.

Beyond the use of the <%@WebService%> directive, the only other distinguishing characteristic of this *.asmx file is the use of the [WebMethod] attribute, which informs the ASP.NET runtime that this method is reachable via incoming HTTP requests and should serialize any return value as XML.

■**Note** Only members that are adorned with [WebMethod] are reachable by HTTP. Members not marked with the [WebMethod] attribute cannot be called by the client-side proxy.

Testing Your XML Web Service Using WebDev.WebServer.exe

Recall (again, from Chapter 23) that WebDev.WebServer.exe is a development ASP.NET web server that ships with the .NET platform 2.0 SDK. While WebDev.WebServer.exe would never be used to host a production-level XML web service, this tool does allow you to run web content directly from a local directory. To test your service using this tool, open a Visual Studio 2005 command prompt and specify an unused port number and physical path to the directory containing your *.asmx file:

```
WebDev.WebServer /port:4000 /path:"C:\HelloWebService"
```

Once the web server has started, open your browser of choice and specify the name of your *.asmx file exposed from the specified port:

```
http://localhost:4000/HelloWorldWebService.asmx
```

At this point, you are presented with a list of all web methods exposed from this URL (see Figure 25-2).

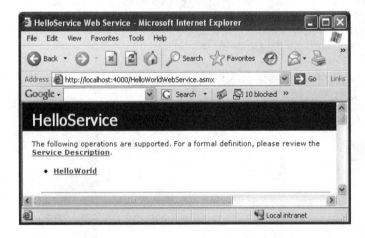

Figure 25-2. *Testing the XML web service*

If you click the HelloWorld link, you will be passed to another page that allows you to invoke the [WebMethod] you just selected. Once you invoke HelloWorld(), you will be returned not a literal .NET-centric System.String, but rather the XML data representation of the textual data returned from the HelloWorld() web method:

```
<?xml version="1.0" encoding="utf-8" ?>
<string xmlns="http://tempuri.org/">Hello!</string>
```

Testing Your Web Service Using IIS

Now that you have tested your XML web service using `WebDev.WebServer.exe`, you'll transfer your `*.asmx` file into an IIS virtual directory. Using the information presented in Chapter 23, create a new virtual directory named HelloWS that maps to the physical folder containing the `HelloWorldWebService.asmx` file. Once you do, you are able to test your web service by entering the following URL in your web browser:

```
http://localhost/HelloWS/HelloWorldWebService.asmx
```

Viewing the WSDL Contract

As mentioned, WSDL is a metalanguage that describes numerous characteristics of the web methods at a particular URL. Notice that when you test an XML web service, the autogenerated test page supplies a link named "Service Description." Clicking this link will append the token `?wsdl` to the current request. When the ASP.NET runtime receives a request for an `*.asmx` file tagged with this suffix, it will automatically return the underlying WSDL that describes each web method.

At this point, don't be alarmed with the verbose nature of WSDL or concern yourself with the format of a WSDL document. For the time being, just understand that WSDL describes how web methods can be invoked using each of the current XML web service wire protocols.

The Autogenerated Test Page

As you have just witnessed, XML web services can be tested within a web browser using an autogenerated HTML page. When an HTTP request comes in that maps to a given `*.asmx` file, the ASP.NET runtime makes use of a file named `DefaultWsdlHelpGenerator.aspx` to create an HTML display that allows you to invoke the web methods at a given URL. You can find this `*.aspx` file under the following directory (substitute `<version>` with your current version of the .NET Framework, of course):

```
C:\Windows\Microsoft.NET\Framework\<version>\CONFIG
```

Providing a Custom Test Page

If you wish to instruct the ASP.NET runtime to make use of a custom `*.aspx` file for the purposes of testing your XML web services, you are free to customize this page with additional information (add your company logo, additional descriptions of the service, links to a help document, etc.). To simplify matters, most developers copy the existing `DefaultWsdlHelpGenerator.aspx` to their current project as a starting point and modify the original HTML and C# code.

As a simple test, copy the `DefaultWsdlHelpGenerator.aspx` file into the directory containing `HelloWorldWebService.asmx` (e.g., C:\HelloWebService). Rename this copy to `MyCustomWsdlHelpGenerator.aspx` and update the some aspect of the HTML, such as the `<title>` tag. For example, change the following existing markup:

```
<title><%#ServiceName + " " + GetLocalizedText("WebService")%></title>
```

to the following:

```
<title>My Rocking <%#ServiceName + " " + GetLocalizedText("WebService")%></title>
```

Once you have modified the HTML content, create a `Web.config` file and save it to your current directory. The following XML elements instruct the runtime to make use of your custom `*.aspx` file, rather than `DefaultWsdlhelpGenerator.aspx`:

```
<!-- Here you are specifying a custom *.aspx file -->
<configuration>
  <system.web>
    <webServices>
      <wsdlHelpGenerator href="MyCustomWsdlHelpGenerator.aspx" />
    </webServices>
  </system.web>
</configuration>
```

When you request your web service, you should see that the browser's title has been updated with your custom content. On a related note, if you wish to disable help page generation for a given web service, you can do so using the following <remove> element within the `Web.config` file:

```
<!-- Disable help page generation -->
<configuration>
  <system.web>
    <webServices>
      <protocols>
        <!-- This element also disables WSDL generation -->
        <remove name="Documentation"/>
      </protocols>
    </webServices>
  </system.web>
</configuration>
```

Source Code The HelloWorldWebService files are included under the Chapter 25 subdirectory.

Building an XML Web Service Using Visual Studio 2005

Now that you have created an XML web service by hand, let's see how Visual Studio 2005 helps get you up and running. Using the File ➤ New ➤ Web Site menu option, create a new C# XML web service project named MagicEightBallWebService and save it to your local file system (see Figure 25-3).

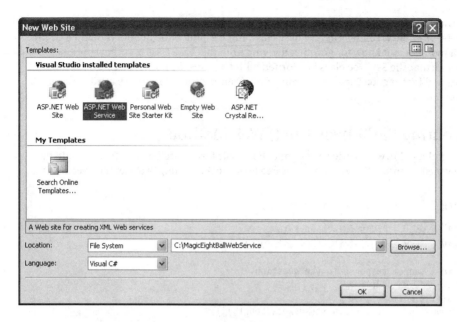

Figure 25-3. *Visual Studio 2005 XML Web Service project*

■**Note** Like an ASP.NET website, XML web service projects created with Visual Studio 2005 place the *.sln file under My Documents\Visual Studio 2005\Projects.

Once you click the OK button, Visual Studio 2005 responds by generating a Service.asmx file that defines the following <%@WebService%> directive:

```
<%@ WebService Language="C#"
CodeBehind="~/App_Code/Service.cs" Class="Service" %>
```

Note that the CodeBehind attribute is used to specify the name of the C# code file (placed by default in your project's App_Code directory) that defines the related class type. By default, Service.cs is defined as so:

```
using System;
using System.Web;
using System.Web.Services;
using System.Web.Services.Protocols;

[WebService(Namespace = "http://tempuri.org/")]
[WebServiceBinding(ConformsTo = WsiProfiles.BasicProfile1_1)]
public class Service : System.Web.Services.WebService
{
    public Service () {
    }

    [WebMethod]
    public string HelloWorld() {
        return "Hello World";
    }
}
```

Unlike the previous HelloWorldWebService example, notice that the Service class now derives from the System.Web.Services.WebService base class. You'll examine the members defined by this type in just a moment, but know for now that deriving from this base class is entirely optional.

Also notice that the Service class is adorned with two (also optional) attributes named [WebService] and [WebServiceBinding]. Again, you'll examine the role of these attributes a bit later in this chapter.

Implementing the TellFortune() Web Method

Your MagicEightBall XML web service will mimic the classic fortune-telling toy. To do so, add the following new method to your Service class (feel free to delete the existing HelloWorld() web method):

```
[WebMethod]
public string TellFortune(string userQuestion)
{
    string[] answers = { "Future Uncertain", "Yes", "No",
        "Hazy", "Ask again later", "Definitely" };

    // Return a random response to the question.
    Random r = new Random();
    return string.Format("{0}? {1}",
        userQuestion, answers[r.Next(answers.Length)]);
}
```

To test your new XML web service, simply run (or debug) the project using Visual Studio 2005. Given that the TellFortune() method requires a single input parameter, the autogenerated HTML test page provides the required input field (see Figure 25-4).

Figure 25-4. *Invoking the* TellFortune() *web method*

Here is a possible response to the question "Will I get the sink fixed this weekend":

```
<?xml version="1.0" encoding="utf-8" ?>
<string xmlns="http://tempuri.org/">
Will I get the sink fixed this weekend? Hazy
</string>
```

So, at this point you have created two simple XML web services: one by hand and the other using Visual Studio 2005. Now that you know the basics, we can dig into the specifics, beginning with the role of the WebService base class.

■**Source Code**   The MagicEightBallWebService files are included under the Chapter 25 subdirectory.

The Role of the WebService Base Class

As you saw during the development of the HelloWorldWebService service, a web service can derive directly from System.Object. However, by default, web services developed using Visual Studio 2005 automatically derive from the System.Web.Service.WebService base class. Table 25-3 documents the core members of this class type.

Table 25-3. *Key Members of the* System.Web.Services.WebService *Type*

Property	Meaning in Life
Application	Provides access to the HttpApplicationState object for the current HTTP request
Context	Provides access to the HttpContext type that encapsulates all HTTP-specific context used by the HTTP server to process web requests
Server	Provides access to the HttpServerUtility object for the current request
Session	Provides access to the HttpSessionState type for the current request
SoapVersion	Retrieves the version of the SOAP protocol used to make the SOAP request to the XML web service; new to .NET 2.0

As you may be able to gather, if you wish to build a *stateful* web service using application and session variables (see Chapter 24), you are required to derive from WebService, given that this type defines the Application and Session properties. On the other hand, if you are building an XML web service that does not require the ability to "remember" information about the external users, extending WebService is not required. We will revisit the process of building stateful XML web services during our examination of the EnableSession property of the [WebMethod] attribute.

Understanding the [WebService] Attribute

An XML web service class may optionally be qualified using the [WebService] attribute (not to be confused with the WebService base class). This attribute supports a few named properties, the first of which is Namespace. This property can be used to establish the name of the XML namespace to use within the WSDL document.

As you may already know, XML namespaces are used to scope custom XML elements within a specific group (just like .NET namespaces). By default, the ASP.NET runtime will assign a dummy XML namespace of http://tempuri.org for a given *.asmx file. As well, Visual Studio 2005 assigns the Namespace value to http://tempuri.org by default.

Assume you have created a new XML web service project with Visual Studio 2005 named CalculatorService that defines the following two web methods, named Add() and Subtract():

```
[WebService(Namespace = "http://tempuri.org/")]
[WebServiceBinding(ConformsTo = WsiProfiles.BasicProfile1_1)]
public class Service : System.Web.Services.WebService
{
    [WebMethod]
    public int Subtract(int x, int y) { return x - y; }

    [WebMethod]
    public int Add(int x, int y) { return x + y; }
}
```

Before you publish your XML web service to the world at large, you should supply a proper namespace that reflects the point of origin, which is typically the URL of the site hosting the XML web service. In the following code update, note that the [WebService] attribute also allows you to set a named property termed Description that describes the overall nature of your web service:

```
[WebService(Description = "The Amazing Calculator Web Service",
    Namespace ="http://www.IntertechTraining.com/")]
[WebServiceBinding(ConformsTo = WsiProfiles.BasicProfile1_1)]
public class Service : System.Web.Services.WebService
{ ... }
```

The Effect of the Namespace and Description Properties

If you run the project, you will find that the warning to replace http://tempuri.org is no longer displayed in the autogenerated test page. Furthermore, if you click the Service Description link to view the underlying WSDL, you will find that the TargetNamespace attribute has now been updated with your custom XML namespace. Finally, the WSDL file now contains a <documentation> element that is based on your Description value:

```
<wsdl:documentation xmlns:wsdl="http://schemas.xmlsoap.org/wsdl/">
    The Amazing Calculator Web Service
</wsdl:documentation>
```

As you might guess, it would be completely possible to build a custom utility that reads the value contained within the <documentation> element (e.g., an XML web service–centric object browser). In most cases, however, this value will be used by DefaultWsdlHelpGenerator.aspx.

The Name Property

The final property of the WebServiceAttribute type is Name, which is used to establish the name of the XML web service exposed to the outside world. By default, the external name of a web service is identical to the name of the class type itself (Service by default). However, if you wish to decouple the .NET class name from the underlying WSDL name, you can update the [WebService] attribute as follows:

```
[WebService(Description = "The Amazing Calculator Web Service",
    Namespace ="http://www.IntertechTraining.com/",
    Name = "CalculatorWebService")]
[WebServiceBinding(ConformsTo = WsiProfiles.BasicProfile1_1)]
public class Service : System.Web.Services.WebService
{ ... }
```

Figure 25-5 shows the test page generated by DefaultWsdlHelpGenerator.aspx based on the [WebService] attribute.

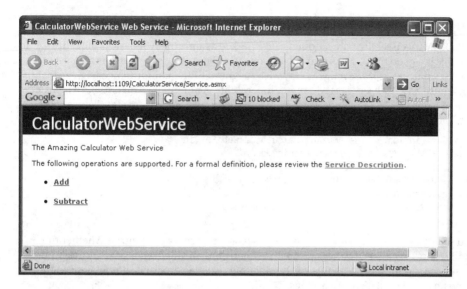

Figure 25-5. *The CalculatorWebService*

Understanding the [WebServiceBinding] Attribute

As of .NET 2.0, an XML web service can be attributed with [WebServiceBinding]. Among other things, this new attribute is used to specify if the XML web service conforms to "Web services interoperability (WSI) basic profile 1.1". So, what exactly does that mean? Well, if you have been actively working with XML web services, you may know firsthand that one of the frustrating aspects of this technology is that early on, WSDL was an evolving specification. Given this fact, it was not uncommon for the same WSDL element (or attribute) to be interpreted in different manners across development tools (IIS, WSAD), web servers (IIS, Apache), and architectures (.NET, J2EE).

Clearly this is problematic for an XML web service, as one of the motivating factors is to simplify the way in which information can be processed in a multiplatform, multi-architecture, and multi-language universe. To rectify the problem, the WSI initiative offers a nonproprietary web services specification to promote the interoperability of web services across platforms. Under .NET 2.0, the ConformsTo property of [WebServiceBinding] can be set to any value of the WsiProfiles enumeration:

```
public enum WsiProfiles
{
    // The web service makes no conformance claims.
    None,
    // The web service claims to conform to the
    // WSI Basic Profile version 1.1.
    BasicProfile1_1
}
```

By default, XML web services generated using Visual Studio 2005 are assumed to conform to the WSI basic profile 1.1. Of course, simply setting the ConformsTo named property to WsiProfiles. BasicProfile1_1 does not guarantee each web method is truly compliant. For example, one rule of BP 1.1 states that every method in a WSDL document must have a unique name (overloading of exposed web methods is not permitted under BP 1.1). The good news is that the ASP.NET runtime is able to determine various BP 1.1 validations and will report the issue at runtime.

Ignoring BP 1.1 Conformance Verification

As of .NET 2.0, XML web services are automatically checked against the WSI basic profile (BP) 1.1. In most cases, this is a good thing, given that you are able to build software that has the greatest reach as possible. In some cases, however, you may wish to ignore BP 1.1 conformance (e.g., if you are building in-house XML web services where interoperability is not much of an issue). To instruct the runtime to ignore BP 1.1 violations, set the ConformsTo property to WsiProfiles.None and the EmitConformanceClaims property to false:

```
[WebService(Description = "The Amazing Calculator Web Service",
    Namespace ="http://www.IntertechTraining.com/",
    Name = "CalculatorWebService")]
[WebServiceBinding(ConformsTo = WsiProfiles.None ,
    EmitConformanceClaims = false)]
public class Service : System.Web.Services.WebService
{...}
```

As you might suspect, the value assigned to EmitConformanceClaims controls whether the conformance claims expressed by the ConformsTo property are provided when a WSDL description of the web service is published. With this, BP 1.1 violations will be permitted, although the auto-generated test page will still display warnings.

Disabling BP 1.1 Conformance Verification

If you wish to completely disable BP 1.1 verification for your XML web service, you may do so by defining the following <conformanceWarnings> element within a proper Web.config file:

```
<configuration>
  <system.web>
    <webServices>
      <conformanceWarnings>
        <remove name='BasicProfile1_1'/>
      </conformanceWarnings>
    </webServices>
  </system.web>
</configuration>
```

■**Note** The [WebServiceBinding] attribute can also be used to define the intended binding for specific methods via the Name property. Consult the .NET Framework 2.0 SDK documentation for further details.

Understanding the [WebMethod] Attribute

The [WebMethod] attribute must be applied to each method you wish to expose from an XML web service. Like most attributes, the WebMethodAttribute type may take a number of optional named properties. Let's walk through each possibility in turn.

Documenting a Web Method via the Description Property

Like the [WebService] attribute, the Description property of the [WebMethod] attribute allows you to describe the functionality of a particular web method:

```
public class Service : System.Web.Services.WebService
{
    [WebMethod(Description = "Subtracts two integers.")]
    public int Subtract(int x, int y) { return x - y; }

    [WebMethod(Description = "Adds two integers.")]
    public int Add(int x, int y) { return x + y; }
}
```

Under the hood, when you specify the Description property within a [WebMethod] attribute, the WSDL contract is updated with a new <documentation> element scoped at the method name level:

```
<wsdl:operation name="Add">
  <wsdl:documentation xmlns:wsdl="http://schemas.xmlsoap.org/wsdl/">
    Adds two integers.
  </wsdl:documentation>
  <wsdl:input message="tns:AddSoapIn" />
  <wsdl:output message="tns:AddSoapOut" />
</wsdl:operation>
```

Avoiding WSDL Name Clashes via the MessageName Property

One of the rules of WSI BP 1.1 is that each method within a WSDL document must be unique. Therefore, if you wish your XML web services to conform to BP 1.1, you should not overload methods in your implementation logic. For the sake of argument, however, assume that you have overloaded the Add() method so that the caller can pass two integer or float data types. You would find the following runtime error:

```
Both Single Add(Single, Single) and Int32 Add(Int32, Int32)
use the message name 'Add'. Use the MessageName property
attribute to specify unique of the WebMethod
custom message names for the methods.
```

Again, the best approach is to simply not overload the Add() method in the first place. If you must do so, the MessageName property of the [WebMethod] attribute can be used to resolve name clashes in your WSDL documents:

```
public class Service : System.Web.Services.WebService
{
...
    [WebMethod(Description = "Adds two float.",
        MessageName = "AddFloats")]
    public float Add(float x, float y) { return x + y; }

    [WebMethod(Description = "Adds two integers.",
        MessageName = "AddInts")]
    public int Add(int x, int y) { return x + y; }
}
```

Once you have done so, the generated WSDL document will internally refer to each overloaded version of Add() uniquely (AddFloats and AddInts). As far as the client-side proxy is concerned, however, there is only a single overloaded Add() method.

Building Stateful Web Services via the EnableSession Property

As you may recall from Chapter 24, the Application and Session properties allow an ASP.NET web application to maintain stateful data. XML web services gain the exact same functionality via the

`System.Web.Services.WebService` base class. For example, assume your CalculatorService maintains an application-level variable (and is thus available to each session) that holds the value of PI, as shown here:

```
public class CalcWebService: System.Web.Services.WebService
{
    // This web method provides access to an app-level variable
    // named SimplePI.
    [WebMethod(Description = "Get the simple value of PI.")]
    public float GetSimplePI()
    { return (float)Application["SimplePI"]; }
    ...
}
```

The initial value of the `SimplePI` application variable could be established with the `Application_Start()` event handler defined in the `Global.asax` file. Insert a new global application class to your project (by right-clicking your project icon within Solution Explorer and selecting Add New Item) and implement `Application_Start()` as so:

```
<%@ Application Language="C#" %>
<script runat="server">
    void Application_Start(Object sender, EventArgs e)
    {
        Application["SimplePI"] = 3.14F;
    }
...
</script>
```

In addition to maintaining applicationwide variables, you may also make use of `Session` to maintain session-centric information. For the sake of illustration, implement the `Session_Start()` method in your `Global.asax` to assign a random number to each user who is logged on:

```
<%@ Application Language="C#" %>
<script runat="server">
...
    void Session_Start(Object sender, EventArgs e)
    {
        // To prove session state data is available from a web service,
        // simply assign a random number to each user.
        Random r = new Random();
        Session["SessionRandomNumber"] = r.Next(1000);
    }
...
</script>
```

For testing purposes, create a new web method in your `Service` class that returns the user's randomly assigned value:

```
public class Service : System.Web.Services.WebService
{
...
    [WebMethod(EnableSession = true,
      Description = "Get your random number!")]
    public int GetMyRandomNumber()
    { return (int)Session["SessionRandomNumber"]; }
}
```

Note that the `[WebMethod]` attribute has explicitly set the `EnableSession` property to true. This step is not optional, given that by default each web method has session state *disabled*. If you were now to launch two or three browsers (to generate a set of session IDs), you would find that each logged-on user is returned a unique numerical token. For example, the first caller may receive the following XML:

```
<?xml version="1.0" encoding="utf-8" ?>
<int xmlns="http://www.IntertechTraining.com/WebServers">931</int>
```

while the second caller may find her value is 472:

```
<?xml version="1.0" encoding="utf-8" ?>
<int xmlns="http://www.IntertechTraining.com/WebServers">472</int>
```

Configuring Session State via Web.config

Finally, recall that a Web.config file may be updated to specify where state should be stored for the XML web service using the <sessionState> element (described in the previous chapter).

```
<sessionState
    mode="InProc"
    stateConnectionString="tcpip=127.0.0.1:42424"
    sqlConnectionString="data source=127.0.0.1;Trusted_Connection=yes"
    cookieless="false"
    timeout="20"
/>
```

■**Source Code** The CalculatorService files are included under the Chapter 25 subdirectory.

Exploring the Web Service Description Language (WSDL)

Over the last several examples, you have been exposed to partial WSDL snippets. Recall that WSDL is an XML-based grammar that describes how external clients can interact with the web methods at a given URL, using each of the supported wire protocols. In many ways, a WSDL document can be viewed as a contract between the web service client and the web service itself. To this end, it is yet another metalanguage. Specifically, WSDL is used to describe the following characteristics for each exposed web method:

- The name of the XML web methods
- The number of, type of, and ordering of parameters (if any)
- The type of return value (if any)
- The HTTP GET, HTTP POST, and SOAP calling conventions

In most cases, WSDL documents are generated automatically by the hosting web server. Recall that when you append the ?wsdl suffix to a URL that points to an *.asmx file, the hosting web server will emit the WSDL document for the specified XML web service:

```
http://localhost/SomeWS/theWS.asmx?wsdl
```

Given that IIS will automatically generate WSDL for a given XML web service, you may wonder if you are required to deeply understand the syntax of the generated WSDL data. The answer typically depends on how your service is to be consumed by external applications. For in-house XML web services, the WSDL generated by your XML web server will be sufficient most of the time.

However, it is also possible to begin an XML web service project by authoring the WSDL document by hand (as mentioned earlier, this is termed the *WSDL first* approach). The biggest selling point for WSDL first has to do with interoperability concerns. Recall that prior to the WSI specification, it was not uncommon for various web service tools to generate incompatible WSDL descriptions. If you take a WSDL first approach, you can craft the document as required.

As you might imagine, taking a WSDL first approach would require you to have a very intimate view of the WSDL grammar, which is beyond the scope of this chapter. Nevertheless, let's get to know the basic structure of a valid WSDL document. Once you understand the basics, you'll better understand the usefulness of the wsdl.exe command-line utility.

Note To see the most recent information on WSDL, visit http://www.w3.org/tr/wsdl.

Defining a WSDL Document

A valid WSDL document is opened and closed using the root <definitions> element. The opening tag typically defines various xmlns attributes. These qualify the XML namespaces that define various subelements. At a minimum, the <definitions> element will specify the namespace where the WSDL elements themselves are defined (http://schemas.xmlsoap.org/wsdl). To be useful, the opening <definitions> tag will also specify numerous XML namespaces that define simple data WSDL types, XML schema types, SOAP elements, and the target namespace. For example, here is the <definitions> section for CalculatorService:

```
<?xml version="1.0" encoding="utf-8"?>
<wsdl:definitions xmlns:soap="http://schemas.xmlsoap.org/wsdl/soap/"
xmlns:tm="http://microsoft.com/wsdl/mime/textMatching/"
xmlns:soapenc="http://schemas.xmlsoap.org/soap/encoding/"
xmlns:mime="http://schemas.xmlsoap.org/wsdl/mime/"
xmlns:tns="http://www.IntertechTraining.com/"
xmlns:s="http://www.w3.org/2001/XMLSchema"
xmlns:soap12="http://schemas.xmlsoap.org/wsdl/soap12/"
xmlns:http="http://schemas.xmlsoap.org/wsdl/http/"
targetNamespace="http://www.IntertechTraining.com/"
xmlns:wsdl="http://schemas.xmlsoap.org/wsdl/">
...
</wsdl:definitions>
```

Within the scope of the root element, you will find five possible subelements. Thus, a bare-bones WSDL document would look something like the following:

```
<?xml version="1.0" encoding="utf-8"?>
<wsdl:definitions ...>
    <wsdl:types>
        <!-- List of types exposed from WS ->
    <wsdl:/types>
    <wsdl:message>
        <!-- Format of the messages ->
    <wsdl:/message>
    <wsdl:portType>
        <!-- Port information ->
    <wsdl:/portType>
    <wsdl:binding>
        <!-- Binding information ->
    <wsdl:/binding>
    <wsdl:service>
        <!-- Information about the XML web service itself ->
```

```
        <wsdl:/service>
< wsdl:/definitions>
```

As you would guess, each of these subelements will contain additional elements and attributes to further describe the intended functionality. Let's check out the key nodes in turn.

The <types> Element

First, we have the <types> element, which contains descriptions of any and all data types exposed from the web service. As you may know, XML itself defines a number of "core" data types, all of which are defined within the XML namespace: http://www.w3.org/2001/XMLSchema (which appears in your <definitions> root element). For example, recall the Subtract() method of CalculatorService took two integer parameters. In terms of WSDL, the CLR System.Int32 is described within a <complexType> element:

```
<s:element name="Subtract">
  <s:complexType>
    <s:sequence>
      <s:element minOccurs="1" maxOccurs="1" name="x" type="s:int" />
      <s:element minOccurs="1" maxOccurs="1" name="y" type="s:int" />
    </s:sequence>
  </s:complexType>
</s:element>
```

The integer that is returned from the Subtract() method is also described within the <types> element:

```
<s:element name="SubtractResponse">
  <s:complexType>
    <s:sequence>
      <s:element minOccurs="1" maxOccurs="1" name="SubtractResult" type="s:int" />
    </s:sequence>
  </s:complexType>
</s:element>
```

If you have a web method that returns or receives custom data types, they will also appear within a <complexType> element. You will see the details of how to expose custom .NET data types via a given web method a bit later in this chapter. For the sake of illustration, assume you have defined a web method that returns a structure named Point:

```
public struct Point
{
    public int x;
    public int y;
    public string pointName;
}
```

The WSDL description of this "complex type" would look like the following:

```
<s:complexType name="Point">
  <s:sequence>
    <s:element minOccurs="1" maxOccurs="1" name="x" type="s:int" />
    <s:element minOccurs="1" maxOccurs="1" name="y" type="s:int" />
    <s:element minOccurs="0" maxOccurs="1" name="pointName" type="s:string" />
  </s:sequence>
</s:complexType>
```

The <message> Element

The <message> element is used to define the format of the request and response exchange for a given web method. Given that a single web service allows multiple messages to be transmitted between the sender and receiver, it is permissible for a single WSDL document to define multiple <message> elements. Typically, these message definitions use the types defined in the <types> element.

Regardless of how many <message> elements are defined within a WSDL document, they tend to occur in pairs. The first definition represents the input-centric format of the message, while the second defines the output-centric format of the same message. For example, the Subtract() method of CalculatorService is defined by the following <message> element:

```
<wsdl:message name="SubtractSoapIn">
  <wsdl:part name="parameters" element="tns:Subtract" />
</wsdl:message>
<wsdl:message name="SubtractSoapOut">
  <wsdl:part name="parameters" element="tns:SubtractResponse" />
</wsdl:message>
```

Here, you are only viewing the SOAP binding of the service. As you may recall from the beginning of this chapter, XML web services can be invoked via SOAP, HTTP GET, and HTTP POST. Thus, if you were to enable HTTP POST bindings (explained later), the generated WSDL would also show the following <message> data:

```
<wsdl:message name="SubtractHttpPostIn">
  <part name="n1" type="s:string" />
  <part name="n2" type="s:string" />
<wsdl:/message>
<wsdl:message name="SubtractHttpPostOut">
  <part name="Body" element="s0:int" />
<wsdl:/message>
```

In reality, <message> elements are not all that useful in and of themselves. However, these message definitions are referenced by other aspects of a WSDL document.

Note Not all web methods require both a request and response. If a web method is a one-way method, then only a request <message> element is necessary. You can mark a web method as a one-way method by applying the [SoapDocumentMethod] attribute.

The <portType> Element

The <portType> element defines the characteristics of the various correspondences that can occur between the client and server, each of which is represented by an <operation> subelement. As you might guess, the most common operations would be SOAP, HTTP GET, and HTTP POST. Additional operations do exist, however. For example, the one-way operation allows a client to send a message to a given web server but does not receive a response (sort of a fire-and-forget method invocation). The solicit/response operation allows the server to issue a request while the client responds (which is the exact opposite of the request/response operation).

To illustrate the format of a possible <operation> subelement, here is the WSDL definition for the Subtract() method:

```
<wsdl:portType name="CalculatorWebServiceSoap">
  <wsdl:operation name="Subtract">
    <wsdl:input message="tns:SubtractSoapIn" />
    <wsdl:output message="tns:SubtractSoapOut" />
  </wsdl:operation>
<wsdl:/portType>
```

Note how the `<input>` and `<output>` elements make reference to the related message name defined within the `<message>` element. If HTTP POST were enabled for the `Subtract()` method, you would find the following additional `<operation>` element:

```
<wsdl:portType name="CalculatorWebServiceHttpPost">
  <wsdl:operation name="Subtract">
    <wsdl:input message="s0:SubtractHttpPostIn" />
    <wsdl:output message="s0:SubtractHttpPostOut" />
  <wsdl:/operation>
<wsdl:/portType>
```

Finally, be aware that if a given web method has been described using the `Description` property, the `<operation>` element will contain an embedded `<documentation>` element.

The `<binding>` Element

This element specifies the exact format of the HTTP GET, HTTP POST, and SOAP exchanges. By far and away, this is the most verbose of all the subelements contained in the `<definition>` root. For example, here is the `<binding>` element definition that describes how a caller may interact with the `MyMethod()` web method using SOAP:

```
<wsdl:binding name="CalculatorWebServiceSoap12"
    type="tns:CalculatorWebServiceSoap">
  <soap12:binding transport="http://schemas.xmlsoap.org/soap/http" />
  <wsdl:operation name="Subtract">
    <soap12:operation soapAction="http://www.IntertechTraining.com/Subtract"
      style="document" />
    <wsdl:input>
      <soap12:body use="literal" />
    </wsdl:input>
    <wsdl:output>
      <soap12:body use="literal" />
    </wsdl:output>
  </wsdl:operation>
</wsdl:binding>
```

The `<service>` Element

Finally we have the `<service>` element, which specifies the characteristics of the web service itself (such as its URL). The chief duty of this element is to describe the set of ports exposed from a given web server. To do so, the `<services>` element makes use of any number of `<port>` subelements (not to be confused with the `<portType>` element). Here is the `<service>` element for CalculatorService:

```
<wsdl:service name="CalculatorWebService">
  <wsdl:documentation xmlns:wsdl="http://schemas.xmlsoap.org/wsdl/">
    The Amazing Calculator Web Service
  </wsdl:documentation>
  <wsdl:port name="CalculatorWebServiceSoap"
    binding="tns:CalculatorWebServiceSoap">
    <soap:address location="http://localhost:1109/CalculatorService/Service.asmx" />
  </wsdl:port>
  <wsdl:port name="CalculatorWebServiceSoap12"
    binding="tns:CalculatorWebServiceSoap12">
    <soap12:address location=
      "http://localhost:1109/CalculatorService/Service.asmx" />
  </wsdl:port>
</wsdl:service>
```

So, as you can see, the WSDL automatically returned by IIS is not rocket science, but given that WSDL is an XML-based grammar, it is a bit on the verbose side. Nevertheless, now that you have a better understanding of WSDL's place in the world, let's dig a bit deeper into the XML web service wire protocols.

Note Recall that the System.Web.Services.Description namespace contains a plethora of types that allow you to programmatically read and manipulate raw WSDL (so check it out if you are so interested).

Revisiting the XML Web Service Wire Protocols

Technically, XML web services can use any RPC protocol to facilitate communication (such as DCOM or CORBA). However, most web servers bundle this data into the body of an HTTP request and transmits it to the consumer using one of three core bindings (see Table 25-4).

Table 25-4. *XML Web Service Bindings*

Transmission Binding	Meaning in Life
HTTP GET	GET submissions append parameters to the query string of the URL.
HTTP POST	POST transmissions embed the data points into the header of the HTTP message rather than appending them to the query string.
SOAP	SOAP is a wire protocol that specifies how to submit data and invoke methods across the wire using XML.

While each approach leads to the same result (invoking a web method), your choice of wire protocol determines the types of parameters (and return types) that can be sent between each interested party. The SOAP protocol offers you the greatest flexibility, given that SOAP messages allow you to pass complex data types (as well as binary files) between the caller and XML web service. However, for completeness, let's check out the role of standard HTTP GET and POST.

HTTP GET and HTTP POST Bindings

Although GET and POST verbs may be familiar constructs, you must be aware that this method of transportation is not rich enough to represent such complex items as structures or classes. When you use GET and POST verbs, you can interact with web methods using only the types listed in Table 25-5.

Table 25-5. *Supported* POST *and* GET *Data Types*

Data Types	Meaning in Life
Enumerations	GET and POST verbs support the transmission of .NET System.Enum types, given that these types are represented as a static constant string.
Simple arrays	You can construct arrays of any primitive type.
Strings	GET and POST transmit all numerical data as a string token. *String* really refers to the string representation of CLR primitives such as Int16, Int32, Int64, Boolean, Single, Double, Decimal, and so forth.

By default, HTTP GET and HTTP POST bindings are not enabled for remote XML web service invocation. However, HTTP POST is enabled to allow a machine to invoke local web services (in fact, this is exactly what the autogenerated help page is leveraging behind the scenes). These settings are established in the machine.config file using the <protocols> element. Here is a partial snapshot:

```
<!-- In the machine.config file! -->
<webServices>
  <protocols>
    <add name="HttpSoap1.2" />
    <add name="HttpSoap" />
    <add name="Documentation" />
    <!-- HTTP GET/POST disabled! -->
    <!-- <add name="HttpPost"/> -->
    <!-- <add name="HttpGet"/> -->
    <!-- Used by the web service test page -->
    <add name="HttpPostLocalhost" />
  </protocols>
</webServices>
```

To re-enable HTTP GET or HTTP POST for a given web service, explicitly add in the HttpPost and HttpGet names within a local Web.config file:

```
<configuration>
  <system.web>
    <webServices>
      <protocols>
        <add name="HttpPost"/>
        <add name="HttpGet"/>
      </protocols>
    </webServices>
  </system.web>
</configuration>
```

Again, recall that if you make use of standard HTTP GET or HTTP POST, you are not able to build web methods that take complex types as parameters or return values (e.g., an ADO.NET DataSet or custom structure type). For simple web services, this limitation may be acceptable. However, if you make use of SOAP bindings, you are able to build much more elaborate XML web services.

SOAP Bindings

Although a complete examination of SOAP is beyond the scope of this text, understand that SOAP itself does not define a specific protocol and can thus be used with any number of existing Internet protocols (HTTP, SMTP, and others). The general role of SOAP, however, remains the same: provide a mechanism to invoke methods using complex types in a language- and platform-neutral manner. To do so, SOAP encodes each complex method with a SOAP message.

A SOAP message defines two core sections. First, we have the SOAP envelope, which can be understood as the conceptual container for the relevant information. Second, we have the rules that are used to describe the information in said message (placed into the SOAP body). An optional third section (the SOAP header) may be used to specify general information regarding the message itself, such as security or transactional information.

```
<soap:Envelope xmlns:xsi="http://www.w3.org/2001/XMLSchema-instance"
xmlns:xsd="http://www.w3.org/2001/XMLSchema"
xmlns:soap="http://schemas.xmlsoap.org/soap/envelope/">
    <soap:Header>
        <!-- Optional header information -->
    </soap:Header>
    <soap:Body>
        <!-- Method invocation information -->
    </soap:Body>
</soap:Envelope>
```

Viewing a SOAP Message

Although you are not required to understand the gory details of SOAP to build XML web services with the .NET platform, you are able to view the format of the SOAP message for each exposed web method using the autogenerated test page. For example, if you were to click the link for the Add() method of CalculatorService, you would find the following SOAP 1.1 request:

```
<soap:Envelope xmlns:xsi="http://www.w3.org/2001/XMLSchema-instance"
xmlns:xsd="http://www.w3.org/2001/XMLSchema"
xmlns:soap="http://schemas.xmlsoap.org/soap/envelope/">
  <soap:Body>
    <Add xmlns="http://www.IntertechTraining.com ">
      <x>int</x>
      <y>int</y>
    </Add>
  </soap:Body>
</soap:Envelope>
```

The corresponding SOAP 1.1 response looks like this:

```
<soap:Envelope xmlns:xsi="http://www.w3.org/2001/XMLSchema-instance"
xmlns:xsd="http://www.w3.org/2001/XMLSchema"
xmlns:soap="http://schemas.xmlsoap.org/soap/envelope/">
  <soap:Body>
    <AddResponse xmlns="http://www.IntertechTraining.com ">
      <AddResult>int</AddResult>
    </AddResponse>
  </soap:Body>
</soap:Envelope>
```

The wsdl.exe Command-Line Utility

Now that you've completed a primer on WSDL and SOAP, let's begin to examine how to build client programs that communicate with remote XML web services using the wsdl.exe command-line tool. In a nutshell, wsdl.exe performs two major tasks:

- Generates a server-side file that functions as a skeleton for implementing an XML web service
- Generates a client-side file that functions as the proxy to a remote XML web service

wsdl.exe supports a number of command-line flags, all of which can be viewed at the command prompt by specifying the -? option. Table 25-6 points out some of the more common arguments.

Table 25-6. *Select Options of* wsdl.exe

Command-Line Flag	Meaning in Life
/appsettingurlkey	Instructs wsdl.exe to build a proxy that does not make use of hard-coded URLs. Instead, the proxy class will be configured to read the URL from a client-side *.config file.
/language	Specifies the language to use for the generated proxy class: CS (C#; default) VB (Visual Basic .NET) JS (JScript) VJS (Visual J#) The default is C#.
/namespace	Specifies the namespace for the generated proxy or template. By default, your type will not be defined within a namespace definition.

Command-Line Flag	Meaning in Life
/out	Specifies the file in which to save the generated proxy code. If the file is not specified, the file name is based on the XML web service name.
/protocol	Specifies the protocol to use within the proxy code; SOAP is the default. However, you can also specify HttpGet or HttpPost to create a proxy that communicates using simple HTTP GET or POST verbs.
/serverInterface	Generates server-side interface bindings for an XML web service based on the WSDL document.

Note The /server flag of wsdl.exe has been deprecated under .NET 2.0. /serverInterface is now the preferred method to generate server-side skeleton code.

Transforming WSDL into a Server-Side XML Web Service Skeleton

One interesting use of the wsdl.exe utility is to generate server-side skeleton code (via the /serverInterface option) based on a WSDL document. Clearly, if you are interested in taking a WSDL first approach to building XML web services, this would be a very important option. Once this source code file has been generated, you have a solid starting point to provide the actual implementation of each web method.

Assume you have created WSDL document (CarBizObject.wsdl) that describes a single method named DeleteCar() that takes a single integer as input and returns nothing. This method is exposed from an XML web service named CarBizObject, which can be invoked using SOAP bindings.

To generate a server-side C# code file from this WSDL document, open a .NET-aware command window and specify the /serverInterface flag, followed by the name of the WSDL document you wish to process. Note that the WSDL document may be contained in a local *.wsdl file:

```
wsdl /serverInterface CarBizObject.wsdl
```

or it can be obtained dynamically from a given URL via the ?wsdl suffix:

```
wsdl /serverInterface http://localhost/CarService/CarBizObject.asmx?wsdl
```

Once wsdl.exe has processed the XML elements, you are presented with interface descriptions for each web method:

```
[System.Web.Services.WebServiceBindingAttribute(Name="CarBizObjectSoap",
  Namespace="http://IntertechTraining.com/")]
public partial interface ICarBizObjectSoap
{
...
    void RemoveCar(int carID);
}
```

Using these interfaces, you can define a class that implements the various methods of the XML web service.

Source Code The CarBizObject.wsdl file is included under the Chapter 25 subdirectory.

Transforming WSDL into a Client-Side Proxy

Although undesirable, it is completely possible to construct a client-side code base that manually opens an HTTP connection, builds the SOAP message, invokes the web method, and translates the incoming stream of XML back into CTS data types. A much-preferred approach is to leverage wsdl.exe to generate a proxy class that maps to the web methods defined by a given *.asmx file.

To do so, you will specify (at a minimum) the name of the proxy file to be generated (via the /out flag) and the location of the WSDL document. By default, wsdl.exe will generate proxy code written in C#. However, if you wish to obtain proxy code in an alternative .NET language, make use of the /language flag. You should also be aware that by default, wsdl.exe generates a proxy that communicates with the remote XML web service using SOAP bindings. If you wish to build a proxy that leverages straight HTTP GET or HTTP POST, you may make use of the /protocol flag.

Another important point to be made regarding generating proxy code via wsdl.exe is that this tool truly needs the *WSDL* of the XML web service, not simply the name of the *.asmx file. Given this, understand that if you make use of WebDev.WebServer.exe to develop and test your services, you will most likely want to copy your project's content to an IIS virtual directory before generating a client-side proxy.

For the sake of illustration, assume that you have created a new IIS virtual directory (CalcService), which contains the content for the CalculatorService project. Once you have done so, you can generate the client proxy code as so:

```
wsdl /out:proxy.cs http://localhost/CalcService/Service.asmx?wsdl
```

As a side note, be aware that wsdl.exe will not define a .NET namespace to wrap the generated C# types unless you specify the /n flag at the command prompt:

```
wsdl /out:proxy.cs /n:CalculatorClient
    http://localhost/CalcService/Service.asmx?wsdl
```

Examining the Proxy Code

If you open up the generated proxy file, you'll find a type that derives from System.Web.Services. Protocols.SoapHttpClientProtocol (unless, of course, you specified an alternative binding via the /protocols option):

```
public partial class CalculatorWebService :
    System.Web.Services.Protocols.SoapHttpClientProtocol
{
    ...
}
```

This base class defines a number of members leveraged within the implementation of the proxy type. Table 25-7 describes some (but not all) of these members.

Table 25-7. *Core Members of the* SoapHttpClientProtocol *Type*

Inherited Members	Meaning in Life
BeginInvoke()	This method starts an asynchronous invocation of the web method.
CancelAsync()	This method (new to .NET 2.0) cancels an asynchronous call to an XML web service method, unless the call has already completed.
EndInvoke()	This method ends an asynchronous invocation of the web method.
Invoke()	This method synchronously invokes a method of the web service.

Inherited Members	Meaning in Life
InvokeAsync()	This method (new to .NET 2.0) is the preferred way to asynchronously invoke a method of the web service.
Proxy	This property gets or sets proxy information for making a web service request through a firewall.
Timeout	This property gets or sets the timeout (in milliseconds) used for synchronous calls.
Url	This property gets or sets the base URL to the server to use for requests.
UserAgent	This property gets or sets the value for the user agent header sent with each request.

The Default Constructor

The default constructor of the proxy hard-codes the URL of the remote web service and stores it in the inherited Url property:

```
public CalculatorWebService()
{
    this.Url = "http://localhost/CalcService/Service.asmx";
}
```

The obvious drawback to this situation is that if the XML web service is renamed or relocated, the proxy class must be updated and recompiled. To build a more flexible proxy type, wsdl.exe provides the /appsettingurlkey flag (which may be abbreviated to /urlkey). When you specify this flag at the command line, the proxy's constructor will contain logic that reads the URL using a key contained within a client-side *.config file.

```
wsdl /out:proxy.cs /n:CalcClient /urlkey:CalcUrl
    http://localhost/CalcService/Service.asmx?wsdl
```

If you now check out the default constructor of the proxy, you will find the following logic (note that if the correct key cannot be found, the hard-coded URL will be used as a backup):

```
public CalculatorWebService()
{
  string urlSetting =
    System.Configuration.ConfigurationManager.AppSettings["CalcUrl"];
    if ((urlSetting != null))
    {
        this.Url = urlSetting;
    }
    else
    {
        this.Url = "http://localhost/CalcService/Service.asmx";
    }
}
```

The corresponding client-side app.config file will look like this:

```
<?xml version="1.0" encoding="utf-8" ?>
<configuration>
  <appSettings>
    <add key="CalcUrl" value="http://localhost/CalcService/Service.asmx"/>
  </appSettings>
</configuration>
```

Synchronous Invocation Support

The generated proxy also defines synchronous support for each web method. For example, the synchronous implementation of the Subtract() method is implemented as so:

```
public int Subtract(int x, int y)
{
    object[] results = this.Invoke("Subtract", new object[] {x, y});
    return ((int)(results[0]));
}
```

Notice that the caller passes in two System.Int32 parameters that are packaged as an array of System.Objects. Using late binding, the Invoke() method will pass these arguments to the Subtract method located at the established URL. Once this (blocking) call completes, the incoming XML is processed, and the result is cast back to the caller as System.Int32.

Asynchronous Invocation Support

Support for invoking a given web method asynchronously has changed quite a bit from .NET 1.*x*. As you might recall from previous experience, .NET 1.1 proxies made use of BeginXXX()/EndXXX() methods to invoke a web method on a secondary thread of execution. For example, consider the following BeginSubtract() and EndSubtract() methods:

```
public System.IAsyncResult BeginSubtract(int x, int y,
    System.AsyncCallback callback, object asyncState)
{
    return this.BeginInvoke("Subtract", new object[] {x, y},
    callback, asyncState);
}
public int EndSubtract(System.IAsyncResult asyncResult)
{
    object[] results = this.EndInvoke(asyncResult);
    return ((int)(results[0]));
}
```

While wsdl.exe still generates these familiar Begin/End methods, under .NET 2.0 they have been deprecated and are replaced by the new XXXAsync() methods:

```
public void SubtractAsync(int x, int y)
{
    this.SubtractAsync(x, y, null);
}
```

These new XXXAsync() methods (as well as a related CancelAsync() method) work in conjunction with an autogenerated helper method (being an overloaded version of a specific XXXAsync() method) which handles the asynchronous operation using C# event syntax. If you examine the proxy code, you will see that wsdl.exe has generated (for each web method) a custom delegate, custom event, and custom "event args" class to obtain the result.

Building the Client Application

Now that you better understand the internal composition of the generated proxy, let's put it to use. Create a new console application named CalculatorClient, insert your proxy.cs file into the project using Project ➤ Add Existing Item, and add a reference to the System.Web.Services.dll assembly. Next, update your Main() method as so:

```
class Program
{
    static void Main(string[] args)
    {
        Console.WriteLine("***** Fun with WS Proxies *****\n");
        // Make the proxy.
        CalculatorWebService ws = new CalculatorWebService();

        // Call the Add() method synchronously.
        Console.WriteLine("10 + 10 = {0}", ws.Add(10, 10));

        // Call the Subtract method asynchronously
        // using the new .NET 2.0 event approach.
        ws.SubtractCompleted += new
            SubtractCompletedEventHandler(ws_SubtractCompleted);
        ws.SubtractAsync(50, 45);

        // Keep console running to make sure we get our subtraction result.
        Console.ReadLine();
    }

    static void ws_SubtractCompleted(object sender, SubtractCompletedEventArgs e)
    {
        Console.WriteLine("Your answer is: {0}", e.Result);
    }
}
```

Notice that the new .NET 2.0 asynchronous invocation logic does indeed directly map to the C# event syntax, which as you might agree is cleaner than needing to work with BeginXXX()/EndXXX() method calls, the IAsyncResult interface, and the AsyncCallback delegate.

Source Code The CalculatorClient project can be found under the Chapter 25 subdirectory.

Generating Proxy Code Using Visual Studio 2005

Although wsdl.exe provides a number of command-line arguments that give you ultimate control over how a proxy class will be generated, Visual Studio 2005 also allows you to quickly generate a proxy file using the Add Web Reference dialog box (which you can activated from the Project menu). As you can see from Figure 25-6, you are able to obtain references to existing XML web services located in a variety of places.

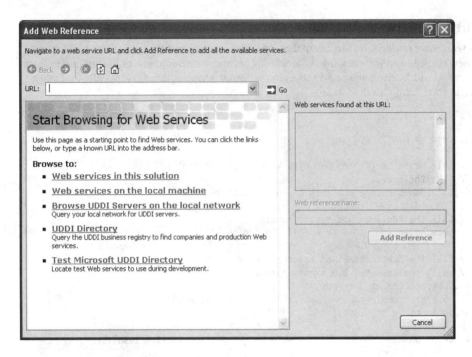

Figure 25-6. *The Add Web Reference dialog box*

■Note The Add Web Reference dialog box cannot reference XML web services hosted with WebDev.WebServer.exe.

Notice that not only are you able to obtain a list of XML web services on your local development machine, but you may also query various UDDI catalogs (which you'll do at the end of this chapter). In any case, once you type a valid URL that points to a given *.wsdl or *.asmx file, your project will contain a new proxy class. Do note that the proxy's namespace (which is based on the URL of origin) will be nested within your client's .NET namespace. Thus, if you have a client named MyClientApp that added a reference to a web service on your local machine you would need to specify the following C# using directive:

```
using MyClientApp.localhost;
```

■Note As of Visual Studio 2005, the Add Web Reference dialog box automatically adds an app.config file to your project that contains the URL of the referenced XML web service or updates an existing app.config file.

Exposing Custom Types from Web Methods

In the final example of this chapter, you'll examine how to build web services that expose custom types as well as more exotic types from the .NET base class libraries. To illustrate this, you'll create a new XML web service that is capable of processing arrays, custom types, and ADO.NET DataSets. To begin, create a new XML web service named CarSalesInfoWS that is hosted under an IIS virtual directory.

Exposing Arrays

Create a web method named GetSalesTagLines(), which returns an array of strings that represent the current sales for various automobiles, and another named SortCarMakes(), which allows the caller to pass in an array of unsorted strings and obtain a new array of sorted strings:

```
[WebService(Namespace = "http://IntertechTraining.com/",
  Description = "A car-centric web service",
  Name = "CarSalesInfoWS")]
[WebServiceBinding(ConformsTo = WsiProfiles.BasicProfile1_1)]
public class Service : System.Web.Services.WebService
{
    [WebMethod(Description = "Get current discount blurbs")]
    public string[] GetSalesTagLines()
    {
        string[] currentDeals = {"Colt prices slashed 50%!",
                "All BMWs come with standard 8-track",
                "Free Pink Caravans...just ask me!"};
        return currentDeals;
    }

    [WebMethod(Description = "Sorts a list of car makes")]
    public string[] SortCarMakes(string[] theCarsToSort)
    {
        Array.Sort(theCarsToSort);
        return theCarsToSort;
    }
}
```

Note The default test page generated by DefaultWsdlHelpGenerator.aspx cannot invoke methods that take arrays of types as parameters.

Exposing Structures

The SOAP protocol is also able to transport XML representations of custom data types (both classes and structures). XML web services make use of the XmlSerializer type to encode the type as XML (see Chapter 17 for details). Recall that the XmlSerializer

- Cannot serialize private data. It serializes only public fields and properties.

- Requires that each serialized class provide a default constructor.

- Does not require the use of the [Serializable] attribute.

This being said, our next web method will return an array of SalesInfoDetails structures, defined as so:

```
// A custom type.
public struct SalesInfoDetails
{
    public string info;
    public DateTime dateExpired;
    public string Url;
}
```

Another point of interest regarding the XmlSerializer is the fact that it allows you to have fine-grained control over how the type is represented. By default, the SalesInfoDetails structure is serialized by encoding each piece of field data as a unique XML element:

```
<SalesInfoDetails>
  <info>Colt prices slashed 50%!</info>
  <dateExpired>2004-12-02T00:00:00.0000000-06:00</dateExpired>
  <Url>http://www.CarsRUs.com</Url>
</SalesInfoDetails>
```

If you wish to change this default behavior, you can adorn your type definitions using attributes found within the System.Xml.Serialization namespace (again, see Chapter 17 for full details):

```
public struct SalesInfoDetails
{
    public string info;
    [XmlAttribute]
    public DateTime dateExpired;
    public string Url;
}
```

This yields the following XML data representation:

```
<SalesInfoDetails dateExpired="2004-12-02T00:00:00">
  <info>Colt prices slashed 50%!</info>
  <Url>http://www.CarsRUs.com</Url>
</SalesInfoDetails>
```

The implementation of GetSalesInfoDetails() returns a populated array of this custom structure as follows:

```
[WebMethod(Description="Get details of current sales")]
public SalesInfoDetails[] GetSalesInfoDetails()
{
    SalesInfoDetails[] theInfo = new SalesInfoDetails[3];
    theInfo[0].info = "Colt prices slashed 50%!";
    theInfo[0].dateExpired = DateTime.Parse("12/02/04");
    theInfo[0].Url= "http://www.CarsRUs.com";
    theInfo[1].info = "All BMWs come with standard 8-track";
    theInfo[1].dateExpired = DateTime.Parse("8/11/03");
    theInfo[1].Url= "http://www.Bmws4U.com";
    theInfo[2].info = "Free Pink Caravans...just ask me!";
    theInfo[2].dateExpired = DateTime.Parse("12/01/09");
    theInfo[2].Url= "http://www.AllPinkVans.com";
    return theInfo;
}
```

Exposing ADO.NET DataSets

To wrap up your XML web service, here is one final web method that returns a DataSet populated with the Inventory table the Cars database you created during our examination of ADO.NET in Chapter 22:

```
// Return all cars in inventory table.
[WebMethod(Description =
  "Returns all autos in the Inventory table of the Cars database")]
public DataSet GetCurrentInventory()
{
    // Fill the DataSet with the Inventory table.
```

```
    SqlConnection sqlConn = new SqlConnection();
    sqlConn.ConnectionString = "data source=localhost; initial catalog=Cars;" +
        "uid=sa; pwd=";
    SqlDataAdapter myDA=
        new SqlDataAdapter("Select * from Inventory", sqlConn);
    DataSet ds = new DataSet();
    myDA.Fill(ds, "Inventory");
    return ds;
}
```

■**Source Code**   The CarsSalesInfoWS files can be found under the Chapter 25 subdirectory.

A Windows Forms Client

To test your new XML web service, create a Windows Forms application and reference CarsSalesInfoWS using the Visual Studio 2005 Add Web References dialog box (see Figure 25-7).

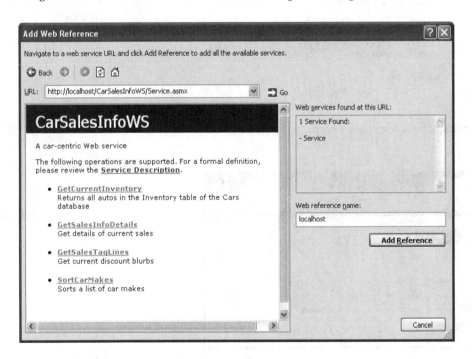

Figure 25-7. *Referencing CarsSalesInfoWS*

At this point, simply make use of the generated proxy to invoke the exposed web methods. Here is one possible Form implementation:

```
using CarsSalesInfoClient.localhost;
...
namespace CarsSalesInfoClient
{
    public partial class MainWindow : Form
    {
```

```
    private CarSalesInfoWS ws = new CarSalesInfoWS();
...
    private void MainWindow_Load(object sender, EventArgs e)
    {
        // Bind DataSet to grid.
        inventoryDataGridView.DataSource
            = ws.GetCurrentInventory().Tables[0];
    }

    private void btnGetTagLines_Click(object sender, EventArgs e)
    {
        string[] tagLines = ws.GetSalesTagLines();
        foreach (string tag in tagLines)
            listBoxTags.Items.Add(tag);
    }
    private void btnGetAllDetails_Click(object sender, EventArgs e)
    {
        SalesInfoDetails[] theSkinny = ws.GetSalesInfoDetails();
        foreach (SalesInfoDetails s in theSkinny)
        {
            string d = string.Format("Info: {0}\nURL:{1}\nExpiration Date:{2}",
                s.info, s.Url, s.dateExpired);
            MessageBox.Show(d, "Details");
        }
    }
  }
}
```

Figure 25-8 shows a possible test run.

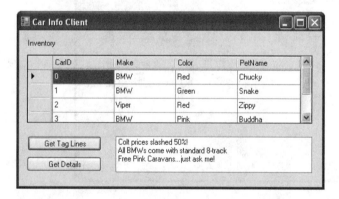

Figure 25-8. *The CarsSalesInfo client*

Client-Side Type Representation

When clients set a reference to a web service that exposes custom types, the proxy class file also contains language definitions for each custom public type. Thus, if you were to examine the client-side representation of SalesInfoDetails (within the generated Reference.cs file), you would see that each field has been encapsulated by a strongly typed property (also note that this type is now defined as a *class* rather than a structure):

```
[System.SerializableAttribute()]
[System.Xml.Serialization.XmlTypeAttribute
  (Namespace="http://IntertechTraining.com/")]
public partial class SalesInfoDetails {
    private string infoField;
    private string urlField;
    private System.DateTime dateExpiredField;

    public string info
    {
        get { return this.infoField; }
        set { this.infoField = value; }
    }
    public string Url
    {
        get { return this.urlField; }
        set { this.urlField = value; }
    }
    [System.Xml.Serialization.XmlAttributeAttribute()]
    public System.DateTime dateExpired
    {
        get { return this.dateExpiredField; }
        set { this.dateExpiredField = value; }
    }
}
```

Now, understand, of course, that like .NET remoting, types that are serialized across the wire as XML do not retain implementation logic. Thus, if the SalesInfoDetails structure supported a set of public methods, the proxy generator will fail to account for them (as they are not expressed in the WSDL document in the first place!). However, if you were to distribute a client-side assembly that contained the implementation code of the client-side type, you would be able to leverage the type-specific logic. Doing so would require a .NET-aware machine, though.

■**Source Code** The CarSalesInfoClient projects can be found under the Chapter 25 subdirectory.

Understanding the Discovery Service Protocol (UDDI)

It is a bit ironic that the typical first step taken by a client to chat with a remote web service is the final topic of this chapter. The reason for such an oddball flow is the fact that the process of identifying whether or not a given web service exists using UDDI is not only optional, but also unnecessary in a vast majority of cases.

Until XML web services becomes the de facto standard of distributed computing, most web services will be leveraged by companies tightly coupled with a given vendor. Given this, the company and vendor at large already know about each other, and therefore have no need to query a UDDI server to see if the web service in question exists. However, if the creator of an XML web service wishes to allow the world at large to access the exposed functionality to any number of external developers, the web service may be posted to a UDDI catalog.

UDDI is an initiative that allows web service developers to post a commercial web service to a well-known repository. Despite what you might be thinking, UDDI is not a Microsoft-specific technology. In fact, IBM and Sun Microsystems have an equal interest in the success of the UDDI initiative. As you would expect, numerous vendors host UDDI catalogs. For example, Microsoft's official UDDI website can be found at `http://uddi.microsoft.com`. The official website of UDDI (`http://www.uddi.org`) provides numerous white papers and SDKs that allow you to build internal UDDI servers.

Interacting with UDDI via Visual Studio 2005

Recall that the Add Web Reference dialog box allows you not only to obtain a list of all XML web services located on your current development machine (as well as a well-known URL) but also to submit queries to UDDI servers. Basically, you have the following options:

- Browse for a UDDI server on your company intranet.
- Browse the Microsoft-sponsored UDDI production server.
- Browse the Microsoft-sponsored UDDI test server.

Assume that you are building an application that needs to discover the current weather forecast on a per–zip code basis. Your first step would be to query a UDDI catalog with the following question:

- "Do you know of any web services that pertain to weather data?"

If it is the case that the UDDI server has a list of weather-aware web services, you are returned a list of all registered URLs that export the functionality of your query. Referencing this list, you are able to pick the specific web service you wish to communicate with and eventually obtain the WSDL document that describes the functionality of the weather-centric functionality.

As a quick example, create a brand-new console application project and activate the Add Web Reference dialog box. Next, select the Test Microsoft UDDI Directory link, which will bring you to the Microsoft UDDI test server. At this point, enter **weather** as a search criterion. Once the UDDI catalog has been queried, you will receive a list of all relevant XML web services. When you find an XML web service you are interested in programming against, add a reference to your current project. As you would expect, the raw WSDL will be parsed by the tool to provide you with a C# proxy.

Note Understand that the UDDI test center is just that: a test center. Don't be too surprised if you find a number of broken links. When you query production-level UDDI servers, URLs tend to be much more reliable, given that companies typically need to pay some sort of fee to be listed.

Summary

This chapter exposed you to the core building blocks of .NET web services. The chapter began by examining the core namespaces (and core types in these namespaces) used during web service development. As you learned, web services developed using the .NET platform require little more than applying the `[WebMethod]` attribute to each member you wish to expose from the XML web service type. Optionally, your types may derive from `System.Web.Services.WebService` to obtain access to the `Application` and `Session` properties (among other things). This chapter also examined three key related technologies: a lookup mechanism (UDDI), a description language (WSDL), and a wire protocol (`GET`, `POST`, or SOAP).

Once you have created any number of `[WebMethod]`-enabled members, you can interact with a web service through an intervening proxy. The `wsdl.exe` utility generates such a proxy, which can be used by the client like any other C# type. As an alternative to the `wsdl.exe` command-line tool, Visual Studio 2005 offers similar functionality via the Add Web Reference dialog box.

PART 6

■■■

Programming with .NET 3.0 Extensions

■ ■ ■

## CHAPTER 26

Establishing a .NET 3.0 Programming Environment

.NET 3.0 can be viewed as an "augmentative release" to the .NET platform. Given this, you will be happy to know that all of the .NET topics, tools, and types described within the previous 25 chapters are still completely relevant under .NET 3.0. The new features contained within the latest release of the platform can happily sit side by side with .NET 2.0, and are strictly speaking entirely optional. Of course, as shown through the remainder of this text, there are many compelling reasons to make use of the functionality found within .NET 3.0. To be sure, the .NET 3.0 technology set is poised to quickly become the preferred approach for developing software targeting the Vista operating system.

The major mission of this chapter is to guide you through the process of installing (and tweaking) the necessary software required to build .NET 3.0 applications. As you will see, configuring your machine to do so requires a bit of time and effort, given the fact that at the time of this writing, many of the development tools are currently in beta. The minor mission of this chapter is to provide an overview of the .NET 3.0 technologies, as well as the forthcoming C# 3.0 language and LINQ programming model. Here, I will only briefly comment on the new APIs and language features, as the remaining chapters of this text will provide much deeper coverage.

Introducing the .NET 3.0 Technologies

With the release of the Vista operating system (OS), Microsoft officially shipped the third version of the .NET base class libraries. Within this release, developers are provided with several new technologies represented by a set of new .NET assemblies. While these .NET 3.0 binaries are automatically installed with the Vista OS, it is completely permissible to run .NET 3.0 software on Windows XP and Windows Server 2003 machines once you have installed the .NET 3.0 runtime. Furthermore, you can develop .NET 3.0 applications on Vista, Windows XP, or Windows Server 2003 once you have installed the correct programming tools.

As you begin to examine the functionality provided by .NET 3.0, you will quickly notice that the overarching themes are unification and symmetry. For example, one particular aspect of .NET 3.0 is termed Windows Communication Foundation (WCF). This API provides a single unified object model for building distributed applications using numerous (and previously unrelated) technologies such as MSMQ, COM+, XML web services, and the .NET remoting framework. From a high level, the .NET 3.0 base class libraries consist of the technologies shown in Table 26-1.

Table 26-1. *Core Functionality of .NET 3.0*

Technology	Meaning in Life
Windows Presentation Foundation (WPF)	WPF provides a symmetrical model for building GUIs by integrating several previously unrelated APIs (2D and 3D rendering, animations, controls, etc.).
Windows Communication Foundation (WCF)	WCF provides a symmetrical programming model for numerous distributed APIs.
Windows Workflow Foundation (WF)	WF provides a way to integrate workflow activities directly within your .NET applications.

The first component of .NET 3.0, Windows Presentation Foundation (WPF), is a completely new approach to building desktop GUI applications. Much like an ASP.NET web program, WPF applications allow you to separate UI design from the functionality that drives it using a "code-behind" mind-set. Using the Extensible Application Markup Language (XAML), graphical designers can author professional-looking front ends that can be tied to a C# class definition. In addition to this separation of concerns, WPF unifies a large number of previously unrelated APIs into a single programming model. Finally, WPF applications support the ability to be hosted by a web server for in-browser rendering. We'll examine WPF further in Chapter 27.

Windows Communication Foundation (WCF) is the second aspect of .NET 3.0. As mentioned earlier, this technology provides a symmetrical approach for building distributed .NET applications using numerous Microsoft-distributed APIs. In some ways, WCF may remind you of the .NET remoting layer examined in Chapter 18, given the abundance of XML configuration descriptors. However, unlike the .NET remoting layer, WCF applications are a blend of numerous distributed technologies, including COM+, MSMQ, and web services. As well, WCF integrates a number of important auxiliary technologies (e.g., security and distributed transactions) within its object model. Chapter 28 provides an introduction to WCF development.

■**Note** Another component of WCF, InfoCard, is a new API that provides for a single method of managing user identity using a business card metaphor. We won't examine InfoCard in this book, so be sure to consult the .NET Framework 3.0 documentation for further details.

The final aspect of .NET 3.0 is termed Windows Workflow Foundation (WF). This particular API allows you to model (and execute) the business processes used by a .NET application directly within the assembly itself. Using various WF designer tools, you are able to create *workflows*, which can then be executed and monitored by the WF runtime engine. One major benefit of WF is the fact that these workflows are represented in a skill set–neutral manner, which allows developers to describe the software to the nontechnical members of the team, without having to use a separate product (such as Visio) to do so. You'll be introduced to Windows Workflow Foundation (WF) in Chapter 29.

■**Note** You may be wondering why Windows Workflow Foundation's acronym isn't WWF (to keep step with WPF and WCF), but simply WF. Despite what you may be thinking, it is not because Microsoft chose not to associate itself with professional wrestling (e.g., the World Wrestling Federation). In reality, the World Wildlife Fund was up in arms at the idea of Microsoft creating a technology named WWF, so the term WF was chosen to keep all parties happy.

Introducing C# 3.0 and LINQ Technologies

When you install the .NET 3.0 base class libraries and the related software development kit, you may naturally assume you are also using "C# 3.0" when you compile your projects, but this is currently not the case. C# 3.0 is not due to be released until mid-2007 (of course, the actual release date remains to be seen). However, interested .NET developers are able to investigate the proposed language enhancements today by installing the Language Integrated Query (LINQ) Community Technology Preview (CTP).

As you will see in Chapter 30, C# 3.0 introduces a good number of new language features (object initialization syntax, implicitly typed local variables, lambda expressions, etc.) that move C# into the realm of other functional languages such as Lisp and Haskell. While these new aspects of the language can most certainly be used out of the box, their usefulness is very apparent when programming against LINQ.

LINQ is a technology that provides a unified model for interacting with various forms of data. As you will see, using LINQ query operators, you can create strongly typed query statements that can be executed against collections of data (including custom objects), relational databases, and XML documents. LINQ technologies will be examined in Chapter 31.

Welcome to Beta Land!

At the time of this writing (fall of 2006), the .NET Framework 3.0 Software Development Kit has been officially released. However, Visual Studio 2005 "Orcas" and the C# 3.0 compiler (with support for LINQ technologies) are currently beta products (again, at least at the time of this writing). As such, you are sure to encounter bugs, crashes, limited documentation, incorrect documentation, and other such issues one encounters when working with prerelease technologies.

Given these facts, you must be aware that installing Visual Studio 2005 "Orcas" and C# 3.0 can be a risky proposition, especially if you install these components on a production machine. Microsoft recommends that you install any prerelease software on a dedicated test machine, which (of course) may not be possible based on your current circumstances.

The short answer is you will need to decide if you are comfortable introducing beta/CTP software onto your development machine before proceeding. If you decide to do so, you will also need to be aware that *uninstalling* beta software can also problematic. In some cases, the uninstallers will simply fail, which is a huge problem, because this may prevent future versions of the same product from installing at all! In these cases, a complete reinstallation of the operating system is the only option.

Disclaimers aside, in the remainder of this chapter I'll walk you through the process of installing all the necessary bits used to build .NET 3.0 and C# 3.0 applications. I assume that your machine is running Windows XP Professional and that Visual Studio 2005 has already been installed. Beyond this, you'll want to make sure your target machine has Microsoft SQL Server (2000 or higher) installed correctly to fully explore the LINQ technology set.

Do be aware that the installation processes described here are identical regardless of the .NET 3.0–aware OS (Windows XP, Windows Vista, or Windows Server 2003) you are running. If there are any major differences, I'll mention them at the appropriate step of the installation procedure.

Installing the .NET Framework 3.0 Runtime Components

■**Note** This step is not required if you are running the Vista OS, because the .NET Framework 3.0 Runtime Components are part of the OS installation. This step is required only if you are running Windows XP or Windows Server 2003.

The first step you must take in order to build .NET 3.0 applications is to install the freely download-able .NET Framework 3.0 Runtime Components. As its name implies, this setup program will equip your machine with the necessary assemblies and runtime engines to host software making use of the WCF, WPF, or WF technologies.

You can download the setup program, dotnetfx3setup.exe, from the Microsoft Vista developer page at http://msdn.microsoft.com/windowsvista/downloads/products. Here, you will find a helpful diagram that illustrates the .NET 3.0 development components, with each sporting a download arrow icon. For this step, select the .NET Framework 3.0 option (see Figure 26-1) and save the setup program to your local machine.

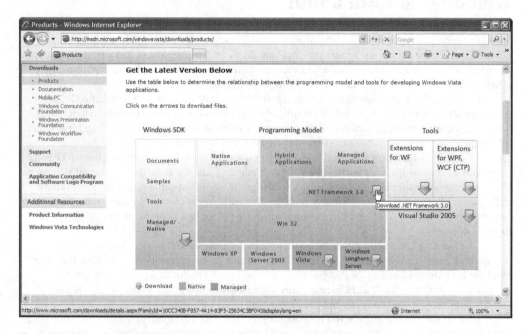

Figure 26-1. *Downloading the .NET Framework 3.0 Framework Runtime Components*

To install the software package, simply double-click the downloaded executable. Once the setup program has completed, you should be able to open your machine's GAC and view the new 3.0 runtime assemblies (see Figure 26-2).

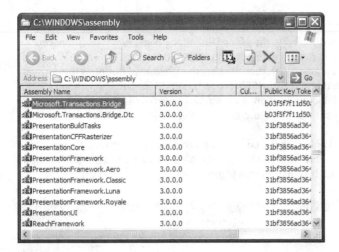

Figure 26-2. *The new .NET Framework 3.0 runtime assemblies*

Installing the Windows Software Development Kit

Now that you have the infrastructure required to run .NET 3.0 applications, the next step is to install the latest version of the Windows Software Development Kit (SDK) in order to build such software. You can download the setup program from the Microsoft Vista developer page (http://msdn. microsoft.com/windowsvista/downloads/products). Figure 26-3 shows the correct option to select.

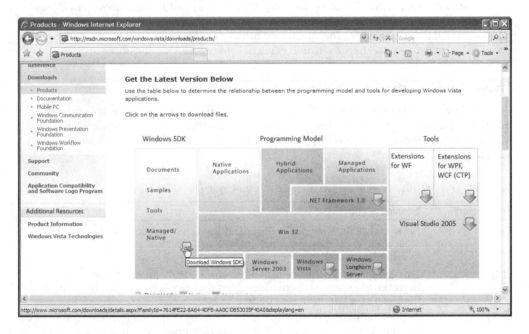

Figure 26-3. *Downloading the Windows SDK*

Choosing an Installation Option

Once you click this link, you will be redirected to the official download page; however, *before you click the Download button*, you need to make a choice. If you wish to download the entire Windows SDK as an ISO image (to burn it on a blank DVD), then clicking the Download button is the correct course of action. Be aware, however, that the entire SDK is over 1,300MB in size. The Windows SDK is so bulky because it includes tools, documentation, and sample code to build managed *and* unmanaged Windows applications using C or C++ and the new Win32 APIs (over 7,000 C-based functions in all).

Given that this text is concerned only with the construction of managed software, I suggest that you do *not* click the Download button, but instead scroll down this page to the Instructions section. Here you will find a link to begin a web installation (see Figure 26-4).

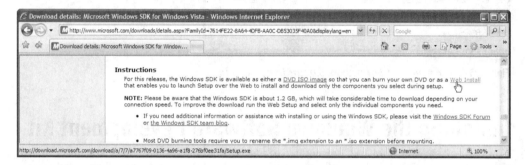

Figure 26-4. *The web installation option provides more flexibility when installing the Windows SDK.*

Using this option, you can deselect all the Win32 options, as well as the Windows Vista Headers and Libraries and Visual C++ Compilers options (see Figure 26-5). This will shorten the installation process and reduce the amount of consumed hard drive space. Of course, if you have the time, hard drive space, and interest, feel free to select all of the possible options before proceeding.

Investigating the SDK's Contents

Once the installation of the Windows SDK has completed (this will take a considerable amount of time), your machine will have a good number of new toys installed under C:\Program Files\ Microsoft SDKs\Windows\v6.0 directory. Table 26-2 documents the role of several of the contained subdirectories.

Table 26-2. *Core Subdirectories of the Windows SDK Installation Directory*

Subdirectory	Meaning in Life
Bin	Here you will find numerous command-line (and GUI-based) development tools, such as xamlpad.exe (a helpful WPF tool) and SvcConfigEditor.exe (a helpful WCF tool).
Help	This subdirectory contains all of the documentation for the Windows SDK. However, as explained shortly, launching the help system is no more difficult than using the Windows Start button.
Samples	As the subdirectory name implies, here you will find numerous samples that illustrate the construction of .NET 3.0 applications.

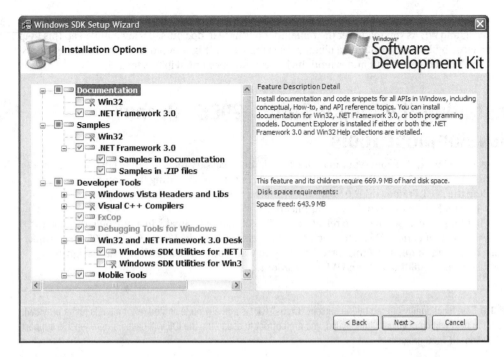

Figure 26-5. *Deselecting the Win32 API elements from the Windows SDK Setup Wizard*

Beyond these subdirectories, you should also be aware that when you click the Start button of the Windows OS and select All Programs, you will find a new entry for a folder named Microsoft Windows SDK. If you examine the Tools pop-up folder, you'll find quick access to several important .NET 3.0 utilities (such as xamlpad.exe and SvcConfigEditor.exe). Moreover, directly within the Windows SDK folder, you will find the Windows SDK documentation. Once you launch this tool, select the .NET Framework 3.0 Development node (see Figure 26-6).

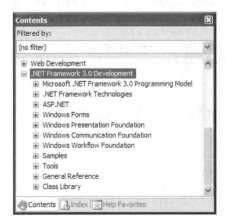

Figure 26-6. *The all-important .NET Framework 3.0 documentation*

As you can see, there is a documentation section for each of the major components of .NET 3.0: WPF, WCF, and WF. As you read over the remainder of this text, do yourself a favor and keep this help system close by. Here you will find a plethora of sample code, high-level overviews, and other necessary details that complement and extend the information presented in this text.

Installing the Visual Studio 2005 "Orcas" Development Tools

Strictly speaking, at this point your machine has all the necessary tools to build .NET 3.0 applications using the C# 2.0 compiler. However, as you saw in Chapter 2 (during the examination of installing the .NET Framework 2.0 SDK), the Windows SDK provides little more than a set of command-line tools used to build .NET 3.0 applications.

Thankfully, Microsoft has also released a CTP code-named "Orcas." In a nutshell, this download will add a set of new .NET 3.0–specific project templates to the Visual Studio 2005 New Project dialog box. In addition, installing "Orcas" will equip Visual Studio 2005 with various design-time tools used when building WPF and WF applications.

Note The functionality offered by the current "Orcas" CTP is actually quite limited (after all, it is just a preview). When the next edition of Visual Studio ships, you are correct in assuming the IDE will have comprehensive support for building .NET 3.0 projects.

Installing WPF and WCF Project Support

Like the previous downloads, the setup program can be found on the Microsoft Vista developer page (http://msdn.microsoft.com/windowsvista/downloads/products), but this time you will want to select the Extensions for WPF, WCF (CTP) download option located under the Tools portion of the web image.

When you run the setup program, simply accept the license agreement and select all defaults. You will find that the installation process takes a bit of time, as this tool is also merging the .NET Framework 3.0 documentation with the other help collections located on your machine.

At this point, you can launch Visual Studio 2005 and open the New Project dialog. If all is well, you should see a new folder named NET Framework 3.0, which has project templates for a WPF and WCF development (see Figure 26-7).

Installing the Visual Studio 2005 Extensions for Windows Workflow Foundation

The next software download, Visual Studio 2005 Extensions for Windows Workflow Foundation (EN).exe (that was a mouthful), updates Visual Studio 2005 with project templates and various designer tools to build workflow-enabled applications. Again, you can download the setup program from the Vista developer homepage, this time by clicking the Extensions for WF link under the Tools section of the web image.

Run the program and select each default option (make sure that Visual Studio 2005 is currently closed). Once the process is complete, you can open the Visual Studio 2005 New Project dialog box and find a new set of project templates for WF (see Figure 26-8).

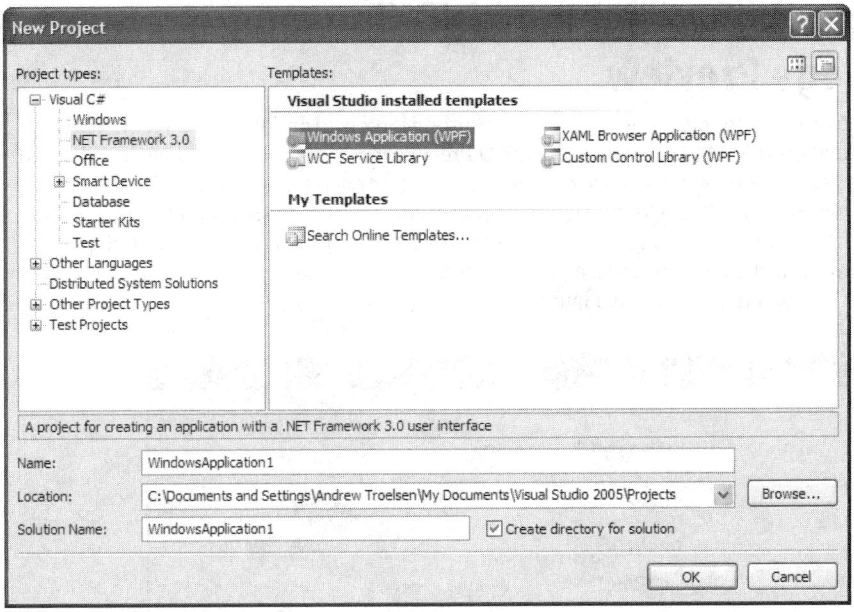

Figure 26-7. *WPF and WCF Visual Studio 2005 "Orcas" IDE support*

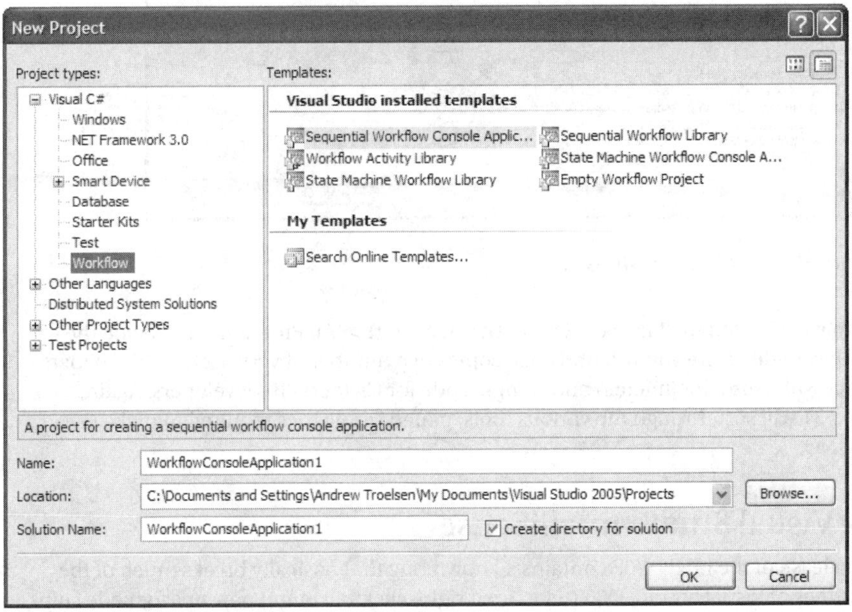

Figure 26-8. *WF Visual Studio 2005 "Orcas" IDE support*

At this point, you are ready to build software using each of the major .NET 3.0 application types (WPF, WCF, and WF) within the friendly confines of Visual Studio 2005. However, you have yet to configure your machine to make use of the C# 3.0 compiler and the LINQ technology suite.

Installing C# 3.0 and the LINQ Community Technology Preview

To explore the forthcoming release of the C# programming language and the LINQ technology set, you have one final download to deal with. The LINQ Preview installer program can be downloaded from the LINQ project homepage at http://msdn.microsoft.com/data/ref/linq.

Ensure Visual Studio 2005 is closed, run the installer and select each default setting (including the request to update the C# language services). Once the installation is complete, open the Visual Studio 2005 New Project dialog box once again, and notice that you now have a new area containing numerous LINQ project templates (see Figure 26-9).

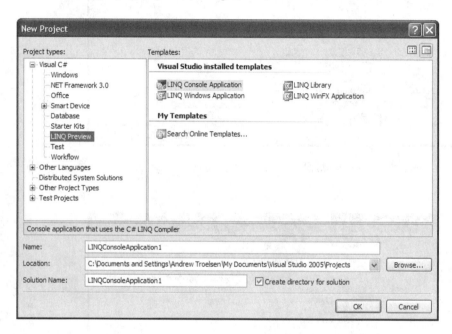

Figure 26-9. *Visual Studio 2005 LINQ support*

Once you have installed the LINQ CTP, you can select Start ➤ All Programs and locate the new LINQ Preview folder. Here you will find local copies of a number of very useful white papers (shipped as Microsoft Word documents) and sample code for C# (and VB) developers. Again, Chapters 30 and 31 will sort through the various tools, papers, and types required to make use of C# 3.0 and LINQ.

Repairing Visual Studio IntelliSense

The May 2006 release of the LINQ CTP contains a known bug that basically breaks much of the IntelliSense settings of Visual Studio 2005 (refactored right-clicking, menu pop-ups for code snippets, etc.). To verify that this is the case, create a new LINQ console application (named whatever you choose). Next, place the mouse cursor within the scope of the Program class and attempt to activate the Prop code snippet (which adds a property and backing field to the current type) by typing the letter **p**. You should *not* find the expected context menu.

■**Note** When you apply the following fix, you must be aware that the Visual Studio 2005 IDE will be reset to its initial default settings. For example, any custom settings (including the current list of recently opened files and solutions) will be wiped clean. If this is not acceptable, you can skip the following fix, but be aware that IntelliSense will be far from functional.

To fix the currently broken IntelliSense support, open the regedit.exe utility by selecting Start ➤ Run (specifying regedit as the application to open). Next, navigate the registry tree structure to highlight the following registry entry:

```
HKEY_LOCAL_MACHINE\
SOFTWARE\
Microsoft\
VisualStudio\
8.0\
Packages\
{A066E284-DCAB-11D2-B551-00C04F68D4DB}\
SatelliteDLL
```

■**Note** To quickly and easily locate the necessary GUID entry ({A066E284-DCAB-11D2-B551-00C04F68D4DB}), simply select the first GUID entry under the Packages folder and quickly type **{A0**. This will bring you to the correct entry.

Once you have selected the SatelliteDLL folder, you should see that the value of the Path entry is (incorrectly) set to C:\Program Files\Microsoft Visual Studio 8\VC#\VCSPackages\1033\. You can verify this by double-clicking on the Path icon for the SatelliteDLL entry. Change the path value to read C:\Program Files\Microsoft Visual Studio 8\VC#\VCSPackages\ (notice you are simply deleting the "1033\" portion of the current entry). At this point, click OK and close regedit.exe.

Before you launch Visual Studio 2005, you must perform one final task. Open a Visual Studio 2005 command prompt (located under Start ➤ All Programs ➤ Microsoft Visual Studio 2005 ➤ Visual Studio Tools) and enter the following command, being sure to specify the arguments in the order shown:

```
devenv /setup /resetuserdata /resetsettings
```

This command will reset the Visual Studio 2005 IDE to the default, out-of-the-box configuration (this process will take a moment or two, so be patient). Now open Visual Studio 2005 once again, create a new LINQ console application (or open the previous test application you made to verify the broken IntelliSense), and again attempt to activate the Prop code snippet. At this point, you should find that all is well (see Figure 26-10).

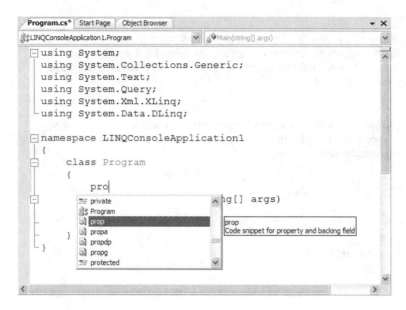

Figure 26-10. *Visual Studio 2005 IntelliSense back in action*

So there you have it! Your machine is now ready to build .NET 3.0 applications, as well as explore the functionality of the upcoming C# 3.0 programming language and LINQ technology.

Summary

This short chapter served two purposes. The primary goal was to walk you through the process of configuring your development machine (or ideally, a test machine) to host and build .NET 3.0/ C# 3.0/LINQ applications. Along the way, I also provided a very brief introduction to the topics that will be covered in detail over the remainder of this text.

I hope your installation process went off without a hitch, and you are now ready to begin your investigation of Windows Presentation Foundation (WPF) in the next chapter.

CHAPTER 27

■ ■ ■

Introducing Windows Presentation Foundation

As you have seen over the course of Chapters 19, 20, and 21, the `System.Windows.Forms.dll` and `System.Drawing.dll` assemblies provide numerous types that can be used to build sophisticated desktop user interfaces using the Windows Forms API. While it is true that Windows Forms/GDI+ is still entirely supported under .NET 3.0, we are now provided with a brand-new desktop API termed Windows Presentation Foundation (WPF; sometimes referred to by its code name, "Avalon").

This chapter provides an introduction to the WPF programming model that will help you understand the motivation behind this new UI framework. You'll check out a number of new assemblies, namespaces, and types, and you'll also examine a brand-new XML-based grammar: Extensible Application Markup Language (XAML). Using XAML (pronounced "zammel"), you are able to separate the look and feel of your desktop application from the logic that drives it. Along the way, this chapter will expose you to a number of important WPF topics such as the control content model, styles, and graphical rendering and animation services. The chapter wraps up with an overview of XAML Browser Applications, or XBAPs.

> ■**Note** Given the scope of WPF, understand that a single introductory chapter cannot cover every aspect of this .NET 3.0 API. If you require a deeper treatment of the topic than presented here, check out *Pro WPF: Windows Presentation Foundation in .NET 3.0* by Matthew MacDonald (Apress, 2007).

The Motivation Behind WPF

Over the years, Microsoft has developed numerous graphical user interface toolkits (raw C/C++/ Win32 API development, VB6, MFC, etc.) to build desktop executables. Each of these GUI APIs provided a code base to represent the basic aspects of a GUI application, including main windows, dialog boxes, controls, menu systems, and other necessities. With the release of the .NET platform, Windows Forms quickly became the preferred model for UI development, given its simple yet very powerful object model.

While many full-featured desktop applications have been successfully created using Windows Forms, the fact of the matter is that the current desktop programming model is very *asymmetrical*. Simply put, `System.Windows.Forms.dll` and `System.Drawing.dll` do not provide direct support for many additional technologies required to build a full-fledged desktop application. To illustrate this point, consider the ad hoc nature of GUI development under .NET 2.0 (see Table 27-1).

Table 27-1. *.NET 2.0 Solutions to Desired Functionalities*

Desired Functionality	.NET 2.0 Solution
Building forms with controls	Windows Forms
2D graphics support	GDI+ (System.Drawing.dll)
3D graphics support	DirectX APIs
Support for streaming video	Windows Media Player APIs
Support for fixed-style documents	Programmatic manipulation of PDF files

As you can see, a .NET 2.0 Windows Forms application must pull in types from a number of different APIs and object models. While it is true that making use of these diverse APIs may look similar syntactically (it is just C# code, after all), you may also agree that each technology requires a radically different mind-set. For example, the skills required to create a 3D rendered animation using DirectX are completely different from those used to display a modal dialog box to gather user input. To be sure, it is very difficult for a .NET 2.0 software professional to master the diverse nature of each API.

WPF was purposely created to merge together these previous unrelated APIs into a single unified object model. Thus, if you need to author a 3D animation, you have no need to manually program against the DirectX API, as this functionality is baked directly into WPF. To see how well things have cleaned up, consider Table 27-2, which illustrates the new .NET 3.0 desktop development model.

Table 27-2. *.NET 3.0 Solutions to Desired Functionalities*

Desired Functionality	.NET 3.0 Solution
Building forms with controls	WPF
2D graphics support	WPF
3D graphics support	WPF
Support for streaming video	WPF
Support for fixed-style documents	WPF

Providing a Separation of Concerns via XAML

In addition to unifying numerous APIs under a single umbrella, you will quickly notice that WPF was designed to leverage the best aspects of web development techniques as well as the best aspects of desktop development techniques. In fact, the WPF team is composed of Microsoft web developers, Windows Forms developers, and Win32 developers. As you might suspect, blending web-centric and desktop-centric programming models together produces some rather interesting end results.

Perhaps one of the most compelling benefits is that WPF provides a way to cleanly separate the look and feel of a Windows application from the programming logic that drives it. Using XAML, it is possible to define the UI of an application via *markup*. This markup (ideally created by those with an artistic mind-set using dedicated tools) can then be connected to a managed code base to provide the guts of the program's functionality. As you will see, this technique makes the process of building a desktop application look and feel like the process of building an ASP.NET application, without the inherent limitations of the web model (limited state management, limited interactivity, etc.).

■**Note** As you may agree, moving the desktop programming model closer to the web model is rather ironic, given that one of the major motivations of ASP.NET was to make the process of building a web application look and feel more like building a Windows application!

Another compelling aspect of WPF is how much flexibility "desktop markup" provides. XAML allows you to define not only simple UI elements (buttons, grids, list boxes, etc.) in markup, but also complex animations, graphical renderings, and multimedia functionality (such as video playback). For example, defining a circular button control that animates a company logo requires just a few lines of markup. Even better, WPF elements can be modified through styles and templates, which allow you to change the overall look and feel of an application with minimum fuss and bother, independent of the core application processing code. Given all these points, the need to build custom controls greatly diminishes under WPF.

Providing an Optimized Rendering Model

Also be aware of the fact that WPF is optimized to take advantage of the new video driver model supported under the Windows Vista operating system. While WPF applications can be developed on and deployed to Windows XP machines (as well as Windows Server 2003 machines), the same application running on Vista will perform much better, especially when making use of animations/multimedia services. This is due to the fact that the display services of WPF are rendered via the DirectX engine, allowing for efficient hardware and software rendering.

WPF applications also tend to behave better under Vista. If one graphics-intensive application crashes, it will not take down the entire OS (à la the blue screen of death); rather, the misbehaving application in question will simply terminate. As you may know, the most common cause of the infamous blue screen of death is misbehaving video drivers. Thankfully, this problem is closer than ever to being "solved" under Vista.

To recap the story thus far, Windows Presentation Foundation (WPF) is a brand-new API to build desktop applications. In addition to the major points previously examined, WPF applications also benefit from the following:

- A number of layout managers (far more than Windows Forms) to provide full control over placement and reposition of content

- Use of an enhanced data-binding engine to bind content to content in a variety of ways

- A built-in style engine, which allows you to define "themes" for a WPF application

- A reliance on vector graphics, which allows an image to be automatically resized to fit the size and resolution of the screen hosting the application

- Support for interoperating with legacy GUI models (e.g., Windows Forms, ActiveX, and Win32 HWNDs)

Again, remember that WPF applications are not limited to the Vista operating system. WPF applications may be created on (and hosted by) Windows XP and Windows Server 2003. To make this point crystal clear, each example in this chapter is built and executed using Windows XP Professional. If you are currently running Vista, all the better!

Investigating the WPF Assemblies

Once you have installed the .NET Framework 3.0 Runtime Components and Windows SDK (as described in Chapter 26), you will find a number of new assemblies have been added to the GAC. Table 27-3 describes the core assemblies used to build WPF applications, each of which must be referenced when creating a new project.

Table 27-3. *Core WPF Assemblies*

Assembly	Meaning in Life
WindowsBase.dll	As the name suggests, this assembly defines the core (and in many cases lower-level) types that constitute the infrastructure of the WPF API.
PresentationCore.dll	This assembly defines numerous types that constitute the foundation of the WPF GUI layer.
PresentationFoundation.dll	This assembly—the "meatiest" of the three—defines the WPF controls types, animation and multimedia support, data binding support, and other WPF services.

■**Note** In addition to the managed assemblies shown in Table 27-3, WPF also makes use (behind the scenes) of an unmanaged binary named milcore.dll. This library is basically a bridge between the managed WPF assemblies and the DirectX runtime layer.

Collectively, these assemblies define a number of new namespaces and hundreds of new .NET types (classes, interfaces, structures, enumerations, and delegates). While you should consult the .NET Framework 3.0 SDK documentation for complete details, Table 27-4 documents the role of some (but certainly not all) of the core namespaces you should be aware of.

Table 27-4. *Core WPF Namespaces*

Namespace	Meaning in Life
System.Windows	This is the root namespace of WPF. Here you will find core types (such as Application and Window) that are required by any WPF desktop project.
System.Windows.Controls	Here you will find all of the expected WPF widgets, including types to build menu systems, tool tips, and numerous layout managers.
System.Windows.Markup	This namespace defines a number of types that allow XAML markup (and the equivalent binary format, BAML) to be parsed.
System.Windows.Media	This is the root namespace to several media-centric namespaces. Within these namespaces you will find types to work with animations, 3D rendering, text rendering, and other multimedia primitives.
System.Windows.Navigation	This namespace provides types to account for the navigation logic employed by XAML browser applications.
System.Windows.Shapes	This namespace defines basic geometric shapes (Rectangle, Polygon, etc.) used by various aspects of the WPF framework.

Beyond the core namespaces shown in Table 27-4, the WPF assemblies also provide a number of namespaces for rendering data to external printers, support for the Ink APIs (for programming against stylus input for Pocket PCs and Tablet PCs), and several lower-level namespaces representing the WPF build engine.

To begin our journey into the WPF programming model, we'll examine two members of the System.Windows namespace that are commonplace to any WPF desktop development effort: Application and Window.

The Role of the Application Class

The System.Window.Application class type represents a global instance of a running WPF application. Like its Windows Forms counterpart, this type supplies a Run() method (to start the application), a series of events that you are able to handle in order to interact with the application's lifetime (such as Startup and Exit), and a number of members that are specific to XAML browser applications.

Beyond the Run() method and Startup and Exit events, the Application type defines other properties of interest, some of which are presented in Table 27-5.

Table 27-5. *Key Properties of the* Application *Type*

Property	Meaning in Life
Current	This static property allows you to gain access to the running Application object from anywhere in your code.
MainWindow	This property allows you to programmatically get or set the main window of the application.
StartupUri	This property gets or sets a URI that specifies a window or page to open automatically when the application starts.
Properties	This property allows you to establish and obtain data that is accessible throughout a WPF application.
Windows	This property returns a WindowCollection type, which provides access to each window created from the thread that created the Application object.

Unlike its Windows Forms counterpart, however, the WPF Application type does not expose its functionality primarily through static members. Rather, WPF programs define a class that extends this type to represent the entry point to the executable. Once you do so, the runtime will allocate a single instance of this type for using during the duration of the application's lifetime, for example:

```
// Define the global application object
// for this WPF program.
class MyApp : Application
{
  [STAThread]
  static void Main()
  {
    // Handle events, run the application,
    // Launch the main window, etc.
  }
}
```

You'll build a complete Application-derived type in an upcoming example. Until then, let's check out the functionality of the Window type.

The Role of the Window Class

The `System.Windows.Window` type represents a single window owned by the `Application`-derived type, including any dialogs displayed by the main window. As you might expect, the `Window` type has a series of parent classes, each of which brings more functionality to the table. Consider Figure 27-1, which shows the inheritance chain (and implemented interfaces) for the `System.Windows.Window` type as seen through the Visual Studio 2005 object browser.

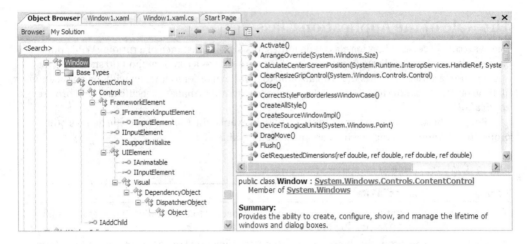

Figure 27-1. *The hierarchy of the* Window *type*

You'll come to understand the functionality provided by these base classes as you naturally progress through this chapter. However, to whet your appetite for the time being, the sections that follow break down the role of each base class (consult the .NET Framework 3.0 SDK documentation for full details).

The Role of System.Windows.Controls.ContentControl

The direct parent of `Window` is `ContentControl`. This base class provides derived types with the ability to host *content*. Under the WPF content model, a content control has the ability to contain a great number of UI elements beyond simple string data. For example, it is entirely possible to define a `Button` that contains a `ScrollBar`. The `ContentControl` base class provides a key property named (not surprisingly) `Content` for this purpose. Consider the following XAML definition, which implicitly sets the `Content` property to a `ScrollBar` type (you'll find more information on XAML later in this chapter, so don't sweat the details just yet):

```
<!-- A Button containing a ScrollBar -->
<Button Height = "80" Width = "100">
  <ScrollBar Width = "75" Height = "40"/>
</Button>
```

Do be aware, however, that not every WPF control derives from `ContentControl`, and therefore only a subset of controls supports this unique content model. Specifically, any class deriving from `Frame`, `GroupItem`, `HeaderedContentControl`, `Label`, `ListBoxItem`, `ButtonBase`, `StatusBarItem`, `ScrollViewer`, `ToolTip`, `UserControl`, or `Window` can make use of this content model. Any other type attempting to do so results in a markup/compile-time error:

```
<!-- Error!  ScrollBars don't derive from ContentControl -->
<ScrollBar Height = "80" Width = "100">
  <Button Width = "75" Height = "40"/>
</ScrollBar >
```

Another important point regarding this new content model is that controls deriving from ContentControl (including the Window type itself) can assign only a *single* value to the Content property. Therefore, the following XAML is also illegal:

```
<!-- Try to add a TextBox and an Ellipse to a Button?  Error! -->
<Button Height = "200" Width = "200">
  <Ellipse Fill = "Green" Height = "80" Width = "80"/>
  <TextBox Width = "50" Height = "40"/>
</Button >
```

At first glance, this code might appear to be extremely limiting (imagine how nonfunctional a dialog box would be with only a single button!). Thankfully, it is indeed possible to add numerous elements to a ContentControl-derived Panel type. To do so, each bit of content must first be arranged into one of the WPF panel types, after which point the panel becomes the single value assigned to the Content property. You'll see more about the various WPF panel types later in this chapter.

The Role of System.Windows.Controls.Control

Unlike ContentControl, all WPF controls share the Control base class as a common parent. This base class provides numerous core members that account for basic UI functionality. For example, Control defines properties to establish the control's size, opacity, tab order logic, cursor to display, background color, and so forth. Furthermore, this parent class provides support for *templating services*. As explained later in this chapter, WPF controls can dynamically change their appearance using templates (aka styles).

The Role of System.Windows.FrameworkElement

This type allows the derived type to support storyboards, which are a key aspect of the WPF animation model. For the time being, you can regard a *storyboard* as a collection of animations. As well, FrameworkElement provides support for WPF data binding services and the ability to participate in the WPF style model.

The Role of System.Windows.UIElement

The UIElement base class provides core animation services as well as a set of members that allows the derived type to receive focus and process input requests. For example, this class provides numerous events to account for drag-and-drop operations, mouse movement, keyboard input, and stylus input (for Pocket PCs and Tablet PCs).

The Role of System.Windows.Media.Visual

The Visual class type provides core rendering support in WPF, which includes hit testing, coordinate transformation, and bounding box calculations. In fact, this type is the connection point between the managed WPF assembly stack and the unmanaged milcore.dll binary that communicates with the DirectX subsystem.

Given your background in Windows Forms programming, you may think that the functionality offered by Visual would only be used for graphical rendering operations such as painting a pie chart on a window's surface. However, WPF allows any UI element to transform the coordinates of the elements it is displaying (e.g., you could easily build a window that displays all of the internal UI elements at a 45-degree angle).

The Role of System.Windows.DependencyObject

As explained later in this chapter, WPF supports a particular flavor of properties termed *dependent properties*. Simply put, this approach allows a type to compute the value of a property based on the value of other properties. In addition, DependencyObject allows derived types to support *attached properties*, which are very useful when programming against the WPF data-binding model.

The Role of System.Windows.Threading.DispatcherObject

The final base class of the Window type (beyond System.Object, which I assume needs no further explanation at this point in the text) is DispatcherObject. This type provides one property of interest, Dispatcher, which returns the associated System.Windows.Threading.Dispatcher object. The Dispatcher type is the entry point to the event queue of the WPF application, and it provides the basic constructs for dealing with concurrency and threading. By and large, this is a lower-level class that can be ignored by the majority of your WPF applications.

Building a (XAML-Free) WPF Application

Given all of the functionality provided by the parent classes of the Window type, it is possible to represent a window in your application by either directly creating a Window type or using this class as the parent to a strongly typed descendent. Let's examine both approaches in the following code example.

Although most WPF applications will make use of XAML, doing so is entirely optional. Anything that can be expressed in XAML can be expressed completely in code and vice versa. If you wish, it is possible to build a complete WPF project using the underlying object model (however, in many cases, the equivalent XAML will require less code).

To illustrate, let's create a minimal and complete application *without* the use of XAML using the Application and Window types directly. Consider the following C# code (defined in SimpleWPFApp.cs), which creates a main window of modest functionality:

```
// A Simple WPF Application, written without XAML.
using System;
using System.Windows;
using System.Windows.Controls;

namespace SimpleWPFApp
{
  // In this first example, we are defining a single class type to
  // represent the application itself and the main window.
  class MyWPFApp : Application
  {
    [STAThread]
    static void Main()
    {
      // Handle the Startup and Exit events, and then run the application.
      MyWPFApp app = new MyWPFApp();
      app.Startup += AppStartUp;
      app.Exit += AppExit;
```

```
    app.Run();  // Fires the Startup event.
  }

  static void AppExit(object sender, ExitEventArgs e)
  {
    MessageBox.Show("App has exited");
  }

  static void AppStartUp(object sender, StartupEventArgs e)
  {
    // Create a Window object and set some basic properties.
    Window mainWindow = new Window();
    mainWindow.Title = "My First WPF App!";
    mainWindow.Height = 200;
    mainWindow.Width = 300;
    mainWindow.WindowStartupLocation = WindowStartupLocation.CenterScreen;
    mainWindow.Show();
  }
 }
}
```

Note that the MyWPFApp class extends the System.Windows.Application type. Within this type's Main() method, we create an instance of our application object and handle the Startup and Exit events using method group conversion syntax. Recall from Chapter 8 that this shorthand notation removes the need to manually specify the underlying delegates. However, if you wish, you can specify the underlying delegates directly by name.

In the following modified Main() method, notice that the Startup event works in conjunction with the StartupEventHandler delegate, which can only point to methods taking an Object as the first parameter and a StartupEventArgs as the second. The Exit event, on the other hand, works with the ExitEventHandler delegate, which demands the method pointed to takes an ExitEventArgs type as the second parameter.

```
static void Main()
{
  // This time, specify the underlying delegates.
  MyWPFApp app = new MyWPFApp();
  app.Startup += new StartupEventHandler(AppStartUp);
  app.Exit += new ExitEventHandler(AppExit);
  app.Run();  // Fires the Startup event.
}
```

The AppStartUp() method has been configured to create a Window type, establish some very basic property settings, and call Show() to display the window on the screen in a modal-less fashion (like Windows Forms, the ShowDialog() method can be used to launch a modal dialog). The AppExit() method simply makes use of the WPF MessageBox type to display a diagnostic message when the application is being terminated.

To compile this C# code into an executable WPF application, assume that we have created a C# response file named build.rsp that references each of the WPF assemblies. Note that the path to each assembly should be defined on a single line (see Chapter 2 for more information on response files and working with the command-line compiler):

```
# build.rsp
#
/target:winexe
/out:SimpleWPFApp.exe
/r:"C:\Program Files\Reference Assemblies\Microsoft\Framework\v3.0\WindowsBase.dll"
/r:"C:\Program Files\Reference Assemblies\Microsoft\Framework
```

```
      \v3.0\PresentationCore.dll"
/r:"C:\Program Files\Reference Assemblies\Microsoft\Framework
      \v3.0\PresentationFramework.dll"
*.cs
```

We can now compile this WPF program at the command prompt as follows:

```
csc @build.rsp
```

Once you run the program, you will find a very simple main window that can be minimized, maximized, and closed. To spice things up a bit, we need to add some user interface elements. Before we do, however, let's refactor our code base to account for a strongly typed and well-encapsulated Window-derived class.

Extending the Window Class Type

Currently, our Application-derived class directly creates an instance of the Window type upon application start-up. Ideally, we would create a class deriving from Window in order to encapsulate its functionality. Assume we have created the following class definition within our current SimpleWPFApp namespace:

```
class MainWindow : Window
{
  public MainWindow(string windowTitle, int height, int width)
  {
    this.Title = windowTitle;
    this.WindowStartupLocation = WindowStartupLocation.CenterScreen;
    this.Height = height;
    this.Width = width;
    this.Show();
  }
}
```

We can now update our Startup event handler to simply directly create an instance of MainWindow:

```
static void AppStartUp(object sender, StartupEventArgs e)
{
  // Create a MainWindow object.
  MainWindow wnd = new MainWindow("My better WPF App!", 200, 300);
}
```

Once the program is recompiled and executed, the output is identical. The obvious benefit is that we now have a strongly typed class to build upon.

■**Note** When you create a Window (or Window-derived) object, it will automatically be added to the application's Windows collection (via some constructor logic found in the Window class itself). Given this fact, the object will be alive in memory until the executable is terminated or is explicitly removed from the collection.

Creating a Simple User Interface

Adding UI elements into a Window-derived type is similar (but not identical) to adding UI elements into a System.Windows.Forms.Form-derived type:

1. Define a member variable to represent the required widget.

2. Configure the variable's look and feel upon Window creation.

3. Add the widget to the Window's client area via a call to AddChild().

Although the process might feel familiar, one obvious difference is that the UI controls used by WPF are defined within the System.Windows.Controls namespace (thankfully, in many cases, they feel quite similar to their Windows Forms counterparts). A more drastic change from Windows Forms is the fact that when a Window-derived type contains multiple UI elements (which will be the case for practically any window), you will make use of various layout managers (such as DockPanel, Grid, Canvas, and StackPanel) to control their positioning.

For this example, we will add single Button type to the Window-derived type. When we click this button, we terminate the application by gaining access to the global application object (via the Application.Current property) in order to call the Shutdown() method. Ponder the following update to the MainWindow class:

```
class MainWindow : Window
{
  // Our UI element.
  private Button btnExitApp = new Button();

  public MainWindow(string windowTitle, int height, int width)
  {
    // Configure button and set the child control.
    btnExitApp.Click += new RoutedEventHandler(btnExitApp_Clicked);
    btnExitApp.Content = "Exit Application";
    btnExitApp.Height = 25;
    btnExitApp.Width = 100;
    this.AddChild(btnExitApp);

    // Configure the window.
    this.Title = windowTitle;
    this.WindowStartupLocation = WindowStartupLocation.CenterScreen;
    this.Height = height;
    this.Width = width;
    this.Show();
  }

  private void btnExitApp_Clicked(object sender, RoutedEventArgs e)
  {
    // Get a handle to the current application and shut it down.
    Application.Current.Shutdown();
  }
}
```

Given your work with Windows Forms over the course of this text, the code within the window's constructor should not look too threatening. Do notice, however, that the Click event of the WPF button works in conjunction with a delegate named RoutedEventHandler, which obviously begs the question, "What is a routed event?" You'll examine the new WPF event model later in this chapter (so hang tight for now). Once you recompile and run this application, you will find the customized window shown in Figure 27-2.

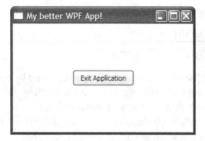

Figure 27-2. *A somewhat interesting WPF application*

At this point in the chapter, WPF might look like nothing more than a new GUI model that is providing (more or less) the same services as System.Windows.Forms.dll. If this were in fact the case, you might question the usefulness of yet another UI toolkit. To truly see what makes WPF so unique requires an understanding of a new XML-based grammar, XAML.

■**Source Code** The SimpleWPFApp project is included under the Chapter 27 subdirectory.

Introducing XAML

Extensible Application Markup Language, or XAML, is a new XML-based grammar that allows you to define the state (and, optionally, the functionality) of a .NET type through markup. While XAML is frequently used when building UIs with WPF, in reality it can be used to describe any tree of *nonabstract* .NET types, provided each supports a default constructor (including your own custom types defined in a custom .NET assembly). As you will see, the markup found within a *.xaml file is transformed into a full-blown object model that maps directly to the types within a related .NET namespace.

Because XAML is an XML-based grammar, we gain all the benefits and drawbacks XML affords us. On the plus side, XAML files are very self-describing (as any XML document should be). By and large, each element in a XAML file represents a type name (such as Button, Window, or Application) within a .NET namespace. Attributes within the scope of an opening element (by and large) map to properties (Height, Width, etc.) and events (Startup, Click, etc.) of the specified type. For example, the following XAML:

```
<!-- Defining a WPF Button in XAML -->
<Button Name = "btnClickMe" Height = "40" Width = "100" Content = "Click Me" />
```

can be represented programmatically as follows:

```
// Defining the same WPF Button in C# code.
Button btnClickMe = new Button();
btnClickMe.Height = 40;
btnClickMe.Width = 100;
btnClickMe.Content = "Click Me";
```

On the negative side, XAML can be verbose and is (like any XML document) case sensitive. As well, complex XAML definitions can result in a good deal of markup. Most developers will not need to manually author a complete XAML description of their WPF applications. Rather, the majority of this task will (thankfully) be relegated to development tools such as Visual Studio 2005, Microsoft Expression Interactive Designer (examined a bit later in this chapter), or any number of third-party products. Once the tools generate the basic markup, you can go in and fine-tune the XAML definitions if necessary.

While tools can generate a good deal of XAML on your behalf, it is important for you to understand the basic workings of XAML syntax and how this markup is eventually transformed into a valid .NET assembly. To illustrate the basics of XAML syntax, our next example will implement the previous WPF application using nothing more than a pair of *.xaml files.

Defining MainWindow in XAML

Currently, our MainWindow has been defined in C# as a class type that extends the System.Windows. Window base class. This class contains a single Button type that calls a registered event handler when clicked. Defining this same Window type in the grammar of XAML can be achieved as so (assume this markup has been defined in a MainWindow.xaml file):

```
<!-- Here is our Window definition -->
<Window x:Class="SimpleXamlApp.MainWindow"
  xmlns="http://schemas.microsoft.com/winfx/2006/xaml/presentation"
  xmlns:x="http://schemas.microsoft.com/winfx/2006/xaml"
  Title="My Xaml App" Height="200" Width="300"
  WindowStartupLocation ="CenterScreen">

  <!--Define our button content -->
  <Button Width="133" Height="24" Name="btnExitApp" Click ="btnExitApp_Clicked">
    Exit Application
  </Button>

  <!--The implementation of our button's Click event handler! -->
  <x:Code>
  <![CDATA[
  private void btnExitApp_Clicked(object sender, RoutedEventArgs e)
  {
    // Get a handle to the current app and shut it down.
    Application.Current.Shutdown();
  }
  ]]>
  </x:Code>
</Window>
```

First of all, notice that the root element, <Window>, defines the name of the derived type via the Class attribute. The x prefix is used to denote that this attribute is defined within the XAML-centric XML namespace, http://schemas.microsoft.com/winfx/2006/xaml (the other XML namespace defines the WPF types themselves). Within the scope of the opening <Window> element we have specified values for the Title, Height, Width, and WindowStartupLocation attributes, which as you can see are a direct mapping to properties of the same name supported by the System.Windows. Window type.

Next up, notice that within the scope of the window's definition, we have authored markup to describe the look and feel of the Button instance, which will be used to set the Content property of the window because it is the value of the Window XML element. Beyond setting up the variable name and its overall dimensions, we have also handled the Click event by assigning the method to delegate to when the Click event occurs.

The final aspect of this XAML file is the <Code> element, which (not too surprisingly) allows us to author event handlers and other methods of this class directly within a *.xaml file. As a safety measure, the code itself is wrapped within a CDATA scope, to prevent XML parsers from attempting to directly interpret the data (although this is not strictly required for the current example). Notice that our method implementation is identical to the previous C# class, in that we are referencing the current Application-derived object to terminate program.

It is important to point out that authoring functionality within a <Code> element is not necessarily recommended. Although this "single file approach" isolates all the action to one location, the current Visual Studio 2005 "Orcas" XAML designer complains vehemently when processing *.xaml files containing <Code> elements. Worse, inline code does not provide us with a clear separation of concerns between markup and logic. In most WPF applications, "real code" will be found within an associated partial C# class (which we will do eventually).

Defining the Application Object in XAML

Remember that XAML can be used to define in markup any nonabstract .NET class that supports a default constructor. Given this, we could most certainly define our application object in markup as well. Consider the following content within a new file, MyApp.xaml:

```
<!-- The main method seems to be missing!
     However, the StartupUri attribute is the
     functional equivalent -->
<Application x:Class="SimpleXamlApp.MyApp"
  xmlns="http://schemas.microsoft.com/winfx/2006/xaml/presentation"
  xmlns:x="http://schemas.microsoft.com/winfx/2006/xaml"
  StartupUri="MainWindow.xaml"
  >
</Application>
```

Here, you might agree, the mapping between the Application-derived C# class type and its XAML description is not as clear-cut as was the case for our MainWindow's XAML definition. Specifically, there does not seem to be any trace of a Main() method. Given that any .NET executable must have a program entry point, you are correct to assume it is generated at compile time, based in part on the StartupUrl property. The assigned *.xaml file will be used to determine which Window-derived class to create when this application starts up.

Although the Main() method is automatically created at compile time, we are free to using the <Code> element to establish our Exit event handler if we so choose, as follows (notice this method is no longer static, as it will be translated into an instance-level member in the MyApp class):

```
<Application x:Class="SimpleXamlApp.MyApp"
  xmlns="http://schemas.microsoft.com/winfx/2006/xaml/presentation"
  xmlns:x="http://schemas.microsoft.com/winfx/2006/xaml"
  StartupUri="MainWindow.xaml" Exit ="AppExit">
  <x:Code>
  <![CDATA[
  private void AppExit(object sender, ExitEventArgs e)
  {
    MessageBox.Show("App has exited");
  }
  ]]>
  </x:Code>
</Application>
```

Processing the XAML Files via msbuild.exe

At this point, we are ready to transform our markup into a valid .NET assembly. When doing so, we cannot make direct use of the C# compiler and a response file. To date, the C# compiler does not have a direct understanding of XAML markup. However, the msbuild.exe command-line utility does understand how to transform XAML into C# code and compile this code on the fly when it is informed of the correct *.targets files.

msbuild.exe is a tool that allows you to define complex build scripts via (surprise, surprise) XML. One interesting aspect of these XML definitions is that they are the same format as Visual Studio 2005 *.csproj files. Given this, we are able to define a single file for automated command-line builds as well as a Visual Studio 2005 project. Consider the following file, SimpleXamlApp.csproj:

```
<Project DefaultTargets="Build"
  xmlns="http://schemas.microsoft.com/developer/msbuild/2003">
  <PropertyGroup>
    <RootNamespace>SimpleXamlApp</RootNamespace>
    <AssemblyName>SimpleXamlApp</AssemblyName>
    <OutputType>winexe</OutputType>
  </PropertyGroup>
  <ItemGroup>
    <Reference Include="System" />
    <Reference Include="WindowsBase" />
    <Reference Include="PresentationCore" />
    <Reference Include="PresentationFramework" />
  </ItemGroup>
  <ItemGroup>
    <ApplicationDefinition Include="MyApp.xaml" />
    <Page Include="MainWindow.xaml" />
  </ItemGroup>
  <Import Project="$(MSBuildBinPath)\Microsoft.CSharp.targets" />
  <Import Project="$(MSBuildBinPath)\Microsoft.WinFX.targets" />
</Project>
```

Here, the <PropertyGroup> element is used to specify some basic aspects of the build, such as the root namespace, the name of the resulting assembly, and the output type (the equivalent of the /target:winexe option of csc.exe).

The first <ItemGroup> specifies the set of external assemblies to reference with the current build, which as you can see are the core WPF assemblies examined earlier in this chapter. The second <ItemGroup> is much more interesting. Notice that the <ApplicationDefinition> element's Include attribute is assigned to the *.xaml file that defines our application object. The <Page>'s Include element can be used to list each of the remaining *.xaml files that define the windows (and pages, which are often used when building XAML browser applications) processed by the application object.

However, the "magic" of this *.csproj file are the final <Import> subelements. Notice that our build script is referencing two *.targets files, each of which contains numerous other instructions used during the build process. The Microsoft.WinFX.targets file contains the necessary build settings to transform the XAML definitions into equivalent C# code files, while Microsoft.CSharp.Targets contains data to interact with the C# compiler itself.

■**Note** A full examination of the msbuild.exe utility is beyond the scope of this chapter. If you'd like to learn more, perform a search for the topic "MSBuild" using the .NET Framework 2.0 (or 3.0) SDK documentation.

At this point, we can pass our `SimpleXamlApp.csproj` file into `msbuild.exe` for processing:

```
msbuild SimpleXamlApp.csproj
```

Once the build has completed, you should be able to find your assembly within the generated \bin\Debug folder. At this point, you can launch your WPF application as expected. As you may agree, is it quite bizarre to generate valid .NET assemblies by authoring a few lines of markup. However, to be sure, if you open `SimpleXamlApp.exe` in `ildasm.exe`, you can see that (somehow) your XAML has been transmogrified into an executable application (see Figure 27-3).

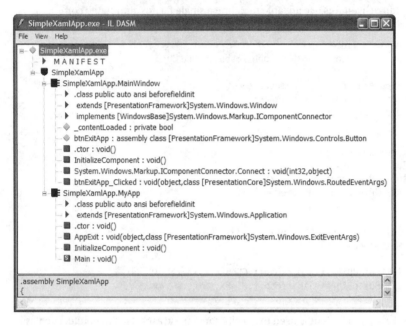

Figure 27-3. *Transforming markup into a .NET assembly? Interesting . . .*

Transforming Markup into a .NET Assembly

To understand exactly how our markup was transformed into a .NET assembly, we need to dig a bit deeper into the `msbuild.exe` process.

Mapping XAML to C# Code

As mentioned, the `*.targets` files specified in an MSBuild script define numerous instructions to translate XAML elements into C# code for compilation. When `msbuild.exe` processed our `*.csproj` file, it produced two files with the form `*.g.cs` (where g denotes auto*generated*), which were saved into the \obj\Debug directory. Based on the names of our `*.xaml` file names, the C# files in question are `MainWindow.g.cs` and `MyApp.g.cs`.

If you open the `MainWindow.g.cs` file, you will find your class extends the `Window` base class and contains the `btnExitApp_Clicked()` method as expected. Also, this class defines a member variable of type `System.Windows.Controls.Button`. Strangely enough, there does *not* appear to be any code that establishes the property settings for the `Button` or `Window` type (`Height`, `Width`, `Title`, etc.). This part of the mystery will become clear in just a moment.

Finally, note that this class defines a private member variable of type Boolean (named _contentLoaded), which was not directly accounted for in the XAML markup. Here is a partial definition of the generated MainWindow type:

```
public partial class MainWindow :
  System.Windows.Window, System.Windows.Markup.IComponentConnector
{
  internal System.Windows.Controls.Button btnExitApp;

  // This member variable will be explained soon enough.
  private bool _contentLoaded;

  private void btnExitApp_Clicked(object sender, RoutedEventArgs e)
  {
    // Get a handle to the current application and shut it down.
    Application.Current.Shutdown();
  }
...
}
```

This Windows-derived class also explicitly implements the WPF IComponentConnector interface defined in the System.Windows.Markup namespace. This interface defines a single method, Connect(), which has been implemented to rig up the event logic as specified within the original MainWindow.xaml file:

```
void System.Windows.Markup.IComponentConnector.Connect(int connectionId,
object target)
{
  switch (connectionId)
  {
  case 1:
    this.btnExitApp = ((System.Windows.Controls.Button)(target));
    this.btnExitApp.Click += new
      System.Windows.RoutedEventHandler(this.btnExitApp_Clicked);
    return;
  }
  this._contentLoaded = true;
}
```

Finally, the MainWindow class also implements a method named InitializeComponent(). This method ultimately resolves the location of an embedded resource within the assembly, given the name of the original *.xaml file. Once the resource is located, it is loaded into the current application object via a call to Application.LoadComponent(). Finally, the private Boolean member variable (mentioned previously) is set to true, to ensure the requested resource is loaded exactly once during the lifetime of this application:

```
public void InitializeComponent() {
  if (_contentLoaded) {
    return;
  }
  _contentLoaded = true;
  System.Uri resourceLocater = new
    System.Uri("/SimpleXamlApp;component/mainwindow.xaml",
    System.UriKind.RelativeOrAbsolute);
  System.Windows.Application.LoadComponent(this, resourceLocater);
}
```

At this point, the question becomes, *What exactly is this embedded resource?*

The Role of BAML

When `msbuild.exe` processed our `*.csproj` file, it generated a file with a `*.baml` file extension, which is named based on the initial `MainWindow.xaml` file. As you might have guessed from the name, Binary Application Markup Language (BAML) is a binary representation of XAML. This `*.baml` file is embedded as a resource (via a generated `*.g.resources` file) into the compiled assembly. Using BAML, WPF assemblies contain within them its complete XAML definition (in a much more compact format). You can verify this for yourself by opening your assembly using Lutz Roeder's .NET Reflector (see Table 2-5 in Chapter 2), as shown in Figure 27-4.

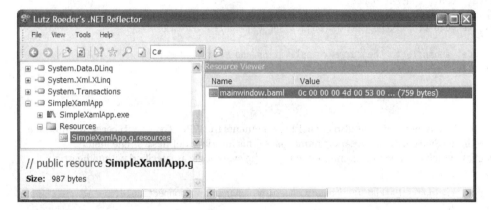

Figure 27-4. *Viewing the embedded* `*.baml` *resource via Lutz Roeder's .NET Reflector*

The call to `Application.LoadComponent()` reads the embedded BAML resource and populates the tree of defined objects with their correct state (again, such as the window's `Height` and `Width` properties). In fact, if you open the `*.baml` or `*.g.resources` file via Visual Studio 2005, you can see traces of the initial XAML attributes. As an example, Figure 27-5 highlights the `StartupLocation.CenterScreen` property.

```
MainWindow.baml                                                        ▾ ✕
00000170  70 3A 2F 2F 73 63 68 65   6D 61 73 2E 6D 69 63 72    p://schemas.micr
00000180  6F 73 6F 66 74 2E 63 6F   6D 2F 77 69 6E 66 78 2F    osoft.com/winfx/
00000190  32 30 30 36 2F 78 61 6D   6C 2F 70 72 65 73 65 6E    2006/xaml/presen
000001a0  74 61 74 69 6F 6E 03 00   01 00 02 00 03 00 35 03    tation........5.
000001b0  00 00 00 03 00 00 00 14   36 01 78 2C 68 74 74 70    ........6.x,http
000001c0  3A 2F 2F 73 63 68 65 6D   61 73 2E 6D 69 63 72 6F    ://schemas.micro
000001d0  73 6F 66 74 2E 63 6F 6D   2F 77 69 6E 66 78 2F 32    soft.com/winfx/2
000001e0  30 30 36 2F 78 61 6D 6C   02 00 01 00 02 00 35 04    006/xaml......5.
000001f0  00 00 00 03 00 00 00 1F   0C 00 00 1D FD 00 05 54    ...............T
00000200  69 74 6C 65 24 11 00 00   0B 4D 79 20 58 61 6D 6C    itle$....My Xaml
00000210  20 41 70 70 99 FD 35 05   00 00 00 03 00 00 00 24     App..5........$
00000220  09 D1 FF 03 32 30 30 A4   FE 36 17 00 00 00 24 09    ....200..6....$.
00000230  C7 FF 03 33 30 30 A4 FE   36 24 00 00 00 1F 1C 01    ...300..6$......
00000240  00 1D FD 00 15 57 69 6E   64 6F 77 53 74 61 72 74    .....WindowStart
00000250  75 70 4C 6F 63 61 74 69   6F 6E 24 12 01 00 0C 43    upLocation$....C
00000260  65 6E 74 65 72 53 63 72   65 65 6E 3D FF 36 30 00    enterScreen=.60.
00000270  00 00 2E F2 FF 35 08 00   00 04 00 00 00 03 C9       .....5..........
00000280  FF 00 2D 01 00 00 00 35   00 00 00 00 00 00 00 00    ..-....5........
00000290  24 10 CA FF 0A 62 74 6E   45 78 6E 74 41 70 70 99    $....btnExitApp.
000002a0  FD 35 08 00 00 00 23 00   00 00 24 09 C7 FF 03 31    .5....#...$....1
000002b0  33 33 A4 FE 36 0B 00 00   00 24 08 D1 FF 02 32 34    33..6....$....24
```

Figure 27-5. *Behold the BAML!*

The final piece of the autogenerated code puzzle occurs in the `MyApp.g.cs` file. Here we see our `Application`-derived class with a proper `Main()` entry point method. The implementation of this method calls `InitializeComponent()` on the `Application`-derived type, which in turn sets the `StartupUri` property, allowing each of the objects to establish its correct property settings based on the binary XAML definition.

```
namespace SimpleXamlApp
{
  public partial class MyApp : System.Windows.Application
  {
    void AppExit(object sender, ExitEventArgs e)
    {
      MessageBox.Show("App has exited");
    }

    [System.Diagnostics.DebuggerNonUserCodeAttribute()]
    public void InitializeComponent() {
      this.Exit += new System.Windows.ExitEventHandler(this.AppExit);
      this.StartupUri = new System.Uri("MainWindow.xaml", System.UriKind.Relative);
    }

    [System.STAThreadAttribute()]
    [System.Diagnostics.DebuggerNonUserCodeAttribute()]
    public static void Main() {
      SimpleXamlApp.MyApp app = new SimpleXamlApp.MyApp();
      app.InitializeComponent();
      app.Run();
    }
  }
}
```

XAML-to-Assembly Process Summary

Whew! So, at this point we have created a full-blown .NET assembly using nothing but three XML documents (one of which was used by the `msbuild.exe` utility). As you have seen, `msbuild.exe` leverages auxiliary settings defined within the `*.targets` file to process the XAML files (and generate the `*.baml`) for the build process. While these gory details happen behind the scenes, Figure 27-6 illustrates the overall picture regarding the compile-time processing of `*.xaml` files.

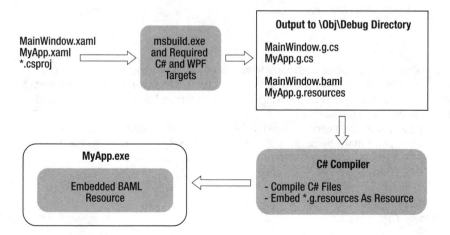

Figure 27-6. *The XAML-to-assembly compile-time process*

Separation of Concerns Using Code-Behind Files

Before we truly begin digging into the details of how to use XAML to build rich user interfaces, we have one final aspect of the basic programming model to address: the separation of concerns. Recall that one of the major motivations for WPF was to separate UI content from programmer logic, which our current examples have not done.

Rather than directly embedding our event handlers (and other custom methods) within the scope of the XAML <Code> element, it is preferable to define a separate C# file to define the implementation logic, leaving the *.xaml files to contain nothing but UI markup content. Assume the following code-behind file, MainWindow.xaml.cs (by convention, the name of a C# code-behind file takes the form *.xaml.cs):

```
// MainWindow.xaml.cs
using System;
using System.Windows;
using System.Windows.Controls;

namespace SimpleXamlApp
{
  public partial class MainWindow : Window
  {
    public MainWindow()
    {
      // Remember!  This method is defined
      // within the generated MainWindow.g.cs file.
      InitializeComponent();
    }

    private void btnExitApp_Clicked(object sender, RoutedEventArgs e)
    {
      // Get a handle to the current application and shut it down.
      Application.Current.Shutdown();
    }
  }
}
```

Here, we have defined a partial class (to contain the event handling logic) that will be merged with the partial class definition of the same type in the *.g.cs file. Given that InitializeComponent() is defined within the MainWindow.g.cs file, our window's constructor makes a call in order to load and process the embedded BAML resource.

If desired, we could also build a code-behind file for our Application-derived type. Given that most of the action takes place in the MyApp.g.cs file, the code within MyApp.xaml.cs is little more than the following:

```
// MyApp.xaml.cs
using System;
using System.Windows;
using System.Windows.Controls;
```

```
namespace SimpleXamlApp
{
  public partial class MyApp : Application
  {
    private void AppExit(object sender, ExitEventArgs e)
    {
      MessageBox.Show("App has exited");
    }
  }
}
```

Before we recompile our files using msbuild.exe, we need to update our *.csproj file to account for the new C# files to include in the compilation process, via the <Compile> elements (shown in bold):

```
<Project DefaultTargets="Build" xmlns=
  "http://schemas.microsoft.com/developer/msbuild/2003">
  <PropertyGroup>
    <RootNamespace>SimpleXamlApp</RootNamespace>
    <AssemblyName>SimpleXamlApp</AssemblyName>
    <OutputType>winexe</OutputType>
  </PropertyGroup>
  <ItemGroup>
    <Reference Include="System" />
    <Reference Include="WindowsBase" />
    <Reference Include="PresentationCore" />
    <Reference Include="PresentationFramework" />
  </ItemGroup>
  <ItemGroup>
    <ApplicationDefinition Include="MyApp.xaml" />
    <Compile Include = "MainWindow.xaml.cs" />
    <Compile Include = "MyApp.xaml.cs" />
    <Page Include="MainWindow.xaml" />
  </ItemGroup>
  <Import Project="$(MSBuildBinPath)\Microsoft.CSharp.targets" />
  <Import Project="$(MSBuildBinPath)\Microsoft.WinFX.targets" />
</Project>
```

Once we pass our build script into msbuild.exe, we find once again the same executable assembly. However, as far as development is concerned, we now have a clean partition of presentation (XAML) from programming logic (C#). Given that this is the preferred method for WPF development, you'll be happy to know that WPF applications created using Visual Studio 2005 "Orcas" always makes use of the code-behind model just presented.

■**Source Code** The CodeBehindXamlApp project can be found under the Chapter 27 subdirectory.

Experimenting with XAML Using XamlPad

Now that you have a better understanding of how XAML eventually results in a .NET assembly, you can begin to build WPF applications through markup. When you are exploring XAML, you will certainly want to author content and quickly see the end result. To facilitate such exploration, the .NET

Framework 3.0 SDK ships with the XamlPad.exe tool. You can launch this tool via the Start ➤ All Programs ➤ Microsoft Windows SDK ➤ Tools menu option. Figure 27-7 shows XamlPad processing markup for a simple animation.

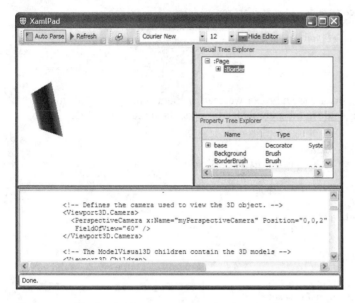

Figure 27-7. *XamlPad provides real-time display of XAML markup.*

Using XamlPad, you are able to author XAML markup in the pane mounted at the bottom of the window. When you first start this tool, you will find little more than an empty <Page> declaration (rather than the <Window> declaration we have seen up until this point):

```
<Page
  xmlns="http://schemas.microsoft.com/winfx/2006/xaml/presentation"
  xmlns:x="http://schemas.microsoft.com/winfx/2006/xaml">
  <Grid>
    <!-- Add your XAML here! -->
  </Grid>
</Page>
```

Recall that WPF supports XAML Browser Applications (XBAPs), which define their markup within a <Page> scope (rather than <Window>). Although XamlPad does not allow you to define a <Window> element without error, the data within the <Page> and <Window> elements make use of identical markup, so you can easily author content for a desktop application via XamlPad and copy the XAML into your <Window> definitions.

■Note XamlPad does not allow you to handle events using the <Code> element, as this requires code compilation (which XamlPad currently cannot do).

As you are authoring markup with XamlPad, you will notice a lack of IntelliSense. However, clicking the Show Visual Tree button opens a UI that mimics the Visual Studio 2005 Properties window to help you visualize the structure of your XAML markup. Sadly, the Visual Tree window cannot (currently) be used change the XAML itself; it is a read-only view of the XAML markup.

Also be aware that XamlPad currently has no way in which you can save individual *.xaml files. Your markup is automatically saved to C:\Program Files\Microsoft SDKs\Windows\v6.0\bin\ XamlPad_Saved.xaml and will be displayed the next time you load the tool. However, as you might guess, you can copy the markup and paste it into your current application.

Building a WPF Application Using Visual Studio 2005 "Orcas"

If you have installed the Visual Studio 2005 "Orcas" Community Technology Preview (see Chapter 26), you can also build WPF applications using Visual Studio 2005. At the time of this writing, the Visual Studio 2005 "Orcas" preview has limited designer support for building WPF GUIs. While you can drag controls onto the designer and configure their XAML attributes using the Properties window, there is currently no support for handling events at design time. Thus, you will need to do so manually using the techniques discussed earlier in this chapter.

Once you open the New Project dialog, you will see a new project category named .NET Framework 3.0 under the Visual C# node, which provides a set of project templates. Assuming you have created a Windows Application (WPF) project, you will find a *.xaml and corresponding code-behind file for the initial window object as well as the application object. If you take a peek at each XAML file and the related code-behind file, you will notice it is more or less the same code base as in the previous CodeBehindXamlApp project.

When you open a *.xaml file (via Solution Explorer), you activate the integrated XAML designer, as shown in Figure 27-8.

Figure 27-8. *The Visual Studio 2005 "Orcas" XAML editor*

Given that the overall process of designing a WPF application is similar to that of a Windows Forms application, I'll assume you are able to dig into the designer tools as you see fit.

■**Note** Remember that the current preview edition of Visual Studio 2005 "Orcas" has no support for handling events at design time. You will be required to add the XAML event declaration and event handler in your code-behind file or entirely in code (using standard C# event registration syntax) within the code file.

Generating XAML Using Microsoft Expression Interactive Designer

While XamlPad.exe is fine for exploring the basics of XAML markup definitions, it is certainly not user-friendly, and it offers very little in the way of productivity. More limiting, XamlPad.exe requires you to already know the correct formatting of the XAML you are authoring. Given these points, it should be clear that graphic designers would be less than enthusiastic if they were told to build a feature-rich UI using this approach.

On a related note, while Visual Studio 2005 "Orcas" does provide a basic XAML editor, Intelli-Sense, and use of some (currently limited) graphic designers, it would be unrealistic to assume nonprogrammers (such as a member of a graphic design team) would feel comfortable using this tool to build front ends.

Given the fact that a major benefit of WPF is a separation of concerns, Microsoft has created a new product lineup that falls under the *Microsoft Expression* nameplate. To date, Microsoft has three different Expression products, all of which are available for free download during their beta cycle from http://www.microsoft.com/products/expression.

The Interactive Designer product is most useful for those interested in WPF, as this tool allows graphic design–minded individuals (typically *not* software developers) to design WPF GUIs in a fashion similar to that of Adobe Photoshop. Once users have completed their design, they can export the design to (surprise, surprise) a XAML file, which can be imported into Visual Studio 2005. To be sure, this approach makes the whole idea of separation of concerns much more than a programming model—it provides a clean way for the graphic design and development teams to collaborate during the construction of WPF application.

I recommend that you download the Microsoft Expression Interactive Designer CTP and take it out for a spin. While this chapter does not provide any real coverage on how to use this tool, be aware that the product ships with a number of samples, templates, and tutorials to get you started. Figure 27-9 shows one such project template.

For the remainder of this chapter, I'll leave it up to you to determine which WPF development technique you'd like to make use of (your text editor of choice and MSBuild, XamlPad, Visual Studio 2005 "Orcas," and/or Microsoft Expression Interactive Designer).

In any case, now that you have a better understanding of the WPF programming model and the tools you have at your disposal, let's turn our attention to working with panels.

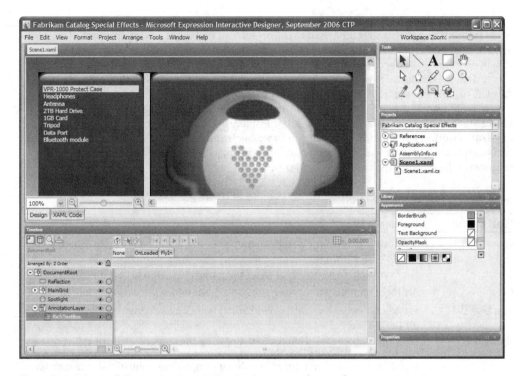

Figure 27-9. *Microsoft Expression Interactive Designer sample template*

Controlling Content Layout Using Panels

A WPF application invariability contains a good number of UI elements (user input controls, graphical content, menu systems, status bars, etc.). As you already observed firsthand during the first example in this chapter, when you place content within a window that does *not* make use of panels, it is positioned dead center within the container. Furthermore, if you attempt to place multiple elements directly within a window, you will receive markup and/or compile-time errors. As you have seen, the reason for these errors is that a window (or any descendant of ContentControl) can assign only a single object to its Content property:

```
<!-- Error! Content property is set more than once!-->
<Window x:Class="MyWPFApp.MainWindow"
  xmlns="http://schemas.microsoft.com/winfx/2006/xaml/presentation"
  xmlns:x="http://schemas.microsoft.com/winfx/2006/xaml"
  Title="Fun with Panels!" Height="285" Width="325">

  <Label Name="lblInstructions"
        Width="328" Height="27" FontSize="15">Enter Car Information</Label>

  <Button Name="btnOK" Width="80">OK</Button>

</Window>
```

When a window needs to contain multiple elements, they must be arranged within any number of panels. The panel itself is then used as the object assigned to the Content property. The System.Windows.Controls namespace provides numerous panel types, each of which controls how subelements are positioned. Using panels, you can establish how the widgets behave when the end user resizes the window, if they remain exactly where placed at design time, if they reflow horizontally left-to-right or vertically top-to-bottom, and so forth.

To build complex user interfaces, panel controls can be intermixed (e.g., a DockPanel that contains a StackPanel) to provide for a great deal of flexibility and control. Furthermore, the panel types often work in conjunction with other controls (such as the ViewBox, TextBlock, TextFlow, and Paragraph types) to further customize how content is arranged within a given panel. Table 27-6 documents the role of some core WPF panel controls.

Table 27-6. *Core WPF Panel Controls*

Panel Control	Meaning in Life
Canvas	Provides a "classic" mode of content placement. Items stay exactly where you put them at design time.
DockPanel	Locks content to a specified side of the panel (Top, Bottom, Left, or Right).
Grid	Arranges content within a series of cells, maintained within a tabular grid.
StackPanel	Stacks content in a vertical or horizontal manner, as dictated by the Orientation property.
WrapPanel	Positions content from left to right, breaking the content to the next line at the edge of the containing box. Subsequent ordering happens sequentially from top to bottom or from right to left, depending on the value of the Orientation property.

To illustrate the use of these panel types, in the next sections we'll build the following UI (Figure 27-10) within various panels and observe how the positioning changes when the window is resized.

Figure 27-10. *Our target user interface*

Positioning Content Within Canvas Panels

By far and away, the simplest panel is Canvas. Most likely, Canvas is the panel you will feel most at home with, as it emulates the default layout of a Windows Forms application. Simply put, a Canvas panel allows for absolute positioning of UI content. If the end user resizes the window to an area that is smaller than the layout maintained by the Canvas panel, the content will not be displayed until the container is stretched to a size equal to or larger than the Canvas area.

To add content to a Canvas, define the required subelements within the scope of the opening <Canvas> and closing </Canvas> tags. If you wish to have the Canvas stretch over the entire surface of the container, simply omit the Height and Width properties. Consider the following XAML markup, which defines the layout shown in Figure 27-10:

```xml
<Window x:Class="MyWPFApp.MainWindow"
  xmlns="http://schemas.microsoft.com/winfx/2006/xaml/presentation"
  xmlns:x="http://schemas.microsoft.com/winfx/2006/xaml"
  Title="Fun with Panels!" Height="285" Width="325">

  <Canvas Background="LightSteelBlue">
    <Button Canvas.Left="212" Canvas.Top="203" Name="btnOK" Width="80">OK</Button>
    <Label Canvas.Left="17" Canvas.Top="14" Name="lblInstructions"
          Width="328" Height="27" FontSize="15">Enter Car Information</Label>
    <Label Canvas.Left="17" Canvas.Top="60" Name="lblMake">Make</Label>
    <TextBox Canvas.Left="94" Canvas.Top="60" Name="txtMake"
          Width="193" Height="25"/>
    <Label Canvas.Left="17" Canvas.Top="109" Name="lblColor">Color</Label>
    <TextBox Canvas.Left="94" Canvas.Top="107" Name="txtColor"
          Width="193" Height="25"/>
    <Label Canvas.Left="17" Canvas.Top="155" Name="lblPetName">Pet Name</Label>
    <TextBox Canvas.Left="94" Canvas.Top="153" Name="txtPetName"
          Width="193" Height="25"/>
  </Canvas>

</Window>
```

Here, each item within the <Canvas> scope is qualified by a Canvas.Left and Canvas.Top value, which control the content's top-left positioning within the panel, using *attached property syntax* (fully explained during our examination of WPF controls). As you may have gathered, vertical positioning is controlled using the Top or Bottom property, while horizontal positioning is established using Left or Right.

Given that each widget has been placed within the <Canvas> element, we find that as the window is resized, widgets are covered up if the container's surface area is smaller than the content (Figure 27-11).

Figure 27-11. *Content in a* Canvas *panel allows for absolute positioning.*

The order you declare content within a Canvas is not used to calculate placement, as this is based on the control's size and the Canvas.Top, Canvas.Bottom, Canvas.Left, and Canvas.Right properties. Given this, the following markup (that groups together like-minded controls) results in an identical rendering:

```
<Canvas Background="LightSteelBlue">
  <TextBox Canvas.Left="94" Canvas.Top="153" Name="txtColor"
          Width="193" Height="25"/>
  <TextBox Canvas.Left="94" Canvas.Top="60" Name="txtPetName"
          Width="193" Height="25"/>
  <TextBox Canvas.Left="94" Canvas.Top="107" Name="txtMake"
          Width="193" Height="25"/>

  <Label Canvas.Left="17" Canvas.Top="14" Name="lblInstructions"
   Width="328" Height="27" FontSize="15">Enter Car Information</Label>
  <Label Canvas.Left="17" Canvas.Top="109" Name="lblColor">Color</Label>
  <Label Canvas.Left="17" Canvas.Top="155" Name="lblMake">Pet Name</Label>
  <Label Canvas.Left="17" Canvas.Top="60" Name="lblPetName">Make</Label>

  <Button Canvas.Left="212" Canvas.Top="203" Name="btnOK" Width="80">OK</Button>
</Canvas>
```

■**Note** If subelements within a Canvas do not define a specific location using attached property syntax, they automatically attach to the upper-left corner of the Canvas.

Although using the Canvas type may seem like a preferable way to arrange content (because it feels so familiar), it does suffer from some limitations. First of all, items within a Canvas do not dynamically resize themselves when applying styles (e.g., their font sizes are unaffected). The other obvious limitation is that the Canvas will not attempt to keep elements visible when the end user resizes the window to a smaller surface.

Perhaps the best use of the Canvas type is to position graphical content. For example, if you were building a custom image using XAML, you certainly would want the lines, shapes, and text to remain where the user placed them, rather than having them dynamically repositioned as the user resizes the window!

■**Source Code** The SimpleCanvas.xaml file can be found under the Chapter 27 subdirectory.

Positioning Content Within WrapPanel Panels

A WrapPanel allows you to define content that will flow across the panel as the window is resized. When positioning elements in a WrapPanel, you do not specify top, bottom, left, and right docking values as you typically do with the Canvas. However, each subelement is free to define a Height and Width value (among other property values) to control its overall size.

Because content within a WrapPanel does not "dock" to a given side of the panel, the order in which you declare the elements is critical (content is rendered from the first element to the last). Consider the following XAML snippet:

```
<WrapPanel Background="LightSteelBlue">
  <Label Name="lblInstruction"
         Width="328" Height="27" FontSize="15">Enter Car Information</Label>
  <Label Name="lblMake">Make</Label>
  <TextBox Name="txtMake" Width="193" Height="25"/>
  <Label Name="lblColor">Color</Label>
  <TextBox Name="txtColor" Width="193" Height="25"/>
  <Label Name="lblPetName">Pet Name</Label>
  <TextBox Name="txtPetName" Width="193" Height="25"/>
  <Button Name="btnOK" Width="80">OK</Button>
</WrapPanel>
```

When you view this markup, the content will look out of sorts, as it is flowing left to right across the window (see Figure 27-12).

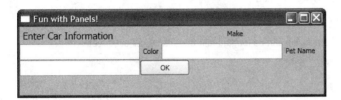

Figure 27-12. *Content in a* WrapPanel *behaves much like a vanilla-flavored HTML page.*

By default, content within a WrapPanel flows left to right. However, if you change the value of the Orientation property to Vertical, you can have content wrap in a top-to-bottom manner:

```
<WrapPanel Background="LightSteelBlue" Orientation ="Vertical">
```

A WrapPanel (as well as some other panel types) may be declared by specifying ItemWidth and ItemHeigth values, which control the default size of each item. If a subelement does provide its own Height and/or Width value, it will be positioned relative to the size established by the panel. Consider the following markup:

```
<WrapPanel Background="LightSteelBlue" ItemWidth ="200" ItemHeight ="30">
  <Label Name="lblInstruction"
         FontSize="15">Enter Car Information</Label>
  <Label Name="lblMake">Make</Label>
  <TextBox Name="txtMake"/>
  <Label Name="lblColor">Color</Label>
  <TextBox Name="txtColor"/>
  <Label Name="lblPetName">Pet Name</Label>
  <TextBox Name="txtPetName"/>
  <Button Name="btnOK" Width ="80">OK</Button>
</WrapPanel>
```

When rendered, we find the output shown in Figure 27-13 (notice the size and position of the Button widget).

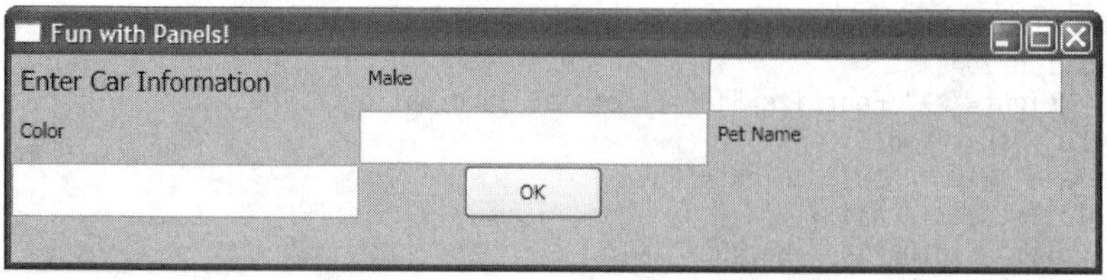

Figure 27-13. *A* WrapPanel *can establish the width and height of a given item.*

As you might agree after looking at Figure 27-13, a WrapPanel is not typically the best choice for arranging content directly in a window, as the elements can become scrambled as the user resizes the window. In most cases, a WrapPanel will be a subelement to another panel type, to allow a small area of the window to wrap its content when resized.

■**Source Code** The SimpleWrapPanel.xaml file can be found under the Chapter 27 subdirectory.

Positioning Content Within StackPanel Panels

A StackPanel control arranges content into a single line that can be oriented horizontally or vertically (the default), based on the value assigned to the Orientation property. For example, the following markup results in the output shown in Figure 27-14:

```
<StackPanel Background="LightSteelBlue">
  <Label Name="lblInstruction"
         FontSize="15">Enter Car Information</Label>
  <Label Name="lblMake">Make</Label>
  <TextBox Name="txtMake"/>
  <Label Name="lblColor">Color</Label>
  <TextBox Name="txtColor"/>
  <Label Name="lblPetName">Pet Name</Label>
  <TextBox Name="txtPetName"/>
  <Button Name="btnOK">OK</Button>
</StackPanel>
```

Figure 27-14. *Vertical stacking of content*

If we assign the Orientation property to Horizontal as follows, the rendered output will match that of Figure 27-15:

```
<StackPanel Background="LightSteelBlue" Orientation ="Horizontal">
```

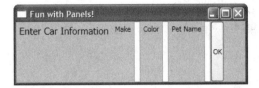

Figure 27-15. *Horizontal stacking of content*

Again, like the WrapPanel, you will seldom want to use a StackPanel to directly arrange content within a window. Rather, a StackPanel is better suited as a subpanel to a master panel.

■**Source Code** The SimpleStackPanel.xaml file can be found under the Chapter 27 subdirectory.

Positioning Content Within Grid Panels

Of all the panels provided with the WPF APIs, Grid is far and away the most flexible. Like an HTML table, the Grid can be carved up into a set of cells, each one of which provides content. When defining a grid, you perform three steps:

1. Define each column in the grid.

2. Define each row in the grid.

3. Assign content to each cell of the grid using attached property syntax.

The first two steps (defining the columns and rows) are achieved by using the <Grid.ColumnDefinitions> and <Grid.RowDefinitions> elements, which contain a collection of <ColumnDefinition> and <RowDefinition> elements, respectively. Because each cell within a grid is indeed a true .NET type, you can configure the look and feel and behavior of each item as you see fit. Here is a rather simple <Grid> definition that arranges our UI content as shown in Figure 27-16:

```
<Grid ShowGridLines ="True" Background ="AliceBlue">
  <!-- Define the rows / columns -->
  <Grid.ColumnDefinitions>
    <ColumnDefinition/>
    <ColumnDefinition/>
  </Grid.ColumnDefinitions>
  <Grid.RowDefinitions>
    <RowDefinition/>
    <RowDefinition/>
  </Grid.RowDefinitions>

  <!-- Now add the elements to the grid's cells-->
  <Label Name="lblInstruction" Grid.Column ="0" Grid.Row ="0"
        FontSize="15">Enter Car Information</Label>
  <Button Name="btnOK"  Height ="30" Grid.Column ="0" Grid.Row ="0" >OK</Button>
  <Label Name="lblMake" Grid.Column ="1" Grid.Row ="0">Make</Label>
```

```
<TextBox Name="txtMake" Grid.Column ="1" Grid.Row ="0" Width="193" Height="25"/>
<Label Name="lblColor" Grid.Column ="0" Grid.Row ="1" >Color</Label>
<TextBox Name="txtColor" Width="193" Height="25" Grid.Column ="0" Grid.Row ="1" />

<!-- Just to keep things interesting, add some color to the pet name cell -->
<Rectangle Fill ="LightGreen" Grid.Column ="1" Grid.Row ="1" />
<Label Name="lblPetName" Grid.Column ="1" Grid.Row ="1" >Pet Name</Label>
<TextBox Name="txtPetName" Grid.Column ="1" Grid.Row ="1"
         Width="193" Height="25"/>
</Grid>
```

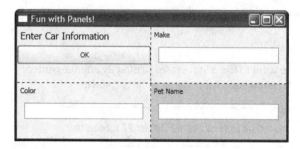

Figure 27-16. *The* Grid *panel in action*

Notice that each element (including a light green Rectangle element, thrown in for good measure) connects itself to a cell in the grid using the Grid.Row and Grid.Column attached properties. By default, the ordering of cells in a grid begins at the upper left, which is specified via Grid.Column = "0" Grid.Row = "0". Given that our grid defines a total of four cells, the bottom right cell can be identified via Grid.Column ="1" Grid.Row ="1".

Source Code The SimpleGrid.xaml file can be found under the Chapter 27 subdirectory.

Positioning Content Within DockPanel Panels

The final type we will examine here is DockPanel, which is typically used as a *master panel* that contains any number of additional panels for grouping of related content. DockPanels make use of attached property syntax as seen with the Canvas type, to control where their upper-left corner (the default) will attach itself within the panel. Here is a very simple DockPanel definition, which results in the output shown in Figure 27-17:

```
<DockPanel LastChildFill ="True">
  <!-- Dock items to the panel -->
  <Label DockPanel.Dock ="Top" Name="lblInstruction"
         FontSize="15">Enter Car Information</Label>
  <Label DockPanel.Dock ="Left" Name="lblMake">Make</Label>
  <Label DockPanel.Dock ="Right" Name="lblColor">Color</Label>
  <Label DockPanel.Dock ="Bottom" Name="lblPetName">Pet Name</Label>
  <Button Name="btnOK">OK</Button>
</DockPanel>
```

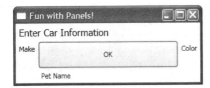

Figure 27-17. *A simple* DockPanel

The benefit of using DockPanel types is that as the user resizes the window, each element remains "connected" to the specified side of the panel (via DockPanel.Dock). Also notice that the opening <DockPanel> element sets the LastChildFill attribute to true. Given that the Button type has not specified any DockPanel.Dock value, it will therefore be stretched within the remaining space.

■**Note** If you add multiple elements to the same side of a DockPanel, they will be stacked along the specified edge in the order that they are declared.

Building a Window's Frame Using Nested Panels

To wrap up our investigation of panels, let's look at one final example that illustrates nested panels. Assume you want to define a UI that establishes a menu system always positioned on the top of the window, a status bar placed on the bottom, a collection of user input elements docked on the left, and some textual (or perhaps graphical) data on the right. In essence, you wish to build the window shown in Figure 27-18.

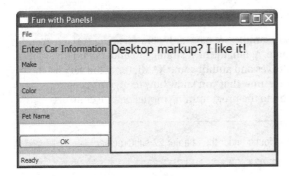

Figure 27-18. *Using nested panels to establish a window's UI*

One possible XAML definition would define an outermost DockPanel that contains a nested StackPanel to contain the UI input elements. Here is the complete markup for this DockPanel type, which also makes use of the <Menu>, <StatusBar>, <Border>, and <TextBlock> elements:

```
<!-- This panel establishes the content for the window -->
<DockPanel LastChildFill ="True">

  <!-- Put a Menu at the top -->
  <Menu DockPanel.Dock ="Top" HorizontalAlignment="Left" Background="White">
    <MenuItem Header="_File">
```

```
      <Separator/>
      <MenuItem Header ="_Exit" />
    </MenuItem>
  </Menu>

  <!-- Put a StatusBar at the bottom -->
  <StatusBar Name="statBar" DockPanel.Dock ="Bottom"
             VerticalAlignment="Bottom" Background="Beige" >
    <StatusBarItem>
      <TextBlock>Ready</TextBlock>
    </StatusBarItem>
  </StatusBar>

  <!-- Put a StackPanel on the left -->
  <StackPanel Background="LightSteelBlue" Orientation ="Vertical"
              DockPanel.Dock ="Left">
    <Label Name="lblInstruction"
            FontSize="15">Enter Car Information</Label>
    <Label Name="lblMake">Make</Label>
    <TextBox Name="txtMake"/>
    <Label Name="lblColor">Color</Label>
    <TextBox Name="txtColor"/>
    <Label Name="lblPetName">Pet Name</Label>
    <TextBox Name="txtPetName"/>
    <Button Name="btnOK">OK</Button>
  </StackPanel>

  <!-- The final area will be a block of text wrapped in a border -->
  <Border BorderThickness ="3" BorderBrush ="DarkRed">
  <TextBlock Background ="LemonChiffon" FontSize ="20">
            Desktop markup?  I like it!</TextBlock>
  </Border>
</DockPanel>
```

Even with this last (slightly more complex) example, we have only scratched the surface regarding the abilities of each panel type examined here. Again, the best strategy to understand the interplay of the panel types is to roll up your sleeves and author some XAML (or at the very least, analyze designer-generated markup). In any case, now that you know how to organize content within logical containers, let's turn our attention to the programming model of WPF controls.

■**Source Code** The `WindowFrame.xaml` file can be found under the Chapter 27 subdirectory.

Understanding WPF Controls

Over the course of many years, developers have been conditioned to see controls as fairly fixed and predictable entities. For example, `Label` widgets always have textual content and seldom have a visible border (although they could). `Buttons` have textual content and may on occasion have an embedded image. When a project demanded that a "standard" widget (such as a `Button`) needed to be customized (such as a `Button` control rendered as a circular image), developers were forced to build a customized control through code.

WPF radically changes the way we look at controls. Not only do we have the option to express a control's look and feel through markup, but also many WPF controls (specifically, any descendant of ContentControl) have been designed to contain any sort of *content* you desire. Thus, rather than assuming that "all Buttons have text and maybe an image," we can describe via XAML the following customized button type:

```
<Button Name="btnClickMe" Height="100" Width = "379">
  <StackPanel Orientation ="Horizontal">
    <Label Height="50">Please Enter Some Text</Label>
    <Canvas Height ="50" Width ="100" >
      <Ellipse Name = "outerEllipse" Fill ="Green" Height ="25"
               Width ="50" Cursor="Hand"
               Canvas.Left="25" Canvas.Top="12"></Ellipse>
      <Ellipse Name = "innerEllipse" Fill ="Yellow" Height = "15" Width ="36"
               Canvas.Top="17" Canvas.Left="32"></Ellipse>
    </Canvas>
    <TextBox Name ="txtUserInput" Height ="25" Width = "100">
      Fancy!
    </TextBox>
  </StackPanel>
</Button>
```

Notice that the <Button> element scope defines a <StackPanel> that arranges the specified subelements in a horizontal fashion. This particular panel contains a Label, two Ellipse controls (placed in a Canvas for absolute positioning), and a TextBox. Furthermore, when the mouse cursor moves over the rendered green oval (but not the yellow oval), it changes to a standard hand cursor. Figure 27-19 shows the rendered output.

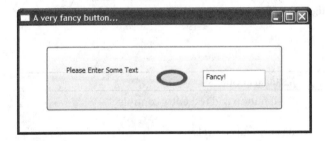

Figure 27-19. *A very fancy button*

By way of a simple compare and contrast, consider how this same control would be built using Windows Forms. Under this API, you could achieve this control only by building a custom Button-derived type that manually handled the rendering of the graphical content, updated the internal controls collection, overrode various event handlers, and so forth.

Given the birth of desktop markup, the only compelling reason to build a custom WPF control using the Custom Control Library (WPF) project template of Visual Studio 2005 "Orcas" is if you need a widget that supports *custom behaviors* (events, overriding of inherited virtual methods, etc.). If you are concerned only with a customized rendering, XAML fits the bill.

Configuring WPF Controls

As you would expect, each WPF control expressed in XAML has its own unique set of attributes that can be specified in the element's opening tag. In the majority of cases, attributes of a XAML element directly map to the properties and events of the control's class representation within the System.Windows.Controls namespace. As such, you always have the option to define a control completely in markup or completely in code, or to use a mix of the two.

If an element has been assigned a Name attribute (such as the Button, Ellipses, and TextBox in the previous example) you can directly access the type in your code file:

```
private void DisplayUserInput()
{
  MessageBox.Show(string.Format("You typed: {0}", txtUserInput.Text));
}
```

This is possible because controls that are given a Name attribute in the XAML definition result in a member variable in the autogenerated *.g.cs file:

```
public partial class MainWindow : System.Windows.Window,
  System.Windows.Markup.IComponentConnector
{
  // Member variables defined based on the XAML markup.
  internal System.Windows.Controls.Button btnClickMe;
  internal System.Windows.Shapes.Ellipse outerEllipse;
  internal System.Windows.Shapes.Ellipse innerEllipse;
  internal System.Windows.Controls.TextBox txtUserInput;
...
}
```

Understand that the purpose of this chapter is not to explain the details of each and every WPF widget, but to explain the overall architecture of WPF itself. Thankfully, the overall functionality of the WPF controls is very similar to that of their Windows Forms counterparts, so you should already feel somewhat comfortable with your choices given your work earlier in this text. Table 27-7 describes many of the built-in WPF widgets, all of which are fully documented within the .NET Framework 3.0 SDK documentation.

Table 27-7. *Sampling of WPF Controls*

Controls	Meaning in Life
Button, RadioButton, RepeatButton, TextBox, and RichTextBox	Push button and text entry controls
ContextMenu, Menu, and Toolbar	Basic menu controls
ComboBox, ListBox, TreeView, CheckBox, and Slider	Controls for list and range selection
Expander, Label, Popup, ProgressBar, StatusBar, and ToolTip	Controls to provide visual information to the user
Frame, ScrollBar, ScrollViewer, TabControl, and Thumb	Controls to allow UI navigation by the end user

Working with WPF Control Properties

As you learned back in Chapter 3, properties are the preferred method of encapsulating data when authoring managed code. In C#, a property can be written quite simply:

```
class Car
{
  private int currSpeed;
  public int Speed
```

```
  {
    get { return currSpeed; }
    set { currSpeed = value; }
  }
}
```

While this property syntax (often called *CLR property syntax*) can be written identically inside a XAML code file, XAML itself has a good number of alternative property formats (such as the attached property syntax seen earlier). The reason for these new flavors of property modeling has to do with the richness we have when using markup as a UI descriptor. As you continue to explore WPF, you will see that the data binding layer, graphics and animation layers, and many other services are greatly simplified using these new methodologies.

The following sections present a brief overview of the various kinds of XAML property syntax.

Dependent Property Syntax

A *dependent property* allows WPF to compute a particular property's value based on other properties. The "other properties" in question could include OS system properties (styles and user preferences), values based on data binding and animation/storyboard logic, resources and styles, or values known through parent/child relationships with other elements. As well, a dependent property can be implemented to provide self-contained validation, default values, callbacks that monitor changes to other properties, and a system that can coerce property values based on potentially runtime information.

As you author XAML (or the equivalent C# code in a code-behind file), you typically are not able to tell that you have set a value to (or received a value from) a dependent property, as these more advanced behaviors have been implemented within the type itself. Therefore, working with the majority of control properties in XAML will simply require you to establish name/value pairs:

```
<!-- A button with FOUR set properties
     placing the string value within the
     button's scope sets the Content property -->
<Button Name="btnClickMe" Height="30" Width = "100">
  Click Me
</Button>
```

Here, the Content value of the Button was indirectly set due to the fact that we have established string data (e.g., "Click Me") within the <Button> XAML scope. If you prefer, you can directly set the Content property as so:

```
<!-- Same output as before -->
<Button Name="btnClickMe" Height="30" Width = "100" Content = "Click Me" />
```

Property-Element Syntax

Some properties on a given control require more than simple string data. Consider for example the Background property of the Brush type. This property can be set on any Brush type found within the WPF APIs. If you simply require a solid brush type, the following markup is all that is required, as the string value assigned to properties requiring a Brush-derived type (such as Background) map directly to a property on the System.Windows.Media.Brushes type:

```
<!-- Here, "Green" maps to Brushes.Green -->
<Button Name="btnClickMe" Height="100" Width = "379" Background ="Green">
  Click Me
</Button>
```

However, if you require a more elaborate brush (such as a LinearGradientBrush), name/value syntax will not suffice. Considering that LinearGradientBrush is a full-blown class type, we need to provide a manner in which we can pass in start-up values to the type (much like passing constructor parameters). For this, we have *property-element syntax*:

```
<Button Name="btnClickMe" Height="100" Width = "379" Content ="Click Me">
  <Button.Background>
    <LinearGradientBrush StartPoint="0,0" EndPoint="1,1">
      <GradientStop Color="Black" Offset="0" />
      <GradientStop Color="Yellow" Offset="0.25" />
      <GradientStop Color="Honeydew" Offset="0.75" />
      <GradientStop Color ="Red" Offset="1" />
    </LinearGradientBrush>
  </Button.Background>
</Button>
```

Here we are using the <Button.Background> (the property) to specify the look and feel of our LinearGradientBrush (the element). As you can see, within the scope of a given widget, we are able to define various subscopes (such as <Button.Background>) to define a complex value setting. Understand that different widgets have unique possible options for their set of property-element syntax. Thankfully, the XAML editor of Visual Studio 2005 provides IntelliSense to show the possibilities.

Attached Property Syntax

You encountered this XAML property form during the examination of the various panel types earlier in the chapter. Using *attached property syntax*, child elements can store unique values of a property that is actually defined in a parent element. For example, consider this XAML definition:

```
<DockPanel>
  <CheckBox DockPanel.Dock="Top">Check me!</CheckBox>
</DockPanel>
```

Here, the child <CheckBox> element is setting the Dock property of its parent element (the DockPanel). This is actually a very helpful simplification, especially when you consider the sort of C# code you would have to author manually:

```
DockPanel myDockPanel = new DockPanel();
CheckBox myCheckBox = new CheckBox();
myCheckBox.Content = "Check Me!";
myDockPanel.Children.Add(myCheckBox);
DockPanel.SetDock(myCheckBox, Dock.Top);
```

In this C# code snippet, the parent type has to define a method with a specific signature: the name of the property prefixed by Set. As you work with XAML, you will surely encounter other unique property formats (including a syntax to reference embedded resources); however, property-element and attached property syntax are two of the most common.

Handling WPF Control Events

Like Windows Forms controls, WPF controls provide a series of events you can handle in your code-behind files (or within a <Code> scope of a XAML file). As you have already seen, it is possible to handle an event using standard C# event syntax, as well as using method group conversion and anonymous methods. Furthermore, when you are building your UI via XAML, you are afforded another simplification in that a given event attribute will instruct the build engine to author the delegate logic on your behalf within the related *.g.cs file. Given this, the most straightforward to handle the Click event for the previous Button is to define the following XAML:

```
<Button Name="btnClickMe" Height="100" Width = "379" Click ="btnClickMe_Clicked">
  <StackPanel Orientation ="Horizontal">
    <Label Height="50">Please Enter Some Text</Label>
    <Canvas Height ="50" Width ="100" >
      <Ellipse Name = "outerEllipse" Fill ="Green" Height ="25"
               Width ="50" Cursor="Hand"
               Canvas.Left="25" Canvas.Top="12"/>
      <Ellipse Name = "innerEllipse" Fill ="Yellow" Height = "15" Width ="36"
               Canvas.Top="17" Canvas.Left="32/">
    </Canvas>
    <TextBox Name ="txtUserInput" Height ="25" Width = "100">
      Fancy!
    </TextBox>
  </StackPanel>
</Button>
```

and update your code-behind file with the following handler:

```
public void btnClickMe_Clicked(object sender, RoutedEventArgs e)
{
  // Do something when button is clicked.
  MessageBox.Show("Clicked the button");
}
```

While the process of handling an event should look very familiar, we do need to address the role of a routed event. Consider again the composition of the previous Button. It contains six nested elements to fully represent the user interface (Canvas, Label, etc.). Now imagine how painful WPF event handling would be if we were forced to handle a Click event for each and every one of these subelements. After all, the end user could click anywhere within the scope of the button's boundaries (on the Label, on the green area of the oval, on the surface of the button, etc.). Under a Windows Forms model, a custom control such as this would require us to handle the Click event for each item on the button. Thankfully, *routed events* take care of this automatically.

Simply put, the routed events model automatically propagates an event up the tree of an object, beginning at the control that received the event and going all the way up to the starting element of the root of the defining element. For example, if the user clicks the yellow oval, the Click event is passed to the <Canvas>, then to the <Label>, then to the <StackPanel>, and finally to the <Button>. Given that our Button is the entity in the tree that handles Click, we are indeed able to have a single handler in our code file to account for the possibility of clicking on any part of the Button type.

However, if you wished to perform custom click logic for a subitem in the tree, you can do so. By way of illustration, assume you need to process a Click event for the outerEllipse control in a unique manner. First, simply handle the MouseDown event for this subelement as expected:

```
<Button Name="btnClickMe" Height="100" Width = "379" Click ="btnClickMe_Clicked">
  <StackPanel Orientation ="Horizontal">
  ...
  <Ellipse Name = "outerEllipse" Fill ="Green" Height ="25"
           Width ="50" Cursor="Hand" Canvas.Left="25" Canvas.Top="12"
           MouseDown ="outerEllipse_MouseDown"/>
  ...
  </StackPanel>
</Button>
```

Then add an appropriate event handler:

```
public void outerEllipse_MouseDown(object sender, RoutedEventArgs e)
{
  // Do something when outer ellipse is clicked.
  MessageBox.Show("Clicked the outer ellipse!");
}
```

As you can see, routed events make it possible to allow a complex group of content to act either as a single logical element (e.g., a Button) or as discrete items (e.g., an Ellipse within the button).

Strictly speaking, routed events can be *bubbling* (as just described) or *tunneling* in nature. Tunneling events (which all begin with the Preview suffix—e.g., PreviewMouseDown) drill down from the outermost element to the originator, while bubbling events drill up from the originator to the outermost element.

By and large, you can ignore a control's tunneling event set. However, one time when this can be helpful is when you wish to prevent an event from being propagated through the control tree, by setting the Handled property of the RoutedEventArgs parameter to false. Look up the topic "Routed Events" within the .NET Framework 3.0 SDK documentation for further details.

Applying Control Styles

ASP.NET 2.0 introduced the concept of server-side themes, which are a new spin on the long-standing use of style sheets. Using ASP.NET themes, it is very simple to apply a common look and feel to elements on a web page. Windows Forms did not (and currently does not) support a similar feature. Thus, under Windows Forms, when you want ensure that the color for all labels on a given window has a similar look and feel, you are required to set the BackColor property for each and every Label maintained by the Form-derived type (or build a custom control). This approach certainly makes it very difficult to make changes down the road, as you need to reset the same set of properties with each change. While you could take this same approach when building a WPF application, you will be happy to find that the ASP.NET-like theme ability is now available to desktop developers.

Earlier in this chapter, you were briefly introduced to the Control base class. Any descendent of Control has the ability to support styles, including, of course, the window itself. When you wish to author a style, one possible approach is to make use of *property-element syntax* that allows you to assign a style inline. Consider the following XAML definition, which establishes a custom style for a button named btnClickMe (but not btnClickMeToo):

```
<Window x:Class="MyWPFApp.MainWindow"
    xmlns="http://schemas.microsoft.com/winfx/2006/xaml/presentation"
    xmlns:x="http://schemas.microsoft.com/winfx/2006/xaml"
    Title="Fun with Controls!" Height="235" Width="451">
  <StackPanel>
    <Button Name="btnClickMe" Height="80" Width = "100" Content ="Click Me">
      <Button.Style>
        <Style>
        <Setter Property ="Button.FontSize" Value ="20"/>
        <Setter Property ="Button.Background">
          <Setter.Value>
            <LinearGradientBrush StartPoint="0,0" EndPoint="1,1">
              <GradientStop Color="Black" Offset="0" />
              <GradientStop Color="Yellow" Offset="0.25" />
              <GradientStop Color="Honeydew" Offset="0.75" />
              <GradientStop Color ="Red" Offset="1" />
            </LinearGradientBrush>
          </Setter.Value>
```

```
        </Setter>
      </Style>
    </Button.Style>
  </Button>

  <!-- No style for this button! -->
  <Button Name="btnClickMeToo" Height="80" Width = "100" Content ="Me Too"/>
  </StackPanel>
</Window>
```

Notice that the style defines what values will be set to properties of the themed element through a set of property name/value pairs using the <Setter> element syntax. Here we have established a font size and background for the btnClickMe Button type. The background is defined using a LinearGradientBrush type that is composed of four interconnected colors.

While this approach to building a style is syntactically correct, one obvious limitation is the fact that the style is bound to this particular Button instance, not each button on the hosting window. In Figure 27-20, notice that the second Button type, btnClickMeToo, is unaffected by the style assigned to btnClickMe.

Figure 27-20. *Inline styles are bound to the control that defined them.*

To define a style that can be used by any UI element, you typically don't make use of inline styles as shown here. Rather, you define the style through XAML and add it into a global dictionary called Resources. Note that you identify it with a name given through the Key property. That way, you define a named theme that can be referenced everywhere in your XAML by using its name. Technically speaking, this is termed a *named style*, as you define and reference it using a defined key:

```
<Window x:Class="MyWPFApp.MainWindow"
    xmlns="http://schemas.microsoft.com/winfx/2006/xaml/presentation"
    xmlns:x="http://schemas.microsoft.com/winfx/2006/xaml"
    Title="Fun with Controls!" Height="223" Width="238">

  <Window.Resources>
    <Style x:Key ="MyFunkyTheme">
      <Setter Property ="Button.FontSize" Value ="20"/>
      <Setter Property ="Button.Background">
        <Setter.Value>
          <LinearGradientBrush StartPoint="0,0" EndPoint="1,1">
            <GradientStop Color="Black" Offset="0" />
            <GradientStop Color="Yellow" Offset="0.25" />
            <GradientStop Color="Honeydew" Offset="0.75" />
            <GradientStop Color ="Red" Offset="1" />
          </LinearGradientBrush>
        </Setter.Value>
```

```
      </Setter>
    </Style>
  </Window.Resources>

  <StackPanel>
    <Button Name="btnClickMe" Height="80" Width = "100"
            Style ="{StaticResource MyFunkyTheme}" Content = "Click Me"/>
    <Button Name="btnClickMeToo" Height="80" Width = "100"
            Style ="{StaticResource MyFunkyTheme}" Content = "Me Too"/>
  </StackPanel>
</Window>
```

This time, note that the style has been defined within the scope of a `<Windows.Resources>` element and has been identified by the name `MyFunkyTheme` via the `Key` attribute. Beyond these points, the style declaration itself is identical to the previous XAML definition.

Also notice that when we want to access a style (as we do within the `<Button>` definitions), we do so using yet another special property syntax. Here the curly brackets are used to establish that we are looking for dictionary entry (via the `StaticResource` token) named according to the defined key (`MyFunkyTheme`). With this update, each button takes on the correct look and feel, as shown in Figure 27-21.

Figure 27-21. *Named themes are embedded as an assembly resource.*

Source Code The `NamedTheme.xaml` file can be found under the Chapter 27 subdirectory.

Introducing WPF Graphical Rendering Services

We'll now examine the new graphical rendering services provided by WPF. As you saw in Chapter 20, GDI+ is a graphical manipulation library that has been part of the .NET base class libraries since version 1.0. Recall that when you wish to render graphical output, your first step is to obtain a `System.Drawing.Graphics` type, typically by handling the `Paint` event of a given control or Form. After this point, you may call any number of methods on the `Graphics` type, passing in icons, bitmaps, pens, and brushes as arguments.

WPF takes a radically different approach. While it is the case that WPF provides namespaces to allow you to directly author C# code to render graphics, it is also possible (and in many cases easier) to do so using XAML. Regardless of your approach, WPF's graphical services provide support for multimedia, vector graphics, animation, and content composition.

WPF's rendering libraries are far more than "just another graphics toolkit." Beyond the fact that WPF blends together a number of graphics technologies under a common API, WPF provides several (major) benefits over the toolkits that preceded it:

- WPF uses device-independent "pixels" to enable screen resolution and device independence that automatically scale with the system's DPI setting.

- WPF graphical elements are true-blue objects, and they can be programmed as such (e.g., they can handle events for mouse activity).

- The WPF rendering engine utilizes DirectX, which can increase overall performance.

- WPF has integrated support for 2D and 3D graphics, as well as a complete animation API.

- WPF has integrated support for audio playback.

The first point in the preceding list may seem like a small feature, but the notion of a "device-independent pixel" (which is 1/96 of an inch in size) makes it possible to define graphics and text that automatically scale as users change their screen resolution and/or DPI settings. Achieving such a feat under GDI+ required a good deal of manual labor. Under WPF, this behavior is available out of the box (provided your content has not been placed within a Canvas, which as you may recall does *not* automatically scale its content).

It is also important to note that the ability to render graphical content is baked directly into the WPF object model. Thus, rather than having to handle a particular event to obtain a "graphics object," we simply author XAML that represents the graphical data. Using this approach, WPF allows us to treat graphical content in a truly object-oriented manner. If, for example, you were to generate a XAML description of a 3D circle and provide the user a way to change the background color, the 3D circle simply updates its state and renders out the new UI. This is another major change from GDI+, where programmers were forced to invalidate a control or surface area to force the widget to redraw itself.

■**Note** Like every other aspect of WPF, graphical data can be represented by XAML or through code. If you are dynamically generating graphical output (e.g., a pie chart that represents data obtained from a relational database), taking a code-based approach is appropriate. Under this model, WPF provides equivalents to the GDI+ Graphics object, rendering events and repainting a surface area.

Breaking Down the Graphical Services of WPF

As you explore graphics support under WPF, it is helpful to remember that the entire API can be broken down into several broad categories, each of which provides a basic service, as described in Table 27-8.

Table 27-8. *Overview of the Core WPF Graphical Services*

Service	Namespace(s)	Meaning in Life
Brushes	System.Windows.Media	Like GDI+, WPF brushes are used to fill an area with a given color, pattern, image, or drawing.
Shapes	System.Windows.Shapes	These primitives are used to create 2D graphical output (as well as to capture user input).

Continued

Table 27-8. *(Continued)*

Service	Namespace(s)	Meaning in Life
Imaging support	`System.Windows.Controls,` `System.Windows.Media`	These are types for image manipulation, including applying special effects to the image itself.
Geometries	`System.Windows.Media`	Geometries allow you to represent nonvisible 2D shapes, which are helpful for defining curves, clipping regions, and hit testing areas.
Transformations	`System.Windows.Media`	Use the `Transform` classes to rotate, translate, scale, and apply other 2D effects to geometries, visuals, brushes, framework elements, and controls.
Animations	`System.Windows.Media.Animation`	These types make WPF objects change color, move, spin, grow, shrink, and so on.
3D graphics	`System.Windows.Media.Media3D`	This namespace defines 3D graphics primitives, transformations, and animations that can be used to create 3D controls and graphics.

Covering all of the bells and whistles incorporated into the WPF graphical system would require a rather hefty book all on its own (and yet another book to fully describe the 3D rendering services). To get you started down the correct path, however, let's check out some basic details behind 2D rendering services and WPF animations. Once you get a handle on the basic process, you should be in a good position for further exploration.

Working with Basic Shapes

The simplest way in which you can render graphical data is to make use of the types within the `System.Windows.Shapes` namespace. Here you will find the `Ellipse`, `Line`, `Path`, `Polygon`, `Polyline`, and `Rectangle` types, all of which extend the abstract base class `Shape`. While the `Shape` parent class provides a good deal of functionally, one property to be particularly aware of is `Fill`. The `Fill` property can be assigned any number of *brushes* to establish how to fill the interior of a geometric image (as you might guess, this value is ignored for `Line` types).

WPF defines a good number of brush types, the simplest of which is `SolidColorBrush`. If you require more exotic fill patterns, you are also free to choose among `LinearGradientBrush` (used in previous examples), `RadialGradientBrush`, `ImageBrush`, `DrawingBrush`, and `VisualBrush`.

Given your exposure to GDI+ earlier in this text, the overall usage of these drawing primitives should look quite familiar. Without belaboring the point, here is some simple XAML that renders out three shapes within a `Canvas`:

```
<Canvas>
  <!-- Draws a diagonal line from (10,10) to (40,50). -->
  <Line
    X1="10" Y1="10" X2="40" Y2="90"
    Stroke="Black" StrokeThickness="15"
    StrokeEndLineCap ="Round" StrokeStartLineCap ="Triangle"/>
```

```
<!-- Draws an oval with a light green interior and a red outline. -->
<Ellipse Width="100" Height="50" Fill="LightGreen"
  Stroke="Red" StrokeThickness="6"
  Canvas.Left="10" Canvas.Top="100"/>

<!-- Draws a polygon. -->
<Polygon Points="150,150 400,125 350,275 250,200"
Stroke="Purple" StrokeThickness="3">
  <Polygon.Fill>
    <SolidColorBrush Color="Blue" Opacity="0.4"/>
  </Polygon.Fill>
</Polygon>
</Canvas>
```

The Shape-derived types typically work in conjunction with other basic drawing primitives such as brushes and images. For example, notice that the attached <Polygon.Fill> property is working with a SolidColorBrush type. As with GDI+, you have several brush types to choose from: ImageBrush, DrawingBrush, VisualBrush, and RadialGradientBrush, among others. Here is a modified polygon, which is now making use of a LinearGradientBrush:

```
<!-- Draw a polygon. -->
<Polygon Points="150,150 400,125 350,275 250,200"
                Stroke="Purple" StrokeThickness="3">
  <Polygon.Fill>
    <LinearGradientBrush StartPoint="0,0" EndPoint="1,1">
      <GradientStop Color="Black" Offset="0" />
      <GradientStop Color="Yellow" Offset="0.25" />
      <GradientStop Color="Honeydew" Offset="0.75" />
      <GradientStop Color ="Red" Offset="1" />
    </LinearGradientBrush>
  </Polygon.Fill>
</Polygon>
```

The output is shown in Figure 27-22.

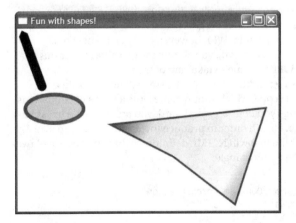

Figure 27-22. *Working with basic* Shape-*derived types*

Beyond simply rendering content, each of these Shape-derived types is capable of detecting user input, such as mouse activity. Consider the following update to the Line's markup:

```
<Line Name="myLine" MouseDown ="myLine_Clicked" Cursor ="Hand"
  X1="10" Y1="10" X2="40" Y2="90"
  Stroke="Black" StrokeThickness="15"
  StrokeEndLineCap ="Round" StrokeStartLineCap ="Triangle"/>
```

Notice that the Line object has the ability to detect a MouseDown event, and it also will automatically change the cursor icon when the user is within its boundaries. Also notice that there is no need to perform any complex hit testing or explicitly author code to monitor the mouse. All we need is an event handler for our registered event:

```
public void myLine_Clicked(Object sender, MouseButtonEventArgs e)
{
  MessageBox.Show("You clicked the line!");
}
```

■**Source Code** The BasicShapes.xaml file can be found under the Chapter 27 subdirectory.

Introducing WPF's Animation Services

When developers hear of WPF's animation support, many assume this feature is used for "classic" animation tasks found in a multimedia or video game applications (e.g., iterating through a sequence of images). While this sort of animation programming is certainly possible, under WPF *animation* simply means changing the values of visual properties (or, if required, other non-UI-specific properties) on a type element over a specified period of time. For example, you could define a specialized button that iterates over a series of colors to provide a "glowing" effect. By way of another example, you might render a polygon that scrolls across the top of a given window to provide a moving "banner."

As you saw in Chapter 20, GDI+ allows you to build simple animations using a Timer type (or a set of threads created manually) and a good amount of elbow grease (handling the Timer's events, manually cycling through a series of images, etc.). Under WPF, however, every element can be directly animated using a declarative manner. Using XAML, you simply assign values to various animation-centric properties and allow the WPF runtime to take care of the rest.

When you are defining an animation using markup (e.g., XAML), you will do so within a <BeginStoryboard>/<EndStoryboard> element scope, which simply represents a series of animations that operate on the elements you specify. Once you define a storyboard, you are then able to associate it to a given WPF element (control, image, etc.) in order to produce the desired result. To take this functionality out for a test drive, ponder the following XAML definition, which makes use of two Button controls to start or stop an animated green rectangle:

```
<Window x:Class="MyWPFApp.Window1"
  xmlns="http://schemas.microsoft.com/winfx/2006/xaml/presentation"
  xmlns:x="http://schemas.microsoft.com/winfx/2006/xaml"
  Title="Simple Animation" Height="165" Width="428">

  <!-- Stuff everything in a stack panel. -->
  <StackPanel Margin="20">
```

```
<!-- Create a simple rectangle to animate. -->
<Rectangle Name="simpleGreenRectangle"
  Fill="Green" Width="50" Height="30" />

<!-- Create a second stack panel to hold
     buttons that start and stop the animations. -->
<StackPanel Orientation="Vertical" Margin="0,20,0,0">
  <Button Name="startButton">Start</Button>
  <Button Name="stopButton">Stop</Button>

  <!-- New!  Here we are associating the clicking of each button
       with a stack of XAML that starts or stops the animation. -->
  <StackPanel.Triggers>
    <EventTrigger SourceName="startButton" RoutedEvent="Button.Click">
      <BeginStoryboard Name="myStoryboard">
        <Storyboard>
          <!-- Create an animation that repeats indefinitely. -->
          <DoubleAnimation
            Storyboard.TargetName="simpleGreenRectangle"
            Storyboard.TargetProperty="Width"
            From="50" To="300" Duration="0:0:2" RepeatBehavior="Forever" />
        </Storyboard>
      </BeginStoryboard>
    </EventTrigger>
    <EventTrigger SourceName="stopButton" RoutedEvent="Button.Click">
      <StopStoryboard BeginStoryboardName="myStoryboard" />
    </EventTrigger>
  </StackPanel.Triggers>

</StackPanel>
</StackPanel>
</Window>
```

First of all, notice that we are making use of a StackPanel to contain each element, one of which is a secondary StackPanel used to position the Button types. Next, notice that our simple green rectangle has been appropriately named simpleGreenRectangle (naming the item to animate is an important step, as the storyboard needs to reference the item to animate by name).

The first real point of interest is the use of property-element syntax to establish a section of XAML marked by the <StackPanel.Triggers> scope. What we are looking at here is termed an *event trigger*. In this case, our trigger has been associated to the inner StackPanel and defines two inner <EventTrigger> scopes. Each of these <EventTrigger> definitions has been configured to execute XAML within its scope when a specified button has been clicked.

Thus, if the user clicks the startButton control, the storyboard begins by creating a DoubleAnimation type to grow the width of our simpleGreenRectangle. Conversely, if the user clicks the stopButton control, the storyboard is stopped. As you can see, these event triggers provide a simple way to inform an animation to start or stop itself (among other things) using XAML definitions.

The final aspect of our example is the use of the DoubleAnimation type, which represents an animation based on manipulation of floating-point numerical data. This is one of many animation types that can be defined within a storyboard, each of which represents the type of item operated upon. Other animation types (all of which are defined within the System.Windows.Media.Animation namespace) include MatrixAnimation, PointAnimation, RectAnimation, Rotation3DAnimation, SizeAnimation, and VectorAnimation.

Here, our DoubleAnimation declaration specified simpleGreenRectangle as the target. On this type, we will change the Width property to cycle indefinitely between 50 and 300 pixels. The length of each cycle has been set to two seconds.

```
<!-- Create an animation that repeats indefinitely. -->
<DoubleAnimation
  Storyboard.TargetName="simpleGreenRectangle"
  Storyboard.TargetProperty="Width"
  From="50" To="300" Duration="0:0:2" RepeatBehavior="Forever" />
```

A static screen shot of this window is a bit anticlimatic, but Figure 27-23 shows the UI of the hosting window. If you click the Start button, sure enough the width of the rectangle grows across the length of the window until you click Stop.

Figure 27-23. *The UI of our animation example*

■**Source Code** The SimpleAnimation.xaml file can be found under the Chapter 27 subdirectory.

Generating XAML Using Microsoft Expression Graphical Designer

Earlier in this chapter, you were briefly exposed to the Microsoft Expression Interactive Designer utility, which allows graphic design–minded individuals to build rich user interfaces that can be saved out as a *.xaml file. At this point, the code-minded individuals can import the XAML definitions and hook up the code that drives the application itself.

In a very similar manner, the Microsoft Expression Graphical Designer allows these same graphic design–minded individuals to build complex graphical output and animation sequences using a dedicated tool. Just like the Interactive Designer, the Graphical Designer tool can export the image data as a *.xaml file that can be imported by the development team. If you are interested in learning more about the XAML used to build complex graphical data and animations, downloading this product is a step in the right direction.

■**Note** Recall that all of the Expression products are currently available as Community Technology Previews from the official Microsoft Expression website (http://www.microsoft.com/products/expression).

A Brief Word Regarding XAML Browser Applications

To close our introductory look at WPF, I feel compelled to briefly mention the role of XAML Browser Applications (XBAPs). As you have seen in this chapter, while you can use WPF to build a traditional desktop executable program, WPF does support an alternative application type, XBAP. As implied by the name, these GUI applications are deployed to an IIS virtual directory and hosted within Internet Explorer. Under this model, the end user can simply enter the URL in the XAML browser application, and the content is downloaded automatically via HTTP.

The major benefit of this model is that, as in a web application, updating content for users is quite simple, because they get the latest and greatest version when they return to the target URL. Another benefit of this model is the fact that WPF browser applications are not limited to HTML and JavaScript to render their content and functionality; Internet Explorer is playing host to the .NET assembly. Finally, browser applications are able to easily maintain state (on the client), unlike in a traditional web program.

One downside to this approach is that when you deploy XBAPs, the receiving web browser must currently be Microsoft Internet Explorer. If you are deploying such applications across a company intranet, browser compatibility should not be a problem (given that system administrators can play dictator regarding which browser should be installed on users' machines). However, if you want the outside world to make use of your XBAP, it is not possible to ensure each end user is making use of Internet Explorer. The other major point to be aware of is that fact that the machine that is hosting the XBAP must be configured with the .NET 3.0 runtime!

■**Note** Microsoft is currently working on a subset of WPF termed WPF/E, where "E" stands for "everywhere." When this subset is released (sometime in 2007), we will be able to access XBAP applications in a browser- and operating system–neutral manner.

Another XBAP limitation is the fact that such an application runs within a security sandbox termed the *Internet zone*. .NET assemblies that are loaded into this sandbox have limited access to system resources (such as the local file system or system registry) and cannot freely use all aspects of specific .NET APIs that might pose a security threat. In stark contrast, a desktop WPF application that has been loaded directly from the user's hard drive runs under *full trust*, meaning that WPF desktop executables have unlimited access to system resources, unless those resources are locked down by a system administrator. Specifically, XBAPs cannot perform the following tasks:

- Create and display stand-alone windows
- Display application-defined dialogs
- Display a Save dialog launched by the XBAP itself
- Access the file system (Isolated Storage is a-OK)
- Make use of legacy UI models (Windows Forms, ActiveX) or call unmanaged code

At first glance, the inability to create secondary windows (or dialogs) may seem very limiting. In reality, an XBAP can, in fact, show users multiple user interfaces by using a page-navigation model. Unlike a desktop WPF application, the XAML Browser Application (WPF) project template of Visual Studio 2005 "Orcas" (see Figure 27-24) makes use of a <Page> element (rather than <Window>) to define the look and feel of a given XBAP page.

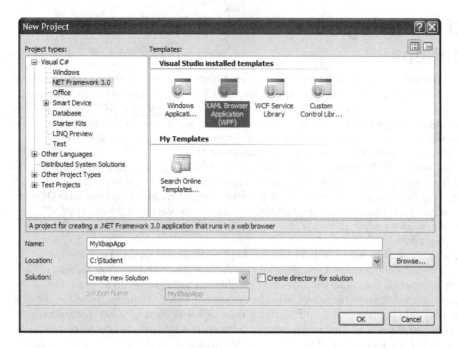

Figure 27-24. *Selecting an XBAP project template using Visual Studio 2005 "Orcas"*

The initial markup is in fact the same markup you see when you launch `XamlPad.exe` for the very first time:

```
<Page x:Class="MyXBapApp.Page1"
  xmlns="http://schemas.microsoft.com/winfx/2006/xaml/presentation"
  xmlns:x="http://schemas.microsoft.com/winfx/2006/xaml"
  Title="Page1" Height="336" Width="510">
  <Grid>

  </Grid>
</Page>
```

If you so choose, your pages can define various navigational controls (Next, Previous, etc.) to allow the user to move between a set of related pages. In this light, XBAPs behave like a "browser within the browser."

■**Note** Traditional WPF desktop applications can also make use of this web-like page navigation. If you wish, your window can also sport Next, Previous, and similar buttons to allow the user to move between views.

In many ways, XBAPs are a new spin on existing .NET technologies—specifically ClickOnce deployment (and the earlier version of this model, Smart Client). If you have deployed executables using either of these models, you should feel right at home with XBAPs. If you are interested in checking out XBAP development in more detail, look up the topic "XAML Browser Applications" in the .NET Framework 3.0 documentation.

Summary

Windows Presentation Foundation (WPF) is a brand-new user interface toolkit introduced with .NET 3.0. The major goal of WPF is to integrate and unify a number of previously unrelated desktop technologies (2D graphics, 3D graphics, window and control development, etc.) into a single programming model. Over the course of this chapter, you learned about the architecture of WPF controls, graphical rendering services, and simple animation services.

You discovered how a WPF application can actually be composed in three distinct manners. If you wish, you can build your WPF applications using nothing but your managed language of choice (such as C#). On the other hand, it is possible to build a WPF application completely with the XAML. However, for all practical purposes, WPF applications make use of a code-behind file mentality, to allow for a separation of concerns.

In addition to examining the use of various WPF controls and panels, you also explored the new Expression product line from Microsoft. Recall that the Expression Interactive Designer allows members of a design team to build a rich user interface that can be exported as a *.xaml file. The Expression Graphics Designer application provides similar functionality for building complex graphical images and animations.

Finally, you were briefly exposed to the role of XAML Browser Applications, or XBAPs. Simply put, XBAPs are WPF applications hosted by a web server and rendered within Internet Explorer. In many ways, XBAPs are simply a new spin on the earlier ClickOnce and Smart Client .NET technologies.

CHAPTER 28

■ ■ ■

Introducing Windows Communication Foundation

.NET 3.0 introduces a brand-new API specifically for the process of building distributed systems: Windows Communication Foundation (WCF). Unlike other distributed APIs you may have used in the past, WCF provides a single, unified (and easily extendable) model to access a number of previously diverse remoting technologies.

This chapter begins by discussing the need for WCF and examining the problems it intends to solve. After we look at the services provided by WCF, we'll turn to examine the .NET assemblies (and core types) that represent this programming model. Over the remainder of this chapter, we will build various WCF services and WCF clients. By the end of the chapter, you should be well versed in the process of building, deploying, and configuring WCF applications, and you will be in a solid position for further investigation.

■Note If you require more complete treatment of Windows Communication Foundation than is provided in this introductory chapter, check out *Pro WCF: Practical Microsoft SOA Implementation* by Chris Peiris et al. (Apress, 2007).

The Motivation Behind WCF

The previous chapter introduced you to Windows Presentation Foundation (WPF), a brand-new GUI toolkit that unifies various desktop-centric programming models under a single API. Similarly, Windows Communication Foundation (WCF) is a brand-new distributed computing toolkit that integrates a number of existing distributed technologies (COM+, .NET remoting, XML web services, and Microsoft Message Queuing service [MSMQ]) into a streamlined API. The motivation for doing so is not due to the fact that the previously mentioned technologies cannot be used successfully within .NET development; rather, it's due to the fact that each API solves *specific* problems of distributed computing instead of offering a single solution.

For example, the .NET remoting layer (examined in Chapter 18) allows multiple computers to distribute types, provided they are all built using the .NET Framework. MSMQ (a Microsoft technology used to build applications that communicate with intermittently connected applications) works very well, provided each machine is from the Windows operating system family. XML web services (see Chapter 25) does allow for interoperability of various operating systems and programming architectures, but if each software agent does not agree upon the same standards, data exchange is limited.

All in all, this wide array of distributed technologies makes it difficult to pick the right tool for the job. This is further complicated by the fact that several of these technologies overlap in the services they provide. Even when a .NET developer has selected what appear to be the "correct" technologies for the task at hand, building, maintaining, and configuring such an application is complex at best.

WCF provides a very clean solution to these problems. At its core, WCF builds on top of the success of service-oriented architectures (SOAs). In fact, many terms and concepts used within the WCF programming API map directly (or very closely) to those of XML web services (such as WSDL and SOAP messages). Given this, interoperability between .NET, J2EE, and COM applications (on a variety of operating systems) can be quite straightforward. In addition, WCF applications also borrow several aspects found when building software making use of .NET remoting (*.config files, choice of transportation layers and data persistence, use of attributes, etc.).

However, it is not quite correct to simply assume that WCF is some sort of wrapper around previous remoting technologies. While WCF does provide a common API to access various distributed computing technologies, it also adds a number of necessary services. For example, unlike a simple XML web service, WCF has been built on top of the latest and greatest industry standards to account for numerous important details such as security and transactional support.

Better yet, WCF has been designed to be easily extendable. Thus, as industry standards grow and change, WCF will be able to adapt intelligently. As well, developers are able to extend the core infrastructure, build custom bindings, and add various custom layers of interception.

Interoperability and integration of diverse APIs are only two high-level (and very important) aspects of WCF. As mentioned, WCF provides a rich software fabric that complements the remoting technologies it exposes. Consider the following list of core WCF services:

- Support for strongly typed *as well as* untyped messages. This approach allows .NET applications to share custom types simply and efficiently, while software created using other platforms (such as Java) can consume streams of loosely typed XML.

- Support for several *endpoints* (raw HTTP, HTTP + SOAP, TCP, MSMQ, and named pipes) to allow you to choose the most appropriate plumbing to transport data to and fro.

- Support for distributed transactions via implementation of the WS-AtomicTransaction (WS-AT) and WS Coordination protocols.

- A fully integrated security model encompassing both native Win32/.NET security protocols and numerous neutral security techniques built upon web service standards.

- The services previously only found in COM+ (aka Enterprise Services) such as management of object lifetime, support for distributed transactions, and publish/subscribe events (among others) are now provided directly from WCF.

- Native support for message queuing (for loosely coupled systems) and reliable session data protocols to ensure message delivery (including the optional ability to receive notification of said delivery).

- Support for sessionlike state management techniques, as well as support for one-way stateless messages.

As impressive as this list of features may be, it really only scratches the surface of the functionality provided by WCF. This chapter introduces the namespaces, types, and tools used to build WCF services and WCF client applications. Given that this edition of the text does not address Enterprise Services (COM+) or MSMQ, I encourage interested readers to dig into these aspects of WCF as they see fit.

Investigating the Core WCF Assemblies

As you would expect, the functionality of WCF is represented by a set of .NET assemblies installed into the GAC once you have configured your development machine with the .NET Framework 3.0 (see Chapter 26). Table 28-1 describes the overall role of each of the WCF assemblies.

Table 28-1. *Core WCF Assemblies*

Assembly	Meaning in Life
System.IdentityModel.dll	Defines a number of namespaces that support the WCF CardSpace API. In a nutshell, this technology allows you to establish and manage digital identities within a WCF application.
System.Runtime.Serialization.dll	Defines namespaces and types that can be used for serializing and deserializing objects within the WCF framework.
System.ServiceModel.dll	Core assembly that contains the core types used to build any sort of WCF application.

These core assemblies define a number of new namespaces and hundreds of new .NET types (classes, interfaces, structures, enumerations, and delegates). While you should consult the .NET Framework 3.0 SDK documentation for complete details, Table 28-2 documents the role of some (but not all) of the core namespaces to be aware of.

Table 28-2. *Core WCF Namespaces*

Namespace	Meaning in Life
System.Runtime.Serialization	Defines numerous types used to control how data is serialized and deserialized within the WCF framework
System.ServiceModel	Core WCF namespace that defines binding and hosting types, as well as basic security, queuing, and transactional types
System.ServiceModel.Configuration	Defines numerous types that provide programmatic access to the core sections of WCF configuration files
System.ServiceModel.Description	Defines types that provide an object model to the addresses, bindings, and contracts defined within WCF configuration files
System.ServiceModel.MsmqIntegration	Contains types to integrate with MSMQ
System.ServiceModel.Security	Defines numerous types to control aspects of the WCF security layers

The ABCs of WCF

The architecture of WCF borrows heavily from that of XML web services, specifically the use of WSDL to describe a given service, the binding protocols used to communicate with it, and the supported list of operations. As you may recall from Chapter 25, a WSDL document describes these aspects of an XML web service using the <service>, <bindings>, and <portType> elements.

WCF employs very similar terms when describing a service: *address*, *binding*, and *contract*, which gives way to a handy acronym, ABC, used to represent the key elements of a WCF service. Do understand that the ABC acronym does not imply that a developer must define the address first, followed by binding, and ending with contract. In many cases, a WCF developer begins with by defining a contract for the service, followed by defining an address and bindings (but any order will do, so long as each aspect is accounted for).

Understanding WCF Contracts

The notion of a *contract* is the key to building a WCF service. Those of you who have a background in classic DCOM and COM technologies might be surprised to know that WCF contracts are expressed using interface-based programming techniques (everything old is new again!). While not mandatory, the vast majority of your WCF applications will begin by defining a set of .NET interface types that are used to represent the set of members a given WCF type will support. Specifically speaking, interfaces that represent a WCF contract are termed *service contracts*. The classes (or structures) that implement them are termed *service types*.

Understanding WCF Bindings

Once a contract (or a set of contracts) has been defined and implemented, the next logical step is to build a hosting agent for the WCF service itself. As you will see, you have a variety of possible hosts to choose from, all of which must specify the *bindings* used by remote callers to gain access to the service type's functionality.

Choosing a set of bindings is one area that makes WCF development quite different from .NET remoting and/or XML web service development. This is not necessary due to the programmatic approach (as you will see, *.config files are used to declare most of the address and binding grunge); rather, it's due to the large number of binding choices at your disposal—well beyond simply HTTP, HTTP + SOAP, or TCP.

Recall that one of the major motivations behind WCF is to offer a unified approach to a number of previously diverse distributed APIs (MSMQ, Enterprise Services, XML web services, etc.). Given this point, WCF offers the bindings shown in Table 28-3 out of the box. As you ponder the table, note that each binding can be represented in code as a class type within the System. ServiceModel namespace or as XML attributes defined within a WCF *.config file.

Table 28-3. *Intrinsic Bindings Provided by WCF*

Binding Class	Binding Element	Meaning in Life
BasicHttpBinding	<basicHttpBinding>	Used when communicating with WS-Basic Profile–conformant .NET web services. This binding uses HTTP as the transport and Text/XML as the default message encoding.
WSHttpBinding	<wsHttpBinding>	A secure and interoperable binding that is suitable for nonduplex service contracts.
WSDualHttpBinding	<wsDualHttpBinding>	A secure and interoperable binding that is suitable for duplex service contracts or communication through SOAP intermediaries.

Binding Class	Binding Element	Meaning in Life
WSFederationHttpBinding	<wsFederationHttpBinding>	A secure and interoperable binding that supports the WS-Federation protocol, enabling organizations that are in a federation to efficiently authenticate and authorize users.
NetTcpBinding	<netTcpBinding>	A secure and optimized binding suitable for cross-machine communication between WCF applications.
NetNamedPipeBinding	<netNamedPipeBinding>	A secure, reliable, optimized binding that is suitable for on-machine communication between WCF applications.
NetPeerTcpBinding	<netPeerTcpBinding>	A binding that enables secure, multimachine communication.
NetMsmqBinding	<netMsmqBinding>	A queued binding that is suitable for cross-machine communication between WCF applications.
MsmqIntegrationBinding	<msmqIntegrationBinding>	A binding that is suitable for cross-machine communication between a WCF application and existing MSMQ applications.

While the number of bindings may look daunting at first glance, we can simplify things a bit by realizing that related options can be grouped together in a number of broad categories. Specifically, the BasicHttpBinding, WSHttpBinding, WSDualHttpBinding, and WSFederationHttpBinding options are geared toward exposing a service type via XML web services. Clearly, if you require the furthest reach possible (multiple operating systems, multiple programming architectures), these are the types to focus on.

If you are building a distributed application involving a set of networked machines that host .NET 3.0 (currently limited to Windows XP, Windows Server 2003, and Windows Vista), you can gain performance benefits by choosing the NetTcpBinding and NetPeerTcpBinding types. As well, if you are looking for the fastest way to push data between WCF applications on the same machine (e.g., cross-application domain communications), then NetNamedPipeBinding is the binding of champions.

Finally, if you are attempting to integrate with a Microsoft MSMQ server, the NetMsmqBinding and MsmqIntegrationBinding bindings are of immediate interest. Do note that there is not a specific binding to interact with COM+ components (e.g., Enterprise Services). Communicating with COM+ components via WCF is entirely possible; however, doing so involves exposing the COM+ types through a XML web service binding via the ComSvcConfig.exe command-line tool that ships with the .NET Framework 3.0 SDK.

As you will see, each of the binding options provided by WCF is in charge of specifying three important bits of information (regardless of whether you do so in code or via configuration elements). Specifically, a WFC binding type defines a protocol, transport, and data encoding:

- The *protocol stack* establishes the security, reliability, and context flow settings to use for messages that are sent to the endpoint.

- The *transport* establishes the underlying transport protocol to use when sending messages to the endpoint (e.g., TCP or HTTP).

- The *encoding* determines how messages are to be sent to the endpoint (pure text, XML, binary, etc.).

Given the flexibility provided by WCF, it is very simple to change the provided bindings (and, therefore, the underlying protocol, transport, and encoding) used by your application. Of course, if none of the default bindings fits the bill for your current programming task, it is possible to build a custom binding type (a task outside the scope of this introductory chapter; check out the .NET Framework 3.0 SDK documentation for details if you're so inclined).

Understanding WCF Addresses

Last but not least, once the contracts and bindings have been established, the final piece of the puzzle is to define an *address* for the WCF service, typically represented in code using the System.Uri type. However, to keep the host as flexible as possible, the actual URI is often stored in a *.config file and programmatically obtained via the ConfigurationManager type.

Building a Complete WCF Application

Now that you have a better understanding of the building blocks of a WCF application, let's create our first sample application to see how the ABCs are accounted for in code.

The Interrelated Assemblies of a WCF Application

Much like the process of building a .NET remoting application, WCF solutions typically revolve around three interrelated assemblies:

- An assembly that defines the service's functionality (including the supported contracts)
- An assembly to host the service and a *.config file to specify the addresses, bindings, and contracts
- An assembly to request use of the service through an intervening proxy (and a client-side *.config file)

As far as the first assembly is concerned, recall that *service contracts* are represented in code using .NET interface types. Therefore, defining service contracts in C# looks just about identical to building any other interface type. However, to advertise that an interface is indeed a WCF service contract (rather than a simple CLR interface), it will need to be adorned with a handful of helpful attributes from the System.ServiceModel namespace. Once the contract has been created, the next step is to build a *service type* to implement its members. Despite the formal-sounding name, a service type is nothing more than a normal C# class or structure implementing a given WCF interface.

The second assembly represents a host for our service types. Again, like the .NET remoting layer, any executable application (console, Windows service, or Windows program) may be used for this purpose. As well, IIS can be configured to host WCF types. In either of these cases, you will find that you can use XML configuration files to simplify the code base and keep your host flexible.

■**Note** The Microsoft Vista OS provides yet another hosting option for WCF services termed Windows Activation Services (WAS). Essentially, WAS is a generalization of IIS features that work with non-HTTP protocols (TCP, named pipes, and MSMQ). Consult the .NET Framework 3.0 SDK documentation for further details.

The process of building the final assembly of a WCF application (the client) will also look quite familiar. For example, the client code makes use of a proxy type to communicate with the remote type, and it will typically make use of XML-based *.config files to establish various WCF settings and so forth.

Defining and Implementing the Contract

To begin, create a new C# Class Library project named CarOrderServiceLib. Then rename your initial class from Class1 to CarOrderService. Finally, set a reference to System.ServiceModel.dll (via the Add References dialog box, which you can access by a right-clicking the References node of the project in Solution Explorer), and in your initial code file, specify that you are using the System. ServiceModel namespace. At this point, your C# file should look like so:

```csharp
using System;
using System.Collections.Generic;
using System.Text;
using System.ServiceModel;

namespace CarOrderServiceLib
{
  public class CarOrderService
  {
  }
}
```

■**Note** The Visual Studio 2005 "Orcas" Community Technology Preview also provides a WCF service project template. The only major benefit of this project type is that it will automatically set references to the WCF assemblies.

Recall that when you are building a WCF service, you begin by modeling the *service contract* using strongly typed interfaces. The interface itself is adorned with the [ServiceContract] attribute, while each interface member is adorned with the [OperationContract] attribute (more details regarding these two attributes in just a moment). Our contract will be named ICarOrder, which defines the following members:

```csharp
[ServiceContract]
public interface ICarOrder
{
  // Allows caller to place an order and obtain
  // an order ID.
  [OperationContract]
  int PlaceOrder(string make, string color, double price);

  // Allows caller to get current status of the order.
  [OperationContract]
  string CheckOrderStatus(int orderID);
}
```

As you know from your study of the interface type (see Chapter 7), interfaces are quite useless until they are implemented by a class or structure, in order to flush out their functionality. To keep focused on WCF itself, the implementation of our service type (CarOrderService) is intentionally simple:

```csharp
public class CarOrderService : ICarOrder
{
  private const int HardCodedOrderNumber = 10;

  public int PlaceOrder(string make, string color, double price)
  {
    // Simply print out the incoming data and return an order ID.
    Console.WriteLine("Thanks for buying a {0} {1} for the low, low price of ${2}.",
```

```
    color, make, price);
    return HardCodedOrderNumber;
  }

  public string CheckOrderStatus(int orderID)
  {
    if (orderID == HardCodedOrderNumber)
    {
      return "Your car has been shipped!";
    }
    else
    {
      return "Sorry, we can't find your order ID.";
    }
  }
}
```

The [ServiceContact] Attribute

In order for an interface to participate in the services provided by WCF, it must be adorned with the [ServiceContract] attribute. Like many other .NET attributes, the ServiceContractAttribute type supports a number of properties to further qualify its intension. Two properties, Name and Namespace, can be set to control how the name of the service type and the XML namespace are defined within the <portType> elements of the WSDL document.

Here, we have not bothered to assign a Name value, given that the default name of the service type is directly based on the C# class name (and there is no potential for name clashes). However, the default name for the underlying XML namespace is (like an XML web service) simply http:// tempuri.org. For this reason, we can update our interface definition with a more fitting definition:

```
[ServiceContract(Namespace = "http://Intertech.com")]
public interface ICarOrder
{
...
}
```

Beyond Namespace and Name, the [ServiceContract] attribute can be configured with the additional properties shown in Table 28-4. You will see many of these in action over the course of this chapter; however, be sure to also check out the .NET Framework 3.0 SDK documentation for full details.

Table 28-4. *Select Properties of the* [ServiceContract] *Attribute*

Property	Meaning in Life
CallbackContract	Establishes if this service contract requires callback functionality for two-way message exchange.
ConfigurationName	The name used to locate the service element in an application configuration file. The default is the name of the service implementation class.
ProtectionLevel	Allows you to specify the degree to which the contract binding requires encryption, digital signatures, or both for endpoints that expose the contract.
SessionMode	Used to establish if sessions are allowed, not allowed, or required by this service contract.

The [OperationContract] Attribute

Methods that wish to be used within the WCF framework must be attributed with the [OperationContract] attribute, which may also be configured with various named properties to control the translation of the method signature into WSDL. Using the properties shown in Table 28-5, you are able to declare a given method is intended to be one-way in nature, supports asynchronous invocation (via the Begin/End .NET delegate pattern), requires encrypted message data, and so forth.

Table 28-5. *Named Properties of the* [OperationContract] *Attribute*

Property	Meaning in Life
Action	Gets or sets the WS-Addressing action of the request message
AsyncPattern	Indicates if the operation is implemented asynchronously using a Begin/End method pair
IsInitiating	Specifies if this operation can be the initial operation in a session
IsOneWay	Indicates if the operation consists of only a single input message (and no associated output)
IsTerminating	Specifies if the WCF runtime should attempt to terminate the current session after the operation completes

Although the methods of ICarOrder do not require additional configuration for the current example, consider the implications of the following updated PlaceOrder() method that makes use of yet another named property, ProtectionLevel:

```
// This method requires encrypted and signed messages,
// and also supports async calls.
[OperationContract(ProtectionLevel =
  System.Net.Security.ProtectionLevel.EncryptAndSign,
  AsyncPattern = true)]
int PlaceOrder(string make, string color, double price);
```

Again, for this initial example, we don't need to configure the PlaceOrder() method with additional traits, so ensure the [OperationContract] attribute is not qualified with additional property values before moving on.

■**Note** It is permissible to define a service contract interface that contains methods not adorned with the [OperationContract] attribute. However, such members will not be exposed through the WCF runtime.

Service Types As Operational Contracts

Before we begin to build a host for our service type, it is worth pointing out that strictly speaking, the use of interfaces are *not* required when building service types. It is in fact possible to apply the [ServiceContract] and [OperationContract] attributes directly on the service type itself:

```
// This is only for illustrative purposes
// and not used for the current example...
[ServiceContract(Namespace = "http://intertech.com")]
public class ServiceTypeAsContract
{
```

```
    [OperationContract]
    void SomeMethod() { }

    [OperationContract]
    void AnotherMethod() { }
}
```

Although this approach is possible, there are many benefits to explicitly defining an interface type to represent the service contract. The most obvious benefit is that a given interface can be applied to multiple service types (authored in a variety of languages and architectures) to achieve a high degree of polymorphism. Another benefit is that a service contract interface can be used as the basis of new contracts (via interface inheritance), without having to carry any implementation baggage.

Finally, by defining strongly typed WCF interfaces (especially if they are contained within a stand-alone .NET assembly), we are able to deploy the interface-only assembly to client machines without having to ship the server's code base to the end user. Given these (and other) benefits, our WCF examples will favor the use of interface types.

■**Source Code** The CarOrderServiceLib project is located under the Chapter 28 subdirectory.

Hosting the WCF Service

We are now ready to define a host for our service type. Although a production-level service would be ideally hosted from a Windows service or an IIS virtual directory, we will create a console-based host named CarOrderServiceHost. Once you have created the project, add a reference to System.ServiceModel.dll and CarOrderServiceLib.dll, and update the using directives to specify you are making use of the System.ServiceModel and CarOrderServiceLib namespaces.

The first step you must take when building a host for a WCF service type is to decide whether you want to define the necessary hosting logic completely in code or you want to relegate several low-level details to an application configuration file. Recall during your examination of the .NET remoting layer that when you make use of *.config files, the host is able to change the underlying plumbing without requiring you to recompile and redeploy the executable. Given this appealing benefit, our host will indeed make use of an application configuration file. However, always remember this is strictly optional, as you can hard-code the hosting logic using the types within the System.ServiceModel.dll assembly.

When you are building a host for a WCF service type, you will follow a very predictable set of steps:

1. Define the endpoint (address, binding, and contract) for the WCF service being hosted within the host's configuration file.

2. Make use of the ServiceHost type to expose the service types available from this endpoint.

3. Ensure the host remains running to service incoming client requests. Obviously, this step is not required if you are hosting your service types using a Windows service or IIS.

To begin, update your initial Program type with the following code (analysis to follow):

```
class Program
{
    static void Main(string[] args)
    {
```

```
// Get the base address from the (yet to be created) *.config file.
Uri baseAddress = new Uri(ConfigurationManager.AppSettings["baseAddress"]);

// Create a ServiceHost, specifying the type information
// of the service and the base address.
using (ServiceHost serviceHost = new
  ServiceHost(typeof(CarOrderService), baseAddress))
{
  // Open the host and start listening for incoming messages.
  serviceHost.Open();

  // Keep the service running until Enter key is pressed.
  Console.WriteLine("The service is ready.");
  Console.WriteLine("Press Enter key to terminate service.");
  Console.ReadLine();

  // Close the ServiceHostBase to shut down the service.
  serviceHost.Close();
}
}
}
```

First off, notice that the Main() method begins by obtaining the value of the baseAddress key from a *.config file in order to create a new System.Uri type. Given this, our next step is to insert a new application configuration file (via the Project ➤ Add New Items menu option) and update the initial content with the following <appSettings> element:

```
<?xml version="1.0" encoding="utf-8"?>
<configuration>
  <!-- Here is the base address of our service -->
  <appSettings>
    <add key = "baseAddress" value = "http://localhost:32469/CarOrderService"/>
  </appSettings>
</configuration>
```

To resolve the location of the ConfigurationManager type, set a reference to the System.Configuration.dll assembly, and update your using statements to specify you are using a type defined in the System.Configuration namespace.

Once the base address has been obtained, you make use of the ServiceHost type (defined in the System.ServiceModel namespace) to perform the grunge work of exposing the CarOrderService type from the (yet to be defined) endpoint. Notice that the constructor used here requires the service's type information and the established base address. If your host must expose a given WCF service using several base addresses (e.g., to account for several specific bindings), you may pass in an array of System.Uri types as the second parameter.

Specifying the ABCs

When the ServiceHost type is allocated into memory, it will automatically read values from the <system.serviceModel> element of the host's *.config file to determine the correct address, binding, and contract. Currently, our configuration file does not specify such endpoint information, and therefore the host executable will throw an invalid operation exception. Here, then, is an updated configuration file that further describes the services exposed from our endpoint, by adding content within the <system.serviceModel> element:

```xml
<?xml version="1.0" encoding="utf-8"?>
<configuration>
  <!-- Here is the base address of our service -->
  <appSettings>
    <add key = "baseAddress" value = "http://localhost:32469/CarOrderService"/>
  </appSettings>

  <!-- Establish the WCF settings for the ServiceHost type -->
  <system.serviceModel>
    <services>
      <!-- The fully qualified name of our service -->
      <service name="CarOrderServiceLib.CarOrderService">
        <!-- Define the ABC of this endpoint -->
        <endpoint address="http://localhost:32469/CarOrderService"
                  binding="basicHttpBinding"
                  contract="CarOrderServiceLib.ICarOrder" />
      </service>
    </services>
  </system.serviceModel>
</configuration>
```

As you can see, each service exposed by the host is represented by a `<service>` element, wrapped within the `<services>` base element. Here, our single `<service>` element makes use of the name attribute to specify the fully qualified name of the service type. The related `<endpoint>` element handles the task of defining the address, the binding model (`basicHttpBinding` in this example), and the fully qualified name of the interface type defining the service contract (the `ICarOrder` interface in this example).

Now the `ServiceHost` object has the necessary information to create the endpoint and receive incoming requests. If all is well, you should be able to compile and run your host project. Figure 28-1 shows the end result.

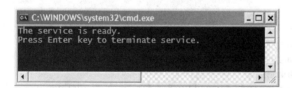

Figure 28-1. *The executing WCF service host*

Before we build a client application to communicate with our service, let's dig a bit deeper into the role of the `ServiceHost` class type.

The Role of the ServiceHost Type

The `ServiceHost` class type (which derives from `ServiceHostBase`) is used to configure and expose a WCF service from the hosting executable. Be aware that you would only make direct use of this type when building a custom `*.exe` to host your services. If you are using IIS or WAS to expose a service, the `ServiceHost` object is created automatically on your behalf.

As you have seen, this type requires a complete service description, which is obtained dynamically through the configuration settings of the host's `*.config` file. While this happens automatically upon object creation, it is possible to manually configure the state of your `ServiceHost` object using the members shown in Table 28-6.

Table 28-6. *Select Members of the* ServiceHost *Type*

Members	Meaning in Life
Authorization	This property gets the authorization level for the service being hosted.
AddServiceEndpoint()	This method allows you to programmatically register an endpoint to the host.
BaseAddresses	This property obtains the list of registered base addresses for the current service.
BeginOpen(), BeginClose()	These methods allow you to asynchronously open and close a ServiceHost object, using the standard asynchronous .NET delegate syntax.
CloseTimeout	This property allows you to set and get the time allowed for the service to close down.
Credentials	This property obtains the security credentials used by the current service.
EndOpen(), EndClose()	These methods are the asynchronous counterparts to BeginOpen() and BeginClose().
OpenTimeout	This property allows you to set and get the time allowed for the service to start up.
State	This property gets a value that indicates the current state of the communication object, represented by the CommunicationState enum (opened, closed, created, etc.).

To illustrate some further functionality of the ServiceHost type, assume the Main() method calls the following helper function directly after calling the Open() method on the ServiceHost object:

```
private static void DisplayHostStats(ServiceHost serviceHost)
{
  Console.WriteLine("***** Stats about your host *****");

  // Display information about the current host.
  Console.WriteLine("Open timeout: {0}", serviceHost.OpenTimeout);
  Console.WriteLine("Close timeout: {0}", serviceHost.CloseTimeout);
  Console.WriteLine();
  foreach (Uri address in serviceHost.BaseAddresses)
  {
    Console.WriteLine("Absolute Uri: {0}", address.AbsoluteUri);
    Console.WriteLine("Absolute Path: {0}", address.AbsolutePath);
  }
  Console.WriteLine();
}
```

When you run the program once again, you can see from Figure 28-2 that the default open timeout setting is one minute, while the default close timeout is ten seconds.

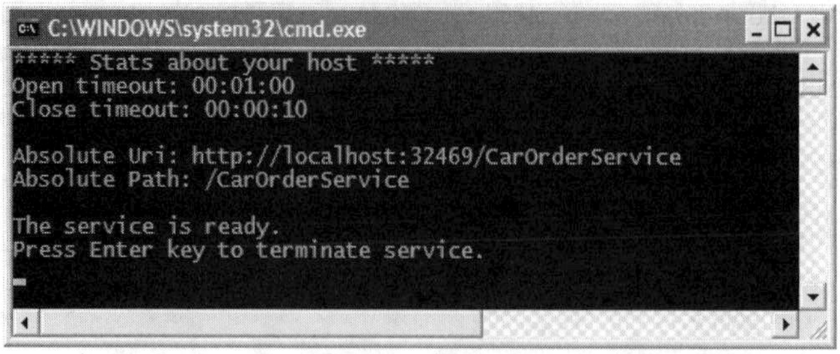

Figure 28-2. *Various statistics of our WCF service host*

Details of the <system.ServiceModel> Element

The current <system.ServiceModel> element consumed by our host is minimalist but complete. As you would guess, the <system.ServiceModel> element can contain many additional subelements beyond <services>, <service>, and <endpoint>, each of which can be fully configured using various attributes. While full details of each option are described within the .NET Framework 3.0 SDK documentation, here is a barebones list of the possible subelements within the <system.ServiceModel> element:

```
<system.ServiceModel>
  <!-- A list of each service exposed by the host -->
  <services>
    <service>
      <endpoint/>
    </service>
  </services>

  <!-- If required, each binding type defined by an endpoint can
       be further qualified within a <binding> element -->
  <bindings>
    <binding />
  </bindings>

  <!-- It is also possible to define a set of 'behaviors' that a
       given service can adhere to -->
  <behaviors>
    <serviceBehaviors>
      <behavior />
    </serviceBehaviors>
  </behaviors>
</system.ServiceModel>
```

As you might guess, each opening element (<binding>, <behavior>, and so on) can be qualified with numerous attributes. Later in this chapter, you'll be introduced to a graphical configuration tool that allows you to author a full-blown host configuration from a friendly user interface. Until then, allow me to introduce the role of service behaviors.

Defining Service Behaviors

An optional element that can be defined within a <system.ServiceModel> element is <behaviors>, which can define any number of *service behaviors*. Simply put, each <behavior> element can define a set of activities a given service can subscribe to. One possible behavior is to enable *metadata exchange* (MEX) for the service. When doing so, you make it possible for remote clients to obtain a WSDL description of the WCF service type.

Consider the following updated host *.config file, which creates a custom <behavior> element (named CarOrderServiceBehavior) that is associated to our CarOrderService service via the behaviorConfiguration attribute within the <service> definition:

```
<?xml version="1.0" encoding="utf-8"?>
<configuration>

  <!-- Here is the base address of our service -->
  <appSettings>
    <add key = "baseAddress" value = "http://localhost:32469/CarOrderService"/>
  </appSettings>

  <system.serviceModel>
    <services>
      <!-- The fully qualified name of our service
           Notice we are now using the behaviorConfiguration element
           to connect the behavior to our service -->
      <service name="CarOrderServiceLib.CarOrderService"
                      behaviorConfiguration = "CarOrderServiceBehaviors">
        <!-- Define the ABC of this endpoint -->
        <endpoint address="http://localhost:32469/CarOrderService"
                  binding="basicHttpBinding"
                  contract="CarOrderServiceLib.ICarOrder" />

        <!-- Enable the metadata exchange endpoint -->
        <endpoint contract="IMetadataExchange"
                  binding="mexHttpBinding" address="mex" />

      </service>
    </services>

    <!-- A behavior definition -->
    <behaviors>
      <serviceBehaviors>
        <behavior name="CarOrderServiceBehaviors" >
          <serviceMetadata httpGetEnabled="true" />
        </behavior>
      </serviceBehaviors>
    </behaviors>

  </system.serviceModel>
</configuration>
```

You are now able to run the service and view its metadata description using the Internet browser of your choice. To do so, while the host is running, simply enter the base address as the URL. Once you are at the homepage for your WCF service, you are provided with basic details regarding how to interact with this service programmatically as well as view the WSDL contract by clicking the hyperlink at the top of the page (Figure 28-3).

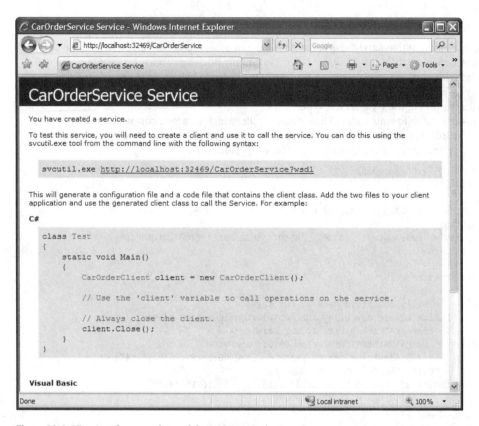

Figure 28-3. *Viewing the metadata of the WCF* CarOrderService *type*

Understand that you would not be able to view this metadata had you not enabled your service to make use of the defined behavior. Thus, if you were to remove the behaviorConfiguration attribute from the <service> element and re-execute your host, you would be shown a page informing you that the service has not enabled metadata exchange.

■**Source Code** The CarOrderServiceHost project is located under the Chapter 28 subdirectory.

Communicating with the WCF Service

Now that our host is in place, the final task is to build a piece of software to communicate with this WCF service type. While we could take the long road and build the necessary infrastructure by hand (a feasible but labor-intensive task), the .NET Framework 3.0 SDK provides several approaches to build a client-side proxy.

Generating Proxy Code Using svcutil.exe

The first manner in which you can build a client-side proxy is to make use of the svcutil.exe command-line tool. Using svcutil.exe, you can generate a new C# language file that represents the proxy code itself as well as a client-side configuration file. To do so, simply specify the service's endpoint as the first parameter. The /out: flag is used to define the name of the *.cs file containing the proxy, while the /config: option specifies the name of the generated client-side *.config file:

```
svcutil http://localhost:32469/CarOrderService /out:myProxy.cs /config:app.config
```

Assuming your service is currently running, svcutil.exe will generate two new files in the working directory. If you open the myProxy.cs file, you will find a client-side representation of the ICarOrder interface, as well as a new class named CarOrderClient, which is the proxy itself.

This class derives from the generic class, System.ServiceModel.ClientBase<T>, where T is the registered service interface. In addition to a number of generated constructors, each method adorned with the [OperationContract] attribute has been implemented to delegate to the parent class's Channels property. Here is a partial snapshot of the proxy type:

```
[System.Diagnostics.DebuggerStepThroughAttribute()]
[System.CodeDom.Compiler.GeneratedCodeAttribute("System.ServiceModel", "3.0.0.0")]
public partial class CarOrderClient : System.ServiceModel.ClientBase<ICarOrder>,
  ICarOrder
{
...
  public int PlaceOrder(string make, string color, double price)
  {
    return base.Channel.PlaceOrder(make, color, price);
  }

  public string CheckOrderStatus(int orderID)
  {
    return base.Channel.CheckOrderStatus(orderID);
  }
}
```

When you create an instance of the proxy type, the base class will establish a connection to the endpoint using the settings specified in the client-side application configuration file. Much like the server-side configuration file, the generated app.config file contains an <endpoint> element and details regarding the basicHttpBinding used to communicate with the service (check out the generated description within app.config if you are interested).

If you include each file into your client project (and reference the Sytem.ServiceModel.dll assembly), you can communicate with your running WCF service quite simply:

```
class Program
{
  static void Main(string[] args)
  {
    // Create the proxy and call the members.
    using(CarOrderClient c = new CarOrderClient())
    {
      int orderID = c.PlaceOrder("BMW", "Silver", 40.303);
      Console.WriteLine(c.CheckOrderStatus(orderID));
    }
    Console.ReadLine();
  }
}
```

Now, assuming your WCF host is currently running, you can execute the client. Figure 28-4 shows the output of the running server window, while Figure 28-5 shows the output of the running client window.

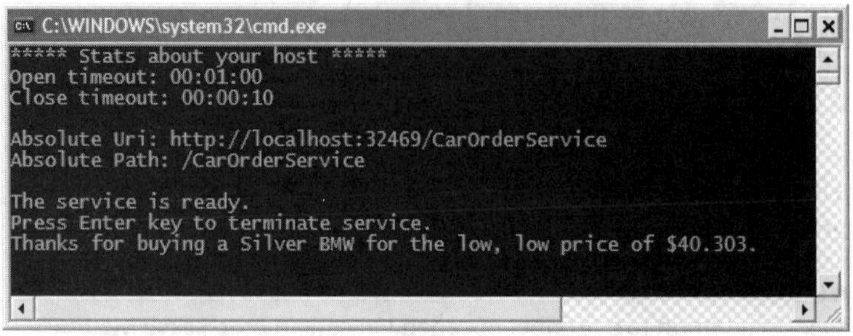
C:\WINDOWS\system32\cmd.exe
***** Stats about your host *****
Open timeout: 00:01:00
Close timeout: 00:00:10
Absolute Uri: http://localhost:32469/CarOrderService
Absolute Path: /CarOrderService
The service is ready.
Press Enter key to terminate service.
Thanks for buying a Silver BMW for the low, low price of $40.303.

Figure 28-4. *The completed WCF service host*

C:\WINDOWS\system32\cmd.exe
Your car has been shipped!

Figure 28-5. *The completed WCF client host*

Generating Proxy Code Using Visual Studio 2005

Like any good command-line tool, `svcutil.exe` provides a great number of options that can be used to control how the client proxy is generated. However, if you do not require these advanced options, you are able to generate the same files using the Visual Studio 2005 IDE. Assuming you have installed the Visual Studio 2005 "Orcas" Community Technology Preview, you can generate the same files (and have them automatically included into your project) by selecting the Add Service Reference option from the Project menu. As well, a reference to the necessary `System.ServiceModel.dll` assembly will be set automatically.

Once you activate this menu option, you will be prompted to enter the service URI, after which point the service reference name field will be automatically set to the name of the machine hosting the service. You are free to change this value if you wish; however, be aware that this will be the name of the .NET namespace defined within the client namespace to define the proxy types (see Figure 28-6).

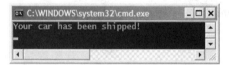

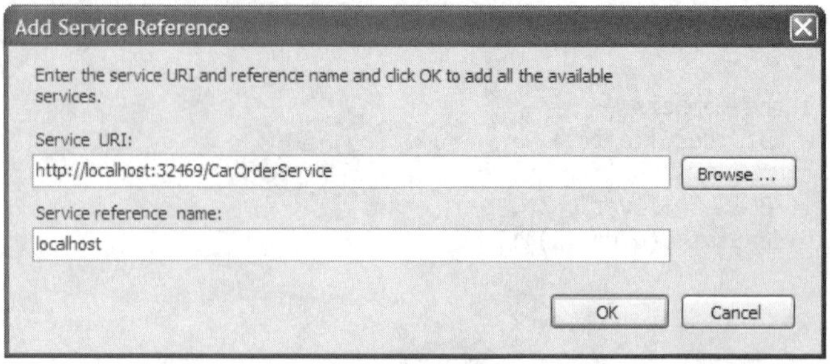
Add Service Reference
Enter the service URI and reference name and click OK to add all the available services.
Service URI:
http://localhost:32469/CarOrderService
Browse ...
Service reference name:
localhost
OK
Cancel

Figure 28-6. *Generating the proxy files using Visual Studio 2005*

At this point, you are ready to interact with the remote service via the proxy type using the code shown previously. The only update is to make sure you are specifying the namespace that contains the proxy types:

```
using System;
using System.Collections.Generic;
using System.Text;

// namespace where the proxy type is defined.
using CarOrderServiceClient.localhost;

namespace CarOrderServiceClient
{
  class Program
  {
    static void Main(string[] args)
    {
      // Create the proxy and call the members.
      using(CarOrderClient c = new CarOrderClient())
      {
        int orderID = c.PlaceOrder("BMW", "Silver", 40.303);
        Console.WriteLine(c.CheckOrderStatus(orderID));
      }
      Console.ReadLine();
    }
  }
}
```

■Source Code   The CarOrderServiceClient project is located under the Chapter 28 subdirectory.

WCF Data Type Representation

Our first WCF example defined a pair of very simple methods that operate on primitive CLR data types. As you created and executed this example, you may have wondered exactly how this data was represented internally. Clearly, it was not represented as a CLR data type (e.g., System.String or System.Int32), as a WCF service could be accessed by a variety of programming architectures (COM, J2EE, etc.) and computer operating systems. On a related note, how does WCF handle moving complex data types (including your custom types) between interested parties? The answer is, *it depends*.

When you are making use of any of the HTTP binding types (BasicHttpBinding, WSHttpBinding, etc.), incoming and outgoing values are automatically mapped into XML elements, using (by default) the new System.Runtime.Serialization.XmlFormatter type, defined within the System.Runtime.Serialization.dll assembly. When you are making use of simple XML/CLR data types (such as numerical and string data), you are not required to take any special measures to ensure the XmlFormatter encodes your data correctly.

However, when you define service contracts that make use of custom types as parameters or return values, these types are defined as data contract. Simply put, a *data contract* is a type adorned with the [DataContract] attribute. Each field you expect to be used as part of the proposed contract (a little bit like a public property) is likewise marked with the [DataMember] attribute.

■**Note** If a data contract contains fields not marked with the [DataMember] attribute, it will not be serialized by the WCF runtime.

Updating the ICarOrder Service Contract

To illustrate the use of these attributes (both of which are defined within the System.Runtime.
Serialization namespace) let's update our previous CarOrderServiceLib project. After you open
this project in Visual Studio 2005, set a reference to the System.Runtime.Serialization.dll assembly. Next, update your existing service contract (ICarOrder) to support the following new member
(note that the parameter is a yet-to-be-defined custom class type):

```
[ServiceContract(Namespace = "http://Intertech.com")]
public interface ICarOrder
{
    // Allows caller to place an order and obtain
    // an order ID.
    [OperationContract]
    int PlaceOrder(string make, string color, double price);

    // This version takes a CarOrderDetails object.
    [OperationContract]
    int PlaceOrder(CarOrderDetails order);

    // Allows caller to get current status of the order.
    [OperationContract]
    string CheckOrderStatus(int orderID);
}
```

The newly overloaded PlaceOrder() method takes a CarOrderDetails object as input,
which defines four private member fields to represent the make, color, and price, as well as a
CarOrderDetails type to represent a backup choice, just in case the first choice is not on the lot:

```
[DataContract]
public class CarOrderDetails
{
    [DataMember]
    public string Make;
    [DataMember]
    public string Color;
    [DataMember]
    public double Price;
    [DataMember]
    public CarOrderDetails SecondChoice;
}
```

The CarOrderService type implements this overloaded method as follows:

```
public int PlaceOrder(CarOrderDetails order)
{
    // Greedy salesperson!
    if (order.SecondChoice.Price < 40000)
    {
        Console.WriteLine("Sorry, your first choice is not on our lot.");
        Console.WriteLine("We do however have a {0} {1}.",
            order.SecondChoice.Color, order.SecondChoice.Make);
```

```
        Console.WriteLine("You will be charged {0}.", order.SecondChoice.Price);
    }
    else
    {
        // Simply print out the incoming data and return an order ID.
        Console.WriteLine("Thanks for buying a {0} {1} for the low, low price of ${2}.",
            order.Color, order.Make, order.Price);
    }
    return HardCodedOrderNumber;
}
```

At this point, compile your assembly to ensure you have no errors. Assuming this is the case, you might be surprised to see that when you load your CarOrderServiceHost project into Visual Studio 2005 (which automatically copies the latest version of CarOrderServiceLib.dll), you receive a runtime exception! The reason is that while method overloading is just fine as far as the CLR is concerned, the rules of WSDL demand that each method is uniquely named within the WCF contract. To disambiguate the name clash, we can set the Name property as so:

```
[ServiceContract(Namespace = "http://Intertech.com")]
public interface ICarOrder
{
    ...
    // This version takes a CarOrderDetails object.
    [OperationContract(Name = "PlaceOrderWithDetails")]
    int PlaceOrder(CarOrderDetails order);
}
```

With this update, you should now be able to rebuild and execute your host.

Recoding the CarOrderServiceClient Assembly

Now, in order for our client to call this new method, we need to regenerate the client-side proxy data, given that the C# code file currently is out of date. To do so, right-click the generated *.map file located under the Service References folder of Solution Explorer. At this point, simply select the Update Service Reference option (see Figure 28-7).

Figure 28-7. *Refreshing the proxy files using Visual Studio 2005*

■Note At the time of this writing, the Visual Studio 2005 "Orcas" Community Technology Preview IDE incorrectly updates the app.config file (by authoring multiple endpoint definitions). If you are having a similar problem, simply delete the entire file from your project before refreshing the server reference.

You can now call the new PlaceOrderWithDetails() method as you would expect:

```
static void Main(string[] args)
{
  // Create the proxy and call the members.
  using(CarOrderClient c = new CarOrderClient())
  {
    CarOrderDetails myOrder = new CarOrderDetails();
    myOrder.Color = "Green";
    myOrder.Make = "BMW";
    myOrder.Price = 15.221;

    CarOrderDetails backUpCar = new CarOrderDetails();
    backUpCar.Make = "Yugo";
    backUpCar.Color = "Pink";
    backUpCar.Price = 5000;
    myOrder.SecondChoice = backUpCar;

    int orderID = c.PlaceOrderWithDetails(myOrder);

    Console.WriteLine(c.CheckOrderStatus(orderID));
  }
  Console.ReadLine();
}
```

When you run the client application, you will find that your original order has been rejected, leaving you with a lovely pink Yugo (see Figure 28-8).

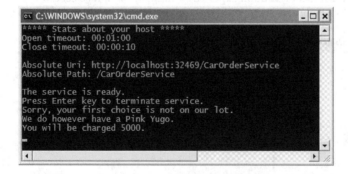

Figure 28-8. *Offer rejected!*

Data Formatting Using the XmlSerializer

As you learned in Chapter 25, XML web services persist data as streams of XML using a completely different formatter named the XmlSerializer in the System.Xml.Serialization namespace. One benefit of this type is that you are able to apply additional attributes to your custom type members to control exactly how each item should be represented in terms of XML. The new WCF XmlFormatter (used by default), on the other hand, uses a fixed XML format for purposes of optimization (some benchmarks place this somewhere in the realm of 10 percent better performance using the WCF XmlFormatter).

If you do need to fine-tune exactly how the fields of your custom types are represented as XML, you can inform the WCF runtime to make use of the XmlSerializer (rather than the default XmlFormatter) by applying the [XmlSerializerFormat] attribute. After this point, you can apply the additional attributes from the System.Xml.Serialization namespace to control the underlying data formatting. Although we have no need to do so, here is a trivial example (see Chapter 25 for further details regarding the use of these attributes):

```
[DataContract]
[XmlSerializerFormat]
public class CarOrderDetails
{
  [DataMember, System.Xml.Serialization.XmlAttribute]
  public string Make;
...
}
```

Transporting Data in Binary Format

The final topic regarding data representation we will examine here is how to instruct the WCF runtime to encode message data in a compact binary format, rather than a stream of XML. Recall that when you specify any of the HTTP or web service–centric binding types, message data is automatically encoded as XML using the XmlFormatter. Again, this is most certainly the best choice when you want your WCF service to be accessible from the greatest number of clients.

However, when you are building WCF services that are accessed directly by WCF clients (and therefore running on the Windows family of operating systems), the overhead of XML encoding is a less-than-perfect solution. If all interested parties are indeed WCF aware, you may prefer to use the NetTcpBinding type, which will encode your message data into a (Microsoft-proprietary) binary format when passing data between machine boundaries.

Moreover, if you are building a WCF service that is accessed by a WCF client *on the same machine*, you can gain even better performance by making use of the NetNamedPipeBinding type. Recall that changing binding is no more difficult than updating the <endpoint> element of the host's application configuration file. Of course, if you do so, you will need to update the client's *.config file as well.

Building WCF Configuration Files Using the Service Configuration Editor

To conclude this introductory look at WCF programming, it is well worth pointing out that the .NET Framework 3.0 SDK ships with the SvcConfigEditor.exe tool (the Microsoft Service Configuration Editor), which allows you to create and edit host-side and client-side configuration files from a friendly graphical editor.

While it is always a good idea to know how to author and modify *.config file by hand, the Service Configuration Editor will save you a great amount of time (and possible typos). Once you launch this tool, you can proceed to the File menu and choose an existing *.config file you wish to update, or you can select a WCF executable to generate a new (properly named) application file (see Figure 28-9).

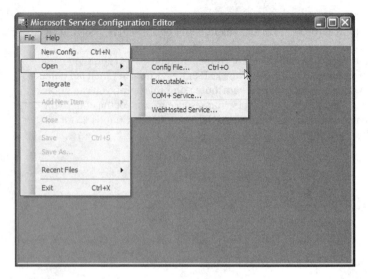

Figure 28-9. *Selecting a target for configuration*

For this example, I suggest opening the host's existing *.config file. Assuming this is the case, you can now select endpoints, behaviors, and diagnostic options for editing using a related Properties window. For example, if you want to change the binding attribute of an endpoint to netNamedPipeBinding, simply select this option from the drop-down (see Figure 28-10).

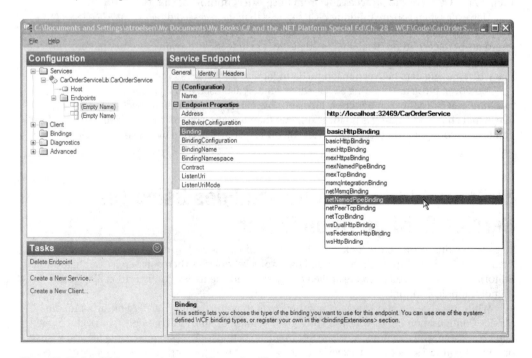

Figure 28-10. *Modifying an existing configuration file*

Beyond simply authoring the necessary XML on your behalf, this tool is an excellent way to learn about the wide variety of options you have at your disposal when configuring WCF services (and clients). As well, the tool itself has a useful help system that can be launched from the Help menu.

Summary

This chapter introduced you to the Windows Communication Foundation (WCF) API, which ships with .NET 3.0. As explained, the major motivation behind WCF is to provide a unified object model that exposes a number of (previously unrelated) distributed computing APIs under a single umbrella. Furthermore, as you saw at the onset of this chapter, a WCF service is represented by specified addresses, bindings, and contracts (easily remembered by the friendly acronym ABC).

As you have seen, a typical WCF application involves the use of three interrelated assemblies. The first assembly defines the service contracts and service types that represent the services functionality. This assembly is then hosted by a custom executable, an IIS virtual directory, or a service, or via the Vista WAS runtime. Finally, the client assembly makes use of a generated code file defining a proxy type (and settings within the application configuration file) to communicate with the remote type.

The chapter wrapped up by mentioning the (very helpful) .NET 3.0 WCF service configuration utility SvcConfigEditor.exe. Using this tool, you (or a system administrator) can alter the functionality of the service host (or client) using a convenient GUI.

## CHAPTER 29

Introducing Windows Workflow Foundation

The final major component of .NET 3.0 is Windows Workflow Foundation (WF). This API allows you to model, configure, and execute the *workflows* (which, for the time being, can simply be regarded as a collection of related tasks) used internally by a given application. The out-of-the-box solution provided by WF is a huge benefit when building production-level software, as we are no longer required to manually develop complex infrastructure to support a workflow-enabled application.

This chapter begins by defining what a business process is and describing how it relates to the WF API, as well as providing a general overview of the WF architecture (and mind-set). Along the way, you will be exposed to the concept of a WF "activity" and the two major flavors of workflows: sequential and state machine.

Once we've covered the basics, we'll build several example programs that illustrate how to leverage the WF programming model to establish business processes that execute under the watchful eye of the WF runtime engine. In addition to learning how to program within the WF object model, you will also examine how to build custom activities and how to make use of the integrated WF designers provided by Visual Studio 2005 "Orcas."

Note The entirety of WF cannot be covered in a single introductory chapter. If you require a deeper treatment of the topic than presented here, check out *Pro WF: Windows Workflow in .NET 3.0* by Bruce Bukovics (Apress, 2007).

The Motivation Behind Windows Workflow Foundation

Any real-world application must be able to model various business processes. Simply put, a *business process* is a conceptual grouping of tasks that logically work as a collective whole. For example, assume you are building an application that allows a user to purchase an automobile online. Once the user submits the order, a large number of activities are set in motion. We might begin by starting a database transaction in order to remove the entry from an inventory table, add a new order in an orders table, and update the customer account information. After the database transaction has completed, we still might need to send a confirmation e-mail to the buyer, and then invoke a remote web service to place the order at the dealership. Collectively, all of these tasks represent a single business process.

Historically speaking, modeling a business process was yet another detail that programmers had to account for, often by authoring custom code to ensure that a business process was not only modeled correctly, but also executed within the application itself. Programmers needed to author additional code to account for points of failure, tracing, and logging support (to see what a given business process is up to); persistence support (to save the state of long-running processes); and whatnot. As you may know firsthand, building this sort of infrastructure under .NET 2.0 entailed a great deal of manual labor.

Assuming that a development team did, in fact, build a custom business process framework for their applications, their work was not yet complete. Simply put, a raw C# code base cannot be easily explained to nonprogrammers on the team who *also* need to understand the business process. The truth of the matter is that subject matter experts (SMEs), managers, salespeople, and members of a graphic design team often do not speak the language of code. Given this, we were required to make use of other modeling tools (such as Microsoft Visio) to graphically represent the process using skill set–neutral terms. The obvious problem here is we now have two entities to keep in sync: If we change the code, we need to update the diagram. If we change the diagram, we need to update the code.

Furthermore, when building a sophisticated software application using the *100% code approach*, the code base has very little trace of the internal "flow" of the application. For example, a typical .NET program might be composed of hundreds of custom types (not to mention the numerous types used by the base class libraries). While programmers may have a feel for which objects are making calls on other objects, the code itself is a far cry from a living document that explains the overall sequence of activity. While the development team may build external documentation and workflow charts, again we run into the problem of multiple representations of the same product.

With the release of .NET 3.0, we are provided with the brand-new Windows Workflow Foundation (WF) API. In essence, WF allows programmers to *declaratively* design business processes using a prefabricated set of *activities*. Thus, rather than building a custom set of assemblies to represent a given business activity and the necessary infrastructure, we can make use of the WF designers of Visual Studio 2005 "Orcas" to create our business process at design time. In this respect, WF allows us to build the skeleton of a business process, which can be fleshed out through code.

When programming with the WF API, a single document can be used to represent the overall business process as well as the code that defines it. Since a single WF document is used to represent the code driving the process in addition to being a friendly visual representation of the process, we no longer need to worry about multiple documents falling out of sync. Better yet, unless you are in the unfortunate position of working for a completely clueless manager, this WF document will clearly illustrate the process itself.

The Building Blocks of WF

As you build a workflow-enabled application, you will undoubtedly notice that it "feels different" from building a traditional application. For example, up until this point in the text, every code example began by creating a new project workspace and authoring custom code to represent the program at large. A WF application also consists of custom code; however, in addition, you are building *directly into the assembly* the business process itself.

Consider Figure 29-1, which illustrates the initial workflow diagram generated by Visual Studio 2005 "Orcas" when selecting a new Sequential Workflow console application.

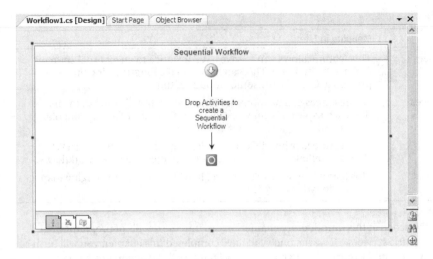

Figure 29-1. *An empty WF sequential diagram*

Using this designer (and various WF-centric tools integrated into Visual Studio 2005 "Orcas") you are able to model your process and eventually author code to execute it under the appropriate circumstances. You'll examine these tools in more detail a bit later in this chapter.

Understand that WF is far more than a pretty designer that allows you to model the activities of a business process. As you are building your WF diagram, the designer tools are (not surprisingly) authoring code to represent the skeleton of your process. Thus, the first thing to be aware of is that a visual WF diagram is executable code, not just simply a Visio-like static image. As such, WF is represented by a set of .NET assemblies, namespaces, and types, just like any other .NET technology.

Given the fact that a WF diagram equates to real types and custom code, the next thing to understand is that WF also consists of a runtime engine to load, execute, unload, and in other ways manipulate the workflow process. The WF runtime engine can be hosted within any .NET application domain. Recall from Chapter 13 that an AppDomain is a partition within a Win32 process that plays host to a .NET application and any external code libraries. As such, the WF engine can be embedded within a simple console program, a GUI desktop application (Windows Forms or Windows Presentation Foundation [WPF]), and an ASP.NET web application.

If you are modeling a business process that needs to be used by a wide variety of systems, you also have the option of authoring your WF within a C# class library project. In this way, new applications can simply reference your *.dll to reuse a predefined collection of business processes. Finally, you are free to build custom hosts for the WF runtime if necessary (which isn't covered in this introductory chapter).

In any case, at this point understand that the WF API provides a full-blown object model that allows you to programmatically interact with the runtime engine as well as the workflows you have designed.

The Integrated Services of WF

In addition to designer tools and a runtime engine, WF provides a set of out-of-the-box services that complete the overall architecture of a workflow-enabled application. This is obviously a good thing, as we can "inherit" a set of necessary services, rather than having to commit time and resources to building our own custom infrastructure. Table 29-1 documents (at a high level) the core services baked into the WF API.

Table 29-1. *Core Services of WF*

Services	Meaning in Life
Persistence services	This feature allows you to save a WF instance to an external source (such as a database). This can be useful if a long-running business process will be idle for some amount of time.
Transaction services	WF instances can be monitored in a transactional context, to ensure that each aspect of your workflow completes (or fails) as a singular atomic unit.
Tracking services	This feature is primarily used for debugging and optimizing a WF activity; it allows you to monitor the activities of a given workflow.
Scheduling services	This feature allows you to control how the WF runtime engine manages threads for your workflows.

It is beyond the scope of this introductory chapter to dive into the details of programming against these WF-centric services. However, once you have completed this chapter, you will be in a perfect position to dive into further details using the .NET Framework 3.0 documentation.

■ **Tip** The official WF website (http://wf.netfx3.com) also provides further resources, sample code, and insights into this new programming model. Be sure to check it out.

A First Look at WF Activities

Recall that the purpose of WF is to allow you to model a business process in a declarative manner, which is then executed by the WF runtime engine. In the vernacular of WF, a business process is composed of any number of *activities*. Simply put, a WF activity is an atomic "step" in the overall process. When you create a new WF-enabled application using Visual Studio 2005 "Orcas," you will find a Windows Workflow toolbox that contains iconic representations of the built-in activities (see Figure 29-2).

Figure 29-2. *The Windows Workflow toolbox*

■**Note** Do be aware that the items within the Windows Workflow toolbox can change based on which WF project
template you select from Visual Studio 2005 "Orcas."

At the time of this writing, the Windows Workflow toolbox provides over 25 default activities
that you can use to model your business process, each of which maps to real types within the
System.Workflow.Activities namespace and therefore can be represented by and driven from
code. You'll make use of several of these baked-in activities over the course of this chapter.
Table 29-2 describes the functionality of some of the core activities' class types, grouped by
related functionality.

Table 29-2. *A Sampling of Intrinsic WF Activities*

Activities	Meaning in Life
CodeActivity	This activity represents a unit of custom code to execute within the workflow.
CallExternalMethodActivity HandleExternalEventActivity	These activities allow your workflow to interact with external services on the local machine.
IfElseActivity WhileActivity	These activities provide basic looping and decision construct support within a workflow.
InvokeWebServiceActivity WebServiceInputActivity WebServiceOutputActivity WebServiceFaultActivity	These activities allow your workflow to interact with XML web services.
ConditionedActivityGroupActivity	This activity allows you to define a group of related activities that execute when a given condition is true.
DelayActivity SuspendActivity TerminateActivity	These activities allow you to define wait periods as well as pause or terminate a course of action within a workflow.
EventDrivenActivity EventHandlingScopeActivity	These activities allow you to associate CLR events to a given activity within the workflow.
ThrowActivity FaultHandlerActivity	These activities allow you to raise and handle exceptions within a workflow.
ParallelActivity SequenceActivity	These activities allow you to execute a set of activities in parallel or in sequence.

While the current number of intrinsic activities is impressive and provides a solid foundation
for many WF-enabled applications, you are also able to create custom activities that seamlessly
integrate into the Visual Studio 2005 "Orcas" IDE and the WF runtime engine.

The Role of Sequential Workflows and State Machine Workflows

WF provides support for modeling two flavors of a business process workflow: sequential workflows
and state machine workflows. Ultimately, both categories are constructed by piecing together any
number of related activities; however, exactly *how* they execute is what sets them apart.

The most straightforward workflow type is *sequential*. As its name implies, a sequential workflow allows you to model a business process where each activity executes in sequence until the final
activity completes. This is not to say that a sequential workflow is necessarily linear or predictable
in nature—it is entirely possible to build a sequential workflow that contains various branching and
looping activities, as well as a set of activities that execute in parallel on separate threads.

The key aspect of a sequential workflow is that it has a crystal-clear beginning and ending point. Within the Visual Studio 2005 "Orcas" workflow designer, the path of execution begins at the top of the WF diagram and proceeds downward to the end point. Figure 29-3 shows a simple sequential workflow that models a partial business process for verifying a given automobile is in stock.

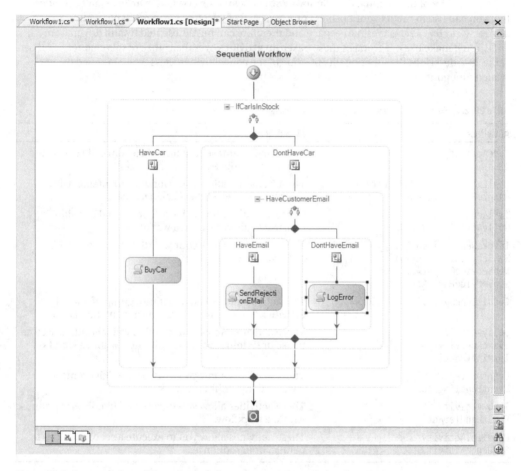

Figure 29-3. *Sequential workflows have a clear starting point and a clear ending point.*

Sequential workflows work well when the workflow model will be shown to a business audience, and when there is no requirement for backtracking in the process. For example, the business process modeled in Figure 29-3 has two possible outcomes: the car is in stock or it isn't. If the car is indeed in stock, the order is processed using some block of custom code (whatever that may be). If the car isn't in stock, we send a notification e-mail, provided that we have the client's e-mail address at our disposal.

In contrast to sequential workflows, *state machine workflows* do not model activities using a simple linear path. Instead, the workflow defines a number of *request states* and a set of related events that trigger transitions between these states. Figure 29-4 illustrates a simple state machine WF diagram that represents the processing of an order. Don't worry about the details of what each activity is doing behind the scenes, but do notice that each request state in the workflow can flow across various states based on some internal event.

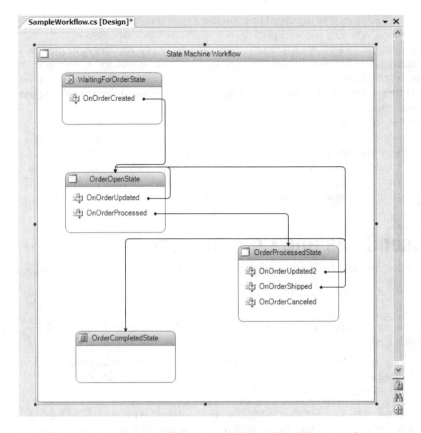

Figure 29-4. *State machine workflows do not follow a fixed, linear path.*

State machine workflows can be very helpful when you need to model a business process that can be in various states of completion. Here, we have a request state that is waiting for an order to be created. Once that occurs, an event forces the flow of activity to the order open state, which may trigger an order processed state (or loop back to the previous open state), and so forth.

■**Note** In this introductory chapter, I don't dig into the details of building state machine workflows. Consult the .NET Framework 3.0 documentation for further details if you are interested.

Getting into the Flow of Workflow

Before we dive into our first code example, allow me point out a few final thoughts regarding the "workflow mind-set."

When programming with the WF API, you must keep in mind that you are ultimately attempting to model a *business process*; therefore, the first step is to investigate the business process itself, including all the substeps within the process and each of the possible outcomes. For example, assume you are modeling the process of registering for a training class online. When a request comes in, what should you do if the salesperson is out of the office? What if the class is currently full? What if the class has been canceled or moved to a new date? How can you determine if the trainer is available, is not on vacation, is not teaching a class that same week, or whatnot?

Depending on your current background, the process of gathering these requirements may be a very new task, as figuring out a business process may be "someone else's problem." However, in small companies, the act of determining the necessary business processes may fall on the shoulders of the developers themselves. Larger organizations typically have business analysts who take on the role of discovering (and often modeling) the business processes.

In any case, do be aware that working with WF is not simply a "jump in and start coding" endeavor. If you do not take the time to clearly analyze the business problem you are attempting to solve before coding, you will most certainly create a good amount of unnecessary pain. In this chapter, you will concentrate on the basic mechanics of workflow design, the use of activities, and how to work with the Visual Studio 2005 "Orcas" WF designers. However, don't be too surprised when your real-world workflows become substantially more complex.

The WF Assemblies and Core Namespaces

From a programmer's point of view, WF is represented by three core assemblies:

- `System.Workflow.Activities.dll`: Defines the intrinsic activities and the rules that drive them

- `System.Workflow.Runtime.dll`: Defines types that represent the WF runtime engine and instances of your custom workflows

- `System.Workflow.ComponentModel.dll`: Defines numerous types that allow for design-time support of WF applications, including definitions for types used by the code-generation services of Visual Studio 2005 "Orcas"

While these assemblies define a number of .NET namespaces, many of them are used behind the scenes by various WF visual design tools. Table 29-3 documents some WF-centric namespaces to be aware of.

Table 29-3. *Core WF Namespaces*

Namespace	Meaning in Life
`System.Workflow.Activities`	This is the core activity-centric namespace, which defines type definitions for each of the items on the Windows Workflow toolbox. Additional subnamespaces define the rules that drive these activities as well as types to configure them.
`System.Workflow.Runtime`	This namespaces defines types that represent the WF runtime engine (such as `WorkflowRuntime`) and an instance of a given workflow (via `WorkflowInstance`).
`System.Workflow.Runtime.Hosting`	This namespace provides types to build a custom host for the WF runtime.

Be aware that when you create a new WF project template using Visual Studio 2005 "Orcas," the IDE will reference each of the WF assemblies and update your namespace imports automatically.

Building a Simple Workflow-Enabled Application

To get your feet wet with the process of building workflow-enabled applications, this first WF example will model a very simple sequential process. The goal is to build a workflow that prompts the user for his or her name and validates the results. If the results do not jibe with our business rules, we will prompt for input again until we reach success.

To begin, create a Sequential Workflow Console Application project named UserDataWFApp (see Figure 29-5).

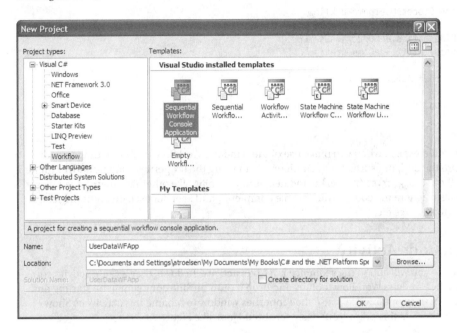

Figure 29-5. *Creating a new Sequential Workflow Console Application project*

Once the project has been created, use Solution Explorer to rename the initial WF designer file from Workflow1.cs to the more fitting ProcessUsernameWorkflow.cs.

Examining the Initial Workflow Code

Before we add activities to represent our business process, let's take a look at how this initial diagram is represented internally. If you examine the ProcessUsernameWorkflow.cs file using Solution Explorer, you will notice that much like other designer-maintained files (forms, windows, web pages), a WF diagram consists of two partial class definitions. When you open the core *.cs file, you will find a class type that extends the SequentialWorkflowActivity type and a default constructor that makes a call to the InitializeComponent() method:

```
public sealed partial class ProcessUsernameWorkflow : SequentialWorkflowActivity
{
  public ProcessUsernameWorkflow()
  {
    InitializeComponent();
  }
}
```

■**Note** One of the tenets of WF development is that workflows are singular, atomic entities. Given this fact, notice that the workflow class type is explicitly sealed, thereby preventing it from functioning as a parent class for derived types.

If you now open the related *.Designer.cs file, you will find that InitializeComponent() has set the Name property accordingly (in addition to a handful of other property settings):

```
partial class ProcessUsernameWorkflow
{
  [System.Diagnostics.DebuggerNonUserCode]
  private void InitializeComponent()
  {
    this.CanModifyActivities = true;
    this.Name = "ProcessUsernameWorkflow";
    this.CanModifyActivities = false;
  }
}
```

As you would expect, when you make use of the Windows Workflow toolbox to drag various activities onto the designer surface and configure them using the Properties window and/or inline smart tags, the *.Designer.cs file will be updated automatically. Like other IDE-maintained files, you can typically ignore the code within this file completely and keep focused on authoring code within the primary *.cs file.

Adding a Code Activity

The first activity you will add in the sequence is a Code activity. To do so, drag a Code activity component from the Windows Workflow toolbox and drop it onto the line connecting the starting and ending points of the workflow. Next, use the Properties window to rename this activity as Show-InstructionsActivity. At this point, your designer should look like Figure 29-6.

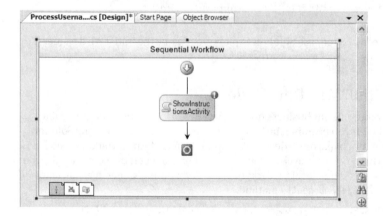

Figure 29-6. *A (not quite ready for prime time) Code activity*

As you can see, the designer is currently reporting an error, which you can view by clicking the red exclamation point on top of the Code activity. The error informs you that the ExecuteCode property has not been set, which is a mandatory step for all Code activity types. Not too surprisingly, this property establishes the name of the method to execute when this task is encountered by the WF runtime engine.

Using the Properties window, set the value of this property to a method named ShowInstructions. Once you press the Enter key, the IDE will update the primary *.cs code file with the following stub code:

```
public sealed partial class ProcessUsernameWorkflow: SequentialWorkflowActivity
{
  public ProcessUsernameWorkflow()
  {
    InitializeComponent();
  }

  private void ShowInstructions(object sender, EventArgs e)
  {

  }
}
```

To implement this method, add a handful of Console.WriteLine() statements that display some basic instructions to the end user:

```
private void ShowInstructions(object sender, EventArgs e)
{
  ConsoleColor previousColor = Console.ForegroundColor;
  Console.ForegroundColor = ConsoleColor.Yellow;
  Console.WriteLine("*****************************************");
  Console.WriteLine("***** Welcome to the first WF Example *****");
  Console.WriteLine("*****************************************");
  Console.WriteLine("\nI will now ask for your name and validate the data...\n");
  Console.ForegroundColor = previousColor;
}
```

Adding a While Activity

Recall that our business process will prompt the end user for his or her name until the input can be validated against a custom business rule (that is yet to be defined), which can be represented using the While activity. Specifically, a While activity allows us to define a set of related activities that will continuously execute until a specified condition is true.

To illustrate, begin by dragging a While activity from the Windows Workflow toolbox directly below the previous Code activity and rename this new activity to AskForNameLoopActivity. The next step is to define the condition that will be used to exit the loop itself by setting the Condition property from the Properties window. Our condition will be based on some custom code that we have yet to author; however, the first step is to select the Code Condition option from the Condition property, and then specify the name of the method that will perform the test. Again using the Properties window, name this method GetAndValidateUserName (see Figure 29-7).

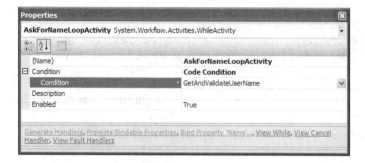

Figure 29-7. *The configured While activity*

As soon as you specify the name of the method used to test the While condition, the IDE will generate a method stub where the second parameter is of type ConditionalEventArgs. This type contains a property named Result, which can be set to true or false based on the success or failure of the condition you are modeling. To do so, add a new string member variable named userName to your ProcessUsernameWorkflow class, and assign to it the value String.Empty. Within the scope of the GetAndValidateUserName() method, simply ask the user to enter his or her name, and if the name length is fewer than ten characters, set the Result property to true. Here are the updates in question:

```
public sealed partial class ProcessUsernameWorkflow : SequentialWorkflowActivity
{
  // User name field and related property.
  private string userName = String.Empty;
  public string UserName
  {
    get { return userName; }
    set { userName = value; }
  }

  private void GetAndValidateUserName(object sender, ConditionalEventArgs e)
  {
    Console.Write("Please enter name, which much be less than 10 chars: ");
    userName = Console.ReadLine();

    // See if name is correct length, and set the result.
    e.Result = (userName.Length > 10);
  }
...
}
```

The final task to complete the While activity involves adding at least a single activity within the scope of the While logic. Here we will add a new Code activity named NameNotValidActivity, which has been connected to a method named NameNotValid via the ExecuteCode property. Figure 29-8 shows the final workflow diagram.

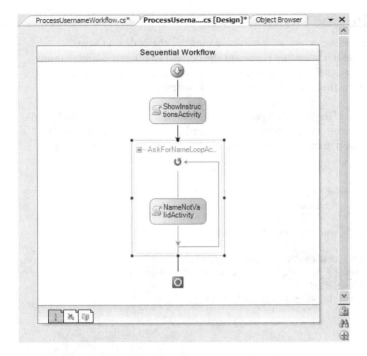

Figure 29-8. *The final WF activity*

The implementation of NameNotValid() is also intentionally simple:

```
private void NameNotValid(object sender, EventArgs e)
{
  Console.WriteLine("Sorry, try again...");
}
```

At this point, you may compile and run this workflow-enabled application. When you execute the program, purposely enter more than ten characters a few times. You will notice that the runtime engine forces the user to reenter data until the business rule (length > 10) is honored. Figure 29-9 shows one possible output.

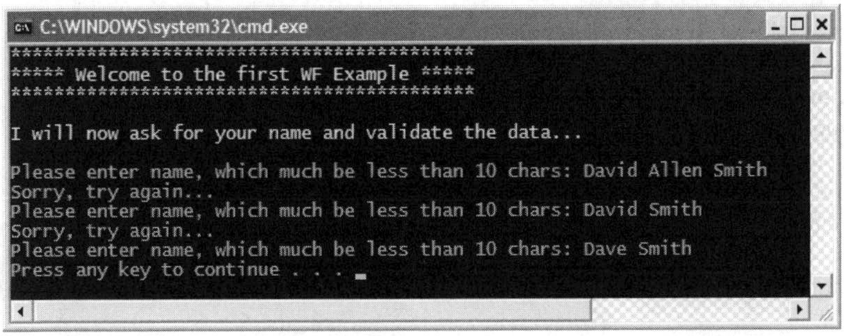

```
C:\WINDOWS\system32\cmd.exe                                       _ □ ×
*************************************
***** Welcome to the first WF Example *****
*************************************

I will now ask for your name and validate the data...

Please enter name, which much be less than 10 chars: David Allen Smith
Sorry, try again...
Please enter name, which much be less than 10 chars: David Smith
Sorry, try again...
Please enter name, which much be less than 10 chars: Dave Smith
Press any key to continue . . . _
```

Figure 29-9. *The workflow-enabled application in action*

Examining the WF Engine Hosting Code

While our first example executes as expected, we have yet to examine the code that actually instructs the WF engine to execute the tasks that represent the current workflow. To understand this aspect of WF, open the `Program.cs` file that was created when you defined your initial project. Within the `Main()` method, you will find code that makes use of two core types, `WorkflowRuntime` and `WorkflowInstance`.

As the names suggest, the `WorkflowRuntime` type represents the WF runtime engine itself, while `WorkflowInstance` is used to represent an instance of a given (pardon the redundancy) workflow instance. Here is the `Main()` method in question, annotated with my various code comments:

```
static void Main(string[] args)
{
  // Ensure the runtime shuts down when we are finished.
  using(WorkflowRuntime workflowRuntime = new WorkflowRuntime())
  {
    AutoResetEvent waitHandle = new AutoResetEvent(false);

    // Handle events that capture when the engine completes
    // the workflow process and if the engine shuts down with an error.
    workflowRuntime.WorkflowCompleted
      += delegate(object sender, WorkflowCompletedEventArgs e)
    {
      waitHandle.Set();
    };
    workflowRuntime.WorkflowTerminated
      += delegate(object sender, WorkflowTerminatedEventArgs e)
    {
      Console.WriteLine(e.Exception.Message);
      waitHandle.Set();
    };

    // Now, create a WF instance that represents our type.
    WorkflowInstance instance =
    workflowRuntime.CreateWorkflow(typeof(UserDataWFApp.ProcessUsernameWorkflow));
    instance.Start();

    waitHandle.WaitOne();
  }
}
```

First of all, notice that the `WorkflowCompleted` and `WorkflowTerminated` events of `WorkflowRuntime` are handled using C# anonymous method syntax. The `WorkflowCompleted` event fires when the WF engine has completed executing a workflow instance, while `WorkflowTerminated` fires if the engine terminates with an error.

Strictly speaking, you are not required to handle these events, although the Visual Studio 2005 "Orcas"–generated code does so in order to inform the waiting thread these events have occurred using the `AutoResetEvent` type. This is especially important for a console-based application, as the WF engine is operating on a secondary thread of execution. If the workflow logic did not make use of some sort of wait handle, the main thread might terminate before the WF instance was able to perform its work.

The next point of interest regarding the code within `Main()` is the creation of the `WorkflowInstance` type. Notice that the `WorkflowRuntime` type exposes a method named `CreateWorkflow()`, which expects type information representing the workflow to be created. At this point, we simply call `Start()` from the returned object reference. This is all that is required to fire up the WF runtime engine and begin the processing of our custom workflow.

Adding Custom Start-up Parameters

Before we move on to a more interesting workflow example, allow me to address how to add application-wide parameters. If you examine the signature of the designer-generated methods used by our Code activities (ShowInstructions() and NameNotValid() specifically), you may have noticed that they are called via WF events that are making use of the System.EventHandler delegate (given the incoming parameter).

Because this .NET delegate demands the registered event handler and takes System.Object and System.EventArgs as arguments, you may wonder how to pass in *custom* parameters to a Code activity. In fact, you may be wondering how to define custom arguments that can be used by any activity within the current workflow instance.

As it turns out, the WF engine supports the use of custom parameters using a generic Dictionary<string, object> type. The name/value pairs added to the Dictionary object must then be associated to (identically named) properties on your workflow instance. Once you've done this, you can pass these arguments into the WF runtime engine when you start your workflow instance. Using this approach, you are able get and set custom parameters throughout a particular workflow instance.

To try this out firsthand, begin by updating the code within Main() to define a Dictionary<string, object> containing two data items. The first item is a string literal that represents the error message to display if the name is too long; the second item is a numeric value that will be used to specify the maximum length of the user name. To register these parameters with the WF runtime engine, pass in your Dictionary object as a second parameter to the CreateWorkflow() method. Here are the relevant updates:

```
using (WorkflowRuntime workflowRuntime = new WorkflowRuntime())
{
...
  // Define two parameters for use by our workflow.
  // Remember!  These must be mapped to identically named
  // properties in our workflow class type.
  Dictionary<string, object> parameters = new Dictionary<string, object>();
  parameters.Add("ErrorMessage", "Ack!  Your name is too long!");
  parameters.Add("NameLength", 5);

  // Now, create a WF instance that represents our type
  // and pass in parameters.
  WorkflowInstance instance =
    workflowRuntime.CreateWorkflow(
        typeof(UserDataWFApp.ProcessUsernameWorkflow), parameters
        );
  instance.Start();
  waitHandle.WaitOne();
}
```

■**Note** In the preceding code, the values assigned to the ErrorMessage and NameLength dictionary items are hard-coded. A more dynamic approach is to read these values from a related *.config file, or perhaps from incoming command-line arguments.

If you try running your program at this point, you will encounter a runtime exception, as you have yet to associate these data points to public properties on your workflow type. Once you have done so, however, the runtime will invoke them upon workflow creation. After this point, you can use these properties to get and set the underlying data values. Here are the relevant updates to the ProcessUsernameWorkflow class type:

```csharp
public sealed partial class ProcessUsernameWorkflow : SequentialWorkflowActivity
{
...
  private string errorMsg;
  private int nameLength;

  public string ErrorMessage
  {
    get { return errorMsg; }
    set { errorMsg = value; }
  }
  public int NameLength
  {
    get { return nameLength; }
    set { nameLength = value; }
  }

  private void GetAndValidateUserName(object sender, ConditionalEventArgs e)
  {
    Console.Write(
        "Please enter name, which much be less than {0} chars: ", NameLength
        );
    userName = Console.ReadLine();

    // See if name is correct length, and set the result.
    e.Result = (userName.Length > NameLength);
  }

  private void NameNotValid(object sender, EventArgs e)
  {
    Console.WriteLine(ErrorMessage);
  }
...
}
```

Beyond the fact that you have added two new properties (and the related member variables), notice that the GetAndValidateUserName() method is now checking for the length specified by the NameLength property, while the error message prints out the value found within the ErrorMessage property. In both cases, these values are determined via the Dictionary object passed in at the time the workflow instance was created. Figure 29-10 shows some possible output for this modified example.

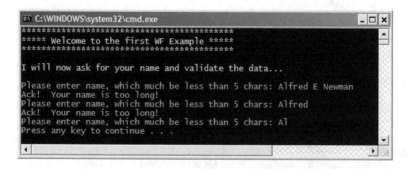

Figure 29-10. *The workflow in action, now with custom parameters*

■Source Code The UserDataWFApp example is included under the Chapter 29 subdirectory.

Invoking Web Services Within Workflows

WF provides several activities that allow you to interact with XML web services during the lifetime of your workflow-enabled application. To illustrate this aspect of WF development (and to examine additional common activities), create a new Sequential Workflow Console Application project named XmlWebServiceWFApp. Then rename your initial `Workflow1.cs` file to the more fitting `CallWebServiceWF.cs`.

Next up, you need to create a web service that can be invoked by your workflow instance. While you are free to use the code for any of the web services created in Chapter 25, you should be aware that the WF designer tools expect the web service you wish to invoke to be hosted by a production web server, rather than the ASP.NET development web server. The reason for this is simply that the InvokeWebService activity will automatically generate proxy code for the remote web service, and therefore it needs to have a fixed URL.

For simplicity, you may wish to add a brand-new XML web service project to your current solution (by right-clicking the solution icon in Solution Explorer, selecting Add ➤ New Web Site, and then selecting the ASP.NET Web Service icon), fittingly named SimpleWebService. When you do so, be sure to create this web service within a new IIS virtual directory. To stay focused on web service/workflow integration, the web service will define a single method that adds two integers and returns the result:

```
[WebService(Namespace = "http://intertech.com/")]
[WebServiceBinding(ConformsTo = WsiProfiles.BasicProfile1_1)]
public class Service : System.Web.Services.WebService
{
  public Service () {}
  [WebMethod]
  public int Add(int x, int y)
  { return x + y; }
}
```

Now, turning back to the WF designer, add a new Code activity named GetDataToAddActivity that is mapped to a method named GetDataToAdd(), by setting the ExecuteCode property via the Properties window. Within this method, prompt the user to enter two numerical values that are stored within appropriately named private member variables and encapsulated by public properties:

```
public sealed partial class CallWebServiceWF : SequentialWorkflowActivity
{
  private int xVal, yVal;
  public int Y
  {
    get { return yVal; }
    set { yVal = value; }
  }
  public int X
  {
    get { return xVal; }
    set { xVal = value; }
  }
}
```

```
public CallWebServiceWF()
{
  InitializeComponent();
}

private void GetDataToAdd(object sender, EventArgs e)
{
  // For simplicity, we are not bothering to verify that
  // the input values are indeed numerical.
  Console.Write("Enter first number: ");
  X = int.Parse(Console.ReadLine());
  Console.Write("Enter second number: ");
  Y = int.Parse(Console.ReadLine());
}
}
```

Next, add a new InvokeWebService activity onto your designer, directly after the previous Code activity. Doing so will immediately open the Add Reference dialog box, where you specify the location of this particular *.asmx file (e.g., http://localhost/Tests/SimpleWebService/Service.asmx). After this point, the IDE will add references to the web service–centric assemblies, insert an app.config file to resolve the specified URL and—most important for this example—assign the InvokeWebService's ProxyClass property to the name of the autogenerated web service proxy type (see Figure 29-11).

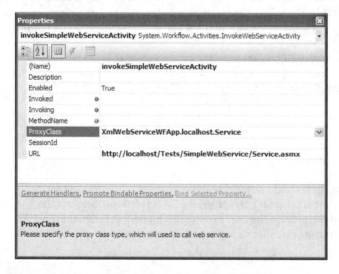

Figure 29-11. *A partially configured InvokeWebService activity*

Before you can invoke the web service, you have a bit of additional configuration to perform for this InvokeWebService activity type. First, you need to select which method to invoke at the specified URL. To do so, use the Properties window to select the Add() method from the MethodName property drop-down box. Next, you need to map the existing X and Y properties of the CallWebServiceWF class type to the input parameters of the Add() method. Again, you can do this using the Properties window. Notice that in Figure 29-12, each input parameter exposed by the Add() method is listed as an option of the editor.

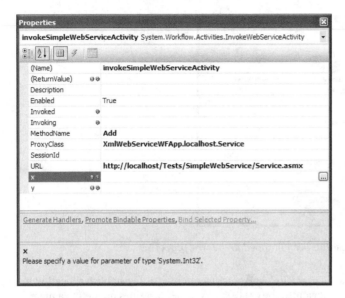

Figure 29-12. *Parameters of a web service must be mapped to members of your WF type.*

Click the ellipsis button next to each parameter property and connect the parameter to the correct property name, as suggested in Figure 29-13.

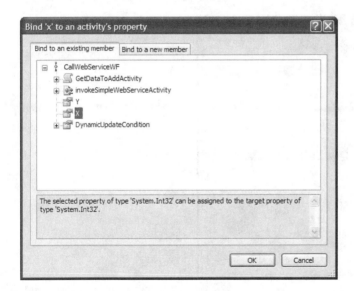

Figure 29-13. *Mapping web service parameters*

Figure 29-14 shows the end result of this parameter mapping.

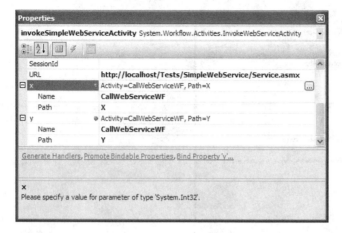

Figure 29-14. *Success! Each parameter has been mapped to the type properties.*

The final task configuration detail of the InvokeWebService activity is to establish a location to hold the web method's return value. Currently, the CallWebServiceWF class does not define a member variable (or property) for this purpose, but using the (ReturnValue) property of the Properties window, you can instruct the IDE to create this infrastructure on your behalf. Once you have clicked the ellipsis button, select the "Bind to a new member" tab and specify a new property named Result, as shown in Figure 29-15.

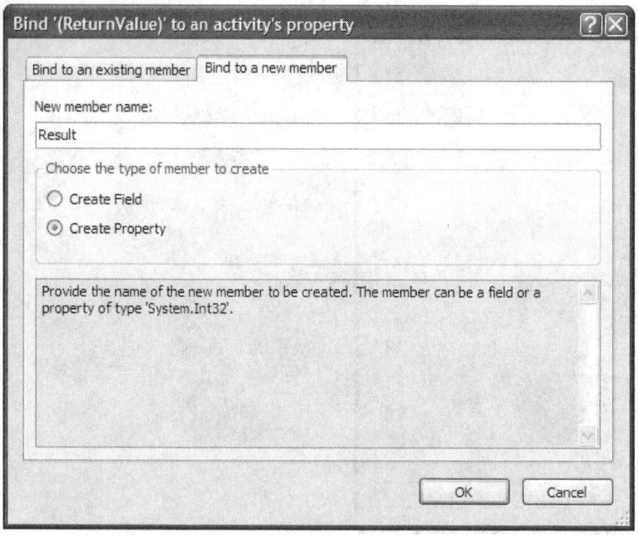

Figure 29-15. *Specifying storage for the web service return value*

Once you click this dialog box's OK button, the IDE will add a property and back field in the CallWebServiceWF class type. At this point, the InvokeWebService activity has been fully configured.

To complete the current example, add a final Code activity (named ShowResultActivity) after the InvokeWebService activity, which maps to a new method named `DisplayResult()`. Implement this method to display the result of adding the two input parameters using each of the properties created during this example:

```
private void DisplayResult(object sender, EventArgs e)
{
  Console.WriteLine("{0} + {1} = {2}", X, Y, Result);
}
```

If you run this workflow-enabled application, sure enough the WF runtime engine will ensure that the external web method is invoked as the workflow executes. Figure 29-16 shows the workflow we have just created.

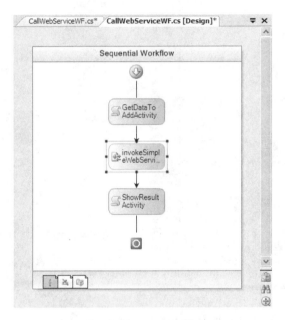

Figure 29-16. *The CallWebService workflow*

Working with the IfElse Activity

To illustrate the use of yet another WF activity, let's add some additional logic that makes use of the IfElse activity. As you might expect, this activity allows you to define a branching condition within your workflow, based on whether a specific condition is true or false.

Add an IfElse activity directly after the previous Code activity and rename it to GreaterThan20Activity. Notice that the IfElse activity expands to two branches, currently called ifElseBranchActivity1 and ifElseBranchActivity2. Using the Properties window, rename ifElse-BranchActivity1 to GreaterThan20 and ifElseBranchActivity2 to NotGreaterThan20. Finally, add a Code activity under each branch named GreaterCodeActivity and LessCodeActivity. Figure 29-17 shows the current state of this modified workflow.

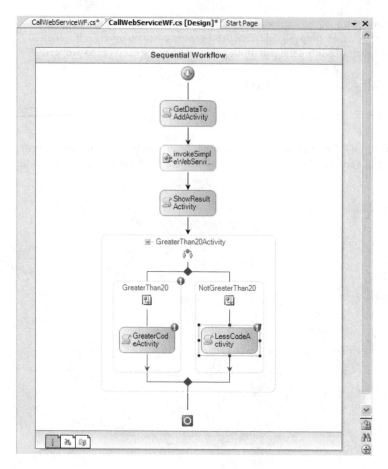

Figure 29-17. *Initial configuration of the IfElse activity*

Next, set the ExecuteCode property of each Code activity to new methods that print out a simple diagnostic message:

```
private void GreaterCode(object sender, EventArgs e)
{
  Console.WriteLine("Your sum is greater than 20.");
}

private void LesserCode(object sender, EventArgs e)
{
  Console.WriteLine("Your sum is less than 20.");
}
```

The final task to perform before you can test the IfElse activity is to define the condition to test against. Using the Properties window (once again), define a new code condition for the GreaterThan20 condition that maps to a method named CheckValue() (see Figure 29-18).

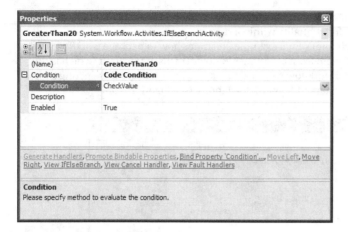

Figure 29-18. *The final IfElse activity configuration detail*

The implementation of CheckValue() is just about what you would expect. Simply set the Result property of the incoming ConditionalEventArgs parameter to true or false, based on the value returned from the web service:

```
private void CheckValue(object sender, ConditionalEventArgs e)
{
  e.Result = Result > 20;
}
```

Now, when you run your application, enter two numbers that result in a sum less than 20. You should see output similar to that of Figure 29-19 (and obviously, if the result is greater than 20, you will see the message specified within the GreaterCode() method).

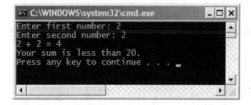

Figure 29-19. *Branching to the right . . .*

■Source Code The XmlWebServiceWFApp example is included under the Chapter 29 subdirectory.

Building a Reusable WF Code Library

Each of the WF examples created thus far in the chapter was defined within the content of a console application. While this fits the bill for the purposes of illustration, I bet you can easily envision building workflow-enabled Windows Forms applications, WPF applications, or ASP.NET web applications. Furthermore, I am sure you can imagine the need to reuse a workflow across numerous applications by packaging the functionality within a reusable .NET code library.

To address these needs, this chapter's final example illustrates how to package workflows into *.dll assemblies and make use of them from a hosting Windows Forms application (which is the same process as hosting an external workflow within a WPF application). Begin by selecting a Sequential Workflow Library project named MyWorkflowLibrary (see Figure 29-20).

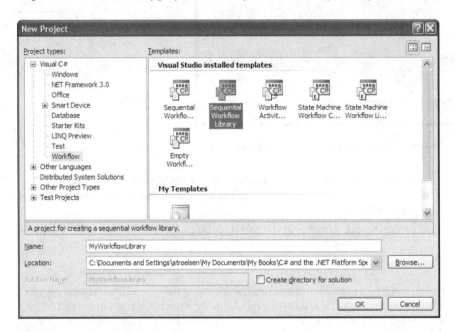

Figure 29-20. *Creating a WF library project*

You are provided with a workflow designer that is identical to the designer you make use of when building a console-based workflow. Using the various designer tools, you can build any sort of workflow to model the business process at hand. As well, a single .NET WF code library can contain multiple workflows, each of which can be inserted using the Project ➤ Add New Item dialog box. Here you can add in any number of sequential workflows, state machine workflows, and custom activities.

Authoring a Simple Workflow

For this illustrative example, simply rename the initial workflow file to SimpleExampleWorkflow.cs, and add a Code activity (named ShowMessageActivity) to the designer that maps to a method named ShowMessage(). This method displays a string literal within a Windows Forms message box (so be sure to reference the System.Windows.Forms.dll assembly in your project):

```
private void ShowMessage(object sender, EventArgs e)
{
  System.Windows.Forms.MessageBox.Show("Success!");
}
```

Next, you'll add a single Delay activity, which allows you to inject a timed wait period within a given branch of a workflow. Using the Properties window, set the TimeoutDuration to 00:00:10, which equates to ten seconds. Finally, add a final Code activity (named ShowEndActivity) that maps to a method named ShowEndMessage, implemented as follows:

```
private void ShowEndMessage(object sender, EventArgs e)
{
  System.Windows.Forms.MessageBox.Show("Time up!");
}
```

Figure 29-21 illustrates the example workflow.

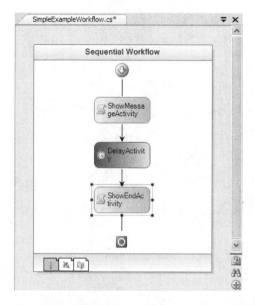

Figure 29-21. *The final (albeit very simple) workflow*

Now compile your code library to ensure you have not injected any typos.

■**Source Code** The MyWorkflowLibrary example is included under the Chapter 29 subdirectory.

Creating a Windows Forms Workflow-Enabled Application

Now that you have authored a reusable .NET code library that contains a custom workflow, you are able to build any sort of .NET application to make use of it. Add a new Windows Forms project (or, if you wish, a WPF project) to your current solution, and ensure you set this project as the start-up project through Solution Explorer. Next, add a reference to each of the following .NET assemblies:

- MyWorkflowLibrary.dll
- System.Workflow.Runtime.dll
- System.Workflow.Activities.dll
- System.Workflow.ComponentModel.dll

Add a single Button type (named btnExecuteWorkflow) on the initial form, and handle the Click event. Within your code file, implement the button-click event handler to fire up the WF runtime engine and create an instance of your custom workflow.

Notice that the following code is identical to that found within a console-based workflow application (minus the threading code required to keep the console program alive until the workflow completes):

```
// Initial using statements removed for simplicity.

// Need the WF runtime!
using System.Workflow.Runtime;

// Be sure to reference our custom WF library.
using MyWorkflowLibrary;

namespace WinFormsWFClient
{
  public partial class MainForm : Form
  {
    public MainForm()
    {
      InitializeComponent();
    }

    private void btnExecuteWorkflow_Click(object sender, EventArgs e)
    {
      // Create the WF runtime.
      WorkflowRuntime wfRuntime = new WorkflowRuntime();

      // Get an instance of our WF.
      WorkflowInstance myWorkflow =
        wfRuntime.CreateWorkflow(typeof(SimpleExampleWorkflow));

      // Start it up!
      myWorkflow.Start();
    }
  }
}
```

Now, when you run your program and click the button, you should see the first message box display instantly, while the final dialog displays after approximately ten seconds. Given that this workflow is launching Windows Forms message boxes, it would not make good sense to use this particular WF code library within an ASP.NET web application, but the overall process is very similar. Look up the topic "Developing ASP.NET Workflow Applications" within the .NET Framework 3.0 documentation for further details.

■**Source Code** The WinFormsWFClient example is included under the Chapter 29 subdirectory.

A Brief Word Regarding Custom Activities

At this point, you have seen how to configure a handful of common WF activities (Code, While, InvokeWebService, etc.). While these built-in activities certainly are a firm starting point for many

WF applications, they do not account for every possible circumstance. Thankfully, since the initial public release of the WF betas, the WF community has been creating new custom activities, some of which are freely downloadable, and others of which are offered through third parties at various price points.

■**Note** If you are interested in examining some additional workflow activities, a good starting point is http://wf.netfx3.com. Here, you can download a good number of additional activities that extend those that ship out of the box with .NET 3.0.

Despite the number of auxiliary activities that can be obtained from the online WF community, it is also entirely possible (and in some cases necessary) to build a custom activity from scratch. As you might guess, Visual Studio 2005 "Orcas" provides a Workflow Activity Library project template for this very purpose. If you select this project type, you will be given a designer surface to create your custom activity, using an identical approach to building a workflow itself (add new activities, connect them to code, etc.).

Much like the process of building a custom Windows Forms control, a custom activity can be adorned with numerous .NET attributes that control how the component should integrate within the IDE—for example, which bitmap image to display on the toolbar, which configuration dialogs (if any) to display when a property is configured within the Properties window, and so forth.

If you are interested in learning more about building custom activities, the .NET Framework 3.0 SDK documentation provides a number of interesting examples, including the construction of a "Send E-mail Activity." For more details, simply browse the Custom Activities samples found under the WF Samples node of the provided documentation (see Figure 29-22).

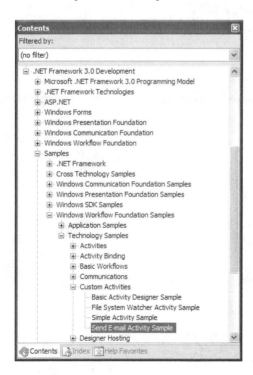

Figure 29-22. *You can find numerous WF code examples within the .NET Framework 3.0 documentation.*

Summary

Windows Workflow Foundation (WF) is the final—and, in some cases, most radical—component of .NET 3.0. In essence, WF allows you to model an application's internal business processes directly within the application itself. Beyond simply modeling the overall workflow, however, WF provides a complete runtime engine and several services that round out this API's overall functionality (transaction services, persistence and tracking services, etc.). While this introductory chapter did not examine these services in any great detail, do remember that a production-level WF application will most certainly make use of these facilities.

When building a workflow-enabled application, Visual Studio 2005 "Orcas" provides several designer tools, including a workflow designer, configuration using the Properties window, and (most important) the Windows Workflow toolbox. Here, you will find numerous built-in *activities* that constitute the overall composition of a particular workflow. And as you have seen, when the baked-in activities don't quite fit the bill, you are free to build your own custom activities.

■ ■ ■

## CHAPTER 30

C# 3.0 Language Features

C# 3.0, the forthcoming release of Microsoft's flagship .NET programming language, introduces a large number of new syntactic constructs. This chapter will introduce you to implicit data typing, extension methods, object initializers, anonymous types, and lambda expressions.

While many of these new language features can be used directly out of the box to help build robust and highly functional .NET software, it is also worth pointing out that many of these new constructs are most helpful when interacting with the LINQ technology set, which we'll examine in Chapter 31. Given this fact, don't be too concerned if the usefulness of some of these new constructs is not immediately obvious. Once you understand the role of LINQ, the role of many of these new features will become clear.

Note At the time of this writing, C# 3.0 is in its beta cycle. Understand that the topics examined in this chapter are subject to change before the final release.

Working with the C# 3.0 Command-Line Compiler

Visual Studio 2005 is "hard-coded" (if you will) to make use of the C# 2.0 compiler when compiling your source code into a .NET assembly. However, the LINQ Community Technology Preview (see Chapter 26) installs a number of new project templates, each of which makes use of the preview C# 3.0 compiler (see Figure 30-1).

These templates automatically set references to a number of LINQ-specific assemblies, use a number of LINQ-specific namespaces, and tend to provide LINQ-specific starter code. In this chapter, we will create all of our examples using the LINQ Console Application project template, to take advantage of the C# 3.0 compiler integration. So simply ignore all the LINQ-specific details for the time being.

As an alternative, you can opt to explicitly compile this chapter's samples at the command line using the C# 3.0 compiler. By default, csc.exe (version 3.0) is installed under C:\Program Files\ LINQ Preview\Bin. Thus, to gain access to this version of the compiler, begin by opening a command prompt and change into the Bin folder using the cd command:

```
cd C:\Program Files\LINQ Preview\Bin
```

As well, to simplify the typing of command-line arguments, I suggest saving all of your code files within a folder named CSharp3 under your C drive. This way, you can compile your code as follows, without having to update your machine's environment variables:

```
csc /out:C:\CSharp3\MyApp.exe C:\CSharp3\MyApp.cs
```

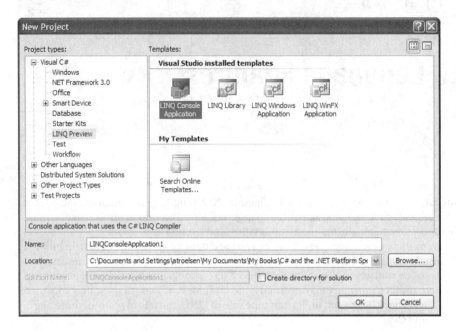

Figure 30-1. *The LINQ project templates of Visual Studio 2005 make use of the C# 3.0 compiler.*

Pick your poison, and let's dive into the new features found in the forthcoming release of the C# programming language, beginning with the concept of implicitly typed data.

Understanding Implicitly Typed Local Variables

As you have learned since the very beginning of this text, local variables (such as variables declared in a method scope) are declared in a very predictable manner:

```
static void Main()
{
  // Local variables are declared as so:
  // dataType variableName = initialValue;
  int myInt = 0;
  bool myBool = true;
  string myString = "Time, marches on...";
  Console.ReadLine();
}
```

C# 3.0 now provides a new keyword, var, which you can use in place of specifying a formal data type (such as int, bool, or string). When you do so, the compiler will automatically infer the underlying data type based on the value used to initialize the data point. For example, the previous Main() method could now be authored as so:

```
static void Main()
{
  // Implicitly typed local variables.
  var myInt = 0;
  var myBool = true;
  var myString = "Time, marches on...";
  Console.ReadLine();
}
```

In this case, the compiler is able to infer that myInt is in fact a System.Int32, myBool is a System. Boolean, and myString is indeed of type System.String, given the assigned value. You can verify this by printing out the type name via reflection:

```
static void Main()
{
  Console.WriteLine("***** Fun with Implicit Typing *****\n");

  // Implicitly typed local variables.
  var myInt = 0;
  var myBool = true;
  var myString = "Time, marches on...";

  // Print out the underlying type.
  Console.WriteLine("myInt is a: {0}", myInt.GetType().Name);
  Console.WriteLine("myBool is a: {0}", myBool.GetType().Name);
  Console.WriteLine("myString is a: {0}", myString.GetType().Name);
  Console.ReadLine();
}
```

Furthermore, be aware that you can use this implicit typing for any type in the base class libraries, including arrays, generics, and custom class types:

```
var evenNumbers = new int[] {2, 4, 6, 8};
var myMinivans = new List<MiniVan>();
var myCar = new SportsCar();
```

If you reflect over each of these implicitly typed local variables, you'll find the output shown in Figure 30-2.

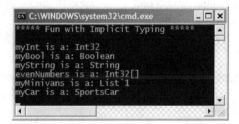

Figure 30-2. *Reflecting over implicitly defined local variables*

It is also possible to make use of the var keyword within a foreach looping construct. As you would expect, the compiler will correctly imply the correct type of type:

```
// Use 'var' in a standard for each loop.
var evenNumbers = new int[] { 2, 4, 6, 8 };

// Here, var is really a System.Int32.
foreach (var item in evenNumbers)
{
  Console.WriteLine("Item value: {0}", item);
}
```

Understand, however, that a foreach loop can make use of a strongly typed iterator when processing an implicitly defined local variable. Thus, the following code is also syntactically correct:

```
// Use 'var' to declare the array of data.
var evenNumbers = new int[] { 2, 4, 6, 8 };

// Use a strongly typed System.Int32 to iterate over contents.
foreach (int item in evenNumbers)
{
  Console.WriteLine("Item value: {0}", item);
}
```

Restrictions on Implicitly Typed Variables

There are, of course, various restrictions regarding the use of the var keyword. First and foremost, implicit typing applies *only* to local variables in a method or property scope. It is illegal to use the var keyword as method return values or parameters, or as field data:

```
class ThisWillNeverCompile
{
  // Error! var cannot be used as field data!
  private var myInt = 10;

  // Error!  var cannot be used as return values
  // or parameter types!
  public var MyMethod(var x, var y){}
}
```

As well, local variables declared with the var keyword *must* be assigned an initial value at the time of declaration and *cannot* be assigned the value of null. The first restriction makes the act of defining an implicitly typed variable look and feel like the process of defining a constant data point. This last restriction should make sense, given that the compiler cannot infer what sort of type in memory the variable would be pointing to based only on null:

```
// Error! Must assign a value!
var myData;

// Error! Must assign value at time of declaration!
var myInt;
myInt = 0;

// Error! Can't assign null!
var myObj = null;
```

It is permissible, however, to assign an inferred object local variable to null after its initial assignment:

```
// OK!
var myCar = new SportsCar();
myCar = null;
```

Furthermore, it is permissible to assign the value of an implicitly typed local variable to the value of other variables, implicitly typed or not:

```
// Also OK!
var myInt = 0;
var anotherInt = myInt;
string myString = "Wake up!";
var myData = myString;
```

Finally, be aware that because var is a new keyword, it is now illegal to define variables and type members using this token:

```
// Compiler error!
int var = 10;
```

Implicitly Typed Local Arrays

Closely related to the topic of implicitly typed local variables is the subject of implicitly typed local arrays. Using this technique, you can allocate a new array type using syntax such as the following:

```
// a is really int[].
var a = new[] { 1, 2, 3, 4000 };

// b is really double[].
var b = new[] { 1, 1.5, 2, 2.5 };

// c is really string[].
var c = new[] { "we", null, "are", null, "family" };

// myCars is really SportsCar[].
var myCars = new[] { new SportsCar(), new SportsCar()};
```

Of course, just as when you allocate an array using traditional C# syntax, the items in the array's initialization list must be of the same underlying type (all ints, all strings, all SportsCars, etc.). Thus, the following generates a compile-time error:

```
// Error!  Mixed types!
var d = new[] { 1, "one", 2, "two" };
```

Final Points Regarding Implicit Data Typing

To wrap up our look at implicitly typed local variables, I'd like to point out that using var as your data type declaration simply for the sake of doing so really brings little to the table. In fact, overuse of this technique can be confusing to others reading your code, as it becomes harder to quickly determine the underlying type of type (and therefore more difficult to understand the overall functionality of the variable).

However, as you will see in Chapter 31, the LINQ technology set makes use of *query expressions* to yield dynamically created result sets based on the format of the query itself. In these cases, implicit typing is extremely helpful, as we do not need to explicitly define the type that a query may return, which saves a lot of tedious typing time.

Furthermore, type inference of local variables is *not* the same technique used with scripting languages (such as VBScript or Perl) or the COM Variant data type, where a variable can hold values of different types over its lifetime in a program. Rather, type inference keeps the strongly typed aspect of the C# language and affects only the declaration of variables at compile time. After that point, the data point is treated as if it was declared with that type; assigning a value of a different type into that variable will result in a compile-time error:

```
// Error!  The compiler knows myVar is a string, not an integer!
var s = "This variable can only hold string data!";
s = "This is fine...";
s = 44; // This is not!
```

■**Source Code** The ImplicitlyTypedLocalVars project can be found under the Chapter 30 subdirectory.

Understanding Extension Methods

As you know, once a type (class, interface, structure, enum, or delegate) is defined and compiled into a .NET assembly, its definition is, more or less, final. The only way to add new members, update members, or remove members is to recode and recompile the code base into an updated assembly (or take more drastic measures, such as using the System.Reflection.Emit namespace to dynamically reshape a compiled type).

Under C# 3.0, it is now possible to define methods as *extension methods*. In a nutshell, extension methods allow existing compiled types (such as classes within an external .NET class library) as well as types currently being compiled (such as types in a project that contains extension methods) to gain new functionality without needing to directly update the type being extended.

As suggested, this technique can be quite helpful when you need to inject new functionality into types for which you do not have an existing code base. It can also be quite helpful when you need to force a type to support a set of members (in the interest of polymorphism), but cannot modify the original type declaration. Using extension methods, you can add functionality to pre-compiled types while providing the illusion these methods were there all along.

When you define extension methods, the first restriction is that they must be defined within a *static class* (see Chapter 3), and therefore each extension method must also be declared as static. The second point is that all extension methods are marked as such by using the this keyword as a modifier on the first (and only the first) parameter of the method in question. The third point is that every extension method can be called either from the correct instance in memory or *statically* via the defining static class. Sound strange? Let's look at a full example to clarify matters.

Defining Extension Methods

Assume you are authoring a utility class named MyExtensions that defines two extension methods. The first method allows any object in the .NET base class libraries to have a brand-new method named DisplayDefiningAssembly() that makes use of types in the System.Reflection namespace. The second extension method, named ReverseDigits(), allows any System.Int32 to obtain a new version of itself where the value is reversed digit by digit. For example, if an integer with the value 1234 called ReverseDigits(), the integer returned is set to the value 4321:

```
static class MyExtensions
{
  // This method allows any object to display the assembly
  // it is defined in.
  public static void DisplayDefiningAssembly(this object obj)
  {
    Console.WriteLine("{0} lives here:\n\t->{1}\n", obj.GetType().Name,
      Assembly.GetAssembly(obj.GetType()));
  }

  // This method allows any integer to reverse its digits.
  // For example, 56 would return 65.
  public static int ReverseDigits(this int i)
  {
    // Translate int into a string, and then
    // get all the characters.
    char[] digits = i.ToString().ToCharArray();
```

```
    // Now reverse items in the array.
    Array.Reverse(digits);

    // Put back into string.
    string newDigits = new string(digits);

    // Finally, return the modified string back as an int.
    return int.Parse(newDigits);
  }
}
```

Again note how the first parameter of each extension method has been qualified with the this keyword, before defining the parameter type. Given that DisplayDefiningAssembly() has been prototyped to extend System.Object, any type in any assembly now has this new member. However, ReverseDigits() has been prototyped to only extend integer types, and therefore if anything other than an integer attempts to invoke this method, you will receive a compile-time error.

Understand that a given extension method could have multiple parameters, but *only* the first parameter can be qualified with this. To illustrate, here is an overloaded extension method defined in another utility class, named simply TesterUtilClass:

```
static class TesterUtilClass
{
  // Every Int32 now has a Foo() method...
  public static void Foo(this int i)
  { Console.WriteLine("{0} called the Foo() method.", i); }

  // ...which has been overloaded to take a string!
  public static void Foo(this int i, string msg)
  { Console.WriteLine("{0} called Foo() and told me: {1}", i, msg); }
}
```

Invoking Extension Methods from an Instance Level

Now that we have these extension methods, look at how all objects (which of course means everything in the .NET base class libraries) have a new method named DisplayDefiningAssembly(), while System.Int32 types (and only integers) have methods named ReverseDigits() and Foo():

```
static void Main(string[] args)
{
  Console.WriteLine("***** Fun with Extension Methods *****\n");

  // The int has assumed a new identity!
  int myInt = 12345678;
  myInt.DisplayDefiningAssembly();

  // So has the DataSet!
  System.Data.DataSet d = new System.Data.DataSet();
  d.DisplayDefiningAssembly();

  // And the SoundPlayer!
  System.Media.SoundPlayer sp = new System.Media.SoundPlayer();
  sp.DisplayDefiningAssembly();

  // Use new integer functionality.
  Console.WriteLine("Value of myInt: {0}", myInt);
  Console.WriteLine("Reversed digits of myInt: {0}", myInt.ReverseDigits());
```

```
myInt.Foo();
myInt.Foo("Ints that Foo?  Who would have thought it!");

// Error!  Booleans don't have the Foo() method!
bool b2 = true;
// b2.Foo();

Console.ReadLine();
}
```

Figure 30-3 shows the output.

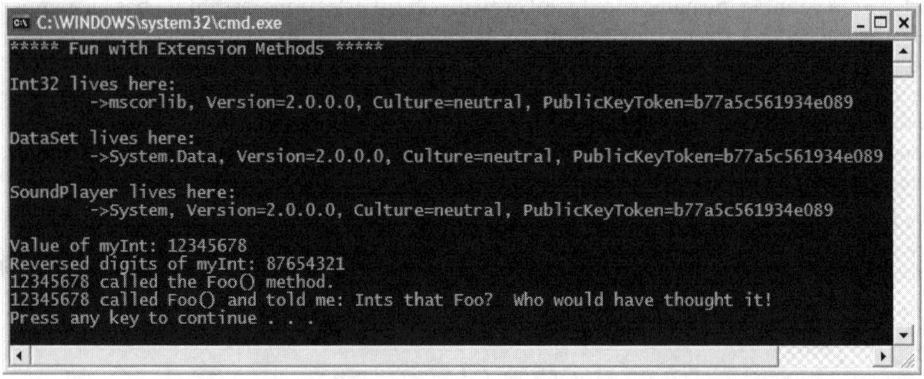

Figure 30-3. *Extension methods in action*

Invoking Extension Methods Statically

Recall that the first parameter of an extension method is marked with the this keyword, followed by the type of item the method is applicable to. If we peek at what is happening behind the scenes (as verified by a tool such as ildasm.exe or Lutz Roeder's Reflector), we will find that the compiler simply calls the "normal" static method, passing in the variable calling the method as a parameter (e.g., it is the this). Consider the following C# code, which approximates the code substitution that took place:

```
private static void Main(string[] args)
{
  Console.WriteLine("***** Fun with Extension Methods *****\n");
  int myInt = 12345678;
  MyExtensions.DisplayDefiningAssembly(myInt);

  DataSet d = new DataSet();
  MyExtensions.DisplayDefiningAssembly(d);

  SoundPlayer sp = new SoundPlayer();
  MyExtensions.DisplayDefiningAssembly(sp);

  Console.WriteLine("Value of myInt: {0}", myInt);
  Console.WriteLine("Reversed digits of myInt: {0}",
    MyExtensions.ReverseDigits(myInt));
  TesterUtilClass.Foo(myInt);
  TesterUtilClass.Foo(myInt, "Ints that Foo?  Who would have thought it!");
}
```

Given that calling an extension method from an object (thereby making it seem that the method were in fact an instance-level method) is just some smoke-and-mirrors effect provided by the compiler, you are always free to call extension methods as normal static methods using the expected C# syntax (as just shown).

Importing Types That Define Extension Methods

When you partition a set of static types with extension methods in a unique namespace (e.g., a namespace termed MyUtilities), other namespaces in that assembly will make use of the standard C# using keyword to import not only the static classes themselves, but also each of the supported extension methods. This is important to remember, because if you do not explicitly import the correct namespace, the extension methods are not available for that C# code file.

In effect, although it can appear that extension methods are "global," they are in fact limited to the namespace that imports them. Thus, if we wrap the MyExtensions and TesterUtilClass types into the namespace named MyUtilities as follows:

```
namespace MyUtilities
{
  static class MyExtensions
  {
  ...
  }

  static class TesterUtilClass
  {
  ...
  }
}
```

the only integers that would have access to Foo() and ReverseDigits() (and the only objects that could call the DisplayDefiningAssembly() method) would be those that explicitly imported the MyUtilities namespace:

```
using System;
using System.Collections.Generic;
using System.Text;

namespace TestNamespace
{
  class JustATest
  {
    void SomeMethod()
    {
      // Error!  Need to use the MyUtilities namespace to extend int with Foo()!
      int i = 0;
      i.Foo();
    }
  }
}
```

Source Code The ExtensionMethods project can be found under the Chapter 30 subdirectory.

Building and Using Extension Libraries

The final aspect of extension methods we will examine here is the construction of extension libraries. Our previous example extended the functionality of various types (such as the System. Int32 type) for use by the current console application. However, I am sure you could imagine the usefulness of building a .NET code library that defines numerous extensions that can be referenced by multiple applications. As luck would have it, doing so is very straightforward.

To illustrate, create a new LINQ library project (named MyExtensionsLibrary) by selecting the LINQ Preview node of the Visual Studio 2005 "Orcas" New Project dialog. Next, rename your initial C# code file to MyExtensions.cs, and copy the DisplayDefiningAssembly() and ReverseDigits() methods into the new class definition. At this point, your namespace should look like the following:

```
namespace MyExtensionsLibrary
{
  public static class MyExtensions
  {
    // Same implementation as before.
    public static void DisplayDefiningAssembly(this object obj)
    {...}

    // Same implementation as before.
    public static int ReverseDigits(this int i)
    {...}
  }
}
```

■**Note** If you wish to export extension methods from a .NET code library, the defining type must be declared publically (recall the default access modifier for a type is internal).

It is worth pointing out that the System.Query.dll assembly (being the core LINQ-centric assembly) defines the [Extension] attribute with the System.Runtime.CompilerServices namespace. This attribute, which can be applied at the assembly, class, or method level, can be used to explicitly mark a member (or class or assembly) as an entity containing extension methods.

While the current LINQ Community Technology Preview does not require you to apply this attribute in order to export extension methods across assembly boundaries, this may change with the final release of C# 3.0. Here is an updated definition of the MyExtensions type, which explicitly marks the extension class and its members:

```
namespace MyExtensionsLibrary
{
  [Extension]
  public static class MyExtensions
  {
    [Extension]
    public static void DisplayDefiningAssembly(this object obj)
    {...}

    [Extension]
    public static int ReverseDigits(this int i)
    {...}
  }
}
```

In any case, at this point you can compile your library and reference the MyExtensionsLibrary. dll assembly within new .NET projects. When you do so, the new functionality provided to System.Object and System.Int32 can be used by any application. To test this out, add a new LINQ console application project (named MyExtensionsLibraryClient) to the current solution.

Next, add a reference to the MyExtensionsLibrary.dll assembly. Within the initial code file, specify that you are using the MyExtensionsLibrary namespace, and author some simple code that invokes these new methods from a local integer:

```
// Get our custom namespace.
using MyExtensionsLibrary;

namespace MyExtnesionsLibraryClient
{
  class Program
  {
    static void Main(string[] args)
    {
      // This time, these extension methods
      // have been defined within an external
      // .NET class library.
      int myInt = 987;
      myInt.DisplayDefiningAssembly();
      Console.WriteLine("{0} is reversed to {1}",
        myInt, myInt.ReverseDigits());
      Console.ReadLine();
    }
  }
}
```

■Source Code The MyExtensionsLibrary and MyExtensionsLibraryClient projects can be found under the Chapter 30 subdirectory.

Understanding Object Initializers

As you may recall from Chapter 12 during our examination of .NET attributes, when you apply attributes, you may make use of *named property syntax* to indirectly set values to properties:

```
// Apply an attribute using named property syntax.
[AttributeUsage(AttributeTargets.Class, Inherited=false, AllowMultiple = false)]
public sealed class SomeInterestingAttribute: Attribute
{ ... }
```

This is obviously very helpful for attribute syntax, as the underlying object (AttributeUsageAttribute in this case) is not directly created when applying the attribute, but rather at runtime when the attribute is reflected upon.

C# 3.0 offers a similar technique termed *object initializer syntax* for objects that you directly create yourself. Using this technique, it is possible to create a new object variable and assign a slew of properties and/or public fields in a few lines of code. Simply put, an object initializer consists of a comma-delimited list of specified values, enclosed by the { and } tokens. Each member in the initialization list maps to the name of a public field or public property of the object being initialized.

To see this new syntax in action, consider the various geometric types created over the course of this text (Point, Rectangle, Hexagon, etc.). For example, recall our simple Point type used throughout this text:

```
public struct Point
{
  private int xPos, yPos;

  public Point(int x, int y)
  { xPos = x; yPos = y; }

  public int X
  {
    get { return xPos; }
    set { xPos = value; }
  }
  public int Y
  {
    get { return yPos; }
    set { yPos = value; }
  }

  public override string ToString()
  { return string.Format("[{0}, {1}]", xPos, yPos); }
}
```

Under C# 3.0, we could now make Points using any of the following approaches:

```
static void Main(string[] args)
{
  // Make a Point by setting each property manually.
  Point firstPoint = new Point();
  firstPoint.X = 10;
  firstPoint.Y = 10;

  // Make a Point via a custom constructor.
  Point anotherPoint = new Point(20, 20);

  // Make some Point types using the new object init syntax.
  var yetAnotherPoint = new Point { X = 30, Y = 30 };
  Point finalPoint = new Point { X = 30, Y = 30 };
}
```

The final two Point types (one of which is implicitly typed) are not making use of a custom type constructor (as one might do traditionally), but are rather setting values to the public X and Y properties. Behind the scenes, the type's default constructor is invoked, followed by setting the values to the specified properties. To this end, yetAnotherPoint and finalPoint are just shorthand notations for the syntax used to create the firstPoint variable (going property by property).

Now recall that this same syntax can be used to set public fields of a type, which Point currently does not support. However, for the sake of argument, assume that the xPos and yPos member variables have been declared publicly. We could now set values to these fields as so:

```
var p = new Point {xPos = 2, yPos = 3};
```

Given that Point now has four public members, the following syntax is also legal. However, try to figure out the actual final values of xPos and yPos:

```
var p = new Point {xPos = 2, yPos = 3, X = 900};
```

As you might guess, xPos is set to 900, while yPos is the value 3. From this, you can correctly assume that object initialization is performed in a left-to-right manner. To clarify, the previous initialization of p using standard object constructor syntax would appear as follows:

```
Point p = new Point();
p.xPos = 2;
p.yPos = 3;
p.X = 900;
```

Calling Custom Constructors with Initialization Syntax

The previous examples initialized Point types by implicitly calling the default constructor on the type:

```
// Here, the default constructor is called implicitly.
Point finalPoint = new Point { X = 30, Y = 30 };
```

If you wish to be very clear about this, it is permissible to explicitly call the default constructor as so:

```
// Here, the default constructor is called explicitly.
Point finalPoint = new Point() { X = 30, Y = 30 };
```

Do be aware that when you are constructing a type using the new initialization syntax, you are able to invoke *any* constructor defined by the class or structure. Our Point type current defines a two-argument constructor to set the (x, y) position. Therefore, the following Point declaration results in an X value of 100 and a Y value of 100, regardless of the fact that our constructor arguments specified the values 10 and 16:

```
// Calling a custom constructor.
Point pt = new Point(10, 16) { X = 100, Y = 100 };
```

Given the current definition of our Point type, calling the custom constructor while using initialization syntax is not terribly useful (and more than a bit verbose). However, if our Point type provides a new constructor that allows the caller to establish a color (via a custom enumeration named PointColor), the combination of custom constructors and object initialization syntax becomes clear. Assume we have updated Point as so:

```
public enum PointColor
{ LightBlue, BloodRed, Gold }

public struct Point
{
  public int xPos, yPos;
  private PointColor c;

  public Point(PointColor color)
  {
     xPos = 0; yPos = 0;
     c = color;
  }

  public Point(int x, int y)
  {
     xPos = x; yPos = y;
     c = PointColor.Gold;
  }
...
```

```
public override string ToString()
{ return string.Format("[{0}, {1}, Color = {2}]", xPos, yPos, c); }
}
```

With this new constructor, we can now create a golden point (positioned at 90, 20) as follows:

```
// Calling a more interesting custom constructor with init syntax.
Point goldPoint = new Point(PointColor.Gold){ X = 90, Y = 20 };
Console.WriteLine("Value of Point is: {0}", goldPoint);
```

Initializing Inner Types

Recall from Chapter 4 that the has-a relationship allows us to compose new types by defining member variables of existing types. For example, assume we now have a Rectangle class, which makes use of the Point type to represent its upper-left/bottom-right coordinates:

```
public class Rectangle
{
  private Point topLeft = new Point();
  private Point bottomRight = new Point();

  public Point TopLeft
  {
    get { return topLeft; }
    set { topLeft = value; }
  }
  public Point BottomRight
  {
    get { return bottomRight; }
    set { bottomRight = value; }
  }

  public override string ToString()
  {
    return string.Format("[TopLeft: {0}, {1}, BottomRight: {2}, {3}]", topLeft.X,
        topLeft.Y, bottomRight.X, bottomRight.Y);
  }
}
```

Using object initialization syntax, we could create a new Rectangle type and set the inner Points as so:

```
// Create and initialize a Rectangle.
Rectangle myRect = new Rectangle
{
  TopLeft = new Point { X = 10, Y = 10 },
  BottomRight = new Point { X = 200, Y = 200}
};
```

Again, the benefit of this new syntax is that it basically decreases the number of keystrokes. Here is the traditional approach to establishing a similar Rectangle:

```
// Old-school approach.
Rectangle r = new Rectangle();
Point p1 = new Point();
p1.X = 10;
p1.Y = 10;
```

```
r.TopLeft = p1;
Point p2 = new Point();
p2.X = 200;
p2.Y = 200;
r.BottomRight = p2;
```

Understanding Collection Initialization

Closely related to the concept of object initialization syntax is *collection initialization*. This syntax makes it possible to populate a generic container (such as List<T>) with items using a syntax that models that of a simple array. Specifically, this syntax can be used only by types that implement the ICollection<T> interface (including custom generic containers you may implement yourself), because the Add() method is used to insert each element into the collection. Given this restriction, the containers within the System.Collection namespace (such as the ArrayList) cannot make use of this new syntax, as they do not implement the required interface. Consider the following examples:

```
// Init a standard array.
int[] myArrayOfInts = { 0, 1, 2, 3, 4, 5, 6, 7, 8, 9 };

// Init a generic List<> of ints.
List<int> myGenericList = new List<int> { 0, 1, 2, 3, 4, 5, 6, 7, 8, 9 };

// Error!  ArrayList does not implement ICollection<T>!
ArrayList myList = new ArrayList { 0, 1, 2, 3, 4, 5, 6, 7, 8, 9 };
```

If your container is managing a collection of object types, you can blend object initialization syntax with collection initialization syntax to provide the following:

```
List<Point> myListOfPoints = new List<Point>
{
  new Point { X = 2, Y = 2},
  new Point { X = 3, Y = 3},
  new Point { X = 4, Y = 4}
};

foreach (var pt in myListOfPoints)
{
  Console.WriteLine(pt);
}
```

Again, the benefit of this syntax is that you save yourself numerous keystrokes. While the nested curly brackets can become difficult to read if you don't mind your formatting, imagine the amount of code that would be required to fill the following List<> of Rectangles if we did not have initialization syntax:

```
List<Rectangle> myListOfRects = new List<Rectangle>
{
  new Rectangle {TopLeft = new Point { X = 10, Y = 10 },
                 BottomRight = new Point { X = 200, Y = 200}},
  new Rectangle {TopLeft = new Point { X = 2, Y = 2 },
                 BottomRight = new Point { X = 100, Y = 100}},
  new Rectangle {TopLeft = new Point { X = 5, Y = 5 },
                 BottomRight = new Point { X = 90, Y = 75}}
};
```

```
foreach (var r in myListOfRects)
{
  Console.WriteLine(r);
}
```

■**Source Code** The ObjectInitializers project can be found under the Chapter 30 subdirectory.

Understanding Anonymous Types

As an OO programmer, you know the benefits of defining classes to represent the state and functionality of a given programming entity. To be sure, whenever you need to define a class that is intended to be reused across projects and provides numerous bits of functionality through a set of methods, events, properties, and custom constructors, creating a new C# class is common practice.

However, there are other times in programming when you would like to define a class simply to model a set of encapsulated (and somehow related) data points without any associated methods, events, or other custom functionality. Furthermore, what if this type is only used internally to your current application, and it's not intended to be reused? If you need such a "temporary" type, C# 2.0 would require you to nevertheless build a new class definition by hand:

```
internal class SomeClass
{
  // Define a set of private member variables...

  // Make a property for each member variable...

  // Override ToString() to account for each member variable...
}
```

While building such a class is not rocket science, it can be rather labor intensive if you are attempting to encapsulate more than a handful of members. As of C# 3.0, we are now provided with a massive shortcut for this very situation termed *anonymous types*, which is a natural extension of C#'s anonymous methods syntax (examined in Chapter 8).

When you define an anonymous type, you do so by making use of the new var keyword in conjunction with the object initialization syntax you have just examined. Consider the following anonymous class, which models a simple car type:

```
// Make an anonymous object representing a car.
var myCar = new {Color = "Bright Pink", Make = "Saab", CurrentSpeed = 55};

// We can now get and set each value using property syntax.
myCar.Color = "Black"; // Ugh! Change the color!
Console.WriteLine("My car is the color {0}.", myCar.Color);
```

Again note that the myCar variable is implicitly typed (this is mandatory), which makes good sense, as we are not modeling the concept of an automobile using a strongly typed class definition. Also notice that we have to specify (using object initialization syntax) the set of properties that model the data we are attempting to encapsulate. Once defined, these properties can then be obtained or changed using standard C# property invocation syntax (as was the case when we changed to Color property from Bright Pink to Black in the previous code snippet).

The Internal Representation of Anonymous Types

All anonymous types are automatically derived from System.Object, and therefore support each of the members provided by this base class. Given this, we could invoke ToString(), GetHashCode(), Equals(), or GetType() on the implicitly typed myCar object. Assume our Program class defines the following static helper function:

```
static void ReflectOverAnonymousType(object obj)
{
  Console.WriteLine("obj is an instance of: {0}", obj.GetType().FullName);
  Console.WriteLine("Base class of {0} is {1}",
    obj.GetType().Name,
    obj.GetType().BaseType);
  Console.WriteLine("obj.ToString() = {0}", obj.ToString());
  Console.WriteLine("obj.GetHashCode() = {0}", obj.GetHashCode());
  Console.WriteLine();
}
```

Now assume we invoke this method from Main(), passing in the myCar object as the parameter:

```
static void Main(string[] args)
{
  Console.WriteLine("***** Fun with Anonymous types *****\n");

  // Make an anonymous object representing a car.
  var myCar = new {Color = "Bright Pink", Make = "Saab", CurrentSpeed = 55};

  // Reflect over what the compiler generated.
  ReflectOverAnonymousType(myCar);
  Console.ReadLine();
}
```

Check out the output shown in Figure 30-4.

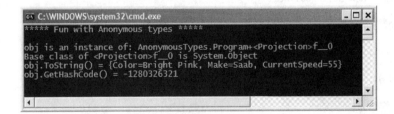

Figure 30-4. *Anonymous types are represented by a compiler-generated class type.*

First of all, notice that in this example, the myCar object is of type <Projection>f__0, which is in fact *nested* within the Program class (recall that the plus symbol is used by the reflection API to denote a nested type). Do understand that the assigned type name is completely determined by the compiler and is not accessible in your C# code base.

Perhaps most important, notice that each name/value pair defined using the object initialization syntax is mapped to an identically named property and a corresponding private backing field. The following C# code approximates the compiler-generated class used to represent the myCar object (which again can be verified using tools such as Lutz Roeder's Reflector or ildasm.exe):

```
[CompilerGenerated]
public sealed class <Projection>f__0
{
  // You are given a default constructor.
  public <Projection>f__0();

  // As well as a canned implementation of each virtual
  // member from System.Object.
  public override bool Equals(object);
  public override int GetHashCode();
  public override string ToString();

  // As well, properties are used to wrap...
  public string Color { get; set; }
  public int CurrentSpeed { get; set; }
  public string Make { get; set; }

  // ... each private member variable.
  private string _Color;
  private int _CurrentSpeed;
  private string _Make;
}
```

The Implementation of ToString() and GetHashCode()

Again note that the compiler-generated type derives directly from System.Object and has been provided with an overridden version of Equals(), GetHashCode(), and ToString(). The ToString() implementation simply builds a string from each name/value pair, for example:

```
public override string ToString()
{
  StringBuilder builder1 = new StringBuilder();
  builder1.Append("{");
  builder1.Append("Color");
  builder1.Append("=");
  builder1.Append(this.Color);
  builder1.Append(", ");
  builder1.Append("Make");
  builder1.Append("=");
  builder1.Append(this.Make);
  builder1.Append(", ");
  builder1.Append("CurrentSpeed");
  builder1.Append("=");
  builder1.Append(this.CurrentSpeed);
  builder1.Append("}");
  return builder1.ToString();
}
```

The GetHashCode() implementation computes a hash value by calling GetHashCode() on each of the anonymous type's member variables:

```
public override int GetHashCode()
{
  int num1 = 0;
  if (this.Color != null)
  {
    num1 ^= this.Color.GetHashCode();
  }
  if (this.Make != null)
  {
    num1 ^= this.Make.GetHashCode();
  }
  return (num1 ^ this.CurrentSpeed.GetHashCode());
}
```

Using this implementation of GetHashCode(), two anonymous types will yield the same hash value if (and only if) they have the same set of properties that have been assigned the same values.

The Semantics of Equality for Anonymous Types

While the implementation of the overridden ToString() and GetHashCode() methods is fairly straightforward, you may be wondering how the Equals() method has been implemented. For example, if we were to define two "anonymous cars" variables that specify the same name/value pairs, would these two variables be considered equal or not? To see the results firsthand, update your Main() method with the following code:

```
// Make 2 anonymous classes with identical name/value pairs.
var firstCar = new { Color = "Bright Pink", Make = "Saab", CurrentSpeed = 55 };
var secondCar = new { Color = "Bright Pink", Make = "Saab", CurrentSpeed = 55 };

// Are they considered equal when using Equals()?
if (firstCar.Equals(secondCar))
    Console.WriteLine("Same anonymous object!");
else
    Console.WriteLine("Not the same anonymous object!");

// Are they considered equal when using ==?
if (firstCar == secondCar)
    Console.WriteLine("Same anonymous object!");
else
    Console.WriteLine("Not the same anonymous object!");

// Are these objects the same underlying type?
if (firstCar.GetType().Name == secondCar.GetType().Name)
    Console.WriteLine("We are both the same type!");
else
    Console.WriteLine("We are different types!");

// Show all the details.
Console.WriteLine();
ReflectOverAnonymousType(firstCar);
ReflectOverAnonymousType(secondCar);
```

Figure 30-5 shows the output.

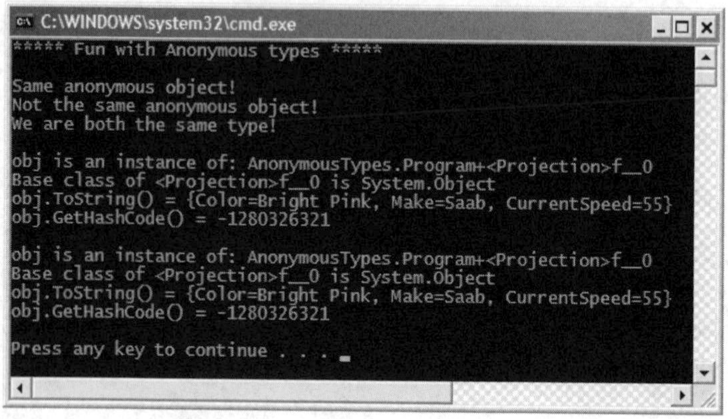

Figure 30-5. *The equality of anonymous types*

When you run this test code, you will see that the first conditional test where you are calling Equals() returns true, and therefore the message "Same anonymous object!" prints out to the screen. This is because the compiler-generated Equals() method makes use of *value-based seman-tics* when testing for equality (e.g., checking the value of each field for the objects being compared). Here is a rough approximation of the compiler-generated Equals() method for the anonymous type:

```
public override bool Equals(object obj1)
{
  Program.<Projection>f__0 f__1 = obj1 as Program.<Projection>f__0;
  if (f__1 == null)
  {
    return false;
  }
  if (!(((this.Color == null) && (f__1.Color == null))
        || this.Color.Equals(f__1.Color)))
  {
    return false;
  }
  if (!(((this.Make == null) && (f__1.Make == null))
        || this.Make.Equals(f__1.Make)))
  {
    return false;
  }
  if (this.CurrentSpeed != f__1.CurrentSpeed)
  {
    return false;
  }
  return true;
}
```

However, the second conditional test (which makes use of the C# equality operator) prints out "Not the same anonymous object!", which may seem at first glance to be a bit counterintuitive. This is due to the fact that anonymous types do *not receive* overloaded versions of the C# equality opera-tors (== and !=). Given this, when you test for equality of anonymous types using the C# equality operators (rather than the Equals() method), the *references*, not the values maintained by the objects, are being tested for equality. Recall from Chapter 9 that this is the default behavior for all class types until you overload the operators directly in your code (something that is not possible for anonymous types).

Last but not least, in our final conditional test (where we are examining the underlying type name), we find that the anonymous types are instances of the same compiler-generated class type (in this example, Program+<Projection>f__0), due to the fact that firstCar and secondCar have the same properties (Color, Make, and CurrentSpeed).

Anonymous Types Containing Anonymous Types

It is possible to create an anonymous type that is composed of additional anonymous types. For example, assume you wish to model a purchase order that consists of a timestamp, a price point, and the automobile purchased. Here is a new (slightly more sophisticated) anonymous type representing such an entity:

```
// Make an anonymous type that is composed of another.
var purchaseItem = new {
  TimeBought = DateTime.Now,
  ItemBought = new {Color = "Red", Make = "Saab", CurrentSpeed = 55},
  Price = 34.000};

ReflectOverAnonymousType(purchaseItem);
```

Here, purchaseItem (internally represented as a class named <Projection>f__1 for this example) maintains three properties, one of which is another anonymous class representing the concept of an automobile. This is represented as a member variable of type .<Projection>f__0 (in other words, <Projection>f__1 *has-a* <Projection>f__0).

If we were to use ildasm.exe (or better yet, Lutz Roeder's Reflector) to view the compiler-generated class, we would find a new type that looks more or less like the following C# code:

```
[CompilerGenerated]
public sealed class <Projection>f__1
{
  public <Projection>f__1();
  public override bool Equals(object);
  public override int GetHashCode();
  public override string ToString();

  public Program.<Projection>f__0 ItemBought { get; set; }
  public double Price { get; set; }
  public DateTime TimeBought { get; set; }

  private Program.<Projection>f__0 _ItemBought;
  private double _Price;
  private DateTime _TimeBought;
}
```

At this point you should understand the syntax used to define anonymous types, but you may still be wondering exactly where (and when) to make use of this new language feature. To be blunt, the use of anonymous type declarations should be used sparingly, typically only when making use of the LINQ technology set (see Chapter 31). You would never want to abandon the use of strongly typed classes/structures simply for the sake of doing so, given anonymous types' numerous limitations, which include the following:

- You don't control the name of the anonymous type.
- Anonymous types always extend System.Object.

- Anonymous types cannot support events, custom methods, or custom overrides.

- Anonymous types are always implicitly sealed.

- Anonymous types are always created using the default constructor.

Again, when you dive into LINQ, you will find that in many cases this syntax can be very helpful when you wish to quickly model the overall shape of an entity rather than its functionality.

■**Source Code** The AnonymousTypes project can be found under the Chapter 30 subdirectory.

Understanding the Role of Lambda Expressions

We will conclude our look at the new C# 3.0 features with an examination of *lambda expressions.* Support for this particular feature has been hotly debated in various C# circles. The reason is not because lambda expressions are not (very) useful, but because the syntax used to interact with them can be quite jarring at first (unless you happen to have a background in another functional language, such as Lisp or Haskell).

Some in the debate feel that lambda expressions are a feature that will be quite ignored by the vast majority of the C# programming community. To this end, if most of your day is concerned with binding relational data to grids, inserting and updating records, or authoring multimedia software, it could very well be the case that this particular language feature will be largely out of sight, out of mind.

Others feel that once developers grasp the basic syntax, they will quickly see how slick this language feature can be. This will be especially true if you have an academic background in computer science (or a related discipline such as formal linguistics, cognitive science, or mathematics), as the lambda calculus is often used in this field.

In any case, if you become comfortable with the basic use of lambda expressions (and you can deal with the slightly terse syntax), these little coding constructs can save you a *lot* of typing time. When you examine LINQ in the next chapter, you'll find that they can also greatly simplify your coding efforts.

■**Note** As you work through the following examples, you may find that Visual Studio 2005 "Orcas" will identify lambda expressions as errors within the code editor (as they are all underlined in red). This is a limitation of the current LINQ Community Technology Preview. When you compile the code, you will not find true compiler errors (unless, of course, you have authored syntactically incorrect code!).

Lambda Expressions As a Better Anonymous Method

Recall from Chapter 8 that C# 2.0 introduced the ability to handle events "inline" by assigning a block of code statements directly to an event (aka anonymous methods). When handling events from various UI elements (Buttons, GridViews, the mouse, etc.), this language feature is not necessarily very useful and it is never mandatory. In these cases, the traditional event handling syntax is typically the best call to decouple the event handling code from the real processing code; the latter being the same for different user actions on a keyboard shortcut, a toolbar button, or a menu item. Consider the following Windows Forms example:

```
class MainForm : Form
{
  public MainForm()
  {
    // Handle the MouseMove event using standard C# event syntax.
    this.MouseMove += new MouseEventHandler(MainForm_MouseMove);
  }
  void MainForm_MouseMove(object sender, MouseEventArgs e)
  {
    // Do something with the mouse data.
  }
}
```

However, many methods in the .NET base class libraries define methods that require delegate types as parameters. When you make use of "traditional" delegate syntax, the code can be on the clunky side. For example, consider the FindAll() method of the generic List<T> type. This method is expecting a generic delegate of type System.Predicate<T>, which is used to wrap any method returning a Boolean and taking a specified T as the only input parameter:

```
class Program
{
  static void Main(string[] args)
  {
    // Make a list of integers using C# 3.0
    // collection initialization syntax.
    List<int> list = new List<int>() {20, 1, 4, 8, 9, 44};

    // Call FindAll() using traditional delegate syntax.
    Predicate<int> callback = new Predicate<int>(CallMeHere);
    List<int> evenNumbers = list.FindAll(callback);

    foreach (int evenNumber in evenNumbers)
    {
      Console.WriteLine(evenNumber);
    }
    Console.ReadLine();
  }

  // Is it an even number?
  static bool CallMeHere(int i)
  {
    return (i % 2) == 0;
  }
}
```

Here, we have a method (CallMeHere) that is in charge of testing the incoming integer parameter to see if it is even or odd, via the C# modulo operator, %. While the code compiles as expected, this method is invoked only under very limited circumstances; specifically, when we call FindAll(), which leaves us with the baggage of a full method definition. If we were to instead use an anonymous method, our code cleans up considerably:

```
static void Main(string[] args)
{
  // Make a list of integers using C# 3.0
  // collection initialization syntax.
  List<int> list = new List<int>() {20, 1, 4, 8, 9, 44};
```

```
    // Now, use an anonymous method.
    List<int> evenNumbers = list.FindAll(delegate(int i) { return (i % 2) == 0; } );

    foreach (int evenNumber in evenNumbers)
    {
        Console.WriteLine(evenNumber);
    }
    Console.ReadLine();
}
```

In this case, rather than directly creating a Predicate<T> delegate type and then authoring a stand-alone method, we are able to supply an anonymous method. While this is a step in the right direction, we are still required to use the delegate keyword (or a strongly typed Predicate<T>), and we must ensure that the parameter list is a dead-on match. Also, as you may agree, the syntax used to define an anonymous method can still be viewed as being somewhat clunky, which is even more apparent here:

```
List<int> evenNumbers = list.FindAll(
  delegate(int i)
  {
    return (i % 2) == 0;
  }
);
```

We can use lambda expressions to further simplify our call to FindAll(). When we make use of this new syntax, there is no trace whatsoever of the underlying delegate. Consider the following update to the same code base:

```
static void Main(string[] args)
{
    // Make a list of integers using C# 3.0
    // collection initialization syntax.
    List<int> list = new List<int>() {20, 1, 4, 8, 9, 44};

    // Now, use a C# 3.0 lambda expression.
    List<int> evenNumbers = list.FindAll(i => (i % 2) == 0);

    foreach (int evenNumber in evenNumbers)
    {
        Console.WriteLine(evenNumber);
    }
    Console.ReadLine();
}
```

If we want to simplify this code base even further, we could make use of type inference with the var keyword. As it turns out, this keyword is quite handy when working with lambda expressions, given that they can typically return various value types. For example, in this case, the hidden Predicate<T> is returning a List<int>; however, other lambdas could return something completely different. Here is the final update:

```
static void Main(string[] args)
{
  // Now using implicit typing.
  var list = new List<int>() {20, 1, 4, 8, 9, 44};
  var evenNumbers = list.FindAll(i => (i % 2) == 0);
```

```
  foreach (var evenNumber in evenNumbers)
  {
    Console.WriteLine(evenNumber);
  }
  Console.ReadLine();
}
```

In either case, notice the rather strange statement of code passed into the FindAll() method, which is, in fact, a lambda expression. In this iteration of the example, there is no trace of the Predicate<T> delegate (or the delegate keyword, for that matter). All we have specified is the lambda expression: i => (i % 2) == 0.

Before we break down this syntax, at this level simply understand that lambda expressions can be used anywhere you would have used an anonymous method, typically with far fewer keystrokes. Under the hood, the C# compiler translates our expression into a normal anonymous method making use of the Predicate<T> delegate type (which can be verified using ildasm.exe).

Dissecting a Lambda Expression

A lambda expression is written by first defining a parameter list, followed by the => token (C#'s token for the lambda operator found in the lambda calculus), followed by an expression. Given our first sample, things break down as so:

```
// 'i' is our parameter list.
// (i % 2) == 0 is our expression.
var evenNumbers = list.FindAll(i => (i % 2) == 0);
```

The parameters of a lambda expression can be explicitly or implicitly typed. Currently, the underlying data type representing the i parameter (an integer) is typed implicitly. The compiler is able to figure out that i is an integer based on the context of the overall lambda expression. However, it is also possible to explicitly define the type of each parameter in the expression, by wrapping the data type and variable name in a pair of parentheses as follows:

```
// Now, explicitly state the parameter type.
var evenNumbers = list.FindAll((int i) => (i % 2) == 0);
```

As you have seen, if a lambda expression has a single, implicitly typed parameter, the parentheses may be omitted from the parameter list. If you wish to be consistent regarding your use of lambda parameters, you are free to *always* wrap the parameter list within parentheses, leaving you with this expression:

```
var evenNumbers = list.FindAll((i) => (i % 2) == 0);
```

Finally, notice that currently our expression has not been wrapped in parentheses (we have, of course, wrapped the modulo statement, to ensure it is executed before the test for equality). Lambda expressions do allow for the statement to be wrapped as so:

```
// Now, wrap the expression as well.
var evenNumbers = list.FindAll((i) => ((i % 2) == 0));
```

Now that you have seen the various ways to build a lambda expression, how can you read this lambda statement in human-friendly terms? Leaving the raw mathematics behind, the following explanation fits the bill:

```
// My list of parameters (in this case, a single integer named i)
// will be processed by the expression (i % 2) == 0.
var evenNumbers = list.FindAll((i) => ((i % 2) == 0));
```

The Two Flavors of Lambda Expressions

Our first lambda expression was a single statement that ultimately evaluated to a Boolean. As you know full well, though, many delegate targets must perform a number of code statements. For this reason, C# 3.0 allows you to define lambda expressions using a set of code statements. When your expression must process the parameters using multiple lines of code, you can denote a scope for these statements using the expected curly brackets. Consider the following example update to the FindAll() invocation:

```
// This time the lambda expression is built with a statement
// block.
var justATest = list.FindAll(i => {
        Console.WriteLine("Called by FindAll()!");
        Console.WriteLine("value of i is currently: {0}", i);
        bool isEven = ((i % 2) == 0);
        return isEven;
        } );
foreach (var evenNumber in justATest)
{
  Console.WriteLine(evenNumber);
}
```

In this case, our parameter list (again, a single integer named i) is being processed by a set of code statements. Beyond the calls to Console.WriteLine(), our modulo statement has been broken into two code statements for increased readability.

Here, then, is the final version of our first lambda expression, whose output can be seen in Figure 30-6:

```
static void Main(string[] args)
{
  Console.WriteLine("***** Fun with Lambda Expressions *****\n");

  // Make a list of integers using C# 3.0
  // collection initialization syntax.
  var list = new List<int>() {20, 1, 4, 8, 9, 44};

  // This time the lambda expression is built with a statement
  // block.
  var justATest = list.FindAll(i =>
    {
      Console.WriteLine("Called by FindAll()!");
      Console.WriteLine("value of i is currently: {0}", i);
      bool isEven = ((i % 2) == 0);
      return isEven;
    }
  );

  Console.WriteLine("\nHere are the even numbers from your list:");
  foreach (var evenNumber in justATest)
  {
    Console.WriteLine(evenNumber);
  }

  Console.ReadLine();
}
```

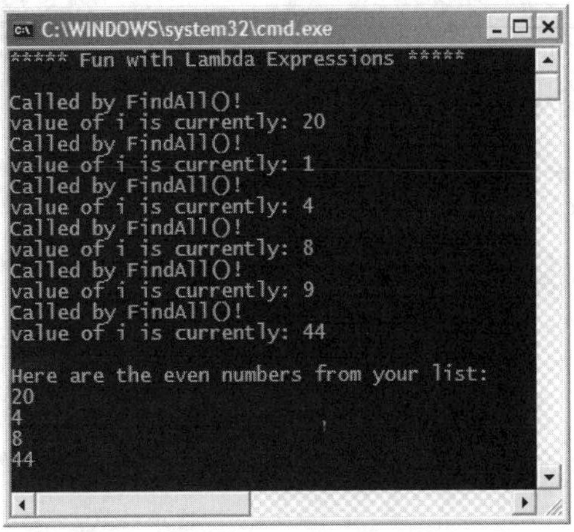

Figure 30-6. *The output of our first lambda expression*

Source Code The SimpleLambdaExpressions project can be found under the Chapter 30 subdirectory.

Retrofitting the CarDelegate Example Using Lambda Expressions

Given that the whole reason for lambda expressions is to provide a clean, concise manner to define an anonymous method (and therefore, indirectly a manner to simplify working with delegates), let's retrofit the CarDelegate project we created in Chapter 8. Recall that this example defined a Car type that defined two custom delegates (AboutToBlow and Exploded), as well as a set of methods (OnAboutToBlow(), RemoveAboutToBlow(), OnExploded(), and RemoveExploded()), which allows the caller to pass in delegate objects as parameters to register with or detach from the event source. Figure 30-7 should jog your memory.

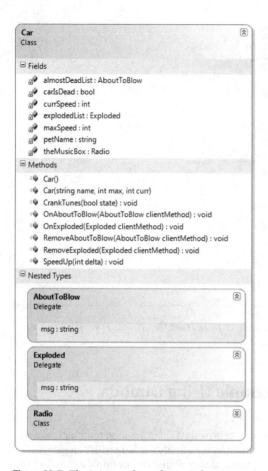

Figure 30-7. *The* Car *type from the* CarDelegate *project in Chapter 8*

Here is a simplified version of that project's Program class that makes use of traditional delegate syntax to respond to each callback:

```
class Program
{
  static void Main(string[] args)
  {
    Console.WriteLine("***** More Fun with Lambdas *****\n");

    // Make a car as usual.
    Car c1 = new Car("SlugBug", 100, 10);

    // Traditional delegate syntax.
    c1.OnAboutToBlow(new Car.AboutToBlow(CarAboutToBlow));
    c1.OnExploded(new Car.Exploded(CarExploded));

    // Speed up (this will generate the events.)
    Console.WriteLine("\n***** Speeding up *****");
    for (int i = 0; i < 6; i++)
      c1.SpeedUp(20);
```

```
    Console.ReadLine();
  }

  // Delegate targets.
  public static void CarAboutToBlow(string msg)
  { Console.WriteLine(msg); }

  public static void CarExploded(string msg)
  { Console.WriteLine(msg); }
}
```

Now, here is a retrofitted version of Main() making use of anonymous method syntax:

```
static void Main(string[] args)
{
  Console.WriteLine("***** More Fun with Lambdas *****\n");

  // Make a car as usual.
  Car c1 = new Car("SlugBug", 100, 10);

  // Now use anonymous methods.
  c1.OnAboutToBlow(delegate(string msg) { Console.WriteLine(msg); });
  c1.OnExploded(delegate(string msg) { Console.WriteLine(msg); });

  // Speed up (this will generate the events).
  Console.WriteLine("\n***** Speeding up *****");
  for (int i = 0; i < 6; i++)
    c1.SpeedUp(20);

  Console.ReadLine();
}
```

And finally, here is a version of the Main() method using lambda expression syntax:

```
static void Main(string[] args)
{
    Console.WriteLine("***** More Fun with Lambdas *****\n");

    // Make a car as usual.
    Car c1 = new Car("SlugBug", 100, 10);

    // Now with lambdas!
    c1.OnAboutToBlow(msg => { Console.WriteLine(msg); });
    c1.OnExploded(msg => { Console.WriteLine(msg); });

    // Speed up (this will generate the events).
    Console.WriteLine("\n***** Speeding up *****");
    for (int i = 0; i < 6; i++)
        c1.SpeedUp(20);

    Console.ReadLine();
}
```

Understand that in each case, the output is identical (see Figure 30-8). While you may agree that the lambda expression syntax is far and away the most compact and functional approach, remember that this technique is always optional.

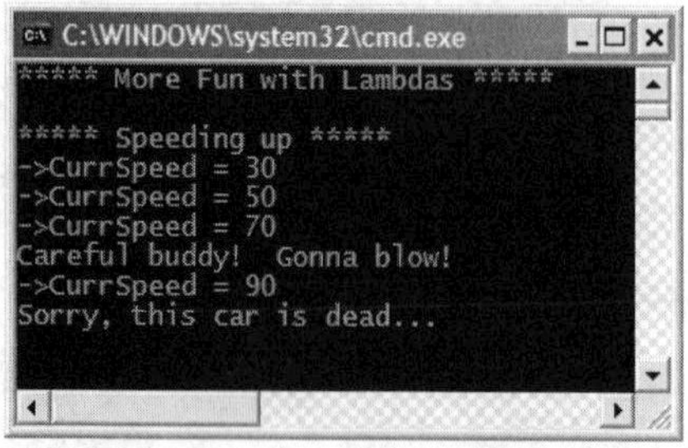

Figure 30-8. *Traditional delegate syntax, anonymous method syntax, and lambda expression syntax each yield the same output.*

■**Source Code** The CarDelegateWithLambdas project can be found under the Chapter 30 subdirectory.

Lambda Expressions with Multiple (or Zero) Parameters

Each of the lambda expressions we have seen here processed a single parameter. This is not a requirement, however: a lambda expression may process multiple arguments or provide no arguments whatsoever. To illustrate the first scenario, assume the following incarnation of the SimpleMath type first seen in Chapter 8:

```
public class SimpleMath
{
  public delegate void MathMessage(string msg, int result);
  private MathMessage mmDelegate;

  public void SetMathHandler(MathMessage target)
  { mmDelegate = target; }

  public void Add(int x, int y)
  {
    if (mmDelegate != null)
      mmDelegate.Invoke("Adding has completed!", x + y);
  }
}
```

Notice that the MathMessage delegate is expecting two parameters. To represent them as a lambda expression, our Main() method might be written as so:

```
static void Main(string[] args)
{
  // Register w/ delegate as a lambda expression.
  SimpleMath m = new SimpleMath();
  m.SetMathHandler((msg, result) =>
    {Console.WriteLine("Message: {0}, Result: {1}", msg, result);});

  // This will execute the lambda expression.
  m.Add(10, 10);

  Console.ReadLine();
}
```

Here, we are leveraging type inference, as our two parameters have not been strongly typed for simplicity. We could, however, call SetMathHandler():

```
m.SetMathHandler(((string msg, int result) =>
  {Console.WriteLine("Message: {0}, Result: {1}", msg, result);}));
```

Finally, if you are using a lambda expression to interact with a delegate taking no parameters at all, you may do so by supplying a pair of empty parentheses as the parameter. For example, assuming you have defined the following delegate type:

```
public delegate string VerySimpleDelegate();
```

you could handle the result of the invocation as follows:

```
// Prints "Enjoy your string!" to the console.
VerySimpleDelegate d = new VerySimpleDelegate( () =>
  {return "Enjoy your string!";} );
Console.WriteLine(d.Invoke());
```

I hope at this point that you can see the overall role of lambda expressions and understand how they provide a "functional manner" to work with anonymous methods and delegate types. Furthermore, as you explore LINQ, you will also find that lambdas are used quite frequently to simplify working with relational data and XML documents.

■**Note** C# 3.0 also allows you to represent lambda expressions as an in-memory object using *expression trees*. This can be very useful for third parties who are building software that needs to extend the functionality of existing lambdas. I suspect that the majority of C# projects will not require this functionality, so check out the .NET Framework SDK documentation for further details if you are interested.

■**Source Code** The LambdaExpressionsMultipleParams project can be found under the Chapter 30 subdirectory.

Summary

C# 3.0 provides a number of very interesting features that bring C# into the family of *functional languages*. This chapter walked you through each of the core updates, beginning with the notion of implicitly typed local variables. While the vast majority of your local variables will not need to be declared with the var keyword, as you will see in the next chapter doing so can greatly simplify your interactions with the LINQ family of technologies.

This chapter also described the role of extension methods (which allow you to add new functionality to a compiled type) and the syntax of object initialization (which can be used to assign property values at the time of construction). The chapter wrapped up by examining the use of anonymous types and numerous examples of lambda expressions. In essence, the new lambda operator (=>) allows us to greatly simplify working with delegate types, and it provides a more elegant solution than the C# 2.0 anonymous method syntax.

■ ■ ■

## CHAPTER 31

An Introduction to LINQ

The previous chapter introduced you to numerous C# 3.0 language constructs. As you have seen, implicitly typed local variables, anonymous types, object initialization syntax, and lambda expressions bring C# into the family of *functional languages*. Recall that while many of these features can be used directly as is, their benefits are much more apparent when used within the context of LINQ.

This chapter will expose you to LINQ and the two major technologies that represent it: LINQ to SQL (previously termed DLinq) and LINQ to XML (previously termed XLinq). As well, you will come to learn the role of *query operators* and *query expressions*, which allow you to define statements that will interrogate a data source to yield the requested result set. Along the way, you will build numerous LINQ examples that interact with data contained within collection types, relational databases, and XML documents.

> **Note** As the LINQ project evolves, related technologies will be released over time. For example, the Blinq prototype makes use of LINQ to generate database-driven ASP.NET websites. I won't cover Blinq here, but be sure to check out http://www.asp.net/downloads/teamprojects for more details.

> **Note** At the time of this writing, LINQ is in its beta cycle. Understand that the topics examined in this chapter are subject to change before the final release.

Defining the Role of LINQ

As software developers, it is hard to deny that the vast majority of our programming time is spent obtaining and manipulating *data*. When speaking of "data," it is very common to automatically envision information contained within relational databases. Another popular format in which data exists is within XML documents (*.config files, locally persisted DataSets, in-memory data returned from XML web services, etc.).

Data can be found in numerous places beyond these two common homes for information. For instance, say you have a generic List<> type containing 300 integers, and you want to obtain a subset that meets a given criterion (e.g., only the odd or even members in the container). Or perhaps you are making use of the reflection APIs and need to obtain only metadata descriptions for each class deriving from a particular parent class from an array of Types. Indeed, data is everywhere.

Under .NET 2.0, interacting with a particular flavor of data required us as programmers to make use of specific types in specific namespaces. Consider, for example, Table 31-1.

Table 31-1. *Ways to Manipulate Various Types of Data*

The Data We Want	How to Obtain It
Relational data	`System.Data.dll`
XML document data	`System.Xml.dll`
Metadata tables	The `System.Reflection` namespace
Collections of objects	`System.Array` and the `System.Collections`/`System.Collections.Generics` namespaces

Of course, nothing is wrong with these approaches to data manipulation. In fact, when programming with .NET 3.0/C# 3.0, you can certainly make direct use of ADO.NET, the XML namespaces, reflection services, and the various collection types. However, the basic problem is that each of these APIs is an island unto itself, which offers very little in the way of integration. True, it is possible (for example) to save an ADO.NET `DataSet` as XML, and then manipulate it via the `System.Xml` namespaces, but nonetheless, today data manipulation remains rather *asymmetrical*.

The Language Integrated Query (LINQ) project is an attempt to provide a consistent, *symmetrical* manner in which programmers can obtain and manipulate "data" in the broad sense of the term. Using LINQ, we are able to create directly within the C# programming language entities called *query expressions*. These query expressions are based on numerous *query operators* and have been intentionally designed to look and feel like SQL expressions.

The twist, however, is that a query expression can be used to interact with numerous types of data—even data that has nothing to do with a relational database. Specifically, LINQ allows query expressions to manipulate any object that implements the `IEnumerable<T>` interface, relational databases, or XML documents in a consistent manner.

■**Note** Strictly speaking, "LINQ" is the term used to describe this overall approach to data access. LINQ to SQL is LINQ over relational data; LINQ to XML is LINQ over XML documents.

It is also very important to point out that a LINQ query expression (unlike a traditional SQL statement) is *strongly typed*. Therefore, the C# compiler will keep us honest and make sure that these expressions are syntactically well formed. On a related note, query expressions have *metadata representation* within the assembly that makes use of them. Tools such as Visual Studio 2005 can use this metadata for useful features such as IntelliSense, autocompletion, and so forth.

Before we dig into the details of LINQ, one final point is that LINQ is designed to be an extendable technology. While this initial release of LINQ is targeted for relational databases, XML documents, and objects implementing `IEnumerable<T>`, third parties can incorporate new query operators (or redefine existing operators) using *extension methods* (see Chapter 30) to account for addition types of data.

■**Note** As you read over this chapter, I wholeheartedly recommend that you first feel comfortable with the material presented in Chapter 30 (C# 3.0). As you will see, LINQ programming makes use of several of the new C# features to simplify coding tasks.

The Core LINQ Assemblies

When you install the Visual Studio 2005 "Orcas" Community Technology Preview (see Chapter 26), you will receive a new set of LINQ-specific project templates, accessible from the LINQ Preview node of the left tree view control (see Figure 31-1).

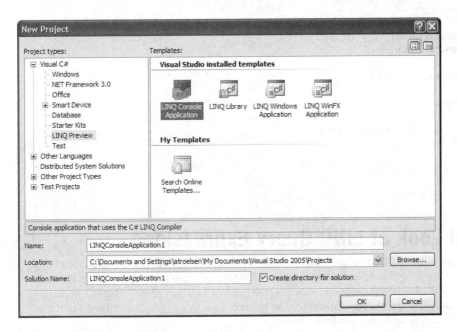

Figure 31-1. *The LINQ-specific project workspaces*

As you can see, you have a template for LINQ-aware console applications, Windows Presentation Foundation/Windows Forms GUI programs, and a simple code library. Regardless of which template you select, Visual Studio 2005 "Orcas" will set references to the core LINQ assemblies, as described in Table 31-2.

Table 31-2. *Core LINQ-centric Assemblies*

Assembly	Meaning in Life
System.Query.dll	Defines types that represent the core LINQ API. This is the one assembly you must have access to.
System.Data.DLinq.dll	Provides functionality for using LINQ with relational databases (LINQ to SQL).
System.Data.Extensions.dll	Defines a number of extension methods for the ADO.NET DataRow and DataTable types to incorporate them into the LINQ programming paradigm.
System.Xml.XLinq.dll	Provides functionality for using LINQ with XML document data (LINQ to XML).

The Visual Studio 2005 "Orcas" LINQ project templates also add a number of using directives for various namespaces. For example, if you were to select a LINQ console application, you would find the following initial setup:

```
using System;
using System.Collections.Generic;
using System.Text;
using System.Query;
using System.Xml.XLinq;
using System.Data.DLinq;

namespace MyLinqConsoleApp
{
  class Program
  {
    static void Main(string[] args)
    {
    }
  }
}
```

A First Look at LINQ Query Expressions

To begin examining the LINQ programming model, let's build simple query expressions to manipulate data contained within various arrays. Create a LINQ console application named LinqOverArray, and define a static helper method within the Program class named QueryOverStrings(). In this method, create a string array containing six or so items of your liking (here, I listed out a batch of video games I am currently attempting to finish).

```
static void QueryOverStrings()
{
  // Assume we have an array of strings.
  string[] currentVideoGames = {"Morrowind", "Dead Rising",
    "Half Life 2: Episode 1", "F.E.A.R.",
    "Daxter", "System Shock 2"};
  Console.ReadLine();
}
```

Finally, update Main() to invoke QueryOverStrings():

```
static void Main(string[] args)
{
    Console.WriteLine("***** Fun with LINQ *****\n");
    QueryOverStrings();
    Console.ReadLine();
}
```

When you have any array of data, it is very common to extract a subset of items based on a given requirement. Maybe you want to obtain only the items with names that contain a number (e.g., System Shock 2), have more than some number of characters, or don't have embedded spaces (e.g., Morrowind). While you could certainly perform such tasks using members of the System.Array type and a bit of elbow grease, LINQ query expressions can greatly simplify the process.

Going on the assumption that we wish to obtain a subset from the array that contains items with names consisting of more than six characters, we could build the following query expression:

```
static void QueryOverStrings()
{
  // Assume we have an array of strings.
  string[] currentVideoGames = {"Morrowind", "Dead Rising",
                   "Half Life 2: Episode 1", "F.E.A.R.",
                   "Daxter", "System Shock 2"};

  // Build a query expression to represent the items in the array
  // that have more than 6 letters.
  IEnumerable<string> subset = from g in currentVideoGames
                 where g.Length > 6 orderby g select g;

  // Print out the results.
  foreach (string s in subset)
    Console.WriteLine("Item: {0}", s);
}
```

Notice that the query expression created here makes use of the from, in, where, orderby, and select query operators. We will dig into the formalities of query expression syntax in just a bit, but even now you should be able to parse this statement as "Give me the games that have more than six characters, ordered alphabetically." Here, each item that matches this criteria has been given the name "g" (as in "game"); however, any valid C# variable name would do:

```
IEnumerable<string> subset = from game in currentVideoGames
  where game.Length > 6 orderby game select game;
```

Finally, notice that the "result set" is represented by an object that implements the generic version of IEnumerable, where T is of type System.String (after all, we are querying an array of strings). Once we obtain the result set, we then simply print out each item using a standard foreach construct.

Before we see the results of our query, assume the Program class defines an additional helper function named ReflectOverQueryResults() that will print out various details of the query result (note the parameter is a System.Object, to account for multiple types of result sets):

```
static void ReflectOverQueryResults(object resultSet)
{
  Console.WriteLine("\n***** Info about your query *****");
  Console.WriteLine("resultSet is of type: {0}", resultSet.GetType().Name);
  Console.WriteLine("resultSet location: {0}", resultSet.GetType().Assembly);
}
```

Assuming you have called this method within QueryOverStrings() directly after printing out the obtained subset, if you run the application, you will see the subset is really an instance of the System.Query.OrderedSequence<T> type (represented in terms of metadata as OrderedSequence`2), which lives in the System.Query.dll assembly (see Figure 31-2).

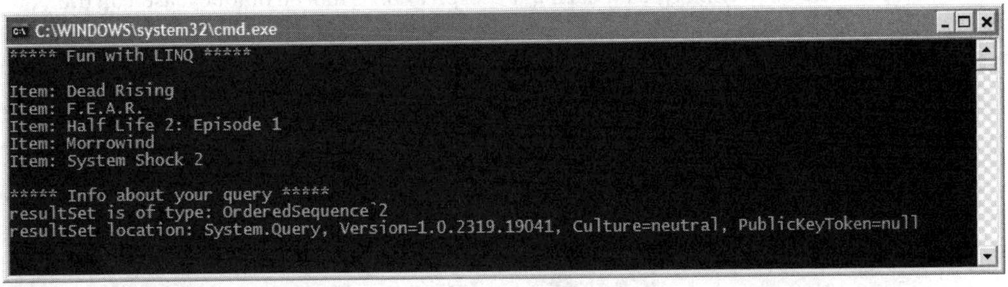

Figure 31-2. *The result of our LINQ query*

Revising Implicitly Typed Local Variables

While the current sample program makes it relatively easy to determine that the result set is enumerable as a string collection, I would guess that it is *not* clear that subset is really of type OrderedSequence<T>. Given the fact that LINQ result sets can be represented using a good number of types from the System.Query namespace (all of which implement IEnumerable<T>), it would be tedious to define the proper type to hold a result set, because in many cases the underlying type may not be obvious.

To further accentuate this point, consider the following additional helper method defined within the Program class (which I assume you will invoke from within the Main() method):

```
static void QueryOverInts()
{
  int[] numbers = {10, 20, 30, 40, 1, 2, 3, 8};

  // Only print items less than 10.
  IEnumerable<int> subset = from i in numbers where i < 10 select i;

  foreach (int i in subset)
    Console.Write("Item: {0} ", i);
  ReflectOverQueryResults(subset);
}
```

In this case, the subset variable is obtained (under the covers) by calling the System.Query. Sequence.Where<T> method, passing in a *compiler-generated anonymous method* as the second parameter. Here is the crux of the internal definition of the subset variable generated by the compiler:

```
// The following LINQ query expression:
//
// IEnumerable<int> subset = from i in numbers where i < 10 select i;
//
// Is transformed into a call to the Squence.Where<int>() method:
//
IEnumerable<int> subset = Sequence.Where<int>(numbers,
  Program.<>9__CachedAnonymousMethodDelegate8);
```

■**Note** If you are interested, you may wish to load this assembly into Lutz Roeder's Reflector (http://www. aisto.com/roeder/dotnet) and analyze the reverse-engineered C# code for the QueryOverInts() method for full details.

Without diving too deeply into the use of Sequence.Where<> at this point, do note that in Figure 31-3, that the underlying type for each query expression is indeed unique, based on the format of our LINQ query expression.

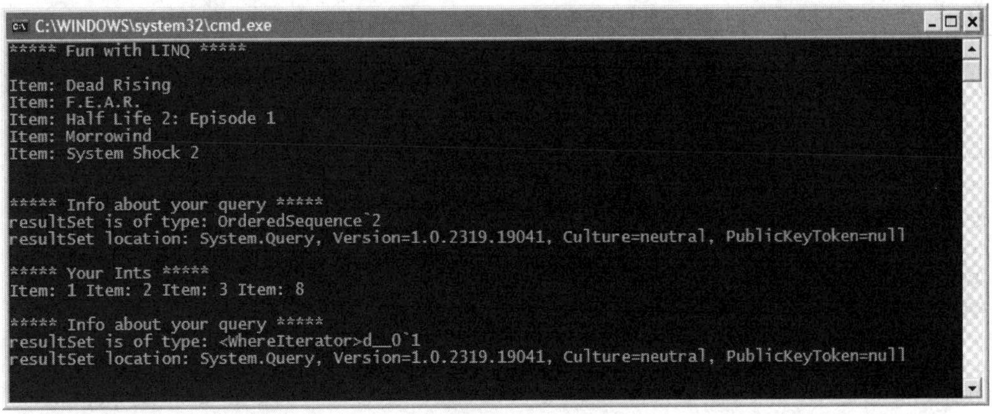

Figure 31-3. *This time our result set is a compiler-generated type!*

Given the fact that the underlying type of a LINQ query is certainly not obvious, the current example has represented the query results as local IEnumerable<T> variable. While this is syntactically correct, use of the var keyword cleans things up considerably when working with LINQ queries:

```
static void QueryOverInts()
{
  int[] numbers = {10, 20, 30, 40, 1, 2, 3, 8};

  // Only print items less than 10.
  var subset = from i in numbers where i < 10 select i;

  // Print out the results.
  foreach (var i in subset)
    Console.Write("Item: {0} ", i);

  ReflectOverQueryResults(subset);
}
```

Recall that the var keyword should not be confused with the legacy COM Variant or loosely typed variable declaration found in many scripting languages. The underlying type is determined by the compiler based on the result of the initial assignment. After that point, it is a compiler error to attempt to change the "type of type." For simplicity, over the remainder of this chapter, we'll make use of the var keyword, although this is technically optional.

Revisiting Extension Methods

Recall from the previous chapter that *extension methods* make it possible to add new members to a previously compiled type. Although the current example does not have you author any extension methods, you are in fact using them seamlessly in the background. Recall that LINQ query expressions can be used to iterate over data containers that implement the generic IEnumerable<T> interface. However, the .NET 2.0 System.Array class type (used to represent our array of strings and array of integers) does *not* implement this behavior:

```
// The System.Array type does not seem to implement the correct
// infrastructure for query expressions!
public abstract class Array : ICloneable, IList, ICollection, IEnumerable
{
   ...
}
```

While System.Array does not directly implement the IEnumerable<T> interface, it indirectly gains the required functionality of this type (as well as many other LINQ-centric members) via the static System.Query.Sequence class type. This type defined a good number of generic extension methods (such as Aggregate<T>(), First<T>(), Max<T>(), etc.), which System.Array (and other types) acquire in the background.

To illustrate, if you apply the dot operator on the currentVideoGames local variable, you will find a good deal of members *not* found within the formal definition of System.Array (see Figure 31-4), including members that take as parameters lambda expressions (also note the lambda operator => of the Aggregate<T>() method).

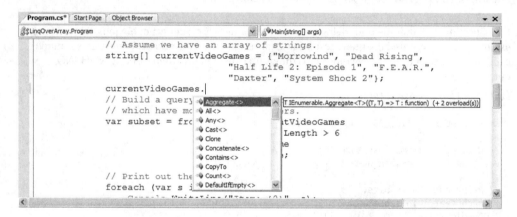

Figure 31-4. *The* System.Array *type has been extended with members of* System.Query.Sequence.

■**Source Code** The LinqOverArray example can be found under the Chapter 31 subdirectory.

Using LINQ to Query Generic Collections

Beyond pulling results from a simple array of data, LINQ query expressions can also manipulate data within members of the System.Collections.Generic namespace, such as the List<T> type.

Create a new LINQ console project named LinqOverCustomObjects, and define a basic Car type that maintains a current speed, color, make, and pet name (public fields used for simplicity; feel free to make use of public properties with private backing fields):

```
class Car
{
   public string PetName;
   public string Color;
   public int Speed;
   public string Make;
}
```

Now, within your `Main()` method, define a local `List<T>` variable of type `Car`, and make use of the new object initialization syntax (see Chapter 30) to fill the list with a handful of new `Car` objects:

```
static void Main(string[] args)
{
  Console.WriteLine("***** More fun with LINQ Expressions *****\n");

  // Make a List<> of Car objects
  // using the new object init syntax.
  List<Car> myCars = new List<Car>() {
    new Car{ PetName = "Henry", Color = "Silver", Speed = 100, Make = "BMW"},
    new Car{ PetName = "Daisy", Color = "Tan", Speed = 90, Make = "BMW"},
    new Car{ PetName = "Mary", Color = "Black", Speed = 55, Make = "VW"},
    new Car{ PetName = "Clunker", Color = "Rust", Speed = 5, Make = "Yugo"},
    new Car{ PetName = "Melvin", Color = "White", Speed = 43, Make = "Ford"}
  };
}
```

Defining LINQ Queries

Our goal is to build a query expression to select only the items within the `myCars` list, where the speed is greater than 55. Once we get the set, we will print out the name of each `Car` object. Here is the complete `Main()` method:

```
static void Main(string[] args)
{
  Console.WriteLine("***** More fun with LINQ Expressions *****\n");

  // Make a List<> of Car objects
  // using the new object init syntax.
  List<Car> myCars = new List<Car>() {
    new Car{ PetName = "Henry", Color = "Silver", Speed = 100, Make = "BMW"},
    new Car{ PetName = "Daisy", Color = "Tan", Speed = 90, Make = "BMW"},
    new Car{ PetName = "Mary", Color = "Black", Speed = 55, Make = "VW"},
    new Car{ PetName = "Clunker", Color = "Rust", Speed = 5, Make = "Yugo"},
    new Car{ PetName = "Melvin", Color = "White", Speed = 43, Make = "Ford"}
  };

  // Create a query expression.
  var fastCars = from c in myCars where c.Speed > 55 select c;

  foreach (var car in fastCars)
  {
    Console.WriteLine("{0} is going too fast!", car.PetName);
  }
}
```

Notice that our query expression is only grabbing items from the `List<>` where the `Speed` property is greater than 55. If we run the application, we will find that "Henry" and "Daisy" are the only two items that match the search criteria.

If we want to build a more complex query, we might wish to only find the BMWs that have a `Speed` value above 90. To do so, simply build a complex Boolean statement using the C# `&&` operator:

```
// Create a query expression.
var fastCars = from c in myCars where
  c.Speed > 90 && c.Make == "BMW" select c;
```

In this case, the only pet name printed out is "Henry".

Revisiting Anonymous Types

C# 3.0 now supports the creation of *anonymous types*. Recall that this construct allows you to define the overall structure (or *shape*) of an entity on the fly, without needing to define a strongly typed class (or structure) definition. In our example, the Car class is really doing nothing more than representing an aggregation of four data points, and it has no special functionality via type members (methods, events, overridden virtual members, etc.).

Given this fact, we would be able to further simplify the current example by removing the Car definition altogether and opting for an anonymous type. Furthermore, rather than using the strongly typed List<>, we could simply make use of an implicitly typed array. Given this, we would update Main() as so (remember, the Car class definition is no longer required):

```
static void Main(string[] args)
{
  Console.WriteLine("***** More fun with LINQ Expressions *****\n");

  // Make an anonymous type using object init syntax.
  var myCars = new[] {
    new { PetName = "Henry", Color = "Silver", Speed = 100, Make = "BMW"},
    new { PetName = "Daisy", Color = "Tan", Speed = 90, Make = "BMW"},
    new { PetName = "Mary", Color = "Black", Speed = 55, Make = "VW"},
    new { PetName = "Clunker", Color = "Rust", Speed = 5, Make = "Yugo"},
    new { PetName = "Melvin", Color = "White", Speed = 43, Make = "Ford"}
  };

  // Create a query expression.
  var fastCars = from c in myCars where
    c.Speed > 90 && c.Make == "BMW" select c;

  foreach (var car in fastCars)
  {
    Console.WriteLine("{0} is going too fast!", car.PetName);
  }
}
```

While the output is identical, we have expressed our code base as a highly functional grammar.

■**Source Code** The LinqOverCustomObjects example can be found under the Chapter 31 subdirectory.

Using LINQ to Query Nongeneric Collections

Recall that the query operators of LINQ are designed to work with any type implementing IEnumerable<T> (either directly or via extension methods). Given that System.Array has been provided with such necessary infrastructure, it may surprise you that the legacy (nongeneric) containers within System.Collections have *not*. Thankfully, it is still possible to iterate over data contained within nongeneric collections using the generic Sequence.OfType<T>() method.

The OfType<T>() method is one of the few members of Sequence that does not extend generic types. When calling this member off a nongeneric container implementing the IEnumerable interface (such as the ArrayList), simply specify the type of item within the container to extract a compatible IEnumerable<T> object. Assume we have a new LINQ console application named LinqOverArrayList that defines the following Main() method (note that we are making use of the previously defined Car type).

```
static void Main(string[] args)
{
  Console.WriteLine("***** LINQ over ArrayList *****\n");

  // Here is a nongeneric collection of cars.
  ArrayList myCars = new ArrayList();
  myCars.Add(new Car{ PetName = "Henry", Color = "Silver",
                      Speed = 100, Make = "BMW"});
  myCars.Add(new Car{ PetName = "Daisy", Color = "Tan", Speed = 90, Make = "BMW"});
  myCars.Add(new Car{ PetName = "Mary", Color = "Black", Speed = 55, Make = "VW"});
  myCars.Add(new Car{ PetName = "Clunker", Color = "Rust",
                      Speed = 5, Make = "Yugo"});
  myCars.Add(new Car{ PetName = "Melvin", Color = "White",
                      Speed = 43, Make = "Ford" });

  // Transform ArrayList into an IEnumerable<T>-compatible type.
  IEnumerable<Car> myCarsEnum = myCars.OfType<Car>();

  // Create a query expression.
  var fastCars = from c in myCarsEnum where c.Speed > 55 select c;

  foreach (var car in fastCars)
  {
    Console.WriteLine("{0} is going too fast!", car.PetName);
  }
}
```

As you know, nongeneric types are capable of containing any combination of items, as the members of these containers (again, such as the ArrayList) are prototyped to receive System. Objects. For example, assume an ArrayList contains a variety of items, only a subset of which are numerical. If we want to obtain a subset that contains only numerical data, we can do so using OfType<T>(), since it filters out each element whose type is different from the given type during the iterations:

```
// Extract the ints from the ArrayList.
ArrayList myStuff = new ArrayList();
myStuff.AddRange(new object[] { 10, 400, 8, false, new Car(), "string data" });
IEnumerable<int> myInts = myStuff.OfType<int>();

// Prints out 10, 400, and 8.
foreach (int i in myInts)
{
  Console.WriteLine("Int value: {0}", i);
}
```

■Source Code The LinqOverArrayList example can be found under the Chapter 31 subdirectory.

Now that you have seen how to use LINQ to manipulate data contained within various arrays and collections, let's dig in a bit deeper to see what is happening behind the scenes.

The Internal Representation of Query Operators

So at this point you have seen that implicit local variables, extension methods, and anonymous types can all be used when building LINQ query expressions. As well, you were briefly introduced to the notion that when building query expressions using various query operators (such as from, in, where, orderby, and select), the C# compiler actually translates these tokens into calls on various methods of the System.Query.Sequence type.

As it turns out, a great many of the methods of Sequence have been prototyped to take delegates as arguments. In particular, many methods require a generic delegate of type Func<>, defined within the System.Query namespace:

```
// Overloaded versions of the Sequence.Where<T>() method.
public static IEnumerable<T> Where<T>(IEnumerable<T> source,
  Func<T, bool> predicate);

public static IEnumerable<T> Where<T>(IEnumerable<T> source,
  Func<T, int, bool> predicate);
```

This delegate (as the name implies) represents a pattern for a given function with a set of arguments and a return value. If you were to examine this type using the Visual Studio 2005 object browser, you'll notice that the Func<> delegate can take between zero and four input arguments (here named A0, A1, A2, and A3), and a return type denoted by T:

```
// The various formats of Func<>.
public delegate T Func<A0,A1,A2,A3,T>(A0 arg0, A1 arg1, A2 arg2, A3 arg3)
public delegate T Func<A0,A1,A2,T>(A0 arg0, A1 arg1, A2 arg2)
public delegate T Func<A0,A1,T>(A0 arg0, A1 arg1)
public delegate T Func<A0,T>(A0 arg0)
public delegate T Func<T>()
```

Given that many members of System.Query.Sequence demand a delegate as input, when invoking them, we can either manually create a new delegate type and author the necessary target methods, make use of a C# anonymous method, or define a proper lambda expression (which is a new option as of C# 3.0). Regardless of which approach you take, the end result is identical.

While it is true that making use of query operators is by far and away the simplest way to build a LINQ query expression, let's walk through each of these possible approaches, just to see the connection between the C# query operators and the underlying Sequence type.

Building Query Expressions with Query Operators (Revisited)

To begin, create a new LINQ console application named LinqOverArrayUsingSequence. The Program class will define a series of static helper methods (each of which is called within the Main() method) to illustrate the various manners in which we can build query expressions. The first method, QueryStringsWithOperators(), offers the most straightforward way to build a query expression and is identical to the code seen in the previous LinqOverArray example:

```
static void QueryStringWithOperators()
{
  string[] currentVideoGames = {"Morrowind", "Dead Rising",
    "Half Life 2: Episode 1", "F.E.A.R.",
    "Daxter", "System Shock 2"};

  // Build a query expression using query operators.
  var subset = from g in currentVideoGames
               where g.Length > 6 orderby g select g;
```

```
// Print out the results.
foreach (var s in subset)
    Console.WriteLine("Item: {0}", s);
}
```

The obvious benefit of using C# query operators to build query expressions is the fact that the Func<> delegates and calls on the Sequence type are out of sight and out of mind, as it is the job of the C# compiler to perform this translation. To be sure, building LINQ expressions using various query operators (from, in, where, orderby, etc.) is the most common and most straightforward approach.

Building Query Expressions Using the Sequence Type and Lambdas

Keep in mind that the LINQ query operators used here are simply shorthand versions for calling various extension methods defined by the Sequence type. Consider the following QueryStringsWithSequenceAndLambdas() method, which is processing the local string array now making direct use of the Sequence extension methods:

```
static void QueryStringsWithSequenceAndLambdas()
{
    Console.WriteLine("***** Using Sequence / Lambda Expressions *****");

    string[] currentVideoGames = {"Morrowind", "Dead Rising",
        "Half Life 2: Episode 1", "F.E.A.R.",
        "Daxter", "System Shock 2"};

    // Build a query expression using extension methods
    // granted to the Array via the Sequence type.
    var subset = currentVideoGames.Where(game => game.Length > 6)
        .OrderBy(game => game).Select(game => game);

    // Print out the results.
    foreach (var game in subset)
        Console.WriteLine("Item: {0}", game);
    Console.WriteLine();
}
```

Here, we are calling the generic Where<T>() method off the string array object, granted to the Array type as an extension method defined by Sequence. In any case, recall that the Sequence.Where<T>() method makes use of System.Query.Func<A0, T> delegate types. The first type parameter of this delegate represents the IEnumerable<T>-compatible data to process (an array of strings in this case), while the second type parameter represents the method that will process said data.

Given that we have opted for a lambda expression (rather than directly creating an instance of Func<T> or crafting an anonymous method), we are specifying that the "game" parameter is processed by the statement game.Length > 6, which results in a Boolean return type.

The return value of the Where<T>() method has been strongly typed as IEnumerable<T>, but under the covers we are operating on an OrderedSequence type. From this resulting object, we call the generic OrderBy<T, K>() method, which also requires a Func<T, K> delegate. Finally, from the result of the specified lambda expression, we select each element, using once again a Func<T, K> under the covers.

It is also worth remembering that extension methods are unique in that they can be called as instance-level members upon the type they are extending (System.Array in this case) or as static members using the type they were defined within. Given this, we could also author our query expression as so:

```
var subset = Sequence.Where(currentVideoGames, game => game.Length > 6)
  .OrderBy(game => game).Select(game => game);
```

As you may agree, building a LINQ query expression using the methods of the Sequence type directly is more verbose than making use of the C# query operators. As well, given that the methods of Sequence require delegates as parameters, you will typically need to author lambda expressions to allow the input data to be processed by the underlying delegate target.

Building Query Expressions Using the Sequence Type and Anonymous Methods

Given that C# 3.0 lambda expressions are simply shorthand notations for working with anonymous methods, consider the third query expression created within the QueryStringsWithAnonymousMethods() helper function:

```
static void QueryStringsWithAnonymousMethods()
{
  Console.WriteLine("***** Using Anonymous Methods *****");

  string[] currentVideoGames = {"Morrowind", "Dead Rising",
    "Half Life 2: Episode 1", "F.E.A.R.",
    "Daxter", "System Shock 2"};

  // Build the necessary Func<> delegates using anonymous methods.
  Func<string, bool> searchFilter =
    delegate(string game) { return game.Length > 6; };
  Func<string, string> itemToProcess = delegate(string s) { return s; };

  // Pass the delegates into the methods of Sequence.
  var subset = currentVideoGames.Where(searchFilter)
    .OrderBy(itemToProcess).Select(itemToProcess);

  // Print out the results.
  foreach (var game in subset)
    Console.WriteLine("Item: {0}", game);
  Console.WriteLine();
}
```

This iteration of the query expression is even more verbose, because we are manually creating the Func<> delegates used by the Where(), OrderBy(), and Select() methods of the Sequence type. On the plus side, the anonymous method syntax does keep all the processing contained within a single method definition. Nevertheless, this method is functionally equivalent to the QueryStringsWithSequenceAndLambdas() and QueryStringsWithOperators() methods created in the previous sections.

Building Query Expressions Using the Sequence Type and Raw Delegates

Finally, if we want to build a query expression using the *really verbose approach*, we could avoid the use of lambdas/anonymous method syntax and directly create delegate targets for each Func<> type. Here is the final iteration of our query expression, modeled within a new class type named VeryComplexQueryExpression:

```
class VeryComplexQueryExpression
{
  public static void QueryStringsWithRawDelegates()
  {
    Console.WriteLine("***** Using Raw Delegates *****");

    string[] currentVideoGames = {"Morrowind", "Dead Rising",
      "Half Life 2: Episode 1", "F.E.A.R.",
      "Daxter", "System Shock 2"};

    // Build the necessary Func<> delegates using anonymous methods.
    Func<string, bool> searchFilter = new Func<string, bool>(Filter);
    Func<string, string> itemToProcess = new Func<string,string>(ProcessItem);

    // Pass the delegates into the methods of Sequence.
    var subset = currentVideoGames
            .Where(searchFilter).OrderBy(itemToProcess).Select(itemToProcess);

    // Print out the results.
    foreach (var game in subset)
      Console.WriteLine("Item: {0}", game);
    Console.WriteLine();
  }

  // Delegate targets.
  public static bool Filter(string s) {return s.Length > 6;}
  public static string ProcessItem(string s) { return s; }
}
```

If you were to now run the application to test each possible approach, it should not be too surprising that the output is identical regardless of the path taken. Keep the following points in mind regarding how LINQ query expressions are represented under the covers:

- Query expressions are created using various query operators.

- Query operators are simply shorthand notations for invoking extension methods defined by the System.Query.Sequence type.

- Many methods of Sequence require delegates (Func<> in particular) as parameters.

- Under C# 3.0, any method requiring a delegate parameter can instead be passed a lambda expression.

- Lambda expressions are simply anonymous methods in disguise.

- Anonymous methods are shorthand notations for allocating a raw delegate and manually building a delegate target method.

Whew! That might have been a bit deeper under the hood than you wish to have gone, but I hope this discussion has helped you understand what query operators are actually doing behind the scenes. Let's now turn our attention to the operators themselves.

──

■**Source Code** The LinqOverArrayUsingSequence example can be found under the Chapter 31 subdirectory.

Investigating the LINQ Query Operators

LINQ defines a good number of query operators out of the box (more than 40 operators at last count). In this introductory chapter, we will explore only a subset of these LINQ tokens, but be aware that when you install the LINQ Community Technology Preview, you will receive a very helpful white paper appropriately named Standard Query Operators.doc. Located by default under C:\Program Files\LINQ Preview\Docs, this document walks you through the details of each operator. While I assume that you will consult this reference for full details, Table 31-3 defines a small subset of these operators.

Table 31-3. *Various LINQ Query Operators*

Query Operators	Meaning in Life
from, in	Used to define the backbone for any LINQ expression.
where	Used to define a restriction for which items to extract from a container.
select	Used to select a sequence from the container.
join, in, on, equals, into	Perform joins based on specified key. Remember, these "joins" do not need to have anything to do with data in a relational database.
orderby, ascending, descending	Allow the resulting subset to be ordered in ascending or descending order.
group, by, into	Yield a subset with data grouped by a specified value.

In addition to the partial list of operators shown in Table 31-3, the Sequence type provides a set of methods that do not have a direct query operator shorthand, but are instead exposed as extension methods. These generic methods can be called to transform a result set in various manners (Reverse<>(), ToArray<>(), ToList<>(), etc.). Some are used to extract singletons from a result set, others perform various set operations (Distinct<>(), Union<>(), Intersect<>(), etc.), and still others aggregate results (Count<>(), Sum<>(), Min<>(), Max<>(), etc.).

Using these query operators (and auxiliary members of the System.Query.Sequence type), you are able to build very expressive query expressions. Again, the interesting aspect of doing so is that the same syntax can be used to interact with a wide variety of data containers. Before we move on to examine LINQ to SQL, let's create some more exotic query expressions.

Building LINQ Query Expressions

To help you become more comfortable with query expression syntax, the next example consists of a series of static helper methods (called from within Main()) that take input a single parameter of type Car[]. These methods display a result set based on numerous query operators.

To begin, create a new LINQ console application named FunWithLinqExpressions. Next, define a trivial Car type, this time sporting a custom ToString() implementation to quickly view the object's state:

```
class Car
{
  public string PetName;
  public string Color;
  public int Speed;
  public string Make;
```

```
  public override string ToString()
  {
    return string.Format("Make={0}, Color={1}, Speed={2}, PetName={3}",
      Make, Color, Speed, PetName);
  }
}
```

Now populate an array with the following Car objects within your Main() method:

```
static void Main(string[] args)
{
  Console.WriteLine("***** Fun with Query Expressions *****\n");

  // This array will be the basis of our testing...
  Car[] myCars = new [] {
    new Car{ PetName = "Henry", Color = "Silver", Speed = 100, Make = "BMW"},
    new Car{ PetName = "Daisy", Color = "Tan", Speed = 90, Make = "BMW"},
    new Car{ PetName = "Mary", Color = "Black", Speed = 55, Make = "VW"},
    new Car{ PetName = "Clunker", Color = "Rust", Speed = 5, Make = "Yugo"},
    new Car{ PetName = "Hank", Color = "Tan", Speed = 0, Make = "Ford"},
    new Car{ PetName = "Sven", Color = "White", Speed = 90, Make = "Ford"},
    new Car{ PetName = "Mary", Color = "Black", Speed = 55, Make = "VW"},
    new Car{ PetName = "Zippy", Color = "Yellow", Speed = 55, Make = "VW"},
    new Car{ PetName = "Melvin", Color = "White", Speed = 43, Make = "Ford"}
  };

  // We will call various methods here!
  Console.ReadLine();
}
```

Basic Selection Syntax

Because LINQ query expressions are validated at compile time, you need to remember that the ordering of these operators is critical. In the simplest terms, every LINQ query expression is built using the from, in, and select operators:

```
var result = from item in container select item;
```

In this case, our query expression is doing nothing more than selecting every item in the container (similar to a Select * SQL statement). Consider the following:

```
static void BasicSelection(Car[] myCars)
{
  // Get everything.
  var allCars = from c in myCars select c;
  foreach (var c in allCars)
  {
    Console.WriteLine(c.ToString());
  }
}
```

Again, this query expression is not entirely useful, given that our subset is identical to that of the data in the incoming parameter. If we wish, we could use this incoming parameter to extract only the PetName values of each car using the following selection syntax:

```
// Now get only the names of the cars.
var names = from c in myCars select c.PetName;
foreach (var n in names)
{
  Console.WriteLine("Name: {0}", n);
}
```

In this case, names is really an internal type that implements IEnumerable<string>, given that we are selecting only the values of the PetName property for each Car object. Again, using implicit typing via the var keyword, our coding task is simplified.

Now consider the following task. What if you'd like to obtain and display the makes of each vehicle? If you author the following query expression:

```
var makes = from c in myCars select c.Make;
```

you will end up with a number of redundant listings, as you will find BMW, Ford, and VW accounted for multiple times. You can use the Sequence.Distinct<T>() method to eliminate such duplication:

```
var makes = (from c in myCars select c.Make).Distinct<string>();
```

When calling any extension method defined by Sequence, you can do so either at the time you build the query expression (as shown in the previous example) or via an extension method on the array type. Thus, the following code yields identical output:

```
var makes = from c in myCars select c.Make;
foreach (var m in makes.Distinct<string>())
{
  Console.WriteLine("Make: {0}", m);
}
```

Figure 31-5 shows the result of calling BasicSelections().

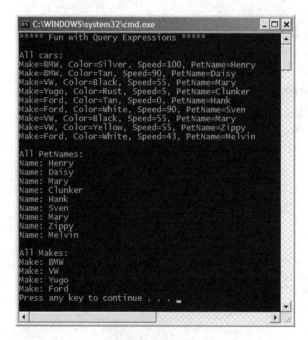

Figure 31-5. *Selecting basic data from the* Car[] *parameter*

Obtaining Subsets of Data

To obtain a specific subset from a container, you can make use of the where operator. When doing so, the general template now becomes as follows:

```
var result = from item in container where Boolean expression select item;
```

Notice that the where operator expects an expression that resolves to a Boolean. For example, to extract from the Car[] parameter only the items that have "BMW" as the value assigned to the Make field, you could author the following code within a method named GetSubsets():

```
// Now get only the BMWs.
var onlyBMWs = from c in myCars where c.Make == "BMW" select c;

foreach (Car c in onlyBMWs)
{
  Console.WriteLine(c.ToString());
}
```

As you might expect, when you are building a where clause, it is permissible to make use of any valid C# operators to build complex expressions. For example, consider the following query that only extracts out the BMWs above the 100 mph mark:

```
// Get BMWs going at least 100 mph.
var onlyFastBMWs = from c in myCars
                   where c.Make == "BMW" && c.Speed >= 100
                   select c;

foreach (Car c in onlyFastBMWs)
{
  Console.WriteLine("{0} is going {1} MPH", c.PetName, c.Speed);
}
```

It is also possible to project new forms of data from an existing data source. Let's assume that you wish to take the incoming Car[] parameter and obtain a result set that accounts only for the make and color of each vehicle. To do so, you can define a select statement that dynamically yields new types via C# 3.0 *anonymous types*. Recall from Chapter 30 that the compiler defines a property and backing field for each specified name, and also is kind enough to override ToString(), GetHashCode(), and Equals():

```
var makesColors = from c in myCars select new {c.Make, c.Color};
foreach (var o in makesColors)
{
  // Could also use Make and Color properties directly.
  Console.WriteLine(o.ToString());
}
```

Figure 31-6 shows the output of each of these new queries.

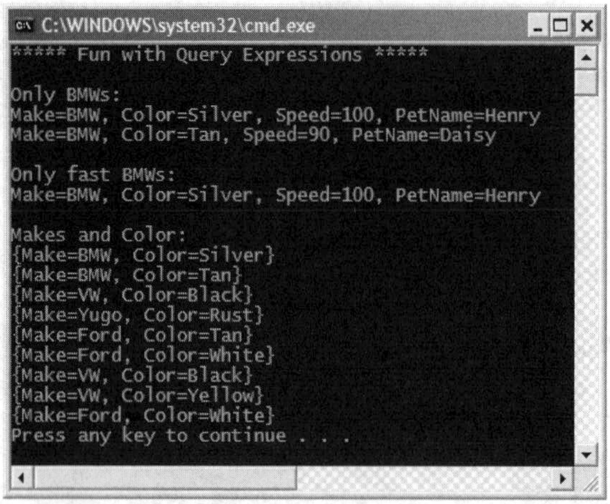

Figure 31-6. *Enumerating over subsets*

Reversing Result Sets

You can reverse the items within a result set quite simply using the generic Reverse<T>() method of the Sequence type. For example, the following method selects all items from the incoming Car[] parameter in reverse:

```
private static void ReversedSelection(Car[] myCars)
{
  // Get everything in reverse.
  Console.WriteLine("\nAll cars in reverse:");
  var subset = (from c in myCars select c).Reverse<Car>();
  foreach (Car c in subset)
  {
    Console.WriteLine("{0} is going {1} MPH", c.PetName, c.Speed);
  }
}
```

Here, we called the Reverse<T>() method at the time we constructed our query. Again, as an alternative, we could invoke this method on the myCars array as so:

```
private static void ReversedSelection(Car[] myCars)
{
  // Get everything in reverse.
  Console.WriteLine("\nAll cars in reverse:");
  var subset = from c in myCars select c;
  foreach (Car c in subset.Reverse<Car>())
  {
    Console.WriteLine(c.ToString());
  }
}
```

Sorting Expressions

As you have seen over this chapter's initial examples, a query expression can take an orderby operator to sort items in the subset by a specific value. By default, the order will be ascending; thus, ordering by a string would be alphabetical, ordering by numerical data would be lowest to highest, and so forth. If you wish to view the results in a descending order, simply include the descending operator. Ponder the following method:

```
private static void OrderedResults(Car[] myCars)
{
  // Order all the cars by PetName.
  var subset = from c in myCars orderby c.PetName select c;

  Console.WriteLine("Ordered by PetName:");
  foreach (Car c in subset)
  {
    Console.WriteLine(c.ToString());
  }

  // Now find the cars that are going less than 55 mph,
  // and order by descending PetName
  subset = from c in myCars
    where c.Speed > 55 orderby  c.PetName descending select c;
  Console.WriteLine("\nCars going faster than 55, ordered by PetName:");
  foreach (Car c in subset)
  {
    Console.WriteLine(c.ToString());
  }
}
```

Although ascending order is the default, you are able to make your intentions very clear by making use of the ascending operator:

```
var subset = from c in myCars
  orderby c.PetName ascending select c;
```

In either case, Figure 31-7 shows the output.

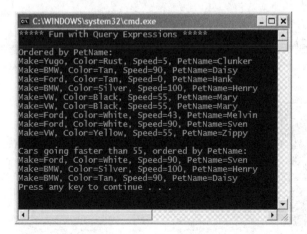

Figure 31-7. *Ascending and descending orders*

Given these examples, you can now understand the format of a basic sorting query expression as so:

```
var result = from item in container orderby value
  ascending/descending select item;
```

If you wish to perform a sort on a subset, you can realize the format of the query as the following:

```
var result = from item in container where boolean expression
  orderby value ascending/descending select item;
```

Transforming Query Results and the Role of Differed Execution

When you build a query expression using your approach of choice (which I would guess is to make use of the query operators rather than members of Sequence, lambda expressions, or anonymous method syntax), the result set is not a fixed constant. Indeed, it is possible for the same query expression to return different results based on the state of the container. This is due to *differed execution* of statements. Simply put, a query expression is not actually executed until you iterate over the results. Consider the following code and the output shown in Figure 31-8.

```
private static void ResultsAsArray(Car[] myCars)
{
  // Get all cars going faster than 55 mph.
  var subset = from c in myCars
    where c.Speed > 55 select c;

  Console.WriteLine("Initial query:");
  foreach (Car c in subset)
  {
    Console.WriteLine("{0} is going {1} MPH", c.PetName, c.Speed);
  }

  // Now change the speed of the 1st item.
  myCars[0].Speed = 5;

  Console.WriteLine("\nSecond query:");
  foreach (Car c in subset)
  {
    Console.WriteLine("{0} is going {1} MPH", c.PetName, c.Speed);
  }
}
```

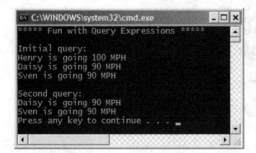

Figure 31-8. *Differed execution in action*

As you can see, the second time we iterate over the incoming Car[] parameter, "Henry" is no longer displayed, so the query is really executed a second time. When you wish to obtain a fixed set of items from a query or execute it only once for performance considerations, you are able to receive the items as a generic List<T> or a standard CLR array type. When you call the generic

ToArray<>() or ToList<>() member of the Sequence type, execution is immediate. Thus, if we were to update our query expression as so:

```
private static void ResultsAsArray(Car[] myCars)
{
  // Get all cars going faster than 55 as array.
  var subset = (from c in myCars
    where c.Speed > 55 select c).ToArray<Car>();
...
}
```

we would find that "Henry" is printed out twice, as we have basically extracted a fixed copy of the data.

These examples should give you just enough knowledge to become dangerous in the world of building LINQ query expressions. As a friendly reminder, don't forget to consult Standard Query Operators.doc (located under C:\Program Files\LINQ Preview\Docs) for further details of query operator syntax. In any case, at this point in the chapter you have more than enough background to begin exploring LINQ to SQL.

■**Source Code** The FunWithLinqExpressions example can be found under the Chapter 31 subdirectory.

Querying Relational Databases Using LINQ to SQL

LINQ to SQL is nothing more than applying well-formed LINQ query expressions to data held within relational databases. In addition to the queries themselves, LINQ to SQL provides a number of types (within the System.Data.DLinq.dll assembly) that facilitate the communication between your code base and the physical database engine.

■**Note** LINQ to SQL is the new, official name (at least for today) to the technology previously termed DLinq. In fact, currently the LINQ to SQL namespace is System.Data.DLinq, rather than the expected System.Data. LinqToSql. This may change in a future release of the LINQ beta.

The major goal of LINQ to SQL is to provide consistency between relational databases and the programming logic that interacts with them. For example, rather than representing database queries using a big clunky string, we can use strongly typed LINQ queries. As well, rather than having to treat relational data as a stream of records, we are able to interact with the data using standard OOP techniques. Because LINQ to SQL allows us to integrate data access directly within our C# code base, the need to manually build dozens of custom classes and data access libraries that hide ADO.NET grunge from view is greatly minimized.

When programming with LINQ to SQL, you see no trace of common ADO.NET types such as SqlConnection, SqlCommand, and SqlDataAdapter, or members of the System.Transactions namespace. Using LINQ query expressions, entity classes (defined shortly), and the DataContext type, you are able to perform all the expected database CRUD (create, remove, update, and delete), as well as define transactional contexts, create new database entities (or entire databases), invoke stored procedures, and perform other database-centric activities.

Furthermore, the LINQ to SQL types (again, such as DataContext) have been developed to integrate with standard ADO.NET data types. For example, one of the overloaded constructors of DataContext takes as input an IdbConnection-compatible object, which as you may recall is a common interface supported by all ADO.NET connection objects. In this way, existing ADO.NET data access libraries can integrate with C# 3.0 LINQ query expressions (and vice versa). In reality, as far as Microsoft is concerned, LINQ to SQL is simply a new member of the ADO.NET family.

The Role of Entity Classes

When you want to make use of LINQ to SQL within your applications, the first step is to define *entity classes*. In a nutshell, entity classes are types that represent the relational data you wish to interact with. Programmatically speaking, entity classes are "normal" C# class definitions that are annotated with various LINQ to SQL attributes (such as [Table] and [Column]) that map to a physical table in a specific database. As you will see in just a bit, the LINQ Community Technology Preview (as well as the Visual Studio 2005 "Orcas" Community Technology Preview) ships with tools that automate the construction of the entity types required by your application. Until that point, our first LINQ to SQL example will illustrate how to build entity classes by hand.

The Role of the DataContext Type

Once you have defined your entity classes, you are then able to pass your query expressions to the relational database using a DataContext type. This LINQ to SQL–specific class type is in charge of translating your LINQ query expressions into proper SQL queries, as well as communicating with the specified database. In some ways, the DataContext looks and feels like an ADO.NET connection object, in that it requires a connection string. However, unlike a typical connection object, the DataContext type has numerous members that map the results of your query expressions back into the entity classes you define.

Furthermore, the DataContext type defines a factory pattern to obtain instances of the entity classes used within your code base. Once you obtain an entity instance, you are free to change its state in any way you desire (add records, update records, etc.) and submit the modified object back for processing. In this way, the DataContext type is similar to an ADO.NET data adapter type.

A Simple LINQ to SQL Example

Before we dive into too many details, let's see a simple example of using LINQ to SQL to interact with the Inventory table of the Cars database created in Chapter 22. Create a new LINQ console application named SimpleDLinqCarsApp and insert a new C# class file named Inventory.cs. This file will define the entity class that requires decorating the type with various LINQ-centric attributes, so be sure to specify you are using the System.Query and System.Data.DLinq namespaces. With this detail out of the way, here is the definition of the Inventory type:

```
[Table]
public class Inventory
{
  [Column] public string Make;
  [Column] public string Color;
  [Column] public string PetName;

  // Identify the primary key.
  [Column(Id = true)] public int CarID;

  public override string ToString()
  {
    return string.Format("ID = {0}; Make = {1}; Color = {2}; PetName = {3}",
      CarID, Make.Trim(), Color.Trim(), PetName.Trim());
  }
}
```

First of all, notice that our entity class has been adorned with the [Table] attribute, while each public field has been marked with [Column]. In both cases, the names are a direct mapping to the physical database table. However, this is not a strict requirement, as the TableAttribute and ColumnAttribute types both support a Name property that allows you to decouple your programmatic representation of the data table from the physical table itself. Also notice that the CarID field has been further qualified by setting the Id of the ColumnAttribute type using named property syntax.

Here, for simplicity, each field has been declared publicly. If you require stronger encapsulation, you could most certainly define private fields wrapped by public properties. When you do so, the *property*, not the fields, will be marked with the [Column] attribute.

It is also worth pointing out that an entity class can contain any number of members that do not map to the data table it represents. As far as the LINQ runtime is concerned, only items marked with LINQ to SQL attributes will be used during the data exchange. For example, this Inventory class definition provides a custom implementation of ToString() to allow the application to quickly display its state.

Now that we have an entity class, we can make use of the DataContext type to submit (and translate) our LINQ query expressions to the specified database. Ponder the following Main() method, which displays the result of all items in the Inventory table maintained by the Cars database:

```
class Program
{
  const string cnStr = "Data Source=localhost;Initial Catalog=Cars;uid='sa';pwd=";

  static void Main(string[] args)
  {
    Console.WriteLine("***** DLinq Sample App *****\n");

    // Create a DataContext object.
    DataContext db = new DataContext(cnStr);

    // Now create a Table<> type.
    Table<Inventory> invTable = db.GetTable<Inventory>();

    // Show all data using a LINQ query.
    Console.WriteLine("-> Contents of Inventory Table from Cars database:\n");
    foreach (var car in from c in invTable select c)
      Console.WriteLine(car.ToString());
  }
}
```

Notice that when you create a DataContext type, you feed in a proper connection string, which is represented here as a simple string constant. Of course, you are free to store this in an application configuration file and/or make use of the SqlConnectionStringBuilder type to treat this string type in a more object-oriented manner.

Next up, we obtain an instance of our Inventory entity class by calling the generic GetTable() method of the DataContext type, specifying the type parameter when doing so. Finally, we build a LINQ query expression and apply it to the invTable object. As you would expect, the end result is a display of each item in the Inventory table.

Building a Strongly Typed DataContext

Although our first example is strongly typed as far as the database query is concerned, we do have a bit of a disconnect between the DataContext and the Inventory entity class it is maintaining. To remedy this situation, it is typically preferable to create a class that extends the DataContext type that defines member variables for each table it operates upon. Insert a new class called CarsDatabase, specify you are using the System.Query and System.Data.DLinq namespaces, and implement the type as follows:

```
class CarsDatabase : DataContext
{
  public Table<Inventory> Inventory;

  public CarsDatabase(string connectionString)
    : base(connectionString){}
}
```

With this new class type, we are now able to simplify the code within Main() quite a bit:

```
static void Main(string[] args)
{
  Console.WriteLine("***** DLinq Sample App *****\n");

  // Create a CarsDatabase object.
  CarsDatabase db = new CarsDatabase(cnStr);

  // Show all data.
  Console.WriteLine("-> Contents of Inventory Table from Cars database:\n");
  foreach (var car in from c in db.Inventory select c)
    Console.WriteLine(car.ToString());
  Console.ReadLine();
}
```

One aspect of building a strongly typed data context that may surprise you is that the DataContext-derived type (CarsDatabase in this example) does not directly create the Table<T> member variables, and it has no trace of the expected GetTable() method call. At runtime, however, when you iterate over your LINQ result set, the DataContext will create the Table<T> type transparently in the background.

Of course, any LINQ query can be used to obtain a given result set. Assume we have authored the following helper method that is called from Main() before exiting (note that this method expects us to pass in a CarsDatabase instance):

```
private static void ShowOnlyBimmers(CarsDatabase db)
{
  Console.WriteLine("\n***** Only BMWs *****");

  // Now use a lambda expression to get only the silver cars.
  var bimmers = from s in db.Inventory
    where s.Make == "BMW"
    orderby s.CarID
    select s;

  foreach (var x in bimmers)
    Console.WriteLine(x.ToString());
}
```

Figure 31-9 shows the output of this first LINQ to SQL example.

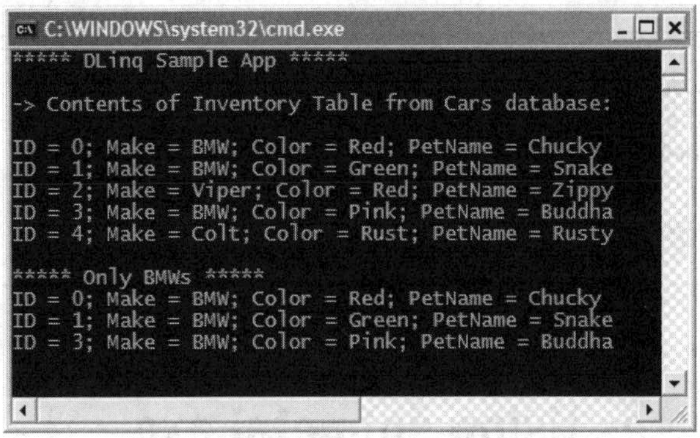

Figure 31-9. *A first look at LINQ to SQL*

■**Source Code** The SimpleDLinqCarsApp example can be found under the Chapter 31 subdirectory.

The [Table] and [Column] Attributes: Further Details

As you have seen, entity classes are adorned with various attributes that are used by LINQ to SQL to translate queries for your objects into SQL queries against the database. At an absolute minimum, you will make use of the [Table] and [Column] attributes; additional attributes exist to mark the methods that perform SQL insert, update, and delete commands. As well, each of the LINQ to SQL attributes defines a set of properties that further qualify to the LINQ to SQL runtime engine how to process the annotated item.

The [Table] attribute is very simple and defines only a single property of interest: Name. As mentioned, this property allows you to decouple of name of the entity class from the physical table. If you do not set the Name property at the time you apply the [Table] attribute, LINQ to SQL assumes the entity class and database table names are one and the same.

The [Column] attribute is a bit meatier than [Table]. Beyond the Id property, ColumnAttribute defines additional members that allow you to fully qualify the details of each field in the entity class and how it maps to a particular column in the physical database table. Table 31-4 documents the additional properties of interest.

Table 31-4. *Select Properties of the* [Column] *Attribute*

Property	Meaning in Life
Name	This property allows you to decouple the name of the entity class field from the physical data table column.
DBType	By default, LINQ to SQL will automatically infer the data types to pass to the database engine based on declaration of your field data. Given this, it is typically only necessary to set DBType directly if you are dynamically creating databases using the CreateDatabase() method of the DataContext type.
AutoGen	This property establishes that a field's value is autogenerated by the database. When setting this property to true, the column in question should also set DBType to the value IDENTITY.

Continued

Table 31-4. *Continued*

Property	Meaning in Life
IsVersion	This property identifies that the column type is a database timestamp or a version number. Version numbers are incremented and timestamp columns are updated every time the associated row is updated.
UpdateCheck	This property controls how LINQ to SQL should handle database conflicts via optimistic concurrency.

Generating Entity Classes Using sqlmetal.exe

Our first LINQ to SQL example was fairly simplistic, partially due to the fact that our DataContext was operating on a single data table. A production-level LINQ to SQL application may instead be operating on multiple interrelated data tables, each of which could define dozens of columns. In these cases, it would be very tedious to author each and every required entity class by hand. Thankfully, we do have two approaches to generate these types automatically.

The first option is to make use of the sqlmetal.exe command-line utility, located by default under the C:\Program Files\LINQ Preview\Bin directory. Simply put, this tool automates the creation of entity classes by generating an appropriate C# class type from the database metadata. While this tool has numerous command-line options, Table 31-5 documents the major flags of interest.

Table 31-5. *Options of the* sqlmetal.exe *Command*

Option	Meaning in Life
/server	Specifies the server hosting the database
/database	Specifies the name of the database to read metadata from
/user	User ID to log into the server
/password	Password to log into the server
/views	Informs sqlmetal.exe to extract database views
/functions	Informs sqlmetal.exe to extract database functions
/sprocs	Informs sqlmetal.exe to extract stored procedures
/code	Informs sqlmetal.exe to output results as C# code (or as Visual Basic code, if the /language flag is set)
/xml	Informs sqlmetal.exe to output results as an XML document
/namespace	Specifies the namespace to define the generated types

By way of an example, the following command set (which should be entered on a single line) will generate entity classes for each table within the Cars database, expose the GetPetName stored procedure, and wrap all generated C# code within a namespace named CarsDatabase:

```
sqlmetal /server:localhost /database:Cars /namespace:CarsDatabase
/code:carsDB.cs /sprocs
```

Once you have executed the command, create a new LINQ console application named LinqWithSqlMetalGenedCode and include the carsDB.cs file into your project using the Project ➤ Add Existing Item menu option. As well, insert a new class diagram into your project (select Project ➤ Add New Item) and expand each of the generated classes (see Figure 31-10).

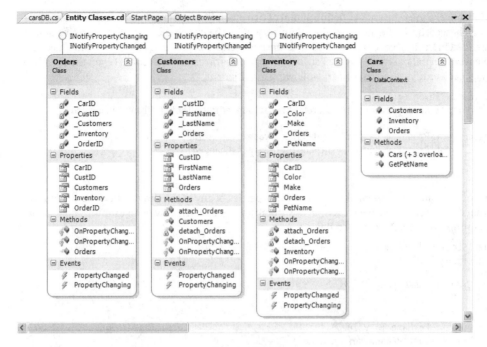

Figure 31-10. *The* sqlmetal.exe-*generated entity classes*

Before we program against these new types, let's examine this autogenerated code in a bit more detail.

Examining the Generated Entity Classes

As you can see, sqlmetal.exe defined a separate entity class for each table in the Cars database (Inventory, Customers, and Orders), with each column encapsulated by a type property. In addition, notice that each entity class implements two interfaces (INotifyPropertyChanging and INotifyPropertyChanged), each of which defines a single event:

```
namespace System.Data.DLinq
{
  public interface INotifyPropertyChanging
  {
    // This event fires when a property is being changed.
    event PropertyChangedEventHandler PropertyChanging;
  }
}

namespace System.ComponentModel
{
  public interface INotifyPropertyChanged
  {
    // This event fires when a property value has changed.
    event PropertyChangedEventHandler PropertyChanged;
  }
}
```

Collectively, these interfaces define a total of two events named PropertyChanging and PropertyChanged, both of which work in conjunction with the PropertyChangedEventHandler delegate defined in the System.ComponentModel namespace. This delegate can call any method, taking an object as the first parameter and a PropertyChangedEventArgs as the second. Given the interface contract, each entity class supports the following members:

```
[Table(Name="Inventory")]
public partial class Inventory : INotifyPropertyChanging, INotifyPropertyChanged
{
  public event PropertyChangedEventHandler PropertyChanging;
  public event PropertyChangedEventHandler PropertyChanged;
...
}
```

If you examine the implementation of the properties of any of the three entity classes, you will note that the set scope fires each event to any interested listener. By way of an example, here is the PetName property of the Inventory type:

```
[Column(Storage="_PetName", DBType="Char(20)")]
public string PetName {
  get {
    return this._PetName;
  }
  set {
    if ((this._PetName != value)) {
      this.OnPropertyChanging("PetName");
      this._PetName = value;
      this.OnPropertyChanged("PetName");
    }
  }
}
```

Notice that the set scope invokes the OnPropertyChanging() and OnPropertyChanged() methods on the entity class type to actually fire the events themselves, passing to the listener the name of the property being manipulated:

```
protected virtual void OnPropertyChanging(string PropertyName) {
  if ((this.PropertyChanging != null)) {
    this.PropertyChanging(this, new PropertyChangedEventArgs(PropertyName));
  }
}

protected virtual void OnPropertyChanged(string PropertyName) {
  if ((this.PropertyChanged != null)) {
    this.PropertyChanged(this, new PropertyChangedEventArgs(PropertyName));
  }
}
```

Defining Relationships Using Entity Classes

Beyond simply defining properties with backing fields to represent data table columns, the sqlmetal.exe utility also models the relationships between interrelated tables using the EntitySet<T> type. Recall from Chapter 22 that the Cars database defined three interrelated tables, connected by primary and foreign keys. Rather than forcing us to author SQL-centric join syntax to navigate between these tables, LINQ to SQL allows us to navigate using the object-centric dot operator.

To account for this sort of table relationship, the parent entity class may encode the child table as property references. This property is marked with the [Association] attribute to establish an *association relationship* made by matching column values between tables. For example, consider the (partially) generated code for the Customer type, which can have any number of orders:

```
[Table(Name="Customers")]
public partial class Customers :
  INotifyPropertyChanging, INotifyPropertyChanged
{
  private EntitySet<Orders> _Orders;

  [Association(Name="FK_Orders_Customers", Storage="_Orders",
              OtherKey="CustID")]
  public EntitySet<Orders> Orders
  {
    get { return this._Orders; }
    set { this._Orders.Assign(value); }
  }
...
}
```

Here, the Orders property is understood by the LINQ to SQL runtime engine as the member that allows navigation *from* the Customers table *to* the Orders table via the column defined by the OtherKey named property. The EntitySet<T> member variable is used to represent the one-to-many nature of this particular relationship. Likewise, if you examine the generated code for the Orders type, you will see a converse relationship between the child and parent tables, using the EntityRef<T> member variable and the ThisKey named property of the [Association] attribute.

The Strongly Typed DataContext

The final aspect of the sqlmetal.exe-generated code to be aware of is the DataContext-derived type. Like the CarsDatabase class we authored in the previous example, each table is represented by a Table<T> member variable. As well, this class has a series of constructors, one of which takes an object implementing IDbConnection, which represents an ADO.NET connection object (remember, LINQ to SQL and ADO.NET can be intermixed within a single application).

As well, this DataContext-derived class is how we are able to interact with the stored procedures defined by the database. Given the fact that we supplied the /sprocs flag as part of our sqlmetal.exe command set, we find a method named (of course) GetPetName(). Here is the complete definition of our custom DataContext:

```
public partial class Cars : DataContext
{
  public Table<Customers> Customers;
  public Table<Inventory> Inventory;
  public Table<Orders> Orders;

  public Cars(string connection) : base(connection) {}
  public Cars(IDbConnection connection) : base(connection) {}
  public Cars(string connection, MappingSource mappingSource) :
    base(connection, mappingSource) {}
  public Cars(IDbConnection connection, MappingSource mappingSource) :
    base(connection, mappingSource) {}

  [StoredProcedure(Name="GetPetName")]
  public int GetPetName(
    [Parameter(DBType="Int")] System.Nullable<int> carID,
```

```
    [Parameter(DBType="Char(20)")] ref string petName)
  {
    StoredProcedureResult result =
      this.ExecuteStoredProcedure(((MethodInfo)(MethodInfo.GetCurrentMethod())),
      carID, petName);
    petName = ((string)(result.GetParameterValue(1)));
    return result.ReturnValue.Value;
  }
}
```

Notice that the GetPetName() method is marked with the [StoredProccedure] attribute, while each parameter is marked with the [Parameter] attribute. The implementation makes use of the inherited ExecuteStoredProcedure() method to take care of the details of invoking the stored procedure and returning the result to the caller.

Programming Against the Generated Types

Now that you have a better idea about the code authored by sqlmetal.exe, consider the following implementation of the Program type that invokes our stored procedure:

```
class Program
{
  const string cnStr = "Data Source=localhost;Initial Catalog=Cars;uid='sa';pwd=";

  static void Main(string[] args)
  {
    Console.WriteLine("***** More Fun with DLinq *****\n");

    Cars carsDB = new Cars(cnStr);
    InvokeStoredProc(carsDB);
    Console.ReadLine();
  }

  private static void InvokeStoredProc(Cars carsDB)
  {
    int carID = 0;
    string petName = "";
    Console.Write("Enter ID: ");
    carID = int.Parse(Console.ReadLine());

    // Invoke stored procedure and print out the pet name.
    carsDB.GetPetName(carID, ref petName);
    Console.WriteLine("Car ID {0} has the petname: {1}",
      carID, petName);
  }
}
```

Notice that LINQ to SQL completely hides the underlying stored procedure logic from view. Here, we have no need to manually create a SqlCommand object, fill the parameters collection, or call ExecuteNonQuery(). Instead, we simply invoke the GetPetName() method of our DataContext-derived type. Do note, however, that output parameters are represented as reference parameters, and therefore must be called using the C# ref keyword.

Now assume we have a second helper function (also called from within Main()) named PrintOrderForCustomer(). This method will print out some order details for the specified customer, as well as the first and last name of the customer:

```
private static void PrintOrderForCustomer(Cars carsDB)
{
  int custID = 0;
  Console.Write("Enter customer ID: ");
  custID = int.Parse(Console.ReadLine());

  var customerOrders =
    from cust in carsDB.Customers
    from o in cust.Orders
    where cust.CustID == custID
    select new { cust, o };

  Console.WriteLine("***** Order Info for Customer ID: {0}. *****", custID);
  foreach (var q in customerOrders)
  {
    Console.WriteLine("{0} {1} is order ID # {2}.",
      q.cust.FirstName.Trim(),
      q.cust.LastName.Trim(),
      q.o.OrderID);
    Console.WriteLine("{0} bought Car ID # {1}.",
      q.cust.FirstName.Trim(), q.o.CarID);
  }
}
```

Given the state of the Cars database at the time of installation, we receive the output shown in Figure 31-11 when querying about the customer assigned the ID of 1.

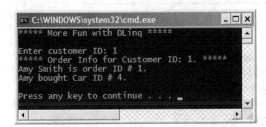

Figure 31-11. *Printing our order details for a specified customer*

Again, the benefit of LINQ to SQL is that we are able to interact with relational databases using a consistent, object-based model. To shed some more light on our LINQ query expression, add the following code statement at the end of the PrintOrderForCustomer() method:

```
Console.WriteLine("\ncustomerOrders as a string: {0}", customerOrders);
```

When you run the program once again, you may be surprised to find that the stringified value of your query expression reveals the underlying SQL query:

```
SELECT [t0].[FirstName], [t0].[LastName], [t0].[CustID],
       [t1].[OrderID], [t1].[CarID], [t1].[CustID] AS [CustID2]
FROM [Customers] AS [t0], [Orders] AS [t1]
WHERE ([t0].[CustID] = @p0) AND ([t1].[CustID] = [t0].[CustID])
```

■**Source Code** The LinqWithSqlMetalGenedCode example can be found under the Chapter 31 subdirectory.

Building Entity Classes Using Visual Studio 2005

To wrap up our look at LINQ to SQL, create a new LINQ console application named DlinqCRUD. This time, rather than running sqlmetal.exe to generate our entity classes, select Project ➤ Add New Item and add a new DLinqObjects item named MyDLinqObjects (see Figure 31-12).

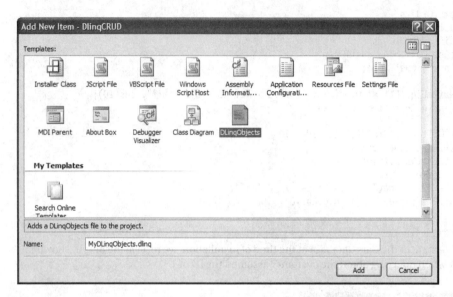

Figure 31-12. *The* DLinqObjects *item performs the same duties as* sqlmetal.exe.

Open Server Explorer and ensure you have an active connection to the Cars database (if not, right-click the Data Connections icon and select Add Connection). At this point, select each table and drag it onto the LINQ to SQL designer surface (see Figure 31-13).

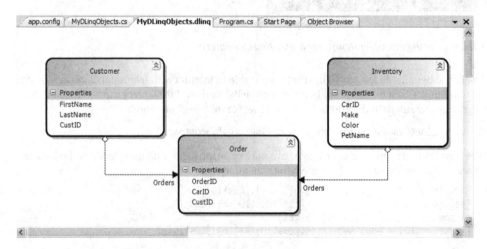

Figure 31-13. *Creating entity classes using the LINQ to SQL designer*

Once you perform your initial compile, go to Solution Explorer and open the related *.cs file (see Figure 31-14). As you look over the generated C# code, you'll quickly notice it is the same overall code generated by the sqlmetal.exe command-line utility. Also note that the visual LINQ to SQL designer added an app.config file to your project to store the necessary connection string data.

Figure 31-14. *Files generated as a result of inserting a* *.dlinq *designer*

Now that all the generated types are accounted for, let's build a Program class that illustrates inserting, updating, and deleting data on the Inventory table.

Inserting New Items

Adding new items to a relational database is as simple as creating a new instance of a given entity class, adding into the Table<T> type maintained by the DataContext, and calling SubmitChanges(). The following InsertNewCars() method adds two new (hard-coded) listings to the Inventory table. The first approach directly sets each field of the Inventory entity class, while the second approach makes use of the more compact object initialization syntax:

```
private static void InsertNewCars(CarsDataContext ctx)
{
  Console.WriteLine("\n***** Adding 2 Cars *****");
  int newCarID = 0;
  Console.Write("Enter ID for Betty: ");
  newCarID = int.Parse(Console.ReadLine());

  // Add a new row using 'longhand' notation.
  Inventory newCar = new Inventory();
  newCar.Make = "Yugo";
  newCar.Color = "Pink";
  newCar.PetName = "Betty";
  newCar.CarID = newCarID;
  ctx.Inventories.Add(newCar);
  ctx.SubmitChanges();

  // Add another row using 'shorthand' object init syntax.
  Console.Write("Enter ID for Henry: ");
  newCarID = int.Parse(Console.ReadLine());

  newCar = new Inventory { Make = "BMW", Color = "Silver",
    PetName = "Henry", CarID = newCarID };
```

```
ctx.Inventories.Add(newCar);
ctx.SubmitChanges();
}
```

Updating Existing Items

Updating an item is also very straightforward. Based on your LINQ query, extract the first item that meets the search criteria. Once you update the object's state, once again call SubmitChanges().

```
private static void UpdateCar(CarsDataContext ctx)
{
  Console.WriteLine("\n***** Updating color of 'Betty' *****");

  // Update Betty's color to light pink.
  var betty = (from c in ctx.Inventories
               where c.PetName == "Betty"
               select c).First();
  betty.Color = "Green";
  ctx.SubmitChanges();
}
```

Deleting Existing Items

And finally, if you want to delete an item from the relational database table, simply build a LINQ query to locate the item you are no longer interested in, and remove it from the correct Table<T> member variable of the DataContext using the Remove method. Once you have done so, again call SubmitChanges():

```
private static void DeleteCar(CarsDataContext ctx)
{
  int carToDelete = 0;
  Console.Write("Enter ID of car to delete: ");
  carToDelete = int.Parse(Console.ReadLine());

  // Remove specified car.
  ctx.Inventories.Remove((from c in ctx.Inventories
                          where c.CarID == carToDelete
                          select c).First());
  ctx.SubmitChanges();
}
```

That wraps up our introductory look at LINQ to SQL. Obviously, there is much more to the story than discussed here, but hopefully at this point you feel you are better equipped to dive into further details as you see fit.

■**Source Code** The DlinqCRUD example can be found under the Chapter 31 subdirectory.

Manipulating XML Documents Using LINQ to XML

In this final section of this chapter, we'll look at the role of LINQ to XML, which as you recall allows you to apply LINQ queries expressions against XML documents. Although the current edition of this text does not provide a chapter dedicated to XML programming, you have likely picked up on the deep extent to which XML data representation has been integrated into the .NET Framework.

Application and web-based configuration files store data as XML. ADO.NET DataSets can easily save out (or load in) data as XML. Windows Presentation Foundation (WPF) makes use of an XML-based grammar (XAML) to represent desktop UIs, and Windows Communication Foundation (WCF), as well as the previous .NET remoting APIs, also store numerous settings as the well-formatted string we call XML.

Although XML is indeed everywhere, programming with XML has historically been very tedious, verbose, and complex, if you are not well versed in a great number of XML technologies (XPath, XQuery, XSLT, DOM, SAX, etc.). Since the inception of the .NET platform, Microsoft has provided a specific assembly devoted to programming with XML documents named System.Xml.dll. Within this binary are a number of namespaces and types to various XML programming techniques, as well as a few .NET-specific XML APIs such as the XmlReader/XmlWriter models.

Just as LINQ to SQL intends to integrate relational database manipulation directly within .NET programming languages, LINQ to XML aspires to the same goals for XML data processing. Not only can you use LINQ to XML as a vehicle to obtain subsets of data from an existing XML document via LINQ queries, but also you can use this same API to create, copy, and parse XML data. To this end, LINQ to XML can be thought of as a "better DOM" programming model. As well, just as LINQ to SQL can interoperate with ADO.NET types, LINQ to XML can interoperate with many members of the System.Xml.dll assemblies.

■**Note** LINQ to XML is the new, official name (at least for today) for the technology previously termed XLinq. In fact, currently the LINQ to XML namespace is System.Xml.XLinq, rather than the expected System.Xml. LinqToXml. This may change in a future release of the LINQ beta.

The System.Xml.XLinq Namespace

Somewhat surprisingly, the core LINQ to XML assembly (System.Xml.XLinq.dll) defines a single namespace: System.Xml.XLinq. Here you will find a manageable set of types that represents various aspects of an XML document, its elements and their attributes, XML namespaces, XML comments and processing instructions, and so on. Table 31-6 documents the core members of System.Xml.XLinq.

Table 31-6. *Select Members of the* System.Xml.XLinq *Namespace*

Member	Meaning in Life
XAttribute	Represents an XML attribute on a given XML element
XComment	Represents an XML comment
XDeclaration	Represents the opening declaration of an XML document
XDocument	Represents the entirety of an XML document
XElement	Represents a given element within an XML document
XName, XNamespace	Provide a very simple manner to define and reference XML namespaces

To begin our investigation of these (and other) types, create a new LINQ console application named XLinqBasics. Like other examples in this chapter, this project will define a set of static helper methods called from within Main() to illustrate core concepts.

Programmatically Creating XML Documents

Unlike the original .NET XML programming model (à la System.Xml.dll), manipulating an XML document using LINQ can be achieved in a *functional manner*. Thus, rather than building a document in memory using the very verbose DOM API, LINQ to XML allows you to do so "DOM-free" if you so choose. Not only does this approach greatly reduce the amount of required code, but also the programming model maps almost directly to the format of well-formed XML data.

To illustrate, add a method to your Program class named CreateFunctionalXmlElement(), implemented as follows:

```
private static void CreateFunctionalXmlElement()
{
  // A 'functional' approach to building an
  // XML element in memory.
  XElement inventory =
    new XElement("Inventory",
      new XElement("Car", new XAttribute("ID", "1"),
        new XElement("Color", "Green"),
        new XElement("Make", "BMW"),
        new XElement("PetName", "Stan")
      )
    );
  // Call ToString() on our XElement.
  Console.WriteLine(inventory);
}
```

Here, notice that the constructor of the inventory XElement object is in fact a tree of additional XElements and XAttributes. When we (indirectly) call ToString() by printing out the object to the console, we find the output shown in Figure 31-15.

Figure 31-15. *A functional approach to XML document creation*

To create an entire XML document in memory (with comments, processing instructions, opening declarations, etc.), you can load the object tree into the constructor of an XDocument type. Consider the following CreateFunctionalXmlDoc() method, which creates an in-memory document that is then saved to a local file:

```
private static void CreateFunctionalXmlDoc()
{
  XDocument inventoryDoc =
    new XDocument(
      new XDeclaration("1.0", "utf-8", "yes"),
      new XComment("Current Inventory of Cars"),
        new XElement("Inventory",
          new XElement("Car", new XAttribute("ID", "1"),
```

```
                new XElement("Color", "Green"),
                new XElement("Make", "BMW"),
                new XElement("PetName", "Stan")
            ),
            new XElement("Car", new XAttribute("ID", "2"),
                new XElement("Color", "Pink"),
                new XElement("Make", "Yugo"),
                new XElement("PetName", "Melvin")
            )
        )
    );
    // Display the document and save it to disk.
    Console.WriteLine(inventoryDoc);
    inventoryDoc.Save("SimpleInventory.xml");
}
```

Figure 31-16 shows the SimpleInventory.xml file opened within Visual Studio 2005.

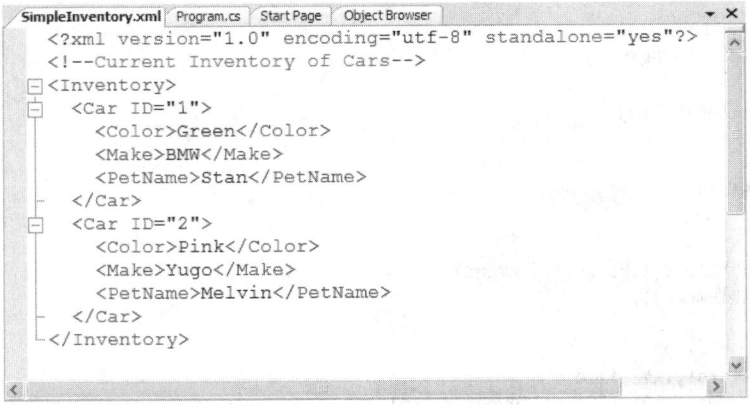

```
SimpleInventory.xml   Program.cs   Start Page   Object Browser                  ▾ ✕
    <?xml version="1.0" encoding="utf-8" standalone="yes"?>
    <!--Current Inventory of Cars-->
⊟<Inventory>
 ⊟   <Car ID="1">
        <Color>Green</Color>
        <Make>BMW</Make>
        <PetName>Stan</PetName>
      </Car>
 ⊟   <Car ID="2">
        <Color>Pink</Color>
        <Make>Yugo</Make>
        <PetName>Melvin</PetName>
      </Car>
 └ </Inventory>
```

Figure 31-16. SimpleInventory.xml

The XElement and XDocument types each define a constructor that takes an XName as the first parameter and a parameter array of objects as the second. The XName type is used in LINQ to SQL to represent (obviously) the name of the item you are creating, while the parameter array of objects can consist of any number of additional LINQ to XML types (XComment, XProcessingInstruction, XElement, XAttribute, etc.) as well as simple strings (for element content) or an object implementing IEnumerable.

As far as that last point is concerned, assume we have a simple Car class that defines a public field for the ID (of type int) and a public field for a pet name (of type string). We could now create an array of these objects and build a LINQ query that will select each name/value pair to dynamically build a new XElement:

```
private static void CreateXmlDocFromArray()
{
    // Create an anonymous array of types.
    var data = new [] {
        new Car { PetName = "Melvin", ID = 10 },
        new Car { PetName = "Pat", ID = 11 },
        new Car { PetName = "Danny", ID = 12 },
        new Car { PetName = "Clunker", ID = 13 }
    };
```

```
    // Now enumerate over the array to build
    // an XElement.
    XElement vehicals =
      new XElement("Inventory",
        from c in data
        select new XElement("Car",
         new XAttribute("ID", c.ID),
         new XElement("PetName", c.PetName)
        )
      );
    Console.WriteLine(vehicals);
}
```

Loading and Parsing XML Content

The XElement and XDocument types both support Load() and Parse() methods, which allow you to hydrate an XML object model from string data or external files. Consider the following method, which illustrates both approaches:

```
private static void LoadExistingXml()
{
  // Build an XElement from string.
  string myElement =
    @"<Car ID ='3'>
      <Color>Yellow</Color>
      <Make>Yugo</Make>
    </Car>";
  XElement newElement = XElement.Parse(myElement);
  Console.WriteLine(newElement);
  Console.WriteLine();

  // Load the SimpleInventory.xml file.
  XDocument myDoc = XDocument.Load("SimpleInventory.xml");
  Console.WriteLine(myDoc);
}
```

■**Source Code** The XLinqBasics example can be found under the Chapter 31 subdirectory.

Navigating an In-Memory Document

So at this point you have seen various ways in which LINQ to XML can be used to create, save, parse, and load XML data. The next aspect of LINQ to XML we need to examine is how to navigate a given document to locate specific elements/attributes. While the LINQ to XML object model provides a number of methods that can be used to programmatically navigate a document, not too surprisingly LINQ query expressions can also be used for this very purpose.

Selecting Elements Using LINQ to XML

Since you have already seen numerous examples of building query expressions, the next example is short and sweet. First, create a new LINQ console application named NavigationWithXLinq. Next, add a new XML document into your current project named Inventory.xml, which supports a small set of Car entries within the root <Inventory> element. Here is one possibility:

```xml
<?xml version="1.0" encoding="utf-8"?>
<Inventory>
  <Car carID ="0">
    <Make>Ford</Make>
    <Color>Blue</Color>
    <PetName>Chuck</PetName>
  </Car>
  <Car carID ="1">
    <Make>VW</Make>
    <Color>Silver</Color>
    <PetName>Mary</PetName>
  </Car>
  <Car carID ="2">
    <Make>Yugo</Make>
    <Color>Pink</Color>
    <PetName>Gipper</PetName>
  </Car>
  <Car carID ="55">
    <Make>Ford</Make>
    <Color>Yellow</Color>
    <PetName>Max</PetName>
  </Car>
  <Car carID ="98">
    <Make>BMW</Make>
    <Color>Black</Color>
    <PetName>Zippy</PetName>
  </Car>
</Inventory>
```

Now, select this file within Solution Explorer and use the Properties window to set the Copy to Output Directory property to Copy Always. Finally, update your Main() method to load this file into memory using XElement.Load(). The local doc variable will be passed into various helper methods to modify the data in various manners:

```csharp
static void Main(string[] args)
{
  Console.WriteLine("***** Fun with XLinq *****\n");

  // Load the Inventory.xml document into memory.
  XElement doc = XElement.Load("Inventory.xml");

  // We will author each of these next...
  PrintAllPetNames(doc);
  Console.WriteLine();
  GetAllFords(doc);
}
```

The PrintAllPetNames() method illustrates the use of the XElement.Descendants() method, which allows you to directly specify a given subelement you wish to navigate to. Here we are selecting each PetName value and printing out the contents to the console window:

```csharp
private static void PrintAllPetNames(XElement doc)
{
  var petNames = from pn in doc.Descendants("PetName")
                 select pn.Value;
```

```
    foreach (var name in petNames)
        Console.WriteLine("Name: {0}", name);
}
```

The GetAllFords() method is similar in nature. Given the incoming XElement, we define a where operator and select the all XElements where the Make element is equal to the value "Ford":

```
private static void GetAllFords(XElement doc)
{
    var fords = from c in doc.Descendants("Make")
                where c.Value == "Ford"
                select c;

    foreach (var f in fords)
        Console.WriteLine("Name: {0}", f);
}
```

Figure 31-17 shows the output of this program.

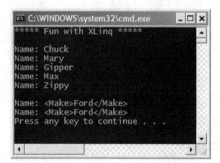

Figure 31-17. *LINQ queries against XML documents*

Modifying Data in an XML Document

Finally, as you would hope, LINQ to XML provides numerous ways to insert, delete, copy, and update XML content. Adding new XElements to an existing XElement (or XDocument) is no more difficult than calling the Add() method, which adds the data to the end of the element/document. As an alternative, you can call AddFirst() to add the item to the top of the element/document or AddAfterThis()/AddBeforeThis() to insert data at a specific location.

Updating or deleting content is also straightforward. After constructing a LINQ query statement to identify the item (or items) you wish to tinker with, call ReplaceContent() (for updating) or Remove()/RemoveContent() (for deletion of data).

By way of a simple example, consider the following code, which adds a set of new <Car> elements to the incoming XElement parameter:

```
private static void AddNewElements(XElement doc)
{
    // Add 5 new purple Fords to the incoming document.
    for (int i = 0; i < 5; i++)
    {
        // Create a new XElement
        XElement newCar =
            new XElement("Car", new XAttribute("ID", i + 1000),
                new XElement("Color", "Green"),
                new XElement("Make", "Ford"),
```

```
        new XElement("PetName", "")
    );

    // Add to doc.
    doc.Add(newCar);
}
// Show the updates.
Console.WriteLine(doc);
}
```

Source Code The NavigationWithXLinq example can be found under the Chapter 31 subdirectory.

Summary

LINQ is a set of related technologies that attempts to provide a single, symmetrical manner to interact with diverse forms of data. As explained over the course of this chapter, LINQ can interact with any type implementing the IEnumerable<T> interface, including simple arrays as well as generic and nongeneric collections of data. LINQ to SQL is this same technology applied to relational databases; LINQ to XML allows you to manipulate XML documents using the functional LINQ syntax.

As you have seen over the course of this chapter, working with LINQ technologies is accomplished using several new C# 3.0 language features. For example, given the fact that LINQ query expressions can return any number of result sets, it is common to make use of the var keyword to represent the underlying data type. As well, lambda expressions, object initialization syntax, and anonymous types can all be used to build very functional and compact LINQ queries. To be sure, as LINQ matures and is eventually officially released, we are all sure to find a number of new LINQ-centric APIs that provide a symmetrical manner to interact with all forms of "data."

Index

Y

You Need the Companion eBook

Your purchase of this book entitles you to buy the companion PDF-version eBook for only $10. Take the weightless companion with you anywhere.

We believe this Apress title will prove so indispensable that you'll want to carry it with you everywhere, which is why we are offering the companion eBook (in PDF format) for $10 to customers who purchase this book now. Convenient and fully searchable, the PDF version of any content-rich, page-heavy Apress book makes a valuable addition to your programming library. You can easily find and copy code—or perform examples by quickly toggling between instructions and the application. Even simultaneously tackling a donut, diet soda, and complex code becomes simplified with hands-free eBooks!

Once you purchase your book, getting the $10 companion eBook is simple:

❶ Visit **www.apress.com/promo/tendollars/**.

❷ Complete a basic registration form to receive a randomly generated question about this title.

❸ Answer the question correctly in 60 seconds, and you will receive a promotional code to redeem for the $10.00 eBook.

2560 Ninth Street • Suite 219 • Berkeley, CA 94710

eBookshop

THE EXPERT'S VOICE™

Offer valid through 7/07.